Carol Peters Martin Braschler
Julio Gonzalo Michael Kluck (Eds.)

Advances in Cross-Language Information Retrieval

Third Workshop of the
Cross-Language Evaluation Forum, CLEF 2002
Rome, Italy, September 19-20, 2002
Revised Papers

Springer

Volume Editors

Carol Peters
Istituto di Scienza e Tecnologie dell'Informazione
Consiglio Nazionale delle Ricerche (ISTI-CNR)
Via G. Moruzzi 1, 56124 Pisa, Italy
E-mail: carol.peters@isti.cnr.it

Martin Braschler
Eurospider Information Technology AG
Schaffhauserstr. 18, 8006 Zürich, Switzerland
E-mail: martin.braschler@eurospider.com

Julio Gonzalo
Universidad Nacional de Educación a Distancia
Lenguajes y Sístemas Informáticos
Ciudad Universitaria, 28040 Madrid, Spain
E-mail: julio@lsi.uned.es

Michael Kluck
Informationszentrum Sozialwissenschaften der
Arbeitsgemeinschaft Sozialwissenschaftlicher Institute e.V. (IZ)
Lennéstr. 30. 53113 Bonn, Germany
E-mail: kluck@bonn.iz-soz.de

Cataloging-in-Publication Data applied for

A catalog record for this book is available from the Library of Congress

Bibliographic information published by Die Deutsche Bibliothek
Die Deutsche Bibliothek lists this publication in the Deutsche Nationalbibliographie; detailed bibliographic data is available in the Internet at <http://dnb.ddb.de>.

CR Subject Classification (1998): H.3, I.2

ISSN 0302-9743
ISBN 3-540-40830-4 Springer-Verlag Berlin Heidelberg New York

Springer-Verlag Berlin Heidelberg New York
a member of BertelsmannSpringer Science+Business Media GmbH

www.springeronline.com

Printed in Germany

Typesetting: Camera-ready by author, data conversion by DA-TeX Gerd Blumenstein
Printed on acid-free paper SPIN: 10931776 06/3142 5 4 3 2 1 0

Lecture Notes in Computer Science 2785
Edited by G. Goos, J. Hartmanis, and J. van Leeuwen

Springer
Berlin
Heidelberg
New York
Hong Kong
London
Milan
Paris
Tokyo

Preface

The third campaign of the Cross-Language Evaluation Forum (CLEF) for European languages was held from January to September 2002. Participation in this campaign showed a slight rise in the number of participants with, 37 groups from both academia and industry and a steep rise in the number of experiments they submitted for one or more of the five official tracks. The campaign culminated in a two-day workshop held in Rome, Italy, 19–20 September, immediately following the Sixth European Conference on Digital Libraries (ECDL 2002), attended by nearly 70 researchers and system developers. The objective of the workshop was to bring together the groups that had participated in CLEF 2002 so that they could report on the results of their experiments. Attendance at the workshop was thus limited to participants in the campaign plus several invited guests with recognized expertise in the multilingual information access field. This volume contains thoroughly revised and expanded versions of the preliminary papers presented at the workshop accompanied by a complete run-down and detailed analysis of the results, and it thus provides an exhaustive record of the CLEF 2002 campaign.

CLEF 2002 was conducted within the framework of a project of the Information Society Technologies programme of the European Commission (IST-2000-31002). The campaign was organized in collaboration with the US National Institute of Standards and Technology (NIST) and with the support of the DELOS Network of Excellence for Digital Libraries. The support of NIST and DELOS in the running of the evaluation campaign is gratefully acknowledged. We would also like to thank the other members of the Workshop Steering Committee for their assistance in the coordination of this event.

June 2003

Carol Peters
Martin Braschler
Julio Gonzalo
Michael Kluck

CLEF 2002 Workshop Steering Committee

Martin Braschler	Eurospider Information Technology AG, Switzerland
Khalid Choukri	Evaluations and Language Resources Distribution Agency, France
Julio Gonzalo Arroyo	Universidad Nacional de Educación a Distancia, Spain
Donna Harman	National Institute of Standards and Technology, USA
Noriko Kando	National Institute of Informatics, Japan
Michael Kluck	IZ Sozialwissenschaften, Bonn, Germany
Patrick Kremer	Institute de Information Scientifique et Technique, Vandoevre, France
Carol Peters	Italian National Research Council, Pisa, Italy
Peter Schäuble	Eurospider Information Technology AG, Switzerland
Laurent Schmitt	Institute de Information Scientifique et Technique, Vandoevre, France
Ellen Voorhees	National Institute of Standards and Technology, USA

Table of Contents

Monolingual Experiments

Mainly Domain-Specific Information Retrieval

Interactive Track

Cross-Language Spoken Document Retrieval

II Cross-Language Systems Evaluation Initiatives, Issues and Results

III Appendix

Introduction

Carol Peters

ISTI-CNR, Area di Ricerca, 56124 Pisa, Italy
carol.peters@isti.cnr.it.

This volume reports theo results of the third campaign of the Cross Language Evaluation Forum (CLEF). The main objectives of CLEF are (i) to provide an infrastructure for the testing and evaluation of information retrieval systems operating on European languages in both monolingual and cross-language contexts, and (ii) to construct test-suites of reusable data that can be employed by system developers for benchmarking purposes. These objectives are achieved through the organization of annual evaluation campaigns. The CLEF 2002 campaign was held from January to September and ended in a workshop held in Rome, Italy, 19-20 September, at which the groups that participated in the campaign had the opportunity to report on their experiments.

However, CLEF has a third objective which goes beyond mere system benchmarking: the creation of a research and development community in the cross-language information retrieval (CLIR) sector. For this reason, although the main part of the Workshop was dedicated to paper and poster sessions in which the results of the different tracks of CLEF 2002 were discussed, additional sessions focused on other issues of interest to groups working in the general domain of multilingual information access. A highlight of the first day was a presentation by two well-known industrial groups on the current limits of cross-language retrieval systems in the commercial world. On the second day, guest speakers presented the results of other international cross-language system evaluation initiatives: the track for Arabic at the Text Retrieval Conference (TREC) series and the activity for Asian languages at the NTCIR workshops. The final session focused on proposals for CLIR on non-textual objects such as images or spoken documents and suggestions for the experimental evaluation of systems working in these areas. The Workshop thus provided an important opportunity for researchers working in the multilingual information access area to get together and exchange ideas and opinions which not only regarded current approaches and techniques but also the future directions for research in this field. Copies of all the presentations are available on the CLEF website in the archives for CLEF 2002.

These proceedings contain thoroughly revised and expanded versions of the preliminary system reports published in the Working Notes and distributed at the workshop. Many of the papers also include descriptions of additional experiments and results as participating groups often further optimize their systems or try out new ideas as a consequence of the discussions held during the workshop. The volume is divided into two parts plus an appendix. The first part provides an exhaustive overview of the CLEF 2002 experiments whereas the second part provides background information on the organization of CLIR system evaluation campaigns.

C.A. Peters (Ed.): CLEF 2002, LNCS 2785, pp. 1-5, 2003.

Readers who have never participated in CLEF or similar evaluation campaigns are probably well advised to begin with the final paper of Part II, which describes the technical infrastructure underlying CLEF and thus provides the necessary contextual information in order to understand the details of the experiments reported in Part I. The appendix provides a complete record of the run statistics for the 2002 campaign, reporting the results for each participating group, track by track, task by task.

1 CLEF 2002 Experiments

Part I of this volume contains papers from the participating groups and provides a complete record of the CLEF 2002 experiments. The CLEF activities are divided into a set of *core tracks* that have been designed specifically to test system performance for monolingual, bilingual, multilingual and domain-specific information retrieval and which are offered regularly each year, and other *additional tracks* that are introduced in order to reflect emerging interests of the CLIR research and development community. The core tracks are coordinated by the CLEF consortium[1], the others are organized by voluntary groups on a more experimental basis. The first paper by Martin Braschler provides an overview of the main results of the core tracks. The rest of Part I is divided into five sections, reflecting the different track characteristics. The fact that not all papers describe experiments belonging to a single track has meant that we have had to be flexible in deciding which section is most appropriate for a particular paper. The first section "Cross-Language and More" thus contains papers that mainly focus on multilingual and/or bilingual retrieval experiments even if they also report other work. Similarly "Mainly Domain-Specific Information Retrieval" contains reports from those groups that gave their main attention to work with the GIRT and /or Amaryllis scientific corpora, even though some other papers in the cross-language section also contain descriptions of domain-specific experiments.

The final two sections of Part I contain reports from the additional tracks: the "Interactive Track" and "Cross-Language Spoken Document Retrieval". Each of these sections begins with a track report by the coordinators, giving an overview of the tasks set and the results obtained. The track overviews are followed by papers describing the individual experiments. These experimental tracks are very important for CLEF. System evaluation cannot be limited to measuring system performance in terms of a ranked list of documents; there are many other issues to consider. These tracks represent the first steps that CLEF is taking towards new types of evaluation, also including non-textual objects.

Overall the papers in Part I provide an important record of the state-of-the-art in the multilingual information access area and of important emerging research trends.

---

[1] Members of the consortium are ISTI-CNR, Italy (coordinators); ELDA, France; Eurospider Information Technology, Switzerland; IZ-Bonn, Germany; LSI-UNED, Spain; NIST, USA. The CLEF 2002 and 2003 campaigns are funded by the EC under the IST programme (IST-2000-31002). More information at: http://www.clef-campaign.org/

2 Evaluation Initiatives, Issues and Results

Part II of these proceedings contains several papers that provide information on the organization of evaluation campaigns. The first paper provides a brief history of the NTCIR workshops, a series of evaluation workshops organized by the National Institute of Informatics in Tokyo with the aim of enhancing research in many different information access technologies for systems using East Asian languages. CLEF and NTCIR intend to coordinate their cross-language activities, exchanging information and data when appropriate. The second paper provides a linguistic and statistic analysis of CLEF topics[2] testing the correlation between topic properties and system performance. The objective is to demonstrate that the CLEF topic sets are balanced and do not influence the results of the retrieval systems. The last paper in this section gives a complete overview of the organization of the CLEF 2002 evaluation campaign, describing the evaluation methodology adopted for the core tracks, the tracks and tasks and the test collection. Finally, the actual results of the systems participating in CLEF 2002 can be found in the Appendix, which provides a summary of the characteristics of all runs for the core tracks together with overview graphs for the different tasks and individual statistics for each run.

3 The Future of CLIR and of CLEF

To some extent, research in the cross-language information retrieval sector is currently at a cross-roads. There has been much interest in and work on system development since SIGIR 1996 when the very first workshop in this area was held[3]. So much so that in a recent workshop at SIGIR 2002 the question asked was whether the CLIR problem can now be considered as solved[4]. The answers given were mixed: the basic technology for cross-language text retrieval systems is now in place as is clearly evidenced by the papers in this volume. But if this is so, why haven't any of the large Web search engines adopted this technology and why don't most commercial information services offer CLIR as a standard service? The already mentioned presentation by Clairvoyance and Irion Technologies at the CLEF 2002 workshop on the current state of the market was very clear. Although there is a strong market potential – with many application sectors showing well-defined requirements – the actual systems are just not ready to meet the needs of the generic user. Most currently available commercial CLIR systems are not sufficiently versatile, they are complex, they are slow when working on-line, they cannot handle "all" languages, they do not present their results in a sufficiently user-friendly fashion, they have been developed for textual applications whereas the real world is multimedia. It is clear that much work remains to be done if the present gap between the CLIR R&D community and the application world is to be bridged satisfactorily.

---

[2] Topics are descriptions of information needs from which participating systems construct their queries.

[3] Workshop on Cross-Linguistic Information Retrieval at SIGIR'96. SIGIR is the ACM Special Interest Group on Information Retrieval

[4] See http://ucdata.berkeley.edu/sigir-2002/ for details on this workshop and, in particular, the position paper by Douglas W. Oard.

It has often been claimed that evaluation campaigns can play an active part in advancing system development. If this is true, what role should CLEF play in this scenario? It seems evident that in the future, we must go further in the extension and enhancement of CLEF evaluation tasks, moving gradually from a focus on cross-language text retrieval and the measurement of document rankings to the provision of a comprehensive set of tasks covering all major aspects of multilingual, multimedia system performance with particular attention to the needs of the end-user. In order to do this we will need to face a number of problems, including:

- What kind of evaluation methodologies need to be developed to address more advanced information requirements?
- How can we cover the needs of all European languages – including minority ones?
- What type of coordination and funding model should be adopted – centralized or distributed?
- How can we best reduce the gap between research and application communities?
- Last but not least – how can we achieve satisfactory agreements with our data providers in order to make our test-suites publicly available at a reasonable cost?

At the moment of writing, CLEF 2003 is well under way and is attempting to move in the direction outlined above. This year, there will be four new tracks on top of the traditional core tracks for mono-, bi- multilingual and domain-specific systems. In addition to continuing with the very successful interactive track, CLEF 2003 includes an activity for multilingual question answering. This track consists of several tasks and offers the possibility to test monolingual question answering systems running on Spanish, Dutch and Italian texts, and cross-language systems using questions in Dutch, French, German, Italian and Spanish to search an English document collection. Two pilot experiments have also been organized to test cross-language spoken document retrieval systems (an extension of the preliminary work reported in this volume), and cross-language retrieval on an image collection. These new tracks have been set up as a result of proposals made at the CLEF 2002 workshop and consequent to the interest expressed in the ensuing discussion. An encouraging number of participants have registered and the preliminary findings will be presented at the CLEF 2003 workshop.

More information on the activities of CLEF and the schedule for CLEF 2003 can be found on our website: http://www.clef-campaign.org/.

Acknowledgements

Many people and organisations must be thanked for their help in the coordination of CLEF 2002. First of all I should like to thank the other members of the CLEF Consortium for all their efforts at making both the campaign and the workshop a great success. In particular, I must express our appreciation to Francesca Borri, who has been responsible for the administrative management of the CLEF initiative, without Francesca we would be quite lost. However, it would be impossible to run CLEF without considerable assistance from many groups, working mainly on a voluntarily basis. Here below we list some of them:

Associated Members of the CLEF Consortium

INIST - INstitute de Information Scientifique et Technique, Vandoeuvre, France – responsible for the Amaryllis task
Department of Information Studies, University of Tampere, Finland – responsible for work on the Finnish collection
Human Computer Interaction and Language Engineering Laboratory, SICS, Kista, Sweden - responsible for work on the Swedish collection
University of Twente, Centre for Telematics and Information Technology, The Netherlands - responsible for work on the Dutch collection
Universitatet Hildesheim, Institut für Angewandte Sprachwissenschaft - Informationswissenschaft, Germany – responsible for checking and revision of the multilingual topic set
College of Information Studies and Institute for Advanced Computer Studies, University of Maryland, College Park, MD, USA – co-organisers of iCLEF
In addition, we should like to thank the following people/organisations for preparing topics in Chinese, Japanese and Portuguese.
Natural Language Processing Lab, Department of Computer Science and Information Engineering, National Taiwan University
National Institute of Informatics (NII), Tokyo
José Borbinha and Eulalia Carvalho of the National Library of Portugal
We also gratefully acknowledge the support of all the data providers and copyright holders, and in particular:
The Los Angeles Times, for the English data collection;
Le Monde S.A. and ELDA: European Language Resources Distribution Agency, for the French data.
Frankfurter Rundschau, Druck und Verlagshaus Frankfurt am Main; Der Spiegel, Spiegel Verlag, Hamburg, for the German newspaper collections.
InformationsZentrum Sozialwissenschaften, Bonn, for the GIRT database.
INIST - INstitute de Information Scientifique et Technique, Vandoeuvre, France, for the Amaryllis data.
Hypersystems Srl, Torino and La Stampa, for the Italian newspaper data.
Agencia EFE S.A. for the Spanish newswire data.
NRC Handelsblad, Algemeen Dagblad and PCM Landelijke dagbladen/Het Parool for the Dutch newspaper data.
Aamulehti Oyj for the Finnish newspaper documents
Tidningarnas Telegrambyrå for the Swedish newspapers
Schweizerische Depeschenagentur, Switzerland, for the French, German and Italian Swiss news agency data.
Without their help, this evaluation activity would be impossible.

Part I

System Evaluation Experiments at CLEF 2002

CLEF 2002 – Overview of Results

Martin Braschler

Eurospider Information Technology AG
Schaffhauserstr. 18, 8006 Zürich, Switzerland
martin.braschler@eurospider.com
Université de Neuchâtel, Institut interfacultaire d'informatique
Pierre-à-Mazel 7, CH-2001 Neuchâtel, Switzerland

Abstract. In its third year, the CLEF campaign has again seen considerable growth on multiple fronts. While the explosive growth in the number of participants has slowed somewhat, the number of actual experiments has grown considerably, as has their complexity (more data to process and more languages to handle). The main tracks of the CLEF 2002 campaign attracted 37 participating groups who submitted nearly 300 different experiments. In this overview, a description of the tracks and tasks, and a summary of the principal research results are given. As for the last two years, we have also examined the multilingual test collection produced as a result of the campaign with respect to the completeness of its relevance assessments, with very favorable findings.

1 Introduction

The third CLEF campaign was held from January to September 2002. Overviews of the results of the two previous campaigns have been published elsewhere (see [4] for CLEF 2000, and [5] for CLEF 2001). CLEF, a successor to the TREC-6-8 cross-language information retrieval (CLIR) tracks [11], had experienced explosive growth in the number of participants in the first two years of its existence. In 2002, the number of participants stabilized somewhat, growing at a slower rate. However, the 2002 campaign saw substantial growth in other notable areas, mainly in the experiments conducted for the campaign – both in terms of the number of experiments submitted, but also in terms of their complexity. This has resulted in the 2002 campaign having what is probably the "richest" set of results produced through CLEF activities so far.

CLEF 2002 offered several different tracks and tasks, and this paper covers the core activities: the multilingual, bilingual, monolingual and domain-specific tracks, which are directly managed by the CLEF consortium. In addition, CLEF 2002 featured an interactive track (expanded from 2001) and a pilot experiment on cross-language speech retrieval. The results of these tracks are discussed elsewhere ([9], [10]). The aim of this paper is to summarize and analyze the main results and research directions, as well as to compare the findings with those of the previous years and

C.A. Peters (Ed.): CLEF 2002, LNCS 2785, pp. 9-27, 2003.

provide a statistical analysis (Sections 2, 3, 4 and 5). We also investigate the CLEF 2002 test collection with respect to the completeness and validity of the relevance assessments (Section 6). The paper closes with a summary and conclusions (Section 7).

2 Tracks and Tasks

The core tracks and tasks offered for the CLEF 2002 campaign were:

- *Multilingual Retrieval.* Retrieval of text documents in any of five languages (English, French, German, Italian, Spanish) using queries formulated in one language (choice of eleven different languages[1]; see also Table 4). Result lists contain items from all five document languages. This was the "main" track, and participants were actively encouraged to tackle it.
- *Bilingual Retrieval.* Retrieval of text documents written in a language different from the query language. Participants could choose one of seven possible target languages (Dutch, Finnish, French, German, Italian, Spanish, Swedish), and from a selection of eleven different query languages. English as a target language was permitted for newcomers only.
- *Monolingual Retrieval.* Retrieval of text documents from a collection written in one of seven languages: Dutch, Finnish, French, German, Italian, Spanish or Swedish. For this track, the query language is identical to document language.
- *Domain-specific Retrieval.* Retrieval on a German or a French document collection containing scientific texts. An accompanying thesaurus/controlled vocabulary was available, and queries were provided in three (German, English, Russian) and two (English, French) languages, respectively.

Participants sent their results in the form of ranked lists containing those documents that best match a given query. They submitted one or several experiments ("runs") for an individual task. For reasons of tractability by the campaign organizers, the maximum number of experiments for each task was limited.

In total, 37 groups from 12 different countries participated in one or more of the tracks and tasks that were offered for CLEF 2002 (see Table 1). Table 2 compares the number of participants and experiments to those of earlier TREC CLIR tracks [11] and earlier CLEF campaigns. While the first two CLEF campaigns in 2000 [4] and 2001 [5] were clearly a breakthrough in promoting larger participation with respect to the CLIR track at TREC, the growth in the number of participants has slowed somewhat. CLEF has a high retention rate of participants (Table 1).

A total of 282 experiments were submitted, an increase of more than 40% compared to last year. A breakdown into the individual tasks can be found in Table 3.

All query languages were used for experiments, including the translations of the queries into Chinese, Portuguese, Russian, and Japanese (post-campaign only), which were provided by independent third parties. English, French, German and Spanish were the most popular query languages, with Dutch and Italian closely behind. By far

[1] After the campaign, queries were also made available in a twelfth language, Japanese.

the most popular query language was English, since many people used it for bilingual experiments, searching on one of the other seven languages. Table 4 shows a summary of the query languages and their use.

Table 1. List of CLEF 2002 participants. One star (*) denotes a participant that has taken part in one previous campaign (2000 or 2001), two stars (**) denote participants that have taken part in both previous campaigns

City University (UK[2])	SINAI/Univ. Jaen (ES) *
Clairvoyance Corp. (US)	Tagmatica (FR)
COLE Group/U La Coruna (ES)	Thomson Legal (US) **
CWI/CNLP (NL/US) *	U Alicante (ES) *
Eurospider (CH) **	U Amsterdam (NL) *
Fondazione Ugo Bordoni (IT)	U Dortmund (DE) *
Hummingbird (CA) *	U Exeter (UK) *
IMBIT (DE)	U Hildesheim (DE)
IMS U Padova (IT)	U Maryland (US) **
IRIT (FR) **	U Montreal/RALI (CA) **
ITC-irst (IT) **	U Neuchâtel (CH) *
JHU-APL (US) **	U Salamanca (ES) **
Lexware (SV)	U Sheffield (UK) **
Medialab (NL) *	U Tampere (FI) **
Middlesex U (UK)	U Twente/TNO (NL) **
National Tawian U (TW) *	UC Berkeley (2 groups) (US) **
OCE Tech. BV (NL) *	UNED (ES) *
SICS/Conexor (SV/FI) *	Xerox (FR) *

Table 2. Development in the number of participants and experiments

Year	# Participants	# Experiments
TREC-6 (1997)	13	(95)[3]
TREC-7 (1998)	9	27
TREC-8 (1999)	12	45
CLEF 2000	20	95
CLEF 2001	34	198
CLEF 2002	37	282

[2] In the following, the paper uses ISO 3166 2-letter country codes to denote countries of origin of participants, and ISO 639 2-letter language codes to abbreviate references to query/topic and document languages.

[3] In TREC6, only bilingual retrieval was offered, which resulted in a large number of runs combining different pairs of languages [[24]]. Starting with TREC7, multilingual runs were introduced [[7]], which usually consist of multiple runs for the individual languages that are merged. The number of experiments for TREC6 is therefore not directly comparable to later years.

Table 3. Experiments listed by track/task

Task	# Participants	# Runs
Multilingual	11	36
Bilingual to DE	6	13
Bilingual to EN	5	16
Bilingual to ES	7	16
Bilingual to FI	2	2
Bilingual to FR	7	14
Bilingual to IT	6	13
Bilingual to NL	7	10
Bilingual to SV	1	1
Monolingual DE	12	21
Monolingual ES	13	28
Monolingual FI	7	11
Monolingual FR	12	16
Monolingual IT	14	25
Monolingual NL	11	19
Monolingual SV	6	9
Domain-specific Amaryllis	3	15
Domain-specific GIRT	5	17

Queries were provided to participants in the form of "topics", which are textual formulations of statements of information need by hypothetical users. Such topics are structured into multiple fields (title, description and narrative), which provide increasingly more detailed representations of a search request. The title typically contains one to three words, whereas the description is usually one sentence long. The narrative, the longest representation, contains an elaborate formulation of several sentences. Participants construct queries for their systems either automatically or manually out of these topic statements, using any combination of the fields.

A large majority of runs (227 out of 282 runs) used only the title and description fields of the topics for query construction, ignoring the narrative part. Participants were required to submit at least one title+description run per task tackled in order to increase comparability. Without doubt, this has contributed to the large number of runs using this combination of topic fields. Furthermore, there may have been a perception by the participants that shorter queries were probably more "realistic" for many operational settings. Even so, using all topic fields (longest possible queries) was the second most popular choice (34 runs). 19 runs used only the title field (resulting in very short queries). The remainder were more "exotic" combinations.

All core tracks used a distinction between "automatic" and "manual" runs, based on the methodology employed for query construction. Only 6 manual experiments were submitted, even less than last year. Manual experiments are useful in establishing baselines and in improving the overall quality of relevance assessment pools. Therefore, an increase in the number of these experiments would be welcome; especially since they also tend to focus on interesting aspects of the retrieval process that are not usually covered by batch evaluations. However, since manual experiments tend to be a resource-intensive undertaking, it seems likely that most of the participants interested in this form of work concentrated their efforts on experiments for the interactive track.

Table 4. Experiments listed by query/topic language

Language	# Runs
DE German	38
EN English	99
ES Spanish	35
FI Finnish	11
FR French	32
IT Italian	26
NL Dutch	20
PT Portuguese *	6
RU Russian *	5
SV Swedish	9
ZH Chinese *	4
(JA Japanese) *	(post-campaign only)

* Query/topic-only language

3 Characteristics of the Experiments

Table 5 gives some key figures for the CLEF 2002 multilingual document collection. The collection was extended over the 2001 version by adding new documents in Finnish and Swedish. As can be seen from the table, the 2002 collection compares well to the widely used TREC-7 and TREC-8 ad-hoc retrieval test collections, both in terms of size and with regard to the amount of topics and relevance assessments. Experiments ("runs") for the multilingual, bilingual and monolingual tasks were conducted by retrieving documents from all or part of this collection.

With CLEF building on earlier campaigns organized both by the same organizers or under different umbrellas (TREC in North America, NTCIR in East Asia), there are participants that have worked on this type of evaluation for several years. Open discussion at the workshop and public availability of the proceedings result in CLEF acting as a "trendsetter", and methods that work well one year are adapted eagerly by other participants in following campaigns. This, and the bringing together of a community of interested researchers, are clearly key contributions that CLEF plays in distributing successful ideas for cross-language retrieval.

Table 5. Characteristics of the CLEF 2001 multilingual document collection

Collection	# Partici-pants.	# Lang.	# Docs.	Size in MB	# Docs. Assessed	# Topic.	# Assessed/ Topic
CLEF 2002	34+3	8	1,138,650	3011	140,043	50	~2900
CLEF 2001	31+3	6	940,487	2522	97,398	50	1948
CLEF 2000	20	4	368,763	1158	43,566	40	1089
TREC-8 CLIR	12	4	698,773	1620	23,156	28	827
TREC-8 AdHoc	41	1	528,155	1904	86,830	50	1736
TREC-7 AdHoc	42+4	1	528,155	1904	~80,000	50	~1600

We have tried to highlight some of the trends that we can discern from the experiments conducted for the 2002 campaign:

- Participants were using fewer "corpus-based" CLIR approaches, i.e. methods that automatically extract translation resources from suitable training data. However, such approaches were still popular especially in combination systems (Latent semantic indexing [20], similarity thesauri [6], [18], statistical models [16], [19]).
- A few MT systems proved to be very popular, mainly for query translation (Systran, e.g. [18], [23], and LH Power Translator, e.g. [8], [13]).
- Participants invested a lot of effort into work on automatic query expansion, such as blind relevance feedback [8], the use of concepts and synonyms [27], random indexing [22] and others.
- A fairly new trend was the added emphasis on fine-tuned weighting per language (as opposed to using the same parameters for all languages, see e.g. [3], [15], [23]). It remains a challenge to prove how the findings based on the CLEF collection generalize to a particular language or to other collections.
- Continuing a trend from the previous year, diverse approaches to stemming were proposed, using simple and elaborate stemming (morphological analyzers), a programming language expressly for stemmers [15], statistical stemming [1] and other ideas. These efforts were supplemented by interesting work on decompounding, such as statistical decompounding [8] (however, different conclusions were reached for different languages on this issue).
- The merging problem, i.e. the combination of multiple translation resources, translation approaches or target languages into a single retrieval result was very much a main focus for participants this year. While simple methods were still widely used in this area, new ideas were proposed as well, such as the use of an unified index [19], reindexing [17], prediction based on translation quality [14], and feedback-based merging [6].

For a detailed discussion of these and other features of the 2002 experiments, please refer to the individual participants' papers in this volume.

4 Results

The following sections describe the results for the core tracks: multilingual, bilingual, monolingual and domain-specific retrieval.

4.1 Multilingual Track

Eleven groups submitted results for the multilingual track. Most of these groups submitted more than one result set. The multilingual track is the main focus of the CLEF campaign, and participants are actively encouraged to tackle it. It was encouraging to see the number of groups for this track grow again in CLEF 2002, after a slight drop in the year before (presumably because the task was made more difficult in the previous year with the addition of the fifth language, and some groups needed the extra year to adapt). We think that the experience gained in previous years has allowed a number of groups to successfully proceed from the monolingual and bilingual tracks to the multilingual track.

Fig. 1 shows the best experiments of the five top groups in the automatic category for this track. The best three groups (U Neuchâtel, UC Berkeley 2 and Eurospider) are the same as last year. Clearly, it is an advantage to have one or more year's worth of experience when tackling this, the most challenging task. Even so, two newcomers to the multilingual track (SINAI/U Jaen and Océ) can be found in the remaining two top-five slots. These two groups had restricted their experiments to bilingual and monolingual retrieval in CLEF 2001. The top three entries all use elaborate combination approaches.

4.2 Bilingual Track

The 2002 campaign offered a bilingual track that was far more extensive than the one offered in previous CLEF campaigns. In 2001, participants were free to choose between two target languages, English and Dutch. In 2002, the CLEF consortium responded to numerous requests from participants and opened the bilingual track to all eight target languages (DE, EN, ES, FI, FR, IT, NL, SV; EN for newcomers or under special conditions only). While allowing for added flexibility in testing the systems on the participant's part, this decision makes comparing different bilingual experiments somewhat harder, since experiments on different target languages use different document sets. It is therefore necessary to investigate eight different result sets, one for each target language. Table 6 shows the best entries by the top five performing participants for each target language, including only runs using the mandatory title+description topic field combination.

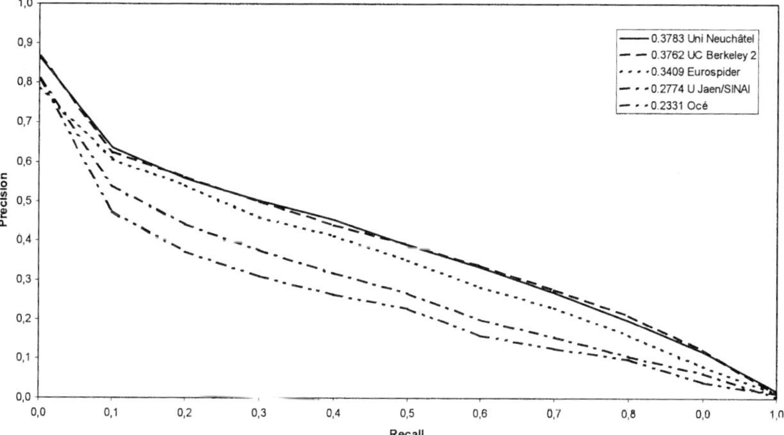

Fig. 1. The best entries of the top five performing groups for the multilingual track. All runs used only the title+description fields of the topics

Table 6. The best entries of the top five performing groups for the bilingual track, sorted by target language. All runs used only the title+description fields of the topics

Target Language	Rank.	Avg. Prec.	Group
DE German	1.	0.4759	UC Berkeley 2
	2.	0.4448	UC Berkeley 1
	3.	0.4129	U Neuchâtel
	4.	0.3137	JHU/APL
	5.	0.2747	SINAI/U Jaen
EN English *	1.	0.4158	JHU/APL
	2.	0.3502	Clairvoyance
	3.	0.3235	Océ
	4.	0.2449	IRIT
	5.	0.2088	Middlesex U
ES Spanish	1.	0.4786	U Neuchâtel
	2.	0.4567	UC Berkeley 2
	3.	0.4202	U Exeter
	4.	0.3699	Océ
	5.	0.3602	JHU/APL
FI Finnish	1.	0.2016	U Tampere
	2.	0.2003	JHU/APL
FR French	1.	0.4935	U Neuchâtel
	2.	0.4773	UC Berkeley 2
	3.	0.4312	UC Berkeley 1
	4.	0.3505	JHU/APL
	5.	0.3467	SINAI/U Jaen
IT Italian	1.	0.4090	UC Berkeley 2
	2.	0.3994	U Exeter
	3.	0.3756	U Neuchâtel
	4.	0.3552	ITC-irst
	5.	0.2794	JHU/APL
NL Dutch	1.	0.3516	JHU/APL
	2.	0.3369	U Twente/TNO
	3.	0.3199	UC Berkeley 2
	4.	0.2933	U Amsterdam
	5.	0.1912	Océ
SV Swedish	1.	0.3003	JHU/APL

* Experiments with English as a target language were restricted to newcomers and certain exceptions.

The five languages of the multilingual track were well represented as target languages for bilingual experiments, as was Dutch. There were fewer experiments using the new languages Finnish and Swedish as targets, possibly due to a lack of available retrieval tools and translation resources (such as stemmers, stopword lists and dictionaries). The smaller number of participants for the new languages, and for English (because of the restrictions), makes it hard to compare results. However, some interesting trends can be derived from the results of the remaining five languages. Firstly, two groups, University of California at Berkeley Group 2 and Université de Neuchâtel, both among the top groups in the multilingual track, performed well for most languages. The differences between the top group and the runner-up are generally more pronounced than in the multilingual track (roughly 5-10%). We conclude that general knowledge of how to build CLIR systems seems to help in performing well across a variety of languages, but the languages still have individual potential for fine-tuning that results in different placement of the groups across the languages. Secondly, it is also interesting to see that for the Dutch target language, where we have an active group of participants from the Netherlands, three Dutch groups performed well. It is well possible that it is advantageous for fine-tuning to have detailed knowledge of the characteristics of a language.

4.3 Monolingual Track

The CLEF 2002 campaign offered monolingual retrieval for all target languages besides English. Table 7 summarizes the best entries of the top five performing groups for the title+description topic field combination.

Again, the results for Finnish and Swedish are somewhat hard to interpret, because these two languages were offered in CLEF for the first time this year. The five "older" languages invite some interesting observations however. For the bilingual track, we have speculated that knowing a language well is an advantage in designing a good retrieval system for it. This speculation receives some further support by the top two entries for Italian, which both come from groups from Italy. We do not observe a similar pattern for the other core languages, but that may well be due to other priorities of the groups taking part in those tasks.

As for bilingual retrieval, there are some groups that do well for many languages, but again the ranking changes from language to language. Competition for the top spots in the monolingual track this year was fierce, with some of the participants that submitted the best performing entries last year dropping six or seven ranks this year for the same language. Generally, results in German, Spanish, French, Italian and Dutch are very close, with the careful fine-tuning of little details accounting for much of the difference. This seems to be a clear indication that monolingual non-English text retrieval for the CLEF core languages has matured, due among other things to the study of these languages in the previous two CLEF campaigns, and the participants having a better understanding of how to squeeze optimum performance out of their systems. It might also indicate, however, that participants are beginning to over-tune for the CLEF document collection. It will be an important challenge in future experiments to investigate how much of the differences seen across the target languages are due to language-specific characteristics, and how much can be attributed to collection-specific artifacts. For new languages, such as Finnish and Swedish, and others yet to be added, the next CLEF campaigns may spark similar progress.

4.4 Domain-Specific Retrieval Track

Continuing the practice started at the TREC-7 cross-language track, and maintained in CLEF 2000 and CLEF 2001, a track dealing with domain-specific data was offered to

CLEF participants. This year, the data collection was substantially extended, by using a new French collection, Amaryllis, in addition to the German "GIRT" texts. The two collections are distinct from the multilingual collection used in the other core tasks. The GIRT texts come from the domain of social science, and are written in German, with 71% of the texts having English titles, and around 8% having English abstracts, while the Amaryllis texts came from a multi-disciplinary scientific database of approximately 150,000 French bibliographic documents. Additional resources were provided that could be used in the retrieval task (a thesaurus in German/English/Russian for the GIRT texts, and a controlled vocabulary in English and French for the Amaryllis texts).

Table 7. The best entries of the top five performing groups for the monolingual track, sorted by target language. All runs used only the title+description fields of the topics

Target Language	Rank.	Avg. Prec.	Group
DE German	1.	0.5234	UC Berkeley 2
	2.	0.4802	U Amsterdam
	3.	0.4672	U Neuchâtel
	4.	0.4663	JHU/APL
	5.	0.4577	Eurospider
ES Spanish	1.	0.5441	U Neuchâtel
	2.	0.5338	UC Berkeley 2
	3.	0.5192	JHU/APL
	4.	0.4993	Thomson Legal
	5.	0.4980	U Alicante
FI Finnish	1.	0.4090	U Neuchâtel
	2.	0.4056	U Twente/TNO
	3.	0.3956	Hummingbird
	4.	0.3280	JHU/APL
	5.	0.3034	U Amsterdam
FR French	1.	0.5191	UC Berkeley 2
	2.	0.4841	U Neuchâtel
	3.	0.4558	UC Berkeley 1
	4.	0.4535	U Amsterdam
	5.	0.4509	JHU/APL
IT Italian	1.	0.5088	F. U. Bordoni
	2.	0.4920	ITC-irst
	3.	0.4750	UC Berkeley 2
	4.	0.4618	U Neuchâtel
	5.	0.4599	JHU/APL
NL Dutch	1.	0.5028	JHU/APL
	2.	0.4878	U Neuchâtel
	3.	0.4847	UC Berkeley 2
	4.	0.4598	U Amsterdam
	5.	0.4447	Hummingbird
SV Swedish	1.	0.4317	JHU/APL
	2.	0.4187	U Amsterdam
	3.	0.3441	Hummingbird
	4.	0.2439	Thomson Legal
	5.	0.1347	SICS/Conexor

Table 8. The best entries of the top five performing groups for the domain-specific track, sorted by target collection and task. All runs used only the title+description fields of the topics

Target Language	Rank.	Avg. Prec.	Group
GIRT Bilingual	1.	0.2330	UC Berkeley 1
	2.	0.0704	U Amsterdam
GIRT Monolingual	1.	0.2587	UC Berkeley 1
	2.	0.1906	U Amsterdam
	3.	0.1890	U Dortmund
	4.	0.1097	U Hildesheim
Amaryllis Bilingual	1.	0.4272	UC Berkeley 1
	2.	0.2660	U Amsterdam
Amaryllis Monolingual	1.	0.4802	U Neuchâtel
	2.	0.4396	UC Berkeley 1
	3.	0.2681	U Amsterdam

The domain-specific track had been sort of a "problem child" with regard to participation in earlier years. Even though there has always been a strong expression of interest by numerous groups, only a few participants actually submitted results in previous years. This year, the number of participants was more encouraging, but still small compared to the amount of expressions of interest that the coordinators of CLEF received. It seems that if in doubt of how to allocate their limited resources, participants still drop the domain-specific track first. Even so, some participants concentrated on this track, and report elaborate experiments (e.g. UC Berkeley 1, U Hildesheim, Xerox).

A summary of the best entries of the top five performing groups for the title+description topic field combination is given in Table 8.

The smaller number of participants makes it difficult to draw overall conclusions. Indeed, the performance obtained by the groups was very dissimilar, probably due to the different degree of tuning for the characteristic of the domain-specific data.

5 Statistical Significance Testing

For reasons of practicality, CLEF uses a limited number of topics (50 in 2002), which are intended to represent an appropriate sample of the population of all possible topics that users would want to ask from the collection. When the goal is to validate how well results can be expected to hold beyond this particular set of topics, statistical testing can help determine what differences between runs appear to be real as opposed to differences that are due to sampling variation. As with all statistical testing, conclusions will be qualified by an error probability, which was chosen to be 0.05 in the following.

Using the IR-STAT-PAK tool [2], a statistical analysis of the results for the multilingual track was carried out for the first time after the 2001 campaign. We have repeated this analysis for 2002. The tool provides an Analysis of Variance (ANOVA) which is the parametric test of choice in such situations but requires that some assumptions concerning the data are checked. Hull [12] provides details of these; in particular, the scores in question should be approximately normally distributed and their variance has to be approximately the same for all runs. IR-STAT-PAK uses the Hartley test to verify the equality of variances. In the case of the CLEF multilingual collection, it indicates that the assumption is violated. For such cases, the program offers an arcsine transformation,

$$f(x) = \arcsin\left(\sqrt{x}\right) \tag{1}$$

which Tague-Sutcliffe [25] recommends for use with Precision/Recall measures, and which we have therefore applied.

The ANOVA test proper only determines if there is at least one pair of runs that exhibits a statistical difference. Following a significant ANOVA, various comparison procedures can be employed to investigate significant differences. IR-STAT-PAK uses the Tukey T test for grouping the runs.

Looking at the results (Table 9), all runs that are included in the same group (denoted by "X") do not have significantly different performance. All runs scoring below a certain group perform significantly worse than at least the top entry of that group. Likewise, all runs scoring above a certain group perform significantly better than at least the bottom entry in that group. To determine all runs that perform significantly worse than a certain run, locate the rightmost group that includes the run. All runs scoring below the bottom entry of that group are significantly worse. Conversely, to determine all runs that perform significantly better than a given run, locate the leftmost group that includes the run. All those runs that score better than the top entry of that group perform significantly better.

It has been observed before that it is fairly difficult to detect statistically significant differences between retrieval runs based on 50 topics [26]. For a recent discussion on the topic set sizes and their implications, see e.g. Voorhess and Buckley [28]. While 50 topics remains a realistic choice based on the time and resources needed to perform a large number of relevance assessments, statistical testing would be one of the areas to benefit most from having additional topics. This fact is addressed by the measures taken to ensure stability of at least part of the document collection across different campaigns, which allows participants to run their system on aggregate sets of topics for post-hoc experiments.

For the 2002 campaign, we have observed a fairly clear division of runs into performance groups for the multilingual track. The top three groups (Université de Neuchâtel (UniNE), University of California at Berkeley (bky2) – Group 2 and Eurospider (EIT)) are within 10% of each other in terms of average precision, but then a considerable gap opens of roughly 20% to the next best group (University of Jaen/SINAI Group (UJA)). The fifth group, Océ (oce), is a further 10% down, while all other groups come in at least a further 10% behind Océ. All in all, there is a performance drop of nearly 50% between the top and the seventh entry.

This considerable variation facilitates the detection of significant differences, and groups with similar performance emerge. Interpreting Table 9, we see that the top three groups significantly outperformed all entries of all other groups except for the University Jaen/SINAI Group. The difference between this group, and the top three is large, but narrowly misses significance. The top four groups significantly outperform all groups ranked eighth and lower, while the best entries of the top seven show a significant difference with at least the bottom three groups.

It is important to note that this table contains experiments conducted with different parameter settings and diverse intentions. Many groups use an evaluation campaign in order to test a new approach. Therefore, it should serve mainly to compare pairs of experiments, considering their individual merits and not to draw more generalized conclusions.

Table 9. Results of statistical analysis (ANOVA) on the experiments submitted for the multilingual track. All experiments, regardless of topic language, topic fields or other characteristics, are included. Results are therefore only valid for comparison of individual pairs of runs, and not in terms of absolute performance

Arcsine-transformed. average precision values, Original mean average precision values, Run IDs			Tukey T test grouping								
0.6415	0.3762	bky2muen1	X								
0.6354	0.3783	UniNEm2	X	X							
0.6323	0.3756	UniNEm4	X	X							
0.6226	0.3552	UniNEm5	X	X							
0.6193	0.3570	bky2muen2	X	X							
0.6181	0.3554	EIT2MNF3	X	X							
0.6154	0.3480	EAN2MDF4	X	X							
0.6096	0.3539	EIT2MNU1	X	X							
0.6069	0.3512	UniNEm3	X	X							
0.6041	0.3488	UniNEm1	X	X							
0.5998	0.3409	EIT2MDF3	X	X							
0.5978	0.3400	EIT2MDC3	X	X							
0.5168	0.2774	UJAMLTDRSV2		X	X						
0.5156	0.2758	UJAMLTD2RSV2		X	X						
0.4696	0.2331	oce02mulMSlo			X	X					
0.4605	0.2210	oce02mulRRlo			X	X					
0.4377	0.2103	oce02mulMSbf			X	X					
0.4375	0.2082	aplmuenb			X	X					
0.4371	0.2049	tlren2multi			X	X					
0.4335	0.2070	aplmuena			X	X					
0.4313	0.2038	UJAMLTDRR			X	X					
0.4279	0.2068	UJAMLTDNORM			X	X	X				
0.4248	0.1973	oce02mulRRbf			X	X	X				
0.3836	0.1720	oce02mulRRloTO				X	X	X			
0.3634	0.1637	tremu1				X	X	X			
0.3054	0.1182	run2					X	X			
0.3006	0.1155	run1						X	X		
0.2972	0.1166	tremu2						X	X		
0.2816	0.0966	UJAMLTDRSV2RR						X	X		
0.2671	0.0945	run3						X	X	X	
0.2309	0.0756	iritMEn2All							X	X	X
0.1572	0.0373	NTUmulti04								X	X
0.1554	0.0361	NTUmulti05								X	X
0.1488	0.0336	NTUmulti03								X	X
0.1317	0.0266	NTUmulti02									X
0.1086	0.0173	NTUmulti01									X

6 Coverage of Relevance Assessments

The results reported in the CLEF campaigns rely heavily on the concept of judging the relevance of documents with respect to given topics. The relevance of a document is judged by human assessors, making this a costly undertaking. These relevance assessments are then used for the calculation of the recall/precision figures that underlie the graphs and figures presented to the participants.

Given their central importance for the calculation of the evaluation measures, critics of relevance assessments are often worried about the "quality" and the "coverage" ("completeness") of the assessments. The first concern stems from the subjective nature of relevance, which can lead to disagreements between different assessors or even when the same assessor judges a document twice. Numerous studies have analyzed the impact of disagreement in judging on the validity of evaluation results. These studies generally conclude that as long as sufficient consistency is maintained during judging, the ranking and comparison of systems is stable even if the absolute performance values calculated on the basis of the assessments change. The quality and consistency of the assessments in CLEF is ensured by following a well-proven methodology based on TREC experience. More details of relevance assessment processes can be found in [21].

The problem of coverage arises from practical considerations in the production of the relevance assessments. While it is comparatively easy to judge a substantial part of the top-ranked results submitted by participants, it is much harder to judge all the documents in a collection against any given topic. This is especially the case with today's large test collections. However, judging the non-retrieved documents is necessary to calculate some evaluation measures such as recall.

In order to keep costs manageable, only documents included and highly ranked in at least one result set (in the top 60 for CLEF 2002) are judged for relevance (with the union of all judged result sets forming a "document pool"). This implies that some relevant documents potentially go undetected if they are not retrieved by any of the participating systems. The assertion is that a sufficient number of diverse systems will turn up most relevant documents this way. Figures calculated based on these "limited" assessments are then a good approximation of theoretical figures based on complete assessments. A potential problem is the (re-)usability of the resulting test collection for the evaluation of a system that did not contribute to this "pool of judged documents". If such a system retrieves a substantial number of unjudged documents that are relevant, but went undetected, it is unfairly penalized when calculating the evaluation measures. An investigation into whether the assessments for the CLEF multilingual collection provide sufficient coverage follows below.

One way to analyze the coverage of the relevance judgments is by focusing on the "unique relevant documents" [30]. For this purpose, a unique relevant document is defined as a document that was judged relevant with respect to a specific topic, but that would not have been part of the pool of judged documents had a certain group not participated in the evaluation, i.e., only one group retrieved the document with a score high enough to have it included in the judgment pool. This addresses the concern that systems not directly participating in the evaluation are unfairly penalized. Subtracting relevant documents only found by a certain group, and then reevaluating the results for this group, simulates the scenario that this group was a non-participant. The smaller the change in performance that is observed, the higher is the probability that the relevance assessments are sufficiently complete.

This kind of analysis has been run by the CLEF consortium since the 2000 campaign for the multilingual track. This year, we have expanded the analysis to include an investigation of the subcollections formed by the individual target languages. A total of $n+1$ sets of relevance assessments are used: the original set, and n sets (n = number of participants) that are built by taking away the relevant documents uniquely found by one specific participant (numbers of uniquely found relevant documents per participant can be found in Fig. 2.). The results for every experiment are then recomputed using the set without the group-specific relevant documents. The key figures obtained after rerunning the evaluations can be found in Table 10 (see also Fig. 3).

The quality of a document pool can therefore be judged by the mean performance difference in terms of average precision that is obtained if the pool had been missing the contribution of a specific group. This difference should be as small as possible, indicating that the pool is "sufficiently exhaustive" and that adding more documents to the pool, such as documents found by an additional participant, does not substantially influence results and/or rankings. As we also found in 2000 and 2001, the pool used in CLEF 2002 for the multilingual track is very stable. The maximum change in performance scores is 1.76%. These small differences influence only direct comparisons between systems that have practically identical performance, and where the original performance differences cannot be considered significant in any case. The value of the multilingual pool for reuse in post-hoc experiments should thus be assured, and the validity of the results reported by CLEF should hold within the inherent limits of interpretation (restricted set of queries/topics, characteristics of evaluation measures and others).

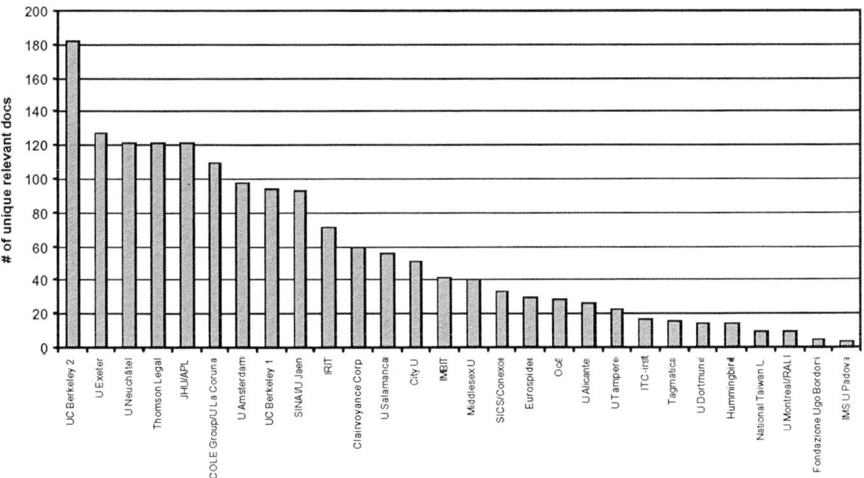

Fig. 2. Number of unique relevant documents contributed by each CLEF participant for the multilingual document collection

Table 10. Key values of the pool quality analysis: mean and maximum change in average precision when removing the pool contribution of one participant, and associated standard deviation

Track	Mean Difference	Max. Difference	Std. Dev. Difference
Multilingual	0.0008 (0.48%)	0.0030 (1.76%)	0.0018 (1.01%)
DE German	0.0025 (0.71%)	0.0095 (5.78%)	0.0054 (1.71%)
EN English	0.0023 (1.14%)	0.0075 (3.60%)	0.0051 (2.60%)
ES Spanish	0.0035 (0.87%)	0.0103 (2.52%)	0.0075 (1.86%)
FI Finnish	0.0021 (0.82%)	0.0100 (4.99%)	0.0049 (2.05%)
FR French	0.0019 (0.54%)	0.0050 (1.86%)	0.0038 (1.08%)
IT Italian	0.0008 (0.22%)	0.0045 (0.93%)	0.0016 (0.46%)
NL Dutch[4]	0.0045 (1.26%)	0.0409 (9.15%)	0.0116 (3.09%)
SV Swedish	0.0082 (3.32%)	0.0306 (10.19%)	0.0182 (7.51%)

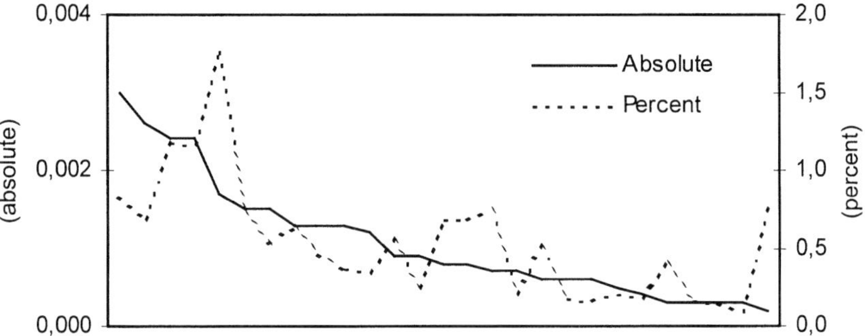

Fig. 3. Changes in mean average precision (absolute values and percentages) for all multilingual runs submitted to CLEF. The majority of runs experienced a change of less than 0.002

The pools for individual target languages are smaller, since they are restricted to the document set of that language. Only runs for that language, and therefore a smaller number than for the multilingual pool, contributed. It is therefore not surprising that differences found for the individual languages are somewhat higher than for the multilingual pool. We feel, however, that they are still comfortably within acceptable limits, and they do indeed compare favorably with numbers reported for comparable collections in the past (e.g. for TREC collections [29]). Not surprisingly, the pool for Swedish is a little less stable than the others, owing to having less contributions and Swedish being a new language in CLEF. For Dutch, we had issues with an outlier that obfuscates the measures somewhat, but we believe that the pool should be of comparable quality to the other languages.

[4] One experiment that was an extreme outlier in terms of performance was removed before calculation of the Dutch figures to avoid a non-representative skew in the numbers.

The ranking of the systems is also very stable: the only systems that switch ranks have an original performance difference of less than 0.0019 (equivalent to 0.93% difference) in average precision, well below any meaningful statistical significance. The differences reported are even slightly lower than the ones observed for the CLEF 2001 campaign [5].

7 Conclusions

CLEF 2002 experienced growth both in the number of participants, and more noticeably, in the number of experiments submitted. This overview summarizes the main characteristics of the 282 experiments submitted for the campaign, and discusses trends observed and the main results. We conclude that people adopt each other's ideas and methods across campaigns, and that those returning groups that have the experience to build complex combination systems have performed well in the main, multilingual track. This demonstrates clearly the learning curve that these participants have experienced. For the bilingual and monolingual track we observe that good performance in a wide variety of target languages requires careful fine-tuning for all these languages. The main challenge is to do this in a manner that respects the characteristics of each language without over-tuning to artifacts of the CLEF document collection. A further encouraging development is a clear trend that many returning groups move from simpler to harder tasks from one campaign to the next. CLEF clearly helps these groups to progress towards more challenging CLIR tasks. This is especially valuable in consideration of the large number of new groups attracted by CLEF in the last campaigns.

The paper also explores the statistical significance of the results for the main, multilingual track. Statistical analysis enables us to qualify and better interpret the results as published by CLEF. As evidenced by an analysis of the multilingual experiments that we present, fairly large performance differences are needed to reach a level of statistical significance. For this kind of testing, having as large a number of queries/topics as possible is of great benefit. The CLEF consortium strives for stability in the test collections to allow post-hoc experiments with combined resources from several campaigns.

Lastly, the validity of the results reported in CLEF depends on measures that are calculated based on the relevance assessments. Consequently, these results are only as good as the data they build on. By investigating the exhaustiveness of the document pool used for the judging, we get an indication of the quality of the relevance assessments. We find that the CLEF relevance assessments seem to be very stable, making them suitable for reuse in post-hoc experiments, and further validating the results published during the campaigns.

Acknowledgements

Thanks go to Carol Peters and Jacques Savoy for helpful hints, suggestions and corrections.

References

[1] Agosti, M., Bacchin, M., Ferro, N., Melucci, M.: Improving the Automatic Retrieval of Text Documents. This volume.

[2] Blustein, J.: IR STAT PAK. URL: http://www.csd.uwo.ca/~jamie/IRSP-overview.html.

[3] Brand, R., Brünner, M.: Océ at CLEF 2002. This volume.

[4] Braschler, M.: CLEF 2000 – Overview of Results. In: Cross-Language Information Retrieval and Evaluation. Workshop of the Cross-Language Evaluation Forum, CLEF 2000, Revised Papers. Pages 89-101, 2001.

[5] Braschler, M.: CLEF 2001 – Overview of Results. In: Evaluation of Cross-Language Information Retrieval Systems. Second Workshop of the Cross-Language Evaluation Forum, CLEF 2001, Revised Papers. Pages 9-26, 2002.

[6] Braschler, M., Göhring, A., Schäuble, P.: Eurospider at CLEF 2002. This volume.

[7] Braschler, M., Krause, J., Peters, C., Schäuble, P.: Cross-Language Information Retrieval (CLIR) Track Overview. In: Proceedings of the Seventh Text REtrieval Conference (TREC-7), NIST Special Publication 500-242, Pages 25-32, 1998.

[8] Chen, A.: Cross-language Retrieval Experiments at CLEF 2002. This volume.

[9] Gonzalo, J., Oard, D.W.: The CLEF 2002 Interactive Track. This volume.

[10] Jones, G.J.F and Federico, M. CLEF2002 Cross-Language Spoken Document Retrieval Pilot Track Report. This volume.

[11] Harman, D., Braschler, M., Hess, M., Kluck, M., Peters, C., Schäuble, P., Sheridan P.: CLIR Evaluation at TREC. In: Cross-Language Information Retrieval and Evaluation. Workshop of the Cross-Language Evaluation Forum, CLEF 2000, Revised Papers. Pages 7-23, 2001.

[12] Hull, D. A: Using Statistical Testing in the Evaluation of Retrieval Experiments. In: Proceedings of the 16th Annual International ACM SIGIR Conference on Research and Development in Information Retrieval, Pittsburg, USA, Pages 329-338, 1993.

[13] Lam-Adesina, A. M., Jones, G. J. F.: Exeter at CLEF 2002: Experiments with Machine Translation for Monlingual and Bilingual Retrieval. This volume.

[14] Lin, W.-C., Chen, H.-H.: Merging Mechanisms in Multilingual Information Retrieval. This volume.

[15] MacFarlane, A.: PLIERS and Snowball at CLEF 2002. This volume.

[16] McNamee, P., Mayfield, J.: Scalable Multilingual Information Access. This volume.

[17] Martinez, F., Ureña, L. A., Martín, M. T.: SINAI at CLEF 2002: Experimenting with Merging Strategies. This volume.

[18] Moulinier, I., Molina-Salgado, H.: Thomson Legal and Regulatory Experiments for CLEF 2002. This volume.

[19] Nie, J.-Y., Jin, F.: A Multilingual Approach to Multilingual Information Retrieval. This volume.

[20] Orengo, V. M., Huyck, C.: Portuguese-English Experiments using Latent Semantic Indexing. This volume.

[21] Peters, C., Braschler, M.: European Research Letter: Cross-language system evaluation: The CLEF campaigns, In: Journal of the American Society for Information Science and Technology, Volume 52, Issue 12, pages 1067-1072, 2001.

[22] Sahlgren, M., Karlgren, J., Cöster, R., Järvinen, T.: SICS at CLEF 2002: Automatic Query Expansion using Random Indexing. This volume.

[23] Savoy, J.: Report on CLEF 2002 Experiments: Combining Multiple Sources of Evidence. This volume.

[24] Schäuble, P. Sheridan, P.: Cross-Language Information Retrieval (CLIR) Track Overview. In: Proceedings of the Sixth Text Retrieval Conference (TREC-6), NIST Special Publication 500-240,Pages 31-43, 1997.

[25] Tague-Sutcliffe, J.: The Pragmatics of Information Retrieval Experimentation, Revisited. In: Readings in Information Retrieval, Morgan Kaufmann Publishers, San Francisco, CA, USA, Pages 205-216, 1997.

[26] Tague-Sutcliffe, J., Blustein, J.: A Statistical Analysis of the TREC-3 Data. In: Proceedings of the Third Text REtrieval Conference (TREC-3), NIST Special Publication 500-226. Page 385ff, 1994.

[27] Vilares, J., Alonso, M. A., Ribadas, F. J., Vilares, M.: COLE Experiments in the CLEF 2002 Spanish Monolingual Track. This volume.

[28] Voorhees, E., Buckley, C.: The Effect of Topic Set Size on Retrieval Experiment Error. In: Proceedings of the 25th Annual International ACM SIGIR Conference on Research and Development in Information Retrieval, Pages 316-323, 2002.

[29] Vorhees, E., Harman, D.: Overview of the Eighth Text REtrieval Conference (TREC-8). In: Proceedings of the Eighth Text Retrieval Conference (TREC-8), NIST Special Publication 500-246, Pages 1-24, 1999.

[30] Zobel, J.: How reliable are the results of large-scale information retrieval experiments? In: Proceedings of the 21st Annual International ACM SIGIR Conference on Research and Development in Information Retrieval, Pages 307-314, 1998.

Cross-Language Retrieval Experiments at CLEF 2002

Aitao Chen

School of Information Management and Systems
University of California at Berkeley, CA 94720-4600, USA
aitao@sims.berkeley.edu

Abstract. This paper describes monolingual, bilingual, and multilingual retrieval experiments using CLEF 2002 test collection. The paper presents a technique for incorporating blind relevance feedback into a document ranking formula based on logistic regression analysis. Both blind relevance feedback and decompounding in German or Dutch are shown to be effective in monolingual and bilingual retrieval. The amount of improvement of performance by decompounding varies from one set of topics to another. The simple raw-score merging strategy in multilingual retrieval can be effective if the individual ranked lists of documents, one for each document language, are produced using the same retrieval system under similar conditions. The performance of English to French bilingual retrieval using a large parallel corpus as the translation resource is comparable to that using machine translation systems.

1 Introduction

Multilingual text retrieval is the task of searching for relevant documents in a collection of documents in more than one language in response to a query, and presenting a unified ranked list of documents regardless of language. Multilingual retrieval is an extension of bilingual retrieval where the collection consists of documents in a single language that is different from the query language. Recent developments on multilingual retrieval are reported in CLEF 2000 [10], and CLEF 2001 [11]. Most of the multilingual retrieval methods fall into one of three groups. The first approach translates the source topics into all the document languages in the document collection. Then monolingual retrieval is carried out separately for each document language, resulting in one ranked list of documents for each document language. Finally the intermediate ranked lists of retrieved documents, one for each language, are merged to yield a combined ranked list of documents regardless of language. The second approach translates a multilingual document collection into the topic language. Then the topics are used to search against the translated document collection. The third approach also translates topics to all document languages as in the first approach. The source topics and the translated topics are concatenated to form a set of multilingual topics. The multilingual topics are then searched against the multilingual document collection, which directly produces a ranked list of documents in all

C.A. Peters (Ed.): CLEF 2002, LNCS 2785, pp. 28–48, 2003.

languages. The latter two approaches do not involve merging two or more ranked lists of documents, one for each document language, to form a combined ranked list of documents in all document languages. Most participating groups of the multilingual retrieval tasks in the TREC or CLEF evaluation conferences applied the first approach. Translating large collections of documents in multiple languages into topic languages requires the availability of machine translation systems that support the necessary language pairs, which is sometimes problematic. For example, if the document collection consists of documents in English, French, German, Italian, and Spanish, and the topics are in English, to perform the multilingual retrieval task using English topics, one would have to translate the French, German, Italian, and Spanish documents into English. In this case, there exist translators, such as Babelfish, that can do the job. However, if the topics are in Chinese or Japanese, it may be more difficult or even impractical at this time to find machine translators capable of direct translation from English, French, German, Italian or Spanish into Chinese or Japanese.

The availability of the translation resources and the need for extensive computation are factors that limit the applicability of the second approach. The third approach is appealing in that it bypasses document translations, and circumvents the difficult merging problem. However, there is some empirical evidence showing that the third approach is less effective than the first one [1].

We believe that three of the core components of the first approach are monolingual retrieval, topic translation, and merging. Performing multilingual retrieval requires many language resources such as stopword lists, stemmers, bilingual dictionaries, machine translation systems, parallel or comparable corpora. The end performance of multilingual retrieval can be affected by many factors such as monolingual retrieval performance of the document ranking algorithm, the quality and coverage of the translation resources, the availability of language-dependent stemmers and stopwords, and the effectiveness of the merging algorithm.

At CLEF 2002, we participated in the *monolingual*, *bilingual*, and *multilingual* retrieval tasks. For the monolingual task, we submitted retrieval runs for Dutch, French, German, Italian, and Spanish. For the bilingual task, we submitted bilingual retrieval runs from English to Dutch, French, German, Italian, and Spanish, one French-to-German run, and one German-to-French run. And for the multilingual task, we submitted two runs using English topics. The document collection for the multilingual task consists of documents in English, French, German, Italian and Spanish. All of our runs used only the *title* and *desc* fields in the topics. We mainly worked on improving the performances of monolingual retrieval and bilingual retrieval by query expansion and word decompounding since we believe that improved performances in monolingual and bilingual retrieval should ultimately lead to better performance in multilingual retrieval. For all of our runs in the bilingual and multilingual tasks, the topics were translated into the document languages. The main translation resources we used are the SYSTRAN-based online *Babelfish translation* and *L&H Power Translator Pro Version 7.0*. We also used parallel English/French texts in one of the English-to-French retrieval runs. The *Babylon* English-Dutch dictionary was used in bilingual retrieval from English to Dutch.

The same document ranking formula developed at Berkeley [3] back in 1993 was used for all retrieval runs reported in this paper. It has been shown that query expansion via blind relevance feedback can be effective in monolingual and cross-language retrieval. The Berkeley formula based on logistic regression has been used for years without blind relevance feedback. We developed a blind relevance feedback procedure for the Berkeley document ranking formula. All of our official runs were produced with blind relevance feedback. We will present a brief overview of the Berkeley document ranking formula in Section 2, and the blind relevance feedback procedure in Section 3.

Of the two official multilingual runs submitted, one used unnormalized raw score to re-rank the documents from intermediate runs to produce the unified ranked list of documents, and the other used normalized score in the same way to produce the final list.

2 Document Ranking

A typical text retrieval system ranks documents according to their relevances to a given query. The documents that are more likely to be relevant are ranked higher than those that are less likely. In this section, we briefly describe a logistic regression-based document ranking formula developed at Berkeley [3]. The log-odds (or the logit transformation) of the probability that document D is relevant with respect to query Q , denoted by $\log O(R|D,Q)$, is given by

$$\begin{aligned}\log O(R|D,Q) &= log\frac{P(R|D,Q)}{1-P(R|D,Q)} = log\frac{P(R|D,Q)}{P(\overline{R}|D,Q)} \\ &= -3.51 + 37.4 * x_1 + 0.330 * x_2 - 0.1937 * x_3 + 0.0929 * x_4\end{aligned}$$

where $P(R|D,Q)$ is the probability that document D is relevant to query Q, $P(\overline{R}|D,Q)$ the probability that document D is irrelevant to query Q, which is 1.0 - $P(R|D,Q)$. The four explanatory variables x_1, x_2, x_3, and x_4 are defined as follows: $x_1 = \frac{1}{\sqrt{n+1}}\sum_{i=1}^{n}\frac{qtf_i}{ql+35}$, $x_2 = \frac{1}{\sqrt{n+1}}\sum_{i=1}^{n}\log\frac{dtf_i}{dl+80}$, $x_3 = \frac{1}{\sqrt{n+1}}\sum_{i=1}^{n}\log\frac{ctf_i}{cl}$, and $x_4 = n$, where n is the number of matching terms between a document and a query, qtf_i is the within-query frequency of the ith matching term, dtf_i is the within-document frequency of the ith matching term, ctf_i is the occurrence frequency in a collection of the ith matching term, ql is query length (i.e., number of terms in a query), dl is document length (i.e., number of terms in a document), and cl is collection length (i.e., number of terms in the test document collection). If stopwords are removed from indexing, then ql, dl, and cl are the query length, document length, and collection length, respectively, after removing stopwords. If the query terms are re-weighted, then qtf_i is no longer the original term frequency, but the new weight, and ql is the sum of the new weight values for the query terms. Note that, unlike x_2 and x_3, the variable x_1 sums the "optimized" relative frequency without first taking the log over the matching terms. The relevance probability of document D with respect to query Q

can be written as $P(R|D,Q) = \frac{1}{1+e^{-logO(R|D,Q)}}$ in terms of the log-odds of the relevance probability. The documents are ranked in decreasing order by their relevance probabilities $P(R|D,Q)$ with respect to a query. The coefficients were determined by fitting the logistic regression model specified in $\log O(R|D,Q)$ to training data using a statistical software package. Readers are referred to reference [3] for more details.

3 Relevance Feedback

It is well known that blind (also called pseudo) relevance feedback can substantially improve retrieval effectiveness. It is commonly implemented in research text retrieval systems. See for example the papers of the groups who participated in the Ad Hoc tasks in TREC-7 [13] and TREC-8 [14]. Blind relevance feedback is typically performed in two stages. First, an initial search using the original query is performed, after which a number of terms are selected from some top-ranked documents that are presumed relevant. The selected terms are merged with the original query to formulate a new query. Finally the new query is searched against the document collection to produce a final ranked list of documents. The techniques for deciding the number of terms to be selected, the number of top-ranked documents from which to extract terms, and ranking the terms vary.

In this section we present a technique for incorporating blind relevance feedback into the logistic regression-based document ranking framework. Some of the issues involved in implementing blind relevance feedback include determining the number of top ranked documents that will be presumed relevant and from which new terms will be extracted, ranking the selected terms and determining the number of terms that should be selected, and assigning weight to the selected terms. We refer readers to [7] for a survey of relevance feedback techniques.

Two factors are important in relevance feedback. The first one is how to select the terms from top-ranked documents after the initial search, the second is how to assign weight to the selected terms with respect to the terms in the initial query. For term selection, we assume some number of top-ranked documents in the initial search are relevant, and the rest of the documents in the collection are irrelevant. For the terms in the documents that are presumed relevant, we compute the ratio of the odds of finding a term in a randomly selected relevant document over the odds of finding the same term in a randomly selected irrelevant document. This is the term relevance weighting formula proposed by Robertson and Sparck Jones in [12]. Table 1 presents a word contingency table, where n is the number of documents in the collection, m the number of top-ranked documents after the initial search that are presumed relevant, m_t the number of documents among the m top-ranked documents that contain the term t, and n_t the number of documents in the collection that contain the term t. Then we see from the above contingency table that the probability of finding the term t in a relevant document is $\frac{m_t}{m}$, because m_t documents out of the m

Table 1. A contingency table for a word

	relevant	irrelevant	
indexed	m_t	$n_t - m_t$	n_t
not indexed	m - m_t	n - n_t - m + m_t	n - n_t
	m	n - m	n

relevant documents contain the term t. Likewise, the probability of not finding the term t in a relevant document is $\frac{m-m_t}{m}$. The odds of finding a term t in a relevant document is $\frac{m_t}{m-m_t}$. Likewise, the odds of finding a term t in an irrelevant document is $\frac{n_t-m_t}{n-n_t-m+m_t}$. The relevance weight of term t is given by

$$w_t = log\frac{\frac{m_t}{m-m_t}}{\frac{n_t-m_t}{n-n_t-m+m_t}} \tag{1}$$

For every term t, except for the stopwords, found in the m top-ranked documents, we compute its weight w_t according to the above formula. Then all the terms are ranked in decreasing order by their weight w_t. The top-ranked k terms are added to the initial query to create a new query. Some of the selected terms may be among the initial query terms. For the selected terms that are not in the initial query, the weight is set to 0.5. The rationale for assigning weights to the selected terms that are not among the initial query terms is that the selected terms are considered not as important as the initial query terms, so the weights assigned to them should fall in the range of 0 to 1, exclusive. In our implementation, we set the weights of the new terms to 0.5, expecting that the query length will be doubled after query expansion. For those selected terms that are in the initial query, the weight is set to 0.5*t_i, where t_i is the occurrence frequency of term t in the initial query. The selected terms are merged with the initial query to formulate an expanded query. When a selected term is one of the query terms in the initial query, its weight in the expanded query is the sum of its weight in the initial query and its weight assigned in the term selection process. For a selected term that is not in the initial query, its weight in the final query is the same as the weight assigned in the term selection process, which is 0.5. The weights for the initial query terms that are not in the list of selected terms remain unchanged. Table 2 presents an example to illustrate how

Table 2. Query expansion

Initial Query	Selected Terms	Expanded Query
t_1 (1.0)		t_1 (1.0)
t_2 (2.0)	t_2 (2*0.5)	t_2 (3.0)
t_3 (1.0)	t_3 (1*0.5)	t_3 (1.5)
	t_4 (0.5)	t_4 (0.5)

the expanded query is created from the initial query and the selected terms. The numbers in parentheses are term weights. For example, the weight for term t_3 in the expanded query is 3.0, since it is in the initial query with a weight value of 2.0 and it is one of the selected terms assigned the weight of 2*0.5.

Three minor changes are made to the blind relevance feedback procedure described above. First, a constant of 0.5 is added to every item in the formula used to compute the weight. Second, the selected terms must occur in at least 3 of the top-ranked m documents that are presumed relevant. Third, the top-ranked two documents in the initial search remain as the top-ranked two documents in the final search. That is, the final search does not affect the ranking of the first two documents in the initial search. The rationale for not changing the top-ranked few documents is that when a query has only a few relevant documents in the entire collection and if they are not ranked in the top in the initial search, it is unlikely these few relevant documents would rise to the top in the second search since most of the documents that are presumed relevant are actually irrelevant. On the other hand, if these few relevant documents are ranked in the top in the initial search, after expansion, they are likely to be ranked lower in the final search for the same reason. We believe a good strategy is to not change the ranking of the top few documents. In our implementation, we chose not to change the ranks of the top two documents in the final search.

Note that in computing the relevance probability of a document with respect to a query in the initial search, ql is the number of terms in the initial query, and qtf_t is the number of times that term t occurs in the initial query. After query expansion, qtf_t is no longer the raw term frequency in the initial query, instead it is now the weight of term t in the expanded query, and ql is the sum of the weight values of all the terms in the expanded query. For the example presented in Table 2, qtf_{t_3} is 1.5, and ql is 6.0 (i.e., $1.0 + 3.0 + 1.5 + 0.5$). The relevance clues related to documents and the collection are the same in computing relevance probability using the expanded query as in computing relevance probability using the initial query. For all the experiments reported below, we selected the top 10 terms ranked by w_t from 10 top-ranked documents in the initial search.

The number of selected terms is approximately twice the average number of unique terms in the original topics. Adding too many terms may decrease the importance of the original query terms since the relative frequencies of the original query terms decrease as the expanded query gets longer.

4 Decompounding

Compounds are words formed by joining two or more short words. For English, one way to create a compound word is to join two or more short words directly together. Another way is to join two or more short words together with hyphens separating them, such as *second-guess*. Compounds occur in natural language texts, frequently in some languages such as German, but less so in others such as English. It is not difficult to find two-word compounds in English texts. Some examples are *breathtaking*, *birthday*, *brainstorm*, *fingerprint*, *greenhouse*, *land-*

mark, *spokeswoman*, *sunrise*, *tiptoe*, and *whereabouts*. However, English compounds of three or more words are much less common. In English, the long compounds are formed by joining words together with hyphens separating the component words, such as *former-astronaut-turned-senator* and *in-between-age-children*. In German texts, unlike English, compound words are common. Most German compounds are formed by directly joining two or more words. Such examples are *Computerviren* (computer viruses), which is the concatenation of *Computer* and *Viren*, and *Sonnenenergie* (solar energy), which is formed by joining *sonnen* and *Energie* together. Sometimes a *linking element* such as *s* or *e* is inserted between two words. For example, the compound *Schönheitskönigin* (beauty queen) is derived from *Schönheit* and *königin* with *s* inserted between them. There are also cases where compounds are formed with the final letter *e* of the first word elided. For example, the compound *Erdbeben* (earthquake) is derived from *Erde* (earth) and *Beben* (trembling). When the word *Erde* is combined with the word *Atmoshpäre* to create a compound, the compound is not *Erdeatmoshpäre*, but *Erdatmoshpäre*. The final letter *e* of the word *Erde* is elided from the compound. We refer readers to, for example, [4] for discussions of German compounds formations.

Chen [1] presents a procedure for splitting German compounds. It first finds all possible ways to break up a German compound into short words with respect to a base dictionary consisting of German words that are not compounds. Then the decomposition that has resulted in the smallest number of component words is chosen to split the compound if there is only one decomposition with the smallest number of component words, otherwise the decomposition that has the highest decomposition probability is chosen. The probability of a decomposition is estimated as the product of the relative frequencies in a German collection of the component words generated from the decomposition. The relative frequency of a word is the ratio of the number of times that the word occurs in a collection over the collection length. Readers are referred to [1] for more details. We will present two examples to demonstrate the decompounding process. For example, when the German base dictionary contains *ball, europa, fuss, fussball, meisterschaft* and others, the German compound *fussballeuropameisterschaft* (European Football Cup) can be decomposed into component words with respect to the base dictionary in two different ways as shown in the table below.

	Decompositions of *fussballeuropameisterschaft*			
1	fuss	ball	europa	meisterschaft
2	fussball	europa	meisterschaft	

The second decomposition has the smallest number of component words, so the German compound *fussballeuropameisterschaft* is split into *fussball*, *europa* and *meisterschaft*. The following table presents another example which shows the decompositions of the German compound *wintersports* (winter sports) with respect to a base dictionary containing *port, ports, s, sport, sports, winter, winters* and other words.

	Decompositions of *wintersports*			log p(D)
1	winter	s	ports	-43.7002
2	winter	sports		-20.0786
3	winters	ports		-28.3584

The compound *wintersports* has three decompositions with respect to the base dictionary. If we ignore the linking element *s*, all three decompositions have two component words, the rule of selecting the decomposition with the smallest number of component words cannot be applied here. We have to compute the probability of decomposition for all the decompositions with the smallest number of component words. The last column in the table shows the log of the decomposition probabilities for all three decompositions that were computed using relative frequencies of the components words in the German test collection. According to the rule of selecting the decomposition of the highest probability, the second decomposition should be chosen as the decomposition of the compound *wintersports.* That is, the compound *wintersports* should be split into *winter* and *sports.* In our implementation, we considered only the case where a compound is the concatenation of component words, and the case where the linking element *s* is present.

It is not always desirable to split up German compounds into their component words. Consider again the compound *Erdbeben.* In this case, it is probably better not to split up the compound. But in other cases like *Gemüseexporteure* (vegetable exporters), *Fußballweltmeisterschaft* (World Soccer Championship), splitting up the compounds probably is desirable since the use of the component words might retrieval additional relevant documents which are otherwise likely to be missed if only the compounds are used. In fact, we noticed that the compound *Gemüseexporteure* does not occur in the CLEF 2002 German document collection.

In general, it is conceivable that breaking up compounds is helpful. The same phrase may be spelled out in words sometimes, but as one compound other times. When a user formulates a German query, the user may not know if a phrase should appear as multi-word phrase or as one compound. An example is the German equivalent of the English phrase "European Football Cup", in the *title* field of topic 113, the German equivalent is spelled as one compound *Fussballeuropameisterschaft*, but in the *description* field, it is *Europameisterschaft im Fußball*, yet in the *narrative* field, it is *Fußballeuropameisterschaft.* This example brings out two points in indexing German texts. First, it should be helpful to split compounds into component words. Second, normalizing the spellings of ss and ß should be helpful. Two more such examples are *Scheidungsstatistiken* (divorce statistics) and *Präsidentschaftskandidaten* (presidential candidates). The German equivalent of "divorce statistics" is *Scheidungsstatistiken* in the *title* field of topic 115, but *Statistiken über die Scheidungsraten* in the *description* field. The German equivalent of "presidential candidates" is *Präsidentschaftskandidaten* in *title* field of topic 135, but *Kandidat für das Präsidentenamt* in the *description* field of the same topic. The German equivalent for "Nobel prize winner for literature" is *Literaturnobelpreisträger.* In the "Der Spiegel" German collection, we find variants of *Literatur-Nobelpreisträger*, *Literaturnobelpreis-Trägerin*. *Literaturnobelpreis* (Nobel prize for literature) sometimes appears as "Nobelpreis für Literatur". One more reason why decompounding is desirable is that when an English phrase is translated into German, the German translation may be a compound, but it could also be a multi-word phrase. For example, when the English phrase "Latin America" was translated into German using Babelfish, its German translation was *lateinischem Amerika*. However, the more common form is the compound *Lateinamerika*. In translating German into English, one may see cases where the German compounds cannot be translated, yet the component words can be translated separately. For example, the German compound *Bronchialasthma* (bronchial asthma) was not translated into English, however the component words were.

5 Test Collection

The document collection for the multilingual retrieval task consists of documents in five languages: English, French, German, Italian, and Spanish. The collection has about 750,000 documents, newspaper articles published mainly in 1994. A set of 50 topics, numbered 91 through 140, was developed and released in more than 10 languages, including English, French, and German. A topic has three parts: *title*, *description*, and *narrative*. Readers are referred to [2] for details on the document collections, topics, tracks and tasks, and evaluations of CLEF 2002.

6 Indexing

Indexing of the texts in our system consists of seven steps: *pre-processing*, *tokenization*, *normalization*, *stopwords removal*, *decompounding*, *stemming*, and *post normalization*. The seven steps are sequentially carried out in the order as presented above. However, not all seven steps are executed in indexing. Some of the steps are optional. For example, pre-processing is only applied to Italian texts to restore the accents from the source Italian texts, and decompounding is applied only to German and Dutch to split German and Dutch compounds into their component words. The indexing procedure is designed to work directly on the source documents. Both topics and documents are indexed in the same way.

The valid character set includes 0 1 2 3 4 5 6 7 8 9 A B C D E F G H I J K L M N O P Q R S T U V W X Y Z a b c d e f g h i j k l m n o p q r s t u v w x y z À Á Â Ã Ä Å Æ Ç È É Ê Ë Ì Í Î Ï Ñ Ò Ó Ô Õ Ö Ø Ù Ú Û Ü Ý ß à á â ã ä å æ ç è é ê ë ì í î ï ñ ò ó ô ö ø ù ú û ü ý ÿ, and the characters with hexadecimal codes of 0xD0, 0xDE, 0xF0, and 0xFE. Characters that are not in the valid character set are treated as word delimiters. A token can contain only valid characters. The source texts are broken into tokens in the tokenization process. The *normalization* step changes upper-case letters into lower case, including the upper-case letters with diacritic marks. Stopwords in both documents and topics are removed from indexing. We have two stoplists for each of the five languages, one for indexing documents and the other for indexing topics. The stoplist for topics contains all the stopwords for documents and some additional stopwords such as *relevant* and *document*. For German and Dutch, compounds are replaced by their component words in both documents and topics. Only the component words are indexed. The Muscat stemmer is applied to the remaining words. The Muscat stemmer set includes stemmers for Dutch, English, French, German, Italian, Spanish, and others. The last step in indexing removes the diacritic marks. The diacritic marks are not removed in the *normalization* step because the stemmers may depend on the diacritic marks.

7 Experimental Results

All retrieval runs reported in this paper used only the *title* and *description* fields in the topics. The ids and average precision values of the official runs are presented in bold face, other runs are unofficial runs.

7.1 Monolingual Retrieval Experiments

In this section we present the results of monolingual retrieval. For automatic query expansion, the top-ranked 10 terms from the top-ranked 10 documents after the initial search were combined with the original query to create the expanded query. For Dutch and German monolingual runs, the compounds were split into their component words, and only their component words were retained in document and topic indexing. All the monolingual runs included automatic query expansion via the relevance feedback procedure described in section 3. Table 3 presents the monolingual retrieval results for six document languages. The last column labeled *change* shows the improvement of average precision with blind relevance feedback compared with not using it. As Table 3 shows, query expansion increased the average precision of the monolingual runs for all six languages, the improvement ranging from 6.42% for Spanish to 19.42% for French.

The third column in Table 3 gives the number of topics with at least one relevant document in the document collection for that language. The average

Table 3. Monolingual IR performance. The *title* and *description* fields in the topics were indexed

			without expansion		with expansion		
run id	language	No. topics	recall	precision	recall	precision	change
bky2moen	English	42	765/821	0.5084	793/821	0.5602	10.19%
bky2monl	Dutch	50	1633/1862	0.4446	1734/1862	**0.4847**	9.02%
bky2mofr	French	50	1277/1383	0.4347	1354/1383	**0.5191**	19.42%
bky2mode	German	50	1696/1938	0.4393	1807/1938	**0.5234**	19.14%
bky2moit	Italian	49	994/1072	0.4169	1024/1072	**0.4750**	13.94%
bky2moes	Spanish	50	2531/2854	0.5016	2673/2854	**0.5338**	6.42%

Table 4. German monolingual retrieval performance. The *title* and *description* fields in the topics were indexed. The total number of German relevant documents for 50 topics is 1938

	1	2	3	4	5	6	7	8
features	none	decomp	stem	expan	decomp+ stem	decomp+ expan	stem+ expan	decomp+ stem+ expan
avg prec	0.3462	0.3859	0.3633	0.4145	0.4393	0.4517	0.4393	**0.5234**
change	baseline	+11.47%	+4.94%	+19.73%	+26.89%	+30.47%	+26.89%	+51.18%
recall	1359	1577	1500	1575	1696	1752	1702	1807

precision and overall recall were computed using the topics having at least one relevant document. There are no relevant Italian documents for topic 120, and no relevant English documents for topics 93, 96, 101, 110, 117, 118, 127 and 132.

Table 4 presents the performance of German monolingual retrieval with three different features which are decompounding, stemming, and query expansion. These features are implemented in that order. For example, when decompounding and stemming are present, the compounds are split into component words first, then the components are stemmed. Stopwords were removed for all runs. When only stopwords were removed, the average precision is 0.3462, which is considered as the baseline performance for the purpose of comparison. The table shows that when any one of the three features is present, the average precision increases from 4.94% to 19.73% over the baseline performance when none of the features is present. When two of the three features are included in retrieval, the improvement in precision ranges from 26.89% to 30.47%. And when all three features are present, the average precision is 51.18% better than the baseline performance. It is interesting to see that the three features are complementary. That is, the improvement brought by each individual feature is not diminished by the presence of the other two features. Without decompounding, stemming alone improved the average precision by 4.94%. However with decompounding, stemming improved the average precision from 0.3859 to 0.4393, an increase of 13.84%. Stemming became more effective because of decompounding. Decompounding alone improved the average precision by 11.47% for German monolingual retrieval.

Table 5 presents some of the German words in the *title* or *desc* fields of the topics that were split into component words. The column labeled *component words* shows the component words of the decomposed compounds. The German word *eurofighter* was split into *euro* and *fighter* since both component words are in the base dictionary, and the word *eurofighter* is not. Including the word *eurofigher* in thc basc dictionary will prevent it from being split into component words. Two topic words, *lateinamerika* (Latin America) and *zivilbevölkerung* (civil population), were not split into component words because both are present in our base dictionary which is far from perfect. For the same

Table 5. Some of the German words in the *title* or *desc* fields of the topics that were split into component words

	compounds	component words		
1	autoindustrie	auto	industrie	
2	bronchialasthma	bronchial	asthma	
3	eurofighter	euro	fighter	
4	europameisterschaft	europa	meisterschaft	
5	goldmedaille	gold	medaille	
6	interessenkonflikts	interessen	konflikts	
7	mobiltelefone	mobil	telefone	
8	präsidentschaftskandidaten	präsidentschafts	kandidaten	
9	literaturnobelpreisträgers	literatur	nobel	preisträgers
10	schönheitswettbewerbe	schönheit	s	wettbewerbe

reason, *preisträgers* was not decomposed into *preis* and *trägers*. An ideal base dictionary should contain all and only the words that should not be further split into smaller component words. Our current decompounding procedure does not split words in the base dictionary into smaller component words. The topic word *südjemen* was not split into *süd* and *jemen* because our base dictionary does not contain words that are three-letters long or shorter. The majority of the errors in decompounding are caused by the incompleteness of the base dictionary or the presence of compound words in the base dictionary. Our current German base dictionary has 762,342 words, some of which are non-German words and some German compounds that should be excluded. It would take a major manual effort to clean up the base dictionary so that it contains only the German words that should not be further decomposed.

We reported a slight decrease in German monolingual performance with German decompounding [1] at CLEF 2001. The slight decline in performance may be attributed to the fact that we kept both the original compounds and the component words resulted from decompounding in the topic index. When we re-ran the same German monolingual retrieval with only the component words of compounds in the topics retained, the average precision was improved by 8.88% with decompounding compared with without it. Further improvements in performance obtained with German decompounding are reported in [1] when a slightly different method was used to compute the relative frequencies of component words. The improved decompounding procedure was used to split German compounds for our CLEF 2002 retrieval experiments.

A Dutch stoplist of 1326 words [15] was used for Dutch monolingual retrieval. After removing stopwords, the Dutch words were stemmed using the muscat Dutch stemmer. For Dutch decompounding, we used a Dutch wordlist of 223,557 words [16]. From this wordlist we created a Dutch base dictionary of 210,639 words by manually breaking up the long words that appear to be compounds. It appears that many Dutch compound words still remain in the base dictionary.

Table 6. Dutch monolingual retrieval performance on CLEF 2002 test set. The *title* and *description* fields in the topics were indexed. The total number of Dutch relevant documents for the 50 topics of CLEF 2002 is 1862

	1	2	3	4	5	6	7	8
features	none	decomp	stem	expan	decomp+ stem	decomp+ expan	stem+ expan	decomp+ stem+ expan
avg prec	0.4021	0.4186	0.4281	0.4669	0.4446	0.4721	0.4770	**0.4847**
change	baseline	+4.10%	+6.47%	+16.12%	+10.57%	+17.41%	+18.63	+20.54%
recall	1562	1623	1584	1614	1633	1727	1702	1734

Like the German base dictionary, an ideal Dutch base dictionary should include all and only the words that should not be further decomposed. Like German decompounding, the words in the Dutch base dictionary are not decomposed. When a compound was split into component words, only the component words were retained in both document and topic indexing.

Table 6 presents the performance of Dutch monolingual retrieval under various conditions. With no stemming and expansion, Dutch decompounding improved the average precision by 4.10%. Together, the three features improved the average precision by 20.54% over the baseline performance when none of the features was implemented and only stopwords were removed.

For comparison, Table 7 presents the Dutch monolingual performance on the CLEF 2001 test set. Decompounding alone improved the average precision by 13.49%. Topic 88 of CLEF 2001 is about *mad cow diseases in Europe.* The Dutch equivalent of *mad cow diseases* is *gekkekoeienziekte* in the topic, but it never occurs in the Dutch collection. Without decompounding, the precision for this topic was 0.1625, and with decompounding, the precision increased to 0.3216. The precision for topic 90 which is about *vegetable exporters* was 0.0128 without decompounding. This topic contains two compound words, *Groenten-exporteurs* and *diepvriesgroenten.* The former one which is perhaps the most

Table 7. Dutch monolingual retrieval performance on CLEF 2001 test set. The *title* and *description* fields in the topics were indexed. The total number of Dutch relevant documents for the 50 topics of CLEF 2001 is 1224

	1	2	3	4	5	6	7	8
features	none	decomp	stem	expan	decomp+ stem	decomp+ expan	stem+ expan	decomp+ stem+ expan
avg prec	0.3239	0.3676	0.3587	0.3471	0.4165	0.3822	0.3887	0.4372
change	baseline	+13.49%	+10.74%	+7.16%	+28.59%	+18.00%	+20.01%	+34.98%

important term for this topic never occurs in the Dutch document collection. After decompounding, the precision for this topic increased to 0.3443. Topic 55 contains two important compound words, *Alpenverkeersplan* and *Alpeninitiatief*. Neither occur in the Dutch document collection. The precision for this topic was 0.0746 without decompounding, and increased to 0.2137 after decompounding.

7.2 Bilingual Retrieval Experiments

A major factor affecting the end performance of both bilingual retrieval and multilingual retrieval is the quality of translation resources. In this section, we evaluate the effectiveness of three different translation resources: automatic machine translation systems, parallel corpora, and bilingual dictionaries. Two of the issues in translating topics are 1) determining the number of translations to retain when multiple candidate translations are available; and 2) assigning weights to the selected translations [6]. When machine translation systems are used to translate topics, these two issues are resolved automatically by the machine translation systems, since they provide only one translation for each word. However, when bilingual dictionaries or parallel corpora are used to translate topics, often for a source word, there may be several alternative translations.

CLIR Using MT. In this section, we evaluate two machine translation systems, the online Babelfish translation [17] and the L&H Power Translator Pro, version 7.0, for topic translation in bilingual retrieval. We used both translators to translate the 50 English topics into French, German, Italian, and Spanish. For each language, both sets of translations were preprocessed in the same way.

Table 8 presents the bilingual retrieval performances for all the official runs and some additional runs. The ids and average precision values for the official runs are in bold face. The last column in Table 8 shows the improvement of average precision with query expansion compared with not using it. When both L&H Translator and Babelfish were used in bilingual retrieval from English to French, German, Italian and Spanish, the translation from L&H Translator and the translation from Babelfish were combined by topic. The term frequencies in the combined topics were reduced by half so that the combined topics were comparable in length to the source English topics. Then the combined translations were used to search against the document collection for relevant documents as in monolingual retrieval. For example, for the English-to-Italian run *bky2bienit*, we first translated the source English topics into Italian using L&H Translator and Babelfish. The Italian translations produced by L&H Translator and the Italian translations produced by Babelfish were combined by topic. Then the combined, translated Italian topics with term frequencies reduced by half were used to search the Italian document collections. The *bky2bienfr*, *bky2biende*, *bky2bienes* bilingual runs from English were all produced in the same way as the *bky2bienit* run. For English or French to German bilingual retrieval runs, the words in the *title* or *desc* fields of the translated German topics were decompounded. For all bilingual runs, words were stemmed after removing stopwords as for monolingual

Table 10. English to French word translation probabilities estimated from parallel corpora using a statistical machine translation toolkit

	English	French translations	Translation probability
1	asthma	asthme	0.902453
		asthma	0.053307
		atteindre	0.044240
2	car	voiturer	0.251941
		automobile	0.214175
		voiture	0.160644
3	fall	automne	0.323739
		tomber	0.081521
		relever	0.064848
4	lead	mener	0.128457
		conduire	0.076652
		amener	0.066278
5	race	race	0.598102
		courser	0.182982
		racial	0.053363
6	rock	rock	0.889616
		rocher	0.015060
		pierre	0.010083
7	star	star	0.624963
		étoile	0.130342
		étoiler	0.077801

the average length ratio. After the preprocessing, only 706,210 pairs of aligned sentences remained. The remaining aligned sentence pairs were fed to GIZA++, a statistical machine translation toolkit [9], for estimating English-to-French word translation probabilities.

Table 10 shows the first three French translations produced by GIZA++ for some of the words in the English topics. In translating an English word into French, we selected only one French word, the one with the highest translation probability, as the translation. The English topics were translated into French word-by-word, then the translated French topics were used to produce the English-to-French run labeld *bky2bienfr5* in Table 8. Without query expansion, the parallel corpus-based English-French CLIR performance was slightly better than when using Babelfish, but slightly lower than when using L&H translator.

The CLEF 2002 English topics contain a number of polysemous words such as *fall*, *interest*, *lead*, *race*, *rock*, *star*, and the like. The word *fall* in the context of *fall in sale of cars* in topic 106 has the meaning of declining. However, the most likely French translation for *fall* as Table 10 shows is *automne*, meaning *autumn* in English. The word *race* in *ski race* in topic 102 or in *race car* in topic 121 has the meaning of contest or competition in speed. Again the French word with the highest translation probability is *race*, meaning human race in

English. The correct French translation for the sense of *race* in *ski race* or *car race* should be *course*. The word *star* in topic 129 means a plant or celestial body, while in topic 123 in the context of *pop star*, it means a famous performer. The correct translation for *star* in topic 129 should be *étoile*, instead of the most likely translation *star*. The word *rock* in topic 130 has the same sense as *rock* in *rock music*, not the sense of *stone*. In the same topic, the word *lead* in *lead singer* means someone in the leading role, not the metal. These examples show that taking the French word with the highest translation probability as the translation for an English word is an overly simplified solution. Choosing the right French translations would require word sense disambiguation.

CLIR Using Bilingual Dictionary. For the only English-to-Dutch run, labeled *bky2biennl*, the English topics were translated into Dutch by looking up each English topic word, excluding stopwords, in an online English-Dutch dictionary [19]. All the Dutch words in the dictionary lookup results were retained except for Dutch stopwords. The Dutch compound words were split into component words. If translating an English topic word resulted in m Dutch words, then all translated Dutch words of the English word received the same weight $\frac{1}{m}$, i.e., the translated Dutch words were weighted uniformly. The average precision of the English-to-Dutch run is 0.3199, which is much lower than 0.4847 for Dutch monolingual retrieval.

7.3 Multilingual Retrieval Experiments

In this section, we describe our multilingual retrieval experiments using the English topics (only *title* and *description* fields were indexed). As mentioned in the bilingual experiments section above, we translated the English topics into the other four document languages which are French, German, Italian, and Spanish using Babelfish and L&H Translator. A separate index was created for each of the five document languages. For the multilingual retrieval runs, we merged five ranked lists of documents, one resulting from English monolingual retrieval and four resulting from bilingual retrieval from English to the other four document languages, to produce a unified ranked list of documents regardless of language.

A fundamental difference between merging in monolingual retrieval or bilingual retrieval and merging in multilingual retrieval is that in monolingual or bilingual retrieval, the documents for individual ranked lists are from the same collection, while in multilingual retrieval, the documents for individual ranked lists are from different collections. For monolingual or bilingual retrieval, if we assume that the documents appearing on more than one ranked list are more likely to be relevant than the ones appearing on a single ranked list, then we should rank the documents appearing on multiple ranked lists in higher position in the merged ranked list of documents. A simple way to accomplish this is to sum the relevance scores of the documents appearing on multiple ranked lists while the relevance scores of the documents appearing on a single list remain the same. After summing up the relevance scores, the documents are re-ranked in descending order by combined relevance scores. In multilingual retrieval merging,

Table 11. Multilingual retrieval performances with two merging strategies

run id	topic language	topic fields	merging strategy	recall	precision
bky2muen1	English	title,desc	raw-score	5880/8068	**0.3762**
bky2muen2	English	title,desc	normalized-score	5765/8068	**0.3570**

since the documents on the individual ranked lists are all different, we cannot use multiple appearances of a document in the ranked lists as evidence to promote its rank in the final ranked list.

There are a few simple ways to merge ranked lists of documents from different collections. Here we will evaluate two of them. The first method is to combine all ranked lists, sort the combined list by the raw relevance score, then take the top 1000 documents per topic. The second method is to normalize the relevance score for each topic, dividing all relevance scores by the relevance score of the top most ranked document for the same topic.

Table 11 presents the multilingual retrieval performances with two merging strategies. The multilingual runs were produced by merging five runs: bky2moen, bky2bienfr, bky2biende, bky2bienit, and bky2bienes. The bky2moen is an English monolingual run, bky2bienfr an English to French bilingual run, bky2biende an English to German bilingual run, bky2bienit an English to Italian bilingual run, and bky2bienes an English to Spanish bilingual run. The run bky2muen1 was produced by ranking the documents by the unnormalized relevance probabilities after combining the individual runs. And the run bky2muen2 was produced in the same way except that the relevance probabilities were normalized before merging. For each topic, the relevance probabilities of the documents was divided by the relevance probability of the highest-ranked document for the same topic. The simplest raw-score merging outperformed the normalized-score merging strategy. We did two things to make the relevance probabilities of documents from different language collections comparable to each other. First, as mentioned in Section 7.2, after concatenating the topic translations from two translators, we reduced the term frequencies by half so that the translated topics are close to the source English topics in length. Second, in query expansion, we took the same number of terms (i.e, 10) from the same number of top-ranked documents (i.e, 10) after the initial search for all five individual runs that were used to produce the multilingual runs.

8 Conclusions

We have presented a technique for incorporating blind relevance feedback into a document ranking formula based on logistic regression analysis. The improvement in average precision brought by query expansion via blind relevance feedback ranges from 6.42% to 19.42% for monolingual retrieval runs, and from 10.85% to 29.36% for bilingual retrieval runs. German decompounding improved the average precision of German monolingual retrieval by 11.47%. Decompounding also increased the average precision for bilingual retrieval to German from English or French. The increase ranges from 8.4% to 11.46%. For Dutch monolingual retrieval, decompounding increased the average precision by 4.10%, which is much lower than the improvement of 13.49% on the CLEF 2001 test set. In summary, both blind relevance feedback and decompounding in German or Dutch have been shown to be effective in monolingual and bilingual retrieval. The amount of improvement in performance by decompounding varies from one set of topics to another. Three different translation resources, machine translators, parallel corpora, and bilingual dictionaries, were evaluated on bilingual retrieval. We found that the English-French CLIR performance using parallel corpora was competitive with that using commercial machine translators. Two different merging strategies in multilingual retrieval were evaluated. The simplest strategy of merging individual ranked lists of documents by unnormalized relevance score worked better than the one where the relevance score was first normalized. To make the relevance scores of the documents from different collections as closely comparable as possible, we selected the same number of terms from the same number of top-ranked documents after the initial search for query expansion in all the runs that were combined to produce the unified ranked lists of documents in multiple languages. We used two machine translators to translate English topics to French, German, Italian and Spanish, and combined by topic the translations from the two translators. We reduced the term frequencies in the combined translated topics by half so that the combined translated topics are close in length to the source English topics.

Acknowledgments

We would like to thank Vivien Petras for improving the German base dictionary. This research was supported by DARPA under research grant N66001-00-1-8911 (PI: Michael Buckland) as part of the DARPA Translingual Information Detection, Extraction, and Summarization Program (TIDES).

References

[1] Chen, A.: Multilingual Information Retrieval Using English and Chinese Queries. In: Peters, C. et al. (eds.): Evaluation of Cross-Language Information Retrieval Systems. Lecture Notes in Computer Science, Vol. 2406. Springer-Verlag, Berlin Heidelberg New York (2002) 44–58.

[2] Braschler, M., Peters, C.: CLEF 2002: Methodology and Metrics. In: this volume.

[3] Cooper, W. S., Chen, A., Gey. F. C.: Full Text Retrieval based on Probabilistic Equations with Coefficients fitted by Logistic Regression. In: Harman, D. K. (ed.): The Second Text REtrieval Conference (TREC-2) (1994) 57–64.

[4] Fox, A.: The Structure of German. Clarendon Press, Oxford (1990).

[5] Gale, W. A., Church, K. W.: A Program for Aligning Sentences in Bilingual Corpora. Computational linguistics. **19** (1993) 75–102.

[6] Grefenstette, G. (ed.): Cross-language information retrieval. Kluwer Academic Publishers, Boston, MA (1998).
[7] Harman, D.: Relevance Feedback and Other Query Modification Techniques. In: Frakes, W., Baeza-Yates. R (eds.): Information Retrieval: Data Structures & Algorithms. Prentice Hall (1992) 241–263.
[8] Karp, D., Schabes, Y., Zaidel, M., Egedi, D.: A Freely Available Wide Coverage Morphological Analyzer for English. Proceedings of COLING (1992).
[9] Och, F. J., Ney, H.: Improved Statistical Alignment Models. In: ACL-2000 (2000) 440–447.
[10] Peters, C. (ed.): Evaluation of Cross-Language Information Retrieval Systems. Lecture Notes in Computer Science, Vol. 2069. Springer-Verlag, Berlin Heidelberg New York (2001).
[11] Peters, C., Braschler, M., Gonzalo, J., Kluck, M. (eds.): Evaluation of Cross-Language Information Retrieval Systems. Lecture Notes in Computer Science, Vol. 2406. Springer-Verlag, Berlin Heidelberg New York (2002).
[12] Robertson, S. E., Sparck Jones, K.: Relevance Weighting of Search Terms. Journal of the American Society for Information Science (1976) 129–146.
[13] Voorhees, E. M., Harman, D. K. (eds.): The Seventh Text Retrieval Conference (TREC-7). NIST (1998).
[14] Voorhees, E. M., Harman, D. K. (eds.): The Eighth Text Retrieval Conference (TREC-8). NIST (1999).
[15] Source: http://clef.iei.pi.cnr.it:2002/.
[16] Source: ftp://archive.cs.ruu.nl/pub/UNIX/ispell/words.dutch.gz.
[17] Available at http://babelfish.altavista.com/.
[18] Source: http://www.parl.gc.ca/.
[19] Available at http://www.babylon.com.

ITC-irst at CLEF 2002: Using N-Best Query Translations for CLIR

Nicola Bertoldi and Marcello Federico

ITC-irst - Centro per la Ricerca Scientifica e Tecnologica
I-38050 Povo, Trento, Italy
{bertoldi,federico}@itc.it

Abstract. This paper reports on the participation of ITC-irst in the Italian monolingual retrieval track and in the bilingual English-Italian track of the Cross Language Evaluation Forum (CLEF) 2002. A cross-language information retrieval system is proposed which integrates retrieval and translation scores over the set of N-best translations of the source query. Retrieval scores result as a combination of a statistical language model and a standard Okapi model. Translations are computed by a hidden Markov model, which is trained on a bilingual dictionary and the target document collection.

1 Introduction

This paper reports on the participation of ITC-irst in two Information Retrieval (IR) tracks of the Cross Language Evaluation Forum (CLEF) 2002: the monolingual retrieval task, and the bilingual retrieval task. The language of the queries was Italian for the monolingual track and English for the bilingual track; Italian documents were searched in both tracks. With respect to the 2001 CLEF evaluation [4], the Cross Language IR (CLIR) system was improved in order to work with multiple translations of queries, and with source and target languages in the reverse order.

The basic IR engine, used for both evaluations, combines scores of a standard Okapi model and of a statistical language model. For CLIR, a light-weight statistical model for translating queries was developed, which also computes a list of N-best translations for each query. In this way, the basic IR engine is used to integrate retrieval and translation scores over multiple alternative translations [4]. Remarkably, training of the system only requires a bilingual dictionary and the target document collection.

This paper is organized as follows. Section 2 introduces the statistical approach to CLIR. Sections 3 to 7 describe, respectively, the query-document model, the query-translation model, the CLIR algorithm, and the modules for preprocessing and query expansion. Section 8 presents experimental results. Finally, Section 9 concludes the paper.

C.A. Peters (Ed.): CLEF 2002, LNCS 2785, pp. 49–58, 2003.

Table 1. List of often used symbols

$\mathbf{q}, \mathbf{f}, \mathbf{e}, d$	generic query, query in French, query in English, and document
q, f, e	generic term, term in French, and term in English
$\mathcal{D}$	collection of documents
$N(\mathbf{q}, q)$	frequency of term q in query $\mathbf{q}$

2 Statistical CLIR Approach

With respect to the ITC-irst CLIR system participating in CLEF 2001, the system of this year features a novel approach for integrating translation and retrieval.

From a statistical perspective, bilingual IR can be formulated as follows. Given a query $\mathbf{f}$, in the source language, e.g. French, one would like to measure the relevance of a documents d, in the target language, e.g. English, by a joint probability $\Pr(\mathbf{f}, d)$. To fill the language gap between query and documents, the hidden variable $\mathbf{e}$ is introduced, which represents a term-by-term translation of $\mathbf{f}$ in the target language. Hence, the following decomposition is derived:

$$\begin{aligned} \Pr(\mathbf{f}, d) &= \sum_{\mathbf{e}} \Pr(\mathbf{f}, \mathbf{e}, d) \\ &\approx \sum_{\mathbf{e}} \Pr(\mathbf{f}, \mathbf{e}) \Pr(d \mid \mathbf{e}) \\ &= \sum_{\mathbf{e}} \Pr(\mathbf{f}, \mathbf{e}) \frac{\Pr(\mathbf{e}, d)}{\sum_{d'} \Pr(\mathbf{e}, d')} \end{aligned} \tag{1}$$

(Main notation used in the following is summarized in Table 1.)

In deriving formula (1), one makes the assumption (or approximation) that the probability of document d given query $\mathbf{f}$ and translation $\mathbf{e}$, does not depend on $\mathbf{f}$. Formula (1) contains probabilities $\Pr(\mathbf{e}, d)$ and $\Pr(\mathbf{f}, \mathbf{e})$, which correspond, respectively, to the query-document and query-translation models, which will be briefly described in the next sections. In principle, the probability $\Pr(\mathbf{f}, d)$ is very expensive to compute; hence, an algorithm will be presented, which through suitable approximations, permits to efficiently compute formula (1).

3 Query-Document Model

A query-document model computes the joint probability of a query $\mathbf{e}$ and a document d written in the same language. Three query-document models were considered in the experiments. The first is based on a statistical language model (LM), the second is derived from the Okapi framework, the last is a combination of the first two.

3.1 Language Model

The relevance of a document d with respect to a query $\mathbf{q}$ can be expressed through a joint probability, which can be decomposed as follows:

$$\Pr(\mathbf{q}, d) = \Pr(\mathbf{q} \mid d) \Pr(d) \tag{2}$$

$\Pr(\mathbf{q} \mid d)$ represents the likelihood of $\mathbf{q}$ given d, and $\Pr(d)$ represents the a-priori probability of d. By assuming no a-priori knowledge about the documents and an order-free multinomial model for the likelihood, the following probability score is derived:

$$\Pr(\mathbf{q}, d) \propto \prod_{i=1}^{n} \Pr(q_i \mid d) \tag{3}$$

By taking the logarithm, we can define the following scoring function:

$$lm(\mathbf{q}, d) = \sum_{q \in \mathbf{q}} N(\mathbf{q}, q) \; \log \Pr(q \mid d) \tag{4}$$

The probability $\Pr(q \mid d)$ that a term q is generated by d can be estimated by applying statistical language modeling techniques [5]. As proposed in previous papers [8, 9], relative frequencies of each document are interpolated with those of the whole collection. In the ITC-irst system, interpolation weights are estimated according to the smoothing method proposed by [15].

3.2 Okapi Model

Okapi [13] is the name of a retrieval system project that developed a family of scoring functions in order to evaluate the relevance of a document d versus a query $\mathbf{q}$. In our IR system the following Okapi function was used:

$$okapi(\mathbf{q}, d) = \sum_{q \in \mathbf{q}} N(\mathbf{q}, q) \, W_d(q) \; \log W_{\mathcal{D}}(q) \tag{5}$$

Formula (5) weighs every word q in the query according to the number of its occurrences in $\mathbf{q}$, $N(\mathbf{q}, q)$, its relevance within a document, $W_d(q)$, and its relevance within the whole collection, $W_{\mathcal{D}}(q)$, which corresponds to the inverted document frequency.

The Okapi and the LM scoring functions present some analogy. In particular, formula (5) can be put in a probabilistic form which maintains the original ranking, thanks to the monotonicity of the exponential function. Hence, a joint probability distribution can be defined, which, disregarding a normalization constant factor, is:

$$\Pr(\mathbf{q}, d) \propto \prod_{i=1}^{n} W_{\mathcal{D}}(q_i)^{W_d(q_i)} \tag{6}$$

In the following, query-document relevance models will be indicated by the joint probability $\Pr(\mathbf{q}, d)$, regardless of the model used, unless differently specified.

3.3 Combined Model

Previous work [1] showed that Okapi and the statistical model rank documents almost independently. Hence, information about the relevant documents can be gained by integrating the scores of both methods. Combination of the two models is implemented by taking the sum of scores. Actually, in order to adjust scale differences, scores of each model are normalized in the range $[0, 1]$ before summation. The resulting query-document model was also applied to the monolingual IR track.

4 Query-Translation Model

The query-translation model [2] computes the probability of any query-translation pair. This probability is modeled by a hidden Markov model (HMM) [12], in which the observable part is the query $\mathbf{f}$ in the source language, e.g. French, and the hidden part is the corresponding query $\mathbf{e}$ in the target language, e.g. English. Hence, the joint probability of a pair $\mathbf{f}, \mathbf{e}$ can be decomposed as follows:

$$\Pr(\mathbf{f} = f_1, \ldots, f_n, \mathbf{e} = e_1, \ldots, e_n) = \prod_{k=1}^{n} \Pr(f_k \mid e_k) \Pr(e_k \mid e_{k-1}) \tag{7}$$

Formula (7) puts in evidence two different conditional probabilities: the term translation probabilities $p(f \mid e)$ and the target LM probabilities $p(e \mid e')$. The former are estimated from a bilingual dictionary. The latter are estimated on the target document collection, through an order-free bigram LM, which tries to compensate for different word positions induced by the source and target languages.

Given a query-translation model and a query $\mathbf{f}$, the most probable translation $\mathbf{e}^*$ can be computed through the well known Viterbi search algorithm [12]. Moreover, intermediate results of the Viterbi algorithm can be used by an A^* search algorithm [10] to efficiently compute the N most probable, or N-best, translations of $\mathbf{f}$ [4].

5 CLIR Algorithm

By looking at formula (1), one can notice that the computation of $\Pr(\mathbf{f}, d)$ is very expensive. In fact, the main summation in (1) is taken over the set of possible translations of $\mathbf{f}$. As terms of $\mathbf{f}$ may typically admit more than one translation, the size of this set can grow exponentially with the length of $\mathbf{f}$. For instance, the Italian-English dictionary used for our experiments returns on average 1.68 Italian words for each English entry. Hence, the number of possible translations for a 45 word long query is in the order of 10^{10}! Finally, the denominator in formula (1) requires summing over all documents in $\mathcal{D}$ and should be computed for every possible translation $\mathbf{e}$.

Two approximations are introduced in order to limit the set of possible translations and documents to be taken into account in formula (1). The first approximation redefines the query-translation probability by limiting its support set to just the N-best translations of $\mathbf{f}$. A second approximation permits to reduce the computational burden of the denominator in equation (1). Hence, the support set of the query-document model is limited to only documents which contain at least one term of the query. Thanks to this approximation, computation of the denominator in formula (1) can be performed by summing up the scores of just the documents accessed through the inverted file index. Detailed explanation of the resulting CLIR algorithm can be found in [4].

Briefly, given an input query $\mathbf{f}$, the N-best translations are computed first. Then, for each translation $\mathbf{e}$, the addenda in formula (1) are computed only for documents containing at least one term of $\mathbf{e}$. This requires one additional loop over the documents in order to compute the normalization term.

It is worth noticing that the cascade approach is a special case of the integrated approach, which corresponds to the 1-best translation case. The cascade method can be used to eliminate the normalization term in equation (1).

On the average, the 100-best translations are generated in about 1.0s and 1.1s for short and long queries, respectively. With respect to the retrieval phase, Table 2 shows that Okapi model is about 10% faster than LM. It can be also seen that the computation time is correlated with the number of different terms in the queries.

Experiments were performed on a Pentium III, 600MHz, 1Gb RAM. Moreover, computation time also depends on the size of inverted index: in particular, on the average number of documents spanned by each term. In our experiments, the index contained 274K terms, each linked to about 52 documents on the average.

Table 2. Computation time (in `sec`) for retrieving N-best translation alternatives

Topics	N-best	Average # of different terms	Model LM	Okapi
TD	1	7.6	2.1s	1.9s
TD	5	10.9	4.1s	3.6s
TD	10	13.1	5.8s	5.2s
TDN	1	17.7	6.8s	6.1s
TDN	5	21.0	10.2s	9.3s
TDN	10	22.9	14.5s	12.8s

6 Document/Query Preprocessing

Text preprocessing was applied on the target documents before indexing, and on the queries before retrieval. More specifically, the following preprocessing steps were carried out:

- *Tokenization* was performed on documents and queries to isolate words from punctuation marks, to recognize abbreviations and acronyms, correct possible word splits across lines, and discriminate between accents and quotation marks.
- *Base forms* were computed for Italian words by means of morphological analysis and POS tagging.
- *Stemming* was performed on English words using Porter's algorithm [11].
- *Stop-terms removal* was applied on the documents by removing terms on the basis either of their POS (if available) or their inverted document frequency [6].
- *Numbers* are not removed.
- *Proper names* in the query were recognized in order to improve coverage of the dictionary, and translated verbatim. However, for these words, there is no guarantee about the correctness of the translation.
- *Out-of-dictionary terms* which are not included in the translation dictionary and have not been recognized either as proper names or numbers were removed from the query.

7 Blind Relevance Feedback

After document ranking, Blind Relevance Feedback (BRF) can be applied. BRF is a well known technique that helps to improve retrieval performance. The basic idea is to perform retrieval in two steps. First, the documents matching the source query $\mathbf{e}$ are ranked, then the B best ranked documents are taken and the R most relevant terms in them are added to the query, and the retrieval phase is repeated. In the CLIR framework, R terms are added to each single translation of the N-best list and the retrieval algorithms is repeated once again.

In this work, new search terms are selected from the top ranked documents according to the Offer Weight proposed in [7]. In all the experiments performed the values $B = 5$ and $R = 15$ were used [1].

8 Experimental Evaluation

Four runs were submitted to CLEF 2002: one for the Italian monolingual track (`IRSTit1`) and 3 for the bilingual English-to-Italian track, using 1-best, 5-best, and 10-best translations (`IRSTen2it1`, `IRSTen2it2`, and `IRSTen2it3`), respectively. The tracks consisted of 49 topics, for a total of 1072 documents to be retrieved, inside a collection of 108,578 Italian newspaper articles from *La Stampa*

Table 3. Results of the official runs

Official Run	N-best	mAvPr
IRSTit1		.4920
IRSTen2it1	1	.3444
IRSTen2it2	5	.3531
IRSTen2it3	10	.3552

Table 4. Official results of the three best systems in all CLEF Italian monolingual tracks

	rank-1	rank-2	rank-3
2000	ITC-irst	Twente	Berkeley
	.4896	.4709	.4601
2001	Neuchatel	ITC-irst	Hummingbird
	.4865	.4642	.4555
2002	Fond. Bordoni	ITC-irst	Berkeley
	.5088	.4920	.4750

Table 5. Detailed results about monolingual track

Model	Topics		+BRF
LM	TD	.3862	.4656
Okapi	TD	.4058	.4703
Combined	TD	.4042	.4920
LM	TDN	.4453	.5271
Okapi	TDN	.4432	.5028
Combined	TDN	.4516	.5304

and *Swiss News Agency*, both of 1994 [3]. All runs used short topics, consisting of only title and description fields. Table 3 shows official results.

As in the previous editions, our monolingual system competed very well with the best performing systems, as shown in Table 4.

A more detailed analysis of results, reported in Table 5, confirmed that the combination of statistical LM approach and Okapi formula is quite effective. Moreover, it is worth noticing that statistical approach performs better when the number of content words in the query increases, i.e. with long topics and after query expansion.

With respect to previous evaluations, this year's bilingual track required performing translation in the reverse order, i.e. from English to Italian. An Italian-English commercial dictionary, containing about 34K English terms and giving about 1.68 alternatives Italian alternatives per entry, was used for query translation.

Table 6. Results with different query translations on English-Italian bilingual IR. All 140 topics provided in the three editions of CLEF were used

Topics	Translation		
	Systran	1-best	human
TD	.3720	.3854	.4811
TDN	.4052	.4395	.5196

By comparing official results obtained by the system with a different number of translations and reported in Table 3, it seems that on the average using more than one translation slightly improves performance. However, these results are not sufficiently consistent to draw any conclusions.

A degradation in `mAvPr` by 13.7% absolute was observed between `IRSTit1` and `IRSTen2it3` runs. This difference is somewhat higher than that observed in Italian-English evaluation of last year [4]. [1]

With respect to the other five groups participating in the English-Italian bilingual track at CLEF, our system ranked 4, but it was the best among those which did not use commercial translation systems.

Further comparative evaluations were then carried out which only focus on the query-translation model. CLIR experiments were performed with translations computed by our statistical model, by a commercial text translation system, and by a human. In the second case, the Babelfish translation service,[2] powered by Systran, was used. As Systran is supposed to work with fluent text, the preprocessing and translation steps were inverted for this second case. In the third case, original Italian versions of the topics were used as provided by CLEF. All 140 topics provided in the three editions of CLEF were used.

Given all the translations, the CLIR algorithm for the 1-best case was applied, for the sake of a better comparison. Results reported in Table 6 show that, on the average, the statistical query-translation method outperforms the Systran translation system over the whole set of CLEF queries. Nevertheless, given the high variations in performance on single query sets, differences cannot be statistically assessed.

9 Conclusion

This paper reported on the participation of ITC-irst in the Italian monolingual retrieval track and in the bilingual English-Italian track of the Cross Language Evaluation Forum (CLEF) 2002. Our CLIR system was improved, with respect to last year, by tightly coupling retrieval and translation models. Moreover, the issue of inverting source and target languages was tackled. Thanks to our

[1] Results in [4] significantly improved those reported in [2], after a software error was fixed.

[2] Available at http://world.altavista.com.

statistical approach, the new system was set up quickly, and no specific problems arose.

Comparative experiments showed that, for the sake of IR, our statistical translation model, which is quite simple to implement, does not perform worse than a state-of-the-art commercial translation engine that has been developed over several decades. In the monolingual track, our retrieval system proved again to be very effective, and ranked very close to the best system.

Future work will be devoted to investigating possible weaknesses in the pre-processing phase, and to improving the statistical translation model.

Acknowledgements

This work was carried out within the project WebFAQ funded under the FDR-PAT program of the Province of Trento.

References

[1] N. Bertoldi and M. Federico. ITC-irst at CLEF 2000: Italian monolingual track. In C. Peters, editor, *Cross-Language Information Retrieval and Evaluation*, LNCS 2069, pages 261–272, Heidelberg, Germany, 2001. Springer Verlag.

[2] N. Bertoldi and M. Federico. ITC-irst at CLEF 2001: Monolingual and bilingual tracks. In C. Peters, M. Braschler, J. Gonzalo, and M. Kluck, editors, *Cross-Language Information Retrieval and Evaluation*, LNCS 2406, pages 94–101, Heidelberg, Germany, 2002. Springer Verlag.

[3] M. Braschler and C. Peters. CLEF2002: Methodology and Metrics. This volume.

[4] M. Federico and N. Bertoldi. Statistical cross-language information retrieval using n-best query translations. In *Proc. of the 25th ACM SIGIR*, pages 167–174, Tampere, Finland, 2002.

[5] M. Federico and R. D. Mori. Language modelling. In R. D. Mori, editor, *Spoken Dialogues with Computers*, chapter 7. Academy Press, London, UK, 1998.

[6] W. B. Frakes and R. Baeza-Yates, editors. *Information Retrieval: Data Structures and Algorithms*. Prenctice Hall, Englewood Cliffs, NJ, 1992.

[7] S. Johnson, P. Jourlin, K. S. Jones, and P. Woodland. Spoken document retrieval for TREC-8 at Cambridge University. In *Proceedings of the 8th Text REtrieval Conference*, Gaithersburg, MD, 1999.

[8] D. R. H. Miller, T. Leek, and R. M. Schwartz. BBN at TREC-7: Using hidden Markov models for information retrieval. In *Proc. of the 7th Text REtrieval Conference*, pages 133–142, Gaithersburg, MD, 1998.

[9] K. Ng. A maximum likelihood ratio information retrieval model. In *Proceedings of the 8th Text REtrieval Conference*, Gaithersburg, MD, 1999.

[10] N. J. Nilsson. *Principles of Artificial Intelligence*. Springer Verlag, Berlin, Germany, 1982.

[11] M. F. Porter. An algorithm for suffix stripping. *Program*, 14(3):130–137, July 1980.

[12] L. R. Rabiner. A tutorial on hidden Markov models and selected applications in speech recognition. In A. Weibel and K. Lee, editors, *Readings in Speech Recognition*, pages 267–296. Morgan Kaufmann, Los Altos, CA, 1990.

[13] S. E. Robertson, S. Walker, S. Jones, M. M. Hancock-Beaulieu, and M. Gatford. Okapi at TREC-3. In *Proc. of the 3rd Text REtrieval Conference*, pages 109–126, Gaithersburg, MD, 1994.
[14] F. K. Soong and E. F. Huang. A tree-trellis based fast search for finding the n-best sentence hypotheses in continuous speech recognition. In *Proc. of the IEEE ICASSP*, pages 705–708, Toronto, Canada, 1991.
[15] I. H. Witten and T. C. Bell. The zero-frequency problem: Estimating the probabilities of novel events in adaptive text compression. *IEEE Trans. Inform. Theory*, IT-37(4):1085–1094, 1991.

Océ at CLEF 2002

Roel Brand and Marvin Brünner

Océ Technologies
P.O. Box 101, NL-5900-MA Venlo, The Netherlands
{rkbr,mbru}@oce.nl

Abstract. This report describes the work done by the Information Retrieval Group at Océ Technologies B.V., for the 2002 edition of the Cross-Language Evaluation Forum (CLEF). We participated in the mono, cross and multi-lingual tasks, using BM25 for ranking, Ergane, Logos and BabelFish for translation and the Knowledge Concepts semantic network for stemming and morphological expansion. We performed a brute-force parameter search using the 2001 topics and relevance assessments to determine for each language the pair of BM25 parameters that yielded the highest average precision. These parameters were used to query the 2002 topics.

1 Introduction

To enlarge our knowledge and experience with information retrieval in multi-lingual document collections, we again participated in the Cross-Language Evaluation Forum (CLEF 2002). In 2001, we only participated in the Dutch monolingual task. Our goals for 2002 were to participate in all of the monolingual tasks, some of the cross-lingual and in the multi-lingual task. Additionally we wanted to explore methods for combining results from different languages to obtain optimal multi-lingual results.

This report describes the details of the retrieval system we built to create our contribution and the results we obtained in the campaign.

2 Experiment Design

Our experiment design is very straight forward. In the following paragraphs we describe the most important elements.

2.1 Indexing

In the indexes we built for each of the languages, documents were split on non-alphanumerical characters and single character words were ignored. We performed no index stemming. For stop word elimination we used the stop list from Knowledge Concepts' Content Enabler semantic network.

C.A. Peters (Ed.): CLEF 2002, LNCS 2785, pp. 59-65, 2003.

2.2 Query Construction

Queries were automatically constructed from the topics. Fields from the topics were split into terms on non-alphanumerical characters. Single character and stopword terms were removed. Because of our decision to index unstemmed words, each query term was expanded with its root form by using morphological collapse (dictionary based stemming) from Knowledge Concepts' Content Enabler semantic network. Using the same semantic network, the root form was then expanded with morphological variations (such as plural form, etc.). We tried query expansion with synonyms but found it did not help.

For the German task, we experienced some difficulties with the semantic network; as a quick work around, a Porter-like stemmer was used to generate a mapping from a term into its stemming variants [3].

2.3 Compound Splitting

For Dutch and German, compound words were split using a simple recursive algorithm that splits a word in all combinations of terms found in the corpus that together compose the word. For instance the word 'waterbeddenfabrikant' is expanded into 'water', 'bed', 'den', 'bedden' and 'fabrikant'. The additional 's' that is sometimes inserted between two parts of a compound for pronunciation is removed by a simple rule in the splitter. On all compound parts we conducted a morphological collapse and expansion, as described in the previous paragraph.

2.4 Topic Translation

For the cross and multi-lingual tasks we used topic translation. We participated in the English to Dutch, Dutch to English, English to Spanish and Spanish to English cross-lingual tasks. For the multi-lingual task we used English as the source language and translated it to German, Spanish, Italian and French.

We experimented with two different translation approaches:

Using a Semantic Network for Translation. We experimented with using the Content Enabler semantic network for word-by-word translation. This yielded very poor results because a word can point to many concepts and we had no way of selecting the proper one, given the topic. For instance, translating the English word 'baby' into Dutch using the semantic network yields the following expansions:

1. Liefje, lieveling, lieverd, schat, schatje, snoesje
2. Baby, dreumes, hummel, jong kind, kind, kleuter, pasgeborene, peuter, puk, uk, wurm, zuigeling
3. Bemoederen, in de watten leggen, koesteren, liefderijk verzorgen, moederen over, vertroetelen, verwekelijken, verwennen

Clearly, only very few terms are correct given the fact that a term in a topic is often used in a specific way. Therefore, this method of translation can not be used in a non-interactive way and hence was abandoned for our CLEF experiment.

Using Logos, BabelFish and Ergane for Translation. For translating Spanish to English and vice versa in the cross-lingual task, we used both Logos and Systran (BabelFish). Keeping all other things the same, we obtained a higher average precision using Logos. The same was observed in the multi-lingual task.

For translating topics between English and Dutch we used the Ergane dictionaries. The number of words in Ergane is rather limited. A positive effect of this is that, unlike the semantic network, we experienced no problematic query expansion. A negative effect is that many essential terms could not be translated using Ergane.

3 Ranking

Instead of using our own model like in 2001[1], we based our system on BM25[2]. Our query terms were expanded with compound parts and morphological variations.

3.1 Adapting BM25 for Expanded Queries

To work with term expansions in our implementation of BM25, we summed term frequencies over the expansion of each term and we defined document frequency as the number of documents in which a term or any of its expansions occurs:

Let q_i be a term in query Q, let $q_{i,0}$, $q_{i,1}$, …, $q_{i,n}$ be the expansion of q_i with $q_{i,0} = q_i$.
We calculate the relevance of document d with BM25:

$$\mathrm{Rel}(d,Q) = \sum_{q_i \in Q} \frac{\log(N) - \log(df(q_i)) \cdot tf(q_i,d) \cdot (k_1+1)}{k_1 \cdot ((1-b) + (b \cdot ndl(d))) + tf(q_i,d)} \tag{1}$$

where

$$tf(q_i,d) = \sum_j tf(q_{i,j},d) \tag{2}$$

df(q_i) = (#d : d is a document
: (Exists j : q_i_j is an expansion term of q_i
: q_i_j occurs in d)
) (3)

nfl(d) is the document length of d, divided by the average document length. (4)

3.2 Picking BM25 Parameters

Picking the right weighting parameters *k1* and *b* has a large influence on the performance of the BM25 model. As an experiment we decided to pick values for *k1* and *b* by means of a brute-force parameter space search on the 2001 topics and relevance assessments to determine the best pair of parameter values. We did this for each language, under the hypothesis that the optimal parameter values might be language or collection related. The result were plots like the one shown in Figure 1 and 2.

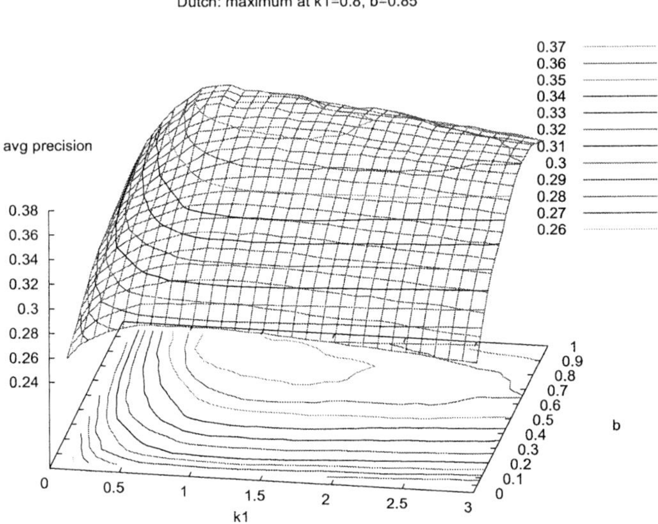

Fig. 1. Surface plot of average precision on 2001 dutch topics at different (k1,b) values

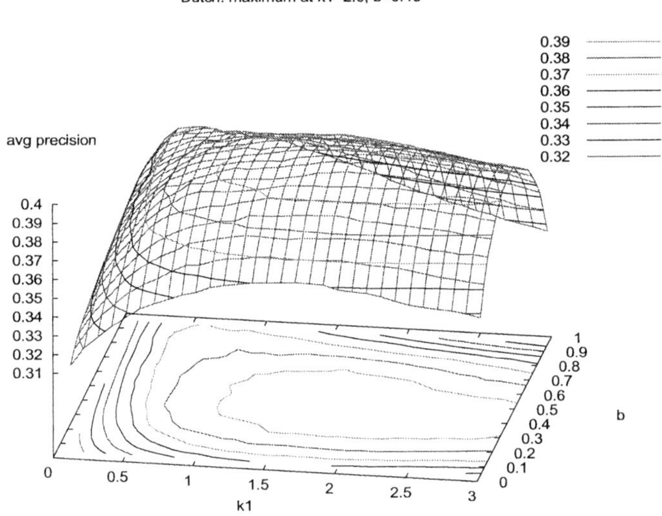

Fig. 2. Surface plot of average precision on 2002 dutch topics at different (k1,b) values

After the 2002 evaluation campaign, when the relevance assessments for 2002 became available, we re-ran our parameter search which yielded entirely different optima. The collections used were the same which leads us to the conclusion that the parameter optima must be strongly query related. Of course, looking at the BM25 ranking formula in Equation 5 this is not surprising since both *k1* and *b* work only on documents in which one of the query terms occurs. In fact, if we look at what parameter values yield the highest precision for each topic (Figure 3 and 4), this is confirmed.

3.3 Result Merging

Due to lack of time we were not able to invest much effort in merging retrieval results from multiple languages into a single multi-lingual result. We therefore choose two basic approaches:

- round robin over all languages in the order ES, FR, IT, DE, EN ;
- merge sort based on document scores, normalized by dividing them by the score of the highest ranked document of the same language.

Of these two strategies, merge sort gave us higher average precision.

3.4 Submitted Runs

We submitted monolingual, cross-lingual and multi-lingual runs. The results of these can be found in the Appendix. Table 1 shows how each run was created.

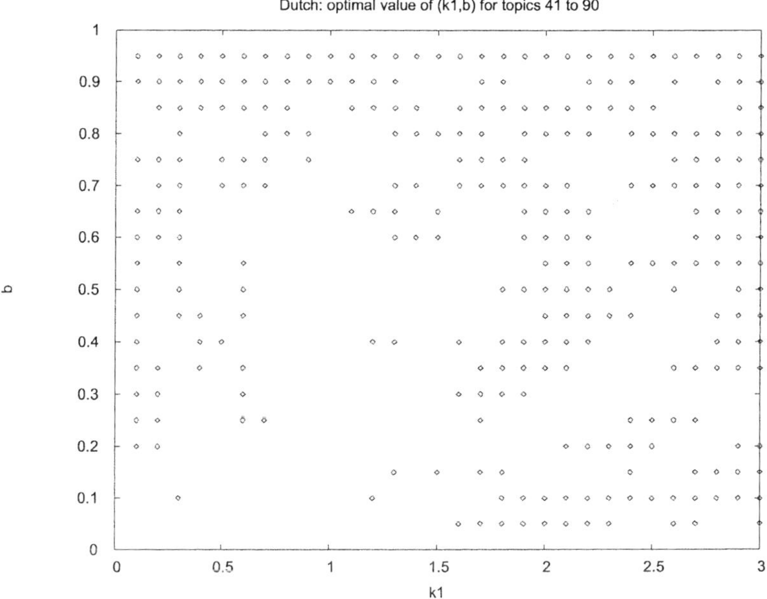

Fig. 3. Scatter plot of (k1,b) optimum for each 2001 topic

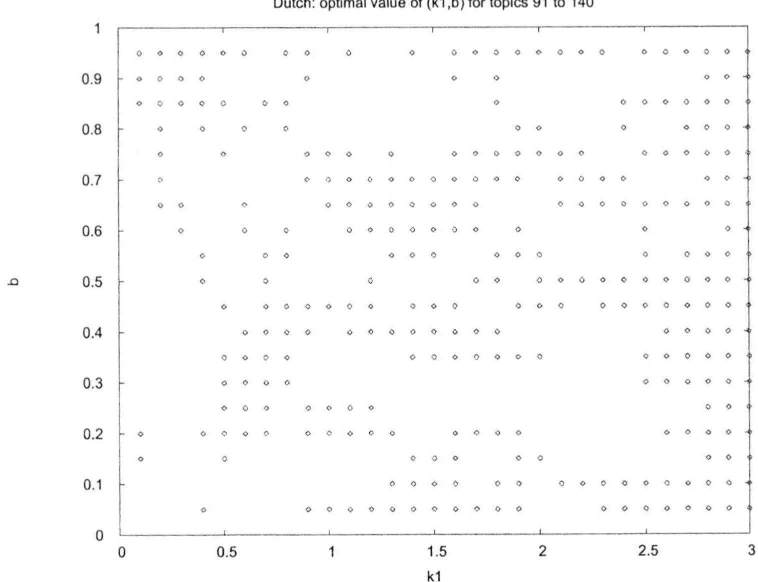

Fig. 4. Scatter plot of (k1,b) optimum for each 2001 topic

Table 1. Description of the submitted runs

Run	Description			
Monolingual	**Language**	**Topic part**		
oce02monNLto	Dutch	Title		
oce02monNL	Dutch	Title, Description		
oce02monITto	Italian	Title		
oce02monIT	Italian	Title, Description		
oce02monFRto	French	Title		
oce02monFR	French	Title, Description		
oce02monESto	Spanish	Title		
oce02monES	Spanish	Title, Description		
oce02monDEto	German	Title		
oce02monDE	German	Title, Description		
Cross-lingual	**Topics**	**Documents**	**Translation**	**Topic part**
oce02nl2enER	Dutch	English	Ergane	Title, Description
oce02en2nlER	English	Dutch	Ergane	Title, Description
oce02es2enBF	Spanish	English	Babelfish	Title, Description
oce02es2enLO	Spanish	English	Logos	Title, Description
oce02en2esBF	English	Spanish	Babelfish	Title, Description
oce02en2esLO	English	Spanish	Logos	Title, Description
Multi-lingual	**Topics**	**Merging**	**Translation**	**Topic part**
oce02mulRRloTO	English	Round Robin	Logos	Title
oce02mulRRbf	English	Round Robin	Babelfish	Title, Description
oce02mulRRlo	English	Round Robin	Logos	Title, Description
oce02mulMSbf	English	Merge Sort	Babelfish	Title, Description
Oce02mulMSlo	English	Merge Sort	Logos	Title, Description

4 Conclusions

Our goals when taking part in the CLEF 2002 were to enter official runs for all tasks and to explore techniques for merging results from different languages. We succeeded in doing the former but we could not spend much time on the latter.

We have participated in many more runs than last year, we have improved our retrieval algorithms and made a more serious implementation of the indexer and ranker. On the other hand, our 2002 contribution was based entirely on "borrowed" techniques, whereas in 2001 we put in a ranking mechanism of our own.

Given that all techniques we used were "borrowed", we could have implemented blind relevance feedback as well. The literature shows that it usually leads to improved results. Unfortunately, time constraints did not allow us to do so.

Our experiment with BM25 parameter optimization teaches us that the optimal parameters are different for each query. We do not have enough information to conclude how the parameter optima are related to the query. More insight in this would maybe allow us to fine-tune parameters for each query.

Finally we have the impression that one of the things which caused us to perform rather well in the bi-lingual and mono-lingual tasks is the fact that we chose "easy" languages. For Spanish to English and vice-versa, good translation resources are available and no extra complexities are present like for instance compound words. This should make it easier to perform Spanish to English retrieval than for instance German to English. Yet in the task evaluation, all bilingual runs with the same target language are compared. A comparable argument can be made for the multilingual task. We chose to use English topics because of the availability of good translation resources from English to the four other languages. Comparing our runs with runs using for instance German topics is not really fair because the difference in translation resources probably weighs heavily on the outcome.

References

[1] Jakob Klok, Marvin Brünner, Samuel Driessen. Some Terms Are More Interchangeable than Others. In Carol Peters, editor, *CLEF 2001 Proceedings, LNCS 2406*, Springer-Verlag 2002.

[2] S. Robertson and K. Jones. Simple proven approaches to text retrieval. *Tech. Rep. TR356*, Cambridge University Computer Laboratory, 1997.

[3] German Stemming Algorithm, http://snowball.sourceforge.net/german/stemmer.html .

Report on CLEF 2002 Experiments: Combining Multiple Sources of Evidence

Jacques Savoy

Institut interfacultaire d'informatique
Université de Neuchâtel, Pierre-à-Mazel 7, 2000 Neuchâtel, Switzerland
jacques.savoy@unine.ch
http://www.unine.ch/info/clef/

Abstract. In our second participation in the CLEF retrieval tasks, our first objective was to propose better and more general stopword lists for various European languages (namely, French, Italian, German, Spanish and Finnish) along with improved, simpler and efficient stemming procedures. Our second goal was to propose a combined query-translation approach that could cross language barriers and also an effective merging strategy based on logistic regression for accessing the multilingual collection. Finally, within the Amaryllis experiment, we wanted to analyze how a specialized thesaurus might improve retrieval effectiveness.

1 Introduction

Taking our experiments of last year as a starting point [1], in CLEF 2002 we participated in the French, Italian, Spanish, German, Dutch and Finnish monolingual tasks, where our information retrieval approaches can work without having to rely on a dictionary. In Section 2, we describe how we improved our stopword lists and simple stemmers for the French, Italian, Spanish and German languages. For German, we also suggest a new decompounding algorithm. For Dutch, we used the available stoplist and stemmer, and for Finnish we designed a new stemmer and stopword list. In order to obtain a better overview of our results, we have evaluated our procedures using ten different retrieval schemes. In Section 3, we discuss how we chose to express the requests in English for the various bilingual tracks, and automatically translated them using five different machine translation (MT) systems and one bilingual dictionary. We study these various translations and, on the basis of the relative merit of each translation device, we investigate various combinations of them. In Section 4, we describe our multilingual information retrieval results, while investigating various merging strategies based on results obtained during our bilingual tasks. Finally, in the last section, we present various experiments carried out using the Amaryllis corpus, which included a specialized thesaurus that could be used to improve the retrieval effectiveness of the information retrieval system.

C.A. Peters (Ed.): CLEF 2002, LNCS 2785, pp. 66–90, 2003.

2 Monolingual Indexing and Search

Most European languages in the Indo-European language family (including French, Italian, Spanish, German and Dutch) can be viewed as flectional languages within which polymorph suffixes are added at the end of a flexed root. However, the Finnish language, a member of the Uralic language family (along with Turkish), is based on a concatenative morphology in which suffixes, more or less invariable, are added to roots that are generally invariable.

Any adaptation for the other languages in the CLEF experiments of indexing or search strategies prepared for English requires the development of stopword lists and fast stemming procedures. Stopword lists are composed of non-significant words that are removed from a document or a request before the indexing process begins. Stemming procedures try to remove inflectional and derivational suffixes in order to conflate word variants into the same stem or root.

This first section will deal with these issues and is organized as follows: Section 2.1 contains an overview of our eight test-collections while Section 2.2 describes our general approach to building stopword lists and stemmers for use with languages other than English. In order to decompound German words, we try a simple decompounding algorithm as described in Section 2.3. Section 2.4 describes the Okapi probabilistic model together with various vector-space models and we evaluate them using eight test-collections written in seven different languages (monolingual track).

2.1 Overview of the Test-Collections

The corpora used in our experiments included newspapers such as the *Los Angeles Times* (1994, English), *Le Monde* (1994, French), *La Stampa* (1994, Italian), *Der Spiegel* (1994/95, German), *Frankfurter Rundschau* (1994, German), *NRC Handelsbald* (1994/95, Dutch), *Algemeen Dagblad* (1995/95, Dutch), and *Tidningarnas Telegrambyrå* (1994/95, Finnish). As a second source of information, we also used various articles edited by news agencies including *EFE* (1994, Spanish) and the Swiss news agency (1994, available in French, German and Italian but without parallel translation). As shown in Tables 1 and 2, these corpora are of various sizes, with the English, German, Spanish and Dutch collections being twice the volume of the French, Italian and Finnish sources. On the other hand, the mean number of distinct indexing terms per document is relatively similar across the corpora (around 120), and this number is a little bit higher for the English collection (167.33). The Amaryllis collection contains abstracts of scientific papers written mainly in French and this corpus contains fewer distinct indexing terms per article (70.418).

An examination of the number of relevant documents per request as shown in Tables 1 and 2 reveals that the mean number is always greater than the median (e.g., the English collection contains an average of 19.548 relevant articles per query and the corresponding median is 11.5). These findings indicate that each collection contains numerous queries with a rather small number of relevant

Table 1. Test-collection statistics

	English	French	Italian	German	Spanish
Size (in MB)	425 MB	243 MB	278 MB	527 MB	509 MB
# of documents	113,005	87,191	108,578	225,371	215,738
# of distinct terms	330,753	320,526	503,550	1,507,806	528,753
Number of distinct indexing terms / document					
Mean	167.33	130.213	129.908	119.072	111.803
Median	138	95	92	89	99
Maximum	1,812	1,622	1,394	2,420	642
Minimum	2	3	1	1	5
Number of queries	42	50	49	50	50
Number of rel. items	821	1,383	1,072	1,938	2,854
Mean rel. items / request	19.548	27.66	21.878	38.76	57.08
Median	11.5	13.5	16	28	27
Maximum	96	177	86	119	321
Minimum	1	1	3	1	3

Table 2. Test-collection statistics

	Dutch	Finnish	Amaryllis
Size (in MB)	540 MB	137 MB	195 MB
# of documents	190,604	55,344	148,688
# of distinct terms	883,953	1,483,354	413,262
Number of distinct indexing terms / document			
Mean	110.013	114.01	70.418
Median	77	87	64
Maximum	2,297	1,946	263
Minimum	1	1	5
Number of queries	50	30	25
Number of rel. items	1,862	502	2,018
Mean rel. items / request	37.24	16.733	80.72
Median	21	8.5	67
Maximum	301	62	180
Minimum	4	1	18

items. For each collection, we encounter 50 queries except for the Italian corpus (for which Query #120 does not have any relevant items) and the English collection (for which Query #93, #96, #101, #110, #117, #118, #127 and #132 do not have any relevant items). The Finnish corpus contains only 30 available requests while only 25 queries are included in the Amaryllis collection.

For our automatic runs we retained only the following logical sections from the original documents during the indexing process: <TITLE>, <HEADLINE>, <TEXT>, <LEAD>, <LEAD1>, <TX>, <LD>, <TI>, and <ST>. On the other hand, we did conduct two experiments (indicated as manual runs): one with the French collection and one with the German corpus, within which we retained the following tags: for the French collection: <DE>, <KW>, <TB>, <SUBJECTS>, <CHA1>, <NAMES>, <NOM1>, <NOTE>, <GENRE>, <ORT1>, <SU11>, <SU21>, <GO11>, <GO12>, <GO13>, <GO14>, <GO24>, <TI01>, <TI02>, <TI03>, <TI04>, <TI05>, <TI06>, <TI07>, <TI08>, <PEOPLE>, <TI09>, <SOT1>, <SYE1>, and <SYF1>; while for the German corpus and for one experiment, we also used the following tags: <KW>, and <TB>.

From the topic descriptions we automatically removed certain phrases such as "Relevant documents report ...", "Find documents that give ...", "Trouver des documents qui parlent ...", "Sono valide le discussioni e le decisioni ...", "Relevante Dokumente berichten ..." or "Los documentos relevantes proporcionan información ...".

To evaluate our approaches, we used the SMART system as a test bed for implementing the Okapi probabilistic model [2] as well as other vector-space models. This year our experiments were conducted on an Intel Pentium III/600 (memory: 1 GB, swap: 2 GB, disk: 6 x 35 GB).

2.2 Stopword Lists and Stemming Procedures

In order to define general stopword lists, we began with lists already available for the English and French languages [3], [4], while for the other languages we established a general stopword list by following the guidelines described in [3]. These lists generally contain the top 200 words most frequently used in the various collections, plus articles, pronouns, prepositions, conjunctions, and very frequently occurring verb forms (e.g., "to be", "is", "has", etc.). Stopword lists used during our previous participation [1] were often extended. For the English language for example we used that provided by the SMART system (571 words). For the other languages we used 431 words for Italian (no change from last year), 462 for French (previously 217), 603 for German (previously 294), 351 for Spanish (previously 272), 1,315 for Dutch (available at CLEF Web site) and 1,134 for Finnish (these stopword lists are available at `www.unine.ch/info/clef/`).

After removing high frequency words, an indexing procedure uses a stemming algorithm that attempts to conflate word variants into the same stem or root. In developing this procedure for the French, Italian, German and Spanish languages, it is important to remember that these languages have more complex morphologies than does the English language [5]. As a first approach, our intention was to remove only inflectional suffixes such that singular and plural word forms or feminine as well as masculine forms conflate to the same root. More sophisticated schemes have already been proposed for the removal of derivational suffixes (e.g., "-ize", "-ably", "-ship" in the English language), such as in the stemmer developed by Lovins [6], based on a list of over 260 suffixes, while that of Porter [7] looks for about 60 suffixes. Figuerola *et al.* [8] for example described two different stemmers for the Spanish language, and the results show that removing only inflectional suffixes (88 different inflectional suffixes were defined) seemed to provide better retrieval levels than did removing both inflectional and derivational suffixes (this extended stemmer included 230 suffixes).

Our stemming procedures can also be found at `www.unine.ch/info/clef/`. This year we improved our stemming algorithms for French, and also removed some derivational suffixes were also removed. For the Dutch language, we use Kraaij & Pohlmann's stemmer(`ruulst.let.ruu.nl:2000/uplift/ulift.html`) [9]. For the Finnish language, our stemmer tries to conflate various word declinations into the same stem. Finnish makes a distinction between partial object(s) and whole object(s) (e.g., "syön leilää" for "I'm eating bread", "syön leivän" for "I'm eating a (whole) bread", or "syön leipiä" for "I'm eating breads", and "syön leivät" for "I'm eating the breads"). This aspect is not currently being taken into consideration.

Finally, diacritic characters are usually not present in English collections (with some exceptions, such as "à la carte" or "résumé"); such characters are replaced by their corresponding non-accentuated letter in the Italian, Dutch, Finnish, German and Spanish collections.

2.3 Decompounding German Words

Most European languages manifest other morphological characteristics for which our approach has made allowances, with compound word constructions being just one example (e.g., handgun, worldwide). In German, compound words are widely used and this causes more difficulties than in English. For example, a life insurance company employee would be "Lebensversicherungsgesellschaftsangestellter" (Leben + s + versicherung + s + gesellschaft + s + angestellter for life + insurance + company + employee). Also the morphological marker ("s") is not always present (e.g., "Bankangestelltenlohn" built as Bank + angestellten + lohn (salary)). In Finnish, we also encounter similar constructions such as "rakkauskirje" (rakkaus + kirje for love + letter) or "työviikko" (työ + viikko for work + week).

According to Monz & de Rijke [10] or Chen [11], including both compounds and their composite parts in queries and documents can result in better performance while according to Molina-Salgado et al. [12], the decomposition of German words seems to reduce average precision.

In our approach we break up any words having an initial length greater than or equal to eight characters. Moreover, decomposition cannot take place before an initial sequence `[V]C`, meaning that a word might begin with a series of vowels that must be followed by at least one consonant. The algorithm then seeks occurrences of one of the models described in Table 3. For example, the last model "gss g s" indicates that when we encounter the character string "gss" the computer is allowed to cut the compound term, ending the first word with "g" and beginning the second with "s". All the models shown in Table 3 can include letter sequences that are impossible to find in a simple German word such as "dtt", "fff", or "ldm". Once it has detected this pattern, the computer makes sure that the corresponding part consists of at least four characters, potentially beginning with a series of vowels (criterion noted as `[V]`), followed by a `CV`

Table 3. Decompounding patterns for German

String sequence			End of previous word			Beginning of next word					
schaften	schaft	.	tion	tion	.	ern	er	.	schg	sch	g
weisen	weise	.	ling	ling	.	tät	tät	.	schl	sch	l
lischen	lisch	.	igkeit	igkeit	.	net	net	.	schh	sch	h
lingen	ling	.	lichkeit	lichkeit	.	ens	en	.	scht	sch	t
igkeiten	igkeit	.	keit	keit	.	ers	er	.	dtt	dt	t
lichkeit	lichkeit	.	erheit	erheit	.	ems	em	.	dtp	dt	p
keiten	keit	.	enheit	enheit	.	ts	t	.	dtm	dt	m
erheiten	erheit	.	heit	heit	.	ions	ion	.	dtb	dt	b
enheiten	enheit	.	lein	lein	.	isch	isch	.	dtw	dt	w
heiten	heit	.	chen	chen	.	rm	rm	.	ldan	ld	an
haften	haft	.	haft	haft	.	rw	rw	.	ldg	ld	g
halben	halb	.	halb	halb	.	nbr	n	br	ldm	ld	m
langen	lang	.	lang	lang	.	nb	n	b	ldq	ld	q
erlichen	erlich	.	erlich	erlich	.	nfl	n	fl	ldp	ld	p
enlichen	enlich	.	enlich	enlich	.	nfr	n	fr	ldv	ld	v
lichen	lich	.	lich	lich	.	nf	n	f	ldw	ld	w
baren	bar	.	bar	bar	.	nh	n	h	tst	t	t
igenden	igend	.	igend	igend	.	nk	n	k	rg	r	g
igungen	igung	.	igung	igung	.	ntr	n	tr	rk	r	k
igen	ig	.	ig	ig	.	fff	ff	f	rm	r	m
enden	end	.	end	end	.	ffs	ff	.	rr	r	r
isten	ist	.	ist	ist	.	fk	f	k	rs	r	s
anten	ant	.	ant	ant	.	fm	f	m	rt	r	t
ungen	ung	.	tum	tum	.	fp	f	p	rw	r	w
schaft	schaft	.	age	age	.	fv	f	v	rz	r	z
weise	weise	.	ung	ung	.	fw	f	w	fp	f	p
lisch	lisch	.	enden	end	.	schb	sch	b	fsf	f	f
ismus	ismus	.	eren	er	.	schf	sch	f	gss	g	s

sequence. If decomposition does prove to be possible, the algorithm then begins working on the right part of the decomposed word.

As an example, the compound word "Betreuungsstelle" (meaning "care center" is made up of "Betreuung" (care) and "Stelle" (center, place)). This word is definitely more than seven characters long. Once this has been verified, the computer begins searching for substitution models starting with the second character. The computer will find a match with the last model described in Table 3, and thus form the words "Betreuung" and "Stelle." This break is validated because the second word has a length greater than four characters. This term also meets criterion `[V]CV` and finally, given that the term "Stelle" has less than eight letters, the computer will not attempt to continue decomposing this term. Our approach for decompounding German words is based on the linguistic rules used to build German compounds. As an alternative, we could decompound German words using a list of German words which may then be used to generate all possible ways to break up a compound and then select the decomposition containing the minimum number of component words as suggested by Chen [13].

2.4 Indexing and Searching Strategy

In order to obtain a broader view of the relative merits of various retrieval models, we first adopted a binary indexing scheme within which each document (or request) was represented by a set of keywords, without any weight. To measure the similarity between documents and requests, we counted the number of common terms, computed according to the inner product (retrieval model denoted "doc=bnn, query=bnn" or "bnn-bnn"). For document and query indexing, binary logical restrictions however are often too limiting. In order to weight the presence of each indexing term in a document surrogate (or in a query), we can take term occurrence frequency (denoted tf) into account, resulting in better term distinction and increasing our indexing flexibility (retrieval model notation: "doc=nnn, query=nnn" or "nnn-nnn").

Those terms that do however occur very frequently in the collection are not considered very helpful in distinguishing between relevant and non-relevant items. Thus we might count their frequency in the collection (denoted df), or more precisely the inverse document frequency (denoted by idf=ln(n/df)), resulting in more weight for sparse words and less weight for more frequent ones. Moreover, a cosine normalization can prove beneficial and each indexing weight

Table 4. Weighting schemes

bnn	$w_{ij} = 1$	npn	$w_{ij} = tf_{ij} \cdot ln\left[\frac{n - df_j}{df_j}\right]$
nnn	$w_{ij} = tf_{ij}$		
ntc	$w_{ij} = \frac{tf_{ij} \cdot idf_j}{\sqrt{\sum_{k=1}^{t}(tf_{ik} \cdot idf_k)^2}}$	atn	$w_{ij} = idf_j \cdot \left[\frac{0.5 + 0.5 \cdot tf_{ij}}{max\ tf_{i.}}\right]$
lnc	$w_{ij} = \frac{ln(tf_{ij})+1}{\sqrt{\sum_{k=1}^{t}(ln(tf_{ik})+1)^2}}$	ltn	$w_{ij} = (ln(tf_{ij}) + 1) \cdot idf_j$
Okapi	$w_{ij} = \frac{(k_1+1) \cdot tf_{ij}}{K + tf_{ij}}$ with $K = k_1 \cdot \left[(1-b) + b \cdot \frac{l_i}{avdl}\right]$		
ltc	$w_{ij} = \frac{(ln(tf_{ij})+1) \cdot idf_j}{\sqrt{\sum_{k=1}^{t}[(ln(tf_{ik})+1) \cdot idf_k]^2}}$		
dtu	$w_{ij} = \frac{(ln(ln(tf_{ij})+1)+1) \cdot idf_j}{(1-slope) \cdot pivot + (slope \cdot nt_i)}$		
dtc	$w_{ij} = \frac{(ln(ln(tf_{ij})+1)+1) \cdot idf_j}{\sqrt{\sum_{k=1}^{t}[(ln(ln(tf_{ik})+1)+1) \cdot idf_k]^2}}$		
Lnu	$w_{ij} = \frac{\frac{ln(tf_{ij})+1}{ln\left(\frac{l_i}{nt_i}\right)+1}}{(1-slope) \cdot pivot + (slope \cdot nt_i)}$		

could vary within the range of 0 to 1 (retrieval model denoted "ntc-ntc"). Table 4 shows the exact weighting formulation w_{ij} for each indexing term T_j in a document D_i in which n indicates the number of documents D_i in the collection, nt_i the number of unique indexing terms in D_i, and l_i the sum of tf_{ij} for a given document D_i.

Other variants of this formula can also be created, especially if we determine the occurrence of a given term in a document to be a rare event. Thus, it may be a good practice to give more importance to the first occurrence of this word as compared to any successive or repeating occurrences. Therefore, the tf component may be computed as 0.5 + 0.5·[tf / max tf in a document] (retrieval model denoted "doc=atn").

Finally, we consider that a term's presence in a shorter document provides stronger evidence than it does in a longer document. To account for this, we integrated document length within the weighting formula, leading to more complex IR models; for example, the IR model denoted by "doc=Lnu" [14], "doc=dtu" [15]. Finally for CLEF 2002, we also conducted various experiments using the Okapi probabilistic model [2] within which K = k_1·[(1-b) + b·(l_i/avdl)], representing the ratio between the length of D_i measured by l_i (sum of tf_{ij}) and the collection mean noted by avdl.

In our experiments, the constants b, k_1, avdl, pivot and slope are fixed according to the values listed in Table 5. To evaluate the retrieval performance of these various IR models, we adopted the non-interpolated average precision technique (computed on the basis of 1,000 retrieved items per request by the TREC-EVAL program [16]), providing both precision and recall with the use of a single number. Brand & Brünner [17] have evaluated in more detail the retrieval effectiveness achieved when modifying the values of these parameters.

Given that French, Italian and Spanish morphology is comparable to that of English, we decided to index French, Italian and Spanish documents based on word stems. For the German, Dutch and Finnish languages and their more complex compounding morphology, we decided to use a 5-gram approach [18], [19]. However, contrary to [19], our generation of 5-gram indexing terms does not span word boundaries. This value of 5 was chosen because it performed better

Table 5. Parameter setting for the various test-collections

Language	b	k_1	avdl	pivot	slope
English	0.8	2	900	100	0.1
French	0.7	2	750	100	0.1
Italian	0.6	1.5	800	100	0.1
Spanish	0.5	1.2	300	100	0.1
German	0.55	1.5	600	125	0.1
Dutch	0.9	3.0	600	125	0.1
Finnish	0.75	1.2	900	125	0.1
Amaryllis	0.7	2	160	30	0.2

with the CLEF 2000 corpora [20]. Using this indexing scheme, the compound "das Hausdach" (the roof of the house) will generate the following indexing terms: "das", "hausd", "ausda", "usdac" and "sdach".

Our evaluation results as reported in Tables 6 and 7 show that the Okapi probabilistic model performs best for the five different languages. In the second position, we usually find the vector-space model "doc=Lnu, query=ltc" and in the third "doc=dtu, query=dtc". Finally, the traditional tf-idf weighting scheme ("doc=ntc, query=ntc") does not exhibit very satisfactory results, and the simple term-frequency weighting scheme ("doc=nnn, query=nnn") or the simple coordinate match ("doc=bnn, query=bnn") results in poor retrieval performance. However, Amati et al. [21] indicate that the PROSIT probabilistic model may result in better performance than the Okapi approach, at least for the Italian collection.

For the German language, we assumed that the 5-gram indexing, decompounded indexing and word-based document representations are distinct and independent sources of evidence about document content. We therefore decided to combine these three indexing schemes and to do so we normalized similarity values obtained from each of these three separate retrieval models, as shown in Equation 1 (see Section 4). The resulting average precision for these four approaches is shown in Table 7, thus demonstrating how the combined model usually results in better retrieval performance.

It has been observed that pseudo-relevance feedback (blind-query expansion) seems to be a useful technique for enhancing retrieval effectiveness. In this study, we adopted Rocchio's approach [14] with $\alpha = 0.75$, $\beta = 0.75$ whereby the system was allowed to add m terms extracted from the k best-ranked documents from the original query. To evaluate this proposition, we used the Okapi probabilistic model and enlarged the query by 10 to 20 terms (or until 300 within the 5-gram

Table 6. Average precision of various indexing and searching strategies (monolingual)

	Average precision			
Query TD Model	English 42 queries	French 50 queries	Italian 49 queries	Spanish 50 queries
doc=Okapi, query=npn	**50.08**	**48.41**	**41.05**	**51.71**
doc=Lnu, query=ltc	48.91	46.97	39.93	49.27
doc=dtu, query=dtc	43.03	45.38	39.53	47.29
doc=atn, query=ntc	42.50	42.42	39.08	46.01
doc=ltn, query=ntc	39.69	44.19	37.03	46.90
doc=ntc, query=ntc	27.47	31.41	29.32	33.05
doc=ltc, query=ltc	28.43	32.94	31.78	36.61
doc=lnc, query=ltc	29.89	33.49	32.79	38.78
doc=bnn, query=bnn	19.61	18.59	18.53	25.12
doc=nnn, query=nnn	9.59	14.97	15.63	22.22

Table 7. Average precision of various indexing and searching strategies (German)

Query TD Model	Average precision German words 50 queries	German decompounded 50 queries	German 5-gram 50 queries	German combined 50 queries
doc=Okapi, query=npn	**37.39**	**37.75**	**39.83**	**41.25**
doc=Lnu, query=ltc	36.41	36.77	36.91	39.79
doc=dtu, query=dtc	35.55	35.08	36.03	38.21
doc=atn, query=ntc	34.48	33.46	37.90	37.93
doc=ltn, query=ntc	34.68	33.67	34.79	36.37
doc=ntc, query=ntc	29.57	31.16	32.52	32.88
doc=ltc, query=ltc	28.69	29.26	30.05	31.08
doc=lnc, query=ltc	29.33	29.14	29.95	31.24
doc=bnn, query=bnn	17.65	16.88	16.91	21.30
doc=nnn, query=nnn	14.87	12.52	8.94	13.49

model, as shown in Table 9) found in the 5 or 10 best-retrieved articles. The results shown in Tables 8 and 9 indicate that the optimal parameter setting seems to be collection dependent. Moreover, performance improvement also seems to be collection dependent (or language dependent). While no improvement was shown for the English corpus, there was an increase of 8.55% for the Spanish corpus (from an average precision of 51.71 to 56.13), 9.85% for the French corpus (from 48.41 to 53.18), 12.91% for the Italian language (41.05 to 46.35) and 13.26% for the German collection (from 41.25 to 46.72, combined model, Table 9).

This year, we also participated in the Dutch and Finnish monolingual tasks, the results of which are given in Table 10, while the average precision obtained using the Okapi model for blind-query expansion is given in Table 11. For these two languages, we also applied our combined indexing model based on the 5-

Table 8. Average precision using blind-query expansion

Query TD Model	Average precision English 42 queries	French 50 queries	Italian 49 queries	Spanish 50 queries
doc=Okapi, query=npn	**50.08**	48.41	41.05	51.71
5 docs / 10 best terms	49.54	53.10	45.14	55.16
5 docs / 15 best terms	48.68	**53.18**	46.07	54.95
5 docs / 20 best terms	48.62	53.13	**46.35**	54.41
10 docs / 10 best terms	47.77	52.03	45.37	55.94
10 docs / 15 best terms	46.92	52.75	46.18	56.00
10 docs / 20 best terms	47.42	52.78	45.87	**56.13**

Table 9. Average precision using blind-query expansion (German corpus)

	Average precision			
Query TD Model	German words 50 queries	German decompounded 50 queries	German 5-gram 50 queries	German combined 50 queries
doc=Okapi, query=npn	37.39	37.75	39.83	41.25
# docs / # terms	5/40 42.90	5/40 42.19	10/200 45.45	**46.72**
# docs / # terms	5/40 **42.90**	5/40 **42.19**	5/300 **45.82**	46.27

gram and word-based document representations. While for the Dutch language, our combined model seems to enhance the retrieval effectiveness, for the Finnish language it does not. This however was a first trial for our proposed Finnish stemmer and this solution seemed to improve average precision over a baseline run without a stemming procedure (Okapi model, unstemmed 23.04, with stemming 30.45, an improvement of +32.16%).

In the monolingual track, we submitted ten runs along with their corresponding descriptions, as listed in Table 12. Seven of them were fully automatic using the request's Title and Description logical sections, while the last three were based on the topic's Title, Description and Narrative sections. In these last three runs, two were labeled "manual" because we used logical sections containing manually assigned index terms. For all runs, however, we did not use any "real" manual intervention during the indexing and retrieval procedures.

Table 10. Average precision for the Dutch and Finnish corpora

	Average precision					
Query TD Model	Dutch words 50 queries	Dutch 5-gram 50 queries	Dutch combined 50 queries	Finnish words 30 queries	Finnish 5-gram 30 queries	Finnish combined 30 queries
Okapi–npn	**42.37**	**41.75**	**44.56**	**30.45**	**38.25**	**37.51**
Lnu–ltc	42.57	40.73	44.50	27.58	36.07	36.83
dtu–dtc	41.26	40.59	43.00	30.70	36.79	36.47
atn–ntc	40.29	40.34	41.89	29.22	37.26	36.51
ltn–ntc	38.33	38.72	40.24	29.14	35.28	35.31
ntc–ntc	33.35	34.94	36.41	25.21	30.68	31.93
ltc–ltc	32.81	31.24	34.46	26.53	30.85	33.47
lnc–ltc	31.91	29.67	34.18	24.86	30.43	31.39
bnn–bnn	18.91	20.87	23.52	12.46	14.55	18.64
nnn–nnn	13.75	10.48	12.86	11.43	14.69	15.56

Table 11. Average precision using blind-query expansion

Query TD Model	Average precision Dutch words 50 queries	 Dutch 5-gram 50 queries	 Dutch combined 50 queries
doc=Okapi, query=npn	42.37	41.75	44.56
# docs/# terms	5/60 47.86	5/75 45.09	48.78
# docs/ # terms	5/100 **48.84**	10/150 **46.29**	**49.28**
	Finnish words 30 queries	Finnish 5-gram 30 queries	Finnish combined 30 queries
doc=Okapi, query=npn	30.45	38.25	37.51
# docs/# terms	5/60 31.89	5/75 40.90	39.33
# docs/ # terms	5/15 **32.36**	5/175 **41.67**	**40.11**

Table 12. Official monolingual run descriptions

Run name	Lang.	Query	Form	Model	Query expansion	Precision
UniNEfr	FR	TD	auto	Okapi	no expansion	48.41
UniNEit	IT	TD	auto	Okapi	10 best docs / 15 terms	46.18
UniNEes	SP	TD	auto	Okapi	5 best docs / 20 terms	54.41
UniNEde	DE	TD	auto	comb	5/40 word, 10/200 5-gram	46.72
UniNEnl	NL	TD	auto	comb	5/60 word, 5/75 5-gram	48.78
UniNEfi1	FI	TD	auto	Okapi	5 best docs / 75 terms	40.90
UniNEfi2	FI	TD	auto	comb	5/60 word, 5/75 5-gram	39.33
UniNEfrtdn	FR	TDN	man	Okapi	5 best docs / 10 terms	59.19
UniNEestdn	SP	TDN	auto	Okapi	5 best docs / 40 terms	60.51
UniNEdetdn	DE	TDN	man	comb	5/50 word, 10/300 5-gram	49.11

3 Bilingual Information Retrieval

In order to overcome language barriers, we based our approach on free and readily available translation resources that automatically translate queries into the desired target language. More precisely, the original queries were written in English and we used no parallel or aligned corpora to derive statistically [22] or semantically related words in the target language. Section 3.1 describes our combined strategy for cross-lingual retrieval while Section 3.2 provides some examples of translation errors.

This year, we used five machine translation systems, namely

1. SYSTRAN™ [23] (`babel.altavista.com/translate.dyn`),
2. GOOGLE.COM (`www.google.com/language_tools`),
3. FREETRANSLATION.COM (`www.freetranslation.com`),
4. INTERTRAN (`www.tranexp.com:2000/InterTran`),
5. REVERSO ONLINE (`translation2.paralink.com`).

As a bilingual dictionary we used the BABYLON™ system (`www.babylon.com`).

3.1 Automatic Query Translation

In order to develop a fully automatic approach, we chose to translate the queries using five different machine translation (MT) systems. We also translated query terms word-by-word using the BABYLON bilingual dictionary, which provides not only one but several terms as the translation of each word submitted. In our experiments, we decided to pick the first translation given (labeled "baby1"), the first two terms (labeled "baby2") or the first three available translations (labeled "baby3").

The first part of Table 13 lists the average precision for each translation device used along with the performance achieved by manually translated queries. For German, we also reported the retrieval effectiveness achieved by the three different approaches, namely using words as indexing units, decompounding the German words according to our approach and the 5-gram model. While the REVERSO system seems to be the best choice for German and Spanish, FREE-TRANSLATION is the best choice for Italian and BABYLON 1 the best for French.

In order to improve search performance, we tried combining different machine translation systems with the bilingual dictionary approach. In this case, we formed the translated query by concatenating the different translations provided by the various approaches. Thus in the line entitled "Comb 1" we combined one machine translation system with the bilingual dictionary ("baby1"). Similarly, in lines "Comb 2" and "Comb 2b", we listed the results of two machine translation approaches, and in lines "Comb 3", "Comb 3b" and "Comb 3b2" the three machine translation systems. With the exception of the performance under "Comb 3b2", we also included terms provided by the "baby1" dictionary look-up in the translated queries. In columns "MT 2" and "MT 3", we evaluated the combination of two or three, respectively, machine translation systems. Finally, we also combined all translation sources (under the heading "All") and all machine translation approaches under the heading "MT all".

Since the performance of each translation device depends on the target language, in the lower part of Table 13 we included the exact specification for each of the combined runs. For German, for each of the three indexing models, we used the same combination of translation resources. From an examination of the retrieval effectiveness of our various combined approaches listed in the middle part of Table 13, a clear recommendation cannot be made. Overall, it seems better to combine two or three machine translation systems with the bilingual dictionary approach ("baby1"). However, combining the five machine translation systems (heading "MT all") or all translation tools (heading "All") did not result in very satisfactory performance.

Table 14 lists the exact specifics of our various bilingual runs. However, when submitting our official results, we used the wrong numbers for Query #130 and #131 (we switched these two query numbers). Thus, both queries have an average precision 0.00 in our official results and we report the corrected performance in Tables 14 and 17 (multilingual runs).

3.2 Examples of Translation Failures

In order to obtain a preliminary picture of the difficulties underlying the automatic translation approach, we analyzed some queries by comparing translations produced by our six machine-based tools with query formulations written by humans (examples are given in Table 15). As a first example, the title of Query #113 is "European Cup". In this case, the term "cup" was analyzed as teacup by all automatic translation tools, resulting in the French translations

Table 13. Average precision of various query translation strategies (Okapi model)

	Average precision					
Query TD Device	French	Italian	Spanish	German word	German decomp.	German 5-gram
Original	48.41	41.05	51.71	37.39	37.75	39.83
Systran	42.70	32.30	38.49	28.75	28.66	27.74
Google	42.70	32.30	38.35	28.07	26.05	27.19
FreeTrans	40.58	**32.71**	40.55	28.85	**31.42**	27.47
InterTran	33.89	30.28	37.36	21.32	21.61	19.21
Reverso	39.02	N/A	**43.28**	**30.71**	30.33	**28.71**
Babylon 1	**43.24**	27.65	39.62	26.17	27.66	28.10
Babylon 2	37.58	23.92	34.82	26.78	27.74	25.41
Babylon 3	35.69	21.65	32.89	25.34	26.03	23.66
Comb 1	46.77	33.31	44.57	34.32	34.66	32.75
Comb 2	48.02	34.70	**45.63**	35.26	34.92	32.95
Comb 2b	48.02		45.53	35.09	34.51	32.76
Comb 3	**48.56**	34.98	45.34	34.43	34.37	**33.34**
Comb 3b	48.49	35.02	45.34	34.58	34.43	32.76
Comb 3b2				**35.41**	**35.13**	33.25
MT 2		**35.82**				
MT 3	44.54	35.57	44.32	33.53	33.05	31.96
All	47.94	35.29	44.25	34.52	34.31	32.79
MT all	46.83	35.68	44.25	33.80	33.51	31.66
Comb 1	Rever-baby1	Free-baby1	Rever-baby1	Reverso-baby1		
Comb 2	Reverso systran-baby1	Free-google baby1	Rever-systran baby1	Reverso-systran-baby1		
Comb 2b	Reverso google-baby1		Rever-google baby1	Reverso-google-baby1		
Comb 3	Reverso-free google-baby1	Free-google inter-baby1	Free-google rever-baby1	Reverso-systran-inter-baby1		
Comb 3b	Reverso-inter google-baby1	Free-google systr-baby1	Free-google rever-baby2	Reverso-google-inter-baby1		
Comb 3b2				Reverso-systran-inter-baby2		
MT 2		Free-google				
MT 3	Reverso systr-google	Free-google inter	Free-google reverso	Reverso-inter-systran		

Table 14. Average precision and description of our official bilingual runs (Okapi model)

	Average precision				
Query TD	French	French	French	Italian	Italian
	UniNEfrBi	UniNEfrBi2	UniNEfrBi3	UniNEitBi	UniNEitBi2
Combined	Comb 3b	MTall+baby2	MT all	Comb 2	Comb 3
#doc/#ter	5 / 20	5 / 40	10 / 15	10 / 60	10 / 100
Corrected	**51.64**	50.79	48.49	38.50	**38.62**
Official	49.35	48.47	46.20	37.36	37.56
Query TD	Spanish	Spanish	Spanish	German	German
	UniNEesBi	UniNEesBi2	UniNEesBi3	UniNEdeBi	UniNEdeBi2
Combined	MT 3	Comb 3b	Comb 2	Comb 3b2	Comb 3
#doc/#ter	10 / 75	10 / 100	10 / 75	5 / 100	5 / 300
Corrected	50.67	**50.95**	50.93	**42.89**	42.11
Official	47.63	47.86	47.84	41.29	40.42

"tasse" or "verre" (or "tazza" in Italian, "Schale" in German ("Pokal" can be viewed as a correct translation alternative) and "taza" or "Jícara" (small teacup) in Spanish).

In Query #118 ("Finland's first EU Commissioner"), the machine translation systems failed to provide the appropriate Spanish term "comisario" for "Commissioner" but returned "comisión" (commission) or "Comisionado" (adjective relative to commission). For this same topic number, the manually translated query seemed to contain a spelling error in Italian ("commisario" instead of "commissario"). For the same topic, the translation provided in German "Beauftragter" (delegate) does not correspond to the appropriate term "Kommissar" (and "-" is missing in the translation "EUBEAUFTRAGTER").

Other examples: for Query #94 ("Return of Solzhenitsyn") which is translated manually in German ("Rückkehr Solschenizyns"), our automatic translation systems fail to translate the proper noun (returning "Solzhenitsyn" instead of "Solschenizyns"). Query #109 ("Computer Security") is translated manually in Spanish as "Seguridad Informática" and our various translation devices return different terms for "Computer" (e.g., "Computadora", "Computador" or "ordenador") but not the more appropriate term "Informática".

4 Multilingual Information Retrieval

Using our combined approach to automatically translate a query, we were able to search target document collections with queries written in a different language. This stage however represents only the first step in the development of multi-language information retrieval systems. We also need to investigate the situation where users write a query in English in order to retrieve pertinent documents in English, French, Italian, German and Spanish, for example. To deal with this

Table 15. Examples of unsuccessful query translations

C113 (query translations failed in French, Italian, German and Spanish)

<EN-TITLE> European Cup

<FR-TITLE manually translated> Coupe d'Europe de football

<FR-TITLE FREETRANSLATION> Tasse européenne

<FR-TITLE BABYLON 1> Européen verre

<FR-TITLE BABYLON 2> Européen résident de verre tasse

<FR-TITLE BABYLON 3> Européen résident de l'Europe verre tasse coupe

<IT-TITLE manually translated> Campionati europei

<IT-TITLE SYSTRAN> Tazza Europea

<IT-TITLE GOOGLE> Tazza Europea

<GE-TITLE manually translated> Fussballeuropameisterschaft

<GE-TITLE SYSTRAN> Europäische Schale

<GE-TITLE REVERSO> Europäischer Pokal

<SP-TITLE manually translated> Eurocopa

<SP-TITLE INTERTRAN> Europea Jícara

<SP-TITLE REVERSO> Taza europea

C118 (query translations failed in Italian, German and Spanish)

<EN-TITLE> Finland's first EU Commissioner

<IT-TITLE manually translated> Primo commisario europeo per la Finlandia

<IT-TITLE GOOGLE> Primo commissario dell'Eu della Finlandia

<IT-TITLE FREETRANSLATION> Finlandia primo Commissario di EU

<GE-TITLE manually translated> Erster EU-Kommissar aus Finnland

<GE-TITLE GOOGLE> Finnlands erster EUBEAUFTRAGTER

<GE-TITLE REVERSO> Finlands erster EG-Beauftragter

<SP-TITLE manually translated> Primer comisario finlandés de la UE

<SP-TITLE GOOGLE> Primera comisión del EU de Finlandia

<SP-TITLE REVERSO> El primer Comisionado de Unión Europea de Finlandia

multi-language barrier, we divided our document sources according to language and thus formed five different collections. After searching in these corpora and obtaining five result lists, we needed to merge them in order to provide users with a single list of retrieved articles.

Recent literature has suggested various solutions to merging separate result lists obtained from different collections or distributed information services. As a first approach, we will assume that each collection contains approximately the same number of pertinent items and that the distribution of the relevant documents is similar across the results lists. Based solely on the rank of the retrieved records, we can interleave the results in a round-robin fashion. According to previous studies [24], the retrieval effectiveness of such an interleaving scheme is around 40% below that achieved from a single retrieval scheme working with a single huge collection, representing the entire set of documents.

To account for the document score computed for each retrieved item (or the similarity value between the retrieved record D_i and the query, denoted rsv_i), we can formulate the hypothesis that each collection be searched by the same or a very similar search engine, and that the similarity values would be therefore directly comparable [25]. Such a strategy, called raw-score merging, produces a final list sorted by the document score computed by each collection. However, collection-dependent statistics in document or query weights may vary widely among collections, and therefore this phenomenon may invalidate the raw-score merging hypothesis [26].

To account for this fact, we could normalize the document scores within each collection by dividing them by the maximum score (i.e. the document score of the retrieved record in the first position). As a variant of this normalized score merging scheme, Powell *et al.* [27] suggested normalizing the document score rsv_i according to the following formula:

$$rsv'_i = (rsv_i - rsv_{min}) \; / \; (rsv_{max} - rsv_{min}) \tag{1}$$

in which rsv_i is the original retrieval status value (or document score), and rsv_{max} and rsv_{min} are the maximum and minimum document score values that a collection could achieve for the current query. In this study, the rsv_{max} is provided by the document score achieved by the first retrieved item and the retrieval status value obtained by the 1,000th retrieved record provides the value of rsv_{min}.

As a fourth strategy, we could use the logistic regression [28], [29] to predict the probability of a binary outcome variable, according to a set of explanatory variables. Based on this statistical approach, Le Calvé and Savoy [30] and Savoy [20] described how to predict the relevance probability for those documents retrieved by different retrieval schemes or collections. The resulting estimated probabilities are dependent on both the original document score rsv_i and the logarithm of the $rank_i$ attributed to the corresponding document D_i (see Equation 2). Based on these estimated relevance probabilities, we sort the records retrieved from separate collections in order to obtain a single ranked list. However, in order to estimate the underlying parameters, this approach requires a training set, which in this case was the CLEF 2001 topics and their relevance assessments.

$$Prob\;[\;D_i \; is \; rel \mid rank_i, \; rsv_i\;] = \frac{e^{\alpha + \beta_1 \cdot ln(rank_i) + \beta_2 \cdot rsv_i}}{1 + e^{\alpha + \beta_1 \cdot ln(rank_i) + \beta_2 \cdot rsv_i}} \tag{2}$$

where $rank_i$ denotes the rank of the retrieved document D_i, ln() is the natural logarithm, and rsv_i is the retrieval status value (or document score) of the document D_i. In this equation, the coefficients α, β_1 and β_2 are unknown parameters that are estimated according the maximum likelihood method (the required computations were programmed using the S system [31]).

When searching multi-lingual corpora using Okapi, both the round-robin and the raw-score merging strategies provide very similar retrieval performance results (see Table 16). Normalized score merging based on Equation 1 provides an

Table 16. Average precision using various merging strategies based on automatically translated queries

	Average precision				
Query TD	English 42 queries 50.08	French 50 queries UniNEfrBi 51.64	Italian 49 queries UniNEitBi 38.50	Spanish 50 queries UniNEesBi 50.67	German 50 queries UniNEdeBi 42.89
Multiling. 50 queries	Round-robin 34.27	Raw-score 33.83	Eq. 1 36.62	Log $\ln(rank_i)$ 36.10	Log reg Eq. 2 **39.49**
	English 42 queries 50.08	French 50 queries UniNEfrBi2 50.79	Italian 49 queries UniNEitBi2 38.62	Spanish 50 queries UniNEesBi2 50.95	German 50 queries UniNEdeBi2 42.11
Multiling. 50 queries	Round-robin 33.97	Raw-score 33.99	Eq. 1 36.90	Log $\ln(rank_i)$ 35.59	Log reg Eq. 2 39.25

enhancement over the round-robin approach (36.62 vs. 34.27, an improvement of +6.86% in our first experiment, and 36.90 vs. 33.97, +8.63% in our second run). Using our logistic model with only the rank as explanatory variable (or more precisely the $\ln(rank_i)$, performance shown under the heading "Log $\ln(rank_i)$"), the resulting average precision was lower than the normalized score merging. The best average precision was achieved by merging the result lists based on the logistic regression approach (using both the rank and the document score as explanatory variables).

Our official and corrected results are shown in Table 17 while some statistics showing the number of documents provided by each collection are given in Table 18. From these data, we can see that the normalized score merging (UniNEm1) extracts more documents for the English corpus (a mean of 24.94 items) than does the logistic regression model (UniNEm2 where a mean of 11.44 documents results from the English collection). Moreover, the logistic regression scheme retrieves more documents from the Spanish and German collections. Finally, we can see that the percentage of relevant items per collection (or language) is relatively similar when comparing CLEF 2001 and CLEF 2002 test-collections.

Table 17. Average precision obtained with our official multilingual runs

Query TD	UniNEm1 Equation 1	UniNEm2 Log reg Eq. 2	UniNEm3 Equation 1	UniNEm4 Log reg Eq. 2	UniNEm5 Equation 1
Corrected	36.62	39.49	36.90	39.25	35.97
Official	34.88	37.83	35.12	37.56	35.52

5 Amaryllis Experiments

For the Amaryllis experiments, we wanted to determine whether a specialized thesaurus might improve the retrieval effectiveness over a baseline, ignoring term relationships. From the original documents and during the indexing process, we retained the following logical sections in our runs: <TEXT>, <TI>, <AB>, <MC>, and <KW>.

From the given thesaurus, we extracted 126,902 terms having a relationship with one or more terms (the thesaurus contains 173,946 entries delimited by the tags <RECORD>...</RECORD>, however only 149,207 entries had at least one relationship with another term. From these 149,207 entries, we found 22,305 multiple entries such as, for example, the term "Poste de travail" or "Bureau poste", see Table 19. In such cases, we stored only the last entry). In building our thesaurus, we removed the accents, wrote all terms in lowercase, and ignored numbers and terms given between parenthesis. For example, the word "poste" appears in 49 records (usually as part of a compound entry in the <TERMFR> field).

From our 126,902 entries, we counted 107,038 TRADENG (English translation) relationships, 14,590 SYNOFRE1 (synonym), 26,772 AUTOP1 relationships and 1,071 VAUSSI1 (See also) relationships (see examples given in Table 19). In a first set of experiments, we did not use this thesaurus and we used the Title and Description logical sections of the topics (second column of Table 20) or the Title, Description and Narrative parts of the queries (last column of Table 20). In a second set of experiments, we included all related words that could be found in the thesaurus using only the search keywords (average precision shown under the label "Qthes"). In a third experiment, we enlarged only document

Table 18. Statistics about the merging schemes based on the top 100 retrieved documents for each query

Statistics \ Language	English	French	Italian	Spanish	German
UniNEm1, based on the top 100 retrieved documents for each query					
Mean	24.94	16.68	19.12	23.8	15.46
Median	23.5	15	18	22	15
Maximum	60	54	45	70	54
Minimum	4	5	5	6	2
Standard deviation	13.14	9.26	9.17	14.15	9.79
UniNEm2, based on the top 100 retrieved documents for each query					
Mean	11.44	15.58	16.18	34.3	22.5
Median	9	14	16	34.5	19
Maximum	33	38	28	62	59
Minimum	1	6	8	10	4
Standard deviation	6.71	7.49	5.18	10.90	11.90
% relevant items CLEF02	10.18%	17.14%	13.29%	35.37%	24.02%
% relevant items CLEF01	10.52%	14.89%	15.31%	33.10%	26.17%

Table 19. Sample of various entries under the word "poste" in the Amaryllis thesaurus

<RECORD> <TERMFR> Analyse de poste <TRADENG> Station Analysis ... <RECORD> <TERMFR> Bureau poste <TRADENG> Post offices <RECORD> <TERMFR> Bureau poste <TRADENG> Post office ... <RECORD> <TERMFR> Isolation poste électrique <TRADENG> Substation insulation ... <RECORD> <TERMFR> Caserne pompier <TRADENG> Fire houses <SYNOFRE1> Poste incendie ... <RECORD> <TERMFR> Habitacle aéronef <TRADENG> Cockpits (aircraft) <SYNOFRE1> Poste pilotage ...	<RECORD> <TERMFR> La Poste <TRADENG> Postal services ... <RECORD> <TERMFR> Poste conduite <TRADENG> Operation platform <SYNOFRE1> Cabine conduite ... <RECORD> <TERMFR> POSTE DE TRAVAIL <TRADENG> WORK STATION <RECORD> <TERMFR> Poste de travail <TRADENG> Work Station <RECORD> <TERMFR> Poste de travail <TRADENG> Work station <RECORD> <TERMFR> Poste de travail <TRADENG> workstations <SYNOFRE1> Poste travail ...

representatives using our thesaurus (performance shown under column heading "Dthes"). In a last experiment, we accounted for related words found in the thesaurus for document surrogates only and under the additional condition that such relationships could be found within at least three terms (e.g. "moteur à combustion" is a valid candidate but not single term like "moteur"). On the other hand, we also included in the query all relationships that could be found using the search keywords (performance shown under the column heading "Dthes3Qthes").

From the average precision shown in Tables 20 and 21, we cannot infer that the available thesaurus is really helpful in improving retrieval effectiveness, at least as implemented in this study.

However, the Amaryllis corpus presents another interesting feature. The logical sections <TI> and <AB> are used to delimit respectively the title and the abstract of each French scientific article written by the author(s) while the logical section <MC> marks the manually assigned keywords extracted from the INIST thesaurus. Finally, the section delimited by the <KW> tags corresponds to the English version of the manually assigned keywords.

Table 20. Average precision for various indexing and searching strategies (Amaryllis)

	Average precision				
Query Model	Amaryllis TD 25 queries	Amaryllis TD Qthes 25 queries	Amaryllis TD Dthes 25 queries	Amaryllis TD Dthes3Qthes 25 queries	Amaryllis TDN 25 queries
Okapi–npn	**45.75**	**45.45**	**44.28**	**44.85**	**53.65**
Lnu–ltc	43.07	44.28	41.75	43.45	49.87
dtu–dtc	39.09	41.12	40.25	42.81	47.97
atn–ntc	42.19	43.83	40.78	43.46	51.44
ltn–ntc	39.60	41.14	39.01	40.13	47.50
ntc–ntc	28.62	26.87	25.57	26.26	33.89
ltc–ltc	33.59	34.09	33.42	33.78	42.47
lnc–ltc	37.30	36.77	35.82	36.10	46.09
bnn–bnn	20.17	23.97	19.78	23.51	24.72
nnn–nnn	13.59	13.05	10.18	12.07	15.94

Table 21. Average precision using blind-query expansion (Amaryllis)

	Average precision				
Query Model	Amaryllis TD 25 queries	Amaryllis TD Qthes 25 queries	Amaryllis TD Dthes 25 queries	Amaryllis TD Dthes3Qthes 25 queries	Amaryllis TDN 25 queries
Okapi–npn	45.75	45.45	44.28	44.85	53.65
5 docs / 10 terms	47.75	47.29	46.41	46.73	55.80
5 docs / 50 terms	**49.33**	48.27	47.84	47.61	**56.72**
5 docs / 100 terms	49.28	48.53	47.78	47.83	56.71
10 docs / 10 terms	47.71	47.43	46.28	47.21	55.58
10 docs / 50 terms	49.04	48.46	48.49	48.12	56.34
10 docs / 100 terms	48.96	**48.60**	**48.56**	**48.29**	56.34
25 docs / 10 terms	47.07	46.63	45.79	46.77	55.31
25 docs / 50 terms	48.02	47.64	47.23	47.85	55.82
25 docs / 100 terms	48.03	47.78	47.38	47.83	55.80

Therefore, using the Amaryllis corpus, we could investigate whether the manually assigned descriptors result in better retrieval performance than the automatically based indexing scheme. To this end, we evaluated the Amaryllis collection using all logical sections (denoted "All" in Table 22), using only the title and the abstract of the articles (denoted "TI & AB") or using only the manually assigned keywords (performance shows under the label "MC & KW").

The conclusions that can be drawn from the data shown in Table 22 are clear. For all retrieval models, the manually assigned keywords result in better average

Table 22. Average precision when comparing manual and automatic indexing procedures

	Average precision					
Query Model	Amaryllis T All	Amaryllis T TI & AB	Amaryllis T MC & KW	Amaryllis TD All	Amaryllis TD TI & AB	Amaryllis TD MC & KW
Okapi–npn	**36.33**	**23.94**	**29.79**	**45.75**	**30.45**	**38.11**
Lnu–ltc	34.79	22.74	25.81	43.07	28.22	32.17
dtu–dtc	31.82	23.89	28.51	39.09	27.23	32.29
atn–ntc	35.01	23.32	29.11	42.19	28.16	35.76
ltn–ntc	31.78	20.42	26.40	39.60	24.58	32.90
ntc–ntc	21.55	16.04	17.58	28.62	21.55	24.16
ltc–ltc	25.85	17.42	20.90	33.59	24.44	26.62
lnc–ltc	26.84	16.77	21.66	37.30	26.12	29.29
bnn–bnn	21.03	11.29	22.71	20.17	11.71	19.80
nnn–nnn	8.99	5.12	8.63	13.59	7.39	11.00

precision than the automatic indexing procedure, using the short queries built only from using the Title section or when using both the Title and Description parts of the topics. However, the best performance was achieved by combining the manually assigned descriptors with the indexing terms extracted from the title and the abstract of the scientific articles.

However, the users usually enter short queries and are concerned with the precision achieved after 5 or 10 retrieved articles. In order to obtain a picture of the relative merits of using various indexing strategies within this context, we reported in Table 23 the precision achieved after retrieving 5 or 10 documents using the Okapi probabilistic model. From this table, we can see that the manually assigned keyword indexing scheme (label "MC & KW") provides better results than does the automatic indexing approach (label "TI & AB") when considering the precision achieved after 5 documents. When comparing the precision after 10 retrieved items, both approaches perform in a very similar manner. Finally, when using both indexing approaches (performances given under the label "All"), we achieve the best performance results.

Table 23. Precision after 5 or 10 retrieved documents

Query Title only Model	Amaryllis All 25 queries	Amaryllis TI & AB 25 queries	Amaryllis MC & KW 25 queries
Precision after 5	71.2%	59.2%	60.8%
Precision after 10	68.8%	54.4%	54.0%

Table 24. Official Amaryllis run descriptions

Run name	Query	Form	Model	Thesaurus	Query expansion	Precision
UniNEama1	TD	auto	Okapi	no	25 docs/50 terms	48.02
UniNEama2	TD	auto	Okapi	query	25 docs/25 terms	47.34
UniNEama3	TD	auto	Okapi	document	25 docs/50 terms	47.23
UniNEama4	TD	auto	Okapi	que & doc	10 docs/15 terms	47.78
UniNEamaN1	TDN	auto	Okapi	no	25 docs/50 terms	55.82

6 Conclusion

For our second participation in the CLEF retrieval tasks, we proposed a general stopword list and stemming procedure for French, Italian, German, Spanish and Finnish. We also tested a simple decompounding approach for German. For Dutch, Finnish and German, our objective was to examine 5-gram indexing and word-based (and decompounding-based) document representation, with respect to their ability to serve as distinct and independent sources of document content evidence, and to investigate whether combining these two (or three) indexing schemes would be a worthwhile strategy.

To improve bilingual information retrieval, we would suggest using not only one but two or three different translation sources to translate the query into the target languages. These combinations seem to improve retrieval effectiveness. In the multilingual environment, we demonstrated that a learning scheme such as logistic regression could perform effectively and as a second best solution, we suggest using a simple normalization procedure based on the document score.

Finally, in the Amaryllis experiments, we compared a manual with an automatic indexing strategy. We found that for French scientific papers manually assigning descriptors result in better performance than does automatic indexing based on the title and abstract. However, the best average precision is obtained when combining both manually assigned keywords and the automatic indexing scheme. With this corpus, we studied various possible techniques in which a specialized thesaurus could be used to improve average precision. However, the various strategies used in this paper do not demonstrate clear enhancement over a baseline that ignores the term relationships found in the thesaurus.

Acknowledgments

The author would like to thank C. Buckley from SabIR for giving us the opportunity to use the SMART system without which this study could not have been conducted. This research was supported in part by the SNSF (Swiss National Science Foundation) under grants 21-58 813.99 and 21-66 742.01.

References

[1] Savoy, J.: Report on CLEF-2001 Experiments: Effective Combined Query-Translation Approach. In: Peters, C., Braschler, M., Gonzalo, J., Kluck, M. (eds.): Evaluation of Cross-Language Information Retrieval Systems. Lecture Notes in Computer Science, Vol. 2406. Springer-Verlag, Berlin Heidelberg New York (2002) 27–43

[2] Robertson, S. E., Walker, S., Beaulieu, M.: Experimentation as a Way of Life: Okapi at TREC. Information Processing & Management **36** (2000) 95–108

[3] Fox, C.: A Stop List for General Text. ACM-SIGIR Forum **24** (1999) 19–35

[4] Savoy, J.: A Stemming Procedure and Stopword List for General French Corpora. Journal of the American Society for Information Science **50** (1999) 944–952

[5] Sproat, R.: Morphology and Computation. The MIT Press, Cambridge (1992)

[6] Lovins, J. B.: Development of a Stemming Algorithm. Mechanical Translation and Computational Linguistics **11** (1968) 22–31

[7] Porter, M. F.: An Algorithm for Suffix Stripping. Program **14** (1980) 130–137

[8] Figuerola, C. G., Gómez, R., Zazo Rodríguez, A. F., Berrocal, J. L. A.: Spanish Monolingual Track: The Impact of Stemming on Retrieval. In: Peters, C., Braschler, M., Gonzalo, J., Kluck, M. (eds.): Evaluation of Cross-Language Information Retrieval Systems. Lecture Notes in Computer Science, Vol. 2406. Springer-Verlag, Berlin Heidelberg New York (2002) 253–261

[9] Kraaij, W., Pohlmann, R.: Viewing Stemming as Recall Enhancement. In Proceedings of the ACM-SIGIR 1996. The ACM Press, New York (1995) 40–48

[10] Monz, C., de Rijke, M.: Shallow Morphological Analysis in Monolingual Information Retrieval for Dutch, German, and Italian. In: Peters, C., Braschler, M., Gonzalo, J., Kluck, M. (eds.): Evaluation of Cross-Language Information Retrieval Systems. Lecture Notes in Computer Science, Vol. 2406. Springer-Verlag, Berlin Heidelberg New York (2002) 262–277

[11] Chen, A.: Multilingual Information Retrieval Using English and Chinese Queries. In: Peters, C., Braschler, M., Gonzalo, J., Kluck, M. (eds.): Evaluation of Cross-Language Information Retrieval Systems. Lecture Notes in Computer Science, Vol. 2406. Springer-Verlag, Berlin Heidelberg New York (2002) 44–58

[12] Molina-Salgado, H., Moulinier, I., Knutson, M., Lund, E., Sekhon, K.: Thomson Legal and Regulatory at CLEF 2001: Monolingual and Bilingual Experiments. In: Peters, C., Braschler, M., Gonzalo, J., Kluck, M. (eds.): Evaluation of Cross-Language Information Retrieval Systems. Lecture Notes in Computer Science, Vol. 2406. Springer-Verlag, Berlin Heidelberg New York (2002) 226–234

[13] Chen, A.: Cross-Language Retrieval Experiments at CLEF 2002. In *this volume*

[14] Buckley, C., Singhal, A., Mitra, M., Salton, G.: New Retrieval Approaches Using SMART. In Proceedings TREC-4. NIST, Gaithersburg (1996) 25–48

[15] Singhal, A., Choi, J., Hindle, D., Lewis, D. D., Pereira, F.: AT&T at TREC-7. In Proceedings TREC-7. NIST, Gaithersburg (1999) 239–251

[16] Braschler, M., Peters, C.: CLEF 2002: Methodology and Metrics. In *this volume*

[17] Brand, R., Brünner, M.: Océ at CLEF 2002. In *this volume*

[18] McNamee, P., Mayfield, J., Piatko, C.: A Language-Independent Approach to European Text Retrieval. In: Peters, C. (ed.): Cross-Language Information Retrieval and Evaluation. Lecture Notes in Computer Science, Vol. 2069. Springer-Verlag, Berlin Heidelberg New York (2001) 131–139

[19] McNamee, P., Mayfield, J.: JHU/APL Experiments at CLEF: Translation Resources and Score Normalization. In: Peters, C., Braschler, M., Gonzalo, J., Kluck, M. (eds.): Evaluation of Cross-Language Information Retrieval Systems. Lecture Notes in Computer Science, Vol. 2406. Springer-Verlag, Berlin Heidelberg New York (2002) 193–208
[20] Savoy, J.: Cross-Language Information Retrieval: Experiments Based on CLEF-2000 Corpora. Information Processing & Management (2002) to appear
[21] Amati, G., Carpineto, C., Romano, G.: Italian Monolingual Information Retrieval with PROSIT. In *this volume*
[22] Nie, J. Y., Simard, M.: Using Statistical Translation Models for Bilingual IR. In: Peters, C., Braschler, M., Gonzalo, J., Kluck, M. (eds.): Evaluation of Cross-Language Information Retrieval Systems. Lecture Notes in Computer Science, Vol. 2406. Springer-Verlag, Berlin Heidelberg New York (2002) 137–150
[23] Gachot, D. A., Lange, E., Yang, J.: The SYSTRAN NLP Browser: An Application of Machine Translation Technology. In: Grefenstette, G. (ed.): Cross-Language Information Retrieval. Kluwer, Boston (1998) 105–118
[24] Voorhees, E. M., Gupta, N. K., Johnson-Laird, B.: The Collection Fusion Problem. In Proceedings of TREC-3. NIST, Gaithersburg (1995) 95–104
[25] Kwok, K. L., Grunfeld, L., Lewis, D. D.: TREC-3 Ad-hoc, Routing Retrieval and Thresholding Experiments Using PIRCS. In Proceedings of TREC-3. NIST, Gaithersburg (1995) 247–255
[26] Dumais, S. T.: Latent Semantic Indexing (LSI) and TREC-2. In Proceedings of TREC-2. NIST, Gaithersburg (1994) 105–115
[27] Powell, A. L., French, J. C., Callan, J., Connell, M., Viles, C. L.: The Impact of Database Selection on Distributed Searching. In Proceedings of ACM-SIGIR'2000. The ACM Press, New York (2000) 232–239
[28] Flury, B.: A First Course in Multivariate Statistics. Springer, New York (1997)
[29] Hosmer, D. W., Lemeshow, S.: Applied Logistic Regression. 2nd edn. John Wiley, New York (2000)
[30] Le Calvé, A., Savoy, J.: Database Merging Strategy Based on Logistic Regression. Information Processing & Management, **36** (2000) 341-359
[31] Venables, W. N., Ripley, B. D.: Modern Applied Statistics with S-PLUS. Springer, New York (1999)

UTACLIR @ CLEF 2002 - Bilingual and Multilingual Runs with a Unified Process

Eija Airio, Heikki Keskustalo, Turid Hedlund, and Ari Pirkola

Department of Information Studies
University of Tampere, Finland
{eija.airio,heikki.keskustalo}@uta.fi
turid.hedlund@shhh.fi
pirkola@tukki.jyu.fi

Abstract. The UTACLIR system of University of Tampere uses a dictionary-based CLIR approach. The idea of UTACLIR is to recognize distinct source key types and process them accordingly. The linguistic resources utilized by the framework include morphological analysis or stemming in indexing, normalization of topic words, stop word removal, splitting of compounds, translation utilizing bilingual dictionaries, handling of non-translated words, phrase composition of compounds in the target language, and constructing structured queries. UTACLIR was shown to perform consistently with different language pairs. The greatest differences in performance are due to the translation dictionary used.

1 Introduction

The cross-language information retrieval (CLIR) task in CLEF is bilingual or multilingual. In the first task, searching is on a target collection of documents written in the same language, while the other searches a collection of documents in written in multiple languages.

One of the main approaches used in CLIR is the dictionary-based strategy, which means utilizing bilingual dictionaries in translation. University of Tampere has developed a translation and query formulation tool, UTACLIR, which is based on the use of bilingual dictionaries and other linguistic resources.

The following kinds of difficulties can occur in dictionary-based CLIR. First, the translation may be problematic. Entries in dictionaries are typically in a normalized form, therefore the source words should also be normalized. However, morphological analyzers are not available for all languages, or they are expensive. Second, poor coverage of a dictionary may cause problems. If important topic words remain untranslated, the retrieval performance will be poor. Third, languages containing compounds (multiword expressions in which component words are written together) are difficult to handle in CLIR. Dictionaries never contain all possible compounds in

C.A. Peters (Ed.): CLEF 2002, LNCS 2785, pp. 91-100, 2003.

compound-rich languages. Therefore, morphological decomposition of compounds into constituents and their proper translation is important [1].

Retrieval topics often contain proper names in inflected form. In some cases even the base form of a proper name varies over languages because of differences in transliteration. Also technical terms are often absent in dictionaries. However, as their appearance tends to be quite similar in different languages, approximate string matching techniques, like n-gram based matching, can be applied when handling them [1].

Translation ambiguity is one of the main problems in dictionary-based CLIR. Dictionaries may contain many possible translation variants for a given source word. This can introduce noise in the query. Since queries tend to have a natural disambiguation effect because of other relevant contextual words, translation variants can be handled and the most relevant documents can still appear first in the result list.

In multilingual information retrieval an additional problem, the merging problem, is encountered. There are two main approaches towards solving this problem: merging result lists and merging indexes. In the first one separate indexes are built for each target language, and retrieval is performed separately from each index. The result lists must then be merged somehow. In the second approach, a common index is built for documents representing different languages. Queries in different languages are merged to one query, and retrieval is performed from the merged index.

2 The UTACLIR Approach

The University of Tampere has developed the UTACLIR translation and query formulation system for cross-language information retrieval. We participated in CLEF 2000 and 2001 utilizing the UTACLIR process, which consisted of separate, but similar programs for three language pairs: Finnish – English, Swedish – English and German – English. In CLEF 2002 we used a new version of UTACLIR: the same program used external language resources for all the different language pairs.

The source word processing of UTACLIR can be described on a general level as follows (see Figure 1). First the topic words are normalized with a morphological analyser, if possible, and after that source stop words are removed. Then translation is attempted. If a translation or translation variants are found, the further handling of the translated words depends on the form of the index. The target query words must be stemmed if the index is stemmed, and accordingly they must be normalized with a morphological analyzer if the index is morphologically normalized. Since stop word lists are in a morphologically normalized form, stop word removal can only be done when using the same method in target language queries.

The untranslatable words are mostly compound words, proper names and technical terms. In many cases these words are spelling variants of each other in different languages, thus allowing the use of approximate string matching techniques. The techniques utilized by the UTACLIR process are language-independent [2]. The best matching strings can be selected from the target index, enveloped with a synonym operator and added to the query.

Structuring of queries using the synonym operator, which means grouping of the target words derived from the same source word into the same facet, is applied in the

UTACLIR system. This has proved to be an effective strategy in CLIR in earlier studies [3].

Finally, UTACLIR has a special procedure for untranslatable compounds. They are first split into their constituents and then the components are translated separately. Translated parts are enveloped with a proximity operator [4].

It is possible to use parallel resources in the UTACLIR system. In that case the input codes denote not only the source and target language, but also specify the resource used. For example, if we have three different English – Finnish bilingual dictionaries in use, we can easily compare their performance as components of UTACLIR.

3 Runs and Results

The University of Tampere participated in CLEF 2002 in the Finnish monolingual task, the English – Finnish, English – French and English – Dutch tasks, and the multilingual task.

In this section, we first describe the language resources used, then the collections, and then the indexing strategy adopted. Finally, we report results of our official runs plus additional monolingual, bilingual and multilingual runs.

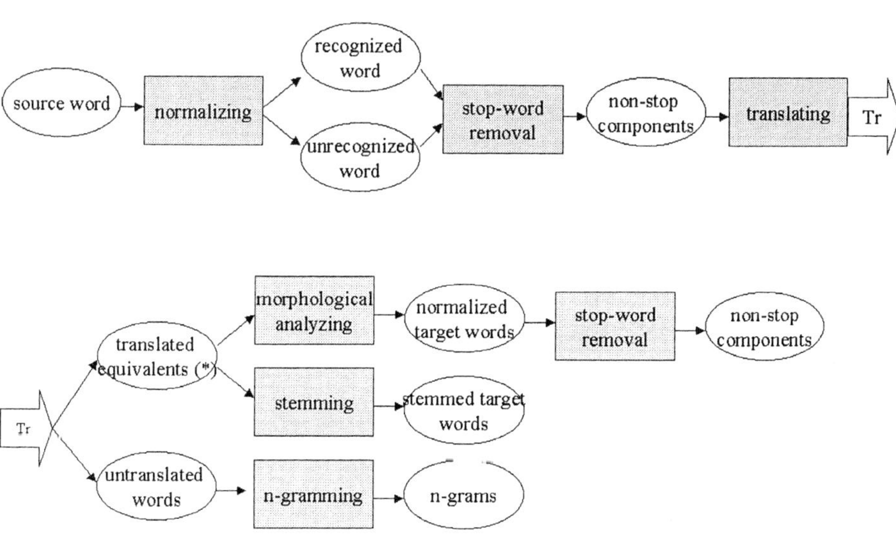

Fig. 1. An overview of processing a word in the UTACLIR process with English as source language. (Depending on the target language, either morphological analysis or stemming is performed.)

3.1 Language Resources

- Motcom GlobalDix multilingual translation dictionary (18 languages, total number of words 665 000) by Kielikone plc. Finland
- Motcom English – Finnish bilingual translation dictionary (110 000 entries) by Kielikone plc. Finland
- Morphological analysers FINTWOL, GERTWOL and ENGTWOL by Lingsoft plc. Finland
- Stemmers for Spanish and French, by ZPrise
- A stemmer for Italian, by the University of Neuchatel
- A stemmer for Dutch, by University of Utrecht
- An English stop word list, created on the basis of InQuery's default stop list for English
- A Finnish stop word list, created on the basis of the English stop list
- A German stop word list, created on the basis of the English stop list

3.2 Test Collections

The following test collections were used in the CLEF 2002 runs: English *LA Times*, Finnish *Aamulehti*, French *Le Monde*, French *SDA*, German *Der Spiegel*, German *SDA*, Italian *La Stampa*, Italian *SDA,* Spanish *EFE,* Dutch *NRC Handelsblad* and Dutch *Algemeen Dagblad.* We had to exclude German *Frankfurter Rundschau* from the official runs because of indexing problems, but we have made additional runs later in which it is present. Next, the indexing of the databases is described.

Lingsoft's morphological analyser FINTWOL was utilized in indexing the Finnish dataset, and GERTWOL in indexing the German datasets. As we did not have morphological analysers for Spanish, Italian, French and Dutch, we indexed those databases by utilizing stemmers. We used Zprise's Spanish stemmer, Zprise's French stemmer, the Italian stemmer granted by the University of Neuchâtel and the Dutch stemmer granted by University of Utrecht.

The *InQuery* system, provided by the Center for Intelligent Information Retrieval at the University of Massachusetts, was utilized in indexing and building the databases, as well as a retrieval system.

3.3 Monolingual Runs

We participated in CLEF 2002 with two monolingual runs, both in Finnish. The approach used in these runs was similar to our bilingual runs, only excluding translation. In the first run topic words were normalized using Lingsoft's morphological analyser FINTWOL. Compounds were split into their constituents. If a word was recognized by FINTWOL, it was checked against the stop word list, and the result (the normalized word, or nothing in the case of stop word) was processed further. If the word was not recognized, it was n-grammed. The n-gram function compares the word with the database index contents. The system utilized returns one best match form among morphologically recognized index words, and one best match form among non-recognized index words, and combines them with InQuery's synonym operator (#syn operator, see [5]).

Table 1. Average precision for Finnish monolingual runs using synonym and uw3 operator

	Average precision (%)	Difference (% units)	Change (%)
N-gramming and Synonym operator	27.0		
N-gramming and uw3 operator	35.2	+8.2	+30.4
No N-gramming, Synonym operator	24.0		
No N-gramming, uw3 operator	32.0	+8.0	+33.3

The second monolingual Finnish run was similar to the first one, except no n-gramming was done. Unrecognised words were added to the query as such. There was no big difference in performance between the results of these two Finnish monolingual runs.

Finnish is a language rich in compounds. Parts of a compound are often content bearing words [6]. Therefore, in a monolingual run it is reasonable to split a compound into its components, normalize the components separately, and envelope the normalized components with an appropriate operator. In the original run, we used the synonym operator in the monolingual runs for this purpose instead of the proximity operator, which turned out to be an inferior approach.

We made an additional run in order to gain a more precise view of the effect of the synonym operator in the compounds compared with the proximity operator. We replaced the synonym operator with InQuery's #uw3 operator (proximity with the window size 3) in order to connect the compound components. We compared these new results to the corresponding results in our CLEF runs (see Table 1). Average precision of this additional run was 30.4 % better in the run using n-grams, and 33.3 % better in the run using no n-grams. We can conclude that requiring all the parts of the compound to be present in the query is essential to get better results.

We made monolingual English, German, Spanish, Dutch, French and Italian runs as baseline runs for the bilingual runs. These monolingual runs are also reported in the next section.

3.4 Bilingual Runs

We participated in CLEF 2002 with three bilingual runs: English – Finnish, English – Dutch and English – French. The English – Dutch run was not reported in the CLEF Working Notes because of a severe failure in the indexing of the Dutch database. In this paper we will report the results of an additional run we made later. Bilingual English – German, English – Italian and English – Spanish runs were also done for CLEF 2002 multilingual task. We also made additional English – German and English – Finnish runs. In the first one the Frankfurter Rundschau dataset, which was not available during the CLEF runs, was added to the index. The average precision of the official run was 13.5 %, and that of the additional run 21.2 % In the additional English – Finnish run untranslatable words were added to the query in two forms: as such and preceded by the character "@" (unrecognised words are preceded by "@" in the index). The average precision of the official run was 20.2 %, and that of the additional run 24.6%.

Next we will report the performance of English – Finnish, English – German, English – Spanish, English – Dutch, English – French and English – Italian runs in order to clarify the performance of UTACLIR. Monolingual Finnish, German, Spanish, Dutch, French and Italian runs were made to provide the baseline runs.

The topics were in English in all cases, so the beginning of the process was similar in every language: topic words were normalized using ENGTWOL and after that the source stop words were removed. The GlobalDix dictionary was then used to translate the normalized source words into the target languages. As we have morphological analysers for Finnish and German (FINTWOL and GERTWOL by Lingsoft), they were used to normalize the translated target words. However, for Spanish, French, Italian and Dutch we did not have morphological analysers, thus we utilized stemmers instead. We used ZPrise's Spanish and French stemmers, the Italian stemmer of the University of Neuchâtel and a Dutch stemmer of the University of Utrecht. Target stop word removal was done only for morphologically analysed target queries (Finnish and German runs), as we did not have stop lists for stemmed word forms.

The average precision of the bilingual runs varies between 20.1 % (English – Italian run) and 24.6 % (English – Finnish run) (Table 2). The performance of UTACLIR is quite similar with all the six language pairs, but there are big differences in the monolingual runs between the languages. The average precision of the monolingual runs varied from 24.5 % (French) to 38.3 % (Spanish). The differences between the baseline run and the bilingual run vary from 0 % (English - French) to – 42.4 % (English – Italian).

We had a beta-version of UTACLIR in use during the runs. There were some deficiencies compared to the old version, because all the features of UTACLIR were not yet implemented in the new one. Splitting of compounds was not yet implemented, and non-translated words were handled by the n-gram method only in German as the target language. We also did not utilize target stop word removal in the case of stemming. Our stop word lists consist of morphologically normalized words at the moment, thus they could not be used as such to remove the stemmed forms. Implementing the Italian and Spanish dictionaries was also not complete when making the runs. Thus, we can expect better results with those languages after some development of UTACLIR.

The translation strings given by the GlobalDix sometimes contained lots of garbage. This had an impact on the result of the bilingual runs. We also have a parallel English – Finnish dictionary in use, which is a MOT dictionary with 110 000 entries (compared to 26 000 entries of GlobalDix). Both dictionaries are from the same producer, Kielikone plc. We made additional English – Finnish runs to clarify the effect of the dictionary on the result. (Table 3). The result was 32.5 % better using another translation source than in the original CLEF result. Thus, as expected, the use of a more extensive dictionary clearly improved the results.

As we did not have parallel resources for all the other languages, we could not compare the effect of the dictionary on these results.

Table 2. Average precision for monolingual and bilingual runs

	Average precision (%)	Difference (% units)	Change (%)
Monolingual Finnish	35.2		
Bilingual English–Finnish	24.6	-10.6	-30.1
Monolingual German	29.9		
Bilingual English–German	21.2	-8.7	-29.1
Monolingual Spanish	38.3		
Bilingual English –Spanish	21.8	-16.5	-43.1
Monolingual Dutch	32.2		
Bilingual English–Dutch	21.3	-10.9	-33.9
Monolingual French	24.5		
Bilingual English–French	23.9	-0.6	0
Monolingual Italian	34.9		
Bilingual English - Italian	20.1	-14.8	-42.4

Table 3. Average precision for English - Finnish bilingual runs using alternative resources

	Average precision (%)	Difference (% units)	Change (%)
GlobalDix	24.6		
MOT bilingual	32.6	+8.0	+32.5

3.5 Multilingual Runs

There are several possible result merging approaches. The simplest of them is *the Round Robin approach*, where a line of every result set is taken, one by one from each. This is the only possibility if only document rankings are available. This is not a very good approach, because collections seldom include the same number of relevant documents. If document scores are available, it is possible to use more advanced approaches. In *the raw score approach* the document scores are used as such as a basis of merging. The disadvantage of this approach is that the scores from different collections are not comparable. *The normalized score approach* tries to overcome this problem. Normalizing can be done for example by dividing the document score by the maximum score of the collection [7].

Table 4. Average precision for official and additional multilingual runs with different merging strategies

	Official CLEF 2002 runs	Additional runs	Difference (% units)	Change (%)
Raw score approach	16.4	18.3	+1.9	+11.6
Round robin approach	11.7	16.1	+4.4	+37.6

In the first official run we applied the raw score merging method, and in the second run the round robin method. In the official CLEF runs the material of Frankfurter Rundschau was not available. We made additional runs where it was included. The results of the additional runs were somewhat better than official runs (see table 4).

The average precision of the bilingual runs present in the multilingual runs can be seen in Table 2. The average precision for the monolingual English run was 47.6 %.

The results of our multilingual runs are quite poor compared to the corresponding bilingual runs. We must concentrate on different result merging techniques to achieve better results.

4 Discussion and Conclusion

The problems of dictionary-based cross-lingual information retrieval include word inflection, translation ambiguity, translation of proper names and technical terms, compound splitting, using of a stop list and query structuring. Multilingual tasks have an additional problem: result merging or index merging. The UTACLIR process can handle the first four problems. The merging problem is independent of the UTACLIR process for query translation and formulation. The merging problem has to be solved, however, when we are dealing with multilingual tasks.

Our test runs showed that the translation dictionary has a significant effect on CLIR performance. The multilingual dictionary we used that included several languages was not as extensive as separate bilingual dictionaries. The result of the multilingual task using a *result merging* approach was always worse than the results of the corresponding bilingual tasks. If the results of bilingual tasks are poor, it is impossible to achieve good multilingual results by merging. If an *index merging* approach is followed, there is no additional merging phase which would ruin results. However, defective translation also causes problems in this case.

Previous research results show that better results should be achieved by applying result merging than by index merging approach [8], [9]. However, as one goal of multilingual information retrieval is also to create functional systems for Internet, the index merging approach should be further studied in the future.

Acknowledgements

The *InQuery* search engine was provided by the Center for Intelligent Information Retrieval at the University of Massachusetts.

References

[1] Hedlund, T., Keskustalo, H., Pirkola, A., Airio, E., Järvelin K.: Utaclir @ CLEF 2001 – Effects of compound splitting and n-gram techniques. Evaluation of Cross-language Information Retrieval Systems. Lecture Notes in Computer Science; Vol. 2406. Springer-Verlag, Berlin Heidelberg New York (2002) 118-136

[2] Pirkola, A., Keskustalo, H., Leppänen, E., Känsälä, A., Järvelin, K.: Targeted s-gram matching: a novel n-gram matching technique for cross- and monolingual word form variants. Information Research, 7(2) (2002), http://InformationR.net/ir/7-2/paper126.html

[3] Pirkola, A.: The effects of query structure and dictionary setups in dictionary-based cross-language information retrieval. Proceedings of the 21st ACM/SIGIR Conference (1998) 55-63

[4] Hedlund, T., Keskustalo, H., Pirkola, A., Airio, E., Järvelin, K.: UTACLIR @ CLEF 2001: New features for handling compound words and untranslatable proper names. Working Notes for the CLEF 2001 Workshop, Italy (2001) 118-136, http://www.ercim.org/publication/ws-proceedings/CLEF2/hedlund.pdf

[5] Kekäläinen, J., Järvelin, K.: The impact of query structure and query expansion on retrieval performance. Proceedings of the 21st ACM/SIGIR Conference (1998) 130–137

[6] Hedlund, T., Pirkola, A., Keskustalo, H., Airio, E.: Cross-language information retrieval: using multiple language pairs. Proceedings of ProLISSA. The Second Biannual DISSAnet Conference, Pretoria (2002) 24-25 October, 2002

[7] Callan, J.P., Lu, Z., Croft, W.B.: Searching distributed collections with inference networks. Proceedings of the 18th ACM/SIGIR Conference (1995) 21-28

[8] Chen, A.: Cross-language retrieval experiments at CLEF 2002. Working Notes for the CLEF 2002 Workshop, Italy (2002) 5-20, http://clef.iei.pi.cnr.it:2002/workshop2002/WN/01.pdf

[9] Nie, J., Jin, F.: Merging different languages in a single document collection. Working Notes for the CLEF 2002 Workshop, Italy (2002) 59-62, http://clef.iei.pi.cnr.it:2002/workshop2002/WN/6.pdf

A Multilingual Approach to Multilingual Information Retrieval

Jian-Yun Nie and Fuman Jin

Laboratoire RALI
Département d'Informatique et Recherche opérationnelle, Université de Montréal
C.P. 6128, succursale Centre-ville, Montréal, Québec, H3C 3J7 Canada
{nie,jinf}@iro.umontreal.ca

Abstract. Multilingual IR is usually carried out by first performing cross-language IR on separate collections, each for a language. Once a set of answers has been found in each language, all the sets are merged to produce a unique answer list. In our experiments of CLEF2002, we propose a truly multilingual approach in which the documents in different languages are mixed in the same collection. Indexes are associated with a language tag so as to distinguish homographs in different languages. The indexing and retrieval processes can then be done once for all the languages. No result merging is required. This paper describes our first tests in CLEF2002.

1 Introduction

Most current approaches to CLIR make a clear separation between different languages. The following approach has been used in most of the previous studies:

1. Query translation: Translate an original query from the source language into all the other languages of interest;
2. Document retrieval: Using the original query and each of the translated queries to separately retrieve documents from the document sub-collection in the corresponding language;
3. Result merging: The results produced in different languages are merged to produce a unique result list.

We refer to this approach as "separate-retrieval-then-merging" approach. We can notice the following two facts in this approach: different languages are processed separately; it is assumed that the documents in each language form a separate document collection. This makes it necessary to carry out a merging step.

The clear separation between different language collections makes it difficult to compare the results in different languages. Previous studies [5] on result merging clearly showed that it is difficult to arrive at the same level of effectiveness in a unique collection with a retrieval-and-merging approach. That is, if a unique docu-

C.A. Peters (Ed.): CLEF 2002, LNCS 2785, pp. 101-110, 2003.

ment collection is separated into several sub-collections (according to whatever criterion), and one uses the "separate-retrieval-then-merging" approach on the sub-collections, the retrieval effectiveness is usually lower than what can be obtained with the unique document collection. Although this conclusion has been made for monolingual IR, we believe that it also applies to multilingual IR: the separation of documents according to languages will produce a similar effect to the separation of a monolingual document collection.

So in order to obtain a better retrieval effectiveness, we define an approach that deals with all the documents together within the same collection, whatever the languages used. In so doing, we can avoid the result-merging step, which usually generates additional problems.

In this paper, we propose a new approach to multilingual IR that deals with a unique document collection, in which all the languages are mixed. This is a multilingual approach to the problem of multilingual IR. Our experiments with CLEF2002 data show that such an approach may be better than the "separate-retrieval-then-merging" approach.

In the following section, we will first describe our approach. Then the experiments in CLEF2002 will be presented. Some analyses will be provided.

2 A Multilingual Approach to Multilingual IR

If we put all the documents into a mixed collection, the first question is how to distinguish words in different languages, especially for homographs such as "but" in English and "but" in French. We propose the following solution: to associate a language tag with every indexing term. For example, the French index "chaise" will be represented as "chaise_f". In such a way, we will also be able to distinguish the English stopword "but_e" from the French non-stopword "but_f". When a query is submitted to the system, and the user indicates the languages of interest, the original query is translated separately into all these languages. All the translations, and the original query, will be grouped into a large query expression for every language of interest. For example, suppose that the user's original query in English is "chair", and the languages of interest are English, French and Italian. Then once we have determined the translations of "chair" in French and Italian, we will arrive at a mixed query containing "chair_e", "chaise_f", "chaire_f", "présidence_f", "presidenza_i", "sedia_i", ... and so on. As both document indexes and query indexes are associated with the appropriate language tags, there is no need to retrieve documents in different languages separately. The retrieval of multilingual documents is no longer different from a monolingual IR problem.

One possible advantage of this approach is that the weights of index terms in different languages may be more comparable, because they are determined in the same way. Although the weights may still be unbalanced because of the unbalanced occurrences of index term in the document collection, the problem is much less severe than if document collections are processed separately.

Another advantage results from the removal of the problematic merging step. The retrieval result naturally contains answers in different languages. One may expect a higher effectiveness.

Finally, we believe that this approach contributes to lowering the barriers between different languages. In fact, documents in different languages often co-exist in the same collection (e.g. the Web). By separating them, we artificially enhance the difference between them. The difference between languages is not more (likely less) than the difference between different areas. In monolingual IR, documents in different areas are grouped into the same collection. Then why not also group documents in different languages in the same collection if they appear naturally together as on the Web?

However, this idea has never been tested in practice. Therefore, our experiments in CLEF2002 aim at obtaining the first experimental results using this idea. The approach we propose is illustrated in Figure 1. It contains the main steps described in the the rest of this section.

2.1 Language Identification

This step aims to identify the language of each document, so that the document can be submitted to the appropriate language-dependent pre-processing. Nowadays, automatic language identification is no longer a difficult problem. There are systems that are able to determine the language accurately using statistical language models. For example, the SILC[1] system developed at RALI (University of Montreal) is one of them. It can determine the language at an accuracy of over 99% when the text is longer than a line.

In CLEF experiments, as the language of each sub-collection is clearly identified, we do not need to use an automatic language identifier. The language is indicated manually in our experiments.

2.2 Language-Dependent Preprocessing

Each document is then submitted to a language-dependent pre-processing. This includes the following steps:

- Stop words in each language are removed separately;
- Each word is stemmed/lemmatized using the appropriate stemmer/lemmatizer of the language,
- Stems/lemmas are associated with the appropriate language tags such as _f, _e, _i, _g, and _s.

All the pre-processed documents form a new document collection, with the words in different languages clearly distinguished with language tags.

[1] http://www-rali.iro.umontreal.ca/

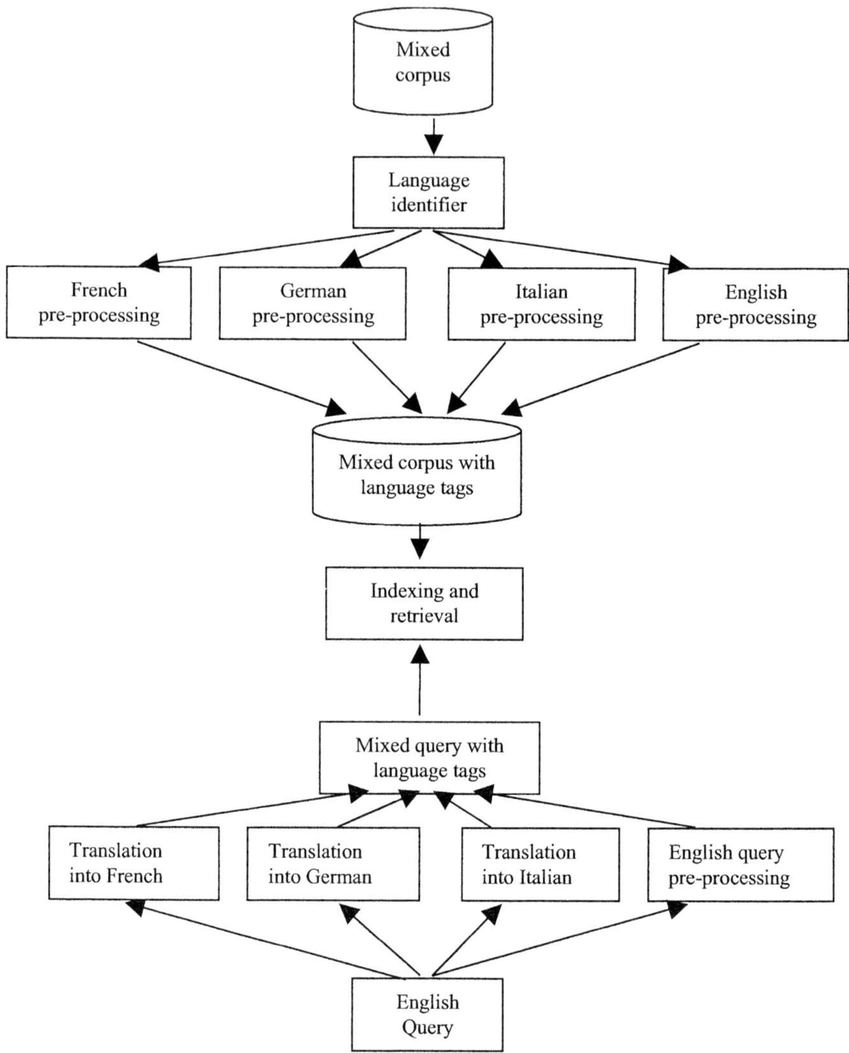

Fig. 1. Multilingual IR approach for a mixed document collection

2.3 Indexing of the Mixed Document Collection

Indexing is performed as for a monolingual document collection. Indexing terms in different languages are weighted according to the same weighting schema. A unique index file is created for all the languages.

In our case, we use the SMART system for indexing and retrieval. Terms are weighted using the following tf*idf schema:

$$tf(t, d) = \log(freq(t, d)+1),$$
$$idf(t) = \log(N/n(t)) ,$$

where freq(t, d) is the frequency of occurrences of term t in document d, N is the total number of documents in the mixed document collection, and n(t) is the number of documents containing t.

2.4 Query Translation

On the query side, similar processes are performed. In our case, the original queries are in English, and the documents to be retrieved are in English, French, Italian, German and Spanish. An original query is translated separately into French, Italian, German and Spanish. The translation words are stemmed and then associated with the appropriate language tag as for document indexes. All the translation words are then put together to form a unique multilingual query, including a part corresponding to the original query.

There is a problem of term weighting in the mixed query expression. As the translations are made independently, the resulting probabilities for different languages may not be comparable. We will discuss this problem in more detail later (section 4).

For query translation from English to the other languages, in our case, we use a set of statistical translation models. These models have been trained on a set of parallel texts. For EN-FR, EN-IT, and EN-DE, the parallel texts are parallel Web pages automatically mined with PTMiner [1]. These are the same translation models as we used last year for CLEF2001 [3]. We add EN-SP model this year. However, the EN-SP training corpus does not come from PTMiner, but from PAHO (Pan-America Health Organization)[2]. This organization holds a large set of parallel documents on public health, including English-Spanish. The total amount of the documents they provided us is about 50 MB for each language. However, at the moment we trained the translation models, only about 4 MB per language were available. So our translation model from English to Spanish was trained on a very small corpus.

2.5 Retrieval

The retrieval is performed in exactly the same way as in monolingual retrieval. The output is a list of documents in different languages.

3 Submitted Results

Three sets of results have been submitted to CLEF 2002. They are produced using the same translation models, but the weights of the terms in the mixed query vary as follows:

1. The weight of a translation word is its translation probability, and the original query terms in English are weighted as 1/n, where n is the number of words in the English query.

---

[2] http://www.paho.org/

2. The weights of translation words are normalized by the maximum probability in that language for the query, and the weights of English query words are assigned a uniform weight varying from 0.1 to 0.7.

The weighting methods we tried do not seem to work well. In fact, with all the three solutions, we observed that very often, one language dominates in the mixed result list: the first 100 documents retrieved are almost only in that language. This shows that we did not reach a reasonable balance between languages. Our intention in mixing the documents in a unique collection is to create a better balance between languages, and we expected to achieve this by the use of the same weighting scheme. However, at a first glance, the results do not seem to confirm this. Figure 2 shows the best performance among the three result sets submitted. We can see that this is well below the medium performance of the participants.

4 Result Analysis

In order to understand why our methods have not performed well, and to separate the multilingual approach from the quality of translations, further analyses have been carried out on the results and on the processes we used.

4.1 CLIR Effectiveness

The first factor that affects the multilingual IR effectiveness is the quality of translation. In order to assess this, we performed a cross-language IR experiment between English and each of the other languages. The following table shows the effectiveness obtained.

As we can see, the effectiveness of SP-EN is much lower than the other cases. This is clearly the main reason why the results we submitted were poor. The EN-DE CLIR does not perform well either. This may be due to the fact that we used a very simple stemmer for German, which is far from sufficient for an agglutinative language such as German. It may also be due to the quality of our training corpus that is mined from the Web. Curiously, using the same translation model last year, we did not observe a difference of the same magnitude between EN-DE and EN-FR, EN-IT. However, we did not carry out an in-depth analysis due to our limited knowledge on German.

In our subsequent experiments, we will not use Spanish for which the translation is clearly not good enough. We will only report the experiments for the other languages for which the translations are done with the parallel texts that we mined from the Web with PTMiner [1].

Table 1. English monolingual and cross-language IR effectiveness in CLEF 2002

Q-D languages	EN-EN	EN-FR	EN-DE	EN-IT	SP-EN
IR effectiveness	0.4228	0.2802	0.1198	0.1990	0.0998

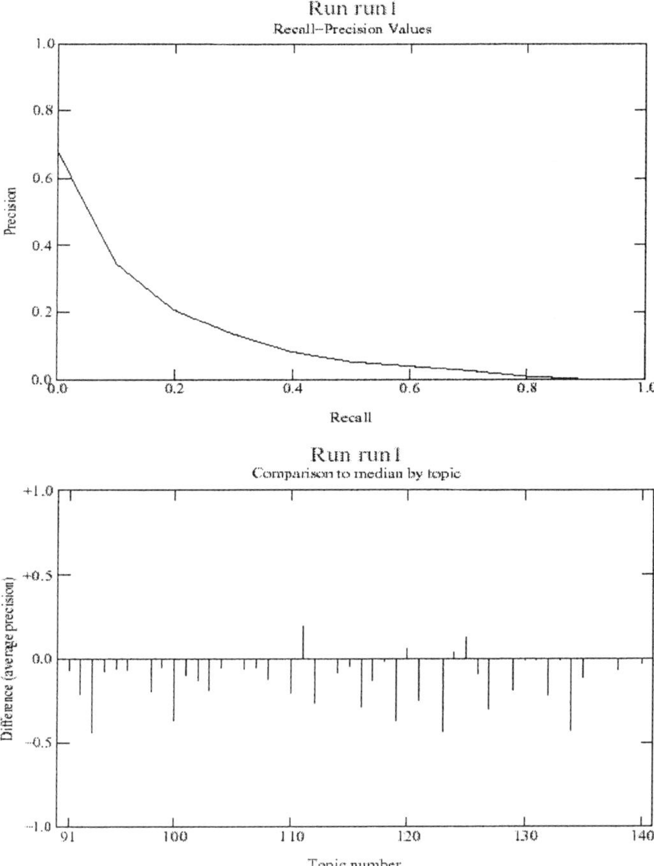

Fig. 2. The best performance we obtained in CLEF 2002 and its comparison with the medium performance

4.2 Using the "Separate-Retrieval-then-Merging" Approach

To have a point of comparison, we implemented the following "separate-retrieval-then-merging" approaches: The original English queries are translated into the other languages using the same translation models; then documents are retrieved in each language (including English) separately; finally, the retrieved documents are merged according to two common strategies – Round-Robin and Raw similarity score [5]. The following table shows the effectiveness with these approaches.

Table 2. Multilingual IR effectiveness with different merging methods

	MLIR effectiveness
Round-Robin	0.1531
Raw similarity score	0.1461

```
america_de              0.282324
ai_de                   0.201025
amerika_de              0.176705
latein_de               0.135495
the_de                  0.077340
lateinamerika_de        0.072702
latin_de                0.054411

amérique_fr             0.546261
latin_fr                0.394064
ai_fr                   0.059675

amer_it                 0.388238
latin_it                0.274379
to_it                   0.172038
the_it                  0.091409

AI_en                   0.250000
in_en                   0.250000
latin_en                0.250000
america_en              0.250000
```

Fig. 3. An example of mixed query

4.3 Multilingual IR with a Mixed Document Collection

Our purpose here is to compare our approach using a mixed document collection with the "separate-retrieval-then-merging" approach. As the translations are performed in the same way, our comparison will directly show the difference between the two methods to multilingual IR.

4.3.1 Using Raw Translation Probabilities

Globally, the raw translation probabilities for a query are relatively balanced, because the sum of the translation probabilities for each field of the query is close to 1 (the difference is assigned to the translation words we did not keep). The translation words with probabilities lower than 0.05 are removed. The key problem is the balance between the original query in the source language and the translated ones. As the translation of each field sums to 1, we assign the weight $1/n$ to each source query word, where n is the number of words in the field of a source query. Such an assignment creates a relatively good balance between the query translations and the original query in the source language: the total weight of words in each field of a query in each language is close to 1. Figure 3 shows the mixed query resulting for the title field of the first query in CLEF 2002 on "AI [Amnesty International] in Latin America".

Table 3. Multilingual IR effectiveness with different weights assigned to English query words

Weight	0.1	0.2	0.3	0.4	0.5	0.7
Avg. P	0.1253	0.1562	0.1694	0.1606	0.1411	0.1078

Notice that several English stopwords (e.g. to, the) have been included in the Italian and German translations. These stopwords will be filtered out during indexing using an enhanced stoplist that includes all the stopwords with language tags, as well as a set of stopwords in the source language that may appear in the translations because of the noise of the translation models. We obtain an average precision of 0.1569 with this method. In comparison with Table 2, we see that the effectiveness is slightly improved (by respectively 2.5% and 7.4%) over Round Robin and Raw Score merging. Although the improvements are not large, we can say that the approach with a mixed collection can at least work as well as approaches using separate collections.

Notice also that the improvements we obtained are in the same magnitude as the difference between the unique collection approach and the "separate-retrieval-then-merging" approach on a monolingual document collection [5]. So this experimental result seems to confirm that separating a mixed document collection into several sub-collections according to languages will produce a degradation similar to the case of monolingual IR.

4.3.2 Using Normalized Weights for Translations

Another way to balance the weights of terms in different languages is to normalize the weights in each language: the raw translation probability of a word is divided by the maximal probability of the translation words for that query in that language. We assigned a uniform value to every query word in the source language, and varied the weight between 0.1 and 0.7. The following table shows the results.

In comparison with the "separate-retrieval-then-merging" approach shown in Table 2, we can see that if the uniform weight is assigned at a reasonable value (in particular, at 0.3), improvements in multilingual IR effectiveness are obtained: respectively 10.6% higher than Round-Robin and 16.0% higher than the raw similarity score method. This figure further confirms the possible advantage we can obtain with an approach on a mixed document collection.

This case also shows that the previous method with raw probabilities does not create the best balance between different languages. A better equilibrium has yet to be found in the mixed query between different languages. Does this mean that by using this approach on a mixed document collection, we are moving the weight-balance problem from the documents in different languages to the query side? Our answer is "probably". Although our experiments do not allow us to formally affirm this, it is our belief that it is easier to create a balance between languages in the mixed query than to create a balance between languages for documents. In fact, all the versions of a query intend to express the same information need and thus aim to contain the same amount of information. This makes it possible to create a balance between different versions of the query. The same balance would be much more difficult to achieve on documents. In some cases, it is even impossible if we do not have the distribution information among documents (this is the case when separate retrievals are carried out with search engines on the Web).

translations of a phrase or word are considered and no attempts to disambiguate the query were made.

One of the main goals of our participation in the GIRT and Amaryllis tasks was to experiment with the keywords used in the collections. Many domain-specific collections, such as the scientific collections of GIRT and Amaryllis, contain keywords. Our strategy for CLEF 2002 was to compute the similarity of keywords based on their occurrence in the collection, and explore whether the resulting keyword space can be used to improve retrieval effectiveness.

The paper is organized as follows. In Section 2 we describe the FlexIR system as well as the approaches used for each of the tasks in which we participated. Section 3 describes our official runs for CLEF 2002, and in Section 4 we discuss the results we have obtained. Finally, in Section 5 we offer some conclusions regarding our document retrieval efforts.

2 System Description

All submitted runs used FlexIR, an information retrieval system developed by the second author. The main goal underlying FlexIR's design is to facilitate flexible experimentation with a wide variety of retrieval components and techniques. FlexIR is implemented in Perl; it is built around the standard UNIX pipeline architecture, and supports many types of preprocessing, scoring, indexing, and retrieval tools, which proved to be a major asset for the wide variety of tasks in which we took part this year.

2.1 Approach

The retrieval model underlying FlexIR is the standard vector space model. All our official mono- and bilingual runs for CLEF 2002 used the Lnu.ltc weighting scheme [2] to compute the similarity between a query and a document. For the experiments on which we report in this note, we fixed *slope* at either 0.1 or 0.2; the pivot was set to the average number of unique words per document.

2.2 Morphological Normalization

Previous retrieval experiments [9] in English have not demonstrated that morphological normalization such as rule-based stemming [17] or lexical stemming [11] consistently yields significant improvements. As to the effect of stemming on retrieval performance for languages that are morphologically richer than English, such as Dutch, German, or Italian, in our experiments for CLEF 2001 we consistently found that morphological normalization does improve retrieval effectiveness [14].

Stemming/Lemmatizing. For this year's monolingual experiments the aim was to improve our existing morphological analysis for languages that we had dealt with before (i.e, Dutch, German, and Italian), and to extend it to languages that we had not dealt with before (i.e., Finnish, French, Spanish, and Swedish). Where available we tried to use a lexical-based stemmer, or lemmatizer: for French, German, and Italian we used lemmatizers that are part of TreeTagger [19]. For Dutch we used a Porter stemmer developed within the Uplift project [21]; for Spanish we also used a version of Porter's stemmer [3]. We did not have access to (linguistically motivated) morphological normalization tools for Finnish or Swedish.

For the GIRT and Amaryllis task, we used TreeTagger for processing the main text. The keywords, i.e., GIRT's controlled-terms and Amaryllis' controlled vocabulary, were indexed as given, indexing the keywords or keyword-phrases as a single token.

Compound Splitting. For Dutch and German, we applied a compound splitter to analyze complex words, such as *Autobahnraststätte* (English: highway restaurant), *Menschenrechte* (English: human rights), *Friedensvertrag* (English: peace agreement), etc. In addition to these noun-noun compounds, there are several other forms of compounding, including verb-noun (e.g., German: *Tankstelle*, English: gas station), verb-verb (e.g., German: *spazierengehen*, English: taking a walk), noun-adjective (e.g., German: *arbeitslos*, English: unemployed), adjective-verb (e.g., German: *sicherstellen*, English: to secure); etc., see [6] for a more detailed overview. In last year's participation we focused on noun-noun compound splitting, but this year we tried to cover the other forms for German as well. This resulted in a much larger compound dictionary for German. Whereas last year's dictionary contained 108,489 entries, it grew up to 772,667 for this year's participation. An entry in the compound dictionary consists of a complex word and its parts, where each part is lemmatized. See [14] for further details on the actual process of compound splitting.

For retrieval purposes, each document in the collection is analyzed and if a compound is identified, both the compound and all of its parts are added to the document. Compounds occurring in a query are analyzed in a similar way: the parts are simply added to the query. Since we expand both the documents and the queries with compound parts, there is no need for compound formation [16].

Ngrams. To obtain a zero-knowledge language independent approach to morphological normalization, we implemented an ngram-based method in addition to our linguistically motivated methods.

Table 1. Average word length and ngram length used for the ngram base runs

	Dutch	*Finnish*	*French*	*German*	*Italian*	*Spanish*	*Swedish*
Avg. word length	5.4	7.3	4.8	5.8	5.1	5.1	5.4
Ngram length	5	6	4	5	5	5	5

For each of the seven non-English languages in the monolingual task we determined the average word length, and set the ngram-length to be the largest integer less than the average word length, except for Finnish, where we set the ngram-length to be 6, while the average word length is 7.3; see Table 1 for the details. For each word we stored both the word itself and all possible ngrams that can be obtained from it without crossing word boundaries. For instance, the Dutch version of Topic 108 contains the phrase *maatschappelijke gevolgen* (English: societal consequences); using ngrams of length 5, this becomes:

> *maatschappelijke maats aatsc atsch tscha schap chapp happe appel ppeli pelij elijk lijke gevolgen gevol evolg volge olgen*

2.3 Blind Feedback

Blind feedback was applied to expand the original query with related terms. Term weights were recomputed by using the standard Rocchio method [18], where we considered the top 10 documents to be relevant and the bottom 500 documents to be non-relevant. We allowed at most 20 terms to be added to the original query. For Dutch and German, the added words are also decompounded, and the complex words and their parts are added to the query.

The text runs for the GIRT and Amaryllis tasks used blind feedback, while it was switched off for the keyword runs. To aid comparison with the monolingual runs, the same feedback settings were used. There is a remarkable difference in the effect of feedback: virtually no words are added for the GIRT and Amaryllis tasks.

2.4 Combined Runs

In addition to our morphological interests we also wanted to experiment with combinations of (what we believed to be) different kinds of runs in an attempt to determine their impact on retrieval effectiveness. More specifically, for each of the languages for which we had access to language specific morphological normalization tools (i.e., stemmers or lemmatizers), we created a base run using those tools. In addition, we used ngrams in the manner described above to create a second base run. We then combined these two base runs in the following manner. First, we normalized the retrieval status values (RSVs), since different runs may have radically different RSVs. For each run we re-ranked these values in $[0.5, 1.0]$ using:

$$RSV_i' = 0.5 + 0.5 \cdot \frac{RSV_i - min_i}{max_i - min_i}$$

and assigned all documents not occurring in the top 1000, the value 0.5; this is a variation of the Min_Max_Norm considered in [13].[1] Next, we assigned new

[1] We also conducted pre-submission experiments with a product combination rule, for which our normalization yielded better results than the standard normalization of [13]. For the combination method used, the $[0.5, 1]$ normalization is identical to the standard $[0, 1]$ normalization.

weights to the documents using a linear interpolation factor λ representing the relative weight of a run:

$$RSV_{new} = \lambda \cdot RSV_1 + (1 - \lambda) \cdot RSV_2.$$

For $\lambda = 0.5$ this is similar to the simple (but effective) summation function used by Fox and Shaw [8], and later by Belkin et al. [1] and Lee [12, 13]. The interpolation factors λ were obtained from experiments on the CLEF 2000 and 2001 data sets (where available).

For the GIRT and Amaryllis task, we created alternative base runs based on the usage of the keywords in the collection, and combined these with the text-based runs.

3 Runs

We submitted a total of 27 runs: 10 for the monolingual task, 7 for the bilingual task, and 5 each for the GIRT and Amaryllis tasks. Below we discuss our runs in some detail.

3.1 Monolingual Runs

All our monolingual runs used the title and description fields of the topics. Table 2 provides an overview of the runs that we submitted for the monolingual task. The third column in Table 2 indicates the type of run:

- *Morphological* — topic and document words are lemmatized and compounds are split (Dutch, German), using the morphological tools described in Section 2.
- *Ngram* — both topic and document words are ngram-ed, using the settings discussed in Section 2.
- *Combined* — two base runs are combined, an ngram run and a morphological run, using the interpolation factor λ given in the fourth column.

Both topics and documents were stopped. First of all, for each language we used a stop phrase list containing phrases such as 'Find documents that discuss ...'; stop phrases were automatically removed from the topics. We then stopped both topics and documents using the same stop word list. We determined the 400 most frequent words, then removed from this list content words that we felt might be important despite their high frequency. For instance, in most of the document collections terms such as 'Europe' and 'dollar' occur with high frequency. We did not use a stop ngram list, but in our *ngram* runs we first used a stop *word* list, and then ngram-ed the topics and documents. For the ngram runs we did not replace diacritic letters by their non-diacritic counterparts, for the morphological runs we did.

3.2 The Bilingual Task

We submitted a total of 7 bilingual runs, using English as the topic language, and Dutch and German as document languages.

For the bilingual runs, we followed a dictionary-based approach. The translations of the words and phrases of the topic are simply added to the query in an unstructured way; see [15] for a more elaborated way of query formulation. The original queries are translated to Dutch using the Ergane dictionary [7], and to German using the Ding dictionary [5], version 1.1. The Ergane dictionary contains 15,103 English head words and 45,068 translation pairs in total. The Ding dictionary contains 103,041 English head words and 145,255 translation pairs in total.

Since the Ergane dictionary is rather small, we used a pattern-based approach to extend the translation dictionary with additional translation pairs. Table 4 shows some of the patterns. Notice that the vast majority of the words that match one or more of these patterns are words that are derived from Latin. If an English word was not in the Ergane dictionary each matching pattern was applied and all translations were added to the query. Of course, this rather adhoc approach to translation is far from perfect. For instance, *privatization* will

Table 2. Overview of the monolingual runs submitted. For combined runs column 3 gives the base runs that were combined, and column 4 gives the interpolation factor λ

Run	*Language*	*Type*	*Factor*
UAmsC02DuDuNGiMO	Dutch	Ngram/Morphological	0.71
UAmsC02DuDuNGram	Dutch	Ngram	–
UAmsC02FiFiNGram	Finnish	Ngram	–
UAmsC02FrFrNGiMO	French	Ngram/Morphological	0.60
UAmsC02GeGeLC2F	German	Morphological	–
UAmsC02GeGeNGiMO	German	Ngram/Morphological	0.285
UAmsC02GeGeNGram	German	Ngram	–
UAmsC02ItItNGiMO	Italian	Ngram/Morphological	0.25
UAmsC02SpSpNGiSt	Spanish	Ngram/Morphological	0.70
UAmsC02SwSwNGram	Swedish	Ngram	–

Table 3. Overview of the bilingual runs submitted

Run	*Topics*	*Documents*	*Type*	*Factor*
UAmsC02EnDuMorph	English	Dutch	Morphological	–
UAmsC02EnDuNGiMO	English	Dutch	Ngram/Morphological	0.71
UAmsC02EnDuNGram	English	Dutch	Ngram	–
UAmsC02EnGeLC2F	English	German	Morphological 1	–
UAmsC02EnGeMOiMO	English	German	Morphological/Morphological 2	0.50
UAmsC02EnGeNGiMO	English	German	Ngram/Morphological 1	0.285
UAmsC02EnGeNGram	English	German	Ngram	–

Table 4. Patterns to extend the English-Dutch dictionary

Patterns	*Example Translation Pairs*	
	English	*Dutch*
(1) `s/acy$/atie/`	democracy	democratie
(2) `s/ency$/entie/`	urgency	urgentie
(3) `s/ency$/ens/`	tendency	tendens
(4) `s/([aeiou])ssion$/$1ssie/`	commission	commissie
(5) `s/zation$/sering/`	privatization	privatisering
(6) `s/zation$/satie/`	realization	realisatie
(7) `s/ation$/atie/`	relation	relatie
(8) `s/ical$/isch/`	medical	medisch
(9) `s/ical$/iek/`	identical	identiek
(10) `s/idal$/idaal/`	suicidal	suicidaal
(11) `s/ic$/iek/`	specific	specifiek
(12) `s/([gmr])y$/$1ie/`	industry	industrie
(13) `s/ty$/teit/`	university	universiteit
(14) `s/ism$/isme/`	realism	realisme

be translated as *privatisering* (correct), by applying pattern (5), and *privatisatie* (incorrect), by applying pattern (6). Although this is unacceptable for machine translation applications, those erroneous translations have virtually no impact on retrieval effectiveness, because almost all of them are non-existing words that do not occur in the inverted index anyway.

Just like our Dutch and German monolingual runs, we prepared morphological and ngram-based runs, and combined these in order to improve effectiveness; see Table 3 for the details.

3.3 The GIRT and Amaryllis Tasks

As pointed out in Section 1, our strategy for the GIRT and Amaryllis tasks in CLEF 2002 was to compute the similarity of keywords based on their occurrence in the collection, and investigate whether the resulting keyword space can be used to improve retrieval effectiveness. We assumed that keywords that are frequently assigned to the same documents, will have similar meaning. We determined the number of occurrence of keywords and of co-occurrences of pairs of keywords used in the collection, and used these to define a distance metric. Specifically, we used the Jaccard similarity coefficient on the log of (co)occurrences, and used 1 minus the Jaccard score as a distance metric [10]. For creating manageable size vectors for each of the keywords, we reduced the matrix using metric multi-dimensional scaling techniques [4]. For all calculations we used the best approximation of the distance matrix on 10 dimensions. This resulted in a 10-dimensional vector for each of the 6745 keywords occurring in the GIRT collection. The Amaryllis collection uses a much richer set of 125360 keywords, which we reduced by selecting the most frequent ones; this resulted in vectors for 10274 keywords occurring ≥ 25 times in the collection. For our official CLEF runs we experimented with

Table 5. Keywords for the GIRT and Amaryllis tasks

(a) GIRT topic 51 (recovered)	(b) Amaryllis topic 1 (monolingual, given)	(c) Amaryllis topic 1 (bilingual, recovered)
Selbstbewußtsein	*Concentration et toxicité des polluants*	*Qualité air*
familiale Sozialisation	*Mécanisme de formation des polluants*	*Moteur diesel*
Junge	*Réduction de la pollution*	*Trafic routier urbain*
Adoleszenz	*Choix du carburant*	*Autobus*
Subkultur	*Réglage de la combustion*	*Azote oxyde*
Erziehungsstil	*Traitement des gaz d'échappement*	*Exposition professionnelle*
soziale Isolation	*Législation et réglementation*	*Véhicule à moteur*
Marginalität		*Carburant diesel*
Bewußtseinsbildung		*Inventaire source pollution*
Pubertät		*Carburant remplacement*

these keywords spaces for two specific purposes: keyword recovery and document re-ranking.

We used the following strategy for determining vectors for the documents and for the topics: we took the top 10 documents from a base run (not using the keywords). For each of these documents we collected the keywords, and determined a document vector by taking the mean of the keyword vectors. Next, we determined a vector for the topic by taking the weighted mean of the vectors for the top 10 documents. For document re-ranking, we simply re-ranked the documents retrieved in the base run by the distance between the document and topic vectors. For keyword recovery, we considered the keywords used in the top 10 documents, and selected the ten keywords that are closest to the topics vector. Table 5(a) shows the keywords recovered for GIRT topic 51.

For the Amaryllis task, we can compare the provided topic keywords in the narrative field (shown in Table 5(b)), with the topic keywords resulting from our automatic keyword recovery (shown in Table 5(c)). The recovered keywords are subsequently used in a keyword-only run.

For the GIRT task, we submitted three monolingual runs and two bilingual (English to German) runs. All our GIRT runs use the title and description fields of the topics. The morphological base run mimics the settings of our monolingual morphological base run for German. Based on the top 10 documents from the base run, we use the keyword space for recovering keywords for the topics as discussed above. The topic vector based on the top 10 documents of the base run is also used for re-ranking the documents retrieved in our base run. Experimentation on topics of CLEF 2000 and CLEF 2001 revealed that the keyword and re-rank runs perform worse than the base text run, yet a combination of the base run with either a keyword or a re-rank run helps to improve the performance. Our runs for the bilingual GIRT task (English topics) used the translation method of the German bilingual task (using the *Ding* dictionary) for translation of the title and description fields. For the rest, the bilingual runs

Table 6. Overview of the runs submitted for the GIRT and Amaryllis tasks

Run	*Task*	*Topics*	*Documents*	*Type*	*Factor*
UAmsC02GeGiTT	GIRT	German	German	Morphological	–
UAmsC02GeGiTTiKW	GIRT	German	German	Morphological/Keyword	0.70
UAmsC02GeGiTTiRR	GIRT	German	German	Morphological/Re-rank	0.60
UAmsC02EnGiTTiKW	GIRT	English	German	Morphological/Keyword	0.70
UAmsC02EnGiTTiRR	GIRT	English	German	Morphological/Re-rank	0.60
UAmsC02FrAmTT	Amaryllis	French	French	Morphological	–
UAmsC02FrAmKW	Amaryllis	French	French	Keyword	–
UAmsC02FrAmTTiKW	Amaryllis	French	French	Morphological/Keyword	0.70
UAmsC02EnAmTTiKW	Amaryllis	English	French	Morphological/Keyword	0.70
UAmsC02EnAmTTiRR	Amaryllis	English	French	Morphological/Re-rank	0.60

mimic the monolingual runs. We made a base morphological run, and recovered keywords for a keyword-only run and a document re-ranking; see Table 6 for the details.

For the Amaryllis task, we submitted three monolingual runs and two bilingual (English to French) runs. Our morphological base run uses the same settings as the monolingual French run. For the keyword-only run, keywords were taken from the narrative fields of the topics. For the bilingual Amaryllis task, we used Systran [20] to translate the title and description fields of the English topics. We did not use the provided English keywords, nor the special dictionary provided. We made a morphological base run (similar to the monolingual task), and collected the keywords from the top 10 documents, which were then used for determining a document re-ranking and for keyword recovery; again, see Table 6 for the details.

4 Results

This section summarizes the results of our CLEF 2002 submissions.

4.1 Monolingual Results

Table 7 contains our non-interpolated average precision scores for all languages. In addition to the scores for our submitted runs, the table also lists the scores for the base runs that were used to generate the combined runs.

We were somewhat surprised by the low scores of our morphological run for Dutch (0.3673) and of the ngram run for Italian (0.3672). The former is probably due to the fact that we used a reasonably crude stemmer, instead of a proper lemmatizer; the latter may be due to the fact that we did not replace diacritic characters by the corresponding non-diacritic letters.

Observe that for all languages for which we submitted combined runs, the combined run outperforms the underlying base runs; in some cases the differences do not seem to be significant, but in others they do. Figure 1 displays the interpolated precision-recall curves for all languages for which we submitted combined runs. The superior performance of the combined runs can again be observed here. Several authors have proposed the following rationale for combining (high

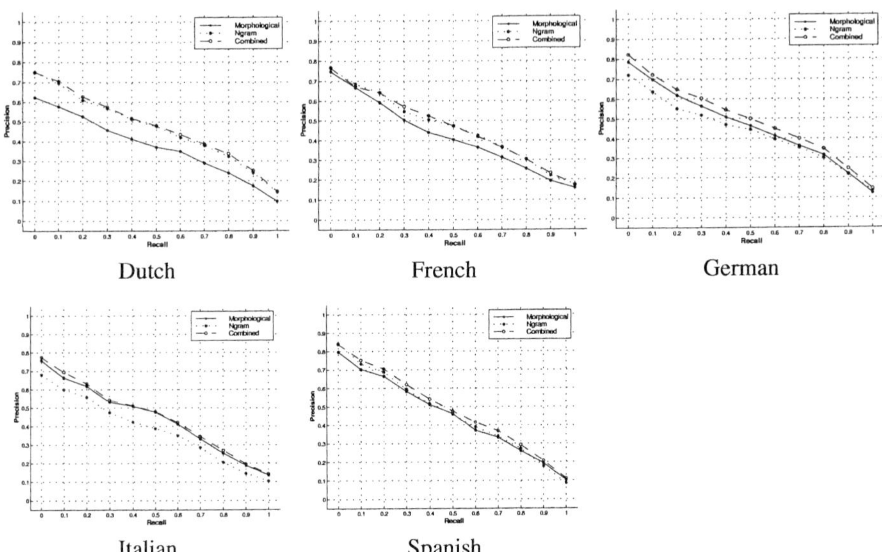

Fig. 1. 11pt interpolated average precision for all combined monolingual runs, and the underlying base runs

quality) runs: one should maximize the overlap of relevant documents between base runs, while minimizing the overlap of non-relevant documents. Lee [12] proposed the following coefficients $R_{overlap}$ and $N_{overlap}$ for determining the overlap between two runs run_1 and run_2:

$$R_{overlap} = \frac{R_{common} \times 2}{R_1 + R_2} \qquad N_{overlap} = \frac{N_{common} \times 2}{N_1 + N_2},$$

where R_{common} (N_{common}) is the number of common relevant (non-relevant) documents, and R_i (N_i) is the number of relevant (non-relevant) documents in run_i. (A document is relevant if, and only if, it receives relevance score equal to

Table 7. Overview of non-interpolated average precision scores for all submitted monolingual runs and for the underlying base runs. Best scores are in boldface; base runs that were not submitted are in italics. The figures in brackets indicate the improvement of the combined run over the best underlying base run

	Dutch	*Finnish*	*French*	*German*	*Italian*	*Spanish*	*Swedish*
Morphological	*0.3673*	–	*0.4063*	0.4476	*0.4285*	*0.4370*	–
Ngram	0.4542	**0.3034**	*0.4481*	0.4177	*0.3672*	*0.4512*	**0.4187**
Combined Ngrm./Mrph.	**0.4598**	–	**0.4535**	**0.4802**	**0.4407**	**0.4734**	–
	(+1.2%)		(+1.2%)	(+7.3%)	(+2.8%)	(+4.9%)	

Table 8. Degree of overlap among relevant and non-relevant documents for the base runs used to form the combined ngram/morphological runs for the monolingual task. The coefficients are computed over all topics

	Dutch	*French*	*German*	*Italian*	*Spanish*
$R_{overlap}$	0.9359	0.9606	0.9207	0.9021	0.9172
$N_{overlap}$	0.4112	0.5187	0.4180	0.4510	0.5264

1 in the qrels provided by CLEF.) Table 8 shows the overlap coefficients for the base runs used to produce combined runs.

A few comments are in order. First, for French and Spanish the base runs are of similar (high) quality, but because the $N_{overlap}$ coefficient is high, the combinations do not improve all that much. Furthermore, we conjecture that the reason for the limited gains of the combined runs over the best base runs for Dutch and Italian is due to the somewhat low quality of one of the base runs for these languages. Finally, the significant improvement obtained by combining the two German base runs may be explained as follows: both base runs are high quality runs, their $R_{overlap}$ coefficient is high, and their $N_{overlap}$ is fairly low — under these circumstances, Lee's rationale predicts that the combined run will be of high quality.

4.2 Bilingual Results

After we had received our results from CLEF, it emerged that one of the base runs submitted for the English to German task (UAmsC02EnGeLC2F) was not the correct one. As a consequence, the combinations in which this base run was used were also incorrect (UAmsC02EnGeNGiMO and UAmsC02EnGeMOiMO). The results and figures below have been obtained with the *correct* version of UAmsC02EnGeLC2F, using the qrels provided by CLEF.

Table 9 shows our non-interpolated average precision scores for both bilingual sub tasks: English to Dutch and English to German. For English to Dutch, we submitted one morphological run, where both stemming and compound splitting were applied. For English to German, we created two morphological runs, one

Table 9. Overview of non-interpolated average precision scores for all correct bilingual runs. Best scores are in boldface. The figures in brackets indicate the improvement of the combined run over the best underlying base run

	English to Dutch	*English to German*
Morphological 1	0.2576	0.3363
Morphological 2	–	*0.3094*
Ngram	0.2807	0.2614
Combined Ngram/Morp. 1	**0.2933** (+4.5%)	**0.3514** (+4.5%)
Combined Morph. 1/Morph. 2	–	0.3451 (+2.6%)

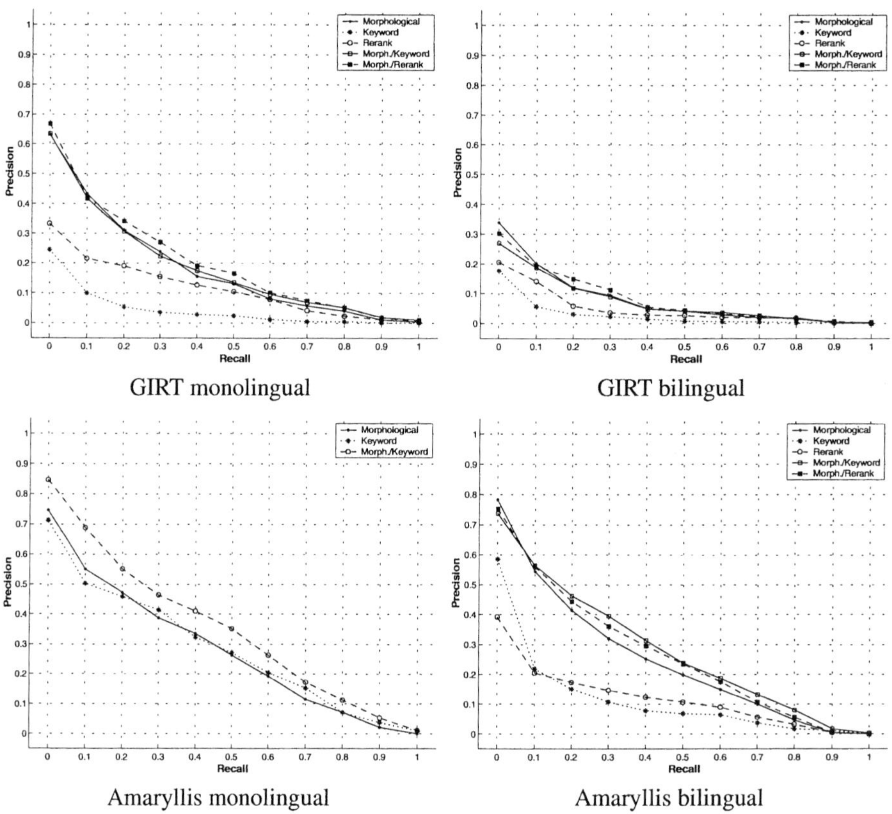

Fig. 3. 11pt interpolated average precision for all submitted GIRT and Amaryllis runs, and the underlying base runs

Figure 3 contains precision-recall plots for the GIRT and Amaryllis tasks. In addition to the scores for our submitted runs, the figure also plots the scores for the base runs that were used to generate the combined runs.

As with the other tasks, we analyzed the overlap coefficients for base runs that were combined; see Table 13. As expected, gains in effectiveness are due to

Table 13. Degree of overlap among relevant and non-relevant documents for the base runs used to form the combined morphological/keyword runs for the GIRT and Amaryllis tasks. The coefficients are computed over all topics

	GIRT (mono)	*GIRT (bi)*	*Amaryllis (mono)*	*Amaryllis (bi)*
$R_{overlap}$	0.4493	0.2984	0.6586	0.6506
$N_{overlap}$	0.1031	0.0756	0.1236	0.1301

Table 8. Degree of overlap among relevant and non-relevant documents for the base runs used to form the combined ngram/morphological runs for the monolingual task. The coefficients are computed over all topics

	Dutch	*French*	*German*	*Italian*	*Spanish*
$R_{overlap}$	0.9359	0.9606	0.9207	0.9021	0.9172
$N_{overlap}$	0.4112	0.5187	0.4180	0.4510	0.5264

1 in the qrels provided by CLEF.) Table 8 shows the overlap coefficients for the base runs used to produce combined runs.

A few comments are in order. First, for French and Spanish the base runs are of similar (high) quality, but because the $N_{overlap}$ coefficient is high, the combinations do not improve all that much. Furthermore, we conjecture that the reason for the limited gains of the combined runs over the best base runs for Dutch and Italian is due to the somewhat low quality of one of the base runs for these languages. Finally, the significant improvement obtained by combining the two German base runs may be explained as follows: both base runs are high quality runs, their $R_{overlap}$ coefficient is high, and their $N_{overlap}$ is fairly low — under these circumstances, Lee's rationale predicts that the combined run will be of high quality.

4.2 Bilingual Results

After we had received our results from CLEF, it emerged that one of the base runs submitted for the English to German task (UAmsC02EnGeLC2F) was not the correct one. As a consequence, the combinations in which this base run was used were also incorrect (UAmsC02EnGeNGiMO and UAmsC02EnGeMOiMO). The results and figures below have been obtained with the *correct* version of UAmsC02EnGeLC2F, using the qrels provided by CLEF.

Table 9 shows our non-interpolated average precision scores for both bilingual sub tasks: English to Dutch and English to German. For English to Dutch, we submitted one morphological run, where both stemming and compound splitting were applied. For English to German, we created two morphological runs, one

Table 9. Overview of non-interpolated average precision scores for all correct bilingual runs. Best scores are in boldface. The figures in brackets indicate the improvement of the combined run over the best underlying base run

	English to Dutch	*English to German*
Morphological 1	0.2576	0.3363
Morphological 2	–	*0.3094*
Ngram	0.2807	0.2614
Combined Ngram/Morp. 1	**0.2933** (+4.5%)	**0.3514** (+4.5%)
Combined Morph. 1/Morph. 2	–	0.3451 (+2.6%)

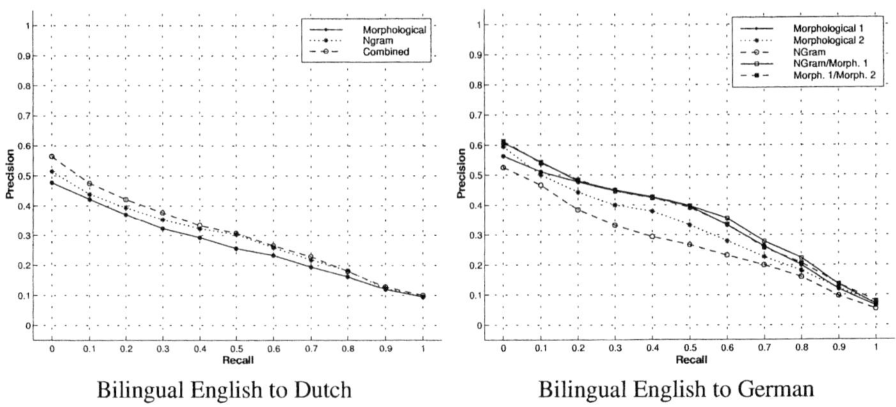

Fig. 2. 11pt interpolated average precision for all correct bilingual runs

with a large decompounding lexicon (*Morphological 1*), and one with last year's settings, i.e., a smaller decompounding lexicon (*Morphological 2*). For both target languages we also submitted a single n-gram run. In addition, we combined the n-gram run with the morphological run for both languages, and for German we also combined the two morphological runs.

Table 10 shows the decrease in effectiveness compared to the best monolingual run for the respective target language.

As to the difference in retrieval effectiveness between monolingual and bilingual, there is a significant difference between Dutch and German. This is probably due to the difference in size between the translation dictionaries that were used to formulate the target queries: the Dutch translation dictionary contained 15,103 head words plus translation rules, whereas the German dictionary contained 103,041 head words; see Section 3.

As with the monolingual runs, we also analyzed the overlap coefficients for base runs that were combined; see Table 11. The gains in effectiveness of the combination over the best base runs is consistent with the coefficients, with comparable gains for the ngram/morphological combinations for Dutch and German; note that both have a fairly low $N_{overlap}$ coefficient. The two (German) morphological runs share many non-relevant documents, and as a consequence the combination of these two runs is less effective than the combination of the ngram run with the morphological 1 run.

Table 10. Decrease in effectiveness for bilingual runs

	Dutch	*German*
Best monolingual	0.4598	0.4802
Best bilingual	0.2933 (−36.2%)	0.3514 (−26.8%)

Table 11. Degree of overlap among relevant and non-relevant documents for the base runs used to form the combined bilingual runs. The coefficients are computed over all topics

	English to Dutch Ngram/Morphological	*English to German Ngram/Morphological 1*	*English to German Morphological 1/Morphological 2*
$R_{overlap}$	0.7737	0.7898	0.9338
$N_{overlap}$	0.2516	0.3588	0.5853

Table 12. Overview of non-interpolated average precision scores for all submitted GIRT and Amaryllis runs, and for the underlying base suns. Best scores are in boldface; base runs that were not submitted are in italics. The figures in brackets indicate the improvement of the combined run over the best underlying base run

	GIRT (mono)	*GIRT (bi)*	*Amaryllis (mono)*	*Amaryllis (bi)*
Morphological	0.1639	*0.0666*	0.2681	*0.2325*
Keyword	*0.0349*	*0.0210*	0.2684	*0.0890*
Re-rank	*0.1015*	*0.0405*	–	*0.1029*
Combined Mrph./KW	0.1687 (+2.9%)	0.0620 (−6.9%)	**0.3401** (+26.7%)	**0.2660** (+14.4%)
Combined Mrph./RR	**0.1906** (+16.3%)	**0.0704** (+5.7%)	–	0.2537 (+9.1%)

4.3 Results for the GIRT and Amaryllis Tasks

Table 12 contains our non-interpolated average precision scores for the GIRT and Amaryllis tasks. In addition to the scores for our submitted runs, the table also lists the scores for the base runs that were used to generate the combined runs.

The results for the GIRT tasks are outright disappointing. Our morphological base run fails to live up to the performance of the corresponding monolingual German runs (average precision 0.1639 for GIRT versus 0.4476 for German). On our pre-submission experiments on the GIRT topics of CLEF 2000 and CLEF 2001, we also noticed a drop in performance, but far less dramatic than for the CLEF 2002 run (average precision around 0.31 for both runs versus 0.1639 this year). Still, the combination of the morphological run with either the keyword run or re-rank run improves retrieval effectiveness. For the English to German GIRT task, only the combination of the morphological and re-rank base runs improves compared to the base runs; this may be due to the extremely low precision at 10 of the bilingual base run (0.1417).

Our runs for Amaryllis are more in line with the results for the monolingual French task (average precision 0.2681 for the base run versus 0.4063 for French). The keyword-only run using the provided keywords even out-performs the morphological base run. The combination of the two runs leads to an impressive improvement in retrieval effectiveness (+26.7%). The English to French Amaryllis task performs fairly well compared to the monolingual Amaryllis task. The combination runs of the morphological base run with the recovered keywords, and of the morphological base run with the re-ranking show significant improvement.

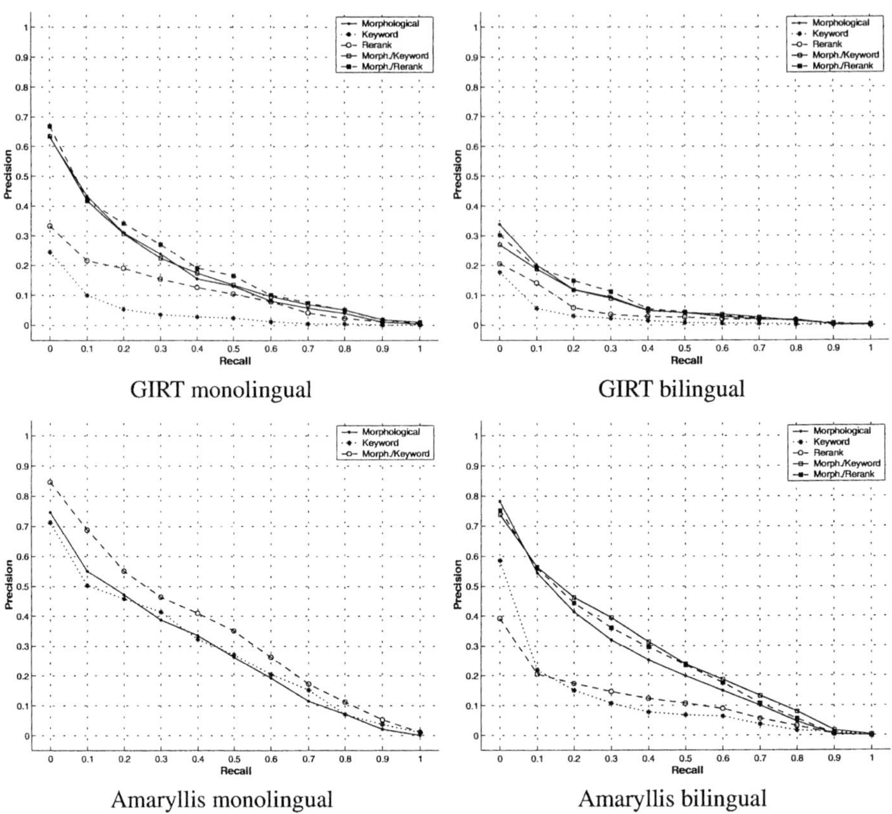

Fig. 3. 11pt interpolated average precision for all submitted GIRT and Amaryllis runs, and the underlying base runs

Figure 3 contains precision-recall plots for the GIRT and Amaryllis tasks. In addition to the scores for our submitted runs, the figure also plots the scores for the base runs that were used to generate the combined runs.

As with the other tasks, we analyzed the overlap coefficients for base runs that were combined; see Table 13. As expected, gains in effectiveness are due to

Table 13. Degree of overlap among relevant and non-relevant documents for the base runs used to form the combined morphological/keyword runs for the GIRT and Amaryllis tasks. The coefficients are computed over all topics

	GIRT (mono)	*GIRT (bi)*	*Amaryllis (mono)*	*Amaryllis (bi)*
$R_{overlap}$	0.4493	0.2984	0.6586	0.6506
$N_{overlap}$	0.1031	0.0756	0.1236	0.1301

a high $R_{overlap}$ coefficient combined with a relatively low $N_{overlap}$ coefficient. It is interesting to note that the coefficients for the combined monolingual Amaryllis runs (using the provided keywords) are similar to those of the bilingual runs (using the recovered keywords). This may provide a partial explanation of why the combination of a base run with a much lower quality run can still improve retrieval effectiveness.

5 Conclusions

The experiments on which report in this paper indicate a number of things. First, morphological normalization does improve retrieval effectiveness significantly, especially for languages such as Dutch and German, which have a more complex morphology than English. We also showed that ngram-based retrieval can be a viable option in the absence of linguistic resources to support deep morphological normalization. Furthermore, combining runs provides a method that can consistently improve base runs, even high quality base runs; moreover, the interpolation factors required for the best gain in performance seem to be fairly robust across topic sets. Finally, our results for the bilingual task indicate that simple word/phrase translation, where all possible translations are used to formulate the target query in an unstructured way, leads to a significant decrease in effectiveness, when compared to the respective monolingual runs. Therefore, we plan to investigate more restrictive ways of formulating target queries.

Acknowledgments

We want to thank Willem van Hage and Vera Hollink for their technical support, and Maarten Marx for useful discussions.

Jaap Kamps was supported by the Netherlands Organization for Scientific Research (NWO, grant # 400-20-036). Christof Monz was supported by the Physical Sciences Council with financial support from the Netherlands Organization for Scientific Research (NWO), project 612-13-001. Maarten de Rijke was supported by grants from the Netherlands Organization for Scientific Research (NWO), under project numbers 612-13-001, 365-20-005, 612.069.006, 612.000.106, 220-80-001, and 612.000.207.

References

[1] N. J. Belkin, P. Kantor, E. A. Fox, and J. A. Shaw. Combining evidence of multiple query representations for information retrieval. *Information Processing & Management*, 31(3):431–448, 1995.

[2] C. Buckley, A. Singhal, and M. Mitra. New retrieval approaches using SMART: TREC 4. In D. Harman, editor, *Proceedings of the Fourth Text REtrieval Conference (TREC-4)*, pages 25–48. NIST Special Publication 500-236, 1995.

[3] CLEF Resources at the University of Neuchâtel. `http://www.unine.ch/info/clef`.

[4] T. F. Cox and M. A. A. Cox. *Multidimensional Scaling*. Chapman & Hall, London UK, 1994.
[5] Ding: A dictionary lookup program. `http://ding.tu-chemnitz.de`.
[6] G. Drosdowski, editor. *Duden: Grammatik der deutschen Gegenwartssprache*. Dudenverlag, fourth edition, 1984.
[7] Ergane: a free multi-lingual dictionary programme. `http://download.travlang.com/Ergane/frames-en.html`.
[8] E. A. Fox and J. A. Shaw. Combination of multiple searches. In *Proceedings TREC-2*, pages 243–252, 1994.
[9] W. Frakes. Stemming algorithms. In W. Frakes and R. Baeza-Yates, editors, *Information Retrieval: Data Strcutures & Algorithms*, pages 131–160. Prentice Hall, 1992.
[10] J. C. Gower and P. Legendre. Metric and Euclidean properties of dissimilarity coefficients. *Journal of Classification*, 3:5–48, 1986.
[11] D. Harman. How effective is suffixing? *Journal of the American Society for Information Science*, 42:7–15, 1991.
[12] J. H. Lee. Analyses of multiple evidence combination. In *Proceedings SIGIR'97*, pages 267–276, 1997.
[13] J. H. Lee. Combining multiple evidence from different relevant feedback methods. In *Database Systems for Advanced Applications*, pages 421–430, 1997.
[14] C. Monz and M. de Rijke. Shallow morphological analysis in monolingual information retrieval for Dutch, German and Italian. In C. Peters, M. Braschler, J. Gonzalo, and M. Kluck, editors, *Proceedings CLEF 2001*, LNCS 2406, pages 262–277. Springer Verlag, 2002.
[15] A. Pirkola, T. Hedlund, H. Keskustalo, and K. Järvelin. Dictionary-based cross-language information retrieval: Problems, methods, and research findings. *Information Retrieval*, 4(3–4):209–230, 2001.
[16] R. Pohlmann and W. Kraaij. Improving the precision of a text retrieval system with compound analysis. In J. Landsbergen, J. Odijk, K. van Deemter, and G. Veldhuijzen van Zanten, editors, *Proceedings of the 7th Computational Linguistics in the Netherlands Meeting (CLIN 1996)*, pages 115–129, 1996.
[17] M. Porter. An algorithm for suffix stripping. *Program*, 14(3):130–137, 1980.
[18] J. Rocchio. Relevance feedback in information retrieval. In G. Salton, editor, *The SMART Retrieval System — Experiments in Automatic Document Processing*. Prentice Hall, 1971.
[19] H. Schmid. Probabilistic part-of-speech tagging using decision trees. In *Proceedings of International Conference on New Methods in Language Processing*, 1994.
[20] Systran Online Translator. `http://www.systransoft.com/`.
[21] UPLIFT: Utrecht project: Linguistic information for free text retrieval. `http://www-uilots.let.uu.nl/ uplift/`.

Exeter at CLEF 2002: Experiments with Machine Translation for Monolingual and Bilingual Retrieval

Adenike M. Lam-Adesina and Gareth J. F. Jones

Department of Computer Science
University of Exeter EX4 4QF, United Kingdom
{a.m.lam-adesina,g.j.f.jones}@ex.ac.uk

Abstract. The University of Exeter participated in the CLEF 2002 monolingual and bilingual tasks for two languages; Italian and Spanish. Our approach for CLEF 2002 was translating the documents and topics into English, and applying our standard retrieval methods. Four ranked results were submitted for each monolingual task and five for each bilingual task. We explored the potential of term weight estimation from a contemporaneous English text collection and show that although this method has been shown to be effective in retrieval from English collections, it cannot be applied effectively to translated document collections in a simple way. This paper also reports our unofficial results for monolingual and bilingual English runs.

1 Introduction

The CLEF 2002 monolingual and bilingual tasks were aimed at encouraging research in the area of Cross-lingual Information Retrieval (CLIR) for non-English document collections. Our approach to CLEF 2002 was to use English as a pivot language by translating documents and topics into English. Our official submissions included results for German, French, English, Italian and Spanish topics using Italian and Spanish documents. Both the collections and the topics were translated from the source language into English; firstly, because we had intended to participate in the multilingual task, and secondly because the retrieval system we used could not deal with accented words. We were ultimately unable to submit results for the multilingual task because of time constraints.

The document collection and the topic statements were submitted to the selected MT system, the output was then collected and applied on the information retrieval (IR) system. For all our submissions and subsequent runs presented in this paper, documents were translated using Systran Version: 3.0 (SYS), and topics translated using both the Systran and the Globalink Power Translation Pro Version: 6.4 (PTP) MT system.

Pseudo-relevance feedback (PRF) has been shown to be an effective approach to improving retrieval performance in IR and also in CLIR [1][2][3]. In our experimental work in [4][5] we demonstrated the effectiveness of a new PRF method using the

C.A. Peters (Ed.): CLEF 2002, LNCS 2785, pp. 127-146, 2003.

Okapi BM25 probabilistic model [6]. In this work we investigated the idea of selecting expansion terms for document summaries and found this method to be more reliable than query expansion from full documents. Since CLEF 2001, we have also explored data combination techniques that merge the output of the two MT systems for the topics, and use this as the initial query set. Furthermore, we have also been investigating the use of a comparable collection (pilot) for expansion terms selection and term weights estimation. The method is described fully below. Our experiments for CLEF 2002 explore the effectiveness of these methods with automatically translated documents and topics. We also report our results for English monolingual and bilingual runs in order to more fully understand the behaviour of the different methods applied in our investigations.

The remainder of this paper is organized as follows: Section 2 reviews the information retrieval methods used, Section 3 gives a brief description of the data processing techniques used, Section 4 describes the different methods of PRF, Section 5 gives the experimental results and section 6 concludes the paper.

2 Retrieval Approach

The experiments were carried out using the City University research distribution version of the Okapi system. A standard set of stopwords were removed from the documents and search queries. All remaining terms were then suffix stripped using Porter stemming [7] and then indexed using a small set of synonyms. Documents terms are weighted using the Okapi BM25 formula [6] reproduced below.

$$cw(i,j) = \frac{cfw(i) \times tf(i,j) \times (K1+1)}{K1 \times ((1-b) + (b \times ndl(j))) + tf(ij)}$$

where cw(i,j) = the weight of term i in document (j),
cfw(i) = the standard collection frequency weight
tf(i,j) = the document term frequency
ndl(j) = the normalized document length calculated as follows

$$ndl(j) = \frac{dl(j)}{Avdl}$$

where dl(j) = the length of j
Avdl = the average document length of all documents in the collection

K1 and b are empirically selected tuning constants for a particular collection. K1 modifies the effect of term frequency and b modifies the effect of document length. All our experiments were done with K1 and b set to 1.4 and 0.6. The parameters were set using the CLEF 2001 data sets.

2.1 Relevance Feedback

Relevance feedback can be used to improve retrieval effectiveness by either modifying the initial query (query modification by adding to or deleting from the initial query set), or the term weights (term-reweighting). All our experiments used our query expansion method, which modifies the initial query by adding new terms selected from a pool of potential expansion terms from the initial retrieval run.

Our query expansion method selects terms from summaries of the top ranked documents. The summaries were generated using the method described in [4]. The summary generation method combines the Luhn's Keyword Cluster Method [8], Title terms frequency method [4], Location/header method [9] and the Query-bias method [10] to form an overall significance score for each sentence. For all our experiments we used the top 6 ranked sentences as the summary of each document. From this summary we collected all non-stopwords and ranked them using a slightly modified version of the Robertson selection value (rsv) [11] reproduced below. A fixed number of the top ranked terms were then added to the initial query in all our experiments.

$$rsv(i) = rw(i) \times rw(i)$$

where r(i) = number of relevant documents containing term i
rw(i) = the standard Robertson/Sparck Jones relevance weight [12]reproduced below

$$rw(i) = \log \frac{(r(i)+0.5)(N \quad n(i) \quad R+r(i)+0.5)}{(n(i) \quad r(i)+0.5)(R \quad r(i)+0.5)}$$

where n(i) = the total number of documents containing term i
r(i) = the total number of relevant documents term i occurs in
R = the total number of relevant documents for this query
N = the total number of documents

In our modified version, although potential expansion terms are selected from the summaries of the top 5 ranked documents, they are ranked using the top 20 ranked documents from the initial run, a method shown to be effective in [4].

3 Data Processing

The two document collections used in our official experiments, Italian and Spanish were translated to English using the Systran Translation Software version 3.0. This was necessitated by the inability of the retrieval system (Okapi) used for our experiments to deal with accented terms as well as languages other than English. All topics were translated from the source language into English using both the Systran Version 3.0 and Globalink Power Translation Pro version 6.4 MT software. All our experiments were done using both the title and description fields of the CLEF topics.

4 Procedures

Our submissions to CLEF 2002 investigated a number of approaches to term weighting and query expansion as described below.

4.1 Standard Method

This method is the same as that used in our CLEF 2001 official submissions [5]. An initial retrieval run using translated queries was performed. The top 5 assumed relevant documents were summarized and the pool of potential expansion terms was generated from the summaries. The top 20 terms were then added to the initial query for the feedback run.

4.2 Pilot Searching

Query expansion is aimed at improving initial search topic in order to make it a better expression of user's information need. This is normally achieved by adding terms selected from assumed relevant document retrieved from the test collection, to the initial query. Another approach that has been shown to be effective is the selection of expansion terms from a larger collection, a subset of which could be the test collection. Based on the assumption that if additional documents from the same corpus as the test collection are available, these can be used for improved query expansion. The larger data collection is likely to enable more accurate parameter estimation and hopefully better retrieval and document ranking. The Okapi submissions for the TREC-7 [13] adhoc tasks used the TREC disks 1-5 of which the TREC-8 data is a subset, for parameter estimation and query expansion. The method was found to be very effective. Our post CLEF 2001 results for bilingual English also demonstrated the effectiveness of this approach [14]. The TREC-8 data collection consisting of more than half a million documents was used as "pilot collection" in our experiments. The Italian and Spanish CLEF document collections are contemporaneous to the TREC-8 data collection and we thus experimented with using it as a pilot collection again for our CLEF 2002 experiments. Two different approaches were taken to the pilot searching procedure as follows:

1. Apply the original query terms to the pilot collection using the Okapi system without feedback. Extract terms from the top R assumed relevant documents; rank the extracted terms and select the desired number of expansion terms from the top of the list. The expansion terms are added to the initial query terms and applied on the test collection. This approach is shown to give an improvement for the CLEF 2001 bilingual task [14].
2. The second method involves using the expansion terms from the pilot collection as above, but this time the cfw(i) weights from the pilot collection are used instead of the term weights from the test collection. This method gave a further improvement for the CLEF 2001 bilingual task [14].

4.3 Combination Methods

MT systems sometimes make translation errors due to the limitations of the dictionaries used in them. However, this problem may be addressed to some extent by combining the outputs of multiple MT systems. This idea is based on the documented notion that combination of evidence from multiple information sources is beneficial to retrieval [16]. In the experiment reported here this method involves the combination of translated queries from the two MT systems into a single query representation consisting of unique terms from each query. These new query representations are then applied to the retrieval systems in two ways:

1. The first method uses the combined queries as the query set without any modification to the term weights (Combined queries).
2. The second uses the combined queries as the query set, but doubling the weight of terms occurring in both translations (Combined queries upweighted).

5 Experimental Results

In this section we report the results of our investigation for the CLEF 2002 Monolingual and Bilingual tasks for Italian, Spanish and English collections. We report the procedures for the selection of system parameters, baseline results without feedback and results after the application of the different methods of feedback. Official submissions are indicated by a *. In all cases the results use the Title and Description fields of the search topics and we present the average precision at various precision cutoff levels (5, 10, 15 and 20 docs), the average precision over all relevant documents (Av. Prec.), the % change in average precision relative to the monolingual run (% chg mono), the % change in average precision compared to the baseline no feedback results (% chg no FB.) and the total number of relevant documents retrieved (R-ret).

5.1 System Parameters

The parameters used in all our experiments were set by carrying out a series of experimental runs on the 2001 query sets using the Italian and Spanish collections (our CLEF 2001 runs used only the English collections). We experimented with different parameter settings using the English, French, German, Italian and Spanish topic sets.

Based on the outcome of the above runs, the Okapi parameters were set as follows: k1=1.4 and b=0.6. For all our feedback runs, potential expansion terms were taken from summaries of the top 5 ranked documents, the top 6 sentences were used as the documents summaries, and the potential expansion terms were then ranked by assuming the top 20 retrieved documents to be relevant. The top 20 terms taken from the summaries was selected as the expansion terms and all original query terms were upweighted by a factor of 3.5 during the feedback process.

5.2 Italian Runs

Tables 1 and 2 above show the Italian baseline results for topic translation using Systran and PTP. The total number of relevant documents available for the Italian collection is 2146. The results show a loss of precision for all language pairs compared to the monolingual results although these results can be classified as reasonable CLIR performance. The Systran translator is shown to give better performance for both Italian and French topics. Performance for German topic translation using Systran is the worse with about 25% degradation in retrieval performance.

The result for the English topics is very surprising, resulting in about 15% loss in precision compared to the monolingual runs. This is interesting since both the documents and the topics have been translated for the monolingual, whereas only the documents have been translated for the English topic runs. This is most likely to be caused by the difference in the linguistics of the translators used on the collection and the English query terms.

Table 1. Baseline retrieval results for Italian task using SYSTRAN

Prec.	Topic Language				
	Italian	English	French	German	Spanish
5 docs	*.465*	*.404*	*.384*	*.355*	*.358*
10 docs	*.425*	*.357*	*.337*	*.314*	*.355*
15 docs	*.382*	*.327*	*.294*	*.283*	*.313*
20 docs	*.352*	*.296*	*.271*	*.253*	*.289*
Av. Prec.	*.388*	*.330*	*.324*	*.293*	*.319*
% chg mono	-	*-14.9%*	*-16.5%*	*-24.5%*	*-17.8%*
R-ret	*966*	*898*	*917*	*830*	*856*

Table 2. Baseline retrieval results for Italian task using Power Translator Pro

Prec.	Topic Language				
	Italian	English	French	German	Spanish
5 docs	*.412*	*.404*	*.371*	*.384*	*.433*
10 docs	*.351*	*.357*	*.333*	*.325*	*.367*
15 docs	*.308*	*.327*	*.295*	*.291*	*.332*
20 docs	*.284*	*.296*	*.275*	*.271*	*.300*
Av. Prec.	*.349*	*0.330*	*.310*	*.305*	*.337*
% chg mono	-	*-5.8%*	*-11.2%*	*-12.6%*	*-3.4%*
R-ret	*853*	*898*	*908*	*777*	*874*

Table 3. Retrieval results for Italian using Systran with summary-based expansion term selection

Prec.	Topic Language				
	Italian*	English*	French	German	Spanish
5 docs	*.552*	*.441*	*.429*	*.396*	*.416*
10 docs	*.480*	*.374*	*.380*	*.341*	*.369*
15 docs	*.434*	*.354*	*.340*	*.306*	*.343*
20 docs	*.384*	*.317*	*.312*	*.280*	*.315*
Av.Prec.	*.453*	*.374*	*.375*	*.341*	*.363*
% chg mono	-	*-17.4%*	*-17.2%*	*-24.7%*	*-19.9%*
% chg noFB	*+16.8%*	*+13.3%*	*+15.7%*	*+16.4%*	*+13.8%*
R-ret	*1004*	*938*	*947*	*869*	*906*

Table 4. Retrieval results for Italian using Power Translation Pro with summary based expansion term selection

Prec.	Topic Language				
	Italian	English*	French	German	Spanish
5 docs	*.441*	*.441*	*.437*	*.437*	*.453*
10 docs	*.392*	*.374*	*.378*	*.386*	*.402*
15 docs	*.350*	*.354*	*.342*	*.337*	*.355*
20 docs	*.316*	*.317*	*.307*	*.307*	*.327*
Av. Prec.	*.394*	*.374*	*.358*	*.377*	*.371*
% chg mono	-	*-5.1%*	*-9.1%*	*-4.3%*	*-5.8%*
% chg no FB	*+12.9%*	*+13.3%*	*+15.5%*	*+23.6%*	*+10.1%*
R-ret	*905*	*938*	*955*	*825*	*922*

Tables 3 and 4 show the retrieval results after the application of our standard feedback method. In all cases feedback improves the absolute average precision over the baseline figures, again results for Systran translated Italian and French topics are better than those for PTP although, PTP results for German and Spanish are better. Overall the best results are for PTP translated German topics which achieved about 24% improvement in average precision over the baseline for the same language pair. The average improvement in performance for all language pairs is about 15%, these results are similar to that achieved in our experiments with the TREC8-8 adhoc tasks [4].

Tables 5-8 shows retrieval results after term expansion and/or term weight estimation from our TREC-8 pilot collection. In all cases except one both methods resulted in improvement in retrieval performance over the baseline results; in the Italian monolingual run with the Systran topic translations for term weight estimation from pilot collection, there was 3% degradation in performance. Careful analysis of this resulted is needed to understand the reason for these.

The average improvement achieved for all language pairs for term expansion from the pilot collection is again about 15%, while on average estimating term weights from the pilot collection resulted in about 10% improvement in retrieval performance over the baseline. Pilot collecting weighting is thus shown to have an adverse effect on retrieval peformance. Overall, these methods however failed to improve over the results for term expansion and weight estimation from test collection. Using pilot collection for query expansion and term weighting gives the worst result for all pairs. This is almost certainly due to the differences in the vocabulary distributions between the pilot and the test collection. The term distributions across the translated test collections are likely to be different to those in the original English pilot collection, but better matched to the translated topics.

It is interesting to note in these cases that the performance for English topic statements improves by the largest percentage, in some cases producing a higher overall average precision than the monolingual Italian result. The well formed initial English queries are presumably better able to exploit the pilot collection for query expansion than the translated topics. However, even in this case use of pilot collection weighting appears to be disadvantageous.

Table 5. Retrieval results for Italian using Systran with summary-based expansion term selection from pilot collection and cfw(i) from test collection

Prec.	Topic Language				
	Italian*	English	French	German	Spanish
5 docs	*.494*	*.474*	*.445*	*.425*	*.465*
10 docs	*.435*	*.410*	*.386*	*.353*	*.390*
15 docs	*.385*	*.392*	*.340*	*.331*	*.342*
20 docs	*.356*	*.355*	*.318*	*.300*	*.311*
Av. Prec.	*.414*	*.407*	*.373*	*.347*	*.362*
% chg mono	-	*-1.7%*	*-9.9%*	*-16.2%*	*-12.6%*
% chg no FB	*+6.7%*	*+23.3%*	*+15.1%*	*+18.4%*	*13.5%*
R-ret	*993*	*976*	*965*	*914*	*904*

Table 6. Retrieval results for Italian using Power Translator Pro with summary-based expansion term selection from pilot collection and cfw(i) from test collection

Prec.	Topic Language				
	Italian	English	French	German	Spanish
5 docs	*.457*	*.474*	*.420*	*.453*	*.490*
10 docs	*.382*	*.410*	*.388*	*.361*	*.412*
15 docs	*.333*	*.392*	*.343*	*.324*	*.369*
20 docs	*.306*	*.355*	*.321*	*.306*	*.329*
Av. Prec.	*.378*	*.407*	*.359*	*.364*	*.379*
% chg mono	-	*+7.7%*	*-5.0%*	*-3.7%*	*+0.3%*
% chg no FB	*+8.3%*	*+23.3%*	*+15.8%*	*+19.3%*	*+12.5%*
R-ret	*910*	*976*	*968*	*867*	*936*

Table 7. Retrieval results for Italian using Systran with summary-based expansion term selection and cfw(i) from pilot collection

Prec.	Topic Language				
	Italian	English*	French	German	Spanish
5 docs	*.461*	*.469*	*.433*	*.420*	*.429*
10 docs	*.388*	*.420*	*.378*	*.337*	*.363*
15 docs	*.359*	*.385*	*.344*	*.309*	*.324*
20 docs	*.335*	*.350*	*.313*	*.285*	*.291*
Av. Prec.	*.376*	*.399*	*.365*	*.335*	*.333*
% chg mono	-	*+6.1%*	*-2.9%*	*-10.9%*	*-11.4%*
% chg no FB	*-3.1%*	*+20.9%*	*+12.7%*	*+14.3%*	*+11.4%*
R-ret	*910*	*968*	*929*	*872*	*830*

Table 8. Retrieval results for Italian using Power Translator Pro with summary-based expansion term selection and cfw(i) from pilot collection

Prec.	Topic Language				
	Italian	English*	French	German	Spanish
5 docs	*.449*	*.469*	*.429*	*.408*	*.433*
10 docs	*.365*	*.420*	*.363*	*.333*	*.388*
15 docs	*.339*	*.385*	*.340*	*.298*	*.346*
20 docs	*.315*	*.350*	*.310*	*.280*	*.320*
Av. Prec.	*.375*	*.399*	*.352*	*.325*	*.360*
% chg mono	-	*+6.0%*	*-6.1%*	*-13.3%*	*-4.0%*
% chg no FB	*+7.4%*	*+20.9%*	*+13.6%*	*+6.6%*	*+6.8%*
R-ret	*880*	*968*	*948*	*851*	*917*

Table 9. Retrieval results for Italian using merged queries from both MT systems with summary-based expansion term selection

Prec.	Combined Topic Language			
	Italian*	French*	German	Spanish*
5 docs	*.498*	*.392*	*.445*	*.449*
10 docs	*.435*	*.363*	*.382*	*.394*
15 docs	*.397*	*.329*	*.351*	*.357*
20 docs	*.365*	*.311*	*.323*	*.328*
Av. Prec.	*.421*	*.348*	*.377*	*.373*
% chg mono	-	*-17.3%*	*-10.5%*	*-11.4%*
% chg no FB SYS	*+8.5%*	*+7.4%*	*+28.7%*	*+16.9%*
% chg no FB PTT	*+20.6%*	*+12.3%*	*+23.6%*	*+10.6%*
R-ret	*1001*	*936*	*901*	*913*

Table 10. Retrieval results for Italian using merged queries from both MT systems with summary-based expansion term selection. Weights of terms occurring in both queries are upweighted by 2

Prec.	Combined Topic Language upweighted			
	Italian*	French	German*	Spanish
5 docs	*.474*	*.425*	*.433*	*.449*
10 docs	*.431*	*.392*	*.363*	*.388*
15 docs	*.395*	*.350*	*.331*	*.358*
20 docs	*.356*	*.307*	*.302*	*.310*
Av. Prec.	*.411*	*.377*	*.368*	*.366*
% chg mono	-	*-8.3%*	*-10.5%*	*-10.9%*
% chg no FB SYS	*+5.9%*	*+16.4%*	*+25.6%*	*+14.7%*
% chg no FB PTP	*+17.8%*	*+21.6%*	*+20.7%*	*+8.6%*
R-ret	*977*	*944*	*890*	*907*

Tables 9 and 10 show retrieval results for the combined queries. All results show improvement in retrieval performance over the baseline results. However the method only resulted in improvements over the standard method for Systran translated German and Spanish topics, and PTP translated Italian and French topics. This shows that careful analysis of the method used for increasing the term weights for common terms from the translators needs to be carried out. However, the results further strengthens the idea that combining the output from two MT systems can help in reducing the effect of poor MT system output on retrieval.

Table 11. Baseline retrieval results for Spanish using SYSTRAN

Prec.	Topic Language				
	Spanish	English	French	German	Italian
5 docs	*.628*	*.524*	*.480*	*.404*	*.468*
10 docs	*.544*	*.452*	*.394*	*.352*	*.372*
15 docs	*.495*	*.411*	*.357*	*.304*	*.336*
20 docs	*.460*	*.375*	*.332*	*.277*	*.311*
Av. Prec.	*.442*	*.372*	*.357*	*.298*	*.331*
% chg mono	-	*-18.8%*	*-19.2%*	*-32.6%*	*-25.1%*
R-ret	*2413*	*2149*	*2041*	*1853*	*1926*

Table 12. Baseline retrieval results for Spanish using Power Translator Pro

Prec.	Topic Language				
	Spanish	English	French	German	Italian
5 docs	*.580*	*.524*	*.528*	*.512*	*.496*
10 docs	*.498*	*.452*	*.454*	*.410*	*.418*
15 docs	*.447*	*.411*	*.407*	*.364*	*.364*
20 docs	*.416*	*.375*	*.377*	*.339*	*.330*
Av. Prec.	*.419*	*.372*	*.377*	*.340*	*.339*
% chg mono	-	*-11.2%*	*-10.0%*	*-18.9%*	*-19.1%*
R-ret	*2235*	*2149*	*2144*	*1868*	*1847*

Table 13. Retrieval results for Spanish using Systran with summary-based expansion term selection

Prec.	Topic Language				
	Spanish*	English*	French	German	Italian
5 docs	*.632*	*.588*	*.488*	*.432*	*.468*
10 docs	*.568*	*.484*	*.414*	*.364*	*.404*
15 docs	*.516*	*.431*	*.375*	*.316*	*.363*
20 docs	*.496*	*.394*	*.350*	*.299*	*.335*
Av. Prec.	*.475*	*.412*	*.382*	*.318*	*.359*
% chg mono	-	*-13.3%*	*-19.6%*	*-33.1%*	*-24.4%*
% chg no FB	*+7.5%*	*+10.8%*	*+7.0%*	*+6.7%*	*+8.5%*
R-ret	*2517*	*2289*	*2069*	*1901*	*2025*

5.3 Spanish Runs

Tables 11 and 12 show Spanish baseline retrieval results. The results show a loss of precision for all language pairs compared to the monolingual results. The PTP is shown to outperform the Systran for all language pairs except for the Spanish topics. This result is perhaps surprising since the documents were translated using Systran. As in the case of the Italian baseline runs, performance for German topic translation using Systran is the worst with about 32% degradation in retrieval performance.

Tables 13 and 14 show feedback results for our standard method. Average improvement in retrieval performance compared to the baseline results for all language pairs is about 9% (lower than that achieved for the Italian runs). The same trend observed in the baseline is again shown in these results, the performance for German topic translation using Systran is the worse with about 33% degradation in retrieval performance compared to the Monolingual run (column 1). It also gave the lowest improvement over the baseline results for all language pairs.

Table 14. Retrieval results for Spanish using Power Translation Pro with summary-based expansion term selection

Prec.	Topic Language				
	Spanish	English*	French	German	Italian
5 docs	*.596*	*.588*	*.532*	*.536*	*.512*
10 docs	*.516*	*.484*	*.482*	*.454*	*.440*
15 docs	*.469*	*.431*	*.441*	*.403*	*.389*
20 docs	*.433*	*.394*	*.407*	*.372*	*.356*
Av. Prec.	*.445*	*.412*	*.414*	*.387*	*.369*
% chg mono	-	*-7.4%*	*-6.9%*	*-13.0%*	*-17.1%*
% chg no FB	*+6.2%*	*+10.8%*	*+9.8%*	*+13.8%*	*+8.9%*
R-ret	*2266*	*2289*	*2326*	*2040*	*1975*

Table 15. Retrieval results for Spanish using for Systran with summary-based expansion term selection from pilot collection and cfw(i) from test collection

Prec.	Topic Language				
	Spanish*	English	French	German	Italian
5 docs	*.624*	*.596*	*.560*	*.480*	*.524*
10 docs	*.580*	*.540*	*.480*	*.400*	*.448*
15 docs	*.529*	*.480*	*.431*	*.360*	*.388*
20 docs	*.490*	*.452*	*.403*	*.340*	*.357*
Av. Prec.	*.473*	*.426*	*.390*	*.329*	*.369*
% chg mono	-	*-9.9%*	*-17.5%*	*-30.4%*	*-21.9%*
% chg no FB	*+7.0*	*+14.5%*	*+9.2%*	*+10.4%*	*+11.5%*
R-ret	*2538*	*2345*	*2237*	*2180*	*2110*

Table 16. Retrieval results for Spanish using Power Translator Pro with summary-based expansion term selection from pilot collection and cfw(i) from test collection

Prec.	Topic Language				
	Spanish	English	French	German	Italian
5 docs	*.608*	*.596*	*.564*	*.532*	*.556*
10 docs	*.548*	*.540*	*.508*	*.462*	*.468*
15 docs	*.497*	*.480*	*.467*	*.412*	*.409*
20 docs	*.469*	*.452*	*.435*	*.385*	*.375*
Av. Prec.	*.466*	*.426*	*.411*	*.379*	*.399*
% chg mono	-	*-8.6%*	*-11.8%*	*-18.7%*	*-14.4%*
% chg no FB	*+11.2%*	*+14.5%*	*+9.0%*	*+11.5%*	*+17.7%*
R-ret	*2412*	*2345*	*2345*	*2156*	*2108*

Table 17. Retrieval results for Spanish using Systran with summary-based expansion term selection and cfw(i) from pilot collection

Prec.	Topic Language				
	Spanish	English	French	German	Italian
5 docs	*.529*	*.592*	*.548*	*.472*	*.500*
10 docs	*.524*	*.528*	*.498*	*.412*	*.422*
15 docs	*.477*	*.499*	*.451*	*.380*	*.377*
20 docs	*.452*	*.469*	*.413*	*.358*	*.344*
Av. Prec.	*.420*	*.420*	*.373*	*.334*	*.342*
% chg mono	-	*0.0%*	*-11.2%*	*-20.5%*	*-18.6%*
% chg no FB	*-4.9%*	*+12.9%*	*+4.5%*	*+12.1%*	*+3.3%*
R-ret	*2249*	*2372*	*2268*	*2152*	*1914*

Table 18. Retrieval results for Spanish using Power Translator Pro with summary-based expansion term selection and cfw(i) from pilot collection

Prec.	Topic Language				
	Spanish	English	French	German	Italian
5 docs	*.572*	*.592*	*.572*	*.476*	*.540*
10 docs	*.516*	*.528*	*.500*	*.432*	*.470*
15 docs	*.480*	*.499*	*.460*	*.395*	*.428*
20 docs	*.446*	*.469*	*.437*	*.366*	*.378*
Av. Preci.	*.431*	*.420*	*.396*	*.350*	*.370*
% chg mono	-	*-2.6%*	*-8.1%*	*-18.8%*	*-14.2%*
% chg no FB	*+2.9%*	*+12.9%*	*+5.0%*	*+2.9%*	*+9.1%*
R-ret	*2295*	*2372*	*2316*	*2124*	*2075*

Tables 15-18 shows retrieval results after term expansion and/or term weights estimation from a pilot collection. In all cases except one both methods resulted in improvement in retrieval performance over the baseline results. In the Spanish monolingual run for term weight estimation from pilot collection, there was 5% degradation in performance. This same trend is observed in the Italian runs (Table 5-8 above). The average improvement achieved for all language pairs for term expansion from the pilot collection is again about 11%, while on average estimating term weights from the pilot collection resulted in about 6% improvement in retrieval performance. Using the pilot collection for expansion term selection resulted in improvement over using the test collection for expansion term selection and term weights estimation. Using the pilot collection for expansion term selection and term weighting is also shown to be less effective than using the test collection for expansion term selection and weighting.

Tables 19 and 20 show retrieval results for the combined queries. All results show improvement in retrieval performance over the baseline results. In all cases this method results in better performance for the MT system with the worst performance. This shows that combining the output of two MT systems might be beneficial and that proper analysis needs to be done to achieve the optimal result for this method.

Table 19. Retrieval results Spanish with merged queries from both MT systems with summary-based expansion term selection

Prec.	Combined Topic Language			
	Spanish	French	German	Italian
5 docs	*.604*	*.564*	*.496*	*.468*
10 docs	*.544*	*.472*	*.448*	*.420*
15 docs	*.504*	*.431*	*.399*	*.376*
20 docs	*.477*	*.390*	*.367*	*.350*
Av. Prec.	*.470*	*.419*	*.359*	*.354*
% chg mono	-	*-10.9%*	*-23.6%*	*-24.7%*
% chg no FB SYS	*+6.3%*	*+17.4%*	*+20.5%*	*+6.9%*
% chg no FB PTP	*+12.2%*	*+11.1%*	*+5.6%*	*+4.4%*
R-ret	*2479*	*2271*	*2065*	*2073*

Table 20. Retrieval results for Spanish with merged queries from both MT systems with summary-based expansion term selection Weights of terms occurring in both queries are upweighted by 2

Prec.	Combined Topic Language upweighted			
	Spanish	French*	German*	Italian*
5 docs	.588	.532	.504	.516
10 docs	.540	.436	.436	.432
15 docs	.500	.409	.381	.404
20 docs	.473	.376	.356	.371
Av. Prec.	.468	.414	354	.379
% chg mono(sys)	-	-11.5%	-24.4%	-19.0%
% chg no FB SYS	+5.9%	+15.9%	+18.8%	+14.5%
% chg no FB PTP	+11.7%	+9.8%	+4.12%	+11.8%
R-ret	2460	2210	2005	2151

5.4 English Runs

Tables 21 and 22 show the baseline retrieval results for English, French, German, Italian and Spanish queries and English documents. The PTP translated topics are shown to outperform the Systran translated topics in all cases except for the French topics. This result is consistent with our results for the English document collection in CLEF 2001 [5].

Table 21. Baseline retrieval results for English run using Systran

Prec.	Topic Language				
	English	French	German	Italian	Spanish
5 docs	*.468*	*.408*	*.368*	*.388*	*.388*
10 docs	*.370*	*.328*	*.320*	*.308*	*.314*
15 docs	*.327*	*.296*	*.276*	*.277*	*.279*
20 docs	*.295*	*.263*	*.237*	*.248*	*.245*
Av. Prec.	*.413*	*.337*	*.297*	*.313*	*.296*
% chg mono	-	*-18.4%*	*-28.1%*	*-24.2%*	*-28.3%*
R-ret	*777*	*747*	*700*	*701*	*708*

Table 22. Baseline retrieval results for English run using Power Translator Pro

Prec.	Topic Language				
	English	French	German	Italian	Spanish
5 docs	*.468*	*.392*	*.396*	*.416*	*.388*
10 docs	*.370*	*.330*	*.320*	*.324*	*.318*
15 docs	*.327*	*.295*	*.277*	*.285*	*.287*
20 docs	*.295*	*.267*	*.248*	*.258*	*.255*
Av. Prec.	*.413*	*.327*	*.303*	*.336*	*.336*
% chg mono	-	*-20.8%*	*-26.6%*	*-18.6%*	*-18.6%*
R-ret	*777*	*752*	*702*	*688*	*727*

Table 23. Retrieval results Englis using Systran with summary-based expansion term selection

Prec.	Topic Language				
	English	French	German	Italian	Spanish
5 docs	*.488*	*.440*	*.416*	*.428*	*.416*
10 docs	*.414*	*.374*	*.340*	*.346*	*.344*
15 docs	*.356*	*.325*	*.289*	*.309*	*.304*
20 docs	*.326*	*.286*	*.264*	*.274*	*.279*
Av. Prec.	*.442*	*.363*	*.326*	*.346*	*.326*
% chg mono	-	*-17.9%*	*-26.2%*	*-21.7%*	*-26.2%*
% chg. No FB	*+7.0%*	*+7.7%*	*+9.8%*	*+10.5%*	*+10.1%*
R-ret	*798*	*776*	*748*	*742*	*727*

Table 24. Retrieval results for English using Power Translation Pro with summary based expansion term selection

Prec.	Topic Language				
	English	French	German	Italian	Spanish
5 docs	*.488*	*.440*	*.416*	*.428*	*.416*
10 docs	*.414*	*.380*	*.348*	*.356*	*.358*
15 docs	*.356*	*.341*	*.311*	*.308*	*.312*
20 docs	*.326*	*.303*	*.275*	*.282*	*.284*
Av. Prec.	*.442*	*.368*	*.345*	*.375*	*.363*
% chg mono	-	*-16.7%*	*-21.9%*	*-15.2%*	*-17.9%*
% chg no FB	*+7.0%*	*+12.5%*	*+13.9%*	*+11.6%*	*+8.0%*
R-re	*798*	*781*	*765*	*746*	*768*

Table 23 and 24 show feedback results using the standard feedback method. Improvements in retrieval performance compared to the absolute baseline for all language pairs are observed in all cases. Again PRF gives improvement over the baseline for all topic languages, with an improvement of about 11% in average precision being observed.

Table 25. Retrieval results for English using Systran with summary-based expansion term selection from pilot collection and cfw(i) from test collection

Prec.	Topic Language				
	English	French	German	Italian	Spanish
5 docs	*.512*	*.472*	*.428*	*.460*	*.396*
10 docs	*.416*	*.382*	*.362*	*.368*	*.356*
15 docs	*.353*	*.335*	*.304*	*.312*	*.304*
20 docs	*.314*	*.289*	*.272*	*.275*	*.273*
Av. Prec.	*.466*	*.405*	*.347*	*.390*	*.369*
% chg mono	-	*-13.1%*	*-25.5%*	*-16.3%*	*-20.8%*
% chg no FB	*+12.8%*	*+20.2%*	*+16.8%*	*+24.6%*	*+24.7%*
R-ret	*787*	*760*	*751*	*732*	*728*

Table 26. Retrieval results for English using Power Translator Pro with summary-based expansion term selection from pilot collection and cfw(i) from test collection

Prec.	Topic Language				
	English	French	German	Italian	Spanish
5 docs	*.512*	*.456*	*.436*	*.432*	*.424*
10 docs	*.416*	*.406*	*.356*	*.352*	*.364*
15 docs	*.353*	*.328*	*.312*	*.320*	*.312*
20 docs	*.314*	*.297*	*.276*	*.289*	*.284*
Av. Prec.	*.466*	*.420*	*.382*	*.391*	*.401*
% chg mono	-	*-9.9%*	*-18.0%*	*-16.1%*	*-13.9%*
% chg no FB	*+12.8%*	*+28.4%*	*+26.1%*	*+16.4%*	*+19.3%*
R-ret	*787*	*775*	*723*	*741*	*755*

Table 27. Retrieval results for English using Systran with summary-based expansion term selection and cfw(i) from pilot collection

Prec.	Topic Language				
	English	French	German	Italian	Spanish
5 docs	*.444*	*.416*	*.376*	*.396*	*.380*
10 docs	*.360*	*.340*	*.298*	*.312*	*.300*
15 docs	*.305*	*.287*	*.257*	*.264*	*.261*
20 docs	*.271*	*.245*	*.229*	*.227*	*.237*
Av. Prec.	*.419*	*.358*	*.313*	*.344*	*.326*
% chg mono	-	*-14.6%*	*-25.3%*	*-17.9%*	*-22.2%*
% chg no FB	*+1.5%*	*+6.2%*	*+5.4%*	*+9.9%*	*+10.1%*
R-ret	*643*	*602*	*607*	*577*	*607*

Table 28. Retrieval results for English using Power Translator Pro with summary-based expansion term selection and cfw(i) from pilot collection

Prec.	Topic Language				
	English	French	German	Italian	Spanish
5 docs	*.444*	*.408*	*.408*	*.412*	*.380*
10 docs	*.360*	*.338*	*.304*	*.302*	*.308*
15 docs	*.305*	*.287*	*.261*	*.261*	*.264*
20 docs	*.271*	*.263*	*.238*	*.230*	*.235*
Av. Prec.	*.419*	*.353*	*.349*	*.346*	*.350*
% chg mono	-	*-15.8%*	*-16.7%*	*-17.4%*	*-16.5%*
% chg no FB	*+1.5%*	*+7.9%*	*+15.2%*	*+2.9%*	*+4.2%*
R-ret	*643*	*621*	*598*	*590*	*612*

Tables 25-28 shows retrieval results for expansion term selection and term weight estimation from our pilot collection. The results show the same trend as observed for the Italian and Spanish collections. Although term expansion selection using the pilot collection resulted in improved retrieval performance for all language pairs compared to both the baseline results and the standard PRF method results, estimating term weights from the pilot collection in addition to expansion term selection resulted in loss in precision compared to the standard method results. Further analysis of the CLEF 2002 query set is needed to understand this retrieval behaviour which is different to our results for CLEF 2001 task where pilot collection cfw(i) estimation led to a further improvement [14].

5.5 Term Weights Estimation from Merged Collections

Query expansion and term weighting from a pilot collection has been shown to be very effective in information retrieval. The results above however suggest that a positive impact on performance is not guaranteed. For the Italian and the Spanish runs, this is probably due to the differences in the language characteristics of the pilot and the translated test collections. To test this theory, we did some further runs; the pilot and the test collection were merged to form a single collection. This merged collection was then used as the pilot collection, i.e. for query expansion and term weighting. The expanded query and the corresponding weight are then applied to the test collection. The tables below show the effect of this method on retrieval. In all cases we present the result for both Systran and PTP translated topics.

Table 29. Retrieval results for Italian using Systran topics with summary-based term selection and cfw(i) from merged collection

Prec.	Topic Language				
	Italian	English	French	German	Spanish
5 docs	*.510*	*.506*	*.433*	*.425*	*.461*
10 docs	*.449*	*.429*	*.392*	*.357*	*.394*
15 docs	*.423*	*.385*	*.361*	*.314*	*.355*
20 docs	*.387*	*.356*	*.327*	*.295*	*.321*
Av. Prec.	*.442*	*.406*	*.371*	*.346*	*.371*
% chg mono	-	*-8.1%*	*-16.1%*	*-21.7%*	*-16.1%*
% chg no FB	*+13.9%*	*+23.0%*	*+14.5%*	*+16.1%*	*+16.3%*
R-ret	*980*	*978*	*952*	*906*	*904*

Table 30. Retrieval results for Italian using PTP with summary-based term selection and cfw(i) from merged collection

Prec.	Topic Language				
	Italian	English	French	German	Spanish
5 docs	*.457*	*.506*	*.461*	*.457*	*.469*
10 docs	*.394*	*.429*	*.394*	*.359*	*.404*
15 docs	*.359*	*.385*	*.346*	*.320*	*.367*
20 docs	*.324*	*.356*	*.314*	*.299*	*.339*
Av. Prec.	*.384*	*.406*	*.366*	*.372*	*.378*
% chg mono	-	*+5.7%*	*-5.2%*	*-3.1%*	*-1.6%*
% chg no FB	*+10.0%*	*+23.0%*	*-3.1%*	*+26.9%*	*+18.5%*
R-ret	*872*	*978*	*970*	*874*	*922*

Table 31. Retrieval results for Spanish using Systran WITH summary-based term selection and cfw(i) from merged collection

Prec.	Topic Language				
	Spanish	English	French	German	Italian
5 docs	*.664*	*.612*	*.544*	*.496*	*.468*
10 docs	*.582*	*.518*	*.458*	*.416*	*.384*
15 docs	*.533*	*.491*	*.416*	*.387*	*.355*
20 docs	*.495*	*.463*	*.383*	*.352*	*.330*
Av. Prec.	*.490*	*.443*	*.383*	*.358*	*.345*
% chg mono	-	*-9.6%*	*-21.8%*	*-26.9%*	*-29.6%*
% chg no FB	*+10.9%*	*+19.1%*	*+7.3%*	*+20.1%*	*+4.2%*
R-ret	*2513*	*2384*	*2186*	*2151*	*2097*

Table 32. Retrieval results for Spanish using PTP with summary-based term selection and cfw(i) from merged collection

Prec.	Topic Language				
	Spanish	English	French	German	Italian
5 docs	*.648*	*.612*	*.568*	*.548*	*.532*
10 docs	*.556*	*.518*	*.498*	*.470*	*.444*
15 docs	*.497*	*.491*	*.457*	*.427*	*.353*
20 docs	*.461*	*.463*	*.419*	*.399*	*.367*
Av. Prec.	*.478*	*.443*	*.407*	*.392*	*.359*
% chg mono	-	*-7.3%*	*-14.9%*	*-17.9%*	*-24.9%*
% chg no FB	*+14.1%*	*+19.1%*	*+7.9%*	*+15.3%*	*+5.9%*
R-ret	*2478*	*2384*	*2288*	*2083*	*2070*

Tables 29-32 show the results for using the merged collection (pilot and test) for query expansion and term weighting. The results show that merging the two collections result in more appropriate estimation of term weights, which results in improved retrieval. On average this method resulted in improvement over using the standard method as shown in Tables 3, 4, 13 and 14, or using the pilot collection alone for term weights estimation. An improvement of about 14% improvement in retrieval compared to the baseline results is achieved in all cases.

6 Conclusions and Further Work

In this paper we have presented our results for the CLEF 2002 monolingual and bilingual Italian and Spanish retrieval tasks. Additional results for English monolingual and bilingual tasks are also presented. The results suggest that good retrieval results can be achieved by merging the output of two commercially available MT systems. It also shows that all language pairs behave differently to different feedback methods, this requires further investigation to determine the causes of such behaviour and how they can be tackled. It also suggests that different methods may have to be adapted to suit different language pairs in order to get the best results. The combined query method is somehow effective in smoothing out the negative effects of bad translations in most cases. Using pilot collection to estimate term weight and for query expansion although shown to be very effective in [13], the results shown here suggests that when there is a difference in the language of the pilot and the test collection the method might not be as effective. The situation is analogous to that found in erroneous documents indexing in multimedia retrieval [15]. We show that further improvements can be achieved by merging the two collections to form a pilot collection. Further investigation is needed to determine the reason for the slightly poor performance of the Systran translated queries compared to the PTP translated queries. We also noticed that some terms were left untranslated by the MT systems, this is more predominant in the Systran translations, and may be the reason for the lower performance achieved using the topics translated using Systran MT compared to that for PTP topic translation in the bilingual results.

References

[1] G.J.F. Jones, T. Sakai, N. H. Collier, A. Kumano and K. Sumita. A Comparison of Query Translation Methods for English-Japanese Cross-Language Information Retrieval. In *Proceedings of the 22nd Annual International ACM SIGIR Conference on Research and Development in Information Retrieval*, pages 269-270, San Francisco, 1999. ACM.

[2] L. Ballesteros and W. B. Croft. Phrasal Translation and Query Expansion Techniques for Cross-Language Information Retrieval. In *Proceedings of the 20th Annual International ACM SIGIR Conference on Research and Development in Information Retrieval*, pages 84-91, Philadelphia, 1997. ACM.

[3] G.Salton and C. Buckley. Improving Retrieval performance by Relevance Feedback. *Journal of the American Society for Information Science*, 41(4):288-297, 1990.

[4] A.M. Lam-Adesina and G.J.F. Jones. Applying Summarization Techniques for Term Selection in Relevance Feedback. In *Proceedings of the 24th Annual International ACM SIGIR Conference on Research and Development in Information Retrieval*, pages 1-9, New Orleans, 2001. ACM.

[5] G.J.F. Jones and A.M. Lam-Adesina. Exeter at CLEF 2001: Experiments with Machine Translation for Bilingual Retrieval. In *Proceedings of the CLEF 2001: Workshop on Cross-Language Information Retrieval and Evaluation*, pages 59-77, Darmstadt, Germany, 2002.

[6] S.E. Robertson and S. Walker. Some simple effective approximations to the 2-Poisson model for probabilistic weighted retrieval. In *Proceedings of the 17th Annual International ACM SIGIR Conference on Research and Development in Information Retrieval*, pages 232-241, Dublin, 1994, ACM.

[7] M. F. Porter. An algorithm for suffix stripping. Program, 14:10-137, 1980.

[8] H.P. Luhn. The Automatic Creation of Literature Abstracts. *IBM Journal of Research and Development*, 2(2):159-165, 1958.

[9] H.P. Edmundson. New Methods in Automatic Abstracting. *Journal of the ACM*, 16(2):264-285, 1969.

[10] Tombros and M. Sanderson. The Advantages of Query-Biased Summaries in Information Retrieval. In *Proceedings of the 21st Annual International ACM SIGIR Conference Research and Development in Information Retrieval*, pages 2-10, Melbourne, 1998. ACM.

[11] S.E. Robertson. On term selection for query expansion. *Journal of Documentation*, 46:359-364, 1990.

[12] S.E. Robertson and K. Sparck Jones. Relevance weighting of search terms. *Journal of the American Society for Information Science*, 27(3):129-146, 1976.

[13] S.E. Robertson, S. Walker, and M. M. Beaulieu. Okapi at TREC-7: automatic ad hoc, filtering, VLS and interactive track. In E. M. Voorhees and D. K. Harman, editors, In *Proceedings of the Seventh Text REtrieval Conference (TREC-7)*, pages 253-264. NIST, 1999.

[14] G.J.F. Jones and A.M. Lam-Adesina. Combination Methods for improving the Reliability of Machine Translation Based Cross-Language Information Retrieval. In *Proceedings of the 13th Irish Conference on Artificial Intelligence and Cognitive Science*, pages 190-196, Limerick, 2002.

[15] A.M. Lam-Adesina, G.J.F. Jones, Examining the Effectiveness of IR Techniques for Document Image Retrieval, In Proceedings of the workshop on Information Retrieval and OCR: From Converting Content to Grasping Meaning at the 25th Annual International ACM SIGIR Conference on Research and Development in Information Retrieval (SIGIR 2002), Tampere 2002.
[16] N.J. Belkin, P. Kantor, E.A Fox, J.A. Shaw. Combining the evidence of multiple query representations for information retrieval. *Information Processing and Mangaement*, 31:431—448, 1995.

Portuguese-English Experiments Using Latent Semantic Indexing

Viviane Moreira Orengo and Christian Huyck

School of Computing Science
Middlesex University, The Burroughs, London NW4 4BT, UK
{v.orengo,c.huyck}@mdx.ac.uk

Abstract. This paper reports the work of Middlesex University in the CLEF bilingual task. We have carried out experiments using Portuguese queries to retrieve documents in English. The approach used was Latent Semantic Indexing, which is an automatic method not requiring dictionaries or thesauri. We have also run a monolingual version of the system to work as a baseline. Here we describe in detail the methods used and give an analysis of the results obtained.

1 Introduction

Middlesex University participated in CLEF for the first time in 2002. We submitted runs for the bilingual task, using Portuguese queries to retrieve English documents. The approach adopted was Latent Semantic Indexing (LSI), which has achieved some promising results in previous experiments using other languages [5,10] and has the great advantage of not requiring expensive resources such as thesauri.

This paper is organised as follows: Section 2 presents some reasons for choosing Portuguese; Section 3 describes LSI and how it can be applied to CLIR; Section 4 reports our experiments and Section 5 analyses our results.

2 Why Portuguese?

Portuguese is the fifth biggest language in terms of native speakers (see Figure 1). It is spoken on 4 continents: Europe (Portugal, Madeira, Azores), South America (Brazil), Africa (Angola, Mozambique, Cape Verde Islands, Guinea-Bissau) and Asia (Goa, Macau, East Timor). There are over 176 million native speakers and another 15 million people use it as a second language.

On the other hand, according to the Internet Software Consortium [4], less than 1% of all web hosts are in Portuguese. In addition, only a small percentage of this population is competent in English, the vast majority (including university students) are not able to formulate good queries (in English) to a search engine like Google, Altavista, Lycos, etc. As a consequence, sources of information for the 8 million Portuguese speakers accessing the Internet are extremely limited compared to the

C.A. Peters (Ed.): CLEF 2002, LNCS 2785, pp. 147-154, 2003.

immense amount of information available to the English speaking population. Moreover, no CLIR research has been carried out using Portuguese. For all those reasons we decided to put Portuguese in the picture, by using it in our experiments.

3 CLIR Using Latent Semantic Indexing

Latent Semantic Indexing [1] is a technique developed in 1990 by Dumais, Derweester, Landauer, Furnas and Harshman. The main goal is to retrieve on the basis of conceptual content rather than the actual terms used in the query. There are several ways of expressing a concept and the terms used in the query may not match the terms used in the documents.

LSI seeks to tackle synonymy and polysemy as they are the main problems with keyword matching. Synonymy stems from the fact that there are many ways to refer to the same object, while polysemy refers to the fact that many words have more than one distinct meaning. Attempts to solve the synonymy problem have been made by using query expansion, which works, e.g., by looking up a thesaurus and augmenting the query with related terms. The polysemy problem is considerably more difficult. Attempts to solve it include research on word sense disambiguation. However, we are not aware of any adequate automatic method for dealing with it.

The main goal of using LSI for CLIR is to provide a method for matching text segments in one language with text segments of similar meaning in another language without needing to translate either, by using a language-independent representation of the words. This means that words are given an abstract description that does not depend on the original language.

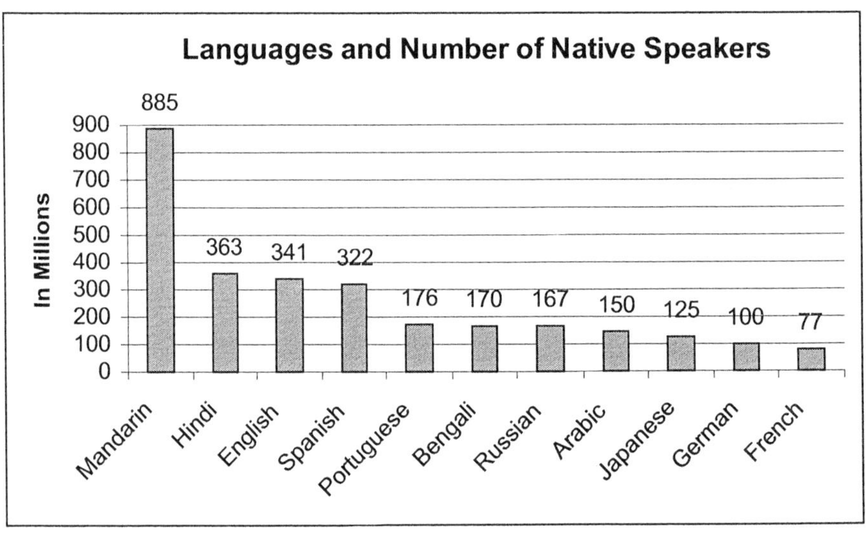

Fig. 1. Languages in terms of native speakers [3]

		D_1	D_2	D_3	D_4	D_5	D_6	D_7	...	D_n
A	água	3	0	4	0	0	1	1	...	0
	casa	0	0	2	1	1	1	0	...	0
	papel	0	0	0	0	0	0	3	...	1
	porta	0	0	1	1	0	1	1	...	0
	...									
B	door	0	0	1	1	0	1	1	...	0
	house	0	0	2	1	1	1	0	...	0
	paper	0	0	0	0	0	0	3	...	1
	water	3	0	4	0	0	1	1	...	0
	...									

Fig. 2. Term by document matrix

LSI is initially applied to a matrix of terms by documents (see Fig. 2.). Therefore, the first step is to build such a matrix based on a set of dual-language documents[1]. The matrix contains the number of occurrences (or weights) of each term in each document. In an ideal situation the pattern of occurrence of a term in language A should be identical to the pattern of occurrence of its match in language B. The resulting matrix tends to be very sparse, since most terms do not occur in every document.

This matrix is then factorised by singular value decomposition[2] (SVD). SVD reduces the number of dimensions, throwing away the small sources of variability in term usage. The *k* most important dimensions are kept. Roughly speaking, these dimensions (or factors) may be thought of as artificial concepts; they represent extracted common meaning components of many different words and documents. Each term or document is then characterised by a vector of weights indicating its strength of association with each of these underlying concepts. Since the number of factors or dimensions is much smaller than the number of unique terms, words will not be independent. For example, if two terms are used in similar documents, they will have similar vectors in the reduced-dimension representation.

It is possible to reconstruct the original term by document matrix from its factor weights with reasonable accuracy. However, it is not advisable to reconstruct it with perfect accuracy, as the original matrix contains noise, which can be eliminated through dimension reduction. LSI implements the vector-space model, in which terms, documents and queries are represented as vectors in a *k*-dimensional semantic space.

The SVD of a sparse matrix A is given by:

$$A = U\Sigma V^T \tag{1}$$

Where U and V are orthogonal matrices and Σ is the diagonal matrix of singular values. The columns of U and V contain the left and right singular vectors, respectively. The $m \times n$ matrix A_k, which is constructed from the k-largest single triplets of A, is the closest rank-k matrix to A (see Fig 3).

1 Dual-language documents are composed by the document in the original language together with its translation in another language.

2 Mathematics are presented in detail in [1].

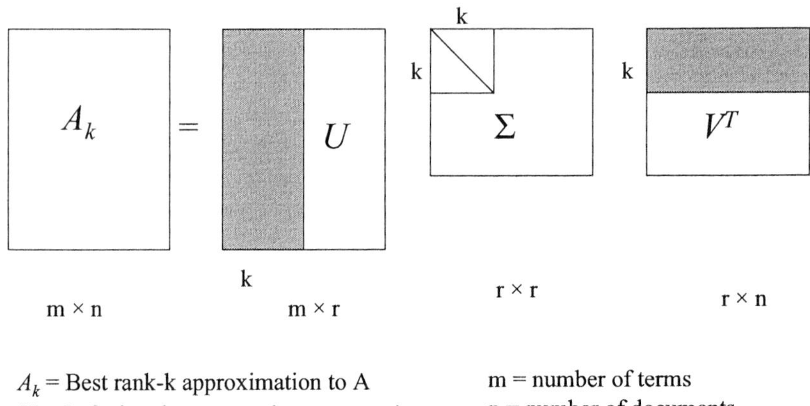

A_k = Best rank-k approximation to A
U = Left singular vectors (term vectors)
Σ = Singular values
V = Right singular vectors (document vectors)

m = number of terms
n = number of documents
k = rank (number of dimensions)
r = number of dimensions of A

Fig. 3. Singular value decomposition

After deriving the semantic space with an initial sample of dual-language documents, new documents can be added. Those new documents will be placed at a location calculated by averaging the vectors of the terms that it contains. This process is known as "folding in". Queries are treated as pseudo-documents and placed at the weighted sum of its component term vectors. The similarity between query and documents is measured using the cosine between their vectors.

SVD causes some synonyms to be represented by similar vectors (since they would have many co-occurrences), which allows relevant documents to be retrieved even if they do not share any terms with the query. This is what makes LSI suitable for CLIR, given that a term in one language will be treated as a synonym to its match in the other language. The main advantages of using LSI for CLIR are:

- There is no traditional-style translation. All terms and documents are transformed to a language-independent representation.
- New languages can be added easily, provided you have training data.
- There is no need for expensive resources such as dictionaries, thesauri or machine translation systems.

As with any method, LSI also has its drawbacks:

- SVD is computationally expensive and it may take several hours to be computed, for a reasonably sized collection.
- Parallel corpora are not always available
- The only currently known way to determine the number of dimensions is through trial and error as there is no automatic way of establishing the optimal number. LSI research suggests a number which is large enough to incorporate important concepts and small enough to not include noise. In previous experiments, this number was typically between 100 and 300.

<DOCNO> LA012394-0072 </DOCNO>	<DOCNO> LA012394-0072 </DOCNO>
TIME TO CARE FOR ROSES	A HORA DE IMPORTAR-SE COM ROSAS
Give attention to roses at this	dá a atenção às rosas neste
time. Prune them before spraying	tempo.Pode-os antes de pulverizar
to reduce the total area that	para reduzir a área total que
needs to be sprayed at this time.	necessita ser pulverizada neste
Remember to drench the **branches**	tempo. Recorde drench as **filiais**
and trunk until the material runs	e o tronco até o material
off the **branches**.	funciona for a das **filiais**.

Fig. 4. Sample dual-language document

4 Experiments

In order to use LSI for a bilingual experiment we needed an initial sample of parallel documents, i.e. the original documents and their translations, to derive the concept space. However, the collection we used, the Los Angeles Times, was in English only. Therefore we used Systran [8] to translate 20% (approximately 22000 documents) of the collection into Portuguese. Figure 4 shows a sample dual-language document used in the experiment. The translation is far from perfect, and many times the incorrect sense of a word was used, e.g. "branch" was translated to "filial" (shop branch), when the correct sense was "ramo" (tree branch). When the system did not have a translation for a term, it remained in the original language. Nevertheless, we did not perform any corrections or modifications on the resulting translations.

We used the Porter stemmer [7] to stem the English documents, and our own stemmer [6] to stem the Portuguese translations. Stop words were also removed. The next step was to run the SVD on the 22,000 dual-language documents. We used a binary version of LSI provided by Telcordia Technologies [9]. An important aspect is the choice of the number of dimensions that will compose the concept space. We chose 700 dimensions since this is the number which gave the best performance, within reasonable indexing time, when using last year's query topics. It was also the highest number that our system could support.

The entries in the term by document matrix were the local weight (frequency of a term in a document) multiplied by the global weight of the term (number of occurrences of a term across the entire collection). The weighting scheme used was "log-entropy" which is given by the formula below. A term whose appearance tends to be equally likely among the documents is given a low weight and a term whose appearance is concentrated in a few documents is given a higher weight. The elements of our matrix will be of the form: $L(i,j) * G(i)$

Local Weighting: $$L(i,j) = \log(tf_{ij} + 1)$$

Global Weighting: $$G(i) = 1 - \sum_{j=1}^{N} \frac{p_{ij} \log(p_{ij})}{\log N} \text{ where } p_{ij} = \frac{tf_{ij}}{gf_i}$$

where:

tf_{ij} = frequency of term i in document j
gf_i = total number of times term i occurs in the entire collection
N = number of documents in the collection

The next step was to "fold in" the remaining 91,000 English-only documents into that semantic space, which means that vector representations were calculated for those remaining documents. The resulting index had 70,000 unique terms, covering both languages. We did not index terms that were less than 3 characters long. We did not use phrases or multiword recognition, syntactic or semantic parsing, word sense disambiguation, heuristic association, spelling checking or correction, proper noun identification, a controlled vocabulary, a thesaurus, or any manual indexing.

All terms and documents from both languages are represented in the same concept space. Therefore a query in one language may retrieve documents in any languages. This situation benefits from cross-linguistic homonyms, i.e. words that have the same spelling and meaning in both languages; e.g. *"singular"* is represented by one vector only, accounting for both languages. On the other hand, it suffers with "false friends", i.e. words that have the same spelling across languages but different meanings; e.g. "data" in Portuguese means "date" instead of "information". The problem in this case is that false friends are wrongly represented by only one point in space, placed at the average of all meanings. The ideal scenario would take advantage of cross-linguistic homonyms while at the same time avoid false friends. We are still looking for a way to do this automatically.

5 Analysis of Results

In an ideal situation the similarity between a term and its translation should be very high (close to 100%). In order to evaluate how accurately LSI represents the correspondence between terms, we calculated the similarities between some randomly picked English words and their counterparts in Portuguese. Table 1 shows the results for this experiment. The scores are generally quite high. However, when cross-linguistic polysemy is present, the similarity decreases significantly (see second column). This happens because term co-occurrences decrease in the presence of polysemy and results in a term and its translation being placed further apart in the concept space.

We submitted three official runs:

- MDXman – keywords manually chosen from title, description and narrative. The average number of words per query was 3.82
- MDXtpc – all terms from title chosen automatically
- MDXtd – all terms from title and description chosen automatically

Our results are summarised at Table 2. Our best score was MDXman, closely followed by MDXtd. The worst result was MDXtpc. We attribute this difference to the fact that shorter queries provide less (or no) context information to the retrieval system. Our performance is consistent with the scores obtained using LSI for a monolingual task [8]. We are less than happy with these results, but we think they are quite reasonable considering that we used machine translation to create a sample of parallel documents. A better quality translation would almost certainly improve the scores.

Table 1. Term Similarity

English	Portuguese	Similarity
baby	bebê	99.67%
England	Inglaterra	99.24%
eat	comer	94.19%
paper	papel	84.38%
book	livro	77.11%
Cyprus	chipre	97.22%
car	carro	91.28%
run	correr	51.03%
find	encontrar	80.06%

English	Portuguese	Similarity
train	trem	12.30%
train	treinar	84.97%
shade	sombra	31.88%
shadow	sombra	31.88%
bank	banco	97.33%
bench	banco	32.94%
match	fósforo	96.72%
match	jogo	36.28%
game	jogo	91.30%

Table 2. Summary of Results

Run	Average Precision	R-Precision
MDXman	20.85%	23.10%
MDXtpc	15.51%	16.76%
MDXtd	20.88%	21.68%

Analysing the sets of documents retrieved for each query, we observed that most highly ranked but irrelevant documents were generally on the query topic, but did not specifically meet the requirements. As an example, for query 121 – "Successes of Ayrton Senna", the documents retrieved were about him, but sometimes did not mention his sporting achievements. We also did not score well in queries 97, 98 and 131 for which there was only one relevant document. We believe that happened because we did not index words that occurred in one document only, and "Kaurismäkis", a name mentioned in one of these topics for example, was one of them.

In comparison with the other groups, we obtained the best score for four topics: 126,130, 137 (MDXman) and 106 (MDXtd). We also obtained the worst result for four topics: 91, 98, 134 (MDXtpc) and 108 (MDXtd). For MDXman, 22 topics were at or above the median and 20 topics were below the median. LSI outperforms keyword based searching in the cases where the words used in the query do not match the terms used in the relevant documents. This was the case of topic 137 – "international beauty contests", both relevant documents did not contain the keywords present in the topic. It had, however, related terms such as "miss world" and "miss universe". Our superior performance in those cases confirms that LSI can efficiently tackle the synonymy problem, modelling relationships between related terms and placing them close together in the vector-space.

In order to evaluate how much cross-linguistic polysemy affects the performance of LSI we have performed a monolingual experiment to compare against the bilingual one. This time we only indexed the English documents and used the English version of the queries. The average precision (with automatic topic +description) was 24 %. A statistical *t-test* revealed that there is no significant difference between the monolingual and bilingual scores. This indicates that LSI is not seriously affected by cross-linguistic polysemy.

An interesting finding is that several bilingual queries had better performance than the monolingual ones (15 out of 42). In query 130, for example, the bilingual version had a precision which was nearly 3 times the monolingual run. This is quite unexpected, as we would imagine that introducing a new language would pose more difficulty for the system.

Future work will include further analysis of these results in order to establish methods for improvement. We also seek reasons for the superiority of some bilingual queries with respect to monolingual ones.

References

[1] Deerwester, S.; Dumais, S.; Furnas, G.; Landauer T. and Harshman,R. Indexing by Latent Semantic Analysis. Journal of the American Society for Information Science, 41(6):1-13, 1990.

[2] Dumais, S. Latent Semantic Indexing (LSI) : TREC–3 Report.

[3] Ethnologue http://www.ethnologue.com.

[4] Internet Software Consortium http://www.isc.org/ds/WWW-200101/dist-bynum.html.

[5] Landauer, Thomas K.; Littman, Michael L. Fully Automatic Cross-Language Document Retrieval Using Latent Semantic Indexing. In: Proceedings of the Sixth Annual Conference of the UW Centre for the New Oxford English Dictionary and Text Research, pages 31-38, Waterloo, Ontario, Oct. 1990.

[6] Orengo, V.M.; Huyck, C.R. A Stemming algorithm for the Portuguese Language. In: Proceedings of SPIRE'2001 Symposium on String Processing and Information Retrieval, Laguna de San Raphael, Chile, November 2001.

[7] Porter, M.F. An Algorithm for Suffix Stripping. Program, 14(3), 130-137, July 1980.

[8] Systran http://www.systransoft.com/.

[9] Telcordia Technologies - http://lsi.research.telcordia.com/.

[10] Yang Yiming et al. Translingual Information Retrieval: Learning from Bilingual Corpora. In: 15th International Joint Conference on Artificial Intelligence IJCAI'97, Nagoya, Japan, August 23-29, 1997.

Thomson Legal and Regulatory Experiments for CLEF 2002

Isabelle Moulinier and Hugo Molina-Salgado

Thomson Legal and Regulatory
Research and Development Group, 610 Opperman Drive, Eagan, MN 55123, USA
{isabelle.moulinier,hugo.salgado}@westgroup.com

Abstract. Thomson Legal and Regulatory participated in the monolingual, the bilingual and the multilingual tracks. Our monolingual runs added Swedish to the languages we had submitted in previous participations. Our bilingual and multilingual efforts used English as the query language. We experimented with dictionaries and similarity thesauri for the bilingual task, and we used machine translations in our multi-lingual runs. Our various merging strategies had limited success compared to a simple round robin.

1 Introduction

For CLEF-2002, Thomson Legal and Regulatory (TLR) participated in monolingual, bilingual, and multilingual retrieval. Our monolingual experiments gained benefit from previous efforts. We added Swedish to the languages we submitted last year (Dutch, French, German, Italian and Spanish). In addition, we tried to improve our Italian runs by refining language resources. Our bilingual runs were from English to either French or Spanish. We translated query concepts using a combination of similarity thesauri and machine-readable dictionaries. Translated queries were structured to take into account multiple translations as well as translations of word pairs rather than words. In our multilingual experiments, we used a machine translation system rather than our bilingual approach. We mostly focused on merging strategies, using CORI, normalization, or round-robin.

We give some background to our experiments in Section 2. Sections 3, 4, and 5 respectively present our monolingual, bilingual, and multilingual experiments.

2 Background

2.1 Previous Research

Our participation at CLEF-2002 benefits from our earlier work, as well as from the work of others. Our bilingual effort relies on similarity thesauri for translating query terms from English to French or Spanish. In addition to translating words [6], we also translate word pairs which loosely capture noun and verb

C.A. Peters (Ed.): CLEF 2002, LNCS 2785, pp. 155–163, 2003.

phrases. This differs from our approach last year when we generated word bigrams rather than pairs [3]. In addition, we follow Pirkola's approach for handling multiple translations. By taking advantage of query structures available in INQUERY, Pirkola [4] has shown that grouping translations for a given term is a better technique than allowing all translations to contribute equally. This has been developed further by Sperer and Oard [7].

One of the main issues in multilingual retrieval remains collection merging. In our experiments, we use simple merging techniques like round robin, normalized scores, as well as a variant of the CORI algorithm [1]. This is similar to Savoy's work at CLEF-2001 [5] and others.

2.2 The WIN System

The WIN system is a full-text natural language search engine, and corresponds to TLR/West Group's implementation of the inference network retrieval model. While based on the same retrieval model as the INQUERY system [2], WIN has evolved separately and focused on the retrieval of legal material in large collections in a commercial environment that supports both Boolean and natural language searches [8].

In addition, WIN has shifted from supporting mostly English content to supporting a large number of Western-European languages as well. This was performed by localizing tokenization rules (mostly for French and Italian) and adopting morphological stemming. Stemming of non-English terms is performed using a third-party toolkit, the LinguistX platform commercialized by Inxight. A variant of the Porter stemmer is used for English.

Document Scoring. WIN supports various strategies for computing term beliefs and scoring documents. We used a standard tf-idf for computing term beliefs in all our runs. The document is scored by combining term beliefs using a different rule for each query operator [2]. The final document score is an average of the document score as a whole and the score of the best portion. The best portion is dynamically computed based on query term occurrences.

Query Formulation. Query formulation identifies concepts in natural language text, and imposes a structure on these queries. In many cases, each term represents a concept, and a flat structure gives the same weight to all concepts. The processing of English queries eliminates stopwords and other noise phrases (such as "Find cases about," or "Relevant documents will include"), identifies (legal) phrases based on a phrase dictionary, and detects common misspellings.

In the experiments reported below, we use our standard English stopword and noise phrase lists, but do not identify phrases or misspellings. We have expanded the English noise phrase list with noise phrases extracted from queries used in previous years. Our German, French, Spanish, and Dutch runs use the same stopword lists as last year, but noise phrase patterns have been updated to cover query sets from CLEF-2001. Our Italian stopword and noise phrase list was validated by a native speaker, while our Swedish resources were extracted from the web and from available query sets.

Concept identification depends on text segmentation. In our experiments, we follow two main definitions for a concept: a concept is an indexing unit (typically a word) or a concept is a construct of indexing units. Constructs are expressed in terms of operators (average, proximity, synonym, etc.) and indexing units. For instance, we use a construct when a term has multiple translations, or when we identify word pairs.

3 Monolingual Experiments

Our approach for monolingual runs is similar to last year's. We have revised the Italian stopword and noise phrase lists with the help of a native speaker. Our stemming procedure, although still based on the LinguistX toolkit, has been altered slightly to limit the occurrence of multiple stems.

German, Dutch, and Swedish are all compounding languages. However, the LinguistX platform does not support compound breaking for Swedish. We therefore index and search only German and Dutch content using compound parts. Swedish is treated as a non-compounding language.

For all languages, we allow the stemmer to generate several stems for each term, as we do not rely on part-of-speech tagging for disambiguation. Multiple stems were grouped under a single concept in the structure query.

Results from our official runs are reported in Table 1. All runs used the title and description fields from the topics. Our results are comparable to those of previous years. Introducing revised stopword and noise phrase lists for Italian allows us to achieve good performance.

While most languages achieve an average precision in the same range (between 0.4 and 0.5), the figures for Swedish are much lower. We suspect that not breaking compounds may be the main cause, since previous work with German and Dutch has shown that retrieval performance was enhanced by compound breaking.

Table 1. Summary of all monolingual experiments using the title and description fields. Comparison to the median is expressed in the number of queries above, equal, and below

Run ID	Lang.	Avg. Prec.	R-Prec.	Above Median	Median	Below Median
tlrde	German	0.4221	0.4294	21	6	23
tlres	Spanish	0.4993	0.4816	31	3	16
tlrfr	French	0.4232	0.4134	17	8	25
tlrit	Italian	0.4159	0.4072	24	7	18
tlrnl	Dutch	0.4141	0.4211	27	3	20
tlrsv	Swedish	0.2439	0.2700	17	11	21

4 Bilingual Experiments

Our bilingual runs were from English queries to Spanish and French collections. As in our previous work [3], we used a combination of similarity thesauri and machine-readable dictionaries. The machine-readable dictionaries were downloaded from the Internet (www.freedict.com).

4.1 Experimental Setting

We implemented a variant of the similarity thesaurus approach described in [6] for multilingual retrieval. We constructed two similarity thesauri: a word thesaurus and a word pair thesaurus. Both similarity thesauri were trained on a collection merging the UN parallel text corpus, of around 20,000 documents, produced by the Linguistic Data Consortium, and an European Union (E.U.) parallel corpus, of over 100,000 documents, that we have at TLR.

Using a part-of-speech tagger, we restricted the set of words to nouns, verbs, adjectives, and adverbs. Word pairs were generated using sliding windows centered only on nouns, and components in pairs were ordered alphabetically. Terms, words, or pairs, were considered as translations when their similarity was above a predefined threshold. This threshold was chosen as it provided the best configuration on CLEF-2001 data.

While we identified noise phrase patterns in our official runs, stopwords were expected to have a different part-of-speech (like auxiliary, prepositions, etc). We later added a stopword list in conjunction with noise phrase patterns.

Finally, we reproduced our bigram experiments from 2001 using a smaller corpus (the UN corpus). This also gave us an insight on the influence of the corpus during the construction of bilingual similarity thesauri.

4.2 Results and Discussion

Table 2 reports our official runs. The translation resources for our official runs were a combination of the word similarity thesaurus and the dictionary.

Our unofficial runs cover several aspects. First, we used the machine readable dictionaries only. Second, we added an explicit stopword list instead of relying on part-of-speech tags. Third, we compared our concept by concept translation approach with automatic translation used in our multilingual runs. Table 3 summarizes these unofficial runs. Finally, we used the smaller UN corpus to build

Table 2. Summary of our official bilingual experiments using the title and description fields. The median was computed from all submitted runs

Run ID	Lang.	Avg. Prec.	R-Prec.	Above Median	Median	Below Median
tlren2es	English/Spanish	0.2873	0.2857	12	4	34
tlren2fr	English/French	0.3198	0.3440	13	3	34

Table 3. Summary of our unofficial bilingual runs using the title and description fields. *Stopwords* is the same as the official runs but we use an explicit stopword list. *Pairs* uses a combination of machine-readable dictionary, word and word pair similarity thesauri. The *Machine Translation* runs use Babelfish

Run Description	Lang.	Avg. Prec.	R-Prec.
Machine Readable Dictionary	English/Spanish	0.2861	0.2755
Stopwords	English/Spanish	0.3123	0.3047
Stopwords + Pairs	English/Spanish	0.3118	0.3038
Machine Translation	English/Spanish	0.3391	0.3414
Machine Readable Dictionary	English/French	0.2565	0.2595
Stopwords	English/French	0.3263	0.3474
Stopwords + Pairs	English/French	0.3257	0.3605
Machine Translation	English/French	0.3513	0.3543

Table 4. Summary of additional unofficial bilingual runs using the title and description fields. An explicit stopword list is used for all runs. The smaller UN corpus is used in building similarity thesauri. *Words* uses a combination of machine readable dictionaries (MRD) and word similarity thesauri. *Pairs* corresponds to the combination of the translations from the MRD, the word and the word pair similarity thesauri, while *Bigrams* corresponds to the combination of the MRD, the word and the bigram similarity thesauri

Run Description	Lang.	Avg. Prec.	R-Prec.
UN corpus + Words	English/Spanish	0.3419	0.3571
UN corpus + Pairs	English/Spanish	0.3377	0.3461
UN corpus + Bigrams	English/Spanish	0.3402	0.3543
UN corpus + Words	English/French	0.3398	0.3459
UN corpus + Pairs	English/French	0.3383	0.3425
UN corpus + Bigrams	English/French	0.3353	0.3422

word, bigram, and word pair similarity thesauri, and we used a combination of machine readable dictionaries and thesauri. These runs are reported in Table 4.

A comparison of Tables 2 and 3 shows that using an explicit list of stopwords helps enhance the average precision. We have identified inaccuracies in part-of-speech tagging as one of the main reasons. Inaccuracies are often caused by inadequate context, or by the lack of a specific tag in one of the languages, e.g. auxiliary versus verb.

In constrast with Table 3, Table 4 shows that building similarity thesauri using only the UN corpus yields to performance improvements for both the Words and the Pairs runs. The improvement is not statistically significant. Using a larger corpus to construct bilingual resources was not helpful. The larger corpus is dominated by E.U. material, and this leads to some E.U.-oriented translations. For instance, *European* is translated[1] into the French terms *européen* and

[1] We consider terms to be translations if the similarity score is above the 0.4 threshold.

communauté, and the Spanish terms *europeo*, *comunidad* and *constitutivo*. One way of addressing that issue may be to filter out corpus-specific terminology.

Unlike our results at CLEF-2001 [3], we find that translating word pairs and bigrams provides little advantage over translating individual words, although it is not harmful. We have not identified the differences between 2001 and 2002 at this point.

Finally, we find that combining resources enhances performance over using a simple machine readable dictionary for translation. We also find little difference between runs using machine translation and runs using our concept by concept translation.

5 Multilingual Experiments

During our multilingual experiments, we translated queries only. We used the indices generated for the monolingual runs for German, French, English, Italian, and Spanish. Queries were translated from English to the other languages using Babelfish[2].

5.1 Merging Techniques

We explored a number of merging approaches based on the ranks or scores of documents in their individual lists, as well as some query-related statistics on each of the collections.

Round-robin merging is a rank-based approach that creates a final list by alternating documents from each individual result list. Documents with identical scores are given the same rank.

Raw score merging is a score-based approach that merges and sorts result lists based on the raw score, even though these scores may not be comparable across collections.

Alternatively, scores can be rendered comparable across results lists by normalization. If D_1 is the top ranked document in collection C_k, then:

$$s_{norm}(Q, D_i) = \frac{bel(Q, D_i, C_k) - 0.4}{bel(Q, D_1, C_k) - 0.4},$$

where s_{norm} is the score used for merging and sorting, $bel(Q, D_i, C_k)$ is the belief score of document D_i for query Q in collection C_k, and 0.4 is the minimal score any document can achieve.

The two remaining merging approaches combine document beliefs with collection scores. In both cases, we estimate the collection score, denoted $bel(Q, C_k)$, as the maximum score the translated query Q could achieve on collection C_k.

The CORI algorithm [1] normalizes document scores as follows:

$$s_{cori}(Q, D_i) = bel(Q, D_i, C_k) * (1 + N * \frac{bel(Q, C_k) - avg\_bel(Q)}{avg\_bel(Q)}),$$

[2] Babelfish can be found at `http://babelfish.altavista.com`.

where $avg\_bel(Q) = \sum_{j=1}^{N} bel(Q, C_j)/N$ and N is the number of collections, assuming one language per collection. Note that the original CORI approach relied on a different collection score.

Collection-weighted score normalizes both the document and collection scores:

$$s_{wnorm}(Q, D_i) = s_{norm}(Q, D_i) * \frac{bel(Q, C_k)}{\max_{j=1..N} bel(Q, C_j)}$$

The merging process uses these new document scores to produce a single result list.

5.2 Results and Analysis

Our official run tlren2multi used round robin. Table 5 reports results from the different merging approaches.

As often reported, we found it hard to outperform the round robin approach. None of the differences observed between round-robin and the raw, norm, and wnorm runs are significant. Our results with the CORI merging strategy are comparable to those obtained by Savoy [5]. It is possible that the CORI algorithm is impacted by our choice of $bel(Q, C_k)$. More analysis is required to assess the difference between the original CORI and our version.

There are two issues with multilingual retrieval, the quality of the individual runs and the effectiveness of the merging strategy. The quality of the individual runs can easily be assessed by comparing their performance to the performance of monolingual runs. As can be seen in Table 6, using translated queries leads to an average degradation of 25% in performance (performance is measured in terms of average precision).

How to quantify the effectiveness of merging strategies remains an open issue. We can observe the following properties in an attempt to measure the effectiveness of merging. In Table 7, we observe that merging better individual runs (the monolingual column vs. the translated column) leads to better performance. We

Table 5. Summary of our multilingual experiments using the title and description fields. English was the query language. Due to a problem in our original English run, the unofficial round-robin and other runs rely on a corrected English run

Run ID	Avg. Prec.	R-Prec.	Prec at 10 docs
tlren2multi (round robin)	0.2049	0.2803	0.4560
Unofficial round robin	0.2382	0.3056	0.4960
raw score	0.2322	0.2861	0.5140
cori	0.1034	0.1510	0.3920
norm	0.2482	0.3120	0.5080
wnorm	0.2449	0.2981	0.4780

Table 6. The impact of translation in multilingual retrieval. The percentages reflect differences in average precision when we compare retrieval using an English query with retrieval using a query in the collection language

Collection language	Monolingual	Translated from English
German	0.4221	0.2849 (-32.5%)
French	0.4232	0.3513 (-17.0%)
Spanish	0.4993	0.3391 (-32.1%)
Italian	0.4159	0.3212 (-22.8%)

can also compare the average of the individual run performances with the performance of the multilingual runs, and find that the average of individual runs is higher that any multilingual run. These observations tend to indicate that merging also deteriorates the effectiveness of multilingual runs, but do not tell us how much so.

Table 5 shows that the R-precision measure is noticeably higher than the average precision. This can be explained by the low recall of multilingual runs and how recall influences average precision. Indeed, to calculate the average precision, one relies on all relevant documents returned. When a system does not retrieve all relevant documents (or most of the relevant documents), the average precision is negatively impacted. The R-precision, on the other hand, is not dependent on recall, just on the number of relevant documents to be found.

In addition, we find that the precision at 10 documents of most multilingual runs is higher than the precision at 10 documents of the translated runs. This shows that merging approaches are able to keep relevant documents at the top of the merged result list. However, merging approaches degrade rapidly when they are unable to find all relevant documents, as we discussed in the previous paragraph.

Table 7. Average precision of merging strategies. The monolingual column uses results from our monolingual runs (English, German, French, Spanish and Italian). The translated column refers to English queries translated to the collection language. The row Average of individual runs does not rely on merging

Merging strategy	Monolingual	Translated
round robin	0.3313	0.2382 (72%)
raw	0.3593	0.2322 (65%)
cori	0.1299	0.1034 (80%)
norm	0.3491	0.2482 (71%)
wnorm	0.3444	0.2449 (71%)
Average of individual runs	0.4517	0.3585 (79%)

6 Conclusion

Our participation at CLEF-2002 produced mixed results. On the one hand, we consider our monolingual runs successful. Future work for monolingual may evaluate how much improvement can be achieved by relevance feedback. On the other hand, our bilingual and multilingual runs did not lead to the expected results. For instance, we did not find any evidence that translating word pairs was helpful in our bilingual runs. We also encountered an over-fitting problem when training similarity thesauri on the E.U. corpus. Finally, the merging strategies we explored are limited by the quality of individual runs. We plan on investigating alternative merging algorithms, since our current approach has shown limited success.

References

[1] J. P. Callan, Z. Lu, and W. B. Croft. Searching distributed collections with inference networks. In *Proceedings of the 18th Annual International ACM SIGIR Conference on Research and Development in Information Retrieval*, pages 21–28, Seattle, WA, 1995.

[2] W. B. Croft, J. Callan, and J. Broglio. The inquery retrieval system. In *Proceedings of the 3rd International Conference on Database and Expert Systems Applications*, Spain, 1992.

[3] H. Molina-Salgado, I. Moulinier, M. Knutson, E. Lund, and K. Sekhon. Thomson legal and regulatory at clef 2001: monolingual and bilingual experiments. In *Workshop Notes for the CLEF 2001 Workshop*, Darmstadt, Germany, 2001.

[4] A. Pirkola. The effects of query structure and dictionary setups in dictionary-based cross-language information retrieval. In *Proceedings of the 21th Annual International ACM SIGIR Conference on Research and Development in Information Retrieval*, pages 55–63, Melbourne, Australia, 1998.

[5] J. Savoy. Report on clef-2001 experiments. In *Workshop Notes for the CLEF 2001 Workshop*, Darmstadt, Germany, 2001.

[6] P. Sheridan, M. Braschler, and P. Schäuble. Cross-lingual information retrieval in a multilingual legal domain. In *Proceedings of the First European Conference on Research and Advanced Technology for Digital Libraries*, pages 253–268, Pisa, Italy, 1997.

[7] R. Sperer and D. W. Oard. Structured translation for cross-language information retrieval. In *Proceedings of the 23th Annual International ACM SIGIR Conference on Research and Development in Information Retrieval*, pages 120–127, Athens, Greece, 2000.

[8] H. Turtle. Natural language vs. boolean query evaluation: a comparison of retrieval performance. In *Proceedings of the 17th Annual International ACM SIGIR Conference on Research and Development in Information Retrieval*, pages 212–220, Dublin, Ireland, 1994.

Eurospider at CLEF 2002

Martin Braschler*, Anne Göhring, and Peter Schäuble

Eurospider Information Technology AG
Schaffhauserstrasse 18, CH-8006 Zürich, Switzerland
{martin.braschler,peter.schauble}@eurospider.com

Abstract. For the CLEF 2002 campaign, Eurospider participated in the multilingual and German monolingual tasks. Our main focus was on trying new merging strategies for our multilingual experiments. In this paper, we describe the setup of our system, the characteristics of our experiments, and give an analysis of the results.

1 Introduction

In the following, we describe our experiments carried out for CLEF 2002. Much of the work for this year's campaign builds again on the foundation laid in the previous two CLEF campaigns [2] [3]. Eurospider participated both in the main multilingual track and in the German monolingual track. The main focus of the work was on the multilingual experiments, continuing our successful practice of combining multiple approaches to cross-language retrieval into one system. Using a combination approach makes our system more robust against deficiencies of any single CLIR approach. The main effort for this year was spent on the problem of merging multiple result lists, such as obtained either from searches on different subcollections (representing the different languages of the multilingual collection) or from searches using different translation resources and retrieval methods. We feel that merging remains an unsolved problem after the first two CLEF campaigns. We introduced a new merging method based on term selection after retrieval, and we also implemented a slightly updated version of our simple interleaving merging strategy.

The remainder of this paper is structured as follows: we first discuss the system setup that we used for all experiments. This is followed by a closer look at the multilingual experiments, including details of this year's new merging strategies. The next section describes our submissions for the German monolingual track. The paper closes with conclusions and an outlook.

---

* Also affiliated with Université de Neuchâtel, Institut Interfacultaire d'Informatique, Pierre-à-Mazel 7, CH-2001 Neuchâtel, Switzerland.

C.A. Peters (Ed.): CLEF 2002, LNCS 2785, pp. 164-174, 2003.

Table 1. Overview of indexing setup for all languages

Language	Stopword removal	Stemming	Convert diacritical chars
English	yes	English "Porter-like" stemmer	-
French	yes	French Spider stemmer	no
German	yes	German Spider stemmer, incl. decompounding	yes
Italian	yes	Italian Spider stemmer	no
Spanish	yes	Spanish Spider stemmer	yes

2 System Setup

2.1 Retrieval System

All experiments used a system consisting of a version of the core software that is included in the "relevancy" system developed by Eurospider Information Technology AG. This core software is used in all commercial products of Eurospider. Prototypical enhancements included in the CLEF system are mainly in the components for multilingual information access (MLIA).

As an additional experiment, we collaborated this year with Université de Neuchâtel in order to produce a special multilingual run. The results for this run are based both on output from the Eurospider system and on output produced by the Neuchâtel group. More details will be given later in this paper.

Indexing: Table 1 gives an overview of indexing methods used for the respective languages.

Ranking: The system was configured to use straight Lnu.ltn weighting, as described in [16]. An exception was made for some of the monolingual runs, which either used BM25 weighting [12] or a mix of both Lnu.ltn and BM25. All runs used a blind feedback loop, expanding the query by the top 10 terms from the 10 best ranked documents.

Individual Language Handling: We decided to make indexing and weighting of all languages as symmetric as possible. We did not use different weighting schemes for different languages, or different policies with regard to query expansion. By choosing this approach, we wanted to both mirror a realistic, scalable approach as well as avoid overtraining to characteristics of the CLEF multilingual collection.

2.2 Submitted Runs

Table 2 summarizes the main characteristics of our official experiments:

Table 2. Main characteristics of official experiments

Run tag	Track Topic lang Topic fields Run type	Translation	Merging strategy	Expansion	Weighting
EIT2MNU1	Multilingual DE TDN Auto	Documents (MT)	-	Blind Feedback 10/10	Lnu.ltn
EIT2MNF3	Multilingual DE TDN Auto	Queries (ST+MT), Documents (MT)	Term selection	Blind Feedback 10/10	Lnu.ltn
EIT2MDF3	Multilingual DE TD Auto	Queries (ST+MT), Documents (MT)	Term selection	Blind Feedback 10/10	Lnu.ltn
EIT2MDC3	Multilingual DE TD Auto	Queries (ST+MT), Documents (MT)	Interleave collection	Blind Feedback 10/10	Lnu.ltn
EAN2MDF4	Multilingual EN TD Auto	Queries (MT+Uni Neuchâtel)	Logrank	Blind Feedback 10/10+Uni Neuchâtel	Lnu.ltn + Uni NE
EIT2GDB1	German Monolingual DE TD Auto	-	-	Blind Feedback 10/10	BM25
EIT2GDL1	German Monolingual DE TD Auto	-	-	Blind Feedback 10/10	Lnu.ltn
EITGDM1	German Monolingual DE TD Auto	-	Logrank	Blind Feedback 10/10	Lnu.ltn + BM25
EITGNM1	German Monolingual DE TDN Auto	-	Logrank	Blind Feedback 10/10	Lnu.ltn + BM25

3 Multilingual Retrieval

3.1 Approach

As for last year, we again spent our main effort on the multilingual track. The goal of this track in CLEF is to select a topic language, and use the queries in that language to retrieve documents in five different languages from a multilingual collection. A single result list has to be returned, potentially containing documents in all languages. For details on the track definition see [1].

A system working on such a task needs to bridge the gap between the language of the search requests and the languages used in the multilingual document collection. For translation, we have successfully used combination approaches, integrating more than one translation method, in the past two campaigns. In 2001, we attempted our most ambitious combination yet [2], combining three forms of query translation (similarity thesauri [11] [15], machine translation and machine-readable dictionaries) with document translation (through machine translation). This year, we shifted the focus of our experiments somewhat, and used a slightly simpler combination approach, concentrating on the pieces that performed well in 2001 and discarding the machine-readable dictionaries from the system. The experiments used either a combination of document translation (DT) and two forms of query translation (QT) - machine translation (MT) and similarity thesaurus (ST) - or document translation only.

More than last year, we concentrated on the problem of producing the final, multilingual result list to be returned by the system in answer to a search request. Our combination approach, as indeed most successful approaches to multilingual retrieval used in the CLEF 2001 campaign, produces several intermediate search results, either due to using different translation methods, or due to handling only a subset of the five languages at a time. These intermediate search results need then be "merged" to produce the multilingual result list necessary for submission to CLEF.

It seems to be generally agreed among the community of active participants in CLEF that merging is an important problem in designing truly multilingual retrieval systems. It was pointed out in the discussions at the CLEF 2001 workshop that not much progress had been made on this topic up to that campaign. This year, several groups have put emphasis either on this issue (e.g. [4], [6], [7], [9], [14]) or alternatively on how to avoid merging altogether (e.g. [8], [10]). The simple merging approaches employed in our experiments are very similar to some of the work described by these groups.

3.2 Merging

In our previous participations in CLEF, we have used two simple merging strategies: rank-based merging, and interleaving. There are two fundamentally different merging scenarios, depending on whether the runs to be merged share the same search space or not. In the case that we merge runs obtained from different translation methods, translation resources or weighting schemes, but using the same target language, there will usually be a substantial overlap in the sets of documents in the respective result lists (this problem is also referred to as "data fusion"). This is not the case when we merge runs that use disjoint search spaces (sometimes referred to as "database merging"), e.g. different target languages. Some merging strategies apply to both these scenarios (e.g. interleaving), while others only operate on one of the two alternatives (e.g. rank-based merging).

The main difficulty in merging is the lack of comparability of scores across different result lists. Result lists obtained from different collections, or through different weightings, are normally not directly comparable. The retrieval status value RSV is only meaningful for sorting the list, and is often only valid in the context of the query, weighting and collection used.

Some merging strategies make use of training data, typically based on relevance assessments for some prior queries. We have decided to avoid reliance on availability of relevance assessments, since we envision many scenarios where it is unfeasible to tune the system to such an extent. We have however used the relevance assessments of this year's collection to evaluate our results against "optimal" merging strategies.

3.3 Simple Merging Strategies

One way of avoiding the problem of non-comparable RSVs is by using a merging strategy that does not make direct use of retrieval scores. The following two simple merging strategies use the position of documents in the result lists to determine a new, merged score.

3.3.1 Rank-Based Merging

For rank-based merging, calculation of a new RSV value for the merged list is based on the ranks of the documents in the original result lists. To calculate the new RSV, the document's ranks in all the result lists are added up. Clearly, the strategy is limited to situations with a shared search space, since a substantial "overlap" in the documents retrieved is necessary to obtain meaningful new scores. We feel that a rank difference between highly ranked documents should be emphasized more than a similar difference among lower ranked documents. As a consequence, we introduced a logarithmic dampening of the rank value that boosts the influence of highly ranked documents. The underlying assumption of this strategy is based on observations made a while back, e.g. by Saracevic and Kantor [13], who report that the probability of relevance of a document increases if that document is found by multiple query representations.

3.3.2 Interleaving

As an alternative that applies for merging scenarios with both a shared search space or disjoint search spaces, we have in the past used interleaving. The merged result list is produced by taking one document in turn from all individual lists. If the collections are not disjoint, duplicates will have to be eliminated after merging, for example by keeping the most highly ranked instance of a document. This very simple strategy, and variants of it, also go by the name of "round-robin" or "uniform merging" (see e.g. [17]).

3.4 New Merging Strategies

We introduced two new merging strategies for this year's experiments. The first one is a slight update of the interleaving strategy. The second one is more elaborate, and presents an attempt at guessing how well the concept of the query is represented in a specific subcollection.

3.4.1 Collection Size-Based Interleaving

One main limitation of interleaving as described above is that all result lists are given equal weight, taking the same number of documents from each. There are many situations, especially in case of disjoint search spaces, where it is unsatisfactory to assume that all result lists will contribute an equal number of relevant items. Clearly, it is extremely difficult to determine the amount of contribution to be expected in the individual subcollections covered by the runs. We have however observed that the average ratio of relevant items is quite stable across the different languages in CLEF when averaged over all queries for a given year. Consequently, we have used a simple update to the straight interleaving method, making use of the fact that the subcollections of the CLEF multilingual collection vary considerably in size, and setting the portion of documents taken from any one result list to be proportional to the size of the corresponding subcollection.

3.4.2 Feedback Merging

The second new strategy aims to predict the amount of relevant information contributed by each subcollection specifically for a given search request. The amount of relevant information contributed by a subcollection can vary widely from query to query. Lifting the limit of using the same merging ratios for every query should help to avoid picking documents from poor retrieval runs too early. In order to achieve this objective, results from an initial retrieval step for every subcollection are collected, and the respective top-ranked documents are then "analyzed" by the system, selecting the best terms to build an "ideal" query to retrieve that set of documents. The system then compares this query to the original query, determining the overlap as an estimate of the degree to which the concepts of the original query are represented in the retrieval result. The underlying assumption is that the better such representation, the higher the likelihood that relevant documents are found. The result lists are then finally merged in proportion to these estimates. No manual intervention with respect to any of the intermediate results takes place. This is the only method we applied that is query-dependent.

3.5 Optimal Retrospective Merging Strategies

We evaluated the effectiveness of our merging strategies by comparing their performance to "baselines" obtained from merging strategies that make retrospective use of the relevance assessments that became available after the evaluation campaign.

3.5.1 Relevance-Ratio Merging

The feedback merging strategy attempts to estimate for a given query how many relevant items are contributed by each of the subcollections. This information can be retrospectively extracted from the relevance assessments, and the merging can be repeated analogous to the interleaving strategy, but with the exact ratios in place of the estimates. While this strategy is query-dependent, it merges using equal ratios for all recall levels.

3.5.2 Optimal Merging

It is possible to improve even on the relevance-ratio merging strategy by lifting the limitation that merging ratios are equal for all recall levels. The idea for optimal merging was presented by Chen at the CLEF 2002 workshop [5]. The strategy works by taking in turn items from those result lists that provide the most relevant items while keeping the number of irrelevant items taken at a minimum. I.e., in every step, the strategy looks in the remainders of the lists to be merged for the shortest uninterrupted sequences of zero or more irrelevant items followed by the longest uninterrupted sequences of relevant items. This sequence is then attached to the merged list, and the corresponding result list is shortened. The resulting final list has different merging ratios both for each query and each recall level.

3.6 Results

The results for our officially submitted multilingual experiments are shown below.

Table 3. Key performance figures for the multilingual experiments

Run tag	Average Precision	Precision @ 10 docs	Relevant retrieved
EIT2MNU1	0.3539	0.6560	5188
EIT2MNF3	0.3554	0.6520	5620
EIT2MDC3	0.3400	0.5860	5368
EIT2MDF3	0.3409	0.6040	5411
EAN2MDF4	0.3480	0.6260	5698

Total number of relevant documents: 8068
"Virtual best performance": 0.4834
"Virtual median performance": 0.2193

Table 4. Comparison of performance against median for multilingual experiments

Run Tag	Best	Above Median	Median	Below Median	Worst
EIT2MNU1	4	34	2	9	1
EIT2MNF3	5	34	3	8	0
EIT2MDC3	1	36	3	10	0
EIT2MDF3	2	37	1	10	0
EAN2MDF4	1	45	0	4	0

As can be seen from Table 3, there is very little difference between runs EIT2MDC3 and EIT2MDF3, which differ only in the merging strategy employed for the combination of the individual language pairs. Additionally to having essentially equivalent average precision values, the two runs also differ only very slightly when compared on a query-by-query basis. Clearly, the merging strategy based on feedback, which we newly introduced for this year, had little impact, even though it allows different merging ratios for different queries. When looking at the ratios which were actually used for merging, we see that the new method indeed chooses fairly different ratios for individual queries. However, we believe that these differences were obscured by later merging steps that combined the various query translation and document translation methods. These further combinations blunted the effect of negative, but unfortunately also of positive "outliers". When concentrating the analysis on merging of a single, specific translation method, larger differences between the simple merging strategies and the feedback method become apparent. Even so, feedback merging did not bring any sustained improvement in retrieval effectiveness, instead even being slightly disadvantageous in several cases. The fact that feedback merging allows different merging ratios for individual queries seems to have resulted in a slight improvement in recall, however.

The run based exclusively on document translation (EIT2MNU1) compares favorably when compared to the equivalent combined DT and QT run (EIT2MNF3). This is analogous to what we observed in earlier campaigns, where DT-based runs outperformed QT-based runs. Indeed, a run based solely on query translation (not officially submitted) performs considerably worse than either the DT-only or the combined run (0.2876 vs. 0.3539 and 0.3554 for TDN queries). However, we think this is probably more due to the imperfect merging strategies we used than due to any superiority of DT over QT. When using the retrospective merging strategies described earlier in the paper it becomes apparent that our best merging results are approximately 20% below what is obtained with the "relevance ratio" method and a sobering 45%-55% below what an optimal merging strategy making full use of the relevance assessments would produce. Since our DT run needs no merging, it is not affected by the substantial loss of performance incurred in this step. There remains clearly much to do with regard to the merging problem.

Even though EIT2MNU1 and EIT2MNF3 show little variation in performance as measured by average precision, closer analysis shows some striking differences. EIT2MNF3, which is based on a combination of query translation and document translation, outperforms EIT2MNU1 in terms of average precision by more than 20% for 14 queries, whereas the reverse is only true for 4 of the queries. Also, EIT2MNF3 retrieves roughly 8% more relevant documents than run EIT2MNU1. We believe that this shows that the combination approach boosts reliability of the system by retrieving extra items, but that we have not found the ideal combination strategy this year that would have maximized this potential.

The potential to retrieve more relevant items by using combination approaches is also demonstrated by our final multilingual entry, EAN2MDF4, which was produced by merging output from the Eurospider system with results kindly provided to us by Université de Neuchâtel (J. Savoy). This run gave the best performance of all our multilingual experiments.

Compared to median performance, all five multilingual runs perform very well. All runs have around 80% of the queries performing on or above the median, with the Eurospider/Neuchâtel combined run outperforming the median in more than 90% of cases (Table 4). The "virtual median performance", obtained by an artificial run that mirrors the median performance among all submissions for every query, is outperformed by more than 50% for all experiments. The best run obtains slightly below 75% of the "virtual best performance", which is obtained by an artificial run combining the best entries for every query.

In absolute terms, our results are among the best reported for the multilingual track in this year's campaign, within 8-10% of the top result submitted by Université de Neuchâtel. Given the sample size of 50 queries, this difference is too small to be statistically significant.

4 Monolingual Retrieval

For monolingual retrieval, we restricted ourselves to the German document collection. We fine-tuned our submissions compared to last year, and experimented with two different weighting schemes.

In contrast to last year, we used blind feedback, which was found to be beneficial in CLEF 2001 by several groups. Our German runs used the Spider German stemmer which includes the splitting of German compound nouns (decompounding). We chose the most aggressive splitting method available in the system, in order to split a maximum number of compound nouns.

Table 5. Key performance figures for the monolingual experiments

Run tag	**Average precision**	**Precision @ 10**	**Relevant retrieved**
EIT2GDB1	0.4482	0.5160	1692
EIT2GDL1	0.4561	0.5420	1704
EIT2GDM1	0.4577	0.5320	1708
EIT2GNM1	0.5148	0.5940	1843

Total number of relevant documents: 1938
Virtual best performance: 0.6587
Virtual median performance: 0.4244

Table 6. Comparison of performance against median for monolingual experiments

Run Tag	**Best**	**Above Median**	**Median**	**Below Median**	**Worst**
EIT2GDB1	1	28	2	19	0
EIT2GDL1	3	27	5	15	0
EIT2GDM1	1	30	5	14	0
EIT2GNM1	6	32	4	8	0

The results show very little difference between EIT2GDB1 and EIT2GDL1, which used the BM25 and Lnu.ltn weighting scheme, respectively (Table 5). Query-by-query analysis confirms little impact from choosing between the two alternatives. Not surprisingly, merging the two runs (into EIT2GDM1) leads again to very similar performance.

On an absolute basis, the runs all perform well, with all runs having around 60%-75% of queries with performance above the median (Table 6). All runs also outperform the "virtual median performance". For German monolingual, this seems to be a harder benchmark than for multilingual, since "virtual median performance" is around 65% of "virtual best performance", compared to roughly 45% for multilingual.

5 Conclusions and Outlook

Our main focus this year was on experiments on the problem of merging multiple result lists coming from different translation resources, weighting schemes, and the different language-specific subcollections in the multilingual task. We introduced a new method based on feedback merging, which however showed little impact in practice. Post-hoc experiments with merging strategies that make use of the relevance assessments show that our merging methods still perform far below what is theoretically possible. We will try to use our new experiences to improve on our merging strategies for next year.

As last year, we again used a combination translation approach for the multilingual experiments. The results confirm last year's good performance. We can again conclude that combination approaches are robust; 80-90% of all queries performed on or above median performance in our systems. This good performance was achieved even though we used no special configuration for individual languages, in order to more accurately reflect situations where only few details about the collections to be searched are known in advance, and to avoid potential overtuning to characteristics of the CLEF collection.

For the monolingual experiments, we compared the impact of choosing between two of the most popular high-performance weighting schemes: BM25 and Lnu.ltn. We could not detect a meaningful difference, either in overall performance or when comparing individual queries. Consequently, combining the two weightings gives no clear advantage over using either one individually.

Acknowledgements

We thank Jacques Savoy from Université de Neuchâtel for providing us with his runs that we used for merging in the experiment labeled "EAN2MDF4".

References

[1] Braschler, M., Peters, C.: CLEF2002: Methodology and Metrics. This volume.

[2] Braschler, M., Ripplinger, B., Schäuble, P.: Experiments with the Eurospider Retrieval System for CLEF 2001. In: Evaluation of Cross-Language Information Retrieval Systems, Second Workshop of the Cross-Language Evaluation Forum, CLEF 2001, Darmstadt, Germany, Lecture Notes in Computer Science 2406, Springer 2002, pages 102-110.

[3] Braschler, M., Schäuble, P.: Experiments with the Eurospider Retrieval System for CLEF 2000. In: Cross-Language Information Retrieval and Evaluation, Workshop of the Cross-Language Evaluation Forum, CLEF 2000, Lisbon, Portugal, Lecture Notes in Computer Science 2069, Springer 2001, pages 140-148.

[4] Chen, A.: Cross-Language Retrieval Experiments at CLEF-2002. This volume.

[5] Chen, A.: Cross-Language Retrieval Experiments at CLEF-2002. In: Results of the CLEF 2002 Cross-Language Systems Evaluation Campaign, Working Notes for the CLEF 2002 Workshop, pages5-20, 2002.

[6] Lin, W.-C., Chen, H.-H.: Merging Mechanisms in Multilingual Information Retrieval. This volume.

[7] Martínez, F., Ureña, L. A., Martín, M. T.: SINAI at CLEF 2002: Experiments with Merging Strategies. This volume.

[8] McNamee, P., Mayfield, J.: Scalable Multilingual Information Access. In: Results of the CLEF 2002 Cross-Language Systems Evaluation Campaign, Working Notes for the CLEF 2002 Workshop, pages 133-140, 2002.

[9] Moulinier, I., Molina-Salgado, H.: Thomson Legal and Regulatory Experiments for CLEF 2002. This volume.

[10] Nie, J.-Y., Jin, F.: Merging Different Languages in a Single Document Collection. In: Results of the CLEF 2002 Cross-Language Systems Evaluation Campaign, Working Notes for the CLEF 2002 Workshop, pages 59-62, 2002.

[11] Qiu, Y., Frei, H.: Concept Based Query Expansion. In: Proceedings of the 16th ACM SIGIR Conference on Research and Development in Information Retrieval, Pittsburgh, PA, pages 160 - 169, 1993.

[12] Robertson, S. E., Walker, S., Jones, S., Hancock-Beaulieu, M. M., Gatford, M.: Okapi at TREC-3. In: Proceedings of the Third Text REtrieval Conference (TREC.3), NIST Special Publication 500-226, pages 109-126, 1994.

[13] Saracevic, T., Kantor, P.: A study of information seeking and retrieving. III. Searchers, searches, overlap. Journal of the American Society for Information Science. 39:3, pages 197-216.

[14] Savoy, J.: Combining Multiple Sources of Evidence. This volume.

[15] Sheridan, P., Braschler, M., Schäuble, P.: Cross-language information retrieval in a multilingual legal domain. In: Proceedings of the First European Conference on Research and Advanced Technology for Digital Libraries, Lecture Notes in Computer Science 1324, Springer 1997, pages 253 - 268.

[16] Singhal, A., Buckley, C., Mitra, M.: Pivoted Document Length Normalization. In: Proceedings of the 19th ACM SIGIR Conference on Research and Development in Information Retrieval, pages 21-29, 1996.

[17] Voorhees, E. M., Gupta, N. K., Johnson-Laird, B.: Learning Collection Fusion Strategies. In: Proceedings of the 18th ACM SIGIR Conference on Research and Development in Information Retrieval, pages 172-179, 1995.

Merging Mechanisms in Multilingual Information Retrieval

Wen-Cheng Lin and Hsin-Hsi Chen

Department of Computer Science and Information Engineering
National Taiwan University, Taipei, Taiwan
denislin@nlg.csie.ntu.edu.tw
hh_chen@csie.ntu.edu.tw

Abstract. This paper considers centralized and distributed architectures for multilingual information retrieval. Several merging strategies, including raw-score merging, round-robin merging, normalized-score merging, and normalized-by-top-*k* merging, were investigated. The effects of translation penalty on merging was also examined. The experimental results show that the centralized approach is better than the distributed approach. In the distributed approach, the normalized-by-top-*k* merging with translation penalty outperforms other merging strategies, except for raw-score merging. Because the performances of English to other languages are similar, raw-score merging gives better performance in our experiments. However, raw-score merging is not workable in practice if different IR systems are adopted.

1 Introduction

Multilingual Information Retrieval [4] uses a query in one language to retrieve documents in different languages. A multilingual data collection is a set of documents written in different languages. There are two types of multilingual data collection. The first one contains several monolingual document collections. The second one consists of multilingual documents. A multilingual document is written in more than one language. Some multilingual documents have a major language, i.e., most of the document is written in the same language. For example, a document can be written in Chinese, but the abstract is in English. Therefore, this document is a multilingual document and Chinese is its major language. The significances of different languages in a multilingual document may be different. For example, the English translation of a Chinese proper noun is a useful clue when using English queries to retrieve Chinese documents. In this case, the English translation should have higher weight. Figure 1 shows these two types of multilingual data collections.

In Multilingual Information Retrieval, queries and documents are in different languages. We can either translate queries, or documents, or both to unify the languages of queries and documents. Figure 2 shows some MLIR architectures when query translation is adopted. The front-end controller processes queries, translates queries,

C.A. Peters (Ed.): CLEF 2002, LNCS 2785, pp. 175-186, 2003.

submits translated queries to monolingual IR systems, collects the relevant document lists reported by IR systems and merges the results. Figure 3 shows another alternative, i.e., architectures for document translation.

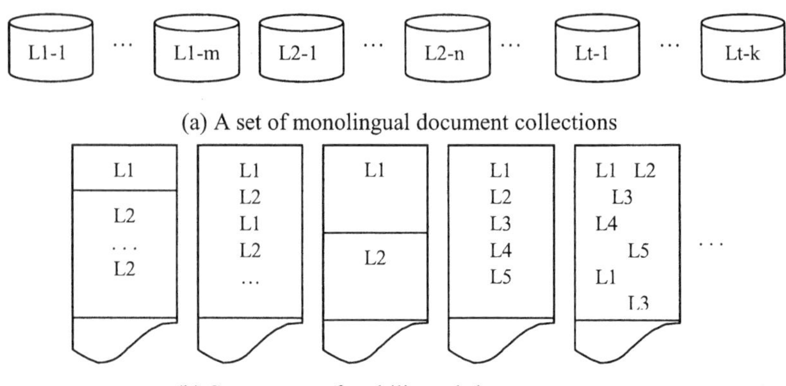

(b) Some types of multilingual-documents

Fig. 1. Multilingual data collections

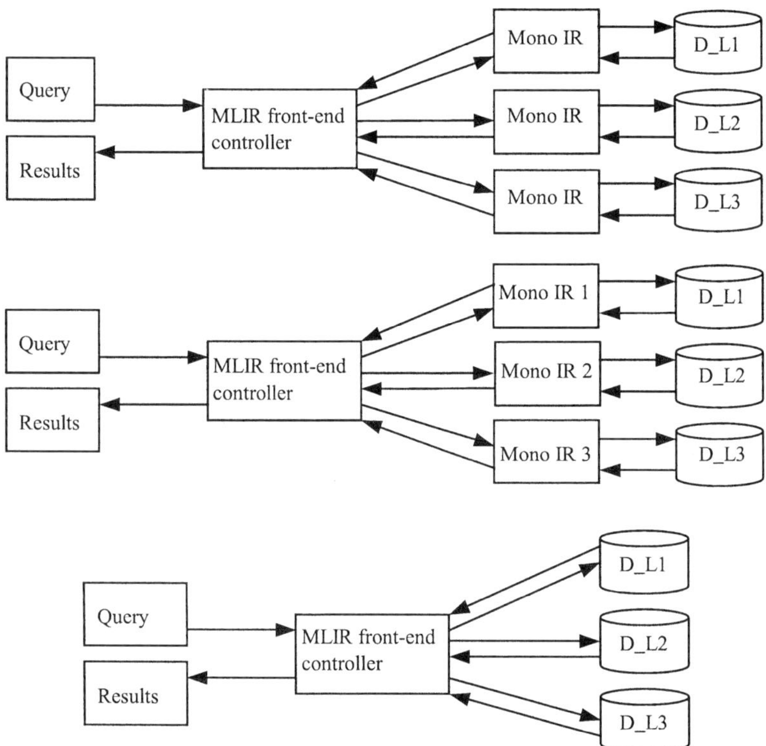

Fig. 2. Architectures of query translation

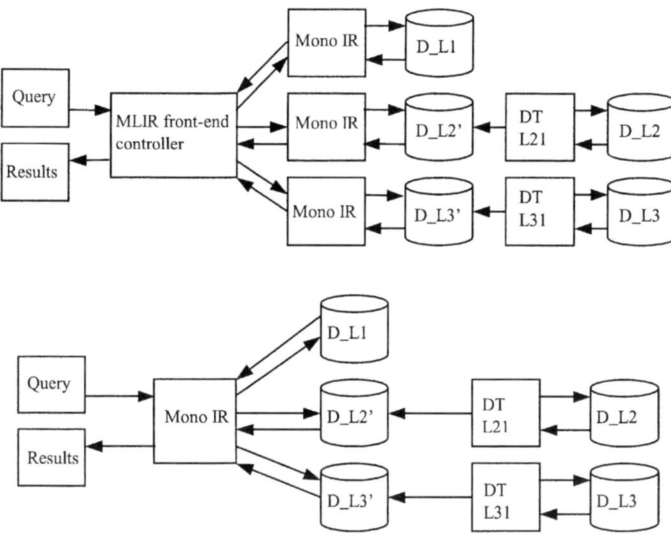

Fig. 3. Architectures for document translation

In addition to the language difference issue, the way in which a ranked list containing documents in different languages from several text collections is produced is also critical. There are two possible architectures in MLIR – let's call them centralized and distributed. The first two architectures in Figure 2 and the first architecture in Figure 3 are distributed architectures. The remaining architectures in Figures 2 and 3 are centralized architectures. In a centralized architecture, a huge collection containing documents in different languages is used. In a distributed architecture, documents in different languages are indexed and retrieved separately. The results of each run are merged into a multilingual ranked list. Several merging strategies have been proposed. Raw-score merging selects documents based on their original similarity scores. Normalized-score merging normalizes the similarity score of each document and sorts all the documents by the normalized score. For each topic, the similarity score of each document is divided by the maximum score in this topic. Round-robin merging interleaves the results in the intermediate runs. In this paper, we adopt distributed architecture and propose several merging strategies to produce the result lists.

The rest of this paper is organized as follows. Section 2 describes the indexing method. Section 3 shows the query translation process. Section 4 describes our merging strategies. Section 5 shows the results of our experiments. Section 6 gives concluding remarks.

2 Indexing

The document set used in CLEF2002 MLIR task consists of English, French, German, Spanish and Italian. The numbers of documents in English, French, German, Spanish and Italian document sets are 113,005, 87,191, 225,371, 215,738 and 108,578, respectively.

The IR model we used is the basic vector space model. Documents and queries are represented as term vectors, and the cosine vector similarity formula is used to measure the similarity of a query and a document. The term weighting function is *tf*idf*. Appropriate terms are extracted from each document in the indexing stage. In the experiment, the <HEADLINE> and <TEXT> sections in English documents were used for indexing. For Spanish documents, the <TITLE> and <TEXT> sections were used. When indexing French, German and Italian documents, the <TITLE>, <TEXT>, <TI>, <LD> and <TX> sections were used. The words in these sections were stemmed, and stopwords were removed. Stopword lists and stemmers developed by University of Neuchatel are available at http://www.unine.ch/info/clef/ [5].

3 Query Translation

English queries were used as source queries and translated into target languages, i.e., French, German, Spanish and Italian. In the past, we used a co-occurrence (abbreviated as CO) model [1, 3] to disambiguate the use of queries. The CO model employed word co-occurrence information extracted from a target language text collection to disambiguate the translations of query terms. In the official runs, we did not have enough time to train the word co-occurrence information for the languages used in the CLEF 2002 MLIR task. Thus, we used a simple method to translate the queries. A dictionary-based approach was adopted. For each English query term, we found its translation equivalents by looking up a dictionary and considered the first two translation equivalents to be the target language query terms. The dictionaries we used are the Ergane English-French, English-German, English-Spanish and English-Italian dictionaries. They are available at http://www.travlang.com/Ergane. There are 8,839, 9,046, 16,936 and 4,595 terms in the Ergane English-French, English-German, English-Spanish and English-Italian dictionaries, respectively.

4 Merging Strategies

There are two possible architectures in MLIR, i.e., centralized and distributed. In a centralized architecture, document collections in different languages are viewed as a single document collection and are indexed in one huge index file. The advantage of a centralized architecture is that it avoids the merging problem. It needs only one retrieval phase to produce a result list that contains documents in different languages. One of the problems of a centralized architecture is that the index terms may be over weighted. In the traditional *tf-idf* scheme, the *idf* of a query term depends on the number of documents in which it occurs. In a centralized architecture, the total number of documents increases but the number of occurrences of a term may not. In such a case, the *idf* of a term is increased and it is over-weighted. This phenomenon is more apparent in a small text collection. For example, the N in the *idf* formula is 87,191 when French document set is used. However, this value is increased to 749,883, i.e., about 8.60 times larger, if the five document collections are merged together. Comparatively, the weights of German index terms are increased 3.33 times due to the size of N. The increments of weights are unbalanced for document collections in different sizes. Thus, an IR system may perform better for documents in small document collections.

The second architecture is a distributed MLIR. Documents in different languages are indexed and retrieved separately. The ranked lists of all monolingual and cross-lingual runs are merged into one multilingual ranked list. How to merge result lists is a problem. Recent literature has proposed various approaches to deal with merging problem. A very simple merging method is the raw-score merging, which sorts all results by their original similarity scores, and then selects the top ranked documents. Raw-score merging is based on the postulation that the similarity scores across collections are comparable. However, collection-dependent statistics for document or query weights invalidates this postulation [2, 6]. Another approach, round-robin merging, interleaves the results based on the rank. This approach postulates that each collection has approximately the same number of relevant documents and the distribution of relevant documents is similar across the result lists. Actually, different collections do not contain equal numbers of relevant documents. Thus, the performance of round-robin merging may be poor. The third approach is normalized-score merging. For each topic, the similarity score of each document is divided by the maximum score in this topic. After adjusting scores, all results are put into a pool and sorted by the normalized score. This approach maps the similarity scores of different result lists into the same range, from 0 to 1, and makes the scores more comparable. But it has a problem. If the maximum score is much higher than the second one in the same result list, the normalized-score of the document at rank 2 would be reduced even if its original score was high. Thus, the final rank of this document would be lower than that of the top ranked documents with very low but similar original scores in another result list.

The similarity score reflects the degree of similarity between a document and a query. A document with a higher similarity score seems to be more relevant to the given query. But, if the query is not formulated well, e.g., inappropriately translated, a document with a high score may still not meet a user's information need. When merging results, such documents that have incorrect high scores should not be included in the final result list. Thus, the effectiveness of each individual run should be considered in the merging stage. The basic idea of our merging strategy is that of adjusting the similarity scores of documents in each result list to make them more comparable and to reflect their confidence. The similarity scores are adjusted using the following formula.

$$\hat{S}_{ij} = S_{ij} \times \frac{1}{\overline{S}_k} \times W_i \ . \tag{1}$$

where

S_{ij} is the original similarity score of the document at rank j in the ranked list of topic i,

$\hat{S}_{ij}$ is the adjusted similarity score of the document at rank j in the ranked list of topic i,

$\overline{S}_k$ is the average similarity score of top k documents, and

W_i is the weight of query i in a cross-lingual run.

We divide the weight adjusting process into two steps. First, we use a modified score normalization method to normalize the similarity scores. The original score of each document is divided by the average score of the top *k* documents instead of the maximum score. We call this normalized-by-top-k. Second, the normalized score multiplies a weight that reflects the retrieval effectiveness of the given topic in each text collection. However, as we do not know the retrieval performance in advance, we have to guess the performance of each run. For each language pair, the queries are translated into the target language and then the target language documents are retrieved. A good translation should perform better. We can predict the retrieval performance based on the translation performance. There are two factors affecting translation performance, i.e., the degree of translation ambiguity and the number of unknown words. For each query, we compute the average number of translation equivalents of query terms and the number of unknown words in each language pair, and use them to compute the weights of each cross-lingual run. The weight can be determined by the following formulas:

$$W_i = c_1 + \left[c_2 \times \left(\frac{51 - T_i}{50}\right)^2\right] + \left[c_3 \times \left(1 - \frac{U_i}{n_i}\right)\right] \cdot \tag{2}$$

$$W_i = c_1 + \left[c_2 \times \left(\frac{1}{\sqrt{T_i}}\right)\right] + \left[c_3 \times \left(1 - \frac{U_i}{n_i}\right)\right] \cdot \tag{3}$$

$$W_i = c_1 + \left[c_2 \times \left(\frac{1}{T_i}\right)\right] + \left[c_3 \times \left(1 - \frac{U_i}{n_i}\right)\right] \cdot \tag{4}$$

where W_i is the weight of query *i* in a cross-lingual run,
T_i is the average number of translation equivalents of query terms in query *i*,
U_i is the number of unknown words in query *i*,
n_i is the number of query terms in query *i*, and
c_1, c_2 and c_3 are tunable parameters, and $c_1+c_2+c_3=1$.

5 Results of Our Experiments

5.1 Official Results

We submitted five multilingual runs. All runs used the title and description fields. The five runs used English topics as source queries. The English topics were translated into French, German, Spanish and Italian. The source English topics and translated French, German, Spanish and Italian topics were used to retrieve the corresponding document collections. We then merged the five result lists. The following different merging strategies were employed.

1. NTUmulti01
   The result lists were merged by normalized-score merging strategy. The maximum similarity score was used for normalization. After normalization, all

results were put in a pool and were sorted by the adjusted score. The top 1000 documents were selected as the final results.

2. NTUmulti02
   In this run, we used the modified normalized-score merging method. The average similarity score of the top 100 documents was used for normalization. We did not consider the performance decrement caused by query translation. That is, the weight W_i in formula (1) was 1 for every sub-run.
3. NTUmulti03
   First, the similarity scores of each document were normalized. The maximum similarity score was used for normalization. We then assigned a weight W_i to each intermediate run. The weight was determined by formula (4). The values of c_1, c_2 and c_3 were 0, 0.4 and 0.6, respectively.
4. NTUmulti04
   We used formula (1) to adjust the similarity score of each document, and then considered the average similarity score of the top 100 documents for normalization. The weight W_i was determined by formula (4). The values of c_1, c_2 and c_3 were 0, 0.4 and 0.6, respectively.
5. NTUmulti05
   In this run, the merging strategy is similar to run NTUmulti04. The difference was that each intermediate run was assigned a constant weight. The weights assigned to English-English, English-French, English-German, English-Italian and English-Spanish intermediate runs were 1, 0.7, 0.4, 0.6 and 0.6, respectively.

The results of our official runs are shown in Table 1. The performance of normalized-score merging is bad. The average precision of run NTUmulti01 is 0.0173. When using our modified normalized-score merging strategy, the performance improves. The average precision increases to 0.0266. Runs NTUmulti03 and NTUmulti04 considered the performance decrement caused by query translation. Table 2 shows the unofficial evaluation of intermediate monolingual and cross-lingual runs. The performance of the English monolingual run is much better than that of cross-lingual runs. Therefore, the cross-lingual runs should have lower weights when merging results. The results show that the performances are improved by decreasing the importance of un-effective cross-lingual runs. The average precisions of runs NTUmulti03 and NTUmulti04 are 0.0336 and 0.0373, which are better than those of runs NTUmulti01 and NTUmulti02. Run NTUmulti05 assigned constant weights to each of the intermediate runs. Its performance is slightly worse than that of run NTUmulti04. All our official runs did not perform well.

Table 1. The results of official runs

Run	Average Precision	Recall
NTUmulti01	0.0173	1083 / 8068
NTUmulti02	0.0266	1135 / 8068
NTUmulti03	0.0336	1145 / 8068
NTUmulti04	0.0373	1195 / 8068
NTUmulti05	0.0361	1209 / 8068

Table 2. The results of intermediate runs

Run	# Topic	Average Precision	Recall
English-English	42	0.2722	741 / 821
English-French	50	0.0497	490 / 1383
English-German	50	0.0066	201 / 1938
English-Italian	49	0.0540	426 / 1072
English-Spanish	50	0.0073	223 / 2854

Table 3. New results after removing a bug

Run	Average Precision	Recall
English-English (fixed)	0.2763	741 / 821
English-French (fixed)	0.1842	735/ 1383
English-German (fixed)	0.1928	972 / 1938
English-Italian (fixed)	0.1905	691 / 1072
English-Spanish (fixed)	0.1084	1021 / 2854
NTUmulti01 (fixed)	0.1206	2689 / 8068
NTUmulti02 (fixed)	0.1311	2651 / 8068
NTUmulti03 (fixed)	0.0992	2532 / 8068
NTUmulti04 (fixed)	0.0954	2489 / 8068
NTUmulti05 (fixed)	0.0962	2413 / 8068

5.2 Post-evaluation

After official evaluation, we checked every step of our experiments, and found that we made a mistake. When indexing documents, the index terms were not transformed into lower case, but the query terms were all in lower case. After fixing this bug, we obtained the new results shown in Table 3. The average precision of each run is much better than that of our official results. Normalized-by-top-*k* (NTUmulti02 (fixed)) is still better than normalized-score merging (NTUmulti01 (fixed)). When considering the query translation penalty, normalized-score merging is slightly better than normalized-by-top-*k*. We used other weighting formulas, i.e. formulas (2) and (3), for further investigations. When using formulas (2) and (3), normalized-by-top-*k* is better. Table 4 shows the results. Compared with NTUmulti01 (fixed) and NTUmulti02 (fixed), average precision decreased when taking performance decrement caused by query translation into consideration.

To compare the effectiveness of our approaches with previous merging strategies, we also conducted several unofficial runs:

1. ntu-multi-raw-score
   We used raw-score merging to merge result lists.
2. ntu-multi-round-robin
   We used round-robin merging to merge result lists.
3. ntu-multi-centralized
   This run adopted a centralized architecture. All document collections were indexed in one index file. The topics contained source English query terms, and other translated query terms.

Table 4. Normalized-score merging and normalized-by-top-100 merging with different merging weighting formulas

Merging strategy	Merging weight	Average Precision	Recall
Normalized-score merging (c_1=0; c_2=0.4; c_3=0.6)	formula 2	0.1124	2683 / 8068
	formula 3	0.1049	2630 / 8068
	formula 4	0.0992	2532 / 8068
Normalized-by-top-100 (c_1=0; c_2=0.4; c_3=0.6)	formula 2	0.1209	2649 / 8068
	formula 3	0.1076	2591 / 8068
	formula 4	0.0954	2489 / 8068

Table 5. Raw-score merging, round-robin merging and centralized architecture

Run	Average Precision	Recall
ntu-multi-raw-score	0.1385	2627 / 8068
ntu-multi-round-robin	0.1143	2551 / 8068
ntu-multi-centralized	0.1531	3024 / 8068

Table 6. Using new translated queries

Merging strategy	Merging weight	Average Precision	Recall	Old translation scheme
English-French		0.1857	800/ 1383	0.1842
English-German		0.2041	1023 / 1938	0.1928
English-Italian		0.1916	700 / 1072	0.1905
English-Spanish		0.1120	999 / 2854	0.1084
Raw-score merging		0.1481	2760 / 8068	0.1385
Round-robin merging		0.1169	2610 / 8068	0.1143
Normalized-score merging		0.1171	2771 / 8068	0.1206
Normalized-score merging (c_1=0; c_2=0.4; c_3=0.6)	formula 2	0.1092	2763 / 8068	0.1124
	formula 3	0.1025	2688 / 8068	0.1049
	formula 4	0.0979	2611 / 8068	0.0992
Normalized-by-top-100		0.1357	2738 / 8068	0.1311
Normalized-by-top-100 (c_1=0; c_2=0.4; c_3=0.6)	formula 2	0.1254	2729 / 8068	0.1209
	formula 3	0.1118	2656 / 8068	0.1076
	formula 4	0.0988	2566 / 8068	0.0954
centralized		0.1541	3022 / 8068	0.1531

Table 7. Number of English query terms without translation but in target language corpora

Run	French	German	Italian	Spanish
# query terms	427	427	427	427
# query terms without translation equivalents	153	157	215	130
# query terms without translation equivalents but in target language corpora	111	120	161	86

Table 8. Considering English query terms without translation but in the target language corpora

Merging strategy	Merging weight	Average Precision	Recall	Table 6*
Normalized-score merging				0.1171
Normalized-score merging (c_1=0; c_2=0.4; c_3=0.6)	formula 2	0.1194	2792 / 8068	0.1092
	formula 3	0.1158	2765 / 8068	0.1025
	formula 4	0.1126	2747 / 8068	0.0979
Normalized-by-top-100				0.1357
Normalized-by-top-100 (c_1=0; c_2=0.4; c_3=0.6)	formula 2	0.1360	2778 / 8068	0.1254
	formula 3	0.1315	2751 / 8068	0.1118
	formula 4	0.1250	2704 / 8068	0.0988

The results are shown in Table 5. The performance of raw-score merging is good. This is because we use the same IR model and term weighting scheme for all text collections, and the performances of English to other languages are similar (see Table 3). When using the round-robin merging strategy, the performance is worse. The best run is ntu-multi-centralized. This run indexes all documents in different languages together.

When translating the queries, we chose the first two translation equivalents in the initial experiments. But the order of translation equivalents in a dictionary is not based on the characteristics of a corpus. We counted the occurrence frequency of each word in the test corpora and selected the first two translation equivalents with the highest frequency. The performances of cross-lingual and multilingual runs are improved by using the new translated queries. Table 6 shows the results.

From Table 6, it can be seen that the centralized architecture gives the best multilingual run. Raw-score merging is slightly worse than the centralized architecture and better than the other merging strategies. Normalized-by-top-*k* is better than normalized-score merging and round-robin merging. When considering the translation penalty, normalized-by-top-*k* is also better than normalized-score merging, but is still worse than raw-score merging. Table 6 also shows that performance decreases when considering the translation penalty. In the query translation phase, if a query term does not have any translation equivalents, the original English query term was retained in the translated query. That is, the English query terms which did not have any translation were used to retrieve target language documents. If such an English term occurs in the target language documents, it is useful in cross-lingual information retrieval and can be considered as a word with just one translation when computing the merging weight. Table 7 lists the number of English query terms that do not have a translation, but occur in the target language corpora. As the number of query terms without a translation is less, the merging weight is higher. The results in Table 8 show that English query terms that do not have a translation but occur in the target language corpus is useful. The average precisions of runs that use formula (2) to compute merging weight (i.e., the third and the seventh rows in Table 8) are slightly better than those of runs which do not consider translation penalty (the second and sixth rows in Table 8). This shows that translation penalty is helpful if a precise translation model is adopted.

6 Concluding Remarks

This paper presents centralized and distributed architectures in MLIR. In the experiments reported, the centralized approach performed well. However, a centralized architecture is not suitable in practice, especially for very huge corpora. A distributed architecture is more flexible. It is easy to add or delete corpora in different languages and employ different retrieval systems in a distributed architecture.

The merging problem is critical in distributed architectures. In this paper, we proposed several merging strategies to integrate the result lists of collections in different languages. Normalized-by-top-*k* avoids the drawback of normalized-score merging. When merging intermediate runs, we also consider the performance drop caused by query translation. The results showed that the performance of our merging strategies was similar to that of raw-score merging and was better than normalized-score and round-robin merging. Considering the degree of ambiguity, i.e., lowering the weights of more ambiguous query terms, improves some performance. We also employ similar experimental designs for Asian language multilingual information retrieval in NTCIR3 [3]. Similarly, we found that a centralized approach is better than a distributed approach. In a distributed approach, normalized-by-top-*k* with consideration of translation penalty outperforms other strategies, including raw-score merging and normalized-score merging. The trend is similar in CLEF2002 and NTCIR3 except that raw-scoring merging in CLEF2002 is better than our approach. The possible reason may be that the performances of English to documents in other languages are similar in CLEF2002, but different in NTCIR3. However, raw-scoring merging is not workable in practice if different search engines are adopted.

References

[1] Chen, H.H., Bian, G.W., and Lin, W.C., 1999. Resolving translation ambiguity and target polysemy in cross-language information retrieval. In *Proceedings of 37th Annual Meeting of the Association for Computational Linguistics*, Maryland, June, 1999. Association for Computational Linguistics, 215-222.

[2] Dumais, S.T., 1992. LSI meets TREC: A Status Report. In *Proceedings of the First Text REtrieval Conference (TREC-1)*, Gaithersburg, Maryland, November, 1992. NIST Publication, 137-152.

[3] Lin, W.C. and Chen, H.H., 2002. NTU at NTCIR3 MLIR Task. In *Working Notes for NTCIR3 workshop*, Tokyo, October, 2002. National Institute of Informatics.

[4] Oard, D.W. and Dorr, B.J., 1996. A Survey of Multilingual Text Retrieval. Technical Report UMIACS-TR-96-19, University of Maryland, Institute for Advanced Computer Studies.

[5] Savoy, J., 2001. Report on CLEF-2001 Experiments: Effective Combined Query-Translation Approach. In Evaluation of Cross-Language Information Retrieval Systems, Lecture Notes in Computer Science, Vol. 2406, Darmstadt, Germany, September, 2001. Springer, 27-43.

[6] Voorhees, E.M., Gupta, N.K., and Johnson-Laird, B., 1995. The Collection Fusion Problem. In *Proceedings of the Third Text REtrieval Conference (TREC-3)*, Gaithersburg, Maryland, November, 1994. NIST Publication, 95-104.

SINAI at CLEF 2002: Experiments with Merging Strategies

Fernando Martínez, L. Alfonso Ureña, and M. Teresa Martín

Dpto. Computer Science
University of Jaén, Avda, Madrid 35, 23071 Jaén, Spain
{dofer,laurena,maite}@ujaen.es

Abstract. For our first participation in the CLEF multilingual task, we present a new approach to obtain a single list of relevant documents for CLIR systems based on query translation. This new approach, which we call two-step RSV, is based on the re-indexing of the retrieval documents according to the query vocabulary, and it performs noticeably better than traditional methods[1].

1 Introduction

A usual approach in CLIR is to translate the query to each language present in the corpus, and then run a monolingual query in each language. It is then necessary to obtain a single ranking of documents merging the individual lists from the separate retrieved documents. However, a problem is how to carry out such a merge? This is known as the merging strategies problem and is not a trivial problem, since the weight assigned to each document (Retrieval Status Value - RSV) is calculated not only according to the relevance of the document and the IR model used, but also with respect to the rest of the monolingual corpus to which the document belongs [1].

There are various approaches to standardise the RSV, but in all cases a large decrease of precision is generated in the process (depending on the collection, between 20% and 40%) [2, 3]. Perhaps for this reason, CLIR systems based on document translation tend to obtain results which are noticeably better than those which only translate the query.

The rest of the paper is organized as follows. Firstly, we present a brief revision of the most extended methods for merging strategies. Sections 3 and 4 describe our proposed method. In Section 5, we detail the experiments carried out with the results obtained. Finally, we present our conclusions and future lines of work.

2 A Brief Review of the Merging Strategies

For each N language, we have N different lists of relevant documents, each obtained independently of the others. The problem is that it is necessary to obtain

[1] This work has been supported by the Spanish Government (MCyT) with grant FIT-150500-2002-416.

C.A. Peters (Ed.): CLEF 2002, LNCS 2785, pp. 187–196, 2003.

a single list by merging all the relevant languages. If we suppose that each retrieved document of each list has the same probability to be relevant and the similarity values are therefore directly comparable, then an immediate approach would be simply to order the documents according to their RSV (this method is known as raw scoring) [4, 5]. However, this method is not adequate, since the document scores computed for each language are not comparable. For example, a document in Spanish that includes the term "información", can calculate a radically different RSV from another document in English with the same term, "information". In general, this is due to the fact that the different indexing techniques take into account not only the term frequency in the document (*tf*),but also consider how frequent such a term is in the rest of the documents, that is, the inverse document frequency (*idf*) [6]. Thus, the *idf* depends on each particular monolingual collection. A first attempt to make these values comparable is to standardise in some way the RSV of each document:

- By dividing each RSV by the maximum RSV obtained in each collection:

$$RSV_i' = \frac{RSV_i}{\max(RSV)}, 1 <= i <= N$$

- A variant of the previous method is to divide each RSV by the difference between the maximum and minimum document score values obtained in each collection [7]:

$$RSV_i' = \frac{RSV_i - \min(RSV)}{\max(RSV) - \min(RSV)}, 1 <= i <= N$$

in which RSV_i is the original retrieval status value, and $\max(RSV)$ and $\min(RSV)$ are the maximum and minimum document score values achieved by the first and last documents respectively. N is the number of documents in the collection.

However, the problem is only solved partially, since the normalization of the document score is accomplished independently of the other collections and, therefore, the differences in the RSV are still great.

Another approach is to apply a round-robin algorithm. In this case, the RSV obtained for each retrieved document is not taken into account, but rather the relative position reached by each document in their collection. A single list of documents is obtained and the document score m is in the position m in the list. Thus for example, if we have five languages and we retrieve five lists of documents, the first five documents of the single result list will coincide with the first document of each list; the next five, with the second document of each list; and so on. This approach is not completely satisfactory because the position reached by each document is calculated exclusively considering the documents of the monolingual collection to the one which belongs.

Finally, another approach, perhaps the most original, is to generate a single index with all the documents without taking into account the multilingual nature of the collection [8, 9, 10]. In this way, a single index is obtained in which the terms from each language are intermixed. In the same way as when all the documents in a single index are merged, we obtain a single query where the terms in several languages are also intermixed. That is, the query must be translated into each of the languages present in the multilingual collection. However, we do not generate a query for each translation, but merge all the translations forming a single query. This query will then be the one which we compare with the document collection. As with the approach based on document translation, in this approach the system will always return a single list of documents for each query. In spite of this, the problem is not eliminated: the ranking of each document is dependent on the language in which it is written. Although a single index is generated, the vocabulary of each language is practically exclusive. Two different languages rarely share terms. For this reason, the weight obtained by each term will refer to the language to which it belongs, and therefore, the similarity between documents will be correct with respect to the documents expressed in the same language. It should be mentioned that a notable exception are proper names, which are frequently invariable in different languages. In this case, this approach proves very effective.

3 A Useful Structure to Describe IR Models

In this section we present a notation that will be used to describe the proposed model. A large number of retrieval methods are based on this structure [11]:

$$< T, \Phi, D; ff, df >$$

where:

- D is the document collection to be indexed.
- Φ is the vocabulary used in the indices generated from D.
- T is the set of all tokens τ present in the collection D, commonly the words or terms. Thus, the function

  $$\varphi : T \rightarrow \Phi, \tau \rightarrow \varphi(\tau)$$

  maps the set of all tokens, T,to the indexing vocabulary Φ. The function φ can be a simple process such as removing accents or another more complex process such as root extraction (stemming), lemmatization...
- ff is the feature frequency and denotes the number of occurrences of φ_i in a document d_j:

  $$ff(\varphi_i, d_j) :=| \{\tau \in T \mid \varphi(\tau) = \varphi_i \wedge d(\tau) = d_j\} |$$

  where d is the function that makes each token τ correspond to its document:

  $$d : T \rightarrow D, \tau \rightarrow d(\tau)$$

- df is the document frequency and denotes the number of documents containing the feature φ_i at least once:

  $$df(\varphi_i) :=| \{d_j \in D \mid \exists \tau \in T : \varphi(\tau) = \varphi_i \wedge d(\tau) = d_j\} |$$

4 Two-Step Retrieval Status Value

The proposed method [12] is a system based on query translation and it calculates RSV in two phases, a pre-selection phase and a re-indexing phase. Although the method is independent of the translation technique, it is necessary to know how each term translates.

1. The document pre-selection phase consists of translating and running the query on each monolingual collection, D_i, as is usual in CLIR systems based on query translation. This phase produces two results:
   - we obtain a single multilingual collection of preselected documents (D' collection) as a result of joining all retrieved documents for each language.
   - we obtain the translation to the other languages for each term of the original query as a result of the translation process. That is, we obtain a T' vocabulary, where each element τ is called "concept" and consists of each term together with its corresponding translation. Thus, a concept is a set of terms expressed independently of the language.
2. The re-indexing phase consists of re-indexing the multilingual collection D', but considering solely the T' vocabulary. That is, only the concepts are re-indexed. Finally, a new query formed by the concepts in T' is generated and this query is executed against the new index. Thus, for example, if we have two languages, Spanish and English, and the term "casa" is in the original query and is translated by "house", both terms represent exactly the same concept. If "casa" occurs a total of 100 times in the Spanish collection, and "house" occurs a total of 150 times in the English collection, then the term frequency would be 250. From a practical point of view, in this second phase each occurrence of "casa" is treated exactly as each occurrence of "house".

Formally, the method can be described as follows:
For each monolingual collection we begin with the already-known structure:

$$< T_i, \Phi_i, D_i, ff, df >, 1 <= i <= N$$

Where N is the number of languages present in the multilingual collection to be indexed. Let $Q = \{Q_i, 1 <= i <= N\}$ be the set formed by the original query together with its translation into the other languages, in such a way that Q_i is the query expressed in the same language as the collection D_i. After each translation Q_i has been run against its corresponding structure $< T_i, \Phi_i, D_i, ff, df >$, it is possible to obtain a new and single structure:

$$< T', \Phi', D, D', ff', df' >$$

where:

- D is the complete multilingual document collection: $D = \{D_i, 1 <= i <= N\}$.

- D' is the set of multilingual documents retrieved inas consequence of running the query Q.
- T' is the set of concepts τ_j, and denotes the vocabulary of the D' collection. Since each query Q_i is a translation of another, it is possible to align the queries at term level.

$$\tau_j := \{\tau_{ij} \in Q_i, 1 <= i <= N\}, 1 <= j = M, M = |Q|$$

  where τ_{ij} represents all the translations of the term j of the query Q to the language i. Thus, τ_j denotes the concept j of the query Q independently of the language.
- Φ' is a new vocabulary to be indexed, such that each $\varphi_j \in \Phi'$ is generated as follows:

$$\varphi_j := \{\varphi(\tau_{ij}), 1 <= i <= N\}, 1 <= j <= M$$

- The ff' function and df' function are interpreted as usual:
  - ff' is the number of occurrences of the concept j in the document k. That is, the sum of the occurrences of the term j in the query, expressed in language i:

$$ff'(\varphi_j, d_k) := ff(\varphi_{ij}, d_k)$$

  - df' is the number of documents with the concept j in the collection D. That is, the sum of the documents with the term j in the query, expressed in language i:

$$\begin{aligned} df'(\varphi_j) :=& \mid \{d_k \in D_i \mid \exists \tau \in T : \varphi(\tau) = \varphi_j \wedge d(\tau) = d_k\} \mid \\ :=& \Sigma df(\varphi_{ij}), \forall \varphi_{ij} \in \varphi_j, d_k \in D, 1 <= i <= N \end{aligned}$$

    where $df(\varphi_{ij})$ is all the documents that contain the concept j in the monolingual collection D_i.

Given this structure, a new index is generated in run time, but only taking into account the documents that are found in D'. The *df* function operates on the whole collection D, not only on the retrieved documents in the first phase, D'. This is because, in practice, we have found that the results obtained were slightly better when the whole collection was considered when calculating the *idf* factor. Once the indices have been generated in this way, the query Q formed by concepts, not by terms, is re-run on the D' collection.

In some ways, this method shares some ideas with CLIR systems based on corpus translation, but instead of translating the complete corpus, it only translates the words that appear in the query and the retrieved documents. These two simplifications allow the development of the system in run-query time since the necessary re-indexing process in the second phase is computationally possible due to the small size of the collection D' and to the scarce vocabulary T' (approximately, the query terms multiplied by the number of present languages in D').

Some relevant aspects of two-step RSV are:

- It is easily scalable to several languages.
- The system requires the term-level alignment of the original query and the translation of its terms. Depending on the approach followed for the translation, this process varies in complexity.
- A term together with its translation are treated in exactly the same way in the proposed model. This is not too realistic since it is not usual for the source term and its translations to be equally weighted. For example, it is possible that for a given language i, we maintain more than one translation for a given concept of the original query. Consequently, the concept frequency will be increased artificially in the documents expressed in the i language. In this case, if we know the translation probability of each term, we can weight each term according to its translation probability with respect to the source term. This can be modelled as follows:

  $$ff'(\varphi_j, d_k) := \Sigma ff(\varphi_{ij}, d_k) * w(\tau_{ij}), \forall \varphi_{ij} \in \varphi_j, \varphi(\tau_{ij}) = \varphi_{ij}, 1 <= i <= N$$

  where $w(\tau_{ij})$ represents the translation probability of each translation of term j in the query to language i, by default it will be 1.

5 Description of Experiments and Results

5.1 Multilingual Experiments

The experiment has been carried out for the five languages of the multilingual task. Each collection has been pre-processed as usual, using the stopword lists and stemming algorithms available for the participants, with the exception of Spanish, where we have used a stemming algorithm provided by the ZPrise system [2]. We have added terms such as "retrieval", "documents", "relevant"... to the stopword lists. Due to the morphological wealth of German, compound words have been reduced to simple words using the MORPHIX package [13]. Once the collections have been pre-processed, they are indexed with the Zprise IR system, using the OKAPI probabilistic model [14]. This OKAPI model has also been used for the on-line re-indexing process required by the calculation of two-step RSV.

For each query, we have used the Title and Description sections. The method for query translation is very simple: we used the Babylon[3] electronic dictionary to translate query terms [15]. For each term, we considered the first two translations given by Babylon. Words not found in the dictionary were been translated. This approach allows us to carry out query alignment at term level easily.

The results obtained show that the calculation of the two-step RSV improves more than seven points (36% more) the precision reached with respect to other approaches (Table 2). This improvement is approximately constant with short, medium and large queries (Table 3).

---

[2] ZPrise, developed by Darrin Dimmick (NIST). Available on demand at http://www.itl.nist.gov/iaui/894.02/works/papers/zp2/zp2.html

[3] Babylon is available at http://www.babylon.com

Table 1. Description of official experiments

x̃periment	Task	Form	Query	Merging Strategy
UJAMLTDRR	Multilingual	automatic	Title+Description	Round-Robin
UJAMLTDNORM	Multilingual	automatic	Title+Description	Normalized score
UJAMLTDRSV2	Multilingual	automatic	Title+Description	2-Step RSV
UJAMLTDRSV2RR	Multilingual	automatic	Title+Description	2-Step RSV+ Round-Robin
UJABITD {SP,DE,FR,IT}	Bilingual	automatic	Title+Description	

Table 2. Performance using different merging strategies (official runs)

Experiment	Avg. prec.	R-Precision	Overall Recall
UJAMLTDRR	0.2038	0.2787	4246/8068
UJAMLTDNORM	0.2068	0.2647	4297/8068
UJAMLTDRSV2	0.2774	0.3280	4551/8068

Table 3. Average precision using different merging strategies and query lengths

Merging strategy	Tit.	Tit.+Desc.	Tit.+Desc.+Narr.
round-robin	0.1593	0.2038	0.2425
normalized score	0.1592	0.2068	0.2554
2-step RSV	0.2159	0.2774	0.3209

Table 4. Bilingual experiments (Title+Description)

Experiment	Language	Avg. prec.	R-Precision
UJABITDSP	english → spanish	0.2991	0.3141
UJABITDDE	english → german	0.2747	0.3077
UJABITDFR	english → french	0.3467	0.3365
UJABITDIT	english → italian	0.2438	0.2620

5.2 Bilingual Experiments

The differences in accuracy between the bilingual experiments may be due to the stemming algorithms used, the quality of which varies according to language. The simplest stemming algorithm is that used for Italian: it removes only inflectional suffixes such as singular and plural word forms or feminine and masculine forms, and it is in this language where the lowest level of accuracy is achieved.

Note that the multilingual document list has been calculated starting from the document lists obtained in the bilingual experiments. The accuracy obtained in the UJAMLTDRSV2 experiment is similar to that obtained in the bilingual

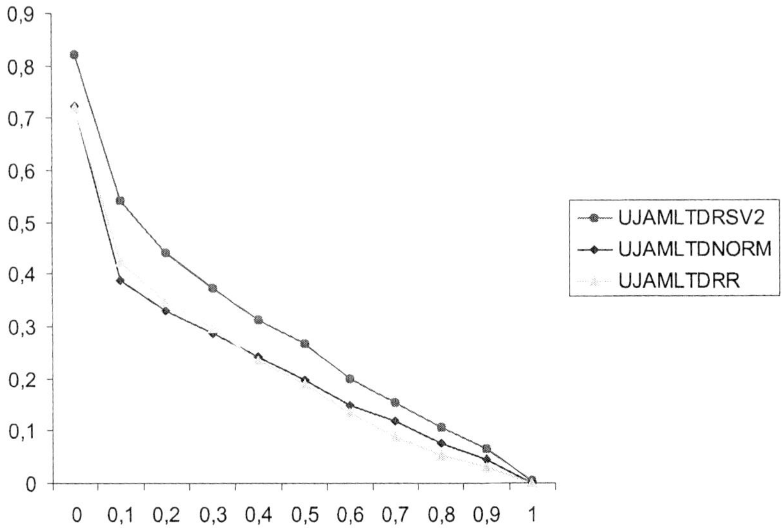

Fig. 1. 11 pt-precision

experiments (Table 4), surpassing even the accuracy for German and Italian, and only two points short of that reached in Spanish.

5.3 Merging Several Approaches

Finally, we carried out an experiment merging several approaches through a simple linear function. We calculated document relevance with the function:

$$Pos_i' = 0.6 * Pos_i^{rsv2} + 0.4 * Pos_i^{merge-approach}$$

Where Pos_i' is the new document position i. Pos_i^{rsv2} is the document position reached using two-step RSV, and $Pos_i^{merge-approach}$ is the document position using the Round-Robin or normalized score approach. As shown in Table 5, not only is there no improvement, but the accuracy even decreases slightly.

Table 5. Merge of two-step RSV and round-robin/normalized score (Title+Description)

Experiment	Merging strategies	Avg. prec.	R-Precision
UJAMLTDRSV2	RSV2	0.2774	0.3280
UJAMLTDRSV2RR	RSV2 and round-robin	0.2758	0.3265
ujamltdrsv2norm	RSV2 and normalized score	0.2631	0.3162

6 Future Work

We have presented a new approach to solve the problem of merging relevant documents in CLIR systems. This approach has performed noticeably better than other traditional approaches. To achieve this performance, it is necessary to align the query with its respective translations at term level. Our next efforts are directed towards three aspects:

- We suspect that with the inclusion of more languages, the proposed method will perform better than other approaches. Our objective is therefore to confirm this suspicion.
- We intend to test the method with other translation strategies. We have a special interest in the Multilingual Similarity Thesaurus, since this provides a measure of the semantic proximity of two terms. This semantic proximity can be used by our method as the translation probability of a term.
- Finally, we could study the effect of pseudo-relevance feedback in the first and second phase of the method proposed.

References

[1] S. T. Dumais. Latent Semantic Indexing (LSI) and TREC-2. In *Proceedings of TREC-2*, pages 105–115, Gaithersburg, 1994.

[2] E. Voorhees. The collection fusion problem. In *Proceedings of TREC-3*, number 225, pages 95–104, Gaithersburg, 1995.

[3] J. Savoy. Report on CLEF-2001 Experiments. In Carol Peters, editor, *Proceedings of the CLEF 2001 Cross-Language Text Retrieval System Evaluation Campaign. Lecture Notes in Computer Science*, pages 10–19. Springer Verlag, 2001.

[4] K. L. Kwok, L. Grunfeld, and D. D. Lewis. TREC-3 ad-hoc, routing retrieval and thresholding experiments using PIRCS. In *Proceedings of TREC-3*, number 215, pages 247–255, Gaithersburg, 1995.

[5] A. Moffat and J. Zobel. Information retrieval systems for large document collections. In *Proceedings of TREC-3*, number 225, pages 85–93, Gaithersburg, 1995.

[6] G. Salton and M. J. McGill. *Introduction to Modern Information Retrieval.* McGraw-Hill, London, U. K., 1983.

[7] A. L. Powell, J. C. French, J. Callan, M. Connell, and C. L. Viles. The impact of database selection on distributed searching. In The ACM Press., editor, *Proceedings of the 23rd International Conference of the ACM-SIGIR'2000*, pages 232–239, New York, 2000.

[8] A. Chen. Multilingual Information Retrieval Using English and Chinese Queries. In Carol Peters, editor, *Proceedings of the CLEF 2001 Cross-Language Text Retrieval System Evaluation Campaign. Lecture Notes in Computer Science.* Springer Verlag, 2002.

[9] F. Gey, H. Jiang, A. Chen, and R. Larson. Manual Queries and Machine Translation in Cross-language Retrieval and Interactive Retrieval with Cheshire II at TREC-7. In E. M. Voorhees and D. K. Harman, editors, *Proceedings of the Seventh Text REtrieval Conference (TREC-7)*, pages 527–540, 2000.

[10] P. McNamee and J. Mayfield. JHU/APL Experiments at CLEF: Translation Resources and Score Normalization. In Carol Peters, editor, *Proceedings of the CLEF 2001 Cross-Language Text Retrieval System Evaluation Campaign. Lecture Notes in Computer Science*. Springer-Verlag, 2001.
[11] P. Sheridan, P. Braschler, and P. Schäuble. Cross-language information retrieval in a multilingual legal domain. In *Proceedings of the First European Conference on Research and Advanced Technology for Digital Libraries*, pages 253–268, 1997.
[12] F. Martínez-Santiago and L. A. Ureña. Proposal for an independient-language CLIR system. In *JOTRI'2002*, pages 141–148, 2002.
[13] G. Neumann. Morphix software package. http://www.dfki.de/~neumann/morphix/morphix.html.
[14] S. E Robertson, S. Walker., and M. Beaulieu. Experimentation as a way of life:okapi at trec. *Information Processing and Management*, 1(36):95–108, 2000.
[15] D. A. Hull and G. Grefenstette. Querying across languages. a dictionary-based approach to multilingual information retrieval. In *Procedings of 19th ACM SIGIR Conference on Research and Development in Information Retrieval*, pages 49–57, 1996.

Cross-Language Retrieval at the University of Twente and TNO

Dennis Reidsma[1], Djoerd Hiemstra[1], Franciska de Jong[1,2], and Wessel Kraaij[2]

[1] University of Twente, Dept. of Computer Science
Parlevink Group, P.O. Box 217, 7500 AE Enschede, The Netherlands
{reidsma,hiemstra,fdejong}@cs.utwente.nl
[2] TNO TPD
P.O. Box 155, 2600 AD Delft, The Netherlands
kraaij@tpd.tno.nl

Abstract. This paper describes the official runs of the Twente/TNO group for CLEF 2002. We participated in the Dutch and Finnish monolingual and the Dutch bilingual tasks. In addition this paper reports on an experiment that was carried out during the assessment of the Dutch results for the CLEF 2002. The goal of the experiment was to examine possible influences on the assessments caused by the use of highlighting in the assessment program.

1 Introduction

This paper has a double focus. The first section describes the CLEF participation of the Twente/TNO group. [1] Section 2 provides the context for the research on multilingual information retrieval carried out at TNO TPD and the University of Twente. Section 3 discusses the applied retrieval model and the results for the Dutch and Finnish runs submitted to CLEF 2002.

The second and main part of the paper starts in section 4. This describes an experiment that has been carried to examine some aspects of the assessment protocol and discusses its results. First the context for the experiment is given and the reasons that led to performing the experiment. After that the experiment itself is described, followed by a summary of results and conclusions.

2 CLIR as an Aspect of Multimedia Retrieval

The work on cross-language information (CLIR) that has been carried out by a joint research group from TNO and the University of Twente since 1997 (TREC 6), is part of a larger research area that can be described as content-based multimedia retrieval. CLIR is just one of the themes in a series of collaborative

[1] The Twente/TNO group used to participate in earlier CLEF-events under the name Twenty-One. Twenty-One was an information retrieval project funded by the TAP programme of the EU. The project was completed in June 1999.

C.A. Peters (Ed.): CLEF 2002, LNCS 2785, pp. 197–206, 2003.

projects on multimedia retrieval. The project Twenty-One provided the name of the search engine that has been developed and used for the participation in TREC and, later on, CLEF. Though the focus on CLIR-aspects is not as strong in all projects as it used to be in Twenty-One, the possibility to search in digital multimedia archives with different query languages and to identify relevant material in other languages than the query language has always been part of the envisaged functionality. Where the early projects exploited mainly the textual material available in multimedia archives (production scripts, cut lists, etc.), the use of timecoded textual information (subtitles, transcripts generated by automatic speech recognition tools, etc.) has become more dominant in the projects running currently, for which video and audio retrieval are the major goals, e.g. DRUID and the IST-projects ECHO and MUMIS[2]. In some projects the CLIR functionality is made available by allowing the users of the demonstator systems to select query terms from a closed list which is tuned to the domain of the media archive to be searched. Translation to other languages is then simply a matter of mapping these query terms to their translation equivalents. Ambiguity resolution and other problems inherent to CLIR-tasks are circumvented in this 'concept search' approach, but there is always the additional user requirement of being able to search for terms that are not in the controlled list. Therefore, even in ontology driven projects such as MUMIS, the type of CLIR functionality that is central to the current CLEF-campaign remains relevant.

3 Retrieval Experiments for the Dutch and Finnish Tasks

The Twenty-One group participated in the Dutch and Finnish monolingual task and the Dutch bilingual task. In this section we present the retrieval model (section 3.1) and discuss the scores for the different tasks (sections 3.2 and 3.3).

3.1 The Retrieval Model

Runs were carried out with an information retrieval system based on a simple unigram language model. The basic idea is that documents can be represented by simple statistical language models. If a query is more probable given a language model based on document d_1, than given e.g. a language model based on document d_2, then we hypothesise that the document d_1 is more likely to be relevant to the query than document d_2. Thus the probability of generating a certain query given a document-based language model can serve as a score to rank the documents.

$$P(T_1, T_2, \cdots, T_n|D)P(D) = P(D)\prod_{i=1}^{n}(1-\lambda)P(T_i) + \lambda P(T_i|D) \qquad (1)$$

Formula 1 shows the basic idea of this approach to information retrieval, where the document-based language model $P(T_i|D)$ is interpolated with a background

[2] For details, cf. http://parlevink.cs.utwente.nl/, http://www.tpd.tno.nl/, and [2]

language model $P(T_i)$ to compensate for sparseness. In the formula, T_i is a random variable for the query term on position i in the query ($1 \leq i \leq n$, where n is the query length), with the set of all terms in the collection as sample space. The probability measure $P(T_i)$ defines the probability of drawing a term at random from the collection, $P(T_i|D_k)$ defines the probability of drawing a term at random from the document; and λ is the smoothing parameter, which is set to $\lambda = 0.15$. Since there is empirical evidence that there is a linear relationship between the probability of relevance of a document and its length, we define the prior $P(D)$ as a constant times the document length [7]. For a description of the embedding of statistical word-by-word translation into our retrieval model, see [4].

3.2 The Dutch Runs

For Dutch three separate runs were submitted. First there was the manual run, in which we had a special interest because of our role in the assessment of the Dutch submissions (cf. section 4). The expected effect of submitting a run for which the queries were manually created from the topics was an increase in the size and quality of the pool of documents to be assessed. The engine applied was a slightly modified version of the NIST Z/Prise 2.0 system.

The Dutch bilingual run is an automatic run done with the TNO retrieval system (also referred to as the Twenty-One engine) as developed and used for previous CLEF participations [4, 6]. Furthermore we used the VLIS lexical database developed by Van Dale Lexicography and the morphological analyzers developed by Xerox Reserch Centre Europe.

For completeness we did a post-evaluation automatic monolingual Dutch run. Mean average precision figures for the three runs are given in Table 1. Figure 1 shows the precision-recall plots for the Dutch experiments.

3.3 The Finnish Run

Since no Finnish morphological analyzer or stemmer was available, it was decided to apply an N-gram approach, which has been advocated as a language independent, knowledge-poor approach by McNamee and Mayfield [9]. After applying a stoplist and lowercasing, documents and queries were indexed by character 5-grams. Unlike the JHU approach, the 5-grams did not span word boundaries. This extremely simple approach turned out to be very effective: for almost all topics the score of this run was at least as high as the median score.

Table 1. Mean average precision of the runs on the Dutch and Finnish dataset

run label	m.a.p.	description
tnoutnl	0.4471	manual monolingual
tnoenl	0.3369	EN-NL dictionary based
tnofifil	0.4056	automatic monolingual (Finnish)
tnonnl	0.4247	automatic monolingual

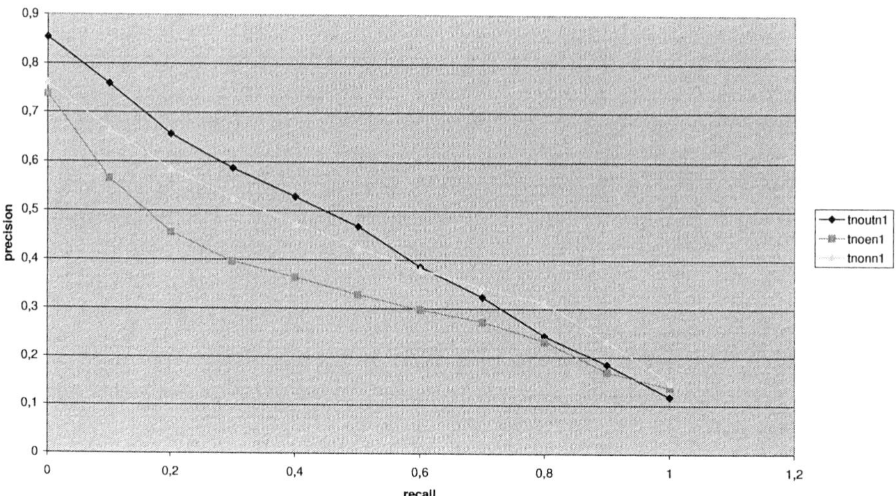

Fig. 1. Precision-recall graphs on the Dutch experiments

4 The Role of Highlighting During Assessment

In a retrieval evaluation campaign such as CLEF, the assessment of the retrieval results plays an important role. For more detail on the methods used to create the test collections on which the evaluations are based and the role of the assessments in this we refer to [1].

The University of Twente was responsible for the assessments of the results for the Dutch CLEF collection, consisting of the 1994-1995 newspaper articles from 'NRC Handelsblad' and 'Algemeen Dagblad'. This meant that for a large number of these articles a judgement had to be made as to whether each article was relevant to the topic for which it was returned as a result by one of the participating retrieval systems.

For the official ranking of the submitted runs the standard assessment protocol was followed. In addition some assessments were repeated under different conditions. The purpose of these additional assessments was to investigate the effect of the use of the highlighting option in the presentation of the retrieved documents on the assessment results. These experiments were kept strictly separate from the official assessments and did not affect the offical rankings presented by the CLEF committee.

This section discusses the motivation for this additional experiment and reports on the findings. First the protocol used to structure the assessment task is discussed. After that some parameters in the protocol are discussed. The last subsections are dedicated to the experiments we carried out on the effect of the highlighting option in the presentation of the documents on the resulting relevance judgments.

4.1 The Assessment Protocol

Within the CLEF campaign the assessment of retrieval results is carried out to produce a high quality, dependable collection of judgments that tell us which documents in the collection are relevant for the given queries. These judgments are used to rank the individual submissions of the participating search engines.

The assessment protocol ensures that the outcomes of the various assessment teams are a solid and reusable basis for the construction of testbeds for the various language specific retrieval tasks.

Variations in several parameters of this protocol can influence the results, such as the number of assessors, the selection of documents that will be manually assessed and the criteria on which a document is judged relevant or non-relevant. The assessment protocol has been standardized based on past research of such parameters, but the fact that the newspaper collections differ for each language and the fact that for each language there is another team doing the assessment task already introduces new variations. On top of that there are several other parameters that are not controlled by the protocol. If experimental results were to indicate that one of these parameters had effects that were previously unknown, the assessment protocol would have to be adapted and the validity of the assessments of previous years would also have to be reconsidered.

The next section discusses some parameters in the assessment protocol and previous research on the influence of variations in these parameters on the resulting system ranking. The rest of the paper is dedicated to our experiments with one of the remaining parameters.

4.2 Protocol Parameters

One of the parameters of the assessments concerns variation in judgement between persons or even for one person on different moments. The question whether this has an adverse effect on the stability of the ranking has been researched for example by Lesk and Salton [8] and Voorhees [13]. For the Dutch testbed similar experiments have been carried out by Hiemstra and Van Leeuwen [5]. Other parameters include pool depth, assessor characteristics, the kind of instruction that the assessors get and the document presentation style. Table 2, taken from [3], gives an overview of variations in the assessment procedures among the various assessment teams for CLEF 2001.

The rest of this paper addresses a parameter that has not yet been researched very extensively: the style of document presentation, more specifically the effect of the use of the highlighting option that the assessment software makes available to the assessors.

Table 2. Aspects of the 2001 judgments [3]

parameter	Dutch	English	French	German	Italian	Spanish
no. of assessors	10	6	5	2	3	4
experienced as user?	yes	some	yes	one	some	no
experienced as assesors?	no	yes	no	one	two	no
written/oral instruction	oral	both	oral	both	both	oral
native topics by assesors	no	yes	yes	one	one	no
translated by assessors	no	no	no	one	one	no
transl. from source lang.?	yes	yes	yes	no	mostly	no
discussion possible?	some	some	yes	yes	yes	yes
single/group opinion?	single	single	?	group	group	group
supervisors involved?	no	no	yes	yes	yes	no
post-assessm. narrative?	no	yes	no	sketchy	sketchy	no

4.3 The Effect of Highlighting

The program used to support the assessment task, developed at NIST, offers the option to highlight terms in the retrieved documents. This functionality serves a clear purpose. For example, the assessor can decide on the relevance of a document more efficiently if words and phrases related to the topic which occur in the document are highlighted.

Usually the assessor will be told explicitly that the presence or absence of highlighted terms in a document should not be taken as a an *a priori* indication that a document relevant. It is therefore assumed that using highlighting will not influence the assessment results, or more specifically the ranking of the search engines that follows from those results. This assumption however can be questioned. The following subsection explains how highlighting can affect the assessments and why the use of highlighting may influence the ranking of search engines. A simple experiment will be described that we applied in an attempt to detect such effects.

4.4 Possible Influences of Highlighting on Assessment Results

We wanted to investigate two different aspects of the assessment results that might be affected by the use of highlighting. The first pertains to the number of documents that are marked as relevant, the second to the ranking of the participating search engines. An effect on the second aspect would clearly have the most impact. We did not expect to find hard statistical evidence for presence or absence of either one of the influences, given the size of the test data. The experiment merely aimed at uncovering possible trends that would warrant further investigation.

The Number of Relevant Documents. Using highlighting might result in more (or less) documents being marked as relevant. Although the assessors are explicitly told not to let the highlighting effect their judgement, it is still possible that this happens unintentionally:

- Assessors might read the documents where terms are highlighted less thoroughly, missing in those documents the relevant parts which do *not* contain highlighted terms.
- Assessors might be biased in favour of documents containing highlighted terms.
- Assessors may uncover documents which they missed because they overlooked the relevant passage without highlighting.

The Scores of Search Engines. If the assessors are biased towards documents containing highlighted terms this might influence the scores of the search engines. After all, many retrieval systems rely on detecting the presence of query words for marking them as relevant. In that case those systems would perform better with the biased assessment than with assessments produced without using highlighting.

4.5 The Experiments

The setup of the experiment was straightforward: 18 topics were each assessed at least twice, once with and once without highlighting. These assessments were assigned randomly over 10 people, in such a way that every assessor did some assessments with and without highlighting and no-one assessed one topic twice. The assessors were instructed not to talk to each other about these assessments until all assessments were finished. The extra assessments were used to produce alternative rankings for 29 submissions.

4.6 Results and Conclusions

The Number of Relevant Documents. Table 3 contains some figures on the extra assessments. For half of the topics, the assessments with highlighting resulted in more relevant documents than the assessments without highlighting. For the rest of the topics it was the other way around. Given the amount of variation between assessors as found by Voorhees [14], these results suggest that variation in the use of highlighting has no significant influence on the number of documents judged to be relevant.

The Rankings. The most important result of the experiments is of course the alternative ranking they produce. As long as the rankings stay more or less the same throughout the variations in the protocol with respect to the highlighting the resulting testbed is still stable and reusable. The official rankings in CLEF are based on the average precision measure shown in figure 2. This figure shows the the influence of *not* using highlighting on the average precision of the submissions as a percentage relative to the average precisions produced using highlighting in

Table 3. Results: no. of relevant found

Topic	no. assessed	rel. w highlighting	rel. w/o highlighting
92	294	38	38
94	412	18	21
100	433	12	14
107	336	5	40
108	217	34,3	48,18
110	296	4	4
115	575	26	25
119	372	31	20
121	274	36	32
125	305	76	124
127	272	20	23
129	390	48	15
130	256	9	20
131	587	40	26
132	481	13	5
135	453	124	128
137	743	5	5
138	564	7,9	7,14
139	416	46	23
140	356	144	109
Total	8032	748	759

the assessment task. The average of the absolute values of these differences is 3.35%.

Table 4 shows two different rankings of some submissions to the Dutch track. The first row shows the official ranking of the 29 submissions that were considered in this experiment. The second row shows the ranking as it would be based on the relevance judgments that were produced *without* using highlighting. Most of the submissions have the same ranking in both cases (though submission 7 and 22 trade places, a minor change). Submission 12 goes 2 places down, but since the initial difference between 11, 12 and 19 was only 0.0144 this is still harmless. Submissions 4 and 16 go 2 places up, but the initial differences in scores between the assessments that are involved are only 0.0127 and 0.0031 respectively. One change is not really trivial anymore: assessment 17 goes 2 places up, 18 goes 3 places up and 21 goes 5 places down. Before the change, the scores of the 6 assessments involved in this change have a difference of 0.0349 between the lowest and the highest (the score of 21 being the highest). After the change this difference is 0.0209 between the score of 21 (the lowest) and the highest. However, the information was not complete enough and the experiments were not extensive enough to permit any fruitful speculation as to the exact causes of this change.

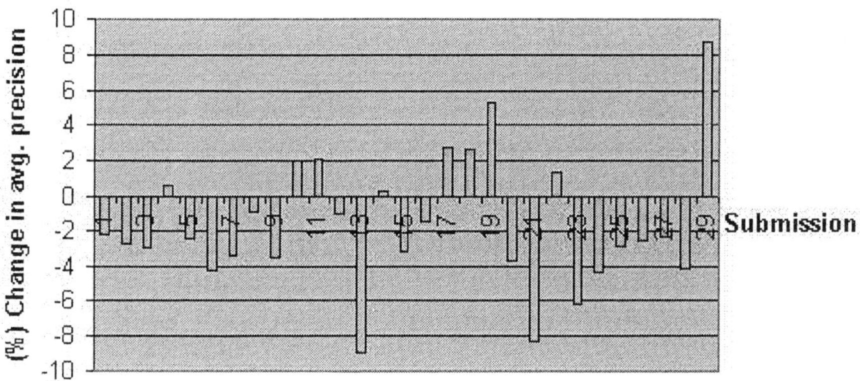

Fig. 2. This figure shows the influence of *not* using highlighting on the average precision of the submissions (percentage relative to the official average precisions)

Table 4. Rankings calculated from assessments using the highlighting functionality vs. rankings calculated from assessments *not* using the highlighting functionality

with highlighting (1-15)	without highlighting (1-15)	with (16-29)	without (16-29)
29	29	23	18
9	9	21	17
14	14	7	7
13	13	15	15
24	24	25	25
3	3	20	20
26	26	1	1
22	22	4	5
10	10	5	27
19	12	27	4
11	19	16	6
12	21	6	28
18	11	28	16
17	23	2	2
8	8		

5 Conclusions

Though these variations in the rankings are not large enough to justify the conclusion that variations in the use of highlighting have an adverse effect on the quality of the relevance judgments, they are certainly large enough to warrant further investigation. It would be advisable to do the experiments described in this paper again, involving more topics and doing the assessments for every topic more than once both with and without highlighting. Another aspect that might be included in these new experiments would be the *speed* with which the assessors work. If the amount of data assessed in the same time using highlighting is for example twice as large as without using highlighting it might be possible that the larger set of relevance judgments compensates for the sligthly lower quality of the individual judgments. We suggest that these experiments be performed to find a definitive answer to the question that has led to this paper: "Does the use of the highlighting option in the NIST system have an unintended effect on the overall quality of the relevance judgments?"

References

[1] M. Braschler and C. Peters. CLEF 2002: Methodology and metrics. *In this volume*, 2002.

[2] F. de Jong, J. L. Gauvain, Dj. Hiemstra, and K. Netter. Language-based multimedia information retrieval. *Content-Based Multimedia Information Access, RIAO 2000 Conference Proceedings, ISBN 2-905450-07-X, C. I. D.-C. A. S. I. S., Paris, 713-722*, 2000.

[3] D. Hiemstra. The CLEF relevance assessments in practice, August 2001. Presentation at the CLEF Workshop 2001, Darmstadt.

[4] D. Hiemstra, W. Kraaij, R. Pohlmann, and T. Westerveld. Translation resources, merging strategies and relevance feedback for cross-language information retrieval. In Peters [10]. LNCS 2069.

[5] D. Hiemstra and D. van Leeuwen. Creating a dutch testbed to evaluate the retrieval from textual databases. Technical report TR-CTIT-02-04, Centre for Telematics and Information Technology, University of Twente, 2002.

[6] W. Kraaij. TNO at CLEF 2001: Comparing translation resources. In Peters [11].

[7] W. Kraaij, T. Westerveld, and D. Hiemstra. The importance of prior probabilities for entry page search. *Proceedings of the 25th Annual International ACM SIGIR Conference on Research and Development in Information Retrieval*, 2002.

[8] M. Lesk and G. Salton. Relevance assessments and retrieval system evaluation. *Information Storage and Retrieval, 4:242359*, 1969.

[9] P. McNamee and J. Mayfield. A language-independent approach to european text retrieval. In Peters [10]. LNCS 2069.

[10] C. Peters, editor. *Cross-language Information Retrieval and Evaluation.* Springer Verlag, 2000. LNCS 2069.

[11] C. Peters, editor. *Working Notes for the CLEF 2001 Workshop.* 2001.

[12] C. Peters, M. Braschler, J. Gonzalo, and M. Kluck, editors. *Evaluation of Cross-Language Information Retrieval Systems.* Springer Verlag, 2001. LNCS 2406.

[13] E. M. Voorhees. Variations in relevance judgements and the measurement of retrieval effectiveness. *Information Processing & Management, 36:697716*, 2000.

[14] E. M. Voorhees. The philosophy of information retrieval evaluation. In Peters et al. [12]. LNCS 2406.

Scalable Multilingual Information Access

Paul McNamee and James Mayfield

Johns Hopkins University Applied Physics Lab
11100 Johns Hopkins Road, Laurel, MD 20723-6099 USA
{mcnamee,mayfield}@jhuapl.edu

Abstract. The third Cross-Language Evaluation Forum workshop (CLEF-2002) provides the unprecedented opportunity to evaluate retrieval in eight different languages using a common set of topics and a uniform assessment methodology. This year the Johns Hopkins University Applied Physics Laboratory participated in the monolingual, bilingual, and multilingual retrieval tasks. We contend that information access in a plethora of languages requires approaches that are inexpensive in developer and run-time costs. In this paper we describe a simplified approach that seems suitable for retrieval in many languages; we also show how good retrieval is possible over many languages, even when translation resources are scarce, or when query-time translation is infeasible. In particular, we investigate the use of character n-grams for monolingual retrieval, CLIR between related languages using partial morphological matches, and translation of document representations to an interlingua for computationally efficient retrieval against multiple languages.

1 Introduction

The number of languages in the CLEF document collection has grown to eight in 2002: Dutch, English, Finnish, French, German, Italian, Spanish, and Swedish. While the Romance languages have a great deal in common with one another, the Teutonic languages and Finnish have different origins; this set of modern languages provide challenges in word decompounding, complex morphology, and handling diacritical marks. For many years research in information retrieval was focused on the English language where these problems are less significant. As a result simple rules for stemming words and case-folding are really the only common improvements to exact string matching used by retrieval systems. The use of stopword lists is also routine, but seems to have little effect except to reduce the size of inverted files and to improve runtime efficiency.

We have been interested in discovering how simple methods can be applied to combat the aforementioned problems. Though their use has not found favor for retrieval in English, we have demonstrated that overlapping character n-grams are remarkably effective for retrieval in many languages, including those most widely used in Europe. This simple technique appears to provide a surrogate means to

C.A. Peters (Ed.): CLEF 2002, LNCS 2785, pp. 207-218, 2003.

normalize word forms, an efficient approximation to word bigrams (when n-grams with interior spaces are formed), and a solution to the problem of decompounding agglutinative languages. For the CLEF-2002 evaluation we continued to use the Hopkins Automated Information Retriever for Combing Unstructured Text (HAIRCUT) system which supports n-gram processing.

We participated in three tasks at this year's workshop, monolingual, cross-language, and multilingual retrieval. All of our official submissions were automated runs. This year we relied on an aligned parallel corpus as our sole translation resource – this resource was automatically mined from the Web and can be used to support retrieval between any pair of E.U. languages, except Greek. In the sections that follow, we first describe the standard methodology used for each language's sub-collection and we then present initial results in monolingual, bilingual, and multilingual retrieval. Highlights include an investigation into the use of parallel corpora in translingual retrieval, a discovery that character n-grams provide a means for effective bilingual retrieval for a close language pair, without translation, and an efficient method for multilingual retrieval that involves no query-time translation.

2 Methodology

For the monolingual tasks we created sixteen indexes, a word and an n-gram (n=6) index for each of the eight languages. For the bilingual and multilingual tasks we used the same indexes but translated topic statements to produce our official runs; however, we also report on another approach for multilingual retrieval that required a separate index. Information about each index is provided in Table 1.

Table 1. Information about indexes for the CLEF-2002 test collection

	# docs	collection size (MB zipped)	type	# terms	index size (MB)
Dutch	190,604	203	words	692,754	160
			6-grams	3,816,580	1133
English	110,282	166	words	235,713	98
			6-grams	2,944,813	889
Finnish	55,344	51	words	981,174	87
			6-grams	2,524,529	383
French	87,191	92	words	248,225	68
			6-grams	2,343,009	511
German	225,371	207	words	1,079,453	221
			6-grams	4,203,047	1,325
Italian	108,578	107	words	338,634	89
			6-grams	2,162,249	607
Spanish	215,737	186	words	382,666	150
			6-grams	3,193,404	1098
Swedish	142,819	94	words	510,245	95
			6-grams	3,254,595	628

Table 2. Example 6-grams produced for the input "the prime minister." Term statistics are based on the LA Times subset of the English collection. Dashes indicate whitespace characters

Term	Document Frequency	Collection Frequency	IDF	RIDF
-the-p	72,489	241,648	0.605	0.434
the-pr	41,729	86,923	1.402	0.527
he-pri	8,701	11,812	3.663	0.364
e-prim	2,827	3,441	5.286	0.261
-prime	3,685	5,635	4.903	0.576
prime-	3,515	5,452	4.971	0.597
rime-m	1,835	2,992	5.910	0.689
ime-mi	1,731	2,871	5.993	0.711
me-min	1,764	2,919	5.966	0.707
e-mini	3,797	5,975	4.860	0.615
-minis	4,243	8,863	4.699	1.005
minist	15,428	33,731	2.838	0.914
iniste	4,525	8,299	4.607	0.821
nister	4,686	8,577	4,557	0.816
ister-	7,727	12,860	3.835	0.651

Index Construction

Our methods for scanning documents, creating an index, and processing queries are essentially unchanged from last year. We include below a description from our CLEF-2001 paper [5]; those already familiar with our previous work using HAIRCUT should skip ahead to a description of this year's experiments.

Documents were processed using only the permitted tags specified in the workshop guidelines. First SGML macros were expanded to their appropriate Unicode character. Then punctuation was eliminated, letters were downcased, and only the first four of a sequence of digits were preserved (e.g., 010394 became 0103##). Diacritical marks were preserved. The result is a stream of words separated by spaces. Exceedingly long words were truncated; the limit was 35 characters in the Dutch and German languages and 20 otherwise. When using n-grams we extract indexing terms from the same stream of words; thus, the n-grams may span word boundaries, but sentence boundaries are noted so that n-grams spanning sentence boundaries are not recorded. N-grams with leading, central, or trailing spaces are formed at word boundaries. For example, given the phrase, "the prime minister," the 6-grams produced can be seen in Table 2.

The use of overlapping character n-grams provides a surrogate form of morphological normalization. For example, in Table 2 above, the n-gram "minist" could have been generated from several different forms like *administer*, *administrative*, *minister*, *ministers*, *ministerial*, or *ministry*. It could also come from an unrelated word like *feminist*. Another advantage of n-gram indexing comes from the fact that n-grams containing spaces can convey phrasal information. In the table above, 6-grams such as "rime-m", "ime-mi", and "me-min" may act much like the phrase "prime minister" in a word-based index using multiple word phrases.

For the 2001 workshop we examined different types of translation resources for bilingual retrieval and espoused a language-neutral approach to retrieval. We continued in this vein and did not utilize stopword lists or morphological analyzers.

Query Processing

HAIRCUT performs rudimentary preprocessing on topic statements to remove stop structure, *e.g.,* phrases such as "... would be relevant" or "relevant documents should....". We have constructed a list of about 1000 such English phrases from previous topic sets (mainly TREC topics) and these have been translated into other languages using commercial machine translation. Other than this preprocessing, queries are parsed in the same fashion as documents in the collection.

3 Monolingual Experiments

We submitted an official run for each target language only using the <title> and <desc> fields and only automatic processing. These official runs were actually the combination of two base-runs, one using words and one using 6-grams; both base-runs also make use of blind relevance feedback. We again relied on a statistical language model of retrieval and used the same parameters as last year. With words as indexing terms we used queries expanded to include 60 terms and a smoothing parameter, alpha, of 0.30. When 6-grams were used instead, queries were expanded to 400 terms and alpha was set to 0.15. In both cases the top 20 documents were used as positive examples and the bottom 75 of 1000 were presumed irrelevant for the purposes of query expansion. Expansion terms were selected by weighting each term using a variant of mutual information and deriving a value for the term based on its occurrence in both the top-ranked and bottom-ranked documents. Then terms were scored using a linear combination of three factors: 2 times the weight based on top-ranked document occurrences, -2 times the weight from bottom-ranked documents, and 3 times the original relative term frequency in the query (if non-zero).

Our official results are shown below in Table 3.

Table 3. Official results for monolingual task. The shaded row contains results for a comparable, unofficial English run

run id	topic fields	average precision	relevant retrieved	# topics
aplmode	TD	0.4663	1792 / 1938	50
aplmoen	TD	0.3957	800 / 821	50
aplmoes	TD	0.5192	2659 / 2854	50
aplmofi	TD	0.3280	483 / 502	30
aplmofr	TD	0.4509	1364 / 1383	50
aplmoit	TD	0.4599	1039 / 1072	49
aplmonl	TD	0.5028	1773 / 1862	50
aplmosv	TD	0.4317	1155 / 1196	49

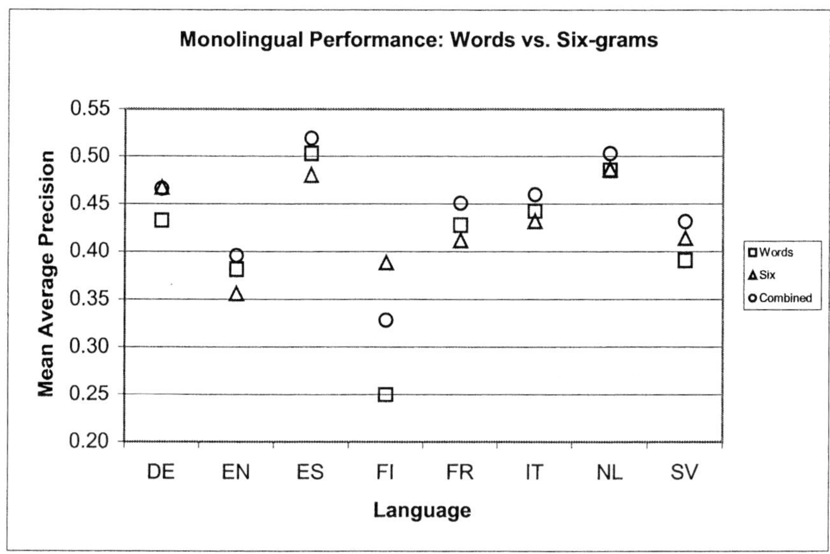

Fig. 1. Comparing words and character n-grams *(n=6)* by language

Since we created runs by combining distinct runs (one using words, one using 6-grams) we should examine the individual performance using each method. Figure 1 contains a plot that shows the mean average precision obtained for each sub-collection using both approaches. We note that in English and the Romance languages, the use of words yields slightly better performance, an improvement of 0.010 to 0.025 in absolute terms. We reported observing the same trend for French and Italian during last year's evaluation [4]. In the Dutch sub-collection, little difference is seen, but 6-grams are clearly advantageous in the remaining languages. A sizeable difference is seen in German (0.035) and Swedish (0.023), and far more significantly. in Finnish (0.13)

In Figure 1 we also plot the performance of the combined runs. Combination was generally beneficial, but due to the large disparity between n-grams and words for Finnish, the technique depressed performance in that language compared to that which would have observed using n-grams alone. No difference due to combination was seen for German, but an improvement of between 0.016 and 0.023 was found in the remaining collections, an improvement of 3-5% in relative terms.

We performed the same analysis when blind relevance feedback was not performed and found similar results. There the performance was generally less than when automated feedback was performed. Also, within each language, differences between techniques were larger without feedback. By averaging across all languages, we saw that feedback improved the microaveraged mean average precision from 0.3479 to 0.4141 when words were used, and from 0.3729 to 0.4295 when 6-grams were used. If, as it seems, n-grams are more effective for retrieval in languages with complex morphology, then the fact that the two approaches achieved more similar performance when feedback was employed would support the notion that automatic relevance feedback improves performance by redressing the effect of inflectional variation. For details about the characteristics of the test collection see the description by Braschler and Peters [1].

4 Bilingual Experiments

Our official bilingual submissions were based on query translation when some attempt at translation was made; we submitted one run for each document collection. For each collection, save English, we created one run using the English query statements and the title and description fields. The runs are named using the template *aplbienxx*. For these 7 runs, we used pre-translation expansion using the L.A. Times collection; queries were expanded to 60 terms and we used statistical word-by-word translations mined from an aligned parallel collection. This collection is an expanded version of the corpus we obtained from the Europa web site (details follow). We used unnormalized words for these bilingual experiments because we have not yet used our parallel collection to generate statistical translations that are character n-grams – we want to investigate this, but for the evaluation, we simply used words. Since 10 runs were permitted under the track guidelines, we did submit three other runs. The first, *aplbipten*, used the Portuguese topic statements to search the English sub-collection; our motivation here was only to submit a run using these statements. The final two runs, *aplbiptesa* and *aplbiptesb*, made no use of translation whatsoever.

The seven runs produced using English queries first performed pre-translation expansion using the L.A. Times sub-collection. The query was expanded to include 60 words, and then each term was translated, if possible, using the Europa corpus for translation. Then two runs were made, one using pre-translation expansion alone and one using both pre- and post-translation query expansion. Scores for these two runs were normalized and merged together to form our official submission. The eighth run, *aplbipten*, used the Portuguese topic statements and no pre-translation expansion was attempted (as we had not suitable indexed collection at hand). However, two runs were still combined, one with no expansion and one that made use of blind relevance feedback. Results for these runs are shown below in Table 4.

Table 4. Official results for the bilingual task. Except for the shaded run, English was used as the source language.

Run id	topic fields	average precision	relevant retrieved	# topics	% mono
aplbiende	TD	0.3137	1535 / 1938	50	67.27%
aplbienes	TD	0.3602	2326 / 2854	50	69.38%
aplbienfi	TD	0.2003	388 / 502	30	61.07%
aplbienfr	TD	0.3505	1275 / 1383	50	77.73%
aplbienit	TD	0.2794	934 / 1072	49	60.75%
aplbiennl	TD	0.3516	1625 / 1862	50	69.93%
aplbiensv	TD	0.3003	1052 / 1196	49	69.56%
aplbipten	TD	0.4158	753 / 821	42	105.07%

The results for each run in Table 4 are not comparable to one another because a different target language collection was involved. Furthermore, the last column, which reports the comparison to a target language monolingual baseline using mean average precision, is not especially meaningful. It is unfair to compare against a monolingual baseline for two reasons. First, Voorhees has pointed out that a comparison between test-sets using different topic statements (as is the case here) is not justified even though the document collections are the same [7]; the various translations of each topic may result in queries that are significantly easier in one language than another. Second, slightly different algorithms were used in our monolingual and bilingual results. Our monolingual runs were formed through merging n-gram and word-based runs while our bilingual results only used words. Also, the bilingual runs all used pre-translation over the English collection, which itself only contained relevant documents for 42 of the 50 topics.

Improved Translation Resource

The quality of translation resources is a critical driver for CLIR performance. Therefore, it is important to select a translation approach that ensures translation of important query terms. At our disposal we had translation software (Systran, L&H Power Translator, and various on-line services), bilingual dictionaries automatically extracted from lists on the Web, and a large parallel corpus. We investigated each of these methods in our 2001 paper and found that when only a single source was used, best performance was obtained by using the parallel collection for translation. We decided to expand the parallel collection and use it for our official runs. Thus, all of our bilingual runs used a single common resource.

The collection was obtained through a nightly crawl of the Europa web site where we targeted the Official Journal of the European Union [8]. The Journal is available in each of the E.U. languages and consists mainly of governmental topics, for example, trade and foreign relations. We had data available from December 2000 through May 2002. Though focused on European topics, the time span is 5-7 years after the CLEF-2002 document collection. So, it is possible that many proper names in 1994 and 1995 will be rarely mentioned, if at all. The Journal is published electronically in PDF format and we wanted to create an aligned collection. Rather than attempt an 11-language, multiple aligned collection, we simply wasted disk space and preformed redundant alignments. At the present we have not aligned all $O(n^2)$ pairs, but instead created n alignments between English and the other languages. We used the publicly available *pdftotext* package [9] to extract text from the PDF, but Greek text is not supported by the software so we neglected this language[1]. Once converted to text, documents were split into pieces using conservative rules for page-breaks and paragraph breaks. Many of the documents are written in outline form, or contain large tables, so this task is not trivial. Approximately 20GB of PDF documents are involved; we find that the PDF files are approximately ten times larger than the plain text versions. Thus we have about 200 MB of text per language that may be aligned.

Once aligned, we indexed each sub-collection using the same technique described for the CLEF-2002 document collections; in particular, unnormalized words were

---

[1] We are interested in seeing Danish and Portuguese collections added to the CLEF test set.

used as indexing terms. We relied on query term translation and extracted candidate translations as follows. First, we took a candidate term as input and identified documents containing this word in the English subset of the aligned data. Up to 5000 documents were considered; we bounded the number for reasons of efficiency and because we felt that performance was not enhanced appreciably when a greater number of documents was used. If no document contained this term, then the word itself was left untranslated. Second, we found the corresponding documents in the target language. Third, using a similarity metric that is similar to mutual information, we extracted a single potential translation using the frequency of occurrence in the whole collection and the frequency in the subset of aligned documents found that are believed to contain a mapping for the original source term.

We found that use of the larger parallel collection containing approximately 200MB of alignable text per language resulted in a roughly 3% improvement in mean average precision compared to when the smaller (100MB / language) collection we used in CLEF 2001. We imagine that the difference is attributable to increased lexical coverage. In our experience when pre-translation query expansion is used, this technique rivals or outperforms CLIR using a single commercial MT system (e.g., Systran); however, a judicious combination of multiple translation resources may yield the best results (e.g., [4]).

CLIR without Translation

In previous work we have shown that reasonably good retrieval between two related languages is possible, without any translation at all. Though the use of cognate matches has been known for some time [2], we found that pre-translation expansion using a comparable expansion corpus enhances performance – in some cases, by 200-300% [6]. During last year's campaign we also noted that n-grams were almost twice as effective as words in this scenario [5]. This year, we wanted to conduct similar work that looked at a variety of language pair in comparison to our pervious work with English as the target language. We looked at several language pairs and hoped to see a difference in performance when this method was used between close languages. Our hypothesis is that translation-less retrieval between related languages (say the Romance group) would be more effective than when this approach was used between, say, German and Spanish.

For these runs, we did not use pre-translation expansion (though we hope to examine this in the future). We did compare performance using words and n-grams. Our two official runs for this experiment we aplbiptesa and aplbiptesb. The first used 6-grams as indexing terms while the later used words. Both urns used blind relevance feedback. Results for these two runs are shown below in Table 5.

Table 5. Official results for the bilingual task using no translation, the Portuguese topic statements, and the Spanish news collection

Run id	topic fields	type	average precision	relevant retrieved	# topics	% mono	%Eng bilingual
Aplbiptesa	TD	6-grams	0.3325	2071 / 2854	50	64.04%	92.31%
Aplbiptesb	TD	words	0.2000	1589 / 2854	50	38.52%	55.52%

Table 6. Results using no translation between other language pairs

Source	target	topic fields	type	average precision	relevant retrieved	# topics	% mono
German	Spanish	TD	6-grams	0.1935	1109 / 2854	50	37.27%
German	Spanish	TD	words	0.2338	951 / 2854	50	45.03%
Finnish	Spanish	TD	6-grams	0.1731	1244 / 2854	50	33.34%
Finnish	Spanish	TD	words	0.1450	837 / 2854	50	27.93%
Dutch	German	TD	6-grams	0.2764	1025 / 1938	50	59.27%
Dutch	German	TD	words	0.1523	610 / 1938	50	32.66%
German	Dutch	TD	6-grams	0.2440	739 / 1862	50	48.53%
German	Dutch	TD	words	0.2444	659 / 1862	50	48.61%
Swedish	Italian	TD	6-grams	0.2216	614 / 1072	49	48.18%
Swedish	Italian	TD	words	0.1867	302 / 1072	49	40.60%

It is interesting to note that with no translation whatsoever and the use of 6-grams as indexing terms, performance was 92% of that when English topics were translated to Spanish and 64% of that for a Spanish monolingual run. This is still not a fair comparison (the English topics might be particularly hard, for example), but, it is surprisingly good. The mean precision at 5 docs for *aplbiptesa* was 0.3920; on average, two out of the five top documents were relevant, despite not translating the queries. We examined several other language pairs as well, but have not looked at all *n(n-1)* cases. These other results were not official runs.

As would be expected, retrieval without translation is more effective in closely related language pairs. In the table above, we see that German retrieval against Dutch is almost 50% as effective as monolingual Dutch retrieval when using 6-grams; similarly, Dutch retrieval against German is about 60% as effective as monolingual German retrieval. This strongly suggests that for language pairs with few direct translation resources, translation to a closely related language for which translation is feasible from the source language, can result in good cross-language retrieval performance. It remains to examine whether small length n-grams result in even greater performance, and whether pre-translation expansion improves this approach. Our previous experiments on the CLEF-2001 collection would suggest the later, but in those we only examined language pairs where English was the target language.

5 Multilingual Experiments

To date, our experiments in multilingual merging have not found a technique that results in producing a high quality, single ranked list from documents in many languages. Last year we experimented with methods that tried to normalize document similarity scores and to produce a single list. This year we submitted two official runs that used either merge-by-score (*aplmuena*) or merge-by-rank (*aplmuenb*). As in the past, we found these two methods comparable, but not tremendously effective. However, no more suitable method has been proposed.

We have been intrigued by work by researchers at the University of California at Berkeley that address this problem in a way that does not require score normalization. Gey et al., create a single inverted file from documents in many languages and then, to score documents, they create a composite query composed of a query statement in a single language concatenated with translations of that query in the other collection languages [3]. This approach results in a single ranked list, and it appears to work well with Berkeley's logistic regression approach to retrieval. In the CLEF-2001 campaign we examined this method using both unnormalized words and character 5-grams. Our results with simple words were disappointing and the 5-grams, though significantly better, did not perform as well as simple merging approaches. We do not yet understand why our results are different than those reported by Berkeley, but the fact that we use a different model of retrieval may be responsible.

This year, we also attempted a dual solution to the approach described above. Rather than translate queries into every language, we created an index that contained a document that was transformed into a single language. We picked English as our interlingua and mapped each document into English using a bag-of-words approach to translation. Strictly speaking, we did not perform translation of the documents. Rather, we took the indexed document representations from our monolingual indexes, loaded a hash-table into memory that contained a bilingual wordlist, and created a new inverted-file where the posting lists were English words (or untranslatable foreign terms) that referred to documents from the different languages. We also included the native English documents. Because we felt lexical coverage was most important, we translated the documentation representations by mapping each source word into all of its candidate (English) translations. We probably should have removed stopwords, but did not do so. This process is linear in the size of the collection since the hash-table lookups are $O(1)$ per word occurrence.

This approach creates an index with several peculiar characteristics. First, it makes the foreign language document representations a bit larger, since on average, a term may have 2 or 3 potential translations. Also, the original English documents are somewhat more focused since they don't have erroneous translations in their representations. Still, we are left with an approach where we can take a query in our preferred language (preferred here because we have good resources for it) and simply run it against our transformed document collection. This approach (*aplmuend*) appears to be 18% more effective than our officially submitted runs using normalization and merging. Interestingly, precision at a small number of documents was greatly enhanced, and recall at 1000 docs suffered; however, a subsequent combination with run *aplmuena* restored the overall recall (*aplmuenq*). Furthermore, this method creates a composite 'English' index in time linear with the collection size and requires no query-time translation or post-retrieval processing (*e.g.*, merging). See Table 7 for a comparison of this and our two official runs.

One final thing we did for this year's multilingual task was to try and isolate the effect of losses due to query translation and multi-collection merging. What we did was to take monolingual runs for each of the collections and attempt to merge them (*aplmuenz*). We found slightly better average precision when doing this, as might be expected. We think this is an interesting way to investigate the multilingual problem; it reduced the problem to that of finding a good merging strategy, which still seems like one of the most viable approaches to MLIR.

Table 7. Multilingual results

run id	topic fields	average precision	relevant retrieved	precision at 5 docs	remarks
aplmuena	TD	0.2070	4729 / 8068	0.4680	official; score-based merge
aplmuenb	TD	0.2082	4660 / 8068	0.4480	official; rank-based merge
aplmuend	TD	0.2447	3394 / 8068	0.5760	translation of document representations
aplmuenq	TD	0.2456	4766 / 8068	0.5600	combination of aplmuena and aplmuend
aplmuenz	TD	0.2265	4772 / 8068	0.4840	score-based merge using monolingual runs

6 Conclusions

We set out to investigate how well a simplified approach to CLIR would work. By applying our language-neutral philosophy, we were able to submit monolingual and bilingual runs for each of the document collections. We repeated previous experiments and confirmed that character n-grams work well in many languages, including Finnish and Swedish which we had not previously studied. N-grams appear to have a decided advantage over words in Finnish retrieval. We also examined retrieval using cognate matches between close, and less close language pairs; as expected, performance is higher (relative to a monolingual baseline) with related pairs. Finally, we implemented a novel approach to multilingual retrieval that is similar to document translation – we transformed a bag-of-words representation of documents in many languages into a corresponding set of English terms using a bilingual dictionary. This processing is efficient and can be done at indexing time. As a result, multilingual queries from a single interlingua can be processed with no additional query-time processing beyond that normal for monolingual retrieval. Our preliminary results indicate that this approach is also 18% more effective than a baseline using score normalization and merging.

References

[1] M. Braschler and C. Peters, 'CLEF-2002: Methodology and Metrics', in this volume.

[2] C. Buckley, M. Mitra, J. Walz, and C. Cardie, 'Using Clustering and Super Concepts within SMART: TREC-6'. In E. Voorhees and D. Harman (eds.), *Proceedings of the Sixth Text REtrieval Conference (TREC-6),* NIST Special Publication 500-240, 1998.

[3] F. Gey, H. Jiang, A. Chen, and R. Larson, 'Manual Queries and Machine Translation in Cross-language Retrieval and Interactive Retrieval with Cheshire II at TREC-7'. In E. M. Voorhees and D. K. Harman, eds., *Proceedings of the Seventh Text REtrieval Conference (TREC-*7), pp. 527-540, 1999.

[4] W. Kraaij, 'TNO at CLEF-2001: Comparing Translation Resources.' In Carol Peters, Martin Braschler, Julio Gonzalo, and Michael Kluck (eds.), *Evaluation of Cross-Language Information Retrieval Systems: Proceedings of the CLEF 2001 Workshop, Lecture Notes in Computer Science 2406*, Springer, pp. 78-93, 2001.

[5] P. McNamee and J. Mayfield, 'JHU/APL Experiments at CLEF: Translation Resources and Score Normalization'. In Carol Peters, Martin Braschler, Julio Gonzalo, and Michael Kluck (eds.), *Evaluation of Cross-Language Information Retrieval Systems: Proceedings of the CLEF 2001 Workshop, Lecture Notes in Computer Science 2406*, Springer, pp. 193-208, 2001.

[6] Paul McNamee and James Mayfield, 'Comparing Cross-Language Query Expansion Techniques by Degrading Translation Resources'. In the *Proceedings of the 25th Annual International Conference on Research and Development in Information Retrieval (SIGIR-2002),* Tampere, Finland, August 2002.

[7] E. M. Voorhees, 'The Philosophy of Information Retrieval Evaluation.' In Carol Peters, Martin Braschler, Julio Gonzalo, and Michael Kluck (eds.), *Evaluation of Cross-Language Information Retrieval Systems: Proceedings of the CLEF 2001 Workshop, Lecture Notes in Computer Science 2406*, Springer, pp. 355-370, 2001.

[8] http://europa.eu.int/.

[9] http://www.foolabs.com/xpdf/.

Some Experiments with the Dutch Collection

Arjen P. de Vries[1] and Anne Diekema[2]

[1] CWI, Amsterdam, The Netherlands
arjen@acm.org
[2] CNLP, Syracuse University, Syracuse NY, USA
diekemar@syr.edu

Abstract. We performed some basic monolingual Dutch and bilingual English–Dutch experiments. The retrieval approach is very basic, without stemming or decompounding, using only a simple language model to rank the documents. In the bilingual task, the English queries have been analyzed by a system for question answering. The resulting queries are translated by dictionary lookup and ranked by the same basic retrieval system used in the monolingual task.

1 Introduction

Inspired by shared observations at the first CLEF workshop[1], the authors decided to initiate work on retrieval experiments that help understand the effect of the quality of the translation process on retrieval results.

We are primarily interested in the problem of multi-lingual retrieval from Dutch collections, and as we believe the quality of the resources for translation a significant factor in the retrieval results, we decided to focus on the bilingual English to Dutch task. Limiting ourselves to this task, we could deploy two high quality resources:

- a natural language processing toolkit aimed at (English) Question Answering, developed at CNLP [1];
- the CD-ROM edition of the (excellent) 'Van Dale Groot woordenboek', a dictionary for English to Dutch translation (and vice versa) [4].

2 Experimental Setup

For topic processing we used the language to logic module from the Center for Natural Language Processing (CNLP) as the front-end of our system. The language to logic (L2L) module converts a natural language query or question into a generic logical representation, which can be interpreted by different search engines. The conversion from language to logic takes place based on an internal query sublanguage grammar, which has been developed by CNLP. Prior to conversion, query processing such as stemming, stopword removal, and phrase

[1] 'We want better resources.'

C.A. Peters (Ed.): CLEF 2002, LNCS 2785, pp. 219–222, 2003.

and named entity recognition take place. Certain terms in the question are expanded with their synonyms or spelling variants, e.g., the term 'Koweit' upon encountering 'Kuwait'.

The terms occuring in the resulting expression are looked up in the dictionary. The Van Dale dictionary has been developed for interactive usage on the desktop only, for example to find a translation while writing a text document with your favourite word processor. Unfortunately, it lacks a command-line interface, which has rendered it unexpectedly difficult to apply as a component in an automatic translation system. As a workaround, we developed a screen-scraping tool based on the Win32 modules for the Perl scripting language: we discovered that the Van Dale application supports requests to lookup query words using DDE (a Windows protocol for data exchange). The results, displayed in the results pane, are copied through the Clipboard into our script by emulating the right sequence of keystrokes. The data captured on the Clipboard is then parsed and converted into a query-specific dictionary. Because some terms generate a large number of alternative translations for many different senses, we set some ad-hoc thresholds: a maximum amount of 10 translations per term, from a maximum of 5 different senses, but taking never more than 3 translations per sense.

The results of these two steps (as well as the documents in the collection) are converted to lower-case and stripped from 'strange' characters, and stopwords are removed. The retrieval backend is a database implementation of the simple – but proven effective – language models developed by Hiemstra [2] (more information about the retrieval backend is given in [3]). We intended to perform our experiments with an improved implementation that processes both phrases and disjunctive queries, but we did not finish our implementation work in time, so we have used the simple term-based model.

3 Analysis

The results of our experiments are summarized in Table 1. We submitted four runs, their names encoding the task – monolingual ('mo') or bilingual ('bi') – and the portion of the topics that has been processed: title only ('t') or title and description ('td').

The difference in mean average precision between title-only and title-and-description topics is surprisingly small in both tasks, especially since the title-only topics are quite short (2.5 word on average). A very large difference is found

Table 1. Results of the submitted runs

Run	Mean average precision
AAmoNLtd	0.399
AAmoNLt	0.348
AAbiENNLtd	0.162
AAbiENNLt	0.133

in topic C110, which is however explained easily since the description gives the name 'Kazem Radjavi' and the title does not. Apparently, only a small number of query terms really help to retrieve relevant documents, and those query terms tend to occur in both title and description.

The significantly decreased mean average precision of the bilingual runs when compared to the monolingual runs demonstrates that the query translation component of our system requires more work. A main cause of our disappointing results is the approach using the Van Dale dictionary through screen-scraping. First, communication via Clipboard cut-and-paste sometimes malfunctioned: the data would not appear on the Clipboard, probably due to timing problems. This makes it particularly difficult to check whether no translation occurred in the dictionary, or, the answer is not there due to communication problems. For example, a term like 'space probe' is found in the Van Dale dictionary, but the translation was unfortunately 'dropped' by our script (other examples are 'telephone', 'administration' and 'fishing'). Second, the Van Dale application performs a fuzzy match if the query term is not found, but checking whether that has happened would require an additional cut-and-paste of a different text pane. Finally, the copied data is not trivially interpreted by a machine, as it does contain instructions aimed at people, such as 'compare to' or 'see also'.

A deeper problem with our current approach lies in the interaction between different process steps. As a simple example, the front-end adds 'Koweit' as an alternative for 'Kuwait', but this alternative does not exist in the dictionary so is ignored further on in the process. In this particular case, it does not hurt effectiveness during the retrieval step, as 'Koweit' will not be found in the Dutch collection. A more interesting example of this problem is exposed when the additional intelligence in the front-end actually reduces effectiveness. A particularly good example of this case is provided by topic 91, *AI in Latin America*. The L2L module makes two wrong assumptions in this case: 'AI' is not 'Artificial Intelligence', and 'America' does not always imply 'United States'. The final result of the process is the following complex query: ('Artificial Intelligence' $\vee$ ('United States' $\vee$ 'United States of America' $\vee$ 'US' $\vee$ 'USA'). Of course, the original untranslated query terms are added, but given that the retrieval model emphasizes frequent query words, most of the results discuss indeed artificial intelligence in the US, and not Amnesty International in Latin America as desired.

4 Next Steps

Summarizing our current experimental results, we must conclude we have not made much progress since the first CLEF workshop. Still, we find ourselves in need of basic resources such as the dictionary; while the chosen 'Van Dale' seems an excellent tool for interactive usage during a word processing session on a Windows desktop, its application in an automatic retrieval system has proven problematic. Although some of the ambiguities in the translation instructions can be interpreted automatically, the current screen-scraping solution is not sufficiently reliable as a basis for further retrieval experiments upon.

to three translations for each word) in the final translated query. The source query languages were Spanish, Chinese, and Japanese; the target language documents were in English. In this report, we describe our translation disambiguation methods and present their performance results.

2 CLARIT Cross-Language Information Retrieval

For cross-language information retrieval, both the documents and the queries need to be represented in the same language at some point in the process [9]. In our experiments, we adopted the query translation approach. First, the query terms in the source languages were translated into all possible terms in the target language using translation lexicons. Some of these translations were retained according to the methods described below. The retained terms in the target language (English, here) were used for retrieving documents from the target collection. For all document processing—including query and document indexing and retrieval—we used the Clarit system [5], in particular, the functions for NLP (morphological analysis and phrase recognition), IR (term weighting and phrasal decomposition), and "thesaurus extraction" (for effecting pseudo-relevance feedback).

2.1 Spanish Topic Processing and Translation

Spanish queries were processed as follows. The text of the Spanish query was tokenized and morphologically analyzed using a Spanish version of Clarit. Only nouns, verbs, adjectives, and adverbs were retained for further treatment. Some additional words were removed via a stop list containing a total of 400 words. This list includes all prepositions, pronouns, and articles (which were already removed using the morphological analyzer); common stop words such as *es* and *cada*; and query metalanguage from previous CLEF queries such as *describir* and *discutir*.

As an example of our processing consider the Spanish query on the Leaning Tower of Pisa (Topic 136): *Torre inclinada de Pisa. ¿En qué estado se encuentra la torre inclinada de Pisa?* After morphological analysis and stop word removal, this query becomes torre, inclinar, pisa, estado, torre, inclinar, pisa. Each of these words is then looked up in a Spanish–English word-to-word dictionary, which contains the translations found in Table 1.

We created our Spanish-English gloss lexicon by combining various lexicons available on the Web. The final collation was not manually edited; stop words were automatically removed from the English translations (unless the only translation was a stop word); and the Spanish side of the dictionary was lemmatized (e.g., an original gloss such as inclinado—apt to was reduced to inclinar—apt in our experimental version). If a source word was not found in the dictionary then the original source word was retained in lieu of a translation. The resulting translations formed the basis of the English queries that were generated by the methods described below.

Table 1. English translations found in our bilingual dictionary for the Spanish words in Topic 136 in one of the CLEF queries

estado	inclinar	pisa	torre
state states statis	apt bow drooping incline inclined inclining sloping stooping titling verging	pisa	high tower towers

We can note here two limitations of our technique: (1) The dictionaries are neither clean nor complete. Notice that *leaning* is missing from the above translations of *inclinar*. (2) We have restricted ourselves to word-to-word translations for engineering reasons, even though we know that phrasal translation results in superior performance in CLIR [8]. If we were to go beyond a research version of our system, investments in reducing these limitations would need to be made.

2.2 Chinese Topic Processing and Translation

Since spaces are not used in Chinese text for word segmentation, we first broke Chinese text into individual words. We used the longest-match method, which greedily recognizes an initial string of characters as a word if the string matches a word in the segmentation dictionary. We obtained a Chinese-to-English wordlist from the Linguistics Data Consortium[1] (LDC). This bilingual wordlist contains a list of Chinese words together with their possible English translations—a total of 188,474 entries. We did not edit or further "clean" the lexicon. Our run-time segmentation dictionary consisted of the Chinese words from this wordlist augmented with all possible single Chinese characters and symbols. By using the words from the bilingual wordlist, we ensured that the words identified during segmentation would have glosses during translation.

Once we obtained the segmented Chinese words, we first removed stop words automatically via a stop word list. The list contains a total of 3,894 entries, including closed-class words (e.g., symbols, prepositions, pronouns, and particles), numerals, and query specific terms such as 报导 and 文章, collected from CLEF 2001 topics. Then we translated the remaining words into English using the LDC bilingual wordlist. Lastly, we used the translation disambiguation methods (described below) to select the best translation for a query word.

As an example of our processing, consider the Chinese version of the *Leaning Tower of Pisa* query (Topic 136): 比萨斜塔; 比萨斜塔的健康情况如何？ First the query is segmented as:

---

[1] http://www.ldc.upenn.edu/Projects/Chinese/LDC_ch.htm#e2cdict

萨 ; 斜 ; 塔 ; 比萨 ; 斜 ; 塔 ; 的 ; 健康 ; 情况 ; 如何 ; ? ;

After the stop-word removal, the query contains unique words: 比萨 ; 斜 ; 塔 ; 健康 ; 情况. Each of these words is then looked up in the Chinese–English bilingual wordlist, which yields the following translations:

比萨	斜	塔	健康	情况
pisa	askant slanting	ter pagoda tower	hygeia exuberance health healthiness	circumstance circumstantiality situation state affairs

We should note that there are several problems with the longest-match method that can cause segmentation errors. First, the greedy algorithm may break words in the wrong places when word boundaries are ambiguous. Generally, a wrong segmentation will result in more subsequent segmentation errors. Second, the coverage of the dictionary will affect segmentation quality. Missing dictionary words will result in single characters being generated during segmentation. For bilingual retrieval, this not only reduces term quality, but also increases ambiguity, since single characters are generally more ambiguous than multiple character words. This is especially a problem with proper names, where the meanings of the single characters in the names bear no relation to the meaning of the name. In the pre-processing of topics, we eliminated any sequence of more than three consecutive single characters. This helped reduce translation noise, but without proper handling of names, we still lost the specific information associated with deleted characters, which tended to render the topics too general.

3 Translation Disambiguation Methods

Given that a source language term can give more than one possible target translation, we want to find the best or the best few translations for each non-stop word in the source topic. Our methods for disambiguating alternative possible translations are based on two observations:

- The correct translation for the query term, given its potential translations in a target language, is generally not ambiguous when context (i.e., other terms in the query) is considered.
- The Web and reference corpora can be used as practical resources for estimating the coherence of the translated terms. Each provides a language model of how words co-occur. In particular, we expect that words that are found to co-occur are lexically-semantically cohesive.

For example, suppose the query terms $s_1,\ldots,s_5$ in the source language have the translations in the target language as follows:

s_1	s_2	s_3	s_4	s_5
t_{11}	t_{21}	t_{31}	t_{41}	t_{51}
t_{12}	t_{22}	t_{32}		t_{52}
t_{13}		t_{33}		
		t_{34}		

Term s_1 has three possible translations: t_{11}, t_{12}, and t_{13}. A context for t_{11} can be constructed as one of the possible sequences including the other translations in the target language, such as,

$<t_{11}, t_{21}, t_{31}, t_{41}, t_{51}>$
$<t_{11}, t_{21}, t_{32}, t_{41}, t_{51}>$
$<t_{11}, t_{21}, t_{33}, t_{41}, t_{51}>$
$<t_{11}, t_{21}, t_{34}, t_{41}, t_{51}>$
...
$<t_{13}, t_{22}, t_{34}, t_{41}, t_{52}>$

In this example, there are a total of $3 \times 2 \times 4 \times 1 \times 2$ (i.e., 48) possible sequences or paths through the translation space. Each path establishes a context for the translated terms with respect to their neighbors. We assume that the best path of all combinations will demonstrate the best coherence among the translated terms.

We have developed several practical methods to measure the quality (or coherence) of translation paths based on evidence of actual word co-occurrence in reference corpora. One of these methods takes advantage of the World Wide Web (WWW) and two use the actual target test collection, as described in the following sections.

3.1 Web Method

The Web method is an elaboration of the ideas explored by Grefenstette [7], namely, using the WWW as the language model for choosing translations. The idea of using the Web to acquire general language models is becoming more popular. (See also [11] for an application for speech.) To exploit the Web, we first create sequences of possible translations. Each sequence is sent to a popular Web portal (here, AltaVista) to discover how often the combination of translations appears. The number of occurrences of a translation is used as the score for the sequence. The complete algorithm is as follows:

1. Get translations for each term in the source language query;
2. Construct a hypothesis space of translated sequences (overlapping word *n*-grams, *n=3* in our experiments) by obtaining all possible combinations of the translations in a source sequence of *n* query words;
3. For each translated sequence in the hypothesis space,
   3.1 Send it to a Web portal (e.g., AltaVista);
   3.2 Call the number of pages on which that translated sequence occurs *the coherence score* for the query;
   3.3 Select the translation for each source word that has the best coherence score.
4. Collate the selected translations into a new target language query.

Since word order is not preserved from one language to another, the query sent to the Web uses an operator that enforces presence of the translated sequence but not sequence order. AltaVista's advanced search supports the operator NEAR, which ensures that the words so linked appear within ten words of each other, in any order. We use this operator to calculate the score of the sequence.

Since the Web searches do not stem search terms, we expanded each translation by linking all surface forms of the search term by OR. For example, if the translated sequence being scored was "big black dogs" then the following, advanced AltaVista query was generated:

(big OR bigger OR biggest) NEAR (black OR blacks OR blacked OR blacking OR blackest OR blacking) NEAR (dog OR dogs)

For the 42 Spanish topics used in the CLEF 2002 experiments, the Web method generates a total of 11,500 word 3-grams for Web search, with each Web access to the AltaVista site taking an average of 7 seconds through a T1 network.

The Web method has the advantage of a massive reference corpus: most candidate translations (paths) will result in some "hits" and the number of hits for meaningful combinations of words will typically be much greater than for meaningless ones. It has the potential disadvantage that the texts on the Web may bear little or no direct relation to the texts (or domain) of the target search. In theory, a narrowly focused target search (e.g., in a technical domain reflected by many documents concentrated in the database to be searched) might be under-represented in the Web corpus compared to alternative, more common documents. To mitigate this possibility, we also explored two methods that use only the target texts for co-occurrence evidence.

3.2 Target Corpus Methods

An alternative reference corpus for language modeling, particularly modeling the coherence of combinations of translation alternatives, is the target corpus itself. We use the target corpus as the basis for choosing a "best" translation of a query, exploiting approaches developed by Evans [3], [4]. We implemented two target-corpus methods ("Corpus1" and "Corpus2").

3.2.1 Corpus1

The Corpus1 method has the following steps:

1. Get translations for each term in the query.
2. Construct a hypothesis space of translated queries by obtaining all possible combinations of the translations.
3. For each translated sequence in the hypothesis space,
   3.1 Send it to the target database;
   3.2 Compute the sum of the similarities scores of the top *N* retrieval documents as the coherence score of the sequence.
4. Select the sequence (or sequences) with the best coherence score.

The Corpus1 method computes the coherence score for every path in the hypothesis space. This can be computationally expensive when the query terms have many possible translations. In our experiments, we reduced the hypothesis space by using a maximum of three translations for each query term. In cases where there were more than three alternative translations, we chose the three terms with the smallest distribution scores in the target corpus. For summing similarity scores, we set N to 100.

3.2.2 Corpus2

The Corpus2 method makes use of the mutual information of two terms based on corpus statistics. The method works as follows:

1. Get translations for each term in the source language query.
2. Construct a hypothesis space of translated sequences (overlapping word n-grams, $n=3$ in our experiments) by obtaining all possible combinations of the translations in a source sequence of n query words.
3. For each translated sequence in the hypothesis space,
   3.1 Compute mutual information (MI) scores for all term pairs in the sequence;
   3.2 Sum up the scores from step 3.1 to give a coherence score for the sequence;
   3.3 Select as a translation of the first source word in the sequence the alternative that gives the best coherence score.
4. Collate the selected translations into a new target language query.

The mutual information between two term t_1 and t_2 is defined as:

$$MI(t_1,t_2) = \log \frac{p(t_1,t_2)}{p(t_1)p(t_2)} . \tag{1}$$

where $p(t_1)$ is the probability of observing term t_1, $p(t_2)$ the probability of observing term t_2, and $p(t_1,t_2)$ the probability of observing both terms together within a text window. $p(t_1)$ is estimated as $C(t_1)/N$, $p(t_2)$ is estimated as $C(t_2)/N$, and $p(t_1,t_2)$ is estimated as $C(t_1,t_2)/N$, where $C(t_1)$, $C(t_2)$, and $C(t_1,t_2)$ represent, respectively, the numbers of occurrences of term t_1, term t_2, and terms t_1 and t_2 together. N is the collection size, with a value of 32,581,138.

To compute the coherence score of each translated sequence at Step 3, we first calculate the mutual information score for each pair of translations in the sequence. Then we take the sum of the mutual information scores of all translation pairs as the score of the sequence. Thus, for a 3-term window consisting of translations t_1, t_2, and t_3, the final coherence score for the sequence is the sum of $MI(t_1,t_2)$, $MI(t_1,t_3)$, and $MI(t_2,t_3)$.

In contrast to the Corpus1 method, which relies on retrieval from the target corpus for computing the coherence score for each hypothetical sequence, the Corpus2 method only needs the frequency counts of term uni-grams and bi-grams, which can be prepared before the translation disambiguation process. Thus, the Corpus2 method is much faster for translation disambiguation and likely to be more desirable in an interactive cross-language retrieval setting.

3.3 An Illustrative Example

As an example, for Topic 136 (as presented in Section 2), we give the target translations for the source query terms as determined by the above three translation disambiguation methods. (This reflects a "combined" method in which all the "best" terms of each method are retained for the final translated query.) In cases where the methods produced different "best" translations, we separate each candidate translation by a comma (",").

Topic 136

English: *Leaning Tower of Pisa. What is the state of health of the Leaning Tower of Pisa?*
English terms: lean tower; pisa; lean; tower; health; state.

Spanish: *Torre inclinada de Pisa . ¿En qué estado se encuentra la torre inclinada de Pisa?*
English translations of the Spanish query terms: pisa; high, tower; state; droop, tilt, bow.

Chinese: 比萨斜塔; 比萨斜塔的健康情况如何？
English translations of the Chinese query terms: pisa; ter, tower; slant; health; affair, situation; health situation

For our actual submissions reflecting a particular method (e.g., Web), we naturally used only those "best" terms that the method itself nominated. In addition to our official runs, our experiments included a combined method that uses the full set of terms (as given above) for the final target query. We describe the performance results of the combined method along with our official and baseline results in the next section.

4 Experiments

Our CLIR experiment labels have the following naming convention:

Cl<source-language>2<target-language><method>

Thus, "Cles2enw" denotes our Spanish-to-English Web-method run. The actual experiments involved separate runs for each of the three translation disambiguation methods described in Section 3 (the "w", "t1", and "t2" runs), and also runs with combined methods ("c1", based on a combination of the Web and Corpus1 methods, and "c2", based on all three methods). In all cases, combinations involved a simple concatenation of the selected translations nominated by each participating method. To establish a baseline for evaluating the quality of translation disambiguation, we used all possible translations in a default run ("all"). We ran English monolingual experiments to obtain the baseline with ideal translations.

All the experiments were run with post-translation pseudo-relevance feedback, as we have observed that post-translation pseudo-relevance feedback produces the best overall performance boost [10]. The feedback-related parameters were based on calibration runs using CLEF 2001 topics. The settings for Spanish-to-English retrieval were: extracting T=50 terms from the top N=25 retrieved documents, with an additional term cutoff percentage set to P=0.1. For Chinese-to-English retrieval: T=50, N=25, P=0.01. For English monolingual retrieval: T=75, N=50, P=0.8. We used a variation of Rocchio weighting to identify terms for selection.

All runs were automatic. All the queries used the title and description fields (Title+Description) of the topics provided by CLEF 2002. The results presented below are based on relevance judgments of 42 topics. The topics not evaluated include 93, 96, 101, 110, 117, 118, 127, and 132, as these were not listed among the official results (because they have no relevant documents in the target corpus).

Table 2 and Table 3 give the results for our submitted runs, together with our other experimental runs for comparative analysis. For Spanish-to-English cross-language retrieval, compared with the baseline of keeping all possible translations, both the Web-based and corpus-based methods improve the average precision by 2.5% to 14.4%. The Web method and the Corpus2 method improve the exact precision by 17.2% and 5%, respectively. Overall recall decreases for the corpus-based methods, while it improves a little (0.6%) for the Web run. By combining the methods, the overall recall, average precision, and exaction precision all improve over the baseline. The combination of all three disambiguation methods produces the best average precision and exact precision, achieving 97.3% and 97.9% of the average precision and exact precision of the English monolingual retrieval results. The best recall is achieved by combining the Web method and the Corpus1 method, reaching 95.7% of that of English monolingual retrieval.

For Chinese-to-English cross-language retrieval, compared with the bilingual baseline of keeping all possible translations, both the Web-based method and the Corpus2 method improve average precision and exact precision, while only the Corpus2 method improves recall. The Corpus1 method did not perform well compared with the baseline. Again, when the methods are combined, we observe improvements over the overall recall, average precision, and exact precision. The best run, with all three translation disambiguation methods combined, reached 89.0%, 59.7%, and 62.9% of the recall, average precision, and exact precision, respectively, of the English monolingual run.

Since pseudo-relevance feedback can affect performance differently depending on the original query terms, in our follow-up experiments, we re-computed the results without using pseudo-relevance feedback to best estimate the quality of the selected translations against the baseline. Table 4 and Table 5 give the results without feedback for both language pairs.

Regardless of whether pseudo-relevance feedback is used or not, the Chinese–English retrieval is generally poor. Beside translation ambiguity, the bilingual translation lexicon is very noisy, with many wrong word choices, occasional misspellings, and interfering descriptive text. In addition, wrong word segmentation resulted from incomplete segmentation dictionary coverage and the greedy longest match segmentation algorithm.

Table 2. Spanish-to-English retrieval performance with post-translation pseudo-relevance feedback. The runs in boldface are our submitted runs

Run ID	Method	Recall (over baseline)	AP (over base)	EP (over base)
Cles2enw	**Web**	**720/821 (+0.6%)**	**0.3502 (+14.4%)**	**0.3399 (+17.2%)**
Cles2ent1	**Corpus1**	**664/821 (-7.3%)**	**0.3137 (+2.5%)**	**0.2871 (-1.0%)**
Cles2ent2	**Corpus2**	**706/821 (-1.4%)**	**0.3310 (+8.2%)**	**0.3046 (+5.0%)**
Cles2encl	**Web, Corpus1**	**750/821 (+4.8%)**	**0.3478 (+13.7%)**	**0.3276 (+12.9%)**
Cles2enc2	Web, Corpus1, Corpus2	744/821 (+3.9%)	0.3583 (+17.1%)	0.3441 (+18.6%)
Cles2enall (baseline)	All possible translations	716/821	0.3060	0.2901
English	*original English topics*	*784/821*	*0.3682*	*0.3514*

Table 3. Chinese-to-English retrieval performance with post-translation pseudo-relevance feedback. The runs in boldface are our submitted runs

Run ID	Method	Recall (over baseline)	AP (over base)	EP (over base)
Clch2enw	**Web**	**591/821 (-9.2%)**	**0.1795 (+2.8%)**	**0.1752 (+3.2%)**
Clch2ent1	**Corpus1**	**558/821 (-14.3%)**	**0.1322 (-24.3%)**	**0.1262 (-25.6%)**
Clch2ent2	**Corpus2**	**655/821 (+0.6%)**	**0.1936 (+10.9%)**	**0.1853 (+9.2%)**
Clch2encl	**Web, Corpus1**	**653/821 (+0.3%)**	**0.1858 (+6.4%)**	**0.1841 (+8.5%)**
Clch2enc2	Web, Corpus1, Corpus2	698/821 (+7.2%)	0.2199 (+25.9%)	0.2209 (+30.2%)
Clch2enall (baseline)	All possible translations	651/821	0.1746	0.1697
English	*original English topics*	*784/821*	*0.3682*	*0.3514*

For Spanish–English cross-language retrieval, all three translation disambiguation methods outperform the baseline in terms of recall, average precision, and exact precision (except recall with the Corpus1 method). The combinations of the methods outperform any individual method participating in the combinations. For Chinese–English cross-language retrieval, both the Web method and the Corpus2 method improve average precision and exact precision, while the Corpus1 method performs less well with these measures compared with the baseline. All three methods resulted in a decrease in recall performance. The combinations generally outperform any individual method participating in the combinations, except for recall of the Clch2enc1-nf run.

Table 4. Spanish-to-English retrieval performance without pseudo-relevance feedback

Run ID	Method	Recall (over baseline)	AP (over base)	EP (over base)
Cles2enw-nf	Web	684/821 (+1.3%)	0.2940 (+27.5%)	0.2776 (+19.2%)
Cles2ent1-nf	Corpus1	620/821 (-8.2%)	0.2608 (+13.1%)	0.2417 (+3.8%)
Cles2ent2-nf	Corpus2	679/821 (+0.6%)	0.3035 (+31.6%)	0.3087 (+32.6%)
Cles2enc1-nf	Web, Corpus1	702/821 (+4.0%)	0.3110 (+34.9%)	0.2948 (+26.6%)
Cles2enc2-nf	Web, Corpus1, Corpus2	695/821 (+3.0%)	0.3079 (+33.5%)	0.2955 (+26.9%)
Cles2enall-nf (baseline)	All possible translations	675/821	0.2306	0.2328
English-nf	*original English topics*	*770/821*	*0.3331*	*0.3156*

A summary of our results focusing on average precision is given schematically in Figure 1. In general, our best results for Spanish-to-English CLIR are virtually indistinguishable from English monolingual performance. Our best results for Chinese-to-English CLIR, suffering from the effects of poor resources, are at about 60% of the monolingual baseline.

Table 5. Chinese-to-English retrieval performance without pseudo-relevance feedback

Run ID	Method	Recall (over baseline)	AP (over base)	EP (over base)
Clch2enw-nf	Web	521/821 (-11.5%)	0.1547 (+20.8%)	0.1630 (+27.5%)
Clch2ent1-nf	Corpus1	534/821 (-9.3%)	0.1094 (-14.6%)	0.1026 (-19.7%)
Clch2ent2-nf	Corpus2	575/821 (-2.4%)	0.1510 (+17.9%)	0.1460 (+14.2%)
Clch2enc1-nf	Web, Corpus1	588/821 (-0.2%)	0.1556 (+21.5%)	0.1608 (+25.8%)
Clch2enc2-nf	Web, Corpus1, Corpus2	613/821 (+4.1%)	0.1761 (+37.5%)	0.1858 (+45.4%)
Clch2enall-nf (baseline)	All possible translations	589/821	0.1281	0.1278
English-nf	*original English topics*	*770/821*	*0.3331*	*0.3156*

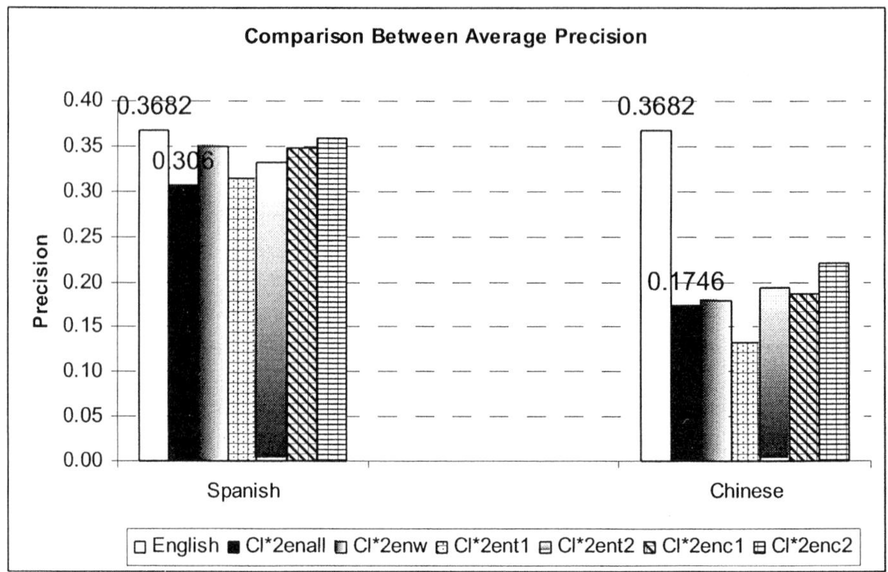

Fig. 1. Comparative analysis of average precision, with the English run as the monolingual retrieval baseline and the Cl*2enall runs as the cross-language retrieval baseline. The best results are achieved by the combination of all three translation disambiguation methods, Cl*2enc2

5 Error Analysis

Comparing the English baseline run to the Spanish-to-English Web run (Cles2enw), we find that 16 of the translated Spanish-to-English queries actually give better or equal results in terms of average precision than the English queries, 26 are worse (of which 12 are much worse, with less than half the average precision of the English queries). (See Figure 2.)

Some of the reasons for improved results are:

- Different word choice, e.g.:
  - Population in the English version of Topic 95 (Conflict in Palestine) becomes town in the Spanish-to-English translation of poblacion.
  - *Ski races* in the English version of Topic 102 becomes *ski competition* in the translations.
  - The English version of Topic 106 (*European car industry*) contains *countermeasures*, whereas the Spanish contains *medidas de recuperacion,* which is translated by the methods described above as *recovery measures*, which are more common words than *countermeasures*, which is usually found in political rather than business contexts in the CLEF documents.

- In Topic 140 (*Mobile phones*), the English version contains *perspectives* and the Spanish version contains *perspectiva*, which can be translated as *outlook, perspective, prospect,* and *vista* via our dictionary, and our method chooses *outlook*, a more common word, which might well account for why this topic scores better after translation.

- Different word ordering: Clarit recognizes noun phrases in the English text; in the Spanish-to-English text, a query is repeated backwards and forwards so that different phrases may be recognized in the reconstituted topic, e.g.:
  - *Weapon destruction* appears in the translation of Topic 119, whereas *weapon* and *destruction* are not found in the same simple noun phrase in the English topic.
  - *Grunge rock* appears in the translation of Topic 130 while the English contains *grunge group*.

- Different formulations of the same topic in English and Spanish, e.g.:
  - Topic 121 (*Successes of Ayrton Senna*) contains the more general terms *success* and *sporting achievements* while the Spanish version contains the more precise word *palmares*, which is not in the Spanish-English dictionary and not translated in the resulting English version of the Spanish topic. It could be that the vaguer English words *successes* and *achievements* lead to the retrieval of a greater number of irrelevant documents that become distractors vis-a-vis relevant documents for Ayrton Senna.
  - Topic 138 (*Foreign words in French*) contains *lengua*, which translates to *language* not present in the English version.

Some of the reasons for worse results are:

- Proper names written differently and not in the dictionary, e.g.:
  - *Solzhenitsyn* (Topic 94) is written *Solzhenitsin* in the Spanish topic and is retained with the same spelling in the translated queries since it is not found in the dictionary.
  - *European Cup* (Topic 113) is written *Eurocopa* in Spanish and is not in the dictionary, so it passes through as-is, but is not found as a string in the English documents.

- Dictionary divergences, e.g.:
  - In Topic 107 (*Genetic Engineering*), *food chain* appears as *cadena alimentaria* in Spanish, but *alimentaria* does not have *food* among its translations.

Comparing the English baseline run to the Chinese-to-English runs, we observe that most of the translated queries are worse in average precision compared with that of the English run. As in Spanish-to-English retrieval, the combination of the three methods (Clch2enc2) produces the best overall performance: 12 of the translated queries give better average precision than the English queries and 30 are worse (Figure 3).

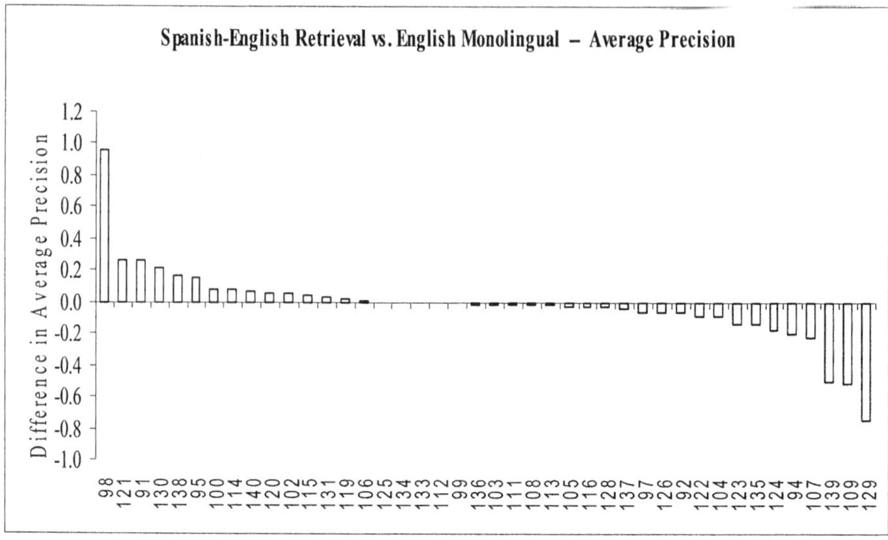

Fig. 2. Query-by-query comparison of precision between the Spanish–English retrieval run (Cles2enw) and English monolingual retrieval

The better performance is due to:

- Reduced ambiguity in translation, e.g.:
  - In Topic 113 (*European Cup*), the English version uses the word *football*, while the target translations include the word *soccer*. Since *football* can mean *soccer* or *American football*, the translation makes the query more relevant to the topic.
- Difference in word choice, e.g.:
  - In Topic 133 (*German Armed Forces Out-of-Area*), the English version uses the word *area*, while the Chinese version uses *border*. As our system throws out *out* and *of* as stop words, the word *area* becomes too general, while *border* implies country boundaries.

Some of the reasons for the poor performance are:

- Improper segmentation of words, e.g.:
  - In Topic 111 (电脑动画), the word 动画 was segmented as two characters 动 (with translations of *act*, *arouse*, *get moving*, *move*, *stir*, *act*, *change*, *use*, *touch*, etc.) and 画 (with translations of *draw*, *painting*, *picture*). As a result, our system produced translations such as *use picture* instead of the correct translation *animation*.
  - Similar segmentation mistakes include: 银河 (galaxy) in Topic 129 as 银 (*silver*) and 河 (*river*); 选美 (beauty contest) in Topic 137 as 选 (*to choose, to elect, to pick, to select*) and 美 (*America, beautiful, pretty*).
  - 欧联渔获 (*EU fishing*) in Topic 139 was rendered as four single characters 欧 , 联 , 渔 , 获 , which were consequently filtered out by the system.

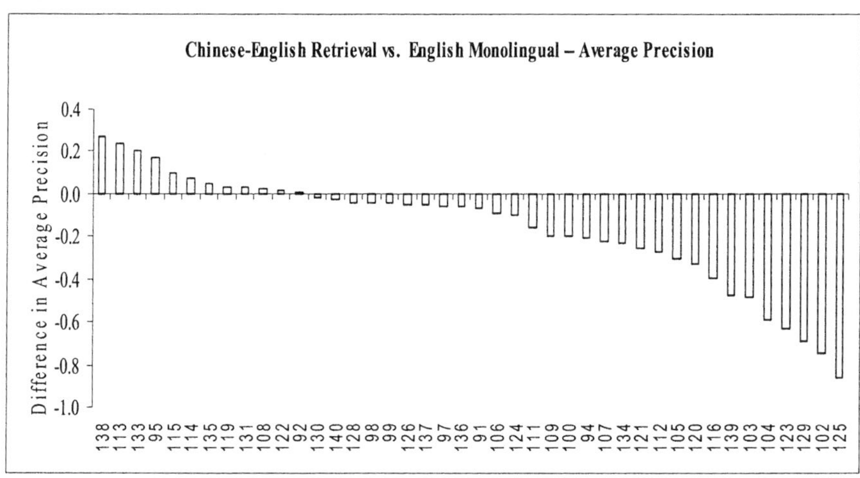

Fig. 3. Query-by-query comparison of precision between the best Chinese–English retrieval run (Clch2enc2) and English monolingual retrieval

- Improper segmentation of transliterated names, e.g.:
  - Topic 102 (阿尔伯特·托姆巴的胜利) is segmented as:

阿；尔；伯 ；特；·；托；姆；巴；的；胜利；
寻找；有关；阿；尔；伯；特；托；姆；巴；获得；滑雪；竞赛的；报导；。；

The name 阿尔伯特·托姆巴 has been incorrectly segmented into seven single characters that have no direct semantic relation to the transliterated name. During pre-processing of the topics, we filtered out the consecutive single characters. As a result, the query contained only general terms such as 胜利 (*victory*), 滑雪 (*ski*), and 竞赛的 (*competition*). The best precision was achieved by the Web run at 0.1078. In contrast, in the English query (*Victories of Alberto Tomba*), the name, *Alberto Tomba*, as a term makes the query very specific, resulting in high precision (0.7491).

  - Other topics that suffered similarly include: Topic 94 (Return of Solzhenitsy), 98 (Films by the Kaurismäkis), 103 (Conflict of interests in Italy), 104 (Super G Gold medal), 120 (Edouard Balladur), 121 (Successes of Ayrton Senna), and 123 (Marriage Jackson-Presley).
- Different word choice, e.g.:
  - The translations of the word 遗传 in Topic 107 (遗传工程) are *transmit*, *transmittal*, and *hereditary*, instead of the desired translation *genetic*.
  - In Topic 99, *Holocaust* is represented in Chinese as 屠杀 (*butchery*, *massacre*).

6 Post-CLEF Experiments

After the CLEF workshop, we obtained the CLEF 2002 Japanese topics and conducted Japanese-to-English retrieval experiments.

As in Chinese, spaces are not used in Japanese text to mark word boundaries. Again, we used the longest-match word segmentation method, based on EDICT[2], a Japanese-to-English wordlist that contains a list of Japanese words and their English translations. The wordlist contains about 179,000 entries. For word segmentation, we used the Japanese words from the EDICT.

Once we obtained the segmented Japanese words, we first removed stop words via a very limited stop word list of a total of 284 entries, which includes functional words (particles, pronouns, etc.) and punctuations. Then we translated the remaining words into English using the EDICT bilingual wordlist. The English translations of the bilingual wordlist were normalized by removing English stop words. Lastly, we used the translation disambiguation methods described in section 3 to select the best translation for a query word.

As an example of our processing, the Japanese version of Topic 136 (*the Leaning Tower of Pisa query*) ピサの斜塔. ピサの斜塔の状態はどうか？ is segmented as:

ピサの斜塔; ピサの斜塔; の; 状態; は; どうか; ？;

After the stop-word removal, the query contains unique words: ピサの斜塔；状態；どうか； After lexicon lookup, this yields the following translations:

ピサの斜塔	情况	どうか
leaning tower pisa	condition situation circumstances state	please somehow or other

As with Chinese, the quality of the translated queries can suffer due to word segmentation errors and missing translations in the bilingual wordlist.

We conducted Japanese-to-English retrieval experiments with the three translation disambiguation methods and the two translation combination methods. All runs used post-translation pseudo-relevance feedback, with T=50, N=25, and P=0.01. Again, a variation of Rocchio weighting was used to identify terms for selection.

Compared with the bilingual baseline of keeping all possible translations, the two corpus-based methods improve average precision, while the average precision for the web-based method is worse than the baseline (Table 5). All three methods resulted in decreased recall. The two combination methods improve recall, average precision, and exact precision over the baseline. The best overall performance is achieved by combining the Web method, the Corpus1 method, and the Corpus2 method, reaching 82.4%, 69.3%, and 74.1% of the recall, average precision, and exact precision of that of English monolingual retrieval, respectively; 17 of the translated queries give better or equal average precision than the English queries and 25 are worse (Figure 4).

---

[2] http://www.csse.monash.edu.au/~jwb/edict.html.

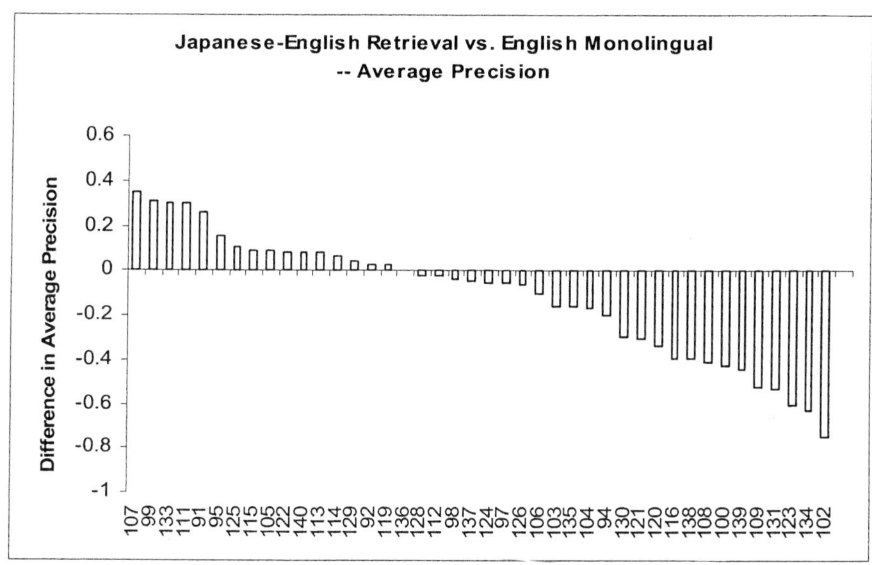

Fig. 4. Query-by-query comparison of precision between the best Japanese-English retrieval run (Cljp2enc2) and English monolingual retrieval

Table 6. Japanese-to-English retrieval performance with post-translation pseudo-relevance feedback

Run ID	Method	Recall (over baseline)	AP (over base)	EP (over base)
Cljp2enw	Web	588/821 (-5.9%)	0.2022 (-12.8%)	0.1942 (-8.6%)
Cljp2ent1	Corpus1	601/821 (-3.8%)	0.2329 (+0.4%)	0.2254 (+6.1%)
Cljp2ent2	Corpus2	607/821 (-1.4%)	0.2541 (+9.5%)	0.2328 (+9.6%)
Cljp2enc1	Web, Corpus1	637/821 (+1.9%)	0.2497 (+7.6%)	0.2494 (+17.4%)
Cljp2enc2	Web, Corpus1, Corpus2	654/821 (+4.6%)	0.2551 (+10.0%)	0.2605 (+22.6%)
Cljp2enal 1 (base-line)	All possi-ble trans-lations	625/821	0.2320	0.2124
English	*original English topics*	*784/821*	*0.3682*	*0.3514*

As in Chinese-to-English runs, the Japanese-to-English runs also suffer from improper segmentation of words and transliterated names and different word choice. In particular, transliteration is more prevalent in Japanese than in Chinese, since, not only names, but many terminological terms are liberally transliterated as katakana, which makes good coverage of a lexicon a challenge. Methods that can take a katakana word and then back transliterate the word to its English original should help.

We have also experimented with different window sizes as the context for translation disambiguation. While we have tested varying window sizes (3-, 4-, and 5-term windows), it is not clear from the empirical results which context size is the best option. The optimal context size is open to further investigation.

7 Conclusions

We have explored three methods for selecting "best" target translations that take advantage of co-occurrence statistics among alternative translations of the source query words. We have demonstrated that, given a wide variety of possible translations that might be generated from a bilingual dictionary, the use of the Web or a local large corpus as a language model can provide a good basis for lexical choice, provided the gloss dictionary covers the source vocabulary. Combining the target words obtained from the different translation disambiguation methods can produce better cross-language retrieval performance, as compared to keeping all possible translations. For Spanish-to-English retrieval, our combined method achieved 95% and 97%, respectively, of the recall and average precision of our English monolingual run. For Chinese-to-English text retrieval, the recall and average precision reached 89% and 60%, respectively, of the English monolingual results. For Japanese-to-English text retrieval, the best recall and average precision reached 82% and 69%, respectively, of the English monolingual results.

Our experiments have shown that the quality of the translation resources has a significant impact on the performance of cross-language retrieval. The poor translation quality and poor coverage of the Chinese-to-English bilingual lexicon we used resulted in relatively poor performance of the Chinese-to-English retrieval. Similarly, we observe poor performance for Japanese-to-English retrieval. Names (transliterated names in CLEF topics, in particular) that are not covered in a translation lexicon need to be recognized and translated correctly for better retrieval performance.

In general, we feel our results demonstrate that it is possible to achieve remarkably high CLIR performance by exploiting relatively simple and available resources. Such approaches hold promise for cross-language retrieval in cases where machine translation, parallel corpora, or other knowledge resources may be difficult or impossible to obtain. We believe that poor coverage of bilingual lexicons remains a bottleneck for better CLIR performance. We have begun to explore techniques for automatically translating phrasal terms and for automatically acquiring name transliterations, and plan to incorporate the acquired resources in future CLIR experiments.

References

[1] Ballesteros, L., and W. B. Croft: Resolving Ambiguity for Cross-Language Retrieval. In Proceedings of ACM SIGIR (1998) 64–71

[2] Davis, M. W., and W. C. Ogden. QUILT: Implementing a Large-Scale Cross-Language Text Retrieval System. In Proceedings of ACM SIGIR (1997) 92-98
[3] Evans, D.A: Method and Apparatus for Cross Linguistic Document Retrieval. U.S. Patent # 6,055,528 (2000)
[4] Evans, D.A.: Method and Apparatus for Cross Linguistic Database Retrieval. U.S. Patent # 6,263,329 (a division of U.S. Patent # 6,055,528) (2001)
[5] Evans, D.A., and R.G. Lefferts: CLARIT–TREC Experiments. Information Processing and Management, Vol.31, No.3 (1995) 385–395
[6] Grefenstette, G.: The Problem of Cross-Language Information Retrieval. In G. Grefenstette, editor, Cross-Language Information Retrieval, Chapter 1. Kluwer Academic Publishers, Boston, (1998) 1-9
[7] Grefenstette, G.: The WWW as a resource for example-based MT tasks. In Proc., ASLIB Translating and the Computer 21 Conference, London (1999)
[8] Hull, D.A. and G. Grefenstette: Experiments in Multilingual Information Retrieval. In Proceedings of the 19th Annual International ACM SIGIR Conference on Research and Development in Information Retrieval, Zurich, Switzerland (1996)
[9] Oard, D.W. and B.J. Dorr: A survey of multilingual text retrieval. Technical Report UMIACS-TR-96-19, University of Maryland, Institute for Advanced Computer Studies (1996)
[10] Qu, Y., A.N. Eilerman, H. Jin, and D.A. Evans. The Effect of Pseudo-relevance Feedback on MT-Based CLIR. In Proceedings of the Recherche d'Informations Assistée par Ordinateur (RIAO 2000) (2000)
[11] Zhu, X. and R. Rosenfeld. Improving Trigram Language Modeling with the World Wide Web. In Proceedings of International Conference on Acoustics, Speech, and Signal Processing (ICASSP) (2001)

Experiments in 8 European Languages with Hummingbird SearchServer™ at CLEF 2002

Stephen Tomlinson

Hummingbird, Ottawa, Ontario, Canada
stephen.tomlinson@hummingbird.com
http://www.hummingbird.com/

Abstract. Hummingbird submitted ranked result sets for all Monolingual Information Retrieval tasks of the Cross-Language Evaluation Forum (CLEF) 2002. Enabling stemming in SearchServer increased average precision by 16 points in Finnish, 9 points in German, 4 points in Spanish, 3 points in Dutch, 2 points in French and Italian, and 1 point in Swedish and English. Accent-indexing increased average precision by 3 points in Finnish and 2 points in German, but decreased it by 2 points in French and 1 point in Italian and Swedish. Treating apostrophes as word separators increased average precision by 3 points in French and 1 point in Italian. Confidence intervals produced using the bootstrap percentile method were found to be very similar to those produced using the standard method; both were of similar width to rank-based intervals for differences in average precision, but substantially narrower for differences in Precision@10.

1 Introduction

Hummingbird SearchServer[1] is an indexing, search and retrieval engine for embedding in Windows and UNIX information applications. SearchServer, originally a product of Fulcrum Technologies, was acquired by Hummingbird in 1999. Founded in 1983 in Ottawa, Canada, Fulcrum produced the first commercial application program interface (API) for writing information retrieval applications, Fulcrum® Ful/Text™. The SearchServer kernel is embedded in many Hummingbird products, including SearchServer, an application toolkit used for knowledge-intensive applications that require fast access to unstructured information.

SearchServer supports a variation of the Structured Query Language (SQL), SearchSQL™, which has extensions for text retrieval. SearchServer conforms to subsets of the Open Database Connectivity (ODBC) interface for C programming language applications and the Java Database Connectivity (JDBC) interface for Java applications. Almost 200 document formats are supported, such as Word, WordPerfect, Excel, PowerPoint, PDF and HTML.

[1] Fulcrum® is a registered trademark, and SearchServer™, SearchSQL™, Intuitive Searching™ and Ful/Text™ are trademarks of Hummingbird Ltd. All other copyrights, trademarks and tradenames are the property of their respective owners.

C.A. Peters (Ed.): CLEF 2002, LNCS 2785, pp. 242–256, 2003.

SearchServer works in Unicode internally [4] and supports most of the world's major character sets and languages. The major conferences in text retrieval evaluation (CLEF [3], NTCIR [6] and TREC [11]) have provided opportunities to objectively evaluate SearchServer's support for a dozen languages. This paper focuses on evaluating SearchServer's options for 8 European languages using the CLEF 2002 test collections.

2 Setup

For the experiments described in this paper, an internal development build of SearchServer 5.3 was used (5.3.500.279).

2.1 Data

The CLEF 2002 document sets consisted of tagged (SGML-formatted) news articles (mostly from 1994) in 8 different languages: German, French, Italian, Spanish, Dutch, Swedish, Finnish and English. For more information on the CLEF collections, see [1] and the CLEF web site [3].

2.2 Text Reader

The custom text reader called cTREC, originally written for handling TREC collections [13], handled expansion of the library files of the CLEF collections and was extended to support the CLEF guidelines of only indexing specific fields of specific documents. The entities described in the DTD files were also converted, e.g. "=" was converted to the equal sign "=".

The documents were assumed to be in the Latin-1 character set, the code page which, for example, assigns e-acute (é) hexadecimal 0xe9 or decimal 233. cTREC passes through the Latin-1 characters, i.e. does not convert them to Unicode. SearchServer's Translation Text Reader (nti), was chained on top of cTREC and the Win_1252_UCS2 translation was specified via its /t option to translate from Latin-1 to the Unicode character set desired by SearchServer.

2.3 Indexing

A separate SearchServer table was created for each language, created with a SearchSQL statement such as the following:

```
CREATE SCHEMA CLEF02DE CREATE TABLE CLEF02DE
(DOCNO VARCHAR(256) 128)
TABLE_LANGUAGE 'GERMAN'
STOPFILE 'LANGDE.STP'
PERIODIC
BASEPATH 'e:\data\clef';
```

The TABLE_LANGUAGE parameter specifies which language to use when performing stemming operations at index time. The STOPFILE parameter specifies a stop file containing typically a couple hundred stop words to not index; the stop file also contains instructions on changes to the default indexing rules, for example, to enable accent-indexing, or to change the apostrophe to a word separator. Here are the first few lines of the stop file used for the French task:

```
IAC = "\u0300-\u0345"
PST = "’‘"
STOPLIST =
a
à
afin
```

The IAC line enables indexing of the specified accents (Unicode combining diacritical marks 0x0300-0x0345). Accent-indexing was enabled for all runs except the Italian and English runs. Accents were known to be specified in the Italian queries but were not consistently used in the Italian documents. The PST line adds the specified characters (apostrophes in this case) to the list of word separators. The apostrophes were changed to word separators except for English runs.

Into each table, we just needed to insert one row, specifying the top directory of the library files for the language, using an Insert statement such as the following:

```
INSERT INTO CLEF02DE ( FT_SFNAME, FT_FLIST ) VALUES
('German','cTREC/E/d=128:s!nti/t=Win_1252_UCS2:cTREC/C/@:s');
```

To index each table, we just executed a Validate Index statement such as the following:

```
VALIDATE INDEX CLEF02DE VALIDATE TABLE;
```

By default, the index supports both exact matching (after some Unicode-based normalizations, such as converting to upper-case and decomposed form) and matching on stems.

3 Search Techniques

The CLEF organizers created 50 "topics" (numbered 91-140) and translated them into many languages. Each topic contained a "Title" (subject of the topic), "Description" (a one-sentence specification of the information need) and "Narrative" (more detailed guidelines for what a relevant document should or should not contain). The participants were asked to use the Title and Description fields for at least one automatic submission per task this year to facilitate comparison of results.

We created an ODBC application, called QueryToRankings.c, based on the example stsample.c program included with SearchServer, to parse the CLEF topics files, construct and execute corresponding SearchSQL queries, fetch the top 1000 rows, and write out the rows in the results format requested by CLEF. SELECT statements were issued with the SQLExecDirect api call. Fetches were done with SQLFetch (typically 1000 SQLFetch calls per query).

3.1 Intuitive Searching

For all runs, we used SearchServer's Intuitive Searching, i.e. the IS_ABOUT predicate of SearchSQL, which accepts unstructured text. For example, for the German version of topic 41 (from last year), the Title was "Pestizide in Babykost" (Pesticides in Baby Food), and the Description was "Berichte über Pestizide in Babynahrung sind gesucht" (Find reports on pesticides in baby food). A corresponding SearchSQL query would be:

```
SELECT RELEVANCE('V2:3') AS REL, DOCNO
FROM CLEF02DE
WHERE FT_TEXT IS_ABOUT 'Pestizide in Babykost Berichte über
Pestizide in Babynahrung sind gesucht'
ORDER BY REL DESC;
```

This query would create a working table with the 2 columns named in the SELECT clause, a REL column containing the relevance value of the row for the query, and a DOCNO column containing the document's identifier. The ORDER BY clause specifies that the most relevant rows should be listed first. The statement "SET MAX_SEARCH_ROWS 1000" was previously executed so that the working table would contain at most 1000 rows.

3.2 Stemming

SearchServer "stems" each distinct word to one or more base forms, called stems. For example, in English, "baby", "babied", "babies", "baby's" and "babying" all have "baby" as a stem. Compound words in German, Dutch and Finnish produce multiple stems; e.g., in German, "babykost" has "baby" and "kost" as stems. SearchServer 5.3 uses the lexicon-based Inxight LinguistX Platform 3.3.1 for stemming operations.

By default, Intuitive Searching stems each word in the query, counts the number of occurrences of each stem, and creates a vector. Optionally some stems are discarded (secondary term selection) if they have a high document frequency or to enforce a maximum number of stems, but we didn't discard any for our CLEF runs. The index is searched for documents containing terms which stem to any of the stems of the vector.

The VECTOR_GENERATOR set option controls which stemming operations are performed by Intuitive Searching. To enable stemming, we used the same setting for each language except for the /lang parameter. For example, for German, the setting was 'word!ftelp/lang=german/base/noalt | * | word!ftelp /lang=german/inflect'. To disable stemming, the setting was just ''.

Besides linguistic expansion from stemming, we did not do any other kinds of query expansion. For example, we did not use approximate text searching for spell-correction because the queries were believed to be spelled correctly. We did not use row expansion or any other kind of blind feedback technique.

3.3 Statistical Relevance Ranking

SearchServer calculates a relevance value for a row of a table with respect to a vector of stems based on several statistics. The inverse document frequency of the stem is estimated from information in the dictionary. The term frequency (number of occurrences of the stem in the row (including any term that stems to it)) is determined from the reference file. The length of the row (based on the number of indexed characters in all columns of the row, which is typically dominated by the external document), is optionally incorporated. The already-mentioned count of the stem in the vector is also used. To synthesize this information into a relevance value, SearchServer dampens the term frequency and adjusts for document length in a manner similar to Okapi [7] and dampens the inverse document frequency in a manner similar to [9]. SearchServer's relevance values are always an integer in the range 0 to 1000.

SearchServer's RELEVANCE_METHOD setting can be used to optionally square the importance of the inverse document frequency (by choosing a RELEVANCE_METHOD of 'V2:4' instead of 'V2:3'). The importance of document length to the ranking is controlled by SearchServer's RELEVANCE_DLEN_IMP setting (scale of 0 to 1000). For all runs in this paper, RELEVANCE_METHOD was set to 'V2:3' and RELEVANCE_DLEN_IMP was set to 750.

3.4 Query Stop Words

Our QueryToRankings program removed words such as "find", "relevant" and "document" from the topics before presenting them to SearchServer, i.e. words which are not stop words in general but were commonly used in the CLEF topics as general instructions. For the submitted runs, the lists were developed by examining the CLEF 2000 and 2001 topics (not this year's topics). For the diagnostic runs in this paper, "finde" was added as a query stop word because it was noticed to be common in the German topics this year. An evaluation of the impact of query stop words is provided below.

4 Results

The evaluation measures are expected to be explained in detail in [1]. Briefly: "Precision" is the percentage of retrieved documents which are relevant. "Precision@n" is the precision after n documents have been retrieved. "Average precision" for a topic is the average of the precision after each relevant document is retrieved (using zero as the precision for relevant documents which are not retrieved). "Recall" is the percentage of relevant documents which have been retrieved. "Interpolated precision" at a particular recall level for a topic is the maximum precision achieved for the topic at that or any higher recall level. For a set of topics, the measure is the average of the measure for each topic (i.e. all topics are weighted equally).

The Monolingual Information Retrieval tasks were to run 50 queries against document collections in the same language and submit a list of the top-1000 ranked documents to CLEF for judging (in June 2002). CLEF produced a "qrels" file for each of the 8 tasks: a list of documents judged to be relevant or not relevant for each topic. From these, the evaluation measures were calculated with Chris Buckley's trec_eval program.

For some topics and languages, no documents were judged relevant. The precision scores are just averaged over the number of topics for which at least one document was judged relevant.

4.1 Impact of Stemming

Table 1 shows two runs for each language. The first run uses the same settings as were used for the submitted runs which used the Title and Description fields; in particular, stemming was enabled. The second run uses the same settings except that VECTOR_GENERATOR was set to the empty string, which disables stemming. Listed for each run are its average precision (AvgP), the precision after 5, 10 and 20 documents retrieved (P@5, P@10 and P@20 respectively), and the interpolated precision at 0% and 30% recall (Rec0 and Rec30 respectively). Additionally listed for the runs with stemming enabled is the number of topics which contained at least one relevant document for that language. The languages are ordered by descending difference in average precision. Stemming increased average precision in Finnish by 69%, German 27%, Spanish 8%, Dutch 8%, French 6%, Italian 4%, Swedish 4% and English 2%.

Most of the remaining tables will focus on one particular precision measure (usually average precision), comparing the scores when a particular feature (such as stemming) is enabled to when it is disabled. The columns of these tables are as follows:

- "Experiment" is the language and topic fields used (for example, "-td" indicates the Title and Description fields were used).
- "AvgDiff" is the average difference in the precision score. In [10], a difference of at least 2 full points (i.e. >=0.020) is considered "noticeable", 4 points "material", 6 points "striking" and 8 points "dramatic".
- "95% Confidence" is an approximate 95% confidence interval for the average difference calculated using the bootstrap percentile method (described in the last section). If zero is not in the interval, the result is "statistically significant" (at the 5% level), i.e. the feature is unlikely to be of neutral impact, though if the average difference is small (e.g. <0.020) it may still be too minor to be considered "significant" in the magnitude sense.

- "vs." is the number of topics on which the precision was higher, lower and tied (respectively) with the feature enabled. These numbers should always add to the number of topics for the language (as per Table 1).
- "2 Largest Diffs (Topic)" lists the two largest differences in the precision score (based on the absolute value), with each followed by the corresponding topic number in brackets (the topic numbers range from 91 to 140).

Table 2 shows the impact of stemming on the average precision measure. The benefit for Finnish and German, for which stemming includes compound-breaking, is dramatic. For example, Finnish topic 115, regarding "avioerotilastoja" (divorce statistics), apparently benefits from compound-breaking. Surprisingly, the other investigated language for which compounds are broken, Dutch, does not similarly stand out, unlike last year [12], though its confidence interval still overlaps the one for German.

Table 3 shows the impact of stemming on the shorter (Title-only) queries. It appears the benefits are a little bigger for the shorter queries in most languages, with English the only language without a noticeable benefit on average. Of course, stemming can hurt precision for some queries, as in English topic 139 (EU fishing quotas), so an application probably should make stemming a user-controllable option.

Table 1. Precision with Stemming Enabled and Disabled

Run	AvgP	P@5	P@10	P@20	Rec0	Rec30	#Topics
Finnish	0.393	44.0%	36.0%	28.2%	0.707	0.502	30
	0.232	29.3%	23.3%	17.7%	0.540	0.299	
German	0.442	64.4%	55.4%	46.7%	0.819	0.538	50
	0.348	55.2%	48.2%	38.7%	0.726	0.426	
Spanish	0.491	68.0%	58.8%	51.2%	0.871	0.617	50
	0.454	64.8%	57.2%	50.9%	0.833	0.586	
Dutch	0.442	58.4%	50.6%	41.3%	0.822	0.529	50
	0.410	54.8%	48.4%	40.6%	0.779	0.516	
French	0.428	52.8%	44.6%	35.6%	0.774	0.554	50
	0.404	49.6%	39.8%	32.6%	0.824	0.488	
Italian	0.409	50.2%	45.3%	36.0%	0.740	0.537	49
	0.395	51.4%	43.3%	35.4%	0.760	0.491	
Swedish	0.348	44.1%	37.6%	29.4%	0.754	0.439	49
	0.334	44.5%	37.1%	28.8%	0.705	0.436	
English	0.508	57.6%	45.2%	34.3%	0.909	0.682	42
	0.500	55.2%	42.9%	33.2%	0.894	0.644	

Table 2. Impact of Stemming on Average Precision

Experiment	AvgDiff	95% Confidence	vs.	2 Largest Diffs (Topic)
Finnish-td	0.161	(0.097, 0.232)	24-5-1	0.753 (115), 0.453 (122)
German-td	0.093	(0.052, 0.136)	35-15-0	0.553 (105), 0.410 (140)
Spanish-td	0.038	(0.012, 0.064)	32-18-0	0.337 (119), 0.248 (137)
Dutch-td	0.032	(0.001, 0.065)	31-17-2	0.437 (116), 0.350 (109)
French-td	0.024	(−0.007, 0.059)	23-24-3	0.406 (115), 0.322 (140)
Italian-td	0.015	(−0.006, 0.037)	27-22-0	0.185 (140), 0.178 (137)
Swedish-td	0.014	(−0.004, 0.032)	27-18-4	−0.217 (93), 0.204 (129)
English-td	0.008	(−0.020, 0.035)	22-16-4	−0.283 (139), 0.213 (129)

Table 3. Impact of Stemming on Average Precision, Title-only queries

Experiment	AvgDiff	95% Confidence	vs.	2 Largest Diffs (Topic)
Finnish-t	0.175	(0.103, 0.259)	26-4-0	0.799 (115), 0.797 (98)
German-t	0.108	(0.057, 0.167)	36-13-1	1.000 (137), 0.521 (140)
Spanish-t	0.036	(0.016, 0.061)	30-8-12	0.485 (119), 0.201 (139)
Italian-t	0.035	(0.012, 0.062)	20-17-12	0.377 (115), 0.263 (137)
Swedish-t	0.033	(0.013, 0.055)	25-7-17	0.323 (129), 0.250 (134)
Dutch-t	0.030	(0.000, 0.065)	26-19-5	0.567 (116), −0.249 (137)
French-t	0.030	(0.005, 0.060)	24-19-7	0.506 (115), 0.261 (103)
English-t	−0.002	(−0.028, 0.025)	20-14-8	0.312 (103), −0.276 (139)

4.2 Impact of Query Stop Words

Table 4 shows the impact of discarding query stop words, such as "find", "relevant" and "documents". Query stop words differ from general stop words (such as "the", "of", "by") in that they do not seem to be noise words in general, but their common use in past CLEF topic sets (particularly the Description and Narrative fields) suggests they are likely not useful terms when encountered in CLEF queries. In the table, a positive difference indicates a benefit from removing query stop words from the topics.

Table 4 shows that the impact of discarding query stop words was always minor (the biggest average benefit was just 1.6 points), though some of the differences are "statistically significant" because of the consistency of the minor benefits. This is a case where a "statistically significant" benefit is still not a "significant" benefit.

Sometimes noise words may occur in relevant documents by chance and scores may fall if the noise words are discarded. Apparently that happened in French topics 123 and 132 (regarding "mariage" and "Kaliningrad" respectively) in which excluding "trouver" and "documents" decreased the scores, even though they don't seem to be meaningful terms for their queries.

Table 4. Impact of Discarding Query Stop Words on Average Precision

Experiment	AvgDiff	95% Confidence	vs.	2 Largest Diffs (Topic)
Spanish-td	0.016	(0.007, 0.027)	24-4-22	0.151 (138), 0.137 (100)
English-td	0.014	(−0.001, 0.032)	17-8-17	0.250 (137), 0.149 (106)
Finnish-td	0.009	(0.002, 0.020)	11-1-18	0.132 (122), 0.050 (114)
Italian-td	0.007	(−0.002, 0.016)	20-8-21	0.113 (93), −0.107 (91)
German-td	0.006	(0.000, 0.014)	19-15-16	0.099 (138), 0.091 (99)
Swedish-td	0.006	(−0.001, 0.015)	17-10-22	0.106 (111), 0.100 (132)
Dutch-td	0.001	(−0.003, 0.006)	15-12-23	0.062 (138), −0.049 (123)
French-td	−0.000	(−0.013, 0.012)	18-10-22	−0.167 (123), −0.150 (132)

Table 5. Impact of Stop Words on Average Precision

Experiment	AvgDiff	95% Confidence	vs.	2 Largest Diffs (Topic)
Spanish-td	0.006	(−0.004, 0.018)	25-24-1	0.186 (99), 0.125 (98)
French-td	0.005	(−0.002, 0.015)	23-22-5	0.167 (123), 0.099 (105)
German-td	0.004	(−0.001, 0.011)	26-21-3	0.064 (106), 0.050 (99)
Finnish-td	0.004	(−0.007, 0.015)	17-9-4	−0.088 (139), 0.083 (132)
Swedish-td	0.002	(−0.003, 0.009)	20-23-6	0.071 (99), −0.054 (130)
Dutch-td	−0.000	(−0.010, 0.009)	28-19-3	−0.117 (138), −0.114 (104)
Italian-td	−0.000	(−0.011, 0.010)	27-22-0	−0.164 (96), −0.083 (139)
English-td	−0.001	(−0.011, 0.011)	14-22-6	0.167 (126), −0.114 (133)

4.3 Impact of Stop Words

Tables 5 and 6 show the impact of using stop words on the average precision measure. To do this experiment, two tables were created for each language, one indexed with a stopfile containing typically a couple hundred stop words, the other with no stop words (though other SearchServer stopfile instructions, such as accent-indexing and apostrophes as word separators, were kept the same as used for the submitted runs). For this experiment, query stop words were not discarded for either run, to isolate the impact of the general stop words on precision. In the tables, a positive difference indicates a benefit to specifying stop words.

Table 5 shows the impact of using stop words for Title plus Description queries was very slight on average, and none of the differences were statistically significant. Table 6 shows there was a noticeable benefit for full topic queries (i.e. when additionally including the Narrative) for some languages, and a statistically significant benefit for most of them. Other benefits of specifying stop words are to reduce search time, indexing time and index size. However, there may be cases when what is usually a stop word is meaningful to a query (e.g. find documents containing "to be or not to be"), so it may be better to make stop

Table 6. Impact of Stop Words on Average Precision, Full Topic Queries

Experiment	AvgDiff	95% Confidence	vs.	2 Largest Diffs (Topic)
Spanish-tdn	0.023	(0.012, 0.034)	36-13-1	0.156 (99), 0.126 (98)
Italian-tdn	0.020	(0.007, 0.034)	33-16-0	0.172 (132), −0.127 (96)
Swedish-tdn	0.017	(0.008, 0.028)	33-14-2	0.163 (102), 0.096 (96)
French-tdn	0.016	(0.004, 0.033)	34-12-4	0.303 (109), 0.094 (128)
German-tdn	0.015	(0.003, 0.029)	33-14-3	0.262 (137), 0.080 (102)
Finnish-tdn	0.012	(0.004, 0.020)	20-7-3	0.083 (132), 0.054 (116)
English-tdn	0.007	(−0.001, 0.018)	20-15-7	0.164 (126), 0.101 (99)
Dutch-tdn	0.005	(−0.013, 0.023)	29-17-4	0.213 (116), −0.177 (109)

Table 7. Impact of Preserving Accents on Average Precision

Experiment	AvgDiff	95% Confidence	vs.	2 Largest Diffs (Topic)
Finnish-td	0.026	(−0.003, 0.060)	17-11-2	0.289 (109), 0.255 (139)
German-td	0.018	(−0.002, 0.040)	29-19-2	0.267 (108), 0.256 (135)
Dutch-td	0.002	(−0.001, 0.005)	12-6-32	0.050 (110), 0.031 (127)
English-td	0.000	(−0.001, 0.001)	0-0-42	0.000 (116), 0.000 (92)
Spanish-td	−0.003	(−0.034, 0.024)	23-25-2	−0.572 (98), 0.298 (103)
Swedish-td	−0.013	(−0.028, 0.000)	15-26-8	−0.167 (134), −0.160 (127)
Italian-td	−0.014	(−0.038, 0.000)	10-25-14	−0.502 (98), −0.109 (101)
French-td	−0.018	(−0.049, 0.009)	16-28-6	−0.474 (98), −0.297 (94)

word elimination an option at search time rather than at index time, depending on the goals of the application.

Stop word lists for many languages are on the Neuchâtel resource page [8]. Our stop word lists may contain differences.

4.4 Impact of Indexing Accents

Tables 7 and 8 show the impact of accent-indexing on the average precision measure. To do this experiment, two tables were created for each language, one preserving accents (e.g. "bébé" and "bebe" would be distinct words) and one which dropped the accents (e.g. "bébé" would be the same as "bebe"). Of course, at search-time SearchServer uses the same rules as at index-time. For this experiment, no stop words were used and no query stop words were discarded. Otherwise, the settings were the same as for the submitted runs; in particular, apostrophes were used as word separators except in English.

Tables 7 and 8 show that topic 98, regarding the Kaurismäki brothers, was strongly affected in many languages by whether or not accents were preserved. Spanish, French and Italian topics 98 included the accent in Kaurismäki, but the

Table 8. Impact of Preserving Accents on Average Precision, Title-only queries

Experiment	AvgDiff	95% Confidence	vs.	2 Largest Diffs (Topic)
Finnish-t	0.061	(0.008, 0.128)	14-14-2	0.703 (98), 0.540 (139)
German-t	0.007	(−0.048, 0.065)	22-16-12	1.000 (137), −0.873 (127)
Dutch-t	0.000	(−0.001, 0.001)	5-2-43	0.007 (127), 0.002 (103)
English-t	0.000	(−0.001, 0.001)	0-0-42	0.000 (116), 0.000 (92)
Spanish-t	−0.002	(−0.045, 0.032)	20-15-15	−0.799 (98), 0.477 (103)
Swedish-t	−0.008	(−0.037, 0.017)	8-10-31	−0.496 (127), 0.329 (129)
Italian-t	−0.014	(−0.041, 0.001)	5-5-39	−0.666 (98), 0.015 (128)
French-t	−0.024	(−0.065, 0.008)	16-19-15	−0.709 (98), −0.462 (94)

Table 9. Impact of Dropping Apostrophes on Average Precision

Experiment	AvgDiff	95% Confidence	vs.	2 Largest Diffs (Topic)
French-td	0.034	(0.007, 0.075)	28-17-5	0.833 (121), 0.220 (105)
Italian-td	0.011	(−0.001, 0.026)	23-18-8	0.211 (93), 0.195 (139)
Dutch-td	0.003	(−0.003, 0.012)	7-8-35	0.188 (98), −0.048 (130)
English-td	0.002	(−0.001, 0.005)	13-18-11	0.039 (103), 0.038 (135)
Spanish-td	0.000	(−0.001, 0.001)	1-4-45	0.004 (101), −0.001 (91)
Swedish-td	0.000	(−0.001, 0.001)	2-0-47	0.004 (130), 0.001 (139)
German-td	−0.000	(−0.001, 0.001)	3-3-44	−0.004 (130), 0.002 (91)
Finnish-td	−0.000	(−0.001, 0.001)	0-3-27	−0.001 (124), −0.000 (92)

documents more often did not include the accent, so accent-indexing hurt precision in those cases. But accent-indexing was helpful for Finnish for this topic, apparently because in Finnish there were variants which required stemming to match (e.g. Kaurismäkien and Kaurismäen), and the stemmer was more effective when given the words with the accents preserved. It appears it would help if the stemmer was modified to be more tolerant of missing accents.

4.5 Impact of Apostrophes as Word Separators

Table 9 shows the impact of treating apostrophes as word separators on the average precision measure. To do this experiment, two tables were created for each language, one treating apostrophes as word separators, the other not. No stop words were used and no query stop words were discarded. Otherwise, the settings were the same as for the submitted runs; in particular, accent-indexing was enabled except in Italian and English.

Table 9 shows that treating apostrophes as word separators had a noticeable benefit for French. For example, French topic 121 may be benefiting from breaking "d'Ayrton" at its apostrophe. The benefit for Italian may have been less because stemming appears to be handling apostrophes. For example, in Italian, if apostrophes are not word separators, "l'ombrello" still matches "ombrello" when stemming is enabled, whereas in French, "l'école" still does not match "école" (again, this difference is moot when apostrophes are treated as word separators). The impact for other languages is slight, including for English.

4.6 Submitted Runs

We submitted 10 monolingual runs (the maximum allowed) in June 2002. Runs humDE02, humFR02, humIT02, humES02, humNL02, humSV02 and humFI02 provided a run for each language using the Title and Description fields as requested by the organizers (note that English monolingual runs were not accepted). For the remaining 3 runs, we submitted an extra run for Finnish, Swedish and Dutch including the Narrative field (runs humFI02n, humSV02n, humNL02n); these languages were expected to have the fewest participants, so additional submissions seemed more likely to be helpful for the judging pools. The precision scores of the submitted runs are expected to be included in an appendix of this volume. Table 10 shows a comparison of the submitted runs with the median scores of submitted monolingual runs for each language. In all but one case, SearchServer scored higher than the median on more topics than it scored lower. Note that the relative performance on different languages may not be meaningful for several reasons, including that the medians are from a mix of runs where some may have used the Narrative field, multiple runs may be submitted by the same group, and the mixture can vary across languages.

The submitted runs of June used an older, experimental build than was used for the diagnostic runs in August, and there may be minor differences in the scores even when the settings are the same.

Table 10. Comparison of Submitted Runs with Medians in Average Precision

Submission	AvgDiff	95% Confidence	vs.	2 Largest Diffs (Topic)
Swedish-tdn	0.125	(0.082, 0.173)	37-6-6	0.762 (101), 0.500 (134)
Swedish-td	0.093	(0.059, 0.132)	37-3-9	0.589 (101), 0.433 (129)
Dutch-tdn	0.080	(0.050, 0.110)	37-7-6	0.366 (138), 0.261 (117)
Finnish-td	0.076	(0.022, 0.138)	20-7-3	0.641 (115), 0.364 (122)
Finnish-tdn	0.068	(0.006, 0.136)	20-8-2	0.618 (126), 0.485 (115)
Spanish-td	0.042	(0.012, 0.070)	37-12-1	−0.326 (138), 0.262 (120)
Dutch-td	0.039	(0.018, 0.059)	35-10-5	0.213 (111), −0.212 (102)
French-td	0.017	(−0.010, 0.049)	24-17-9	0.500 (121), −0.274 (94)
German-td	0.013	(−0.013, 0.039)	26-20-4	0.297 (105), 0.244 (137)
Italian-td	−0.001	(−0.025, 0.025)	20-25-4	0.254 (98), 0.240 (137)

5 Confidence Intervals for Precision Differences

The 95% confidence intervals presented in this paper have been produced using Efron's Bootstrap (percentile method). If there are 50 topics (i.e. 50 precision differences), then precision differences are chosen randomly (with replacement) 50 times, producing a "bootstrap sample", and a mean (average) is computed from this sample. This step is repeated B times (e.g. B=100,000). The B sample means are sorted, the bottom and top 2.5% are discarded, and the endpoints of the remaining range of sample means are an approximate 95% confidence interval for the average difference in precision (we always rounded so that the listed endpoints are not actually in the produced interval). The bootstrap percentile method is considered to work well in more cases than the standard method of using the mean plus/minus 1.96 times the standard error, though there are more complicated bootstrap methods which are considered even more general [2].

Table 11 shows the bootstrap confidence intervals produced for the impact of stemming on average precision with different numbers of iterations. Even at just 1000 iterations the values are fairly close to the values at 1 million iterations. When comparing 1,000,000 iterations to 100,000, very few of the endpoints changed, and they only changed by 0.001. For the confidence intervals in this paper, we used B=100,000.

Tables 12 and 13 contain side-by-side comparisons of the approximate 95% confidence intervals produced by the bootstrap percentile method and the standard method. It turns they are very similar. There is a disagreement on statistical significance (i.e. when zero is not in the interval) in the case of Dutch in Table 12, but it is a borderline case.

Tables 12 and 13 also include an estimator and 95% confidence interval based on the Wilcoxon signed rank test (the 2 rightmost columns). (We implemented an exact computation, including for the case of ties in the absolute values of the differences [5]). For differences in average precision, the widths of the intervals are very similar (the bootstrap intervals are a little smaller than the Wilcoxon intervals for the Finnish and German results, and the Wilcoxon intervals are a little smaller for the others); the methods agree on which differences are statistically

Table 11. Impact of Number of Bootstrap Iterations on Confidence Intervals

Experiment	B=1000	B=10,000	B=100,000	B=1,000,000
Finnish-td	(0.102, 0.232)	(0.099, 0.232)	(0.097, 0.232)	(0.097, 0.231)
German-td	(0.054, 0.136)	(0.053, 0.137)	(0.052, 0.136)	(0.052, 0.137)
Spanish-td	(0.012, 0.066)	(0.012, 0.064)	(0.012, 0.064)	(0.012, 0.065)
Dutch-td	(0.002, 0.060)	(0.001, 0.065)	(0.001, 0.065)	(0.001, 0.065)
French-td	(−0.006, 0.058)	(−0.007, 0.059)	(−0.007, 0.059)	(−0.007, 0.058)
Italian-td	(−0.005, 0.036)	(−0.006, 0.037)	(−0.006, 0.037)	(−0.006, 0.037)
Swedish-td	(−0.005, 0.032)	(−0.004, 0.032)	(−0.004, 0.032)	(−0.004, 0.032)
English-td	(−0.021, 0.035)	(−0.020, 0.036)	(−0.020, 0.035)	(−0.020, 0.035)

Table 12. Comparison of Confidence Intervals for Impact of Stemming on Average Precision

Experiment	AvgDiff	Bootstrap 95% Confidence	+/− (1.96 * StdErr)	Wilcoxon EstDiff	95% Confidence
Finnish-td	0.161	(0.097, 0.232)	(0.093, 0.229)	0.150	(0.073, 0.215)
German-td	0.093	(0.052, 0.136)	(0.050, 0.136)	0.077	(0.032, 0.133)
Spanish-td	0.038	(0.012, 0.064)	(0.011, 0.064)	0.028	(0.008, 0.053)
Dutch-td	0.032	(0.001, 0.065)	(−0.001, 0.064)	0.017	(0.000, 0.040)
French-td	0.024	(−0.007, 0.059)	(−0.009, 0.057)	0.008	(−0.009, 0.042)
Italian-td	0.015	(−0.006, 0.037)	(−0.007, 0.037)	0.010	(−0.007, 0.034)
Swedish-td	0.014	(−0.004, 0.032)	(−0.004, 0.032)	0.009	(−0.001, 0.026)
English-td	0.008	(−0.020, 0.035)	(−0.019, 0.036)	0.005	(−0.013, 0.027)

Table 13. Comparison of Confidence Intervals for Impact of Stemming on Precision@10

Experiment	AvgDiff	Bootstrap 95% Confidence	+/− (1.96 * StdErr)	Wilcoxon EstDiff	95% Confidence
Finnish-td	0.127	(0.046, 0.211)	(0.044, 0.210)	0.100	(0.000, 0.250)
German-td	0.072	(0.013, 0.133)	(0.011, 0.133)	0.050	(0.000, 0.150)
French-td	0.048	(0.015, 0.083)	(0.015, 0.081)	0.050	(0.000, 0.100)
English-td	0.024	(−0.005, 0.055)	(−0.006, 0.054)	0.000	(−0.050, 0.050)
Dutch-td	0.022	(−0.016, 0.063)	(−0.017, 0.062)	0.000	(−0.050, 0.100)
Italian-td	0.020	(−0.004, 0.045)	(−0.005, 0.046)	0.000	(−0.050, 0.050)
Spanish-td	0.016	(−0.012, 0.045)	(−0.012, 0.044)	0.000	(−0.050, 0.050)
Swedish-td	0.004	(−0.033, 0.041)	(−0.032, 0.041)	0.000	(−0.050, 0.050)

significant. However, for differences in Precision@10, the bootstrap intervals are a lot smaller than the Wilcoxon intervals (because the Wilcoxon is based on ranks, it cannot distinguish between a shift of 0.01 and 0.09 (they have the same effect on the ranks because every difference is a multiple of 0.10)); the methods still agree on statistically significant results (for the 8 cases listed).

References

[1] M. Braschler and C. Peters. CLEF2002: Methodology and Metrics. This volume

[2] Michael R. Chernick. Bootstrap Methods: A Practitioner's Guide. 1999. John Wiley & Sons

[3] Cross-Language Evaluation Forum web site. http://www.clef-campaign.org/

[4] Andrew Hodgson. Converting the Fulcrum Search Engine to Unicode. In Sixteenth International Unicode Conference, Amsterdam, The Netherlands, March 2000

[5] Myles Hollander and Douglas A. Wolfe. Nonparametric Statistical Methods. Second Edition, 1999. John Wiley & Sons
[6] NTCIR (NII-NACSIS Test Collection for IR Systems) Home Page. http://research.nii.ac.jp/~ntcadm/index-en.html
[7] S.E. Robertson, S. Walker, S. Jones, M.M. Hancock-Beaulieu, M. Gatford. (City University.) Okapi at TREC-3. In D.K. Harman, editor, Overview of the Third Text REtrieval Conference (TREC-3). NIST Special Publication 500-226. http://trec.nist.gov/pubs/trec3/t3_proceedings.html
[8] Jacques Savoy. (Université de Neuchâtel.) CLEF and Multilingual information retrieval resource page. http://www.unine.ch/info/clef/
[9] Amit Singhal, John Choi, Donald Hindle, David Lewis and Fernando Pereira. AT&T at TREC-7. In E.M. Voorhees and D.K. Harman, editors, Proceedings of the Seventh Text REtrieval Conference (TREC-7). NIST Special Publication 500-242. http://trec.nist.gov/pubs/trec7/t7_proceedings.html
[10] K. Sparck Jones, S. Walker and S.E. Robertson. (City University.) A probabilistic model of information retrieval: development and status. August 1998. Page 15
[11] Text REtrieval Conference (TREC) Home Page. http://trec.nist.gov/
[12] Stephen Tomlinson. Stemming Evaluated in 6 Languages by Hummingbird SearchServer™ at CLEF 2001. In C. Peters, M. Braschler, J. Gonzalo, M. Kluck, editors, Evaluation of Cross-Language Information Retrieval Systems: Second Workshop of the Cross-Language Evaluation Forum, CLEF 2001, Darmstadt, Germany, September 3-4, 2001. Revised Papers. Springer LNCS 2406. http://link.springer.de/link/service/series/0558/tocs/t2406.htm
[13] Stephen Tomlinson and Tom Blackwell. Hummingbird's Fulcrum SearchServer at TREC-9. In E.M. Voorhees and D.K. Harman, editors, Proceedings of the Ninth Text REtrieval Conference (TREC-9). NIST Special Publication 500-249. http://trec.nist.gov/pubs/trec9/t9_proceedings.html

Italian Monolingual Information Retrieval with PROSIT

Gianni Amati, Claudio Carpineto, and Giovanni Romano

Fondazione Ugo Bordoni
via B. Castiglione 59, 00142 Rome, Italy
{gba,carpinet,romano}@fub.it

Abstract. PROSIT (PRObabilistic Sifting of Information Terms) is a novel probabilistic information retrieval system that combines a term-weighting model based on deviation from randomness with information-theoretic query expansion. We report on the application of PROSIT to the Italian monolingual task at CLEF. We experimented with both standard PROSIT and with enhanced versions. In particular, we studied the use of bigrams and coordination level-based retrieval within the PROSIT framework. The main findings of our research are that (i) standard PROSIT was quite effective, with an average precision of 0.5116 on CLEF 2001 queries and 0.5019 on CLEF 2002 queries, (ii) bigrams were useful provided that they were incorporated into the main algorithm, and (iii) the benefits of coordination level-based retrieval were unclear.

1 Introduction

Recent research has shown the effectiveness of deviation from randomness [2] and information-theoretic query expansion [6]. We combined these techniques into a comprehensive document ranking system named PROSIT, which stands for PRObabilistic Sifting of Information Terms.

The best features of PROSIT are that it is fast, it can be easily understood and replicated, it requires virtually no training or parameter tuning, it does not employ any ad hoc linguistic manipulations, and, perhaps even more important, it has shown to be surprisingly effective.

An earlier version of PROSIT was tested at the web track of TREC-10 [1], where it was ranked as the best system in the topic relevance task. Subsequently, we developed a web version of PROSIT to act as the search engine of the web site of the Italian Ministry of Communications (http://www.comunicazioni.it). The search engine has been running on the site since the end of July 2002.

The study reported in this paper is a follow up on this previous research, aiming at extending the scope of applications of PROSIT and improving its performance. As the site search engine based on PROSIT receives queries typically expressed in Italian and retrieves relevant documents mostly from Italian web pages, we were particularly interested in evaluating the effectiveness of PROSIT for the Italian language. This was the first goal of our participation in CLEF.

C.A. Peters (Ed.): CLEF 2002, LNCS 2785, pp. 257–264, 2003.

In addition, as PROSIT performs single-word indexing and does not take advantage of the structure of queries and documents, we intended to investigate the use of multi-word indexing and text structure to improve its performance. This was our second main goal.

In the rest of the paper, we first describe the indexing stage and the two main components of PROSIT. Then we discuss how to enhance PROSIT with bigrams and coordination level-based retrieval. Finally, we present the performance results and draw some conclusions.

2 Indexing

Our system first identified the individual words occurring in the documents, considering only the admissible sections and ignoring punctuation and case. The system then performed word stemming and word stopping.

Similar to earlier results reported at CLEF 2001, we found that stemming improves performance. We used a simple form of stemming for conflating singular and plural words to the same root [8]. It is likely that the use of a more sophisticated stemmer such as the Italian version of Porter's stemmer would produce better results, but we did not have a chance to try it. To remove common words, we used the stop list provided by Savoy [8].

We did not use any ad hoc linguistic manipulation such as removing certain words from the query text, e.g., "trova" (find), "documenti" (documents), etc., or expanding acronyms, e.g., does AI stand for Amnesty International or Artificial Intelligence?, or using lists of proper nouns, e.g, Alberto Tomba.

The use of such manipulations makes it difficult to evaluate the overall results and makes it even more difficult to replicate the experiments. We think that it would be better to discourage their use unless it is supported by some linguistic resources which are public or which are made available by the authors.

3 Description of PROSIT

PROSIT consists of two main components: the retrieval-matching function module and the automatic query expansion module. The system has been implemented in ESL, a Lisp-like language that is automatically translated into ANSI C and then compiled by gcc compiler. PROSIT is able to index two gigabytes of documents per hour and allows sub-seconds searches on a 550 MHz Pentium III with 256 megabytes of RAM running Linux. PROSIT has been released as an application for searching documents on WEB collections. In the following two sections we explain in detail the two main components of the system.

3.1 Term Weighting

PROSIT can implement different matching functions which have similar and excellent performance. These basic retrieval functions are generated from a unique probabilistic framework [2]. The appealing feature of the basic term weighting models is the absence of parameters which should be learned and tuned using a training set. In addition, the framework is easy to implement since the models use up a total number of 6 random variables which are given by the collection statistics, namely:

tf	the within document term frequency
N	the size of the collection
n_t	the size of the elite set E_t of the term (see below)
F_t	the total number of term occurrences in its elite set
l	the length of the document
avg_l	the average length of documents

However, for both TREC-10 and CLEF collections we have introduced a parameter for document length normalization which enhances the retrieval results.

The framework is based on computing the information gain for each query term. The information gain is obtained by a combination of three distinct probabilistic processes: the probabilistic process computing the amount of the information content of the term with respect to the entire collection, the probabilistic process computing a conditional probability of occurrence of the term with respect to an "Elite" set of documents, which is the set of documents containing the query term, and the probabilistic process deriving the term frequency within the document normalized to the document average length. The framework thus consists of three independent components: the "information content" component relative to the entire data collection, the "information gain" normalization factor component relative to the elite set of the observed term, and the "term frequency normalization function" component relative to the document length.

Our formulation of informative gain is:

$$w = (1 - Prob_1) \cdot (-log_2 Prob_2) \tag{1}$$

In our experiments we have instantiated our framework choosing Laplace's law of succession for $Prob_1$ as the gain normalization factor and the Bose-Einstein statistics for $Prob_2$:

$$Prob_1 = \frac{tfn}{tfn + 1} \tag{2}$$

$$Prob_2 = \left(\frac{1}{1+\lambda}\right) \cdot \left(\frac{\lambda}{1+\lambda}\right)^{tfn} \tag{3}$$

where:

λ is the term frequency in the collection $\frac{F_t}{N}$

tfn is the normalized term frequency $tf \cdot \log_2\left(1 + \frac{avg\_l}{l}\right)$.

The correcting factor $c = 3$ may be inserted in the term frequency normalization and obtain $tfn = tf \cdot \log_2\left(1 + \frac{c \cdot avg\_l}{l}\right)$. The system displayed in Formulas 1, 2 and 3 was used in our experiments and is called $B_E L2$ (B_E stands for Bose-Einstein and L for Laplace).

3.2 Relevance Feedback

Formulas 1, 2 and 3 produce a first ranking of possible relevant documents. The topmost ones are candidates to be assessed relevant and therefore we might consider them to constitute a second different "Elite set T of documents", namely documents which best describe the content of the query. We have considered in our experiments only 10 documents as pseudo-relevant documents and extracted from them the first 40 most informative terms which were then added to the original query. The most informative terms are selected by using the information-theoretic Kullback-Leibler divergence function:

$$KL = f \cdot \log_2 \frac{f}{p} \tag{4}$$

where:

f is the term frequency in the set T,
p is the prior, e.g. the term frequency in the collection.

Once the computation of the Kullback-Leibler values KL are obtained and the new terms selected, we combine the initial term frequency of the term within the query (possibly equal to 0) with the score KL as follows:

$$tfq_{exp} = \frac{tfq}{Max_{tfq}} + \beta \cdot \frac{KL}{Max_{KL}} \tag{5}$$

where:

Max_{tfq} is the maximum number of occurrences of a term in the query
Max_{KL} is the highest KL value in the set T
β was set to 0.5

In the second retrieval experiment we used the term weighting function:

$$w = tfq_{exp} \cdot (1 - Prob_1) \cdot (-log_2 Prob_2) \tag{6}$$

where $Prob_1$ and $Prob_2$ were defined as for the first retrieval experiment, that is according to Formulas 2 and 3.

4 Augmenting PROSIT with Word Proximity

PROSIT, like most information retrieval systems, is based on index units consisting of single keywords, or unigrams, and it ignores word proximity. We attempted to improve its performance by using two-word index units (bigrams).

Bigrams are good for disambiguating terms and for handling topic drift, i.e., when the results of queries on specific aspects of wide topics contain documents that are relevant to the general topic but not to the requested aspect of it. This phenomenon can also be seen as some query terms matching out of context of their relationships to other terms [4]. For instance, using unigrams, most documents found for the CLEF query "Kaurismaki films" were about other famous films, whereas using bigrams considerably improved the precision of search.

On the other hand, some bigrams that are generated automatically may, in turn, over-emphasize concepts that are common to both relevant and nonrelevant documents [9]. So far, the results about the effectiveness of bigrams versus unigrams have not been conclusive.

We used a simple technique known as lexical affinities. Lexical affinities are identified by finding pairs of words that occur close to each other in a window of some predefined small size. For the CLEF experiments, we used the title query and chose a distance of 5 words. All the bigrams generated this way are seen as new index units and are used to increase the relevance of those documents that have the same pair of words occurring within the specified window. The score assigned to bigrams is computed using the same weighting function used for unigrams.

From an implementation point of view, in order to efficiently compute the bigram scores it is necessary to encode the information about the position of each term in each document into the inverted file. During query evaluation, for each bigram extracted from the query, the posting lists associated with the bigram words in the inverted file are merged and a new pseudo posting list is created that contains all documents that contain the bigram along with the relevant occurrence information.

The lexical affinity technique was reported to produce very good results on the TREC web collection, even better than those obtained using unigrams [5]. However, we were not able to obtain such good results on the CLEF collection, at least using queries with title and descriptions. In fact, we found that the bigram performance was considerably worse than the unigram performance; even when combining the scores, the performance remained lower than that obtainable by using just unigram scores.

Based on these observations, we decided to use bigrams in addition to, not in place of, single words. Second, instead of running two separate ranking systems, one for unigrams and the other for bigrams, and then combining their scores, we tried to incorporate the bigram component directly into PROSIT's main algorithm.

The bigram scores were thus combined with the unigram score to produce the first-pass ranking of PROSIT. In this way one can hope to increase the quality of the documents on which the subsequent query expansion step is based. This may happen because more top relevant documents are retrieved or because the nonrelevant documents which contribute to query expansion are more similar to the query.

After the first ranking was computed using unigram and bigram scores, the top documents were used to generate the expanded query and PROSIT computed the second ranking as if it were just using unigrams. We chose to not expand the original query with two-word units due to the dimensionality problem, and we did not use the bigram method during the second-pass ranking of PROSIT because the order of words in the expanded query is not relevant.

We submitted one run to CLEF 2002, labelled "fub02l", which was produced using PROSIT augmented with the bigrams procedure just described.

It should also be noted that we experimented with other types of multi-word index units, by using windows of different size and by selecting a larger number of words. However, we found that using just two words with a window of size 5 was the optimal choice.

5 Reranking PROSIT Results Using Coordination Level-Based Retrieval

Consistent with earlier effectiveness results, most information retrieval systems are based on best-matching algorithms between query and documents.

However, the use of very short queries by most of the users and the prevailing interest in precision rather than recall have fostered new research on exact matching retrieval, seen as an alternative or as a complementary technique to traditional best-matching retrieval. In particular, it has been shown that taking into account the number of query words matched by the documents to rerank retrieval results may improve performance in certain situations (e.g.,[7], [3]).

For the CLEF experiments, we focused on the query title. The goal was to prefer documents that matched all of the query keywords above documents that matched all but one of the keywords, and so on. To implement this strategy, we modified the standard best-matching similarity score between query and documents, computed as explained in Section 2, by adding a much larger addendum to it which was proportional to the number of distinct terms shared by the document and the query title. In this way, the documents were partially ordered according to their coordination level-based retrieval score with the query title, with ties being broken using their best-matching similarity score to the query.

However, the results were somewhat disappointing. We obtained a much better retrieval effectiveness by simply preferring the documents that contained all the words of the query title, without paying attention to lower levels of coordination matching. This was our choice (run fub02b).

Finally, we submitted a fourth run by using a fully enhanced version of PROSIT, i.e., bigrams + coordination level-based retrieval (run fub02lb)

6 Results

We tested PROSIT and its three variants (i.e., PROSIT with bigrams, PROSIT with coordination level-based retrieval, and PROSIT with both bigrams and

Table 1. Retrieval performance of PROSIT and its variants

CLEF	PROSIT	PROSIT+bigrams	PROSIT+CLM	PROSIT+bigrams+CLM
CLEF 2001	0.5116	0.5208	0.5127	0.5223
CLEF 2002	0.5019	0.5088	0.4872	0.4947

coordination level-based retrieval) on the CLEF 2001 and CLEF 2002 Italian monolingual tasks. Table 1 shows the retrieval performance of the four systems on the two test collections using the average precision as evaluation measure. The results of Table 1 show that the performance of standard PROSIT was excellent on both test collections, with the value obtained for CLEF 2001 (0.5116) higher than the result of the best system at CLEF 2001 (0.4865). This result is a confirmation of the high effectiveness of the probabilistic ranking model implemented in PROSIT, which is exclusively based on simple document and query statistics.

Table 1 also shows that, in general, the variations in performance when passing from basic PROSIT to enhanced PROSIT were small. More specifically, the use of bigrams improved performance across both test collections, whereas the use of coordination level-based retrieval was slightly beneficial for CLEF 2001 and detrimental for CLEF 2002. Combining both enhancements improved the retrieval performance over using CLM alone on both test collections but it was still worse than baseline performance on the CLEF 2002 collection and worse than using bigrams alone on CLEF 2002.

Overall, the results for the enhanced versions of PROSIT are inconclusive. More work is needed to collect further evidence about their effectiveness, e.g., by using a more representative sample of performance measures or by considering other query scenarios. Besides a more robust evaluation of retrieval performance, a better understanding of why the use of bigrams into PROSIT's main algorithm yielded positive results in the experiments reported in this paper would be useful. This might be achieved, for instance, by analysing the variations in quality of the top ranked documents used for query expansion or by performing a query by query analysis of concept drift in the final retrieved documents.

7 Conclusions

We have experimented with the PROSIT system on the Italian monolingual task and have explored the use of bigrams and coordination level-based retrieval within PROSIT's main algorithm. From our experimental evaluation, the following main conclusions can be drawn.

- The novel probabilistic model implemented in PROSIT achieved high retrieval effectiveness on both the CLEF 2001 and CLEF 2002 Italian monolingual tasks. These results are even more remarkable considering that the system employs very simple indexing techniques and does not rely on any specialised or ad hoc natural language processing techniques.

- Using bigrams in the place of unigrams hurts performance; the combination of bigram scores and unigram scores performed better but it was still inferior to the results obtained by using unigrams alone. However, using the bigram scores in the first-pass ranking only to rank the documents used for query expansion, resulted in a performance improvement. These results held across both test collections.
- Using coordination level-based retrieval to rerank the retrieval results did not, in general, improve performance. Favouring the documents that contained all the keywords in the query title worked better on one test collection and worse on the other collection, whereas ordering the documents according to their level of coordination matching hurt performance on both test collections.

We regret that due to tight schedule we were not able to test PROSIT on the other CLEF monolingual tasks. However, as the application of PROSIT to the Italian task did not require any special work, we are confident that with a small effort we could obtain similar results for the other languages. This is left for future work.

References

[1] Gianni Amati, Claudio Carpineto, and Giovanni Romano. FUB at TREC-10 web track: a probabilistic framework for topic relevance term weighting. In E. M. Voorhees and D. K. Harman, editors, *In Proceedings of the 10th Text Retrieval Conference TREC 2001*, pages 182-191, Gaithersburg, MD, 2002. NIST Special Pubblication 500-250.

[2] Gianni Amati and Cornelis Joost van Rijsbergen. Probabilistic models of information retrieval based on measuring divergence from randomness. *ACM Transactions on Information Systems*, (to appear), 2002.

[3] E. Berenci, C. Carpineto, V. Giannini, S. Mizzaro. Effectiveness of keyword-based display and selection of retrieval results for interactive searches. *International Journal On Digital Libraries*, 3(3):249-260, 2000.

[4] D. Bodoff, A. Kambil. Partial coordination. I. The best of pre-coordination and post-coordination. *JASIS*, 49(14):1254-1269,1998.

[5] D. Carmel, E. Amitay, M. Herscovici, Y. Maarek, Y. Petruschka, A. Soffer, Juru at TREC-10 - Experiments with index pruning. In E. M. Voorhees and D. K. Harman, editors, *In Proceedings of the 10th Text Retrieval Conference TREC 2001*, pages 228-236, Gaithersburg, MD, 2002. NIST Special Pubblication 500-250.

[6] C. Carpineto, R. De Mori, G. Romano, and B. Bigi. An information theoretic approach to automatic query expansion. *ACM Transactions on Information Systems*, 19(1):1-27, 2001.

[7] C. Clarke, G. Cormack, E. Tudhope, (1997). Relevance ranking for one to three term queries. *Proceedings of RIAO'97*, 388-400, 1997.

[8] J Savoy. Reports on CLEF-2001 experiments. In *Working notes of CLEF*, Darmstadt, 2001.

[9] C.M Tan, Y. F. Wang, C.D Lee. The use of bigrams to enhance text categorization. *IP&M*, 38(4):529-546,2002.

COLE Experiments in the CLEF 2002 Spanish Monolingual Track

Jesús Vilares[1], Miguel A. Alonso[1], Francisco J. Ribadas[2], and Manuel Vilares[2]

[1] Departamento de Computación
Universidade da Coruña, Campus de Elviña s/n, 15071 La Coruña, Spain
jvilares@mail2.udc.es
alonso@udc.es
[2] Escuela Superior de Ingeniería Informática
Universidade de Vigo, Campus de As Lagoas, 32004 Orense, Spain
ribadas@ei.uvigo.es
vilares@uvigo.es
http://www.grupocole.org/

Abstract. In this our first participation in CLEF, we applied Natural Language Processing techniques for single word and multi-word term conflation. We tested several approaches at different levels of text processing in our experiments: first, we lemmatized the text to avoid inflectional variation; second, we expanded the queries through synonyms according to a fixed similarity threshold; third, we employed morphological families to deal with derivational variation; and fourth, we tested a mixed approach based on the employment of such families together with syntactic dependencies to deal with the syntactic content of the document.

1 Introduction

In Text Retrieval, since the information is encoded as text, the task of deciding whether a document is relevant or not to a given information need can be viewed as a Natural Language Processing (NLP) problem, in particular for languages with rich lexical, morphological and syntactical structures, such as Spanish. In recent years, progress in the field of NLP has resulted in the development of a new generation of more efficient, robust and precise tools. These advances, together with the increasing power of new computers, facilitate the application of NLP systems in real IR environments.

However, when applying NLP to Spanish texts, we face a severe problem, the lack of adequate linguistic resources for Spanish: large tagged corpora, tree-banks and advanced lexicons are not available. Therefore, while waiting for such resources to become available, we have to attempt simple solutions, employing a minimum of linguistic resources.

In this paper, we present a set of NLP tools designed to deal with different levels of linguistic variation in Spanish: morphological, lexical and syntactical.

C.A. Peters (Ed.): CLEF 2002, LNCS 2785, pp. 265–278, 2003.

The effectiveness of our solutions has been tested during this our first participation in the CLEF Spanish monolingual track.

This article is structured as follows. Section 2 describes the techniques used for single word term conflation. Expansion of queries by means of synonyms is introduced in Section 3. Multi-word term conflation through syntactic dependencies is described in Section 4. Section 5 describes our module for recovering uppercase phrases. In Section 6, the results of our experiments using the CLEF Spanish corpus are shown. Finally, in Section 7 we explain our conclusions and future work.

2 Conflation of Words Using Inflectional and Derivational Morphology

Our proposal for single word term conflation is based on exploiting the lexical level in two phases: first, by lemmatizing the text to solve inflectional variation, and second, by employing morphological families to deal with derivational morphology.

In this process, the first step consists in tagging the document. Document processing starts by applying our linguistically motivated preprocessor module [10, 3], performing tasks such as format conversion, tokenization, sentence segmentation, morphological pretagging, contraction splitting, separation of enclitic pronouns from verbal stems, phrase identification, numeral identification and proper noun recognition. It is interesting to observe that classical techniques do not deal with many of these phenomena, resulting in erroneous simplifications during the conflation process.

The output of the preprocessor is taken as input by the tagger-lemmatizer. Although any kind of tagger could be applied, in our system we have used a second order Markov model for part-of-speech tagging. The elements of the model and the procedures to estimate its parameters are based on Brant's work [5], incorporating information from external dictionaries [11] which is implemented by means of numbered minimal acyclic finite-state automata [9].

Once the text has been tagged, the lemmas of the content words (nouns, verbs, adjectives) are extracted for indexing. In this way, we solve the problems derived from inflection in Spanish and, as a result, recall is increased. With regard to the computational cost, the running cost of a lemmatizer-disambiguator is linear with respect to the length of a word, and cubic with respect to the size of the tagset, which is a constant. As we only need to know the grammatical category of the word, the tagset is small and therefore the increase in cost with respect to classical approaches (stemmers) is negligible.

When inflectional variation has been solved, the next logical step is to solve the problems caused by derivational morphology. Spanish has a great productivity and flexibility in its word formation mechanisms, using a rich and complex productive morphology, and preferring derivation to other mechanisms of word formation. We have considered the derivational morphemes, the allomorphic variants of such morphemes and the phonological conditions they must satisfy to automatically generate the set of morphological families from a large lexicon of Spanish words [16]. The resulting morphological families can be used as a kind of advanced and linguistically motivated stemmer for Spanish, where every lemma is substituted by a fixed representative of its morphological family. Since the set of morphological families is generated statically, there is no increment in the running cost.

3 Using Synonymy to Expand Queries

The use of synonymy relations in the task of automatic query expansion is not a new subject, but the approaches presented until now do not assign a weight to the degree of synonymy that exists between the original terms present in the query and those produced by the process of expansion [12]. As our system has access to this information, a threshold of synonymy can be set in order to control the degree of query expansion.

The most frequent definition of synonymy identifies it as a relation between two expressions with identical or similar meaning. The controversy as to whether synonymy should be understood as a precise relationship or as an approximate relationship, i.e. as a relationship of identity or as a relationship of similarity, has existed from the beginning of the study of this semantic relation. In our system, synonymy is understood as a gradual relation between words.

We have used as a starting point a computer-readable dictionary obtained from the Blecua's Spanish dictionary of synonyms [4], which contains 27,029 entries and 87,762 synonymy relations. In order to calculate the degree of synonymy, we have used *Jaccard's coefficient* as measure of similarity applied to the sets of synonyms provided by the dictionary for each of its entries. Given two sets X and Y, their *similarity* is measured as:

$$sm(X,Y) = \frac{|X \cap Y|}{|X \cup Y|}$$

Let us consider a word w with m_i possible meanings, and another word w' with m_j possible meanings, where $dc(w, m_i)$ represents the function that gives us the set of synonyms provided by the dictionary for every entry w in the concrete meaning m_i. The degree of synonymy of w and w' in the meaning m_i of w is calculated as $dg(w, m_i, w') = \max_j \ sm[dc(w, m_i), dc(w', m_j)]$. Furthermore, by calculating $k = \arg\max_j \ sm[dc(w, m_i), dc(w', m_j)]$ we obtain in m_k the meaning of w' closest to the meaning m_i of w. The details of the implementation are given in [7].

4 Extracting Dependencies between Words by Means of a Shallow Parser

Our system is not only able to process the content of the document at word level, it can also process its syntactic structure. For this purpose, a parser module obtains from the tagged document the *head-modifier* pairs corresponding to the most relevant syntactic dependencies: *noun-modifier*, relating the head of a noun phrase with the head of a modifier; *subject-verb*, relating the head of the subject with the main verb of the clause; and *verb-complement*, relating the main verb of the clause with the head of a complement.

The kernel of the grammar used by this shallow parser is inferred from the basic trees corresponding to noun phrases[1] and their syntactic and morpho-syntactic variants [13, 15]:

- *Syntactic variants* result from the inflection of individual words and from modifying the syntactic structure of the original noun phrase by means of:
  - *Synapsy:* this corresponds to a change of preposition or the addition or removal of a determiner, e.g. *una caída de ventas* (a drop in sales).
  - *Substitution:* this consists of employing modifiers to make a term more specific, e.g. *una caída inusual de ventas* (an unusual drop in sales).
  - *Permutation:* this refers to the permutation of words around a pivot element, e.g. *una inusual caída de ventas* (an unusual drop in sales).
  - *Coordination:* this consists of employing coordinating constructions (copulative or disjunctive) with the modifier or with the modified term, e.g. *una inusual caída de ventas y de beneficios* (an unusual drop in sales and profits).
- *Morpho-syntactic variants* differ from syntactic variants in that at least one of the content words of the original noun phrase is transformed into another word derived from the same morphological stem, e.g. *las ventas han caído* (sales have dropped).

We note that syntactic variants involve inflectional morphology but not derivational morphology, whereas morpho-syntactic variants involve both inflectional and derivational morphology. In addition, syntactic variants have a very restricted scope (the noun phrase) whereas morpho-syntactic variants can span a whole sentence, including a verb and its complements.

Once the basic trees of noun phrases and their variants have been established, they are compiled into a set of regular expressions, which are matched against the tagged document in order to extract its dependencies in the form of pairs which are used as index terms after conflating their components through morphological families, as is described in [15]. In this way, we are identifying dependency pairs through simple pattern matching over the output of the tagger-lemmatizer, solving the problem by means of finite-state techniques, leading to a considerable reduction in the running cost.

5 The Uppercase-to-Lowercase Module

An important characteristic of IR test collections that may have a considerable impact on the performance of linguistically motivated indexing techniques is the

[1] At this point we will take as example the noun phrase *una caída de las ventas* (a drop in sales).

large number of typographical errors present in documents, as has been reported in the case of the Spanish CLEF corpus, by [8]. In particular, words in news titles and subsection headings are generally written in capital letters without accents, and cannot be correctly managed by the preprocessor and tagger modules, thus leading to incorrect conflations. We must, however, remember that these titles are usually very indicative of the topic of the document.

In an attempt to solve this problem, we have incorporated an *uppercase-to-lowercase* module in our system to process uppercase sentences, converting them to lowercase and restoring the existent diacritics when necessary. Other approaches, such as [18], deal with documents where absolutely all diacritics have been eliminated. Our situation is different because the main body of the document is written in lowercase and preserves the diacritics; only some sentences are written in capital letters. Moreover, for our purposes we only need the grammatical category and lemma of the word, not the form.

We can thus employ the lexical context of an uppercase sentence, either forms or lemmas, to recover this lost information. The first step of this process is to identify the uppercase phrases. We consider that a sequence of words forms an *uppercase phrase*, when it consists of three or more words written in capital letters and at least three of them have more than three characters. For each of these uppercase phrases we do the following:

1. We obtain its surrounding context.
2. For each of the words in the phrase:
   (a) We examine the context looking for terms with the same flattened form [2]. Each of these terms become candidates.
   (b) If a number of candidates are found, that with the most occurrences is chosen, and in the case of a draw, the closest to the term in the phrase is chosen.
   (c) If no candidates are found, the lexicon is examined:
      i. We obtain from the lexicon all entries with the same flattened form, grouping them according to their category and lemma (we are not interested in the form, just in the category and the lemma of the word).
      ii. If no entries are found, we keep the actual tag and lemma.
      iii. If only one entry is found, we choose that one.
      iv. If more than one entry is found, we choose the most numerous in the context (according to the category and the lemma). Again, in the case of a draw, we choose the closest to the sentence.

Sometimes, some words of the uppercase phrase preserve some of their diacritics, for example the ˜ of the Ñ. In this situations the candidates from the context or the lexicon must observe this restriction.

[2] That is, after both words been converted to lowercase, and after eliminating all diacritics from them

6 Experiments with the CLEF Spanish Corpus

The Spanish CLEF corpus used for these experiments is formed by 215,738 documents corresponding to the news provided by EFE, a Spanish news agency, in 1994. Documents are formatted in SGML, with a total size of 509 Megabytes. After deleting SGML tags, the size of the text corpus is reduced to 438 Megabytes. Each query consists of three fields: a brief title statement, a one-sentence description, and a more complex narrative specifying the relevance assessment criteria.

The techniques proposed in this article are independent of the indexing engine we choose to use. This is because we first conflate each document to obtain its index terms; the engine then receives the conflated version of the document as input. So, any standard text indexing engine can be employed, which is a great advantage. Nevertheless, each engine will behave according to its own features, that is, its indexing model, ranking algorithm, etc. [17]. In our case, we have worked with the vector-based engine SMART.

We have compared the results obtained using five different indexing methods:

- Stemming text after eliminating stopwords (*stm*). In order to apply this technique, we have tested several stemmers for Spanish. The best results we obtained were for the stemmer used by the open source search engine Muscat[3], based on Porter's algorithm [2]. This process eliminates accents from text before converting it to lowercase.
- Conflation of content words via lemmatization (*lem*), i.e. each form of a content word is replaced by its lemma. This kind of conflation only takes into account inflectional morphology.
- Conflation of content words via lemmatization and expansion of queries by means of synonymy (*syn*). We considered two words to be synonyms if their similarity measure is greater or equal to 0.80. Previous experiments have shown that the expansion of the narrative field introduces too much noise in the system; for this reason we only expand title and description fields.
- Conflation of content words by means of morphological families (*fam*), i.e. each form of a content word is replaced by the representative of its morphological family. This kind of conflation takes into account both inflectional and derivational morphology.
- Text conflated by means of the combined use of morphological families and syntactic dependency pairs (*f-sdp*).

The methods *lem*, *syn*, *fam*, and *f-sdp* are linguistically motivated. Therefore, they are able to deal with some complex linguistic phenomena such as clitic pronouns, contractions, idioms, and proper name recognition. By contrast, the method *stm* works simply by removing a given set of suffixes, without taking into account such linguistic phenomena, and yielding incorrect conflations that

[3] Currently, Muscat is not an open source project, and the web site `http://open.muscat.com` used to download the stemmer is not operating. Information about a similar stemmer for Spanish (and other European languages) can be found at `http://snowball.sourceforge.net/spanish/stemmer.html`.

Table 1. CLEF 2002 (submitted): performance measures

	TD*lem*	TDN*lem*	TDN*syn*	TDN*f-sdp*
Documents retrieved	50,000	50,000	50,000	50,000
Relevant docs retrieved (2854 expected)	2,495	2,634	2,632	2,624
R-precision	0.3697	0.4466	0.4438	0.3983
Average precision per query	0.3608	0.4448	0.4423	0.4043
Average precision per relevant docs	0.3971	0.4665	0.4613	0.4472
11-points average precision	0.3820	0.4630	0.4608	0.4205

introduce noise in the system. For example, clitic pronouns are simply considered as a set of suffixes to be removed. Moreover, the employment of finite-state techniques in the implementation of our methods allows us to reduce the computational cost, making their application feasible in a real world context.

6.1 CLEF 2002 Original Experiments

The original results submitted to CLEF 2002 consisted of four different runs:

- TD*lem*: Conflation of title + description content words via lemmatization (*lem*).
- TDN*lem*: The same as above, but using title + description + narrative.
- TDN*syn*: Conflation of title + description + narrative via lemmatization and expansion by means of synonymy (*syn*). It should be noted that only title and description fields were expanded.
- TDN*f-sdp*: Text conflated by means of the combined use of morphological families and syntactic dependency pairs (*f-sdp*), and using title + description + narrative to construct the queries.

For this set of experiments, the following conditions were applied:

1. Employment of the `lnc-ltc` weighting scheme [6].
2. Stopword list obtained from the content word lemmas of the Spanish stopword list provided by SMART [4].
3. Employment of the uppercase-to-lowercase module to recover uppercase sentences.
4. Except for TD*lem*, the terms extracted from the title section were considered to be twice as important with respect to the description and narrative.

As shown in Table 1, all NLP-based methods performed better than standard stemming, but lemmatization (TDN*lem*) appeared to be the best option, even when only dealing with inflectional variation. Expansion through synonymy

[4] `ftp://ftp.cs.cornell.edu/pub/smart/`

(TDN*syn*) did not improve the results because the expansion was *total*, that is, all synonyms of all terms of the query were added, and no word sense disambiguation procedures were available; thus, too much noise was introduced into the system. When the syntactic dependency pairs (TDN*f-dsp*) were employed, the results did not show any improvement with respect to the other NLP-based techniques considered, except in the case of average precision at N documents, where this method performed best for the first 10 retrieved documents.

6.2 New Experiments: Tuning the System with CLEF 2001 Queries

After our participation in the CLEF 2002 campaign, we decided to improve our system by applying some extra processing and by using a better weighting scheme, the `atn-ntc` [14]. Before testing our conflation techniques with these changes, we tuned our system using CLEF 2001 queries. During this training phase, we only tested the *lem* conflation technique because, as was shown in the original CLEF 2002 runs and other previous experiments [17], this approach was shown to be a good starting point for our NLP techniques. For these training experiments, we used all the three fields of each topic: title + description + narrative. However, the same results were obtained for parallel experiments using just the title + description fields, as is required in the CLEF mandatory run.

Table 2 shows the performance measures obtained during this tuning phase with CLEF 2001 topics. The monolingual Spanish task in 2001 provided a set of 50 queries; however, there were no relevant documents in the corpus for one of these queries, thus the performance measures were computed over 49 queries.

In our initial tests we did not apply the uppercase-to-lowercase module, and we used a very restricted stopword list formed by the lemmas of the most common verbs in Spanish[5]. The results obtained for this base run are shown in the column *step 1* of Table 2.

Our first improvement consisted in enlarging the stopword list using the list employed in the submitted results, i.e., the lemmas of the content words of the Spanish stopword list provided with SMART engine. The results are shown in the column *step 2* of Table 2 and are very similar to the previous ones, although they do show a slight improvement and an extra reduction of 6% in the size of the inverted file of the index. Therefore, we decided to continue using the SMART stopword list.

The next step consisted in employing our uppercase-to-lowercase module. The results, shown in the column *step 3* of Table 2, show that the performance of the system improves when the lemmas of uppercase sentences are recovered. At this point, all the conditions considered were those that were applied to produce the original CLEF 2002 results.

Nevertheless, there were still many typographical errors in the body of the documents, many of them consisting in unaccented vowels; part of this problem can be solved by eliminating the accents from the conflated text. The rationale for this solution is that once the lemma of a word has been identified there is

[5] i.e. *ser*, *estar*, *haber*, *tener*, *ir* and *hacer*

Table 2. CLEF 2001: training process using conflation through lemmatization (*lem*)

	step 1	*step 2*	*step 3*	*step 4*	*step 5*	*step 6*
Documents retrieved	49,000	49,000	49,000	49,000	49,000	49,000
Rel. docs retrieved (2694 exp.)	2,602	2,602	2,607	2,609	2,621	2,623
R-precision	0.5067	0.5115	0.5094	0.5156	0.5250	0.5269
Avg. non-interpolated precision	0.5231	0.5240	0.5312	0.5403	0.5512	0.5535
Avg. document precision	0.6279	0.6272	0.6339	0.6385	0.6477	0.6483
11-points avg. precision	0.5289	0.5301	0.5380	0.5467	0.5571	0.5600
3-points avg. precision	0.5422	0.5444	0.5513	0.5613	0.5727	0.5735

no reason to keep the accents. It can be argued that we will lose the *diacritical accents*[6], but if we are working with content word lemmas this problem is irrelevant. However, we keep the character *'ñ'* in the texts, i.e. not converting it to *'n'*, because it may introduce more noise in the system by conflating words, e.g. *cana* (grey hair) and *caña* (cane), into the same term. Moreover, in Spanish, although it is quite common to forget an accent when writing, confusion between *'ñ'* and *'n'* is extremely rare. In the column *step 4* of Table 2 we see the improvements obtained with this adjustment .

Similarly, an additional experiment was made in which the resulting text was also converted to lower-case as in the case of stemming, and the results obtained showed a further improvement, as can be seen in column *step 5* of Table 2.

As in the original submitted runs, our final test case considered the title field of the topic to be twice as important with respect to the description and narrative, as we presume that it contains the main information of the query. The improvement obtained with this measure can be seen in column *step 6* of Table 2.

The conditions employed in this last run will be retained for further experiments:

1. Employment of the `atn-ntc` weighting scheme.
2. Stopword list obtained from the content word lemmas of the SMART stopword list.
3. Employment of the uppercase-to-lowercase module to recover uppercase sentences.
4. Elimination of accents after conflation to reduce typographical errors.
5. Conversion to lowercase after conflation.
6. Title statement considered as twice as important.

[6] Accents that distinguish between words with the same graphical form but different meaning, e.g. *mí* (me) - *mi* (my).

Table 3. CLEF 2001: performance measures

	stm	*lem*	*syn*	*fam*	*f-sdp*
Documents retrieved	49,000	49,000	49,000	49,000	49,000
Relevant docs retrieved (2694 expected)	2,628	2,623	2,620	2,611	2,575
R-precision	0.5221	0.5269	0.5170	0.5139	0.4839
Average non-interpolated precision	0.5490	0.5535	0.5420	0.5360	0.5046
Average document precision	0.6277	0.6483	0.6326	0.6128	0.5370
11-points average precision	0.5574	0.5600	0.5486	0.5431	0.5187
3-points average precision	0.5691	0.5735	0.5660	0.5552	0.5306

Table 4. CLEF 2001: average precision at 11 standard recall levels

Recall	Precision				
	stm	*lem*	*syn*	*fam*	*f-sdp*
0.00	0.8895	0.8975	0.8693	0.8616	0.8648
0.10	0.7946	0.7951	0.7802	0.7672	0.7603
0.20	0.7393	0.7532	0.7426	0.7212	0.6975
0.30	0.6779	0.6994	0.6779	0.6684	0.6217
0.40	0.6394	0.6526	0.6367	0.6137	0.5712
0.50	0.5867	0.5878	0.5781	0.5559	0.5359
0.60	0.5299	0.5228	0.5145	0.4988	0.4707
0.70	0.4411	0.4412	0.4357	0.4355	0.4029
0.80	0.3814	0.3794	0.3772	0.3886	0.3585
0.90	0.2952	0.2831	0.2766	0.2956	0.2663
1.00	0.1561	0.1477	0.1459	0.1678	0.1563

6.3 New Experiments with CLEF 2001 and CLEF 2002 Topics

In Tables 3 and 4 we show the results obtained for CLEF 2001 topics using our NLP-based conflation techniques (*lem*, *syn*, *fam*, *f-sdp*) compared with stemming (*stm*) when applying the new conditions.

In contrast with the results obtained in [1] for the same topics using the `lnc-ltc` scheme, only the *lem* conflation method beats *stm* now. This is due to a performance change in the system when using the new weighting scheme. This new scheme improves the results obtained for all the conflation methods considered with respect to the previous scheme, but considerably more with stemming and lemmatization than when employing synonymy and morphological families. The reason for this may be due to a higher sensitivity to the noise introduced by badly constructed families in the case of *fam*, and therefore also in *f-sdp*, and to the noise introduced by our approach for expansion through synonymy in the case of *syn*.

Table 5. CLEF 2002: performance measures

	stm	*lem*	*syn*	*fam*	*f-sdp*	TD*lem*
Documents retrieved	50,000	50,000	50,000	50,000	50,000	50,000
Rel. docs retrieved (2854 exp.)	2,570	2,593	2,582	2,624	2,577	2504
R-precision	0.4892	0.4924	0.4721	0.4772	0.4317	0.4443
Aveg. non-interpolated precision	0.5097	0.5186	0.5057	0.4971	0.4546	0.4592
Avg. document precision	0.5255	0.5385	0.5264	0.5170	0.4560	0.4910
11-points avg. precision	0.5239	0.5338	0.5192	0.5155	0.4733	0.4764
3-points avg. precision	0.5193	0.5378	0.5249	0.5109	0.4605	0.4764

Table 6. CLEF 2002: average precision at 11 standard recall levels

Recall	Precision					
	stm	*lem*	*syn*	*fam*	*f-sdp*	TD*lem*
0.00	0.8887	0.8859	0.8492	0.8783	0.8758	0.8446
0.10	0.7727	0.7888	0.7753	0.7637	0.7664	0.7210
0.20	0.6883	0.7096	0.6965	0.6721	0.6704	0.6420
0.30	0.6327	0.6417	0.6246	0.6108	0.5936	0.5740
0.40	0.5909	0.6025	0.5848	0.5724	0.5265	0.5506
0.50	0.5465	0.5628	0.5447	0.5310	0.4458	0.4945
0.60	0.5041	0.4918	0.4720	0.4708	0.3861	0.4226
0.70	0.4278	0.4214	0.4109	0.4144	0.3309	0.3608
0.80	0.3231	0.3410	0.3336	0.3296	0.2654	0.2928
0.90	0.2456	0.2595	0.2547	0.2647	0.2131	0.2103
1.00	0.1422	0.1666	0.1653	0.1628	0.1322	0.1276

Nevertheless, as we can see in Tables 3 and 4, *lem* continues to perform better than *stm*, even though it is the simpler approach.

The behavior of the system with CLEF 2002 topics, see Tables 5 and 6, is very similar to 2001, but with a lower recall for stemming (*stm*) with respect to NLP-based techniques. This difference shows more clearly in the case of the morphological families approach (*fam*), which also covers derivational morphology. Nevertheless, only lemmatization continues to perform better than stemming. The column TD*lem* contains the results we would now submit to the CLEF campaign, that is, the results obtained using the *lem* technique with the new conditions and employing only the title + description topic fields.

7 Conclusions

According to the results we have obtained for CLEF 2001 and CLEF 2002 topics, content word lemmatization (*lem*) seems to be the best conflation option, even when it only covers inflectional morphology. It performs better than standard stemming (*stm*), which also covers derivational variation.

Our approach towards lexical variation by means of query expansion through synonymy (*syn*) does not improve system performance, due to the noise introduced. A different approach, similar to relevance feedback, based on the expansion of the most relevant terms in the most relevant documents, may be more appropriate. Traditional automatic relevance feedback, followed by a phase of filtering and re-weighting of synonyms in the terms generated during expansion is another possibility.

In the case of derivational variation, the use of morphological families seems to introduce too much noise into the system due to badly constructed families, giving a worse performance than expected for single word term conflation (*fam*). The tuning of the morphological families approach, or similar approaches to those proposed for synonymy may solve this problem.

The same problem is inherited by our proposal for dealing with syntactical variation through the employment of syntactic dependency pairs and morphological families (*f-sdp*).

These results, together with previous ones obtained in other experiments using different weighting schemes and retrieval models [1, 15, 17], suggest that mere lemmatization is a good starting point. It should be investigated whether an initial search using lemmatization should be followed by a relevance feedback process based on expansion through synonymy and/or morphological families. Another alternative for post-processing could be the re-ranking of the results by means of syntactic information obtained in the form of syntactic dependency pairs.

Acknowledgements

The research reported in this article has been supported in part by Plan Nacional de Investigación Científica, Desarrollo e Innovación Tecnológica (grant TIC2000-0370-C02-01), Ministerio de Ciencia y Tecnología (grant HP2001-0044), FPU grants of Secretaría de Estado de Educación y Universidades, Xunta de Galicia (grants PGIDT01PXI10506PN, PGIDIT02PXIB30501PR and PGIDIT02SIN01E) and Universidade da Coruña.

References

[1] Miguel A. Alonso, Jesús Vilares, and Víctor M. Darriba. On the usefulness of extracting syntactic dependencies for text indexing. In Michael O'Neill, Richard F.E. Sutcliffe, Conor Ryan, Malachy Eaton, and Niall J.L. Griffith, editors, *Artificial Intelligence and Cognitive Science*, volume 2464 of *Lecture Notes in Artificial Intelligence*, pages 3–11. Springer-Verlag, Berlin-Heidelberg-New York, 2002.

[2] Ricardo Baeza-Yates and Berthier Ribeiro-Neto. *Modern Information Retrieval*. Addison-Wesley, Harlow, England, 1999.

[3] Fco. Mario Barcala, Jesús Vilares, Miguel A. Alonso, Jorge Graña, and Manuel Vilares. Tokenization and proper noun recognition for information retrieval. In A Min Tjoa and Roland R. Wagner (eds.), *Thirteen International Workshop on Database and Expert Systems Applications. 2-6 September 2002. Aix-en-Provence, France*, pp. 246-250, IEEE Computer Society Press, Los Alamitos, California, 2002.

[4] J. M. Blecua (dir.), *Diccionario Avanzado de Sinónimos y Antónimos de la Lengua Española*, Vox, Barcelona, Spain, 1997.

[5] Thorsten Brants. TnT - a statistical part-of-speech tagger. In *Proceedings of the Sixth Applied Natural Language Processing Conference (ANLP'2000)*, Seattle, 2000.

[6] Chris Buckley, James Allan, and Gerard Salton. Automatic routing and ad-hoc retrieval using SMART: TREC 2. In D. K. Harman, editor, *NIST Special Publication 500-215: The Second Text REtrieval Conference (TREC-2)*, pages 45–56, Gaithersburg, MD, USA, 1993.

[7] Santiago Fernández, Jorge Graña, and Alejandro Sobrino. A Spanish e-dictionary of synonyms as a fuzzy tool for information retrieval. In *Actas del XI Congreso Español sobre Tecnologías y Lógica Fuzzy (ESTYLF-2002)*, León, Spain, September 2002.

[8] Carlos G. Figuerola, Raquel Gómez, Angel F. Zazo, and José Luis Alonso. Stemming in Spanish: A first approach to its impact on information retrieval. In Carol Peters, editor, *Working notes for the CLEF 2001 Workshop*, Darmstadt, Germany, September 2001.

[9] Jorge Graña, Fco. Mario Barcala, and Miguel A. Alonso. Compilation methods of minimal acyclic automata for large dictionaries. In Bruce W. Watson and Derick Wood, editors, *Proc. of the 6th Conference on Implementations and Applications of Automata (CIAA 2001)*, pages 116–129, Pretoria, South Africa, July 2001.

[10] Jorge Graña, Fco. Mario Barcala, and Jesús Vilares. Formal methods of tokenization for part-of-speech tagging. In Alexander Gelbukh, editor, *Computational Linguistics and Intelligent Text Processing*, Volume 2276 of *Lecture Notes in Computer Science*, pages 240–249. Springer-Verlag, Berlin-Heidelberg-New York, 2002.

[11] Jorge Graña, Jean-Cédric Chappelier, and Manuel Vilares. Integrating external dictionaries into stochastic part-of-speech taggers. In *Proceedings of the Euroconference Recent Advances in Natural Language Processing (RANLP 2001)*, pages 122–128, Tzigov Chark, Bulgaria, 2001.

[12] Jane Greenberg. Automatic query expansion via lexical-semantic relationships. *Journal of the American Society for Information Science and Technology*, 52(5):402–415, 2001.

[13] Christian Jacquemin and Evelyne Tzoukermann. NLP for term variant extraction: synergy between morphology, lexicon and syntax. In Tomek Strzalkowski, editor, *Natural Language Information Retrieval*, volume 7 of *Text, Speech and Language Technology*, pages 25–74. Kluwer Academic Publishers, Dordrecht/Boston/London, 1999.

[14] J. Savoy, A. Le Calve, and D. Vrajitoru. Report on the TREC-5 experiment: Data fusion and collection fusion. Proceedings of TREC'5, NIST publication #500-238, pages 489–502, Gaithersburg, MD, 1997.

[15] Jesús Vilares, Fco. Mario Barcala, and Miguel A. Alonso. Using syntactic dependency-pairs conflation to improve retrieval performance in Spanish. In Alexander Gelbukh, editor, *Computational Linguistics and Intelligent Text Processing*, Volume 2276 of *Lecture Notes in Computer Science,*, pages 381–390. Springer-Verlag, Berlin-Heidelberg-New York, 2002.

[16] Jesús Vilares, David Cabrero, and Miguel A. Alonso. Applying productive derivational morphology to term indexing of Spanish texts. In Alexander Gelbukh, editor, *Computational Linguistics and Intelligent Text Processing*, Volume 2004 of *Lecture Notes in Computer Science*, pages 336–348. Springer-Verlag, Berlin-Heidelberg-New York, 2001.

[17] Jesús Vilares, Manuel Vilares, and Miguel A. Alonso. Towards the development of heuristics for automatic query expansion. In Heinrich C. Mayr, Jiri Lazansky, Gerald Quirchmayr, and Pavel Vogel, editors, *Database and Expert Systems Applications*, Volume 2113 of *Lecture Notes in Computer Science*, pages 887–896. Springer-Verlag, Berlin-Heidelberg-New York, 2001.

[18] David Yarowsky. A comparison of corpus-based techniques for restoring accents in Spanish and French text. In *Natural Language Processing Using Very Large Corpora*, pages 99–120. Kluwer Academic Publishers, 1999.

Improving the Automatic Retrieval of Text Documents

Maristella Agosti, Michela Bacchin, Nicola Ferro, and Massimo Melucci

Department of Information Engineering
University of Padua, Via Gradenigo, 6/a – 35031 Padova, Italy
{maristella.agosti,michela.bacchin,nicola.ferro,massimo.melucci}@unipd.it

Abstract. This paper reports on a statistical stemming algorithm based on link analysis. Considering that a word is formed by a prefix (stem) and a suffix, the key idea is that the interlinked prefixes and suffixes form a community of sub-strings. Thus, discovering these communities means searching for the best word splits that give the best word stems. The algorithm has been used in our participation in the CLEF 2002 Italian monolingual task. The experimental results show that stemming improves text retrieval effectiveness. They also show that the effectiveness level of our algorithm is comparable to that of an algorithm based on a-priori linguistic knowledge.

Keywords: Italian Text Retrieval; Information Retrieval; Web Information Gathering; Stemming; Link-based Analysis

1 Introduction

The main objective of the research reported in this paper is to design, implement and evaluate a language-independent stemming algorithm based on statistical and link-analysis methods. To accomplish this objective, we designed our experiments to investigate whether stemming does not deteriorate or even enhances the effectiveness of retrieval of documents written in Italian, using both a linguistic and a statistical stemmer. We then investigated whether a statistical and language-independent stemming algorithm can perform as effectively as an algorithm developed on the basis of a-priori linguistic knowledge.

The paper is organized as follows: Section 2 illustrates our previous work in multilingual information retrieval. We report on a background activity for the building of test collections of documents written in Italian – the seed work that has led us to investigate and concentrate on stemming as a fundamental building block in the retrieval of textual documents written in Italian. Using our experience in the construction of a document collection for the retrieval of Italian documents as a starting point, we realized that a real weakness in text retrieval is dependence on the specific languages used in the documents of interest. Thus we concentrate on efforts for developing stemming methods and algorithms that can be independent of the specific languages of interest. The second part of the paper reports on results obtained in this area. In particular, Section 3 introduces

C.A. Peters (Ed.): CLEF 2002, LNCS 2785, pp. 279–290, 2003.

the stemming process, Section 4 reports on the methodological approach we followed to build a new statistical and language-independent stemming algorithm, Section 5 describes our runs and the results obtained, and Section 6 reports some conclusions and future work.

2 Background

One of the essential tools needed to conduct research in information retrieval for a language other than English is a test collection of documents written in the language of interest. The purpose of such a collection is to make research results repeatable and available for evaluation by different research groups, with different systems, and in different contexts. At the Department of Information Engineering of the University of Padua, research work on multilingual information retrieval dates back to 1998, when we started to design and implement a test collection for the retrieval of documents written in Italian in order to perform experiments using stemming algorithms [1]. Unfortunately, the test collection is not yet publicly available due to copyright constraints.

When we started the investigation, we decided to select a large set of full-text documents, representing one year's publication of an Italian newspaper. We chose a newspaper that publishes the complete collection of articles for each year on CD-ROM together with an information retrieval system that can be used to search it. The collection we chose has almost seventy thousand documents, so its size is comparable to the size of one of the TREC sub-collections, such as WSJ, distributed on TREC disk 2, which contains 74,520 newspaper documents taken from the "Wall Street Journal, 1990-1992".

Examining the content of the source collection of documents, some information needs were identified and corresponding topics were written in natural language in order to create a query set. Our objectives were twofold:

- to build up a set of "real" queries, i.e. reflecting queries a hypothetical "real" final user would submit to a system providing access to the collection, and
- to ensure that some of the queries constructed refer to real events or facts being reported in newspapers, other than general subjects.

Therefore, the test queries refer to specific facts, and include specific words, such as proper names or dates. The final requirement concerned the query size: queries were similar in size to real ones as formulated by real final users of the source collection. In order to be able to create sufficiently specific queries, referring to real facts or events, it was decided to use the classification scheme provided on the CD-ROM, as a way to "suggest" potential reasonable test queries. The class names were used as a starting point for the definition of the queries, and each query was compiled using one of a set of selected categories from the classification scheme.

The task of assessing the relevance of test documents with respect to test queries should in principle be exhaustive, i.e. should be made for every document-query pair in order to have the total number of relevant documents of the entire collection for each query. However, such a exhaustive task is clearly impossible, and this is why sampling methods have been proposed [21].

We developed a new method that combines the experience of TREC with the exploitation of the classification system which was used to classify all the documents of the set. The main contributions were provided by (1) the different tools and evidence used to compile the relevance assessments, and (2) the assignment of relevance assessments to different document parts to enable the evaluation of tasks that are different from classical document retrieval, such as passage retrieval.

The methodology we set up to build document set samples was based on the combined use of a classification system and of a query tool. In fact, each year during the preparation of the CD-ROM of the newspaper articles, a group of experts manually classifies all the documents using a classification system that has the following characteristics: it has been built by experts in the domain of the source database; it is a specialized classification; it allows overlapping, so a document can be classified in two or more classes. The query tool available on the CD-ROM provides quite sophisticated Boolean searching capabilities, since the tool has been tuned to the available set of documents in order to provide effective retrieval.

At relevance assessment time, our human assessors were asked first to find relevant documents in some predefined categories which were likely to include relevant material. Then, they had to find additional relevant documents from the whole document collection using the query tool. While the classification system helped to increase retrieval precision, the query tool made it possible to increase recall by retrieving many other relevant documents outside the categories in which it was thought that the newly retrieved relevant documents should have been classified.

Moreover, as newspaper documents have different lengths and structures, it was quite common to have long documents in the retrieved set. Therefore, it was necessary to give relevance judgments on different document parts in order to capture different relevant portions of the documents. Specifically, assessors were asked to assess distinctly the relevance of the title, first paragraph, and whole text. In this way, there are three levels of assessment for each document. The resulting test collection is endowed with relevance judgments at a level of granularity which allows us to design document structuring-based applications. One of the problems that remained open after the design of this Italian test collection was the availability of an effective stemming algorithm, preferably an algorithm that adopted a methodology that could be reusable for languages other than Italian. Thus we decided to focus our attention on stemming, and we decided to participate in the CLEF 2002 campaign with the aim of evaluating a language-independent algorithm.

3 Stemming

Stemming is used to reduce variant word forms to a common root. The assumption is that if two words have the same root, then they represent the same concept. Hence stemming permits an IR system to match query and document terms which are related to the same meaning but which can appear in different morphological variants.

The effectiveness of stemming is a debated issue, and there are different results and conclusions. If effectiveness is measured by the traditional precision and recall measures, it seems that for a language with a relatively simple morphology, like English, stemming influences the overall performance little [7]. In contrast, stemming can significantly increase retrieval effectiveness [14] and can also increase precision for short queries [9], for languages with a more complex morphology, like the Romance languages. Finally, as system performance must reflect user's expectations it must be remembered that the use of a stemmer is apparently assumed by many users [7], who express a query to a system using a specific word without taking into account that only a variant of this word may appear in a relevant document. Hence, stemming can also be viewed as a feature that is related to the user-interaction interface of an IR service.

When designing a stemming algorithm, it is possible to follow a linguistic approach, using prior knowledge of the morphology of the specific language, or a statistical approach using methods based on statistical principles to infer the word formation rules in the language studied from a corpus of documents in that language. The former implies manual labor which has to be done by linguistic experts – in fact, it is necessary to formalize the word formation rules and this is hard work, especially for those languages with a complex morphology. Stemming algorithms based on statistical methods imply low costs to insert new languages in the system, and this is an advantage that can become crucial, especially for multilingual IR systems.

4 Methodology

We will consider a special case of stemming, which belongs to the category known as *affix removal stemming* [4]. In particular our approach follows a suffix stripping paradigm which is adopted by most stemmers currently in use by IR, such as those reported in [10, 13, 16]. This stemming process splits each word into two parts, prefix and suffix, and considers the stem as the sub-string corresponding to the prefix obtained.

Let us consider a finite collection of unique words $W = \{w_1, ..., w_N\}$ and a word $w \in W$ of length $|w|$, then w can be written as $w = xy$ where x is a prefix and y is a suffix. If we split each word w into all the $|w| - 1$ possible pairs of sub-strings, we build a collection of sub-strings, and each sub-string may be either a prefix, a suffix, or both, of at least an element $w \in W$. Let X be the set of the prefixes of the collection and $S \subseteq X$ be the set of the stems. We are interested in detecting the prefix x that is the most probable stem for the observed word w. Hence, we have to determine the prefix x^* such that:

$$x^* = \arg\max_x Pr(x \in S \mid w \in W) \quad (1)$$

$$= \arg\max_x \frac{Pr(w \in W \mid x \in S) Pr(x \in S)}{Pr(w \in W)} \quad (2)$$

where (2) is obtained applying Bayes' theorem which lets us swap the order of dependence between events. We can ignore the denominator, which is the same for all splits of w. $Pr(w \in W \mid x \in S)$ is the probability of observing w given that the stem x has been observed. A reasonable estimation of that probability would be the reciprocal of the number of words beginning with that stem if the stems were known. However note that the stems are unknown – indeed stem detection is the target of this method – and the number of words beginning with a stem cannot be computed. Therefore we estimated that probability by the reciprocal of the number of words beginning by that prefix. With regard to $Pr(x \in S)$ we estimated this probability using an algorithm that discloses the mutual relationship between stems and derivations in forming the words of the collection.

The rationale of using mutual reinforcement is based on the idea that stems extracted from W are those sub-strings that:

- are very frequent, and
- form words together with very frequent suffixes.

This means that very frequent prefixes are candidate stems, but they are discarded if they are not followed by very frequent suffixes; for example, all initials are very frequent prefixes but they are unlikely stems because the corresponding suffixes are rather rare, if not unique – the same holds for suffixes corresponding to ending vowels or consonants. Thus, there are prefixes that are less frequent than initials, but followed by suffixes that are frequent but less frequent than ending characters: these suffixes and prefixes correspond to candidate correct word splits and we label them as "good". The key idea is that interlinked good prefixes and suffixes form a community of sub-strings whose links correspond to words, i.e. to splits. Discovering these communities is like searching for the best splits.

To compute the best split, we used the quite well-known algorithm called HITS (Hyperlink Induced Topic Search) reported in [8] and often discussed in research papers as a paradigmatic algorithm for Web page retrieval. It considers a mutually reinforcing relationship among good authorities and good hubs, where an authority is a web page pointed to by many hubs and a hub is a web page which points to many authorities. The parallel with our context will be clear when we associate the concept of a hub with a prefix and that of an authority with a suffix. The method belongs to the larger class of approaches based on frequencies of sub-strings to decide the goodness of prefixes and suffixes, often used in statistical morphological analysis [12, 5], and in pioneer work [6]. The contribution of this paper is the use of the mutual reinforcement notion applied

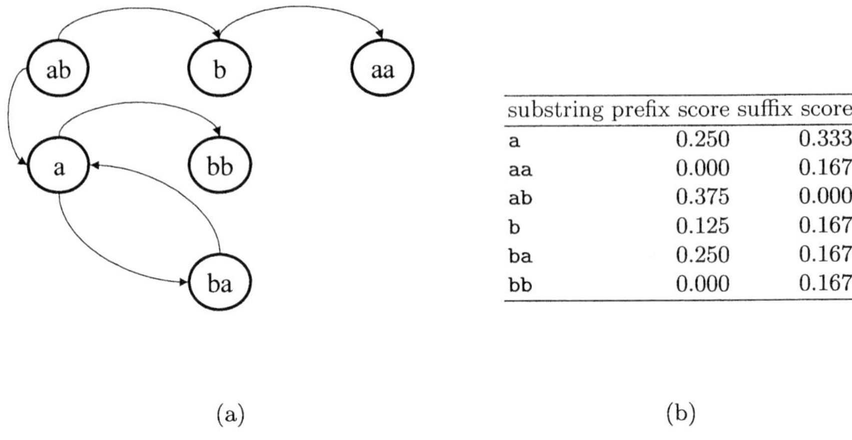

substring	prefix score	suffix score
a	0.250	0.333
aa	0.000	0.167
ab	0.375	0.000
b	0.125	0.167
ba	0.250	0.167
bb	0.000	0.167

(a) (b)

Fig. 1. (a) The graph obtained from W. (b) The prefix and suffix scores from W

to prefix frequencies and suffix frequencies, to compute the best word splits which give the best word stems as explained in the following.

Using a graphical notation, the set of prefixes and suffixes can be written as a graph $g = (V, E)$ such that V is the set of sub-strings and $w = (x, y) \in E$ is an edge w that occurs between nodes x, y if $w = xy$ is a word in W. By definition of g, no vertex is isolated. As an example, let us consider the following toy set of words: W={`aba`, `abb`, `baa`}; splitting these into all the possible prefixes and suffixes produces the graph reported in Figure 1a.

If a directed edge exists between x and y, the mutual reinforcement notion can be stated as follows:

> good prefixes point to good suffixes, and good suffixes are pointed to by good prefixes.

Let us define $P(y) = \{x \in V : \exists w, w = xy\}$ and $S(x) = \{y \in V : \exists w, w = xy\}$ as, respectively, the set of all prefixes of a given suffix y and the set of all suffixes of a given prefix x. If p_x and s_x indicate, respectively, the prefix score and the suffix score, the criteria can be expressed as:

$$p_x = \sum_{y \in S(x)} s_y \qquad s_y = \sum_{x \in P(y)} p_x \tag{3}$$

under the assumption that scores are expressed as sums of scores and splits are equally weighed.

The mutual reinforcement method has been formalized through the HITS iterative algorithm. Here we map HITS in our study context, as follows:

Compute suffix scores and prefix scores from W

V: the set of substrings extracted from all the words in W

$P(y)$: the set of all prefixes of a given suffix y

$S(x)$: the set of all suffixes of a given prefix x

N: the number of all substrings in V

n: the number of iterations

$\mathbf{1}$: the vector $(1, ..., 1) \in \mathcal{R}^{|V|}$

$\mathbf{0}$: the vector $(0, ..., 0) \in \mathcal{R}^{|V|}$

$\mathbf{s}^{(k)}$: suffix score vector at step k

$\mathbf{p}^{(k)}$: prefix score vector at step k

$\mathbf{s}^{(0)} = \mathbf{1}$

$\mathbf{p}^{(0)} = \mathbf{1}$

for each iteration $k = 1, ..., n$

$\mathbf{s}^{(k)} = \mathbf{0}$

$\mathbf{p}^{(k)} = \mathbf{0}$

for each $y \in V$

$$s_y^{(k)} = \sum_{x \in P(y)} p_x^{(k-1)};$$

for each $x \in V$

$$p_x^{(k)} = \sum_{y \in S(x)} s_y^{(k)};$$

normalize $\mathbf{p}^{(k)}$ and $\mathbf{s}^{(k)}$ so that $1 = \sum_x p_x^{(k)} = \sum_y s_y^{(k)}$

end.

Using the matrix notation, graph g can be described with a $|V| \times |V|$ matrix $\mathbf{M}$ such that

$$m_{ij} = \begin{cases} 1 & \text{if prefix } i \text{ and suffix } j \text{ form a word} \\ 0 & \text{otherwise} \end{cases}$$

As explained in [8], the algorithm computes two matrices: $\mathbf{A} = \mathbf{M}^T\mathbf{M}$ and $\mathbf{B} = \mathbf{M}\mathbf{M}^T$, where the generic element a_{ij} of $\mathbf{A}$ is the number of vertices that are pointed by both i and j, whereas the generic element b_{ij} of $\mathbf{B}$ is the number of vertices that point to both i and j. The n-step iteration of the algorithm corresponds to computing $\mathbf{A}^n$ and $\mathbf{B}^n$. In the same paper, it was argued that $\mathbf{s} = [s_y]$ and $\mathbf{p} = [p_x]$ converge to the eigenvectors of $\mathbf{A}$ and $\mathbf{B}$, respectively. The scores computed for the toy set of words are reported in Table 1.

As explained previously, we argue that the probability that x is a stem can be estimated with the prefix score p_x just calculated. The underlying assumption is that the scores can be seen as probabilities, and, in effect, it has been shown in a recent paper that HITS scores can be considered as a stationary distribution of a random walk [2]. In particular, the authors proved the existence of a Markov chain, which has the stationary distribution equal to the hub vector after the nth iteration of Kleinberg's algorithm, which is, in our context, the prefix score vector $\mathbf{p}^{(n)}$. The generic element $q_{ij}^{(n)}$ of the transition matrix referred to the chain is the probability that, starting from i, one reaches j after n "bouncing" to one

Table 1. The candidate splits from W={aba, baa, abb}

word	prefix	suffix	words beginning by prefix	words ending by suffix	probability	choice
baa	b	aa	1	1	0.1250	
baa	ba	a	1	2	0.2500	*
aba	a	ba	2	1	0.1250	
aba	ab	a	2	2	0.1875	*
abb	a	bb	2	1	0.1250	
abb	ab	b	2	1	0.1875	*

of the suffixes which is associated with both i and j. To interpret the result in a linguistic framework, p_i can be seen as the probability that i is judged as a stem by the same community of substrings (suffixes) resulting from the process of splitting the words of a language. In Table 1, all the possible splits for all the words are reported and measured using the estimated probability.

5 Experiments

The aim of our CLEF 2002 experiments has been to compare the retrieval effectiveness of the link analysis-based algorithm illustrated in the previous section with that of an algorithm based on a-priori linguistic knowledge; the hypothesis is that a language-independent algorithm, such as the one we propose, might effectively replace one developed on the basis of manually coded derivational rules. Before comparing the algorithms, we assessed the impact of both stemming algorithms by comparing their effectiveness with that reached without any stemmer. In fact, we wanted to test whether system performance is not significantly hurt by the application of stemming, as hypothesized in [7]. If, on the contrary, stemming improved effectiveness, and the effectiveness of the tested algorithms were comparable, the link-based algorithm could be extended to other languages inexpensively, which is of crucial importance in multilingual settings. To evaluate stemming, we decided to compare the performance of an IR system when different stemming algorithms were used for different runs, all other things being equal.

5.1 Experimental Prototype System

For indexing and retrieval, we used an experimental IR system, called IRON, which has been developed by our research group in order to have a robust tool for carrying out IR experiments. IRON is built on top of the Lucene 1.2 RC4 library, which is an open-source library for IR written in Java and publicly available at [11]. The system implements the vector space model [17], and a (tf · idf)-based weighting scheme [18]. The stop-list which was used consists of 409 Italian frequent words and is publicly available at [19].

In order to develop the statistical stemming algorithm, we built a suite of tools, called Stemming Program for Language Independent Tasks (SPLIT), which implements the link-based algorithm and chooses the best stem, according to the probabilistic criterion described in Section 4. From the vocabulary of the Italian CLEF sub-collection, SPLIT spawns a 2,277,297-node and 1,215,326-edge graph, which is processed to compute prefix and suffix scores – SPLIT took 2.5 hours for 100 iterations on a personal computer equipped with Linux, 800 MHz CPU and 256MB RAM.

5.2 Runs

We tested four different stemming algorithms:

1. `NoStem`: No stemming algorithm was applied.
2. `Porter-like`: We used the stemming algorithm for Italian, which is freely available on the Snowball Web Site [15] edited by M. Porter. Besides being publicly available for research purposes, we chose this algorithm because it uses a kind of a-priori knowledge of the Italian language. Thus, comparing our SPLIT algorithm with this particular "linguistic" algorithm could provide some information with respect to the feasibility of estimating linguistic knowledge from statistically inferred knowledge.
3. `SPLIT`: We implemented our first version of the stemming algorithm based on a link-analysis with 100 iterations.
4. `SPLIT-L3`: We included in our stemming algorithm a minimum of linguistic knowledge, inserting a heuristic rule which forces the length of the stem to be at least 3.

5.3 A Global Evaluation

We carried out a macro evaluation by averaging the results over all the queries of the test collection. Table 2 shows a summary of the figures related to the macro analysis of the stemming algorithm for 2001 topics, while Table 3 reports data on 2002 topics, which are our official runs submitted at CLEF.

Table 2. Macro comparison of runs for 2001 topics

Algorithm	N. Relevant Retrieved	Av. Precision	R-Precision
`NoStem`	1093	0.3387	0.3437
`Porter-like`	1169	0.3753	0.3619
`SPLIT`	1143	0.3519	0.3594
`SPLIT-L3`	1149	0.3589	0.3668

Table 3. Macro comparison among runs for 2002 topics

Run ID	Algorithm	N. Relevant Retrieved	Av. Precision	R-Precision
PDDN	`NoStem`	887	0.3193	0.3367
PDDP	`Porter-like`	914	0.3419	0.3579
PDDS2PL	`SPLIT`	913	0.3173	0.3310
PDDS2PL3	`SPLIT-L3`	911	0.3200	0.3254

Note that both for 2001 and 2002 topics, all the stemming algorithms considered improve recall, since the number of retrieved relevant documents is larger than the number of retrieved relevant documents observed in the case of retrieval without any stemmer; this increase has been observed for all the stemming algorithms. With regard to precision, while for 2002 topics stemming does not hurt the overall performances of the system, for 2001 data stemming actually increases precision, and overall performance is higher thanks to the application of stemming.

Figure 2 shows the Averaged Recall-Precision curve at different levels of recall for the 2001 and 2002 topic sets. With respect to the use of link-based stemming algorithms, it is worth noting that SPLIT can attain levels of effectiveness that are comparable to algorithms based on linguistic knowledge. This is surprising if you know that SPLIT was built without any sophisticated extension to HITS and that neither heuristics nor linguistic knowledge was used to improve effectiveness, except for the slight constraint of `SPLIT-L3`. The result should also be considered good bearing in mind that it has been obtained for Italian, which is morphologically more complex than English.

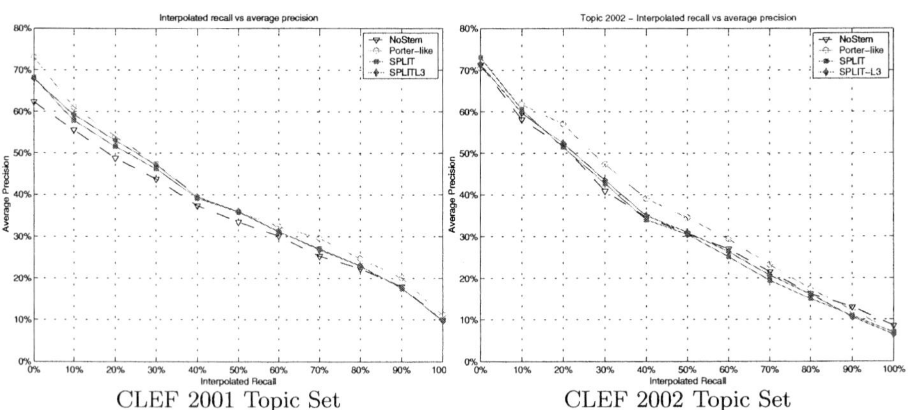

CLEF 2001 Topic Set CLEF 2002 Topic Set

Fig. 2. Average Precision curves for four stemming algorithms

6 Conclusions and Future Work

The objective of this research was to investigate a stemming algorithm based on link analysis procedures. The idea is that prefixes and suffixes, which are stems and derivations, form communities once extracted from words. We tested this hypothesis by comparing the retrieval effectiveness of SPLIT, a link analysis based algorithm derived from HITS, with a linguistic knowledge based algorithm, on a relatively morphologically complex language such as Italian.

The results are encouraging because the effectiveness of SPLIT is comparable to the algorithm developed by Porter. The results should be considered even better since SPLIT does not incorporate any heuristics nor linguistic knowledge. Moreover, both stemming and then SPLIT have been shown to improve effectiveness with respect to not using any stemmer.

We are carrying out further analysis at a micro level to understand the conditions under which SPLIT performs better or worse than other algorithms. Further work is in progress to improve the probabilistic decision criterion and to insert linguistic knowledge directly in the link-based model in order to weight links among prefixes and suffixes with a probabilistic function that could capture available information on the language, such as, for example, the minimum length of a stem. Finally, further experimental work is in progress with other languages.

Acknowledgements

The authors wish to express their thanks to Carol Peters for the fruitful discussions on multilingual retrieval and for her support during their participation in the CLEF 2002 campaign. The authors have been partially supported by a grant of the Department of Information Engineering of the University of Padua. Massimo Melucci has been partially supported by the Young Researchers programme of the University of Padua.

References

[1] M. Agosti, M. Bacchin, and M. Melucci. Report on the Construction of an Italian Test Collection. Position paper at the *Workshop on Multi-lingual Information Retrieval* at the *ACM International Conference on Research and Development in Information Retrieval (SIGIR)*, Berkeley, CA, USA, 1999.

[2] A. Borodin, G. O. Roberts, J. S. Rosenthal, and P. Tsaparas. Finding authorities and hubs from link structures on the World Wide Web. In *Proceedings of the World Wide Web Conference*, pages 415–429, Hong Kong, 2001. ACM Press.

[3] C. Cleverdon. The Cranfield Tests on Index Language Devices. In K. Sparck Jones and P. Willett (Eds.). *Readings in Information Retrieval*, pages 47-59, Morgan Kaufmann, 1997.

[4] W. B. Frakes and R. Baeza-Yates. *Information Retrieval: data structures and algorithms.* Prentice Hall, 1992.

[5] J. Goldsmith. Unsupervised learning of the morphology of a natural language. *Computational Linguistics*, 27(2):154–198, 2001.

[6] M. Hafer and S. Weiss. Word segmentation by letter successor varieties. *Information Storage and Retrieval*, 10:371–385, 1994.

[7] D. Harman. How effective is suffixing? *Journal of the American Society for Information Science*, 42(1):7–15, 1991.

[8] J. Kleinberg. Authoritative sources in a hyperlinked environment. *Journal of the ACM*, 46(5):604–632, September 1999.

[9] R. Krovetz. Viewing Morphology as an Inference Process,. In *Proceedings of the ACM International Conference on Research and Development in Information Retrieval (SIGIR)*, 1993.

[10] J. Lovins. Development of a stemming algorithm. *Mechanical Translation and Computational Linguistics*, 11:22–31, 1968.

[11] The Jakarta Project. Lucene. `http://jakarta.apache.org/lucene/docs/index.html`, 2002.

[12] C. D. Manning and H. Schütze. *Foundations of statistical natural language processing*. The MIT Press, 1999.

[13] C. D. Paice. Another Stemmer. In *ACM SIGIR Forum*, 24, 56–61, 1990.

[14] M. Popovic and P. Willett. The effectiveness of stemming for natural-language access to Slovene textual data. *Journal of the American Society for Information Science*, 43(5):383–390, 1992.

[15] M. Porter. Snowball: A language for stemming algorithms. `http://snowball.sourceforge.net`, 2001.

[16] M. F. Porter. An algorithm for suffix stripping. *Program*, 14(3):130–137, 1980.

[17] G. Salton and M. McGill. *Introduction to Modern Information Retrieval*. McGraw-Hill, New York, NY, 1983.

[18] G. Salton and C. Buckley. Term weighting approaches in automatic text retrieval. *Information Processing & Management*, 24(5):513–523, 1988.

[19] Institut interfacultaire d'informatique. CLEF and Multilingual information retrieval. University of Neuchatel. `http://www.unine.ch/info/clef/`, 2002.

[20] C. Buckley. Trec_eval. `ftp://ftp.cs.cornell.edu/pub/smart/`, 2002.

[21] E. M. Voorhees. Special Issue on the Sixth Text Retrieval Conference (TREC-6). *Information Processing and Management*. Volume 36, Number 1, 2000.

IR-n System at CLEF-2002

Fernando Llopis, José L. Vicedo, and Antonio Ferrández

Grupo de investigación en Procesamiento del Lenguaje y Sistemas de Información
Departamento de Lenguajes y Sistemas Informáticos, University of Alicante, Spain
{llopis,vicedo,antonio}@dlsi.ua.es

Abstract. Passage Retrieval is an alternative to traditional document-oriented Information Retrieval. These systems use contiguous text fragments (or passages) instead of full documents as the basic unit of information. The IR-n system is a passage retrieval system that uses groups of contiguous sentences as units of information. This paper reports on experiments with the IR-n system at CLEF-2002 where it has obtained considerably better results than in the previous participation in CLEF-2001.

1 Introduction

Information Retrieval (IR) systems receive as input a user's query and as result they return a set of documents ranked by their relevance to the query. There are different techniques for measuring the relevance of a document to a query, but most of them take into account the number of times that query terms appear in documents, the importance or discrimination value of these terms in the document collection, as well as the size of each document.

One of the main problems related to document-oriented retrieval systems is that they do not consider the proximity of appearance of query terms in the documents [5] (see Figure 1).

A possible alternative to these models consists in computing the similarity between a document and a query in accordance with the relevance of the passages each document is divided into (see Figure 2). This approach, called Passage Retrieval (PR), is not so affected by the length of the documents and, moreover, adds the concept of proximity to the similarity measure by analysing small pieces of text instead of whole documents. Figures 1 and 2 show the main differences between both approaches.

PR systems can be classified in accordance with the way that documents are divided into passages. The PR community generally agrees with the classification proposed in [1], where the author distinguishes between discourse models, semantic models, and window models. The first one uses structural properties of the documents, such as sentences or paragraphs [8] in order to define the passages. The second one divides each document into semantic pieces according to the different topics in the document [2]. The last one uses windows of a fixed size (usually a number of terms) to determine passage boundaries [4].

C.A. Peters (Ed.): CLEF 2002, LNCS 2785, pp. 291–300, 2003.

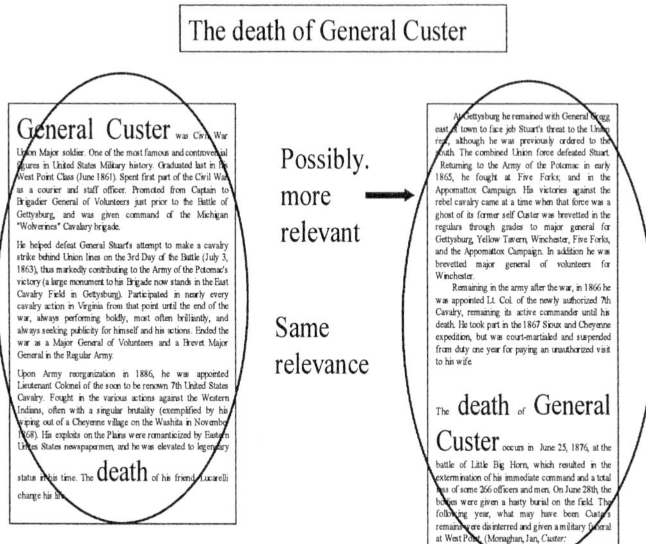

Fig. 1. Document-oriented retrieval

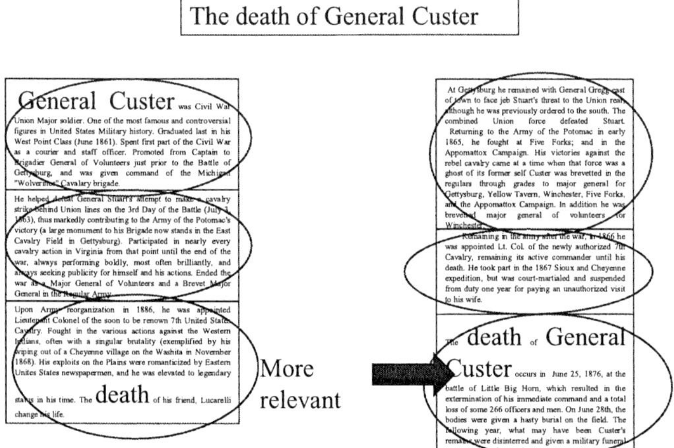

Fig. 2. Passage retrieval

At first glance, it could seem that discourse-based models would be the most effective in retrieval terms, since they use the structure of the document itself. However, the main problem with this type of model is that of detecting passage boundaries since this depends on the writing style of the author of each document. On the other hand, window models have as their main advantage that they are simpler to implement since the passages have a previously known size, whereas the other models have to support the variable size of each passage. Nevertheless, discourse-based and semantic models have the main advantage that they return full information units of the document, which is quite important if these units are used as input by other applications.

The passage extraction model that we propose (IR-n) allows us to benefit from the advantages of discourse-based models since self-contained information units of text, such as sentences, are used for building passages. Moreover, the relevance measure, unlike other discourse-based models, is not based on the number of passage terms, but on a fixed number of passage sentences. This fact allows a simpler calculation of this measure. Although each passage is made up of a fixed number of sentences, we consider that our proposal differs from the window model since our passages do not have a fixed size (i.e. a fixed number of words) as we use sentences with a variable size.

This paper is structured as follows. The following section presents the basic features of the IR-n system. The third section describes the main improvements introduced for the CLEF-2002 Conference. The fourth section describes the different runs performed for this campaign and discusses the results obtained. Finally, the last section presents initial conclusions and opens directions for future work.

2 The IR-n System

The system proposed has the main following features:

1. A document is divided into passages that are made up of a number N of sentences.
2. Passages overlap. The first passage contains from sentence *1* to N, the second passage contains from sentence *2* to $N+1$, etc.
3. The similarity between a passage p and a query q is computed as follows:

$$Passage\_similarity = \sum_{t \in p \wedge q} W_{p,t} \cdot W_{q,t} \qquad (1)$$

Where
$W_{p,t} = log_e(f_{p,t} + 1)$,
$f_{p,t}$ is the number of appearances of term t in passage p,
$W_{q,t} = log_e(f_{q,t} + 1) \cdot idf$,
$f_{q,t}$ represents the number of appearances of term t in query q,
$idf = log_e(n/f_t + 1)$,
n is the number of documents of the collection and
f_t is the number of documents term t appears in.

As can be observed, this formula is similar to the cosine measure defined in [9]. The main difference is that length normalisation is omitted. Instead, our proposal performs length normalisation by defining passage size as a fixed number of textual discourse units. In this case, the discourse unit selected is the sentence and a passage is defined as a fixed number N of sentences. This way, although the number of terms of each passage may vary, the number of sentences is constant.

The IR-n system has been developed in C++ and runs on a cheap Linux machine, without additional software requirements.

3 The IR-n System from CLEF-2001 to CLEF-2002

In the last CLEF campaign, the IR-n system [7] was used in two retrieval tasks: monolingual (Spanish) and bilingual (Spanish-English). The results of the bilingual task were satisfactory. However, the monolingual results were very poor, ranging below the average of the results obtained by all the other participating systems.

After analysing those results we arrived at a series of conclusions, summed up in the following points:

- We had several problems when processing the original SGML files. Consequently, some documents were not indexed correctly.
- The Spanish lemmatizer that we selected (Conexor) produced a high number of errors.
- The type of document collection used, small sized press agencies, meant that big differences between the passage retrieval and document retrieval approaches were not evident. This fact was confirmed when we saw that the results obtained by our system were similar to the baseline system (cosine model) whereas, with retrieval from the Los Angeles Times, collection the improvement achieved by the passage approach was considerable.
- We could not make any previous experiments to determine the optimum size of the passage since it was the first time this approach was applied.

The main adaptations to the system for CLEF-2002 were studied to solve these problems. The following changes were introduced:

- Document and query preprocessing was improved.
- The Spanish lemmatizer was replaced by a simple stemmer.
- A series of experiments was performed to determine the most suitable size of the passages (the number N of sentences).
- The relevance measure was modified in order to increase the score of the passages when a sentence contained two or more consecutive words appearing in the query.
- Treatment of long queries was changed.
- We added a query expansion module that could be optionally applied.

3.1 Training Process

We ran a series of experiments in order to optimize system performance. These experiments were carried out on the same document collection (EFE agency), but using the 49 test topics proposed for CLEF-2001.

Table 1. Results for short queries

		Precision at N documents						
	Recall	5	10	20	30	200	AvgP	Inc
Baseline	94.02	0.6000	0.5408	0.4582	0.4054	0.1826	0.4699	0.00
IR-n 7 sentences	94.54	0.6612	0.5796	0.4939	0.4490	0.1917	**0.5039**	7.23%
IR-n 8 sentences	94.95	0.6735	0.6061	0.4929	0.4537	0.1924	0.5017	6.76%

Table 2. Results for long queries

		Precision at N documents						
	Recall	5	10	20	30	200	AvgP	Inc
Baseline	95.62	0.6163	0.5612	0.4857	0.4367	0.1943	0.5010	0.00
IR-n 6 sentences	96.18	0.6653	0.5918	0.5020	0.4469	0.1995	**0.5156**	2.92%
IR-n 7 sentences	95.99	0.6816	0.5939	0.4990	0.4490	0.1983	0.5150	2.79%

As baseline system, we selected the well-known document retrieval model based on the cosine similarity measure [9]. The experiments were designed to detect the best value for N (the number of sentences that make up a passage). Initially, we detected the interval where the best results were obtained and then proceeded to determine the optimum value for N. System performance was measured using the standard average interpolated precision (AvgP).

For short queries, best results were obtained when passages were 7 or 8 sentences long. For long queries, best results were achieved for passages of 6 or 7 sentences. Tables 1 and 2 show these results for short and long queries respectively.

In both cases improved results are obtained although the difference with the baseline is more considerable when using long queries. After analysing these results, we decided to fix the size of passages to 7 sentences since this length achieved the best results for short queries and was also nearly the best for long queries.

Once we had determined the optimum length for passages, we designed a second experiment in order to adapt the similarity measure described before so that the measure could be increased when more than one query term was found in a sentence and these terms appeared in the same order in both query and sentence. This experiment consisted in optimizing the value α that increases the score of a query term when this situation occurs. Thus, the passage similarity formula given above changed as follows:

$$Passage\_similarity = \Big(\sum_{t \in p \wedge q} W_{p,t} \cdot W_{q,t}\Big) \cdot \alpha \quad (2)$$

Factor α takes value 1 when a given query term appears in a sentence in which the terms that appear immediately before and following this term in the query are not present; otherwise, it takes a different value. We experimented

Table 3. Results for short queries

		Precision at N documents						
	Recall	5	10	20	30	200	AvgP	Inc
IR-n base	94.54	0.6612	0.5796	0.4939	0.4490	0.1917	0.5039	0.00
IR-n factor 1.1	94.95	0.6653	0.5918	0.5041	0.4497	0.1935	0.5102	1.25%
IR-n factor 1.2	94.84	0.6694	0.5878	0.5010	0.4510	0.1933	0.5127	1.74%
IR-n factor 1.3	94.47	0.6735	0.5857	0.4990	0.4537	0.1930	0.5100	1.21%

Table 4. Results for long queries

		Precision at N documents						
	Recall	5	10	20	30	200	AvgP	Inc
IR-n base	95.99	0.6816	0.5939	0.4990	0.4490	0.1983	0.5150	0.00
IR-n factor 1.1	95.88	0.6735	0.5898	0.5010	0.4510	0.1969	0.5098	-1.00%
IR-n factor 1.2	95.47	0.6694	0.5898	0.5082	0.4510	0.1959	0.5047	-2.00%
IR-n factor 1.3	95.40	0.6490	0.5959	0.5031	0.4524	0.1945	0.4975	-3.39%

a number of coefficients in order to obtain the optimum value for α. Tables 3 and 4 shows the results obtained for short and long queries respectively.

In these tables it can be observed that, for short queries, results improve for α values of 1.1 and 1.2 whereas results get slightly worse for long queries.

4 CLEF-2002: Experiments and Results

As the results obtained in CLEF-2001 for the monolingual task were not as expected, our participation this year was focused on improving our results for the Spanish monolingual task.

4.1 Runs Description

We carried out four runs for the monolingual task. Two with *title + description* and two with *title + description + narrative*. For all the runs, passage length was set to 7 sentences and the value 1.1 was assigned to the α proximity coefficient. These runs are described below.

To illustrate the differences between the four runs we will consider the following example topic:

<top>
<num> C103 </num>
<ES-title> *Conflicto de intereses en Italia* </ES-title>
<ES-desc> *Encontrar documentos que discutan el problema del conflicto de interes es del primer ministro italiano, Silvio Berlusconi.* </ES-desc>

<ES-narr> *Los documentos relevantes se referirán de forma explícita al conflicto de intereses entre el Berlusconi político y cabeza del gobierno italiano, y el Berlusconi hombre de negocios. También pueden incluir información sobre propuestas o soluciones adoptadas para resolver este conflicto.* </ES-narr>
</top>

IR-n1. This run takes only short queries (*title + description*). The example topic was processed as follows:

Conflicto de intereses en Italia. Encontrar documentos que discutan el problema del conflicto de intereses del primer ministro italiano, Silvio Berlusconi.

IR-n2. This run is a little more complex. The topic is divided into several queries. Each query contains an isolated idea appearing within the whole topic. Each query is formulated for retrieval, in order to evaluate how passages respond to each of them. This approach is fully described in [6], the basic steps can be summed up as follows:

1. The topic narrative is divided according to the sentences it contains.
2. The system generates as many queries as sentences detected in the narrative. Each query contains title, description and a sentence from the narrative.
3. Each generated query is processed separately retrieving the best 5,000 documents.
4. Relevant documents are scored with the maximum similarity value obtained for all the generated queries processed and the best 1,000 relevant documents are finally retrieved.

In this case, from the example topic described above the system generates the following two queries:

Query 1. *Conflicto de intereses en Italia. Encontrar documentos que discutan el problema del conflicto de interes es del primer ministro italiano, Silvio Berlusconi. Los documentos relevantes se referirán de forma explícita al conflicto de intereses entre el Berlusconi político y cabeza del gobierno italiano, y el Berlusconi hombre de negocios.*

Query 2. *Conflicto de intereses en Italia. Encontrar documentos que discutan el problema del conflicto de interes es del primer ministro italiano, Silvio Berlusconi.También pueden incluir información sobre propuestas o soluciones adoptadas para resolver este conflicto.*

IR-n3. This run is similar to IR-n1 but applies query expansion according to the model defined in [3]. This expansion consists in detecting the best 10 terms of the first 5 retrieved documents, and adding them to the original query.

Table 5. Results comparison

		Precision at N documents						
	Recall	5	10	20	30	200	AvgP	Inc
Average CLEF2002							0.4490	0.00
IR-n1	90.08	0.6800	0.5820	0.5140	0.4620	0.1837	0.4684	+4.32%
IR-n2	92.64	0.7200	0.6380	0.5600	0.4813	0.1898	0.5067	+12.85%
IR-n3	93.51	0.6920	0.5920	0.5190	0.4667	0.2018	0.4980	+10.91%
IR-n4	91.83	0.7120	0.6120	0.5380	0.4867	0.1936	0.4976	+10.82%

IR-n4. This run uses long queries formed by title, description and narrative. The example queries were formulated for retrieval as follows.

Conflicto de intereses en Italia. Encontrar documentos que discutan el problema del conflicto de interés es del primer ministro italiano, Silvio Berlusconi. Los documentos relevantes se referirán de forma explícita al conflicto de intereses entre el Berlusconi político y cabeza del gobierno italiano, y el Berlusconi hombre de negocios. También pueden incluir información sobre propuestas o soluciones adoptadas para resolver este conflicto.

4.2 Results

The results achieved by our four runs are compared with those obtained by all the systems that participated in the evaluation campaign. Table 5 shows the average precision for monolingual runs and computes the precision increase achieved. This increase was calculated by taking as base the median average precision of all the participating systems. As can be observed, our four runs performed better than the median results. Our baseline (IR-n1) improved around 4% and the other runs performed between 11% and 13% better.

Tables 6 and 7 show the best results obtained by all the participants using short queries (title and description) and long queries (title, description and narrative), respectively. They are ordered by the standard average precision measure (AvgP).

In addition to having obtained good results with both kinds of queries, we want to highlight that our approach is near to the best performing one if we consider precision at the first five retrieved documents.

5 Conclusions and Future Work

Our general conclusions are positive. We have obtained considerably better results than in the previous CLEF campaign. This is a result of three main factors: first, the better preprocessing of documents; second, the system was correctly trained to obtain the optimum passage size; third, the errors introduced by the Spanish lemmatizer were avoided by using a simple stemmer.

Table 6. CLEF-2002 official results. Spanish monolingual task with short queries

		Precision at N documents					
	Rec.	5	10	20	30	200	AvgP
U.Neuchatel	93.13	0.6920	0.6200	0.5350	0.4787	0.2056	0.5441
U.Berkeley	93.65	0.6600	0.6020	0.5200	0.4780	0.2096	0.5338
U. Johns Hopkins	93.16	0.6120	0.5920	0.5090	0.4700	0.2056	0.5192
Thomson L&R	89.66	0.6600	0.5960	0.5130	0.4593	0.1966	0.4993
U. Alicante	91.83	0.6920	0.5920	0.5190	0.4667	0.2018	0.4980
Hummingbird	89.73	0.6760	0.5900	0.5150	0.4687	0.1988	0.4909
U.Exeter	88.19	0.6320	0.5680	0.4960	0.4387	0.1872	0.4745
U.Amsterdam	86.22	0.6440	0.5480	0.4720	0.4207	0.1812	0.4734
Océ	88.57	0.6520	0.5760	0.5050	0.4367	0.1905	0.4557
U.La Coruña	87.42	0.4600	0.4540	0.4050	0.3693	0.1645	0.3697
U.Tolouse	72.17	0.4360	0.4100	0.3730	0.3380	0.1424	0.3305
U.Salamanca	81.49	0.4400	0.3940	0.3460	0.3100	0.1494	0.3143
City University	61.70	0.3200	0.2940	0.2540	0.2320	0.1129	0.2173

Table 7. CLEF-2002 official results. Spanish monolingual task with long queries

		Precision at N documents					
	Recall	5	10	20	30	200	AvgP
U. de Neuchatel	93.41	0.7760	0.6920	0.5960	0.5307	0.2128	0.6051
U. Alicante	92.64	0.7200	0.6380	0.5600	0.4813	0.1898	0.5067
U. La Coruña	92.22	0.5440	0.5280	0.4690	0.4280	0.1825	0.4423
U. Salamanca	89.13	0.5360	0.4900	0.4310	0.3967	0.1697	0.4051

After this new experiment, we are examining several lines of future work. We want to analyse the improvements that could be obtained by using another type of lemmatizer instead of the simple stemmer that we have used this year. On the other hand, we are going to continue studying adjustments to the relevance formula in order to improve the application of proximity factors.

Acknowledgements

This work has been partially supported by the Spanish Government (CICYT) with grant TIC2000-0664-C02-02 and (PROFIT) with grant FIT-150500-2002-416.

References

[1] James P. Callan. Passage-Level Evidence in Document Retrieval. In *Proceedings of the 17th Annual International Conference on Research and Development in Information Retrieval*, pages 302–310, London, UK, July 1994. Springer Verlag.

[2] M. Hearst and C. Plaunt. Subtopic structuring for full-length document access. In SIGIR [10], pages 59–68.
[3] P. Jourlin, S. E. Johnson, K. Spärck Jones, and P. C. Woodland. General query expansion techniques for spoken document retrieval. In *Proc. ESCA Workshop on Extracting Information from Spoken Audio*, pages 8–13, Cambridge, UK, 1999.
[4] Marcin Kaszkiel and Justin Zobel. Passage Retrieval Revisited. In *Proceedings of the 20th Annual International ACM SIGIR Conference on Research and Development in Information Retrieval*, Text Structures, pages 178–185, Philadelphia, PA, USA, 1997.
[5] Marcin Kaszkiel and Justin Zobel. Effective Ranking with Arbitrary Passages. *Journal of the American Society for Information Science (JASIS)*, 52(4):344–364, February 2001.
[6] Fernando Llopis, Antonio Ferrández, and José L. Vicedo. Using Long Queries in a Passage Retrieval System. In O. Cairo, E. L. Sucar, and F. J. Cantu, editors, *Proceeding of Mexican International Conference on Artificial Intelligence*, volume 2313 of *Lectures Notes in Artificial Intelligence*, Mérida, Mexico, 2002. Springer-Verlag.
[7] Fernando Llopis and José L. Vicedo. IR-n system, a passage retrieval system at CLEF 2001. In *Workshop of Cross-Language Evaluation Forum (CLEF 2001)*, volume 2406 of *Lecture Notes in Computer Science*, pages 244–252, Darmstadt, Germany, 2001. Springer-Verlag.
[8] G. Salton, J. Allan, and C. Buckley. Approaches to passage retrieval in full text information systems. In SIGIR [10], pages 49–58.
[9] Gerard A. Salton. *Automatic Text Processing: The Transformation, Analysis, and Retrieval of Information by Computer.* Addison Wesley, New York, 1989.
[10] *Sixteenth International ACM SIGIR Conference on Research and Development in Information Retrieval*, Pittsburgh, PA, June 1993.

Experiments in Term Expansion Using Thesauri in Spanish

Ángel F. Zazo, Carlos G. Figuerola, José L.A. Berrocal, Emilio Rodríguez, and Raquel Gómez

Grupo de Recuperación Automatizada de la Información (REINA)
Dpto. Informática y Automática, Universidad de Salamanca, 37008 Salamanca, Spain
http://reina.usal.es

Abstract. This paper presents some experiments carried out this year in the Spanish monolingual task at CLEF2002. The objective is to continue our research on term expansion. Last year we presented results regarding stemming. Now, our effort is centred on term expansion using thesauri. Many words that derive from the same stem have a close semantic content. However other words with very different stems also have semantically close senses. In this case, the analysis of the relationships between words in a document collection can be used to construct a thesaurus of related terms. The thesaurus can then be used to expand a term with the best related terms. This paper describes some experiments carried out to study term expansion using association and similarity thesauri.

1 Introduction

A major problem in word based information retrieval (IR) systems is the *word-mismatch or vocabulary problem* [1]. Lexical phenomena such as synonymy and polysemy mean that the same concept can be expressed with different words and the same word can appear in documents that deal with different topics. The performance of IR systems depends on the number of query terms. The problem is less severe for long queries because more index terms are included, and thus there is more possibility to find query terms in the relevant documents. In addition, short queries are poor for recall and precision: they do not take into account the variety of words used to describe a topic, and they are too broad to retrieve relevant documents on specific topics. Our interest is centred on queries with very few terms. This kind of query has special importance in Web search engines, where queries are typically of one to three terms in length [2].

Many techniques have been used to try to reduce this problem, inter alia automatic query expansion. Query expansion methods have been investigated for almost as long as the history of information retrieval. This technique involves two basic steps: expanding the original query with new terms, and reweighting the terms in the expanded query. With query expansion, the retrieval performance can improve but the computational cost or the response time may increase. In

C.A. Peters (Ed.): CLEF 2002, LNCS 2785, pp. 301–310, 2003.

order to expand the query, words or phrases with similar meaning to those of the initial query must be added. There are several possible approaches to this task, and the use of a thesaurus is the most important. A thesaurus is a system composed of words or phrases and of a set of related words for each of them. In information retrieval, thesauri are used to help with with the query formation process. Likewise, stemming can be thought of as a mechanism for query expansion, and can be seen as similar to using a thesaurus. Some stemmers can be created or modified using the same techniques as for thesaurus construction [3].

This paper explores the association and similarity thesauri approach to term expansion. Additionally, an experiment in term expansion using stemming has been carried out. This is useful for comparison purposes with our last year's paper. We assume the well-known vector space model, but queries are first expanded to help improve retrieval performance.

2 Stemming

The impact of our stemmers for the Spanish monolingual track at CLEF2001 was presented in [4]. For all query fields (title + narrative + descriptive), the improvement is only about 3% for inflectional stemming over non-stemming. Derivational stemming is even a little worse than no stemming. At CLEF2002 we have corrected small bugs in our stemmers, and only inflectional stemming was applied. The objective is to measure the improvement, taking into account only the `ES-title` field of the queries. We then compare the results with those derived from applying thesauri.

3 Thesaurus

One of the most important methods for query expansion is the application of a thesaurus. A general thesaurus could be used, but this usually does not give good results (e.g. [5]). The relations among entries in a general thesaurus are usually not valid in the scope of the document collection being used. Better results are obtained if thesauri, or other expansion techniques, are constructed from the document collection. When the thesaurus is constructed automatically, without additional user feedback information, several approaches can be used [6]: automatic term classification (term co-occurrences statistics) [7], use of document classification [8], concept based query expansion [9, 10], phrase-finder expansion [11] or expansion based on syntactic information [12]. We have tested approaches that use association (term co-occurrence statistics) and similarity (conceptually-based query expansion) thesauri, because they are relatively simple and effective.

A thesaurus is a matrix that measures term relations [13]. This matrix is used to expand the query terms with related terms. The matrix can be seen as a semantic description of terms, which reflects the impact of terms in the conceptual descriptions of other terms [14]. We note two fundamental aspects to apply the matrix in our tests. First, the expansion is made only with *best* related terms. No threshold values are taken into consideration: terms with highly related values are selected for each original query term. Secondly, the entire query, i.e., the query concept [10], is taken into account. The top ranked terms for the entire query are considered.

We must state at this point that results for term expansion using thesauri may be differ considerably. Several of the papers cited previously show acceptable results. On the other hand, for example, [15] offers perhaps the most critical study of term co-occurrence based models. Indeed, earlier studies [16] showed even better results with randomly selected terms than when using term co-occurrence statistics. However, we have obtained satisfactory results, which perhaps helps to confirm the two observations just made.

3.1 Association Matrix

Term co-occurrence has been frequently used in IR to identify some of the semantic relationships that exist among terms. In fact, this idea is based on the Association Hypothesis [17, p.104]. If query terms are useful to identify relevant and non relevant documents, then their associated terms will also be useful, and can be added to the original query.

Several coefficients have been used to calculate the degree of relationship between two terms. All of them measure the number of documents in which they occur separately, in comparison with the number of documents in which they co-occur. In our tests three well-known coefficients have been used [9]:

$$\text{Tanimoto}(t_i, t_j) = \frac{c_{ij}}{c_i + c_j - c_{ij}}$$

$$\text{Cosine}(t_i, t_j) = \frac{c_{ij}}{\sqrt{c_i \cdot c_j}}$$

$$\text{Dice}(t_i, t_j) = \frac{2 \cdot c_{ij}}{c_i + c_j}$$

where c_i and c_j are the number of documents in which terms t_i and t_j occur, respectively, and c_{ij} is the number of documents in which t_i and t_j co-occur. The coefficients have values between 0 and 1: if two terms occur only in the same documents, the associated coefficient is 1. If there is no document in which they co-occur, the value is 0.

3.2 Similarity Matrix

The similarity matrix measures term-term similarities, instead of term-term co-occurrences. To compute the values of the elements, each term is indexed by the documents in which it occurs, i.e., the roles of terms and documents are switched. This theory is fully explained in [10]. The broad outlines are: first, each term in the document vector space is represented by a vector, whose elements are computed adapting the normalized *tf·idf* weighting scheme to this new situation.

We use the same calculus as in [10]. Second, to compute the similarity between two terms the simple scalar product of vectors is used. We have also used it. Computation for every term produces the similarity matrix.

Both the association and the similarity matrices produce comparable results. Table 1 shows the 20 best related terms with the Spanish word *terremoto.*

3.3 Expansion of the Query

The aim of using the association or the similarity matrices is to expand the entire query, not only separate terms. A term can be included in the list of expanded terms only if it has a high relationship value with all query terms. To obtain the expanded terms with the highest potential, each term of the original query should be expanded with all related terms. A new value is computed multiplying the weight of the original query term by the corresponding association/similarity value of related terms. For all original query terms, all values are added for each term that could be included in the list of expanded terms. The sum represents the value of the relationship of that term with the entire query. The list of expanded terms is then sorted in decreasing order. Only top ranked terms are used to expand the original query.

Table 1. Example for the Spanish entry *terremoto* in the expansion matrices

Association Matrix						**Similarity Matrix**	
Tanimoto		Cosine		Dice			
terremoto	1.0000	terremoto	1.0000	terremoto	1.0000	terremoto	1.0000
richter	0.4058	richter	0.5827	richter	0.5773	richter	0.6192
seismo	0.3502	seismo	0.5288	seismo	0.5188	seismo	0.5491
epicentro	0.2800	epicentro	0.4569	epicentro	0.4375	epicentro	0.4833
temblor	0.2045	temblor	0.3626	temblor	0.3395	escala	0.3993
escala	0.1855	escala	0.3488	escala	0.3130	grados	0.3716
grados	0.1844	grados	0.3289	grados	0.3113	temblor	0.3696
sacudio	0.1725	sacudio	0.3255	sacudio	0.2943	sacudio	0.3525
magnitud	0.1704	terremotos	0.3018	magnitud	0.2912	magnitud	0.3380
terremotos	0.1407	magnitud	0.2935	terremotos	0.2467	terremotos	0.3173
temblores	0.1205	sismico	0.2792	temblores	0.2151	temblores	0.2860
intensidad	0.1137	temblores	0.2721	intensidad	0.2041	sismico	0.2798
sismico	0.1080	seismos	0.2591	sismico	0.1949	seismos	0.2603
seismos	0.1022	sismica	0.2424	seismos	0.1854	sismica	0.2538
sismica	0.0929	daños	0.2130	sismica	0.1700	intensidad	0.2405
daños	0.0913	northridge	0.2126	daños	0.1673	northridge	0.2400
damnificados	0.0833	intensidad	0.2092	damnificados	0.1537	daños	0.2379
sacude	0.0737	tsunami	0.2056	sacude	0.1373	tsunami	0.2221
telurico	0.0729	maremoto	0.2026	telurico	0.1358	sismicos	0.2121
sintio	0.0706	sismicos	0.2006	sintio	0.1318	maremoto	0.2099
olas	0.0674	sacude	0.1879	olas	0.1263	sacude	0.2061

Finally, it is necessary to calculate the weight of the term added to the query. Obviously this depends on the relationship value with the entire query. In [10] the sum of the weight of the original query is used to reduce this value, but other criteria may be applied. The aim in this paper is not only to show whether these expansion techniques are valid to increase retrieval performance, but also to study the expansion technique itself. Therefore, as shown in Table 2, we have experimented with coefficients to compute the weight of expanded terms (n and mod are respectively the number of terms and modulus of the original query). The coefficient denoted 'Magic' has no special meaning in information retrieval, we use it merely as another coefficient for test purposes.

At this point, it is necessary to comment on the normalization of document and query vectors. Normalization in document vectors prevents large documents from being considered more relevant than short ones. Normalization in query vectors is only used to obtain similarity values between 0 and 1 (we use standard scalar product for similarity function), but it does not affect the ranking. The coefficients in Table 2 have a different behaviour regarding normalization. 'Average' and 'Unit' coefficients have the same value with normalized and non-normalized query vectors. The other coefficients have different values.

Previous work [18] shows that normalization in query vectors has an impact when the original query is expanded with a few terms (about 0 to 50 terms). If more terms are added to the original query hardly any difference exists between a normalized query and a non-normalized one, except perhaps for the fact that the latter performs slightly better than the former. Thus, in our experiments, we have used non-normalized query vectors.

4 Experiments

Table 3 shows the collection used for our test. Only the `TITLE` and `TEXT` fields of the documents are used. For queries, the table indicates the average number of unique index terms for the `ES-title` field and for all fields. For our tests, we converted all words to lowercase, suppressed the stress signs, and included numbers as index terms. The number of stop words was 573. We used the well-known *tf*·idf scheme and recommendations in [19], and the simple scalar product to calculate the similarity between query vector and document vectors. Only the document vectors were normalized.

The results were evaluated taking into account three measures (averaged over all queries): average non-interpolated precision, average R-Precision and

Table 2. Coefficients for weighting expanded terms

Qiu-Frei	Average	Magic	Unit
$\frac{1}{\sum_{t_i \in q} q_i}$	$\frac{1}{n}$	$\frac{1}{mod * sqrt(n)}$	1

Table 3. Collection

Collection	Spanish (EFE)
Documents	215,738 (513 MB raw)
Queries	50 (C091 to C140)
Total index terms (`TEXT` and `TITLE`)	352,777
Averaged doc length (words)	333.68 (max. 2,210, min. 9)
Averaged doc length (unique index terms)	120.48
Averaged query length (unique index terms)	2.62 (`ES-title`) 20.48 (all)

Table 4. Results with 100 terms added to original query (`ES-title` field)

	No expansion	Association Thesauri			Similarity	Inflectional
Measurement	no stemming	Tanimoto	Cosine	Dice	Thesaurus	Stemming
avg. precision	0.2618	0.2993	0.3281	0.3163	0.3342	0.2733
avg. R-Precision	0.2752	0.3095	0.3261	0.3121	0.3274	0.2866
avg. prec. at 10 docs	0.3320	0.3660	0.4160	0.3900	0.4100	0.3460

average precision when 10 documents have been retrieved (precision at 10 docs). We include this last measurement because the user's interface normally shows documents in groups of 10.

We compute the association and the similarity thesauri from the document collection. The objective is to improve retrieval performance taking into account only the `ES-title` field of queries. For the sake of efficiency, only the terms in original queries were selected as entries in the thesauri. We do not use word or text windows, as other studies usually do. The whole document (`TEXT` and `TITLE` fields) is treated as a single word window. Neither do we apply stemming. For comparison purposes, we have calculated recall-precision values for only the `ES-title` query field without applying expansion or stemming.

A first set of tests was carried out to verify whether thesauri expansion techniques have better retrieval results than no expansion techniques. In this case, we use the weighting coefficient 'Average' for expanded terms. Table 4 shows the measurements for 100 terms added to the original query. This table also includes results for the experiment in inflectional stemming with no expansion. In all cases we have obtained positive improvement, but the improvement obtained with Cosine or Similarity thesauri is higher than the others. Very little improvement (about 4%) is obtained with inflectional stemming. Table 5 shows that a similar improvement is obtained using inflectional stemming for all query fields.

A second set of experiments was carried out to compare the efficiency for coefficients in Table 2. Figure 1 shows the way in which the number of additional terms affects the retrieval effectiveness. The improvement increases quickly with very few terms added to the original query. After 50 or 100 additional terms the

Table 5. Improvement using inflectional stemming (all query fields)

Measurement	No stemming	Inflectional stemming	Improvement
avg. precision	0.3908	0.4051	3.66%
avg. R-Precision	0.3844	0.4076	6.04%
avg. prec. at 10 docs	0.4840	0.4900	1.24%

improvement remains about constant. This figure shows improvement in average non-interpolated precision for association and similarity thesauri expansion. Similar results are obtained for average R-precision and average precision at 10 docs. In all cases, 'Unit' coefficient has the highest improvement, and 'Average' coefficient also shows a good performance. 'Qiu-Frei' and 'Magic' coefficients show some improvements, but their performance is the lowest. Figure 1 also shows that improvement with Cosine or Similarity thesauri is better (about 30%) than the others.

Figure 2 shows the evolution of Cosine and Similarity thesauri expansion. The results for average precision at 10 docs are very important since this is the number usually shown in the user's interface for Web search engines or OPACs. For this measurement the improvement is from 35 to 40 percent.

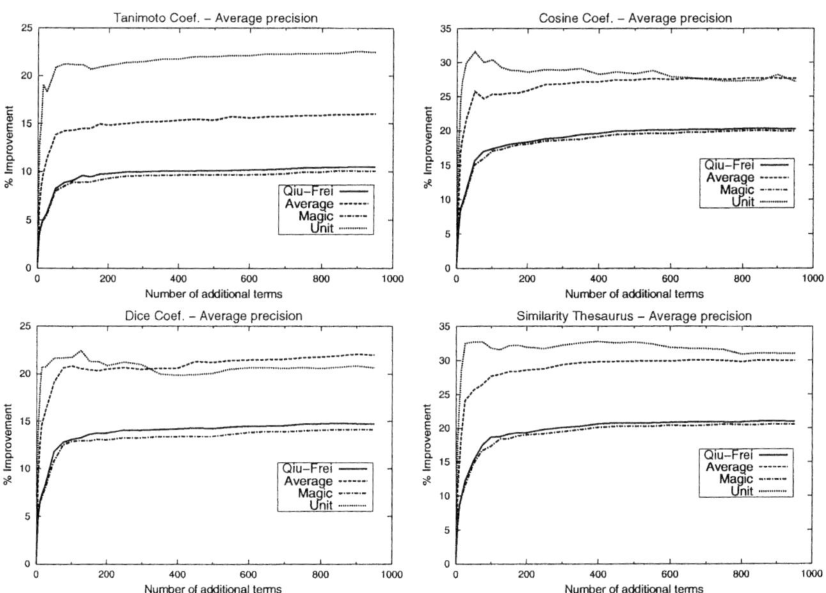

Fig. 1. Results for average precision non-interpolated

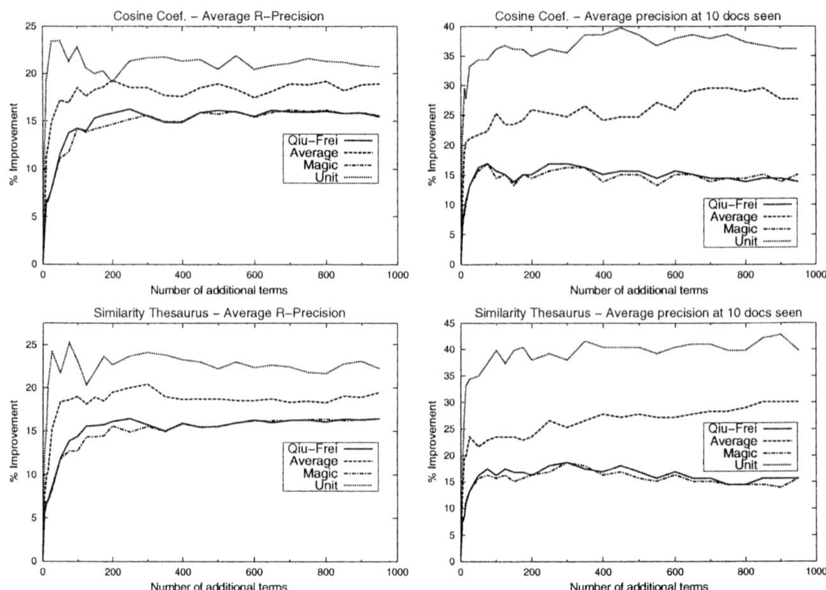

Fig. 2. R-precision and Precision at 10 docs for Cosine and Similarity thesauri expansion

5 Conclusions

In this paper we have explored association and similarity thesauri approaches to query or term expansion: queries are expanded to help improve retrieval performance. The results show that these techniques are valid. The expansion was carried out using only the terms in the `ES-title` field of the queries. No stemming was applied to documents or queries in this expansion. For comparison with the CLEF2001 evaluation campaign, we have carried out an additional test on term expansion using inflectional stemming over documents and queries.

The best results are obtained with thesauri expansion. Improvement with stemming expansion is only about 4% for the `ES-title` field of the queries. For all query fields the improvement is similar. Stemming is a very expensive process, which includes some morphological and semantical information, hard to implement automatically. Simple measures of co-occurrence data as in association thesauri are cheap processes, and appear to give better results than stemming. The construction of the similarity thesaurus is also computationally expensive, but gives the best results.

Results indicate that query expansion using thesauri is a valid tool to improve retrieval performance. However, it should be noted that there is a disadvantage: as the number of query terms increases the response time of the information retrieval system also increases.

It is important to emphasize that thesauri are constructed automatically from the document collection. No user feedback information is used to select terms for expansion. When using relevance feedback information the number of additional terms is about 20. These terms are selected from retrieved documents marked as relevant. On the contrary, when the added terms are selected from an automatically constructed thesaurus, 50 to 100 terms is a reasonable figure.

For query expansion using association thesauri, the best results are obtained with the Cosine coefficient. With the similarity thesaurus a little improvement is obtained compared with to Cosine coefficient, but the construction of the former is computationally more expensive than that of the latter.

Our interest is centred on queries with very few terms. They have special importance in Web search engines, which typically use one to three terms per query. In our query set the average query length is 2.62 for `ES-title`. Expansion with association or similarity thesauri may be an instrument to improve retrieval effectiveness in Web search engines, but the information in Internet is very dynamic, and this implies that thesauri should be continually updated. Thus, we think that this type of expansion performs best when applied to more static document collections.

References

[1] Furnas, G. W., Landauer, T. K., Gomez, L. M., Dumais, S. T.: The vocabulary problem in human-system communication. Comunications of the ACM **30** (1987) 964–971.

[2] Wolfram, D., Spink, A., Janses, B. J., Saracevic, T.: Vox populi: The public searching of the web. Journal of the American Society for Information Science and Technology **52** (2001) 1073–1074.

[3] Xu, J., Croft, W. B.: Corpus-based stemming using cooccurrence of word variants. ACM Transactions on Information Systems **16** (1998) 61–81.

[4] Figuerola, C. G., Gómez Díaz, R., Zazo Rodríguez, Á.F., Alonso Berrocal, J. L.: Spanish monolingual track: the impact of stemming on retrieval. In Peters, C., Braschler, M., Gonzalo, J., Kluck, M., eds.: Evaluation of Cross-Language Information Retrieval Systems. Second Workshop of the Cross-Languge Evaluation Forum, CLEF 2001. Darmstadt, Germany, September 2001. Revised Papers. Volume 2406 of Lecture Notes in Computer Science. Springer, Berlin, etc. ISBN: 3-540-44042-9 (2002) 253–261.

[5] Voorhees, E.: Query expansion using lexical-semantic relations. In Croft, W. B., van Rijsbergen, C., eds.: Proceedings of the 17th Annual International ACM-SIGIR Conference on Research and Development in Information Retrieval. Dublin. Ireland, 3 6 July 1994 (Special Issue of the SIGIR Forum), ACM/Springer-Verlag (1994) 61–69.

[6] Han, C., Fujii, H., Croft, W.: Automatic query expansion for japanese text retrieval. Technical Report UM-CS-1995-011, Department of Computer Science, Lederle Graduate Research Center, University of Massachusetts (1995) On line: `ftp://ftp.cs.umass.edu/pub/techrept/techreport/1995/UM-CS-1995-011%.ps`.

[7] Minker, J., Wilson, G., Zimmerman, B.: An evaluation of query expansion by the addition of clustered terms for a document retrieval system. Information Storage and Retrieval **8** (1972) 329–348.
[8] Crouch, C. J., Yang, B.: Experiments in automatic statistical thesaurus construction. [20] 77–88.
[9] Salton, G., McGill, M.: Introduction to Modern Information Retrieval. McGraw-Hill, New-York (1983).
[10] Qiu, Y., Frei, H. P.: Concept-based query expansion. In Korfhage, R., Rasmussen, E. M., Willett, P., eds.: Proceedings of the 16th Annual International ACM-SIGIR Conference on Research and Development in Information Retrieval. Pittsburgh, PA, USA, June 27 - July 1, 1993, ACM Press (1993) 160–169.
[11] Jing, Y., Croft, W. B.: An association thesaurus for information retrieval. In: Proceedings of RIAO-94, 4th International Conference "Recherche d'Information Assistee par Ordinateur", New York, US (1994) 146–160.
[12] Grefenstette, G.: Use of syntactic context to produce term association lists for text retrieval. [20] 89–97.
[13] Schutze, H.: Dimensions of meaning. In: Proceedings of Supercomputing '92, Minneapolis, 1992. (1992) 787–796.
[14] Billhardt, H., Borrajo, D., Maojo, V.: A context vector model for information retrieval. Journal of the American Society for Information Science and Technology **53** (2002) 236–249.
[15] Peat, H. J., Willet, P.: The limitations of term co-occurrence data for query expansion in document retrieval systems. Journal of the American Society for Information Science **42** (1991) 378–383.
[16] Smeaton, A., van Rijsbergen, C.: The retrieval effects of query expansion on a feedback document retrieval system. The Computer Journal **26** (1983) 239–246.
[17] van Rijsbergen, C.: Information Retrieval. Second edn. Dept. of Computer Science, University of Glasgow (1979).
[18] Zazo Rodríguez, Á.F., Figuerola, C. G., Berrocal, J. L. A., Rodríguez, E.: Tesauros de asociación y similitud para la expansión automática de consultas: Algunos resultados experimentales. Technical Report DPTOIA-IT-2002-007, Departamento de Informática y Automática - Universidad de Salamanca (2002) On line: `http://tejo.usal.es/inftec/2002/DPTOIA-IT-2002-007.pdf`.
[19] Salton, G., Buckley, C.: Term-weighting approaches in automatic text retrieval. Information Processing & Management **24** (1988) 513–523.
[20] Belkin, N. J., Ingwersen, P., Pejtersen, A. M., eds.: Proceedings of the 15th Annual International ACM-SIGIR Conference on Research and Development in Information Retrieval. Copenhagen, Denmark, June 21-24. In Belkin, N. J., Ingwersen, P., Pejtersen, A. M., eds.: Proceedings of the 15th Annual International ACM-SIGIR Conference on Research and Development in Information Retrieval. Copenhagen, Denmark, June 21-24, ACM Press (1992).

SICS at CLEF 2002: Automatic Query Expansion Using Random Indexing

Magnus Sahlgren[1], Jussi Karlgren[1], Rickard Cöster[1], and Timo Järvinen[2]

[1] Swedish Institute of Computer Science
SICS, Box 1263, SE-164 29 Kista, Sweden
{mange,jussi,rick}@sics.se
[2] Connexor oy
Helsinki Science Park, Koetilantie 3, 00710 Helsinki, Finland
timo@connexor.com

Abstract. Vector space techniques can be used for extracting semantically similar words from the co-occurrence statistics of words in large text data collections. We have used a technique called Random Indexing to accumulate context vectors for Swedish, French and Italian. We have then used the context vectors to perform automatic query expansion. In this paper, we report on our CLEF 2002 experiments on Swedish, French and Italian monolingual query expansion.

1 Introduction: Queries and Query Expansion

Arguably, query formulation is the major bottleneck for satisfying user needs in information access applications. This problem is aggravated in a cross-lingual context; finding the right word in a non-native language is even more of a problem than in one's first language.

The fundamental problem in the query formulation process is what has become known as the *vocabulary* problem, since it concerns people's choice of words to express their information need. There are two facets to this dilemma; the *synonymy* and *polysemy* problems. The synonymy problem consists in the fact that people might choose different words to express the same information. For example, one person might use the word "boat" to refer to water craft, while another person might use the word "ship". The polysemy problem, on the other hand, is the problem that one "word" (or, rather, one orthographic construction) can have several meanings — the cardinal example here being "bank" (as in "sandbank", "monetary institution" etc.). In other words, words are both too specific and too vague at the same time. If the retrieval system does not attempt to handle these vocabulary discrepancies, it might miss relevant documents, or, it might retrieve totally irrelevant documents.

One common solution to the vocabulary problem is to add additional terms to the query. This methodology is generally known as *query expansion*, and it can be used to tackle both the synonymy and polysemy problems. For example,

C.A. Peters (Ed.): CLEF 2002, LNCS 2785, pp. 311–320, 2003.

we can add additional terms to a query in order to disambiguate a polysemous word (e.g. if the query contains "bank", it might be wise to add an additional term specifying whether it is sandbanks (e.g. "sand") or monetary institutions (e.g. "money") that is being referred to), or, which is the more common reason for performing a query expansion, we can add additional terms to a query in order to ensure adequate recall for the query (e.g. by adding "ship" to a query containing "boat").

We deal with the vocabulary problem by using a statistical technique for automatic query expansion. The idea is to use a vector space model to extract context vectors for the words in the data. The context vectors represent the distributional profiles of words, which means that they can be used to calculate semantic similarity between words [6]. We use the context vectors to perform automatic query expansion. For example, if "boat" is in the query, the system will expand the query with words that have context vectors similar to that of "boat". Hopefully, this will be words such as "ship," "vessel," "craft," "water" and so on.

In this paper, we report on our CLEF 2002 experiments using statistically based automatic query expansion.

2 An Overview of the Vector Space Methodology

Vector space models use co-occurrence statistics to generate context vectors that can be used to calculate similarity between words. Traditionally, this is done by representing the text data as an $n \times m$ co-occurrence matrix, where each row n represents a unique word and each column m represents a document or a word. Latent Semantic Analysis/Latent Semantic Indexing (LSA/LSI) [8], [2] uses a words-by-*document* matrix, whereas Hyperspace Analogue to Language (HAL) [9] uses a words-by-*words* matrix. The cells of the co-occurrence matrix are the (normalized) frequency counts of a particular word in a particular context (document or word). The rows of the co-occurrence matrix can be interpreted as *context vectors* for the words in the vocabulary, making it straight-forward to express the distributional similarity between words in terms of vector similarity.

We have chosen a somewhat different methodology to construct the co-occurrence matrix. The technique, which we call *Random Indexing* [5], [6], uses *distributed* representations to accumulate context vectors from the distributional statistics of words. This is accomplished by first assigning a unique high-dimensional sparse random *index vector* to each word type in the text data. Then, every time a word occurs in the text data, we add the index vectors of the n surrounding words to the context vector for the word in question. Mathematically, this technique is equivalent to the Random Mapping approach described in [7].

The resulting high-dimensional context vectors thus represent the distributional profiles of words, by effectively being the sum of (the representations of) every word that the target word has co-occurred with. Now, according to the *Distributional Hypothesis*, which states that two words are semantically similar to the extent that they share contexts [4], the context vectors can be used to calculate (distributional) similarity between words. We do this by simply calculating the cosine of the angles between the context vectors.

3 The CLEF 2002 Query Expansion Experiments

In the CLEF 2002 monolingual retrieval task, we have used Random Indexing to construct context vectors for words in Swedish, French and Italian. We have then used the context vectors to extract semantically similar words to the words in the CLEF queries. In effect, what we have produced is a series of automatically generated thesauri.

3.1 Training Data

The system was trained using the CLEF 2002 collections for Swedish, French and Italian. The data files were preprocessed and morphologically analyzed and normalized to base form using syntactic analysis tools from Connexor.[1] The same morphological analysis and normalization procedure was applied to the topic texts.

3.2 Applying the Random Indexing Technique

In order to generate context vectors for the words in the Swedish, French and Italian training data, we first assigned a 1,800-dimensional sparse random index vector to each word type in the three different training data. The 1,800-dimensional random index vectors consisted of 8 randomly distributed -1s and $+1$s (4 of each), with the rest of the elements in the vectors set to zero. We used these parameters since they have been verified in other experiments to be viable for extracting semantically related words from co-occurrence information [6]. However, it should be noted that the technique does perform better the higher the dimensionality of the vectors. Of course, there is a trade-off between performance and efficiency, since using very high-dimensional vectors would be computationally demanding.

As previously described, the 1,800-dimensional random index vectors were then used to accumulate context vectors for the words in the data. This was done by adding the index vectors of the n surrounding words to the context vector for a given word every time the word occurred in the training data. In these experiments, we used $n = 6$ (i.e. the three preceding and the three succeeding words), since this has proven to be a viable context size to capture distributional distinctiveness [6]. Also, the context windows were weighted by the function 2^{1-d}, where d is the distance (in word units) to the target word. Finally, we used a frequency threshold for the vector additions to exclude words with a frequency less than 3, since low frequency words give unreliable statistical estimates.

[1] http://www.connexor.com

3.3 Query Construction and Expansion

The queries were constructed by removing stop words and some query specific terms (e.g. "find", "documents", "relevant" etc.) from the <title> and <description> fields of the CLEF 2002 topics.

For the query expansion runs, we expanded every word in the queries with the 5 words whose context vectors were most similar to the context vector of the original query word. Vector similarity was computed as the cosine of the angle between the context vectors:

$$d_{cos}(x,y) = \frac{\boldsymbol{x} \cdot \boldsymbol{y}}{\mid \boldsymbol{x} \mid\mid \boldsymbol{y} \mid} = \frac{\sum_{i=1}^{n} x_i y_i}{\sqrt{\sum_{i=1}^{n} x_i^2}\sqrt{\sum_{i=1}^{n} y_i^2}}$$

This measure gives an estimate of the amount of correlation between the vectors, ranging from 1 (which is a perfect match) to -1 (which means that the vectors are totally uncorrelated).[2] To ensure that only sufficiently correlated words were included in the expanded queries, we used a threshold that only included words with a correlation above 0.2.

4 Search Engine

The text retrieval engine used for our experiments is the first version of a system being developed at SICS. It currently supports vector space, boolean and structured queries. In the following sections, we provide a detailed description of the index structure and query methods.

4.1 Document Format

Documents are converted from their original format to a common XML format prior to indexing. Each XML document contains several meta-data tags such as creation date, author and original location as well as a list of sections (structured fields). A section has a name, a weight and a block of textual content. The XML file as well as the index is stored in Unicode format, a prerequisite for cross-language indexing and retrieval.

We use a simple procedure for term extraction from the XML documents, since the document content has already been formatted by lexical analysis and stemming.

4.2 Index Construction

For the inverted index, we use a Simple Prefix B^+-tree [1], [3]. To construct the index and the inverted lists, we use sort-based inversion [13] where the sort phase is implemented as an external (disk-based) k-way merge sort [3], [13]. The

[2] In practice, two distributionally unrelated words get a correlation around 0. Negative correlations are merely the result of noise.

inverted lists of document id and term frequency pairs $(d_i, tf_{d_i,t})$ are compressed for each term t. The d_i numbers are run-length encoded and the $(d_i, tf_{d_i,t})$ pairs are further compressed using integer compression.

A number of different integer compression algorithms have been proposed in the literature: Golomb coding, Elias delta coding, Elias gamma coding etc. [12], [13]. We use Golomb coding for the d_i values and Elias delta coding for the $tf_{d_i,t}$ values.

4.3 Queries

The query language supports Vector Space, Boolean and structured queries. All queries in the experiments were evaluated as full-text Vector Space queries.

Vector Space Queries. For Vector Space queries, we use an approximate cosine measure, where documents are normalized by the square root of the number of terms in the document, instead of the Euclidean length of the document's vector of $tf * idf$ values. The similarity between a query q and document d is

$$sim(q,d) = \frac{\sum_{t \in T_q} w_{t,q} * w_{t,d}}{\sqrt{\text{number of terms in } d}}$$

where T_q is the set of terms in the query.

The term weighting scheme $w_{t,d}$ for term t in document d follows a classical model of the product of term frequency tf and inverse document frequency idf:

$$tf * idf = (0.5 + 0.5 \frac{tf_{t,d}}{\max tf_d}) * \log_2 \frac{N}{n(t)}$$

where N is the total number of documents in the collection and $n(t)$ is the number of documents containing term t. The query term weight $w_{t,q}$ is set to 1 in our experiments.

5 Results

We used the preprocessed Swedish, French and Italian CLEF 2002 collections for the automatic monolingual task. A separate index was created for each language, and queries were submitted twice to the retrieval engine; with and without query expansion.

The top 1000 documents were taken as the result list for each query. We report the non-interpolated average precision as well as R-precision scores for each run in Table 5. The suffix X for languages denotes the automatic semantic query expansion result for the query. Rel. is the number of relevant documents for the queries, Ret. is how many relevant documents we found. Avg. p. is the non-interpolated average precision for all relevant documents, R-Prec. is the precision after our system had retrieved Rel. number of documents.

The results are decidedly mixed. Our expanded runs show consistently lower results than the unexpanded ones; all runs are below median on most queries, but all also score at least some queries over the median.

5.1 Lexical Factors

It is clear that we need to rethink the utility of statistically based and lexically agnostic expansion. We should be able to typologize terminology so that expansion will be performed by term type rather than blindly. Person names, for instance, most likely should not be expanded to other names. Place names, on the other hand, could be expanded to hypernyms or related places names with less risk of introducing noise. To demonstrate the problem, consider query no. 123, which features a number of person names, which get expanded with other names:

Marie → *Claude Pierre Gabin Harlow Francois*

in the Italian expansion, and

Marie → *Helsén Helsen Hedborg Cardesjö Fritthioff*

in the Swedish expansion.

Arguably, expansion of person names merely introduce noise into the query. On the other hand, consider query no. 118, which features a place name:

Finland → *Funlandia Norvegia Islanda Svezia Danimarca*

in the Italian expansion, and

Finland → *Norge Danmark Sverige Österrike Island*

in the Swedish expansion.

These expansion terms show better promise of usefulness, as they all refer to (geographically, culturally, politically and economically) similar countries.

Table 1. Results from SICS automatic monolingual runs

	Rel	Ret	Avg. p.	R-Prec.
Swedish	1196	836	0.1347	0.1432
SwedishX	1196	850	0.1053	0.1170
Italian	1072	871	0.2239	0.2344
ItalianX	1072	844	0.1836	0.1799
French	1383	1117	0.2118	0.2155
FrenchX	1383	1072	0.1775	0.2030

We will investigate the possibility to automatically understand the lexical category of a term from its statistical properties; we would prefer to use as little hand-compiled lexical resources as possible so as not to limit the generality of the results to high-density languages.

5.2 Query Term Selection

Another important issue that we need to consider when performing automatic query expansion is the selection of query terms. In the present experiments, we simply expanded the queries word by word. As demonstrated above, this proved to be an inefficient approach, as many of the distributionally related words were clearly unsuitable as expansion terms in the given search context. This problem derives from the fact that the similarity relations between the context vectors merely reflect the distribution of words in the training data. In other words, the context vectors are highly domain specific, and reflect the topicality of the collection they were extracted from.

To demonstrate the domain specificity of the context vectors, we trained the system on two different text data: the 60-million-word Los Angeles Times TREC collection and the 10-million-word Touchstone Applied Science Associates (TASA) corpus. We then extracted the 5 nearest neighbors to "invasion", and compared the results to those produced by training on the CLEF 2002 collections:

These examples clearly demonstrate the fact that the correlations extracted from co-occurrence information reflect the topicality of the training data. The LA Times and TASA corpora produce fairly generic expansion terms, whereas the CLEF 2002 collections generate highly domain specific correlations.

One way to remedy the problem with domain specificity could be to select query terms by measuring similarity, not to individual query terms, but to the entire query concept, as suggested by [11]. This means that we would first produce a query vector by, e.g., summing the context vectors of the words in the query, and then calculate similarity between the query vector and the context vectors of the words in the vocabulary. Qiu & Frei (1993) demonstrate that this

Table 2. Nearest neighbors (NN) to "invasion" in 5 different corpora

Corpus	1st NN	2nd NN	3rd NN	4th NN	5th NN
LA Times	withdrawal	aggression	invading	invaded	troops
TASA	revolt	discriminated	rebelled	rebelling	immunized
CLEF 2002 Swedish collection	invadera	Haiti	haitiinvasion	kuwaitkonflikt	haitijunta
CLEF 2002 Italian collection	Iraq	city	Baghdad	invadere	Haiti
CLEF 2002 French collection	Bahrain	Irak	indépendance	Bahraïn	mouuik

methodology performs better on three standard test collections than traditional term based expansion.

5.3 Query Typology

Queries are usually very compact, but in their structure and in anticipated user needs we should be able to find types of anticipated retrieval. Some queries are to the point; others more vague. In a CLEF-type evaluation the query surface structure is of limited use, since all have purposely been formulated similarly; in a real-life setting variation will be more noticeable and give more information for typologization.

5.4 Combining Runs

An interesting alternative to merely comparing the results of the unexpanded and expanded runs is to merge the results of these runs, as suggested in this volume by Monz, Kamps and de Rijke [10]. If a combined run performs better than an unexpanded run, this implies that the expansion does provide valuable information after all. Jaap Kamps at the University of Amsterdam kindly performed a combination of our runs using the combination algorithm described in their paper in this volume.

The results of the (best) combined runs in comparison with the unexpanded and expanded runs are given in Table 5.4. The factor $0.X$ indicates the relative weight of the unexpanded run, so Combined (0.6) means that the unexpanded run had a weight of 0.6 in the combination (consequently, the expanded run then had a weight of 0.4). The improvements (2.52% for the Swedish runs, 3.08% for the Italian runs, and an improvement of 7.65% for the French runs) indicate that there is valuable information in the expansions after all.

Table 3. Results from combined and uncombined runs

	Avg. p.	**R-Prec.**
Swedish	0.1347	0.1432
SwedishX	0.1053	0.1170
Combined (0.6)	0.1381	0.1475
Italian	0.2239	0.2344
ItalianX	0.1836	0.1799
Combined (0.7)	0.2308	0.2351
French	0.2118	0.2155
FrenchX	0.1775	0.2030
Combined (0.6)	0.2280	0.2314

6 Conclusions

Using state-of-the-art morphological tools is necessary for compounding and inflecting languages such as those treated in this paper. The utility of higher level linguistic analysis for information retrieval is yet unproven; in further experiments we plan to investigate the utility of clause-internal dependency relations for this purpose.

Our baseline retrieval method must be improved, primarily by adding a mechanism for query term weighting. One possibility is to use information about typological features to derive different weighting schemes. We also noted that the retrieval function promotes short documents over longer ones, i.e. the normalization method should also be improved. Normalization is especially important in this domain since corpora of news articles usually contain a large number of very short articles.

Co-occurrence-based query expansion gives patchy results when used without domain-specific and general linguistic guidance. Lexical resources or domain models would undoubtedly improve results. However, the major aim for our conceptual clustering experiments is to model human information processing — we wish to find data-driven models that can be trained on the data at hand, whatever it is, to discover and build such tools rather than make use of existing ones. This means we need a finer-grained model of co-occurrence, term distribution, and textual progression.

Acknowledgements

The work reported here is partially funded by the European Commission under contracts IST-2000-29452 (DUMAS) and IST-2000-25310 (CLARITY) which is hereby gratefully acknowledged. We thank Tidningarnas TelegrambyråAB, Stockholm, for providing us with the Swedish text collection.

References

[1] R. Bayer and K. Unterauer. Prefix B-trees. *ACM Transactions on Database Systems*, 2(1):11–26, March 1977.

[2] S. Deerwester, S. Dumais, G. Furnas, T. Landauer, and R. Harshman. Indexing by latent semantic analysis. *Journal of the Society for Information Science*, 41(6):391–407, 1990.

[3] M. J. Folk, B. Zoellick, and G. Riccardi. *File Structures. An Object-Oriented Approach with C++*. Addison-Wesley, 3rd edition, 1998.

[4] Z. Harris. *Mathematical Structures of Language*. Interscience publishers, 1968.

[5] P. Kanerva, J. Kristofersson, and A. Holst. Random indexing of text samples for latent semantic analysis. In *Proceedings of the 22nd Annual Conference of the Cognitive Science Society*, page 1036. Erlbaum, 2000.

[6] J. Karlgren and M. Sahlgren. From words to understanding. In Y. Uesaka, P. Kanerva, and H. Asoh, editors, *Foundations of Real World Intelligence*, pages 294–308. CSLI publications, 2001.

[7] S. Kaski. Dimensionality reduction by random mapping: Fast similarity computation for clustering. In *Proceedings of the IJCNN'98, International Joint Conference on Neural Networks*, pages 413–418. IEEE Service Center, 1998.
[8] T. Landauer and S. Dumais. A solution to Plato's problem: The latent semantic analysis theory of acquisition, induction and representation of knowledge. *Psychological Review*, 104(2):211–240, 1997.
[9] K. Lund and C. Burgess. Producing high-dimensional semantic spaces from lexical co-occurrence. *Behavior Research Methods, Instruments and Computers*, 28(2):203–208, 1996.
[10] C. Monz, J. Kamps, and M. de Rijke. Combining Evidence for Cross-language Information Retrieval. *This volume.*
[11] Y. Qiu and H. P. Frei. Concept based query expansion. In *Proceedings of the 16th ACM SIGIR Conference on Research and Development in Information Retrieval*, pages 160–169, 1993.
[12] H. E. Williams and J. Zobel. Compressing integers for fast file access. *The Computer Journal*, 42(3):193–201, 1999.
[13] I. H. Witten, A. Moffat, and T. C. Bell. *Managing Gigabytes: Compressing and Indexing Documents and Images.* Morgan Kaufmann Publishing, 2nd edition, 1999.

Pliers and Snowball at CLEF 2002

A. MacFarlane

Centre for Interactive Systems Research
Department of Information Science, City University, UK
andym@soi.city.ac.uk

Abstract: We test the utility of European language stemmers created using the Snowball language. This allows us to experiment with PLIERS in languages other than English. We also report on some experiments on tuning BM25 constants conducted in order to find the best settings for our searches.

1 Introduction

In this paper we briefly describe our experiments at CLEF 2002. We address a number of issues as follows. The Snowball language was recently created by Porter [1,2] in order to provide a generic mechanism for creating stemmers. The main purpose of the experiments was to investigate the utility of these stemmers and whether a reasonable level of retrieval effectiveness could be achieved by using Snowball in an information retrieval system. This allowed us to port the PLIERS system [3] for use on languages other than English. We also investigate the variation of tuning constants for the BM25 weighting function for the chosen European languages. The languages used for our experiments are as follows: German, French, Dutch, Italian, Spanish and Finnish. All experiments were conducted on a Pentium 4 machine with 256 MB of memory and 240 GB of disk space. The operating system used was Red Hat Linux 7.2. All search runs were done using the Robertson/Sparck Jones Probabilistic model – the BM25 weighting model was used. All our runs are in the monolingual track. All queries derived from topics are automatic.

The paper is organised as follows. Section 2 describes our motivation for doing this research. In Section 3 we describe our indexing methodology and results. In Section 4 we describe some preparatory results using CLEF 2001 data. Section 5 describes our CLEF 2002 results, and a conclusion is given at the end in Section 6.

2 Motivation for the Research

We have several different strands in our research agenda. The most significant of these is the issue of using Snowball stemmers in information retrieval, both in terms of retrieval effectiveness and retrieval efficiency. In terms of retrieval efficiency we want to quantify the cost of stemming both for indexing collections and servicing queries over them. How expensive is stemming in terms of time when processing

C.A. Peters (Ed.): CLEF 2002, LNCS 2785, pp. 321-335, 2003.

words? Our hypothesis for search would be that stemming will increase inverted list size and that this would in turn lead to slower response times for queries. Stemming will slow down indexing, but by how much? Due to time constraints we restrict our discussion on search efficiency to CLEF 2002 runs. With respect to retrieval effectiveness we hope to demonstrate that using Snowball stemmers leads to an increase in retrieval effectiveness for all languages, and any deterioration in results should not be significantly worse. Our hypothesis is therefore: "stemming using Snowball will lead to an increase in retrieval effectiveness". A further issue that we wish to address is that of tuning constants for the BM25 weighting model. Our previous research on this issue has been done on collections of English [3], but we want to investigate the issue on other types of European languages. A hypothesis is formulated in Section 4 where the issue is discussed in more detail.

3 Indexing Methodology and Results

3.1 Indexing Methodology

We used a simple and straightforward methodology for indexing: parsing, remove stop words, stemming in the given language. The PLIERS HTML/SGML parser needed to be altered to detect non-ascii characters such as those with umlauts, accents, circumflexes etc. The stemmers were easily incorporated into the PLIERS library. We used various stop word lists for the language, gathered from the internet. The official runs for Finnish did not use stemming, as no stemmer was available for that language while experiments were being conducted.

Table 1. Indexing results for builds using stemmers

Language	Elapsed Time (mins)	Dictionary file size MB	Postings file size MB	Map file size MB	% of text
German	34.3	22.58	149.83	7.29	34%
French	23.6	4.36	48.16	3.13	23%
Dutch	36.1	12.49	138.98	6.00	30%
Italian	33.2	6.04	62.37	3.49	26%
Spanish	44.3	8.14	135.46	7.35	30%
Finnish	10.2	21.07	37.17	1.91	45%

Table 2. Indexing results for builds without using stemmers

Language	Elapsed Time (mins)	Dictionary file size MB	Postings file size MB	Map file size MB	% of text
German	8.28	28.6	159.3	7.29	37%
French	3.28	5.93	67.3	3.13	32%
Dutch	7.72	15.6	145.1	6.00	32%
Italian	4.05	8.09	87.2	3.49	36%
Spanish	6.78	9.95	140.6	7.35	31%
Finnish	2.30	21.1	37.2	1.91	45%

3.2 Indexing Results

The indexing results are given in Tables 1 and 2. We report the following information: elapsed time in minutes, dictionary file size in MB, postings file size in MB, data file size in MB, and the size of the build files compared with the text file. The dictionary file contains keywords detected in the indexing process together with a link to the inverted lists contained in the postings file, while the data (or map) file contains information such as the CLEF document identifier and location on disk.

The key results here are that stemmed builds take up slightly less space for most languages (it is a significant saving for French and Italian) and that builds with stemming take significantly longer than builds with no stemming. Builds with no stemming index text at a rate of 3.7 to 4.5 GB per hour compared with 0.48 to 0.89 GB per hour for stemmed builds. The results for stemmed builds are acceptable however.

4 Preparatory Experiments: Working with CLEF 2001 Data

In order to find the best tuning constants for our CLEF 2002 runs we conducted tuning constant variation experiments on the CLEF 2001 data for the following languages: French, German, Dutch, Spanish and Italian. We were unable to conduct experiments with Finnish data as this track was not run in 2001: we arbitrarily chose K1=1.5 and B=0.8 for our Finnish runs.

We give a brief description of the BM25 tuning constants being discussed here [4]. The K1 constant alters the influence of term frequency in the BM25 function, while the B constant alters the influence of normalised average document length. Values of K1 can range from 0 to infinity, whereas the values of B are with the range 1 (document lengths used unaltered) to 0 (document length data not used at all).

We used the following strategy for tuning constant variation. For K1 we start with a value of 0.25 with increments of 0.25 to a maximum of 3.0, stopping when it was obvious that no further useful data could be gathered. For B we used a range of 0.1 to 0.9 with increments of 0.1. A maximum of 135 experiments were therefore conducted for each language.

Table 3 show the best tuning constants found for CLEF 2002 together with the query type used for that tuning constants combination [Note: T = Title only queries, TD=Title and Description]. Note that these tuning constants were found by running experiments on the stemming builds, for application on runs of both type of build.

Table 3. CLEF 2002 experiment results with chosen tuning constants (builds with stemming)

Language	K1 Constant	B Constant	Query Type
German	1.75	0.5	T and TD
French	2.0	0.5	T and TD
Dutch	2.75	0.8	T and TD
Italian	2.5	0.6	TD
Spanish	2.75	0.5	TD
Finnish	1.75	0.6	T

Table 4. CLEF 2001 experiment results on builds without stemming

Language	Average precision	Precision @5	Precision @10	Query Type
German	.213	.363	.326	T
	.269	.392	.373	TD
French	.243	.253	.226	T
	.254	.302	.265	TD
Dutch	.207	.268	.208	T
	.242	.336	.238	TD
Italian	.242	.260	.260	T
	.253	.306	.289	TD
Spanish	.210	.286	.273	T
	.225	.375	.322	TD

Table 5. CLEF 2001 experiment results on builds with stemming

Language	Average precision	Precision @5	Precision @10	Query Type
German	.192	.335	.300	T
	.207	.367	.342	TD
French	.238	.269	.247	T
	.256	.286	.249	TD
Dutch	.193	.236	.208	T
	.228	.360	.292	TD
Italian	.266	.315	.300	T
	.305	.379	.336	TD
Spanish	.264	.343	.322	T
	.255	.427	.365	TD

Tables 4 and 5 show the best results using CLEF 2001 data: using the tuning constants declared in Table 3. We formulate the following hypothesis for tuning constants on the CLEF collections: "the best tuning constants are independent of a given query set, if and only if the two sets are roughly the same size". In other words the best tuning constants found in our CLEF 2001 experiments should also be the best for our CLEF 2002 experiments for title only or title/description runs (we concentrate on title/description runs).

Due to lack of time, our aim in these experiments was to achieve a better than baseline retrieval effectiveness for our preparatory CLEF 2001 experiments. For the most part we succeeded in doing this for both types of build. However we can separate our results into three main groups:

- For Dutch and German we were able to better six systems with our runs.
- For French and Italian, we were unable to better more than one run, but our effectiveness is considerably better than the official baseline runs.
- For Spanish we were unable to show much of an improvement over the baseline run.

Table 6. CLEF 2002 experiment results with chosen tuning constants (official runs)

Language	Average elapsed Time (secs)	Average Query Size	Query Type	Run Identifier
German	0.97	16.1	TD	plge02td
	0.22	3.84	T	plge02t
French	0.05	10.2	TD	plfr02td
Dutch	1.51	34.5	TD	ptdu02td
	0.28	4.50	T	ptdu02t
Italian	0.33	12.0	TD	plit02td
Spanish	1.23	17.2	TD	plsp02td
	0.52	5.06	T	plsp02t
Finnish	0.12	13.6	TD	plfn02td
	0.01	12.2	T	plfn02t

Having said that we have a long way to go before our runs achieve the levels of performance of groups such as the University of Neuchatel particularly for languages such as French and Spanish.

We were unable to investigate the reason for the levels of performance achieved because of time constraints, but it is believed that the automatic query generator used to select terms for queries is simplistic and needs to be replaced with a more sophisticated mechanism. Our reason for believing that this might be the problem is that our results for Title only queries on the Spanish run are superior to those queries that were derived from Title and Description: this is counter to what we would expect.

When comparing experiments on those builds which used stemming and those that did not, we can separate our runs into three main groups:

- Stemming is an advantage: We were able to demonstrate that stemming was a positive advantage for both Italian and Spanish runs.
- Stemming makes no difference: Using stemming on French made very little difference either way.
- Stemming is a disadvantage: Stemming proved to be problematic for both Dutch and German.

We need to investigate the reason for these results. We are surprised that stemming is a disadvantage for any language.

5 CLEF 2002 Results

5.1 Retrieval Efficiency Results

Table 6 shows timings for each official run together with the average sizes of each query. All our runs have met the one to ten second response time criteria specified by Frakes [5], and all bar one have sub second response times. Title and description runs are significantly slower than title only.

Table 7. CLEF 2002 experiment results with chosen tuning constants (alternative runs)

Language	Average elapsed Time (secs)	Average Query Size	Query Type
German	1.07	16.6	TD
	0.19	3.82	T
French	0.05	10.4	TD
Dutch	1.47	34.9	TD
	0.03	2.80	T
Italian	0.28	12.1	TD
Spanish	1.09	16.9	TD
	0.47	4.90	T
Finnish	0.11	13.2	TD
	0.01	3.50	T

Table 8. CLEF 2002 official runs

Language	Average precision	Precision @5	Precision @10	Query Type
German	0.147	0.228	0.210	T
	0.173	0.284	0.254	TD
French	0.248	0.340	0.298	TD
Dutch	0.193	0.308	0.282	T
	0.259	0.396	0.346	TD
Italian	0.266	0.384	0.318	TD
Spanish	0.217	0.320	0.294	T
	0.255	0.376	0.354	TD
Finnish	0.123	0.200	0.143	T
	0.171	0.240	0.190	TD

Table 7 show the alternative runs which means that searches were conducted on builds with no stemming, apart from Finnish where we did have a stemmer available. As with our official runs the response times are acceptable. With respect to the difference in response time between the two types of build, we can separate the results into three main groups:

- Runs on Stemmed builds are faster: German (TD).
- Runs on No-Stemmed builds are faster: German (T), Dutch, Italian, and Spanish.
- No significant difference in response times: French, Finnish.

In general this is what we would expect as inverted lists on stemmed builds tend to be larger than those of builds with no stemming. It is interesting to examine the exceptions and outliers, however. The reason German (TD) runs are faster on stemmed builds, is that the average query size is slightly larger by about half a term (more inverted lists are being processed on average). The Dutch no stem run is significantly faster on average than the stemmed runs, but this is largely due to query size: queries with no stems on the Dutch collection have 1.7 less terms on average than those of stemmed queries (fewer inverted lists are being processed). An interesting result with title only Finnish runs is that queries with no stems are nearly 3.5 times smaller than stemmed queries, but run times are virtually identical: execution speeds are so small here it is difficult to separate them. It should be noted when we compared the size of queries with stems to those without stems, there is no clear pattern. We think therefore that a simple hypothesis which suggested that runs on builds without stemming is faster on average than runs on stemmed builds cannot be supported with the evidence given here. It is clear that the number of inverted lists processed is an important factor as well as the size of the inverted lists.

5.2 Retrieval Effectiveness Results

Table 8 shows our official results for CLEF 2002. In general the results are quite disappointing and much lower in terms of average precision than our CLEF 2001 runs. We believe that our results are on the low side compared with other participants.

Table 9 shows the results on comparative runs, all using builds without stemming apart from Finnish where we did have a stemmer available. When comparing runs on different types of build we can separate our results into two main groups:

- Stemming is an advantage: French and Italian.
- Stemming is a disadvantage: German, Dutch, Spanish and Finnish.

The status for German and Dutch is unchanged from our CLEF 2001 results (stemming runs produced worse results), and also for Italian where the stemmer runs produced better results. Our results for French have improved comparatively, but for Spanish the results have deteriorated. The runs on the Finnish collection are particularly disappointing: the results for average precision on builds with stemming being about 40% worse for title only queries and nearly 60% worse on title/description queries than experiments on builds without stemming. The reason for this loss in performance could be because of the morphological complexity of Finnish and merits significant further investigation. It is also interesting that the initial version of the Finnish stemmer did slightly better in terms of average precision than the final version: this is offset with a slight loss in precision at 5 and 10 documents retrieved. The reduced effectiveness found on title/description queries compared with title only queries in our Spanish CLEF 2001 experiments was not repeated in our CLEF 2002 runs. However there is a slight loss in performance on the second version of the Finnish stemmer when comparing title/description queries to title only queries: this loss is consistent across all shown precision measures.

After reviewing these results, we decided to investigate the reduced retrieval effectiveness with respect to other participants in the CLEF monolingual track. On investigation we found that there were several errors which affected the overall retrieval performance, some of which we tackled, others which we did not. They are as follows:

- Our query generator, as well as being naïve, also contained errors which generated terms not existing in the topic file.
- In not indexing dates, we were at a significant disadvantage with some topics which actually require the use of dates for best retrieval.
- Some of the languages required larger stop word lists to filter out frequent terms (this was particularly true for German).

Table 9. CLEF 2002 Comparative runs (* run on first stemmer attempt)

Language	Average precision	Precision @5	Precision @10	Query Type
German	0.159	0.292	0.253	T
	0.240	0.404	0.344	TD
French	0.237	0.271	0.244	TD
Dutch	0.246	0.384	0.334	T
	0.315	0.456	0.410	TD
Italian	0.198	0.282	0.239	TD
Spanish	0.235	0.388	0.344	T
	0.268	0.432	0.382	TD
Finnish	0.078	0.147	0.133	T*
	0.074	0.160	0.140	T
	0.069	0.147	0.123	TD

Table 10. Post CLEF 2002 results: Average precision results

Language	Stemmed Builds	Increase on Official Run	No Stem Builds	Increase on Official Run
French	0.279	12%	0.291	22%
German	0.196	12.7%	0.255	5%
Italian	0.282	5%	0.255	28%
Spanish	0.283	11%	0.292	8%
Dutch	0.328	27%	0.298	-5%
Finnish	0.074	7%	0.224	82%

We did some further runs to address the first problem, removing words from the batch query files which were either generated in error by the query program or we felt should have been included in the original stop word list. This simple technique was used for German, French, Italian and Spanish. For Dutch and Finnish we decided to manually choose the terms, inspecting the index to choose those which we felt may be the best descriptors for a given topic. The results of these extra runs are shown in Table 10 (average precision only).

We were able to increase the average precision on all of our runs, apart from the No Stem builds for Dutch. The increases range from modest (5% for Italian Stemmed, German No Stem builds) to the spectacular (82% for Finnish No Stem builds). Only two of our revised runs show any demonstrable benefit for stemming: Italian and Dutch. Italian is the only language which has been consistently shown to have positive benefits when using Snowball stemmers. We are encouraged by the improvement in our Dutch runs, where using the same terms we can show there is a definite improvement for that language as well: albeit for manually generated queries. The one big disappointment is that the gap between runs on stemmed and no stemmed builds on Finnish has increased, largely due to the significant gain found in runs on no stemmed builds. It is clear that we have some way to go before our system is able to handle these languages satisfactorily.

Table 11. Best values for tuning constant variation experiments – CLEF 2002 collection

Language	K1 Constant	B Constant	Average precision
German	1.75	0.5	0.173
French	1.75	0.3	0.256
Dutch	2.5	0.6	0.263
Italian	2.0	0.6	0.268
Spanish	2.75	0.5	0.264

5.3 Tuning Constant Variation Experiments

We present the results of our tuning constant experiments using the queries we used for our official runs. All runs are done with title/description queries only. No runs were done on Finnish data as we did not have data from 2001. Graphs showing a three-dimensional view of the data can be seen in the Appendix, and the best yielding runs are shown in Table 11.

What is interesting about our tuning constant experiments is that the graphs in both 2001 and 2002 runs for each individual language have much the same shape (that is within a language the graphs look the same). The results for the best individual pair of tuning constants show that either the chosen values from 2001 are the best for 2002, or there is no significant difference in terms of average precision. Details for each language are as follows.

Spanish: 2001 values are best for 2002 runs.

- Italian: Only K1 value varied (2.0 for 2002, 2.5 for 2001) and the difference in average precision is 0.002.
- French: K1 and B values are different, but are actually in the same area of the graph. Difference is not significant between 2001 and 2002 values: 0.008.
- German: 2001 values are best for 2002 runs.
- Dutch: Chosen constants were very close on the graph, and the difference in average precision is only 0.004.

Recall our hypothesis on these tuning constants in Section 4. We have shown that for the particular query sets used on the given collections the hypothesis does hold i.e. we have not been able to refute the conjecture with the data available.

6 Conclusion

A number of research questions have been raised during this investigation of the effectiveness of stemming utilitising Snowball. They are as follows:

- Why are results using Snowball stemmers compared with builds inconsistent?
- Why are the results using the Finnish Snowball stemmer significantly worse?

Our hypothesis that suggested that the use of Snowball stemmers is always beneficial has not been confirmed. It may be possible to investigate this hypothesis further when we have investigated the problems with our software and indexing schemes described above. We also have some conclusions with regard to retrieval efficiency and stemming:

- Stemming using the Snowball stemmers is costly when indexing, but does not slow down the process of inverted file generation to an unacceptable level.
- We have confirmed that inverted file size is not the only factor in search speed, query size which requires processing of more inverted lists plays an important part as well.

As far as our hypothesis with respect to tuning constants goes, we have not be able to refute it using the data available. It would be worthwhile investigating this issue further – particularly when we have solved some of the problems detailed above with our system.

Acknowledgements

The author is grateful to Martin Porter for his efforts to produce a Snowball stemmer for Finnish.

References

[1] Snowball web site [http://snowball.sourceforge.net] – visited 19th July 2002.

[2] Porter. M., Snowball: A language for stemming algorithms, [http://snowball.sourceforge.net/texts/introduction.html] – visited 19th July 2002.

[3] MacFarlane, A., Robertson, S.E.., McCann, J.A., PLIERS AT TREC8, In: Voorhees, E.M., and Harman, D.K., (eds), The Eighth Text Retrieval Conference (TREC-8), NIST Special Publication 500-246, NIST: Gaithersburg, 2000, p241-252.

[4] Robertson, S.E., and Sparck Jones, K., Simple, proven approaches to text retrieval, University of Cambridge Technical report, May 1997, TR356, [http://www.cl.cam.ac.uk/Research/Reports/TR356-ksj-approaches-to-text-retrieval.html] – visited 22nd July 2002.

[5] Frakes, W.B., Introduction to information storage and retrieval systems. In: Frakes, W.B. and Baeza-Yates, R. (eds), Information retrieval; data structures and algorithms, Prentice Hall, 1992, p1-12.

Appendix – Graphs for Tuning Constant Variation Runs

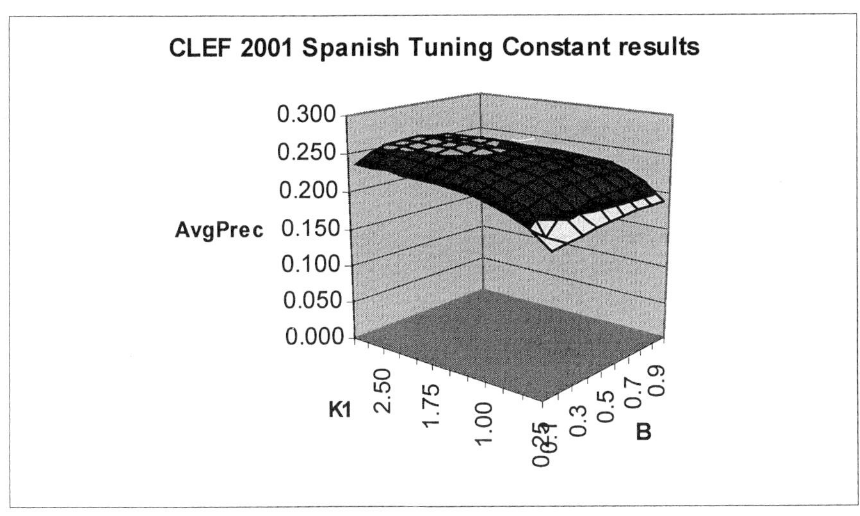

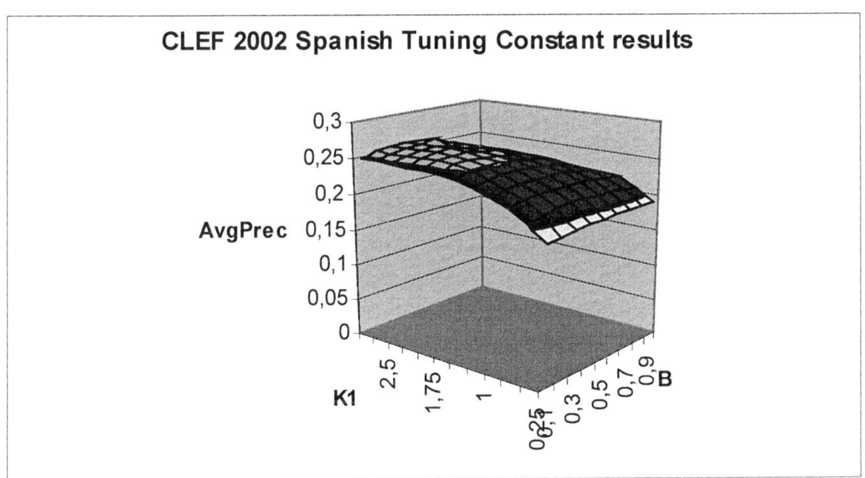

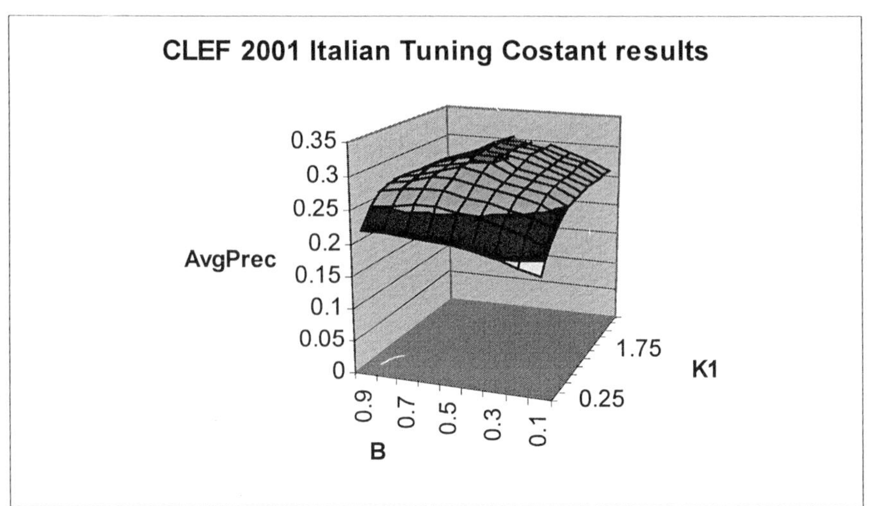
CLEF 2001 Italian Tuning Costant results
AvgPrec
0.35
0.3
0.25
0.2
0.15
0.1
0.05
0
0.9
0.7
0.5
0.3
0.1
B
1.75
0.25
K1

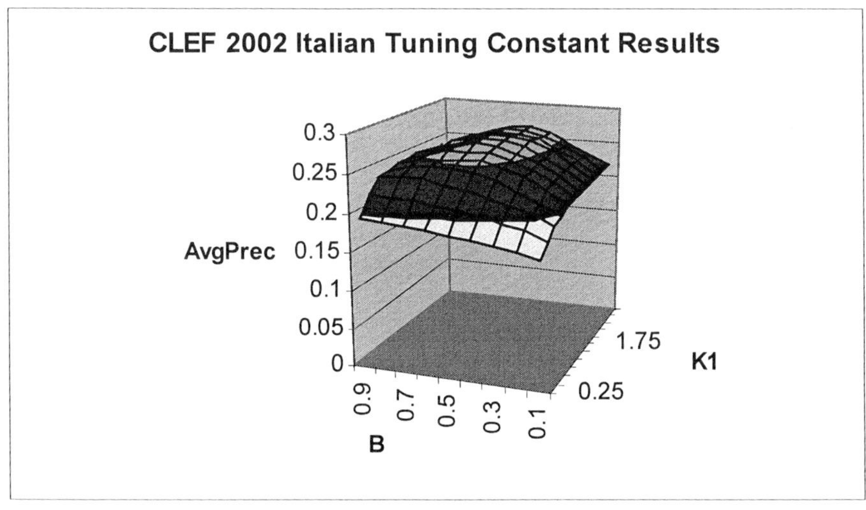
CLEF 2002 Italian Tuning Constant Results
AvgPrec
0.3
0.25
0.2
0.15
0.1
0.05
0
0.9
0.7
0.5
0.3
0.1
B
1.75
0.25
K1

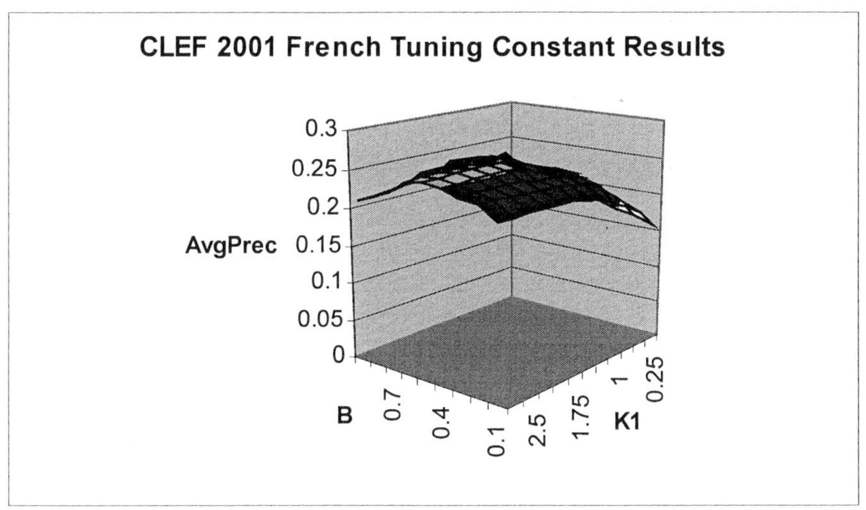
CLEF 2001 French Tuning Constant Results
AvgPrec
0.3
0.25
0.2
0.15
0.1
0.05
0
B
0.7
0.4
0.1
2.5
1.75
1
0.25
K1

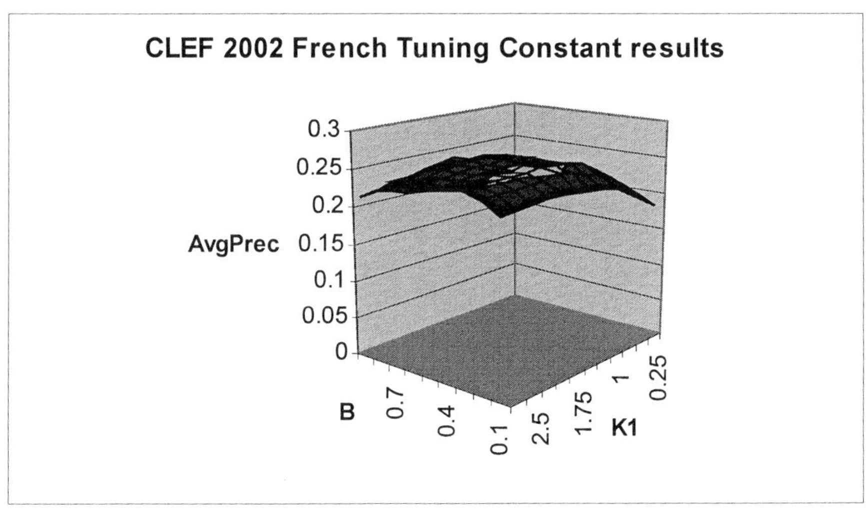
CLEF 2002 French Tuning Constant results
AvgPrec
0.3
0.25
0.2
0.15
0.1
0.05
0
B
0.7
0.4
0.1
2.5
1.75
1
0.25
K1

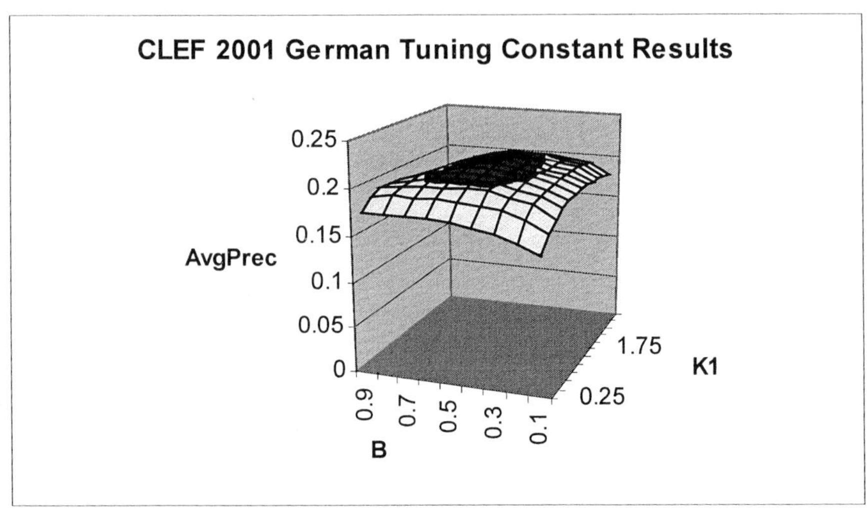
CLEF 2001 German Tuning Constant Results
AvgPrec
0.25
0.2
0.15
0.1
0.05
0
B
0.9
0.7
0.5
0.3
0.1
K1
1.75
0.25

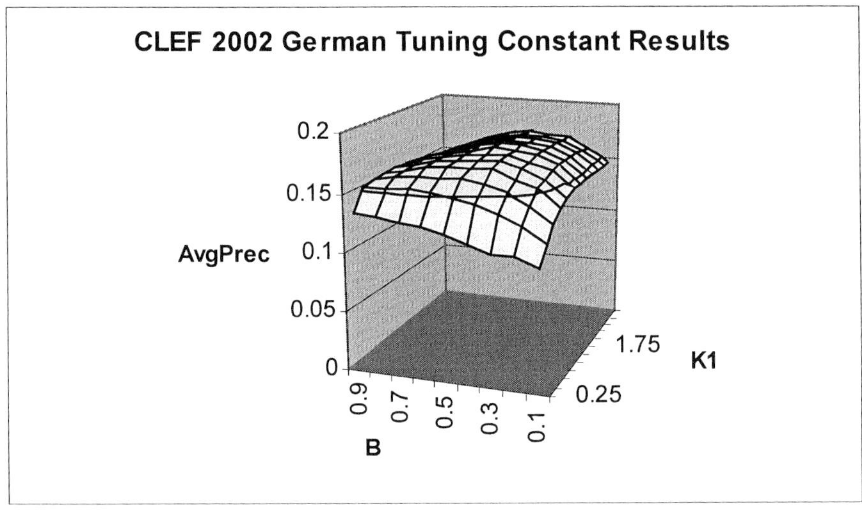
CLEF 2002 German Tuning Constant Results
AvgPrec
0.2
0.15
0.1
0.05
0
B
0.9
0.7
0.5
0.3
0.1
K1
1.75
0.25

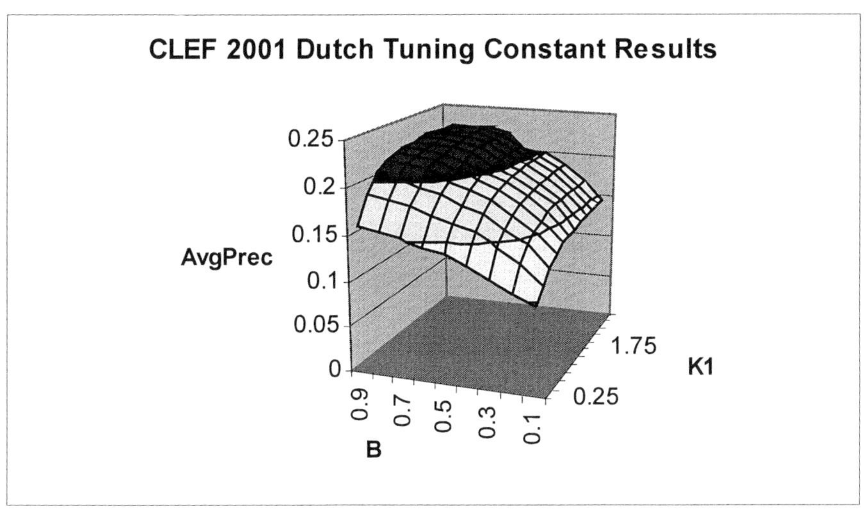
CLEF 2001 Dutch Tuning Constant Results
AvgPrec
0.25
0.2
0.15
0.1
0.05
0
0.9
0.7
0.5
0.3
0.1
B
1.75
0.25
K1

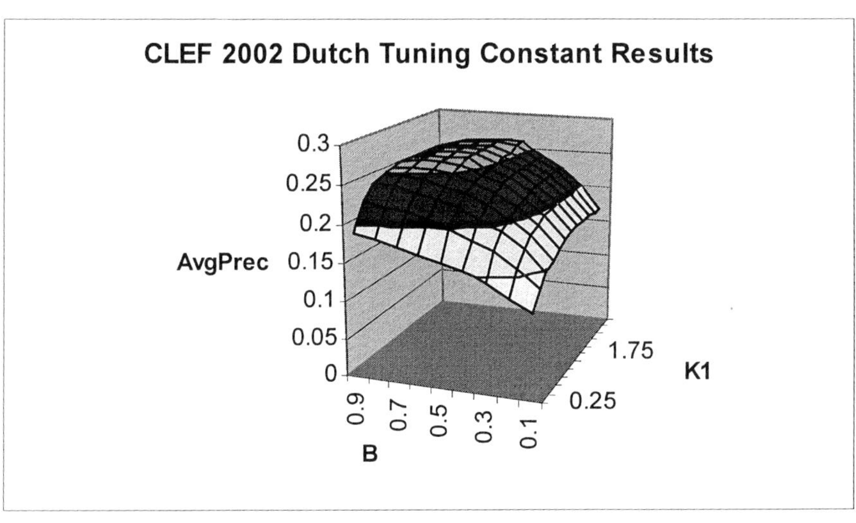
CLEF 2002 Dutch Tuning Constant Results
AvgPrec
0.3
0.25
0.2
0.15
0.1
0.05
0
0.9
0.7
0.5
0.3
0.1
B
1.75
0.25
K1

Experiments with a Chunker and Lucene

Gil Francopoulo

TAGMATICA 101 avenue de Saint-Mandé
75012 Paris France
gil.francopoulo@tagmatica.com
www.tagmatica.com

Abstract. The present paper describes the way we participated in the French track of CLEF-2002. We used a morphological analyser and a syntactic chunker in order to disambiguate words and to filter out certain categories of words. We then built a global index using the Lucene Indexor. For the search process, we wrote boolean queries manually and tested them using the Lucene query evaluator.

1 Introduction

This paper describes the way Tagmatica participated in the French (monolingual) track of CLEF-2002 during 3 weeks in Spring 2002, using an in-house morphological analyser and syntactic chunker.

The collection for the French track was composed of two parts. The first part consisted of a one-year production of a Swiss news agency whose name in French is "Agence Télégraphique Suisse" (part of the SDA collection) and the second part of one year of the "Le Monde" newspaper.

The task was to run 50 queries on an index built from the two corpora.

2 Indexing

We took two decisions. The first was to improve our «picking up» module that corrects written mistakes. We note that these mistakes are numerous in news texts. The goal was to avoid the "silence" caused by the fact that a miswritten word cannot be found and so is not considered as a candidate during search. The second decision was to apply a natural language process on the input corpora during indexing.

We had the following reasons for this:

1. We wanted to recognize compound words as truly compound words in order to a) avoid noise due to false interpretation of components: a "pomme de terre" is not a "pomme". and b) to identify words that are interesting to index which makes it interesting to identify the document in which they appear. It should be

C.A. Peters (Ed.): CLEF 2002, LNCS 2785, pp. 336-337, 2003.

noted that we have a lot of compound words recorded in our lexicon (30,000 compound words).
2. We wanted to filter out certain grammatical categories, for instance, we wanted to avoid indexing empty words and adverbs.
3. We wanted to include only the lemmatized forms in the index and not the full forms in order to group together the various occurrences of the same lemmatized form, and compute a weight for all the occurrences of the various full forms. This criteria held for both simple and compounds words.
4. We wanted to disambiguate certain difficult (and frequent) French words such as "tu" as "Pronoun" vs. "Past participle of the verb taire".
5. We needed to use local grammars in order to recognize dates, times, numbers etc. and our morphological analyzer already had these algorithms.

In other words, we needed to parse the whole sentence.

We proceeded as follows:

1. Sentence segmentation,
2. Morphological analyses for simple and compound words,
3. If the word was unknown, a "picking up" was tried. A rapid visual control has been made on this process. We verified all unknown words that begin with a lower case and appear more than five times plus unknown words that begin with an upper case and appear more that 50 times. The check showed that most of the frequent mistakes were corrected.
4. A syntactic and partial parsing was applied by the means of a chunker (see www.tagmatica.com). We did not use the syntactic information labelled by the chunker, we just used the word level disambiguation.
5. The lemmatized form is given to the Lucene Indexor (see jakarta.apache.org/lucene).

3 Search

We translated the topics manually into boolean expressions. As we indexed only lemmatized forms, we entered the query terms according to their lemmatized form. We did not use the title tag. We used only the descriptive and narrative tags.

4 Conclusions

We do not know exactly how our results can be compared with the results of the other participants. We indexed the whole SDA corpus but we only had sufficient time to index 70% of the "Le Monde" corpus (we had a hardware problem). This means that we certainly have a lot of "silence" compared with the other results., but with respect to noise, we probably are not very noisy.

Information Retrieval with Language Knowledge

Elzbieta Dura and Marek Drejak

Lexware Labs, Göteborg, Sweden
elzbieta@lexwarelabs.com

Abstract. The introduction of Swedish made it possible for Lexware® to be tested for the first time in CLEF. Lexware is a natural language system applied in an information retrieval task and not an information retrieval system using NLP techniques. Therefore it is interesting to compare its results with other less unusual IR systems. From our experience, we believe that separate evaluation of document description and query building would provide even better testing for our system.

1 A Natural Language System for Swedish

Lexware is a natural language system applied in an information retrieval task and not an information retrieval system using NLP techniques, like e.g. NLIR [4]. It can be also be considered unusual as a natural language processing system, if such systems are assumed to focus on syntactic analysis (c.f. [3]). Text-analysis is shallow and is not demanding in terms of computing power and storage [1]. The strength of the system is its rich lexicon and the possibility to expand the lexicon with external items without negative impact on access time [2]. The vocabulary of about 80 000 lexical items is richly interconnected by relations of form and content: derivational origin, synonymy, components for complex items, hyponymy. Content words are categorized into about 100 content categories. There are also supplementary word lists which include about 50 000 terms such as names of people, places, organizations, etc. plus basic glossaries of English, French, German, and Latin. 400 word formation rules cope with inflection, compounding and derivation, 500 general phrase rules plus 700 collocation patterns are used to disambiguate and to determine modifier–head roles.

2 Lexware in Another Information Retrieval Task

Lexware has been extensively tested in another information retrieval task. The library of the Swedish parliament – Riksdagsbiblioteket, designed and conducted an evaluation of software that could supplement or even substitute manual indexing of the documents of the parliament. The task was to select appropriate keywords among descriptors in a thesaurus specially created for this kind of document. The keywords were limited in number, from 2-10 and not only were supposed to identify the main subject but also to do so at the correct level of generality in the thesaurus hierarchy.

C.A. Peters (Ed.): CLEF 2002, LNCS 2785, pp. 338-342, 2003.

For instance, when a document refers to university education the term *university education* and not *education* should be picked from the thesaurus.

Software from Connexor, Lingsoft, Kungliga Tekniska Högskola and LexWare Labs participated in the tests. The evaluation was based on a comparison of keywords assigned manually to the same documents by two different indexers. The overlap in keywords assigned by the two indexers was only 34%. LexWare obtained the best F-value: 36%, Kungliga Tekniska Högskola 32%, Connexor 22%, Lingsoft 19%.

Recent tests of the fully developed Lexware application for indexing parliamentary documents have shown very high coverage with full precision. Automatically assigned keywords were compared with manually assigned ones in 1400 documents obtained from Riksdagsbiblioteket. 80% of keywords assigned by LexWare are the same or very closely related in the thesaurus to those assigned manually.

Lexware is also applied in retrieval of parliamentary documents without the thesaurus. All content words are used in document description and are made available for search. The screen dump shows a list of content words presented to the user for the search word *kompetens* (*competence*). Each word is presented with the number of documents it occurs in. Compounds and synonymous expressions for *kompetens* (*behörighet*, *befogenhet*) are included in the list (c.f. http://www.lexwarelabs.com).

Fig. 1. Content words presented to user searching *kompetens*

This type of two step query is meant to assist an "average user" of a search engine, who according to Google statistics does not look over more than one result screen (85%), leaves the query unmodified (78%), is very "concise" (2.35 terms on average), does not use much syntax (80% queries are without operator).

One role of the lexicon is to provide abstract terms another one is to provide these with precise relevance weights. Each lexical item has its specific semantic load. For instance content words used as part of lexicalised compounds or set expressions are often devoid of all content. Verbs of the kernel vocabulary contribute with little or no content, even those which are not function words at all. This kind of lexical knowledge used by Lexware (together with corpus statistics) is decisive for precision.

3 Lexware in CLEF

The CLEF task was approached in a similar way. Lexware participated in the monolingual track for Swedish. Documents were analysed and provided with a description in weighted abstract terms: lexemes, lexical phrases and named items. Each query text was analysed linguistically in a similar way as the documents. Vocabulary items recognized as meaningful content words were included together with items related to them, like synonyms, derivations, etc. Weights were assigned to each item in a query depending also on where the item appeared in the query text: in the title, description or narration part. The total relevance of a document for a given query is simply calculated as a sum of the weights of each query item matched in the document description. Only documents that pass a relevance threshold are selected.

A query is created as a list of weighted terms subdivided into the following groups: *exists* – must occur in a document, *not_exists* – must not occur in a document, *plus_intersection* – contributes to relevance, *minus_intersection* – counteracts relevance. Proper names and meaningful content words of the title part of a query text are classified as *exists*. Other words in non-negating contexts constitute *plus_intersection*.

4 Evaluation of Query Building

Even if query building is not evaluated separately, it is fairly obvious to us that it is the quality of the queries that is primarily lacking in Lexware and not the quality of document description. On the other hand we find it highly improbable that queries in practical applications will ever have the form of the queries in the CLEF task.

A query about bronchial asthma is a good example of how trivially easy retrieval is made impossible by an improper query. In the case of *bronchial asthma* the modifier is almost devoid of content because the default use of the word *asthma* is exactly *bronchial asthma* but Lexware excludes documents on *asthma* as not sufficiently specific. A similar example of default use assumption, this time on the part of the test-suite, is the belief that documents on gold medals in the Paraolympics in Lillehammer are not relevant for the subject "gold medals in the Olympics in Lillehamer". It is not obvious at all how default use should be coped with.

Some misses in query construction depend on lack of world knowledge. Some world knowledge is necessary and not difficult to include in the system. For instance, if country and city names were linked with the name of the continent in the Lexware representation, no documents about reports from Amnesty International in Latin America would be missed. The disregard of important meta-information about documents, like publication dates, is also an example of Lexware mistakes which are rather easy to repair. But there are problems that are not easy to eliminate. Queries which involve some kind of meta-information are difficult to cope with lexically. For instance, one query requires that the reasons for an event should be mentioned. How does one expand *reasons* into a list of vocabulary items? Very general concepts are also difficult: which lexical items are counterparts of *immaterial property*?

5 Evaluation of Retrieval

We set the threshold of relevance high in order to maximize precision. Documents were rejected even in cases when only a few were retrieved. For instance, proper name identification was not sufficient by itself. Another example of too sharp cutting off are documents on many topics, such as "foreign affairs in short", all of which were rejected. The same example goes for documents with only a mention of the subject, in parenthesis, or as an example, etc. It would be reasonable to have a flexible relevance metric dependent on the availability of documents on a subject. This approach is adopted in the test-suite. Documents are qualified for a query even on a mention in cases when only few ones are available otherwise, but not when many documents are available on the subject.

It is difficult to determine whether negative information should be deemed relevant. For instance, Lexware selects a document in which it is stated that Germany refuses to provide armed forces for a mission abroad when German forces in foreign assignments are queried. A similar example is a document in which it is assessed that cellular telephones cannot be used by people with pace makers, selected by Lexware in response to a query about possible uses of cellular phones. Is a document stating that a spy affair was not taken up during some top meeting relevant for a query about whether and how a spy affair had an impact on Soviet-US relations? Metaphors are also difficult to cope with. For instance, a document about a divorce between Renault and Volvo is qualified by Lexware as a document on divorces. This problem borders on the problem of default language use – divorces are for people not for cars.

6 Evaluation of Evaluation

There is a minor bug in the evaluation program. Whenever Lexware retrieves 0 documents the program counts 1 document as retrieved and 0 documents as relevantly retrieved (queries: 91, 105, 110, 111, 121). 0 documents was retrieved for query 109 both in the test suite and by Lexware – this result is missing in the result list.

Since there are only 50 queries it is easy to go through the results of query building manually. One can see directly which queries are properly constructed and which are almost worthless. Therefore it was surprising for us to see poor retrieval results when queries were very good, which in turn made us check manually some of the results. We made checks only in cases in which our queries seemed to be properly built, which is the case for about half of the queries. The list of our findings can be made available for corrections of the test-suite. Only extremely obvious misses are considered: documents explicitly on a topic not marked as relevant or documents without the slightest mention of the topic qualified as relevant. 53 documents are marked as relevant by mistake, while 19 fully relevant documents are left out. There are less documents than texts because some documents are repeated - we encountered 3 pairs of the same documents. After corrections the total number of relevant documents is 1219, 281 of which were retrieved by Lexware of 463 totally retrieved documents.

7 Conclusions

Evaluation is perhaps the most efficient way to improve both NLP and IR systems but it seems to be appreciated mainly by IR practitioners. It is crucial that monolingual systems for small languages like Swedish can also be tested, even more for NLP than for IR systems. The Swedish test-suite initiated by Jussi Karlgren is extremely valuable to all researchers working with Swedish and it is very important to improve it and develop further.

It would be desirable for Lexware if query construction could be tested and evaluated separately from retrieval. The type of querying that should also find its place in testing are queries closer to the ones stated by an average user of search engines. Testing Lexware in the present task helped us to appreciate the difficulties in query construction, some of which are notoriously difficult for our lexical approach. In some cases there can be no meaningful expansion of a query with content words that are lexically related to the ones present in the query. Perhaps the completion required for Lexware in such cases is statistic language modelling.

Considering the deficiencies in our query construction and the too highly set threshold, the results of Lexware are not bad: the average F-value for all topics is 41% with corrections of test-suite, and 37% without the corrections.

References

[1] Dura, E. 1998. Parsing Words. Data linguistica 19. Göteborg: Göteborgs universitet.

[2] Dura, E. 2000. Lexicon-based Information Extraction with Lexware. In: PALC99 Proceedings.

[3] Sparck Jones, K. 1999. What is the Role of NLP in Text Retrieval?. In: Strzalkowski, T. (ed.): Natural Language Information Retrieval.

[4] Strzalkowski, T., Perez-Carballo, J., Karlgren, J., Hulth, A., Tapanainen, P., T. Lahtinen, T. 2000. Natural Language Information Retrieval: TREC-8 Report. Online at: http://trec.nist.gov/pubs/trec8/t8_proceedings.html

Domain Specific Retrieval Experiments with MIMOR at the University of Hildesheim

René Hackl, Ralph Kölle, Thomas Mandl, and Christa Womser-Hacker

University of Hildesheim, Information Science, Marienburger Platz 22
D-31141 Hildesheim, Germany
{koelle,mandl,womser}@uni-hildesheim.de

Abstract. For our first participation in CLEF we chose the domain specific GIRT corpus. We implemented the adaptive fusion model MIMOR (Multiple Indexing and Method-Object Relations) which is based on relevance feedback. The linear combination of several retrieval engines was optimized. As a basic retrieval engine, IRF from NIST was employed. The results are promising. For several topics, our runs achieved a performance above the average. The optimization based on topics and relevance judgements from CLEF 2001 proved to be a fruitful strategy.

1 Introduction

In the CLEF 2002 campaign, we tested an adaptive fusion system based on the MIMOR model [1, 2]. The experiments are carried out fully automatically and deal with the domain specific corpus of social science documents. We choose the GIRT track for our first participation because we are especially interested in the challenges of the domain specific task and because it allows monolingual retrieval. As the basic retrieval engine for our fusion system, we used the IRF package from NIST.

2 Fusion in Information Retrieval

The basic idea behind fusion is to delegate a task to different algorithms and consider all the results returned. These single results are then combined to give one final result. This approach is especially promising, when the single results are very different.

As investigations on the outcome of the TREC conferences have shown, the results of information retrieval systems performing similarly well are often different. This means, the systems find the same percentage of relevant documents, however, the overlap between their ranked lists is sometimes low [2].

An overview of fusion methods in information retrieval is given by [3]. Research concentrates on issues like which methods can be combined, how the retrieval status

C.A. Peters (Ed.): CLEF 2002, LNCS 2785, pp. 343-348, 2003.

values of two or more systems can be treated mathematically and which features of collections indicate that a fusion might lead to positive results.

Different retrieval methods can be defined according to various parameters. One possibility is using different indexing approaches, like word and phrase indexing.

The values are combined statically by taking the sum, the minimum or the maximum of the results from the individual systems [4]. Linear combinations assign a weight to each method which determines its influence on the final result. These weights may be improved for example by heuristic optimization or learning methods [5].

In experimental systems, the methods to be fused are applied to the same collection. However, fusion has also been applied to collections without overlap as well. A corpus can be split into artificial sub-sets which are treated by a retrieval system. In this case, the goal of the fusion can be regarded as an attempt to derive knowledge as to which collection leads to good results. For internet meta search engines, fusion usually means elimination of documents returned by at least two search engines.

3 MIMOR

MIMOR (Multiple Indexing and Method-Object Relations) represents a learning approach to the fusion task, which is based on results of information retrieval research which show that the overlap between different systems is often small [2]. On the other hand, relevance feedback is a very promising strategy for improving retrieval quality. As a consequence, the linear combination of different results is optimized through learning from relevance feedback. MIMOR represents an information retrieval system managing poly-representation of queries and documents by selecting appropriate methods for indexing and matching [1]. By learning from user feedback on the relevance of documents, the model adapts itself by assigning weights to the different basic retrieval engines. Therefore, MIMOR follows a long term learning strategy in which the relevance assessments are not just used for the current query. MIMOR is not limited to text documents but open to other data types such as structured data and multimedia objects. Learning is implemented as a delta rule. More complex learning schemes should be evaluated [6,7,8].

4 CLEF Retrieval Experiments with the GIRT Corpus

The GIRT data is part of a digital library for the social sciences. The domain specific task is described in [9]. We did not use the intellectually assigned thesaurus terms.

4.1 Tools

Our main tool was the IRF retrieval package available from NIST[1]. IRF is an object oriented retrieval framework, which is programmed in JAVA. The sample IR application proved to meet our retrieval needs sufficiently, which means ranked results, setting of parameters etc. Thus, only a few changes were necessary.

---

[1] http://www.itl.nist.gov/iaui/894.02/projects/irf/irf.html

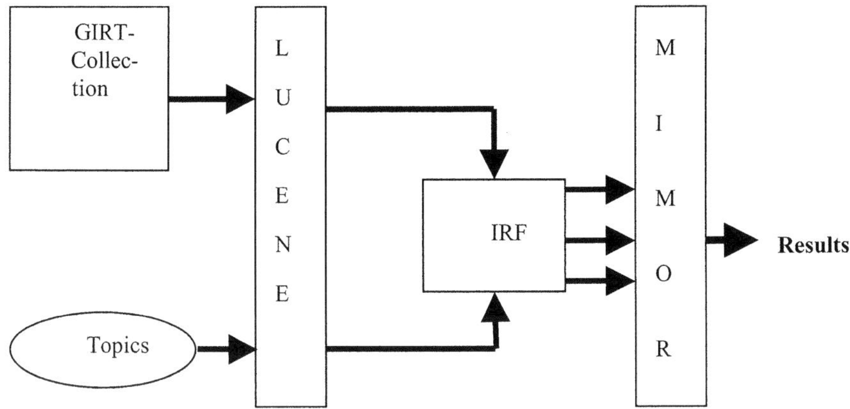

Figure 1. Sequence of operations

In addition we used the Lucene package for topic and data preprocessing. It is written in JAVA, too, and can be obtained from the Jakarta Apache Project's homepage[2]. Lucene comprises both a built-in German analyzer and a German stemmer apart from many other features. Both may easily be altered as desired. The indexing application could be run without major changes, so we slightly modified the filter settings and provided a different, more thorough stop word list[3].

4.2 Processing Steps

The current MIMOR implementation of the University of Hildesheim could only partly be employed for our processing steps. Therefore, several steps were carried out with AWK4 scripts. We cut off all information except for the document number, the title and the text. The most important function was to simulate MIMOR's merging algorithm (cf. Figure 1); this was done by several scripts.

IRF allows the indexing methods *keyword* and *inverse document frequency*. For both, text and title may be weighted differently. Our three runs with IRF used the following settings:

Table 1. Basic runs

Run	Index	Text weight	Title weight
IRF Run 1	inverse document frequency	1	1
IRF Run 2	inverse document frequency	1	3
IRF Run 2	Keyword	1	1

[2] http://jakarta.apache.org/lucene/docs/index.html

[3] http://www.unine.ch/info/clef/

[4] http://members.cox.net/dos/txtfrmt.htm

Table 2. Result overview

Run	Retrieved	Relevant	Rel_ret	Avg. prec.
UHi02r1 (fusion)	23.751	961	387	0.1093
UHi02r2 (optimized)	23.751	961	397	0.1097

We ran the topics from 2001 with the same setup. Subsequently, we compared the results obtained with the relevant documents assessed for last years campaign. Based on these results we globally optimized the fusion by assigning a higher weight to the system with better results.

For comparison we submitted two runs:

- Run with equal weights for individual systems
- Run with optimized weights derived from last year's results

4.3 Results

As Table 1 shows, the average precision for both runs is almost equal. Speaking in absolute figures, run UHi02r2 (where optimized fusion was applied) produced ten more relevant documents.

Query 67 – where out of five possible relevant documents none was retrieved – is considered an outlier and is left out for the following operations.

Comparing the difference between the two precision scores, the fused result was better on nine, equal on two and worse for twelve topics. However the sum of differences produced a slight advantage in favor of the optimized fusion.

The precision at five documents is at 0.2667 and 0.2750 for fused and optimal runs, respectively, which we consider not too bad for our first participation. Some of our results were above the average of all participants, others were below.

We also analyzed the performance of the IRF runs without fusion to see whether the fusion had improved the retrieval quality. The results are shown in Table 3 and Figure 2. They show an amazingly strong improvement for the fused runs. However, the improvement may be partly due to the evaluation methodology used in CLEF. Only a few runs were submitted in 2002 for GIRT and consequently not very many documents were assessed by human judges. As a result, the three single runs may actually contain relevant documents which were not found by any other participating system. Nevertheless, the experiment shows that the performance of low performance runs can be improved significantly by fusion. This is especially interesting for web information retrieval where results are often of poor quality.

To summarize, the results show that fusion and MIMOR are effective approaches. We gained valuable experience from the CLEF experiments and expect that a learning process over some cycles will eventually lead to a good improvement in system performance.

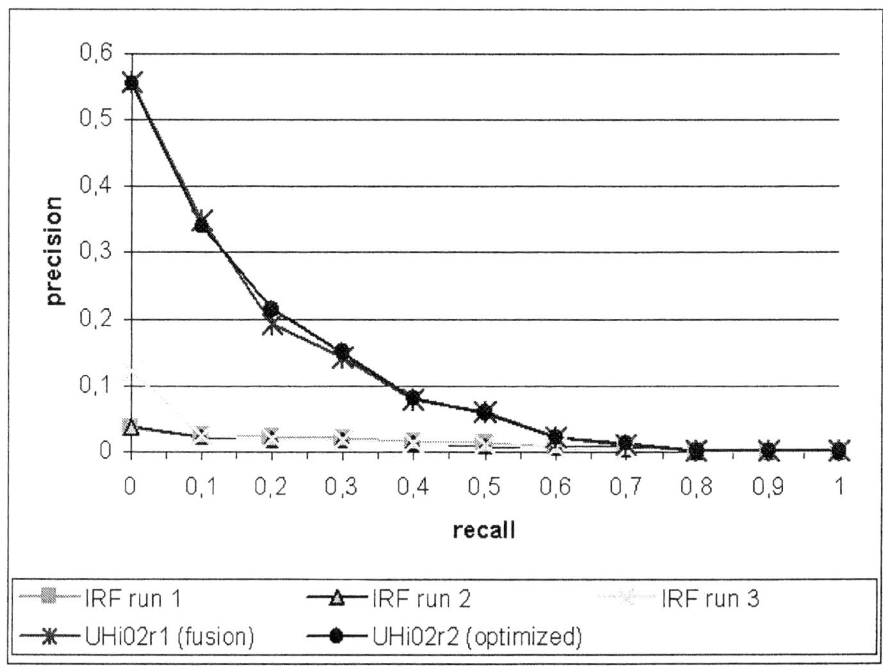

Figure 2. Retrieval quality of IRF and fused runs

Table 3. Results of individual and fused runs

Run	**Average Precision**
IRF Run 1	0.0134
IRF Run 2	0.0126
IRF Run 2	0.0206
UHi02r1 (fusion)	0.1294
UHi02r2 (optimized)	0.1313

5 Outlook

For our participation in CLEF next year we are planning the following improvements:

- More basic retrieval systems need to be integrated
- The optimization process needs to be refined
- MIMOR needs to be further automated

Furthermore, we plan to further extend our work on the CLEF challenge and participate also in the multilingual track with our fusion system.

Acknowledgements

We would like to thank NIST and especially Paul Over and Darrin Dimmick for providing the source code of the IRF package.

We also thank the Jakarta and Apache project teams for sharing Lucene with a wide community.

Furthermore, we acknowledge the work of several students from the University of Hildesheim who implemented MIMOR as part of their course work.

References

[1] Mandl, T., Womser-Hacker, C.: Probability Based Clustering for Document and User Properties. In: Ojala, T. (ed.): Infotech Oulo International Workshop on Information Retrieval (IR 2001). Oulo, Finland. Sept 19-21 2001. 100-107

[2] Womser-Hacker, C.: Das MIMOR-Modell. Mehrfachindexierung zur dynamischen Methoden-Objekt-Relationierung im Information Retrieval. Habilitationsschrift. Universität Regensburg, Informationswissenschaft (1997)

[3] McCabe, M., Chowdhury, A., Grossmann, D., Frieder, O.: A Unified Framework for Fusion of Information Retrieval Approaches. In: Eigth ACM Conference on Information and Knowledge Management (CIKM) ACM Press, New York, NY, USA (1999) 330-334

[4] Mandl, T., Womser-Hacker, C.: Fusion Approaches for Mappings Between Heterogeneous Ontologies. In: Constantopoulos, Panos; Sølvberg, Ingeborg (eds.): Research and Advanced Technology for Digital Libraries: 5th European Conference (ECDL) Lecture Notes in Computer Science, Vol. 2163 Springer-Verlag, Berlin Heidelberg New York (2001) 83-94

[5] Vogt, C., Cottrell, G.: Predicting the Performance of Linearly Combined IR Systems. In: 21th Annual Intl ACM SIGIR Conference on Research and Development in Information Retrieval (SIGIR)) ACM Press, New York, NY, USA (1998) 190-196

[6] Drucker, H., Wu, D., Vapnik, V.: Support Vector Machines for Spam Categorization. IEEE Trans. on Neural Networks 10 (1999) 1048-1054

[7] Joachims, T.: Text Categorization with Support Vector Machines: Learning with Many Relevant Features. In: European Conference on Machine Learning (ECML 1998) 137-142

[8] Iyer, R., Lewis, D., Schapire, R., Singer, Y., Singhal, A.: Boosting for Document Routing. In: Ninth ACM Conference on Information and Knowledge Management (CIKM) ACM Press, New York, NY, USA (2000) 70-77

[9] Kluck, M., Gey, F.: The Domain-Specific Task of CLEF - Specific Evaluation Strategies in Cross-Language Information Retrieval. In: Peters, Carol (ed.): Cross-Language Information Retrieval and Evaluation. Workshop of the Cross-Language Information Evaluation Forum (CLEF) Lecture Notes in Computer Science, Vol. 2069 Springer-Verlag, Berlin Heidelberg New York (2000) 48-56

Using Thesauri in Cross-Language Retrieval of German and French Indexed Collections

Vivien Petras[1], Natalia Perelman[1], and Fredric Gey[2]

[1] School of Information Management and Systems
[2] UC Data Archive & Technical Assistance
University of California, Berkeley, CA 94720 USA

Abstract. For CLEF 2002, Berkeley's Group One experimented with Russian, French and English as query languages, and investigated thesaurus-aided retrieval for the special CLEF collections GIRT and Amaryllis. Two techniques were used to locate source language topic terms within the controlled vocabulary and replace them with the document language thesaurus terms to form the query sent against the collection index. This form of controlled vocabulary-aided translation is called thesaurus matching. Results show that thesaurus-aided cross-language retrieval performs slightly worse than machine translation retrieval on average, but can yield decidedly better results for particular queries.
In addition, Berkeley submitted runs to the monolingual and bilingual (French and German) CLEF main tasks. We found that bilingual retrieval sometimes outperforms monolingual retrieval and postulate reasons to explain this phenomenon.

1 Introduction

Digital libraries relating to particular subject domains have invested a great deal of human effort in developing metadata in the form of subject area thesauri. This effort has emerged more recently in artificial intelligence as ontologies or knowledge bases which organize particular subject areas. The purpose of subject area thesauri is to provide organization of the subject into logical, semantic divisions as well as to index document collections for effective browsing and retrieval. Prior to free-text indexing (i.e. the bag-of-words approach to information retrieval), subject area thesauri provided the only point of entry (or 'entry vocabulary') to retrieve documents. A debate began over thirty years ago about the relative utility of the two approaches to retrieval:

- to use index terms assigned by a human indexer, drawn from the controlled-vocabulary, or
- to use automatic free-text indexing from the words or phrases contained in the document text.

This debate continues to this day and the evidence seems to have been mixed. In performance studies thesaurus-aided retrieval performs worse than free-text over a group of queries, while it performs better for particular queries [5].

C.A. Peters (Ed.): CLEF 2002, LNCS 2785, pp. 349–362, 2003.

It is an interesting question to evaluate what utility and performance can be obtained in cross-language information retrieval (CLIR) with the use of multilingual thesauri. The two domain-specific CLEF tasks, Amaryllis and GIRT, provide the opportunity to examine CLIR performance for such thesauri. The GIRT task provides a thesaurus for the social sciences in German, English, and (by translation) Russian, and Berkeley has studied it for three years. Amaryllis does not have a thesaurus per se (i.e. it does not identify broader terms, narrower terms or related terms), but it does have a specialized controlled vocabulary for its domain of coverage in both the French and English languages.

We have been evaluating thesaurus-aided retrieval by comparing traditional machine translation with our thesaurus matching techniques. We match a non-source-collection language search topic against the non-source-collection language version of our thesaurus (e.g. look up English query words in the English version of the GIRT thesaurus). Once a match is found, we replace the non-source-collection language thesaurus term with the source-collection language thesaurus term (e.g. the English GIRT thesaurus term is replaced with the associated German GIRT thesaurus term) and search those against the collection.

In addition we have been investigating the viability of Russian as a query language for the CLEF collections and continue this research for the CLEF bilingual (Russian to German and Russian to French) main tasks and the GIRT task (Russian to German).

For monolingual retrieval the Berkeley group has used the technique of logistic regression from the beginning of the TREC series of conferences. In the TREC-2 conference [2] we derived a statistical formula for predicting probability of relevance based upon statistical clues contained within documents, queries and collections as a whole.

2 Amaryllis

The Amaryllis task consisted of retrieving documents from the Amaryllis collection of approximately 150,000 French documents which were abstracts of articles in a broad range of disciplines (e.g. biological sciences, chemical sciences, engineering sciences, humanities and social sciences, information science, medical sciences, physical and mathematical sciences, etc). There were twenty-five topics and the primary goal was French-French monolingual retrieval under multiple conditions (primarily testing retrieval with or without concept words from the Amaryllis controlled vocabulary). An auxiliary task was to test out English to French cross-language information retrieval.

The first French topic is found below as Figure 1. Note that in distinction from previous CLEF tasks, the narrative field (FR-narr) consists only of controlled vocabulary concepts taken from the Amaryllis controlled vocabulary rather than the usual narration which expands upon the description.

For the Amaryllis task, we experimented with the effects of translation, inclusion of concept words and thesaurus matching. We indexed all fields in the

```
<top>
  <num>001</num>
  <FR-title>Impact sur l'environnement des moteurs diesel</FR-title>
  <FR-desc>Pollution de l'air par des gaz d'échappement des moteurs diesel
    et méthodes de lutte antipollution. Emissions polluantes (NOX, SO2,
    CO, CO2, imbrûlés, ...) et méthodes de lutte antipollution</FR-desc>
- <FR-narr>
    <c>Concentration et toxicité des polluants</c>
    <c>Mécanisme de formation des polluants</c>
    <c>Réduction de la pollution</c>
    <c>Choix du carburant</c>
    <c>Réglage de la combustion</c>
    <c>Traitement des gaz d'échappement</c>
    <c>Législation et réglementation</c>
  </FR-narr>
</top>
<top>
  <num>001</num>
  <EN-title>The impact of diesel engine on environment</EN-title>
  <EN-desc>Air pollution by the exhaust of gas from diesel engines and
    methods of controlling air pollution. Pollutant emissions (NOX, SO2, CO,
    CO2, unburned product, ...) and air pollution control</EN-desc>
- <EN-narr>
    <c>Concentration and toxicity of pollutant</c>
    <c>Pollutant formation mechanism</c>
    <c>Pollution prevention and reduction</c>
    <c>Motor fuel selection</c>
    <c>Combustion control</c>
    <c>Exhaust gas treatment</c>
    <c>Legislation and regulation</c>
  </EN-narr>
</top>
```

Fig. 1. Amaryllis Topic 01 (French and English xml)

document collection and used a stop word list, the latin-to-lower normalizer (changes capitals into lower case) and the Muscat French stemmer.

2.1 Amaryllis Controlled Vocabulary Matching

For Amaryllis controlled vocabulary matching we first extracted individual words and phrases from the English topics. Phrases were identified by finding the longest matching word sequences in the Amaryllis vocabulary file that was used as a segmentation dictionary. This method identified phrases such as "air pollution" and "diesel engine" in the first topic. The individual words and phrases were then searched in the Amaryllis vocabulary and if a match was found the words were replaced with their French equivalents.

Table 1. Results of official Amaryllis runs for CLEF 2002

Run Name	BKAMFF1	BKAMFF2	BKAMEF1	BKAMEF2	BKAMEF3
Qry ndx	TDN	TD	TD	TD	TD
Retrieved	25000	25000	25000	25000	25000
Relevant	2018	2018	2018	2018	2018
Rel Ret	1935	1863	1583	1897	1729
Precision					
at 0.00	0.9242	0.8175	0.6665	0.8079	0.6806
at 0.10	0.8011	0.7284	0.5198	0.7027	0.6497
at 0.20	0.7300	0.6296	0.4370	0.6114	0.5874
at 0.30	0.6802	0.5677	0.3791	0.5612	0.5337
at 0.40	0.6089	0.5159	0.3346	0.5033	0.4983
at 0.50	0.5458	0.4722	0.2942	0.4489	0.4452
at 0.60	0.4784	0.4035	0.2481	0.3825	0.3848
at 0.70	0.4242	0.3315	0.1874	0.3381	0.3114
at 0.80	0.3326	0.2682	0.1251	0.2664	0.2414
at 0.90	0.2193	0.1788	0.0501	0.1888	0.1570
at 1.00	0.0596	0.0396	0.0074	0.0300	0.0504
Avg Prec.	0.5218	0.4396	0.2792	0.4272	0.4038

2.2 Amaryllis Runs

Our Amaryllis results are summarized in Table 1. The runs are described below. The performance is computed over the top ranked 1000 documents for 25 queries.

BKAMFF1, our monolingual run including the concepts in the queries (title, description and narrative) yielded the best results. Our second monolingual run, BKAMFF2, where we excluded the concepts from the query indexes (only title and description) resulted in a 20% drop in average precision. Blind feedback improved the performance for both runs.

In comparing thesaurus matching and translation, this year the translation runs yielded better results. As a baseline, we run the English Amaryllis queries (without concepts or translation) against the French Amaryllis collection (BKAMEF1). As expected, average precision was not very high, but it is still greater than 50 percent of the best monolingual run. Using machine translation for the second bilingual run (BKAMEF2) improved precision over 50%. For translating the English topics, we used the Systran and L & H Power translator. By using only the Amaryllis thesaurus to match English words with French thesaurus terms (the BKAMEF3 run), we improved our average precision 44% compared to the baseline. For all runs, the query indexes only included the title and description fields, but we used blind feedback for BKAMEF2 and BKAMEF3.

3 GIRT Task and Retrieval

The GIRT collection consists of reports and papers (grey literature) in the social science domain. The collection is managed and indexed by the GESIS organization (http://www.social-science-gesis.de). GIRT is an excellent example of a collection indexed by a multilingual thesaurus, originally German-English, recently translated into Russian. The GIRT multilingual thesaurus (German-English), which is based on the Thesaurus for the Social Sciences [3], provides the vocabulary source for the indexing terms within the GIRT collection of CLEF. There are 76,128 German documents in the GIRT subtask collection. Almost all the documents contain manually assigned thesaurus terms. On average, there are about 10 thesaurus terms assigned to each document. More detail about the GIRT task may be found in [6].

For the GIRT task, we experimented with the effects of different thesaurus matching techniques and the inclusion of thesaurus terms. The German GiIRT collection was indexed using the German decompounding algorithm to split compounds (see section 4). For all runs, we used our blind feedback algorithm to improve the runs' performance.

3.1 GIRT Thesaurus Matching

Similar to the Amaryllis thesaurus-based translation, we initially identified some phrases in the English GIRT topics by finding the longest matching entries in the English-German GIRT thesaurus. This method produced phrases such as "right wing extremism" and "drug abuse". Then individual topic words and phrases were matched against the thesaurus and replaced with their German translations.

For the thesaurus-based translation of Russian GIRT topics we first transliterated both Russian topics and Russian entries in the German-Russian GIRT thesaurus by replacing Cyrillic characters with their Roman alphabet equivalents. Then two different approaches were used to find matches in the thesaurus.

In the first approach (run BKGRRG1 below) we identified phrases by finding the longest sequences of exact word matches to the terms in the thesaurus. The second approach was to follow the exact match with a fuzzy matching method to match both phrases and individual words that were not identified by the exact match method. This method, previously employed by our group in CLEF 2001, identified thesaurus terms in Russian by determining Dice's coefficient of similarity between the topic words and phrases and the thesaurus entries [4]. Since fuzzy matching sometimes finds commonality between unrelated words, in our second approach, in order to deal with Russian inflectional morphology, we normalized Russian words by removing the most common Russian inflectional suffixes. Then we identified phrases as in the previous method and translated both phrases and individual words by finding their matches in the thesaurus.

The following examples delineate the differences between the fuzzy match and longest match:

While fuzzy matching finds more matches, it sometimes overgenerates: for example, it matched the original topic word "shkol'nik" (schoolboy) with "doshkol'nik" (preschool aged child).

Russian word	Fuzzy Thesaurus Match	Exact match	German translation
uverennost'	samouverennost'	(no match)	Selbstsicherheit
devushek	devushka	(no match)	weibliche Jugendliche
uchebnye	uchebnik	ucheba	Lehrbuch–Lernen
sotsial'noi	sotsial'nyi sloi	(no match)	soziale Schicht
polov	(no match)	pol	Geschlecht
shkol'nikov	doshkol'nik	(no match)	Vorschulkind
obshchestvennye	obshchestvennye nauki	(no match)	Gesellschaftswissenschaft

3.2 GIRT Results and Analysis

Our GIRT results are summarized in Table 2. We had five runs, two monolingual and three cross-language, two with Russian topics, and one with English topics. The runs are described below. Only 24 of the 25 GIRT queries had relevant documents, consequently the performance is computed over the top ranked 1000 documents for 24 queries. Except for the second monolingual run (BKGRGG2), we indexed all allowed fields (including the controlled terms) in the document collection.

Using all query fields and indexing the controlled terms resulted in a 45% improvement in average precision for the monolingual GIRT run BKGRGG1 compared to BKGRGG2 (which only indexed the title and description query fields).

For Russian-German retrieval, the positive effect of including the narrative fields for the query indexing was countered by the different thesaurus matching techniques for the Russian GIRT run. Although the BKGRRG1 run used all

Table 2. Results of official GIRT runs for CLEF 2002

Run Name	BKGRGG1	BKGRGG2	BKGREG1	BKGRRG1	BKGRRG2
Qry ndx	TDN	TD	TD	TDN	TD
Retrieved	24000	24000	24000	24000	24000
Relevant	961	961	961	961	961
Rel. Ret	853	665	735	710	719
Precision					
at 0.00	0.7450	0.6227	0.5257	0.5617	0.5179
at 0.10	0.6316	0.4928	0.3888	0.3595	0.3603
at 0.20	0.5529	0.4554	0.3544	0.3200	0.3233
at 0.30	0.5112	0.3551	0.3258	0.2705	0.2867
at 0.40	0.4569	0.3095	0.2907	0.2275	0.2263
at 0.50	0.4034	0.2462	0.2345	0.1793	0.1932
at 0.60	0.3249	0.1953	0.2042	0.1451	0.1553
at 0.70	0.2753	0.1663	0.1432	0.0945	0.1105
at 0.80	0.2129	0.1323	0.1188	0.0679	0.0858
at 0.90	0.1293	0.0497	0.0713	0.0413	0.0606
at 1.00	0.0826	0.0216	0.0454	0.0256	0.0310
Avg Prec.	0.3771	0.2587	0.2330	0.1903	0.1973

query fields for searching, its fuzzy thesaurus matching technique resulted in a 3% drop in average precision compared to the BKGRRG2 run, which only used the title and description topic fields for searching but used a different thesaurus matching technique. Both runs pooled 2 query translations (Systran and Promt) and the thesaurus matching results into one file.

Comparing the Russian GIRT runs (translation plus thesaurus matching) to the Russian to German bilingual runs with translation only (also: different collection), one can see a 36% and 70% improvement in average precision for the title and description only and the title, description and narrative runs, respectively.

Our final GIRT run was BKGREG1 (Berkeley GIRT English to German automatic run 1) where we used machine translation (L & H Power and the Systran translator) combined with our normalized thesaurus matching technique. This run had better results than the Russian runs, but did not perform comparably to the bilingual main task English-to-German runs.

4 Submissions for the CLEF Main Tasks

For the CLEF main tasks, we concentrated on French and German as the collection languages and English, French, German and Russian as the topic languages. We participated in 2 tasks: monolingual and bilingual for French and German document collections. We experimented with several translation programs, German decompounding and blind feedback. Two techniques are used almost universally:

Blind Feedback

For our relevance feedback algorithm, we initially searched the collections using the original queries. Then, for each query, we assumed the 20 top-ranked documents to be relevant and selected 30 terms from these documents to add to the original query for a new search.

German decompounding

To decompound the German compounds in the German and GIRT collections, we first created a wordlist that included all words in the collections and queries. Using a base dictionary of component words and compounds, we then split the compounds into their components. During indexing, we replaced the German compounds with the component words found in the base dictionary. This technique was first successfully applied by Aitao Chen in the 2001 CLEF competition [1].

4.1 Monolingual Retrieval of the CLEF Collections

For CLEF 2002, we submitted monolingual runs for the French and German collections. Our results for the French bilingual runs were slightly better than those for the German runs. In both languages, adding the narrative to the query indexes improved average precision about 6% and 7% for the German and French runs, respectively.

BKMLFF1 (Berkeley Monolingual French against French Automatic Run 1). The original query topics (including title, description and narrative) were searched against the French collection. We applied a blind feedback algorithm for performance improvement. For indexing the French collection, we used a stop word list, the latin-to-lower normalizer and the Muscat French stemmer.

BKMLFF2 (Berkeley Monolingual French against French Automatic Run 2). For indexing and querying the collections, we used the same procedure as in BKMLFF1. For indexing the topics, we only included the title and description.

BKMLGG1 (Berkeley Monolingual German against German Automatic Run 1). The query topics were searched against the German collection. For indexing both the document collection and the queries, we used a stop word list, the latin-to-lower normalizer and the Muscat German stemmer. We used Aitao Chen's decompounding algorithm to split German compounds in both the document collection and the queries. We applied our blind feedback algorithm to the results for performance improvement. All query fields were indexed.

BKMLGG2 (Berkeley Monolingual German against German Automatic Run 2). For this run, we used the same indexing procedure as for BKMLGG1. From the queries, only the title and description were searched against the collections.

4.2 Bilingual Retrieval of the CLEF Collections

We submitted 10 bilingual runs for search against the French and German collections. Overall, the Russian to German or French runs yielded decidedly worse results than the other language runs. Submitting English without any translation yielded much worse results than the same experiment in the Amaryllis collection – this was an error in processing where the French stop word list and stemmer were applied to the English topic descriptions instead of the appropriate English ones. Correcting this error (unofficial run BKBIEF2c below) results in an overall precision of 0.2304 instead of the official result of 0.0513.

The English to French runs yielded slightly better results than the English to German runs, whereas the French to German run did better than the German to French run.

4.3 Bilingual to French Documents

Our runs for the CLEF bilingual-to-French main task (as well as monolingual French runs) are summarized in Table 3.

BKBIEF1 (Berkeley Bilingual English against French Automatic Run 1). We translated the English queries with two translation programs: the Systran translator (Altavista Babelfish) and L & H's Power translator. The translations were pooled together and the term frequencies of words occurring twice or more divided (to avoid overemphasis of terms that were translated the same by both programs). The title and description fields of the topics were indexed and searched against the French collections. For indexing the collection, we used the

Table 3. Results of Berkeley Bilingual to French runs for CLEF 2002

Run Name	bkmlff1	bkmlff2	bkbief1	bkbief2	bkbief2c	bkbigf1	bkbirf1
Retrieved	50000	50000	50000	50000	50000	50000	50000
Relevant	1383	1383	1383	1383	1383	1383	1383
Rel. ret.	1337	1313	1285	162	874	1303	1211
Precision							
at 0.00	0.8125	0.7475	0.6808	0.0840	0.3137	0.6759	0.5686
at 0.10	0.7747	0.6990	0.6284	0.0795	0.3084	0.6271	0.5117
at 0.20	0.6718	0.6363	0.5642	0.0695	0.2952	0.5582	0.4726
at 0.30	0.5718	0.5358	0.5210	0.0693	0.2817	0.4818	0.4312
at 0.40	0.5461	0.5068	0.4962	0.0672	0.2737	0.4589	0.3841
at 0.50	0.5017	0.4717	0.4702	0.0669	0.2634	0.4389	0.3312
at 0.60	0.4647	0.4332	0.4260	0.0612	0.2462	0.3986	0.3022
at 0.70	0.3938	0.3752	0.3713	0.0481	0.2275	0.3428	0.2656
at 0.80	0.3440	0.3301	0.3302	0.0411	0.1878	0.2972	0.2283
at 0.90	0.2720	0.2666	0.2626	0.0242	0.1401	0.2330	0.1674
at 1.00	0.1945	0.1904	0.1868	0.0188	0.1113	0.1686	0.1093
Avg prec.	0.4884	0.4558	0.4312	0.0513	0.2304	0.4100	0.3276

same procedures as in the monolingual runs. For performance improvement, we applied our blind feedback algorithm to the query results.

BKBIEF2 (Berkeley Bilingual English against French Automatic Run 2). We submitted the English queries (all fields) without any translation to the French collections and used the blind feedback algorithm for performance improvement. Collection indexing remained the same.

BKBIGF1 (Berkeley Bilingual German against French Automatic Run 1). We translated the German queries with two translation programs: the Systran translator (Altavista Babelfish) and L & H's Power translator. The translations were pooled together and the term frequencies of words occurring twice or more divided. The title and description fields of the topics were indexed and searched against the French collections. Again, a blind feedback algorithm was applied. Collection indexing remained the same.

BKBIRF1 (Berkeley Bilingual Russian against French Automatic Run 1). We translated the Russian queries with two translation programs: the Systran translator (Altavista Babelfish) and the Promt (http://www.translate.ru/) translator. The Promt translator translated the queries directly from Russian to French, whereas in the Systran translation, we used an intermediate step from the Russian translation to an English translation to then translate further to French (i.e. English is used as a pivot language). The translations were pooled and the title and description fields submitted to the collection. Our blind feedback algorithm was applied. Collection indexing remained the same.

Table 4. Results of official Bilingual to German runs for CLEF 2002

Run name	bkmlgg1	bkmlgg2	bkbifg1	bkbifg2	bkbieg1	bkbieg2	bkbirg1	bkbirg2
Retrieved	50000	50000	50000	50000	50000	50000	50000	50000
Relevant	1938	1938	1938	1938	1938	1938	1938	1938
Rel Ret.	1705	1734	1798	1760	1628	1661	1351	1260
Precision								
at 0.00	0.7686	0.7670	0.8141	0.8122	0.7108	0.6625	0.5638	0.5051
at 0.10	0.6750	0.6161	0.7345	0.6959	0.6190	0.6011	0.5055	0.4029
at 0.20	0.6257	0.5836	0.6959	0.6219	0.5594	0.5595	0.4565	0.3779
at 0.30	0.5654	0.5352	0.5947	0.5565	0.5207	0.5075	0.4141	0.3417
at 0.40	0.5367	0.4983	0.5490	0.5174	0.4741	0.4642	0.3761	0.3202
at 0.50	0.5018	0.4753	0.4851	0.4596	0.4358	0.4359	0.3408	0.2923
at 0.60	0.4722	0.4426	0.4465	0.4226	0.4090	0.4105	0.3122	0.2685
at 0.70	0.4239	0.4027	0.3833	0.3637	0.3647	0.3588	0.2687	0.2375
at 0.80	0.3413	0.3406	0.3084	0.3010	0.2972	0.3061	0.2253	0.1906
at 0.90	0.2642	0.2445	0.2289	0.2191	0.2204	0.2172	0.1659	0.1366
at 1.00	0.1681	0.1451	0.1271	0.1256	0.1441	0.1140	0.0927	0.0720
Bky Avg.	0.4696	0.4404	0.4722	0.4448	0.4150	0.4060	0.3254	0.2691

4.4 Bilingual to German Documents

Our runs for the CLEF bilingual-to-German main task (as well as monolingual German runs) are summarized in Table 4.

BKBIEG1 (Berkeley Bilingual English against German Automatic Run 1). We translated the English queries with two translation programs: the Systran translator (Altavista Babelfish) and L & H's Power translator. The translations were pooled together and the term frequencies of words occurring twice or more divided (to avoid overemphasis of terms that were translated the same by both programs). We used the German decompounding procedure to split compounds in the collections and the queries. All query fields were indexed and searched against the German collections. A blind feedback algorithm was applied.

BKBIEG2 (Berkeley Bilingual English against German Automatic Run 1). This resembles BKBIEG1, except that we only submitted the title and description fields of the topics to the German collections.

BKBIFG1 (Berkeley Bilingual French against German Automatic Run 1). We used the same procedures as for the BKBIEG1 run.

BKBIFG2 (Berkeley Bilingual French against German Automatic Run 2). We used the same procedures as for the BKBIEG2 run.

BKBIRG1 (Berkeley Bilingual Russian against German Automatic Run 1). We translated the Russian queries with two translation programs: the Systran translator (Altavista Babelfish) and the Prompt translator (http://www.translate.ru). The Promt translator translated the queries directly from Russian to German, whereas Systran can only translate from Russian to English. For this Systran translation we then further translated from the English translation into German. Both translation results were pooled and the topics (all fields) submitted to the collection. As before, we used German decompounding for indexing the collections and blind feedback to improve our results.

BKBIRG2 (Berkeley Bilingual Russian against German Automatic Run 2). This resembles BKIRG1, except that we only submitted the title and description fields of the topics to the German collections.

5 Further Analysis of Bilingual Results by Query

After the CLEF workshop we undertook to do some further analysis of the results by query. Of particular interest to us was why our French-to-German Run (BKB-IFG1) seemed to have higher average precision (0.4722) than our best German monolingual run (BKMLGG1 which had overall precision of 0.4696). A table of the Bilingual-to-German Runs by Query can be found below as Table 5.

For certain queries, the retrieval performance from a French or Russian language version of the topic (after being translated into German) was much higher than the original German version of the topic. We postulate three reasons for why the automatic translations of a topic language query to obtain a collection language query might yield better results than the original collection-language version of the topic:

(i) In the machine translation process particular query words might be emphasized through repetition. If those query terms are discriminating, then the ranking will yield better results.

(ii) The translation of the query topics might introduce more specific terms or more general terms (for specific compounds) that help the algorithm in matching more relevant documents.
For example, the translation from French of query 111 had a precision of 0.2807 whereas the monolingual German version only yielded 0.0453. Where the German version of the topic only mentions the compound "Computeranimation" in its phrasing, while the translation from French also introduces the more general terms "Computer" and "Rechner" which found more relevant documents.

(iii) The translation of some query topics might introduce additional important terms or variations of important terms that do not occur in the original query.

For example, topic 139 which asks about EU fishing quotes, had a precision of 0.4059 for the French-German run, where it only yielded 0.0467 for the monolingual German run. Whereas the monolingual query mentions two German compound words "EU-Fischfangquoten" and "Fischereiquoten", the translation from French offers more variety with the phrases "Fangquoten" and "Quoten des Fischens" and "EU" and "Europäische Union". It is very likely that our decompounding algorithm could not split the two compounds in the monolingual query version, which would mean that any relevant document must have have exactly these two compounds to be retrieved The translated terms, being somewhat less

Table 5. Bilingual-to-German Precision by Query (* Best performance for topic)

Qry	bkbiegl	bkbieg2	bkbifgl	bkbifg2	bkbirgl	bkbirg2	bkmlggl	bkmlgg2
91	0.4179	0.3662	0.3936	0.4342*	0.2043	0.0437	0.3080	0.3434
92	0.2481	0.2426	0.2950	0.2700	0.2434	0.2413	0.3299	0.3334
93	0.8737	0.8805	0.8577	0.8806	0.8388	0.0000	0.9098	0.8868
94	0.0040	0.0995	0.1738	0.4649	0.0198	0.3738	0.8850	0.9008
95	0.1624	0.0609	0.1861	0.1893	0.1652	0.1350	0.1490	0.1486
96	0.5341	0.5400	0.6107	0.5772	0.4131	0.4492	0.6141	0.7040
97	0.6633	0.2730	0.7112*	0.3412	0.7095	0.1571	0.8464	0.5706
98	0.6400*	0.6371	0.6184	0.6223	0.5794	0.1927	0.6179	0.6335
99	0.0515	0.2921	0.5770	0.5146	0.0036	0.0113	0.6241	0.4569
100	0.5899	0.6037	0.5416	0.5488	0.5963	0.7601	0.6057	0.5964
101	0.5730	0.7378	0.6448	0.7378	0.4726	0.7216	0.5057	0.7420
102	0.4682	0.4680	0.3962	0.4018	0.4051	0.1371	0.4255	0.4258
103	0.5153	0.5313	0.4106	0.5301	0.2644	0.2290	0.4666	0.5045
104	0.1166	0.1500	0.1553	0.1771	0.0916	0.0471	0.3366	0.2810
105	0.6316	0.6717	0.6110	0.6681	0.5339	0.5826	0.4665	0.2042
106	0.0496	0.0907	0.1156	0.0730	0.0968	0.1290	0.1309	0.2375
107	0.0350	0.0959	0.0952	0.1338	0.0206	0.0186	0.0719	0.1126
108	0.3834	0.3545	0.4146	0.4459*	0.0000	0.0000	0.4175	0.4233
109	0.2370	0.1352	0.4032	0.0202	0.3397	0.0056	0.1793	0.0006
110	0.6333	0.5794	0.6351	0.6194	0.6614	0.6535	0.5800	0.5573
111	0.2629	0.0620	0.2526	0.2807*	0.0726	0.0010	0.0825	0.0453
112	0.6317	0.6203	0.7129	0.6168	0.5901	0.6051	0.6229	0.6194
113	0.2819*	0.0020	0.2167	0.0279	0.0002	0.0001	0.1216	0.2623
114	0.4456	0.4315	0.4932	0.4330	0.5178	0.5273*	0.4547	0.4261
115	0.3325	0.2794	0.4024	0.4120	0.3109	0.2368	0.3580	0.2034
116	0.7387	0.7100	0.7497	0.6823	0.0169	0.0000	0.7008	0.7067
117	0.0000	0.0000	0.0000	0.0000	0.3035	0.3834*	0.5523	0.6375
118	0.0065	0.0095	0.2845	0.0870	0.0059	0.0422	0.4267	0.1233
119	0.8539	0.8770	0.8368	0.8477	0.8707	0.8734	0.8477	0.8198
120	0.0444	0.0274	0.0500	0.0355	0.0188	0.0494	0.0183	0.0426
121	0.2535	0.4556	0.3500	0.3687	0.1682	0.0387	0.4514	0.3833
122	0.0306	0.0804	0.0972	0.1992	0.0195	0.0557	0.0389	0.0241
123	0.9571	0.8833	0.8755	0.8929	1.0000*	0.9571	0.8833	0.8929
124	0.2980	0.2875	0.5175*	0.4557	0.0202	0.0279	0.5805	0.4533
125	0.5580	0.5283	0.5445	0.5511	0.6788*	0.6069	0.6196	0.5425
126	0.0479	0.0435	0.4758	0.0438	0.4062	0.0435	0.2315	0.0437
127	0.8892	0.8157	0.8864	0.8913	0.0077	0.0010	0.8973	0.8996
128	0.1193	0.0488	0.2852*	0.1776	0.0076	0.0092	0.0372	0.1307
129	0.6476	0.7195*	0.7183	0.6855	0.5968	0.7132	0.6964	0.6890
130	0.6743	0.5810	0.6740	0.5824	0.5862	0.5686	0.8487	0.7301
131	0.4329	0.5522	0.5366	0.5514	0.7779*	0.6080	0.0295	0.0114
132	0.7223	0.7353	0.4720	0.5506	0.7904	0.7724	0.6380	0.7202
133	0.5709	0.4913	0.6386*	0.5993	0.0210	0.0004	0.7521	0.7082
134	0.6060	0.5667	0.6573	0.5612	0.2952	0.0632	0.5802	0.6619
135	0.0762	0.2821	0.3388	0.2472	0.4585	0.2393	0.6250	0.3091
136	1.0000	0.9683	1.0000	1.0000	0.0000	0.0000	1.0000	0.9481
137	0.0164	0.0417	0.0019	0.0000	0.0175	0.0256	0.0000	0.0000
138	0.8533	0.8514	0.7679	0.7024	0.8404	0.8607*	0.8772	0.8052
139	0.0102	0.0685	0.3312	0.4059*	0.2110	0.2438	0.0386	0.0467
140	0.0002	0.0005	0.0716	0.0516	0.0020	0.0148	0.0004	0.0718
Avg.	0.4150	0.4060	0.4722	0.4448	0.3254	0.2691	0.4696	0.4404

specific, seem to have a much higher chance of matching to relevant German documents.

In another case, topic 131 about intellectual property rights, the German queries perform poorly with the Russian topic (in translation) runs the best performing. This is because the Russian phrase авторских прав (copyright) is translated to the German term Urheberrecht which is missing from the original German formulation of the topic. The Russian-German cross-language performance for this topic is 0.7779 versus the best German monolingual performance of 0.0295.

6 Summary and Acknowledgments

For CLEF 2002, Berkeley Group One concentrated on two collection languages, French and German, and three document collections, Amaryllis, GIRT and CLEF main (French and German newspapers). We worked with four topic languages: English, French, German and Russian. For the three tasks where we worked with Russian as a topic language (GIRT, bilingual Russian to French, and bilingual Russian to German) Russian bilingual consistently underperformed other bilingual topic languages. Why this is the case needs further in-depth investigation. Interestingly enough in the bilingual-to-German documents task, our French topics slightly outperformed our monolingual German runs, retrieving considerably more relevant documents in the top 1000.

Another major focus of our experimentation was to determine the utility of controlled vocabulary and thesauri in cross-language information retrieval. We did experiments with both the Amaryllis and GIRT collections utilizing thesaurus matching techniques. Our results do not show any particular advantage to thesaurus matching over straight translation when machine translation is available; however examination of individual queries shows that thesaurus matching can be a big win sometimes. We are beginning a detailed analysis of individual queries in the CLEF tasks.

This research was supported by research grant number N66001-00-1-8911 (Mar 2000-Feb 2003) from the Defense Advanced Research Projects Agency (DARPA) Translingual Information Detection Extraction and Summarization (TIDES) program, within the DARPA Information Technology Office. We thank Aitao Chen supplying us with his German decompounding software.

References

[1] A. Chen. Multilingual Information Retrieval using English and Chinese Queries. In C. Peters, M. Braschler, J. Gonzalo, and M. Kluck, editors, *Evaluation of Cross-Language Information Retrieval Systems Second Workshop of the Cross-Language Evaluation Forum, CLEF 2001, Darmstadt, Germany, September 3-4, 2001*, pages 44–58. Springer Computer Science Series LNCS 2406, 2001.

[2] W. Cooper, A. Chen, and F. Gey. Full text retrieval based on probabilistic equations with coefficients fitted by logistic regression. In D. K. Harman, editor, *The Second Text REtrieval Conference (TREC-2)*, pages 57–66, March 1994.

[3] H. Schott (ed.). *Thesaurus for the Social Sciences. [Vol. 1:] German-English. [Vol. 2:] English-German. [Edition] 1999.* InformationsZentrum Sozialwissenschaften Bonn, 2000.

[4] H. Jiang F. Gey and N. Perelman. Working with Russian queries for the GIRT, bilingual and multilingual CLEF tasks. In Carol Peters, Martin Braschler, Julio Gonzalo, and Michael Kluck, editors, *Cross Language Retrieval Evaluation, Proceedings of the CLEF 2001 Workshop*, pages 235–243. Springer Computer Science Series LNCS 2406, 2002.
[5] W. Hersh, S. Price, and L. Donohoe. Assessing Thesaurus-Based Query Expansion Using the UMLS Metathesaurus. In *Proceedings of the 2000 American Medical Informatics Association (AMIA) Symposium*, 2000.
[6] M. Kluck and F. Gey. The domain-specific task of CLEF - specific evaluation strategies in Cross-language Information Retrieval. In *Cross Language Retrieval Evaluation, Proceedings of the CLEF 2000 Workshop*, pages 48–56. Springer Computer Science Series LNCS 2069, 2001.

Assessing Automatically Extracted Bilingual Lexicons for CLIR in Vertical Domains: XRCE Participation in the GIRT Track of CLEF 2002

Jean-Michel Renders, Hervé Déjean, and Éric Gaussier

Xerox Research Centre Europe
6, chemin de Maupertuis, 38240 Meylan, France
Firstname.Lastname@xrce.xerox.com

Abstract. In this paper, we describe the approach we used in the Cross-Language Evaluation Forum CLEF 2002, and more specifically in the GIRT Task. The approach is based on (1) the extraction of two bilingual lexicons, one from parallel corpora and the other one from comparable corpora, (2) the optimal combination of these bilingual lexicons for Cross-Language Information Retrieval and (3) the combination with monolingual IR on parallel corpora. While our original submission to CLEF2002 was restricted to short queries (using only the title field), we present here the results extended to complete queries.

1 Introduction

The GIRT Task of CLEF 2002 [1] consists of retrieving documents in a German corpus dedicated to Social Science, starting from English queries. For this cross-language task, resources such as the ELRA bilingual dictionary and the GIRT bilingual thesaurus are available. The corpus contains scientific articles, whose titles are translated in English. Several articles (about 6%) have their body translated as well.

When using English queries on this corpus, the most obvious approach is the monolingual one, and to consider only the translated parts of the German documents. Of course, this approach may not be satisfying because the translated titles are a poor representation of the original content (actually, more than 20% of the documents do not even have their titles translated).

A more complex approach is to use bilingual resources to translate the queries. However, it is well known that using such resources can introduce problems of coverage (entries are missing, translations are not domain-specific, etc.). It is therefore necessary to extend these resources by extracting specialized bilingual lexicons for the corpus. This can be done by alignment from parallel or comparable corpora.

The titles and the translated bodies constitute a parallel corpus. Starting from classical techniques of alignment from parallel corpora, a bilingual lexicon

C.A. Peters (Ed.): CLEF 2002, LNCS 2785, pp. 363–371, 2003.

can be extracted, which gives $P_{par}(t|s)$, the probability of selecting target word t as translation of source word s. However, we could enrich the derived lexicon by extracting another one from a comparable corpus. Besides being of more general use, a lexicon built from a comparable corpus can provide more reliable translation candidates when terms are of very low frequency in the parallel corpus. We describe later in the paper a technique that can be used to extract a bilingual lexicon from a comparable corpus, which results in providing $P_{comp}(t|s)$, the probability of selecting target word t as translation of source word s following this model.

The main idea of our technique is to optimize a combination of the following approaches:

- the monolingual approach
- the use of a lexicon extracted from the parallel corpus
- the use of a lexicon extracted from the comparable corpus.

Each approach has different strengths and weaknesses and combining them should provide better performance than using one on its own.

This paper is organized as follows: Sections 2 and 3 briefly describe the methods for bilingual lexicon extraction from parallel and comparable corpora that we used in the CLEF 2002 GIRT task. Section 4 is dedicated to optimizing the combination of the methods when performing Cross-Language Information Retrieval tasks. The corresponding experimental results are presented in Section 5. These results involve not only what we submitted to CLEF2002 (at that time, we restricted ourselves to the "short query problem"), but also the extension of the work to the more general problem (dealing with the complete topics, i.e. all fields of the queries).

2 Bilingual Lexicon Extraction: Alignment from Parallel Corpora

Bilingual lexicon extraction from parallel corpora has received much attention since the seminal works of [2, 3, 4] on sentence alignment. Recent research has demonstrated that statistical alignment models can be highly successful at extracting word correspondences from parallel corpora, [5, 6, 7, 8] among others. We follow the approach proposed by [6] and [9], and represent co-occurrences between words across translations by a matrix, the rows of which represent the source language words[1], the columns the target language words, and the elements of the matrix the expected alignment frequencies for the words appearing in the corresponding row and column.

The estimation of the expected alignment frequency is based on the Iterative Proportional Fitting Procedure (IPFP), [10], which, given an initial estimate of

[1] We use "source" and "target" to refer to elements of different languages, which does not imply, in our case, any privileged direction.

all cell counts, consists in the following two computations at the kth iteration, for each element of the matrix n_{ij}:

$$n_{ij}^{(k,1)} = n_{ij}^{(k-1,2)} \times \frac{m_{i.}}{n_{i.}^{(k-1,2)}}$$

$$n_{ij}^{(k,2)} = n_{ij}^{(k,1)} \times \frac{m_{.j}}{n_{.j}^{(k,1)}}$$

where $n_{i.}$ and $n_{.j}$ are the current row and column marginals, whereas $m_{i.}$ and $m_{.j}$ are the observed row and column term frequencies. Empty words are added in both languages in order to deal with words with no equivalent in the other language.

At each iteration, the algorithm considers each pair of aligned sentences, and updates local expected counts of the source and target words they contain using the previous equations. The local expected counts are then summed up into global expected counts for the whole corpus, that will serve as intial values for local expected counts at the next iteration. Once the global expected counts are stable, they are normalized so as to yield probabilistic translation lexicons, where each source word is associated with a target word through a score. In the remainder of the paper, we will use $P_{par}(t|s)$ to denote the probability of selecting target word t as translation of source word s.

The corpus used for extracting this bilingual lexicon is the bilingual part of the GIRT corpus, namely the German/English titles of each entry of the collection and the German/English bodies when an English translation was present in the collection (6% of the entries).

3 Bilingual Lexicon Extraction: Alignment from Comparable Corpora

Bilingual lexicon extraction from non-parallel but comparable corpora has been studied by a number of researchers, [11, 12, 13, 14, 15] among others. Their work relies on the assumption that if two words are mutual translations, then their more frequent collocates (taken here in a very broad sense) are likely to be mutual translations as well. Based on this assumption, a standard approach consists in building context vectors, for each source and target word, which aim at capturing the most significant collocates. The target context vectors are then translated using a general bilingual dictionary, and compared with the source context vectors. This approach is reminiscent of the way similarities between terms are built in information retrieval, through the use of the cosine measure between term vectors extracted from the term-document matrix [16].

Our implementation is somehow different. We still use bilingual resources (here the ELRA dictionary and the GIRT thesaurus), but no vector translation is performed. Instead, we compute the similarity between each word of the source corpus with each class in the bilingual resource. The same computation is done on the target side. The similarity between source words and target words is based on the following probabilistic model:

$$P(t|s) = \sum_C P(C|s)P(t|C,s) \approx \sum_C P(C|s)P(t|C) \tag{1}$$

where C stands for a bilingual entry in our resource. The approximation used in the above equation is based on the fact that we do not want to privilege any of the possible lexicalisations on the target side of the bilingual entry C.

The different steps followed are:

- for each word w occuring in the corpus, build a context vector by considering all the words occurring in a window encompassing several sentences that is run through the corpus. Each word i in the context vector of w is then weighted with a measure of its association with w. We chose the log-likelihood ratio test to measure this association that we will denote v_{wi}.
- for each class of the general lexicon and of the GIRT thesaurus, build a context vector using the context vectors previously computed. A class can have a context vector if and only if it has terms occurring in the corpus. If a class has several terms occurring in the corpus, the vector of this class corresponds to the intersection of the vectors of each term.
- the similarity of each source word s, for each class c, is computed on the basis of the cosine measure:

$$sim(s,C) = \frac{\sum_i v_{si}v_{Ci}}{\sqrt{\sum_i v_{si}^2 \sum_i v_{Ci}^2}} \tag{2}$$

  where the context word i ranges over the set of source words.
- the same is done on the target side, resulting in $sim(t,C)$.
- the similarities are then normalized to yield a probabilistic translation lexicon.

$$P_{comp}(t|s) = \sum_C p(C|s)p(C|t) = \sum_C \frac{sim(t,C).sim(s,C)}{\sum_i sim(i,C).\sum_{Kj} sim(s,K)} \tag{3}$$

The German part of the collection was used in order to constitute the German corpus. The comparable English corpus was built with the English side. As this part was too small compared to the German oside, we added parts of the British National Corpus (BNC) in order to reach the same amount of data. This part of the BNC was selected from texts which contained all words occurring in the queries with a similar relative frequency. Both corpora can then be considered as comparable according to the definition given in [17].

We refer the reader to [18] for more details on our procedure (note however that we do not make use of model combination for extracting bilingual lexicons from comparable corpora in the present case).

4 Optimization

Three approaches are combined here: the monolingual approach, the bilingual approach based on the parallel corpus, and the one based on the comparable corpus.

The monolingual retrieval method basically returns relevant German documents just by considering the similarity of the English queries with the (translated) English titles of the documents constituting the parallel corpus. In our case, German documents are here indexed by the English words (in a lemmatized form) of their translated titles. Adopting the Vector Space model, let us note:

- q_e: the vector of (normalized) words of the English queries (NB. A stoplist is applied, which removes non relevant words)
- d_e: the vector representing a GIRT document, indexed by the normalized English terms of the titles.

Then, after applying standard weighting schemes on both query and document vectors, a first monolingual score can be computed and associated with each document:

$$s_{english} = \tilde{q}_e^t . \tilde{d}_e \tag{4}$$

where the "~" denotes weighted vector (see the experimental part for the weighting schemes applied).

When adopting the bilingual lexicon extracted from the parallel corpus and using it as a probabilistic translation lexicon, the new vector representing the query in the target language is given by $P_{par}(t|s)$.qe. Similarly, when adopting the bilingual lexicon extracted from the comparable corpus, the new vector representing the query in the target language is given by $P_{comp}(t|s).qe$.

The first stage of the combination is to combine the lexicons extracted from parallel and comparable corpora. This can be done by a simple convex linear combination: the new vector representing the query in the target language is then given by:

$$q_g = [\alpha(s)P_{par}(t|s) + (1 - \alpha(s))P_{comp}(t|s)].qe \tag{5}$$

Note that we introduced a dependence of the combining factor (α) on the particular word (s). To make the approach feasible, we divided the set of normalized English words into 3x3 subsets. The first dimension of the division is the frequency of the word in the (English) parallel corpus, discretized by 3 values (HIGH, MEDIUM, LOW). The second dimension is the proximity of the word to the thesaurus, defined by (the similarity is given by equation 3) and discretized as well. The dependence on s is now reduced to the dependence on these features (HIGH/MEDIUM/LOW frequency; HIGH/MEDIUM/LOW proximity). The choice of optimal values for $\alpha(s)$ is our first set of degrees of freedom.

In practice, the vector qg can be limited to its k largest components (in order to take a "finite" and small enough number of translation candidates). The value of the k threshold should be optimized as well (there is some trade-off between recall and precision when varying k).

After applying the probabilistic translation lexicons, the translated queries qg and the vectors representing the documents indexed by the segmented and normalized German terms dg are weighted, respectively, by a traditional SMART-like weighting scheme, in order to provide our second score:

$$s_{german} = \tilde{q}_g^t.\tilde{d}_g \tag{6}$$

Then both scores can be combined. This is the second stage of the combination:

$$s_{final} = \beta s_{english} + (1 - b) s_{german} \tag{7}$$

Once again, the value of b must be optimized.

To briefly summarize the method, we have to find the optimum values of $\alpha(s)$, the k threshold, the b coefficient, as well as the weighting schemes for German documents, English titles, English queries and translated (German) queries. We have decided to optimize this with respect to the average precision (non interpolated) for the 50 queries of GIRT 2000 and GIRT 2001.

5 Experiments and Results

As described above, there are a lot of parameters to be optimized. Therefore, we have adopted the following heuristic (non necessarily optimal) strategy. We began to search for the optimal weighting scheme for both queries and documents (b=0 or 1; a=1 ; k=100). Next we optimized the threshold (k retained candidate translations). We then searched for a constant a, which resulted in the optimal value of the criterion (average non-interpolated precision), and tried to find independently the values of a for each of the nine classes of features. Finally, we optimized b, keeping all other parameters at their optimal value found so far. Of course, this search strategy assumes some independence between the parameters. The experiments we have conducted so far seem to confirm this assumption.

The experiments are separated into two groups. The first one deals with "short" queries (queries limited to the "title" field). This group of experiments constituted our official submission to GIRT in June 2002. The second group considers "long" queries (all fields are used, even if some parts of the "narrative" field are automatically filtered).

The performance measure that we used here is the non-interpolated average precision. This measure is given:

- for the training setting (which consists of 48 queries of GIRT 2000 and 2001, and of a set of 16000 documents for which the relevance judgments were known)
- for the GIRT 2002 setting (23 English queries and the complete set of about 80.000 documents constituting the GIRT corpus).

The main results are given Table 1.

The weighting scheme "nin" only consists in applying the IDF (inverse document frequency) weighting, the "lin" scheme performs a logarithmic transformation of the term frequencies before the IDF weighting, while the "lic" scheme also performs a final normalization (cosine transformation).

Table 1. Evaluation according to the different settings

Query Type	β	Weigthing scheme query	document	k	$\alpha*$	Average precision on training	on GIRT 2002	Setting Num
Short	0	nin	lic	200	1	0.308	0.114	1
Short	0	nin	lic	200	0	0.105	0.081	2
Short	0	nin	lic	200	0.06	0.332	0.126	3
Long	0	nin	lic	25	1	0.327	0.166	4
Long	0	nin	lic	25	0.15	0.330	0.194	5
Long	0	nin	lic	25	$\alpha*$	0.332	0.206	6
Long	1	lin	lic	–	–	0.212	0.09	7
Long	0.01	lin(e)/nin(g)	lic	25	$\alpha*$	0.360	0.212	8

Table 2. Optimized values of $\alpha*$

	HIGH frequency	MEDIUM frequency	LOW frequency
HIGH similarity	0.10	0.13	0.18
MEDIUM similarity	0.13	0.15	0.21
LOW similarity	0.15	0.20	0.21

The relatively low values of α are due to the difference between the distribution of $P_{par}(t|s)$ and $P_{comp}(t|s)$. The distribution obtained with the comparable corpus is flatter, with lower values for the most likely translation candidates when compared with the best candidates obtained with the parallel corpus. So, in order to take into account the influence of the lexicon extracted from the comparable corpus, α must be kept small.

The optimal values of α can be explained intuitively at least for the evolution with the "similarity" feature: the lexicon originated from the comparable corpus is less reliable for words with lower similarity with respect to the thesaurus. On the other hand, the dependency of α along the "frequency" dimension seems to be less obvious and needs more investigations.

The following chart summarizes the progression of the average precision (non-interpolated) on GIRT2002, when adopting the different stages of the combination.

6 Conclusions

Starting from three single approaches to address Cross-Linguage Information Retrieval tasks, we have shown how to combine them in an optimal way. Experimental results show that such a combination gives a performance in the GIRT2002 task which is better than the performance obtained by each approach taken in isolation. Significant improvement was achieved for the queries of the 2002 GIRT task, where it appears that taking the complete query into account and enriching lexicons by exploiting comparable corpora can bring important benefits.

Table 3.

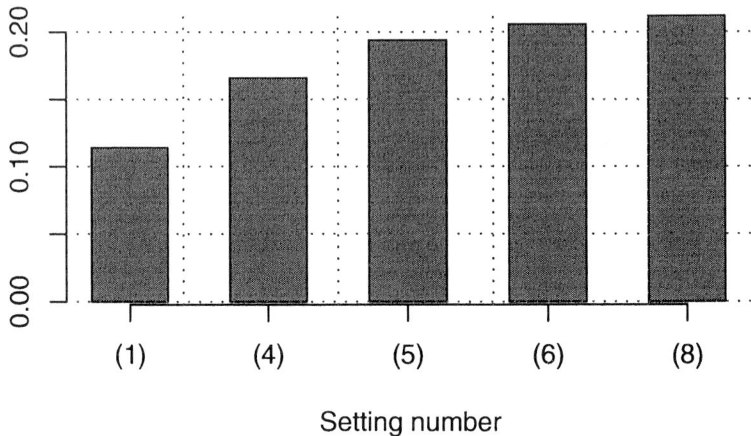

References

[1] Braschler, M., Peters, C.: CLEF 2002: Methodology and Metrics. Lecture Notes for Computer Science Series. This volume.

[2] Gale, W. A., Church, K. W.: A program for aligning sentences in bilingual corpora. In: Meeting of the Association for Computational Linguistics. (1991) 177–184

[3] Brown, P., Lai, J., Mercer, R.: Aligning sentences in parallel corpora. In: Proceedings of the 29th Annual Meeting for the Association of Computational Linguistics. (1996) 169–176

[4] Kay, M., Röscheisen, M.: Test-translation alignment. Computational Linguistics **19** (1993) 121–142

[5] Brown, P., Pietra, S. D., Pietra, V. D., Mercer, R.: The mathematics of statistical machine learning translation: Parameter estimation. Computational Linguistics **19** (1993) 263–311

[6] Hiemstra, D.: Using statistical methods to create a bilingual dictionary. Master's thesis, Universiteit Twente (1996)

[7] Melamed, I. D.: A word-to-word model of translational equivalence. In: Proceedings of the Thirty-Fifth Annual Meeting of the Association for Computational Linguistics and Eighth Conference of the European Chapter of the Association for Computational Linguistics. (1997) 490–497

[8] Gaussier, E.: Flow network models for word alignment and terminology extraction from bilingual corpora. In: Proceedings of the joint 17th International Conference on Computational Linguistics and 26th Annual Meeting of the Association for Computational Linguistics. (1998) 444–450

[9] Hull, D.: Automating the constuction of bilingual terminology lexicons. Terminlogy **5** (1997)
[10] Bishop, Y., Fienberg, S., Holland, P.: Discrete Multivariate Analysis. MIT Press (1975)
[11] Rapp, R.: Identifying word translations in nonparallel texts. In: Proceedings of the Annual Meeting of the Association for Computational Linguistics. (1995)
[12] Peters, C., Picchi, E.: Capturing the comparable: A system for querying comparable text corpora. In: JADT'95 - 3rd International Conference on Statistical Analysis of Textual Data. (1995) 255–262
[13] Tanaka, K., Iwasaki, H.: Extraction of lexical translations from non-aligned corpora. In: International Conference on Computational Linguistics, COLING'96. (1996)
[14] Shahzad, I., Ohtake, K., Masuyama, S., Yamamoto, K.: Identifying translations of compound nouns using non-aligned corpora. In: Proceedings of the Workshop MAL'99. (1999) pp. 108–113
[15] Fung, P.: A statistical view on bilingual lexicon extraction: From parallel corpora to non-parallel corpora. In Véronis, J., ed.: Parallel Text Processing. (2000)
[16] Salton, G., McGill, J.: Introduction to Modern Information Retrieval. New York, McGraw-Hill (1983)
[17] Déjean, H., Gaussier, E.: Une nouvelle approche l'extraction de lexiques bilingues partir de corpus comparables. lexicometrica (2002)
[18] Déjean, H., Gaussier, E., Sadat, F.: Bilingual terminology extraction: An approach based on multilingual thesaurus applicable to comparable corpora. In: International Conference on Computational Linguistics, Coling'02. (2002)

The CLEF 2002 Interactive Track

Julio Gonzalo and Douglas W. Oard

[1] Departamento de Lenguajes y Sistemas Informáticos
Universidad Nacional de Educación a Distancia
E.T.S.I Industriales, Ciudad Universitaria s/n, 28040 Madrid, Spain
julio@lsi.uned.es
http://sensei.lsi.uned.es/~julio/
[2] Human Computer Interaction Laboratory
College of Information Studies and
Institute for Advanced Computer Studies
University of Maryland, College Park, MD 20742, USA
oard@glue.umd.edu.edu
http://www.glue.umd.edu/~oard/

Abstract. In the CLEF 2002 Interactive Track, research groups interested in the design of systems to support interactive Cross-Language Retrieval used a shared experiment design to explore aspects of that question. Participating teams each compared two systems, both supporting a full retrieval task where users had to select relevant documents given a (native language) topic and a (foreign language) document collection. The two systems being compared at each site should differ in (at least) one of these aspects: a) support for document selection (how the system describes the content of a document written in a foreign language), b) support for query translation (how the system interacts with the user in order to obtain an optimal translation of the query), and c) support for query refinement (how the system helps the user refine their query based on previous search results). This paper describes the shared experiment design and summarizes preliminary results from the five teams that submitted runs.

1 Introduction

A Cross-Language Information Retrieval (CLIR) system, as that term is typically used, takes a query in some natural language and finds documents written in one or more other languages. From a user's perspective, that is only one component of a system to help a user search foreign-language collections and recognize relevant documents. We generally refer to this situated task as *Multilingual Information Access*. To emphasize the importance of interactive mechanisms in a situated, user-centered cross-language search, we might refer to systems that support that task as *Cross-Language Search Assistants*.

The Cross-Language Evaluation Forum's (CLEF) interactive track (iCLEF) aims to develop shared experiment designs that will allow research teams to compare their strategies for cross-language search assistance. In the first year of

C.A. Peters (Ed.): CLEF 2002, LNCS 2785, pp. 372–382, 2003.

the track, iCLEF 2001 focused on comparing document selection strategies (i.e., approaches to facilitate fast and accurate relevance judgments for documents that the user could not read without assistance). The experiment guidelines combined CLEF resources (including the CLEF documents and topic descriptions, ranked lists from CLEF 2000, and relevance assessments made by native speakers in every document language) with the within-subject quantitative user study design that was used for many years in the TREC interactive track. The success of that evaluation [3] led to a decision to continue the track in the CLEF 2002 evaluation campaign. This paper describes the design of the iCLEF 2002 evaluation and presents results on the relevance assessment process.

The CLEF 2002 interactive track retained provisions for studying document selection, but added a new focus on comparing interactive query formulation and reformulation. Unlike document selection, which can reasonably be studied as an isolated process, query formulation and reformulation only make sense as part of a larger process; queries have no inherent value beyond their effect on search results. We therefore chose an experiment design that supported comparison of complete interactive CLIR systems, while retaining provisions for more focused experiments. Each participating team compared two systems that differed in one or more aspects of the interaction with the user. Five groups submitted results: Swedish Institute of Computer Science (SICS, Sweden), University of Sheffield (UK), University of Alicante and University of Jaen (Spain), University of Maryland (USA) and Universidad Nacional de Educación a Distancia (UNED, Spain).

In Section 2 we describe the experiment design in detail, and in Section 3 we enumerate the participants and the hypotheses that they sought to test. In Section 4, we summarize the experiments run by each team and briefly discuss the suitability of our current experiment design. Finally, in Section 5 we draw some conclusions and describe the prospects for future iCLEF evaluations.

2 Experiment Design

The basic design for an iCLEF 2002 experiment consists of:

- Two systems to be compared, usually one of which is intended as a reference system;
- A set of searchers, in groups of 4;
- A set of topic descriptions, written in a language in which the searchers are fluent;
- A document collection in a different language (usually one in which the searchers lack language skills);
- A standardized procedure to be followed in every search session;
- A presentation order (i.e., a list of user/topic/system combinations that defines every search session and their relative order); and
- A set of evaluation measures for every search session and for the overall experiment, to permit comparison between systems.

In the remainder of this section, we describe these aspects in detail.

2.1 Topics

Topics for iCLEF 2002 were selected from those used for evaluation of fully automated ranked retrieval systems in the CLEF 2001 evaluation campaign. The main reason that we selected a previous year's topics was that it allowed more time between topic release and the submission deadline, an important factor when performing user studies.

The criteria for topic selection were:

- Select only broad (i.e., multi-faceted) topics. In iCLEF 2001, we observed that narrow (single-faceted) topics tended to have very few relevant documents, which made evaluation measures based on the fraction of relevant documents retrieved less insightful.
- Select topics that had at least 8 relevant documents in every document language, according to CLEF 2001 assessments.
- Select topics that could reasonably be expected to be found in collections from different years. This provided a degree of assurance that the new CLEF 2002 document collections could also be used by participating teams (the Finnish collection is mainly news from 1995, while the others are mainly 1994).

These restrictions were satisfied by eight topics, from which four were selected as iCLEF 2002 topics:

```
<num> C053 </num>
<EN-title> Genes and Diseases </EN-title>
<EN-desc> What genes have been identified that are the source of or
contribute to the cause of diseases or developmental disorders in
human beings? </EN-desc>
<EN-narr> A~document that identifies a~gene or reports that a~gene
has been discovered that is the source of any type of disease,
syndrome, behavioral or developmental disorder in humans is
relevant. Any document that reports the discovery of a~defective
gene that causes problems in humans is relevant, but reports of
diseases and disorders that are caused by the absence of a~gene are
not relevant. </EN-narr>

<num> C056 </num>
<EN-title> European Campaigns against Racism </EN-title>
<EN-desc> Find documents that talk about campaigns against racism in
Europe. </EN-desc>
<EN-narr> Relevant documents describe informative or educational
campaigns against racism (ethnic or religious, or against
immigrants) in Europe. Documents should refer to organized campaigns
rather than reporting mere opinions against racism. </EN-narr>

<num> C065 </num>
<EN-title> Treasure Hunting </EN-title>
<EN-desc> Find documents about treasure hunters and treasure hunting
```

```
activities. </EN-desc>
<EN-narr> Identify types of current treasure hunting activities such
as searching for gold, digging for buried relics, or searching
underwater for sunken galleons. </EN-narr>

<num> C080 </num>
<EN-title> Hunger Strikes </EN-title>
<EN-desc> Documents will report any information relating to a~hunger
strike attempted in order to attract attention to a~cause. </EN-desc>
<EN-narr> Identify instances where a~hunger strike has been
initiated, including the reason for the strike, and the outcome if
known. </EN-narr>
```

and one was selected as a training topic:

```
<num> C086 </num>
<EN-title> Renewable Power </EN-title>
<EN-desc> Find documents describing the use of or policies regarding
"green" power, i.e., power generated from renewable energy
sources. </EN-desc>
<EN-narr> Relevant documents discuss the use of renewable energy
sources such as solar, wind, biomass, hydro, and geothermal sources.
Low emission vehicles as for example electric or CNG cars are not
relevant. Fuel cells are not relevant unless their fuel qualifies as
renewable. </EN-narr>
```

The number of relevant documents for these topics in the CLEF 2001 pools can be seen in Table 1.

We did not impose any restriction on the topic language. Participants could pick any topic language provided by CLEF, or could prepare their own manual translations into any additional language that would be appropriate for their searcher population.

2.2 Document Collection

We allowed participants to search any CLEF document collection (Dutch, English, French, German, Italian, Spanish, Finnish and Swedish). To facilitate

Table 1. Number of relevant documents for iCLEF 2002 topics in previous pools

Topic	Dutch	English	French	German (SDA + Spiegel)	Italian	Spanish
53	27	36	13	17	37	33
56	8	10	44	20	24	137
65	69	15	13	47	15	74
80	93	56	31	62	84	245
86	50	82	36	58	31	56

cross-site comparisons, we provided standard Machine Translations of the German collection (into English) and of the English collection (into Spanish) for use by teams that found those language pairs convenient, in each case using Systran Professional 3.0. A fraction of the German collection (the Frankfurter Rundschau set) was discarded for iCLEF experiments because both Systran and an alternative system that we tried produced no output for a significant fraction of those documents. The other collections were used in their entirety.

2.3 Search Procedure

For teams that chose the end-to-end experiment design, searchers were given a topic description written in a language that they could understand and asked to use one of the two systems to find as many relevant documents as possible in the foreign-language document collection. Searchers were instructed to favor precision rather than recall by asking them to envision a situation in which they might need to pay for a high-quality professional translation of the documents that they selected, but that they wished to avoid paying for translation of irrelevant documents.

The searchers were asked to answer some questions at specific points during their session:

- Before the experiment, about computer/searching experience and attitudes, and their language skills.
- After completing the search for each topic (one per topic).
- After completing the use of each system (one per system).
- After the experiment, about system comparison and general feedback on the experiment design.

These questions were normally posed using questionnaires that closely followed the design of the questionnaires used in iCLEF 2001. This year, however, we did not require the use of standardized questionnaires; Participating teams could adapt the examples that we provided to their particular experiment conditions in whatever way they wished.

Every searcher performed four searches, first for two topics using one system and for the remaining two topics with the other system. Each search was limited to 20 minutes. The overall time required for one session was approximately three hours, including initial training with both systems, four 20-minute searches, all questionnaires, and two breaks (one following training, one between systems).

For teams that chose to focus solely on document selection, the experiment design was similar, but searchers were asked only to scan a frozen list of documents (returned by for some standard query by some automatic system) and select the ones that were relevant to the topic description from which the query had been generated. This is essentially the iCLEF 2001 task.

2.4 Searcher/Topic/System Combinations

The presentation order for topics, searchers and systems was standardized to facilitate comparison between systems. We chose an order that was counterbal-

Table 2. Presentation order for topics and association of topics with systems

Searcher	Block 1	Block 2	Searcher	Block 1	Block 2
1	System 1: 1-4	System 2: 3-2	5	System 1: 4-2	System 2: 1-3
2	System 2: 2-3	System 1: 4-1	6	System 2: 3-1	System 1: 2-4
3	System 2: 1-4	System 1: 3-2	7	System 2: 4-2	System 1: 1-3
4	System 1: 2-3	System 2: 4-1	8	System 1: 3-1	System 2: 2-4

anced in a way that sought to minimize user/system and topic/system interactions when examining averages. We adopted a Latin square design similar to that used in the TREC interactive track. The presentation order for topics was varied systematically, with participants that saw the same topic-system combination seeing those topics in a different order. An eight-participant presentation order matrix is shown in Table 2.[1] The minimum number of participants was set at 4, in which case only the top half of the matrix would be used. Additional participants could be added in groups of 8, with the same matrix being reused as needed.

2.5 Evaluation

In this section we describe the common evaluation measure used by all teams, and the data that was available to individual teams to support additional evaluation activities.

Data Collection For every search (searcher/topic/system combination), two types of data were collected:

- The set of documents selected as relevant by the searcher. Optional attributes are the *duration* of the assessment process, the *confidence* in the assessment, and judgment values other than "relevant" (such as "somewhat relevant," "not relevant," or "viewed but not judged."
- The ranked lists of document identifiers created by the ranked retrieval system. One list was submitted by teams focusing on document selection; teams focusing on query formulation and reformulation were asked to submit one ranked list for every query refinement iteration.

Official Evaluation Measure The set of documents selected as relevant was used to produce the official iCLEF measure, an unbalanced version of van Rijsbergen's F measure that we called F_α:

$$F_\alpha = \frac{1}{\alpha/P + (1-\alpha)/R}$$

[1] This table was prepared before the topics were chosen, and some participating teams refer to topics numbered 1–4 in their papers. The mapping for iCLEF 2002 is 1=C053, 2=C065, 3=C056, 4=C080.

where P is precision and R is recall [4]. Values of α above 0.5 emphasize precision, values below 0.5 emphasize recall [2]. As in CLEF 2001, $\alpha = 0.8$ was chosen, modeling the case in which missing some relevant documents would be less objectionable than finding too many documents that (after perhaps paying for professional translations) turn out not to be relevant. For the same reason, documents judged as "somewhat relevant" are treated as not relevant for computing $\alpha = 0.8$.

The comparison of average $F_{\alpha=0.8}$ measures for both systems provides the official, first order differentiation of systems. All complementary material (ranked lists for each iteration, assessment duration, assessment confidence, questionnaire responses, observational notes, etc.) can be used by participating groups as a basis for further analysis.

Relevance assessments We provided relevance assessments by native speakers of the document languages for at least:

- All documents manually selected by searchers (to compute $F_{\alpha=0.8}$).
- The first 20 documents in all iterative rankings produced along every search process.

For the CLEF 2001 document languages (English, German, Italian, Spanish, Dutch, and French) we already had some assessments available from the CLEF 2001 pools. In the case of Finnish and Swedish, all assessments had to be done from scratch. All iCLEF 2002 relevance judgments were done by CLEF assessors immediately after assessing the CLEF 2002 pools.

3 Participants

Six teams expressed interest in participating, and five teams submitted experiment results: three that had participated in iCLEF 2001 (Sheffield, Maryland, and UNED), and two new teams (SICS and Alicante/Jaen). Both newcomers focused on the document selection subtask:

- **Alicante/Jaen** compared full machine translations (as the reference condition) with topic-oriented summaries of the same translations, containing the title and the most relevant paragraph for the topic being searched (as the contrastive condition). They used Spanish as the topic language, and English as the document language.
- **SICS** tested a hypotheses that assessing documents in one's native language would be less work than assessing documents in another language, even if that language is relatively well mastered. Therefore they used one topic language (Swedish) and two document languages: English and Swedish. Twelve Swedish users with high English skills participated in the experiment. The users were presented with prefabricated ranked lists of search results in an

interface which allowed them to view each document and assess it for relevance. The ranked lists were either from the Swedish or the English CLEF collection, forming the two conditions being tested (native language versus foreign language assessments).

The other three groups focused on the query formulation and refinement aspects of interactive searches:

- **Maryland** used four searchers in their official submission to compare user-assisted query translation with a fully automatic approach. An additional eight searchers performed the same experiment with a smaller collection. The hypothesis being tested was that user-assisted query translation could improve search effectiveness. The document language was German, and the topic language was English. For the user-assisted query translation condition, searchers were provided two types of cues about the meaning of each translation: a list of other words sharing a common translation (potential synonyms) and a sentence in which the word was used in a translation-appropriate context selected from a word-aligned parallel corpus.
- **Sheffield** used four users with a prototype system being developed jointly by Sheffield, SICS, and the University of Tampere (Finland) to compare user-assisted translation with a fully automatic approach. The hypothesis being tested was that user-assisted query translation could improve search effectiveness. The search engine was created by Tampere using a modified version of the Inquery search system. The interface was designed by SICS and Sheffield based on interviews and observations of users with CLIR needs.
- **UNED** used eight searchers to compare a reference system using words as units for query formulation and refinement with a contrastive system using phrases. The hypothesis being tested was that phrases as interactive query formulation units could provide enough context information for accurate automatic translation, as an alternative to word-by-word user-assisted translation.

4 Results and Discussion

The official $F_{\alpha=0.8}$ measure for all systems is shown in Table 3[2]. A detailed discussion of each of the experiments can be found elsewhere in these proceedings. Most experiments showed substantial differences between the systems being compared, suggesting that there is a good deal to be learned from the detailed analysis reported in each team's paper.

German and English are the two languages for which a) there were available pools from CLEF 2001, and b) participants ran end-to-end interactive cross-language sessions to contribute new documents to the assessment pools (either

[2] The Sheffield results shown here are based on recomputation at Sheffield. Format problems in the submitted results precluded automatic official scoring.

Table 3. Official iCLEF 2002 results

Group	Experiment Condition	$F_{\alpha=0.8}$
Experiments in Query formulation and refinement		
Maryland	automatic query translation	0.34
Maryland	user-assisted query translation	0.50
Sheffield	automatic query translation	0.20
Sheffield	user-assisted query translation	0.26
UNED	word-based query translation	0.23
UNED	phrase-based query translation	0.37
Experiments in Document selection		
SICS	foreign language docs	0.36
SICS	native language docs	0.65
Alicante/Jaen	Systran full translations	0.22
Alicante/Jaen	Systran title + best passage	0.32

because they were selected by the searchers as relevant or because they appeared near the top of some ranked lists during the search processes).

Voorhees has found that manual TREC runs (those which include any form of human intervention in the search process) often find documents that are not present in assessment pools generated from the output of automatic systems [5]. The CLEF 2001 pools (produced from 198 submitted runs) were already large and stable [1], so the iCLEF 2002 assessment pools provided us with an opportunity to explore this issue in a cross-language search context. We observed a similar effect. Table 4 summarizes the additional assessments and the additional relevant documents found with the new assessments.

In the case of the SDA and Der Spiegel subset of the German collection used in our evaluation, the large number of query reformulation iterations produced enormous pools, but only increased the set of known relevant documents by 10%. The newly judged pools were substantially smaller for English, but the set of known relevant documents still was increased by 12%. A plausible explanation is that, when a query formulation produces seemingly good results, searching time is primarily spent in the process of selecting documents from the ranked list returned by the system. When the query does not produce good results, time is spent in iterative query reformulations which enlarge the document pool. Hence, the harder the query, the larger the pool.

From this, we can conclude that although human searchers do find relevant documents that automatic systems miss, the search strategies that they employed resulted in many more non-relevant documents. This is a classic recall-precision tradeoff. It is important, of course, to caveat this observation by point-

Table 4. Contribution of interactive runs to CLEF 2001 pools

Topic	German CLEF (SDA+Der Spiegel)		iCLEF add-on (SDA+Der Spiegel)	
	assessed	relevant	assessed	relevant
53	220	17	225	5 (+30%)
56	230	20	465	5 (+25%)
65	249	47	835	0 (=)
80	118	62	450	6 (+10%)

Topic	English CLEF		iCLEF add-on	
	assessed	relevant	assessed	relevant
53	456	36	22	1 (+3%)
56	626	10	419	1 (+10%)
65	613	15	233	10 (+67%)
80	578	56	250	2 (+4%)

ing out that we explored only a limited range of conditions (in particular, 20 minute searches for broad topics).

Another question that we might ask is whether number of documents added to the assessment pools is correlated with the number of relevant documents contained in those pools. As Table 4 indicates, there does seem to be a weak negative correlation; the topic with the fewest newly discovered relevant documents generated the largest assessment pools, for example. Our experiment design required relevance assessments for only 4 topics, so the assessment costs were not prohibitive in this case. But these observations may be helpful as we design future interactive CLIR studies.

5 Conclusions

Together, the five teams that participated in iCLEF 2002 had 38 searchers perform 158 searches in four document languages to test a broad range of hypotheses related to the design of cross-language search assistance systems. To the best of our knowledge, this is the largest multilingual information access user study ever performed. We therefore believe that the results obtained by the participating teams will be a rich source of evidence from which we can learn more about the way cross-language information retrieval technology will ultimately be used. Perhaps even more importantly, we have enriched our understanding of the design of user studies for end-to-end cross-language search assistance systems, and have expanded the community of researchers that share an interest in this important question.

Acknowledgements

We are indebted to many people that helped along the organization of this iCLEF track: Fernando López wrote the evaluation scripts and maintained the web site and distribution list; Martin Braschler created the assessment pools; Ellen Voorhees, Michael Kluck, Eija Airio and Jorun Kugelberg provided native relevance assessments; and Jianqiang Wang and Dina Demner-Fushman provided Systran translations for the German and English collections. Finally, we also want to thank Carol Peters for her continued support and encouragement.

References

[1] M. Braschler. CLEF 2001 - overview of results. In *Evaluation of Cross-Language Information Retrieval Systems. Proceedings of CLEF 2001: revised papers*, Springer-Verlag LNCS 2406, 2002.

[2] Douglas Oard. Evaluating cross-language information retrieval: Document selection. In Carol Peters, editor, *Cross-Language Information Retrieval and Evaluation: Proceedings of CLEF 2000*, Springer-Verlag Lecture Notes in Computer Science 2069, 2001.

[3] Douglas W. Oard and Julio Gonzalo. The CLEF 2001 interactive track. In Carol Peters, Martin Braschler, Julio Gonzalo, and Michael Kluck, editors, *Proceedings of CLEF 2001, Springer-Verlag LNCS Series 2069*, 2002.

[4] C. J. van Rijsbergen. *Information Retrieval.* Butterworths, London, second edition, 1979.

[5] Ellen Voorhees. Variations in relevance judgments and the measurement of retrieval effectiveness. In *Proceedings of the 21st Annual International ACM SIGIR Conference on Research and Development in Information Retrieval*, 1998.

SICS at iCLEF 2002: Cross-Language Relevance Assessment and Task Context

Jussi Karlgren and Preben Hansen

Swedish Institute of Computer Science, SICS
Box 1263, SE-164 29 Kista, Sweden
{jussi,preben}@sics.se

Abstract. An experiment on how users assess relevance in a foreign language they know well is reported. Results show that relevance assessment in a foreign language takes more time and is prone to errors compared to assessment in the readers' first language. The results are related to task and context and an enhanced methodology for performing context-sensitive studies is reported.

1 Cross-Linguality and Reading

1.1 People Are Naturally Multi-lingual

For people in cultures all around the world competence in more than one language is quite common and the European cultural area is typical in that respect. Many people, especially those engaged in intellectual activities are familiar with more than one language and have some acquaintance with several.

1.2 People Are Good at Making Relevance Assessments

Information access systems deliver results which on a good day hold up to forty per cent relevant items. It is up to the reader to winnow out the good stuff from the bad.

We know that readers are excellent at making relevance assessments for texts. Both assessment efficiency and precision are very impressive. But we know very little about how they go about it. Practice seems to improve both assessment speed, assessment precision, and assessor confidence, but what features a reader focuses on and how they are combined has not been studied in any great detail.

1.3 Linguistic Competence Is a Continuum

Languages are tools tied to tasks. For any one task, typically people have one language they prefer to perform it in. In general, while people may have working knowledge of more than one language, it is not common for people to have equal competence in many; the first language, or the school language, or the

C.A. Peters (Ed.): CLEF 2002, LNCS 2785, pp. 383–391, 2003.

workplace language will tend to be stronger for whatever task they are engaged in. Linguistic competence is not a binary matter: people know a language to some extent, greater or lesser. What bits of competence are important in any given situation is an ongoing discussion in the field of language teaching — we will here concentrate on some aspects of reading, related to situation, task, and domain.

1.4 Assessing Relevance in a Strange Language Is Hard – and Important

We do know that reading about strange things in strange genres takes more time than familiar genres, and that reading a language we do not know well is hard work, and something we only attempt if we believe it is worth the effort.

Judging trustworthiness and usefulness of documents in a foreign language is difficult and a noticeably less reliable process than doing it in a language and cultural context we are familiar with.

These starting points have immediate ramifications for the design of cross-lingual and multi-lingual information access systems. Presenting large numbers of documents to users if it is likely they will not be able to determine their usefulness is a waste at best and a trustworthiness and reliability risk at worst.

1.5 Finding out More – Does Language Make a Difference?

We need more data about reading and related processes. To find out more we set up an experiment where Swedish-speaking subjects, fluent in English as determined by self-report, were presented with retrieval results in both languages, and given the task of rating the results by relevance. Our hypotheses were that results for a foreign language would be more time-consuming and less competent than those for the first language.

1.6 Task-Based Approach to Query Construction and Relevance Assessment

Generally, topicality has been the main criteria for relevance in information retrieval experiments. Our approach suggests that other criteria may come into play, especially criteria related to the task and domain at hand. For interactive information retrieval experiments, we propose to expand the original query with information about context. In this study, we want to relate the relevance assessment to a specific task situation, i.e. the subject will be given a semi-realistic situation including a domain description, and then we will investigate if the relevance assessment situation involves criteria beyond topicality.

2 Experiment

2.1 Set-Up

Participants: The study involved 12 participants divided into 3 groups. Groups A and B were given a workplace scenario and a description involving a domain with relevant work-tasks. Group C was given the i-CLEF queries without context information.
Scenario: Each scenario had 4 participants.
Language: 2 languages were used: English and Swedish.
Queries: The four CLEF queries used in this year's interactive track were used in both languages: queries 53, 56, 65, and 80. Query 86 was used for a practice run.
Result List: Sets of ranked result lists of length between one and two hundred were produced in Swedish using Siteseeker, a commercial web-based search system by Euroseek AB, on the Swedish TT CLEF corpus and English using Inquery on the LA Times CLEF corpus.
Presentation: The ranked lists were presented to the participants, varied by order and language (cf. Table 1) in a simulated search interface.
System: The experiment infrastructure was built using HTTP and was deployed over the WWW. The canned ranked results were put up as html pages and linked to the actual documents, which were displayed with four buttons to be used for the relevance ranking. A simple cgi-bin based logging tool noted the relevance assessment made and the time taken to make the assessment after display of the document.
Questionnaires: The participants also filled out a questionnaire at various points in the study. The data was collected either by semi-structured questions or measured by a Likert scale of 1 to 5 or 1 to 3.
Relevance Categories: The participants could in the interface indicate for each document one of four assessments: "not relevant" "somewhat relevant", "relevant", and "don't know".

2.2 Simulated Domain and Work-Task Scenarios

In this study we use the Simulated Domain and Work-Task Scenario (SDWS) methodology, an evaluation methodology with simulated contexts that include description of domains and work-tasks. The method is an extension of the notion of simulated work-tasks, e. g. [1], [2], [4]. Borlund and Ruthven enhanced the context of standard queries using two fields with descriptive information. We extend this design to include a domain description and a general work-task description. The goal of the method is to give the experimental query a context closer to a real-life information-seeking situation. In this way, the SDWS would allow the user a) a broader understanding of the situation, and b) a subjective interpretation of the relevance.

Constructing a SDWS query within a context was done by creating two levels of description (cf. Figure 2): a general description including a short description

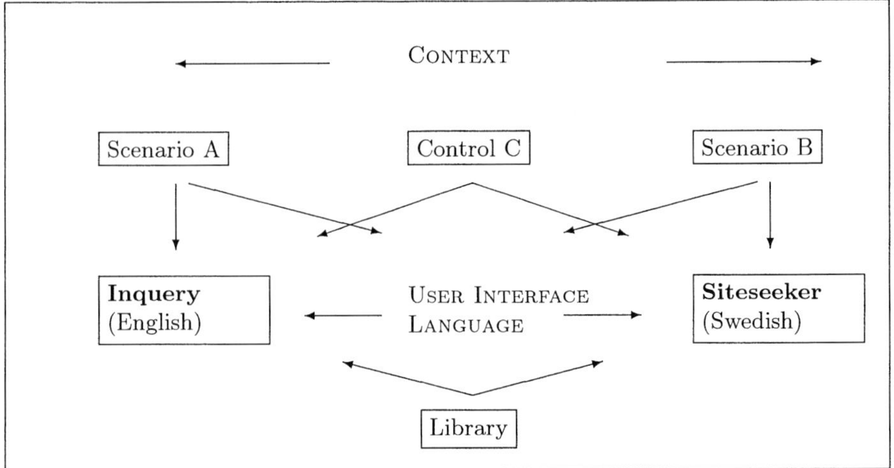

Fig. 1. Task and scenario-based experiment design

General descriptions:	
	Domain:
	Work-task description:
Situational description:	
	Topic:
	Search task description:

Fig. 2. Design of the simulated Domain and Work-Task scenario

Scenario	Domain
A	Monitoring news and translation services
B	Information specialist / Consultant
C	Control - CLEF Scenario

Fig. 3. Scenarios

of the domain and a short description of general work-tasks or routines that are performed. The next level contains a situational description including the topic of the query (in this case the i-CLEF query) and a search task description, which also include parts of the description field of the actual i-CLEF query (cf. appendix A for a SDWS for query CO53).

The scenarios were designed on the basis of a real work domain including real but rather general work descriptions. The designed domains for scenario A and B (see Figure 3), were assigned randomly to the participants.

2.3 Procedure

The participants were asked to answer some initial questions. After that, participants in groups A or B were asked to read through a workplace scenario carefully

Scenario A			Scenario B			Control C		
User			User			User		
1	L:SE Q:1+3	L:EN Q:2+4	5	L:SE Q:1+3	L:EN Q:2+4	9	L:SE Q:1+3	L:EN Q:2+4
2	L:EN Q:1+3	L:SE Q:2+4	6	L:EN Q:1+3	L:SE Q:2+4	10	L:EN Q:1+3	L:SE Q:2+4
3	L:SE Q:3+1	L:EN Q:4+2	7	L:SE Q:3+1	L:EN Q:4+2	11	L:SE Q:3+1	L:EN Q:4+2
4	L:EN Q:3+1	L:SE Q:4+2	8	L:EN Q:3+1	L:SE Q:4+2	12	L:EN Q:3+1	L:SE Q:4+2

Fig. 4. Matrix of scenarios, queries and languages used in experiment

and try to act within the assigned scenario as well as possible. Then participants were asked to read through the first work-task related query and to assess the ranked list for it, pursuant time constraints as per the scenario, or in the case of group C, to keep the time about constant around fifteen to twenty minutes per query. After the assessment, participants were asked to answer a fixed set of questions related to the query and the work task. This fixed set of questions was repeated after each of the four queries. Finally, after the last query, participants were asked to answer a last set of questions.

2.4 Participants

The 12 participants in this study had a variety of academic and professional backgrounds. 5 participants were male and 7 female, with an average age of 36,5. The participants had an overall high experience searching web-based search engines such as Google (4,33) and an overall low experience in searching commercial databases (2,16) and using machine translation tools such as Babelfish (2.00). 2/3 of the participants used some kind of search engine 1-2 times every day. Average on overall knowledge in English was 4,25. Note that this information is based on the participants' own subjective judgments.

3 Results

3.1 Foreign-Language Texts Took Longer to Assess and Were Assessed Less Well

Assessing texts in English (30 s average assessment time) took longer than for Swedish (19 s). Given the extra effort invested into reading the English texts it is somewhat surprising to find that the results of the assessments were significantly less reliable for English than for Swedish (cf. Figure 5; all differences between English and Swedish significant by Mann Whitney U; $p > 0,95$). Assessments were judged by how well they correspond to the CLEF official assessments; precision and recall are calculated with respect to the known relevant documents found in the retrieved and presented set of documents. In general, the precision is reasonably high for both languages, which can be taken to indicate that

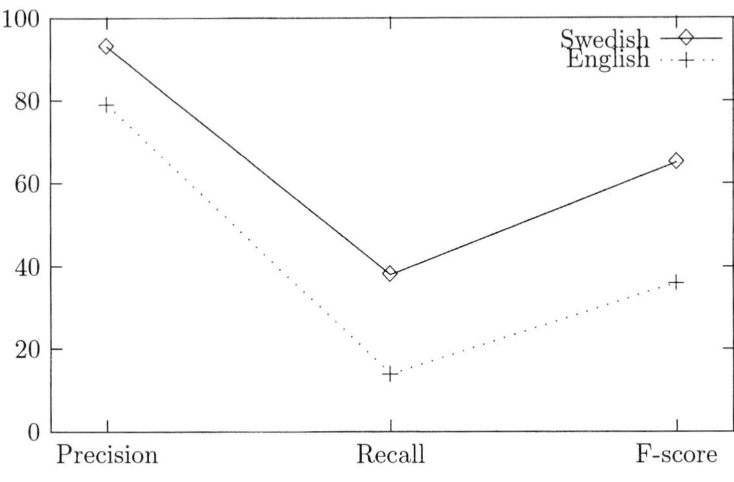

Fig. 5. Retrieval results

participants went through the list and found most relevant documents in the presented list.

All documents are very short. The Swedish documents are from a wire service and the English documents from a newspaper. The average length of an English article is over seven hundred words, whereas the Swedish articles are of an average length of just over four hundred. The difference in averages is partially due to the English average being highly skewed by a few very long feature articles, a genre almost entirely missing from the Swedish corpus. The length difference could account for part of the assessment time difference, but since the length of the article correlates very weakly with assessment time (Spearman's Rho = 0,3) that explanation can be discounted.

3.2 Task Focus May Have an Effect on Assessment Performance

No significant differences between scenarios (cf. Figure 6) could be found, other than a tendency for group B to perform better ($p > 0,75$; Mann Whitney U) than group A or the control group. As found by questionnaire, group B invested less effort in topic and more in task related aspects of relevance than did group A, which may be a tentative explanation for the tendency; this relation needs to be investigated further before any conclusions can be drawn, however.

3.3 Relevance Judgment Aspects

We assumed that aspects of the relevance judgment considered would extend beyond traditional topicality. In order to see if aspects other than topicality were taken into account, we added two more levels related to our domain and task-based scenario approach. After each query, the participants were asked what

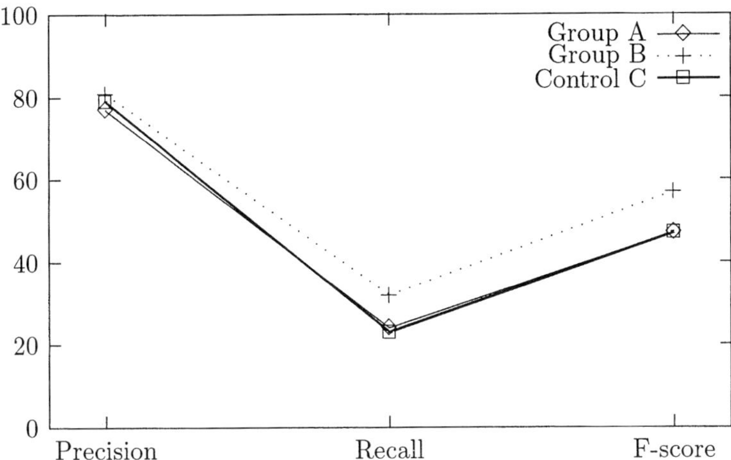

Fig. 6. Retrieval result by task

aspects of relevance judgments were of any importance for their assessment. We present the results for groups A and B in Table 7. Merged, the two groups used the domain related aspect in 12% of the cases, the task related aspect in 46% of the cases, and the topic-related aspect in 42% of the cases. All observations were done over all four i-CLEF queries given to the participants. Notable is that 36% in the A-group and 61 % in the B-group marked that their assessments were related to task. Another interesting observation is that nobody in the group B reported using the domain-related aspect in assessments. Group A had a level of 44% on topic-related aspect and 36% on task-related aspects.

	Scenario A				**Scenario B**				**Both A + B**			
	R1	R2	R3	SUM	R1	R2	R3	SUM	R1	R2	R3	TSUM
Q53	1	2	1	4	0	2	3	5	1	4	4	9
Q56	2	2	4	8	0	4	1	5	2	6	5	13
Q65	1	3	3	7	0	2	1	3	1	5	4	10
Q80	1	2	3	6	0	3	2	5	1	5	5	11
TSUM	5	9	11	25	0	11	7	18	5	20	18	43
Mean				1,56				1,12				1,34

R1 Relevance judgement aspects related to the task domain (translator and news agents)
R2 Relevance judgement aspects related to the task given to the participant
R3 Relevance judgement aspects related to the topic of the query

Fig. 7. Type of relevance judgement aspect by scenario, for both languages combined

4 Discussion

The results are quite convincing. Time matters. Relevance assessment in a foreign language, even a familiar one, is more time-consuming and more difficult than in one's first language. Tasks seem to matter. Generally, traditional information retrieval experiments are based on algorithmic and topical relevance. In this study we have seen that other aspects do count in the relevance assessment. Furthermore, we have a weak but interesting indication that the Simulated Domain and Work-Task Scenario applied may have an effect on the assessment performance. This is but a first step in this direction; we intend to pursue this avenue of inquiry further, and investigate its effects on design. Specifically, during the coming year we will investigate if adding more information to the interface will improve results for the foreign language assessment task.

Acknowledgements

We thank Tidningarnas Telegrambyrå AB, Stockholm, for providing us with the Swedish text collection, and Heikki Keskustalo, University of Tampere, Johan Carlberger and Hercules Dalianis, Euroling AB, for kind support in producing the ranked lists of documents. Furthermore, we gratefully acknowledge funding provided to us by the European Commission under contracts IST-2000-29452 (DUMAS) and IST-2000-25310 (CLARITY). And finally we thank our patient subjects for the time they spent reading really old news.

References

[1] Borlund, P. (2000). *Evaluation of Interactive Information Retrieval Systems.* Doctoral dissertation. Turku, Finland: Åbo Akademi.

[2] Brajnik, G., Mizzaro, S and Tasso, C. Evaluating user interfaces to information retrieval systems. A case study on user support. In: Frei, H-P., Harman, D., Schäuble, P., and Wilkinson, R. (eds.). *Proc. ACM-SIGIR'96*, pp. 128-136. 1996.

[3] Hansen, P., and Järvelin, K. (2000). The Information Seeking and Retrieval Process at the Swedish Patent- and Registration Office. Moving from Lab-based to real life work-task environment. *Proc. ACM-SIGIR 2000 Workshop on Patent Retrieval*, pp. 43-53.

[4] Ruthven, I., Lalmas, M. and van Rijsbergen, K. (2002). Ranking Expansion Terms with Partial and Ostensive Evidence. *Proc. Fourth Int. Conf. on Conceptions of Library and Information Science — CoLIS4*, Seattle, USA, July, 2002, pp. 199-220.

Appendix A

The SDWS Framework Description

The following is a full version of a simulated Domain and Work-task Scenario (SDWS) (translated from the Swedish original) for iCLEF query C053.

General descriptions:		
	Domain:	Monitoring news and translation services
	Work-task description:	Among your daily work-tasks you monitor and translate news information within a specific areas based on profiles set up by external customers. Your customers are usually companies and public institutions.
Situational description:		
	Topic:	Genes and Diseases
	Search task description:	You have been assigned to monitor incoming news items that describe genes, which cause disease on humans. The customer especially wants documents that identify or report the discovery of a gene that is the source of any type of disease, syndrome, behavioural or developmental disorder in humans. Any information or document that reports the discovery of a defective gene that causes problems in humans is relevant. Documents that describe diseases and disorders caused by the absence of a gene are not relevant.

Universities of Alicante and Jaen at iCLEF

Fernando Llopis[1], José L. Vicedo[1], Antonio Ferrández[1], Manuel C. Díaz[2], and Fernando Martínez[2]

[1] Departamento de Lenguajes y Sistemas Informáticos
University of Alicante, Spain
{llopis,vicedo,antonio}@dlsi.ua.es
[2] Departamento de Ciencias de la Computación
University of Jaen, Spain
{mcdiaz,dofer}@ujaen.es

Abstract. We present the results obtained at iCLEF-2002. This is the first time that we have participated in the iCLEF task, and we have used our Passage Retrieval approach (IR-n). This system previously divides the document in fragments or passages, and the similarity of each passage with the query is then measured. Finally, the document that contains the most similar passage is returned as the most relevant. In the interactive document selection task, we have experimented with this system by showing the most relevant passage of each returned document instead of the entire document. In this paper, we present the results obtained with this system, where the relevant passages have been automatically translated into Spanish by means of Systran. The results are compared with those obtained using the Z-Prise system where the entire document is read to establish relevance.

1 Introduction

The focus of this paper is the interactive document selection task. The main objective of this task is to design a system to facilitate users to find relevant documents about their information needs. Classical Information Retrieval (IR) systems use the whole document in order to determine the relevance of the document with reference to a query. The main problem with this kind of system is that they can return entire relevant documents, but they cannot locate the most relevant piece of text in the document. For example, a document about the "Biography of Felipe II" is relevant for the query "the town were Felipe II was born", but only a part of this document is relevant for the information required. In this way, when users have to determine whether a document is relevant or not, they probably have to read the entire document. A new IR proposal that tries to overcome this problem is called Passage Retrieval (PR). PR systems divide the document into pieces of text that are called passages. A similarity measure is obtained for each passage and then the document will be given the similarity value of its most relevant passage. The IR system used in this paper, called IR-n, employs the PR strategy. The IR-n system was used as an IR system in CLEF 2001 [2], and as a module in a Question Answering (QA) system in

C.A. Peters (Ed.): CLEF 2002, LNCS 2785, pp. 392–399, 2003.

TREC-10 [7], where it reduces the amount of text in which the QA system works. In this paper, the results obtained with the IR-n system for the iCLEF task are presented, with the user determining whether a document is relevant or not by reading only the most relevant passages returned by this system. These relevant passages are automatically translated into Spanish by Systran.

This paper is structured in the following way. First, an introduction of PR systems and the architecture of IR-n system are presented. Second, the interactive document selection task is introduced. Third, the experiments for tuning the IR-n system for this task are described and results achieved are analysed and compared with those obtained with the Z-Prise system, which is based on the IR approach that uses the entire document to determine the relevance to a query. Finally, the conclusions obtained from this experiment and plans for future work are presented.

2 The State of the Art in Passage Retrieval

Previous work [4] shows that PR systems can improve the precision of IR systems by from 20% to 50%. PR systems can be classified according to the way they define the passages in a document. A general classification usually quoted by researchers is that proposed in [1], where the PR systems are divided into those based on discourse, those based on semantic properties and those based on a window model. The first one uses the structural properties of the documents, such as sentences, paragraphs or HTML marks in order to define the passages. The second one divides each document in semantic pieces, according to the different topics in the document. The last one uses windows with a fixed size to form the passages. We can find a further taxonomy of window models in [4], which distinguishes between those that use the structure of the document when defining the passages, and those that do not use this kind of information. On the one hand, it seems plausible that discourse-based models are more effective since they are using the structure of the document itself. However, their greatest problem is that the results could depend on the writing style of the document author. Furthermore, this kind of model produces a very heterogeneous set of passages, with reference to the size of each passage. On the other hand, window models have the great advantage that they are simpler to create since the passages have a previously known size, whereas the other models have to support variable sized passages. However, they have the problem that as the passage can start with any word in the sentence, such passages may not be adequate for presentation to the user as the most relevant passage, since they are not logical and coherent fragments of the document.

3 IR-n System Architecture

The IR-n system [2] is based on a window model that uses the structure of the document when defining the passages. The main characteristics of this system are the following:

1. A document is divided into passages, which are formed by a fixed number of sentences. This is because a sentence usually represents an idea in the document, whereas the paragraphs can be used just to give a visual structure to the document. Moreover, sentences are logical and complete units of information, whereas window models that start with any word in the document can return incoherent fragments of text.
2. The number of sentences that form a passage can be separately determined for each set of documents. Previous experiments for the documents of Los Angeles Times show that the best results are obtained with passages of seven sentences.
3. The system uses windows with overlapped pieces of text in order to fine-tune the results. For example, with passages of seven sentences, the first passage is formed by sentences from 1 to 7, the second one from 2 to 8, and so on. We have used these overlapping passages because we have obtained better results in the experiments presented in [5], than when using other kinds of passages (e.g. those with no overlapping, or with other degrees of overlapping). The overlapping process increments the running time, but this increment is not very high, since the first passage starts in the first sentence where a key word of the query appears, and the last passage in the last sentence where a key word appears.
4. We are using the cosine measure but with no normalization with reference to the size of the passage, because the passages are quite homogeneous (the same number of sentences with a similar number of words).

4 The Interactive Document Selection Task in CLEF-2002

The aim of the interactive document selection (IDS) task in CLEF-2002 is to evaluate the systems that allow multilingual interactive information retrieval. The idea of interactivity is related to the issues involved in displaying documents appropriately so that users can decide whether they are relevant or not. Multilinguality means that the answer is presented in one language while the document collection is written in a different one. The set-up of this task is the following:

1. Each participant has to compare two IDS systems. One of them will be taken as baseline.
2. Two four-user groups are selected by each participant.
3. Each individual user has to process a set of four queries written in their native language.
4. The document collection where the search has to be performed is written in a different language to the queries.
5. The relevant documents obtained by an IR system are shown to the user for each query. These documents are sorted by relevance.
6. Each user should decide which of these documents are relevant for him/her.

7. Each participant in the task should submit the list of documents that have been selected by the users.

The organization evaluates if the documents that have been selected by iCLEF users are really relevant or not. After that, precision, recall and F_α measures are calculated for each participant. F_α [6] is defined as follows:

$$F_\alpha = \frac{1}{\alpha/P + (1-\alpha)/R} \quad (1)$$

Where $\alpha = 0.8$ since it is considered more valuable to obtain higher precision (P) than recall (R).

5 IR-n System in the Interactive Document Selection Task

The participation of the IR-n system in this task has been based on a set of Spanish queries, and a document collection written in English, the LA Times collection.

The query collection was made up by some of the CLEF-2001 queries, specifically numbers 53, 56, 65 and 80. Moreover, there was an additional query (number 86) that was used for system training. It is important to note that we have only processed short versions (title + description) of the queries.

A number of experiments were carried out with two main aims. First, in order to present the documents to the user, we designed an HTML interface as is shown in Figure 1. This interface presented the most relevant passage (seven sentences) of each document and allowed an easy selection of relevant or non-relevant documents. In addition, it collected other useful information for the task, such as the number of the question and the name of the user.

Second, as the IR-n system does not have multilingual capabilities, and in order to facilitate the document reading process, we translated the documents into Spanish using Systran[1].

5.1 System Training

The system was trained using the query supplied by the iCLEF organisation. The objective was to adapt the process by taking into account the comments and suggestions of two non-experimented users in order to investigate the best way to show the information to the user.

The main problems detected in this experiment were the following:

1. Document translation was not good enough, and produced some unreadable pieces of text that made it difficult to understand the passage presented.

[1] http://www.systransoft.com

2. Sometimes, the passage did not include some important information, because the IR-n system started building relevant passages from the first sentence that contained a query term.
3. Even when the translation was reasonable, sometimes reading only the passage was not enough to decide if it was relevant because user lacked information about the context in which the passage was included.
4. Usually, when users did not understand these pieces of text or doubted their relevance because contextual information was lacking, they discarded them and tried to read the following piece of text.

After this first experiment, several changes were introduced to the interface in order to minimize these problems and facilitate user decisions:

1. As our system lacks of translation capabilities nothing was done to improve translation. Instead, we increased readability by presenting the passages in different lines to the user. This facilitated the comprehension of the passages, and was quite easy to achieve since IR-n performs an indexing on sentences.
2. In order to avoid missing important information, the previous sentence to the relevant passage was also presented. By including this sentence, the comprehension of the passage is highly increased.
3. In order to provide important context information, the system always shows the title of the document to which the relevant passage belongs. This way, the

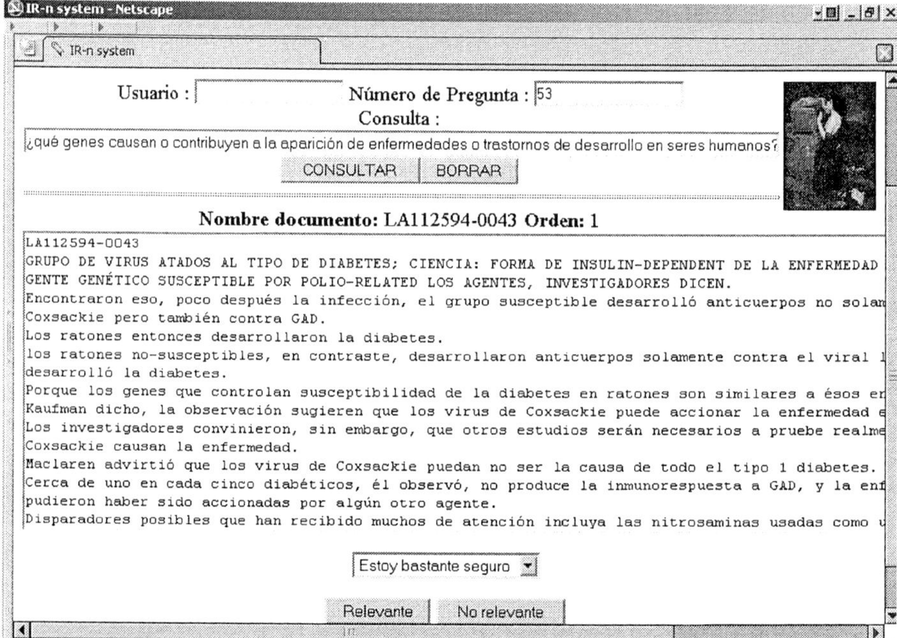

Fig. 1. HTML interface for presenting documents to the user

user knows the main subject the passage talks about and enhances passage understanding. This title is presented in capital letters.

All these changes, tested by two different users to those who performed training, produced a better readability and comprehension of passages. Moreover, the amount of discarded or skipped passages was drastically reduced.

5.2 System Evaluation

The experiments were carried out by eight final course university students. All of them processed relevant passages returned by IR-n system and full documents retrieved by the Z-Prise IR system [3] which was used as baseline.

Instead of explaining to the students what the IR community considered to be a "relevant" or a "non-relevant" document, we decided to adopt a different strategy with the aim of coordinating relevance criteria between them. They were told to select all those documents that, in their opinion, provided useful information about the topic of the query since they would later be requested to write a paper on this topic. The experiments were carried out in the following way:

- All students (users) processed all the questions in both systems (IR-n and Z-Prise).
- The 25 most relevant documents selected by the IR system were presented to the user. The IR-n system only showed the more relevant passage of each document, whereas the Z-Prise system displayed the whole document.
- The user classified each document as relevant or non-relevant.
- The time for each query was not limited.

5.3 Results

The results achieved are presented in Table 1. This table compares IR-n system results with those obtained with Z-Prise. Only the first 25 most relevant documents have been used for each query, which could explain the low recall results.

Given that only 25 relevant documents were retrieved for each topic, it is interesting to study the precision results. Table 2 presents the precision achieved for each topic. First, the low results obtained for Topic 3 should be pointed out because no relevant document was retrieved by any system. Second, we should note the high precision achieved in two of the three remaining topics, which was obtained with just the most relevant passage.

Table 1. Results comparison

System	Average F_alpha
Z-Prise	0.2166
IR-n	0.3248

Table 2. Results by topic

Average Precision	IR-n	Z-Prise
Topic 1	0.4601	0.6371
Topic 2	0.8098	0.5925
Topic 3	0	0
Topic 4	0.7643	0.3748
Average	0.5085	0.4011

6 Conclusions and Future Work

In this paper, we have described an experiment that studies the ability of users to judge the relevance of documents, in which the users can only read the most relevant passages of these documents. The results were quite good, because the users took only a short time to judge relevance since they had to read short pieces of text. However, these short pieces of text contain the most relevant data about the information required, therefore the precision results were high, even higher than those obtained by means of reading the entire document. There are some points to note, once the individual results and the opinions of the users have been analysed:

- Users become very anxious when they do not find the relevant document in the list of relevant passages. This occurred for one of the queries in which only one relevant document appeared in the 25 documents presented by our system. In this case, the users judged as relevant some non-relevant documents that were not selected in other cases.
- The users find the automatic translations into Spanish quite unreadable most of the times (more than was expected).
- We think that the results have been influenced by using just the title and description fields of the queries, which have raised some doubts about the relevance of the passages.
- It has been difficult to find users to carry out the experiments, which explains the reduction of the number of documents to study (only 25) for each query. This has highly decreased the recall of the IR-n system, although we are quite happy with the results obtained, since the users found a high percentage of relevant documents in not much time (an average between 8 and 9 minutes per query). This is because the piece of text that has to be read is only formed by seven sentences.

In the future, we plan to improve the automatic translations. Systran has been used in order to translate the passages presented to the user. Given that the automatic translation of the Los Angeles Times collection was imperfect, and even at times unreadable, we will try to present the results to the user in a more structured way. This task will be carried out by retrieving information from a collection similar to the Los Angeles Times, specifically, the EFE news of the same year, which is available in Spanish.

Secondly, we have to improve the interactivity with the system by using user relevance decisions to learn about question expansion techniques.

Acknowledgements

This work has been partially supported by the Spanish Government (CICYT) with grant TIC2000-0664-C02-02 and (PROFIT) with grant FIT-150500-2002-416.

References

[1] James P. Callan. Passage-Level Evidence in Document Retrieval. In Proceedings of the 17th Annual International Conference on Research and Development in Information Retrieval, London, UK, July 1994. Springer Verlag, pages 302-310.
[2] CLEF2001. Evaluation of Cross-Language Information Retrieval Systems. In Proceedings of the Workshop of the Cross-Language Evaluation Forum, Darmstadt, Germany, 2001. Lecture Notes in Computer Science 2406, Springer-Verlag.
[3] Darrin Dimmick. ZPrise information retrieval system. Available on demand at NIST. http://www.itl.nist.gov/iaui/849.02/works/papers/zp2/zp2.html.
[4] Marcin Kaszkiel and Justin Zobel. Effective Ranking with Arbitrary Passages. Journal of the American Society for Information Science (JASIS), 52(4):344–364, February 2001.
[5] Fernando Llopis, José L. Vicedo, and Antonio Ferrández. Text Segmentation for efficient Information Retrieval. In Third International Conference on Intelligent Text Processing and Computational Linguistics (CICLing 2002), Mexico City, Mexico, 2002. Lecture Notes in Computer Science, Springer-Verlag, pages 373-380.
[6] C. J. Van Rijsbergen. Information Retrieval, 2nd edition. Butterworths, London, 1979.
[7] José Luis Vicedo, Antonio Ferrández, and Fernando Llopis. University of Alicante at TREC-10. In Tenth Text REtrieval Conference (Notebook), volume 500-250 NIST Special Publication, Gaithersburg, USA, Nov 2001. National Institute of Standards and Technology.

Comparing User-Assisted and Automatic Query Translation

Daqing He[1], Jianqiang Wang[2], Douglas W. Oard[2], and Michael Nossal[1]

[1] Institute for Advanced Computer Studies
University of Maryland, College Park, MD 20742 USA
{daqingd,nossal}@umiacs.umd.edu

[2] College of Information Studies & Institute for Advanced Computer Studies
University of Maryland, College Park, MD 20742 USA
{wangjq,oard}@glue.umd.edu

Abstract. For the 2002 Cross-Language Evaluation Forum Interactive Track, the University of Maryland team focused on query formulation and reformulation. Twelve people performed a total of forty eight searches in the German document collection using English queries. Half of the searches were with user-assisted query translation, and half with fully automatic query translation. For the user-assisted query translation condition, participants were provided two types of cues about the meaning of each translation: a list of other terms with the same translation (potential synonyms), and a sentence in which the word was used in a translation-appropriate context. Four searchers performed the official iCLEF task, the other eight searched a smaller collection. Searchers performing the official task were able to make more accurate relevance judgments with user-assisted query translation for three of the four topics. We observed that the number of query iterations seems to vary systematically with topic, system, and collection, and we are analyzing query content and ranked retrieval measures to obtain further insight into these variations in search behavior.

1 Introduction

Interactive Cross Language Information Retrieval (CLIR) is an iterative process in which searcher and system collaborate to find documents that satisfy an information need, regardless of whether they are written in the same language as the query. Humans and machines bring complementary strengths to this process. Machines are excellent at repetitive tasks that are well specified; humans bring creativity and exceptional pattern recognition capabilities. Properly coupling these capabilities can result in a synergy that greatly exceeds the ability of either human or machine alone. The design of the fully automated components to support cross-language searching (e.g., structured query translation and ranked retrieval) has been well researched, but achieving true synergy requires that the machine also provide tools that will allow its human partners to exercise their skills to the greatest possible degree. Such tools are the focus of our work in

C.A. Peters (Ed.): CLEF 2002, LNCS 2785, pp. 400–415, 2003.

the Cross-Language Evaluation Forum's (CLEF) interactive track (iCLEF). In 2001, we began by exploring support for document selection [5]. This year, our focus is on query formulation.

Cross-language retrieval techniques can generally be classified as query translation, document translation, or interlingual designs [2]. We adopted a query translation design because the query translation stage provides an additional interaction opportunity not present in document translation based systems. Our searchers first formulate a query in English, then the system translates that query into the document language (German, in our case). The translated query is used to search the document collection, and a ranked list of document surrogates (first 40 words, in our case) is displayed. The searcher can examine individual documents, and can optionally repeat the process by reformulating the query. Although there are only three possible interaction points (query formulation, query translation, and document selection), the iterative nature of the process introduces significant complexity. We therefore performed extensive exploratory data analysis to understand how searchers employ the systems that we provided.

Our study was motivated by the following questions:

1. What strategies do searchers apply when formulating their initial query and when reformulating that query? In what ways do their strategies differ from those used in monolingual applications? How do individual differences in subject knowledge, language skills, search experience, and other factors affect this process?
2. What information do searchers need when reformulating their query, and how do they obtain that information?
3. Can searchers find documents more effectively if we give them some degree of control over the query translation process? Do searchers prefer to exercise control over the query translation process? What reasons do they give for their preference?
4. What measures can best illuminate the effect of interactive query reformulation on retrieval effectiveness?

These questions are, of course, far too broad to be answered completely by any single experiment. For the experiments reported in this paper, we chose to provide our searchers with two variants on a single retrieval system, one with support for interaction during query translation (which we call "manual"), and the other with fully automatic query translation (which we call "auto"). This design allowed us to test a hypothesis derived from the third question above. We relied on observations, questionnaires, semi-structured interviews, and exploratory data analysis to augment the insight gained through hypothesis testing, and to begin our exploration of the other questions.

In the next section, we describe the design of our system. Section 3 then describes our experiment, and Section 4 presents the results that we obtained. Section 5 concludes the paper with a brief discussion of future work.

2 System Design

In this section, we describe the resources that we used, the design of our cross-language retrieval system, and our user interface design.

2.1 Resources

We chose English as the query language and German as the document language because our population of potential searchers was generally skilled in English but not German. The full German document collection contained 71,677 news stories from the Swiss News Agency (SDA) and 13,979 news stories from Der-Spiegel. We used the German-to-English translations provided by the iCLEF organizers for construction of document surrogates (for display in a ranked list) and for display of full document translations (when selected for viewing by the searcher). The translations were created using Systran Professional 3.0.

We obtained a German-English bilingual term list from the Chemnitz University of Technology[1], and used the German stemmer from the "Snowball" project[2]. Our Keyword in Context (KWIC) technique requires parallel (i.e., translation-equivalent) German/English texts – we obtained those from the Foreign Broadcast Information Service (FBIS) TIDES data disk, release 2.

2.2 CLIR System

We used the InQuery text retrieval system (version 3.1p1) from the University of Massachusetts, along with locally implemented extensions to support cross-language retrieval between German and English. We used Pirkola's structured query technique for query translation [4], which aggregates German term frequencies and document frequencies separately before computing the weight for each English query term. This tends to suppress the contribution to the ranking computations of those English terms that have at least one translation that is a common German word (i.e., that occurs in many documents). For the automatic condition, all known translations were used. For the manual condition, only translations selected by the searcher were used. We employed a backoff translation strategy to maximize the coverage of the bilingual term list [3]. If no translation was found for the surface form of an English term, we stemmed the term (using the Porter stemmer) and tried again. If that failed, we also stemmed the English side of the bilingual term list and tried a third time. If that still failed, we treated the untranslated term as its own translation in the hope that it might be a proper name.

2.3 User Interface Design

For our automatic condition, we adopted an interface design similar to that of present Web search engines. Searchers entered English query terms in a one-line

[1] http://dict.tu-chemnitz.de/
[2] http://snowball.sourceforge.net

text field, based on their understanding of a full CLEF topic description (title, description, and narrative). We provided that topic description on paper in order to encourage a more natural query formulation process than might have been the case if cut-and-paste from the topic description were available. When the search button was clicked, a ranked list of document surrogates was displayed below the query field, thus allowing the query to serve as context when interpreting the ranked list. Ten surrogates were displayed simultaneously as a page, and up to 10 pages (in total 100 surrogates) could be viewed by clicking "next" button. Our surrogates consisted of the first 40 words in the TEXT field of the translated document. English words in the surrogate that shared a common stem with any query term (using the Porter stemmer) were highlighted in red. See Figure 1 for an illustration of the automatic user interface.

Each surrogate is labeled with a numeric rank (1, 2, 3, ...), which is displayed as a numbered button to the left of the surrogate. If the searcher selected the button, the full text of that document would be displayed in a separate window, with query terms highlighted in the same manner. In order to provide context, we repeated the numeric rank and the surrogate at the top of the document examination window. Figure 2 illustrates a document examination window.

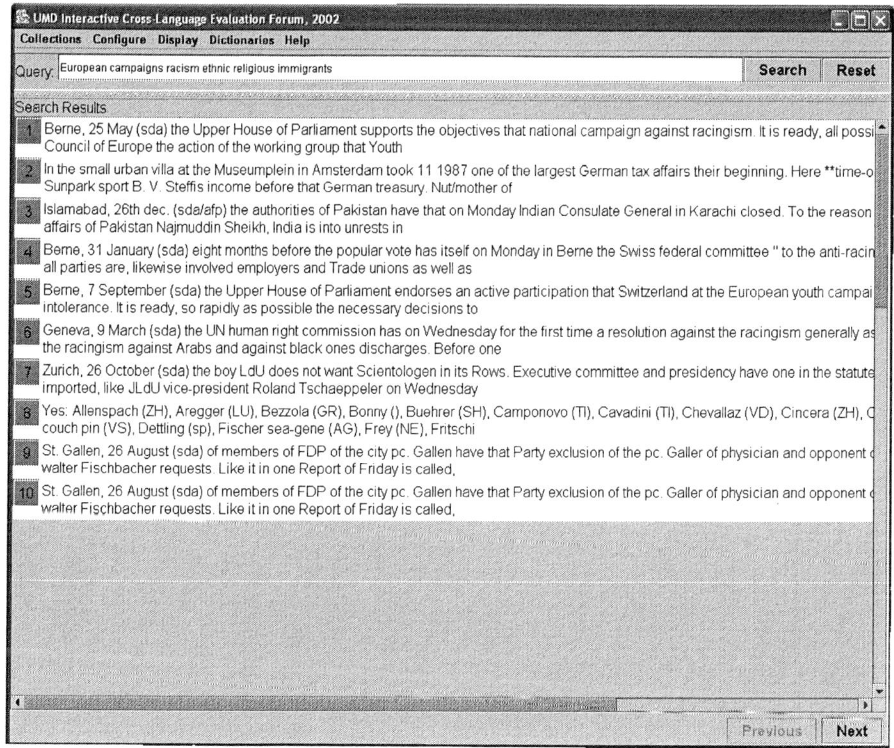

Fig. 1. User interface, automatic condition

We collected three types of information about relevance judgments. First, searchers could indicate whether the document was not relevant ("N"), somewhat relevant ("S"), or highly relevant ("H"). A fourth value, "?" (indicating unjudged), was initially selected by the system. Second, searchers could indicate their degree of confidence in their judgment as low ("L"), medium ("M"), or high ("H"), with a fourth value ("?") being initially selected by the system. Both relevance judgments and confidence values were recorded incrementally in a log file. Searchers could record relevance judgments and confidence values in either the main search window or in a document examination window (when that window was displayed). Finally, we recorded the times at which documents were selected for examination and the times at which relevance judgments for those documents were recorded. This allowed us to later compute the (approximate) examination time for each document. For documents that were judged without examination (e.g., based solely on the surrogate), we assigned zero as the examination time.

For the manual interface, we used a variant of the same interface with two additional items: 1) term-by-term control over the query translation process, and 2) a summary of the translations chosen for all query terms. We used a tabbed pane to allow the user to examine alternative translations for one English query term at a time. Each possible translation was shown on a separate line, and a check-box to the left of each line allowed the user to deselect or reselect that

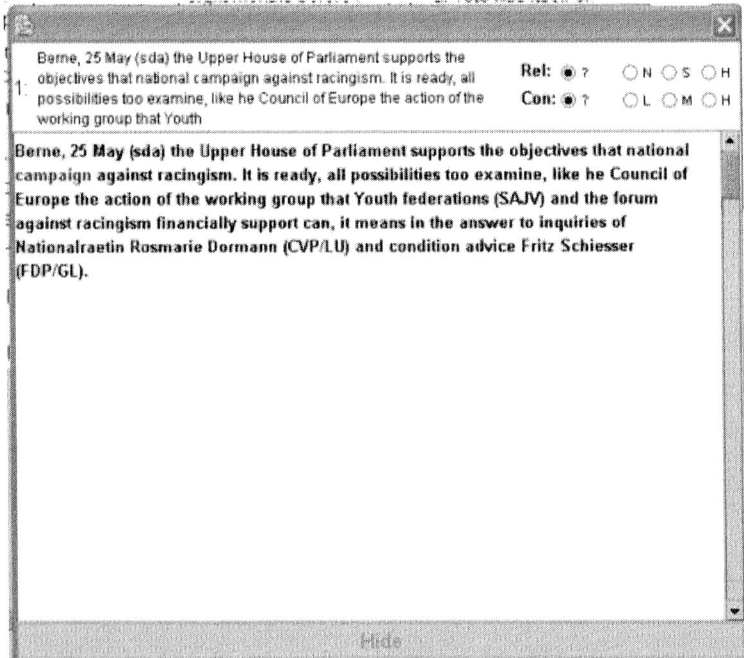

Fig. 2. Document examination window

translation. All translations were initially selected, so the manual and automatic conditions would be identical if the user did not deselect any translation.

Since we designed our interface to support searchers with no knowledge of German, we provided cues in English about the meaning of each German translation. For these experiments, searchers were able to view two types of cues: (1) back translation, and (2) Keyword In Context (KWIC). Each was created automatically, using techniques described below. Searchers were able to alternate between the two types of cues using tabs. The query translation summary area provided additional context for interpretation of the ranked list, simultaneously showing all selected translations (with one back translation each). In order to emphasize that two steps were involved (query translation, followed by search), we provided both "translate query" and "search" buttons. All other functions were identical to the automatic condition. Figure 3 illustrates the user interface for the manual condition.

Back Translation Ideally, we would prefer to provide the searcher with English definitions for each German translation alternative. Dictionaries with these types of definitions do exist for some language pairs (although rights management considerations may limit their availability in electronic form), but bilingual term lists are much more easily available. What we call "back translations" are English terms that share a specific German translation, something

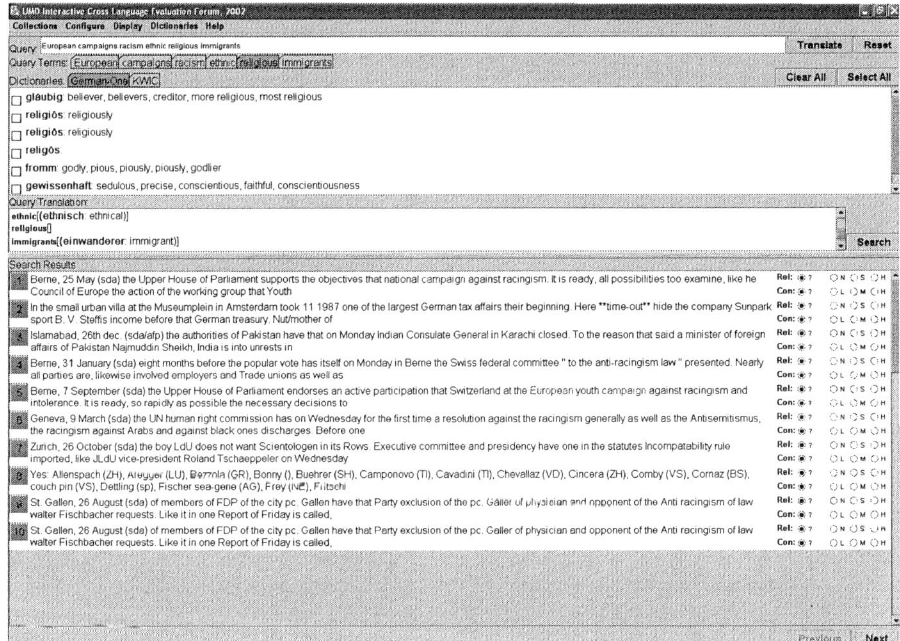

Fig. 3. User interface, manual condition

that we can determine with a simple bilingual term list. For example, the English word religious has several German translations in the term list that we used, two of which are fromm and gewissenhaft. Looking in the same term list for cues to the meaning of fromm, we see that it can be translated into English as religious, godly, pious, piously, or godlier. Thus fromm seems to clearly correspond to the literal use of religious. By contrast, gewissenhaft's back translations are religious, sedulous, precise, conscientious, faithful, or conscient-iousness. This seems as if it might correspond with a more figurative use of religious, as in "he rode his bike to work religiously." Of course, many German translations will themselves have multiple senses, so detecting a reliable signal in the noisy cues provided by back translation sometimes requires common-sense reasoning. Fortunately, that is a task for which humans are uniquely well suited. The original English term will always be its own back translation, so we supress its display. Sometimes this results in an empty (and therefore uninformative) set of back translations. Figure 4 shows the back translation display for "religious" in our manual condition.

Keyword in Context One way to compensate for the weaknesses of back translation is to draw additional evidence from examples of usage. In keeping with the common usage in monolingual contexts [1], we call this approach "keyword in context" or "KWIC." For each German translation of an English term, our goal is to find a brief passage in which the English term is used in a manner appropriate to the translation in question. To do this, we started with a

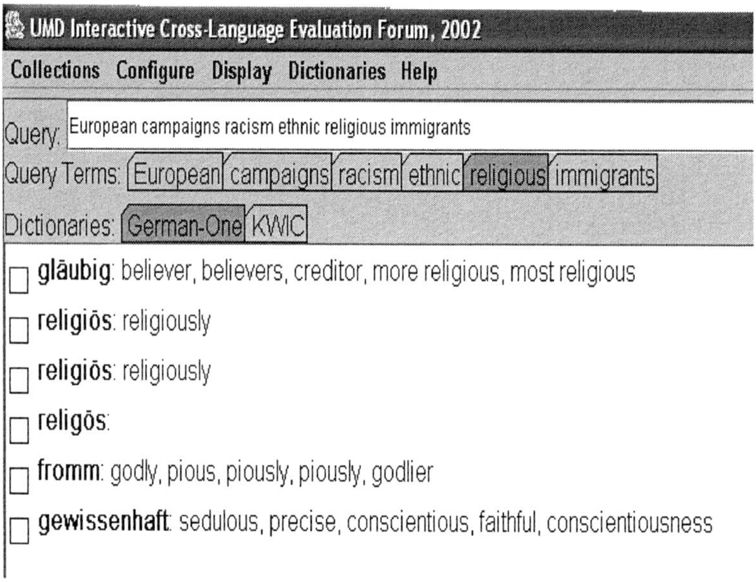

Fig. 4. Back translations of "religious."

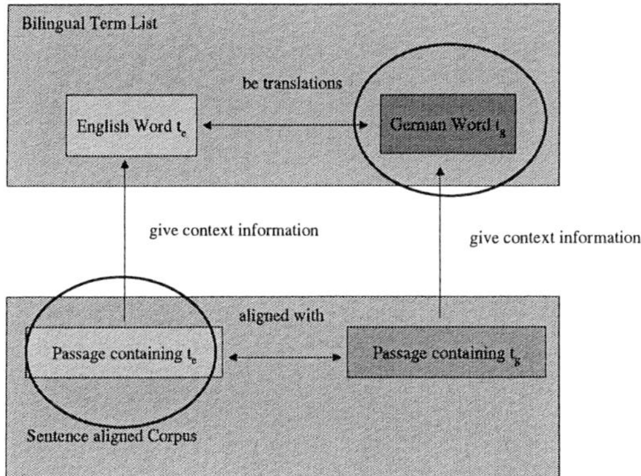

Fig. 5. Constructing cross-language KWIC using a sentence-aligned parallel corpus

collection of document pairs that are translations of each other. We used German news stories that had previously been manually translated into English by the Foreign Broadcast Information Service (FBIS) and distributed as a standard research corpus. We segmented the FBIS documents into sentences using rule-based software based on punctuation and capitalization patterns, and then produced aligned sentence pairs using the GSA algorithm (which uses dynamic programming to discover a plausible mapping of sentences within a paired documents based upon known translation relationships from the bilingual term list, sentence lengths and relative positions in each document). We presented the entire English sentence, favoring the shortest one if multiple sentence pairs contained the same English term.[3]

Formally, let t_e be an English term for which we seek an example of usage, and let t_g be the German translation from the bilingual term list that is of interest. Let S_e and S_g be the shortest pair of sentences that contain t_e and t_g respectively. We then present S_e as the example of usage for translation t_g. Figure 5 illustrates this process.

3 Experiment Design

Our experiment is designed to test the utility of user-assisted query translation in an interactive cross-language retrieval system. We were motivated to explore this question by two potential benefits that we foresaw:

- The effectiveness of ranked retrieval might be improved if a more refined set of translations for key query terms were known.

[3] We did not highlight the query term in the current version due to time constraints. Another limitation of the current implementation is that a briefer passage may serve our purpose better in some cases.

- The searcher's ability to employ the retrieval system might be improved by providing greater transparency for the query translation process.

Formally, we sought to reject the null hypotheses that there is no difference between the $F_{\alpha=0.8}$ achieved using the automatic and manual systems. The F measure is an outcome measure, however, and we were also interested in understanding process issues. We used exploratory data analysis to improve our understanding of how the searchers used the cues we provided.

3.1 Procedure

We followed the standard protocol for iCLEF 2002 experiments. Searchers were sequentially given four topics (stated in English), two for use with the manual system and two for use with the automatic system. Presentation order for topics and system was varied systematically across searchers as specified in the track guidelines. After an initial training session, they were given 20 minutes for each search to identify relevant documents using the radio buttons provided for that purpose in our user interface. The searchers were asked to emphasize precision over recall (by telling them that it was more important that the document that they selected be truly relevant than that they find every possible relevant document). We asked each searcher to fill out brief questionnaires before the first search (for demographic data), after each search, and after using each system. Each searcher used the same system at a different time, so we were able to observe each individually and make extensive observational notes. We also conducted a semi-structured interview (in which we tailored our questions based on our observations) after all searches were completed.

We conducted a pilot study with a single searcher (umd01) to exercise our new system and refine our data collection procedures. Eight searchers (umd02-umd09) then performed the experiment using the eight-subject design specified in the track guidelines [4]. While preparing our results for submission, we noticed that no SDA document appeared in any ranked list. Investigation revealed that InQuery had failed to index those documents because we had not configured the SGML parsing correctly for that collection. We therefore corrected that problem, recruited four new searchers (umd10-umd13), and repeated the experiment, this time using the four-subject design specified in the track guidelines.

We submitted all twelve runs for use in forming relevance pools, but designated the second experiment as our official submission because the first experiment did not comply with one requirement of the track guidelines (the collections to be searched). Our results from the first experiment are, however, interesting for several reasons. First, it turned out that topic 3 had no relevant documents in the collection searched in the first experiment.[5] This happens in real applications, of course, but the situation is rarely studied in information retrieval experiments because the typical evaluation measures are unable to discriminate

[4] http://terral.lsi.uned.es/iclef/2002/

[5] In this paper, we number the topics 1, 2, 3, and 4 in keeping with the track guidelines. These correspond to CLEF topic numbers c053, c065,c056 and c080, respectively.

between systems when no relevant documents are exist. Second, the number of relevant documents for the remaining three topics was smaller in the first experiment than the second. This provided an opportunity to study the effect of collection characteristics on searcher behavior.

For convenience, we refer to the first experiment as the *small collection* experiment, and the second as the *large collection* experiment.

3.2 Measures

We computed the following measures in order to gain insight into search behavior and search results:

- $F_{\alpha=0.8}$, as defined in the track guidelines (with "somewhat relevant" documents treated as not relevant). We refer to this condition as "strict" relevance judgments. This value was computed at the end of each search session.
- $F_{\alpha=0.8}$, but with "somewhat relevant" documents treated as relevant. We refer to this condition as "loose" relevance judgments. This value was also computed for each session.
- Mean uninterpolated Average Precision (MAP) for the ranked list returned by each iteration of a search process.
- A variant of MAP in which documents already marked as "highly relevant" are placed at the top of the ranked list (in an arbitrary order). We refer to this measure as "MAP-S" (for "strict").
- A second variant of MAP in which documents already marked as "highly relevant" or "somewhat relevant" are placed at the top of the ranked list (in an arbitrary order). We refer to this measure as "MAP-L" (for "loose").
- A third variant of MAP in which only the documents statisfying the two conditions – 1) they are already marked as "highly relevant" by the subject; 2) they are the real relevant documents according to "ground truth" – are placed at the top of the ranked list (in an arbitrary order). We refer to this measure as "MAP-R" (for "real").
- The total examination time (in seconds) for each document, summed over all instances of examination for the same document. If the full text of a document was never examined, an examination time of zero was recorded.
- The total number of query iterations for each search.

The set oriented measures (strict and loose F) are designed to characterize end-to-end task performance using the system. The rank-oriented measures (MAP, MAP-S, MAP-L and MAP-R) are designed to offer indirect insight into the query formulation process by characterizing the effect of a query based on the density of relevant documents near the top of the ranked list produced for that query (or for queries up through that iteration by either viewing from the point of the subject's own sense of performance, in the case of MAP-S and MAP-L, or viewing from the actual performance, in the case of MAP-R). Examination time is intended for use in conjunction with relevance judgment categories, in order to gain some insight into the relevance judgment process. We have not yet finished our trajectory analysis or the analysis of examination duration, so in this paper we report results only for the final values of $F_{\alpha=0.8}$ and for the number of iterations.

4 Results

4.1 Searchers

Our searcher population was relatively homogeneous. Specifically, they were:

Affiliated with a University. Every one of our searchers was a student, staff member or faculty member at the University of Maryland.

Highly Educated. Ten of the 12 searchers are either enrolled in a Masters degree program or had earned a Masters degree or higher. The remaining two were undergraduate students, and they are both in the small collection experiment.

Mature. The average age over all 12 searchers was 31, with the youngest being 19 and the oldest being 43. The average age of the four searchers in the large collection experiment was 32.

Mostly Female. There were three times as many female searchers as males, both overall and in the large collection experiment.

Experienced Searchers. Six of the 12 searchers held degrees in library science. The searchers reported an average of about 6 years of on-line searching experience, with a minimum of 4 years and maximum of 10 years. Most searchers reported extensive experience with Web search services, and all reported at least some experience searching computerized library catalogs (ranging from "some" to "a great deal"). Eleven of the 12 reported that they search at least once or twice a day. The search experience data for the four participants in the large collection experiment was slightly greater than for the 12 searchers as a whole.

Not Previous Study Participants. None of the 12 subjects had previously participated in a TREC or iCLEF study.

Inexperienced with Machine Translation. Nine of the 12 participants reported never having used any machine translation software or free Web translation service. The other 3 reported “very little experience” with machine translation software or services. The four participants in the large collection experiment reported the same ratio.

Native English Speakers. All 12 searchers were native speakers of English.

Not Skilled in German. Eight of the 12 searchers reported no reading skills in German at all. Another 3 reported poor reading skills in German, and one (umd12) reported good reading skill in German. Among the four searchers in the large collection experiment, 3 reported no German skills, with the fourth reporting good reading skills in German.

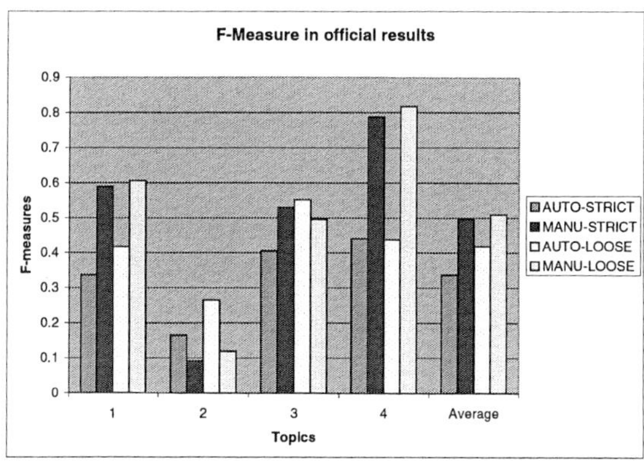

Fig. 6. $F_{\alpha} = 0.8$, large collection, by condition and topic

4.2 Large Collection Experiment

Our official results on the large collection experiment found that the manual system achieved a 48% larger value for $F_{\alpha=0.8}$ than the automatic system (0.4995 vs. 0.3371). However, the difference is not statistically significant, and the most likely reason is the small sample size. The presence of a searcher with good reading skills in German is also potentially troublesome given the hypothesis that we wished to test. We have not yet conducted searcher-by-searcher analysis to determine whether searcher umd12 exhibited search behaviors markedly different from the other 11 searchers. For contrast, we recomputed the same results with loose relevance. In that case, the searchers in our large collection experiment achieved a 22% increase in $F_{\alpha=0.8}$ over the automatic system (0.5095 vs. 0.4176).

As Figure 6 shows, the manual system achieved the largest improvements for topics 1 (Genes and Diseases) and 4 (Hunger Strikes) with strict relevance, but the automatic system actually outperformed the manual system on topic 2 (Treasure Hunting). Loose relevance judgments exhibited a similar pattern. Searchers that were presented with topic 2 in the manual condition reported (in the questionnaire) that it was more difficult to identify appropriate translations for topic 2 than for any other topic, and searchers generally indicated that they were less familiar with topic 2 than with other topics. We have not yet completed our analysis of observational notes, so we are not able to say whether this resulted in any differences in search behavior. But it seems likely that without useful cues, searchers removed translations that they would have been better off keeping. If confirmed through further analysis, this may have implications for user training.

4.3 Small Collection Experiment

The results of the small collection experiment shown in Figure 7 are quite different. The situation is reversed for topic 1, with automatic now outperforming

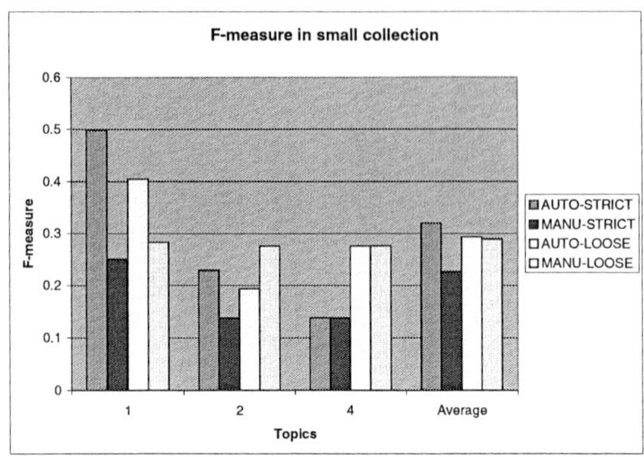

Fig. 7. $F_\alpha = 0.8$, small collection group, by conditions

manual, and topic 4 no longer discriminates between the two systems.[6] Overall, the manual and automatic systems could not be distinguished using loose relevance (0.2889 vs 0.2931), but the automatic system seemed to do better with strict relevance (0.2268 vs 0.3206). Again, we did not find that the difference is statistically significant. The data that we have analyzed does, however, seem to suggest that our manual system is better suited to cases in which there are a substantial number of relevant documents. We plan to use this question to guide some of our further data analysis.

4.4 Subjective Assessment

We analyzed questionnaire data and interview responses in an effort to understand how participants employed the systems and to better understand their impressions about the systems. Questionnaire responses are on a 1-5 scale (with 1 being "not at all," and 5 being "strongly agree").

Searchers in the large collection experiment reported that the manual and automatic systems were equally easy to search with (average 3.5), but searchers in the small collection experiment reported that the automatic system was easier to use than the manual system (3.4 vs. 2.75).

Searchers in the large collection experiment reported an equal need to reformulate their initial queries with both systems (average 3.25), but searchers in the small collection experiment reported that this was somewhat less necessary with the automatic system (3.9 vs. 4.1). One searcher, umd07 reported that it was "extremely necessary" to reformulate queries with both systems. We notice from his/her answers to our open questions that he/she thought the query translations were "usually very poor," and he/she would like both systems to support Boolean queries, proximity operators and truncations so that "noise" could be removed.

[6] Topic 3, with no relevant documents in the small collection, is not shown.

Searchers in the large collection experiment reported that they were able to find relevant documents more easily using the manual system than the automatic system (4.0 vs. 3.5), but searchers in the small collection experiment had the opposite opinion (2.6 vs. 3.0).

For questions unique to the manual system, the large collection group reported positive reactions to the usefulness of user-assisted query translation (with everyone choosing a value of 4). They generally felt that it was possible to identify unintended translations (an average of 3.5), and that most of the time the system provided appropriate translations (average of 3.9).

Most participants reported that they were not familiar with the topics, with topic 3 (European Campaigns against Racism) having the most familiarity, and topics 1 and 2 having the least.

4.5 Query Iteration Analysis

We determined the number of iterations for each search through log file analysis. In the large collection experiment, searchers averaged 9 query iterations per search across all conditions. Topic 2 had the largest number of iterations (averaging 16), topic 4 had the fewest (averaging 6). Topics 1 and 2 exhibited little difference in the average number of iterations across systems, but topics 3 and 4 had substantially fewer iterations with the manual system. In the small collection experiment, searchers performed substantially more iterations per search than in the large collection experiment, averaging 13 iterations per search across all conditions. Topic 2 again has the greatest number of iterations (averaging 16), while topic 1 had the fewest (averaging 8).

4.6 The Effect of the Number of Relevant Documents

The unexpected problem with indexing the SDA collection reduced the number of searchers that contributed to our official results, but it provided us with an extra dimension for our analysis. Searchers in the large collection and small collection experiments were generally drawn from the same population, were given the same topics, used the same systems, and performed the same tasks. The main difference is the nature of the collection that they searched, and in particular the number of relevant documents that were available to be found. Summarizing the results above from this perspective, we observed the following differences between the two experiments:

- Objectively, searchers seemed to achieve a better outcome measure with the manual system in the large collection experiment, but they seemed to do better with the automatic system in the small collection experiment.
- Subjectively, searchers preferred using the manual system in the large collection experiment, but they preferred the automatic system in the small collection experiment.
- Examining search behavior, we found that the average number of query refinement iterations per search was inversely correlated with the number of relevant documents.

We have not yet finished our analysis, but the preponderance of the evidence that is presently available suggests that collection characteristics may be an important variable in the design of interactive CLIR systems. We believe that this factor should receive attention in future work on this subject.

5 Conclusion and Future Work

We focused on supporting user participation in the query translation process, and tested the effectiveness of two types of cues—*back translation* and *keyword in context* in an interactive CLIR application. Our preliminary analysis suggests that together these cues can sometimes be helpful, but that the degree of utility that is obtained is dependent on the characteristics of the topic, the collection, and the available translation resources.

Our experiments suggest a number of promising directions for future work. First, mean average precision is a commonly reported measure for the quality of a ranked list (and, by extension, for the quality of the query that led to the creation of that ranked list). We have found that it is difficult to draw insights from MAP trajectories (variations across sequential query refinement iterations), in part because we do not yet have a good way to describe the strategies that a searcher might employ. We are presently working to characterize these strategies in a useful way, and to develop variants of the MAP measure (three of which were described above) that may offer additional insight. Second, our initial experiments with using KWIC for user-assisted query translation seem promising, but there are several things that we might improve. For example, it would be better if we could find the examples of usage in a comparable corpus (or even the Web) rather than a parallel corpus because parallel corpora are difficult to obtain. Finally, we observed far more query reformulation activity in this study than we had expected to see. Our present system provides some support for reformulation by allowing the user to see which query term translations are being used in the search. But we do not yet provide the searcher with any insight into the second half of that process—which German words correspond to potentially useful English terms that are learned by examining the translations? If we used the same resources for document translation as for query translation, this might not be a serious problem. But we don't, so it is an issue that we need to think about how to support.

The CLEF interactive track has proven to be an excellent source of insight into both system design and experiment design. We look forward to next year's experiments!

Acknowledgments

The authors would like to thank Julio Gonzalo and Fernando López-Ostenero for their tireless efforts to coordinate iCLEF. This work has been supported in part by DARPA cooperative agreement N660010028910.

References

[1] Ricardo Baeza-Yates and Berthier Ribeiro-Neto. *Modern Information Retrieval.* Addison Wesley, 1999.

[2] Douglas W. Oard and Anne Diekema. Cross-Language Information Retrieval. *Annual Review of Information Science and Technology*, 33:223–256, 1998.

[3] Douglas W. Oard, Gina-Anne Levow, and Clara I. Cabezas. CLEF Experiments at Maryland: Statistical Stemming and backoff translation. In C. Peters, editor, *Cross-Language Information Retrieval and Evaluation: Workshop of Cross-Language Evaluation Forum, CLEF 2000*, pages 176–187, Lisbon, Portugal, 2000.

[4] Ari Pirkola. The Effects of Query Structure and Dictionary Setups in Dictionary-Based Cross-Language Information Retrieval. In *Proceedings of the 21st Annual International ACM SIGIR Conference on Research and Development in Information Retrieval*, Melbourne, Australia, 1998. ACM.

[5] Jianqiang Wang and Douglas W. Oard. iCLEF 2001 at Maryland: Comparing Word-for-Word Gloss and MT. In C. Peters, M. Braschler, J. Gonzalo, and Kluck M, editors, *Evaluation of Cross-Language Information Retrieval Systems: Second Workshop of the Cross-Language Evaluation Forum, CLEF 2001*, pages 336–354, Darmstadt, Germany, 2001.

Interactive Cross-Language Searching: Phrases Are Better than Terms for Query Formulation and Refinement

Fernando López-Ostenero, Julio Gonzalo, Anselmo Peñas, and Felisa Verdejo

Departamento de Lenguajes y Sistemas Informáticos
Universidad Nacional de Educación a Distancia
Edificio Interfacultativo, C/ Juan del Rosal 16. 28040 Madrid, Spain
{flopez,julio,anselmo,felisa}@lsi.uned.es
http://nlp.uned.es/

Abstract. This paper summarizes the participation of the UNED group in the CLEF 2002 Interactive Track. We focused on interactive query formulation and refinement, comparing two approaches: a) a reference system that assists the user to provide adequate translations for terms in the query; and b) a proposed system that assists the user to formulate the query as a set of relevant phrases, and to select promising phrases in the documents to enhance the query. All collected evidence indicates that the phrase-based approach is preferable: the official $F_{\alpha=0.8}$ measure is 65% better for the proposed system, and all users in our experiment preferred the phrase-based system as a simpler and faster way of searching.

1 Introduction

In our second participation in the CLEF Interactive track, we have focused on assisted query formulation and refinement for cross-language searching. Previous experiments in this area have mainly concentrated on assisted query translation [4, 1]: for every term in the query, the system displays its possible translations with some information about the meaning of each candidate (via definitions in the source language or inverse translations). The user then selects the most appropriate translations, interacting with the system to overcome translation ambiguity.

Our hypothesis to be tested in iCLEF 2002 was twofold:

- Examining translations in an (unknown) foreign language is a high-load cognitive task, and therefore it is worth exploring alternative ways of assisting cross-language query formulations.
- Selecting relevant phrases for a topic should be easier and faster than selecting translations, and without human intervention phrases can be translated more accurately than individual terms.

In order to test our hypothesis, we have used:

C.A. Peters (Ed.): CLEF 2002, LNCS 2785, pp. 416–429, 2003.

- An Interactive Cross-Language system that helps users to provide accurate translations for query terms, based on the information provided by a reverse dictionary. This system is used as the reference one.
- An Interactive Cross-Language system that helps users to select appropriate phrases to describe their user needs, and translates phrases in a completely automatic way.
- A common document translation strategy for both systems based on our previous iCLEF findings [3].

In Section 2, we describe our experiment design. In Section 3, we discuss the outcome of the experiment, and in Section 4 we provide some conclusions.

2 Experiment Design

Our experiment consists of:

- Eight native Spanish speakers with null or very low English skills.
- The Spanish version of the four official iCLEF topics.
- The English CLEF 2002 document collection (LA Times 1994).
- A reference interactive cross-language search system based on assisted term translation (System WORDS).
- A proposed system based on noun-phrase selections (System PHRASES).
- The official iCLEF latin square to combine topics, searchers and systems into 32 different searching sessions.
- The official iCLEF search procedure.

In this section we describe the most relevant aspects of the above items.

2.1 Reference System

The reference system (WORDS) uses assisted query term translation and refinement throughout the search process:

- **Initial Query Formulation.** The system translates all content words in the Spanish iCLEF topic using a bilingual dictionary, and displays possible English translations to the user. When the user points to an English term, the system displays inverse translations into Spanish. This information can be used by the searcher to decide which translations to keep and which translations to discard before performing the first search. Figure 1 illustrates this initial step.
- **Cross-Language Search.** The system performs a monolingual search of the LA Times collection with the English terms selected by the user.
- **Ranked Document List.** The ranked list of documents displays the (translated) title of the document and a colour code to indicate whether each document has already been marked as *relevant*, *not relevant* or *unsure*. Figure 2 A shows a retrieved ranked list.

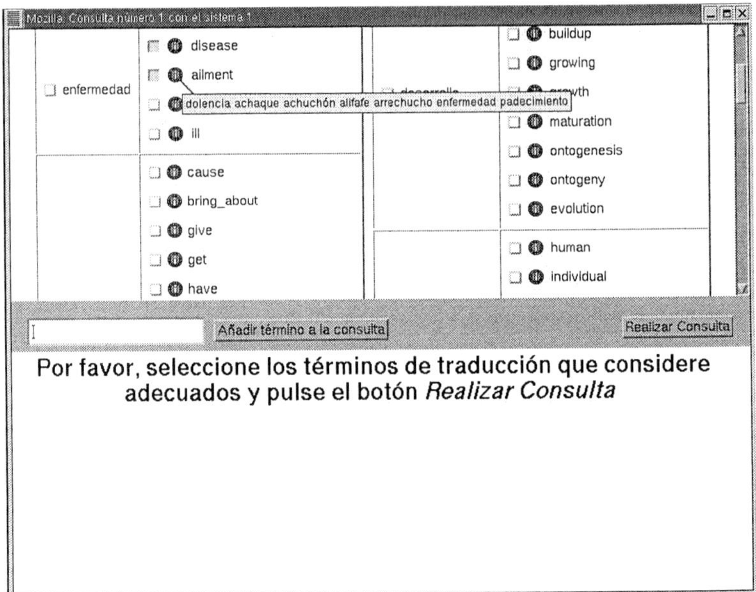

Fig. 1. Reference system (WORDS), initial assisted translation

- **Document Selection.** Instead of using Machine Translation to display the contents of a document, the system displays a cross-language summary consisting of the translation of all noun phrases in the body of the document, plus an MT (Systran Professional 3.0) translation of the title. The user can select the document as *relevant*, mark the document as *non-relevant* or *unsure*, or leave it unmarked.
- **Query Refinement by Selection.** When a Spanish term in a document translation corresponds to an original English term already in the query, the user can point to the Spanish term (highlighted); then the system points to the English query term, allowing for de-selection or selection of the English term (or some of its companion translations) or the original Spanish term (then all translations are disabled). Figure 2 B illustrates this process.
- **Additional Query Refinement.** Additionally, the user can also enter a single term at any time during the search. Again, the system displays its possible translations to the target language, along with their inverse translations, and permits individual selection and de-selection of translations.

2.2 Phrase-Based Searching

Our proposed system uses noun phrasal information throughout the Cross-Language assisted search process:

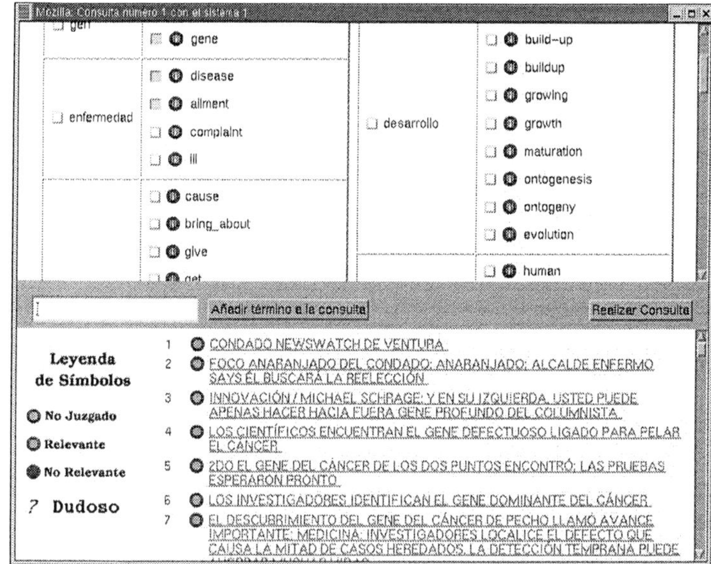

A) Colour codes in the ranked list indicate already judged documents.

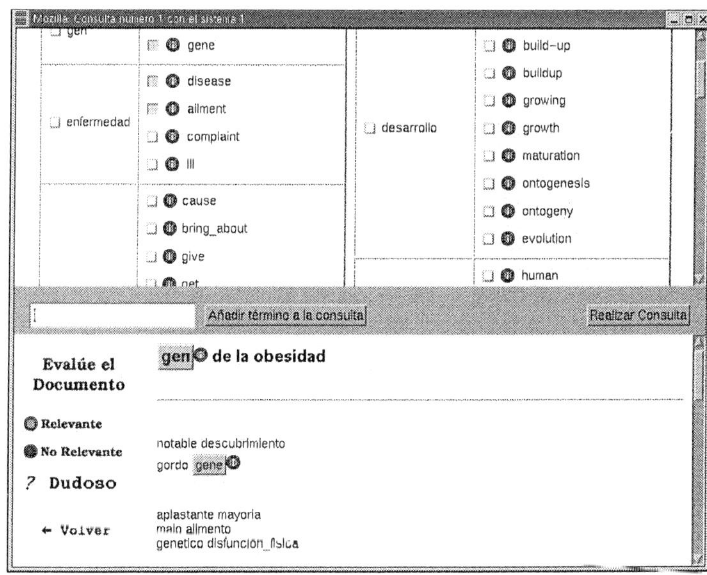

B) Clicking on a Spanish term in the document takes the user to the source English keyword matched.

Fig. 2. Reference system (WORDS): visualization of rankings and single documents

- **Initial Query Formulation.** The system extracts noun phrases from the full iCLEF topic, filters phrases with optimal translations, and displays the resulting set of phrases for user selection.
- **Cross-Language Search.** The system translates automatically the phrases selected by the user, and performs a monolingual search in the document collection.
- **Ranked Document List.** The ranked list is identical for both systems (see reference system above).
- **Document Selection.** Again, document selection is identical for both systems (see WORDS system above).
- **Query Refinement by Term Suggestion.** Optimally translated noun phrases in the documents can be selected to enrich the original query. When a user clicks on a noun-phrase in a document, the system automatically translates the noun-phrase and performs a new monolingual search with the enlarged query, updating the list of ranked documents. This process is illustrated in Figure 3.
- **Additional Query Refinement.** Identical in both systems (see system WORDS above).

In order to obtain this functionality, there is a pre-processing phase using shallow Natural Language Processing techniques, which has been described in detail in [3]. The essential steps are:

- Phrase indexing. Shallow parsing of two comparable collections (the CLEF Spanish and English collections in this case) to obtain an index of all noun phrases in both languages and their statistics.
- Phrase Alignment. Spanish and English noun phrases (up to three lemmas) are aligned for translation equivalents using only a bilingual dictionary and statistical information about phrases (see [3] for details). As a result of this step, aligned phrases receive a list of candidate phrase translations in decreasing order of frequency. The result is a pseudo bilingual dictionary of phrases that is used in all other translation steps. The statistics for the CLEF English-Spanish collection can be seen in Table 1.
- Document translation. All noun phrases are extracted and translated. Translation of each noun phrase is performed in two steps: first, maximal aligned subphrases are translated according to the alignment information. Then, the rest of the terms are translated using an estimation that selects target terms which overlap maximally with the set of related subphrases.

Only an additional step is required at searching time:

- Query translation. All Spanish phrases selected by the user are replaced by: 1) the most frequent aligned English phrase and 2) the second most frequent aligned phrase, if its frequency reaches a threshold of 80% of the most frequent one. The INQUERY `phrase` operator is used to formulate the final monolingual query with all English phrases. The search is then performed using the INQUERY search engine.

Mozilla: Consulta número 4 con el sistema 2

Seleccione las expresiones que desea incluir en la consulta

La consulta contiene 5 expresiones

atención al paciente
consecuencia de la huelga
caso de ataque
motivo de la huelga
huelga de hambre

Si lo desea puede añadir nuevos términos individuales a la consulta

Añadir término a la consulta
Realizar Consulta

Evalúe el Documento
Relevante
No Relevante
? Dudoso
← Volver

huelga de hambre en guatemala
derechos humanos
criminal acusaciones contra oficiales del ejército
jornada de trabajo
abogados estadounidenses

A) Clicking on best-aligned phrases incorporates them to the query.

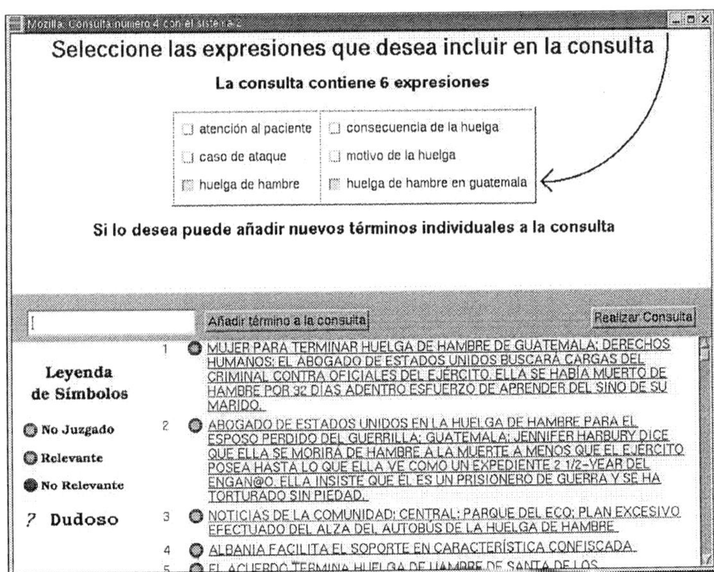

B) Results of clicking the phrase "huelga de hambre en Guatemala". The phrase is added to the query and a new ranked list is displayed.

Fig. 3. Proposed system (PHRASES): query expansion by clicking a phrase in a document

Table 1. Statistics of the phrase alignment algorithm (English-Spanish CLEF collection)

Phrase set	Extracted	Aligned
Spanish, 2 lemmas	6,577,763	2,004,760
Spanish, 3 lemmas	7,623,168	252,795
English, 2 lemmas	3,830,663	1,456,140
English, 3 lemmas	3,058,698	198,956

2.3 Data Collected

Every searcher performed 4 searches, one per iCLEF topic, alternating systems and topics according to the iCLEF latin square design. The time for each search was 20 minutes, and the overall time per searcher was around three hours, including training, questionnaires and searches (see [2] for details). For every user/topic/system combination, the following data were collected:

- The set of documents retrieved by the user, and the time at which every selection was made.
- The ranked lists produced by the system in each query refinement.
- The questionnaires filled-in by the user.
- An observational study of the search sessions.

3 Results

3.1 Official $F_{\alpha=0.8}$ Scores

The official iCLEF score for both systems is $F_{\alpha=0.8}$, which combines precision and recall over the set of manually retrieved documents, favoring precision. The results of our experiment can be seen in Table 3.1. Our proposed system (PHRASES) improves the reference system (WORDS) by a 65% increment. In a more detailed analysis per topic, it can be seen that topic 3 was too difficult and did not contribute to the results (no searcher found relevant documents with any of the systems). All the other topics receive a better F measure with the PHRASES system than with the WORDS system. The difference is not dramatic for topics 1 (+11%) and 2 (+8%), but it is very drastic for topic 4, which seemed easy using the PHRASES system and almost impossible with the WORDS system.

The most important expression in Topic 4 is "hunger strikes" (the description is "documents will report any information relating to a hunger strike attempted in order to attract attention to a cause"). Searchers using the PHRASES system easily select "huelga de hambre" (the Spanish equivalent) from the displayed options, and the aligned translation (which is, in turn, "hunger strikes") will retrieve useful documents. Searchers using the WORDS system, however, find that

Table 2. Official results

Overall $F_{\alpha=0.8}$ per system

System	$F_{\alpha=0.8}$
WORDS	.23
PHRASES	**.37 (+65%)**

Average $F_{\alpha=0.8}$ per topic/system

Topic	WORDS	**PHRASES**
1	.57	**.64 (+11%)**
2	.28	**.31 (+8%)**
3	0	**0**
4	.0005	**.55 (+110400%)**

$F_{\alpha=0.8}$ per topic/searcher/system combination

Searcher\Topic	**1**	**2**	**3**	**4**	**Av.**
1	0.62	**0.44**	**0**	0.07	0.28
2	0.55	**0**	**0**	0	0.14
3	**0.62**	0.35	0	**0.56**	0.38
4	**0.64**	0.49	0	**0.65**	0.45
5	**0.66**	0.15	**0**	0.08	0.22
6	**0.62**	0.14	**0**	0.08	0.21
7	0.56	**0.51**	0	**0.44**	0.38
8	0.56	**0.27**	0	**0.56**	0.35
Av.	0.6	0.29	0	0.31	0.3

(System WORDS in normal font, System **PHRASES** in **bold font**)

"huelga" (strike) and "hambre" (hunger) may receive many possible translations into English. Looking at the average F_α, it is obvious that they do not manage to find the appropriate translations for both terms, failing to match relevant documents.

3.2 Additional Data

Besides the official F_α result, there are many other sources of evidence to compare both systems: additional quantitative data (time logs, ranked results for every query refinement), questionnaires filled by participants, and the observation study of their search sessions. We discuss that additional evidence here.

Searching Behavior over Time. The plot of document selections against time in Figure 4 provides interesting evidence about search behavior:

Searchers begin selecting documents much faster with the PHRASES system (8 selections made in minute one) than with the WORDS system (the first selection for any topic is made in minute 3). The obvious explanation is that initial query formulation is very simple in the PHRASES system (select a few phrases in the native language), compared to the WORDS system (examining many foreign-language candidate translations per term and selecting them using inverse dictionary evidence).

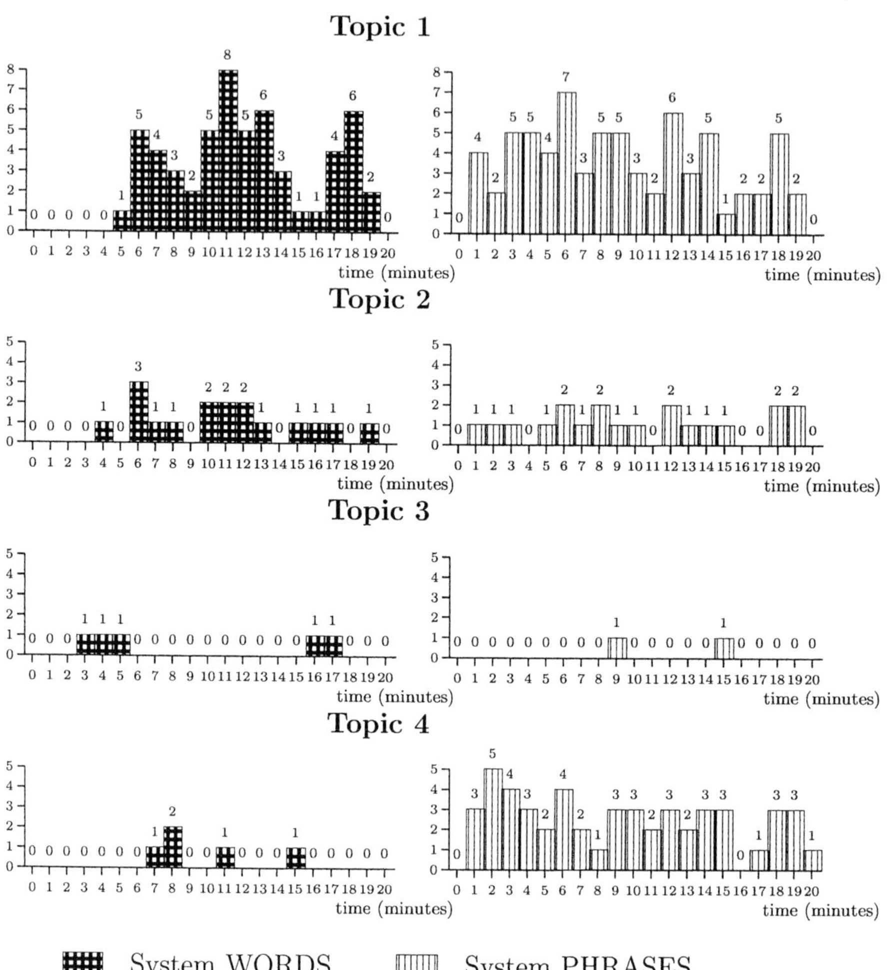

Fig. 4. Distribution of number of documents selected by users across time

Evolution of Query Refinements. In Table 3 we can see the average time used by the searchers to construct the initial query, the average precision of the top-20 documents retrieved by this first query and the number of query refinements made by the searchers for both systems.

In Figures 5, 6 and 7, the precision of the top-20 ranked documents retrieved at every refinement step is shown for topics 1, 2 and 4 (no relevant document was found for topic 3).

Some observations can be made:

– The initial precision (i.e. the precision after initial query formulation) is 50% higher for the PHRASES system, in spite of the substantially larger

Table 3. Time versus Precision

System	Avg.Time first query	Initial precision	# of Refinements
WORDS	286.13 seconds	.19%	70
PHRASES	44.25 seconds **(-85%)**	.29% (+**50.82%**)	142 (+**102%**)

time spent by searchers in the WORDS query formulation. This confirms that a good initial selection of native-language phrases can provide accurate translations of the topic terms.
- Searchers perform many more query refinements with the PHRASES system, confirming that it is easier to enhance the query using phrases selected from documents.
- Searchers obtain occasional precision figures of 1, .95, .90, etc. using the PHRASES system, while the highest precision obtained with WORDS is .75 for topic 1, searcher 1.

Overall, the additional quantitative data strongly support our initial hypothesis.

Analysis of Questionnaires. The answers supplied by the eight searchers strongly support our hypothesis. All of them stated that the PHRASES system was easier to learn, easier to user and better overall. They appreciated both the possibility to select phrases rather than individual terms, and most of them added that it was much better not to see English terms at any moment. A general claim was that the dictionary had too many translations for each term.

Observational Study. A careful observation of searchers' behavior is in agreement with the above results. Some points are worth commenting:

- Users get discouraged with terms that have a lot of alternative translations in the WORDS system. Even if a term is important for the topic, they try to avoid its translation when there are many options available.
- Selecting foreign-language terms is perceived as a hard task; when no relevant documents are found after a few iterations, users get discouraged with the WORDS system.
- The refinement loop works well for the PHRASES system once relevant documents begin to appear. However, if relevant documents do not appear soon, the initial query refinements are not obvious and both systems are equally hard. This is the case of topic 3.
- The automatic translation of phrases may be harmful when the aligned equivalent is incorrect. This is the case of "búsqueda de tesoros", which does not receive a correct translation ("treasure hunting") and it is the most important concept for Topic 2. The problem is that users do not detect that

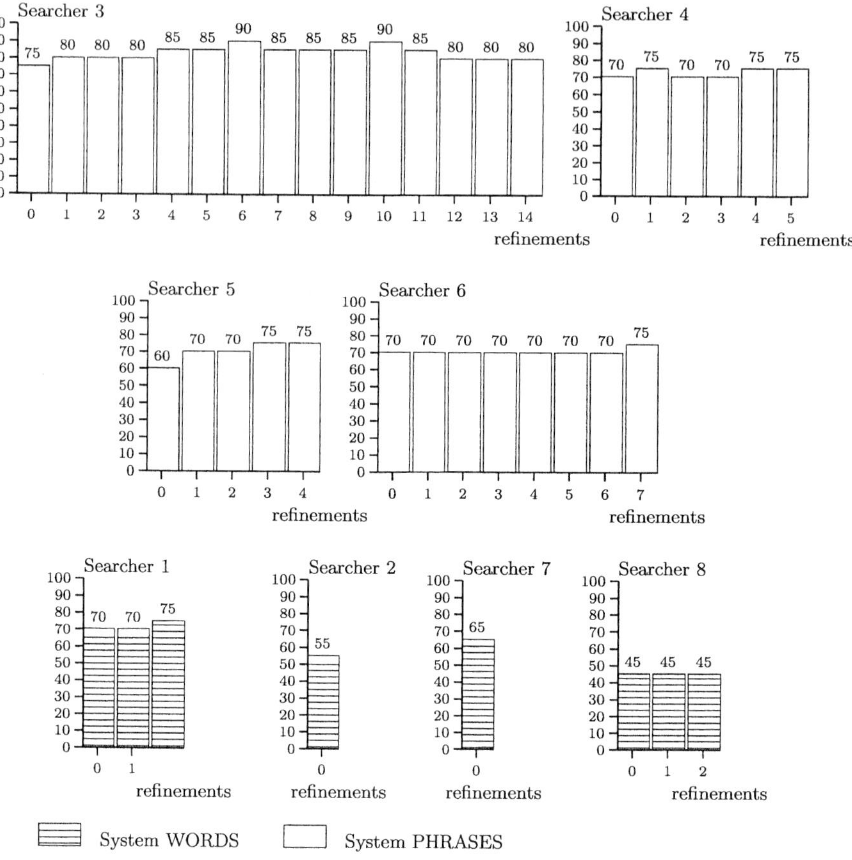

Fig. 5. Precision across iterative refinements for Topic 1

the translation is incorrect; they simply think that there is no match in the collection for such concept.
- The difficulty of topic 3 (campaigns against racism in Europe) comes from the fact that the LA Times collection does not refer to any of such campaigns as generically "European", and the overwhelming majority of documents about racism are US-centered.

Statistical Analysis. A non trivial issue is how to measure statistical significance on our data. We have chosen linear mixed-effects models [5] as the most adequate to describe iCLEF data. Linear mixed effects models are similar to linear models, but permit to distinguish between the system effect that we seek to detect (a *fixed effect* of the model) and the combined searcher/topic/system effect that we wish to suppress (*random effects* in the model).

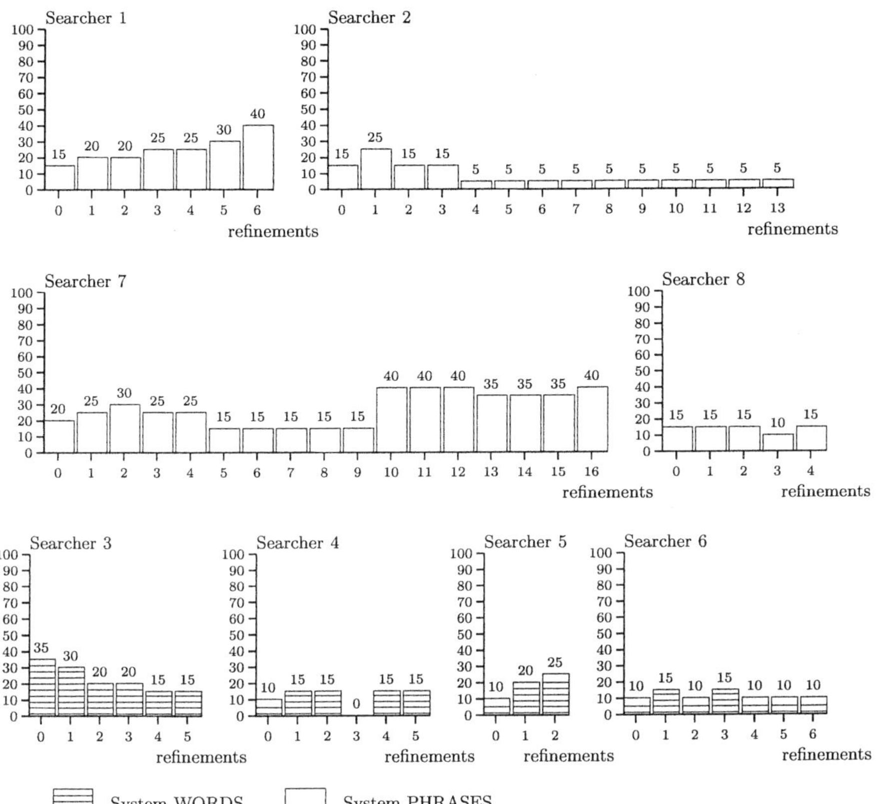

Fig. 6. Precision across iterative refinements for Topic 2

The linear mixed-effects model that best fits the data according to standard normality tests is

$$F_{\alpha=0.8}\tilde{}Query * System, random = \tilde{}1 + Query|User$$

where $F_{\alpha=0.8}$, as outcome variable, depends on two coupled fixed effects of $Query$ and $System$, and the $User$ is a random effect coupled with the $Query$.

The prediction of this model has a 0.995 correlation with the data, once topic 3 and user 2 (which are clear outliers) are removed from the data. The application of ANOVA on the model gives $p = 0.039$ for the difference in $F_{\beta=0.5}$ between both systems, hence the result is statistically significant at the standard $p < 0.05$ level.

4 Conclusions

We have obtained multiple evidence (quantitative data, user opinions and observational study confirming) that a phrase-based approach to cross-language query

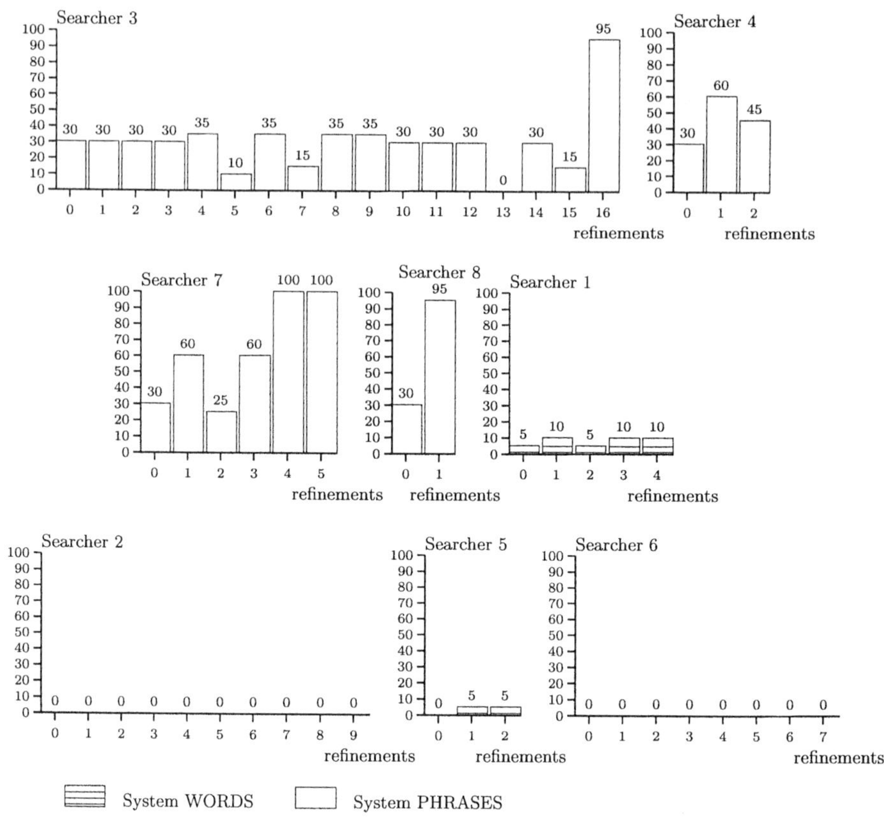

Fig. 7. Precision across iterative refinements for Topic 4

formulation and refinement, without user-assisted translation, can be easier to use and more effective than assisted term by term translation. Of course, this is not an absolute conclusion, if only because our reference system offered only crude help for term-by-term translation (inverse translations using a bilingual dictionary). Probably a more sophisticated translation assistance would stretch the differences between approaches. But we believe that a valid conclusion, in any case, is that language barriers are perceived as a strong impediment by users, and it is worth studying strategies of Cross-Language Search Assistance keeping a strictly monolingual interface for the user.

Acknowledgements

This work has been funded by the Spanish *Comisión Interministerial de Ciencia y Tecnología*, project *Hermes* (TIC2000-0335-C03-01).

References

[1] G. Erbach, Günter Neumann, and Hans Uszkoreit. MULINEX: Multilingual indexing, navigation and editing extensions for the world-wide web. In *AAAI Symposium on Cross-Language Text and Speech Retrieval*, 1997.
[2] J. Gonzalo and D. Oard. The CLEF 2002 interactive track. In *Evaluation of Cross-Language Information Retrieval Systems. Proceedings of CLEF 2001: revised papers*, Springer-Verlag LNCS 2406, 2002.
[3] F. López-Ostenero, J. Gonzalo, A. Peñas, and F. Verdejo. Noun-phrase translations for cross-language document selection. In *Proceedings of CLEF 2001*, 2001.
[4] W. Ogden, J. Cowie, M. Davis, E. Ludovic, S. Nirenburg, H. Molina-Salgado, and N. Sharples. Keizai: An interactive cross-language text retrieval system. In *Proceeding of the MT SUMMIT VII Workshop on Machine Translation for Cross Language Information Retrieval*, 1999.
[5] José C. Pinheiro and Douglas M. Bates. *Mixed-Effects Models in S and S-PLUS*. Springer, 2000.

Exploring the Effect of Query Translation when Searching Cross-Language

Daniela Petrelli, George Demetriou, Patrick Herring, Micheline Beaulieu, and Mark Sanderson

University of Sheffield
Regent Court - 211 Portobello Street, S10 4DP, Sheffield, UK
{d.petrelli,m.beaulieu,m.sanderson}@shef.ac.uk
{g.demetriou,p.herring}@dcs.shef.ac.uk

Abstract. A usability study of Clarity, a cross language information retrieval system for rare languages, is presented. Clarity aims at investigating CLIR for so-called *low-density* languages, those with few translation resources. The usability study explored two different levels of feedback and control over the query translation mechanism. Techniques like word-by-word translation of title and keywords were also tested. Although it would appear that a greater control over query translation enables users to retrieve more relevant documents a great difference among participants, topics, and tasks was discovered. Indeed the user engagement with the searching task is extremely subjective and variable, thus affecting the homogeneity of the results and preventing any statistical validity. A revision of the current evaluation schema is important to get a better understanding of user-CLIR interaction and some issues on different ways of measuring user's performance are outlined in this perspective.

1 Introduction

The user interface is the means by which the user controls the IR system: decisions and supervision has to be left to the human. This statement seems also well supported by empirical evidence in query expansion [6], and relevance feedback [2]. In CLIR, researchers assume that users will type the query in their own language (*source language*), the system translates it to the document language (*target language*) and performs the retrieval [7]. Controlling a CLIR system means that the user checks the query translation first and searches next; thus there are two separated tasks. This vision has been implemented in CLIR systems so far (e.g. Arctos [8] and Mulinex [4]) and the user's main job is to disambiguate translations coming from words with multiple senses.

Following this well traced path, the first Clarity interface design adopted this two steps CLIR interaction. A transparent user interface would show how the system translates the query terms and would allow users to modify, update and correct the

C.A. Peters (Ed.): CLEF 2002, LNCS 2785, pp. 430-445, 2003.

translation before the search would be actually performed. However before implementing this solution, a user study was conducted to understand users and uses of CLIR [9]. Requiring the user to check the query translation was often criticized. A full control was not a requirement by most of the observed/interviewed users and they seemed to care about the system's internal mechanisms only when the retrieval was unsuccessful. Only in those situations users seemed to be interested in discovering what the system did and to eventually correct its behavior (or modify their query).

New system features were listed as important and the user interface was redesigned. The new interface contradicted the first solution by hiding the query translation. Moreover query translation and search were collapsed in a single step. This decision was supported by the observation that if a CLIR engine works fine, it is able to disambiguate the query by itself and to retrieve mainly the relevant documents. In the unlucky case of a single word query with multiple senses the user can identify the problem by browsing the result and reformulate the query exactly as it happens in all current search engines.

The new design was considered to be more effective, but the choice of hiding the query translation was discordant respect to the unusual practice [7, 8, 4]. Thus the participation of the University of Sheffield in Interactive CLEF aimed at ascertain if the query translation should be "hided" or "shown" considering both the system performance and the user preference. A user experiment was set up in the context of the Clarity system, described in the next section 2. Section 3 presents the experiment planning while the procedure used follows in section 4. Results are presented and discussed in section 5. Finally conclusions are drawn in section 6.

2 The System Test-Bed

The University of Sheffield participated in the Interactive track of CLEF 2002 with the prototype under development in the Clarity project. Clarity is a EU funded project aiming at investigating cross-language information retrieval for so-called *low-density* languages, those with few translation resources. CLIR between English and Finnish is considered here even though Clarity includes also Swedish, Latvian and Lithuanian.

The whole Clarity prototype was used and this session outlines its architecture and user interface at the time of the experiment.

2.1 The Architecture

Accessing and analysing data in different languages requires integration of a variety of physically distributed information sources and software services. Clarity is physically distributed with the user interface and few correlated services in the UK (at the University of Sheffield) and the cross-language retrieval core in Finland (query translation and searching performed at the University of Tampere). SOAP[1] services facilitated communication between the two sites. The tested prototype can translate queries from English into Finnish and search documents in both English and Finnish

---

[1] SOAP is Simple Object Access Protocol: http://www.w3.org/TR/soap12/

at the same time. For iCLEF, the search was limited to only Finnish documents, thus the user typed a query in English and retrieved documents in Finnish.

Clarity is designed as a three-layer system (Figure 1) with the user interface as a front-end (*Interface Layer*), the data sources and services on the back-end (*Application Layer*) and a middle layer that separates the interface from the system services and provides the communication between them (*Communication Layer*).

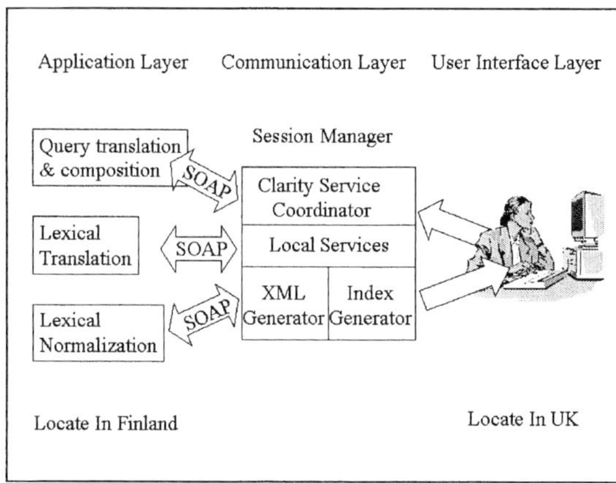

Fig. 1. Clarity architecture

The Application Layer incorporates all the processes necessary for efficient CLIR interaction. These processes are modelled as web services (i.e. services that can be accessed over the Internet using HTTP) - henceforth called Clarity services - and included:

- Document retrieval services: Clarity uses the Inquery retrieval engine developed by the University of Massachusetts for text collections in Finnish and English.
  - Query processing services: These include services for the translation and formulation of the source query. For example, the query "mad cow disease BSE" is translated to Finnish and formulated using Inquery operators as:

```
#sum( #syn( hullu mielipuolinen mielenvikainen mieletön järjetön
            kaistapäinen pähkähullu sekapäinen hurja äkäinen
            raivostunut raivopäinen raivo suuttua julmistua)
      #syn( lehmä naaras pelotella ikuisesti)
      #syn( sairaus tauti vika vitsaus)
      #syn( bse hullu))
```

- Term information services: These include services about the translation of a term from one language to another, its normalisation (in terms of lemmatisation or compound morphology) as well as frequency information about the occurrence of the term in the document collection.

The services in the Application layer (provided by the University of Tampere) have been modelled as SOAP services that are accessed by SOAP clients in the Communication Layer.

The Communication Layer acts as a communicator and a data integrator between the interface and the Clarity services. At its core is the *Clarity Session Manager* that currently consists of four components:

- **Service Coordinator** analyses the interface requests and route transactions to the appropriate Clarity services; for example, the request for "100 documents in English and Finnish for the English query X" would result in the original query X being routed to the translation service first and then to the retrieval service in order to retrieve the texts.
- **XML Generator:** the information generated during a Clarity interaction is stored locally in XML; XML serves to provide a uniform representation of session data that may be extensible in future and which can also act as a local 'cache' in order to speed up the interaction[2].
- **Interface Content Generator** generates the necessary information to the user interface, for instance, the document language, the document title and its translation, the query terms found in the document, the document location in the file system etc.
- **Local Services Component**: for efficiency reasons some of the Clarity services have been moved from the Application Layer (where they were initially) to the Communication Layer so that repetitive tasks, such as tokenisation, term normalisation and translation, will not cause significant delays to the system interaction[3].

The User Interface Layer includes the Clarity graphical interface and the associated indexes and temporary files created during the interaction. The interface component parses the meta-data index generated by the Interface Content Generator and dynamically reformats the corresponding information to HTML for display on a web browser.

---

[2] At the time of writing (November 2002), the use of XML in Clarity has been rather limited as CLIR is restricted to two target languages only, but we believe that XML will prove to be useful as more languages, text databases and services are gradually added to the system.

[3] As an example, for a set of 500 Finnish texts approximately 150,000 terms may need to be morphologically analysed, translated and transported over HTTP per request.

2.2 The User Interface

The Clarity user interface (figure 2) is composed of two parts: query formulation and result presentation. The query formulation area on the top allows the user to select the source and the target languages, to limit the search to documents produced in a certain time period, and to decide the number of documents to be retrieved (10, 20, 50 or 100). For the experiment discussed in this paper English was used as source language while Finnish was the target language. However Clarity can search many languages at the same time and retrieve, for example, English and Finnish documents simultaneously. The query formulation area includes the display of the query translation when this is shown, see figure 3 below.

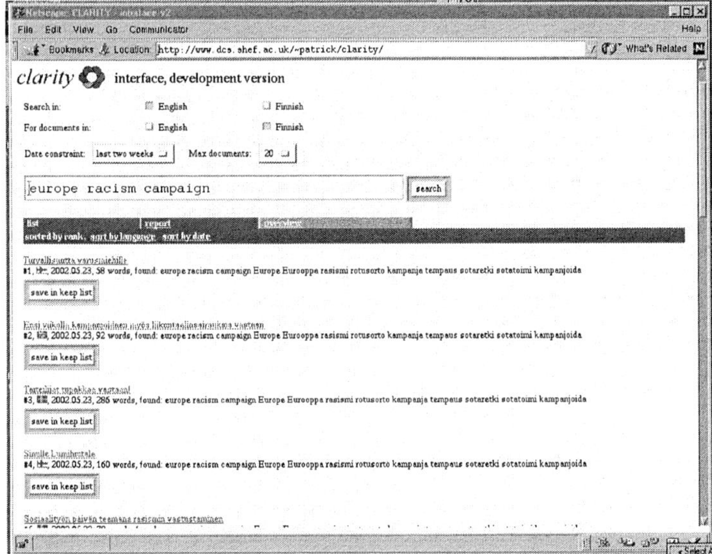

Fig. 2. The Clarity User Interface

The search result is displayed immediately below the query formulation area. Clarity target users are polyglots, people who know the languages they are searching, thus document or title translation are not needed. As a result the ranked list is minimalistic and encompasses the title and few other essential information.

However, one of the Interactive CLEF requirements was to recruit participants who do not know the language they are searching. Therefore the result presentation was modified to support this user class and further information on the document was introduced, as shown in figure 3 and 4. The original title in Finnish was complemented with a translation into English. The translation used a word-by-word mechanism; multiple translations for a single word were displayed in sequence separated by commas. This pseudo-translation could be long and not very precise, for example with polysemic words, since all the possible translations were displayed independently from how plausible they were. As a further aid for relevance judgement a list of keywords was extracted from the Finnish documents; those keywords were displayed with the corresponding translation into English for each document in the ranked list. Keywords were selected in the index file among those highly frequent in the document but rare in the collection. Finally a list of supposed proper names was provided; the criteria adopted was to select words that were not in the dictionary and had some graphics features, e.g. start with a capital letter.

3 Planning the Experiment

3.1 Questions

The Clarity interface designed after the user study hides the translation mechanisms in favour of a simpler layout and interaction. The CLIR engine was trusted to be robust enough to support a *delegation* from the user to the system and did not require a *supervision* of the user over the system query translation. Delegation and supervision imply different interaction styles and a different philosophy for CLIR:

- **Delegation**: the user inputs the query, the system translates the query and searches without any user intervention (1 step CLIR), showed in fig. 3.
- **Supervision**: the user inputs the query, the query translation is shown by the system, the user verifies and/or modifies the query, and the system searches (2 steps CLIR), showed in fig.4 [4].

The choice of a delegation paradigm for Clarity was well motivated by the result of the study, but it might be that the cross-language technology is not yet robust enough to support a fully automatic CLIR. On the user side, supervising the query translation offers a minimum understanding of the CLIR process and could mitigate the uncertainty related to not knowing the target language.

On the contrary, if the system would perform equally well in both delegation or supervision mode (i.e. no significant difference) the simpler interaction (i.e. delegation) should be considered as the best design choice.

3.2 Conditions

Two different interfaces were implemented for the test. Both layouts were based on the Clarity interface described in 2.2 and were kept as much similar as possible to avoid the interface design biasing the result. The only difference was in the control the user had on the query-translation process.

---

[4] This layout keeps the essence of the query translation check-and-revision step though, if revision is required, the user has to go back to the query input line and re-type the query.

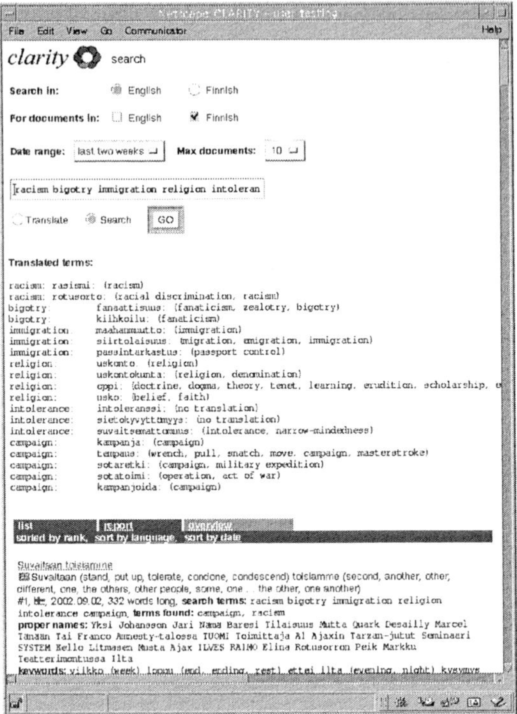

Fig. 3. The layout that forces translation check (Supervision)

In the supervision condition (S) (Figure 3) the user's first task is to check the query translated from English into Finnish; changes have to be done by writing in the query box. Each query term is English is listed below the search box; each term is translated in Finnish and back-translation into English (in brackets) to show alternative meanings for the same word. Multiple senses of the same word are listed one after the other. Figure 3 shows such an interface with the query "racism bigotry immigration religion intolerance campaign" translated and listed.

When the user is satisfied with the query translation, they select "search" and click "go" for the actual retrieval. The retrieved documents are displayed in a tab as described above in 2.2.

In the delegation condition (D) (Figure 4), the query translation is not displayed and the search runs immediately. To reduce the differences between the two layouts, a button to display the query translation on top of the ranked list was added. When clicked the query translation is displayed (as in fig. 3), however the search is automatically performed and cannot be interrupted.

3.3 Design

As required by iCLEF, a within subject design was adopted (i.e. each participant used both interfaces) and a Latin square matrix was used to counterbalance the learning effect.

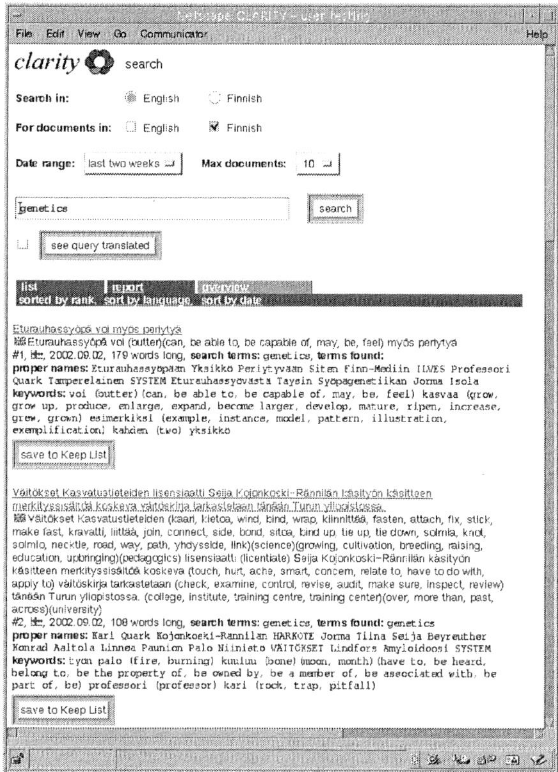

Fig. 4. The layout that hides the translation (Delegation)

Participants were required to type query in English and retrieve documents written in Finnish; from the retrieved set they were required to select those relevant for the topic in hand. This relevance judgement (e.g. documents marked as relevant) was the main measure required by iCLEF. However other objective and subjective measures were collected. A log containing queries, translations, retrieved documents, relevance judgements, and a few other data was automatically recorded while the interaction was going on. Time was not considered a reliable measure for performance due to the fact that accessing a remote service in Finland did not assure a constant time across users, however a time stamp was recorded in the log.

Several questionnaires were used throughout the experiment to collect subjective data. All were designed to get the strength of agreement with a clear statement (a 5 point Likert scale), as for "I always understand why a document has been retrieved" with the scale from "strongly disagree" to "strongly agree". While the questionnaires filled after the tasks completion aimed at collecting opinions on topics and systems, the preliminary one was designed to gather information about user expertise with computer and search and to figure out their general attitude to IR.

Whenever possible, participants were videotaped or observed by the experimenter in order to collect additional information about the interaction.

4 Running the Experiment

4.1 Participants

Four people (students and research associates) recruited at the departments of Information Studies and Computer Sciences participated in the experiment. They were paid £15 for their participation. All participants were English native speakers and none of them had any (passive or active) knowledge of Finnish. All considered themselves good or expert computer users (mean= 4.26, sd= 0.96) and fair searchers (mean= 3.75, sd= 0.5), searched the web often (mean= 4.50, sd= 1), seldom the library (mean= 3.75, sd= 0.5), and rarely other DB (mean= 2.25, sd= 1.26).

Participant attitude toward searching seems to be positive with respect to the search task: they were confident they would find what they were looking for (mean=4.33, sd=0.52), and feel in control of the search process (mean=3.83, sd=0.41). Opinions were less homogeneous when addressing the need for help in formulating a query (mean=2.5, sd=1.05) or the understanding of the reason for retrieving a certain document (mean=3.5, sd=1.05). Also the perception of the "advanced" or "Boolean" search was not straightforward: it seemed those were considered powerful tools (mean=3.84, sd=0.75) but rarely used (mean=3.5, sd=0.84).

4.2 Procedure

Participants used the computers available in the student laboratory and used the system in parallel. At arrival, users received a page describing the experiment and its purpose, and a questionnaire to measure their attitude to IR (commented briefly above). Subjects were required to use English as source language and Finnish as target language. A training query with both systems was done first, then participants conducted two searches on each system. Users were provided with a context-based scenario that described the task [3]. They were asked to move interesting documents from the ranked list to a "keep list" and then to judge those as "highly relevant", "somewhat relevant", or "not relevant".

After each search, participants filled in a questionnaire: topic familiarity, difficulties in query formulation or judgment, and confidence were the questions addressed. Opinions about the system were collected after the two tasks were completed; a further questionnaire comparing the two systems was filled at the end.

5 Results and Discussion

A great variation in performance among users and topics was discovered and is discussed below. For clearness the 4 participants are addressed as P_1, P_2, ... and the topic as T_1 for C053 on "genes and disease", T_2 for C065 on "treasure hunting", T_3 for C056 on "European campaign against racism", and T_4 for C080 on "hunger strike".

5.1 Precision, Recall, and F-measure

Results returned by iCLEF are in Table 1 below showing low *F* scores for both interface conditions. On closer examination, it was discovered that our submission was wrongly formatted, which had a profound affect on the official result.

Table 1. Official iCLEF results

System	F
Delegation	0.081
Supervised	0.061

Fortunately, sufficiently detailed logs of all user interactions were available and a recalculation was possible. Differently from the official result that considered only "highly relevant" documents, those judged as "somewhat relevant" were included in the measurement. Table 2 summarises the mean P and R for the two systems.

Table 2. Precision, Recall and F measure respect to the system

System	P	R	$F_{0.8}$
Delegation	0.21	0.16	0.20
Supervised	0.24	0.43	0.26

From this table it seems that the condition S slightly overcomes D. However P and R consider the interaction as a single unit, whereas it is important to distinguish the query formulation by the relevance judgement step. Indeed to identify relevant documents in the pool of retrieved can be challenging when the target language is unknown to the user and the document translation is limited. In our case the word-by-word translation of the title and of the extracted keywords may not be sufficient to support an accurate judgement of the Finnish documents. Therefore there is the need to measure the two steps separately.

Now precision and recall have been calculated for the query formulation step respect to the pool of documents retrieved. The result is reported in Table 3.

Table 3. Precision and Recall of the query formulation task

	Topic 1	Topic 2	Topic 3	Topic 4
Participant 1	(with S) P=0.5 R=0.7	(with D) P=0.11 R=0.18	(with D) P=0.31 R=0.35	(with S) 0
Participant 2	(with S) P=0.13 R=0.17	(with D) P=0.03 R=0.01	(with D) P=0.2 R=0.23	(with S) 0
Participant 3	(with D) P=0.14 R=0.05	(with S) P=0.17 R=0.36	(with S) P=0.2 R=0.23	(with D) 0
Participant 4	(with D) P=0.5 R=0.17	(with S) P=0.26 R=0.54	(with S) P=0.18 R=0.58	(with D) 0

It should be noted that none of the users were able to retrieve any relevant documents for T_4. This of course negatively affected the global rating but do not affect the comparison. But the variability is not limited to the topics, it affects users too. The same user can be very effective while searching a topic (e.g. P_1 in T_1) whereas performing very poorly in another (e.g. P_1 in T_2). Variation is not related to a system in particular, since it T_1 participant P_1 was successful with system S while participant P_4 was successful using system D. This high variability prevented any statistics. However a quantitative analysis offer a useful insight on the user-CLIR interaction.

To analyse the user performance in the relevance judgement task only the retrieved set of document was used and the following measures were applied:

- **Correct Selection**: relevant document properly detected out of the set retrieved (indicated with $+R_j$ in Table 4).
- **Mistaken Selection**: non-relevant document judged as relevant (indicated with $-R_j$ in Table 4).

Table 4 below reports these data (the number of relevant documents per topic is reported in the top row). It shows that users correctly detected only 28 relevant documents out of the 55 retrieved. Worst, the number of non-relevant documents selected as relevant is high (61 mistaken selections) and double the number of relevant documents correctly identified (28). It is clear from this result that selecting a document in a unknown language is a big problem and the solution adopted, title and keywords translated, was not sufficient.

This result is also important from a methodological point of view. In fact the correct selection is at the basis of the calculation of P and R for the general system performance. Thus it might appear a system is very poor in retrieving while the problem is limited to the document display and does not affect the retrieval mechanisms. In other words a problem at the interface level may be mistaken for a problem in the search.

Table 4. Successes and failures in relevance judgement

	Topic 1 (RD=17)	**Topic 2 (RD=11)**	**Topic 3 (RD=17)**	**Topic 4 (RD=11)**
Participant 1	(with S) $+R_j$= 10/12 $-R_j$=6	(with D) $+R_j$= 0/2 $-R_j$=8	(with D) $+R_j$= 2/6 $-R_j$= 9	(with S) 0 $-R_j$=4
Participant 2	(with S) $+R_j$= 0/2 $-R_j$=2	(with D) $+R_j$= 0/1 $-R_j$=3	(with D) $+R_j$= 2/4 $-R_j$= 4	(with S) 0 $-R_j$=0
Participant 3	(with D) $+R_j$= 1/1 $-R_j$=4	(with S) $+R_j$= 1/4 $-R_j$=1	(with S) $+R_j$= 2/4 $-R_j$ = 2	(with D) 0 $-R_j$=5
Participant 4	(with D) $+R_j$= 1/3 $-R_j$= 2	(with S) $+R_j$=4/6 $-R_j$= 4	(with S) $+R_j$= 5/10 $-R_j$= 3	(with D) 0 $-R_j$= 4

Table 4 also highlight differences among searchers and tasks. Two participants were extremely successful in searching specific tasks: P_1 in T_1 and P_4 in T_3. Looking at the log it is clear P_1 and P_4 found a "killer query" that retrieved an high number of relevant documents. However, an extremely successful query can be very similar to an unsuccessful one. For example the query used by P_1 in T_1 was "gene DNA disease" that retrieved 9 relevant documents out of 10 while "DNA genetics disorders" formulated by P_4 retrieved only 2 relevant documents out of 10. This analysis done at the query is important to understand what went wrong in the interaction and how Clarity could be improved, e.g. by introducing a query expansion.

5.2 Other Measures

The logs give the possibility of analysing the interaction from a different perspective than P and R alone. Here for each task we consider:

- number of queries, Q;
- number of different terms used, T;
- average query length, L;
- total number of documents retrieved (including duplications), D;
- number of relevant document retrieved, D_r;
- number of relevant document detected (correctly judged), D_j;
  as a measure of the engagement of participants with the search task.

Table 5 reports these engagement measures; for each participant the sequence of the tasks as performed is given. It shows that there is a great variation among the different participants, as between P_1 and P_2 for example. Variation occurs also for the same user between tasks done earlier or later, as for P_3 who has a high engagement in task T_1 and T_4 done at the beginning and far less in task T_3 and T_2 done at the end. Similarly participant P_4 has a good performance in the first two tasks (T_2 and T_3) that drops for the last two (T_4 and T_1). The variation between participants can be due to a different search expertise, however the answers of P_3 in the IR attitude questionnaire do not differ from those of the other participants. The variation of behaviour in the same user is easily explained considering that the whole experiment lasted 3 hours and tiredness and boredom become important issues as time passed. It would be interesting to see if any correlation exists between low-engagement and poor performances. For this some criteria to summarise user performance and user engagement in a single value needs to be defined first. This is considered future work.

5.3 Observations

An analysis of the queries formulated by the participants showed the training session, not used in iCLEF, was a good representation of what the users try when approaching an unknown search system. Specifically, the 2 participants who trained with the D system first both modified the query before any search was run, for example "green power" was discarded in favour of "wind turbine". The reason can be the fact that both "green" and "power" have many senses; the long list of possible meanings pushed participants to be more precise. In other cases good words were discarded because the translation dictionary did not have the entry, e.g. for "Alzheimer"; if this term had been used, the system would have successfully retrieved relevant documents since proper names are passed unchanged to the search engine.

Table 5. Engagement with the search task

	Topic 1 (RD=17)	Topic 2 (RD=11)	Topic 3 (RD=17)	Topic 4 (RD=11)
Participant 1	(with S)	(with D)	(with D)	(with S)
T1	Q= 8	Q= 13	Q= 8	Q= 14
T4	T= 9	T= 17	T= 10	T= 14
T3	L= 2.5	L= 2.07	L= 1.87	L= 2.78
T2	D= 80	D= 130	D= 80	D= 140
	D_r= 12	D_r= 2	D_r= 6	D_r= 0
	D_i= 10	D_i= 0	D_i= 2	D_i= 0
Participant 2	(with S)	(with D)	(with D)	(with S)
T2	Q= 3	Q= 3	Q= 3	Q= 3
T3	T= 3	T=3	T= 3	T= 3
T4	L= 1.3	L= 1.3	L= 1	L= 1.6
T1	D= 50	D=50	D= 30	D= 30
	D_r= 2	D_r= 1	D_r= 4	D_r= 0
	D_i= 0	D_i= 0	D_i= 2	D_i= 0
Participant 3	(with D)	(with S)	(with S)	(with D)
T1	Q= 7	Q= 3	Q= 3	Q= 7
T4	T= 9	T= 4	T= 4	T= 7
T3	L= 1.85	L= 1.3	L= 1.3	L= 3
T2	D= 70	D= 30	D= 30	D= 70
	D_r= 1	D_r= 4	D_r= 4	D_r= 0
	D_i= 1	D_i= 1	D_i= 2	D_i= 0
Participant 4	(with D)	(with S)	(with S)	(with D)
T2	Q= 4	Q= 8	Q= 10	Q= 4
T3	T= 5	T= 12	T=16	T=5
T4	L= 2	L= 3.62	L= 2.9	L= 2.3
T1	D= 70	D= 80	D= 110	D= 80
	D_r= 3	D_r= 6	D_r= 10	D_r= 0
	D_i=1	D_i= 4	D_i= 5	D_i= 0

Whatever the reasons, the consequences of not using some words could be positive as well as negative. Indeed the fact that some queries are not used might result in relevant documents not retrieved; on the contrary more specific queries could be the killer query for subtopics. Unfortunately the data we have is not enough to measure the positive or negative effect of different behaviour (the training task does not have any relevant assessment, the phenomenon disappears with the use and it does not occur with participants trained with the S system first).

In an effort to be more precise, users used Boolean operators, e.g. inverted commas, "+" and "AND". With the same disambiguation intention participants typed words in Finnish picked-up from the translation list. This wrong behaviour could be avoided with a different interface layout where the users could simply tick the desired sense of the translation.

Another interesting phenomenon is the use of proper names. Half the subjects used proper names to search. Many had a corresponding entry in the dictionary, like

"Europe" or "Jew"; others are not included, as "Alzheimer". Finally some proper names are culturally biased; P_1 and P_3 used "Burnley", "Sangatte", and "Bobby Sands", two refugee centres and the name of a hunger striker. This observation is important for the effectiveness of CLIR since states the importance of properly translate proper names but also shows how searching cross-language is deeply routed into the culture.

6 Conclusions and Future Work

Despite the fact that the study is rich with interesting results, the basic question if the user supervised query translation is more effective than a fully automatic one is still open. It would appear that having greater translation control enables users to retrieve more relevant documents, but there is too much variation among users, topics, and tasks to consider the data collected robust enough for a general assertion. We think that a more strict framework for usability evaluation is needed to assure that good data is collected. In this study we have shown how performance varies greatly from user to user: P_2 always made 3 queries for each task with only 1 term in each while P_1 interacted on average 10.75 times using 12.5 different terms. It is therefore essential to minimize this difference by selecting people with similar skills. Questionnaires are not enough since from the IR attitude one all our participants appeared to be equally skilled.

Another condition to be revised is the length of the experiment. Two participants had a strong decrease in engagement as time passed and this affected their performance. Reducing the time required of users seems to be another revision needed.

Retrieval in cross-language means being able to formulate the query in such a way that the system can retrieve relevant documents but also being able to detect them once retrieved. A global measure (F) of the performance does not take this difference into account. Indeed participants were able to retrieve many more documents than what appears from F (or even from P and R) because they were not able to detect those relevant. Evaluating the query formulation as separate from the relevance judgement sub-task has the advantage of showing more clearly where the problem is.

Similarly the observed behaviour inferred from the log suggests a decrease in potential effectiveness when query translation is seen; being more specific without having seen any documents might prevent the retrieval of relevant documents. This intuition seems to contradict the result that shows better performances with S than with D. We intend to analyse the queries and the evolution of the interaction to better clarify this point. It is also our intention to run the experiment again with more users and a better designed interface.

When faced with ambiguous terms, participants tried to disambiguate the query by using the Finnish word. This made the system perform worse and the user frustrated. This could probably be avoided by offering a layout that allows users to dynamically select the right sense. However this solution does not guarantee a better performance.

Both query translation and document presentation will be improved. The poor results in the retrieval sub-task can be explained by the odd translations returned sometimes by the dictionary used, as discovered by the Finnish colleagues in their

CLEF2002 experiment [1]. It is our hope this would improve the system effectiveness, however cases where similar queries do not retrieve the same documents should be carefully considered since it is unrealistic to expect users to formulate synonyms or lexical variations by themselves.

Improving the relevance judgement seems less critical. When the users know the target language they can bridge with their knowledge the poor system translation of keywords and make sense of the documents retrieved. In this respect, it is our intention to involve only participants who can fluently read the target language in the next evaluations.

Finally we think that a more precise framework for user evaluation is needed. The three usability elements of efficiency, effectiveness, and user satisfaction have to be exploited in the context of CLIR search to get the best and widest possible understanding from user evaluations.

Acknowledgements

Our gratitude to Heikki Keskustalo and Bemmu Sepponen from the University of Tampere for the promptness, patience and help in setting-up the CLIR core module for the experiment. A special acknowledgement to Steve Levin for the help with the data. Finally we thank the European Commission for funding Clarity (contract number IST-2000-25310).

References

[1] Airio, E, Keskustalo, H., Hedlund, T., Pirkola, A.: UTACLIR @ CLEF 2002: Towards a unified translation process model. Working notes CLEF2002, (2002), 51-58.

[2] Beaulieu, M., Jones, S.: Interactive searching and interface issues in the Okapi best match probabilistic retrieval system. Interacting with computers, 10(3), (1998) 237-248.

[3] Borlund, P., and Ingwersen, P. Experimental components for the evaluation of interactive information retrieval systems. Journal of Documentation, (53)3, (2000) 225-250.

[4] Capstick, J., Diagne, A. K. Erbach, G., Uszkoreit, H., Laisenberg, A., Leisenberg, M.A.: A system for supporting cross-lingual information retrieval. Information Processing and Management, 36 (2), (2000) 275-289.

[5] He, D., Wang, J., Oard, D., and Nossal, M.: Comparing User-assisted and Automatic Query Translation. Working notes CLEF 2002, (2002) 267-278.

[6] Koenemann, J., and Belkin, N.J.: A case for interaction: A study of interactive information retrieval behaviour and effectiveness. Proceedings of CHI96, (1996) 205-212

[7] Oard, D.: Serving users in many languages cross-language information retrieval for digital libraries, D-Lib Magazine, December 1997.

[8] Ogden, W. C., and Davis, M.W.: Improving cross-language text retrieval with human interactions. Proceedings of the Hawaii International Conference on System Science – HICSS-33, 2000.

[9] Petrelli, D., Hansen, P., Beaulieu, M. Sanderson M.: User Requirement Elicitation for Cross-Language Information Retrieval. Proceedings of International Conference on Information Seeking and Retrieval in Context – ISIC 2002, Lisbon, September 2002.

CLEF 2002 Cross-Language Spoken Document Retrieval Pilot Track Report

Gareth J. F. Jones[1] and Marcello Federico[2]

[1] Department of Computer Science, University of Exeter, EX4 4QF, UK
G.J.F.Jones@exeter.ac.uk
[2] ITC-irst – Centro per la Ricerca Scientifica e Tecnologica
I-38050 Povo, Trento, Italy
federico@itc.it

Abstract. The current expansion in collections of natural language based digital documents in various media and languages is creating challenging opportunities for automatically accessing the information contained in these documents. This paper describes the CLEF 2002 pilot track investigation of Cross-Language Spoken Document Retrieval (CLSDR) combining information retrieval, cross-language translation and speech recognition. The experimental investigation is based on the TREC-8 and TREC-9 SDR evaluation tasks, augmented to form a CLSDR task. The original task of retrieving English language spoken documents using English request topics is compared with cross-language retrieval using French, German, Italian and Spanish topic translations. The results of the pilot track establish baseline performance levels and indicate that pseudo relevance feedback and contemporaneous text document collections can be used to improve CLSDR performance.

1 Introduction

The current rapid expansion in the availability of multilingual digital material, increasingly contained in different media, is creating many demands for technology to automate access to the information contained within these archives. If the documents are contained in media other than text or are in a language in which the user is not fluent then a more complex IR approach is required.

In recent years much independent research has been carried out on multimedia and multilingual retrieval. The most extensive work in multimedia retrieval has concentrated on spoken document retrieval from monolingual (almost exclusively English language) collections, generally using text search requests to retrieve spoken documents. Speech recognition technologies have made impressive advances in recent years and these have proven to be effective for indexing spoken documents for spoken document retrieval (SDR). The TREC SDR track ran for 4 years from TREC-6 to TREC-9 and demonstrated very good performance levels for SDR [1]. There has also been more limited work on the retrieval of scanned document images [2] [3] and an increasing interest in retrieval of video material [4]. In parallel with this, there has been much progress in cross-language

C.A. Peters (Ed.): CLEF 2002, LNCS 2785, pp. 446–457, 2003.

information retrieval (CLIR) as exemplified by the CLEF workshops [5]. Good progress in these separate areas means that it is now timely to explore integrating these technologies to provide multilingual multimedia IR systems.

This overview paper describes the preliminary investigation of cross-language retrieval of spoken documents carried out as part of the CLEF 2002 campaign. The English language TREC-8 and TREC-9 SDR tasks were adapted to explore cross-language document retrieval using topic statements in French, German, Italian and Spanish. The aim of this initial study is to establish baseline figures for Cross-Language Spoken Document Retrieval (CLSDR), and to identify areas requiring research in further detailed investigations of CLSDR.

This paper is organised as follows: Section 2 outlines existing work in spoken document retrieval, Section 3 introduces issues in cross-language spoken document retrieval, Section 4 describes the test collection used for the CLEF 2002 CLSDR evalation, Section 5 summarises the participants experimental results, and finally Section 6 gives concluding remarks and suggestions for further investigations.

2 Spoken Document Retrieval

Spoken document retrieval (SDR) is usually taken to mean the use of textual search requests to locate potentially relevant spoken documents. SDR was developed initially within a number of early studies using small independently developed document collections, for example [6] [7] [8] [9]. Interest in SDR expanded very rapidly with the establishment of the SDR tracks at the recent TREC workshops [1]. The TREC SDR track made standard collections available to all participants enabling the potential of different proposed techniques for SDR to be compared directly for the first time. Although larger than the early independent collections, even the largest TREC SDR collections are much smaller than current text retrieval test collections.

The cost of developing new test collections for IR research is considerable even for text documents. The effort involved includes selecting a suitable document set for the research, the development of the search requests and collection of corresponding relevance assessments for each request, the last stage of which is particularly expensive since the assessments must be made by manual judgment of each document. Although methods such as pooling are typically used to reduce the number of documents which must be checked for relevance, the cost is still very high for more than very small collections. The price of developing multimedia retrieval collections is higher still since in addition to the steps required for text collections, the document set must be manually verified to check the contents, and usually it will also need to be manually indexed to enable the effectiveness of automatic indexing techniques on retrieval performance to be explored.

A key issue for SDR is making the contents of the documents available for indexing. Although spoken documents could be indexed manually, in practice this is impracticably expensive and identification must be performed using a process of automatic speech recognition. A problem with this is that speech recognition systems all make errors in identifying the words spoken; such errors will impact on retrieval behaviour. Speech recognition errors may arise from various sources. For example, the speech may be inherently hard to transcribe due to effects such as poor articulation, spontaneous speech issues such as phrase and word restarts, and acoustic channel noise, However, an important issue in speech recognition systems in the context of SDR is the indexing vocabulary. Standard word-based transcription speech recognition systems (termed *large vocabulary recognisers*) have a restricted recognition vocabulary meaning that any words present in a spoken document, but not in the recognition vocabulary, cannot, by definition, be recognised correctly. In the case of any speech recognition error arising from vocabulary limitations, the correct word in the document is transcribed as one or more words from the available recognition vocabulary.

Several approaches to addressing this problem based on subword-based indexing have been explored including including keyword spotting [6], subword feature indexing [7] [10] [11], and phone lattice spotting [8] [9]. Keyword spotting attempts to identify one of a limited number of words from a fixed list of keywords, the systems seeks to map all non-keywords to a background filler model designed to account for non-keyword sounds and silence [6]. These systems enable the vocabulary to be changed easily, but the spoken data must be re-recognised every time the vocabulary is changed. Phone lattice spotting (PLS) constructs an open-vocabulary subword lattice in the main recognition pass, the lattice can then be searched for the subword phone string corresponding to any word [8] [9]. This system has the advantage of an unrestricted open-vocabulary, but the lattices are physically very large and huge amounts of RAM are required for efficient operation. While PLS has been shown to be effective on a small retrieval task [9], it has never been investigated for a larger task such as those in the TREC evaluations.

Fortunately the out-of-vocabulary problem has not been found to be a significant issue in the TREC SDR tasks where LVR transcriptions have shown the best retrieval results. The TREC SDR tracks provided participants with baseline LVR transcriptions of the TREC documents, as well as giving them access to the original spoken document sources enabling them to make their own transcriptions using their own speech recognition systems.

In addition to the problems related to vocabulary limitations, SDR performance is affected by recognition mistakes for words that are in the vocabulary. Errors may either be *misses*, where a word spoken in the soundtrack is not recognised correctly, or *false alarms* where words not spoken are output by the recogniser. Both of these error types can affect the accuracy of SDR; misses may result in failure to retrieve relevant documents and false alarms may cause retrieval of non-relevant documents. Co-occurrence or redundancy effects of terms in a search request often reduce the impact of transcription errors, but the problem can be severe, particularly if the transcription error rate is very high or topic statements are very short.

SDR has a number of similarities with text CLIR in relation to problems with matching topic statements and document representations used for retrieval, and techniques used to overcome these. It is thus not surprising to find that techniques that have proved useful in CLIR have also been shown to be effective for SDR. The methods found to compensate for the general problem of reduced retrieval performance due to recognition errors, include pseudo (or blind) relevance feedback (PRF) for query expansion [12] and document expansion [13]. In both cases an initial retrieval run is used to select query or document expansion terms respectively before carrying out a final retrieval run. Some participants in the final SDR tracks at TREC-8 and TREC-9 combined these techniques to achieve SDR performance comparable to the available manual text transcriptions. These manual transcriptions were not strictly accurate (as described in Section 4.2), so the comparison may not be completely accurate - 100% accurate transcriptions could be expected to achieve at least marginally better retrieval performance. However, given these unquestionably good SDR results relative to text transcription, it was not felt that it was worthwhile to pursue SDR within TREC further at this time, and the TREC-8 and TREC-9 collections remain the largest tasks available for SDR evaluation.

Some relevant practical observations with regard to the final TREC SDR tracks are as follows. The volume of spoken data that needed to be transcribed (more than 500 hours of audio material) meant that only very few participants were able to generate their own automatic document transcriptions. Other participants thus either made use of the baseline transcriptions provided by NIST or transcriptions provided by other participants. Thus most participants were really only exploring the development of IR techniques for SDR. It is thus vital that any CLSDR evaluation makes common baseline transcripts available to participants.

3 Cross-Language Spoken Document Retrieval

CLSDR combines the challenges of monolingual SDR and text CLIR. Errors in speech recognition for SDR and translation for CLIR individually reduce the effectiveness of retrieval. When these technologies are combined in CLSDR, it can be expected that these errors will be additive. The initial study carried out at CLEF 2002 concentrates on establishing baseline CLSDR retrieval behaviour. The results are thus likely to represent a lower bound on CLSDR performance achievable. Further investigations may then enable closer and more effective integration to yield improvements in overall system performance.

As stated earlier in Section 2, for the TREC SDR tasks out-of-vocabulary words have been shown not to a significant issue, but there is scope for problems in CLSDR, particularly when the language translation and speech recognition systems are drawn from entirely different sources, which will generally be the case, and their models and composition and low-level operating parameters must be treated as black boxes which cannot be accessed or modified. In CLSDR we are thus faced with a situation of a limited translation vocabulary in the translation system and potentially in the speech recognition system. Even "correct" translations will be expressed in terms of the linguistic and lexical knowledge of the translation system. Thus concepts may not be expressed in language well related to the index of the document collection. This is a general problem of CLIR, and to a lesser extent for IR in general. In the case of CLSDR this issue is compounded by a vocabulary limitations in the speech recognition system. Words outside the recognition vocabulary cannot be recognised correctly. Thus, we may face situations where the knowledge of the translation system leads to translations which are not well matched with the active recognition vocabulary of the speech recognition system.

There is very little existing work in CLSDR. Two existing sets of experiments are reported in [14] [15]. Both of these investigations used very small document collections, and the TREC SDR collections used in this study are much larger. The previous experiments concentrated on using only a single language pair. The general conclusion from these investigations is that the reduction in retrieval performance associated with the SDR and CLIR components of the overall system was largely additive.

4 The TREC-8 SDR Spoken Document Retrieval Collection

The cost of developing a brand new test collection was beyond the resources of this initial CLSDR investigation. However, the TREC SDR evaluations have left a large legacy of data and tools which can be exploited for further evaluation exercises. It was thus decided to extend the existing TREC-8 and TREC-9 SDR evaluation collections to CLIR. The TREC-8 and TREC-9 SDR collections are based on the English broadcast news portion of the TDT-2 News Corpus which was originally collected by the US Linguistic Data Consortium (LDC) to support the DARPA Topic Detection and Tracking Evaluations [16]. This section outlines the features of the TDT-2 document sets, the TREC SDR retrieval task, and its extension to CLSDR.

4.1 TDT-2

Document Collection Overview The TDT-2 data used in the TREC SDR tasks contains news data collected from 4 English language news sources over a period of 6 months from January to June 1998. The broadcast news sources are as follows:

CNN_HDL	Cable News Network "Headline News"
ABC_WNT	American Broadcasting Company "World News Tonight"
PRI_TWD	Public Radio International "The World"
VOA_END	Voice of America, English news programmes

The news data is broken down as follows:

CNN_HDL	about 80 stories per day, in four sample files
ABC_WNT	about 15 stories per day, in one sample file
PRI_TWD	about 20 stories per day, in one sample file, 5 days each week
VOA_ENG	about 40 stories per day, in two sample files

These sampling frequencies are approximate and all sources were prone to some failures in the data collection process. To avoid overlap with related speech recognition evaluation tasks, which allowed the January 1998 data to be used in training the parameters of the speech recognition systems, only the data from the 5 month period February to June 1998 is used in the SDR evaluation document collection.

Broadcast Structure Each sample file represents a contiguous collection of stories from a given source on a given date over a specific period of time. Each broadcast is manually segmented into a number of individual news stories which form the basic document unit of the corpus. Each story unit was manually classified as either a "NEWS STORY" or a "MISCELLANEOUS TEXT". A unit was classified as a "NEWS STORY" if it contained two or more declarative statements about a single event. Miscellaneous text units include commercial breaks, music interludes, and introductory portions of broadcasts where an anchor person is providing a list of upcoming stories. The SDR data contained a total of around 500 hours of audio data.

There are two TREC SDR tasks designed using this data set. One version is the "Story Known" task where the audio transcription was manually segmented into the separate "NEWS STORY" and "MISCELLANEOUS TEXT" units. The other is the "Unknown Story Boundary" task where the audio file is simply passed through the recogniser without any manual labelling of the story boundaries. The task then is to locate and retrieve relevant stories from the unlabeled transcription. The CLEF 2002 pilot CLSDR evaluation considers only the Story Known task. In the Story Known TREC SDR task only the data labelled as "NEWS STORY" is used as the retrieval collection [1]. This comprises around 385 hours of speech from the total audio data and contain a total of 21,754 stories with an average length of 180 words. The total numbers of broadcasts and stories for each source are as follows:

	Source			
	ABC	CNN	PRI	VOA
No of Broadcasts	139	550	102	111
No of Stories	1834	13526	2407	3992

4.2 TREC SDR Documents and Transcriptions

This section outlines the features of the document sources from the TDT-2 document set.

Text Documents There is no high-quality human reference transcription available for TDT-2 - only "closed-caption" quality transcriptions for the television sources and rough manual transcripts quickly made for the radio sources by commercial transcription services. These transcriptions are used as a baseline against which retrieval performance of the automatic spoken document transcriptions can be compared.

In order to accurately assess speech recognition performance over the document collection a 10 hour subset of the data was randomly selected by the LDC and a detailed manual transcription carried out. As well as enabling the accuracy of speech recognisers to be evaluated, these accurate transcriptions also permitted the error rate of the closed-caption quality transcriptions to be evaluated. These evaluations showed the television closed-caption sources to have a Word Error Rate of approximately 14.5% and radio sources to have a Word Error Rate of around 7.5%. These error rates are significant with the television closed caption error rates approaching those for state-of-the-art broadcast news recognisers with clearly recorded well structured speech data [1].

Spoken Documents The baseline transcription set provided for the TREC SDR evaluation used is designated 'B2" in the official NIST TREC-8 SDR documentation and "B1" in the corresponding TREC-9 SDR documentation. This was generated by NIST using the BBN BYBLOS Rough'N'Ready transcription system using a dynamically updated rolling language model. Full details of this recognition system are contained in [17]. The recognition performance of this transcription is recorded as:

Correct	Substitutions	Deletions	Insertions	Word Error Rate
76.5%	17.2%	6.2%	3.2%	26.7%

4.3 TREC SDR Test Collections

The TREC-8 SDR retrieval test collections were completed by forming sets of 50 search topics and corresponding relevance assessments. A team of 6 NIST assessors created the ad hoc topics for the evaluation set. The goal in creating the topics was to devise topics with a few (but not too many) relevant documents in the collection to appropriately challenge test retrieval systems. Prior to commencing work at NIST, the assessors were told to review the news for the first half of 1998 and to come up with 10 possible topics each. The assessors then tested their putative topics against the Reference Transcriptions in the SDR collection using the NIST PRISE search engine [18]. If a topic was found to retrieve 1 to 20 relevant documents in the top 25, it was considered for inclusion in the test collection. Otherwise, the assessors were required to refine (broaden or narrow) or replace the topic to retrieve the appropriate number of relevant documents using PRISE. The assessors created approximately 60 topics. Topics with similar subjects or which were considered malformed were then excluded to yield a final test set containing 50 topics.

Retrieval runs submitted by the TREC SDR participants were used to form a document pool for each topic which was then passed on for manual relevance assessment [1]. For the TREC-8 SDR task, the average topic length was 13.7 words and the mean number of relevant documents for each topic was 36.4. Note: only 49 of the topics were ultimately adjudged to have relevant documents within the TREC-8 SDR corpus.

A similar procedure was followed to form a set of search topics for the TREC-9 SDR task. For TREC-9 SDR the average short topic length was 11.7 words, and the mean number of relevant documents for each topic was 44.3. Note: the TREC-9 SDR task introduced a shorter *terse* statement of each topic to better simulate typical user search requests. The CLSDR tasks currently only use the original longer *short* form topic statements [19].

4.4 Cross-Language SDR Test Collection

The TREC-8 and TREC-9 SDR topic sets both use the same document collection. In order to extend the English language TREC SDR collections for CLSDR evaluation, the topic statements for the TREC-8 and TREC-9 tasks were translated into French, German, Italian, Spanish and Dutch by native speakers at IRST, Italy. The translators were aware of the task for which the topic translations were intended. There was no separate authentication of the suitability or accuracy of each translation. The translations were performed independently for each language, and so are not directly comparable.

Translators were not given instructions on the use of structures such as proper names, neologisms and idioms in the translation. Some of these were reported verbatim without translation, others were translated literally between the languages and others were converted into native language equivalents of the expression. On some occasions where the appropriate action was not clear, the translator included alternative translations. Overall the translations contain some small idiosyncrasies of the translators, these could however be those of real users, particularly those knowing that their request was being submitted to a CLIR system. In order to explore the impact of alternative translations on retrieval behaviour, it is hoped that further sets of manual topic translations will be collected in the future.

5 Summary of Pilot Study Results

Two sets of results were submitted for the CLSDR pilot study by IRST, Italy and University of Exeter, U.K.

5.1 IRST Results

IRST submitted results for both the TREC-8 and TREC-9 CLSDR tasks. They used an Okapi type retrieval system which they showed to be competitive with previous TREC SDR systems. Their CLSDR results illustrated that PRF for query expansion using either a parallel text collection or the test collection itself improved average retrieval performance, and that this was enhanced when these procedures were applied to the topics sequentially [20]. Their results also indicated a strong correlation between retrieval performance and dictionary coverage.

They also compared retrieval performance for topic translation using their own statistical translation system and the online *AltaVista Babelfish* system based on *Systran*. Results show that at present Systran gave better retrieval results, but there is considerable scope for improvement with their statistical system, as shown by their results for text CLIR [21].

5.2 University of Exeter Results

University of Exeter also used an Okapi retrieval system. Their results compare topic translation using *Systran Version 3* and *Globalink Power Translator Pro Version: 6.4*. They only report results for the TREC-8 CLSDR tasks and use a later release of the TDT-2 corpus than that used for the original TREC-8 SDR evaluation [22]. Their results indicate improvement in retrieval precision from the application of their summary-based PRF method for topic expansion [23]. They report further improvements from the use of a combined test and parallel text document collection for PRF. They also show good improvements in the number of relevant documents retrieved from the use of data fusion to combine the separate runs from the two translation systems.

Their results indicate a reduction of between 20% and 25% in average precision for the baseline spoken document transcription relative to the baseline spoken document transcriptions relative to the TDT-2 version 3 reference text transcriptions. This is a much larger difference than typically noted for the monolingual SDR task [12]. However, while this difference must be examined, it can be noted that there was little processing of the LVR transcription to a form more similar to written text, and this will account for at least some of the lower SDR performance.

6 Plans for Further Investigation

The pilot study has demonstrated baseline performance levels for CLSDR tasks and illustrated that results can be improved by the use of PRF and parallel document collections. There are many potential further investigations that can be carried out for this task. This section gives some possible extensions to the current studies.

The existing experiments suggest that the degree of improvement associated with a parallel collection is related to the amount of data used, a useful further investigation would be to examine the maximum degree of improvement can that be achieved using this method and how much parallel data is required to do this.

Planned new investigations are to collect further manual translations of the English topic to explore the sensitivity of translation methods to different topic statements and to explore ways to minimise the sensitivity of CLSDR itself to variations in retrieval behaviour arising from these different translations.

It is also intended to run the alternative TREC SDR unknown story boundary evaluation task outline in Section 4.1 on the CLSDR collections.

A further task could be to extend the TDT-2 collection itself to a cross-language task. The TDT task starts with a topic statement and aims to detect and track documents related to this topic over time. In order to work on this CL-TDT task, these topic statements will need to be manually translated into alternative starting languages.

We need to translate the *terse* topic statements provided for the TREC-9 SDR tasks for the CLSDR evaluation to examine any significant differences in behaviour associated with very short topic statements.

While the TDT document collection provides a good starting point for CLSDR evaluations, it has several limitations. Importantly the collection itself in all transcriptions forms and the associated parallel document collections are all maintained by the LDC and are only available under licence. This means that they are generally only available to organisations who are members of the LDC for the periods in which the collection was published. In addition, these documents are all in English. It is thus desirable to be able to make use of document collections which can be made available to all groups interested in participating in the CLSDR tracks, and non-English documents to enable investigation of CLSDR for other languages and multilingual SDR.

Acknowledgement

The CLEF 2002 Cross-Language Spoken Document Retrieval pilot track was supported by the DELOS Network of Excellence on Digital Libraries.

References

[1] J. S. Garafolo, C. G. P. Auzanne, and E. M. Voorhees. The TREC Spoken Document Retrieval Track: A Success Story. In *Proceedings of the RIAO 2000 Conference: Content-Based Multimedia Information Access*, pages 1–20, Paris, 2000.

[2] K. Taghva, J. Borsack, and A. Condit. Results of applying probabilistic IR to OCR text. In *Proceedings of the 17th Annual International ACM SIGIR Conference on Research and Development in Information Retrieval*, pages 202–211, Dublin, 1994. ACM.

[3] P. B. Kantor and E. M. Voorhees. The TREC-5 Confusion Track: Comparing Retrieval Methods for Scanned Text. *Information Retrieval*, 2:165–176, 2000.

[4] A. F. Smeaton, P. Over, and R. Taban. The TREC-2001 Video Track Report. In *Proceedings of the Tenth Text REtrieval Conference (TREC-2001)*, pages 52–60, Gaithersburg, MD, 2002. NIST.

[5] Carol Peters el al., editor. *Workshop of the Cross-Language Evaluation Forum, CLEF 2001*, Darmstadt, September 2001. Springer.

[6] R. C. Rose. Techniques for information retrieval from speech messages. *Lincoln Laboratory Journal*, 4(1):45–60, 1991.

[7] U. Glavitsch and P. Schäuble. A System for Retrieving Speech Documents. In *Proceedings of the 15th Annual International ACM SIGIR Conference on Research and Development in Information Retrieval*, pages 168–176. ACM, 1992.

[8] D. A. James. *The Application of Classical Information Retrieval Techniques to Spoken Documents.* PhD thesis, Cambridge University, February 1995.

[9] G. J. F. Jones, J. T. Foote, K. Sparck Jones, and S. J. Young. Retrieving Spoken Documents by Combining Multiple Index Sources. In *Proceedings of the 19th Annual International ACM SIGIR Conference on Research and Development in Information Retrieval*, pages 30–38, Zürich, August 1996. ACM.

[10] M. Wechsler, E. Munteanu, and P. Schauble. New Techniques for Open-Vocabulary Spoken Document Retrieval. In *Proceedings of the 21st Annual International ACM SIGIR Conference on Research and Development in Information Retrieval*, pages 20–27, Melbourne, 1998. ACM.

[11] K. Ng and V. Zue. Phonetic Recognition for Spoken Document Retrieval. In *Proceedings of ICASSP 98*, volume I, pages 325–328, Seattle, WA, May 1998. IEEE.

[12] S. E. Johnson, P. Jourlin, K. Sparck Jones, and P. C. Woodland. Spoken Document Retrieval for TREC-8 at Cambridge University. In D. K. Harman and E. M. Voorhees, editors, *Proceedings of the Eighth Text REtrieval Conference (TREC-8)*, pages 157–168, Gaithersburg, MD, 2000. NIST.

[13] A. Singhal and F. Pereira. Document Expansion for Speech Retrieval. In *Proceedings of the 22nd Annual International ACM SIGIR Conference on Research and Development in Information Retrieval*, San Francisco, 1999. ACM.

[14] P. Sheridan, M. Wechsler, and P. Schäuble. Cross-Language Speech Retrieval: Establishing a Baseline Performance,. In *Proceedings of the 20th Annual International ACM SIGIR Conference on Research and Development in Information Retrieval*, pages 99–108, Philadelphia, 1997. ACM.

[15] G. J. F. Jones. Applying Machine Translation Resources for Cross-Language Information Access from Spoken Documents. In *Proceedings of the MT2000: Machine Translation and Multilingual Applications in the New Millennium*, pages 4–(1–9), Exeter, 2000.

[16] D. Graff, C. Cieri, S. Strassel, and N. Martey. Linguistic Data Consortium the TDT-3 Text and Speech corpus. In *Proceedings of the Topic Detection and Tracking (TDT) Workshop*, Vienna, Virginia, USA, 1999. NIST.

[17] C. Auzanne, J. S. Garafolo, J. G. Fiscus, and W. M. Fisher. Automatic Language Model Adaptation for Spoken Document Retrieval. In *Proceedings of the RIAO 2000 Conference: Content-Based Multimedia Information Access*, pages 1–20, Paris, 2000.

[18] D. Dimmick, G. O'Brien, P. Over, and W. Rogers. Guide to Z39.50/Prise 2.0: Its Installation, Use, & Modification. `http://www-nlpir.nist.gov/works/papers/zp2/zp2.html`, 1998.

[19] S.E. Johnson, P. Jourlin, K. Sparck Jones, and P. C. Woodland. Spoken Document Retrieval for TREC-9 at Cambridge University. In E. M.Voorhees and D. K.Harman, editors, *Proceedings of the Ninth Text REtrieval Conference (TREC-9).* NIST, 2001.

[20] N. Bertoldi and M. Federico. Cross-Language Spoken Document Retrieval on the TREC SDR Collection. In *Proceedings of the CLEF 2002: Workshop on Cross-Language Information Retrieval and Evaluation*, Rome, September 2002. Springer Verlag.

[21] M. Federico and N. Bertoldi. Statistical Cross-Language Information Retrieval using N-Best Query Translation. In *Proceedings of the 25th Annual International ACM SIGIR Conference on Research and Development in Information Retrieval*, pages 167–174, Tampere, 2002. ACM.

[22] G. J. F. Jones and A. M. Lam-Adesina. Exeter at CLEF 2002: Cross-Language Spoken Document Retrieval Experiments. In *Proceedings of the CLEF 2002: Workshop on Cross-Language Information Retrieval and Evaluation*, Rome, September 2002. Springer Verlag.

[23] A. M. Lam-Adesina and G. J. F. Jones. Applying Summarization Techniques for Term Selection in Relevance Feedback. In *Proceedings of the 24th Annual International ACM SIGIR Conference on Research and Development in Information Retrieval*, pages 1–9, New Orleans, 2001. ACM.

Exeter at CLEF 2002: Cross-Language Spoken Document Retrieval Experiments

Gareth J. F. Jones and Adenike M. Lam-Adesina

Department of Computer Science, University of Exeter, EX4 4QF, UK
{G.J.F.Jones,A.M.Lam-Adesina}@exeter.ac.uk

Abstract. Cross-Language Spoken Document Retrieval (CLSDR) combines the need for language translation and the retrieval of spoken documents. CLSDR baseline retrieval performance is established for the TREC-8 SDR task using two machine translation tools (*Systran* and *Power Translator Pro*) combined with the Okapi probabilistic retrieval system. Our CLSDR results show that pseudo relevance feedback and combination with contemporaneous text collections both lead to improved absolute retrieval performance, but that there is little improvement in cross-language retrieval losses relative to monolingual text retrieval. Further experiments show that significant loss in retrieval performance arises separately due to both cross-language topic translation weaknesses and errors in automatic transcription of the spoken documents, and that these losses are almost exactly additive for our current CLSDR system. The use of data fusion to combine the output from retrieval runs carried out using separate topic translations from the two MT systems gives a large increase in the number of relevant documents retrieved, but has mixed results for retrieval precision.

1 Introduction

This paper gives results and analysis for our participation in the CLEF 2002 pilot track investigation of Cross-Language Spoken Document Retrieval (CLSDR). The aim of the track was to develop an initial standard CLSDR collection and to establish baseline performance metrics and observe retrieval behaviour for this task. The CLSDR task used in the evaluation is an extension of the SDR tasks used at TREC-8 and TREC-9 [1]. The English language topics were translated into French, German, Italian and Spanish by IRST, Italy [2].

Our approach to this track was to use methods which we have found to be effective for the CLEF text retrieval bilingual tracks, and combine these with techniques that we have found to be effective for the monolingual TREC-8 SDR track modified to a corrupted data OCR retrieval task [3].

Details of the test collection are given separately in [2]. The remainder of this paper first outlines our approach to cross-language information retrieval (CLIR) in Section 2, Section 3 summarises the CLSDR evaluation task, Section 4 outlines our retrieval methods, Section 5 then gives detailed results and analysis and the paper ends with concluding remarks in Section 6.

C.A. Peters (Ed.): CLEF 2002, LNCS 2785, pp. 458–475, 2003.

2 Cross-Language Information Retrieval

In order to perform CLIR a process of translation is required between the documents and the search requests. Whether to translate the topics or the documents has been the focus of a number of research studies. However, it is generally held that in practice topic translation is the more practical option, since topics are translated into the target document language as they are entered. This means that document index files only need to be maintained once for each document in its original language. This approach is followed here.

Topics can be translated using a number of different methods. We have achieved good performance for text CLIR at CLEF using commercial machine translation systems. In order to establish a CLSDR baseline, we use these tools again in this pilot investigation [4]. The study described in this paper uses two commercial MT systems: *Systran Version 3*, and the *Globalink Power Translator Pro Version: 6.4*. All topics are translated independently using both systems.

A number of methods have been shown to improve retrieval performance for monolingual IR and CLIR [5] [6], including pseudo relevance feedback (PRF). In this paper we investigate the use of PRF, which has also been shown to be effective for monolingual SDR.

A further method that has been shown to be useful for CLIR is *data fusion* [7]. Data fusion methods [8] combine the output of multiple document retrieval runs to form a single output. In this investigation data fusion is implemented by merging the output of retrieval runs for the two MT systems used in our work. The matching scores for the documents retrieved in each list are summed and a single re-ranked retrieval list output. This has the effect of making use of the translation resources and dictionaries of both the MT systems, by combining information from independent translation resources. The full theory underlying this approach for CLIR is described in [9]. In general, the combination of PRF and data fusion has been shown to be effective in our earlier work on text CLIR [7]. The matching scores can be normalised prior to merging, but in general we have found the unnormalised strategy to be more effective for CLIR.

3 CLSDR Test Collection

The CLSDR test collection is based on the SDR tasks used at TREC-8 and TREC-9 [1]. The document collection is taken from the spoken audio data of the news documents used for the TDT-2 evaluation, further details are given in [2]. We did not have the original document transcript files used in the TREC SDR evaluations (TDT-2 Version 2) available to us for this evaluation, and so used the version of TDT-2 which we did have (Version 3).

The TDT-2 corpus has been modified incrementally by NIST since its initial release to correct mistakes and improve story segmentation. These changes have affected the story IDs which are based on the start and end times of the stories, and produced some reclassification and deletion of "NEWS STORY" and "MISCELLANEOUS" stories. Overall, the correction process included deletions, insertions and substitutions of docnos. The total number of "NEWS STORY" items in this revised collection is 21,759.

There is no simple table giving correspondence between the TDT-2 Version 2 (current at December 1998) story labelling used in the TREC SDR collections and TDT-2 Version 3. The change in formatting between Versions 2 and 3 is further complicated by the correction of timing information. We decided to develop an alternative relevance file for the TREC-8 SDR task relabelling all relevant documents from Version 2 to Version 3 story label format. All story label revisions were manually verified to ensure that documents actually appeared to be those relevant to the topic statement.

4 Information Retrieval Methods

The basis of our experimental information retrieval system is the City University research distribution version of the Okapi system [10]. The retrieval model used in Okapi has been shown to be very effective in a number comparative evaluation exercises in recent years, including SDR [11] and CLIR [9].

The retrieval strategy adopted in this investigation follows standard practice for best-match ranked retrieval. The documents and search topics are first processed to remove common stop words from a list of around 260 words, suffix stripped using the Okapi implementation of Porter stemming [12] to encourage matching of different word forms, and further indexed using a small set of synonyms. Following preprocessing document terms are weighted using the Okapi BM25 *combined weight* (cw) [10].

The performance of IR systems can often be improved by the application of Pseudo Relevance Feedback (PRF). This assumes a number of top ranked documents from the initial retrieval run to be relevant, from which a number of terms are selected to expand the initial query. The main implementational issue for PRF is the selection of appropriate expansion terms for the topic statement. In the standard Okapi approach potential expansion terms from the relevant documents are ranked using the Robertson selection value $(rsv(i))$ [13], and the top ranking terms are then added to the topic.

Problems can arise in PRF when terms taken from assumed relevant documents that are actually non-relevant, are added to the query causing a drift in the focus of the query. A further problem can arise in PRF where documents may be multi-topic, i.e. they deal with several different topics. In this case only a portion of a document may actually be relevant. Standard PRF methods treat the whole document as relevant, the implication of this being that using terms from non-relevant sections of these documents for expansion may also cause a drift in the focus of the query. In an attempt to exclude terms from non-relevant material that may cause query drift, we have developed a term selection method for PRF based on document summaries [14]. Results using this method have been very encouraging and we adopt this method in this investigation.

Summary Length In order to generate an appropriate summary it is essential to place a limit on the number of sentences to be used as the summary content. The objective of the summary is to provide terms to be used for query expansion. Hence the optimal summary length is a compromise between maintaining terms that can be beneficial to the retrieval process, while ensuring that the summary length is such that the number of non-relevant terms is minimised. The optimal summary length for the TREC SDR task was determined empirically from the monolingual text collection.

Spoken Document Summaries The automatic spoken document transcriptions do not have any punctuation, there are thus no sentence boundary markers. However, the transcriptions do have silence markers indicating points where the speaker stops talking. These break points are most often between sentences or phrases, but not are guaranteed to be so. The summary generation system for SDR uses these silence marker segmented units instead of sentences. In general, these units are shorter in length than the sentence units, so the resulting summaries will typically be slightly shorter. There will, of course, be a small difference in the expansion terms selection parameters values and ranking of potential expansion terms; however any problems arising from this effect are likely to be much less important than problems arising from recognition errors in the document transcriptions.

4.1 Modification to the *rsv*

The *rsv* has generally been based on taking an equal number of relevant documents for both the available expansion terms and ranking of the terms. Our earlier investigation, described in [14], explored the use of an alternative approach which takes a smaller number of top ranked assumed relevant documents to determine the pool of potential expansion terms rather than the number of documents used to determine the *rsv* ranking. Again this technique was shown to be very effective for PRF and is adopted here.

4.2 Collection Combination

The reliability of IR term weight estimates improves as the size of the document collection used to estimate them increases. In order to improve the performance of IR systems previous studies have combined a retrieval test collection with an additional related, often contemporaneous, collection of text documents. This larger *pilot* collection is used to estimate term weights for retrieval from the test collection and for PRF [15]. In PRF the additional documents can be used only to enhance term weights in the test collection or additionally as a contributory source of expansion terms by using the combined collection in the initial PRF run.

There is a further issue in the case of multimedia data where recognition errors result not only in matching problems with requests and documents, but also degrade the quality of term weights estimates. Combining multimedia retrieval collections with text document collections can thus be beneficial not just by increasing the quantity of data used for parameter estimation, but also their

Table 1. Baseline retrieval results for text transcriptions with topic translation using Systran topic

		Topic Language				
		English	French	German	Italian	Spanish
Prec.	5 docs	0.633	0.539	0.498	0.478	0.502
	10 docs	0.551	0.478	0.453	0.420	0.441
	15 docs	0.494	0.427	0.403	0.382	0.388
	20 docs	0.433	0.386	0.347	0.344	0.344
Av Precision		0.468	0.402	0.363	0.330	0.351
% chg. CLIR		—	-14.1%	-22.4%	-29.5%	-25.0%
Rel. Ret.		1608	1292	1415	1395	1268
chg. CLIR		—	-316	-193	-213	-340

Table 2. Baseline retrieval results for text transcription with topic translation using Power Translator Pro

		Topic Language				
		English	French	German	Italian	Spanish
Prec.	5 docs	0.633	0.502	0.486	0.469	0.547
	10 docs	0.551	0.431	0.439	0.414	0.463
	15 docs	0.494	0.396	0.395	0.371	0.414
	20 docs	0.433	0.358	0.345	0.341	0.367
Av Precision		0.468	0.361	0.366	0.325	0.378
% chg. CLIR		—	-22.9%	-21.8%	-30.6%	-19.2%
Rel. Ret.		1608	1375	1422	1406	1341
chg. CLIR		—	-233	-186	-202	-267

quality by smoothing the values arising from the multimedia data. Combining collections for parameter estimation has been used successfully for SDR in previous evaluations [11] [16].

In this investigation we examine the combination of the TREC SDR collection with a small contemporaneous text document collection. The combined term weights are used for retrieval ranking and also PRF. However, in these experiments only the test documents are used as the source of expansion terms for PRF.

5 Experimental Investigations

This section describes our current investigation of CLSDR for the TREC-8 SDR collection. Experiments compare retrieval performance for the text baseline data set and the "B2" automatic speech transcription. Results are reported for baseline retrieval without feedback, retrieval with PRF using only the test collection, and PRF using the contemporaneous text collection to modify the test collection term weights.

Table 3. Baseline retrieval results for automatic spoken document transcriptions with topic translation using Systran

		Topic Language				
		English	French	German	Italian	Spanish
Prec.	5 docs	0.482	0.425	0.359	0.347	0.359
	10 docs	0.420	0.367	0.322	0.316	0.302
	15 docs	0.377	0.317	0.286	0.286	0.280
	20 docs	0.337	0.284	0.259	0.259	0.263
Av Precision		0.349	0.303	0.252	0.226	0.251
% chg. media		-25.4%	-24.6%	-30.6%	-31.5%	-28.5%
% chg. CLIR		—	-13.2%	-27.8%	-35.2%	-28.1%
% chg. media + CLIR		—	-35.3%	-46.2%	-51.7%	-46.4%
Rel. Ret.		1471	1210	1280	1235	1155
chg. media		-137	-82	-135	-160	-113
chg. CLIR		—	-261	-191	-236	-316
chg. media + CLIR		—	-398	-328	- 373	-453

The Okapi system parameters were selected using a series of baseline runs for the text collection. Based on the results of these runs the parameter values were set $K1 = 1.4$ and $b = 0.6$. These values were used for all experiments reported in this paper.

Results are shown for retrieval precision at 5, 10, 15, and 20 document cutoff, standard TREC average precision and the total number of relevant documents retrieved. The total number of relevant documents retrieved in each case can be compared to the total number of relevant documents in the TREC-8 SDR test set of 1818.

5.1 Baseline Results

Tables 1 and 2 show baseline retrieval results for the document text transcriptions using Systran and Power Translator Pro topic translation respectively. For all cross-language pairs it can be seen that there is a large reduction in retrieval precision relative to the monolingual result. The smallest reduction is for Systran French to English translation and the largest reduction is for Italian to English translation for both translation systems. In general there is less variation in performance for the Power Translator Pro than for Systran translation. All these patterns of behaviour have been observed previously for the CLEF 2001 bilingual CLIR text retrieval task [9]. In addition, there is a loss of relevant documents retrieved for each language. The total loss of relevant documents retrieved varies between about 200 and 350, i.e. on average between 4 and 7 relevant documents per topic statement. However, interestingly there does not seem to be any direct correlation between the performance in terms of precision and the number of relevant documents retrieved. For example, with French to English Systran

Table 4. Baseline retrieval results for automatic spoken document transcriptions with topic translation using Power Translator Pro

		Topic Language				
		English	French	German	Italian	Spanish
Prec.	5 docs	0.482	0.392	0.380	0.327	0.376
	10 docs	0.418	0.349	0.345	0.304	0.335
	15 docs	0.377	0.298	0.302	0.272	0.302
	20 docs	0.337	0.266	0.280	0.257	0.283
Av Precision		0.349	0.277	0.270	0.238	0.270
% chg. media		-25.4	-23.3%	-26.2%	-26.8%	-29.6%
% chg. CLIR		—	-20.6%	-22.6%	-31.8%	-22.6%
% chg. media + CLIR		—	-40.8%	-42.3%	-49.1%	-42.3%
Rel. Ret.		1471	1265	1285	1254	1234
chg. media		-137	-110	-137	-152	-107
chg. CLIR		—	-206	-186	-217	-237
chg. media + CLIR		—	-343	-323	-354	-374

topic translation, while the reduction in average precision is by far the lowest at only -14.1%, the loss in relevant documents is one of the largest at -316.

Tables 3 and 4 show corresponding results for automatic spoken document transcriptions. Comparison between retrieval precision for the language pairs shows identical trends to those observed for the text transcriptions in Tables 1 and 2. Overall the precision values are individually between 25% and 30% lower than those for the text transcriptions. The loss of retrieved relevant documents between CLSDR and monolingual varies between about 200 and 300, although these figures are all between 80 and 160 lower in absolute terms compared to the text transcription results. Once again there is no clear correlation between the number of relevant documents retrieved and the corresponding precision values. The loss in relevant documents between monolingual text retrieval and CLSDR varies between -323 and -453, i.e. on average between 6.5 and 9 relevant documents per topic.

5.2 Feedback Results

The following section gives results for experiments using PRF. Based on preliminary experiments the parameters of the PRF stage were set as follows: 20 expansion terms were added to each topic statement in the feedback run, based on selecting terms from the top 5 ranked documents from the baseline run using summaries composed of the top 6 ranked sentences. The top 20 baseline run documents were assumed relevant for evaluation of the $rsv(i)$ for each term [3]. The first set of experiments report results using only the test collection to computer term weights. Subsequent experiments show results for experiments combining the test collection with the contemporaneous text collection.

Table 5. Retrieval results incorporating PRF for text transcriptions with topic translation using Systran

		Topic Language				
		English	French	German	Italian	Spanish
Prec.	5 docs	0.670	0.604	0.534	0.539	0.551
	10 docs	0.598	0.529	0.474	0.467	0.482
	15 docs	0.540	0.467	0.426	0.420	0.435
	20 docs	0.486	0.413	0.379	0.381	0.391
Av Precision		0.514	0.463	0.396	0.397	0.398
% chg. no FB		+9.8%	+15.2%	+9.1%	+20.3%	+13.4%
% chg. CLIR		—	-9.9%	-23.0%	-22.8%	-22.6%
Rel. Ret.		1631	1462	1417	1446	1429
chg. no FB		+23	+170	+2	+51	+61
chg CLIR		—	-169	-214	-185	-202

Table 6. Retrieval results incorporating PRF for text transcriptions with topic translation using Power Translator Pro

		Topic Language				
		English	French	German	Italian	Spanish
Prec.	5 docs	0.670	0.555	0.539	0.478	0.612
	10 docs	0.598	0.486	0.471	0.437	0.527
	15 docs	0.540	0.430	0.420	0.405	0.461
	20 docs	0.486	0.403	0.377	0.374	0.413
Av Precision		0.514	0.422	0.404	0.360	0.440
% chg. no FB		+9.8%	+16.9%	+10.4%	+10.8%	+16.4%
% chg. CLIR		—	-17.9%	-21.4%	-30.0%	-14.4%
Rel. Ret.		1631	1568	1396	1434	1490
chg. no FB		+23	+193	-26	+28	+149
chg CLIR		—	-63	-235	-197	-141

Text Document Results Tables 5 and 6 show PRF results for text document transcriptions again using Systran and Power Translator Pro topic translation respectively. The first observation that can be made is that there is an average increase of between 10% and 20% in average precision performance arising from the application of PRF. The monolingual result of +9.8% is very nearly the smallest improvement, in all but one case cross-language results improve by more than 10%. In consequence the loss in precision for cross-language results relative to monolingual is now generally about 5% better in absolute terms compared to the text baseline results in Tables 1 and 2. Perhaps the most disappointing result is the Italian-English performance for Power Translator Pro, this result remains at -30% the same as the baseline result.

There is a wide variation in the effect of PRF on the number of relevant documents retrieved. For French-English Power Translator Pro there is an increase

Table 7. Retrieval results incorporating PRF for automatic spoken document transcriptions with topic translation using Systran

		Topic Language				
		English	French	German	Italian	Spanish
Prec.	5 docs	0.522	0.465	0.376	0.380	0.371
	10 docs	0.482	0.400	0.367	0.361	0.351
	15 docs	0.423	0.352	0.313	0.336	0.328
	20 docs	0.388	0.316	0.290	0.312	0.289
Av Precision		0.404	0.344	0.278	0.295	0.283
% chg. no FB		+15.8%	+13.5%	+10.3%	+30.5%	+12.7%
% chg. media		-21.4%	-25.7%	-29.8%	-25.7%	-28.9%
% chg. CLIR		—	-14.9%	-31.2%	-27.0%	-30.0%
% chg. media + CLIR		—	-33.1%	-45.9%	-42.6%	-44.9%
Rel. Ret.		1546	1242	1356	1341	1220
chg. no FB		+75	+32	+76	+106	+65
chg. media		-85	-220	-115	-105	-209
chg. CLIR		—	-304	-190	-205	-326
chg. media + CLIR		—	-389	-275	-290	-411

of +193, whereas for the corresponding German-English results there is a loss of -26, despite an increase in average precision of +10.4%. For Systran translated German-English there is an increase of only +2 with a corresponding average precision increase of +9.1%. The total number of relevant documents retrieved in each case is the lowest for German translation, although in each case the average precision results are generally similar to those for the other language pairs. Since the document collection is the same in each case, it is not clear why there should be such large variations in behaviour with respect to changes in the number of relevant documents retrieved associated with the application of PRF. It is not apparent whether there is a significant underlying reason for these differences, and these results need to subjected to further investigation. Thus while the topic expansion is improving the rank of retrieved documents, it does not enable the system to effectively retrieve additional relevant items. The reasons for this need to be explored carefully, but the result suggests that while the expanded topics are a better description of retrieved relevant documents, they may not describe non-retrieved relevant items well.

Spoken Document Results Tables 7 and 8 show corresponding results for CLSDR. In this case the improvement in retrieval performance is between +10% and +30% for the application of PRF. In this case the average improvement is similar for monolingual and CLSDR, overall the degradation in performance arising from topic translation is not reduced by PRF since the improvement on monolingual SDR is +15.8%.

With respect to the number of relevant documents retrieved there is an improvement in all cases of between +32 and +106. The increase in the number of documents retrieved is more consistent for the spoken documents than for the

Table 8. Retrieval results incorporating PRF for automatic spoken document transcriptions for topic translation using Power Translator Pro

		Topic Language				
		English	French	German	Italian	Spanish
Prec.	5 docs	0.522	0.400	0.412	0.355	0.392
	10 docs	0.482	0.369	0.382	0.325	0.376
	15 docs	0.423	0.336	0.339	0.310	0.355
	20 docs	0.388	0.310	0.317	0.292	0.325
Av Precision		0.404	0.305	0.318	0.282	0.315
% chg. no FB		+15.8%	+10.1%	+17.8%	+18.5%	+16.7%
% chg. media		-21.4%	-27.7%	-21.3%	-21.7%	-28.4%
% chg. CLIR		—	-24.5%	-21.3%	-30.2%	-22.0%
% chg. media + CLIR		—	-40.7%	-38.1%	-45.1%	-38.7%
Rel. Ret.		1546	1341	1362	1323	1272
chg. no FB		+75	+76	+75	+69	+38
chg. media		-85	-227	-34	-111	-218
chg. CLIR		—	-205	-184	-223	-274
chg. media + CLIR		—	-290	-269	-308	-359

text transcription results shown in Tables 5 and 6; while the largest increases are lower than those for text transcriptions, the lower increases are better. Again, it is not clear whether there is a substantive reason for these differences and further investigation is required. The loss in relevant documents retrieved for CLSDR relative to monolingual text now varies between -264 and -411, comparing these figures with the earlier results without PRF in Table 4, it can be seen that the loss is reduced by an average of about 50.

Merged Collections In this section we report results for experiments utilizing a contemporaneous text document collection together with the test collections to explore the extent to which improved retrieved parameters can be computed from non-parallel text document sources. The text document data used here is also taken from the TDT-2 New Corpus. In addition to the broadcast data sources mentioned in Section 3, the collection also includes 2 text document sources taken from the same time period as the broadcast news material. These are taken from New York Times Newswire Service (excluding non-NYT sources) and Associated Press Worldstream Service (English content only), and include a total of around 20,000 news stories.

The collections are combined for computation of the $cfw(i)$ parameters. Retrieval is then carried out using only the test collection. More sophisticated merging strategies are possible using pilot searching for PRF query expansion (and term weighting) [15]. The runs in this section use the same parameters for Okapi retrieval and PRF as used in the previous section for the test collection only runs.

Table 9. Retrieval results incorporating PRF with merged collection weights for text transcriptions with topic translation using Systran

		Topic Language				
		English	French	German	Italian	Spanish
Prec.	5 docs	0.718	0.580	0.494	0.543	0.559
	10 docs	0.620	0.516	0.451	0.465	0.500
	15 docs	0.548	0.469	0.399	0.422	0.459
	20 docs	0.490	0.427	0.362	0.393	0.410
Av Precision		0.538	0.460	0.379	0.401	0.418
% chg. no FB		+15.0%	+14.4%	+4.4%	+21.5%	+19.1%
% chg. CLIR		—	-14.5%	-29.6%	-25.5%	-22.3%
Rel. Ret.		1656	1429	1446	1492	1443
chg. no FB		+48	+137	+31	+97	+175
chg CLIR		—	-227	-210	-164	-213

Table 10. Retrieval results incorporating PRF with merged collection weights for text transcriptions with topic translation using Power Translator Pro

		Topic Language				
		English	French	German	Italian	Spanish
Prec.	5 docs	0.718	0.502	0.535	0.498	0.584
	10 docs	0.620	0.482	0.469	0.474	0.541
	15 docs	0.548	0.427	0.414	0.419	0.464
	20 docs	0.490	0.402	0.367	0.383	0.417
Av Precision		0.538	0.408	0.406	0.404	0.438
% chg. no FB		+15.0%	+13.0%	+10.9%	+24.9%	+15.9%
% chg. CLIR		—	-24.2%	-24.5%	-24.9%	-18.6%
Rel. Ret.		1656	1523	1432	1476	1383
chg. no FB		+48	+148	+10	+70	+42
chg CLIR		—	-133	-224	-180	-273

Text Document Results Tables 9 and 10 show retrieval results for text transcriptions with combined collection weights and the application of PRF. Comparing these with the baseline results in Tables 1 and 2, and the test collection only PRF results in Tables 5 and 6, the following observations can be made. In all cases there is improvement in the average precision relative to the baseline ranging from about +11% to +25%. For monolingual retrieval the result is +15.0% vs +9.8% for the test collection only weighting PRF result. The cross-language results are more varied, in some cases the merged collection produces better results (Spanish-English with Systran +13.4% vs +19.1%, Italian-English with Power Translator Pro +10.8% vs +24.9%), for others there is little difference (Spanish-English with Power Translator Pro, +16.4% vs 15.9%), while for others the result is lower (French-English with Power Translator Pro +16.9% vs +13.0%, German-English with Systran +9.1% vs +4.4%). The document collection parameters are the same in each case. The differences in effectiveness of

Table 11. Retrieval results incorporating PRF with merged collection weights for automatic spoken document transcriptions with topic translation using Systran

		Topic Language				
		English	French	German	Italian	Spanish
Prec.	5 docs	0.588	0.510	0.408	0.461	0.445
	10 docs	0.502	0.461	0.347	0.402	0.398
	15 docs	0.460	0.410	0.320	0.361	0.346
	20 docs	0.404	0.359	0.304	0.322	0.325
Av Precision		0.431	0.392	0.299	0.332	0.325
% chg. no FB		+23.5%	+29.4%	+10.7%	+46.9%	+29.4%
% chg. media		-19.9%	-14.8%	-21.1%	-17.2%	-22.2%
% chg. CLIR		—	-9.0%	-30.6%	-23.0%	-24.6%
% chg. media + CLIR		—	-27.1%	-44.4%	-38.3%	-39.6%
Rel. Ret.		1590	1289	1416	1352	1226
chg. no FB		+119	+79	+136	+117	+71
chg. media		-66	-140	-30	-140	-217
chg. CLIR		—	-301	-174	-238	-364
chg. media + CLIR		—	-367	-240	-304	-430

the merged collection weights for the different topic translations require further investigation.

Looking at the number of relevant documents retrieved, it can be seen that while there is an improvement in all cases, there is again no correlation between the average precision values and the increase in the number of relevant documents retrieved. Overall while the merged collection results are mixed in absolute terms, the variation between different language pairs is lower than that for the test collection only system. This indicates that the retrieval behaviour of the system is less sensitive to the initial topic translation. The amount of additional text data used here is quite small, and it would be interesting to see the effect of using progressively larger sets of contemporaneous (or even different) text data.

Spoken Document Results Tables 11 and 12 show the corresponding results for spoken document retrieval. In this case it can be seen that there are significant increases in average precision in all cases ranging from +10.7% to +46.9% (although only one figure is less than +20%). The difference in performance between spoken document retrieval and the text transcription varies between -14.0% and -22.2%, compared with the differences for the text collection only results in Tables 7 and 8 which vary from -21.3% to -29.8%. One effect of merging the extra text data with the test collection is to decrease the difference between the text document and spoken document retrieval. This improvement is derived from improved term weighting since the baseline run in each case is identical in other regards. The differences in the final PRF run are slightly more complicated, since an improved baseline run may give better feedback terms accounting for part of the improvement in the final PRF result. This result is to be expected

Table 12. Retrieval results incorporating PRF with merged collection weights for automatic spoken document transcriptions with topic translation using Power Translator Pro

		Topic Language				
		English	French	German	Italian	Spanish
Prec.	5 docs	0.588	0.474	0.449	0.441	0.469
	10 docs	0.502	0.429	0.376	0.402	0.443
	15 docs	0.460	0.380	0.342	0.362	0.386
	20 docs	0.404	0.341	0.311	0.328	0.340
Av Precision		0.431	0.351	0.325	0.334	0.373
% chg. no FB		+23.5%	+26.7%	+20.4%	+40.3%	+38.1%
% chg. media		-19.9%	-14.0%	-20.0%	-17.3%	-14.8%
% chg. CLIR		—	-18.6%	-24.6%	-22.5%	-13.5%
% chg. media + CLIR		—	-35.2%	-39.6%	-37.9%	-30.7%
Rel. Ret.		1590	1371	1406	1433	1333
chg. no FB		+119	+106	+121	+179	+99
chg. media		-66	-152	-26	-43	-50
chg. CLIR		—	-219	-184	-157	-257
chg. media + CLIR		—	-285	-250	-223	-323

since recognition errors for spoken document indexing will produce poor $cfw(i)$ estimates which can be improved by incorporating additional text data. We have previously demonstrated the importance of this factor for retrieval of scanned document images in [3]. Again it would be interesting to explore the effects of using a larger amount of additional text data. The decrease in performance for cross-language as opposed to monolingual retrieval remains in the range -9.0% to -30.6%.

Considering the number of relevant documents retrieved, the following observations can be made. In all cases there is a large increase compared to the SDR baseline, this varies between +71 and +179. In all cases there is an increase in the number of relevant documents retrieved compared to the results for test collection only PRF shown in Tables 7 and 8.

Thus, comparing the merged text and spoken document transcriptions it can be seen that merging is effective in all cases for the spoken documents whereas the results are mixed for text transcriptions. In both cases the retrieval system starts with an identical topic statement. The difference in retrieval behaviour clearly relates to query-document matching and term weighting. Indexing errors in spoken documents mean that improving the weights using contemporaneous text is on average always beneficial, for text transcriptions the modification of weights arising from merging is clearly not always useful. The exact reasons for this effect require further investigation of separate runs. As part of this investigation a further set of experiments needs to be carried out to give baseline results for the merged collections to contribute to the understanding of the effects of changes in term weighting. In addition, analysis of individual topics, their

Table 13. Data Fusion retrieval results incorporating PRF for text transcriptions

		Topic Language				
		English	French	German	Italian	Spanish
Prec.	5 docs	0.670	0.604	0.567	0.527	0.588
	10 docs	0.598	0.535	0.496	0.451	0.506
	15 docs	0.540	0.468	0.441	0.395	0.449
	20 docs	0.486	0.424	0.396	0.360	0.405
Av Precision		0.514	0.467	0.419	0.378	0.425
% chg. CLIR		—	-9.1%	-18.5%	-26.4%	-17.3%
% chg. Systran		—	+0.9%	+5.8%	-4.8%	+6.8%
% chg. PTP		—	+10.7%	+3.7%	+5.0%	-3.4%
Rel. Ret.		1631	1622	1473	1452	1529
% chg. CLIR		—	-9	-158	-179	-102
% chg. Systran		—	+160	+56	+6	+100
% chg. PTP		—	+54	+77	+18	+39

different translations and the effects of different term weights associated with individual terms needs to be carried out.

5.3 Data Fusion

Experiments in the following section explore the use of data fusion combining the output from retrieval runs carried out using the separate Systran and PTP translations. Initial results show data fusion for the test collection only retrieval systems, and subsequent experiments the corresponding results for merged collection retrieval.

Test Collection Only Results Table 13 shows document text transcription retrieval results and Table 14 corresponding results for automatic spoken document transcriptions for data fusion with PRF and test collection only term weighting. Considering first the average precision results, it can be seen that for text transcriptions results are mixed with some small losses over single translation performance, although increases observed for the other cases are generally larger than the losses, and overall the results appear more stable when data fusion is applied. The loss compared to monolingual retrieval now varies between -9.1% and -26.4%, whereas for the single translation results in Tables 7 and 8 the variation is from -9.7% to -30.0% . The results in terms of the number of relevant documents retrieved are very encouraging, in all cases there is improvement compared to single translations, and the losses compared to monolingual retrieval now vary between -9 and -102 whereas previously the loss varied from -63 to -235. The system is thus nearer to monolingual performance than either of the single translation systems in isolation.

From the spoken document results in Table 14 it can be seen that while average precision results are still somewhat mixed, data fusion appears to be more

Table 14. Data Fusion retrieval results incorporating PRF for automatic spoken document transcriptions

		Topic Language				
		English	French	German	Italian	Spanish
Prec.	5 docs	0.522	0.482	0.437	0.420	0.376
	10 docs	0.482	0.408	0.388	0.357	0.365
	15 docs	0.423	0.354	0.343	0.347	0.347
	20 docs	0.388	0.327	0.314	0.327	0.312
Av Precision		0.404	0.351	0.315	0.308	0.302
% chg. Systran		—	+2.0%	+13.3%	+4.4%	+6.7%
% chg. PTP		—	+15.1%	-0.9%	+9.2%	-4.1%
% chg. CLIR		—	-13.1%	-22.0%	-23.8%	-25.2%
% chg. media + CLIR		—	-31.7%	-38.7%	-40.1%	-41.2%
Rel. Ret.		1546	1407	1415	1414	1325
% chg. Systran		—	+165	+59	+73	+105
% chg. PTP		—	+66	+53	+91	+53
% chg. CLIR		—	-139	-131	-132	-221
% chg. media + CLIR		—	-224	-216	-217	-306

useful for the errorful automatic spoken document transcriptions than for the accurate manual text transcriptions. The loss compared to monolingual SDR now varies from -13.1% to -25.2% compared to the single translation variation from -14.9% to -31.2%. The results for the number of relevant documents retrieved show even larger gains than for text transcriptions, increasing by between +53 and +165. The loss compared to monolingual retrieval now varies between -131 and -221 which is again an improvement on the single translation results in Tables 7 and 8 which vary from -184 to -326.

Combined Collection Results Tables 15 and 16 show the corresponding data fusion results for the test collections merged with the contemporaneous text data. The results in these tables show that in all cases data fusion again leads to an increase in the overall number of relevant documents retrieved compared to retrieval with the individual translation systems. For the text transcriptions the results in Table 15 show that the loss compared to monolingual retrieval is now between -66 and -221 compared to a variation of between -133 and -275 for the separate translations, and for automatic spoken document transcriptions in Table 16 the variation is from -91 to -203 compared to -157 and -364. In terms of average precision the results are more mixed, for the text transcriptions results are lower than either separate translation for Italian and Spanish topics, in the case of Spanish by a considerable margin (merged 0.392, Systran 0.418, Power Translator Pro 0.438). This is unusual for data fusion where combination of similarly performing systems usually leads to an overall improvement in precision values. The results are more positive for the automatic spoken document transcriptions where data fusion in general gives an overall improvement.

Table 15. Data Fusion retrieval results incorporating PRF with merged collection weights for text transcriptions

		Topic Language				
		English	French	German	Italian	Spanish
Prec.	5 docs	0.718	0.551	0.547	0.510	0.474
	10 docs	0.620	0.494	0.486	0.457	0.443
	15 docs	0.548	0.450	0.426	0.403	0.401
	20 docs	0.490	0.418	0.384	0.369	0.377
Av Precision		0.538	0.451	0.416	0.392	0.392
% chg. Systran		—	-2.0%	+9.8%	-2.2%	-6.2%
% chg. PTP		—	+10.5%	+2.5%	-1.2%	-10.5%
% chg. CLIR		—	-16.2%	-22.7%	-27.1%	-27.1%
Rel. Ret.		1656	1590	1483	1509	1451
% chg. Systran		—	+161	+37	+17	+8
% chg. PTP		—	+67	+51	+33	+68
% chg. CLIR		—	-139	-131	-132	-221

Table 16. Data Fusion retrieval results incorporating PRF with merged collection weights for automatic spoken document transcriptions

		Topic Language				
		English	French	German	Italian	Spanish
Prec.	5 docs	0.588	0.498	0.465	0.474	0.461
	10 docs	0.502	0.453	0.394	0.422	0.404
	15 docs	0.460	0.399	0.355	0.378	0.366
	20 docs	0.404	0.359	0.326	0.354	0.332
Av Precision		0.431	0.393	0.333	0.349	0.350
% chg. Systran		—	+0.3%	+11.4%	+5.1%	+7.7%
% chg. PTP		—	+12.0%	+2.5%	+4.5%	-6.2%
% chg. CLIR		—	-8.8%	-22.7%	-19.0%	-18.8%
% chg. media + CLIR		—	-28.2%	-38.1%	-35.1%	-34.9%
Rel. Ret.		1590	1436	1482	1499	1387
% chg. Systran		—	+147	+66	+147	+161
% chg. PTP		—	+65	+76	+66	+54
% chg. CLIR		—	-154	-108	-91	-203
% chg. media + CLIR		—	-220	-174	-157	-269

6 Conclusions and Further Work

The following conclusions can be drawn from this initial study. Indexing errors in the automatic spoken document transcriptions and inappropriate word translations in the topics both lead to reductions in precision and the number of relevant documents retrieved. It is clear also that PRF is effective for this test collection both for the text transcriptions and the spoken document transcriptions. There is generally an increase in both precision values and the number of relevant documents retrieved. Combining the test collection with a small contemporaneous text document collection shows little benefit for the text transcriptions, but gives consistent improvements for the spoken document transcriptions. Data fusion has mixed results for precision with text documents, but is again more reliable for spoken document retrieval. In both cases it has a positive impact on the number of relevant documents retrieved. This presumably relates to the combination of the different words appearing in the two query translations locating more relevant documents.

The study described in this report establishes a baseline for CLSDR for the TREC-8 SDR collection. Further studies are required to build on this work to seek to improve CLSDR performance relative to the monolingual text baseline. There are a number of techniques which have been developed to improve performance in existing SDR and CLIR studies. These techniques may also offer improvements for CLSDR and need to be investigated. For example, further investigation of the use of contemporaneous text collections to improve term weighting; the small one used here has been shown to be effective particularly with spoken documents. The extent to which this can improve performance can be investigated by using progressively larger sets of text documents. Use of a pilot collection as a source of expansion terms for PRF, not just for term weighting – on its own or in combination with the test collection needs to be explored. In addition, it may be possible to develop further techniques specifically applicable to CLSDR.

References

[1] J. S. Garafolo, C. G. P. Auzanne, and E. M. Voorhees. The TREC Spoken Document Retrieval Track: A Success Story. In *Proceedings of the RIAO 2000 Conference: Content-Based Multimedia Information Access*, pages 1–20, Paris, 2000.

[2] G. J. F. Jones and M. Federico. CLEF 2002 Cross-Language Spoken Document Retrieval Pilot Track Report. In *Proceedings of the CLEF 2002: Workshop on Cross-Language Information Retrieval and Evaluation*, Rome, September 2002. Springer Verlag.

[3] G. J. F.Jones and A. M.Lam-Adesina. Examining the Effectiveness of IR Techniques for Document Image Retrieval. In *Proceedings of the Workshop on Information Retrieval and OCR: From Converting Content to Grasping Meaning at Twenty-Fifth Annual International ACM SIGIR Conference on Research and Development in Information Retrieval (SIGIR 2002)*, Tampere, 2002.

[4] G. J. F. Jones and A. M. Lam-Adesina. Exeter at CLEF 2001: Experiments with Machine Translation for bilingual retrieval. In *Proceedings of the CLEF 2001: Workshop on Cross-Language Information Retrieval and Evaluation*, pages 59–77, Darmstadt, September 2001. Springer Verlag.

[5] L. Ballesteros and W. B. Croft. Phrasal Translation and Query Expansion Techniques for Cross-Language Information Retrieval. In *Proceedings of the 20th Annual International ACM SIGIR Conference on Research and Development in Information Retrieval*, pages 84–91, Philadelphia, 1997. ACM.

[6] G. J. F. Jones, T. Sakai, N. H. Collier, A. Kumano, and K. Sumita. A Comparison of Query Translation Methods for English-Japanese Cross-Language Information Retrieval. In *Proceedings of the 22nd Annual International ACM SIGIR Conference on Research and Development in Information Retrieval*, pages 269–270, San Fransisco, 1999. ACM.

[7] G. J. F.Jones and A. M.Lam-Adesina. Combination Methods for Improving the Reliability of Machine Translation Based Cross-language Information Retrieval. In *Proceedings of the 13th Irish Conference on Artificial Intelligence & Cognitive Science*, pages pp190–196, Limerick, 2002. Springer Verlag.

[8] N. J. Belkin, P. Kantor, E. A. Fox, and J. A. Shaw. Combining the Evidence of Multiple Query Representations for Information Retrieval. *Information Processing and Management*, 31:431–448, 1995.

[9] G. J. F.Jones and A. M.Lam-Adesina. An Investigation of Techniques for Improving Machine Translation Based Cross-Language Information Retrieval. Technical Report 404, Department of Computer Science, University of Exeter, October 2002.

[10] S. E. Robertson, S. Walker, S. Jones, M. M. Hancock-Beaulieu, and M. Gatford. Okapi at TREC-3. In D. K. Harman, editor, *Overview of the Third Text REtrieval Conference (TREC-3)*, pages 109–126. NIST, 1995.

[11] S. E. Johnson, P. Jourlin, K. Sparck Jones, and P. C. Woodland. Spoken Document Retrieval for TREC-8 at Cambridge University. In D. K. Harman and E. M. Voorhees, editors, *Proceedings of the Eighth Text REtrieval Conference (TREC-8)*, pages 157–168, Gaithersburg, MD, 2000. NIST.

[12] M. F. Porter. An algorithm for suffix stripping. *Program*, 14:130–137, 1980.

[13] S. E. Robertson. On term selection for query expansion. *Journal of Documentation*, 46:359–364, 1990.

[14] A. M. Lam-Adesina and G. J. F. Jones. Applying Summarization Techniques for Term Selection in Relevance Feedback. In *Proceedings of the 24th Annual International ACM SIGIR Conference on Research and Development in Information Retrieval*, pages 1–9, New Orleans, 2001. ACM.

[15] S. E. Robertson, S. Walker, and M. M. Beaulieu. Okapi at TREC-7: automatic ad hoc, filtering, vls and interactive track. In E. Voorhees and D. K. Harman, editors, *Proceedings of the Seventh Text REtrieval Conference (TREC-7)*, pages 253–264. NIST, 1999.

[16] D. Abberley, S. Renals, D. Ellis, and T. Robinson. The THISL SDR System At TREC-8. In E. Voorhees and D. K. Harman, editors, *Proceedings of the Eighth Text REtrieval Conference (TREC-8)*, pages 699–706. NIST, 2000.

Cross-Language Spoken Document Retrieval on the TREC SDR Collection

N. Bertoldi and M. Federico

ITC-irst – Centro per la Ricerca Scientifica e Tecnologica
I-38050 Povo, Trento, Italy
{bertoldi,federico}@itc.it

Abstract. This paper presents preliminary experiments on cross-language spoken document retrieval (SDR) carried out on a benchmark assembled at ITC-irst. The benchmark is based on resources used in the last two spoken document retrieval tracks at the TREC conference, which are available on the Internet. They include automatic transcripts of American English broadcast news, short topics written in English, and relevance assessments. The extension from monolingual to cross-language SDR was obtained by translating all topics into five European languages: Dutch, French, German, Italian, and Spanish. In this paper preliminary experiments on the last four languages are presented. Translations of the topics will be used to run a pilot track in CLEF 2003.

1 Introduction

Digital audiovisual archives represent a relevant sector of the digital library landscape. Cross-language (CL) information retrieval (IR) provides an important way to access multi-lingual documents. CL spoken document retrieval (SDR) extends the IR framework by assuming that queries and target documents are not in the same language, and that the target documents are in spoken form, e.g. recordings of broadcast news.

In the recent years, speech recognition technology has made impressive advances and has proven to be effective for indexing the audio trace of broadcast news programs. At the TREC Conference in 2000, the best text retrieval systems showed no significant degradation in performance when applied to automatically generated transcripts of broadcast news[4]. Although SDR seems to be a solved problem, the same is not necessarily true for CL-SDR. This paper reports preliminary experiments on CL-SDR performed at ITC-irst by exploiting American English topics and automatic transcripts used in the last TREC SDR tracks. In particular, retrieval was performed on manually segmented stories by means of translations of the original topics into several European languages.

This paper is organized as follows. Section 2 briefly introduces the CL-SDR benchmark used here. Section 3 summarizes the main features of the ITC-irst statistical CL-IR system. Section 4 describes preliminary experiments. Finally, Section 5 presents some conclusions.

C.A. Peters (Ed.): CLEF 2002, LNCS 2785, pp. 476–481, 2003.

2 CL-SDR Benchmark

A CL-SDR benchmark [9] was assembled by ITC-irst, and is based on the collection of American English broadcast news prepared by NIST for two SDR evaluations, namely under TREC 8 and TREC 9.

Briefly, broadcast news shows were automatically transcribed by NIST, for a total of 389 hours of speech, with an estimated word error rate of 26.7%. The resulting time-aligned transcripts were manually segmented into stories, commercials, and fillers. The result is a collection of 21,754 stories. Two sets of short topics were developed for two subsequent SDR tracks, for a total of 100 topics. Participants of the tracks were either invited to use their in-house broadcast news transcription system, or to use the automatic transcripts provided by NIST.

In order to perform CL-SDR, ITC-irst managed the translation of each topic into five other European languages: Dutch, French, German, Italian and Spanish. Translations were made by native speakers.

In TREC, two retrieval conditions were defined: one assuming the story boundaries are given, the other assuming the story boundaries to be unknown. Although only the second hypothesis sounds realistic, preliminary experiments were only conducted under the known-story boundary condition. In this way, SDR can be approached similarly to document retrieval.

3 Statistical CL-IR

The ITC-irst CL-IR system [3, 2] integrates a retrieval model and a translation model in a single statistical framework. The retrieval model relies on the combination of a statistical language model, and the well-known Okapi formula. The query-translation model is based on a hidden Markov model. The observable part of it is the input query, while the hidden part is the translation of the query into the document language. Parameters of the translation model are trained on a bilingual dictionary and the target document collection. Finally, cross-language retrieval scores results as an expectation of monolingual retrieval scores taken over the N most probable translations of the query [2]

Queries and documents are preprocessed in order to normalize words, remove functional words, and reduce the size of the index file. As the CL-IR system should work with any language pair, the preprocessing procedure was uniformed to reduce cost of porting to new languages. Hence, texts are stemmed by Porter-like algorithms [5], and stop-terms are removed by means of available language dependent lists [7].

Multi-words occurring in the bilingual dictionary are joined only for the sake of topic translation. Proper names, which are automatically spotted in the topics, are translated verbatim if not translated differently by the dictionary. Of course, the result is just a reasonable guess which may succeed in some cases, e.g. names of people, and eventually fail in others e.g. names of countries.

Major improvements in text retrieval performance are obtained by expanding the query on the same target collection through a blind relevance feedback (BRF)

Table 1. Statistics about dictionaries and queries

Language	Dictionary entries	Mean query length	Coverage words	Coverage +proper names
French	44,727	6.23	85.87%	92.94%
German	131,428	5.85	79.83%	—
Italian	44,194	6.51	84.49%	92.17%
Spanish	47,304	6.26	91.21%	96.49%

procedure [3]: 15 terms, with the highest Offer Weights [8] in the 5 top rank retrieved documents, are added to the original query. As the number of stories in the SDR target collection is quite small, a double query expansion policy was chosen: first query expansion was performed on a parallel text collection (see next section) and then on the target collection.

4 Language Resources

4.1 Parallel Text Collection

A larger document collection was used both for topic translation and query expansion. In particular, a slightly smaller collection was employed than that used by participants oin the TREC SDR tracks. It consists of the target collection of automatic transcripts and of a parallel corpus of written news, extracted from *Los Angeles Times*, *Washington Post*, *New York Times*, and *Associated Press Worldstream*, and issued between September 1997 and April 1998[1]. Unfortunately, we were not able to acquire the full parallel text collection, which entirely covers the test period, i.e. until June 1998.

4.2 Bilingual Dictionaries

Bilingual dictionaries used for topic translation were gathered from the Internet, and their statistics are reported in Table 1. Unfortunately, Dutch could not be included because the available dictionary resulted too small. Coverage of the dictionaries with respect to the queries are given before and after proper name recognition. As proper name recognition is not as straightforward for German, mainly because common nouns are also capitalized, in this preliminary work proper name recognition was not performed for German.

[1] These corpora are distributed by LDC.

5 Experimental eEvaluation

5.1 Monolingual SDR

A first English monolingual run was carried out to compare performance of our IR model with those who participated tin the TREC SDR tracks. In particular, the first 50 available topics were used at TREC 1999, while the latter 50 at TREC 2000. Results in mean average precision (`mAvPr`) are reported in Table 2. By taking into account the different conditions under which the TREC systems and our system were developed, these results, together with those achieved in the CLEF campaigns [1, 2, 3], confirm that our monolingual retrieval system is comparable with the state-of-the-art.

Table 2. Results on TREC 1999 and 2000 SDR tasks.

System	1999	2000
Sheffield	.5335	—
CUHTK	.5302	.4831
LIMSI	.4839	.4620
IRST	.5640	.4372

5.2 CL-SDR Results

The experiments carried out are summarized in Table 3. Reported figures are the `mAvPr` before query expansion (base), after expansion on the target collection (trg), after expansion on the parallel collection (par), and after sequential query expansion on both (par+trg). Results are given using the 1-best, 5-best, and 10-best translations. For the sake of comparison, the same figures are also given for the English monolingual run.

The results in Table 3 suggest the following remarks. Double query expansion is effective, and outperforms single expansions both on the target and on the parallel collection alone. The final gain with respect to the "base" runs is little less than the sum of the gains with the single expansions. Moreover, using more than one translation improves performance of our CL-SDR system, at least on average. Nevertheless, in order to measure significant differences a much larger set of queries would be needed. Furthermore, a strong correlation between retrieval performance and dictionary coverage was observed. Indeed, the best performances were achieved with Spanish, whose dictionary also provides the best coverage.

5.3 Translation Quality

Finally, comparative experiments were made to evaluate our statistical query-translation model. CL-IR experiments were performed with translations computed by our statistical approach and by a commercial text translation system.

Table 3. Results on CL-SDR task for French, German, Italian, and Spanish, and on SDR task on English

Language	Translation	Base	BRF		
			trg	par	par+trg
`English`		.3620	.4584	.4582	.5033
`French`	1-best	.2016	.2658	.2707	.2950
`French`	5-best	.1980	.2818	.2814	.3123
`French`	10-best	.1967	.2817	.2823	.3172
`German`	1-best	.2015	.2569	.2700	.2920
`German`	5-best	.2016	.2688	.2620	.2993
`German`	10-best	.2030	.2700	.2607	.2867
`Italian`	1-best	.1898	.2586	.2529	.2669
`Italian`	5-best	.1917	.2640	.2548	.2811
`Italian`	10-best	.1912	.2660	.2463	.2723
`Spanish`	1-best	.2389	.2694	.3092	.3328
`Spanish`	5-best	.2438	.2945	.3293	.3609
`Spanish`	10-best	.2448	.2938	.3306	.3644

In particular, the Babelfish translation service [6] was used, which is powered by Systran and is available on the Internet. Results on the whole set of topics are reported in Table 4 for French, German, Italian, and Spanish. Moreover, the percentages of mean average precision of the monolingual (ML) system which are covered by each cross-language (CL) system are also reported.
It results that, on the average, our system performs significantly worse than Systran. In fact, a closer look at the rankings of single topics, showed that about 70% of the times our translations resulted in a `mAvPr` lower than that of Systran. Again, the smallest gap was achieved with Spanish.

Table 4. Results with different query translations, and comparison with the monolingual system

Language	Translation	Base		+BRF	
		mavpr	CL/ML%	mavpr	CL/ML %
`French`	Systran	.2691	74.34	.4101	81.48
`French`	N-best	.1967	54.34	.3172	63.02
`German`	Systran	.2569	70.97	.3520	69.94
`German`	N-best	.2016	55.69	.2993	59.47
`Italian`	Systran	.2375	65.61	.3650	72.52
`Italian`	N-best	.1917	52.96	.2811	55.85
`Spanish`	Systran	.2757	76.16	.3960	78.68
`Spanish`	N-best	.2448	67.62	.3644	72.40

6 Conclusion

This paper has presented preliminary experiments on cross-language IR with several European languages. Automatic transcripts of American English broadcast news were used as the document collection. The results reported are very preliminary; however they can give some ideas about the task peculiarities.

- The known story boundary condition allows the same approaches to be used for CL-SDR as for written documents. Results reported at TREC show that recognition errors seem to have marginal impact on retrieval performance.
- Major performance improvements can be obtained by applying query expansion not only on the target collection, but also on a larger comparable corpus of written news.
- Experiments on several languages have shown strong correlation between dictionary coverage and retrieval performance.
- The comparison against Systran showed the weakness of our translation model on short topics. Previous experiments on longer topics showed that our translation model compares well with Systran.

Future work will go in three directions: (i) to develop dictionaries with a better coverage; to improve translation of short queries (ii) by exploiting query expansion in the source language, and (iii) by better statistical modelling.

Acknowledgements

This work was carried out within the project WebFAQ funded under the FDR-PAT program of the Province of Trento.

References

[1] N. Bertoldi and M. Federico. ITC-irst at CLEF 2000: Italian monolingual track. In C. Peters, editor, *Cross-Language Information Retrieval and Evaluation*, LNCS 2069, pages 261–272, Heidelberg, Germany, 2001. Springer Verlag.

[2] N. Bertoldi and M. Federico. ITC-irst at CLEF 2001: Monolingual and bilingual tracks. In C. Peters, et al, (eds.), *Evaluation of Cross-Language Information Retrieval Systems*, LNCS 2406, pages 94–101, Springer Verlag 2002.

[3] N. Bertoldi and M. Federico. ITC-irst at CLEF 2002: Using N-best query translations for CL-IR. This volume.

[4] J. Garofolo, G. Auzanne, and E. Voorhees. The TREC spoken document retrieval track: A success story. In *Proc. of the RIAO: Content Based Multimedia Information Access Conference*, Paris, France, 2000.

[5] http://snowball.tartarus.org.

[6] http://world.altavista.com.

[7] http://www.unine.ch/info/clef.

[8] S. Johnson, P. Jourlin, K. S. Jones, and P. Woodland. Spoken document retrieval for TREC-8 at Cambridge University. In *TREC-8 Proceedings*, Gaithersburg, MD, 1999.

[9] G. J. F. Jones, and M. Federico. CLEF2002 Cross-Language Spoken Document Retrieval Pilot Track Report. This volume.

Part II

Cross-Language Systems Evaluation Initiatives, Issues and Results

CLIR at NTCIR Workshop 3: Cross-Language and Cross-Genre Retrieval

Noriko Kando

National Institute of Informatics
Tokyo 101-8430, Japan
kando@nii.ac.jp

Abstract: This paper introduces the NTCIR Workshops, a series of evaluation workshops that are designed to enhance research in information access technologies, such as information retrieval, text summarization, question answering, information extraction, and text mining, by providing large-scale test collections and a forum for researchers. A brief history and descriptions of tasks, participants, test collections and CLIR evaluation at the workshops, and a brief overview of the third NTCIR Workshop are given. To conclude, some thoughts on future directions are suggested.

1 Introduction

The *NTCIR Workshops* [1] are a series of evaluation workshops designed to enhance research in information access (IA) technologies including information retrieval (IR), cross-lingual information retrieval (CLIR), information extraction (IE), automatic text summarization, and question answering.

The aims of the NTCIR project are:

1. to encourage research in information access technologies by providing large-scale test collections reusable for experiments, and common evaluation infrastructures,
2. to provide a forum for research groups interested in cross-system comparisons and exchanging research ideas in an informal atmosphere, and
3. to investigate methodologies and metrics for evaluation of information access technologies and methods for constructing large-scale reusable test collections.

The importance of large-scale standard test collections in IA research has been widely recognized. Fundamental text processing procedures for IA such as stemming and indexing are language-dependent. In particular, processing texts written in Japanese or other East Asian languages such as Chinese is quite different from processing English, French or other European languages, because there are no explicit boundaries (*i.e.*, no spaces) between words in a sentence. The NTCIR project therefore started in late 1997 with emphasis on, but not limited to, Japanese or other

C.A. Peters (Ed.): CLEF 2002, LNCS 2785, pp. 485-504, 2003.

East Asian languages, and its series of workshops has attracted international participation.

1.1 Information Access

The term "information access" (IA) embraces an entire process aimed at making information in the documents usable. A traditional IR system returns a ranked list of retrieved documents, possibly from a vast document collection, that are likely to contain information relevant to the user's needs. This is one of the most fundamental and core processes of IA. It is however not the end of the story for the users. After obtaining a ranked list of retrieved documents, the user skims the documents, performs relevance judgments, locates the relevant information, reads, analyses, compares the contents with other documents, integrates, summarizes and performs information-based work such as decision making, problem solving, writing, etc., based on the information obtained from the retrieved documents. We have looked at IA technologies to help users utilize the information in large-scale document collections.

In the following, the next section provides a brief history of *NTCIR* and term definitions. Section 3 describes the third *NTCIR* Workshop, the latest in the series, and test collections with a focus on CLIR-related tasks. Section 4 summarizes the discussion on the future direction of CLIR evaluation focusing on the East Asian language context.

2 *NTCIR*

2.1 Brief History of *NTCIR*

The *NTCIR Workshops* are periodical events that have taken place at about 18-month intervals since 1997. They had been co-sponsored by the Japan Society for Promotion of Science (JSPS) as part of the JSPS "*Research for the Future" Program* (JSPS-RFTF 96P00602) and by the National Center for Science Information Systems (NACSIS). In April 2000, NACSIS was reorganized and changed its name to the National Institute of Informatics (NII). NTCIR was co-sponsored by the JSPS and the Research Center for Information Resources at NII (RCIR/NII,) in FY2000, and by the RCIR/NII and *Japanese MEXT*[1] *Grant-in-Aid for Scientific Research on Informatics (#13224087)* in and after FY2001. The tasks, test collections constructed, and participants of the previous workshops are summarized in Table 1.

For the First NTCIR Workshop, the process started with the distribution of the training data set on 1 November 1998, and ended with the workshop meeting, which was held from 30 August to 1 September 1999 in Tokyo, Japan [2]. NTCIR and IREX [3], another evaluation workshop of IR and IE (named entities) that uses Japanese newspaper articles, joined forces in 2000 and have worked together to organize the NTCIR Workshops since then. The challenging tasks of Text Summarization and Question Answering became feasible with this collaboration.

[1] MEXT: Ministry of Education, Culture, Sports, Science and Technology

Table 1. Previous NTCIR Workshops

	period	tasks	subtasks	test collections	participants* (attribute)					count-ries
							co.	nat.	univ	
1	Nov.1998- Sept.1999	Ad Hoc IR	J-JE	NTCIR-1	18	28	9	4	15	6
		CLIR	J-E		10					
		Term Extraction	term extraction		9					
			role analysis							
2	June 2000- March 2001	Chinese Text Retrieval	monolingual IR: C-C	CIRB010	11	36	12	4	20	8
			CLIR: E-C							
		Japanese&English IR	monolingual IR: J-J, E-E	NTCIR-1, -2	25					
			CLIR J-E, E-J, J-JE, E-JE							
		Text Summarization	task A-1: intrinsic - extraction	NTCIR-2Summ	9					
			task A-2: intrinsic - abstract							
			task B: extrinsic - IR task-based							
3	Aug. 2001- Oct. 2002	CLIR	single lang IR:C-C,K-K,J-J	NTCIR-3CLIR, CIRB020, KEIB010	23	65	14	7	44	9
			bilingual CLIR:x-J,x-C, x-K							
			mulilingual CLIR:x-CJE							
		Patent Retrieval	cross genre	NTCIR-3Patent	10					
			CLIR x-J, x-JEabst							
			optional task: alignments, readability							
		Question Answering	task1- 5 candidate answers	NTCIR-3QA	16					
			task2-one set of all the answers							
			task3-series of questions							
		Text Summarization	task A: single text	NTCIR-3Summ	8					
			task B: multiple texts							
		Web Retrieval	survey retrieval	NTCIR-3Web	7					
			target retrieval							
			optional task: search result classification, speech-driven retrieval							

"n-m" for CLIR: n=query language, m=document language(s), J:Japanese, E:English, C:Chinese, K:Korean, x:any of CJKE

*: number of active participating groups that submitted task results; co:company, nat:national/independent research institut univ:unviersity

An international collaboration to organize Asian-language IR evaluation was proposed at the 4th International Workshop on Information Retrieval with Asian Languages (IRAL '99). In accordance with the proposal, Hsin-Hsi Chen and Kuang-hua Chen, National Taiwan University, organized the Chinese Text Retrieval Task at the second workshop and Cross-Lingual Information Retrieval of Asian languages at the third workshop.

For the Second Workshop, the process was started in June 2000 and the meeting was held on 7–9 March 2001 at NII [4]. The process of the Third NTCIR Workshop started in October, 2001 and the meeting was held on 8–10 October 2002 at NII, Tokyo [5].

2.2 Focus of *NTCIR*

Through the series of the NTCIR Workshops, we have looked at both traditional laboratory-type IR system testing and the evaluation of challenging technologies. For the laboratory-type testing, we placed emphasis on 1) information retrieval (IR) with Japanese or other Asian languages and 2) cross-lingual information retrieval. For the challenging issues, 3) the shift from document retrieval to technologies that utilize "information" in documents, and 4) investigation of evaluation methodologies, including the evaluation of: automatic text summarization; multi-grade relevance judgments for IR; and evaluation methods appropriate to the retrieval and processing of a particular document genre and its usage by the user group.

From the beginning, CLIR has been one of the central interests of *NTCIR*, because CLIR between English and own-languages is critical for international information transfer in Asian countries, and it was challenging to perform CLIR between languages with completely different structures and origins such as English and Chinese or English and Japanese. CLIR techniques may also be needed even for monolingual text retrieval [6]. For example, a part of a document is sometimes written in English (e.g., a Japanese document often contains an English abstract or figure captions, but no Japanese abstract or captions). Technical terms or new terms can be represented in four different forms: English terms with original spelling; acronyms of the English terms using roman alphabets; transliterated forms of the English terms in Japanese characters; and Japanese terms. This variety in term expression often causes a decline in search effectiveness, and CLIR techniques are effective in overcoming the problem. In these years, interest towards social and cultural aspects in other East Asian countries has been acutely increasing especially among the younger generation. The importance of technological information transfer within Asia has sharply increased in the business and industrial sectors. In response to such social needs, the CLIR task has changed from English-Japanese Scientific documents to multilingual newspapers and patent documents in the latest NTCIR workshop.

Table 2. Test collections constructed through NTCIR

collection	task	documents			topic		relevance judgment
		genre	size	lang	lang	#	
NTCIR-1	IR	sci. abstract	577MB	JE	J	83	3 grades
CIRB010	IR	newspaper 98-9	210MB	C	CE	50	4 grades
NTCIR-2	IR	sci. abstract	800MB	JE	JE	49	4 grades
NTCIR-2 SUMM	Summ	newspaer94,95,98	180 doc	J	J	-	-
NTCIR-2TAO	Summ	newspaper98	1000 doc	J	J	-	-
KEIB010	IR	newpaper94	74MB	K	CKJE	30	4 grades
CIRB011+020, NTCIR-3CLIR	IR	newspaper 98-9	870MB	CJE		50	4 grades
NTCIR-3PAT	IR	patent full'98-9	17GB	J	CCKJE	31	3 grades
		+abstract'95-9	4GB	JE			
NTCIR-3 QA	QA	newspaper 98-9	282MB	J	J	240+60+ about 900	2 grades
NTCIR-3 SUMM	Summ	newspaper 98-9	30 docs + 30 sets of docs	J	J	-	-
NTCIR-3Web	IR	HTML	100GB	J(E)	J	47	5 grades

J:Japanese, E:English, C:Chinese, K:Korean

2.3 Test Collections

A test collection is a data set used in system testing or experiments. In the NTCIR project the term "test collection" is used for any kind of data set usable for system testing and experiments though it often means an IR test collection used in search experiments. The test collections constructed for the NTCIR Workshops are listed in Table 2.

2.3.1 Documents

Documents were collected from various domains or genres. Each task carefully selected the appropriate domain of document collection. The task (experiment) design and relevance judgment criteria were set according to the document collection and the user community of the type of documents. Figure 1 shows a sample record in NTCIR-3 CLIR. Documents are plain text with SGML-like tags in the NTCIR collections. The collection consists of news articles published in Taiwan, ROC, Korea and Japan in the languages of Chinese (Traditional), Korean, Japanese, and English.

```
<DOC>
<DOCNO>ctg_xxx_19990110_0001</DOCNO>
<LANG>EN</LANG>
<HEADLINE> Asia Urged to Move Faster in Shoring Up Shaky Banks </HEADLINE>
<DATE>1999-01-10</DATE>
<TEXT>
<P>HONG KONG, Jan 10 (AFP) - Bank for International Settlements (BIS) general manager Andrew Crockett has urged Asian economies to move faster in reforming their shaky banking sectors, reports said Sunday. Speaking ahead of Monday's meeting at the BIS office here of international central bankers including US Federal Reserve chairman Alan Greenspan, Crockett said he was encouraged by regional banking reforms but "there is still some way to go." Asian banks shake off their burden of bad debt if they were to be able to finance recovery in the crisis-hit region, he said according to the Sunday Morning Post. Crockett added that more stable currency exchange rates and lower interest rates had paved the way for recovery. "Therefore I believe in the financial area, the crisis has in a sense been contained and that now it is possible to look forward to real economic recovery," he was quoted as saying by the Sunday Hong Kong Standard.</P>
<P>"It would not surprise me, given the interest I know certain governors have, if the subject of hedge funds was discussed during the meeting," Crockett said. </P>
<P>He reiterated comments by BIS officials here that the central bankers would stay tight-lipped about their meeting, the first to be held at the Hong Kong office of the Swiss-based institution since it opened last July. </P>
</TEXT>
</DOC>
```

Fig. 1. Sample document (NTCIR-3 CLIR)

2.3.2 Topics

A sample topic record used in the CLIR task at the NTCIR Workshop 3 is shown in Fig. 2. Topics are defined as statements of "user's requests" rather than "queries", which are the strings actually submitted to the system, because we wish to allow both manual and automatic query construction from the topics.

The topics contain SGML-like tags. A topic consists of the title of the topic, a description (question), a detailed narrative, and a list of concepts and field(s). The title is a very short description of the topic and can be used as a very short query that resembles those often submitted by users of Internet search engines[2]. Each narrative may contain a detailed explanation of the topic, term definitions, background knowledge, the purpose of the search, criteria for judgment of relevance, etc.

Task organizers chose a specific set of topic field or fields as "mandatory runs" and every participant must submit at least one set of mandatory runs. The purpose of the mandatory runs is to enhance the cross-system comparison on the common condition of experiments. As optional runs, participants could submit runs using any topic fields and reported the topic fields used. The topic field(s) specified for the mandatory runs may vary according to the purpose and nature of the experiments of each task. "<DESC> only" is the mandatory run we have used in the previous NTCIR Workshops and CLIR at the NTCIR Workshop 3. Both <DESC> only and <TITLE> only are the mandatory runs for WEB task.

```
<TOPIC>
<NUM>002</NUM>
<SLANG>CH</SLANG>
<TLANG>EN</TLANG>
<TITLE>Joining WTO </TITLE>
<DESC>
Find possible problems that industries will meet after Taiwan's joining WTO.
</DESC>
<NARR>
It has taken Taiwan 10 years to get in to WTO. The Council For Economic Planning and
Development, Chung-Hua Institution for Economic Research and Taiwan Institution for Economic
Research evaluated the beneficial result of joining WTO. Related contents are supposed to include
the evaluation contents, the advantages and disadvantages and the effects on agriculture, industry and
business. If the documents only describe the opinions, comments, and attitudes of the America and
other countries, or the political and diplomatic issues, they will be regarded irrelevant.
</NARR>
<CONC>
Taiwan, WTO, agriculture, industry, benefits, economy, World Trade Organization
</CONC>
</TOPIC>
```

Fig. 2. Sample topic (CLIR at NTCIR WS 3)

2.3.3 Relevance Judgments (Right Answers)

The relevance judgments were conducted using multiple grades. Relevance judgment files contained not only the relevance of each document in the pool, but also contained extracted phrases or passages showing the reason the analyst assessed the document as "relevant". These statements were used to confirm the judgments, and also in the hope of future use in experiments related to extracting answer passages.

In addition, we proposed new measures, *weighted R precision* and *weighted average precision*, for IR system testing with ranked output based on multi-grade

[2] In the Web Retrieval task at the NTCIR Workshop 3, <TITLE> was clearly defined as a list of query terms put in the search engine by the user. It contains up to three terms, separated by commas. Terms are arranged in descending order of importance to express the search request, and the relation between the terms are specified as an attribute.

relevance judgments [7]. Intuitively, highly relevant documents are more important for users than partially relevant ones, and the documents retrieved with higher ranks in the ranked list are more important. Therefore, the systems producing search results in which higher-relevance documents are in higher ranks in the ranked list, should be rated as better. Based on the review of existing IR system evaluation measures, it was decided that both of the proposed measures should be single numbers, and could be averaged over a number of topics.

Most IR systems and experiments have assumed that the highly relevant items are useful to all users. However, some user-oriented studies have suggested that partially relevant items may be important for specific users and they should not be collapsed into relevant or irrelevant items, but should be analyzed separately [8]. More investigation is required.

2.3.4 Linguistic Analysis (Additional Data)

NTCIR–1 contains a "Tagged Corpus". This contains detailed hand-tagged part-of-speech (POS) tags for 2000 Japanese documents selected from NTCIR–1 Japanese document collection. Spelling errors were manually corrected. Because of the absence of explicit boundaries between words in Japanese sentences, we set three levels of lexical boundaries (*i.e.*, word boundaries, and strong and weak morpheme boundaries).

In NTCIR–2, segmented data for the whole J (Japanese document) collection are provided. They were segmented into three levels of lexical boundaries using a commercially available morphological analyzer called *HAPPINESS*. An analysis of the effect of segmentation is reported in Yoshioka et al. [9].

2.3.5 Robustness of System Evaluation Using the Test Collections

The test collections *NTCIR–1* and *–2* have been tested for the following aspects, to enable their use as a reliable tool for IR system testing:

- exhaustiveness of the document pool
- inter-analyst consistency and its effect on system evaluation
- topic-by-topic evaluation.

The results have been reported on various occasions [10–13]. In terms of exhaustiveness, pooling the top 100 documents from each run worked well for topics with fewer than 100 relevant documents. For topics with more than 100 relevant documents, although the top 100 pooling covered only 51.9 % of the total relevant documents, coverage was higher than 90 % if combined with additional interactive searches. Therefore, we conducted additional interactive searches for topics with more than 50 relevant documents in the first workshop, and those with more than 100 relevant documents in the second workshop.

When the pool size was larger than 2500 for a topic, the number of documents collected from each run was reduced to 90 or 80. This was done to keep the pool size practical and manageable for assessors to keep consistency in the pool. Even though the numbers of documents collected in the pool were different for each topic, the number of documents collected from each run is exactly the same for a specific topic.

A strong correlation was found to exist between the system rankings produced using different relevance judgments and different pooling methods, regardless of the inconsistency of the relevance assessments between analysts and regardless of the different pooling methods used [1–12, 14]. These results serve as an additional support to the analysis reported by Voorhees [15].

2.4 NTCIR Workshop 1 (Nov. 1998 – Sept. 1999)

The first NTCIR Workshop [2] hosted the following three tasks:

1. *Ad Hoc Information Retrieval Task*: to search a static set of documents using new search topics (J -> JE).
2. *Cross-Lingual Information Retrieval Task*: an ad hoc task in which the documents are in English and the topics are in Japanese (J -> E).
3. *Automatic Term Recognition and Role Analysis Tasks*: (1) to extract terms from titles and abstracts of Japanese documents, and (2) to identify the terms representing the "object", "method", and "main operation" of the main topic of each document.

In the Ad Hoc Information Retrieval Task, the documents collection containing Japanese, English and Japanese-English paired documents was retrieved by Japanese search topics, therefore, it was substantially CLIR, although some of the participants discarded the English part and performed the task as a Japanese monolingual IR. In Japan, document collections often naturally consist of such a mixture of Japanese and English.

Table 3. Active participants for the first NTCIR Workshop

Communications Research Laboratory (Japan)	RMIT and CSIRO (Australia)
Fuji Xerox (Japan)	Tokyo Univ. of Technology (Japan)
Fujitsu Laboratories (Japan)	Toshiba (Japan)
Central Research Laboratory, Hitachi Co. (Japan)	Toyohashi Univ. of Technology (Japan)
JUSTSYSTEM Corp. (Japan)	Univ. of California Berkeley (US)
Kanagawa Univ. (2) (Japan)	Univ. of Lib. and Inf. Science (Tsukuba, Japan)
KAIST/KORTERM (Korea)	Univ. of Maryland (US)
Manchester Metropolitan Univ. (UK)	Univ. of Tokushima (Japan)
Matsushita Electric Industrial (Japan)	Univ. of Tokyo (Japan)
NACSIS (Japan)	Univ. of Tsukuba (Japan)
National Taiwan Univ. (Taiwan ROC)	Yokohama National Univ. (Japan)
NEC (2) (Japan)	Waseda Univ. (Japan).
NTT (Japan)	

2.5 NTCIR Workshop 2 (June 2000 – March 2001)

The second workshop [4] hosted three tasks, and each task was proposed and organized by a research group of that topic.

1. *Chinese Text Retrieval Task (CHTR):* including English-Chinese CLIR (ECIR; E -> C) and Chinese monolingual IR (CHIR tasks, C -> C) using the test collection CIRB010, consisting of Chinese (traditional) newspaper articles from five newspapers in Taiwan R.O.C.
2. *Japanese-English IR Task (JEIR):* using the test collections NTCIR–1 and –2, including monolingual retrieval of Japanese and English (J -> J, E -> E), and CLIR of Japanese and English (J -> E, E -> J, J -> JE, E -> JE).
3. *Text Summarization Task (TSC: Text Summarization Challenge):* text summarization of Japanese newspaper articles of various kinds. The NTCIR–2 Summ Collection was used.

Each task was proposed and organized by a different research group in a relatively independent manner, while maintaining good contact and discussion with the NTCIR Project organizing group, headed by the author. Evaluation and what should be evaluated were thoroughly discussed in a discussion group.

Table 4. Active participants for the second NTCIR Workshop

ATT Labs and Duke Univ. (US)	National Institute of Informatics (Japan)
Communications Research Laboratory (Japan),	NTT–CS and NAIST (Japan)
Fuji Xerox (Japan)	OASIS, Aizu Univ. (Japan)
Fujitsu Laboratories (Japan)	Osaka Kyoiku Univ. (Japan)
Fujitsu R&D Center (China PRC)	Queen College–City Univ. of New York (US)
Central Research Laboratory, Hitachi Co. (Japan)	Ricoh Co. (2) (Japan)
Hong Kong Polytechnic (Hong Kong, China PRC)	Surugadai Univ. (Japan)
Institute of Software, Chinese Academy of Sciences (China PRC)	Trans EZ Co. (Taiwan ROC)
Johns Hopkins Univ. (US)	Toyohashi Univ. of Technology (2) (Japan)
JUSTSYSTEM Corp. (Japan)	Univ. of California Berkeley (US)
Kanagawa Univ. (Japan)	Univ. of Cambridge/Toshiba/Microsoft (UK)
Korea Advanced Institute of Science and Technology (KAIST/KORTERM) (Korea)	Univ. of Electro-Communications (2) (Japan)
Matsushita Electric Industrial (Japan)	Univ. of Library and Information Science (Japan)
National TsinHua Univ. (Taiwan, ROC)	Univ. of Maryland (US)
NEC Media Research Laboratories (Japan)	Univ. of Tokyo (2) (Japan),
	Yokohama National Univ. (Japan)
	Waseda Univ. (Japan).

3 *NTCIR* Workshop 3 (Oct. 2001 - Oct. 2002)

The third NTCIR Workshop started with document data distribution in October 2001 and the workshop meeting was held in October 2002. We selected five areas of research as tasks; (1) Cross-lingual information retrieval of Asian languages (CLIR), (2) Patent retrieval (PATENT), (3) Question answering (QAC), (4) Automatic text summarization (TSC2), and (5) Web retrieval (WEB). Sixty-five research groups from nine countries and areas shown in Table 5 participated and submitted the results. This section describes the design of each task and major results in CLIR-related tasks, *i.e.*, CLIR and PATENT tasks. The updated information is available at http://research.nii.ac.jp/ntcir/workshop/.

Table 5. Active participats for the third NTCIR Workshop

Chungnam National University (Korea) & ETRI+ (Korea)	NTT DATA* (Japan)
Carnegie Mellon University (USA)	New York University (USA) & CRL+ (Japan)
Communication Research Laboratory+ (3 groups) (Japan)	Oki Electric* (Japan)
CRL+ (Japan) & New York University (USA)	Osaka Kyoiku Univeristy (3 groups) (Japan)
Fu Jen Catholic University (Taiwan ROC)	POSTECH (2 groups) (Korea)
Hitachi* (Japan)	Queen College City University of New York (USA)
Hong Kong Polytechnic University (Hong Kong)	RICOH* (Japan)
Hummingbird* (Canada)	Ritsumeikan University (2 groups) (Japan)
Institute of Software, Chinese Academy of Sciences+ (China, PRC)	SICS+ (Sweden)
Johns Hopkins University (USA)	Surugadai University (Japan)
Keio University (2 groups) (Japan)	Thomson Legal and Regulatory* (USA)
Kent Ridge Digital Labs+ (Singapore)	Tianjin University (China PRC)
Kochi University of Technology (Japan)	Tokyo Institute of Technology (Japan)
Korea University (Korea)	Tokai University & Beijin Japan Center (China PRC)
Matsushita Electric Industrial* (Japan)	Toshiba* (Japan)
Microsoft Research Asia* (China PRC)	Toyohashi University of Technology (4 groups) (Japan)
Mie University (Japan)	ULIS & AIST+ (2 groups) (Japan)
Nara Advanced Institute of Science and Technology (Japan)	University Aizu (2 groups)
NAIST & CRL+ (Japan)	University of California Berkeley (2 groups) (USA)
National Taiwan University (Taiwan ROC)	University of Tokyo (2 groups) (Japan)
NEC Kansai* (Japan)	University of Lib and Information Science (2 groups) (Japan)
NEC MRL* (Japan)	University of Tokyo (Japan) & RICOH* (Japan)
NTT Data Technology* (Japan)	Waterloo University (Canada)
NTT-CS* (Japan)	Yokohama National University (2 groups) (Japan)
NTT-CS* (Japan) & NAIST (Japan)	

65 groups from 9 countries, *: company, +: national or independent research institute, without-symbol: university

3.1 Cross-Lingual Information Retrieval Task (CLIR) [16]

An executive committee consisting of eight researchers from Japan, Korea, and Taiwan was organized. These members met four times in Japan to discuss the details of the CLIR Task, to make the schedule, and to arrange the agenda. Topic creation and relevance judgments on documents in each language were performed by each country group. Evaluation and report writing were done by Kuang-hua Chen and pooling was done by Kazuko Kuriyama.

Documents and topics are in four languages: Chinese, Korean, Japanese and English. Fifty topics were selected for the collections of 1998–1999 (Topic98) and 30 topics for the collection of 1994 (Topic94). English topics for Topic98 were prepared by National Institute of Standards and Technology and those for Topic94 were selected from CLEF 2001 topics[24]. Both topic sets contain all four languages. The context of the experimental design is "report writing".

- *Multilingual CLIR (MLIR)*: Search the document collection consisting of more than one language except the Korean documents because of the time-range difference. Any topic language can be used from Topic98 set (Xtopic98>CEJ).
- *Bilingual CLIR (BLIR):* Search any two different languages as documents and topics, except for searching English documents (Xtopic98>C, Xtopic94>K, Xtopic98>J).
- *Single Language IR (SLIR)*: Monolingual Search of Chinese, Korean, or Japanese (Ctopic98>C, Ktopic94>K, Jtopic98>J).

where, C: Chinese, E: English, K: Korean, J: Japanese, X: any language of C, E, K, or J.

When we think of the "*layers of CLIR technologies*" shown in Table 8, the CLIR of newspaper articles relates to the "pragmatic layer (social, cultural convention, etc)" and cultural/social differences between countries is the issue we should attack. The problem of identification and transliteration of proper names is one of the challenges for CLIR among Asian languages and English. Therefore topics were selected with the consideration of the balance of local and international ones as well as the balance of those with and without proper names.

The number of relevant documents for a topic was small on particular document sub-collections. Then the **NTCIR–3 CLIR Formal Test Collection** was constructed based on the "3-in-S+A" criterion for each document collection as shown in Tables 6 and 7. This means that a qualified topic has at least three relevant documents with 'S (highly relevant)' or 'A (relevant)' scores on the document collection.

Table 6. NTCIR–3 CLIR Formal Test Collection and its Eight Sub-Collections

Sub-Collection	Documents			Topics		
	Lang	Number	Year	Lang	#	TopicSet
Chinese	C	381,681	1998-99	CJKE	42	Topic98
Japanese	J	220,078	1998-99	CJKE	42	Topic98
English	E	22,927	1998-99	CJKE	32	Topic98
CJ	CJ	601,759	1998-99	CJKE	50	Topic98
CE	CE	404,608	1998-99	CJKE	46	Topic98
JE	JE	243,005	1998-99	CJKE	45	Topic98
CJE	CJE	624,686	1998-99	CJKE	50	Topic98
Korean	K	66,146	1994	CJKE	30	Topic94

C:Chinese, J:Japanese, E:English, K:Korea

Table 7. Topics usable for Each Sub-Collection in the NTCIR–3 CLIR

Collection (DocmentLang)	Topic Number																																																	
	0									1										2										3										4										5
	1	2	3	4	5	6	7	8	9	0	1	2	3	4	5	6	7	8	9	0	1	2	3	4	5	6	7	8	9	0	1	2	3	4	5	6	7	8	9	0	1	2	3	4	5	6	7	8	9	0
C	Y	Y	Y	Y	Y	Y	Y	Y	Y	Y	Y	Y	Y	Y	Y		Y	Y	Y	Y	Y	Y	Y	Y	Y		Y					Y	Y	Y	Y	Y	Y	Y	Y	Y		Y	Y		Y	Y	Y	Y	Y	Y
JE		Y		Y	Y		Y	Y		Y		Y		Y	Y	Y	Y	Y	Y	Y	Y	Y	Y	Y	Y	Y	Y	Y	Y	Y	Y	Y	Y	Y	Y	Y	Y	Y	Y	Y	Y	Y	Y	Y	Y	Y	Y			Y
E		Y		Y	Y		Y		Y			Y	Y	Y				Y	Y	Y	Y	Y		Y		Y	Y	Y	Y	Y	Y	Y		Y	Y	Y	Y	Y	Y			Y	Y		Y	Y				Y
CJ	Y	Y	Y	Y	Y	Y	Y	Y	Y	Y	Y	Y	Y	Y	Y	Y	Y	Y	Y	Y	Y	Y	Y	Y	Y	Y	Y	Y	Y	Y	Y	Y	Y	Y	Y	Y	Y	Y	Y	Y	Y	Y	Y	Y	Y	Y	Y	Y	Y	Y
CE	Y	Y	Y	Y	Y	Y	Y	Y	Y	Y	Y	Y	Y	Y	Y		Y	Y	Y	Y	Y	Y	Y	Y	Y	Y	Y	Y	Y	Y	Y	Y		Y	Y	Y	Y	Y	Y	Y		Y	Y		Y	Y	Y	Y	Y	Y
JE		Y		Y	Y		Y	Y	Y	Y		Y	Y	Y	Y	Y	Y	Y	Y	Y	Y	Y	Y	Y	Y	Y	Y	Y	Y	Y	Y	Y	Y	Y	Y	Y	Y	Y	Y	Y	Y	Y	Y	Y	Y	Y	Y	Y		Y
CJE	Y	Y	Y	Y	Y	Y	Y	Y	Y	Y	Y	Y	Y	Y	Y	Y	Y	Y	Y	Y	Y	Y	Y	Y	Y	Y	Y	Y	Y	Y	Y	Y	Y	Y	Y	Y	Y	Y	Y	Y	Y	Y	Y	Y	Y	Y	Y	Y	Y	Y

C:Chinese, J:Japanese, E:English, K:Korea, 'Y' indicates the topic usable for the target document collection

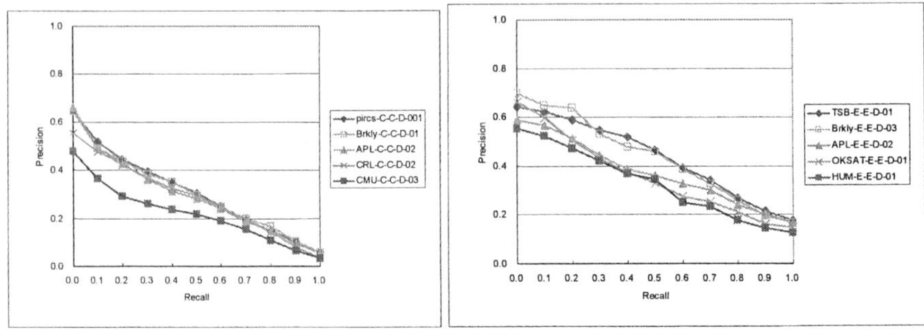

Fig. 3. SLIR (Monolingual) Mandatory Top Runs with Rigid Relevance: C-C and E-E[3]

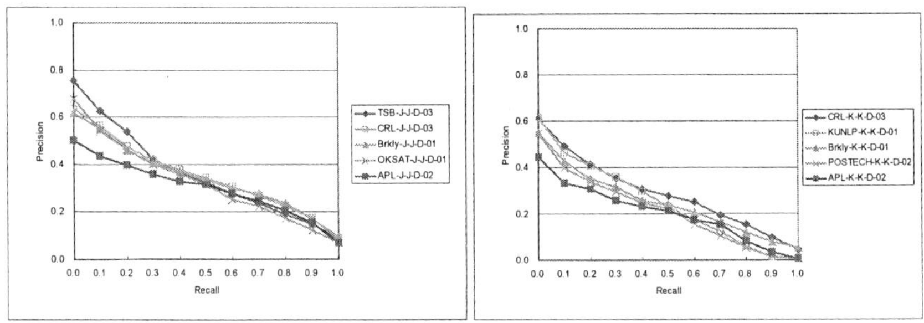

Fig. 4. SLIR (Monolingual) Mandatory Top Runs with Rigid Relevance: J-J and K-K

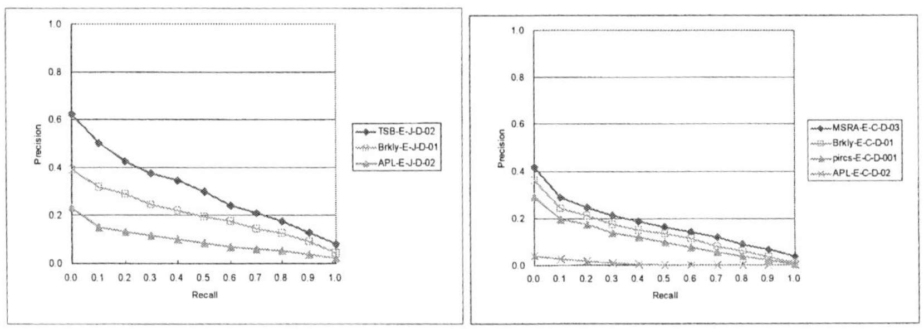

Fig. 5. BLIR Mandatory Top Runs with Rigid Relevance: E-J and E-C

Many participants worked on every combination of SLIR runs then tested strategies most appropriate for each language. These results should represent a good preparation for the MLIR task at the next NTCIR although small numbers of MLIR runs were submitted to this NTCIR. Use of word or word-and-phrase query segmentation increased on Japanese and performed better than bi-gram or other character-based segmentation in each of the comparison done by multiple participants. The problems of segmentation of Chinese and Korean queries seem not

---

3 Note that the document collection for English is smaller. A run-ID consists of five parts, Group's ID - TopicLanguage - DocumentLanguage - TopicFields - Priority

to have been settled yet. Regarding CLIR approaches, the corpus-based only approaches were less used, but the combination of a corpus-based approach with an MT-based approach showed an improvement of search effectiveness.

As shown in Figs. 3-6, overall SLIR and BLIR runs with English or Japanese topics obtained better effectiveness. BLIR with Chinese or Korean topics and MLIR in general show that there is still need for further research in these areas. One of the biggest problems for CLIR among Asian languages is the limited availability of resources from which translation knowledge can be extracted although the situation has been improving and several MT commercial products for these languages were released in late 2002, in accordance with the social needs for information transfer among those languages. Proper-name identification and their appropriate transliteration or translation, and translation of highly technical or out-of-dictionary vocabulary are other serious problems that need to be attacked. Newspaper articles published in 1998–99 in both the English and Korean languages in Korea will be added for the next NTCIR Workshop.

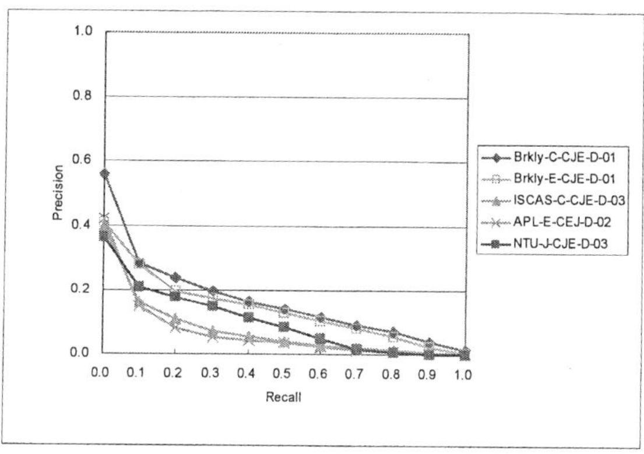

Fig. 6. MLIR Mandatory Top Runs with Rigid Relevance

3.2 Patent Retrieval Task (PATENT) [18]

The context for this task is: "search for a technological trend survey" and patents were treated as ordinary technical documents rather than legal documents. If any part of a patent mentioned relevant information to the search request, the patent was judged as "relevant" regardless of whether it was included in the "claim", the central focus of the patent as a legal document to protect the intellectual property of an invention. Regarding "Cross-Genre Retrieval", we assumed that someone (for example, a business manager) would send a newspaper clipping to a patent search intermediary and ask to retrieve the related patents. Searches using ordinary topic fields such as <DESC>, <NARR>, etc. were accepted as non-mandatory runs. Topic creation and relevance judgments were conducted by professional patent intermediaries who were members of the Intellectual Property Search Committee of the Japanese Intellectual Property Association. The task was designed in close collaboration with these professionals.

Main Task

- *Cross-language Cross-Genre Retrieval*: retrieve patents associated with technology and commercial products in response to newspaper articles. A topic contains a query article and short descriptions of the search request. Thirty-one topics were available in Japanese, English, Chinese (simplified and traditional), and Korean.
- *Monolingual Associative Retrieval:* retrieve related patents with a Japanese patent as an input query. Thirty-one query patents were used with short descriptions of the search requests.

Optional Task

- Other research reports were invited on patent processing using the above data, including, but not limited to: generating patent maps, paraphrasing claims, aligning claims and examples, summarization for patents, clustering patents.

Documents:

- Japanese patents: 1998–1999 (ca. 18GB, ca. 697K docs)
- Patent abstracts (Japanese and literally translated English; Prepared by professional abstractors): 1995–1999 (ca. 4GB, ca.1701K docs)
- Newspaper articles (included in topics, 31 articles)

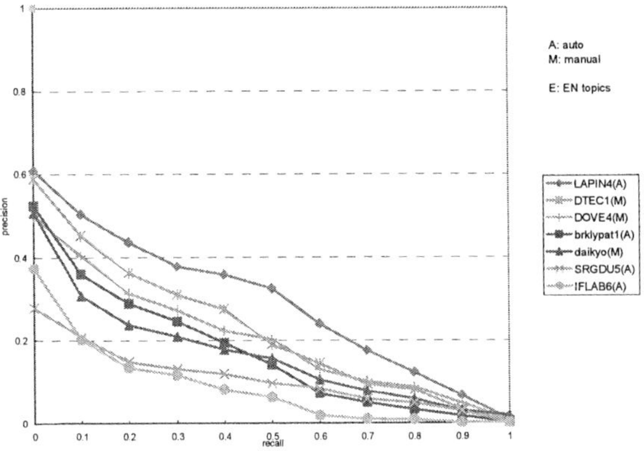

Fig. 7. Patent Main Task (Cross-Genre Retrieval) Mandatory Top Runs with Rigid Relevance

The top performing group in the Cross-Genre Retrieval subtask proposed a model capable of mapping different word-spaces of newspaper articles and patents, and proposed this as a flexible model extensible for retrieval on different user models for each user (Fig. 7) [19]. When dealing with cross-lingual aspects, identification of highly technical terms is an important challenge because if the technical terms divide into multiple parts, the translation that results from a combination of each single part may represent a completely different concept. The UC Berkeley group proposed a "Treat Japanese technical terms as a misspelling of Chinese" approach by identifying technical terms and proper names in queries and converting character codes of them, and combined this with an ordinary dictionary or MT-based CLIR strategy, showing an improvement of search effectiveness [20].

3.3 Other Tasks of NTCIR Workshop 3

3.3.1 Question Answering Challenge (QAC) [21]

This was the first evaluation of question answering on Japanese documents; it was an open-domain fact-type question answering from Japanese newspaper articles published in 1998-1999. The answers are "exact answers", *i.e.,* nouns or noun phrases accompanied with document IDs as support information. About 900 questions were also provided as additional runs and evaluated. There were three subtasks:

- *Task 1*: System extracts five possible answers from the documents in some order. 100 questions.
- *Task 2*: System extracts only one set of all the answers from the documents. 100 questions.
- *Task 3*: A series of questions. The related questions are given for 40 of the questions from Task 2.

3.3.2 Text Summarization Challenge (tsc2) [22]

This was the second NTCIR workshop for text summarization of Japanese documents. The focus of this workshop is "intrinsic evaluation" both for single and multiple document abstract-type summarization, and a novice evaluation methodology based on revision was proposed. Various reference summaries and assessments were done by professional captionists for summarization of the document type. There were two subtasks:

- *Task A (single-document summarization)*: Given the texts to be summarized and summarization lengths, the participants submit summaries for each text in plain-text format.
- *Task B (multi-document summarization):* Given a set of texts, the participants produce a summary of them in plain-text format. The information that was used to produce the document set, such as queries, as well as the required summarization lengths, was given to the participants.

3.3.3 Web Retrieval Task (Web) [23]

Four different subtasks were included. *Survey retrieval* is a search for a survey and aims to retrieve as many relevant documents as possible. *Target retrieval* is a search aiming to retrieve a few highly relevant documents to deliver a quick answer to the search request represented as a topic. "Topic retrieval" is a search in response to a search request and "similarity retrieval" is a search by given relevant document(s). In the relevance judgments, one-hop linked documents were also taken into consideration. Topics contained several extra fields specialized to Web retrieval such as a) known relevant documents, b) information on the topic authors, who were basically the relevance assessors.

A. Survey Retrieval (both recall and precision are evaluated)
  A1. Topic Retrieval
  A2. Similarity Retrieval
B. Target Retrieval (precision-oriented)
C. Optional Task
  C1.Search Results Classification
  C2. Speech-Driven Retrieval

3.4 Features of the NTCIR Workshop 3 Tasks

The characteristic features of evaluation for the third NTCIR Workshop can be summarized including:

1. Multilingual CLIR (CLIR)
2. Search by Document (PATENT, Web)
3. Optional Task (PATENT, WEB)
4. Multi-grade Relevance Judgments (CLIR, PATENT, WEB)
5. Various Relevance Judgments (WEB)
6. Precision-Oriented Evaluation (QA, WEB)
7. Various types of relevance judgments

It should be noted that the document collections used for the PATENT and WEB tasks are unique and many interesting characteristics were included, and we invited any research groups who were interested in using the document collections to participate. For PATENT, automatic alignment identification and rhetorical structure analysis were proposed and experimented as optional tasks. The former utilized various types of "alignments" found in the document collection, such as those for fulltext and abstract, English and Japanese abstracts, author abstracts and professional prepared abstracts, complicated longer sentences in the "claim" of the patents and ordinary, technical document-like sentences in the "example" sections in the patents, etc. The latter, the complicated structure of the "claim" section, was analyzed as an initial stage of the bigger research plan on automatic patent map creation. This subtask was selected and extended as a subtask for the next NTCIR Workshop with a 4-year research roadmap for the problem of automatic creation of patent maps.

Passage-based relevance judgments were proposed in PATENT, QAC and WEB. It was proposed that the most relevant passage in the retrieved documents should be identified when retrieving longer documents such as Web documents or patents. The primary evaluation was done from the document base, but we planned to use the submitted passages as secondary information for further analysis. However, these trials were all cancelled because it was too hard for participants in the short time period, especially tackling to the new types of larger-scale document collection.

4 Discussion

This Workshop was our first trial of the *CLEF* [24] model for Multilingual CLIR evaluation for Asian languages at NTCIR. The social needs for CLIR in East Asia

were previously focused on CLIR between a user's own language and English. However, mutual interest in each other's cultures has increased recently in Asia, especially among the younger generation. Information transfer in the technological and industrial domains has also increased in importance rapidly both in Asian and global context. For example, Japanese technological information is of great interest to Korean industry while on the other hand Korea is the second largest patent importing country, just after the United States, to Japan.
However, each language is quite different. Even though Taiwan, Japan and the People's Republic of China (PRC) use “Chinese Characters”, the pronunciation and sentence structures are completely different between Chinese and Japanese, and the characters are simplified and modified in different ways in PRC and Japan, so that we cannot understand each other using our own languages. Furthermore, there are no umbrella organizations like the European Union in Asia. The need for CLIR among these languages is increasing in a rather informal, or grass roots, way.

In response to this situation, some search engines provide simple CLIR functionalities, and operational information providers specializing in patents started CLIR for Asian languages late 2002. We are now at a stage to initiate multilingual CLIR for East Asian languages although several years behind the situation in Europe.

Multilingual CLIR for East Asian languages must tackle new problems, such as character codes (there are four standards for Japanese character codes and two in Korea, and the character codes used in simplified Chinese and traditional Chinese are different and cannot be converted with 100 % certainty), less available resources, and limited research staff who can understand the contents of other languages or transliteration of proper names in English documents. Additionally, the structures of the various Asian languages are quite different from each other. In summary, the barriers for cross-language information access in East Asia are serious in every layer of the CLIR technologies, as shown below, and this bring new challenges to CLIR research and to CLIR evaluation design and organization as well.

Table 8. Layers of CLIR technologies

pragmatic layer: cultural and social aspects, convention
semantic layer: concept mapping
lexical layer: language identification, indexing
symbol layer: character codes
physical layer: network

For one future direction, we may think of the possibility of the following CLIR tasks, which are rather aimed towards the application of operational CLIR systems. In the following, focus is placed on directions that have implications in operational or real life CLIR systems.

Table 9. Future directions in CLIR at NTCIR Workshops

Pivot language CLIR
Task/genre-oriented CLIR
Pragmatic layer of CLIR technologies and identifying the differences
Towards CL information access

Pivot (Switching) language CLIR: In the Internet environment, which includes a wide variety of languages, the limited resources for translation knowledge is one of the critical problems for CLIR. In the real world environment, we can often find parallel or quasi-parallel document collections for the native language and English in non-English speaking countries. Many CLIR researchers have proposed utilizing such parallel document collections and connecting them by using English as a switch to obtain translation knowledge, but this idea has seldom been evaluated, partly because relevance judgments on such multilingual document collections are difficult for an individual research group.

A *pragmatic layer of CLIR technologies* that cope with social and cultural aspects of languages is one of the most challenging issues of real world CLIR. CLIR research has so far placed emphasis on technologies that provide access to relevant information across different languages. Identifying the differences of viewpoints expressed in different languages or in documents produced in different cultural or social backgrounds is also critical to improve realistic global information transfer across languages.

Towards CL information access: To widen the scope of CLIR in the whole process of information access, we can think of technologies to make information in the document more usable for users, for example, cross-language question answering, and cross-language text mining. Technologies to enhance the interaction between systems and users or to support query construction in CLIR systems are included in this direction.

References

[1] NTCIR Project: http://research.nii.ac.jp/ntcir/

[2] NTCIR Workshop 1: Proceedings of the First NTCIR Workshop on Research in Japanese Text Retrieval and Term Recognition. Tokyo Japan ISBN 4-924600-77-6 (30 Aug–1 Sept 1999) (http://research.nii.ac.jp/ntcir/workshop/Online Proceedings/)

[3] IREX URL: http://cs.nyu.edu/cs/projects/proteus/irex/

[4] NTCIR Workshop 2: Proceedings of the Second NTCIR Workshop on Research in Chinese and Japanese Text Retrieval and Text Summarization. Tokyo Japan ISBN 4-924600-96-2 (June 2000 – March 2001) (http://research.nii.ac.jp/ntcir/ workshop/OnlineProceedings/)

[5] Kando, N., Oyama, K., Ishida, E. (eds): NTCIR Workshop 3: Proceedings of the Third NTCIR Workshop on Research in Information Retrieval, Automatic Text Summarization, and Question Answering. Tokyo Japan ISBN: 4-86049-016-9 (Oct 2002–Oct 2003) (to appear)

[6] Kando, N.: Cross-linguistic scholarly information transfer and database services in Japan. Presented in the panel on Multilingual Database in the Annual Meeting of the American Society for Information Science, Washington DC USA (Nov 1997)

[7] Kando, N., Kuriyama, K., Yoshioka, M.: Evaluation based on multi-grade relevance judgments. IPSJ SIG Notes, Vol. 2001-FI-63 [in Japanese with English abstract] (Jul 2001) 105–112

[8] Spink, A., Greisdorf, H.: Regions and levels: Measuring and mapping users' relevance judgments. Journal of the American Society for Information Sciences 52(2) (2001) 161–173

[9] Yoshioka, M., Kuriyama, K., Kando, N.: Analysis of the usage of Japanese segmented texts in the NTCIR Workshop 2. In: NTCIR Workshop 2: Proceedings of the Second NTCIR Workshop on Research in Chinese and Japanese Text Retrieval and Text Summarization. Tokyo Japan (Jun 2000–Mar 2001)

[10] Kando, N., Nozue, T., Kuriyama, K., Oyama, K.: NTCIR-1: Its policy and practice. IPSJ SIG Notes, Vol. 99, No. 20 [in Japanese with English abstract] (1999) 33–40

[11] Kuriyama, K., Nozue, T., Kando, N., Oyama, K.: Pooling for a large scale test collection: Analysis of the search results for the pre-test of the NTCIR-1 Workshop. IPSJ SIG Notes, Vol. 99-FI-54 [in Japanese] (May 1999) 25–32

[12] Kuriyama, K., Kando, N: Construction of a large scale test collection: Analysis of the training topics of the NTCIR-1. IPSJ SIG Notes, Vol. 99-FI-55 [in Japanese with English abstract] (Jul 1999) 41–48

[13] Kando, N., Eguchi, K., Kuriyama, K.: Construction of a large scale test collection: Analysis of the test topics of the NTCIR-1. In: Proceedings of IPSJ Annual Meeting [in Japanese] (30 Sept–3 Oct 1999) 3-107–3-108

[14] Kuriyama, K., Yoshioka, M., Kando, N.: Effect of cross-lingual pooling. In: NTCIR Workshop 2: Proceedings of the Second NTCIR Workshop on Research in Chinese and Japanese Text Retrieval and Text Summarization. Tokyo Japan (Jun 2000–Mar 2001)

[15] Voorhees, E.M.: Variations in relevance judgments and the measurement of retrieval effectiveness. In: Proceedings of 21st Annual International ACM-SIGIR Conference on Research and Development in Information Retrieval. Melbourne Australia (Aug 1998) 315–323

[16] Chen, K.H., Chen, H.H., Kando, N., Kuriyama, K., Lee, S.H., Myaeng, S.H., Kishida, K., Eguchi, K., Kim, H.: Overview of CLIR task at the third NTCIR Workshop. In: Working Notes of the Third NTCIR Workshop Meeting. Tokyo Japan (8–10 Oct 2002) (to appear)

[17] Kando, N.: Towards real multilingual information discovery and access. ACM Digital Libraries and ACM-SIGIR Joint Workshop on Multilingual Information Discovery and Access. Panel on the Evaluation of the Cross-Language Information Retrieval. Berkeley CA (15 Aug 1999) (http://www.clis2.umd.edu/conferences/midas/papers/kando2.ppt)

[18] Iwayama, M., Fujii, A., Takano, A., Kando, N.: Overview of patent retrieval task at NTCIR -3, In NTCIR Workshop 3: Proceedings of the Third NTCIR Workshop on Research in Information Retrieval, Automatic Text Summarization, and Question Answering. Tokyo Japan (Oct 2002–Oct 2003) (to appear)

[19] Itoh, H., Mano, H., Ogawa, Y. Term Distillation for Cross-DB Retrieval. In: NTCIR Workshop 3: Proceedings of the Third NTCIR Workshop on Research in Information Retrieval, Automatic Text Summarization, and Question Answering. Tokyo Japan (Oct 2002–Oct 2003) (to appear)

[20] Chen, A., Gey, F.C. Experiments on Cross-language and Patent Retrieval at NTCIR-3 Workshop. In: NTCIR Workshop 3: Proceedings of the Third NTCIR Workshop on Research in Information Retrieval, Automatic Text Summarization, and Question Answering. Tokyo Japan (Oct 2002–Oct 2003) (to appear)

[21] Fukumoto, J., Kato, T., Masui, F.: Question Answering Challenge (QAC-1) Question answering evaluation at NTCIR Workshop. In: NTCIR Workshop 3: Proceedings of the Third NTCIR Workshop on Research in Information Retrieval, Automatic Text Summarization, and Question Answering. Tokyo Japan (Oct 2002–Oct 2003) (to appear)

[22] Fukusima, T., Nanba, H., Okumura, M.: Text Summarization Challenge 2/ Text Summarization evaluation at NTCIR Workshop3. In: NTCIR Workshop 3: Proceedings of the Third NTCIR Workshop on Research in Information Retrieval, Automatic Text Summarization, and Question Answering. Tokyo Japan (Oct 2002–Oct 2003) (to appear)

[23] Eguchi, K., Oyama, K., Ishida, E., Kando, K., Kuriyama, K.: Overview of Web retrieval task at the third NTCIR Workshop. In: NTCIR Workshop 3: Proceedings of the Third NTCIR Workshop on Research in Information Retrieval, Automatic Text Summarization, and Question Answering. Tokyo Japan (Oct 2002–Oct 2003) (to appear)

[24] Cross-Language Evaluation Forum: http://www.clef-campaign.org/

Linguistic and Statistical Analysis of the CLEF Topics

Thomas Mandl and Christa Womser-Hacker

University of Hildesheim, Information Science
Marienburger Platz 22, D-31141 Hildesheim, Germany
{mandl,womser}@uni-hildesheim.de

Abstract. This paper reports on an analysis of the CLEF 2001 topics. In particular, we investigated potential correlations between features of the topics and the performance of retrieval systems. Although there are some weak relations, we claim that the properties of the CLEF topics do not influence the results of the retrieval systems. We found just one correlation for the English topics. The more linguistic challenges contained in the topic texts, the better the systems performed. However, no correlation for the length of a topic could be found.

1 Introduction

The significant effort invested in large scale evaluation studies can only be justified when the results are valid and can serve as a measure for the performance of the systems in real environments. One critical question has been the reliability of the assessors` relevance judgements. Reservations about the objectivity of these assessments have been discussed widely. One study showed that judgements made by different assessors are in fact different. However, TREC and also CLEF are comparitive evaluations which aim at presenting a ranked list of systems. The absolute numbers of the performance values are not meant to exactly represent the quality of the systems. A study which assigned documents to several human relevance assessors showed the absolute numbers of the recall precision values are indeed affected by different judgements. However, the overall ranking of the systems does not change [1].

In research on information retrieval evaluation, it has been pointed out, that "the quality of requests (and hence queries) appears very important" [2]. In CLEF, there might be greater uncertainty about assessments made by different people for the same topic as these are over collections in different languages, as well as about a bias-free translation of the topics.

Topic creation for a multilingual environment requires especial care in order to avoid that cultural aspects influence the meaning [3]. A thorough translation check of all translated topics was introduced in CLEF to assure that the translators who are only aware of two language versions of the topics do not omit or add any thematic aspects accidentally [7]. Another study has focused on the size of the topic set [4].

C.A. Peters (Ed.): CLEF 2002, LNCS 2785, pp. 505-511, 2003.

2 Topics in Information Retrieval Evaluation

Topics in information retrieval evaluation should express an information need. The topics are always formulated in natural language. In a real usage scenario, the information need is a state of mind. As a consequence, the transformation of the information need to the query is not tested in evaluation initiatives. The systems are confronted with a natural language formulation presumed to approximate the information need.

The creation of appropriate topics or queries for testing systems has been a major concern in the research on the evaluation of information retrieval. In one of the first studies which was based on the Cranfield collection the queries led to considerable objections against the validity of the results. The queries were derived from the documents and basically each pointed to one document [5].

TREC and subsequently CLEF have devoted considerable effort to topic generation. TREC has seen a shift from elaborate topics to increasingly shorter topics between TREC-3 and TREC-4 [6]. This may have been a result of the Web where information retrieval systems are available mostly for free and are widely used and where the queries are usually very short. In the Web-track at TREC, only a few words are used as the topic while the narrative is only used for the assessment [6].

Retrieval systems can be optimized for short queries by relying more on term expansion techniques [7]. Even proper similarity calculation functions have been developed for short queries [8].

An investigation on TREC-1 topics has come to the conclusion that the topics are lexically distant from the relevant documents [9]. All judged documents for a topic were plotted in a two dimensional display in a way that the similarities in a similarity matrix were expressed as far as possible by their distances. Multidimensional scaling was used in this study. Relevant documents lay closer to each other and appeared denser than non relevant documents. However, when the topics was plotted in the same display, there was usually a relatively large distance between the relevant clusters. It can be concluded that relevance judgements require more than simply counting appearances of words. However, relevant documents do exhibit some formally detectable similarities.

3 Topics of CLEF 2001

As in previous years, the topics in CLEF 2001 have not been constructed e.g. from documents. Rather, they have been created in a natural way in order to closely resemble potential information needs [10].

Our research has been mainly directed toward the following questions:

- What are the important and typical characteristics of the CLEF topics?
- Do these features have any influence on the quality of the retrieval results?
- Can this knowledge be exploited for the development of retrieval systems?
- Should the design of the CLEF topics be altered to eliminate a potential bias for the systems?

When looking at individual CLEF topics, we find striking differences. For example, when we consider run EIT01M3N in CLEF 2001, we see that it has a fairly good average precision of 0.341. However, for topic 44, which had an average difficulty, this run performs far below (0.07) the average for that topic (0.27). An analysis of the topics revealed that two of the most difficult topics contained no proper names and were both about sports (Topic 51 and 54).

More specifically, we want to find out whether there are linguistic characteristics of the CLEF topics which may lead to a better or worse performance of the systems. The rationale for this assumption lies in the retrieval systems. It is known that some system developers invest great effort in language processing capabilities. As a result, topics with more linguistic challenges may pose greater problems for some systems. In this context, it may be interesting to look at systems which perform well but demonstrate weaknesses for topics which are generally solved with good quality (or vice versa). Such an analysis seems to be especially interesting because the deviation of results between topics is larger than between systems and runs as the following table shows. Some features of the topics may have a higher influence on the result than the retrieval system's parameters. This phenomena is well known from TREC [5].

Table 1. Overall statistics of average precision

	Average	**Std. Deviation**	**Maximum**	**Minimum**
All Runs	0.273	0.111	0.450	0.013
Topics over all languages	0.273	0.144	0.576	0.018
English Runs	0.263	0.074	0.373	0.104
English Topics	0.263	0.142	0.544	0.018
German Runs	0.263	0.092	0.390	0.095
German Topics	0.263	0.142	0.612	0.005

Table 1 shows that the average of all systems surprisingly neither differs much from the average of all runs for English nor from all runs with German as topic language. For further analysis we can consider the performance for the topics (all systems for one topic) and the performance of the systems (one system for all topics). In this case the deviation for topics is higher (>0.14) than the deviation for the systems (<0.12) regardless of whether we consider only English topics, German topics or all languages.

However, overall there do not seem to be easy topics nor superior runs. The correlation between the average precision and the deviation for a topic over all runs is 0.83. That means, the better a topic is handled on average, the higher is the deviation of systems for that topic. Not all systems have achieved a similar quality for these easier topics. The same is true for runs. The average precision and the deviation for a run over all topics correlate with 0.84. We can draw the conclusion that no run performs well on all topics. On the contrary, the better a run performed overall, the higher are the differences between its performance for single topics.

We assume that linguistic phenomena like morphological modifications, abbreviations or proper names pose challenges to the retrieval systems which might be handled with different approaches and consequently give different quality of results. For example, a system performing generally very well may have difficulties when confronted with topics containing abbreviations and numbers. In such cases, these difficult queries could be better handled by another system because they can be easily recognized automatically.

We carried out an analysis of the topics and assessed the values for different propertiesas shown in Table 2. For some of the features, types as well as tokens were assessed.

Table 2. Topic Properties

German topics:	English topics:
• original topic language	• original topic language
• length	• length
• compound words	• abbreviations
• abbreviations	• nominal phrases
• nominal phrases	• proper names
• proper names	• negations
• negations	• subordinate clauses
• subordinate clauses	• foreign words
• foreign words	• parenthesis
• numbers or dates	• numbers of dates

At first, we looked at the relation between topic features and the average precision of all runs for that topic without considering system characteristics. The overall quality of the run was measured by the following properties:

- Average precision (non- interpolated) for all relevant documents
- Precision at five documents
- For some of our analysis, the runs were grouped into five buckets

The correlation calculation between linguistic phenomena and average precision of all runs revealed the following. The only properties that had a correlation higher than 0.2 or lower than -0.2 for the number of phenomena and precision were proper names. This indicates that the existence of proper names in the topic and consequently in the query makes a topic easier. Maybe proper names have a low frequency in the corpus and the same is true for other low frequency terms.

Table 3. Correlation between number of proper names and precision

	Types	Tokens	Sum of all linguistic phenomena
English	0.446	0.473	0.293
German	0.440	0.464	0.286

The sum of all linguistic phenomena also has a positive but lower correlation with the precision. However, if we consider the bucket analysis where the runs are grouped in five buckets, the correlation reaches 0.96 for the English topics. Each bucket contains 20% of all runs. Bucket one has the worst runs and so forth. The relation can be seen in Figure 1. The reported relations are not statistically significant since only 50 topics and 70 runs were analyzed.

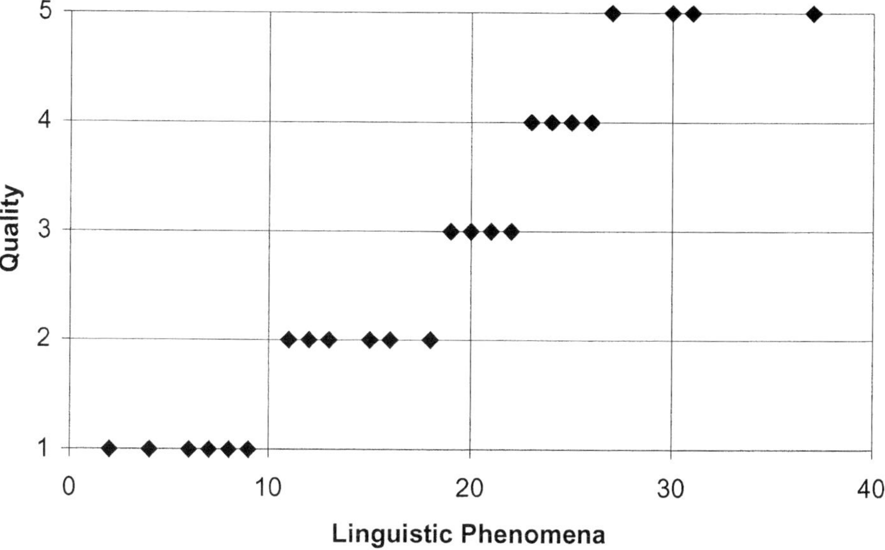

Fig. 1. Relation between sum of number of linguistic phenomena and the runs' performance bucket

However, no correlation was found for the length of the topics. Although CLEF topics do not differ too much in length, it appears that linguistic complexity has a greater effect and needs to be considered more than the number of words. We assume that the systems have a greater chance of finding a correct interpretation when they are confronted with a high linguistic variety.

4 Topics and Runs of CLEF 2001

The global analysis of topics and runs needs to be refined by a more detailed inspection on the relation between topic and run properties. To perform this investigation, some properties of the runs were also considered in the analysis. They can be found in the CLEF proceedings:

- Multi- or bilingual run
- Topic language
- Topic fields used (title, description, narrative)
- Used for the pool or not

A statistical analysis was not carried out beforehand, because there is relatively little evidence for a statistical analysis. There were only 600 combinations of runs and German topics and 900 for English topics. As a consequence, we first used machine learning methods to find out whether a formal model could be built to establish any relation between topic properties and system performance. If any relations were detected, a subsequent statistical analysis could have been applied.

We used the Waikato Environment for Knowledge Analysis (WEKA[1]) which allows the testing of many machine learning algorithms within the same framework. WEKA is implemented in JAVA and is provided as open source software. As target of a machine learning model, we used the average precision of the run for the topic being examined.

Neither the German nor the English training data resulted in a satisfying model. This was true for linear algorithms like Naive Bayes as well as for non linear models like neural networks. That means, the existing data cannot be used to build any predictive model to map from system and topic properties to the quality of the run measured by the average precision.

5 Outlook

The investigations reported in this article have found no bias in the topics of the CLEF campaign. As a result, no reservations toward the validity of the results arise from this research.

At this point, in order to obtain more conclusive data, the topics of the 2002 campaign must be evaluated and their features should be assessed. Further languages should also be included in the analysis. Relevance assessment requires human judgement and therefore, we want to eliminate possible individual bias. Additional machine assessable properties like sentence complexity and part of speech frequency analysis must also be considered. Domain specific words may also be worth an analysis. Another interesting question could be the comparison of topics with similar difficulty. Are these similar topics?

In other areas of TREC and CLEF, the tuning of systems towards topic properties might play an even more crucial role. In the web track, two different types of topics have been developed. In addition to the topical searches adopted by the ad hoc track, homepage finding has been defined as a task. In multimedia retrieval, topic creation is more difficult. For example, the video track in TREC comprises several dimensions of topic properties. Topics are characterized formally by the multimedia elements contained. In addition to the mandatory text description, topics may embrace graphic, video or audio files. Furthermore, the topic content is far more diverse than for text retrieval. The semantics differs greatly. Some users seekvideo with certain graphical features, others require objects, others look for certain people during a search session [5]. These issues deserve further study.

---

[1] http://www.cs.waikato.ac.nz/~ml/weka/index.html

References

[1] Voorhees, E.: Variations in relevance judgments and the measurement of retrieval effectiveness. In: Proc of the 21st Annual Intl ACM SIGIR Conference on Research and Development in Information Retrieval (SIGIR) ACM Press, New York, NY, USA (1998) 315-223.

[2] Sparck Jones, Karen: Reflections on TREC. Information Processing & Management 31(1995) 291-314

[3] Kluck, M., Womser-Hacker, C: Inside the Evaluation Process of the Cross-Language Evaluation Forum (CLEF): Issues of Multilingual Topic Creation and Multilingual Relevance Assessment. In: 3rd International Conference on Language Resources and Evaluation, Las Palmas, Spain (2002) 573-576

[4] Voorhees, E., Buckley, C.: The effect of topic set size on retrieval experiment error. In: Proc of the 25th Annual Intl ACM SIGIR Conference on Research and Development in Information Retrieval (SIGIR) ACM Press, New York, NY, USA (2002) 316-323

[5] Womser-Hacker, C.: Das MIMOR-Modell. Mehrfachindexierung zur dynamischen Methoden-Objekt-Relationierung im Information Retrieval. Habilitationsschrift. Universität Regensburg, Informationswissenschaft (1997)

[6] Hawking, D., Craswell, N.: Overview of the TREC-2001 Web Track. In: Voorhees E, Harman, D. (eds.): The Ninth Text Retrieval Conference (TREC-9). NIST Special Publication. Gaithersburg, Maryland (2001) http://trec.nist.gov/pubs/

[7] Kwok, K. L., Chan, M.: Improving Two-Stage Ad-Hoc Retrieval for Short Queries. In: Proc of the 21st Annual Intl ACM SIGIR Conference on Research and Development in Information Retrieval (SIGIR) ACM Press, New York, NY, USA (1998) 250-256

[8] Wilkinson, R., Zobel, J., Sacks-Davis, R.: Similarity Measures for Short Queries. In: Harman, D. (ed.) The Fourth Text REtrieval Conference (TREC-4). NIST Special Publication. Gaithersburg, Maryland (1995) http://trec.nist.gov/pubs/

[9] Rorvig, M., Fitzpatri, S.: Visualization and Scaling of TREC Topic Document Sets. Information Processing and Management 34 (1998) 135-149

[10] Womser-Hacker, C.: Multilingual Topic Generation within the CLEF 2001 Experiments. In: Peters, C, Braschler, M., Gonzalo, J., Kluck, M. (eds.): Evaluation of Cross-Language Information Retrieval Systems. Workshop of the Cross-Language Information Evaluation Forum (CLEF) Lecture Notes in Computer Science, Vol. 2406 Springer-Verlag, Berlin Heidelberg New York (2002) 389-393

[11] Smeaton, A., Over, P., Taban, R.: The TREC-2001 Video Track Report. In: Voorhees E, Harman, D. (eds.): The Tenth Text Retrieval Conference (TREC-10). NIST Special Publication. Gaithersburg, Maryland (2002) http://trec.nist.gov/pubs/

CLEF 2002 Methodology and Metrics

Martin Braschler[1,2] and Carol Peters[3]

[1] Eurospider Information Technology AG
Schaffhauserstr. 18, 8006 Zürich, Switzerland
[2] Université de Neuchâtel, Institut interfacultaire d'informatique
Pierre-à-Mazel 7, CH-2001 Neuchâtel, Switzerland
martin.braschler@eurospider.com
[3] ISTI-CNR, Area di Ricerca, 56124 Pisa, Italy
carol@isti.cnr.it

Abstract. We give a detailed presentation of the organization of the CLEF 2002 evaluation campaign, focusing mainly on the core tracks. This includes a discussion of the evaluation approach adopted, explanations of the tracks and tasks and the underlying motivations, a description of the test collections, and an outline of the guidelines for the participants. The paper concludes with indications of the techniques used for results calculation and analysis.

1 Introduction

The Cross-Language Evaluation Forum (CLEF) uses a comparative evaluation approach. Comparative evaluation consists of deciding on a control task - which may correspond either to the function of a complete system or to that of a single component, of defining the protocol and metrics to be used, of identifying system or component developers interested in participating, and of organizing an evaluation campaign - which includes the acquisition and distribution of appropriate data for training and testing the systems. In the case of CLEF, performance measures are calculated on the basis of a test collection of documents, sample queries and relevance assessments for these queries with respect to documents in the collection.

CLEF adopts a corpus-based, automatic scoring method in the assessment of system performance, based on ideas first introduced in the Cranfield experiments [1] in the late 1960s. This methodology is widely used and accepted in the information retrieval community. Its properties have been thoroughly investigated and are well understood. This approach is also used by the popular series of TREC conferences [2], which are the "gold standard" for this form of evaluation campaign. The implications of adopting the Cranfield paradigm are discussed in detail in [3].

In this paper, we describe the organization of the CLEF 2002 campaign, focusing mainly on the core tracks. The aim is to give an exhaustive record of the technical setup for these tracks in order to provide readers, who have never participated in CLEF or similar evaluation campaigns, with the necessary background information in order to understand the details of the experiments described in Part I of this volume

C.A. Peters (Ed.): CLEF 2002, LNCS 2785, pp. 512-525, 2003.

and to be able to interpret the result pages in the Appendix. The paper is thus a revised and updated version of a similar paper included in the Proceedings to CLEF2001 and is considered essential reading for newcomers to the CLEF campaigns.

The rest of the paper is organized as follows. In Section 2 we describe the tracks, tasks and the data collections provided for CLEF 2002 – distinguishing between core and additional tracks - and briefly outline the instructions given to the participants, Section 3 describes the techniques and measures used for result calculation and analysis, and Section 4 explains how the results of the participating groups are presented in the appendix.

2 Agenda for CLEF 2002

CLEF campaigns are organized according to a predefined schedule, with a series of strict deadlines. The dates are determined in order to be as compatible as possible with those of two other major Information Retrieval system evaluation activities: that organized by TREC and sponsored by the National Institute of Standards and Technology [4], and the NACSIS Test Collection for Information Retrieval (NTCIR) sponsored by the National Institute for Informatics of Tokyo [5]. The dates vary slightly from year to year, mainly in order to respect the tradition of holding the annual workshop in conjunction with the European Digital Library Conference (ECDL).

The main dates for 2002 were:

- First release of Call for Participation - November 2001
- Data Collection Release - 1 February 2002
- Topic Release - from 1 April 2002
- Receipt of runs from participants - 16 June 2002
- Release of relevance assessments and individual results – 1 August 2002
- Submission of paper for Working Notes – 1 September 2002
- Workshop – 19-20 September 2002, Rome, Italy, following ECDL2002.

2.1 Evaluation Tracks

Over the years, the range of activities offered to participants in the initial cross-language information retrieval (CLIR) track at TREC and subsequent CLEF campaigns has expanded and been modified in order to meet the needs of the research community. Consequently, the campaign is structured into several distinct tracks[1] (see also [6]). Some of these tracks are in turn structured into multiple tasks. From its beginning, the main focus of CLEF is the *multilingual retrieval track*, in which systems must use queries in one language to retrieve items from a test collection that contains documents written in a number of different languages (five for CLEF 2002).

---

[1] While the cross-language activities in earlier TREC campaigns were organized as a single track (the CLIR track at TREC), the larger CLEF campaigns are themselves structured into multiple tracks.

Participants are actively encouraged to work on this, the hardest task offered. A stated goal of the CLEF campaign is to allow groups to gradually move from "easier" tracks/tasks in their first participation to eventually work with as many languages as possible, joining the multilingual track. For this reason, *bilingual* and *monolingual tracks* are also offered. These smaller tracks serve additional important purposes, for example in terms of helping to better understand the characteristics of individual languages, and to fine-tune methods. In recognition of the fact that cross-language retrieval systems face many interesting challenges supplementary to the handling of multiple languages and maximum effectiveness during retrieval, CLEF 2002 also featured a *domain-specific track*, an *interactive track* and a *speech retrieval pilot experiment*. In CLEF, we distinguish between the ***core tracks***, which are those that are offered regularly each year (the monolingual, bilingual, multilingual and domain-specific tracks) and ***additional tracks***, which tend to be organized on a more experimental basis and have the objective of identifying new requirements and appropriate methodology for their testing. Here below we describe the tracks and tasks offered by CLEF 2002.

For each of the core tracks, the participating systems construct their queries (automatically or manually) from a common set of statements of information needs (known as topics) and search for relevant documents in the collections provided, listing the results in a ranked list.

Multilingual Information Retrieval. This is the main track in CLEF. It requires searching a multilingual collection of documents for relevant items, using a selected query language. Multilingual information retrieval is a complex problem, testing the capability of a system to handle a number of different languages simultaneously, ordering the results according to relevance. As in CLEF 2001, the multilingual collection for this track in CLEF 2002 contained English, German, French, Italian and Spanish documents. Using a selected topic (query) language, the goal was to retrieve documents for all languages in the collection, rather than just a given pair, listing the results in a single ranked list. Topics in eleven different languages were made available to participants: Dutch, English, Finnish, French, German, Italian, Spanish, Swedish, Russian, Portuguese and Chinese. Japanese was added to the test collection subsequently.

Bilingual Information Retrieval. In this track, any query language can be used to search a single target document collection. Many newcomers to CLIR system evaluation prefer to begin with the simpler bilingual track before moving on to tackle the more complex issues involved in truly multilingual retrieval. CLEF 2001 offered two distinct bilingual tracks with either English or Dutch target collections. In response to considerable pressure from the participants, in CLEF 2002 we decided to extend the choice to all of the target document collections, with the single limitation that only newcomers to a CLEF cross-language evaluation task could use the English target document collection. This decision had the advantage of encouraging experienced groups to experiment with "different" target collections, rather than concentrating on English, but it had the strong disadvantage that the results were harder to assess in a comparative evaluation framework. There were simply too many topic-target language combinations. Consequently, a very different choice has been made for CLEF2003 (see [7]).

Monolingual (Non-english) IR. Until recently, most IR system evaluation focused on English. However, many of the issues involved in IR are language dependent. CLEF provides the opportunity for monolingual system testing and tuning, and for building test suites in other European languages apart from English. In CLEF 2002, we provided the opportunity for monolingual system testing and tuning in Dutch, Finnish, French, German, Italian, Spanish and Swedish.

Domain-Specific Mono- and Cross-Language Information Retrieval. The rationale for this task is to study CLIR on other types of collections, serving a different kind of information need. The information that is provided by domain-specific scientific documents is far more targeted than news stories and contains much terminology. It is claimed that the users of this type of collection are typically interested in the completeness of results. This means that they are generally not satisfied with finding just some relevant documents in a collection that may contain many more. Developers of domain-specific cross-language retrieval systems need to be able to tune their systems to meet this requirement. See [8] for a discussion of this point. In CLEF 2002, this track was based on two scientific data collections: the GIRT and Amaryllis corpora. Each collection had an associated controlled vocabulary: in English, German and Russian for GIRT, and in English and French for Amaryllis. Each collection could be queried either monolingually or cross-language. Topics were prepared in English, German and Russian for the GIRT task, and in English and French for Amaryllis.

Interactive CLIR. The aim of the tracks listed so far is to measure the performance of a system mainly in terms of its effectiveness in document ranking. However, this is not the only issue that interests the user. User satisfaction with an IR system is based on a number of factors, depending on the functionality of the particular system. For example, the ways in which a system can help the user when formulating a query or the ways in which the results of a search are presented are of great importance in CLIR systems where it is common to have users retrieving documents in languages with which they are not familiar. An interactive track that focused on both user-assisted query formulation and document selection was experimented with success in CLEF 2002 [9].

Cross-Language Spoken Document Retrieval. The current growth of multilingual digital material in a combination of different media (e.g. image, speech, video) means that there is an increasing interest in systems capable of automatically accessing the information available in these archives. For this reason, the DELOS Network of Excellence for Digital Libraries [10] supported a preliminary investigation aimed at evaluating systems for cross-language spoken document retrieval. The aim was to establish baseline performance levels and to identify those areas where future research was needed. The results of this pilot investigation were first presented at the CLEF 2002 Workshop and are reported in [11].

2.2 The Test Collections

The main CLEF test collection is formed of sets of documents in different European languages but with common features (same genre and time period, comparable content); a single set of topics rendered in a number of languages; relevance judgments determining the set of relevant documents for each topic. A separate test collection has been created for systems tuned for domain-specific tasks.

Document Collections for CLEF 2002. The main document collection consisted of well over one million documents in eight languages – Dutch, English, Finnish French, German, Italian, Spanish and Swedish. It contained both newswires and national newspapers. Swedish and Finnish, both Scandinavian languages, were introduced for the first time in CLEF 2002, but for different reasons. Swedish was chosen as a representative of the North-Germanic languages, whereas Finnish was included both because it was a Uralic language rather than a member of the Indo-European family and also because its complex morphology makes it a particularly challenging language from the text processing viewpoint. Parts of this collection were used for the mono-, bi- and multilingual tracks and also for the interactive track.

There were two scientific collections for the domain-specific track: the GIRT database of about 80,000 German social science documents, which has controlled vocabularies for English-German and German-Russian and the Amaryllis scientific database of approximately 150,000 French bibliographic documents, plus a controlled vocabulary in English and French. The cross-language spoken document retrieval track used the TREC-8 and TREC-9 spoken document collections.

Table 1 gives further details with respect to the source and dimensions of the main multilingual document collection used in CLEF 2002. It gives the overall size of each subcollection, number of documents contained, and three key figures indicating some typical characteristics of the individual documents: the median length in bytes, tokens and features. Tokens are "word" occurrences, extracted by removing all formatting, tagging and punctuation, and the length in terms of features is defined as the number of distinct tokens occurring in a document. Table 2 shows which parts of the multilingual collection are used in the various CLEF 2002 multilingual, bilingual and monolingual tasks.

Topics. The groups participating in the multilingual, bilingual and monolingual tracks derive their queries in their preferred language from a set of topics created to simulate user information needs. Following the TREC philosophy, each topic consists of three parts: a brief title statement; a one-sentence description; a more complex narrative specifying the relevance assessment criteria. The title contains the main keywords, the description is a “natural language” expression of the concept conveyed by the keywords, and the narrative adds extra syntax and semantics, stipulating the conditions for relevance assessment. Queries can be constructed from one or more fields. Here below we give the English version of a typical topic from CLEF 2002.

```
<top>
<num> C091 </num>
<EN-title> AI in Latin America </EN-title>
<EN-desc> Amnesty International reports on human rights
in Latin America. </EN-desc>
<EN-narr> Relevant documents should inform readers
about Amnesty International reports regarding human
rights in Latin America, or on reactions to these
reports. </EN-narr>
</top>
```

Table 1. Sources and dimensions of the main CLEF 2002 document collection

Collection	Size (KB)	No. of Docs	Median Size of Docs. (Bytes)	Median Size of Docs. (Tokens)[2]	Median Size of Docs . (Features)
Dutch: Algemeen Dagblad	247141	106483	1282	166	112
Dutch: NRC Handelsblad	306207	84121	2153	354	203
English: LA Times	435112	113005	2204	421	246
Finnish: Aamulehti	140793	55344	1712	217	150
French: Le Monde	161423	44013	1994	361	213
French: SDA	88005	43178	1683	227	137
German: Frankfurter Rundschau	327652	139715	1598	225	161
German: Der Spiegel	64429	13979	1324	213	160
German: SDA	147494	71677	1672	186	131
Italian: La Stampa	198112	58051	1915	435	268
Italian: SDA	87592	50527	1454	187	129
Spanish: EFE	523497	215738	2172	290	171
Swedish: TT	352 MB	142,819			

SDA = Schweizerische Depeschenagentur (Swiss News Agency)
EFE = Agencia EFE S.A (Spanish News Agency)
TT = Tidningarnas Telegrambyrå (Swedish newspaper)

2 The number of tokens extracted from each document can vary slightly across systems, depending on the respective definition of what constitutes a token. Consequently, the number of tokens and features given in this table are approximations and may differ from actual implemented systems.

Table 2. Use of the main document collection in the CLEF 2002 monolingual, bilingual, and multilingual tracks

	Dutch Algemeen Dagblad	*Dutch NRC Handelsblad*	*English LA Times*	*Finnish Aamulethi*	*French Le Monde*	*French SDA*	*German Frankfurter Rundschau*	*German Der Spiegel*	*German SDA*	*Italian La Stampa*	*Italian SDA*	*Spanish EFE*	*Swedish - TT*
Multilingual			X		X	X	X	X	X	X	X	X	
Bilingual Dutch	X	X											
Bilingual English			X										
Bilingual Finnish				X									
Bilingual French					X	X							
Bilingual German							X	X	X				
Bilingual Italian										X	X		
Bilingual Spanish												X	
Bilingual Swedish													X
Monoling. Dutch	X	X											
Monoling. Finnish				X									
Monoling.French					X	X							
Monoling.German							X	X	X				
Monoling.Italian										X	X		
Monoling.Spanish												X	
Monoling.Swedish													X

The motivation behind using structured topics is to simulate query "input" for a range of different IR applications, ranging from very short to elaborate query formulations, and representing keyword-style input as well as natural language formulations. The latter potentially allows sophisticated systems to make use of morphological analysis, parsing, query expansion and similar features. In the cross-language context, the transfer component must also be considered, whether dictionary or corpus-based, a fully-fledged MT system or other. Different query structures may be more appropriate for testing one or the other approach.

CLEF topics are developed on the basis of the contents of the multilingual document collection. For each language, native speakers propose a set of topics covering events of local, European and general importance. The topics are then compared over the different sites to ensure that a high percentage of them will find some relevant documents in all collections, although the ratio can vary considerably. The fact that the same topics are used for the mono-, bi-, and multilingual tracks is a significant constraint. While in the multilingual task, it is of little importance if a given topic does not find relevant documents in all of the collections, in both the bilingual and monolingual tracks, where there is a single target collection, a significant number of the queries must retrieve relevant documents. Once the topics have been selected, they are prepared in all the collection languages by skilled translators translating into their native language. They can then be translated into additional languages, depending on the demand from the participating systems.

For CLEF 2002, 50 such topics were developed on the basis of the contents of the multilingual collection and topic sets were produced in all eight document languages. Additional topic sets in Russian, Portuguese, Chinese and Japanese were also prepared Separate topic sets were developed for the GIRT task in German, English and Russian for the GIRT task, The CLEF topic generation process and the issues involved are described in detail in [12,13].

Relevance Judgments. The relevance assessments for these core tracks are produced in the same distributed setting and by the same groups who work on the topic creation. CLEF uses methods adapted from TREC to ensure a high degree of consistency in the relevance judgments. All assessors follow the same criteria when judging the documents. An accurate assessment of relevance of retrieved documents for a given topic implies a good understanding of the topic. This is much harder to achieve in the distributed scenario of CLEF where understanding is influenced by language and cultural factors. A continual exchange of e-mail for discussion and verification between the assessors at each site is thus necessary during the relevance assessment stage to ensure, as far as possible, that the decisions taken as to relevance are consistent over sites, and over languages.

The practice of assessing the results on the basis of the "Narrative" means that only using the "Title" and/or "Description" parts of the topic implicitly assumes a particular interpretation of the user's information need that is not (explicitly) contained in the actual query that is run in the experiment. The fact that the information contained in the title and description fields could have additional possible interpretations has influence only on the absolute values of the evaluation measures, which in general are inherently difficult to interpret. However, comparative results across systems are usually stable when considering different interpretations. These considerations are important when using the topics to construct very short queries to evaluate a system in a web-style scenario.

The number of documents in large test collections such as CLEF makes it impractical to judge every document for relevance. Instead, approximate recall figures are calculated by using pooling techniques. The results submitted by the participating groups are used to form a "pool" of documents for each topic and for each language by collecting the highly ranked documents from all the submissions. The pooling procedure is discussed later in this paper.

2.3 Instructions to Participants

Guidelines for the main tracks were made available to CLEF 2002 participants shortly after the data release date[3]. These guidelines provide a definition of the system data structures and stipulate the conditions under which they can be used.

System Data Structures. To carry out the retrieval tasks of the CLEF campaign, systems have to build supporting data structures. Allowable data structures can consist of the original documents, or any new structures built automatically (such as inverted files, thesauri, conceptual networks, etc.) or manually (such as thesauri, synonym lists, knowledge bases, rules, etc.) from the documents. They may not be modified in response to the topics. For example, participants are not allowed to add topic words that are not already in the dictionaries used by their systems in order to extend coverage. The CLEF tasks are intended to represent the real-world problem of an ordinary user posing a question to a system. For cross-language tasks, the question is posed in one language and relevant documents must be retrieved in whatever language they have been written. If an ordinary user could not make the change to the system, the participating groups must not make it after receiving the topics.

There are several parts of the CLEF data collections that contain manually-assigned, controlled or uncontrolled index terms. These fields are delimited by specific SGML tags. Since the primary focus of CLEF is on retrieval of naturally occurring text over language boundaries, these manually-indexed terms must not be indiscriminately used as if they are a normal part of the text. If a group decides to use these terms, they should be part of a specific experiment that utilizes manual indexing terms, and these runs should be declared as manual runs. However, learning from (e.g. building translation sources from) such fields is permissible.

Constructing the Queries. There are many possible methods for converting the topics into queries that a system can execute. CLEF defines two broad categories, "automatic" and "manual", based on whether any manual intervention is used. When more than one set of results are submitted, the different sets may correspond to different query construction methods, or if desired, can be variants within the same method. The manual query construction method includes both runs in which the queries are constructed manually and then executed without looking at the results and runs in which the results are used to alter the queries using some manual operation. Manual runs should be appropriately motivated in a CLIR context, e.g. a run using manual translations of the topic into the document language(s) is not what most people consider cross-language retrieval. Allowing different kinds of manual intervention in the manual query construction method makes it harder to do comparisons between experiments. CLEF encourages groups strongly to determine what constitutes a base run for their experiments and to include these runs (officially or unofficially) to allow useful interpretations of the results. Unofficial runs are those not submitted to CLEF but evaluated using thc trec_eval package available from Cornell University [14].

Submission of Results. At CLEF 2002, as a consequence of limited evaluation resources, we accepted a maximum of 5 runs for the multilingual task and a maximum

[3] The additional tracks provided their own guidelines for participants.

of 10 runs overall for the bilingual tasks, including all language combinations. We also accepted a maximum of 10 runs for the monolingual tasks (there were seven languages to choose from). As an additional side constraint – and in order to encourage diversity, we did not allow more than 4 runs for any one language combination. A final restriction was that participants were allowed to submit a maximum of 25 runs altogether for the multilingual, bilingual and monolingual tasks. We also accepted a maximum of 5 runs each for the GIRT and Amaryllis tasks.

In all, a participating group doing all tasks could submit at most 35 runs by submitting a maximum number of runs for each of the individual tasks and their respective language combinations. Typically, the maximum number was lower, due to the choice of tasks by each group. In order to facilitate comparison between results, there was a mandatory run: Title + Description (per experiment, per topic language).

3 Result Calculation

3.1 Measures

The effectiveness of IR systems can be objectively evaluated by an analysis of a set of representative sample search results. To this end, test queries are used to retrieve the best matching documents. Effectiveness measures are then calculated based on the relevance assessments. Popular measures usually adopted for exercises of this type are Recall and Precision.

$$\text{Recall } \rho_r(q) := \frac{\left|D_r^{rel}(q)\right|}{\left|D^{rel}(q)\right|} \text{ and Precision } \pi_r(q) := \frac{\left|D_r^{rel}(q)\right|}{\left|D_r(q)\right|},$$

where $D_r(q) := \{d_1, \ldots, d_r\}$ is the answer set to query q containing the first r documents. The choice of a specific value for r is necessary because recall and precision are set-based measures, and evaluate the quality of an unordered set of retrieved documents. Choosing a low value for r implies that the user is interested in few, high-precision documents, whereas a high value for r means that the user conducts an exhaustive search. $D^{rel}(q)$ is the set of all relevant documents, and $D_r^{rel}(q) := D^{rel}(q) \cap D_r(q)$ is the set of relevant documents contained in the answer set [10]. When precision and recall are determined for every possible size of the answer set, a plot of the corresponding values results in a saw tooth curve (see Table 3). In the next step, typically a replacement curve is defined by assigning for every recall value $\rho \in [0,1]$ a precision value as follows:

$$\Pi_q(\rho) := \max\{\pi_r(q) \mid \rho_r(q) \geq \rho\}$$

Using this "interpolation step", we obtain a monotonically decreasing curve where each recall value corresponds to a unique precision value (see Figure 1). This "ceiling operation" can be interpreted as looking only at the theoretically optimal answer sets for which recall and precision cannot be improved simultaneously by inspecting further documents.

When evaluating a system with a set of queries (typically 50 in CLEF), an averaging step is introduced that produces the final recall/precision curve:

$$\Pi(\rho) := \frac{1}{|Q|} \sum_{q \in Q} \Pi_q(\rho)$$

where $|Q|$ denotes the number of queries.

Often people prefer single value measures to a more complex performance indicator, such as a recall/precision curve. The advantage of such single value measures lies in easy comparison, their danger in too much abstraction: if relying exclusively on a single value, the ability to judge a system's effectiveness for different user preferences, such as exhaustive search or high-precision results, is lost.

Table 3. Precision/recall figures for sample query and corresponding relevance assessments.

rank r	relevant to q.	$\rho_r(q)$	$\pi_r(q)$
1	+	0.20	1.00
2	-	0.20	0.50
3	-	0.20	0.33
4	+	0.40	0.50
5	-	0.40	0.40
6	-	0.40	0.33
7	+	0.60	0.43
8	+	0.80	0.50
9	-	0.80	0.44
10	+	1.00	0.50

The most popular single value measure for assessing the effectiveness of information retrieval systems is average precision. To calculate the average precision value, the precision after each relevant document found in the result list is determined as outlined above. The list of precision values that is obtained is then used to calculate an average. No interpolation is used to calculate the final average.

3.2 Pooling

All evaluations in the CLEF campaigns are based on the use of relevance assessments, i.e. judgments made by human "assessors" with respect to the usefulness of a certain document to answer a user's information need. CLEF uses a set of topics as a sample of possible information needs that could be formulated by real users. Theoretically, for each of these topics, all documents in the test collection would have to be judged for relevance. Since this judging ("assessment") involves an assessor reading the complete document, this is a laborious process. With the size of today's test collections, which contain hundreds of thousands or even millions of documents (the CLEF multilingual track used around 750,000 documents for 2002), this becomes impractical.

Therefore, evaluation campaigns such as CLEF often use an alternative strategy, only assessing a fraction of the document collection for any given topic. This implies – for every query – eliminating all those documents from consideration that were not retrieved by any participant high up in their ranked list of results. The reasoning behind this strategy is discussed in detail in [6]. The remaining documents, which share the property of having been retrieved as a highly ranked document by at least one participant, form a "document pool" that is then judged for relevance. The number of result sets per participant that are used for pooling, and the establishing of the line between "highly ranked" and other documents (the so-called "pool depth") are dictated to a large extent by practical needs (i.e. available resources for assessment).

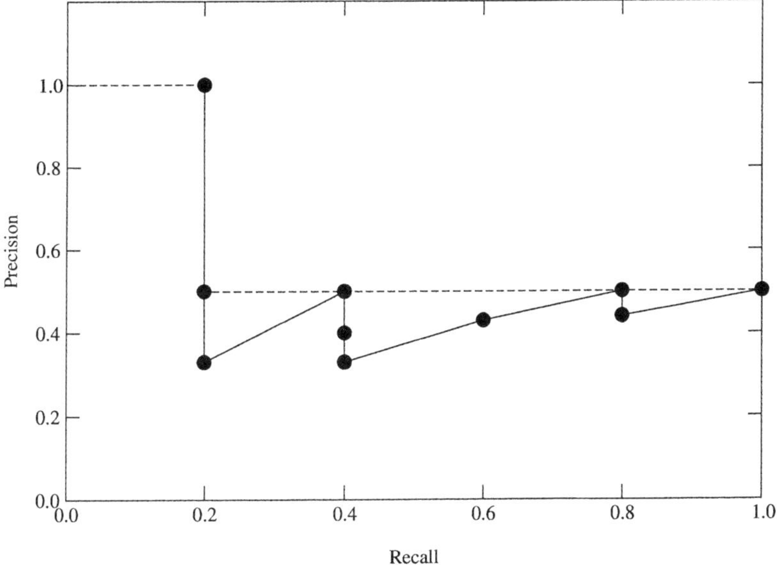

Fig. 1. Interpolation of recall/precision values

In the CLEF 2002 campaign, only selected results sets (slightly more than half of all results sets) were included in the pool. From these sets, the top 60 documents were used for pool formation. In [6] we discuss the implications of using a document pool vs. judging all documents in a collection

4 Results Presentation

4.1 Structure of Result Page

The Appendix contains one page for each result set submitted by a participating group for the core tracks. The page contains a set of tables and two graphs:

1. The tables provide the following information:
   - Average precision figures for every individual query. This allows comparison of system performance for single queries, which is important since variation of performance across queries is often very high and can be significant.
   - Overall statistics, giving:
     - the total number of documents retrieved by the system
     - the total number of overall relevant documents in the collection, and
     - the total number of relevant documents actually found by the system
     - interpolated precision averages at specific recall levels (see above)
     - non-interpolated average precision over all queries (see above)
     - precision numbers after inspecting a specific number of documents (see above)
     - R-precision: precision after the last relevant document was retrieved.
2. The graphs consist of:
   - a recall/precision graph, providing a plot of the precision values for various recall levels. This is the standard statistic and is the one most commonly reported in the literature.
   - a comparison to median performance. For each query, the difference in average precision, when compared to the median performance for the given task, is plotted. This graph gives valuable insight into which type of queries is handled well by different systems.

The results page for a specific experiment can be most quickly located by using the table at the beginning of the appendix. This table is sorted by group, and gives the name of the track/task, run identifier, topic language, topic fields, run type (automatic/manual), and whether the run was used for pooling prior to producing the relevance assessment. The individual results pages are sorted by track/task, and further sorted by run identifier, as can be seen from the overview table.

Acknowledgments

As mentioned, CLEF began its life as a track for cross-language information retrieval systems within TREC. When setting up a larger, independent initiative, the CLEF organizers have benefited considerably from the experiences gained at TREC. Much of the methodology employed in the CLEF campaigns is based on TREC, and the authors would like to express their gratitude in particular to Donna Harman and Ellen Voorhees.

Section 3.1 of this paper is based on a description contained in [15]. We thank Peter Schäuble for his contribution.

References

[1] Cleverdon, C.: The Cranfield Tests on Index Language Devices. In K. Sparck-Jones and P. Willett (Eds.): Readings in Information Retrieval, pages 47-59. Morgan Kaufmann, 1997.

[2] Harman, D.: The TREC Conferences. In R. Kuhlen and M. Rittberger (Eds.): Hypertext - Information Retrieval - Multimedia: Synergieeffekte Elektronischer Informationssysteme, Proceedings of HIM '95, pages 9-28. Universitätsverlag Konstanz

[3] Voorhees, E.: The Philosophy of Information Retrieval Evaluation. In Peters, C., Braschler, M., Gonzalo, J., and Kluck, M. (Eds.): Evaluation of Cross-Language Information Retrieval Systems. Second Workshop of the Cross-Language Evaluation Forum, CLEF 2001, Revised Papers, 2002, Pages 355-370.

[4] Text REtrieval Conference (TREC) Series: http://trec.nist.gov/

[5] NTCIR (NII-NACSIS Test Collection for IR Systems): http://research.nii.ac.jp/ntcir/

[6] Braschler, M. CLEF 2002 - Overview of Results: This volume.

[7] Peters, C. Introduction: This volume.

[8] Gey, F.C. & Kluck, M.: The Domain-Specific Task of CLEF – Specific Evaluation Strategies in Cross-Language Information Retrieval. In C. Peters (Ed.). Cross-Language Information Retrieval and Evaluation. Lecture Notes in Computer Science 2069, Springer Verlag, pp 48-56.4.

[9] Gonzalo, J and Oard, D.W.: The CLEF 2002 Interactive Track. This volume.

[10] DELOS Network of Excellence on Digital Libraries: http://delos-noe.iei.pi.cnr.it/

[11] Jones, G.J.F., Federico, M.: CLEF2002 Cross-Language Spoken Document Retrieval Pilot Track Report. This volume.

[12] Womser-Hacker, C.: Multilingual Topic Generation within the CLEF 2001 Experiments.

[13] Mandl, T., Womser-Hacker, C.: Linguistic and Statistical Analysis of the CLEF Topics. This volume.

[14] ftp://ftp.cs.cornell.edu/pub/smart/

[15] Schäuble, P.: Content-Based Information Retrieval from Large Text and Audio Databases. Section 1.6 Evaluation Issues, Pages 22-29, Kluwer Academic Publishers, 1997.

Part III

Appendix

Institution	Country	Run Tag	Task	Top. Lang.	Top. Fld.	Run Type	Judged?
City University	United Kingdom	plge02t	Mono	DE	T	Auto	
City University	United Kingdom	plge02td	Mono	DE	TD	Auto	Y
City University	United Kingdom	plsp02t	Mono	ES	T	Auto	
City University	United Kingdom	plsp02td	Mono	ES	TD	Auto	Y
City University	United Kingdom	plfn02t	Mono	FI	T	Auto	Y
City University	United Kingdom	plfn02td	Mono	FI	TD	Auto	Y
City University	United Kingdom	plfr02td	Mono	FR	TD	Auto	Y
City University	United Kingdom	plit02td	Mono	IT	TD	Auto	Y
City University	United Kingdom	pldu02t	Mono	NL	T	Auto	
City University	United Kingdom	pldu02td	Mono	NL	TD	Auto	Y
Clairvoyance Corp.	USA	cles2enw	Bi-EN	ES	TD	Auto	Y
Clairvoyance Corp.	USA	cles2ent1	Bi-EN	ES	TD	Auto	Y
Clairvoyance Corp.	USA	cles2ent2	Bi-EN	ES	TD	Auto	Y
Clairvoyance Corp.	USA	cles2enc1	Bi-EN	ES	TD	Auto	
Clairvoyance Corp.	USA	clch2enw	Bi-EN	ZH	TD	Auto	Y
Clairvoyance Corp.	USA	clch2ent1	Bi-EN	ZH	TD	Auto	Y
Clairvoyance Corp.	USA	clch2ent2	Bi-EN	ZH	TD	Auto	Y
Clairvoyance Corp.	USA	clch2enc1	Bi-EN	ZH	TD	Auto	
COLE Group Univ. La Coruna	Spain	coleTDlem02	Mono	ES	TD	Auto	
COLE Group Univ. La Coruna	Spain	coleTDNlem02	Mono	ES	TDN	Auto	Y
COLE Group Univ. La Coruna	Spain	coleTDNpds02	Mono	ES	TDN	Auto	Y
COLE Group Univ. La Coruna	Spain	coleTDNsyn02	Mono	ES	TDN	Auto	
CWI/CNLP	Netherlands/USA	AAbiENNLt	Bi-NL	EN	T	Auto	
CWI/CNLP	Netherlands/USA	AAbiENNLtd	Bi-NL	EN	TD	Auto	Y
CWI/CNLP	Netherlands/USA	AAmoNLt	Mono	NL	T	Auto	
CWI/CNLP	Netherlands/USA	AAmoNLtd	Mono	NL	TD	Auto	Y
Eurospider IT AG	Switzerland	EIT2GDM1	Mono	DE	TD	Auto	Y
Eurospider IT AG	Switzerland	EIT2GDL1	Mono	DE	TD	Auto	Y
Eurospider IT AG	Switzerland	EIT2GDB1	Mono	DE	TD	Auto	
Eurospider IT AG	Switzerland	EIT2GNM1	Mono	DE	TDN	Auto	
Eurospider IT AG	Switzerland	EIT2MDF3	Multi	DE	TD	Auto	Y
Eurospider IT AG	Switzerland	EIT2MDC3	Multi	DE	TD	Auto	
Eurospider IT AG	Switzerland	EIT2MNF3	Multi	DE	TDN	Auto	Y
Eurospider IT AG	Switzerland	EIT2MNU1	Multi	DE	TDN	Auto	
Eurospider IT AG	Switzerland	EAN2MDF4	Multi	EN	TD	Auto	
Fondazione Ugo Bordini	Italy	fub02bl	Mono	IT	TD	Auto	Y
Fondazione Ugo Bordini	Italy	fub02l	Mono	IT	TD	Auto	Y
Fondazione Ugo Bordini	Italy	fub02b	Mono	IT	TD	Auto	
Fondazione Ugo Bordini	Italy	fub02	Mono	IT	TD	Auto	
Hummingbird	Canada	humDE02	Mono	DE	TD	Auto	Y
Hummingbird	Canada	humES02	Mono	ES	TD	Auto	Y
Hummingbird	Canada	humFI02	Mono	FI	TD	Auto	Y
Hummingbird	Canada	humFI02n	Mono	FI	TDN	Auto	Y
Hummingbird	Canada	humFR02	Mono	FR	TD	Auto	Y
Hummingbird	Canada	humIT02	Mono	IT	TD	Auto	Y
Hummingbird	Canada	humNL02	Mono	NL	TD	Auto	Y
Hummingbird	Canada	humNL02n	Mono	NL	TDN	Auto	
Hummingbird	Canada	humSV02	Mono	SV	TD	Auto	Y
Hummingbird	Canada	humSV02n	Mono	SV	TDN	Auto	Y
IMBIT Inst., Univ. Hildesheim	Germany	IMBIT	Mono	DE	TDN	Manual	Y
IMS Univ. Padova	Italy	PDDS2PLL3	Mono	IT	TD	Auto	Y
IMS Univ. Padova	Italy	PDDP	Mono	IT	TD	Auto	Y
IMS Univ. Padova	Italy	PDDS2PL	Mono	IT	TD	Auto	
IMS Univ. Padova	Italy	PDDN	Mono	IT	TD	Auto	
IRIT, Toulouse	France	iritBFr2En	Bi-EN	FR	TD	Auto	Y
IRIT, Toulouse	France	RunMonoSp	Mono	ES	TD	Auto	Y
IRIT, Toulouse	France	RunMonFrench	Mono	FR	TD	Auto	Y
IRIT, Toulouse	France	RunMonoIt	Mono	IT	TD	Auto	Y
IRIT, Toulouse	France	iritMEn2All	Multi	EN	TD	Auto	Y
ISU, Univ. Hildesheim	Germany	UHi02r1	GIRT	DE	TD	Auto	Y
ISU, Univ. Hildesheim	Germany	UHi02r2	GIRT	DE	TD	Auto	Y
ITC-IRST	Italy	IRSTen2it1	Bi-IT	EN	TD	Auto	Y
ITC-IRST	Italy	IRSTen2it2	Bi-IT	EN	TD	Auto	
ITC-IRST	Italy	IRSTen2it3	Bi-IT	EN	TD	Auto	
ITC-IRST	Italy	IRSTit1	Mono	IT	TD	Auto	Y
JHU/APL	USA	aplbiende	Bi-DE	EN	TD	Auto	Y
JHU/APL	USA	aplbiptena	Bi-EN	PT	TD	Auto	Y
JHU/APL	USA	aplbienes	Bi-ES	EN	TD	Auto	
JHU/APL	USA	aplbiptesa	Bi-ES	PT	TD	Auto	
JHU/APL	USA	aplbiptesb	Bi-ES	PT	TD	Auto	
JHU/APL	USA	aplbienfi	Bi-FI	EN	TD	Auto	Y

C.A. Peters (Ed.): CLEF 2003, LNCS 2785, pp. 529-825, 2003.

JHU/APL	USA	aplbienfr	Bi-FR	EN	TD	Auto	
JHU/APL	USA	aplbienit	Bi-IT	EN	TD	Auto	
JHU/APL	USA	aplbiennl	Bi-NL	EN	TD	Auto	
JHU/APL	USA	aplbiensv	Bi-SV	EN	TD	Auto	Y
JHU/APL	USA	aplmode	Mono	DE	TD	Auto	Y
JHU/APL	USA	aplmoes	Mono	ES	TD	Auto	Y
JHU/APL	USA	aplmofi	Mono	FI	TD	Auto	Y
JHU/APL	USA	aplmofr	Mono	FR	TD	Auto	Y
JHU/APL	USA	aplmoit	Mono	IT	TD	Auto	Y
JHU/APL	USA	aplmonl	Mono	NL	TD	Auto	Y
JHU/APL	USA	aplmosv	Mono	SV	TD	Auto	Y
JHU/APL	USA	aplmuena	Multi	EN	TD	Auto	Y
JHU/APL	USA	aplmuenb	Multi	EN	TD	Auto	Y
Lexware Labs Ltd.	Sweden	lexware2002	Mono	SV	TDN	Auto	Y
MediaLab BV	Netherlands	medialab4	Mono	NL	TD	Auto	Y
MediaLab BV	Netherlands	medialab3	Mono	NL	TD	Auto	
MediaLab BV	Netherlands	medialab2	Mono	NL	TD	Auto	
MediaLab BV	Netherlands	medialab5	Mono	NL	TD	Auto	Y
Middlesex Univ.	United Kingdom	MDXtpc	Bi-EN	PT	T	Auto	
Middlesex Univ.	United Kingdom	MDXtd	Bi-EN	PT	TD	Auto	Y
Middlesex Univ.	United Kingdom	MDXman	Bi-EN	PT	TDN	Manual	Y
National Taiwan Univ.	Taiwan	NTUmulti01	Multi	EN	TD	Auto	
National Taiwan Univ.	Taiwan	NTUmulti02	Multi	EN	TD	Auto	Y
National Taiwan Univ.	Taiwan	NTUmulti03	Multi	EN	TD	Auto	
National Taiwan Univ.	Taiwan	NTUmulti04	Multi	EN	TD	Auto	Y
National Taiwan Univ.	Taiwan	NTUmulti05	Multi	EN	TD	Auto	
Océ	Netherlands	oce02es2enLO	Bi-EN	ES	TD	Auto	Y
Océ	Netherlands	oce02es2enBF	Bi-EN	ES	TD	Auto	
Océ	Netherlands	oce02nl2enER	Bi-EN	NL	TD	Auto	Y
Océ	Netherlands	oce02en2esLO	Bi-ES	EN	TD	Auto	
Océ	Netherlands	oce02en2esBF	Bi-ES	EN	TD	Auto	
Océ	Netherlands	oce02en2nlER	Bi-NL	EN	TD	Auto	Y
Océ	Netherlands	oce02monDEto	Mono	DE	T	Auto	
Océ	Netherlands	oce02monDE	Mono	DE	TD	Auto	Y
Océ	Netherlands	oce02monESto	Mono	ES	T	Auto	
Océ	Netherlands	oce02monES	Mono	ES	TD	Auto	Y
Océ	Netherlands	oce02monFRto	Mono	FR	T	Auto	
Océ	Netherlands	oce02monFR	Mono	FR	TD	Auto	Y
Océ	Netherlands	oce02monITto	Mono	IT	T	Auto	
Océ	Netherlands	oce02monIT	Mono	IT	TD	Auto	Y
Océ	Netherlands	oce02monNLto	Mono	NL	T	Auto	
Océ	Netherlands	oce02monNL	Mono	NL	TD	Auto	Y
Océ	Netherlands	oce02mulRRloTO	Multi	EN	T	Auto	
Océ	Netherlands	oce02mulRRlo	Multi	EN	TD	Auto	Y
Océ	Netherlands	oce02mulMSlo	Multi	EN	TD	Auto	Y
Océ	Netherlands	oce02mulRRbf	Multi	EN	TD	Auto	
Océ	Netherlands	oce02mulMSbf	Multi	EN	TD	Auto	
RALI U Montreal	Canada	run1	Multi	EN	TDN	Auto	Y
RALI U Montreal	Canada	run2	Multi	EN	TDN	Auto	Y
RALI U Montreal	Canada	run3	Multi	EN	TDN	Auto	
SICS/Conexor	Sweden/Finland	sicsFRFR0	Mono	FR	TD	Auto	
SICS/Conexor	Sweden/Finland	sicsFRFRX0	Mono	FR	TD	Auto	Y
SICS/Conexor	Sweden/Finland	sicsITIT	Mono	IT	TD	Auto	
SICS/Conexor	Sweden/Finland	sicsITITX	Mono	IT	TD	Auto	Y
SICS/Conexor	Sweden/Finland	siteseeker	Mono	SV	T	Auto	Y
SICS/Conexor	Sweden/Finland	sicsSVSV	Mono	SV	TD	Auto	Y
SICS/Conexor	Sweden/Finland	sicsSVSVX	Mono	SV	TD	Auto	Y
Tagmatica	France	runA	Mono	FR	DN	Manual	Y
TLR Research	USA	tlren2es	Bi-ES	EN	TD	Auto	Y
TLR Research	USA	tlren2fr	Bi-FR	EN	TD	Auto	
TLR Research	USA	tlrde	Mono	DE	TD	Auto	Y
TLR Research	USA	tlres	Mono	ES	TD	Auto	Y
TLR Research	USA	tlrfr	Mono	FR	TD	Auto	Y
TLR Research	USA	tlrit	Mono	IT	TD	Auto	Y
TLR Research	USA	tlrnl	Mono	NL	TD	Auto	Y
TLR Research	USA	tlrsv	Mono	SV	TD	Auto	Y
TLR Research	USA	tlren2multi	Multi	EN	TD	Auto	Y
Univ. Dortmund	Germany	GIRTsppc	GIRT	DE	TD	Auto	Y
Univ. Dortmund	Germany	GIRTstem	GIRT	DE	TD	Auto	Y
Univ. Dortmund	Germany	MLstem	Mono	DE	TD	Auto	Y
Univ. Exeter	United Kingdom	exespgemgcntbi	Bi-ES	DE	TD	Auto	
Univ. Exeter	United Kingdom	exespengorgbi	Bi-ES	EN	TD	Auto	

Univ. Exeter	United Kingdom	exespengpiwgt	Bi-ES	EN	TD	Auto	Y
Univ. Exeter	United Kingdom	exespfrmgcntbi	Bi-ES	FR	TD	Auto	
Univ. Exeter	United Kingdom	exespitmgcntbi	Bi-ES	IT	TD	Auto	
Univ. Exeter	United Kingdom	exeitgemgcntbi	Bi-IT	DE	TD	Auto	
Univ. Exeter	United Kingdom	exeitengorgbi	Bi-IT	EN	TD	Auto	
Univ. Exeter	United Kingdom	exeitengpiwgt	Bi-IT	EN	TD	Auto	
Univ. Exeter	United Kingdom	exeitspmgbi	Bi-IT	ES	TD	Auto	Y
Univ. Exeter	United Kingdom	exeitfrmgbi	Bi-IT	FR	TD	Auto	
Univ. Exeter	United Kingdom	exespmgcntmn	Mono	ES	TD	Auto	
Univ. Exeter	United Kingdom	exespmgmn	Mono	ES	TD	Auto	Y
Univ. Exeter	United Kingdom	exesporgmn	Mono	ES	TD	Auto	
Univ. Exeter	United Kingdom	exespwtpimn	Mono	ES	TD	Auto	
Univ. Exeter	United Kingdom	exeitmgcntmn	Mono	IT	TD	Auto	
Univ. Exeter	United Kingdom	exeitmgmn	Mono	IT	TD	Auto	
Univ. Exeter	United Kingdom	exeitorgmn	Mono	IT	TD	Auto	Y
Univ. Exeter	United Kingdom	exeitwtpimn	Mono	IT	TD	Auto	
Univ. Jaen/SINAI	Spain	UJABIDE	Bi-DE	EN	TD	Auto	Y
Univ. Jaen/SINAI	Spain	UJABISP	Bi-ES	EN	TD	Auto	Y
Univ. Jaen/SINAI	Spain	UJABIFR	Bi-FR	EN	TD	Auto	Y
Univ. Jaen/SINAI	Spain	UJABIIT	Bi-IT	EN	TD	Auto	Y
Univ. Jaen/SINAI	Spain	UJAMLTDRSV2RR	Multi	EN	TD	Auto	
Univ. Jaen/SINAI	Spain	UJAMLTDNORM	Multi	EN	TD	Auto	
Univ. Jaen/SINAI	Spain	UJAMLTDRR	Multi	EN	TD	Auto	
Univ. Jaen/SINAI	Spain	UJAMLTDRSV2	Multi	EN	TD	Auto	Y
Univ. Jaen/SINAI	Spain	UJAMLTD2RSV2	Multi	EN	TD	Auto	Y
Univ. of Ca. at Berkeley 1	USA	BKAMEF1	Amaryllis	EN	TD	Auto	Y
Univ. of Ca. at Berkeley 1	USA	BKAMEF2	Amaryllis	EN	TD	Auto	Y
Univ. of Ca. at Berkeley 1	USA	BKAMEF3	Amaryllis	EN	TD	Auto	Y
Univ. of Ca. at Berkeley 1	USA	BKAMFF2	Amaryllis	FR	TD	Auto	Y
Univ. of Ca. at Berkeley 1	USA	BKAMFF1	Amaryllis	FR	TDN	Auto	Y
Univ. of Ca. at Berkeley 1	USA	BKBIEG2	Bi-DE	EN	TD	Auto	
Univ. of Ca. at Berkeley 1	USA	BKBIEG1	Bi-DE	EN	TDN	Auto	
Univ. of Ca. at Berkeley 1	USA	BKBIFG2	Bi-DE	FR	TD	Auto	
Univ. of Ca. at Berkeley 1	USA	BKBIFG1	Bi-DE	FR	TDN	Auto	
Univ. of Ca. at Berkeley 1	USA	BKBIRG2	Bi-DE	RU	TD	Auto	Y
Univ. of Ca. at Berkeley 1	USA	BKBIRG1	Bi-DE	RU	TDN	Auto	Y
Univ. of Ca. at Berkeley 1	USA	BKBIGF1	Bi-FR	DE	TD	Auto	
Univ. of Ca. at Berkeley 1	USA	BKBIEF1	Bi-FR	EN	TD	Auto	
Univ. of Ca. at Berkeley 1	USA	BKBIEF2	Bi-FR	EN	TDN	Auto	
Univ. of Ca. at Berkeley 1	USA	BKBIRF1	Bi-FR	RU	TD	Auto	
Univ. of Ca. at Berkeley 1	USA	BKGRGG2	GIRT	DE	TD	Auto	Y
Univ. of Ca. at Berkeley 1	USA	BKGRGG1	GIRT	DE	TDN	Auto	Y
Univ. of Ca. at Berkeley 1	USA	BKGREG1	GIRT	EN	TD	Auto	Y
Univ. of Ca. at Berkeley 1	USA	BKGRRG2	GIRT	RU	TD	Auto	Y
Univ. of Ca. at Berkeley 1	USA	BKGRRG1	GIRT	RU	TDN	Auto	Y
Univ. of Ca. at Berkeley 1	USA	BKMLGG2	Mono	DE	TD	Auto	
Univ. of Ca. at Berkeley 1	USA	BKMLGG1	Mono	DE	TDN	Auto	Y
Univ. of Ca. at Berkeley 1	USA	BKMLFF2	Mono	FR	TD	Auto	
Univ. of Ca. at Berkeley 1	USA	BKMLFF1	Mono	FR	TDN	Auto	Y
Univ. of Ca. at Berkeley 2	USA	bky2biende	Bi-DE	EN	TD	Auto	Y
Univ. of Ca. at Berkeley 2	USA	bky2bifrde	Bi-DE	FR	TD	Auto	
Univ. of Ca. at Berkeley 2	USA	bky2bienes	Bi-ES	EN	TD	Auto	Y
Univ. of Ca. at Berkeley 2	USA	bky2bidefr	Bi-FR	DE	TD	Auto	
Univ. of Ca. at Berkeley 2	USA	bky2bienfr	Bi-FR	EN	TD	Auto	Y
Univ. of Ca. at Berkeley 2	USA	bky2bienfr2	Bi-FR	EN	TD	Auto	
Univ. of Ca. at Berkeley 2	USA	bky2bienit	Bi-IT	EN	TD	Auto	
Univ. of Ca. at Berkeley 2	USA	bky2biennl	Bi-NL	EN	TD	Auto	Y
Univ. of Ca. at Berkeley 2	USA	bky2mode	Mono	DE	TD	Auto	Y
Univ. of Ca. at Berkeley 2	USA	bky2moes	Mono	ES	TD	Auto	Y
Univ. of Ca. at Berkeley 2	USA	bky2mofr	Mono	FR	TD	Auto	Y
Univ. of Ca. at Berkeley 2	USA	bky2moit	Mono	IT	TD	Auto	Y
Univ. of Ca. at Berkeley 2	USA	bky2monl	Mono	NL	TD	Auto	Y
Univ. of Ca. at Berkeley 2	USA	bky2muen1	Multi	EN	TD	Auto	Y
Univ. of Ca. at Berkeley 2	USA	bky2muen2	Multi	EN	TD	Auto	Y
Univ. of Twente	Netherlands	tnoen1	Bi-NL	EN	TD	Auto	
Univ. of Twente	Netherlands	tnofifi1	Mono	FI	TD	Auto	Y
Univ. of Twente	Netherlands	tnoutn1	Mono	NL	TDN	Manual	Y
Univ. Tampere, Dept. IS	Finland	finbi2	Bi-FI	EN	TD	Auto	Y
Univ. Tampere, Dept. IS	Finland	bifren	Bi-FR	EN	TD	Auto	Y
Univ. Tampere, Dept. IS	Finland	dualge	Bi-NL	EN	TD	Auto	Y
Univ. Tampere, Dept. IS	Finland	finmo1	Mono	FI	TD	Auto	Y
Univ. Tampere, Dept. IS	Finland	finmo2	Mono	FI	TD	Auto	Y

Univ. Tampere, Dept. IS	Finland	tremu1	Multi	EN	TD	Auto	Y
Univ. Tampere, Dept. IS	Finland	tremu2	Multi	EN	TD	Auto	Y
Université de Neuchâtel	Switzerland	UniNEama1	Amaryllis	FR	TD	Auto	Y
Université de Neuchâtel	Switzerland	UniNEama2	Amaryllis	FR	TD	Auto	Y
Université de Neuchâtel	Switzerland	UniNEama3	Amaryllis	FR	TD	Auto	Y
Université de Neuchâtel	Switzerland	UniNEama4	Amaryllis	FR	TD	Auto	Y
Université de Neuchâtel	Switzerland	UniNEamaN1	Amaryllis	FR	TDN	Auto	Y
Université de Neuchâtel	Switzerland	UniNEdeBi	Bi-DE	EN	TD	Auto	Y
Université de Neuchâtel	Switzerland	UniNEdeBi2	Bi-DE	EN	TD	Auto	
Université de Neuchâtel	Switzerland	UniNEesBi	Bi-ES	EN	TD	Auto	
Université de Neuchâtel	Switzerland	UniNEesBi3	Bi-ES	EN	TD	Auto	
Université de Neuchâtel	Switzerland	UniNEesBi2	Bi-ES	EN	TD	Auto	
Université de Neuchâtel	Switzerland	UniNEfrBi	Bi-FR	EN	TD	Auto	
Université de Neuchâtel	Switzerland	UniNEfrBi3	Bi-FR	EN	TD	Auto	
Université de Neuchâtel	Switzerland	UniNEfrBi2	Bi-FR	EN	TD	Auto	
Université de Neuchâtel	Switzerland	UniNEitBi	Bi-IT	EN	TD	Auto	Y
Université de Neuchâtel	Switzerland	UniNEitBi2	Bi-IT	EN	TD	Auto	
Université de Neuchâtel	Switzerland	UniNEde	Mono	DE	TD	Auto	
Université de Neuchâtel	Switzerland	UniNEdetdn	Mono	DE	TDN	Manual	Y
Université de Neuchâtel	Switzerland	UniNEes	Mono	ES	TD	Auto	
Université de Neuchâtel	Switzerland	UniNEestdn	Mono	ES	TDN	Auto	Y
Université de Neuchâtel	Switzerland	UniNEfi1	Mono	FI	TD	Auto	Y
Université de Neuchâtel	Switzerland	UniNEfi2	Mono	FI	TD	Auto	Y
Université de Neuchâtel	Switzerland	UniNEfr	Mono	FR	TD	Auto	
Université de Neuchâtel	Switzerland	UniNEfrtdn	Mono	FR	TDN	Manual	Y
Université de Neuchâtel	Switzerland	UniNEit	Mono	IT	TD	Auto	Y
Université de Neuchâtel	Switzerland	UniNEnl	Mono	NL	TD	Auto	Y
Université de Neuchâtel	Switzerland	UniNEm1	Multi	EN	TD	Auto	Y
Université de Neuchâtel	Switzerland	UniNEm2	Multi	EN	TD	Auto	Y
Université de Neuchâtel	Switzerland	UniNEm3	Multi	EN	TD	Auto	
Université de Neuchâtel	Switzerland	UniNEm4	Multi	EN	TD	Auto	
Université de Neuchâtel	Switzerland	UniNEm5	Multi	EN	TD	Auto	
University of Alicante	Spain	irn1	Mono	ES	TD	Auto	Y
University of Alicante	Spain	irn3	Mono	ES	TD	Auto	
University of Alicante	Spain	irn2	Mono	ES	TDN	Auto	
University of Alicante	Spain	irn4	Mono	ES	TDN	Auto	Y
University of Amsterdam	Netherlands	UAmsC02EnAmTTiKW	Amaryllis	EN	TD	Auto	Y
University of Amsterdam	Netherlands	UAmsC02EnAmTTiRR	Amaryllis	EN	TD	Auto	Y
University of Amsterdam	Netherlands	UAmsC02FrAmKW	Amaryllis	FR	N	Auto	Y
University of Amsterdam	Netherlands	UAmsC02FrAmTT	Amaryllis	FR	TD	Auto	Y
University of Amsterdam	Netherlands	UAmsC02FrAmTTiKW	Amaryllis	FR	TDN	Auto	Y
University of Amsterdam	Netherlands	UAmsC02EnGeNGram	Bi-DE	EN	TD	Auto	
University of Amsterdam	Netherlands	UAmsC02EnDuMorph	Bi-NL	EN	TD	Auto	
University of Amsterdam	Netherlands	UAmsC02EnDuNGiMO	Bi-NL	EN	TD	Auto	
University of Amsterdam	Netherlands	UAmsC02EnDuNGram	Bi-NL	EN	TD	Auto	
University of Amsterdam	Netherlands	UAmsC02GeGiTT	GIRT	DE	TD	Auto	Y
University of Amsterdam	Netherlands	UAmsC02GeGiTTiKW	GIRT	DE	TD	Auto	Y
University of Amsterdam	Netherlands	UAmsC02GeGiTTiRR	GIRT	DE	TD	Auto	Y
University of Amsterdam	Netherlands	UAmsC02EnGiTTiKW	GIRT	EN	TD	Auto	Y
University of Amsterdam	Netherlands	UAmsC02EnGiTTiRR	GIRT	EN	TD	Auto	Y
University of Amsterdam	Netherlands	UAmsC02GeGeLC2F	Mono	DE	TD	Auto	
University of Amsterdam	Netherlands	UAmsC02GeGeNGiMO	Mono	DE	TD	Auto	Y
University of Amsterdam	Netherlands	UAmsC02GeGeNGram	Mono	DE	TD	Auto	
University of Amsterdam	Netherlands	UAmsC02SpSpNGiSt	Mono	ES	TD	Auto	Y
University of Amsterdam	Netherlands	UAmsC02FiFiNGram	Mono	FI	TD	Auto	Y
University of Amsterdam	Netherlands	UAmsC02FrFrNGiMO	Mono	FR	TD	Auto	Y
University of Amsterdam	Netherlands	UAmsC02ItItNGiMO	Mono	IT	TD	Auto	Y
University of Amsterdam	Netherlands	UAmsC02DuDuNGiMO	Mono	NL	TD	Auto	Y
University of Amsterdam	Netherlands	UAmsC02DuDuNGram	Mono	NL	TD	Auto	
University of Amsterdam	Netherlands	UAmsC02SwSwNGram	Mono	SV	TD	Auto	Y
University of Salamanca	Spain	usalNST	Mono	ES	T	Auto	
University of Salamanca	Spain	usalNAT	Mono	ES	T	Auto	
University of Salamanca	Spain	usalNNTDN	Mono	ES	TDN	Auto	Y
University of Salamanca	Spain	usalFNTDN	Mono	ES	TDN	Auto	Y
XRCE Xerox	France	xrcegirt1	GIRT	EN	T	Auto	Y
XRCE Xerox	France	xrcegirt3	GIRT	EN	T	Auto	Y
XRCE Xerox	France	xrcegirt4	GIRT	EN	T	Auto	Y

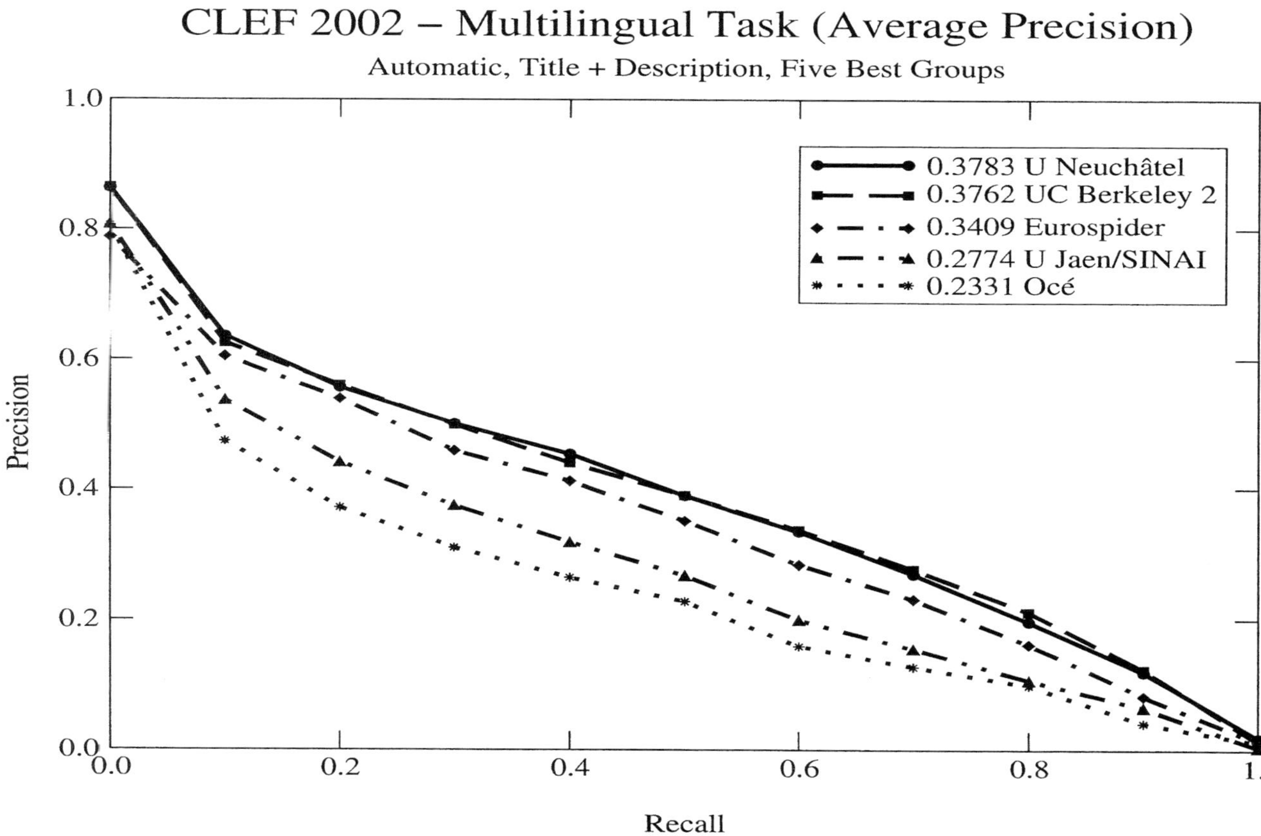
CLEF 2002 – Multilingual Task (Average Precision)
Automatic, Title + Description, Five Best Groups
0.3783 U Neuchâtel
0.3762 UC Berkeley 2
0.3409 Eurospider
0.2774 U Jaen/SINAI
0.2331 Océ
Precision
1.0
0.8
0.6
0.4
0.2
0.0
Recall
0.0
0.2
0.4
0.6
0.8
1.0

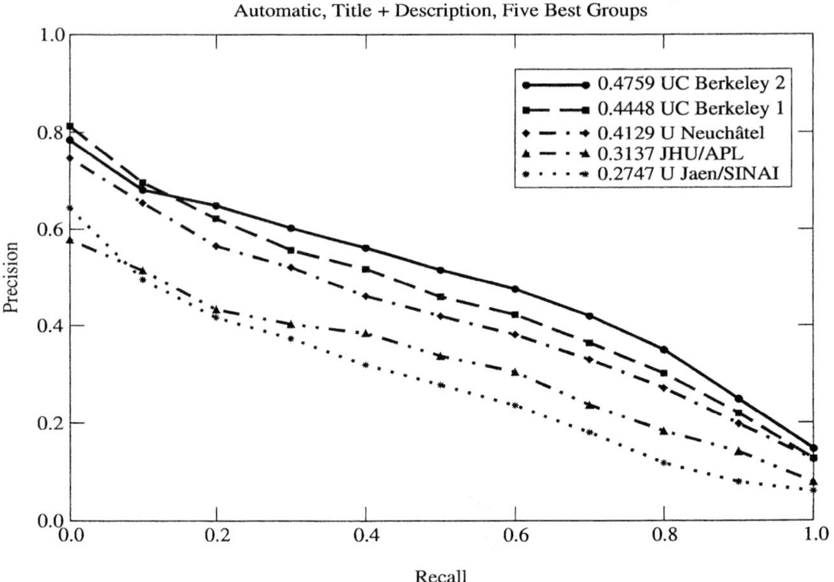
CLEF 2002 – Bilingual to German Task (Average Precision)
Automatic, Title + Description, Five Best Groups
0.4759 UC Berkeley 2
0.4448 UC Berkeley 1
0.4129 U Neuchâtel
0.3137 JHU/APL
0.2747 U Jaen/SINAI
Precision
Recall
0.0
0.2
0.4
0.6
0.8
1.0

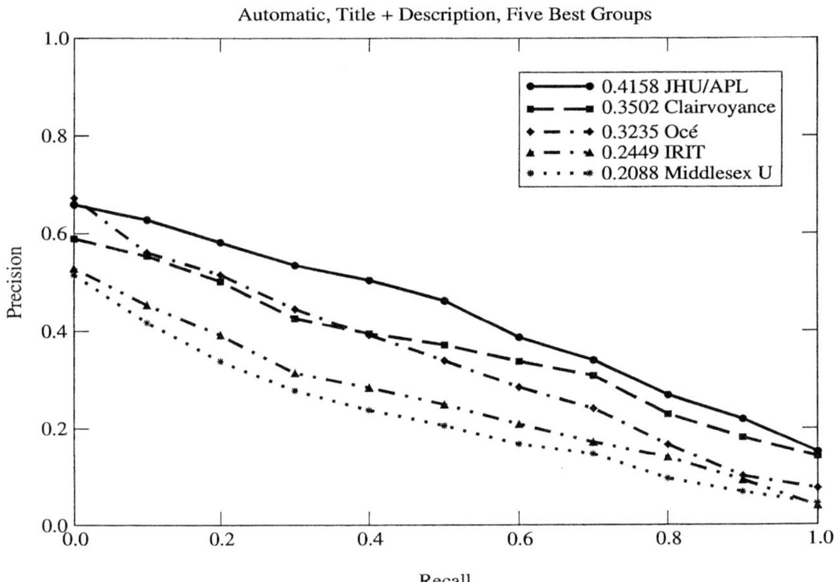
CLEF 2002 – Bilingual to English Task (Average Precision)
Automatic, Title + Description, Five Best Groups
0.4158 JHU/APL
0.3502 Clairvoyance
0.3235 Océ
0.2449 IRIT
0.2088 Middlesex U
Precision
Recall
0.0
0.2
0.4
0.6
0.8
1.0

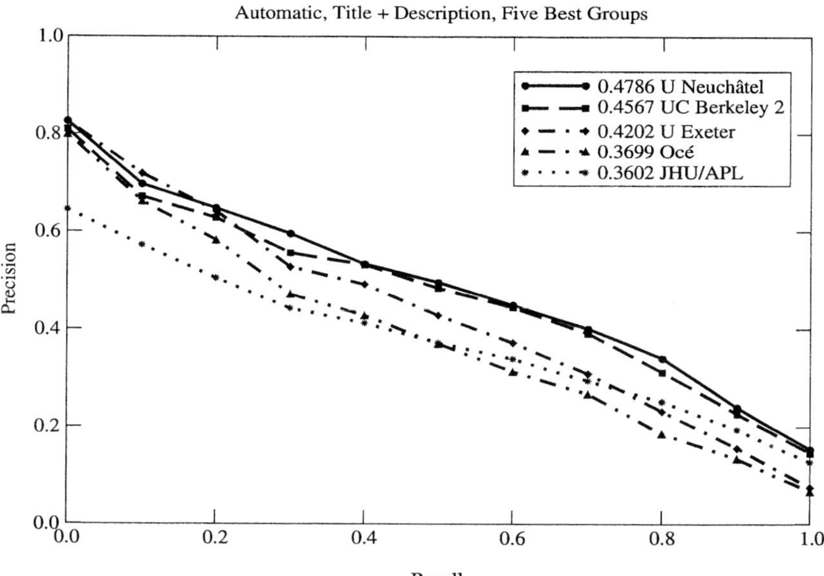
CLEF 2002 – Bilingual to Spanish Task (Average Precision)
Automatic, Title + Description, Five Best Groups
0.4786 U Neuchâtel
0.4567 UC Berkeley 2
0.4202 U Exeter
0.3699 Océ
0.3602 JHU/APL
Precision
Recall
0.0
0.2
0.4
0.6
0.8
1.0

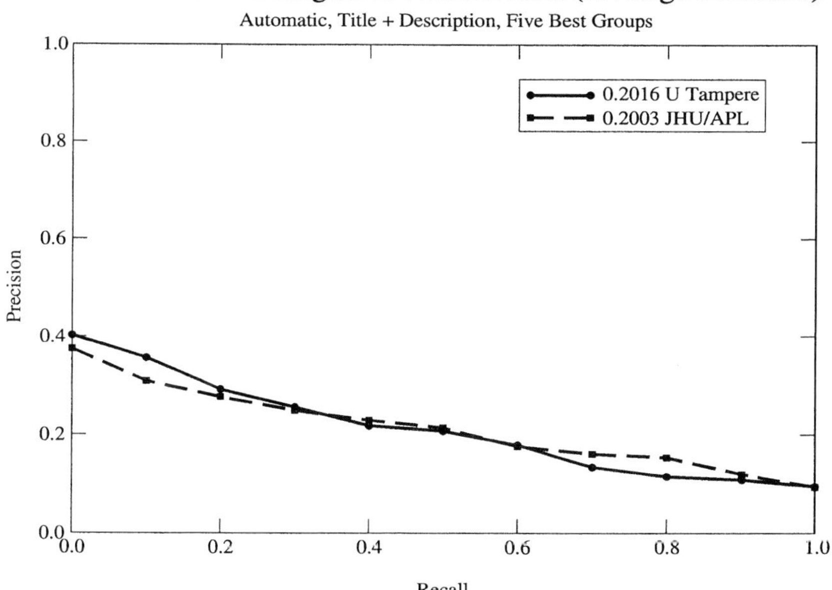
CLEF 2002 – Bilingual to Finnish Task (Average Precision)
Automatic, Title + Description, Five Best Groups
0.2016 U Tampere
0.2003 JHU/APL
Precision
Recall
0.0
0.2
0.4
0.6
0.8
1.0

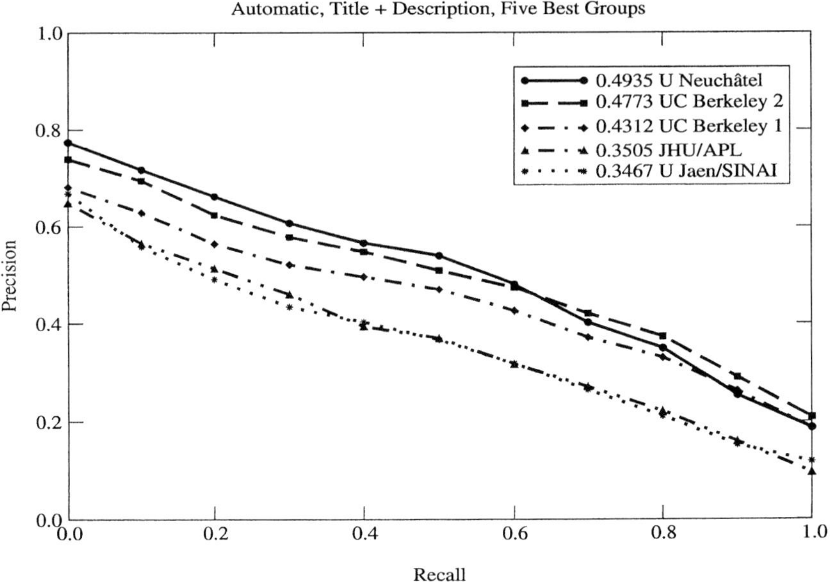
CLEF 2002 – Bilingual to French Task (Average Precision)
Automatic, Title + Description, Five Best Groups
0.4935 U Neuchâtel
0.4773 UC Berkeley 2
0.4312 UC Berkeley 1
0.3505 JHU/APL
0.3467 U Jaen/SINAI
Precision
Recall
0.0
0.2
0.4
0.6
0.8
1.0

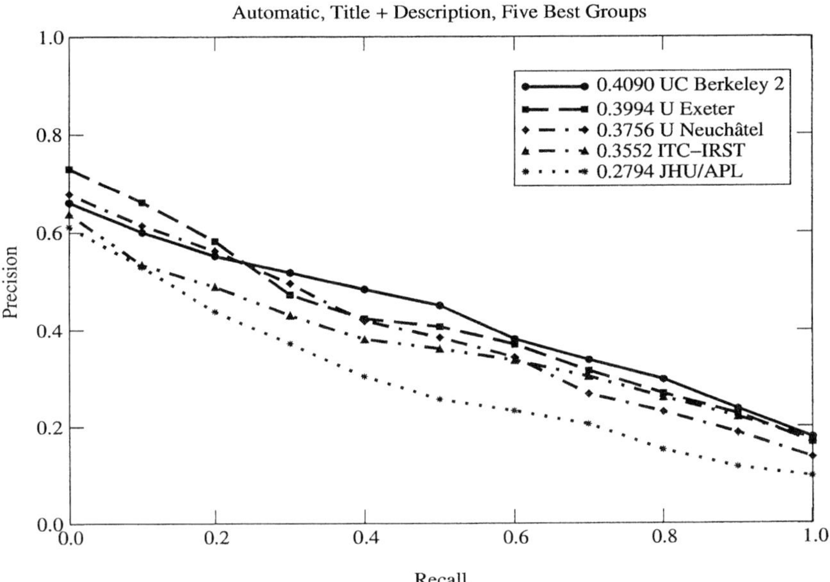
CLEF 2002 – Bilingual to Italian Task (Average Precision)
Automatic, Title + Description, Five Best Groups
0.4090 UC Berkeley 2
0.3994 U Exeter
0.3756 U Neuchâtel
0.3552 ITC–IRST
0.2794 JHU/APL
Precision
Recall
0.0
0.2
0.4
0.6
0.8
1.0

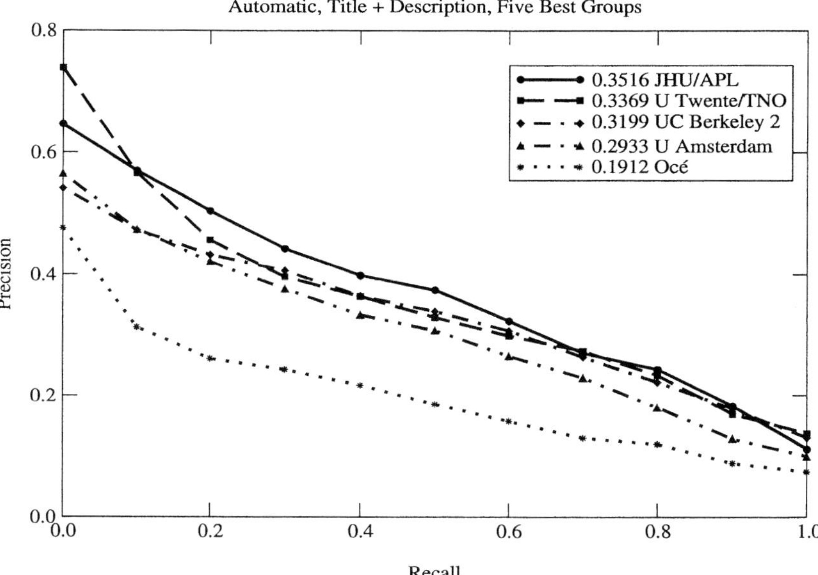
CLEF 2002 – Bilingual to Dutch Task (Average Precision)
Automatic, Title + Description, Five Best Groups
0.3516 JHU/APL
0.3369 U Twente/TNO
0.3199 UC Berkeley 2
0.2933 U Amsterdam
0.1912 Océ
Precision
Recall
0.0
0.2
0.4
0.6
0.8
1.0

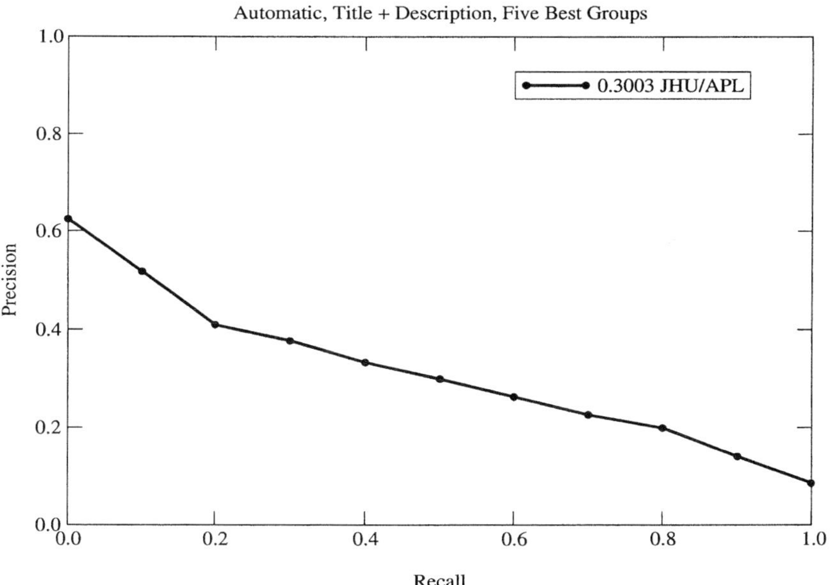
CLEF 2002 – Bilingual to Swedish Task (Average Precision)
Automatic, Title + Description, Five Best Groups
0.3003 JHU/APL
Precision
Recall
0.0
0.2
0.4
0.6
0.8
1.0

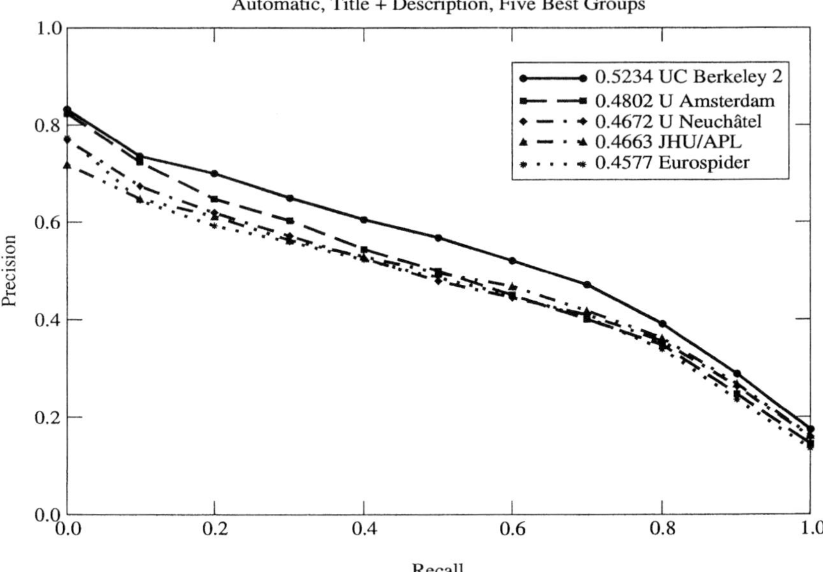
CLEF 2002 – German Monolingual Task (Average Precision)
Automatic, Title + Description, Five Best Groups
0.5234 UC Berkeley 2
0.4802 U Amsterdam
0.4672 U Neuchâtel
0.4663 JHU/APL
0.4577 Eurospider
Precision
Recall
0.0
0.2
0.4
0.6
0.8
1.0

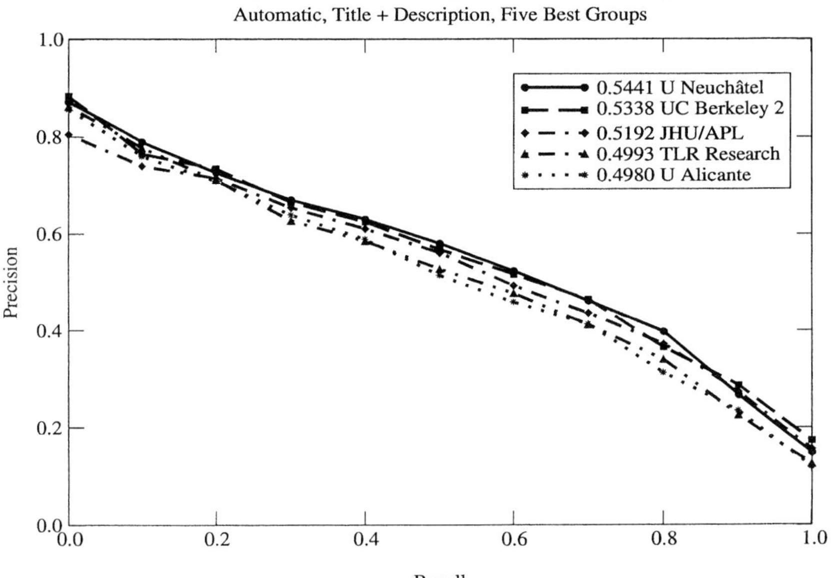
CLEF 2002 – Spanish Monolingual Task (Average Precision)
Automatic, Title + Description, Five Best Groups
0.5441 U Neuchâtel
0.5338 UC Berkeley 2
0.5192 JHU/APL
0.4993 TLR Research
0.4980 U Alicante
Precision
Recall
0.0
0.2
0.4
0.6
0.8
1.0

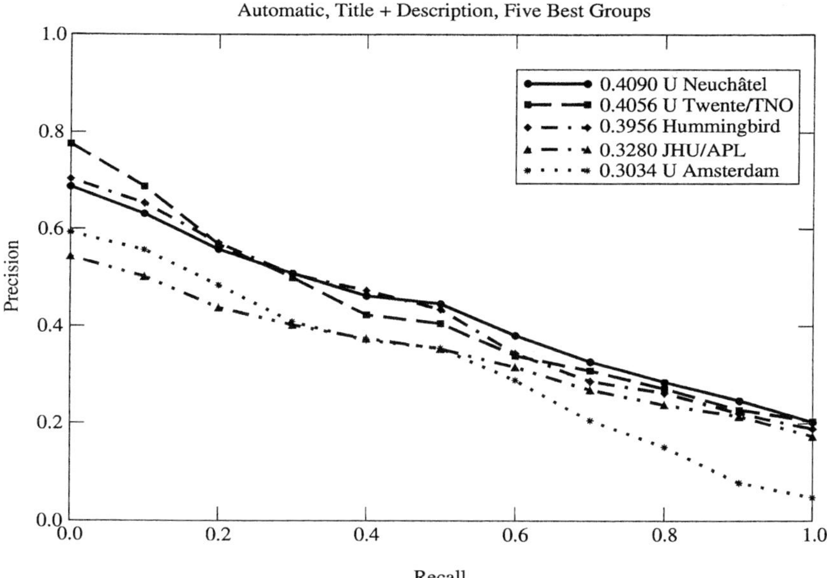
CLEF 2002 – Finnish Monolingual Task (Average Precision)
Automatic, Title + Description, Five Best Groups
0.4090 U Neuchâtel
0.4056 U Twente/TNO
0.3956 Hummingbird
0.3280 JHU/APL
0.3034 U Amsterdam
Precision
Recall
0.0
0.2
0.4
0.6
0.8
1.0

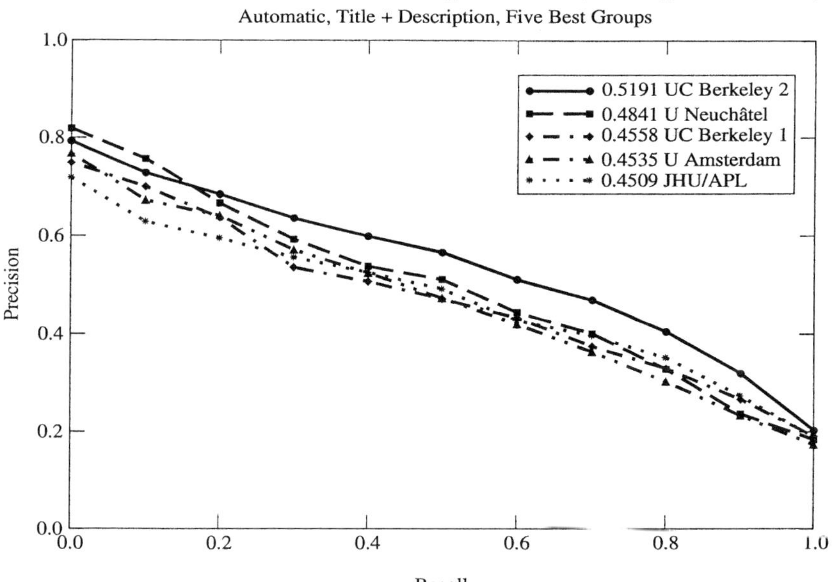
CLEF 2002 – French Monolingual Task (Average Precision)
Automatic, Title + Description, Five Best Groups
0.5191 UC Berkeley 2
0.4841 U Neuchâtel
0.4558 UC Berkeley 1
0.4535 U Amsterdam
0.4509 JHU/APL
Precision
Recall
0.0
0.2
0.4
0.6
0.8
1.0

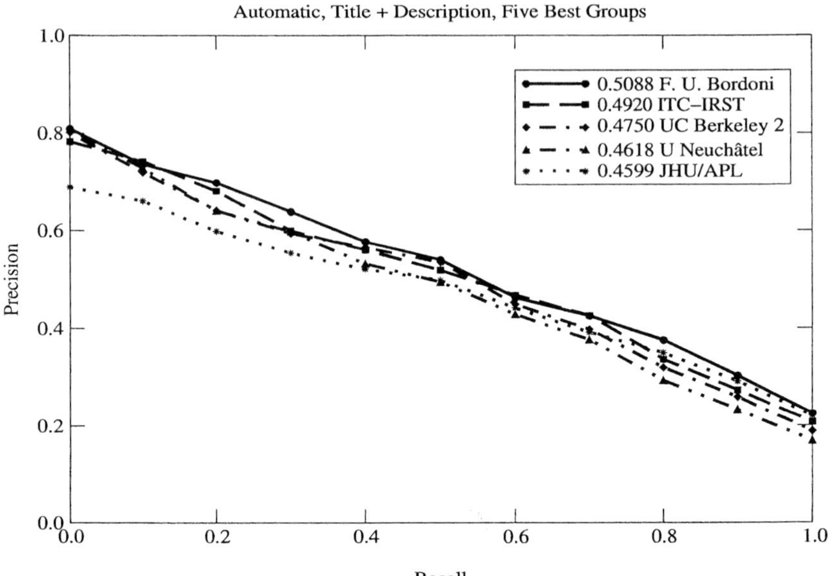
CLEF 2002 – Italian Monolingual Task (Average Precision)
Automatic, Title + Description, Five Best Groups
0.5088 F. U. Bordoni
0.4920 ITC–IRST
0.4750 UC Berkeley 2
0.4618 U Neuchâtel
0.4599 JHU/APL
Precision
Recall
0.0
0.2
0.4
0.6
0.8
1.0

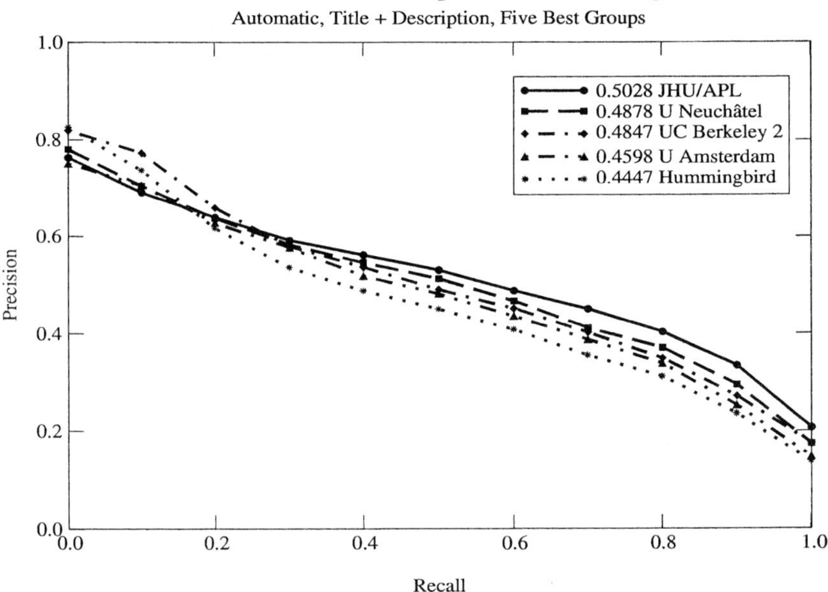
CLEF 2002 – Dutch Monolingual Task (Average Precision)
Automatic, Title + Description, Five Best Groups
0.5028 JHU/APL
0.4878 U Neuchâtel
0.4847 UC Berkeley 2
0.4598 U Amsterdam
0.4447 Hummingbird
Precision
Recall
0.0
0.2
0.4
0.6
0.8
1.0

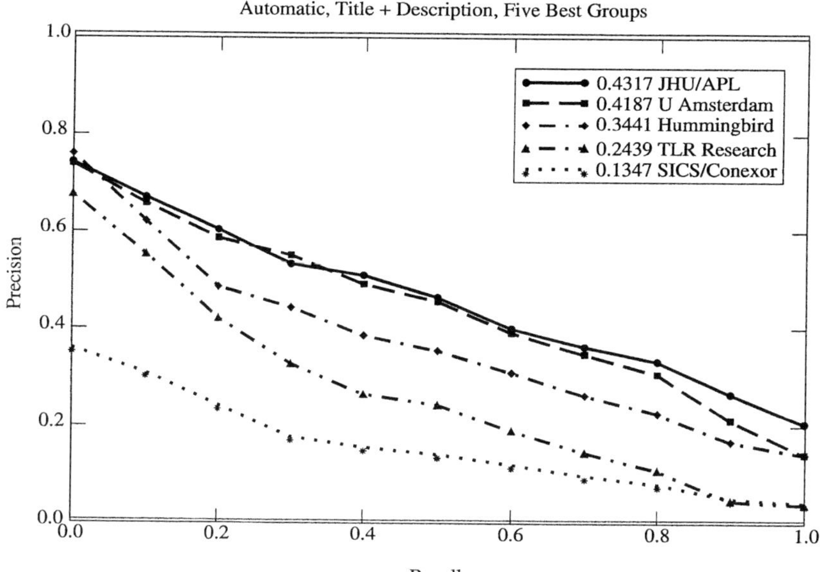
CLEF 2002 – Swedish Monolingual Task (Average Precision)
Automatic, Title + Description, Five Best Groups
0.4317 JHU/APL
0.4187 U Amsterdam
0.3441 Hummingbird
0.2439 TLR Research
0.1347 SICS/Conexor
Precision
Recall
0.0
0.2
0.4
0.6
0.8
1.0

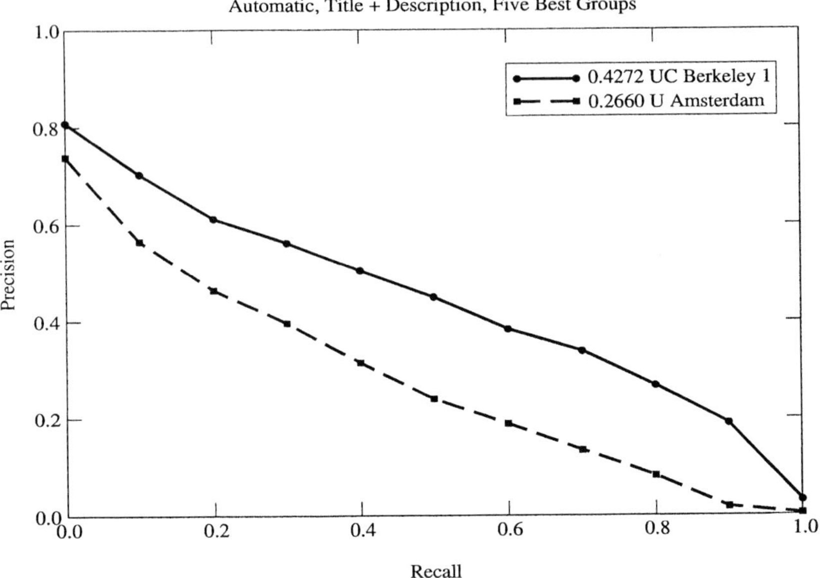
CLEF 2002 – Amaryllis Bilingual Task (Average Precision)
Automatic, Title + Description, Five Best Groups
0.4272 UC Berkeley 1
0.2660 U Amsterdam
Precision
Recall
0.0
0.2
0.4
0.6
0.8
1.0

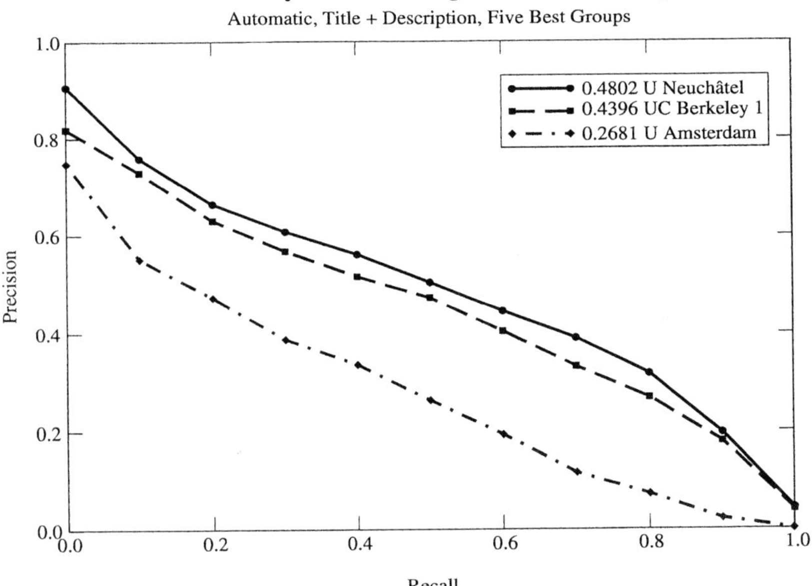
CLEF 2002 – Amaryllis Monolingual Task (Average Precision)
Automatic, Title + Description, Five Best Groups
0.4802 U Neuchâtel
0.4396 UC Berkeley 1
0.2681 U Amsterdam
Precision
Recall
0.0
0.2
0.4
0.6
0.8
1.0

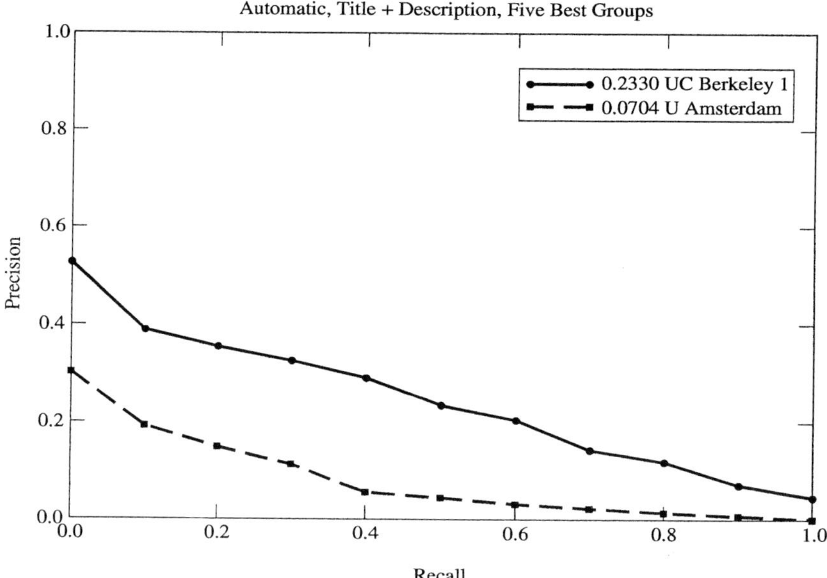
CLEF 2002 – GIRT Bilingual Task (Average Precision)
Automatic, Title + Description, Five Best Groups
0.2330 UC Berkeley 1
0.0704 U Amsterdam
Precision
Recall
0.0
0.2
0.4
0.6
0.8
1.0

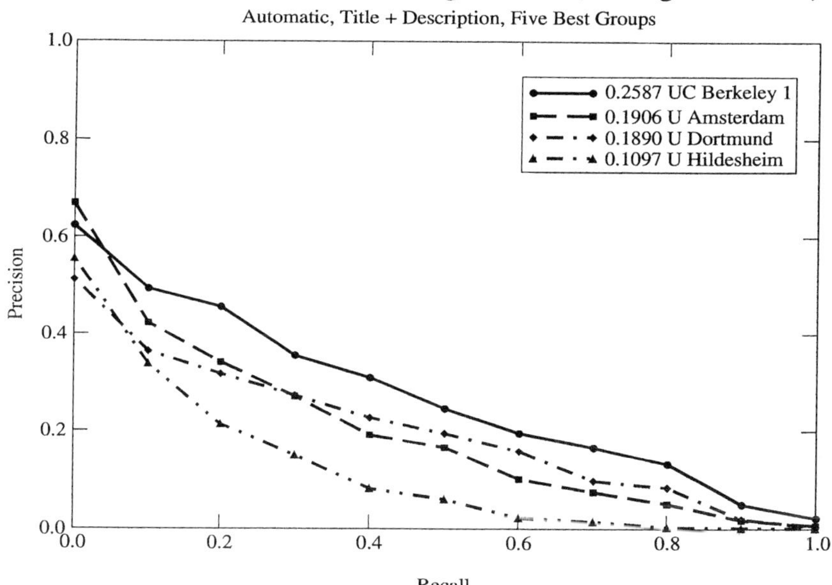
CLEF 2002 – GIRT Monolingual Task (Average Precision)
Automatic, Title + Description, Five Best Groups
0.2587 UC Berkeley 1
0.1906 U Amsterdam
0.1890 U Dortmund
0.1097 U Hildesheim
Precision
Recall
0.0
0.2
0.4
0.6
0.8
1.0

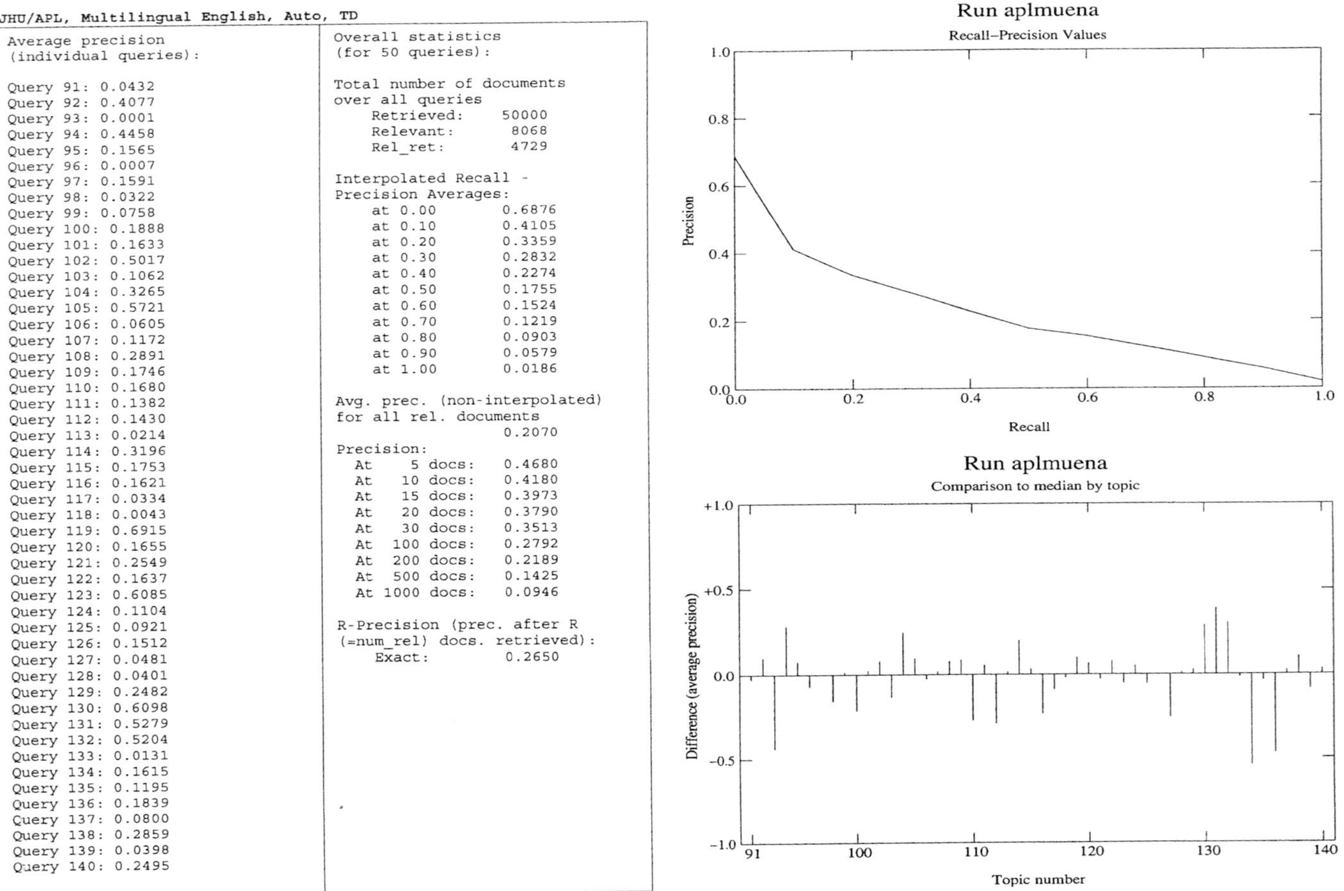

JHU/APL, Multilingual English, Auto, TD

```
Average precision                Overall statistics
(individual queries):            (for 50 queries):

Query 91: 0.0432                 Total number of documents
Query 92: 0.4077                 over all queries
Query 93: 0.0001                     Retrieved:     50000
Query 94: 0.4458                     Relevant:       8068
Query 95: 0.1565                     Rel_ret:        4729
Query 96: 0.0007
Query 97: 0.1591                 Interpolated Recall -
Query 98: 0.0322                 Precision Averages:
Query 99: 0.0758                     at 0.00        0.6876
Query 100: 0.1888                    at 0.10        0.4105
Query 101: 0.1633                    at 0.20        0.3359
Query 102: 0.5017                    at 0.30        0.2832
Query 103: 0.1062                    at 0.40        0.2274
Query 104: 0.3265                    at 0.50        0.1755
Query 105: 0.5721                    at 0.60        0.1524
Query 106: 0.0605                    at 0.70        0.1219
Query 107: 0.1172                    at 0.80        0.0903
Query 108: 0.2891                    at 0.90        0.0579
Query 109: 0.1746                    at 1.00        0.0186
Query 110: 0.1680
Query 111: 0.1382                Avg. prec. (non-interpolated)
Query 112: 0.1430                for all rel. documents
Query 113: 0.0214                                   0.2070
Query 114: 0.3196                Precision:
Query 115: 0.1753                  At    5 docs:    0.4680
Query 116: 0.1621                  At   10 docs:    0.4180
Query 117: 0.0334                  At   15 docs:    0.3973
Query 118: 0.0043                  At   20 docs:    0.3790
Query 119: 0.6915                  At   30 docs:    0.3513
Query 120: 0.1655                  At  100 docs:    0.2792
Query 121: 0.2549                  At  200 docs:    0.2189
Query 122: 0.1637                  At  500 docs:    0.1425
Query 123: 0.6085                  At 1000 docs:    0.0946
Query 124: 0.1104
Query 125: 0.0921                R-Precision (prec. after R
Query 126: 0.1512                (=num_rel) docs. retrieved):
Query 127: 0.0481                    Exact:         0.2650
Query 128: 0.0401
Query 129: 0.2482
Query 130: 0.6098
Query 131: 0.5279
Query 132: 0.5204
Query 133: 0.0131
Query 134: 0.1615
Query 135: 0.1195
Query 136: 0.1839
Query 137: 0.0800
Query 138: 0.2859
Query 139: 0.0398
Query 140: 0.2495
```

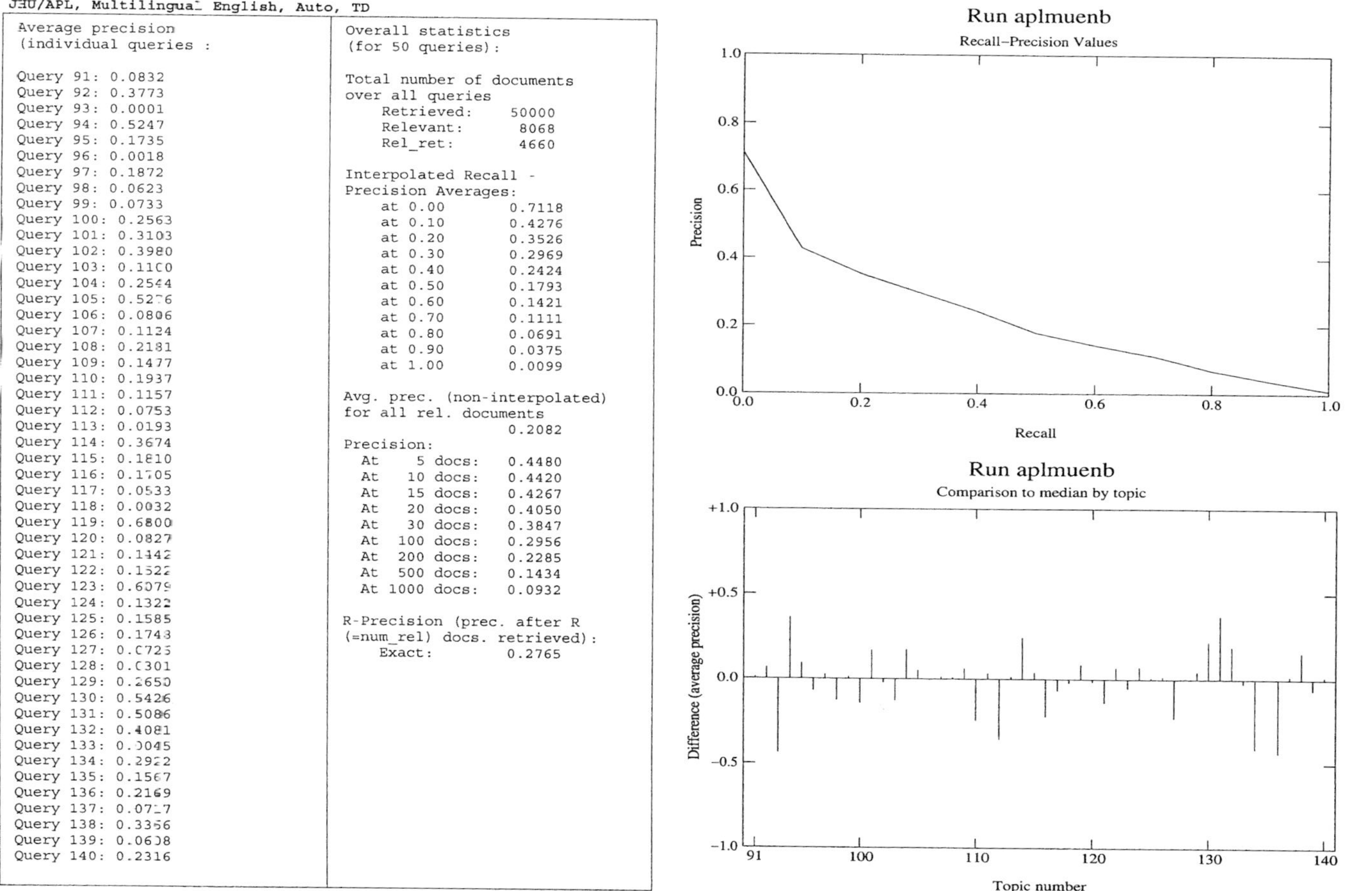

JHU/APL, Multilingual English, Auto, TD

```
Average precision                 Overall statistics
(individual queries :             (for 50 queries):

Query 91: 0.0832                  Total number of documents
Query 92: 0.3773                  over all queries
Query 93: 0.0001                      Retrieved:    50000
Query 94: 0.5247                      Relevant:      8068
Query 95: 0.1735                      Rel_ret:       4660
Query 96: 0.0018
Query 97: 0.1872                  Interpolated Recall -
Query 98: 0.0623                  Precision Averages:
Query 99: 0.0733                      at 0.00       0.7118
Query 100: 0.2563                     at 0.10       0.4276
Query 101: 0.3103                     at 0.20       0.3526
Query 102: 0.3980                     at 0.30       0.2969
Query 103: 0.1100                     at 0.40       0.2424
Query 104: 0.2544                     at 0.50       0.1793
Query 105: 0.5276                     at 0.60       0.1421
Query 106: 0.0806                     at 0.70       0.1111
Query 107: 0.1124                     at 0.80       0.0691
Query 108: 0.2181                     at 0.90       0.0375
Query 109: 0.1477                     at 1.00       0.0099
Query 110: 0.1937
Query 111: 0.1157                 Avg. prec. (non-interpolated)
Query 112: 0.0753                 for all rel. documents
Query 113: 0.0193                                   0.2082
Query 114: 0.3674                 Precision:
Query 115: 0.1810                   At    5 docs:   0.4480
Query 116: 0.1705                   At   10 docs:   0.4420
Query 117: 0.0533                   At   15 docs:   0.4267
Query 118: 0.0032                   At   20 docs:   0.4050
Query 119: 0.6800                   At   30 docs:   0.3847
Query 120: 0.0827                   At  100 docs:   0.2956
Query 121: 0.1442                   At  200 docs:   0.2285
Query 122: 0.1522                   At  500 docs:   0.1434
Query 123: 0.6079                   At 1000 docs:   0.0932
Query 124: 0.1322
Query 125: 0.1585                 R-Precision (prec. after R
Query 126: 0.1743                 (=num_rel) docs. retrieved):
Query 127: 0.0725                     Exact:        0.2765
Query 128: 0.0301
Query 129: 0.2650
Query 130: 0.5426
Query 131: 0.5086
Query 132: 0.4081
Query 133: 0.0045
Query 134: 0.2922
Query 135: 0.1567
Query 136: 0.2169
Query 137: 0.0717
Query 138: 0.3356
Query 139: 0.0608
Query 140: 0.2316
```

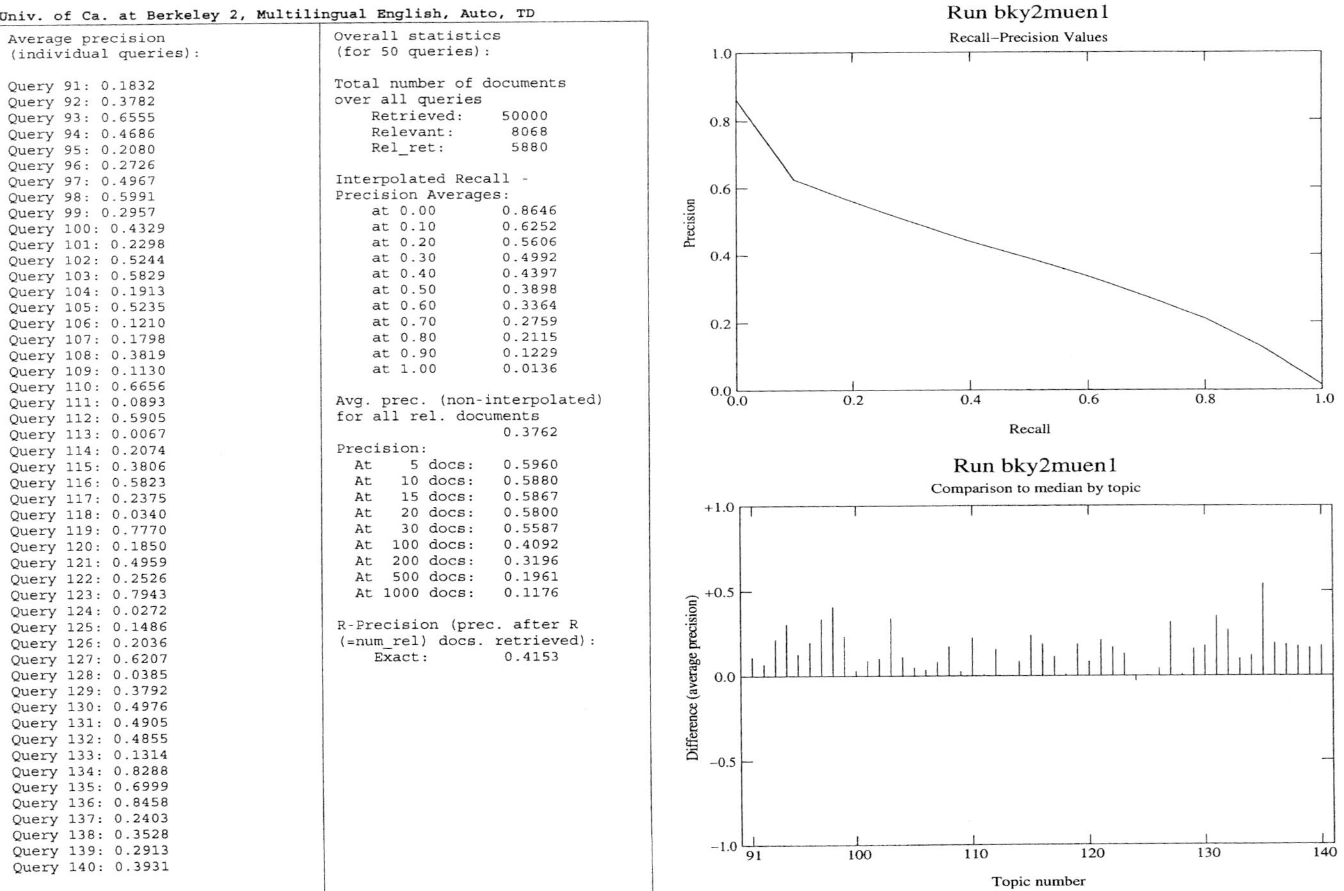

Univ. of Ca. at Berkeley 2, Multilingual English, Auto, TD

Average precision
(individual queries):

Query	Average precision
Query 91:	0.1832
Query 92:	0.3782
Query 93:	0.6555
Query 94:	0.4686
Query 95:	0.2080
Query 96:	0.2726
Query 97:	0.4967
Query 98:	0.5991
Query 99:	0.2957
Query 100:	0.4329
Query 101:	0.2298
Query 102:	0.5244
Query 103:	0.5829
Query 104:	0.1913
Query 105:	0.5235
Query 106:	0.1210
Query 107:	0.1798
Query 108:	0.3819
Query 109:	0.1130
Query 110:	0.6656
Query 111:	0.0893
Query 112:	0.5905
Query 113:	0.0067
Query 114:	0.2074
Query 115:	0.3806
Query 116:	0.5823
Query 117:	0.2375
Query 118:	0.0340
Query 119:	0.7770
Query 120:	0.1850
Query 121:	0.4959
Query 122:	0.2526
Query 123:	0.7943
Query 124:	0.0272
Query 125:	0.1486
Query 126:	0.2036
Query 127:	0.6207
Query 128:	0.0385
Query 129:	0.3792
Query 130:	0.4976
Query 131:	0.4905
Query 132:	0.4855
Query 133:	0.1314
Query 134:	0.8288
Query 135:	0.6999
Query 136:	0.8458
Query 137:	0.2403
Query 138:	0.3528
Query 139:	0.2913
Query 140:	0.3931

Overall statistics
(for 50 queries):

Total number of documents
over all queries

Retrieved:	50000
Relevant:	8068
Rel_ret:	5880

Interpolated Recall -
Precision Averages:

at 0.00	0.8646
at 0.10	0.6252
at 0.20	0.5606
at 0.30	0.4992
at 0.40	0.4397
at 0.50	0.3898
at 0.60	0.3364
at 0.70	0.2759
at 0.80	0.2115
at 0.90	0.1229
at 1.00	0.0136

Avg. prec. (non-interpolated)
for all rel. documents
0.3762

Precision:

At 5 docs:	0.5960
At 10 docs:	0.5880
At 15 docs:	0.5867
At 20 docs:	0.5800
At 30 docs:	0.5587
At 100 docs:	0.4092
At 200 docs:	0.3196
At 500 docs:	0.1961
At 1000 docs:	0.1176

R-Precision (prec. after R
(=num_rel) docs. retrieved):
Exact: 0.4153

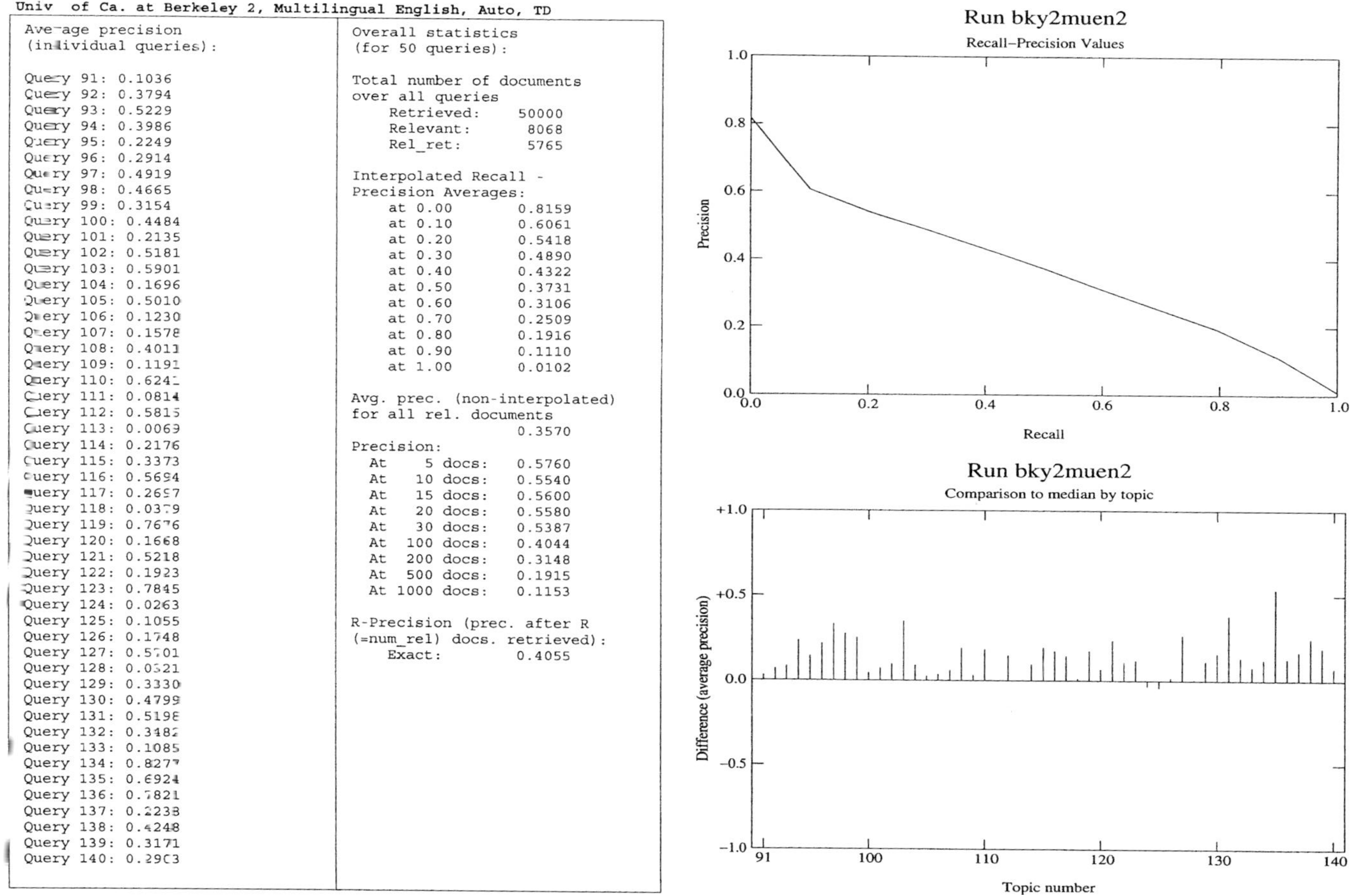

Univ of Ca. at Berkeley 2, Multilingual English, Auto, TD

```
Average precision                Overall statistics
(individual queries):            (for 50 queries):

Query 91: 0.1036                 Total number of documents
Query 92: 0.3794                 over all queries
Query 93: 0.5229                     Retrieved:    50000
Query 94: 0.3986                     Relevant:      8068
Query 95: 0.2249                     Rel_ret:       5765
Query 96: 0.2914
Query 97: 0.4919                 Interpolated Recall -
Query 98: 0.4665                 Precision Averages:
Query 99: 0.3154                     at 0.00       0.8159
Query 100: 0.4484                    at 0.10       0.6061
Query 101: 0.2135                    at 0.20       0.5418
Query 102: 0.5181                    at 0.30       0.4890
Query 103: 0.5901                    at 0.40       0.4322
Query 104: 0.1696                    at 0.50       0.3731
Query 105: 0.5010                    at 0.60       0.3106
Query 106: 0.1230                    at 0.70       0.2509
Query 107: 0.1578                    at 0.80       0.1916
Query 108: 0.4011                    at 0.90       0.1110
Query 109: 0.1191                    at 1.00       0.0102
Query 110: 0.6241
Query 111: 0.0814                Avg. prec. (non-interpolated)
Query 112: 0.5815                for all rel. documents
Query 113: 0.0069                                  0.3570
Query 114: 0.2176                Precision:
Query 115: 0.3373                  At    5 docs:   0.5760
Query 116: 0.5694                  At   10 docs:   0.5540
Query 117: 0.2697                  At   15 docs:   0.5600
Query 118: 0.0379                  At   20 docs:   0.5580
Query 119: 0.7676                  At   30 docs:   0.5387
Query 120: 0.1668                  At  100 docs:   0.4044
Query 121: 0.5218                  At  200 docs:   0.3148
Query 122: 0.1923                  At  500 docs:   0.1915
Query 123: 0.7845                  At 1000 docs:   0.1153
Query 124: 0.0263
Query 125: 0.1055                R-Precision (prec. after R
Query 126: 0.1748                (=num_rel) docs. retrieved):
Query 127: 0.5701                    Exact:        0.4055
Query 128: 0.0521
Query 129: 0.3330
Query 130: 0.4799
Query 131: 0.5198
Query 132: 0.3482
Query 133: 0.1085
Query 134: 0.8277
Query 135: 0.6924
Query 136: 0.7821
Query 137: 0.2238
Query 138: 0.4248
Query 139: 0.3171
Query 140: 0.2903
```

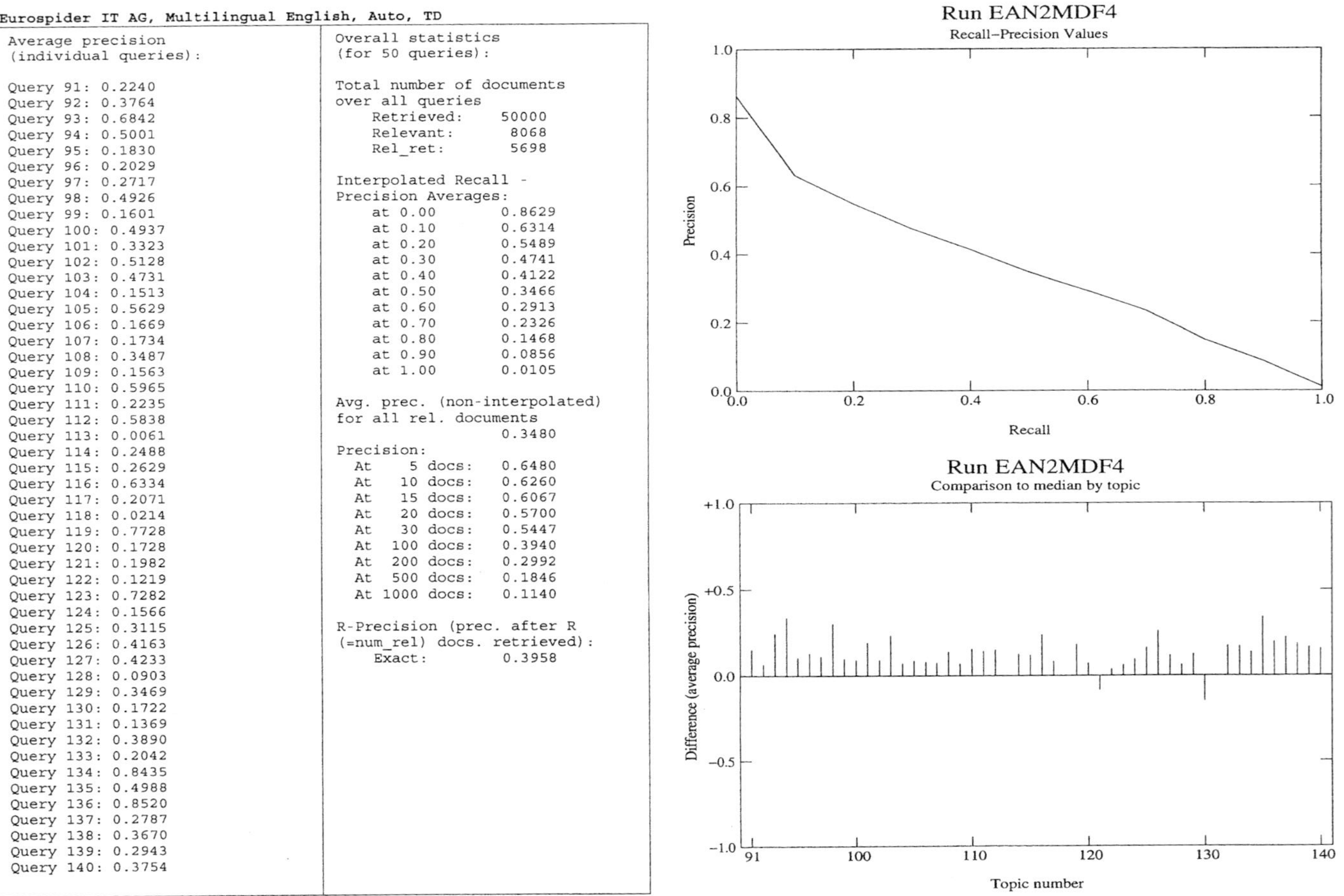

Eurospider IT AG, Multilingual English, Auto, TD

Average precision (individual queries):	Overall statistics (for 50 queries):
Query 91: 0.2240	Total number of documents over all queries
Query 92: 0.3764	Retrieved: 50000
Query 93: 0.6842	Relevant: 8068
Query 94: 0.5001	Rel_ret: 5698
Query 95: 0.1830	
Query 96: 0.2029	Interpolated Recall - Precision Averages:
Query 97: 0.2717	at 0.00 0.8629
Query 98: 0.4926	at 0.10 0.6314
Query 99: 0.1601	at 0.20 0.5489
Query 100: 0.4937	at 0.30 0.4741
Query 101: 0.3323	at 0.40 0.4122
Query 102: 0.5128	at 0.50 0.3466
Query 103: 0.4731	at 0.60 0.2913
Query 104: 0.1513	at 0.70 0.2326
Query 105: 0.5629	at 0.80 0.1468
Query 106: 0.1669	at 0.90 0.0856
Query 107: 0.1734	at 1.00 0.0105
Query 108: 0.3487	
Query 109: 0.1563	Avg. prec. (non-interpolated) for all rel. documents 0.3480
Query 110: 0.5965	
Query 111: 0.2235	Precision:
Query 112: 0.5838	At 5 docs: 0.6480
Query 113: 0.0061	At 10 docs: 0.6260
Query 114: 0.2488	At 15 docs: 0.6067
Query 115: 0.2629	At 20 docs: 0.5700
Query 116: 0.6334	At 30 docs: 0.5447
Query 117: 0.2071	At 100 docs: 0.3940
Query 118: 0.0214	At 200 docs: 0.2992
Query 119: 0.7728	At 500 docs: 0.1846
Query 120: 0.1728	At 1000 docs: 0.1140
Query 121: 0.1982	
Query 122: 0.1219	R-Precision (prec. after R (=num_rel) docs. retrieved):
Query 123: 0.7282	Exact: 0.3958
Query 124: 0.1566	
Query 125: 0.3115	
Query 126: 0.4163	
Query 127: 0.4233	
Query 128: 0.0903	
Query 129: 0.3469	
Query 130: 0.1722	
Query 131: 0.1369	
Query 132: 0.3890	
Query 133: 0.2042	
Query 134: 0.8435	
Query 135: 0.4988	
Query 136: 0.8520	
Query 137: 0.2787	
Query 138: 0.3670	
Query 139: 0.2943	
Query 140: 0.3754	

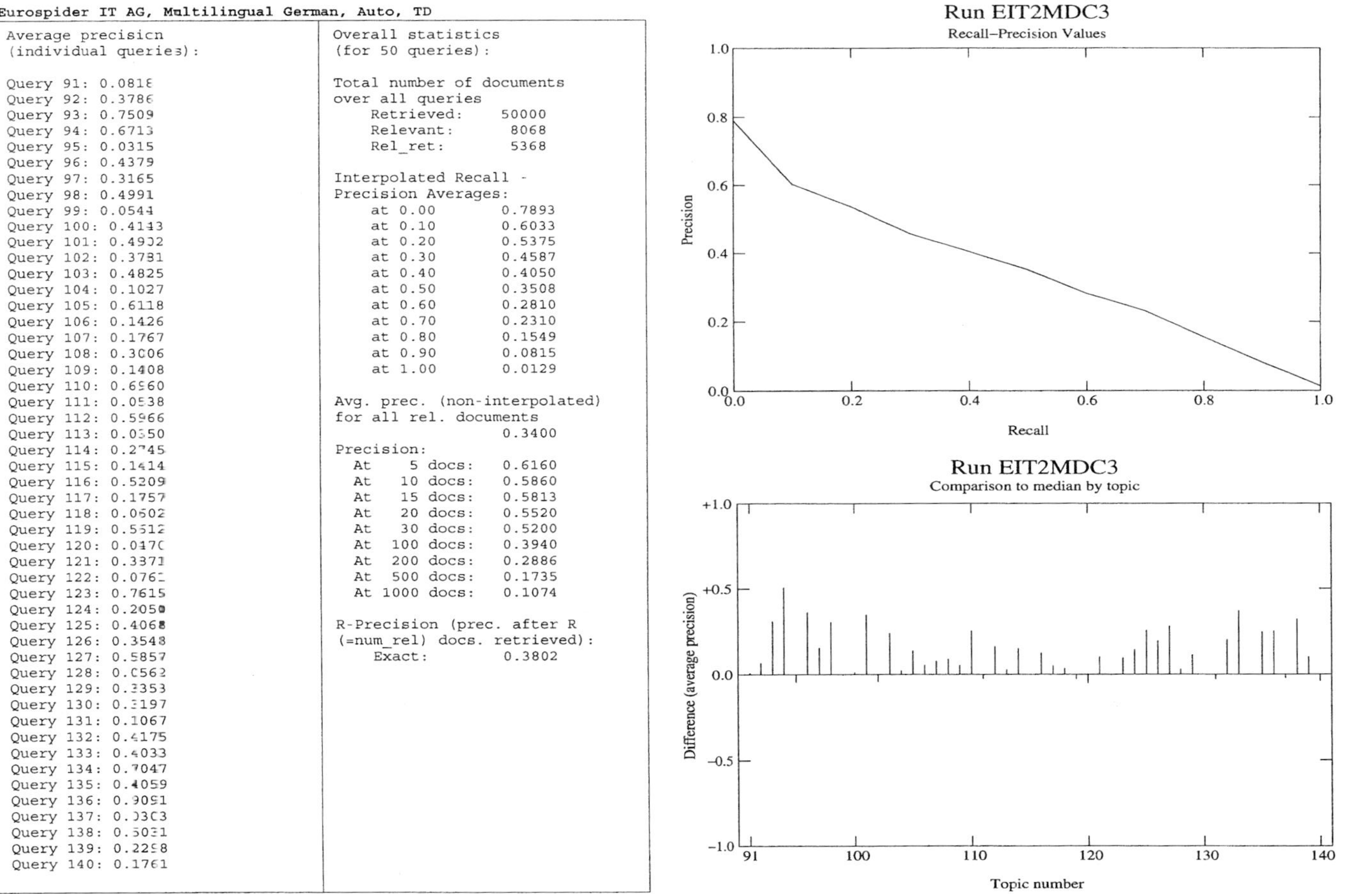

```
Eurospider IT AG, Multilingual German, Auto, TD

Average precision                Overall statistics
(individual queries):            (for 50 queries):

Query 91: 0.0818                 Total number of documents
Query 92: 0.3786                 over all queries
Query 93: 0.7509                     Retrieved:    50000
Query 94: 0.6713                     Relevant:      8068
Query 95: 0.0315                     Rel_ret:       5368
Query 96: 0.4379
Query 97: 0.3165                 Interpolated Recall -
Query 98: 0.4991                 Precision Averages:
Query 99: 0.0544                     at 0.00        0.7893
Query 100: 0.4143                    at 0.10        0.6033
Query 101: 0.4932                    at 0.20        0.5375
Query 102: 0.3731                    at 0.30        0.4587
Query 103: 0.4825                    at 0.40        0.4050
Query 104: 0.1027                    at 0.50        0.3508
Query 105: 0.6118                    at 0.60        0.2810
Query 106: 0.1426                    at 0.70        0.2310
Query 107: 0.1767                    at 0.80        0.1549
Query 108: 0.3006                    at 0.90        0.0815
Query 109: 0.1408                    at 1.00        0.0129
Query 110: 0.6560
Query 111: 0.0538                Avg. prec. (non-interpolated)
Query 112: 0.5966                for all rel. documents
Query 113: 0.0350                                   0.3400
Query 114: 0.2745                Precision:
Query 115: 0.1414                  At    5 docs:   0.6160
Query 116: 0.5209                  At   10 docs:   0.5860
Query 117: 0.1757                  At   15 docs:   0.5813
Query 118: 0.0502                  At   20 docs:   0.5520
Query 119: 0.5512                  At   30 docs:   0.5200
Query 120: 0.0470                  At  100 docs:   0.3940
Query 121: 0.3371                  At  200 docs:   0.2886
Query 122: 0.0761                  At  500 docs:   0.1735
Query 123: 0.7615                  At 1000 docs:   0.1074
Query 124: 0.2050
Query 125: 0.4068                R-Precision (prec. after R
Query 126: 0.3548                (=num_rel) docs. retrieved):
Query 127: 0.5857                    Exact:         0.3802
Query 128: 0.0562
Query 129: 0.3353
Query 130: 0.3197
Query 131: 0.1067
Query 132: 0.4175
Query 133: 0.4033
Query 134: 0.7047
Query 135: 0.4059
Query 136: 0.9051
Query 137: 0.0303
Query 138: 0.5031
Query 139: 0.2258
Query 140: 0.1761
```

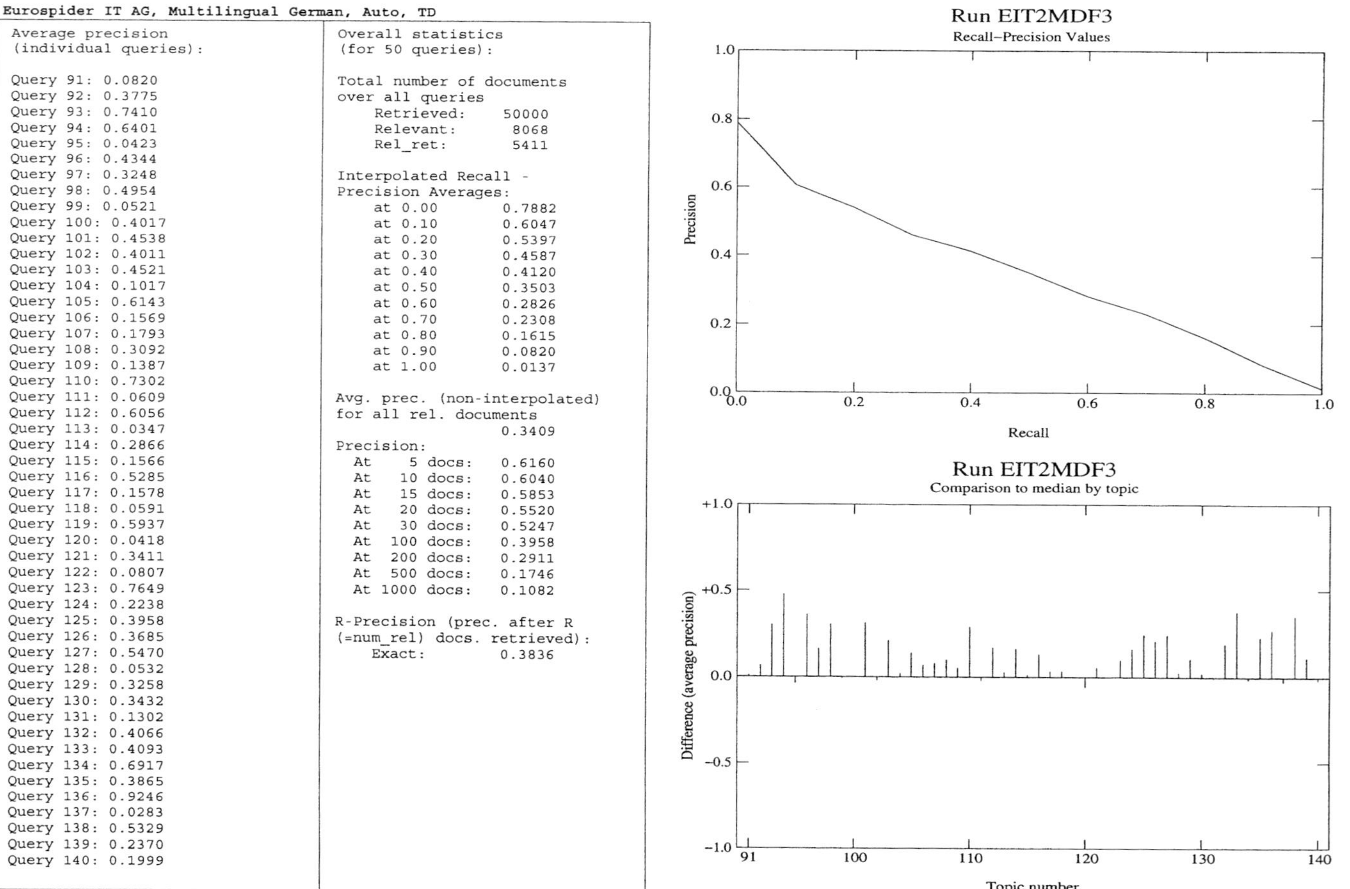

Eurospider IT AG, Multilingual German, Auto, TD

```
Average precision                Overall statistics
(individual queries):            (for 50 queries):

Query 91: 0.0820                 Total number of documents
Query 92: 0.3775                 over all queries
Query 93: 0.7410                     Retrieved:     50000
Query 94: 0.6401                     Relevant:       8068
Query 95: 0.0423                     Rel_ret:        5411
Query 96: 0.4344
Query 97: 0.3248                 Interpolated Recall -
Query 98: 0.4954                 Precision Averages:
Query 99: 0.0521                     at 0.00        0.7882
Query 100: 0.4017                    at 0.10        0.6047
Query 101: 0.4538                    at 0.20        0.5397
Query 102: 0.4011                    at 0.30        0.4587
Query 103: 0.4521                    at 0.40        0.4120
Query 104: 0.1017                    at 0.50        0.3503
Query 105: 0.6143                    at 0.60        0.2826
Query 106: 0.1569                    at 0.70        0.2308
Query 107: 0.1793                    at 0.80        0.1615
Query 108: 0.3092                    at 0.90        0.0820
Query 109: 0.1387                    at 1.00        0.0137
Query 110: 0.7302
Query 111: 0.0609                Avg. prec. (non-interpolated)
Query 112: 0.6056                for all rel. documents
Query 113: 0.0347                                   0.3409
Query 114: 0.2866                Precision:
Query 115: 0.1566                  At    5 docs:    0.6160
Query 116: 0.5285                  At   10 docs:    0.6040
Query 117: 0.1578                  At   15 docs:    0.5853
Query 118: 0.0591                  At   20 docs:    0.5520
Query 119: 0.5937                  At   30 docs:    0.5247
Query 120: 0.0418                  At  100 docs:    0.3958
Query 121: 0.3411                  At  200 docs:    0.2911
Query 122: 0.0807                  At  500 docs:    0.1746
Query 123: 0.7649                  At 1000 docs:    0.1082
Query 124: 0.2238
Query 125: 0.3958                R-Precision (prec. after R
Query 126: 0.3685                (=num_rel) docs. retrieved):
Query 127: 0.5470                    Exact:         0.3836
Query 128: 0.0532
Query 129: 0.3258
Query 130: 0.3432
Query 131: 0.1302
Query 132: 0.4066
Query 133: 0.4093
Query 134: 0.6917
Query 135: 0.3865
Query 136: 0.9246
Query 137: 0.0283
Query 138: 0.5329
Query 139: 0.2370
Query 140: 0.1999
```

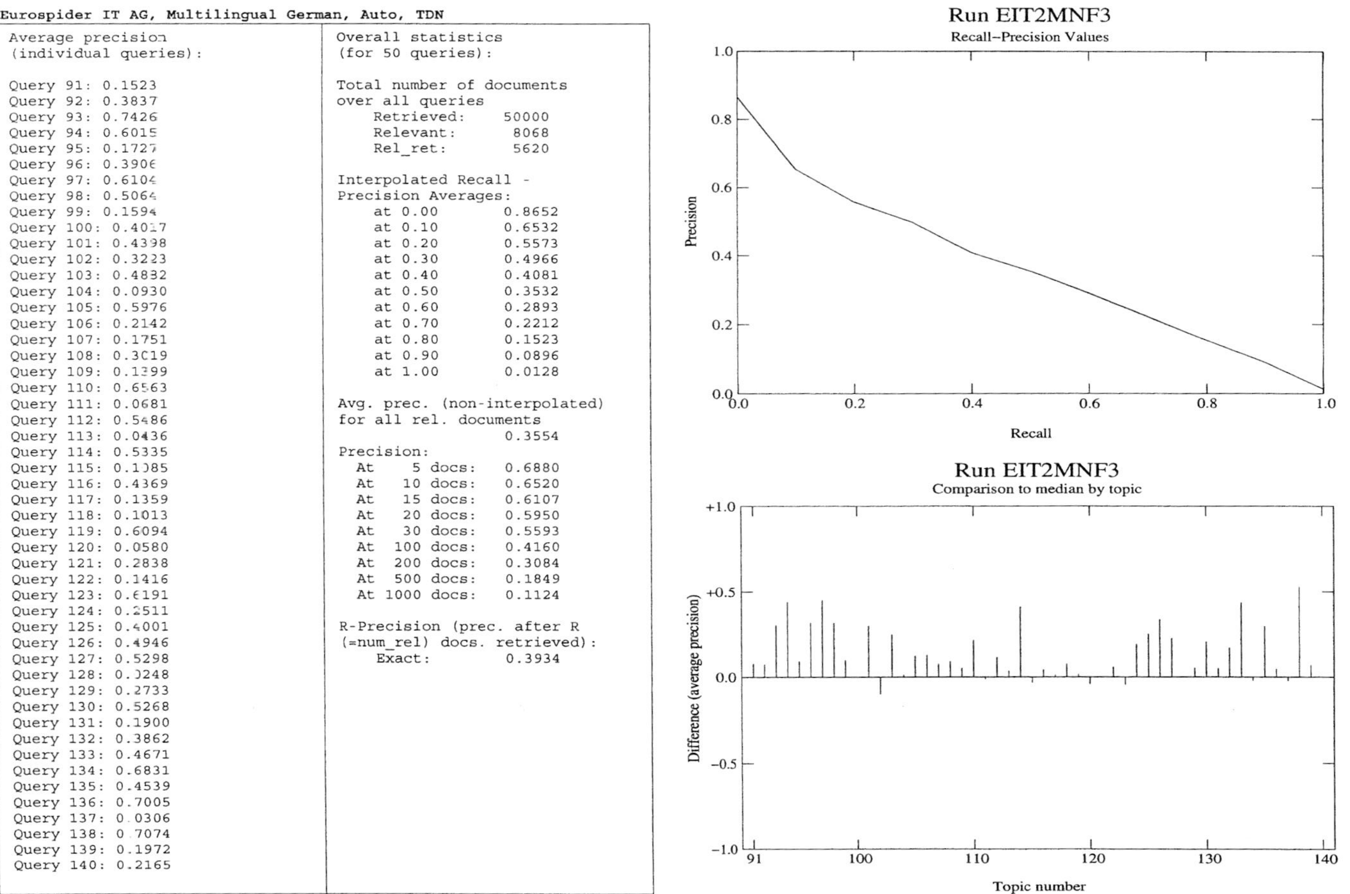

Eurospider IT AG, Multilingual German, Auto, TDN

```
Average precision                   Overall statistics
(individual queries):               (for 50 queries):

Query 91: 0.1523                    Total number of documents
Query 92: 0.3837                    over all queries
Query 93: 0.7426                        Retrieved:     50000
Query 94: 0.6015                        Relevant:       8068
Query 95: 0.1727                        Rel_ret:        5620
Query 96: 0.3906
Query 97: 0.6104                    Interpolated Recall -
Query 98: 0.5064                    Precision Averages:
Query 99: 0.1594                        at 0.00        0.8652
Query 100: 0.4017                       at 0.10        0.6532
Query 101: 0.4398                       at 0.20        0.5573
Query 102: 0.3223                       at 0.30        0.4966
Query 103: 0.4832                       at 0.40        0.4081
Query 104: 0.0930                       at 0.50        0.3532
Query 105: 0.5976                       at 0.60        0.2893
Query 106: 0.2142                       at 0.70        0.2212
Query 107: 0.1751                       at 0.80        0.1523
Query 108: 0.3019                       at 0.90        0.0896
Query 109: 0.1399                       at 1.00        0.0128
Query 110: 0.6563
Query 111: 0.0681                   Avg. prec. (non-interpolated)
Query 112: 0.5486                   for all rel. documents
Query 113: 0.0436                                      0.3554
Query 114: 0.5335                   Precision:
Query 115: 0.1085                     At    5 docs:    0.6880
Query 116: 0.4369                     At   10 docs:    0.6520
Query 117: 0.1359                     At   15 docs:    0.6107
Query 118: 0.1013                     At   20 docs:    0.5950
Query 119: 0.6094                     At   30 docs:    0.5593
Query 120: 0.0580                     At  100 docs:    0.4160
Query 121: 0.2838                     At  200 docs:    0.3084
Query 122: 0.1416                     At  500 docs:    0.1849
Query 123: 0.6191                     At 1000 docs:    0.1124
Query 124: 0.2511
Query 125: 0.4001                   R-Precision (prec. after R
Query 126: 0.4946                   (=num_rel) docs. retrieved):
Query 127: 0.5298                       Exact:         0.3934
Query 128: 0.0248
Query 129: 0.2733
Query 130: 0.5268
Query 131: 0.1900
Query 132: 0.3862
Query 133: 0.4671
Query 134: 0.6831
Query 135: 0.4539
Query 136: 0.7005
Query 137: 0.0306
Query 138: 0.7074
Query 139: 0.1972
Query 140: 0.2165
```

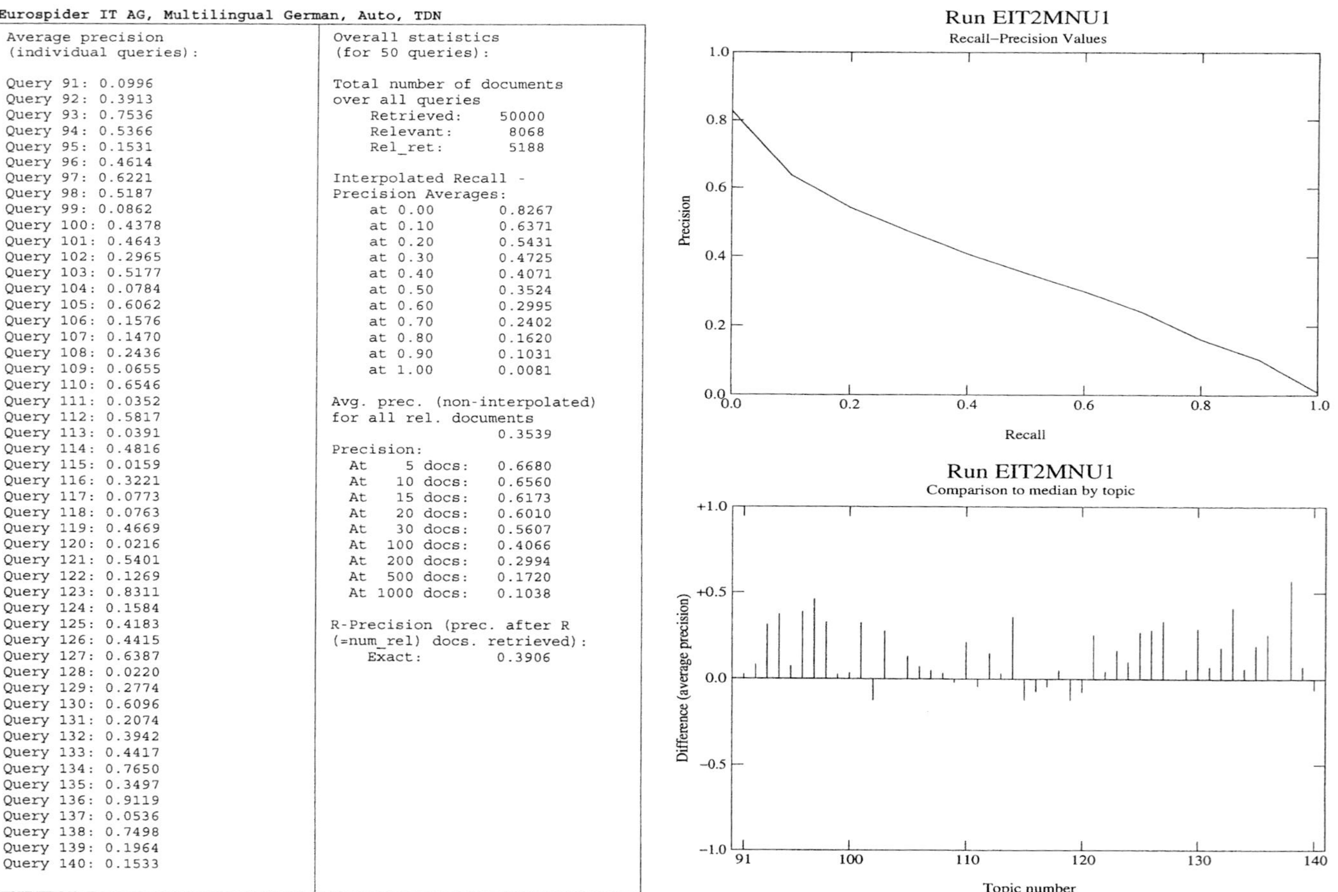

Eurospider IT AG, Multilingual German, Auto, TDN

Average precision (individual queries):	Overall statistics (for 50 queries):
Query 91: 0.0996	Total number of documents over all queries
Query 92: 0.3913	Retrieved: 50000
Query 93: 0.7536	Relevant: 8068
Query 94: 0.5366	Rel_ret: 5188
Query 95: 0.1531	
Query 96: 0.4614	Interpolated Recall - Precision Averages:
Query 97: 0.6221	at 0.00 0.8267
Query 98: 0.5187	at 0.10 0.6371
Query 99: 0.0862	at 0.20 0.5431
Query 100: 0.4378	at 0.30 0.4725
Query 101: 0.4643	at 0.40 0.4071
Query 102: 0.2965	at 0.50 0.3524
Query 103: 0.5177	at 0.60 0.2995
Query 104: 0.0784	at 0.70 0.2402
Query 105: 0.6062	at 0.80 0.1620
Query 106: 0.1576	at 0.90 0.1031
Query 107: 0.1470	at 1.00 0.0081
Query 108: 0.2436	
Query 109: 0.0655	Avg. prec. (non-interpolated) for all rel. documents 0.3539
Query 110: 0.6546	
Query 111: 0.0352	Precision:
Query 112: 0.5817	At 5 docs: 0.6680
Query 113: 0.0391	At 10 docs: 0.6560
Query 114: 0.4816	At 15 docs: 0.6173
Query 115: 0.0159	At 20 docs: 0.6010
Query 116: 0.3221	At 30 docs: 0.5607
Query 117: 0.0773	At 100 docs: 0.4066
Query 118: 0.0763	At 200 docs: 0.2994
Query 119: 0.4669	At 500 docs: 0.1720
Query 120: 0.0216	At 1000 docs: 0.1038
Query 121: 0.5401	
Query 122: 0.1269	R-Precision (prec. after R (=num_rel) docs. retrieved):
Query 123: 0.8311	Exact: 0.3906
Query 124: 0.1584	
Query 125: 0.4183	
Query 126: 0.4415	
Query 127: 0.6387	
Query 128: 0.0220	
Query 129: 0.2774	
Query 130: 0.6096	
Query 131: 0.2074	
Query 132: 0.3942	
Query 133: 0.4417	
Query 134: 0.7650	
Query 135: 0.3497	
Query 136: 0.9119	
Query 137: 0.0536	
Query 138: 0.7498	
Query 139: 0.1964	
Query 140: 0.1533	

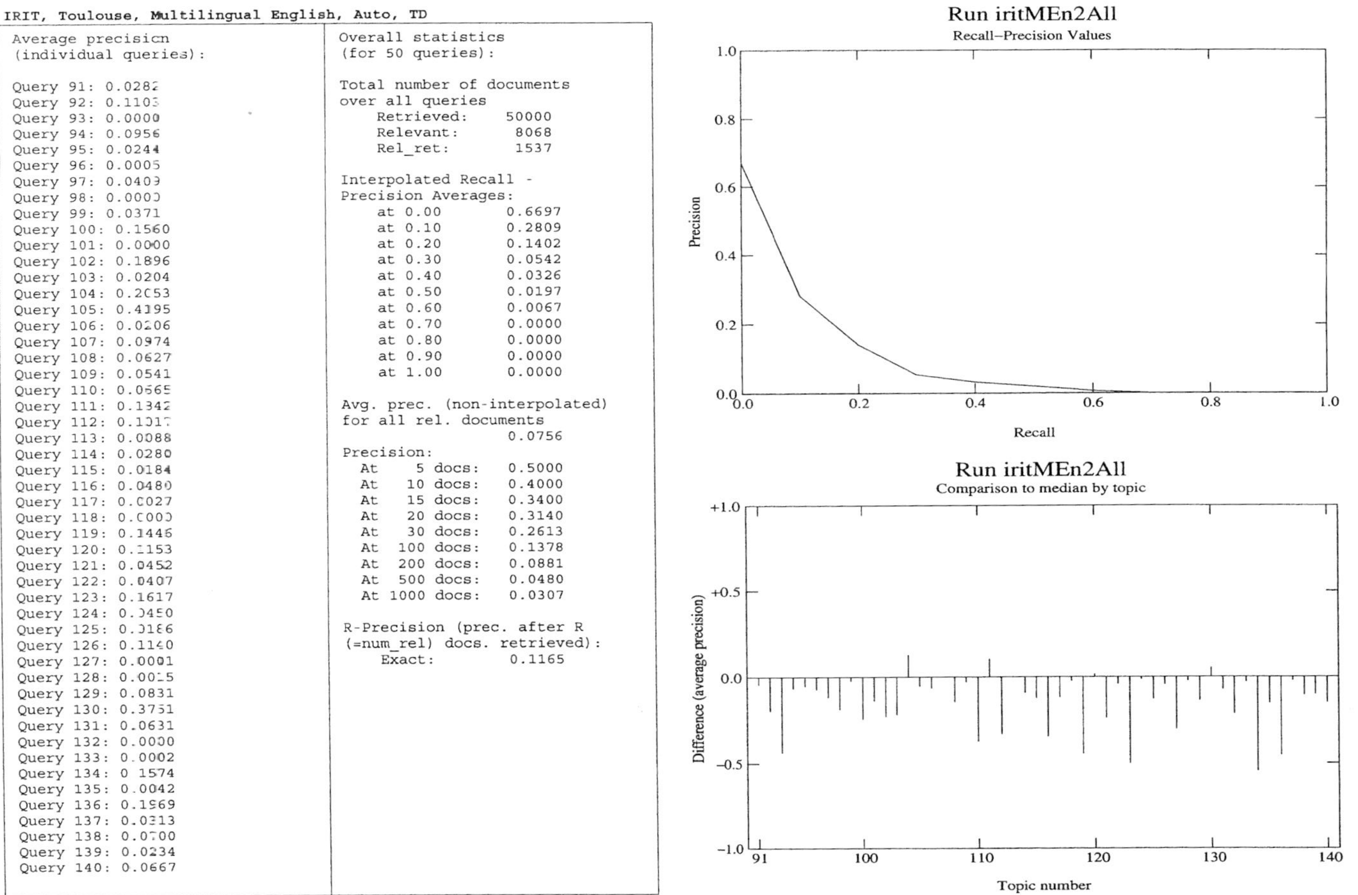

IRIT, Toulouse, Multilingual English, Auto, TD

```
Average precision              Overall statistics
(individual queries):          (for 50 queries):

Query 91: 0.0282               Total number of documents
Query 92: 0.1103               over all queries
Query 93: 0.0000                   Retrieved:    50000
Query 94: 0.0956                   Relevant:      8068
Query 95: 0.0244                   Rel_ret:       1537
Query 96: 0.0005
Query 97: 0.0409               Interpolated Recall -
Query 98: 0.0000               Precision Averages:
Query 99: 0.0371                   at 0.00        0.6697
Query 100: 0.1560                  at 0.10        0.2809
Query 101: 0.0000                  at 0.20        0.1402
Query 102: 0.1896                  at 0.30        0.0542
Query 103: 0.0204                  at 0.40        0.0326
Query 104: 0.2053                  at 0.50        0.0197
Query 105: 0.4195                  at 0.60        0.0067
Query 106: 0.0206                  at 0.70        0.0000
Query 107: 0.0974                  at 0.80        0.0000
Query 108: 0.0627                  at 0.90        0.0000
Query 109: 0.0541                  at 1.00        0.0000
Query 110: 0.0565
Query 111: 0.1342              Avg. prec. (non-interpolated)
Query 112: 0.1017              for all rel. documents
Query 113: 0.0088                                 0.0756
Query 114: 0.0280              Precision:
Query 115: 0.0184                At    5 docs:    0.5000
Query 116: 0.0480                At   10 docs:    0.4000
Query 117: 0.0027                At   15 docs:    0.3400
Query 118: 0.0000                At   20 docs:    0.3140
Query 119: 0.1446                At   30 docs:    0.2613
Query 120: 0.1153                At  100 docs:    0.1378
Query 121: 0.0452                At  200 docs:    0.0881
Query 122: 0.0407                At  500 docs:    0.0480
Query 123: 0.1617                At 1000 docs:    0.0307
Query 124: 0.0450
Query 125: 0.0186              R-Precision (prec. after R
Query 126: 0.1140              (=num_rel) docs. retrieved):
Query 127: 0.0001                  Exact:         0.1165
Query 128: 0.0015
Query 129: 0.0831
Query 130: 0.3751
Query 131: 0.0631
Query 132: 0.0000
Query 133: 0.0002
Query 134: 0 1574
Query 135: 0.0042
Query 136: 0.1969
Query 137: 0.0313
Query 138: 0.0700
Query 139: 0.0234
Query 140: 0.0667
```

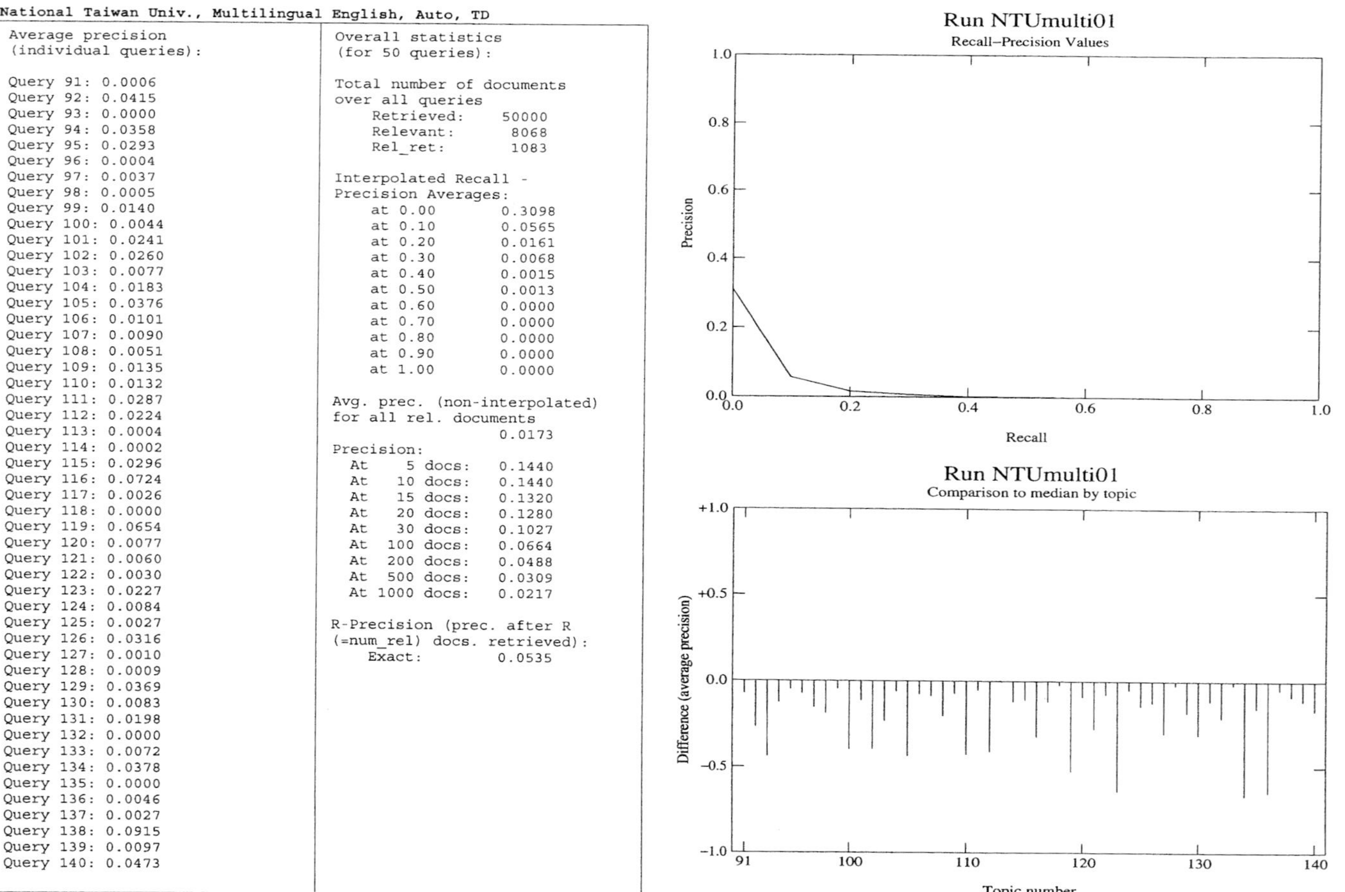

National Taiwan Univ., Multilingual English, Auto, TD

Average precision (individual queries):	Overall statistics (for 50 queries):
Query 91: 0.0006	Total number of documents over all queries
Query 92: 0.0415	Retrieved: 50000
Query 93: 0.0000	Relevant: 8068
Query 94: 0.0358	Rel_ret: 1083
Query 95: 0.0293	
Query 96: 0.0004	Interpolated Recall - Precision Averages:
Query 97: 0.0037	at 0.00 0.3098
Query 98: 0.0005	at 0.10 0.0565
Query 99: 0.0140	at 0.20 0.0161
Query 100: 0.0044	at 0.30 0.0068
Query 101: 0.0241	at 0.40 0.0015
Query 102: 0.0260	at 0.50 0.0013
Query 103: 0.0077	at 0.60 0.0000
Query 104: 0.0183	at 0.70 0.0000
Query 105: 0.0376	at 0.80 0.0000
Query 106: 0.0101	at 0.90 0.0000
Query 107: 0.0090	at 1.00 0.0000
Query 108: 0.0051	
Query 109: 0.0135	Avg. prec. (non-interpolated) for all rel. documents 0.0173
Query 110: 0.0132	Precision:
Query 111: 0.0287	At 5 docs: 0.1440
Query 112: 0.0224	At 10 docs: 0.1440
Query 113: 0.0004	At 15 docs: 0.1320
Query 114: 0.0002	At 20 docs: 0.1280
Query 115: 0.0296	At 30 docs: 0.1027
Query 116: 0.0724	At 100 docs: 0.0664
Query 117: 0.0026	At 200 docs: 0.0488
Query 118: 0.0000	At 500 docs: 0.0309
Query 119: 0.0654	At 1000 docs: 0.0217
Query 120: 0.0077	
Query 121: 0.0060	R-Precision (prec. after R (=num_rel) docs. retrieved):
Query 122: 0.0030	Exact: 0.0535
Query 123: 0.0227	
Query 124: 0.0084	
Query 125: 0.0027	
Query 126: 0.0316	
Query 127: 0.0010	
Query 128: 0.0009	
Query 129: 0.0369	
Query 130: 0.0083	
Query 131: 0.0198	
Query 132: 0.0000	
Query 133: 0.0072	
Query 134: 0.0378	
Query 135: 0.0000	
Query 136: 0.0046	
Query 137: 0.0027	
Query 138: 0.0915	
Query 139: 0.0097	
Query 140: 0.0473	

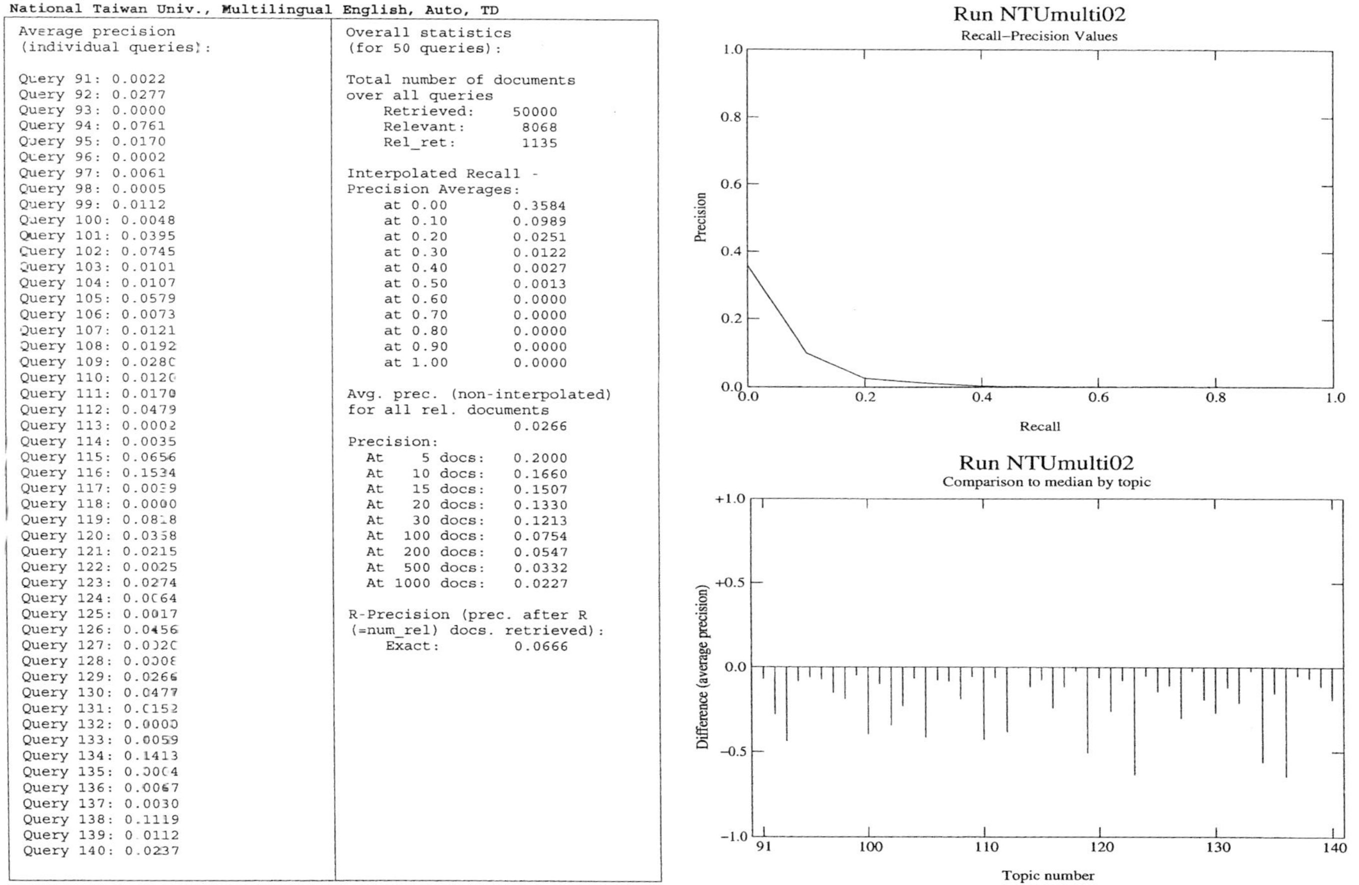

National Taiwan Univ., Multilingual English, Auto, TD

Average precision (individual queries):	Overall statistics (for 50 queries):
Query 91: 0.0022	Total number of documents over all queries
Query 92: 0.0277	Retrieved: 50000
Query 93: 0.0000	Relevant: 8068
Query 94: 0.0761	Rel_ret: 1135
Query 95: 0.0170	
Query 96: 0.0002	Interpolated Recall - Precision Averages:
Query 97: 0.0061	at 0.00 0.3584
Query 98: 0.0005	at 0.10 0.0989
Query 99: 0.0112	at 0.20 0.0251
Query 100: 0.0048	at 0.30 0.0122
Query 101: 0.0395	at 0.40 0.0027
Query 102: 0.0745	at 0.50 0.0013
Query 103: 0.0101	at 0.60 0.0000
Query 104: 0.0107	at 0.70 0.0000
Query 105: 0.0579	at 0.80 0.0000
Query 106: 0.0073	at 0.90 0.0000
Query 107: 0.0121	at 1.00 0.0000
Query 108: 0.0192	
Query 109: 0.0280	Avg. prec. (non-interpolated) for all rel. documents 0.0266
Query 110: 0.0120	
Query 111: 0.0170	Precision:
Query 112: 0.0479	At 5 docs: 0.2000
Query 113: 0.0002	At 10 docs: 0.1660
Query 114: 0.0035	At 15 docs: 0.1507
Query 115: 0.0656	At 20 docs: 0.1330
Query 116: 0.1534	At 30 docs: 0.1213
Query 117: 0.0039	At 100 docs: 0.0754
Query 118: 0.0000	At 200 docs: 0.0547
Query 119: 0.0818	At 500 docs: 0.0332
Query 120: 0.0358	At 1000 docs: 0.0227
Query 121: 0.0215	
Query 122: 0.0025	R-Precision (prec. after R (=num_rel) docs. retrieved):
Query 123: 0.0274	Exact: 0.0666
Query 124: 0.0064	
Query 125: 0.0017	
Query 126: 0.0456	
Query 127: 0.0020	
Query 128: 0.0008	
Query 129: 0.0266	
Query 130: 0.0477	
Query 131: 0.0152	
Query 132: 0.0000	
Query 133: 0.0059	
Query 134: 0.1413	
Query 135: 0.0004	
Query 136: 0.0067	
Query 137: 0.0030	
Query 138: 0.1119	
Query 139: 0.0112	
Query 140: 0.0237	

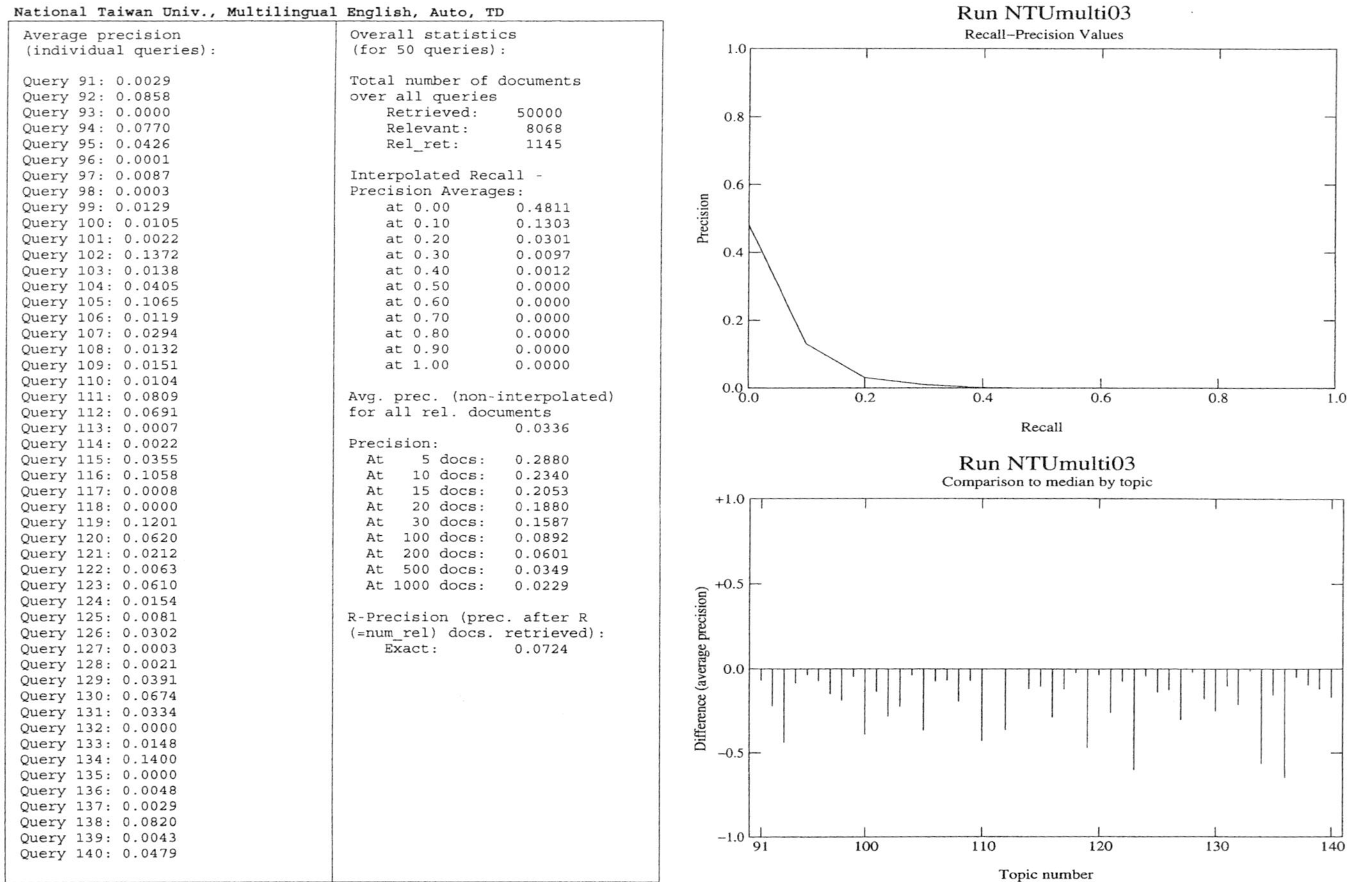

National Taiwan Univ., Multilingual English, Auto, TD

Average precision (individual queries):	Overall statistics (for 50 queries):
Query 91: 0.0029	Total number of documents over all queries
Query 92: 0.0858	Retrieved: 50000
Query 93: 0.0000	Relevant: 8068
Query 94: 0.0770	Rel_ret: 1145
Query 95: 0.0426	
Query 96: 0.0001	Interpolated Recall - Precision Averages:
Query 97: 0.0087	at 0.00 0.4811
Query 98: 0.0003	at 0.10 0.1303
Query 99: 0.0129	at 0.20 0.0301
Query 100: 0.0105	at 0.30 0.0097
Query 101: 0.0022	at 0.40 0.0012
Query 102: 0.1372	at 0.50 0.0000
Query 103: 0.0138	at 0.60 0.0000
Query 104: 0.0405	at 0.70 0.0000
Query 105: 0.1065	at 0.80 0.0000
Query 106: 0.0119	at 0.90 0.0000
Query 107: 0.0294	at 1.00 0.0000
Query 108: 0.0132	
Query 109: 0.0151	Avg. prec. (non-interpolated) for all rel. documents 0.0336
Query 110: 0.0104	
Query 111: 0.0809	Precision:
Query 112: 0.0691	At 5 docs: 0.2880
Query 113: 0.0007	At 10 docs: 0.2340
Query 114: 0.0022	At 15 docs: 0.2053
Query 115: 0.0355	At 20 docs: 0.1880
Query 116: 0.1058	At 30 docs: 0.1587
Query 117: 0.0008	At 100 docs: 0.0892
Query 118: 0.0000	At 200 docs: 0.0601
Query 119: 0.1201	At 500 docs: 0.0349
Query 120: 0.0620	At 1000 docs: 0.0229
Query 121: 0.0212	
Query 122: 0.0063	R-Precision (prec. after R (=num_rel) docs. retrieved):
Query 123: 0.0610	Exact: 0.0724
Query 124: 0.0154	
Query 125: 0.0081	
Query 126: 0.0302	
Query 127: 0.0003	
Query 128: 0.0021	
Query 129: 0.0391	
Query 130: 0.0674	
Query 131: 0.0334	
Query 132: 0.0000	
Query 133: 0.0148	
Query 134: 0.1400	
Query 135: 0.0000	
Query 136: 0.0048	
Query 137: 0.0029	
Query 138: 0.0820	
Query 139: 0.0043	
Query 140: 0.0479	

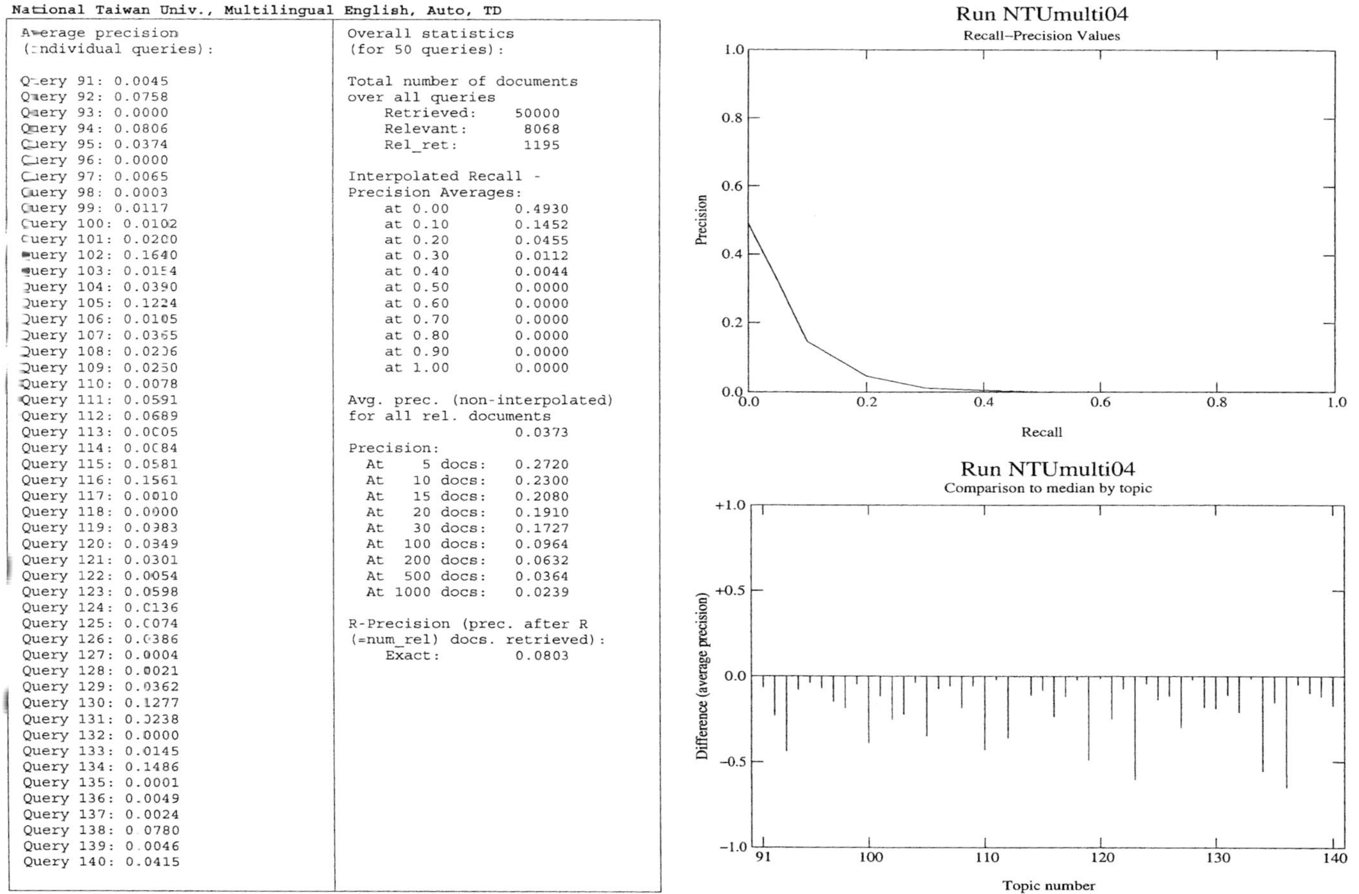

National Taiwan Univ., Multilingual English, Auto, TD

Average precision (individual queries):

Query	Average precision
Query 91:	0.0045
Query 92:	0.0758
Query 93:	0.0000
Query 94:	0.0806
Query 95:	0.0374
Query 96:	0.0000
Query 97:	0.0065
Query 98:	0.0003
Query 99:	0.0117
Query 100:	0.0102
Query 101:	0.0200
Query 102:	0.1640
Query 103:	0.0154
Query 104:	0.0390
Query 105:	0.1224
Query 106:	0.0105
Query 107:	0.0365
Query 108:	0.0206
Query 109:	0.0250
Query 110:	0.0078
Query 111:	0.0591
Query 112:	0.0689
Query 113:	0.0005
Query 114:	0.0084
Query 115:	0.0581
Query 116:	0.1561
Query 117:	0.0010
Query 118:	0.0000
Query 119:	0.0383
Query 120:	0.0349
Query 121:	0.0301
Query 122:	0.0054
Query 123:	0.0598
Query 124:	0.0136
Query 125:	0.0074
Query 126:	0.0386
Query 127:	0.0004
Query 128:	0.0021
Query 129:	0.0362
Query 130:	0.1277
Query 131:	0.0238
Query 132:	0.0000
Query 133:	0.0145
Query 134:	0.1486
Query 135:	0.0001
Query 136:	0.0049
Query 137:	0.0024
Query 138:	0.0780
Query 139:	0.0046
Query 140:	0.0415

Overall statistics (for 50 queries):

Total number of documents over all queries

Retrieved:	50000
Relevant:	8068
Rel_ret:	1195

Interpolated Recall - Precision Averages:

at 0.00	0.4930
at 0.10	0.1452
at 0.20	0.0455
at 0.30	0.0112
at 0.40	0.0044
at 0.50	0.0000
at 0.60	0.0000
at 0.70	0.0000
at 0.80	0.0000
at 0.90	0.0000
at 1.00	0.0000

Avg. prec. (non-interpolated) for all rel. documents 0.0373

Precision:

At 5 docs:	0.2720
At 10 docs:	0.2300
At 15 docs:	0.2080
At 20 docs:	0.1910
At 30 docs:	0.1727
At 100 docs:	0.0964
At 200 docs:	0.0632
At 500 docs:	0.0364
At 1000 docs:	0.0239

R-Precision (prec. after R (=num_rel) docs. retrieved):
Exact: 0.0803

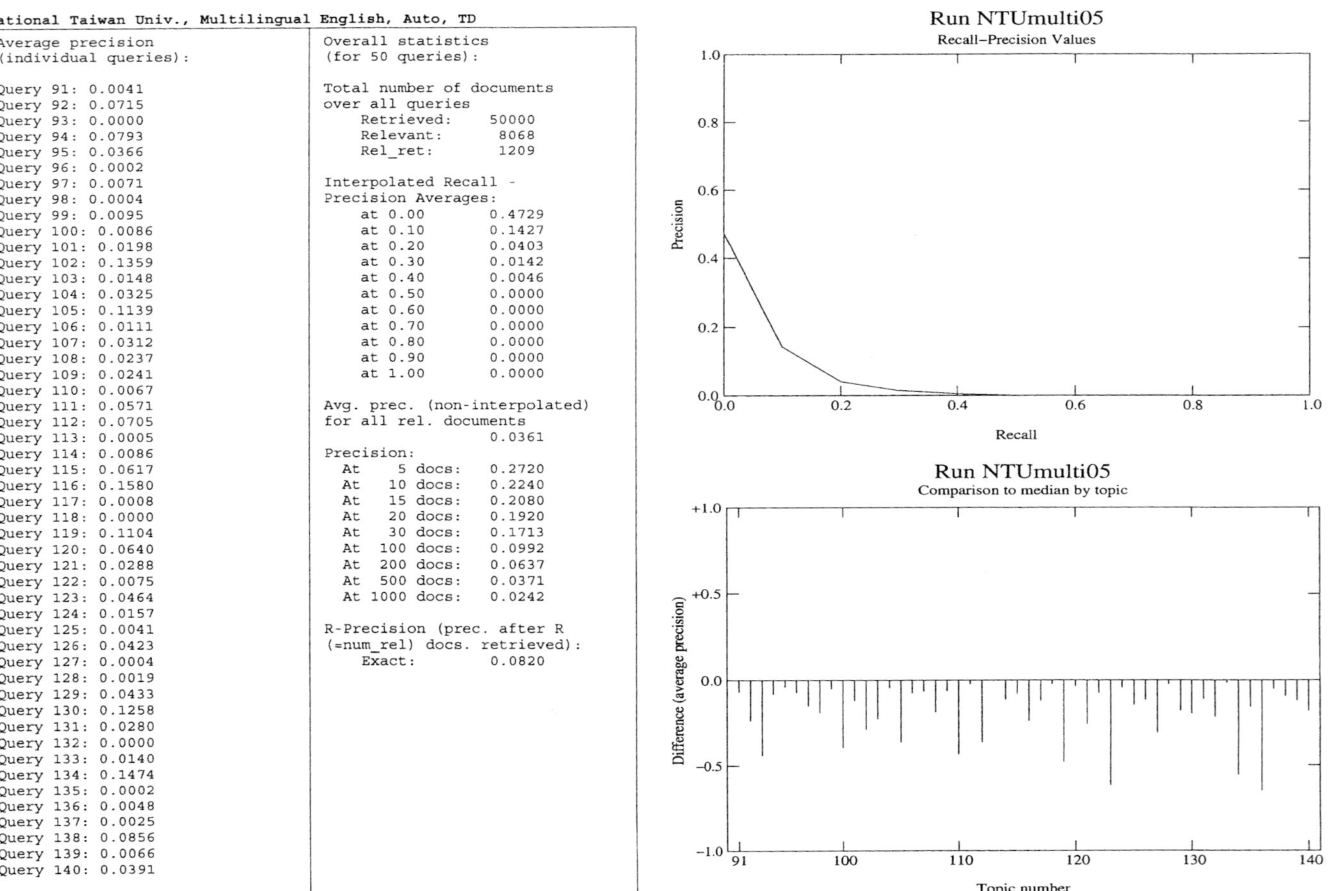

National Taiwan Univ., Multilingual English, Auto, TD

```
Average precision                Overall statistics
(individual queries):            (for 50 queries):

Query 91: 0.0041                 Total number of documents
Query 92: 0.0715                 over all queries
Query 93: 0.0000                     Retrieved:    50000
Query 94: 0.0793                     Relevant:      8068
Query 95: 0.0366                     Rel_ret:       1209
Query 96: 0.0002
Query 97: 0.0071                 Interpolated Recall -
Query 98: 0.0004                 Precision Averages:
Query 99: 0.0095                     at 0.00        0.4729
Query 100: 0.0086                    at 0.10        0.1427
Query 101: 0.0198                    at 0.20        0.0403
Query 102: 0.1359                    at 0.30        0.0142
Query 103: 0.0148                    at 0.40        0.0046
Query 104: 0.0325                    at 0.50        0.0000
Query 105: 0.1139                    at 0.60        0.0000
Query 106: 0.0111                    at 0.70        0.0000
Query 107: 0.0312                    at 0.80        0.0000
Query 108: 0.0237                    at 0.90        0.0000
Query 109: 0.0241                    at 1.00        0.0000
Query 110: 0.0067
Query 111: 0.0571                Avg. prec. (non-interpolated)
Query 112: 0.0705                for all rel. documents
Query 113: 0.0005                                   0.0361
Query 114: 0.0086                Precision:
Query 115: 0.0617                  At    5 docs:    0.2720
Query 116: 0.1580                  At   10 docs:    0.2240
Query 117: 0.0008                  At   15 docs:    0.2080
Query 118: 0.0000                  At   20 docs:    0.1920
Query 119: 0.1104                  At   30 docs:    0.1713
Query 120: 0.0640                  At  100 docs:    0.0992
Query 121: 0.0288                  At  200 docs:    0.0637
Query 122: 0.0075                  At  500 docs:    0.0371
Query 123: 0.0464                  At 1000 docs:    0.0242
Query 124: 0.0157
Query 125: 0.0041                R-Precision (prec. after R
Query 126: 0.0423                (=num_rel) docs. retrieved):
Query 127: 0.0004                    Exact:         0.0820
Query 128: 0.0019
Query 129: 0.0433
Query 130: 0.1258
Query 131: 0.0280
Query 132: 0.0000
Query 133: 0.0140
Query 134: 0.1474
Query 135: 0.0002
Query 136: 0.0048
Query 137: 0.0025
Query 138: 0.0856
Query 139: 0.0066
Query 140: 0.0391
```

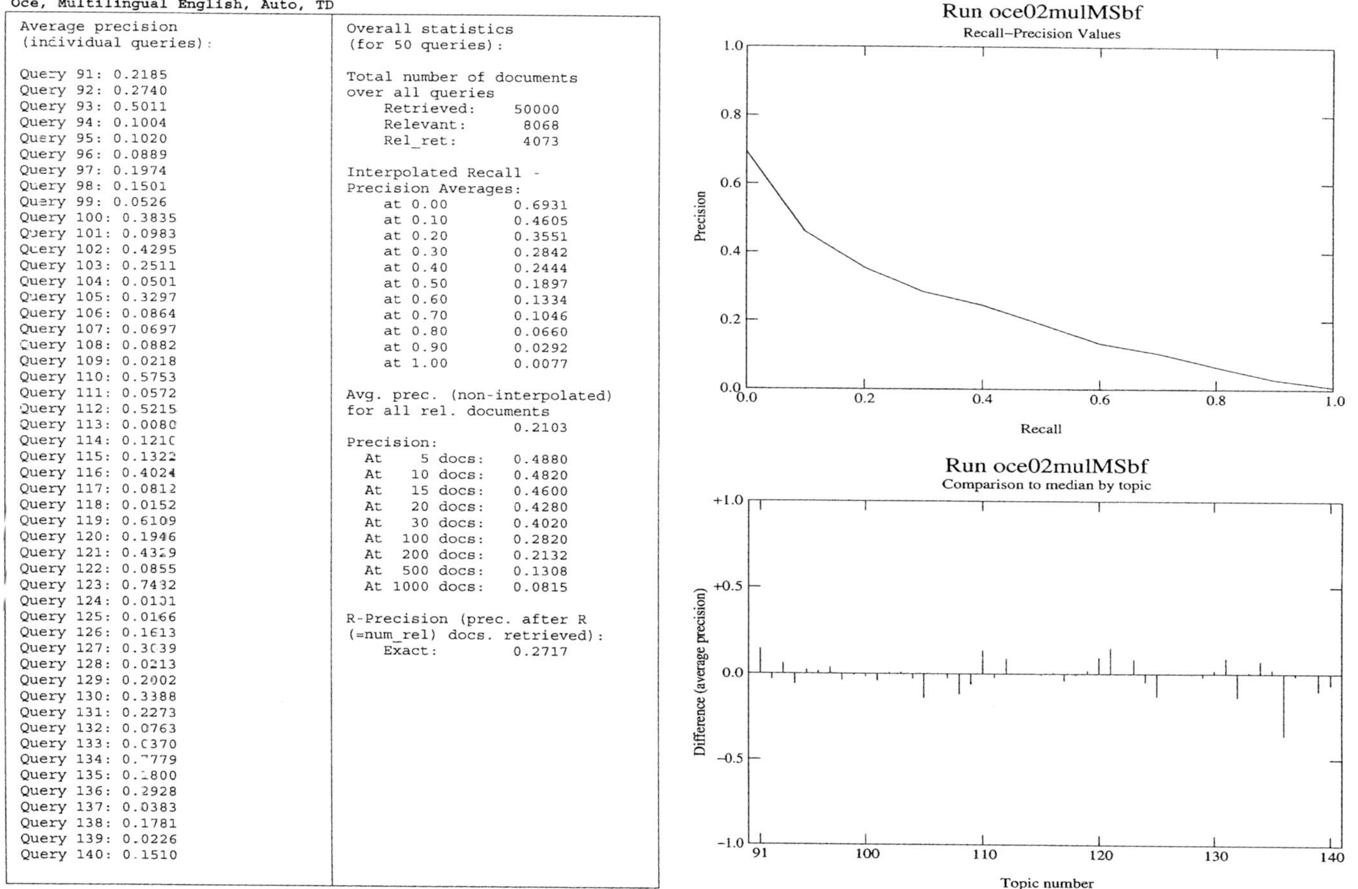

Océ, Multilingual English, Auto, TD

```
Average precision                 Overall statistics
(individual queries):             (for 50 queries):

Query 91: 0.2185                  Total number of documents
Query 92: 0.2740                  over all queries
Query 93: 0.5011                      Retrieved:     50000
Query 94: 0.1004                      Relevant:       8068
Query 95: 0.1020                      Rel_ret:        4073
Query 96: 0.0889
Query 97: 0.1974                  Interpolated Recall -
Query 98: 0.1501                  Precision Averages:
Query 99: 0.0526                      at 0.00        0.6931
Query 100: 0.3835                     at 0.10        0.4605
Query 101: 0.0983                     at 0.20        0.3551
Query 102: 0.4295                     at 0.30        0.2842
Query 103: 0.2511                     at 0.40        0.2444
Query 104: 0.0501                     at 0.50        0.1897
Query 105: 0.3297                     at 0.60        0.1334
Query 106: 0.0864                     at 0.70        0.1046
Query 107: 0.0697                     at 0.80        0.0660
Query 108: 0.0882                     at 0.90        0.0292
Query 109: 0.0218                     at 1.00        0.0077
Query 110: 0.5753
Query 111: 0.0572                 Avg. prec. (non-interpolated)
Query 112: 0.5215                 for all rel. documents
Query 113: 0.0080                                    0.2103
Query 114: 0.1210                 Precision:
Query 115: 0.1322                   At    5 docs:    0.4880
Query 116: 0.4024                   At   10 docs:    0.4820
Query 117: 0.0812                   At   15 docs:    0.4600
Query 118: 0.0152                   At   20 docs:    0.4280
Query 119: 0.6109                   At   30 docs:    0.4020
Query 120: 0.1946                   At  100 docs:    0.2820
Query 121: 0.4329                   At  200 docs:    0.2132
Query 122: 0.0855                   At  500 docs:    0.1308
Query 123: 0.7432                   At 1000 docs:    0.0815
Query 124: 0.0101
Query 125: 0.0166                 R-Precision (prec. after R
Query 126: 0.1613                 (=num_rel) docs. retrieved):
Query 127: 0.3039                     Exact:         0.2717
Query 128: 0.0213
Query 129: 0.2002
Query 130: 0.3388
Query 131: 0.2273
Query 132: 0.0763
Query 133: 0.0370
Query 134: 0.7779
Query 135: 0.1800
Query 136: 0.2928
Query 137: 0.0383
Query 138: 0.1781
Query 139: 0.0226
Query 140: 0.1510
```

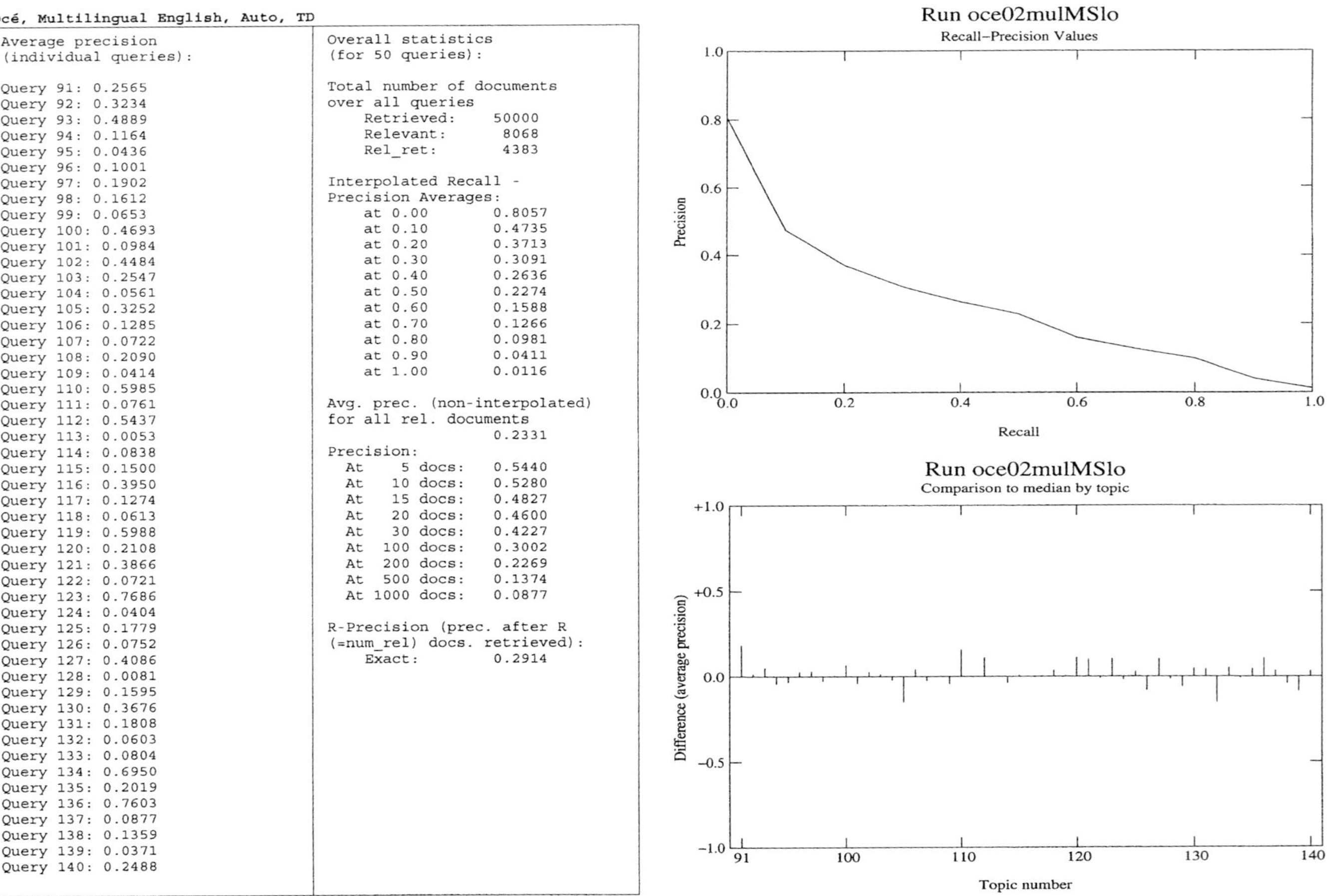

Océ, Multilingual English, Auto, TD

Average precision
(individual queries):

Query	Average precision
Query 91:	0.2565
Query 92:	0.3234
Query 93:	0.4889
Query 94:	0.1164
Query 95:	0.0436
Query 96:	0.1001
Query 97:	0.1902
Query 98:	0.1612
Query 99:	0.0653
Query 100:	0.4693
Query 101:	0.0984
Query 102:	0.4484
Query 103:	0.2547
Query 104:	0.0561
Query 105:	0.3252
Query 106:	0.1285
Query 107:	0.0722
Query 108:	0.2090
Query 109:	0.0414
Query 110:	0.5985
Query 111:	0.0761
Query 112:	0.5437
Query 113:	0.0053
Query 114:	0.0838
Query 115:	0.1500
Query 116:	0.3950
Query 117:	0.1274
Query 118:	0.0613
Query 119:	0.5988
Query 120:	0.2108
Query 121:	0.3866
Query 122:	0.0721
Query 123:	0.7686
Query 124:	0.0404
Query 125:	0.1779
Query 126:	0.0752
Query 127:	0.4086
Query 128:	0.0081
Query 129:	0.1595
Query 130:	0.3676
Query 131:	0.1808
Query 132:	0.0603
Query 133:	0.0804
Query 134:	0.6950
Query 135:	0.2019
Query 136:	0.7603
Query 137:	0.0877
Query 138:	0.1359
Query 139:	0.0371
Query 140:	0.2488

Overall statistics
(for 50 queries):

Total number of documents
over all queries

Retrieved:	50000
Relevant:	8068
Rel_ret:	4383

Interpolated Recall -
Precision Averages:

at 0.00	0.8057
at 0.10	0.4735
at 0.20	0.3713
at 0.30	0.3091
at 0.40	0.2636
at 0.50	0.2274
at 0.60	0.1588
at 0.70	0.1266
at 0.80	0.0981
at 0.90	0.0411
at 1.00	0.0116

Avg. prec. (non-interpolated)
for all rel. documents
0.2331

Precision:

At 5 docs:	0.5440
At 10 docs:	0.5280
At 15 docs:	0.4827
At 20 docs:	0.4600
At 30 docs:	0.4227
At 100 docs:	0.3002
At 200 docs:	0.2269
At 500 docs:	0.1374
At 1000 docs:	0.0877

R-Precision (prec. after R
(=num_rel) docs. retrieved):
Exact: 0.2914

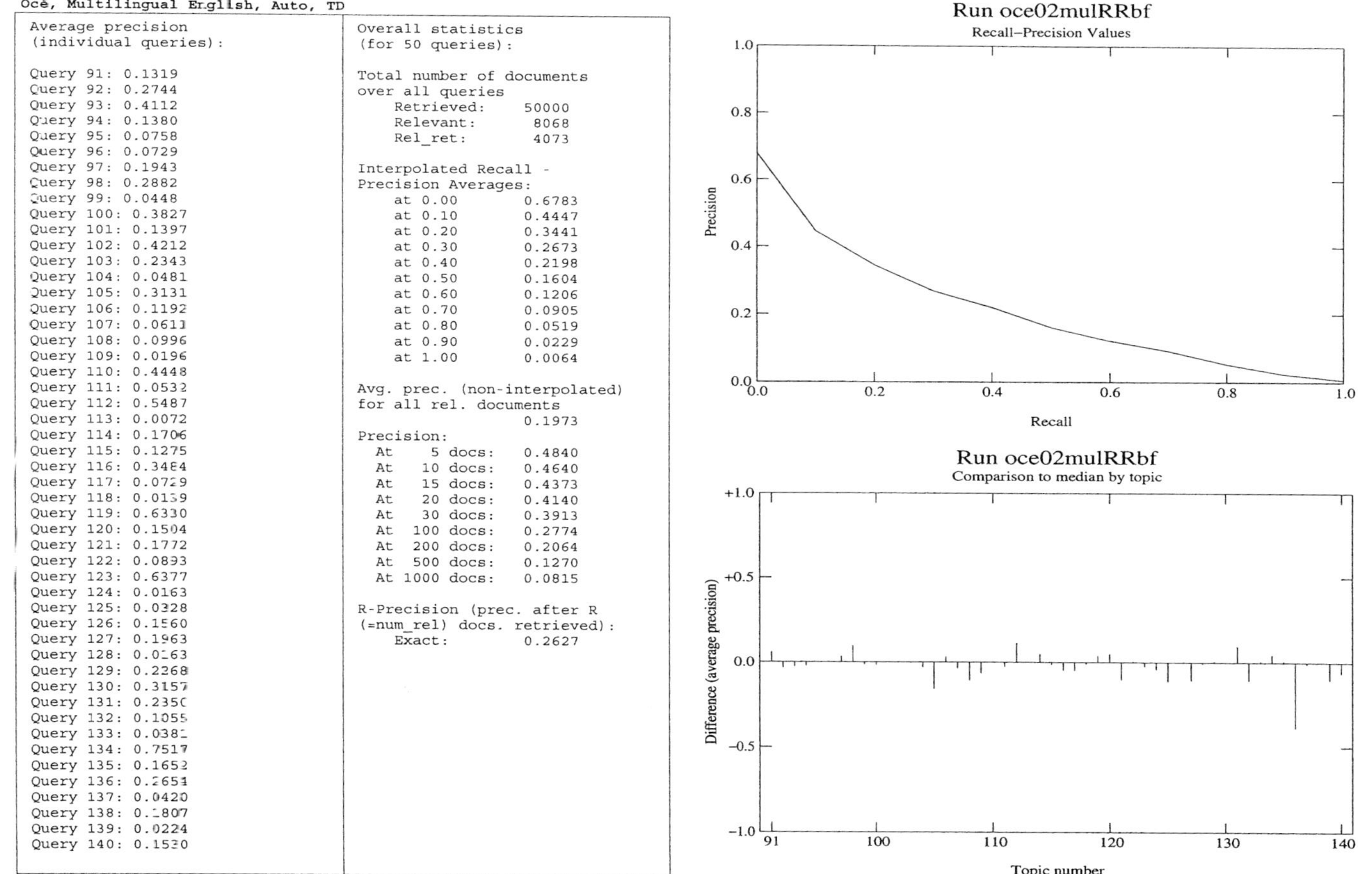

Océ, Multilingual English, Auto, TD

```
Average precision
(individual queries):

Query 91: 0.1319
Query 92: 0.2744
Query 93: 0.4112
Query 94: 0.1380
Query 95: 0.0758
Query 96: 0.0729
Query 97: 0.1943
Query 98: 0.2882
Query 99: 0.0448
Query 100: 0.3827
Query 101: 0.1397
Query 102: 0.4212
Query 103: 0.2343
Query 104: 0.0481
Query 105: 0.3131
Query 106: 0.1192
Query 107: 0.0611
Query 108: 0.0996
Query 109: 0.0196
Query 110: 0.4448
Query 111: 0.0532
Query 112: 0.5487
Query 113: 0.0072
Query 114: 0.1706
Query 115: 0.1275
Query 116: 0.3484
Query 117: 0.0729
Query 118: 0.0159
Query 119: 0.6330
Query 120: 0.1504
Query 121: 0.1772
Query 122: 0.0893
Query 123: 0.6377
Query 124: 0.0163
Query 125: 0.0328
Query 126: 0.1560
Query 127: 0.1963
Query 128: 0.0163
Query 129: 0.2268
Query 130: 0.3157
Query 131: 0.2350
Query 132: 0.1055
Query 133: 0.0381
Query 134: 0.7517
Query 135: 0.1652
Query 136: 0.2654
Query 137: 0.0420
Query 138: 0.1807
Query 139: 0.0224
Query 140: 0.1530
```

```
Overall statistics
(for 50 queries):

Total number of documents
over all queries
    Retrieved:     50000
    Relevant:       8068
    Rel_ret:        4073

Interpolated Recall -
Precision Averages:
    at 0.00        0.6783
    at 0.10        0.4447
    at 0.20        0.3441
    at 0.30        0.2673
    at 0.40        0.2198
    at 0.50        0.1604
    at 0.60        0.1206
    at 0.70        0.0905
    at 0.80        0.0519
    at 0.90        0.0229
    at 1.00        0.0064

Avg. prec. (non-interpolated)
for all rel. documents
                   0.1973
Precision:
  At    5 docs:    0.4840
  At   10 docs:    0.4640
  At   15 docs:    0.4373
  At   20 docs:    0.4140
  At   30 docs:    0.3913
  At  100 docs:    0.2774
  At  200 docs:    0.2064
  At  500 docs:    0.1270
  At 1000 docs:    0.0815

R-Precision (prec. after R
(=num_rel) docs. retrieved):
    Exact:         0.2627
```

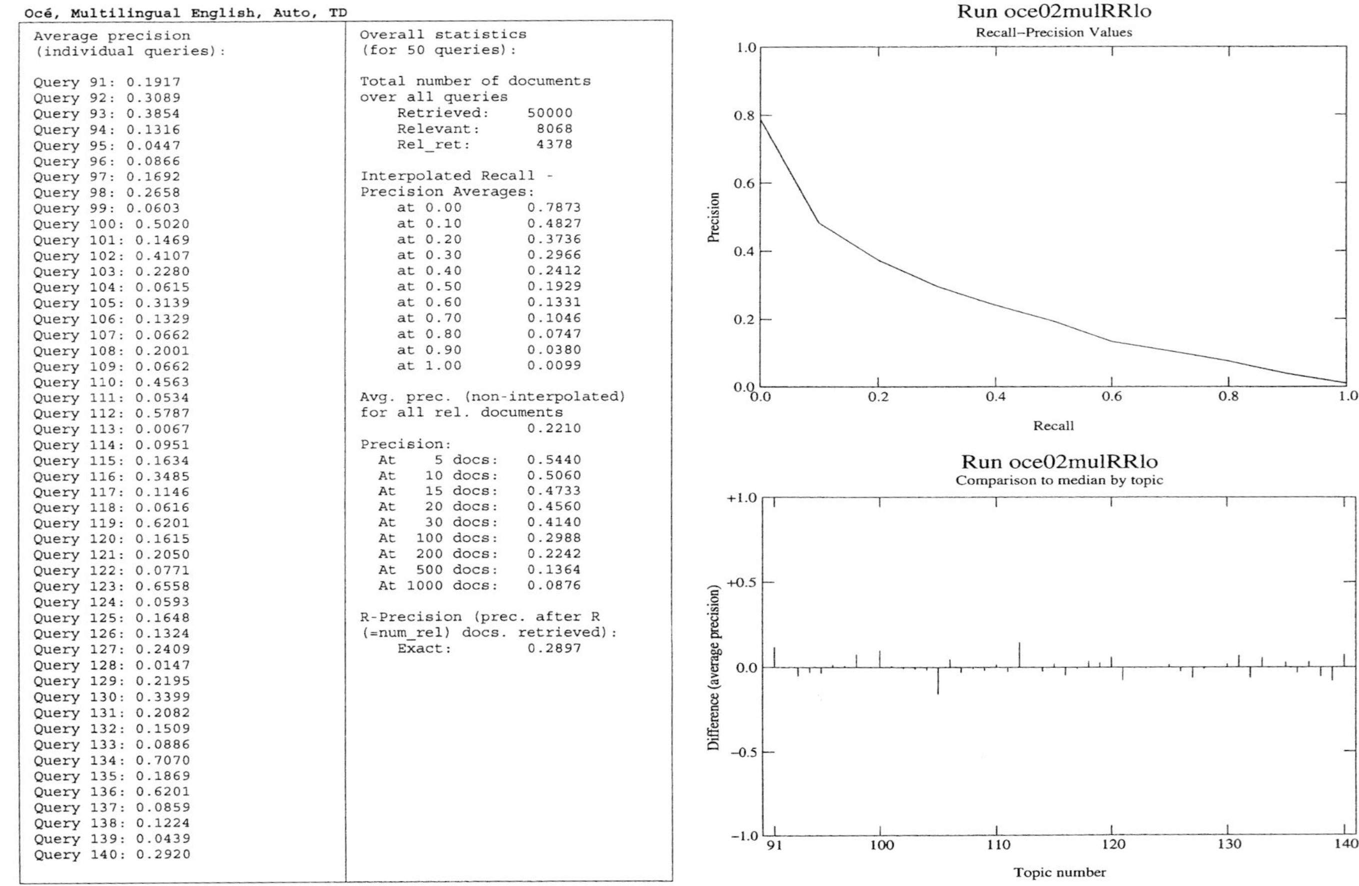

Océ, Multilingual English, Auto, TD

```
Average precision               Overall statistics
(individual queries):           (for 50 queries):

Query 91: 0.1917                Total number of documents
Query 92: 0.3089                over all queries
Query 93: 0.3854                    Retrieved:    50000
Query 94: 0.1316                    Relevant:      8068
Query 95: 0.0447                    Rel_ret:       4378
Query 96: 0.0866
Query 97: 0.1692                Interpolated Recall -
Query 98: 0.2658                Precision Averages:
Query 99: 0.0603                    at 0.00       0.7873
Query 100: 0.5020                   at 0.10       0.4827
Query 101: 0.1469                   at 0.20       0.3736
Query 102: 0.4107                   at 0.30       0.2966
Query 103: 0.2280                   at 0.40       0.2412
Query 104: 0.0615                   at 0.50       0.1929
Query 105: 0.3139                   at 0.60       0.1331
Query 106: 0.1329                   at 0.70       0.1046
Query 107: 0.0662                   at 0.80       0.0747
Query 108: 0.2001                   at 0.90       0.0380
Query 109: 0.0662                   at 1.00       0.0099
Query 110: 0.4563
Query 111: 0.0534               Avg. prec. (non-interpolated)
Query 112: 0.5787               for all rel. documents
Query 113: 0.0067                                 0.2210
Query 114: 0.0951               Precision:
Query 115: 0.1634                 At    5 docs:   0.5440
Query 116: 0.3485                 At   10 docs:   0.5060
Query 117: 0.1146                 At   15 docs:   0.4733
Query 118: 0.0616                 At   20 docs:   0.4560
Query 119: 0.6201                 At   30 docs:   0.4140
Query 120: 0.1615                 At  100 docs:   0.2988
Query 121: 0.2050                 At  200 docs:   0.2242
Query 122: 0.0771                 At  500 docs:   0.1364
Query 123: 0.6558                 At 1000 docs:   0.0876
Query 124: 0.0593
Query 125: 0.1648               R-Precision (prec. after R
Query 126: 0.1324               (=num_rel) docs. retrieved):
Query 127: 0.2409                   Exact:        0.2897
Query 128: 0.0147
Query 129: 0.2195
Query 130: 0.3399
Query 131: 0.2082
Query 132: 0.1509
Query 133: 0.0886
Query 134: 0.7070
Query 135: 0.1869
Query 136: 0.6201
Query 137: 0.0859
Query 138: 0.1224
Query 139: 0.0439
Query 140: 0.2920
```

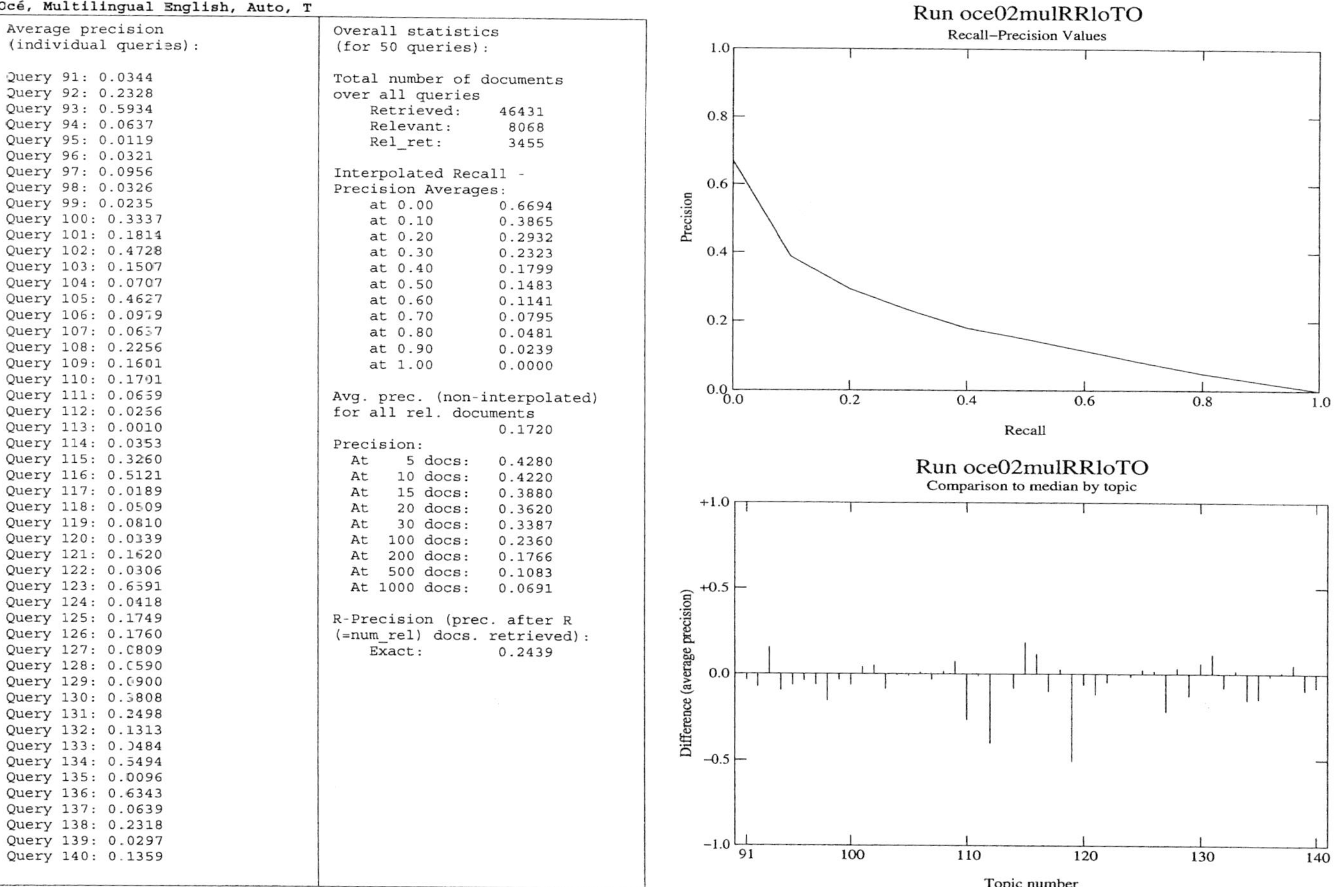

Océ, Multilingual English, Auto, T

```
Average precision
(individual queries):

Query 91: 0.0344
Query 92: 0.2328
Query 93: 0.5934
Query 94: 0.0637
Query 95: 0.0119
Query 96: 0.0321
Query 97: 0.0956
Query 98: 0.0326
Query 99: 0.0235
Query 100: 0.3337
Query 101: 0.1814
Query 102: 0.4728
Query 103: 0.1507
Query 104: 0.0707
Query 105: 0.4627
Query 106: 0.0979
Query 107: 0.0637
Query 108: 0.2256
Query 109: 0.1601
Query 110: 0.1701
Query 111: 0.0659
Query 112: 0.0256
Query 113: 0.0010
Query 114: 0.0353
Query 115: 0.3260
Query 116: 0.5121
Query 117: 0.0189
Query 118: 0.0509
Query 119: 0.0810
Query 120: 0.0339
Query 121: 0.1620
Query 122: 0.0306
Query 123: 0.6591
Query 124: 0.0418
Query 125: 0.1749
Query 126: 0.1760
Query 127: 0.0809
Query 128: 0.0590
Query 129: 0.0900
Query 130: 0.3808
Query 131: 0.2498
Query 132: 0.1313
Query 133: 0.0484
Query 134: 0.5494
Query 135: 0.0096
Query 136: 0.6343
Query 137: 0.0639
Query 138: 0.2318
Query 139: 0.0297
Query 140: 0.1359
```

```
Overall statistics
(for 50 queries):

Total number of documents
over all queries
    Retrieved:    46431
    Relevant:      8068
    Rel_ret:       3455

Interpolated Recall -
Precision Averages:
    at 0.00        0.6694
    at 0.10        0.3865
    at 0.20        0.2932
    at 0.30        0.2323
    at 0.40        0.1799
    at 0.50        0.1483
    at 0.60        0.1141
    at 0.70        0.0795
    at 0.80        0.0481
    at 0.90        0.0239
    at 1.00        0.0000

Avg. prec. (non-interpolated)
for all rel. documents
                   0.1720
Precision:
  At    5 docs:    0.4280
  At   10 docs:    0.4220
  At   15 docs:    0.3880
  At   20 docs:    0.3620
  At   30 docs:    0.3387
  At  100 docs:    0.2360
  At  200 docs:    0.1766
  At  500 docs:    0.1083
  At 1000 docs:    0.0691

R-Precision (prec. after R
(=num_rel) docs. retrieved):
    Exact:         0.2439
```

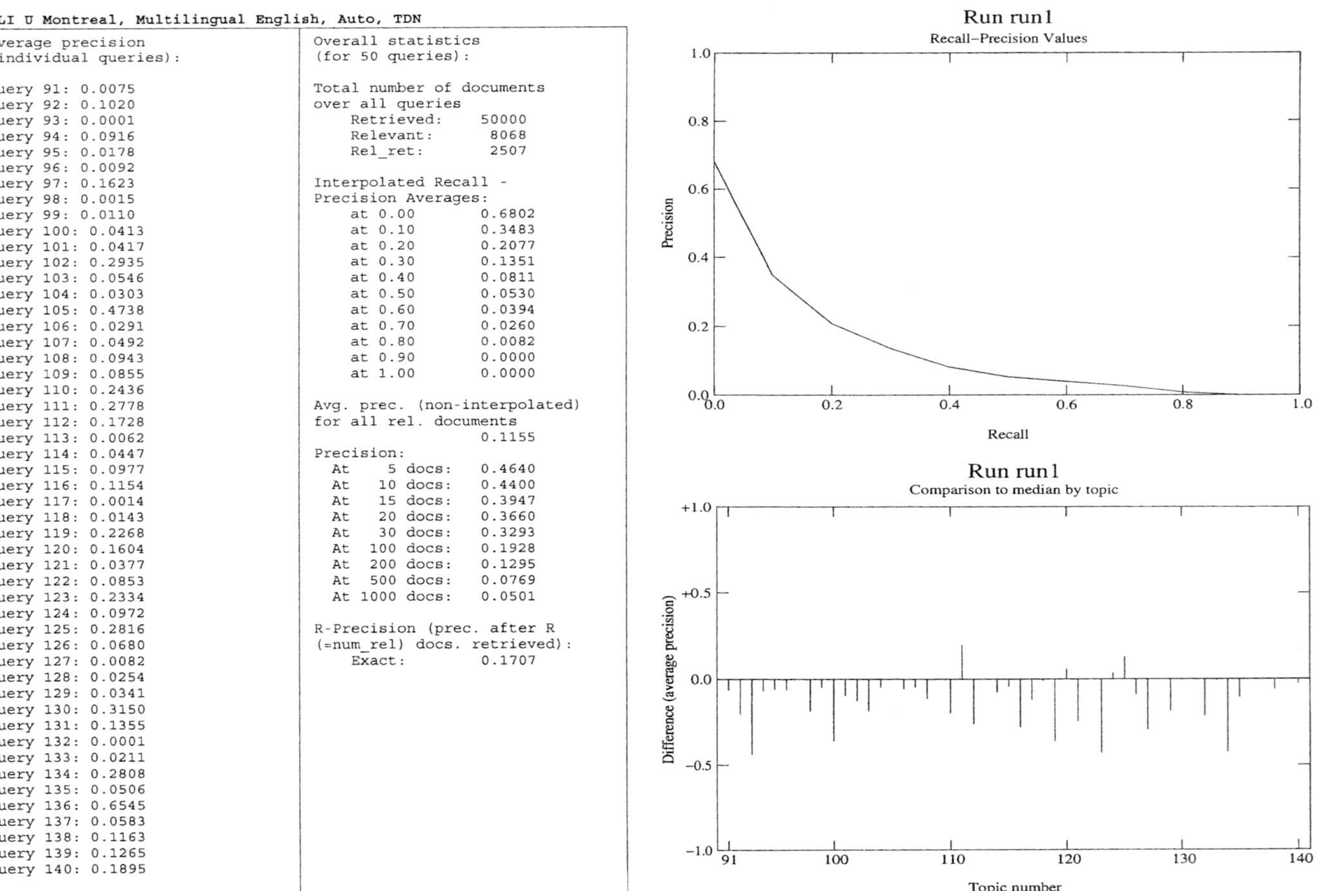

RALI U Montreal, Multilingual English, Auto, TDN

```
Average precision                 Overall statistics
(individual queries):             (for 50 queries):

Query  91: 0.0075                 Total number of documents
Query  92: 0.1020                 over all queries
Query  93: 0.0001                   Retrieved:     50000
Query  94: 0.0916                   Relevant:       8068
Query  95: 0.0178                   Rel_ret:        2507
Query  96: 0.0092
Query  97: 0.1623                 Interpolated Recall -
Query  98: 0.0015                 Precision Averages:
Query  99: 0.0110                    at 0.00       0.6802
Query 100: 0.0413                    at 0.10       0.3483
Query 101: 0.0417                    at 0.20       0.2077
Query 102: 0.2935                    at 0.30       0.1351
Query 103: 0.0546                    at 0.40       0.0811
Query 104: 0.0303                    at 0.50       0.0530
Query 105: 0.4738                    at 0.60       0.0394
Query 106: 0.0291                    at 0.70       0.0260
Query 107: 0.0492                    at 0.80       0.0082
Query 108: 0.0943                    at 0.90       0.0000
Query 109: 0.0855                    at 1.00       0.0000
Query 110: 0.2436
Query 111: 0.2778                 Avg. prec. (non-interpolated)
Query 112: 0.1728                 for all rel. documents
Query 113: 0.0062                                  0.1155
Query 114: 0.0447                 Precision:
Query 115: 0.0977                   At    5 docs:  0.4640
Query 116: 0.1154                   At   10 docs:  0.4400
Query 117: 0.0014                   At   15 docs:  0.3947
Query 118: 0.0143                   At   20 docs:  0.3660
Query 119: 0.2268                   At   30 docs:  0.3293
Query 120: 0.1604                   At  100 docs:  0.1928
Query 121: 0.0377                   At  200 docs:  0.1295
Query 122: 0.0853                   At  500 docs:  0.0769
Query 123: 0.2334                   At 1000 docs:  0.0501
Query 124: 0.0972
Query 125: 0.2816                 R-Precision (prec. after R
Query 126: 0.0680                 (=num_rel) docs. retrieved):
Query 127: 0.0082                   Exact:         0.1707
Query 128: 0.0254
Query 129: 0.0341
Query 130: 0.3150
Query 131: 0.1355
Query 132: 0.0001
Query 133: 0.0211
Query 134: 0.2808
Query 135: 0.0506
Query 136: 0.6545
Query 137: 0.0583
Query 138: 0.1163
Query 139: 0.1265
Query 140: 0.1895
```

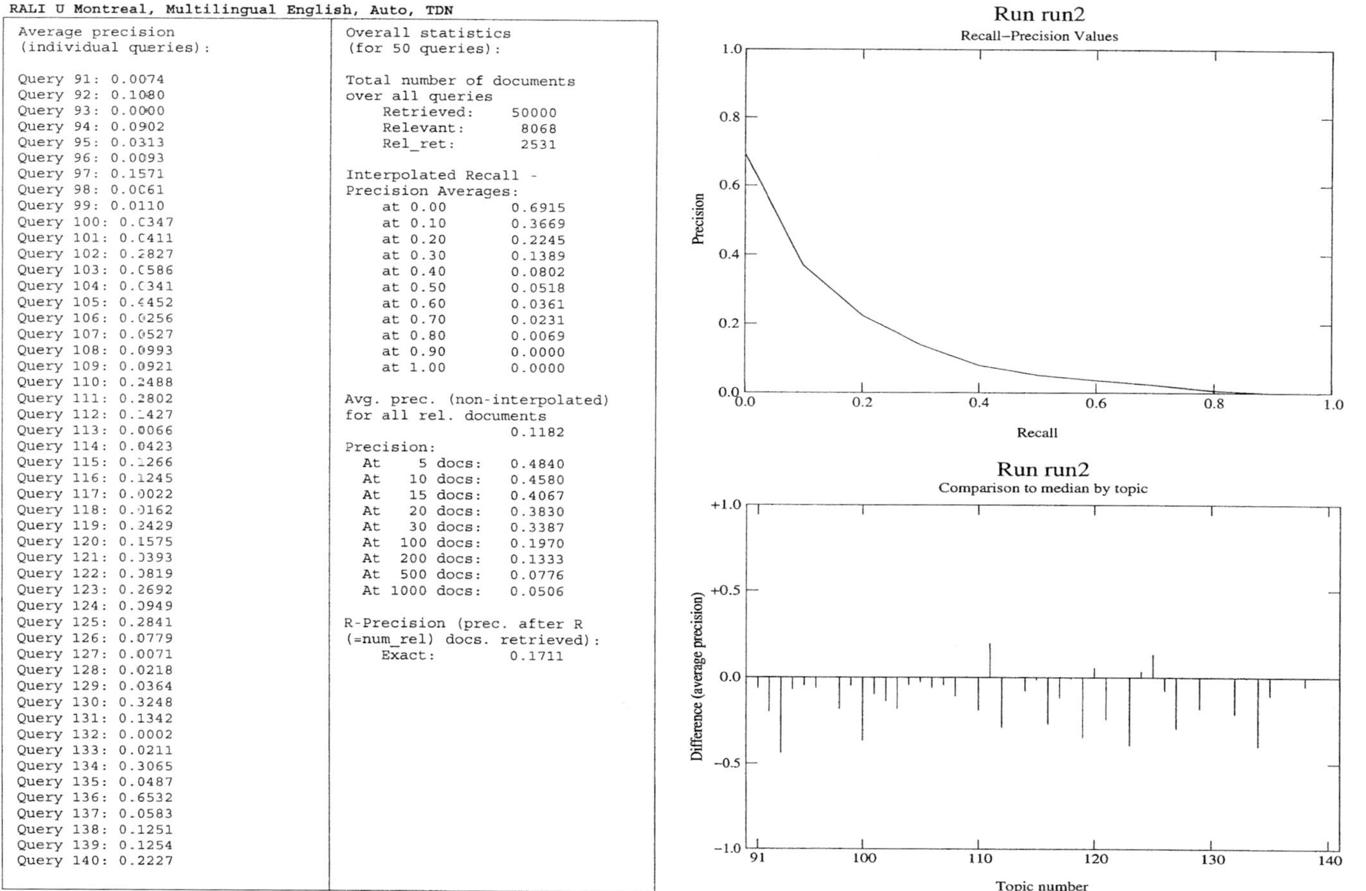

RALI U Montreal, Multilingual English, Auto, TDN

```
Average precision            Overall statistics
(individual queries):        (for 50 queries):

Query 91: 0.0074             Total number of documents
Query 92: 0.1080             over all queries
Query 93: 0.0000                 Retrieved:    50000
Query 94: 0.0902                 Relevant:      8068
Query 95: 0.0313                 Rel_ret:       2531
Query 96: 0.0093
Query 97: 0.1571             Interpolated Recall -
Query 98: 0.0061             Precision Averages:
Query 99: 0.0110                 at 0.00       0.6915
Query 100: 0.0347                at 0.10       0.3669
Query 101: 0.0411                at 0.20       0.2245
Query 102: 0.2827                at 0.30       0.1389
Query 103: 0.0586                at 0.40       0.0802
Query 104: 0.0341                at 0.50       0.0518
Query 105: 0.4452                at 0.60       0.0361
Query 106: 0.0256                at 0.70       0.0231
Query 107: 0.0527                at 0.80       0.0069
Query 108: 0.0993                at 0.90       0.0000
Query 109: 0.0921                at 1.00       0.0000
Query 110: 0.2488
Query 111: 0.2802            Avg. prec. (non-interpolated)
Query 112: 0.1427            for all rel. documents
Query 113: 0.0066                              0.1182
Query 114: 0.0423            Precision:
Query 115: 0.1266              At    5 docs:   0.4840
Query 116: 0.1245              At   10 docs:   0.4580
Query 117: 0.0022              At   15 docs:   0.4067
Query 118: 0.0162              At   20 docs:   0.3830
Query 119: 0.2429              At   30 docs:   0.3387
Query 120: 0.1575              At  100 docs:   0.1970
Query 121: 0.0393              At  200 docs:   0.1333
Query 122: 0.0819              At  500 docs:   0.0776
Query 123: 0.2692              At 1000 docs:   0.0506
Query 124: 0.0949
Query 125: 0.2841            R-Precision (prec. after R
Query 126: 0.0779            (=num_rel) docs. retrieved):
Query 127: 0.0071                Exact:        0.1711
Query 128: 0.0218
Query 129: 0.0364
Query 130: 0.3248
Query 131: 0.1342
Query 132: 0.0002
Query 133: 0.0211
Query 134: 0.3065
Query 135: 0.0487
Query 136: 0.6532
Query 137: 0.0583
Query 138: 0.1251
Query 139: 0.1254
Query 140: 0.2227
```

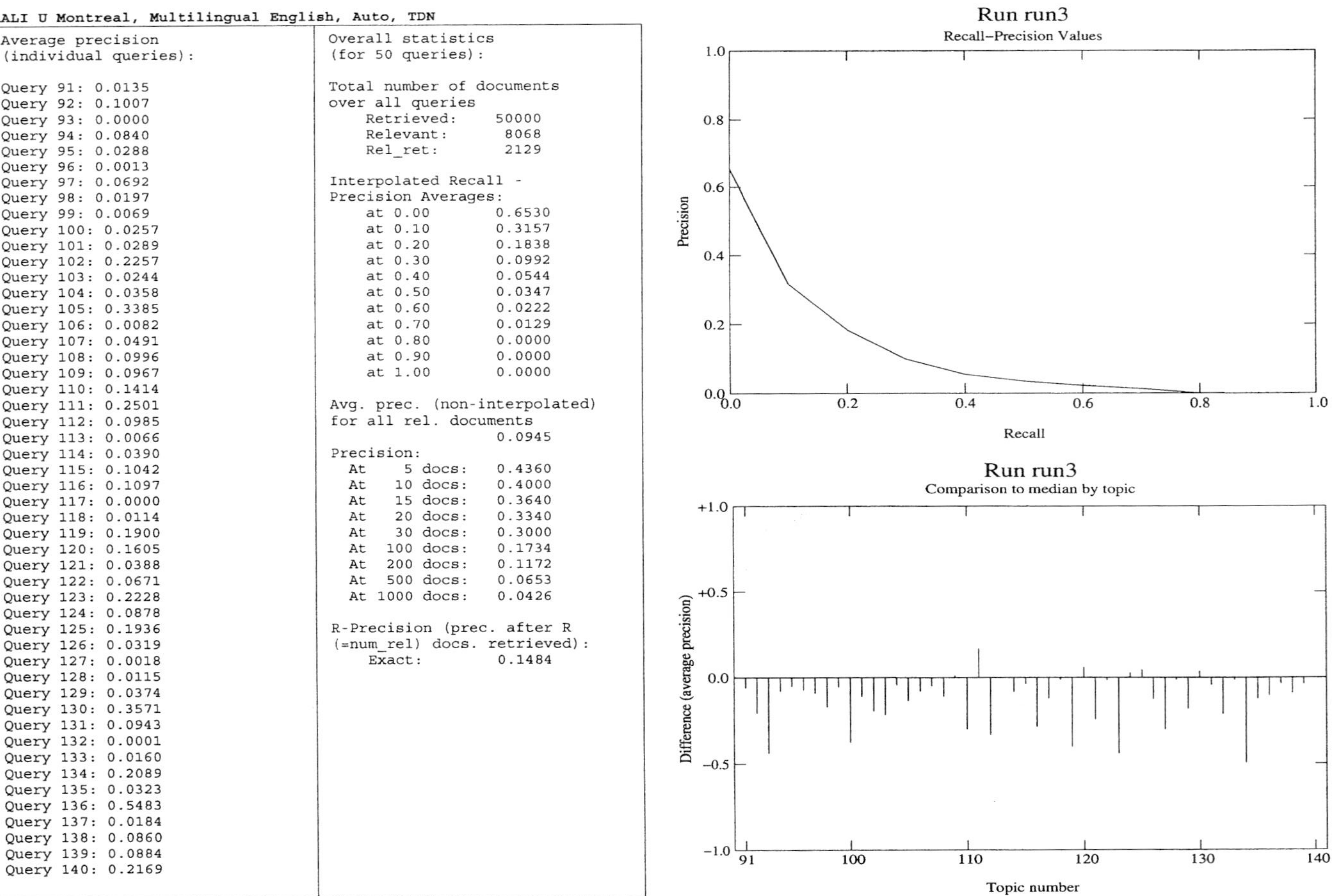

RALI U Montreal, Multilingual English, Auto, TDN

```
Average precision              Overall statistics
(individual queries):          (for 50 queries):

Query 91: 0.0135               Total number of documents
Query 92: 0.1007               over all queries
Query 93: 0.0000                   Retrieved:    50000
Query 94: 0.0840                   Relevant:      8068
Query 95: 0.0288                   Rel_ret:       2129
Query 96: 0.0013
Query 97: 0.0692               Interpolated Recall -
Query 98: 0.0197               Precision Averages:
Query 99: 0.0069                   at 0.00       0.6530
Query 100: 0.0257                  at 0.10       0.3157
Query 101: 0.0289                  at 0.20       0.1838
Query 102: 0.2257                  at 0.30       0.0992
Query 103: 0.0244                  at 0.40       0.0544
Query 104: 0.0358                  at 0.50       0.0347
Query 105: 0.3385                  at 0.60       0.0222
Query 106: 0.0082                  at 0.70       0.0129
Query 107: 0.0491                  at 0.80       0.0000
Query 108: 0.0996                  at 0.90       0.0000
Query 109: 0.0967                  at 1.00       0.0000
Query 110: 0.1414
Query 111: 0.2501              Avg. prec. (non-interpolated)
Query 112: 0.0985              for all rel. documents
Query 113: 0.0066                                0.0945
Query 114: 0.0390              Precision:
Query 115: 0.1042                At    5 docs:   0.4360
Query 116: 0.1097                At   10 docs:   0.4000
Query 117: 0.0000                At   15 docs:   0.3640
Query 118: 0.0114                At   20 docs:   0.3340
Query 119: 0.1900                At   30 docs:   0.3000
Query 120: 0.1605                At  100 docs:   0.1734
Query 121: 0.0388                At  200 docs:   0.1172
Query 122: 0.0671                At  500 docs:   0.0653
Query 123: 0.2228                At 1000 docs:   0.0426
Query 124: 0.0878
Query 125: 0.1936              R-Precision (prec. after R
Query 126: 0.0319              (=num_rel) docs. retrieved):
Query 127: 0.0018                  Exact:        0.1484
Query 128: 0.0115
Query 129: 0.0374
Query 130: 0.3571
Query 131: 0.0943
Query 132: 0.0001
Query 133: 0.0160
Query 134: 0.2089
Query 135: 0.0323
Query 136: 0.5483
Query 137: 0.0184
Query 138: 0.0860
Query 139: 0.0884
Query 140: 0.2169
```

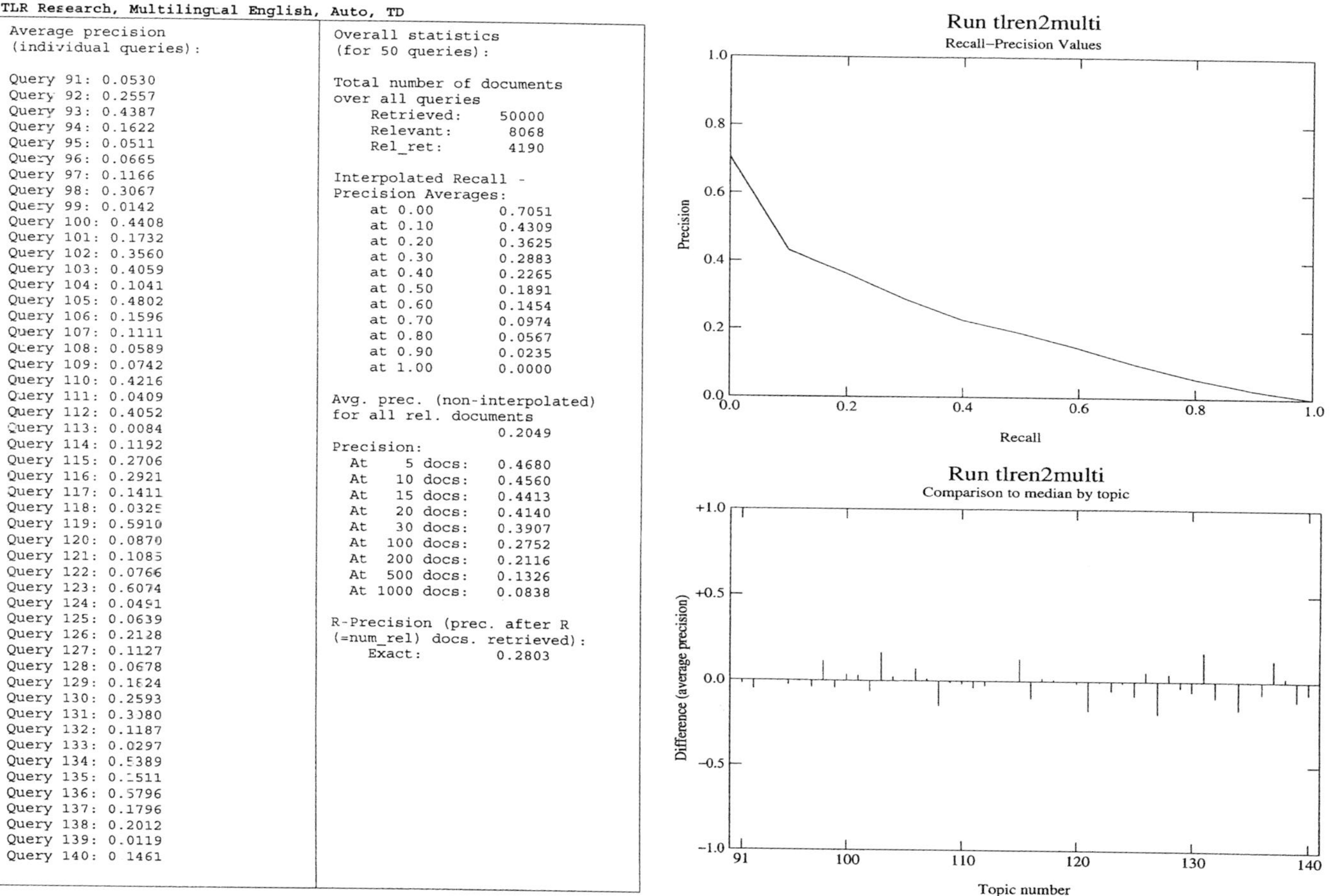

TLR Research, Multilingual English, Auto, TD

```
Average precision
(individual queries):

Query 91: 0.0530
Query 92: 0.2557
Query 93: 0.4387
Query 94: 0.1622
Query 95: 0.0511
Query 96: 0.0665
Query 97: 0.1166
Query 98: 0.3067
Query 99: 0.0142
Query 100: 0.4408
Query 101: 0.1732
Query 102: 0.3560
Query 103: 0.4059
Query 104: 0.1041
Query 105: 0.4802
Query 106: 0.1596
Query 107: 0.1111
Query 108: 0.0589
Query 109: 0.0742
Query 110: 0.4216
Query 111: 0.0409
Query 112: 0.4052
Query 113: 0.0084
Query 114: 0.1192
Query 115: 0.2706
Query 116: 0.2921
Query 117: 0.1411
Query 118: 0.0325
Query 119: 0.5910
Query 120: 0.0870
Query 121: 0.1085
Query 122: 0.0766
Query 123: 0.6074
Query 124: 0.0491
Query 125: 0.0639
Query 126: 0.2128
Query 127: 0.1127
Query 128: 0.0678
Query 129: 0.1624
Query 130: 0.2593
Query 131: 0.3080
Query 132: 0.1187
Query 133: 0.0297
Query 134: 0.5389
Query 135: 0.1511
Query 136: 0.5796
Query 137: 0.1796
Query 138: 0.2012
Query 139: 0.0119
Query 140: 0.1461
```

```
Overall statistics
(for 50 queries):

Total number of documents
over all queries
    Retrieved:     50000
    Relevant:       8068
    Rel_ret:        4190

Interpolated Recall -
Precision Averages:
    at 0.00        0.7051
    at 0.10        0.4309
    at 0.20        0.3625
    at 0.30        0.2883
    at 0.40        0.2265
    at 0.50        0.1891
    at 0.60        0.1454
    at 0.70        0.0974
    at 0.80        0.0567
    at 0.90        0.0235
    at 1.00        0.0000

Avg. prec. (non-interpolated)
for all rel. documents
                   0.2049
Precision:
  At    5 docs:    0.4680
  At   10 docs:    0.4560
  At   15 docs:    0.4413
  At   20 docs:    0.4140
  At   30 docs:    0.3907
  At  100 docs:    0.2752
  At  200 docs:    0.2116
  At  500 docs:    0.1326
  At 1000 docs:    0.0838

R-Precision (prec. after R
(=num_rel) docs. retrieved):
   Exact:          0.2803
```

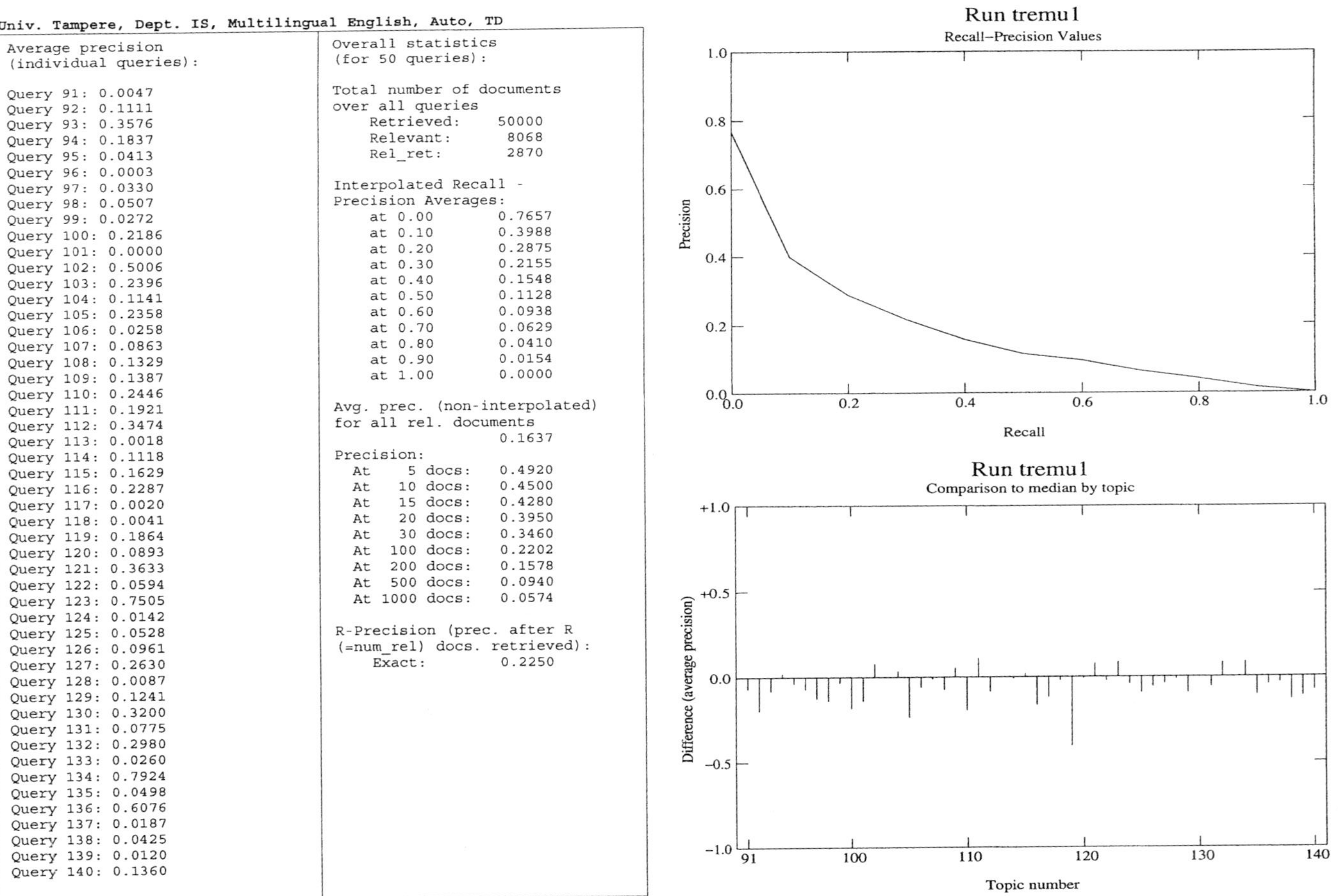

Univ. Tampere, Dept. IS, Multilingual English, Auto, TD

```
Average precision
(individual queries):

Query 91: 0.0047
Query 92: 0.1111
Query 93: 0.3576
Query 94: 0.1837
Query 95: 0.0413
Query 96: 0.0003
Query 97: 0.0330
Query 98: 0.0507
Query 99: 0.0272
Query 100: 0.2186
Query 101: 0.0000
Query 102: 0.5006
Query 103: 0.2396
Query 104: 0.1141
Query 105: 0.2358
Query 106: 0.0258
Query 107: 0.0863
Query 108: 0.1329
Query 109: 0.1387
Query 110: 0.2446
Query 111: 0.1921
Query 112: 0.3474
Query 113: 0.0018
Query 114: 0.1118
Query 115: 0.1629
Query 116: 0.2287
Query 117: 0.0020
Query 118: 0.0041
Query 119: 0.1864
Query 120: 0.0893
Query 121: 0.3633
Query 122: 0.0594
Query 123: 0.7505
Query 124: 0.0142
Query 125: 0.0528
Query 126: 0.0961
Query 127: 0.2630
Query 128: 0.0087
Query 129: 0.1241
Query 130: 0.3200
Query 131: 0.0775
Query 132: 0.2980
Query 133: 0.0260
Query 134: 0.7924
Query 135: 0.0498
Query 136: 0.6076
Query 137: 0.0187
Query 138: 0.0425
Query 139: 0.0120
Query 140: 0.1360
```

```
Overall statistics
(for 50 queries):

Total number of documents
over all queries
    Retrieved:    50000
    Relevant:      8068
    Rel_ret:       2870

Interpolated Recall -
Precision Averages:
    at 0.00       0.7657
    at 0.10       0.3988
    at 0.20       0.2875
    at 0.30       0.2155
    at 0.40       0.1548
    at 0.50       0.1128
    at 0.60       0.0938
    at 0.70       0.0629
    at 0.80       0.0410
    at 0.90       0.0154
    at 1.00       0.0000

Avg. prec. (non-interpolated)
for all rel. documents
                 0.1637

Precision:
  At    5 docs:   0.4920
  At   10 docs:   0.4500
  At   15 docs:   0.4280
  At   20 docs:   0.3950
  At   30 docs:   0.3460
  At  100 docs:   0.2202
  At  200 docs:   0.1578
  At  500 docs:   0.0940
  At 1000 docs:   0.0574

R-Precision (prec. after R
(=num_rel) docs. retrieved):
    Exact:        0.2250
```

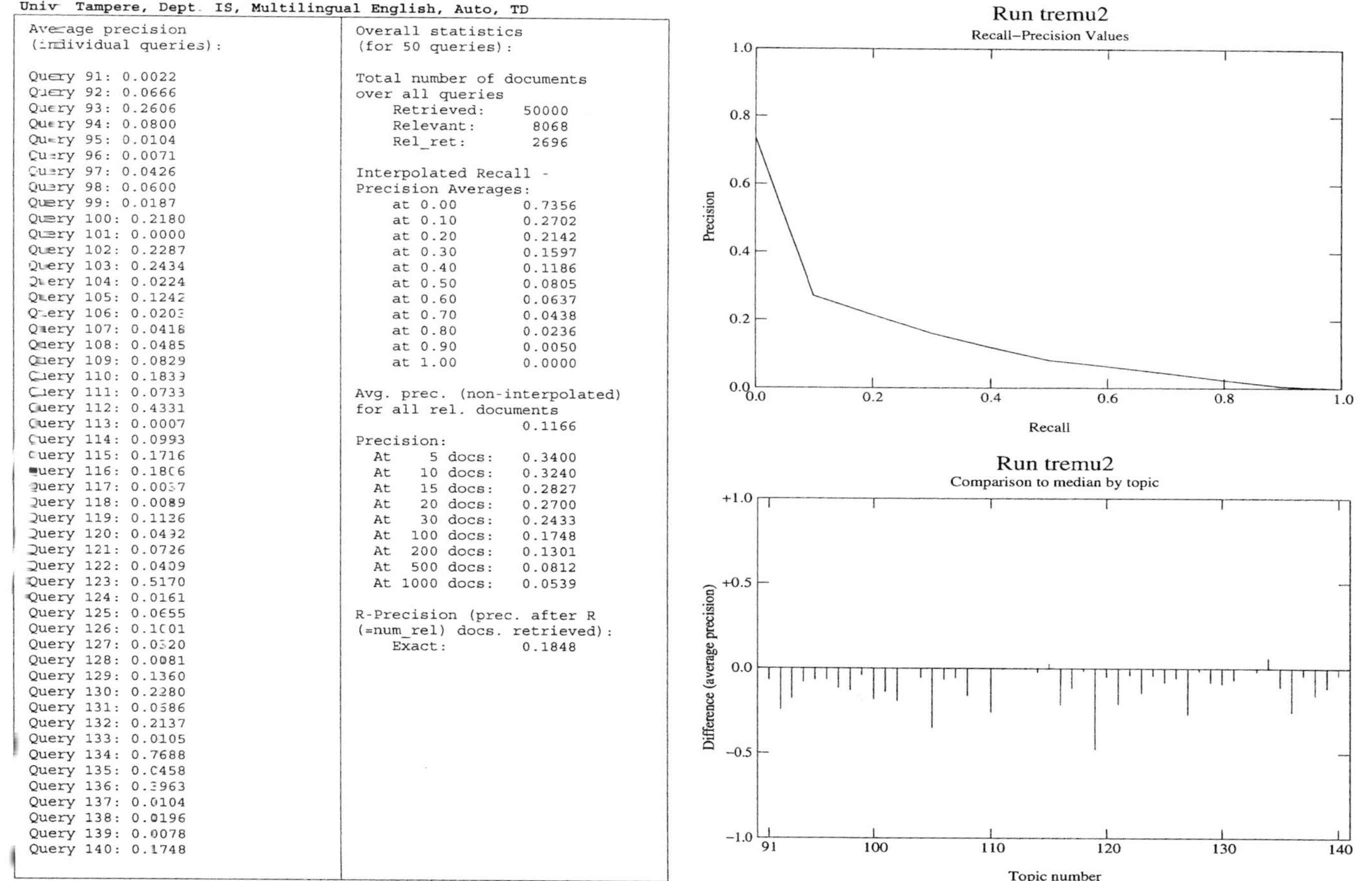

Univ. Tampere, Dept. IS, Multilingual English, Auto, TD

Average precision (individual queries):	Overall statistics (for 50 queries):
Query 91: 0.0022	Total number of documents over all queries
Query 92: 0.0666	Retrieved: 50000
Query 93: 0.2606	Relevant: 8068
Query 94: 0.0800	Rel_ret: 2696
Query 95: 0.0104	
Query 96: 0.0071	Interpolated Recall - Precision Averages:
Query 97: 0.0426	at 0.00 0.7356
Query 98: 0.0600	at 0.10 0.2702
Query 99: 0.0187	at 0.20 0.2142
Query 100: 0.2180	at 0.30 0.1597
Query 101: 0.0000	at 0.40 0.1186
Query 102: 0.2287	at 0.50 0.0805
Query 103: 0.2434	at 0.60 0.0637
Query 104: 0.0224	at 0.70 0.0438
Query 105: 0.1242	at 0.80 0.0236
Query 106: 0.0203	at 0.90 0.0050
Query 107: 0.0418	at 1.00 0.0000
Query 108: 0.0485	
Query 109: 0.0829	Avg. prec. (non-interpolated) for all rel. documents 0.1166
Query 110: 0.1839	
Query 111: 0.0733	Precision:
Query 112: 0.4331	At 5 docs: 0.3400
Query 113: 0.0007	At 10 docs: 0.3240
Query 114: 0.0993	At 15 docs: 0.2827
Query 115: 0.1716	At 20 docs: 0.2700
Query 116: 0.1806	At 30 docs: 0.2433
Query 117: 0.0037	At 100 docs: 0.1748
Query 118: 0.0089	At 200 docs: 0.1301
Query 119: 0.1126	At 500 docs: 0.0812
Query 120: 0.0492	At 1000 docs: 0.0539
Query 121: 0.0726	
Query 122: 0.0409	R-Precision (prec. after R (=num_rel) docs. retrieved):
Query 123: 0.5170	Exact: 0.1848
Query 124: 0.0161	
Query 125: 0.0655	
Query 126: 0.1001	
Query 127: 0.0320	
Query 128: 0.0081	
Query 129: 0.1360	
Query 130: 0.2280	
Query 131: 0.0586	
Query 132: 0.2137	
Query 133: 0.0105	
Query 134: 0.7688	
Query 135: 0.0458	
Query 136: 0.3963	
Query 137: 0.0104	
Query 138: 0.0196	
Query 139: 0.0078	
Query 140: 0.1748	

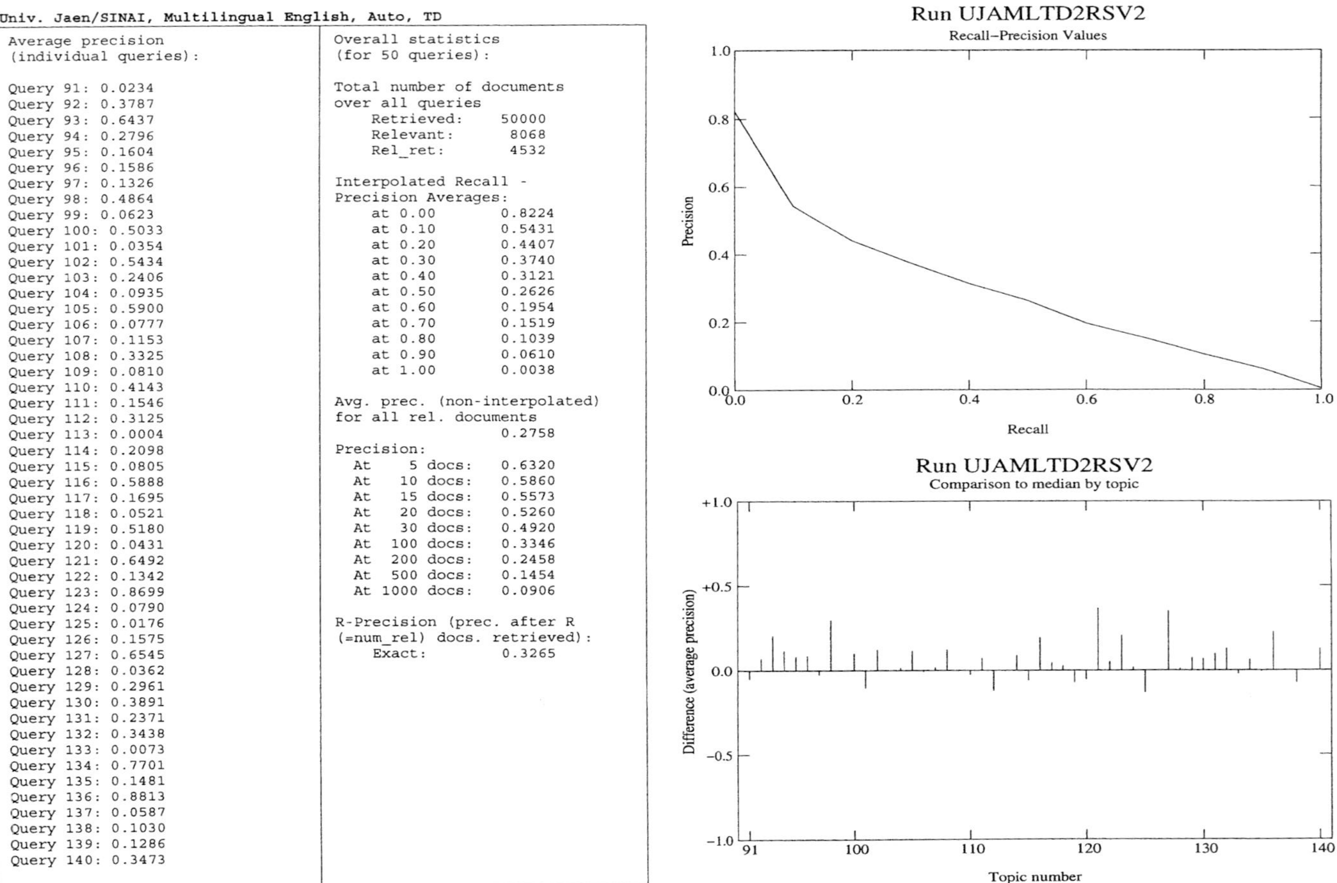

Univ. Jaen/SINAI, Multilingual English, Auto, TD

Average precision (individual queries):	Overall statistics (for 50 queries):
Query 91: 0.0234	Total number of documents over all queries
Query 92: 0.3787	Retrieved: 50000
Query 93: 0.6437	Relevant: 8068
Query 94: 0.2796	Rel_ret: 4532
Query 95: 0.1604	
Query 96: 0.1586	Interpolated Recall - Precision Averages:
Query 97: 0.1326	at 0.00 0.8224
Query 98: 0.4864	at 0.10 0.5431
Query 99: 0.0623	at 0.20 0.4407
Query 100: 0.5033	at 0.30 0.3740
Query 101: 0.0354	at 0.40 0.3121
Query 102: 0.5434	at 0.50 0.2626
Query 103: 0.2406	at 0.60 0.1954
Query 104: 0.0935	at 0.70 0.1519
Query 105: 0.5900	at 0.80 0.1039
Query 106: 0.0777	at 0.90 0.0610
Query 107: 0.1153	at 1.00 0.0038
Query 108: 0.3325	
Query 109: 0.0810	Avg. prec. (non-interpolated) for all rel. documents 0.2758
Query 110: 0.4143	
Query 111: 0.1546	Precision:
Query 112: 0.3125	At 5 docs: 0.6320
Query 113: 0.0004	At 10 docs: 0.5860
Query 114: 0.2098	At 15 docs: 0.5573
Query 115: 0.0805	At 20 docs: 0.5260
Query 116: 0.5888	At 30 docs: 0.4920
Query 117: 0.1695	At 100 docs: 0.3346
Query 118: 0.0521	At 200 docs: 0.2458
Query 119: 0.5180	At 500 docs: 0.1454
Query 120: 0.0431	At 1000 docs: 0.0906
Query 121: 0.6492	
Query 122: 0.1342	R-Precision (prec. after R (=num_rel) docs. retrieved):
Query 123: 0.8699	Exact: 0.3265
Query 124: 0.0790	
Query 125: 0.0176	
Query 126: 0.1575	
Query 127: 0.6545	
Query 128: 0.0362	
Query 129: 0.2961	
Query 130: 0.3891	
Query 131: 0.2371	
Query 132: 0.3438	
Query 133: 0.0073	
Query 134: 0.7701	
Query 135: 0.1481	
Query 136: 0.8813	
Query 137: 0.0587	
Query 138: 0.1030	
Query 139: 0.1286	
Query 140: 0.3473	

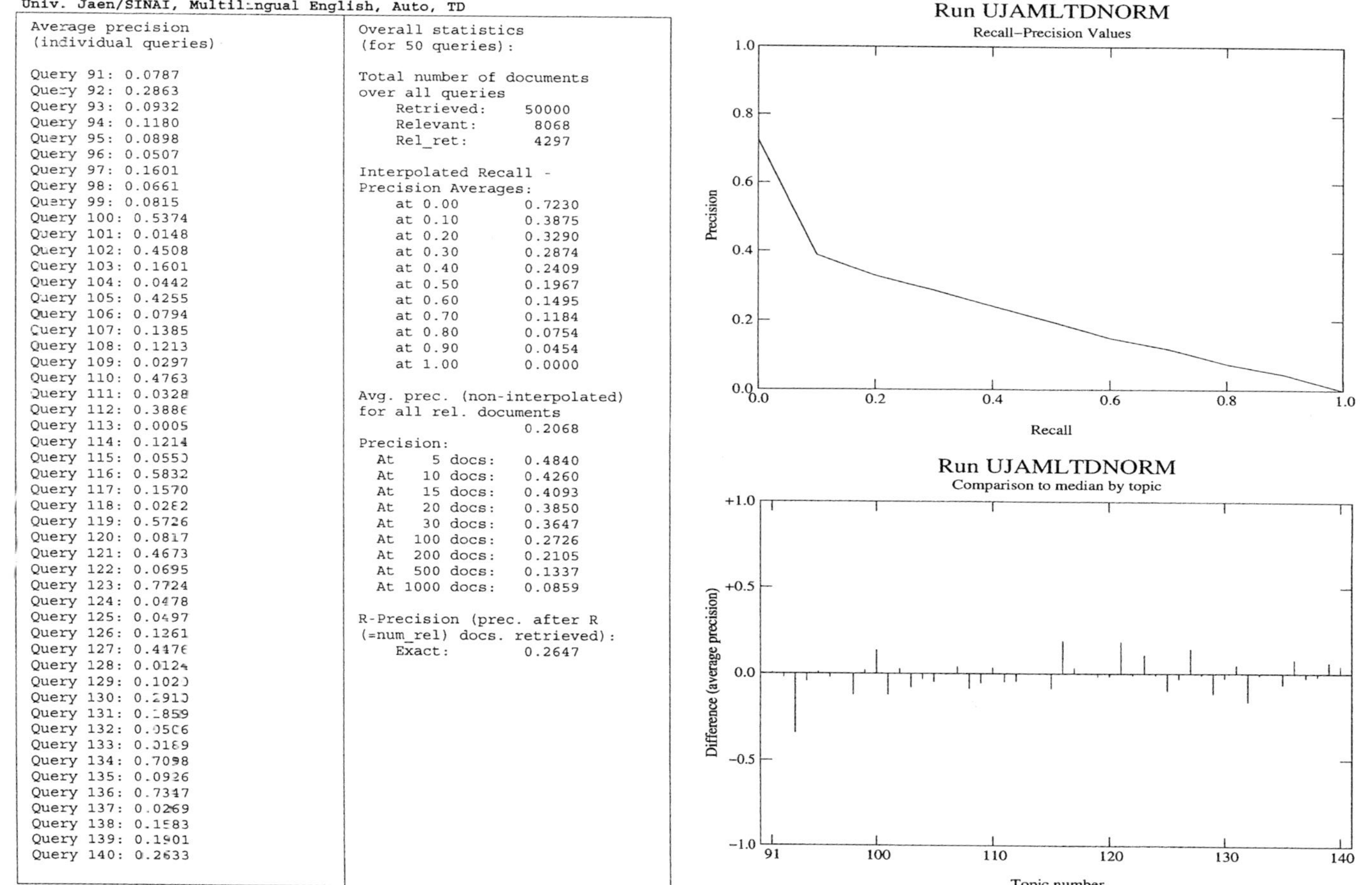

Univ. Jaen/SINAI, Multilingual English, Auto, TD

Average precision (individual queries)	
Query 91:	0.0787
Query 92:	0.2863
Query 93:	0.0932
Query 94:	0.1180
Query 95:	0.0898
Query 96:	0.0507
Query 97:	0.1601
Query 98:	0.0661
Query 99:	0.0815
Query 100:	0.5374
Query 101:	0.0148
Query 102:	0.4508
Query 103:	0.1601
Query 104:	0.0442
Query 105:	0.4255
Query 106:	0.0794
Query 107:	0.1385
Query 108:	0.1213
Query 109:	0.0297
Query 110:	0.4763
Query 111:	0.0328
Query 112:	0.3886
Query 113:	0.0005
Query 114:	0.1214
Query 115:	0.0550
Query 116:	0.5832
Query 117:	0.1570
Query 118:	0.0282
Query 119:	0.5726
Query 120:	0.0817
Query 121:	0.4673
Query 122:	0.0695
Query 123:	0.7724
Query 124:	0.0478
Query 125:	0.0497
Query 126:	0.1261
Query 127:	0.4476
Query 128:	0.0124
Query 129:	0.1020
Query 130:	0.2910
Query 131:	0.1859
Query 132:	0.0506
Query 133:	0.0169
Query 134:	0.7098
Query 135:	0.0926
Query 136:	0.7347
Query 137:	0.0269
Query 138:	0.1583
Query 139:	0.1901
Query 140:	0.2633

Overall statistics (for 50 queries):

Total number of documents over all queries

Retrieved:	50000
Relevant:	8068
Rel_ret:	4297

Interpolated Recall - Precision Averages:

at 0.00	0.7230
at 0.10	0.3875
at 0.20	0.3290
at 0.30	0.2874
at 0.40	0.2409
at 0.50	0.1967
at 0.60	0.1495
at 0.70	0.1184
at 0.80	0.0754
at 0.90	0.0454
at 1.00	0.0000

Avg. prec. (non-interpolated) for all rel. documents 0.2068

Precision:

At 5 docs:	0.4840
At 10 docs:	0.4260
At 15 docs:	0.4093
At 20 docs:	0.3850
At 30 docs:	0.3647
At 100 docs:	0.2726
At 200 docs:	0.2105
At 500 docs:	0.1337
At 1000 docs:	0.0859

R-Precision (prec. after R (=num_rel) docs. retrieved):
Exact: 0.2647

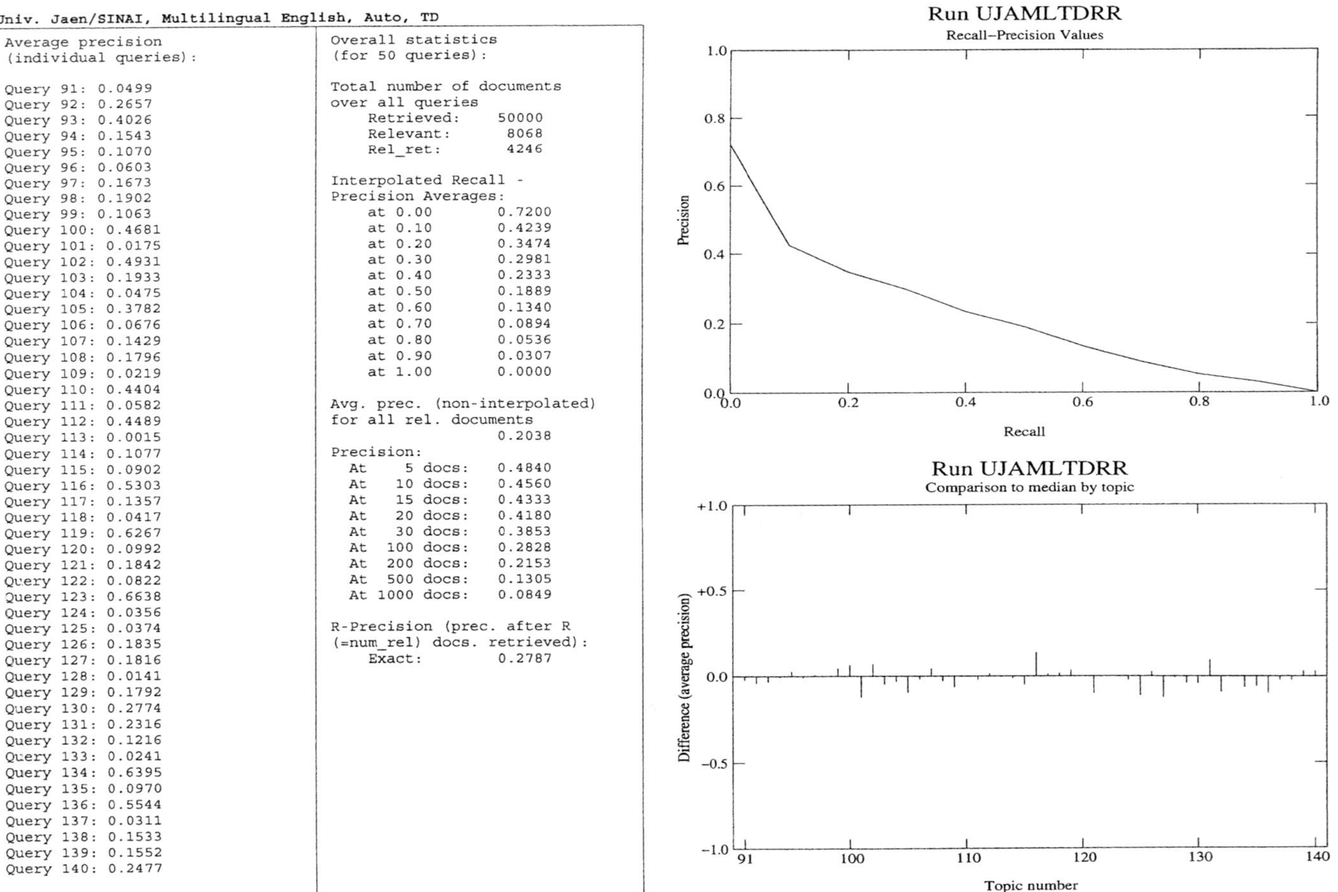

Univ. Jaen/SINAI, Multilingual English, Auto, TD

Average precision (individual queries):	Overall statistics (for 50 queries):	
Query 91: 0.0499	Total number of documents over all queries	
Query 92: 0.2657	Retrieved:	50000
Query 93: 0.4026	Relevant:	8068
Query 94: 0.1543	Rel_ret:	4246
Query 95: 0.1070		
Query 96: 0.0603	Interpolated Recall - Precision Averages:	
Query 97: 0.1673	at 0.00	0.7200
Query 98: 0.1902	at 0.10	0.4239
Query 99: 0.1063	at 0.20	0.3474
Query 100: 0.4681	at 0.30	0.2981
Query 101: 0.0175	at 0.40	0.2333
Query 102: 0.4931	at 0.50	0.1889
Query 103: 0.1933	at 0.60	0.1340
Query 104: 0.0475	at 0.70	0.0894
Query 105: 0.3782	at 0.80	0.0536
Query 106: 0.0676	at 0.90	0.0307
Query 107: 0.1429	at 1.00	0.0000
Query 108: 0.1796		
Query 109: 0.0219	Avg. prec. (non-interpolated) for all rel. documents	0.2038
Query 110: 0.4404		
Query 111: 0.0582	Precision:	
Query 112: 0.4489	At 5 docs:	0.4840
Query 113: 0.0015	At 10 docs:	0.4560
Query 114: 0.1077	At 15 docs:	0.4333
Query 115: 0.0902	At 20 docs:	0.4180
Query 116: 0.5303	At 30 docs:	0.3853
Query 117: 0.1357	At 100 docs:	0.2828
Query 118: 0.0417	At 200 docs:	0.2153
Query 119: 0.6267	At 500 docs:	0.1305
Query 120: 0.0992	At 1000 docs:	0.0849
Query 121: 0.1842		
Query 122: 0.0822	R-Precision (prec. after R (=num_rel) docs. retrieved):	
Query 123: 0.6638	Exact:	0.2787
Query 124: 0.0356		
Query 125: 0.0374		
Query 126: 0.1835		
Query 127: 0.1816		
Query 128: 0.0141		
Query 129: 0.1792		
Query 130: 0.2774		
Query 131: 0.2316		
Query 132: 0.1216		
Query 133: 0.0241		
Query 134: 0.6395		
Query 135: 0.0970		
Query 136: 0.5544		
Query 137: 0.0311		
Query 138: 0.1533		
Query 139: 0.1552		
Query 140: 0.2477		

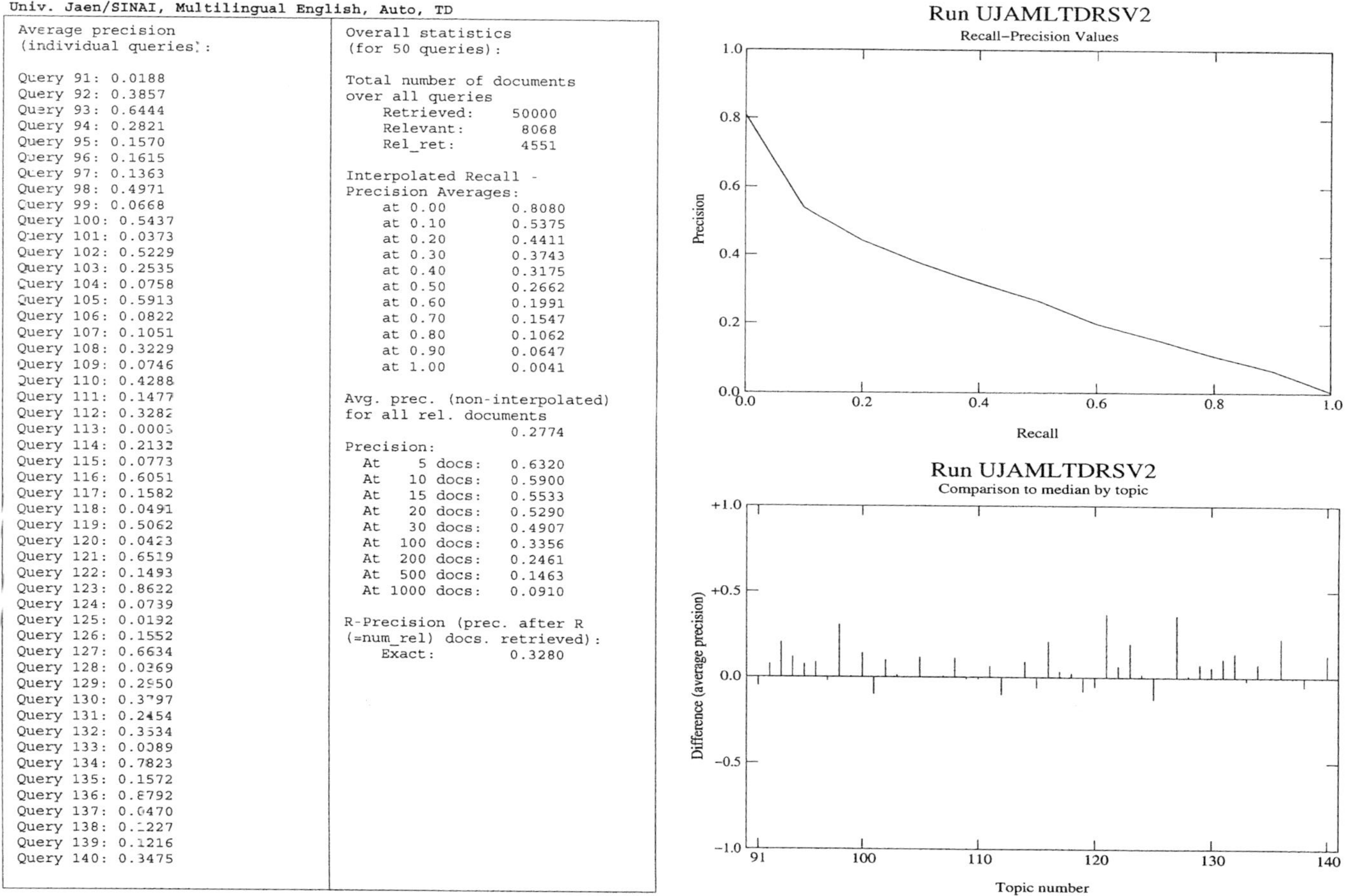

Univ. Jaen/SINAI, Multilingual English, Auto, TD

Average precision (individual queries):	Overall statistics (for 50 queries):
Query 91: 0.0188	Total number of documents over all queries
Query 92: 0.3857	Retrieved: 50000
Query 93: 0.6444	Relevant: 8068
Query 94: 0.2821	Rel_ret: 4551
Query 95: 0.1570	
Query 96: 0.1615	Interpolated Recall - Precision Averages:
Query 97: 0.1363	at 0.00 0.8080
Query 98: 0.4971	at 0.10 0.5375
Query 99: 0.0668	at 0.20 0.4411
Query 100: 0.5437	at 0.30 0.3743
Query 101: 0.0373	at 0.40 0.3175
Query 102: 0.5229	at 0.50 0.2662
Query 103: 0.2535	at 0.60 0.1991
Query 104: 0.0758	at 0.70 0.1547
Query 105: 0.5913	at 0.80 0.1062
Query 106: 0.0822	at 0.90 0.0647
Query 107: 0.1051	at 1.00 0.0041
Query 108: 0.3229	
Query 109: 0.0746	Avg. prec. (non-interpolated) for all rel. documents 0.2774
Query 110: 0.4288	
Query 111: 0.1477	Precision:
Query 112: 0.3282	At 5 docs: 0.6320
Query 113: 0.0005	At 10 docs: 0.5900
Query 114: 0.2132	At 15 docs: 0.5533
Query 115: 0.0773	At 20 docs: 0.5290
Query 116: 0.6051	At 30 docs: 0.4907
Query 117: 0.1582	At 100 docs: 0.3356
Query 118: 0.0491	At 200 docs: 0.2461
Query 119: 0.5062	At 500 docs: 0.1463
Query 120: 0.0423	At 1000 docs: 0.0910
Query 121: 0.6519	
Query 122: 0.1493	R-Precision (prec. after R (=num_rel) docs. retrieved):
Query 123: 0.8622	Exact: 0.3280
Query 124: 0.0739	
Query 125: 0.0192	
Query 126: 0.1552	
Query 127: 0.6634	
Query 128: 0.0369	
Query 129: 0.2950	
Query 130: 0.3797	
Query 131: 0.2454	
Query 132: 0.3534	
Query 133: 0.0089	
Query 134: 0.7823	
Query 135: 0.1572	
Query 136: 0.8792	
Query 137: 0.0470	
Query 138: 0.1227	
Query 139: 0.1216	
Query 140: 0.3475	

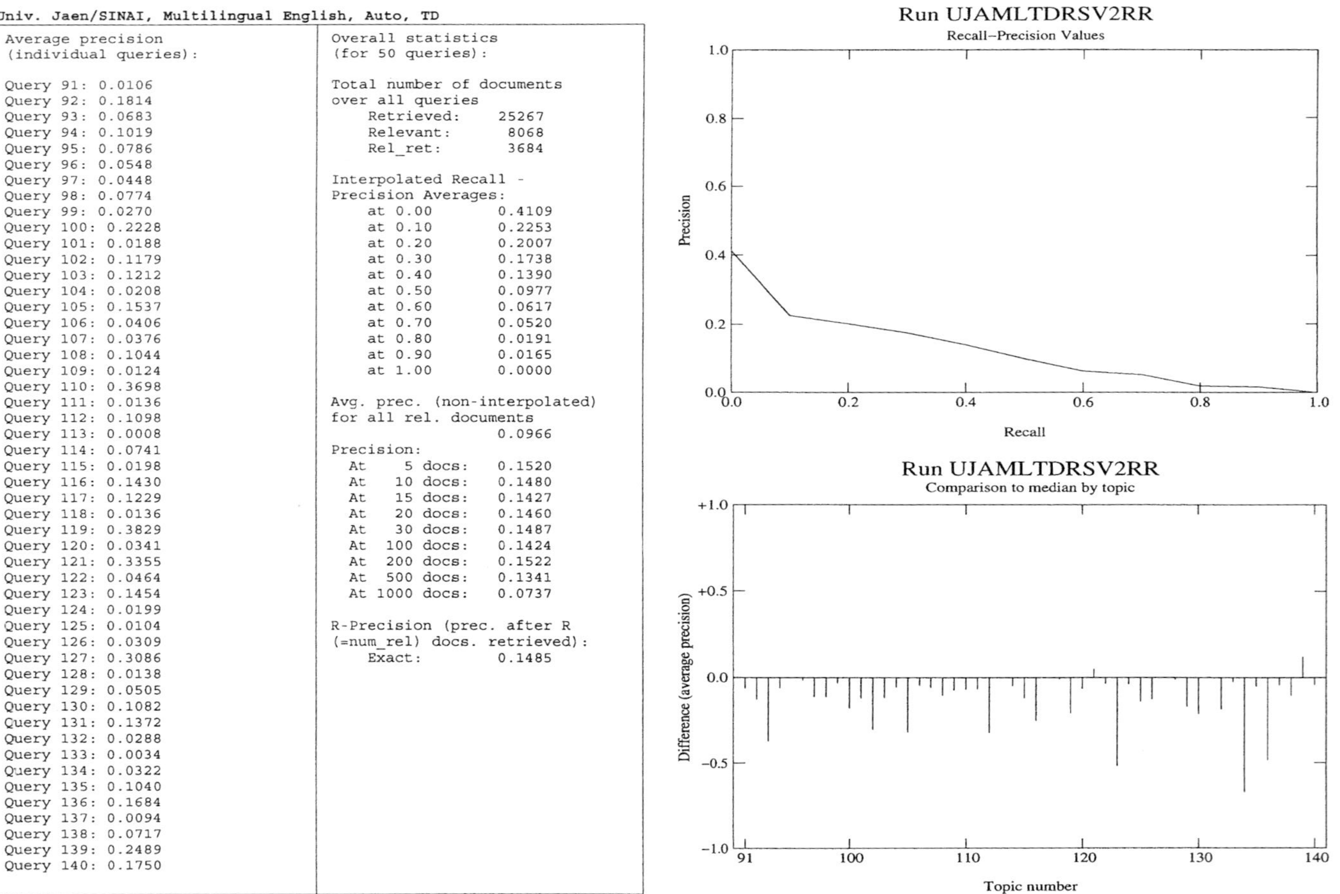

Univ. Jaen/SINAI, Multilingual English, Auto, TD

```
Average precision                 Overall statistics
(individual queries):             (for 50 queries):

Query 91: 0.0106                  Total number of documents
Query 92: 0.1814                  over all queries
Query 93: 0.0683                      Retrieved:    25267
Query 94: 0.1019                      Relevant:      8068
Query 95: 0.0786                      Rel_ret:       3684
Query 96: 0.0548
Query 97: 0.0448                  Interpolated Recall -
Query 98: 0.0774                  Precision Averages:
Query 99: 0.0270                      at 0.00        0.4109
Query 100: 0.2228                     at 0.10        0.2253
Query 101: 0.0188                     at 0.20        0.2007
Query 102: 0.1179                     at 0.30        0.1738
Query 103: 0.1212                     at 0.40        0.1390
Query 104: 0.0208                     at 0.50        0.0977
Query 105: 0.1537                     at 0.60        0.0617
Query 106: 0.0406                     at 0.70        0.0520
Query 107: 0.0376                     at 0.80        0.0191
Query 108: 0.1044                     at 0.90        0.0165
Query 109: 0.0124                     at 1.00        0.0000
Query 110: 0.3698
Query 111: 0.0136                 Avg. prec. (non-interpolated)
Query 112: 0.1098                 for all rel. documents
Query 113: 0.0008                                    0.0966
Query 114: 0.0741                 Precision:
Query 115: 0.0198                   At    5 docs:    0.1520
Query 116: 0.1430                   At   10 docs:    0.1480
Query 117: 0.1229                   At   15 docs:    0.1427
Query 118: 0.0136                   At   20 docs:    0.1460
Query 119: 0.3829                   At   30 docs:    0.1487
Query 120: 0.0341                   At  100 docs:    0.1424
Query 121: 0.3355                   At  200 docs:    0.1522
Query 122: 0.0464                   At  500 docs:    0.1341
Query 123: 0.1454                   At 1000 docs:    0.0737
Query 124: 0.0199
Query 125: 0.0104                 R-Precision (prec. after R
Query 126: 0.0309                 (=num_rel) docs. retrieved):
Query 127: 0.3086                     Exact:         0.1485
Query 128: 0.0138
Query 129: 0.0505
Query 130: 0.1082
Query 131: 0.1372
Query 132: 0.0288
Query 133: 0.0034
Query 134: 0.0322
Query 135: 0.1040
Query 136: 0.1684
Query 137: 0.0094
Query 138: 0.0717
Query 139: 0.2489
Query 140: 0.1750
```

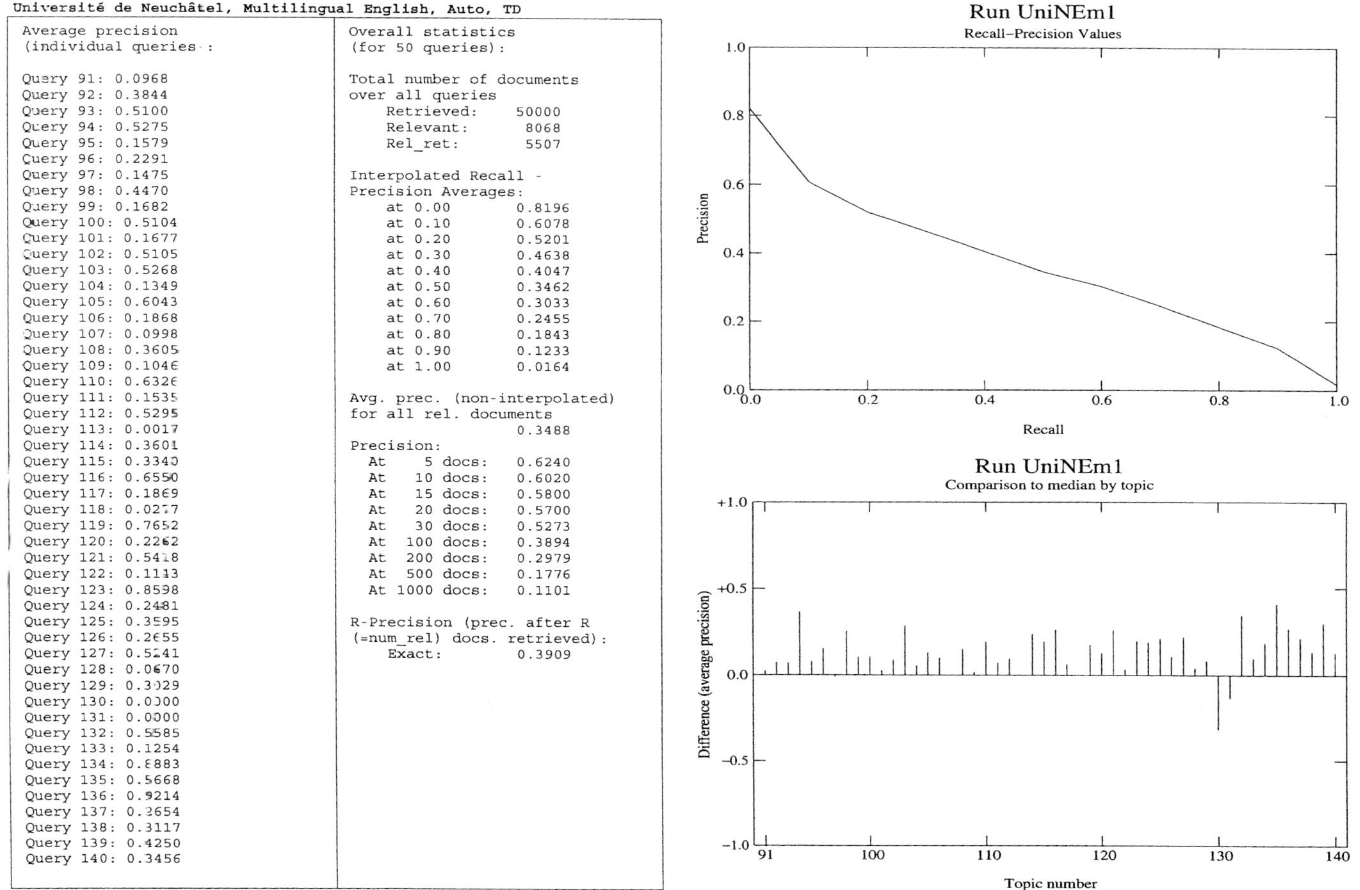

Université de Neuchâtel, Multilingual English, Auto, TD

Average precision (individual queries):	Overall statistics (for 50 queries):
Query 91: 0.0968	Total number of documents over all queries
Query 92: 0.3844	Retrieved: 50000
Query 93: 0.5100	Relevant: 8068
Query 94: 0.5275	Rel_ret: 5507
Query 95: 0.1579	
Query 96: 0.2291	Interpolated Recall - Precision Averages:
Query 97: 0.1475	at 0.00 0.8196
Query 98: 0.4470	at 0.10 0.6078
Query 99: 0.1682	at 0.20 0.5201
Query 100: 0.5104	at 0.30 0.4638
Query 101: 0.1677	at 0.40 0.4047
Query 102: 0.5105	at 0.50 0.3462
Query 103: 0.5268	at 0.60 0.3033
Query 104: 0.1349	at 0.70 0.2455
Query 105: 0.6043	at 0.80 0.1843
Query 106: 0.1868	at 0.90 0.1233
Query 107: 0.0998	at 1.00 0.0164
Query 108: 0.3605	
Query 109: 0.1046	Avg. prec. (non-interpolated) for all rel. documents 0.3488
Query 110: 0.6326	
Query 111: 0.1535	Precision:
Query 112: 0.5295	At 5 docs: 0.6240
Query 113: 0.0017	At 10 docs: 0.6020
Query 114: 0.3601	At 15 docs: 0.5800
Query 115: 0.3340	At 20 docs: 0.5700
Query 116: 0.6550	At 30 docs: 0.5273
Query 117: 0.1869	At 100 docs: 0.3894
Query 118: 0.0277	At 200 docs: 0.2979
Query 119: 0.7652	At 500 docs: 0.1776
Query 120: 0.2262	At 1000 docs: 0.1101
Query 121: 0.5418	
Query 122: 0.1113	R-Precision (prec. after R (=num_rel) docs. retrieved):
Query 123: 0.8598	Exact: 0.3909
Query 124: 0.2481	
Query 125: 0.3595	
Query 126: 0.2655	
Query 127: 0.5241	
Query 128: 0.0670	
Query 129: 0.3029	
Query 130: 0.0000	
Query 131: 0.0000	
Query 132: 0.5585	
Query 133: 0.1254	
Query 134: 0.8883	
Query 135: 0.5668	
Query 136: 0.9214	
Query 137: 0.3654	
Query 138: 0.3117	
Query 139: 0.4250	
Query 140: 0.3456	

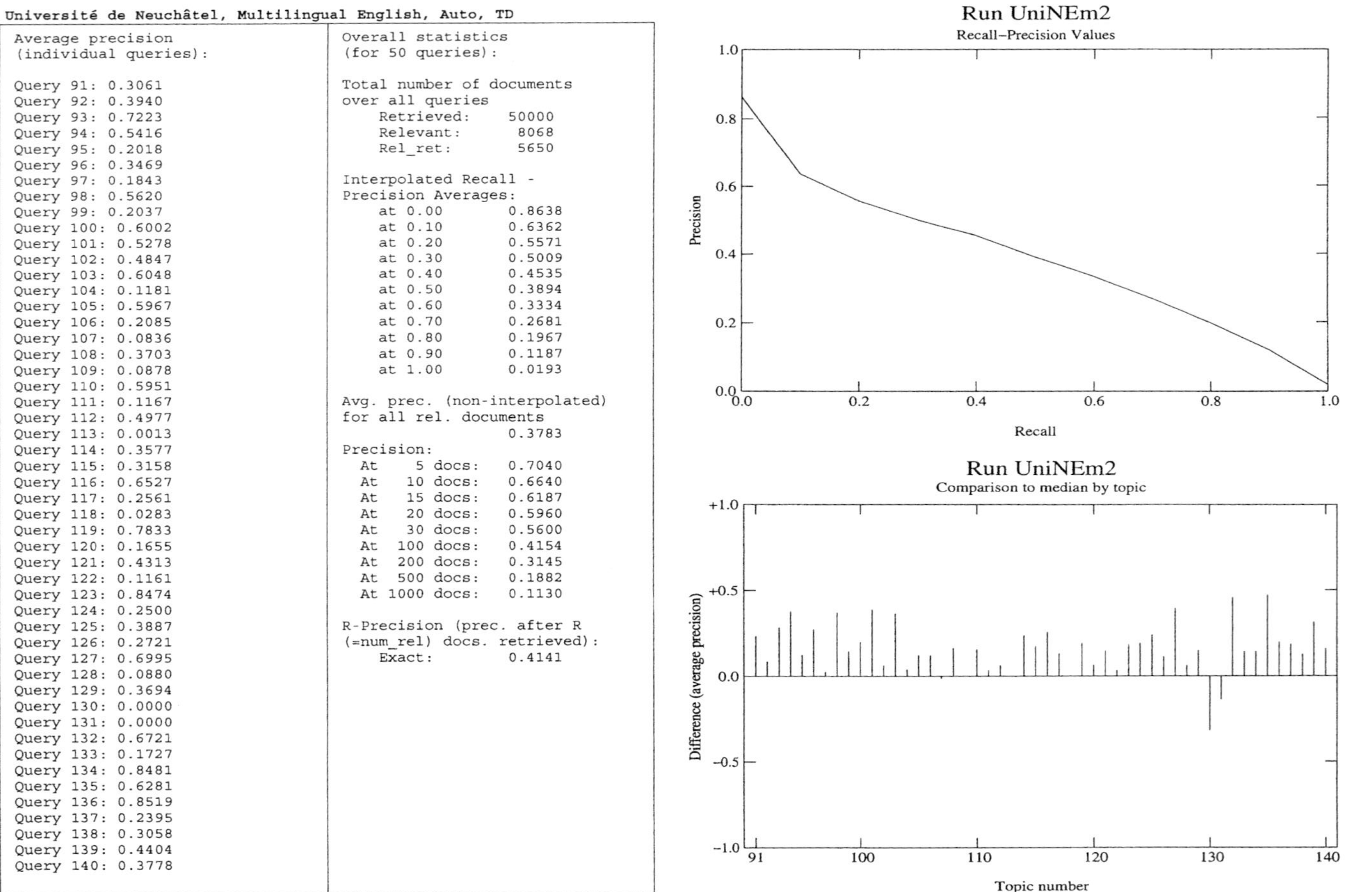

Université de Neuchâtel, Multilingual English, Auto, TD

```
Average precision                 Overall statistics
(individual queries):             (for 50 queries):

Query 91: 0.3061                  Total number of documents
Query 92: 0.3940                  over all queries
Query 93: 0.7223                      Retrieved:    50000
Query 94: 0.5416                      Relevant:      8068
Query 95: 0.2018                      Rel_ret:       5650
Query 96: 0.3469
Query 97: 0.1843                  Interpolated Recall -
Query 98: 0.5620                  Precision Averages:
Query 99: 0.2037                       at 0.00       0.8638
Query 100: 0.6002                      at 0.10       0.6362
Query 101: 0.5278                      at 0.20       0.5571
Query 102: 0.4847                      at 0.30       0.5009
Query 103: 0.6048                      at 0.40       0.4535
Query 104: 0.1181                      at 0.50       0.3894
Query 105: 0.5967                      at 0.60       0.3334
Query 106: 0.2085                      at 0.70       0.2681
Query 107: 0.0836                      at 0.80       0.1967
Query 108: 0.3703                      at 0.90       0.1187
Query 109: 0.0878                      at 1.00       0.0193
Query 110: 0.5951
Query 111: 0.1167                 Avg. prec. (non-interpolated)
Query 112: 0.4977                 for all rel. documents
Query 113: 0.0013                                    0.3783
Query 114: 0.3577                 Precision:
Query 115: 0.3158                   At    5 docs:    0.7040
Query 116: 0.6527                   At   10 docs:    0.6640
Query 117: 0.2561                   At   15 docs:    0.6187
Query 118: 0.0283                   At   20 docs:    0.5960
Query 119: 0.7833                   At   30 docs:    0.5600
Query 120: 0.1655                   At  100 docs:    0.4154
Query 121: 0.4313                   At  200 docs:    0.3145
Query 122: 0.1161                   At  500 docs:    0.1882
Query 123: 0.8474                   At 1000 docs:    0.1130
Query 124: 0.2500
Query 125: 0.3887                 R-Precision (prec. after R
Query 126: 0.2721                 (=num_rel) docs. retrieved):
Query 127: 0.6995                     Exact:         0.4141
Query 128: 0.0880
Query 129: 0.3694
Query 130: 0.0000
Query 131: 0.0000
Query 132: 0.6721
Query 133: 0.1727
Query 134: 0.8481
Query 135: 0.6281
Query 136: 0.8519
Query 137: 0.2395
Query 138: 0.3058
Query 139: 0.4404
Query 140: 0.3778
```

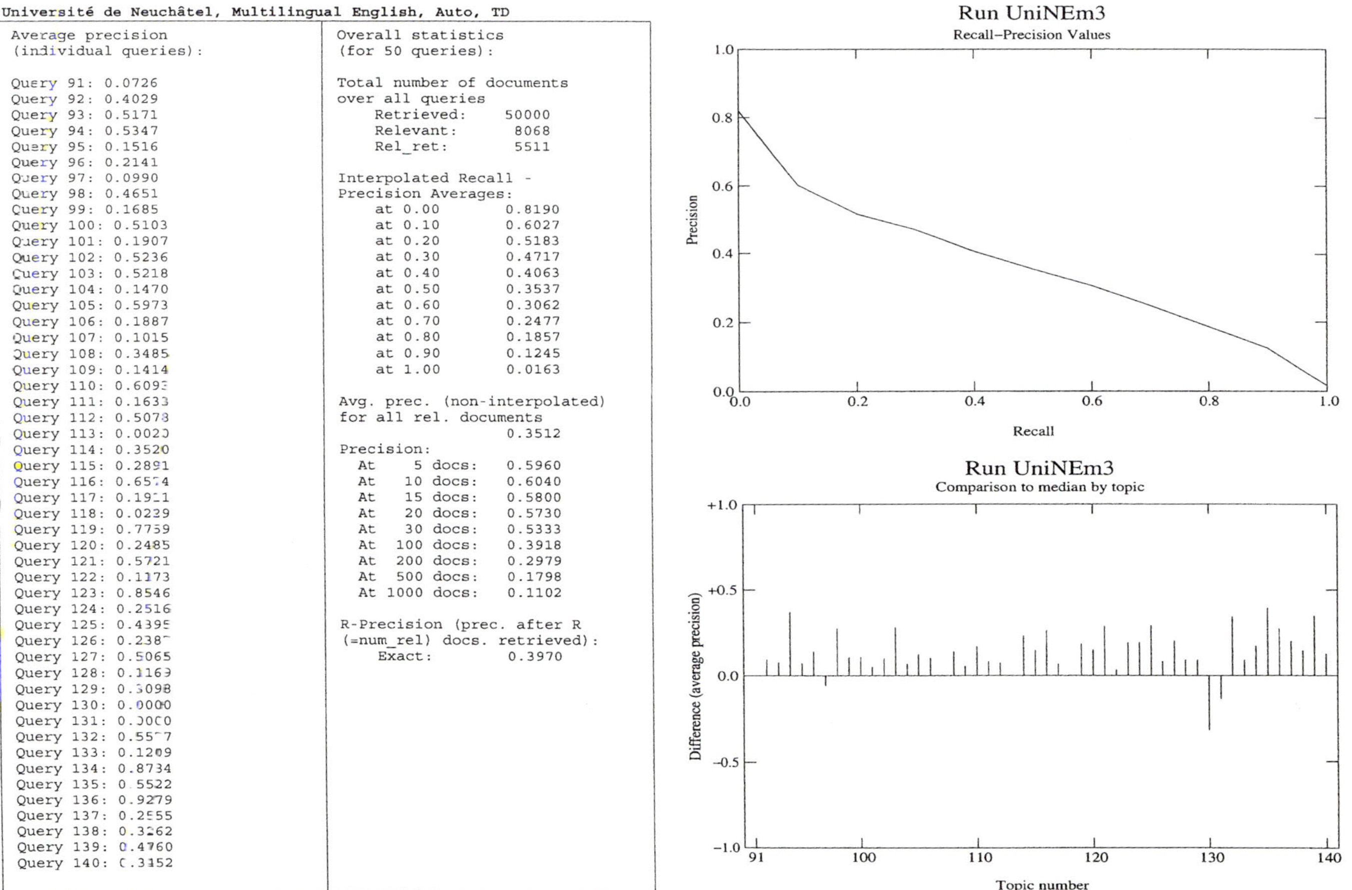

Université de Neuchâtel, Multilingual English, Auto, TD

```
Average precision             Overall statistics
(individual queries):         (for 50 queries):

Query 91: 0.0726              Total number of documents
Query 92: 0.4029              over all queries
Query 93: 0.5171                  Retrieved:    50000
Query 94: 0.5347                  Relevant:      8068
Query 95: 0.1516                  Rel_ret:       5511
Query 96: 0.2141
Query 97: 0.0990              Interpolated Recall -
Query 98: 0.4651              Precision Averages:
Query 99: 0.1685                  at 0.00       0.8190
Query 100: 0.5103                 at 0.10       0.6027
Query 101: 0.1907                 at 0.20       0.5183
Query 102: 0.5236                 at 0.30       0.4717
Query 103: 0.5218                 at 0.40       0.4063
Query 104: 0.1470                 at 0.50       0.3537
Query 105: 0.5973                 at 0.60       0.3062
Query 106: 0.1887                 at 0.70       0.2477
Query 107: 0.1015                 at 0.80       0.1857
Query 108: 0.3485                 at 0.90       0.1245
Query 109: 0.1414                 at 1.00       0.0163
Query 110: 0.6093
Query 111: 0.1633             Avg. prec. (non-interpolated)
Query 112: 0.5078             for all rel. documents
Query 113: 0.0020                               0.3512
Query 114: 0.3520
Query 115: 0.2891             Precision:
Query 116: 0.6574               At    5 docs:   0.5960
Query 117: 0.1911               At   10 docs:   0.6040
Query 118: 0.0239               At   15 docs:   0.5800
Query 119: 0.7759               At   20 docs:   0.5730
Query 120: 0.2485               At   30 docs:   0.5333
Query 121: 0.5721               At  100 docs:   0.3918
Query 122: 0.1173               At  200 docs:   0.2979
Query 123: 0.8546               At  500 docs:   0.1798
Query 124: 0.2516               At 1000 docs:   0.1102
Query 125: 0.4395
Query 126: 0.2387             R-Precision (prec. after R
Query 127: 0.5065             (=num_rel) docs. retrieved):
Query 128: 0.1169                 Exact:        0.3970
Query 129: 0.3098
Query 130: 0.0000
Query 131: 0.0000
Query 132: 0.5577
Query 133: 0.1209
Query 134: 0.8734
Query 135: 0.5522
Query 136: 0.9279
Query 137: 0.2555
Query 138: 0.3262
Query 139: 0.4760
Query 140: 0.3152
```

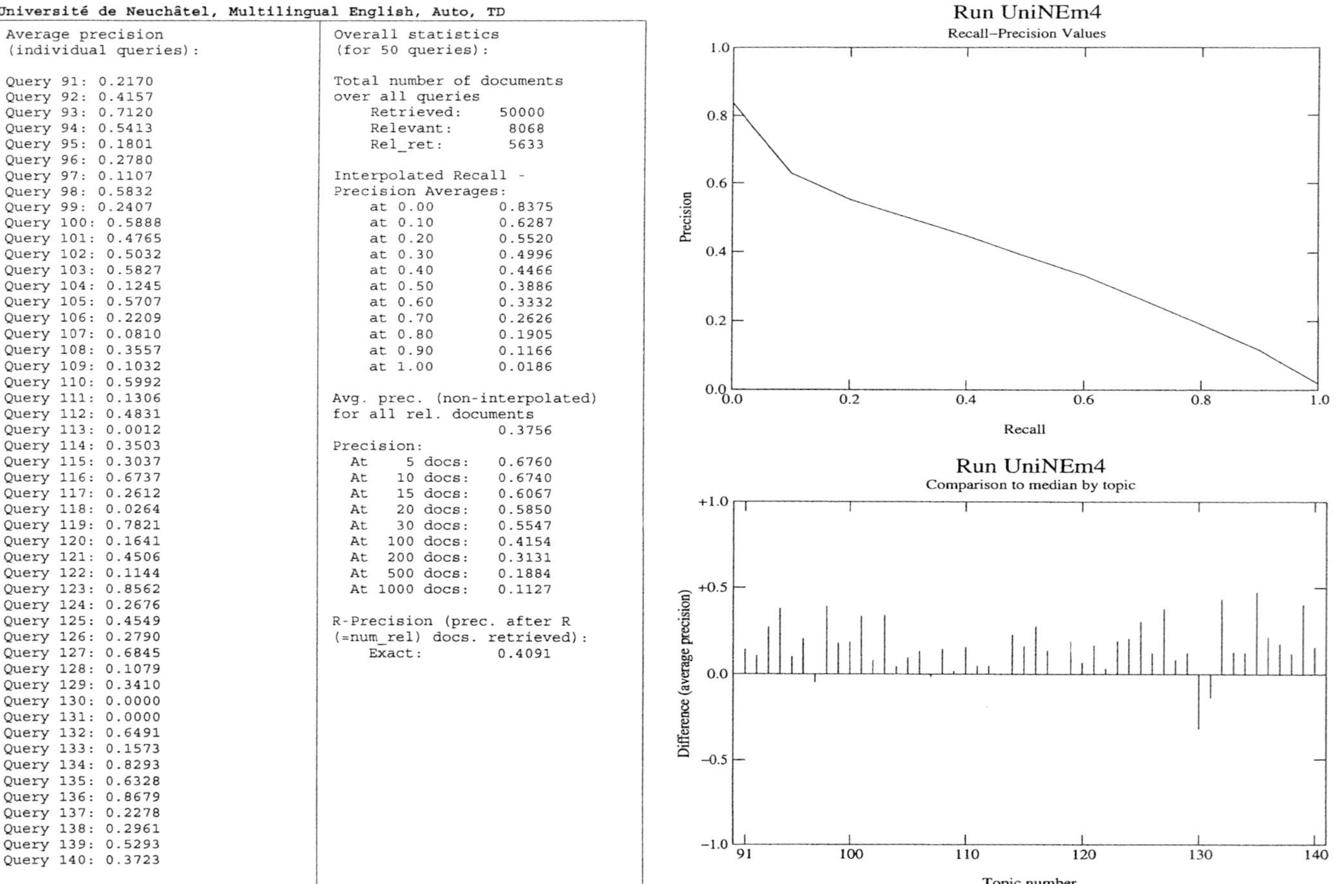

Université de Neuchâtel, Multilingual English, Auto, TD

```
Average precision                   Overall statistics
(individual queries):               (for 50 queries):

Query 91: 0.2170                    Total number of documents
Query 92: 0.4157                    over all queries
Query 93: 0.7120                        Retrieved:     50000
Query 94: 0.5413                        Relevant:       8068
Query 95: 0.1801                        Rel_ret:        5633
Query 96: 0.2780
Query 97: 0.1107                    Interpolated Recall -
Query 98: 0.5832                    Precision Averages:
Query 99: 0.2407                        at 0.00       0.8375
Query 100: 0.5888                       at 0.10       0.6287
Query 101: 0.4765                       at 0.20       0.5520
Query 102: 0.5032                       at 0.30       0.4996
Query 103: 0.5827                       at 0.40       0.4466
Query 104: 0.1245                       at 0.50       0.3886
Query 105: 0.5707                       at 0.60       0.3332
Query 106: 0.2209                       at 0.70       0.2626
Query 107: 0.0810                       at 0.80       0.1905
Query 108: 0.3557                       at 0.90       0.1166
Query 109: 0.1032                       at 1.00       0.0186
Query 110: 0.5992
Query 111: 0.1306                   Avg. prec. (non-interpolated)
Query 112: 0.4831                   for all rel. documents
Query 113: 0.0012                                     0.3756
Query 114: 0.3503                   Precision:
Query 115: 0.3037                     At    5 docs:   0.6760
Query 116: 0.6737                     At   10 docs:   0.6740
Query 117: 0.2612                     At   15 docs:   0.6067
Query 118: 0.0264                     At   20 docs:   0.5850
Query 119: 0.7821                     At   30 docs:   0.5547
Query 120: 0.1641                     At  100 docs:   0.4154
Query 121: 0.4506                     At  200 docs:   0.3131
Query 122: 0.1144                     At  500 docs:   0.1884
Query 123: 0.8562                     At 1000 docs:   0.1127
Query 124: 0.2676
Query 125: 0.4549                   R-Precision (prec. after R
Query 126: 0.2790                   (=num_rel) docs. retrieved):
Query 127: 0.6845                       Exact:        0.4091
Query 128: 0.1079
Query 129: 0.3410
Query 130: 0.0000
Query 131: 0.0000
Query 132: 0.6491
Query 133: 0.1573
Query 134: 0.8293
Query 135: 0.6328
Query 136: 0.8679
Query 137: 0.2278
Query 138: 0.2961
Query 139: 0.5293
Query 140: 0.3723
```

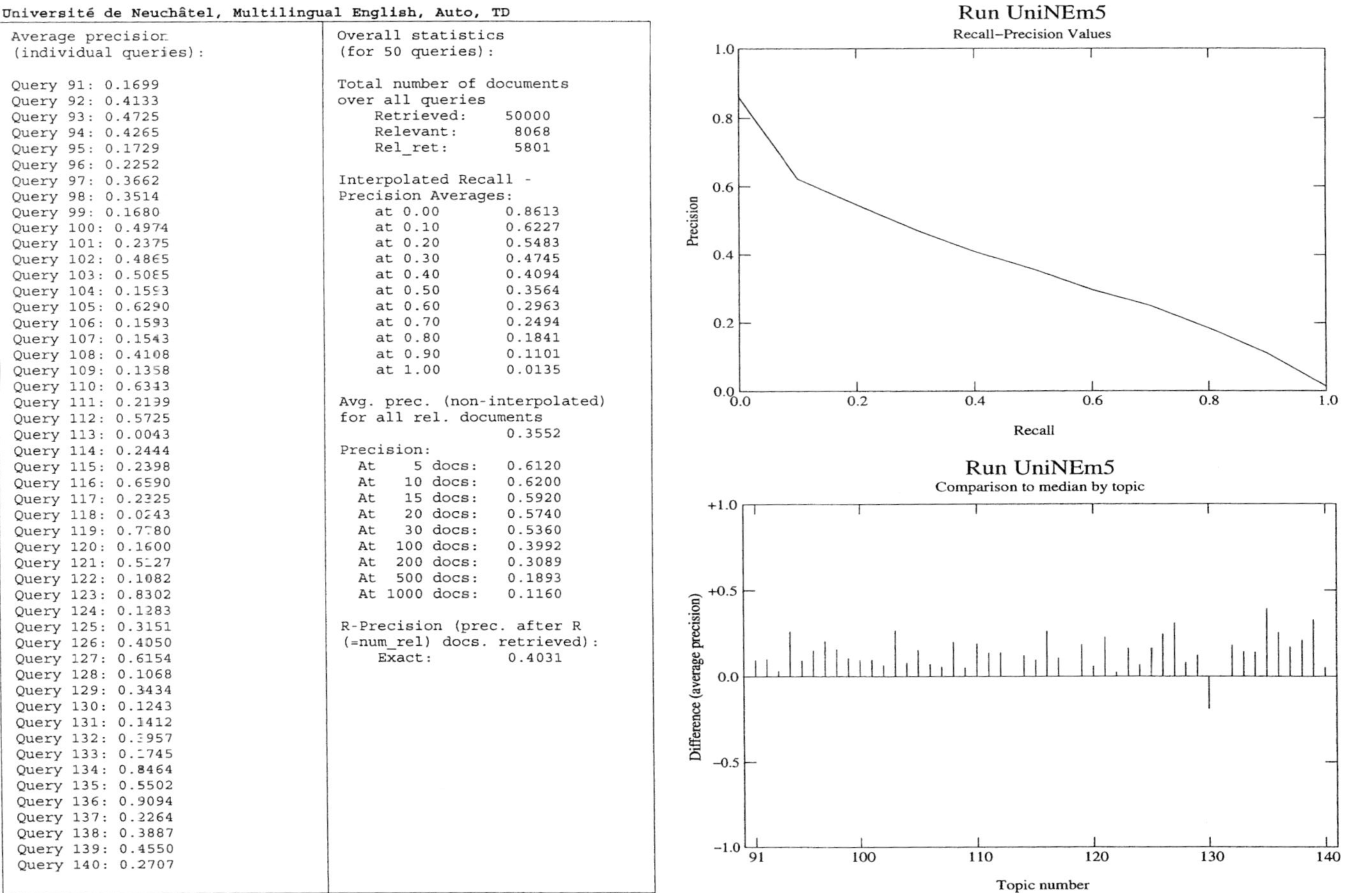

Université de Neuchâtel, Multilingual English, Auto, TD

```
Average precision                    Overall statistics
(individual queries):                (for 50 queries):

Query 91: 0.1699                     Total number of documents
Query 92: 0.4133                     over all queries
Query 93: 0.4725                         Retrieved:     50000
Query 94: 0.4265                         Relevant:       8068
Query 95: 0.1729                         Rel_ret:        5801
Query 96: 0.2252
Query 97: 0.3662                     Interpolated Recall -
Query 98: 0.3514                     Precision Averages:
Query 99: 0.1680                         at 0.00        0.8613
Query 100: 0.4974                        at 0.10        0.6227
Query 101: 0.2375                        at 0.20        0.5483
Query 102: 0.4865                        at 0.30        0.4745
Query 103: 0.5085                        at 0.40        0.4094
Query 104: 0.1593                        at 0.50        0.3564
Query 105: 0.6290                        at 0.60        0.2963
Query 106: 0.1593                        at 0.70        0.2494
Query 107: 0.1543                        at 0.80        0.1841
Query 108: 0.4108                        at 0.90        0.1101
Query 109: 0.1358                        at 1.00        0.0135
Query 110: 0.6343
Query 111: 0.2139                    Avg. prec. (non-interpolated)
Query 112: 0.5725                    for all rel. documents
Query 113: 0.0043                                       0.3552
Query 114: 0.2444                    Precision:
Query 115: 0.2398                      At    5 docs:    0.6120
Query 116: 0.6590                      At   10 docs:    0.6200
Query 117: 0.2325                      At   15 docs:    0.5920
Query 118: 0.0243                      At   20 docs:    0.5740
Query 119: 0.7780                      At   30 docs:    0.5360
Query 120: 0.1600                      At  100 docs:    0.3992
Query 121: 0.5127                      At  200 docs:    0.3089
Query 122: 0.1082                      At  500 docs:    0.1893
Query 123: 0.8302                      At 1000 docs:    0.1160
Query 124: 0.1283
Query 125: 0.3151                    R-Precision (prec. after R
Query 126: 0.4050                    (=num_rel) docs. retrieved):
Query 127: 0.6154                        Exact:         0.4031
Query 128: 0.1068
Query 129: 0.3434
Query 130: 0.1243
Query 131: 0.1412
Query 132: 0.3957
Query 133: 0.1745
Query 134: 0.8464
Query 135: 0.5502
Query 136: 0.9094
Query 137: 0.2264
Query 138: 0.3887
Query 139: 0.4550
Query 140: 0.2707
```

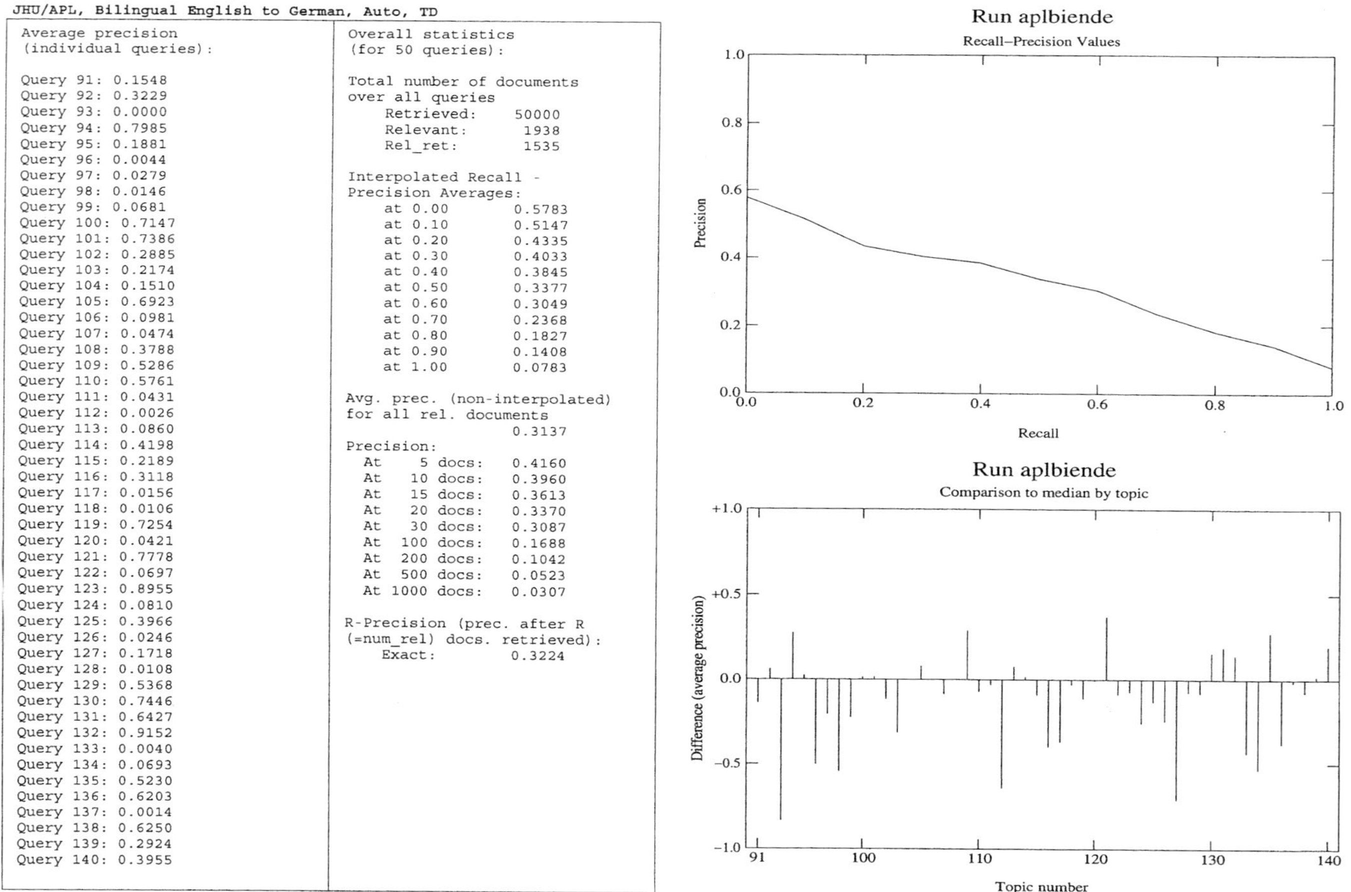

JHU/APL, Bilingual English to German, Auto, TD

Average precision (individual queries):

Query	Average precision
Query 91:	0.1548
Query 92:	0.3229
Query 93:	0.0000
Query 94:	0.7985
Query 95:	0.1881
Query 96:	0.0044
Query 97:	0.0279
Query 98:	0.0146
Query 99:	0.0681
Query 100:	0.7147
Query 101:	0.7386
Query 102:	0.2885
Query 103:	0.2174
Query 104:	0.1510
Query 105:	0.6923
Query 106:	0.0981
Query 107:	0.0474
Query 108:	0.3788
Query 109:	0.5286
Query 110:	0.5761
Query 111:	0.0431
Query 112:	0.0026
Query 113:	0.0860
Query 114:	0.4198
Query 115:	0.2189
Query 116:	0.3118
Query 117:	0.0156
Query 118:	0.0106
Query 119:	0.7254
Query 120:	0.0421
Query 121:	0.7778
Query 122:	0.0697
Query 123:	0.8955
Query 124:	0.0810
Query 125:	0.3966
Query 126:	0.0246
Query 127:	0.1718
Query 128:	0.0108
Query 129:	0.5368
Query 130:	0.7446
Query 131:	0.6427
Query 132:	0.9152
Query 133:	0.0040
Query 134:	0.0693
Query 135:	0.5230
Query 136:	0.6203
Query 137:	0.0014
Query 138:	0.6250
Query 139:	0.2924
Query 140:	0.3955

Overall statistics (for 50 queries):

Total number of documents over all queries

Retrieved:	50000
Relevant:	1938
Rel_ret:	1535

Interpolated Recall - Precision Averages:

at 0.00	0.5783
at 0.10	0.5147
at 0.20	0.4335
at 0.30	0.4033
at 0.40	0.3845
at 0.50	0.3377
at 0.60	0.3049
at 0.70	0.2368
at 0.80	0.1827
at 0.90	0.1408
at 1.00	0.0783

Avg. prec. (non-interpolated) for all rel. documents 0.3137

Precision:

At 5 docs:	0.4160
At 10 docs:	0.3960
At 15 docs:	0.3613
At 20 docs:	0.3370
At 30 docs:	0.3087
At 100 docs:	0.1688
At 200 docs:	0.1042
At 500 docs:	0.0523
At 1000 docs:	0.0307

R-Precision (prec. after R (=num_rel) docs. retrieved):
Exact: 0.3224

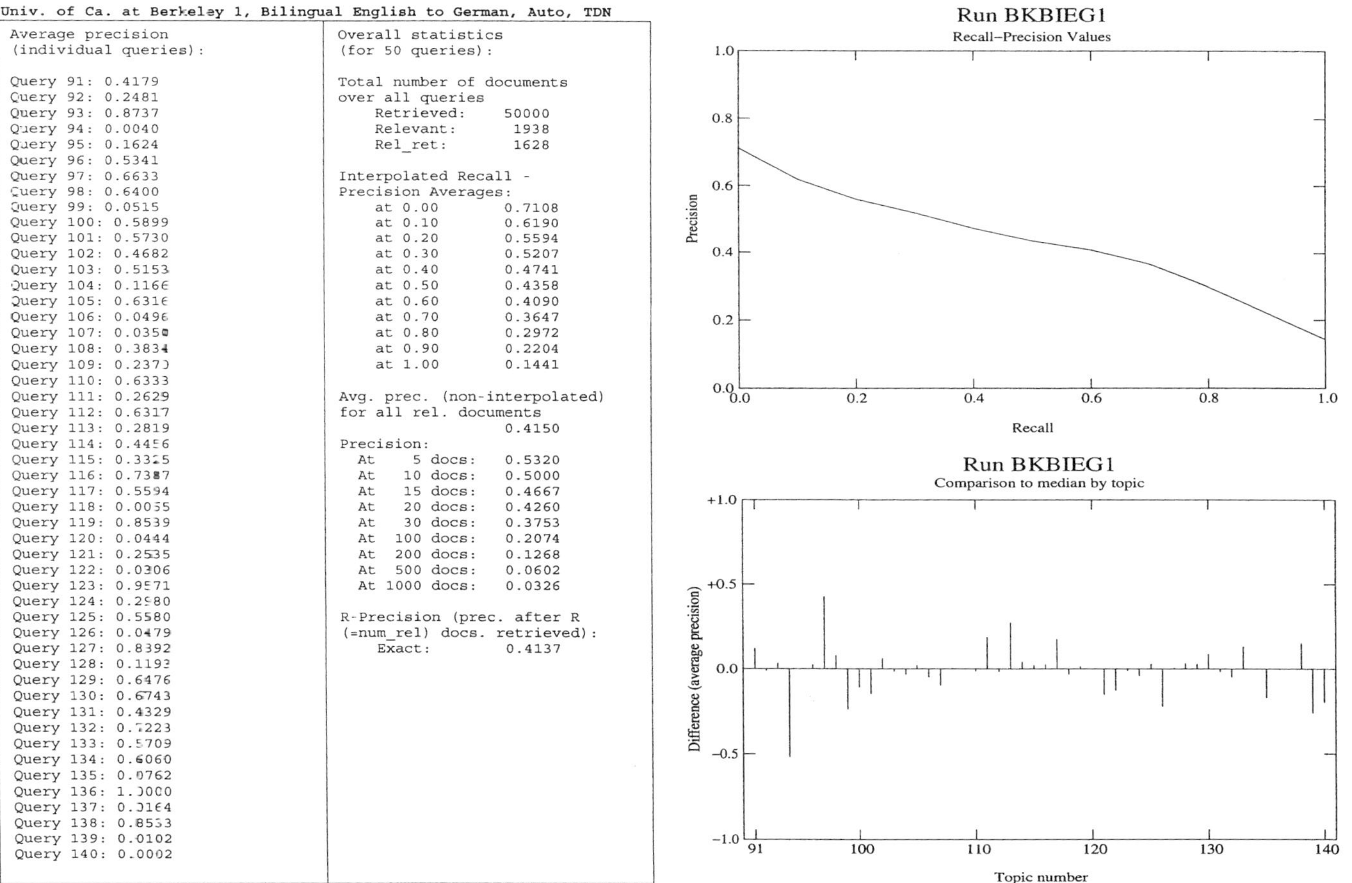

Univ. of Ca. at Berkeley 1, Bilingual English to German, Auto, TDN

Average precision (individual queries):

Query	Average precision
Query 91	0.4179
Query 92	0.2481
Query 93	0.8737
Query 94	0.0040
Query 95	0.1624
Query 96	0.5341
Query 97	0.6633
Query 98	0.6400
Query 99	0.0515
Query 100	0.5899
Query 101	0.5730
Query 102	0.4682
Query 103	0.5153
Query 104	0.1166
Query 105	0.6316
Query 106	0.0496
Query 107	0.0350
Query 108	0.3834
Query 109	0.2370
Query 110	0.6333
Query 111	0.2629
Query 112	0.6317
Query 113	0.2819
Query 114	0.4456
Query 115	0.3325
Query 116	0.7387
Query 117	0.5594
Query 118	0.0055
Query 119	0.8539
Query 120	0.0444
Query 121	0.2535
Query 122	0.0306
Query 123	0.9571
Query 124	0.2980
Query 125	0.5580
Query 126	0.0479
Query 127	0.8392
Query 128	0.1193
Query 129	0.6476
Query 130	0.6743
Query 131	0.4329
Query 132	0.7223
Query 133	0.5709
Query 134	0.6060
Query 135	0.0762
Query 136	1.0000
Query 137	0.0164
Query 138	0.8553
Query 139	0.0102
Query 140	0.0002

Overall statistics (for 50 queries):

Total number of documents over all queries

Retrieved:	50000
Relevant:	1938
Rel_ret:	1628

Interpolated Recall - Precision Averages:

at 0.00	0.7108
at 0.10	0.6190
at 0.20	0.5594
at 0.30	0.5207
at 0.40	0.4741
at 0.50	0.4358
at 0.60	0.4090
at 0.70	0.3647
at 0.80	0.2972
at 0.90	0.2204
at 1.00	0.1441

Avg. prec. (non-interpolated) for all rel. documents 0.4150

Precision:

At 5 docs:	0.5320
At 10 docs:	0.5000
At 15 docs:	0.4667
At 20 docs:	0.4260
At 30 docs:	0.3753
At 100 docs:	0.2074
At 200 docs:	0.1268
At 500 docs:	0.0602
At 1000 docs:	0.0326

R-Precision (prec. after R (=num_rel) docs. retrieved):
Exact: 0.4137

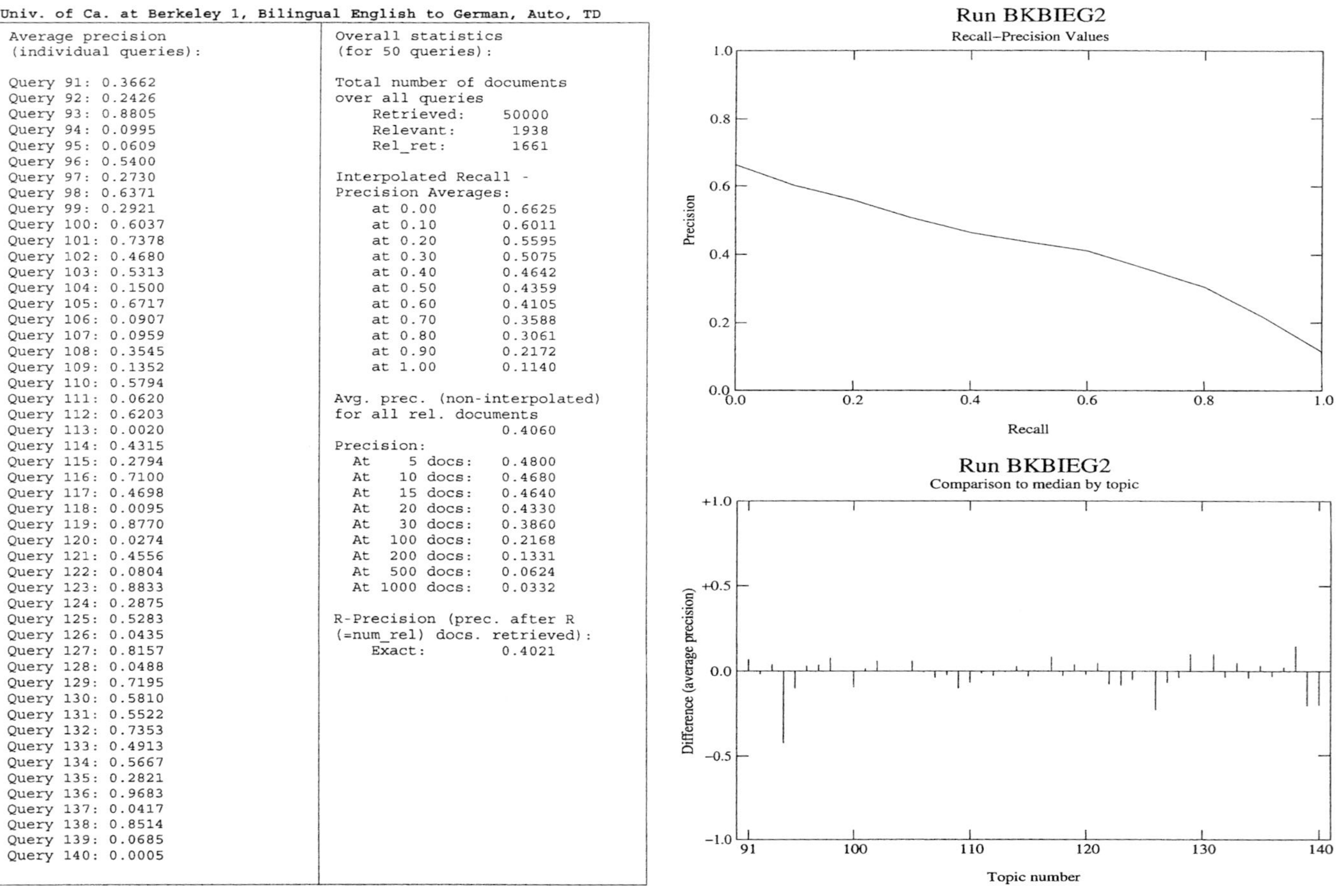

Univ. of Ca. at Berkeley 1, Bilingual English to German, Auto, TD

Average precision
(individual queries):

Query 91: 0.3662
Query 92: 0.2426
Query 93: 0.8805
Query 94: 0.0995
Query 95: 0.0609
Query 96: 0.5400
Query 97: 0.2730
Query 98: 0.6371
Query 99: 0.2921
Query 100: 0.6037
Query 101: 0.7378
Query 102: 0.4680
Query 103: 0.5313
Query 104: 0.1500
Query 105: 0.6717
Query 106: 0.0907
Query 107: 0.0959
Query 108: 0.3545
Query 109: 0.1352
Query 110: 0.5794
Query 111: 0.0620
Query 112: 0.6203
Query 113: 0.0020
Query 114: 0.4315
Query 115: 0.2794
Query 116: 0.7100
Query 117: 0.4698
Query 118: 0.0095
Query 119: 0.8770
Query 120: 0.0274
Query 121: 0.4556
Query 122: 0.0804
Query 123: 0.8833
Query 124: 0.2875
Query 125: 0.5283
Query 126: 0.0435
Query 127: 0.8157
Query 128: 0.0488
Query 129: 0.7195
Query 130: 0.5810
Query 131: 0.5522
Query 132: 0.7353
Query 133: 0.4913
Query 134: 0.5667
Query 135: 0.2821
Query 136: 0.9683
Query 137: 0.0417
Query 138: 0.8514
Query 139: 0.0685
Query 140: 0.0005

Overall statistics
(for 50 queries):

Total number of documents
over all queries
Retrieved: 50000
Relevant: 1938
Rel_ret: 1661

Interpolated Recall -
Precision Averages:
at 0.00 0.6625
at 0.10 0.6011
at 0.20 0.5595
at 0.30 0.5075
at 0.40 0.4642
at 0.50 0.4359
at 0.60 0.4105
at 0.70 0.3588
at 0.80 0.3061
at 0.90 0.2172
at 1.00 0.1140

Avg. prec. (non-interpolated)
for all rel. documents
0.4060

Precision:
At 5 docs: 0.4800
At 10 docs: 0.4680
At 15 docs: 0.4640
At 20 docs: 0.4330
At 30 docs: 0.3860
At 100 docs: 0.2168
At 200 docs: 0.1331
At 500 docs: 0.0624
At 1000 docs: 0.0332

R-Precision (prec. after R
(=num_rel) docs. retrieved):
Exact: 0.4021

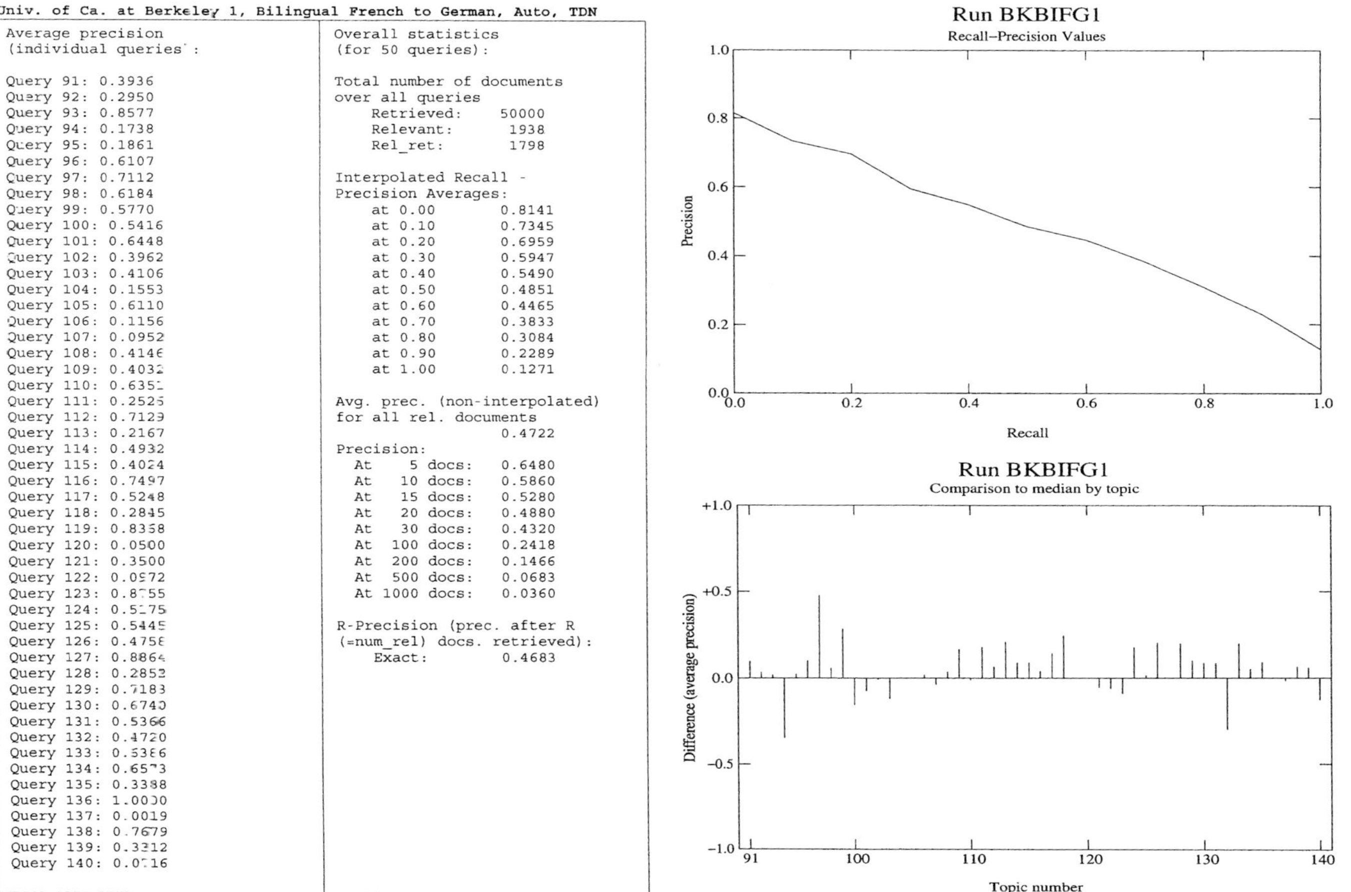

Univ. of Ca. at Berkeley 1, Bilingual French to German, Auto, TDN

```
Average precision                 Overall statistics
(individual queries):             (for 50 queries):

Query 91: 0.3936                  Total number of documents
Query 92: 0.2950                  over all queries
Query 93: 0.8577                      Retrieved:     50000
Query 94: 0.1738                      Relevant:       1938
Query 95: 0.1861                      Rel_ret:        1798
Query 96: 0.6107
Query 97: 0.7112                  Interpolated Recall -
Query 98: 0.6184                  Precision Averages:
Query 99: 0.5770                      at 0.00        0.8141
Query 100: 0.5416                     at 0.10        0.7345
Query 101: 0.6448                     at 0.20        0.6959
Query 102: 0.3962                     at 0.30        0.5947
Query 103: 0.4106                     at 0.40        0.5490
Query 104: 0.1553                     at 0.50        0.4851
Query 105: 0.6110                     at 0.60        0.4465
Query 106: 0.1156                     at 0.70        0.3833
Query 107: 0.0952                     at 0.80        0.3084
Query 108: 0.4146                     at 0.90        0.2289
Query 109: 0.4032                     at 1.00        0.1271
Query 110: 0.6351
Query 111: 0.2525                 Avg. prec. (non-interpolated)
Query 112: 0.7129                 for all rel. documents
Query 113: 0.2167                                    0.4722
Query 114: 0.4932                 Precision:
Query 115: 0.4024                   At    5 docs:   0.6480
Query 116: 0.7497                   At   10 docs:   0.5860
Query 117: 0.5248                   At   15 docs:   0.5280
Query 118: 0.2845                   At   20 docs:   0.4880
Query 119: 0.8358                   At   30 docs:   0.4320
Query 120: 0.0500                   At  100 docs:   0.2418
Query 121: 0.3500                   At  200 docs:   0.1466
Query 122: 0.0572                   At  500 docs:   0.0683
Query 123: 0.8755                   At 1000 docs:   0.0360
Query 124: 0.5175
Query 125: 0.5445                 R-Precision (prec. after R
Query 126: 0.4758                 (=num_rel) docs. retrieved):
Query 127: 0.8864                     Exact:         0.4683
Query 128: 0.2852
Query 129: 0.7183
Query 130: 0.6740
Query 131: 0.5366
Query 132: 0.4720
Query 133: 0.5386
Query 134: 0.6573
Query 135: 0.3388
Query 136: 1.0000
Query 137: 0.0019
Query 138: 0.7679
Query 139: 0.3212
Query 140: 0.0716
```

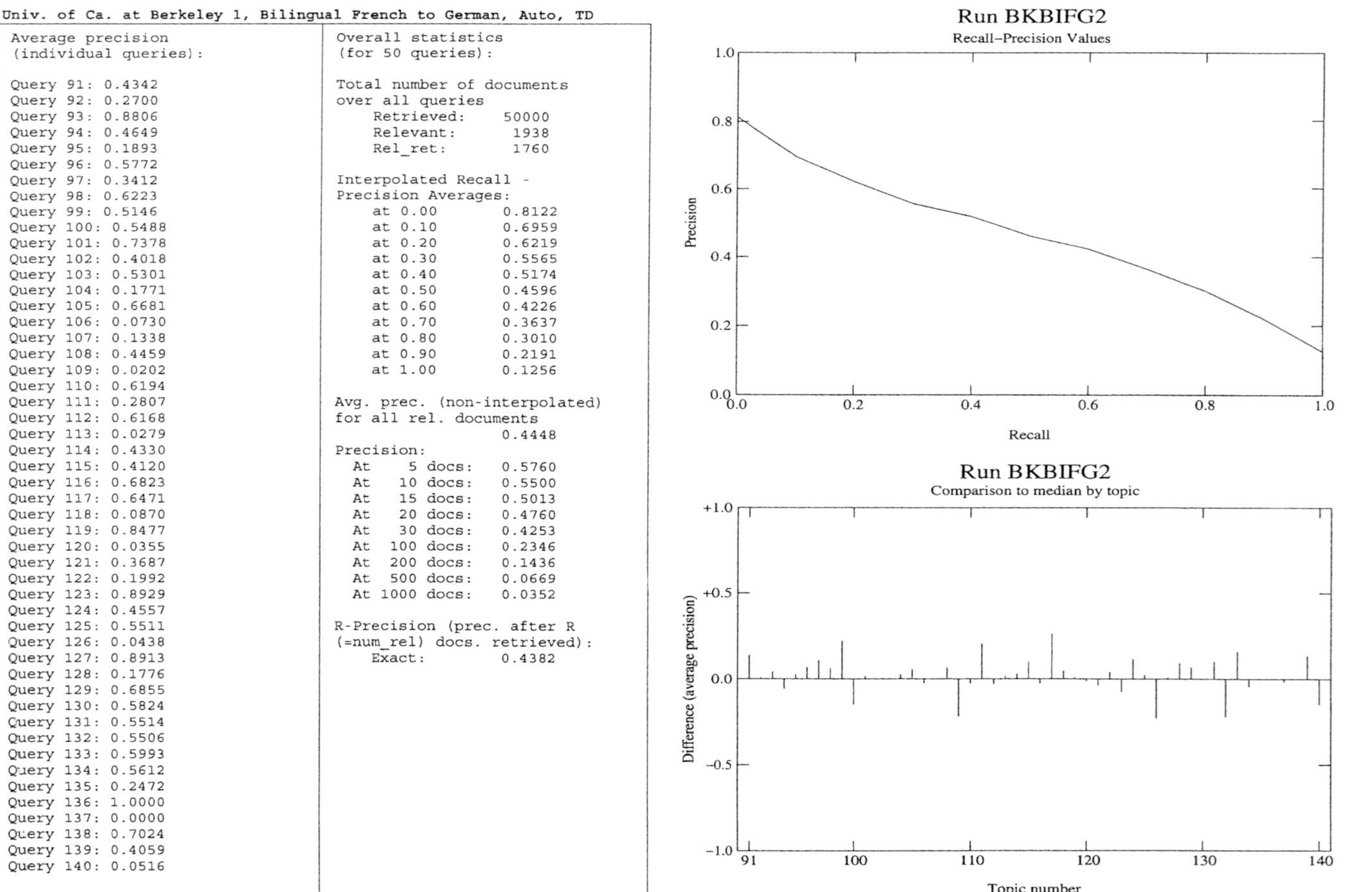

Univ. of Ca. at Berkeley 1, Bilingual French to German, Auto, TD

```
Average precision            Overall statistics
(individual queries):        (for 50 queries):

Query 91: 0.4342             Total number of documents
Query 92: 0.2700             over all queries
Query 93: 0.8806                 Retrieved:    50000
Query 94: 0.4649                 Relevant:      1938
Query 95: 0.1893                 Rel_ret:       1760
Query 96: 0.5772
Query 97: 0.3412             Interpolated Recall -
Query 98: 0.6223             Precision Averages:
Query 99: 0.5146                 at 0.00       0.8122
Query 100: 0.5488                at 0.10       0.6959
Query 101: 0.7378                at 0.20       0.6219
Query 102: 0.4018                at 0.30       0.5565
Query 103: 0.5301                at 0.40       0.5174
Query 104: 0.1771                at 0.50       0.4596
Query 105: 0.6681                at 0.60       0.4226
Query 106: 0.0730                at 0.70       0.3637
Query 107: 0.1338                at 0.80       0.3010
Query 108: 0.4459                at 0.90       0.2191
Query 109: 0.0202                at 1.00       0.1256
Query 110: 0.6194
Query 111: 0.2807            Avg. prec. (non-interpolated)
Query 112: 0.6168            for all rel. documents
Query 113: 0.0279                              0.4448
Query 114: 0.4330            Precision:
Query 115: 0.4120              At    5 docs:   0.5760
Query 116: 0.6823              At   10 docs:   0.5500
Query 117: 0.6471              At   15 docs:   0.5013
Query 118: 0.0870              At   20 docs:   0.4760
Query 119: 0.8477              At   30 docs:   0.4253
Query 120: 0.0355              At  100 docs:   0.2346
Query 121: 0.3687              At  200 docs:   0.1436
Query 122: 0.1992              At  500 docs:   0.0669
Query 123: 0.8929              At 1000 docs:   0.0352
Query 124: 0.4557
Query 125: 0.5511            R-Precision (prec. after R
Query 126: 0.0438            (=num_rel) docs. retrieved):
Query 127: 0.8913                Exact:        0.4382
Query 128: 0.1776
Query 129: 0.6855
Query 130: 0.5824
Query 131: 0.5514
Query 132: 0.5506
Query 133: 0.5993
Query 134: 0.5612
Query 135: 0.2472
Query 136: 1.0000
Query 137: 0.0000
Query 138: 0.7024
Query 139: 0.4059
Query 140: 0.0516
```

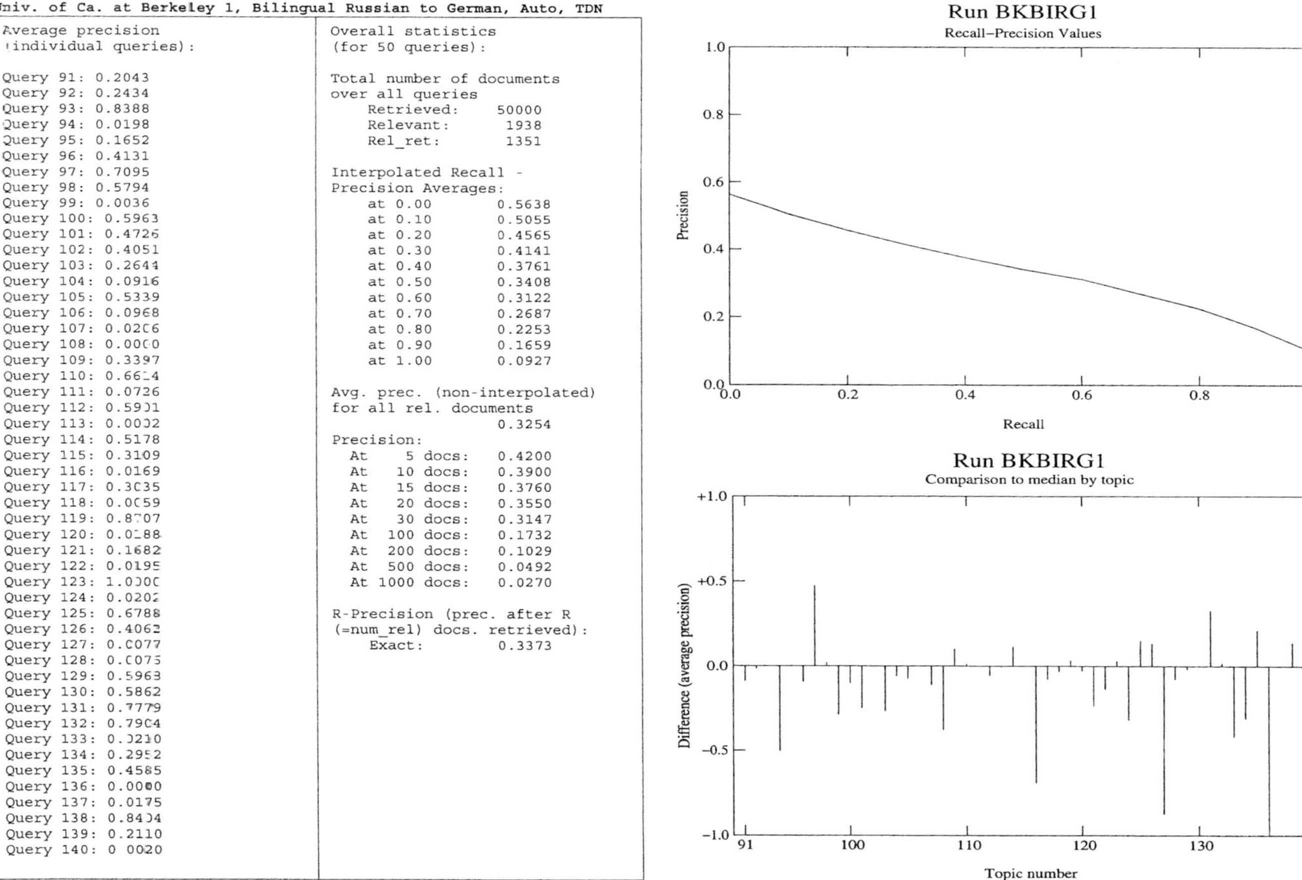

Univ. of Ca. at Berkeley 1, Bilingual Russian to German, Auto, TDN

Average precision (individual queries):

Query 91:	0.2043
Query 92:	0.2434
Query 93:	0.8388
Query 94:	0.0198
Query 95:	0.1652
Query 96:	0.4131
Query 97:	0.7095
Query 98:	0.5794
Query 99:	0.0036
Query 100:	0.5963
Query 101:	0.4726
Query 102:	0.4051
Query 103:	0.2644
Query 104:	0.0916
Query 105:	0.5339
Query 106:	0.0968
Query 107:	0.0206
Query 108:	0.0000
Query 109:	0.3397
Query 110:	0.6614
Query 111:	0.0726
Query 112:	0.5901
Query 113:	0.0002
Query 114:	0.5178
Query 115:	0.3109
Query 116:	0.0169
Query 117:	0.3035
Query 118:	0.0059
Query 119:	0.8707
Query 120:	0.0188
Query 121:	0.1682
Query 122:	0.0195
Query 123:	1.0000
Query 124:	0.0202
Query 125:	0.6788
Query 126:	0.4062
Query 127:	0.0077
Query 128:	0.0075
Query 129:	0.5963
Query 130:	0.5862
Query 131:	0.7779
Query 132:	0.7904
Query 133:	0.0210
Query 134:	0.2952
Query 135:	0.4585
Query 136:	0.0000
Query 137:	0.0175
Query 138:	0.8404
Query 139:	0.2110
Query 140:	0.0020

Overall statistics (for 50 queries):

Total number of documents over all queries

Retrieved:	50000
Relevant:	1938
Rel_ret:	1351

Interpolated Recall - Precision Averages:

at 0.00	0.5638
at 0.10	0.5055
at 0.20	0.4565
at 0.30	0.4141
at 0.40	0.3761
at 0.50	0.3408
at 0.60	0.3122
at 0.70	0.2687
at 0.80	0.2253
at 0.90	0.1659
at 1.00	0.0927

Avg. prec. (non-interpolated) for all rel. documents 0.3254

Precision:

At 5 docs:	0.4200
At 10 docs:	0.3900
At 15 docs:	0.3760
At 20 docs:	0.3550
At 30 docs:	0.3147
At 100 docs:	0.1732
At 200 docs:	0.1029
At 500 docs:	0.0492
At 1000 docs:	0.0270

R-Precision (prec. after R (=num_rel) docs. retrieved):
Exact: 0.3373

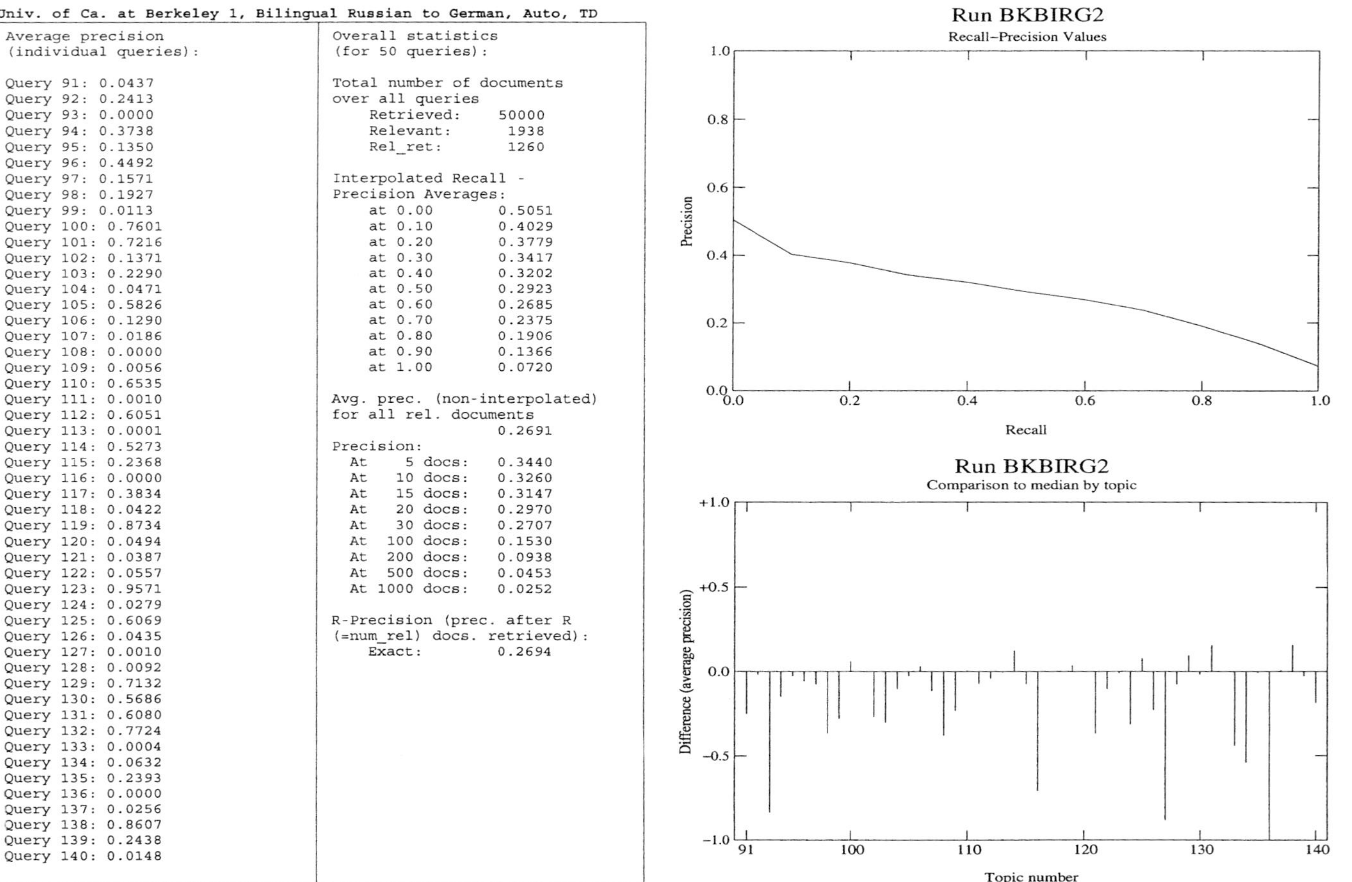

Univ. of Ca. at Berkeley 1, Bilingual Russian to German, Auto, TD

Average precision (individual queries):	
Query 91:	0.0437
Query 92:	0.2413
Query 93:	0.0000
Query 94:	0.3738
Query 95:	0.1350
Query 96:	0.4492
Query 97:	0.1571
Query 98:	0.1927
Query 99:	0.0113
Query 100:	0.7601
Query 101:	0.7216
Query 102:	0.1371
Query 103:	0.2290
Query 104:	0.0471
Query 105:	0.5826
Query 106:	0.1290
Query 107:	0.0186
Query 108:	0.0000
Query 109:	0.0056
Query 110:	0.6535
Query 111:	0.0010
Query 112:	0.6051
Query 113:	0.0001
Query 114:	0.5273
Query 115:	0.2368
Query 116:	0.0000
Query 117:	0.3834
Query 118:	0.0422
Query 119:	0.8734
Query 120:	0.0494
Query 121:	0.0387
Query 122:	0.0557
Query 123:	0.9571
Query 124:	0.0279
Query 125:	0.6069
Query 126:	0.0435
Query 127:	0.0010
Query 128:	0.0092
Query 129:	0.7132
Query 130:	0.5686
Query 131:	0.6080
Query 132:	0.7724
Query 133:	0.0004
Query 134:	0.0632
Query 135:	0.2393
Query 136:	0.0000
Query 137:	0.0256
Query 138:	0.8607
Query 139:	0.2438
Query 140:	0.0148

Overall statistics (for 50 queries):	
Total number of documents over all queries	
Retrieved:	50000
Relevant:	1938
Rel_ret:	1260
Interpolated Recall - Precision Averages:	
at 0.00	0.5051
at 0.10	0.4029
at 0.20	0.3779
at 0.30	0.3417
at 0.40	0.3202
at 0.50	0.2923
at 0.60	0.2685
at 0.70	0.2375
at 0.80	0.1906
at 0.90	0.1366
at 1.00	0.0720
Avg. prec. (non-interpolated) for all rel. documents	0.2691
Precision:	
At 5 docs:	0.3440
At 10 docs:	0.3260
At 15 docs:	0.3147
At 20 docs:	0.2970
At 30 docs:	0.2707
At 100 docs:	0.1530
At 200 docs:	0.0938
At 500 docs:	0.0453
At 1000 docs:	0.0252
R-Precision (prec. after R (=num_rel) docs. retrieved):	
Exact:	0.2694

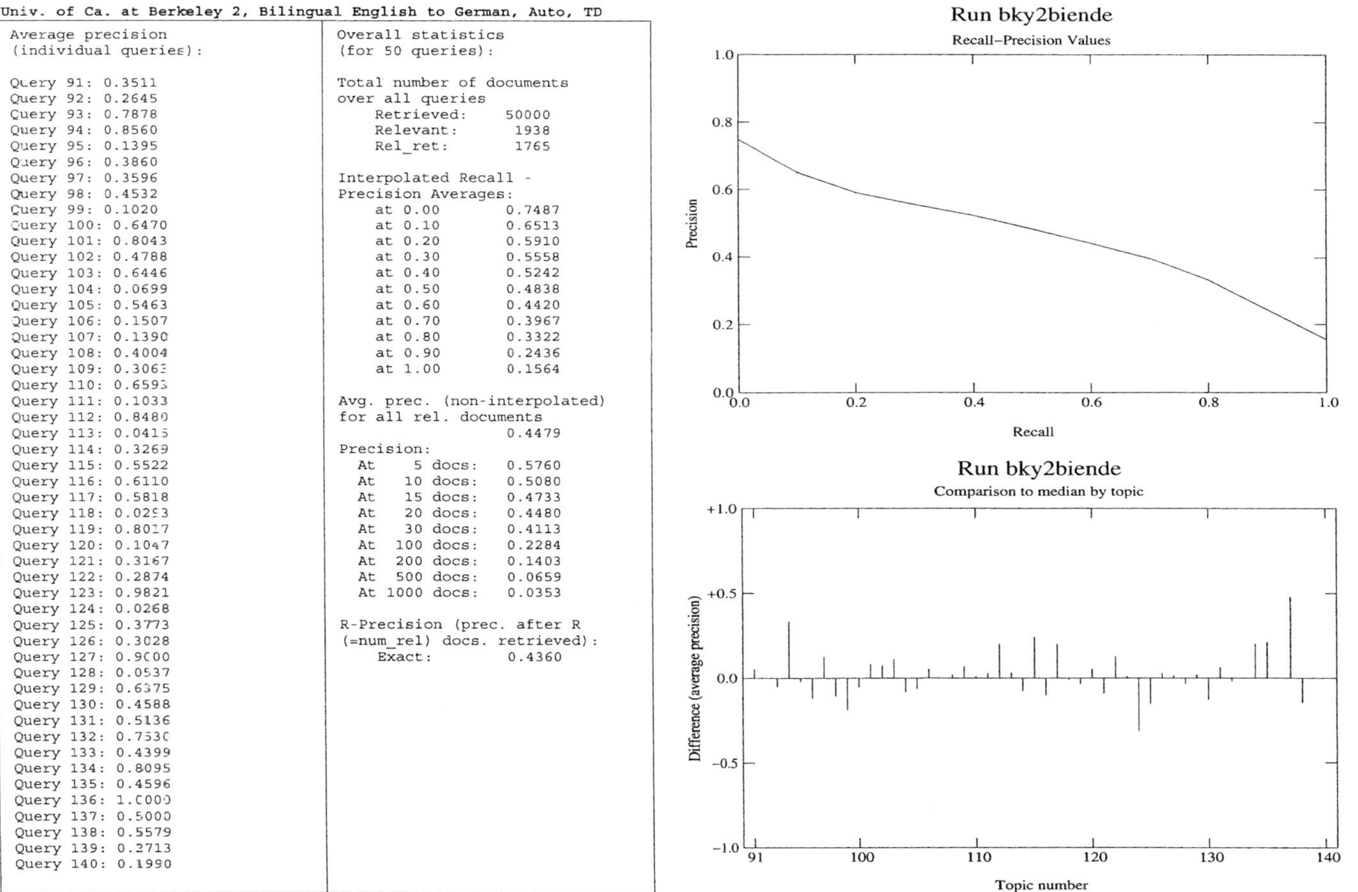

Univ. of Ca. at Berkeley 2, Bilingual English to German, Auto, TD

```
Average precision                Overall statistics
(individual queries):            (for 50 queries):

Query 91: 0.3511                 Total number of documents
Query 92: 0.2645                 over all queries
Query 93: 0.7878                     Retrieved:    50000
Query 94: 0.8560                     Relevant:      1938
Query 95: 0.1395                     Rel_ret:       1765
Query 96: 0.3860
Query 97: 0.3596                 Interpolated Recall -
Query 98: 0.4532                 Precision Averages:
Query 99: 0.1020                     at 0.00       0.7487
Query 100: 0.6470                    at 0.10       0.6513
Query 101: 0.8043                    at 0.20       0.5910
Query 102: 0.4788                    at 0.30       0.5558
Query 103: 0.6446                    at 0.40       0.5242
Query 104: 0.0699                    at 0.50       0.4838
Query 105: 0.5463                    at 0.60       0.4420
Query 106: 0.1507                    at 0.70       0.3967
Query 107: 0.1390                    at 0.80       0.3322
Query 108: 0.4004                    at 0.90       0.2436
Query 109: 0.3063                    at 1.00       0.1564
Query 110: 0.6593
Query 111: 0.1033                Avg. prec. (non-interpolated)
Query 112: 0.8480                for all rel. documents
Query 113: 0.0415                                  0.4479
Query 114: 0.3269                Precision:
Query 115: 0.5522                  At    5 docs:   0.5760
Query 116: 0.6110                  At   10 docs:   0.5080
Query 117: 0.5818                  At   15 docs:   0.4733
Query 118: 0.0293                  At   20 docs:   0.4480
Query 119: 0.8017                  At   30 docs:   0.4113
Query 120: 0.1047                  At  100 docs:   0.2284
Query 121: 0.3167                  At  200 docs:   0.1403
Query 122: 0.2874                  At  500 docs:   0.0659
Query 123: 0.9821                  At 1000 docs:   0.0353
Query 124: 0.0268
Query 125: 0.3773                R-Precision (prec. after R
Query 126: 0.3028                (=num_rel) docs. retrieved):
Query 127: 0.9000                    Exact:        0.4360
Query 128: 0.0537
Query 129: 0.6375
Query 130: 0.4588
Query 131: 0.5136
Query 132: 0.7530
Query 133: 0.4399
Query 134: 0.8095
Query 135: 0.4596
Query 136: 1.0000
Query 137: 0.5000
Query 138: 0.5579
Query 139: 0.2713
Query 140: 0.1990
```

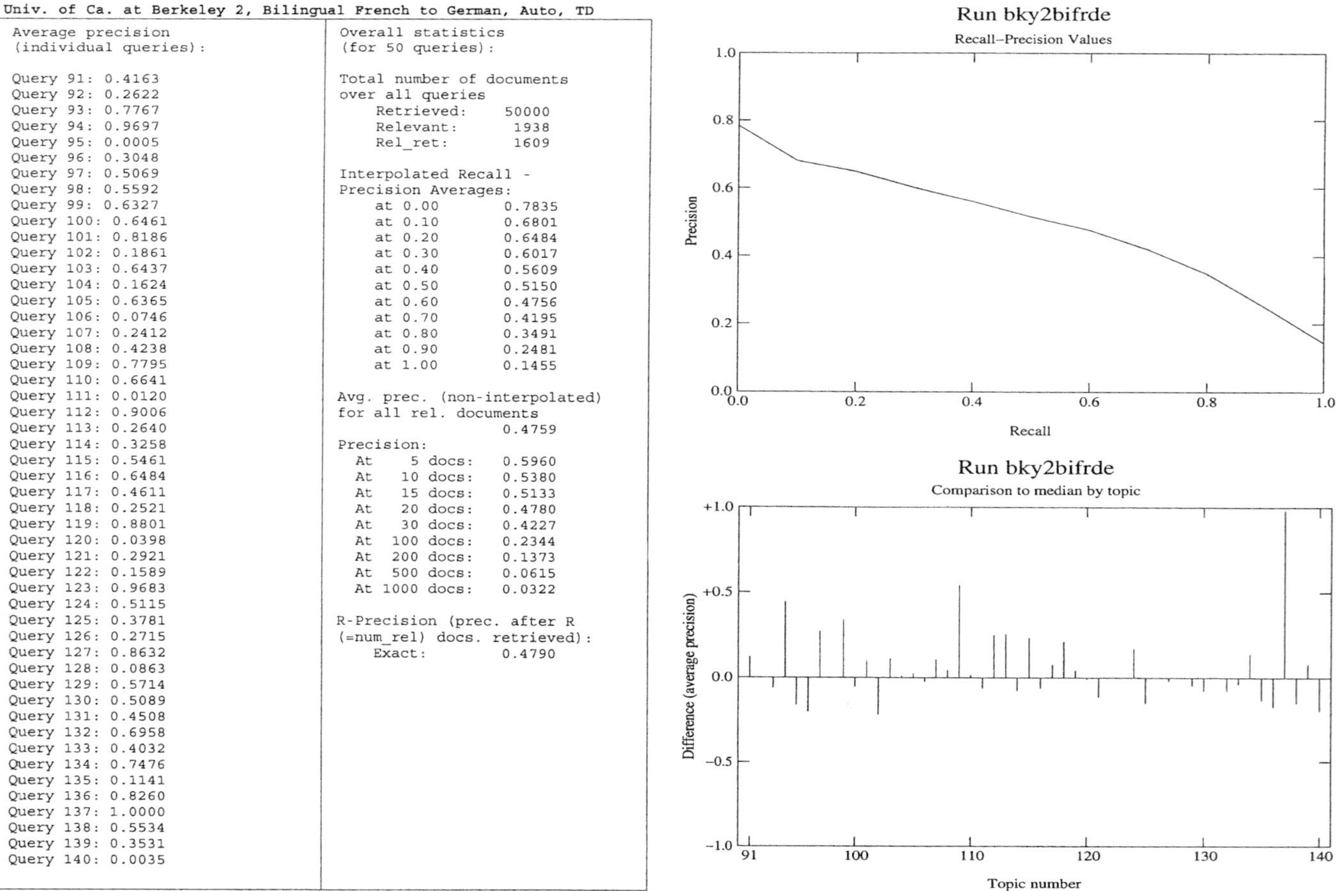

Univ. of Ca. at Berkeley 2, Bilingual French to German, Auto, TD

Average precision (individual queries):

Query	Avg. precision
Query 91:	0.4163
Query 92:	0.2622
Query 93:	0.7767
Query 94:	0.9697
Query 95:	0.0005
Query 96:	0.3048
Query 97:	0.5069
Query 98:	0.5592
Query 99:	0.6327
Query 100:	0.6461
Query 101:	0.8186
Query 102:	0.1861
Query 103:	0.6437
Query 104:	0.1624
Query 105:	0.6365
Query 106:	0.0746
Query 107:	0.2412
Query 108:	0.4238
Query 109:	0.7795
Query 110:	0.6641
Query 111:	0.0120
Query 112:	0.9006
Query 113:	0.2640
Query 114:	0.3258
Query 115:	0.5461
Query 116:	0.6484
Query 117:	0.4611
Query 118:	0.2521
Query 119:	0.8801
Query 120:	0.0398
Query 121:	0.2921
Query 122:	0.1589
Query 123:	0.9683
Query 124:	0.5115
Query 125:	0.3781
Query 126:	0.2715
Query 127:	0.8632
Query 128:	0.0863
Query 129:	0.5714
Query 130:	0.5089
Query 131:	0.4508
Query 132:	0.6958
Query 133:	0.4032
Query 134:	0.7476
Query 135:	0.1141
Query 136:	0.8260
Query 137:	1.0000
Query 138:	0.5534
Query 139:	0.3531
Query 140:	0.0035

Overall statistics (for 50 queries):

Total number of documents over all queries

Retrieved:	50000
Relevant:	1938
Rel_ret:	1609

Interpolated Recall - Precision Averages:

at 0.00	0.7835
at 0.10	0.6801
at 0.20	0.6484
at 0.30	0.6017
at 0.40	0.5609
at 0.50	0.5150
at 0.60	0.4756
at 0.70	0.4195
at 0.80	0.3491
at 0.90	0.2481
at 1.00	0.1455

Avg. prec. (non-interpolated) for all rel. documents 0.4759

Precision:

At 5 docs:	0.5960
At 10 docs:	0.5380
At 15 docs:	0.5133
At 20 docs:	0.4780
At 30 docs:	0.4227
At 100 docs:	0.2344
At 200 docs:	0.1373
At 500 docs:	0.0615
At 1000 docs:	0.0322

R-Precision (prec. after R (=num_rel) docs. retrieved):
Exact: 0.4790

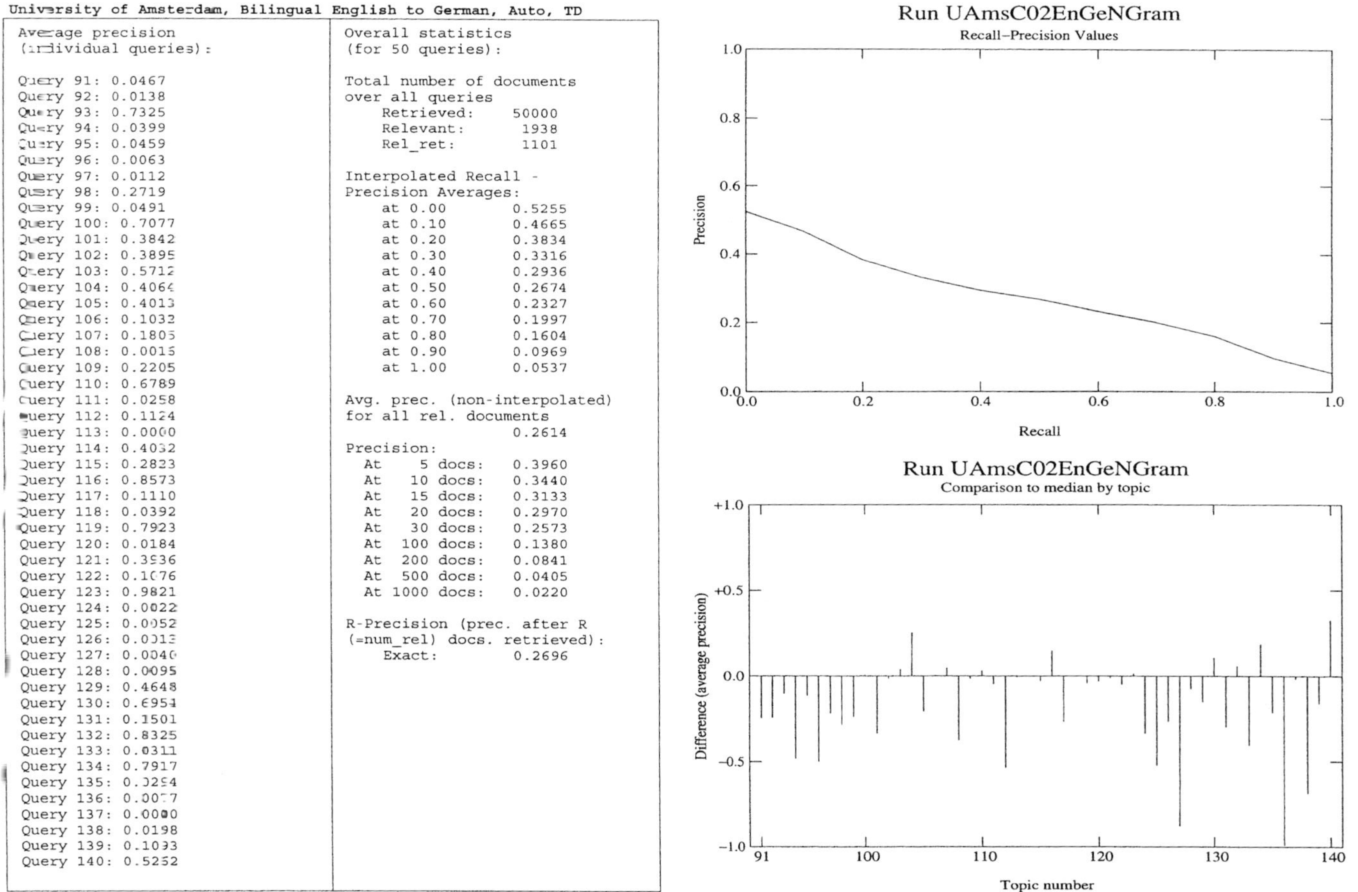

University of Amsterdam, Bilingual English to German, Auto, TD

Average precision (individual queries):

Query	Average precision
Query 91:	0.0467
Query 92:	0.0138
Query 93:	0.7325
Query 94:	0.0399
Query 95:	0.0459
Query 96:	0.0063
Query 97:	0.0112
Query 98:	0.2719
Query 99:	0.0491
Query 100:	0.7077
Query 101:	0.3842
Query 102:	0.3895
Query 103:	0.5712
Query 104:	0.4064
Query 105:	0.4013
Query 106:	0.1032
Query 107:	0.1805
Query 108:	0.0015
Query 109:	0.2205
Query 110:	0.6789
Query 111:	0.0258
Query 112:	0.1124
Query 113:	0.0000
Query 114:	0.4032
Query 115:	0.2823
Query 116:	0.8573
Query 117:	0.1110
Query 118:	0.0392
Query 119:	0.7923
Query 120:	0.0184
Query 121:	0.3936
Query 122:	0.1076
Query 123:	0.9821
Query 124:	0.0022
Query 125:	0.0052
Query 126:	0.0013
Query 127:	0.0040
Query 128:	0.0095
Query 129:	0.4648
Query 130:	0.6954
Query 131:	0.1501
Query 132:	0.8325
Query 133:	0.0311
Query 134:	0.7917
Query 135:	0.0254
Query 136:	0.0077
Query 137:	0.0000
Query 138:	0.0198
Query 139:	0.1033
Query 140:	0.5252

Overall statistics (for 50 queries):

Total number of documents over all queries

Retrieved:	50000
Relevant:	1938
Rel_ret:	1101

Interpolated Recall - Precision Averages:

at 0.00	0.5255
at 0.10	0.4665
at 0.20	0.3834
at 0.30	0.3316
at 0.40	0.2936
at 0.50	0.2674
at 0.60	0.2327
at 0.70	0.1997
at 0.80	0.1604
at 0.90	0.0969
at 1.00	0.0537

Avg. prec. (non-interpolated) for all rel. documents 0.2614

Precision:

At 5 docs:	0.3960
At 10 docs:	0.3440
At 15 docs:	0.3133
At 20 docs:	0.2970
At 30 docs:	0.2573
At 100 docs:	0.1380
At 200 docs:	0.0841
At 500 docs:	0.0405
At 1000 docs:	0.0220

R-Precision (prec. after R (=num_rel) docs. retrieved):
Exact: 0.2696

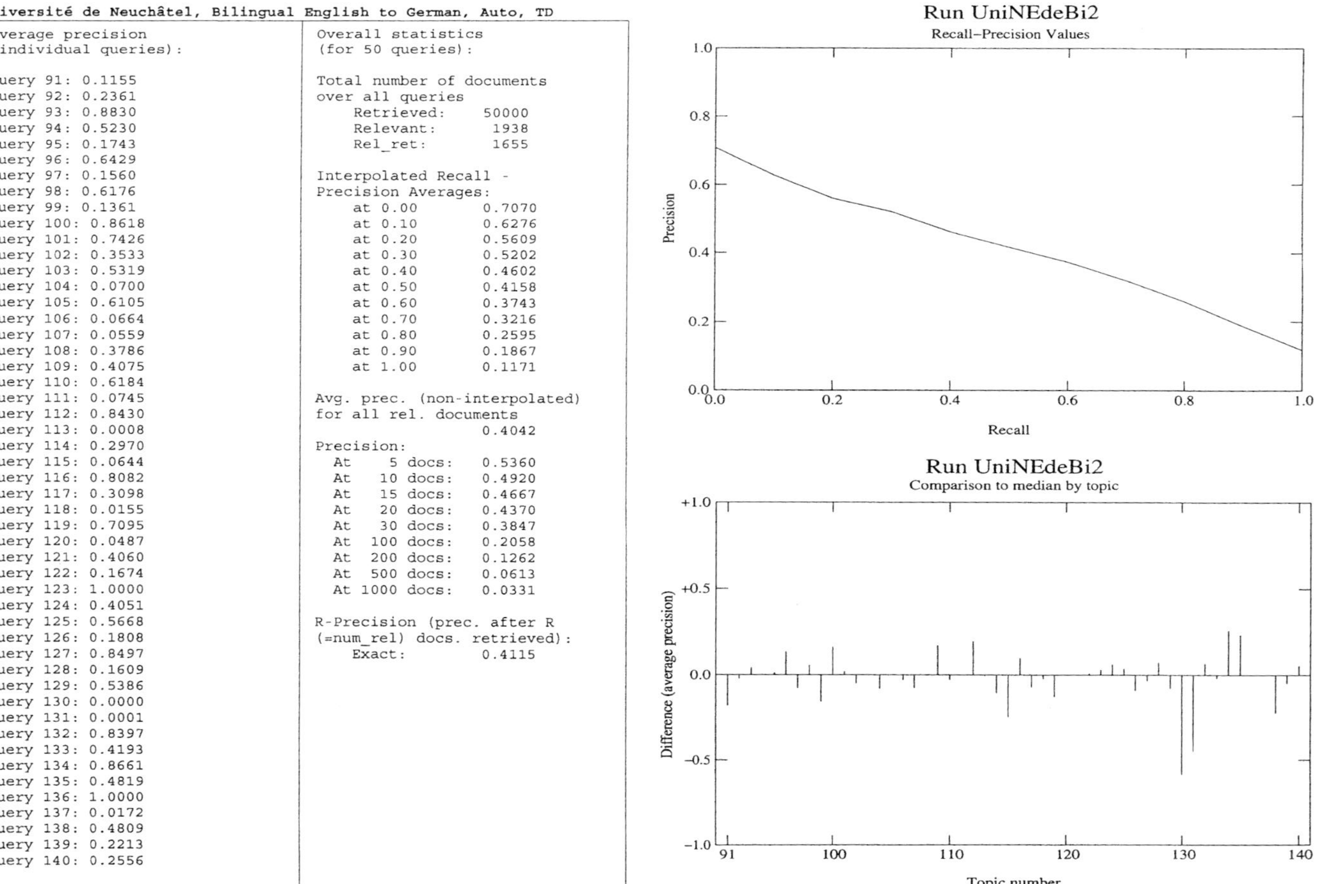

Université de Neuchâtel, Bilingual English to German, Auto, TD

Average precision (individual queries):

Query	Average precision
Query 91:	0.1155
Query 92:	0.2361
Query 93:	0.8830
Query 94:	0.5230
Query 95:	0.1743
Query 96:	0.6429
Query 97:	0.1560
Query 98:	0.6176
Query 99:	0.1361
Query 100:	0.8618
Query 101:	0.7426
Query 102:	0.3533
Query 103:	0.5319
Query 104:	0.0700
Query 105:	0.6105
Query 106:	0.0664
Query 107:	0.0559
Query 108:	0.3786
Query 109:	0.4075
Query 110:	0.6184
Query 111:	0.0745
Query 112:	0.8430
Query 113:	0.0008
Query 114:	0.2970
Query 115:	0.0644
Query 116:	0.8082
Query 117:	0.3098
Query 118:	0.0155
Query 119:	0.7095
Query 120:	0.0487
Query 121:	0.4060
Query 122:	0.1674
Query 123:	1.0000
Query 124:	0.4051
Query 125:	0.5668
Query 126:	0.1808
Query 127:	0.8497
Query 128:	0.1609
Query 129:	0.5386
Query 130:	0.0000
Query 131:	0.0001
Query 132:	0.8397
Query 133:	0.4193
Query 134:	0.8661
Query 135:	0.4819
Query 136:	1.0000
Query 137:	0.0172
Query 138:	0.4809
Query 139:	0.2213
Query 140:	0.2556

Overall statistics (for 50 queries):

Total number of documents over all queries

Retrieved:	50000
Relevant:	1938
Rel_ret:	1655

Interpolated Recall - Precision Averages:

at 0.00	0.7070
at 0.10	0.6276
at 0.20	0.5609
at 0.30	0.5202
at 0.40	0.4602
at 0.50	0.4158
at 0.60	0.3743
at 0.70	0.3216
at 0.80	0.2595
at 0.90	0.1867
at 1.00	0.1171

Avg. prec. (non-interpolated) for all rel. documents 0.4042

Precision:

At 5 docs:	0.5360
At 10 docs:	0.4920
At 15 docs:	0.4667
At 20 docs:	0.4370
At 30 docs:	0.3847
At 100 docs:	0.2058
At 200 docs:	0.1262
At 500 docs:	0.0613
At 1000 docs:	0.0331

R-Precision (prec. after R (=num_rel) docs. retrieved):
Exact: 0.4115

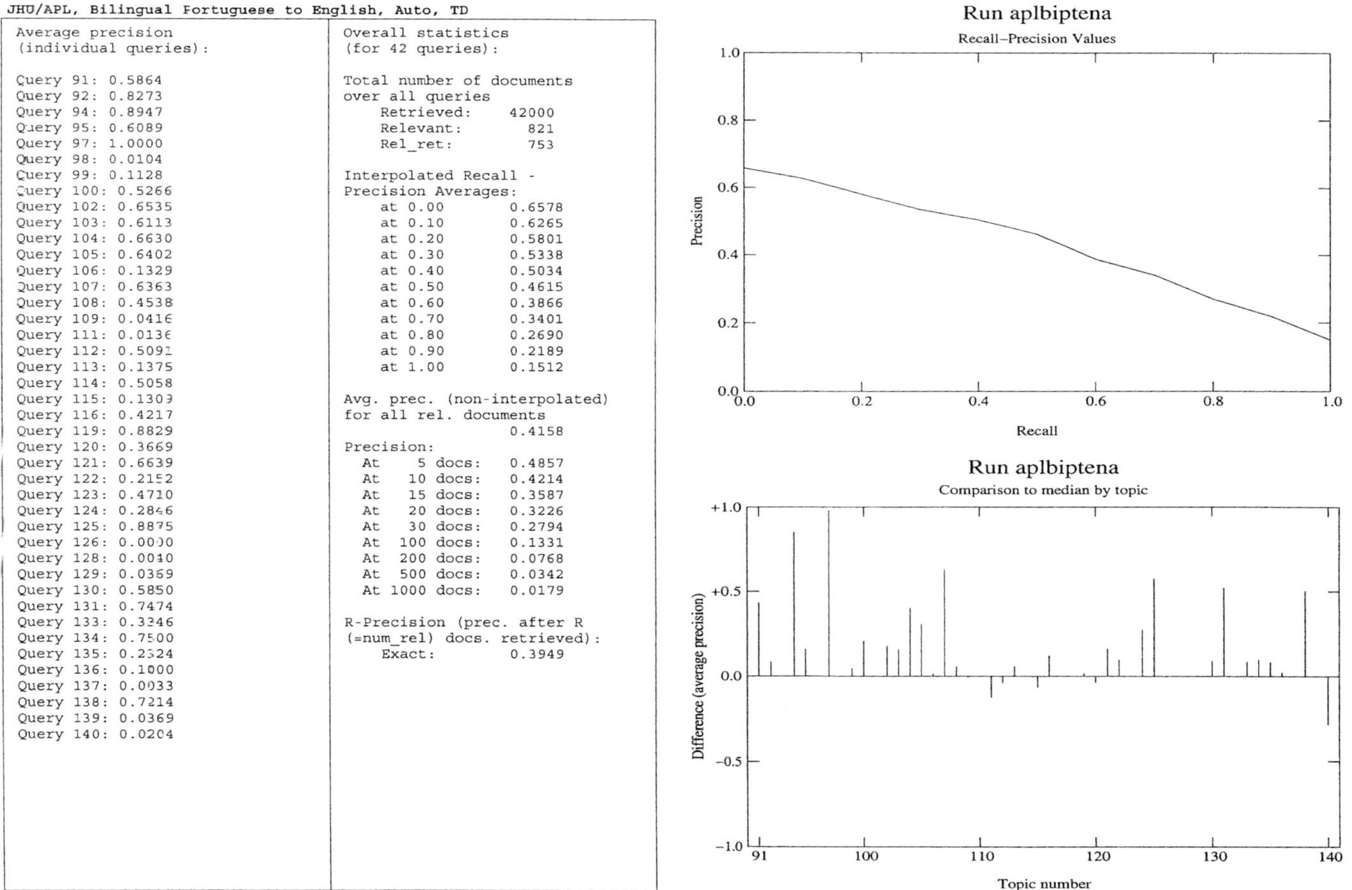

JHU/APL, Bilingual Portuguese to English, Auto, TD

```
Average precision                Overall statistics
(individual queries):            (for 42 queries):

Query 91: 0.5864                 Total number of documents
Query 92: 0.8273                 over all queries
Query 94: 0.8947                     Retrieved:     42000
Query 95: 0.6089                     Relevant:        821
Query 97: 1.0000                     Rel_ret:         753
Query 98: 0.0104
Query 99: 0.1128                 Interpolated Recall -
Query 100: 0.5266                Precision Averages:
Query 102: 0.6535                    at 0.00         0.6578
Query 103: 0.6113                    at 0.10         0.6265
Query 104: 0.6630                    at 0.20         0.5801
Query 105: 0.6402                    at 0.30         0.5338
Query 106: 0.1329                    at 0.40         0.5034
Query 107: 0.6363                    at 0.50         0.4615
Query 108: 0.4538                    at 0.60         0.3866
Query 109: 0.0416                    at 0.70         0.3401
Query 111: 0.0136                    at 0.80         0.2690
Query 112: 0.5091                    at 0.90         0.2189
Query 113: 0.1375                    at 1.00         0.1512
Query 114: 0.5058
Query 115: 0.1303                Avg. prec. (non-interpolated)
Query 116: 0.4217                for all rel. documents
Query 119: 0.8829                                    0.4158
Query 120: 0.3669                Precision:
Query 121: 0.6639                  At    5 docs:     0.4857
Query 122: 0.2152                  At   10 docs:     0.4214
Query 123: 0.4710                  At   15 docs:     0.3587
Query 124: 0.2846                  At   20 docs:     0.3226
Query 125: 0.8875                  At   30 docs:     0.2794
Query 126: 0.0000                  At  100 docs:     0.1331
Query 128: 0.0010                  At  200 docs:     0.0768
Query 129: 0.0369                  At  500 docs:     0.0342
Query 130: 0.5850                  At 1000 docs:     0.0179
Query 131: 0.7474
Query 133: 0.3246                R-Precision (prec. after R
Query 134: 0.7500                (=num_rel) docs. retrieved):
Query 135: 0.2524                    Exact:          0.3949
Query 136: 0.1000
Query 137: 0.0033
Query 138: 0.7214
Query 139: 0.0369
Query 140: 0.0204
```

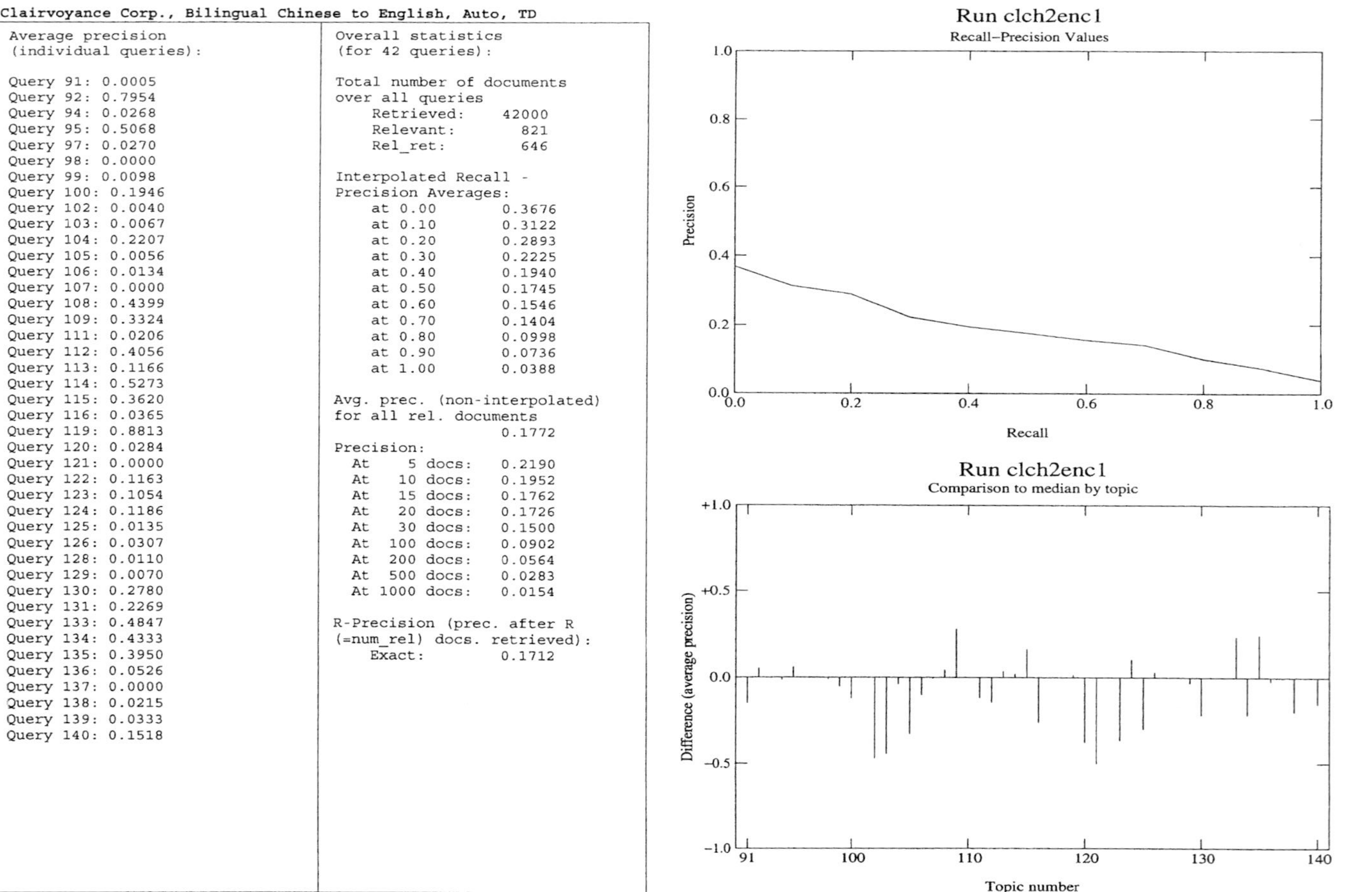

Clairvoyance Corp., Bilingual Chinese to English, Auto, TD

```
Average precision              Overall statistics
(individual queries):          (for 42 queries):

Query 91: 0.0005               Total number of documents
Query 92: 0.7954               over all queries
Query 94: 0.0268                   Retrieved:    42000
Query 95: 0.5068                   Relevant:       821
Query 97: 0.0270                   Rel_ret:        646
Query 98: 0.0000
Query 99: 0.0098               Interpolated Recall -
Query 100: 0.1946              Precision Averages:
Query 102: 0.0040                  at 0.00       0.3676
Query 103: 0.0067                  at 0.10       0.3122
Query 104: 0.2207                  at 0.20       0.2893
Query 105: 0.0056                  at 0.30       0.2225
Query 106: 0.0134                  at 0.40       0.1940
Query 107: 0.0000                  at 0.50       0.1745
Query 108: 0.4399                  at 0.60       0.1546
Query 109: 0.3324                  at 0.70       0.1404
Query 111: 0.0206                  at 0.80       0.0998
Query 112: 0.4056                  at 0.90       0.0736
Query 113: 0.1166                  at 1.00       0.0388
Query 114: 0.5273
Query 115: 0.3620              Avg. prec. (non-interpolated)
Query 116: 0.0365              for all rel. documents
Query 119: 0.8813                                0.1772
Query 120: 0.0284              Precision:
Query 121: 0.0000                At    5 docs:   0.2190
Query 122: 0.1163                At   10 docs:   0.1952
Query 123: 0.1054                At   15 docs:   0.1762
Query 124: 0.1186                At   20 docs:   0.1726
Query 125: 0.0135                At   30 docs:   0.1500
Query 126: 0.0307                At  100 docs:   0.0902
Query 128: 0.0110                At  200 docs:   0.0564
Query 129: 0.0070                At  500 docs:   0.0283
Query 130: 0.2780                At 1000 docs:   0.0154
Query 131: 0.2269
Query 133: 0.4847              R-Precision (prec. after R
Query 134: 0.4333              (=num_rel) docs. retrieved):
Query 135: 0.3950                  Exact:        0.1712
Query 136: 0.0526
Query 137: 0.0000
Query 138: 0.0215
Query 139: 0.0333
Query 140: 0.1518
```

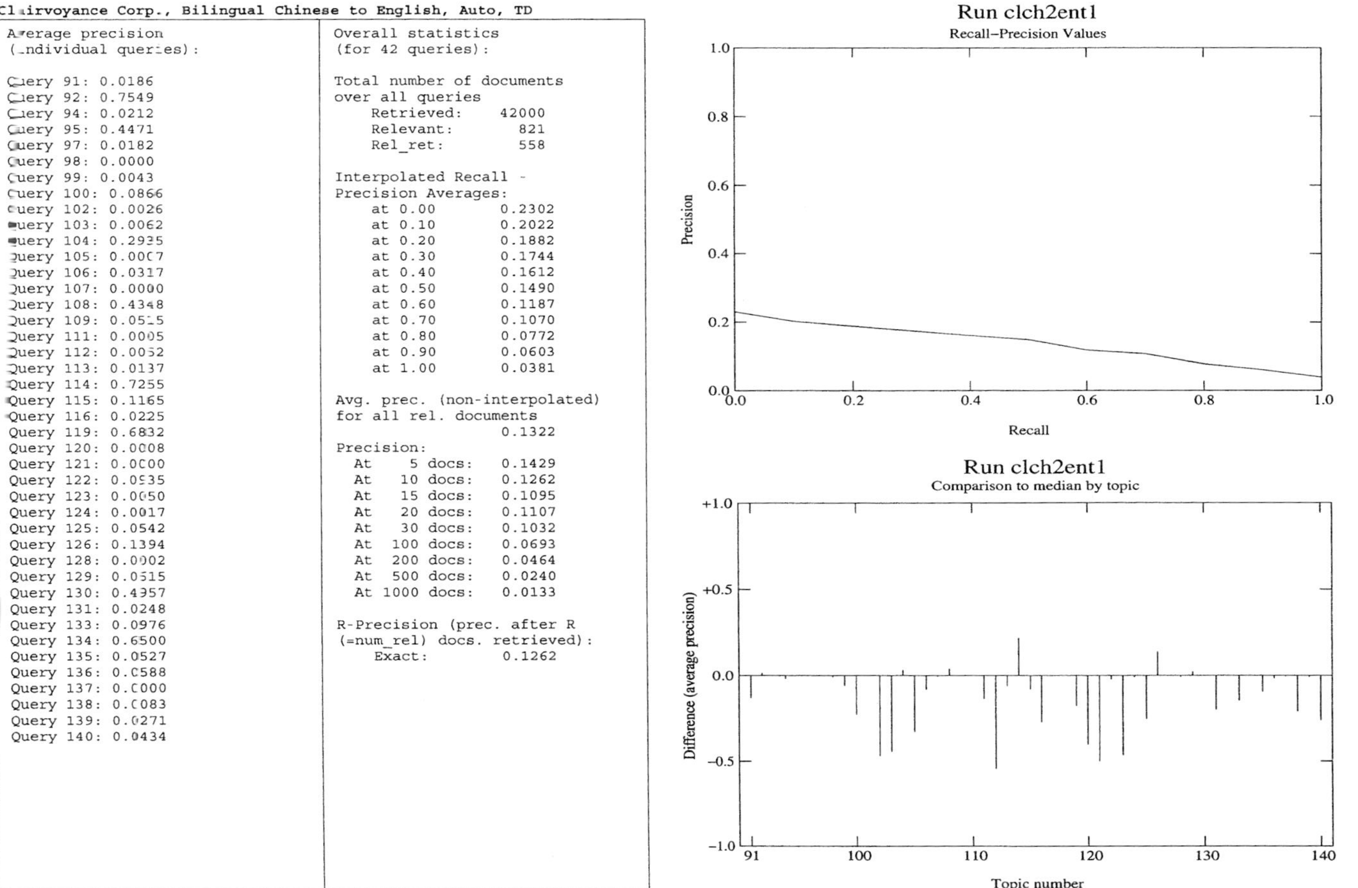

Clairvoyance Corp., Bilingual Chinese to English, Auto, TD

```
Average precision                 Overall statistics
(individual queries):             (for 42 queries):

Query 91: 0.0186                  Total number of documents
Query 92: 0.7549                  over all queries
Query 94: 0.0212                      Retrieved:    42000
Query 95: 0.4471                      Relevant:       821
Query 97: 0.0182                      Rel_ret:        558
Query 98: 0.0000
Query 99: 0.0043                  Interpolated Recall -
Query 100: 0.0866                 Precision Averages:
Query 102: 0.0026                     at 0.00       0.2302
Query 103: 0.0062                     at 0.10       0.2022
Query 104: 0.2935                     at 0.20       0.1882
Query 105: 0.0007                     at 0.30       0.1744
Query 106: 0.0317                     at 0.40       0.1612
Query 107: 0.0000                     at 0.50       0.1490
Query 108: 0.4348                     at 0.60       0.1187
Query 109: 0.0515                     at 0.70       0.1070
Query 111: 0.0005                     at 0.80       0.0772
Query 112: 0.0052                     at 0.90       0.0603
Query 113: 0.0137                     at 1.00       0.0381
Query 114: 0.7255
Query 115: 0.1165                 Avg. prec. (non-interpolated)
Query 116: 0.0225                 for all rel. documents
Query 119: 0.6832                                   0.1322
Query 120: 0.0008                 Precision:
Query 121: 0.0000                   At     5 docs:   0.1429
Query 122: 0.0535                   At    10 docs:   0.1262
Query 123: 0.0050                   At    15 docs:   0.1095
Query 124: 0.0017                   At    20 docs:   0.1107
Query 125: 0.0542                   At    30 docs:   0.1032
Query 126: 0.1394                   At   100 docs:   0.0693
Query 128: 0.0002                   At   200 docs:   0.0464
Query 129: 0.0515                   At   500 docs:   0.0240
Query 130: 0.4357                   At  1000 docs:   0.0133
Query 131: 0.0248
Query 133: 0.0976                 R-Precision (prec. after R
Query 134: 0.6500                 (=num_rel) docs. retrieved):
Query 135: 0.0527                     Exact:        0.1262
Query 136: 0.0588
Query 137: 0.0000
Query 138: 0.0083
Query 139: 0.0271
Query 140: 0.0434
```

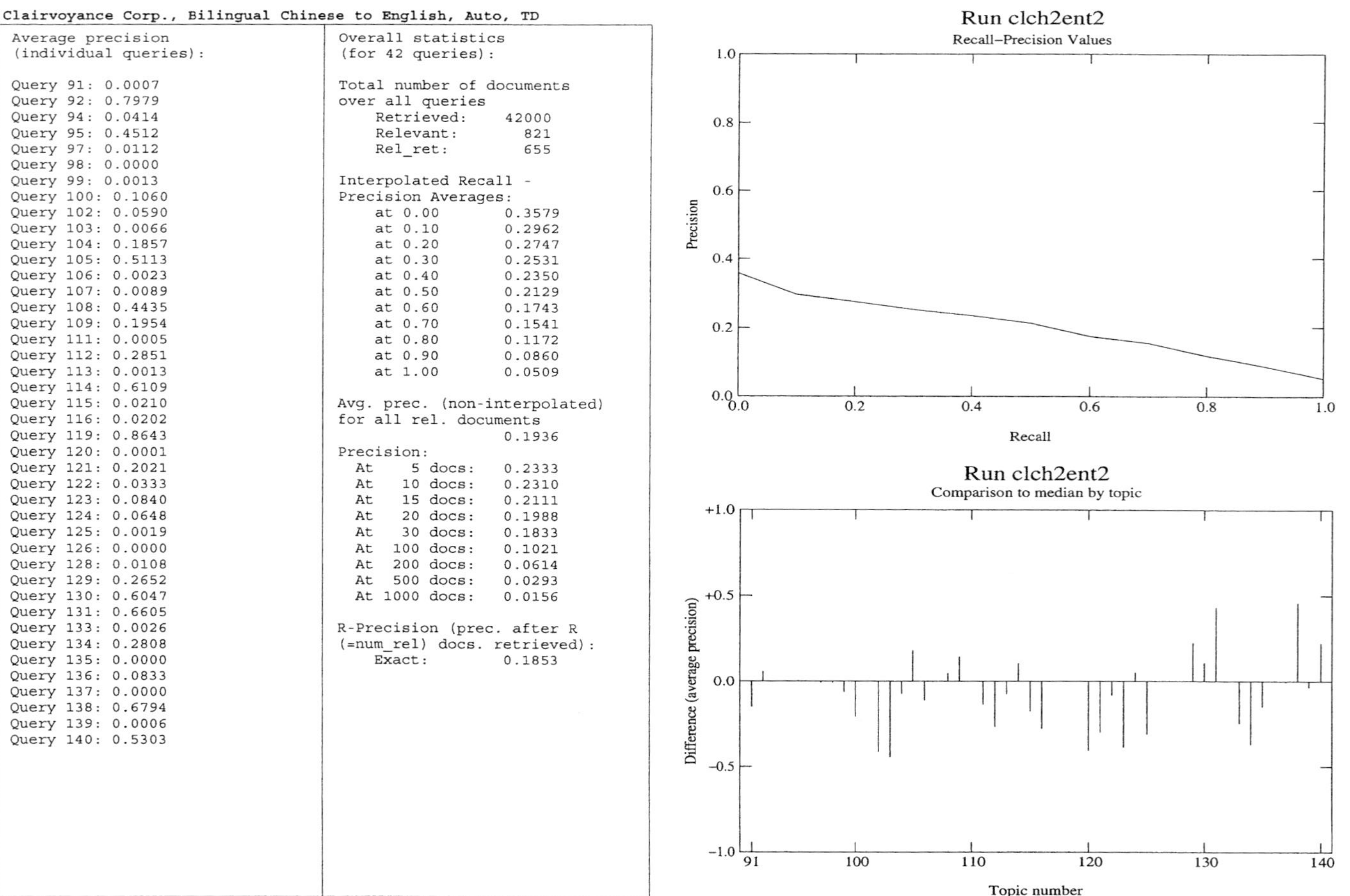

Clairvoyance Corp., Bilingual Chinese to English, Auto, TD

Average precision (individual queries):	Overall statistics (for 42 queries):
Query 91: 0.0007	Total number of documents over all queries
Query 92: 0.7979	Retrieved: 42000
Query 94: 0.0414	Relevant: 821
Query 95: 0.4512	Rel_ret: 655
Query 97: 0.0112	
Query 98: 0.0000	Interpolated Recall - Precision Averages:
Query 99: 0.0013	at 0.00 0.3579
Query 100: 0.1060	at 0.10 0.2962
Query 102: 0.0590	at 0.20 0.2747
Query 103: 0.0066	at 0.30 0.2531
Query 104: 0.1857	at 0.40 0.2350
Query 105: 0.5113	at 0.50 0.2129
Query 106: 0.0023	at 0.60 0.1743
Query 107: 0.0089	at 0.70 0.1541
Query 108: 0.4435	at 0.80 0.1172
Query 109: 0.1954	at 0.90 0.0860
Query 111: 0.0005	at 1.00 0.0509
Query 112: 0.2851	
Query 113: 0.0013	Avg. prec. (non-interpolated) for all rel. documents 0.1936
Query 114: 0.6109	
Query 115: 0.0210	Precision:
Query 116: 0.0202	At 5 docs: 0.2333
Query 119: 0.8643	At 10 docs: 0.2310
Query 120: 0.0001	At 15 docs: 0.2111
Query 121: 0.2021	At 20 docs: 0.1988
Query 122: 0.0333	At 30 docs: 0.1833
Query 123: 0.0840	At 100 docs: 0.1021
Query 124: 0.0648	At 200 docs: 0.0614
Query 125: 0.0019	At 500 docs: 0.0293
Query 126: 0.0000	At 1000 docs: 0.0156
Query 128: 0.0108	
Query 129: 0.2652	R-Precision (prec. after R (=num_rel) docs. retrieved):
Query 130: 0.6047	Exact: 0.1853
Query 131: 0.6605	
Query 133: 0.0026	
Query 134: 0.2808	
Query 135: 0.0000	
Query 136: 0.0833	
Query 137: 0.0000	
Query 138: 0.6794	
Query 139: 0.0006	
Query 140: 0.5303	

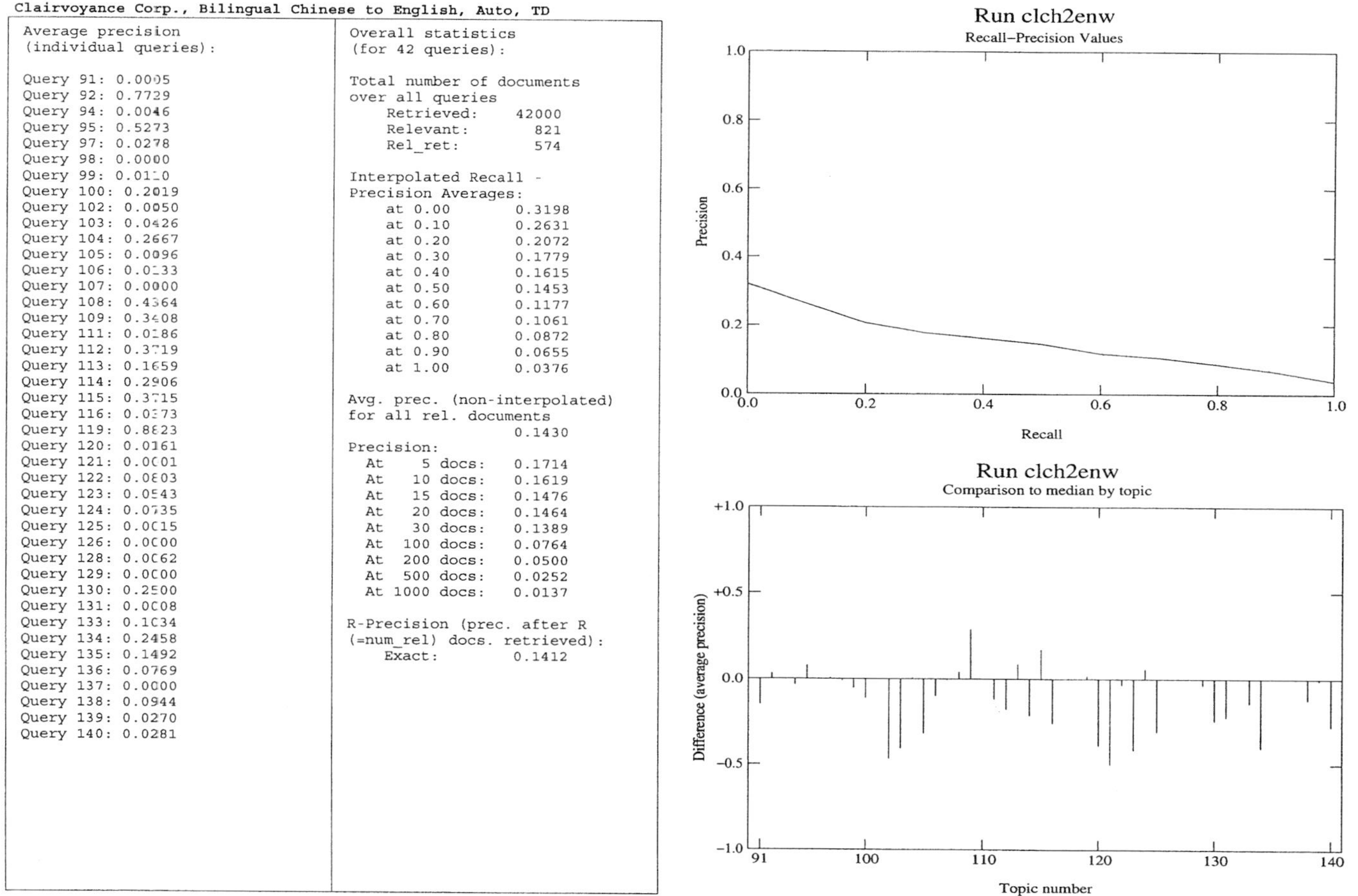

Clairvoyance Corp., Bilingual Chinese to English, Auto, TD

Average precision (individual queries):

Query	Average precision
Query 91:	0.0005
Query 92:	0.7729
Query 94:	0.0046
Query 95:	0.5273
Query 97:	0.0278
Query 98:	0.0000
Query 99:	0.0110
Query 100:	0.2019
Query 102:	0.0050
Query 103:	0.0426
Query 104:	0.2667
Query 105:	0.0096
Query 106:	0.0133
Query 107:	0.0000
Query 108:	0.4364
Query 109:	0.3408
Query 111:	0.0186
Query 112:	0.3719
Query 113:	0.1659
Query 114:	0.2906
Query 115:	0.3715
Query 116:	0.0373
Query 119:	0.8823
Query 120:	0.0161
Query 121:	0.0001
Query 122:	0.0803
Query 123:	0.0543
Query 124:	0.0735
Query 125:	0.0015
Query 126:	0.0000
Query 128:	0.0062
Query 129:	0.0000
Query 130:	0.2500
Query 131:	0.0008
Query 133:	0.1034
Query 134:	0.2458
Query 135:	0.1492
Query 136:	0.0769
Query 137:	0.0000
Query 138:	0.0944
Query 139:	0.0270
Query 140:	0.0281

Overall statistics (for 42 queries):

Total number of documents over all queries

Retrieved:	42000
Relevant:	821
Rel_ret:	574

Interpolated Recall - Precision Averages:

at 0.00	0.3198
at 0.10	0.2631
at 0.20	0.2072
at 0.30	0.1779
at 0.40	0.1615
at 0.50	0.1453
at 0.60	0.1177
at 0.70	0.1061
at 0.80	0.0872
at 0.90	0.0655
at 1.00	0.0376

Avg. prec. (non-interpolated) for all rel. documents 0.1430

Precision:

At 5 docs:	0.1714
At 10 docs:	0.1619
At 15 docs:	0.1476
At 20 docs:	0.1464
At 30 docs:	0.1389
At 100 docs:	0.0764
At 200 docs:	0.0500
At 500 docs:	0.0252
At 1000 docs:	0.0137

R-Precision (prec. after R (=num_rel) docs. retrieved):
Exact: 0.1412

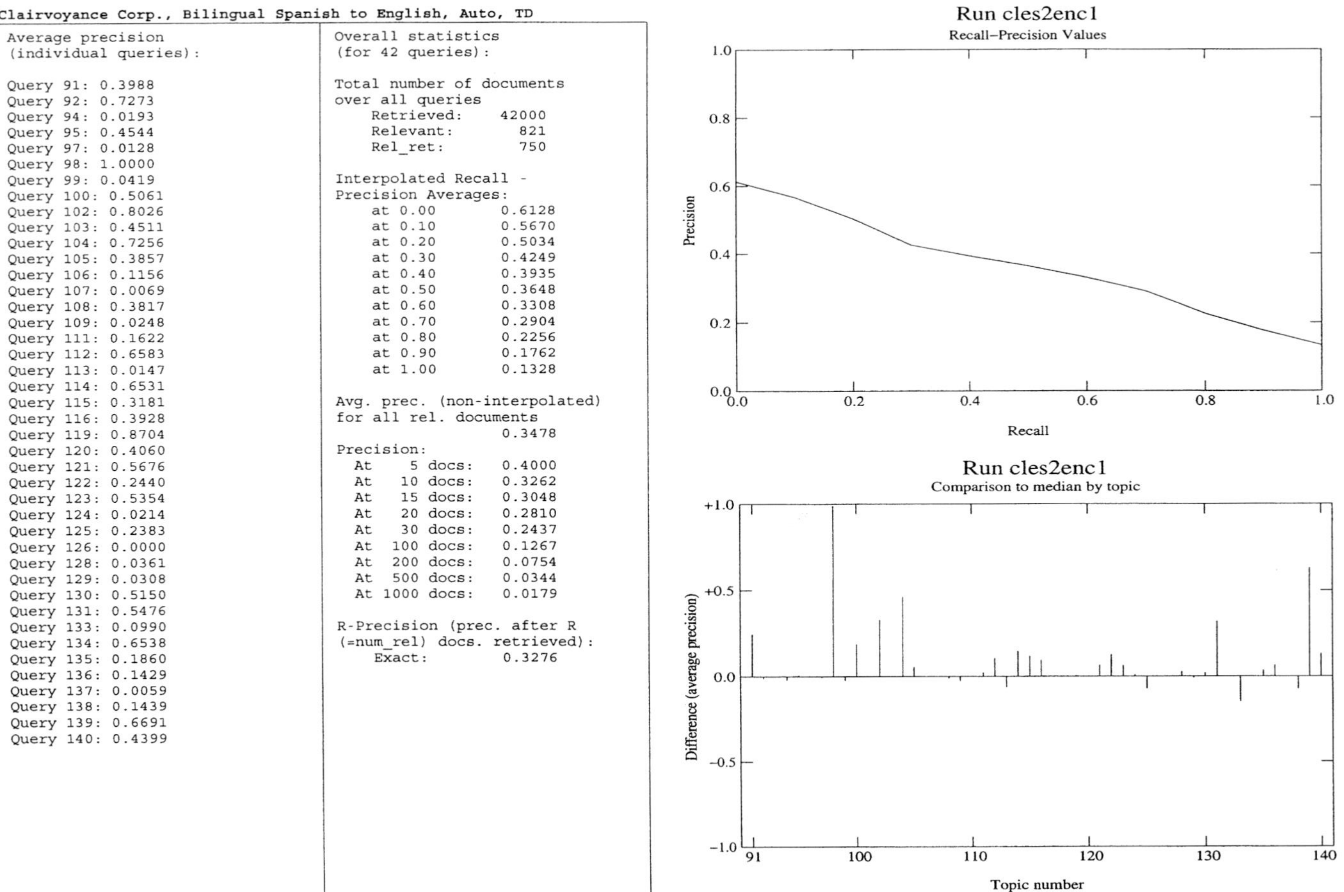

Clairvoyance Corp., Bilingual Spanish to English, Auto, TD

Average precision
(individual queries):

Query 91: 0.3988
Query 92: 0.7273
Query 94: 0.0193
Query 95: 0.4544
Query 97: 0.0128
Query 98: 1.0000
Query 99: 0.0419
Query 100: 0.5061
Query 102: 0.8026
Query 103: 0.4511
Query 104: 0.7256
Query 105: 0.3857
Query 106: 0.1156
Query 107: 0.0069
Query 108: 0.3817
Query 109: 0.0248
Query 111: 0.1622
Query 112: 0.6583
Query 113: 0.0147
Query 114: 0.6531
Query 115: 0.3181
Query 116: 0.3928
Query 119: 0.8704
Query 120: 0.4060
Query 121: 0.5676
Query 122: 0.2440
Query 123: 0.5354
Query 124: 0.0214
Query 125: 0.2383
Query 126: 0.0000
Query 128: 0.0361
Query 129: 0.0308
Query 130: 0.5150
Query 131: 0.5476
Query 133: 0.0990
Query 134: 0.6538
Query 135: 0.1860
Query 136: 0.1429
Query 137: 0.0059
Query 138: 0.1439
Query 139: 0.6691
Query 140: 0.4399

Overall statistics
(for 42 queries):

Total number of documents
over all queries
Retrieved: 42000
Relevant: 821
Rel_ret: 750

Interpolated Recall -
Precision Averages:
at 0.00 0.6128
at 0.10 0.5670
at 0.20 0.5034
at 0.30 0.4249
at 0.40 0.3935
at 0.50 0.3648
at 0.60 0.3308
at 0.70 0.2904
at 0.80 0.2256
at 0.90 0.1762
at 1.00 0.1328

Avg. prec. (non-interpolated)
for all rel. documents
0.3478

Precision:
At 5 docs: 0.4000
At 10 docs: 0.3262
At 15 docs: 0.3048
At 20 docs: 0.2810
At 30 docs: 0.2437
At 100 docs: 0.1267
At 200 docs: 0.0754
At 500 docs: 0.0344
At 1000 docs: 0.0179

R-Precision (prec. after R
(=num_rel) docs. retrieved):
Exact: 0.3276

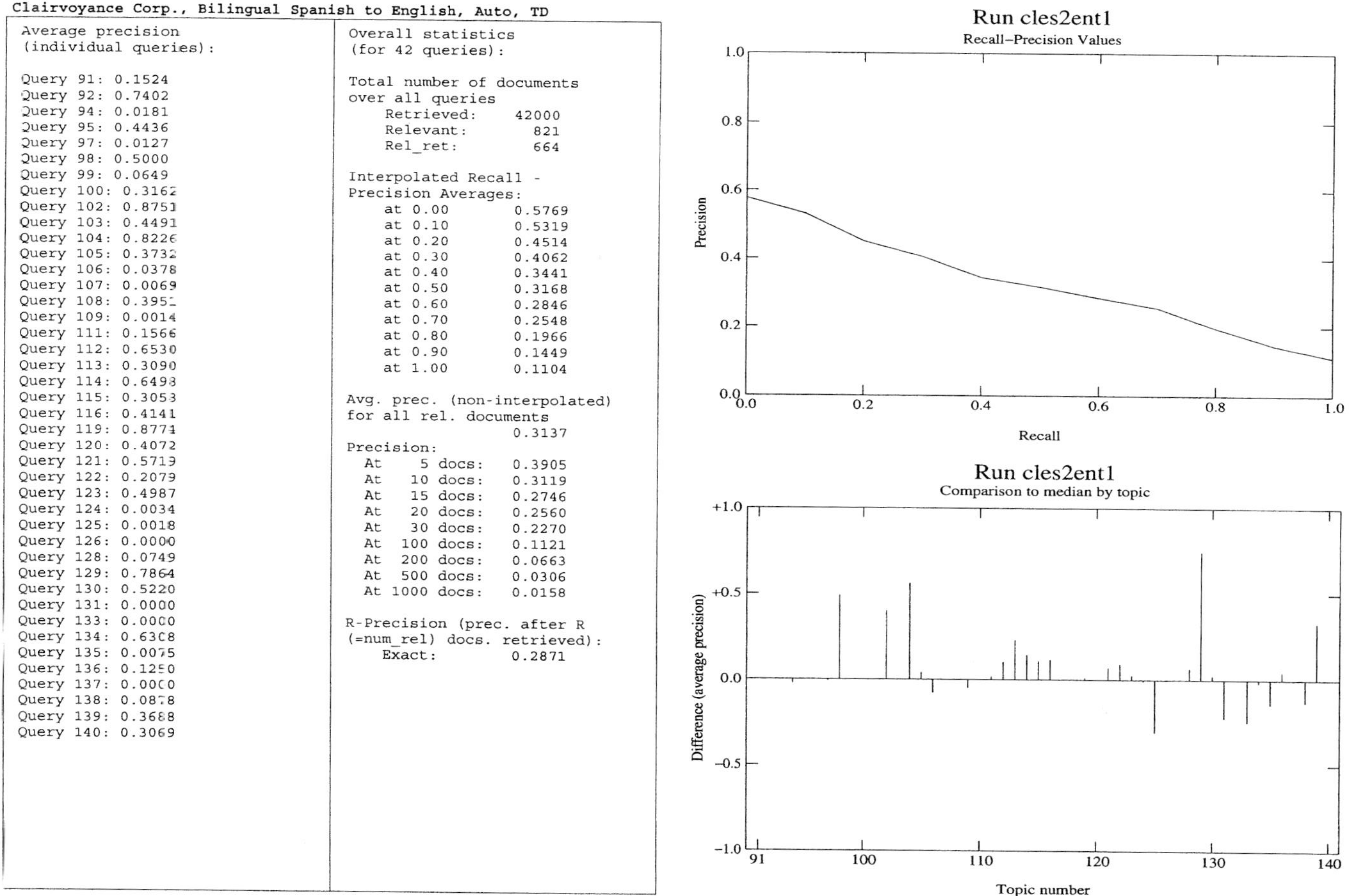

Clairvoyance Corp., Bilingual Spanish to English, Auto, TD

```
Average precision                 Overall statistics
(individual queries):             (for 42 queries):

Query 91: 0.1524                  Total number of documents
Query 92: 0.7402                  over all queries
Query 94: 0.0181                      Retrieved:    42000
Query 95: 0.4436                      Relevant:       821
Query 97: 0.0127                      Rel_ret:        664
Query 98: 0.5000
Query 99: 0.0649                  Interpolated Recall -
Query 100: 0.3162                 Precision Averages:
Query 102: 0.8751                     at 0.00       0.5769
Query 103: 0.4491                     at 0.10       0.5319
Query 104: 0.8226                     at 0.20       0.4514
Query 105: 0.3732                     at 0.30       0.4062
Query 106: 0.0378                     at 0.40       0.3441
Query 107: 0.0069                     at 0.50       0.3168
Query 108: 0.3951                     at 0.60       0.2846
Query 109: 0.0014                     at 0.70       0.2548
Query 111: 0.1566                     at 0.80       0.1966
Query 112: 0.6530                     at 0.90       0.1449
Query 113: 0.3090                     at 1.00       0.1104
Query 114: 0.6498
Query 115: 0.3053                 Avg. prec. (non-interpolated)
Query 116: 0.4141                 for all rel. documents
Query 119: 0.8774                                   0.3137
Query 120: 0.4072                 Precision:
Query 121: 0.5719                   At    5 docs:   0.3905
Query 122: 0.2079                   At   10 docs:   0.3119
Query 123: 0.4987                   At   15 docs:   0.2746
Query 124: 0.0034                   At   20 docs:   0.2560
Query 125: 0.0018                   At   30 docs:   0.2270
Query 126: 0.0000                   At  100 docs:   0.1121
Query 128: 0.0749                   At  200 docs:   0.0663
Query 129: 0.7864                   At  500 docs:   0.0306
Query 130: 0.5220                   At 1000 docs:   0.0158
Query 131: 0.0000
Query 133: 0.0000                 R-Precision (prec. after R
Query 134: 0.6308                 (=num_rel) docs. retrieved):
Query 135: 0.0075                    Exact:         0.2871
Query 136: 0.1250
Query 137: 0.0000
Query 138: 0.0878
Query 139: 0.3688
Query 140: 0.3069
```

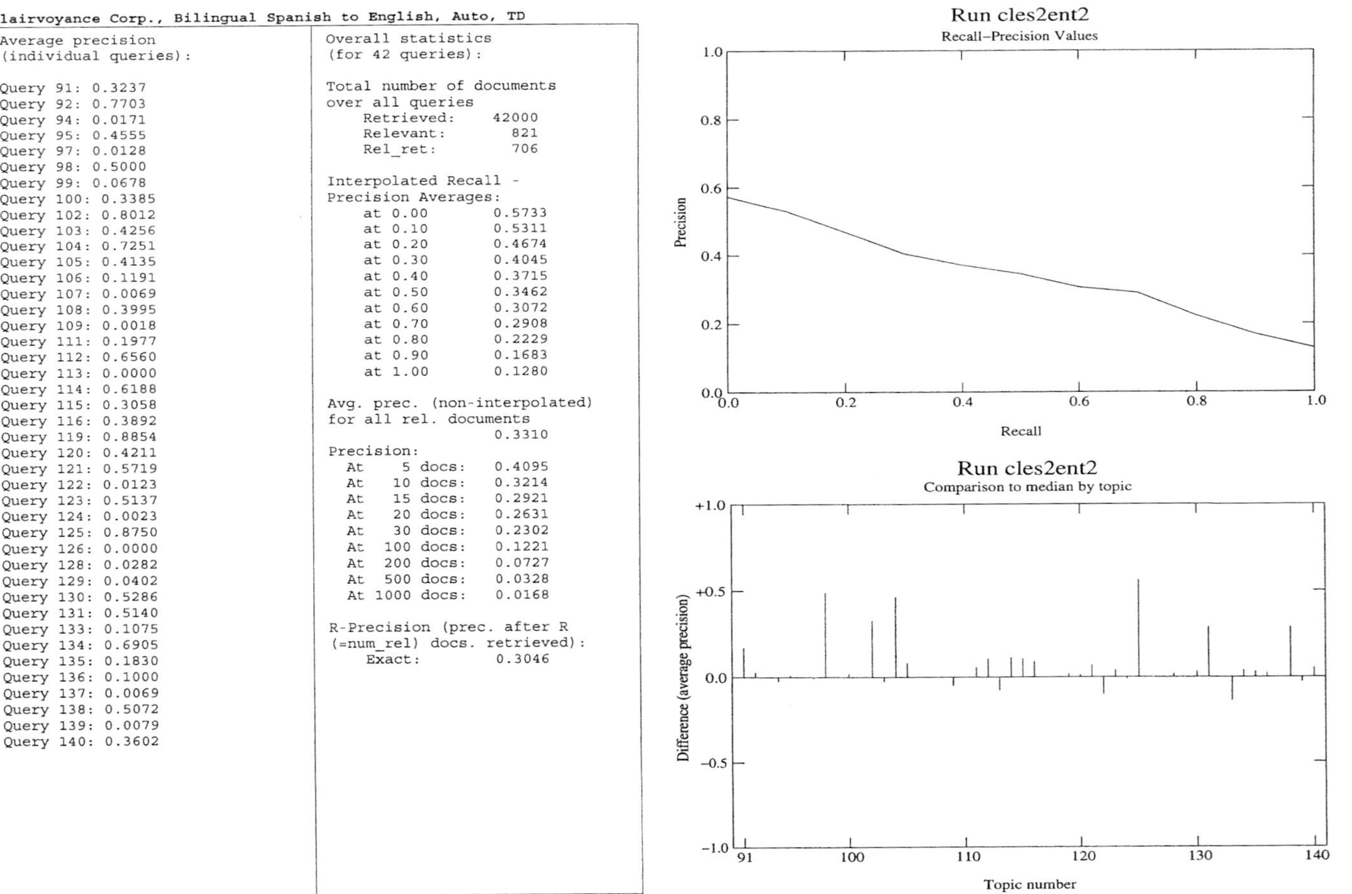

Clairvoyance Corp., Bilingual Spanish to English, Auto, TD

Average precision (individual queries):	Overall statistics (for 42 queries):
Query 91: 0.3237	Total number of documents over all queries
Query 92: 0.7703	Retrieved: 42000
Query 94: 0.0171	Relevant: 821
Query 95: 0.4555	Rel_ret: 706
Query 97: 0.0128	
Query 98: 0.5000	Interpolated Recall - Precision Averages:
Query 99: 0.0678	at 0.00 0.5733
Query 100: 0.3385	at 0.10 0.5311
Query 102: 0.8012	at 0.20 0.4674
Query 103: 0.4256	at 0.30 0.4045
Query 104: 0.7251	at 0.40 0.3715
Query 105: 0.4135	at 0.50 0.3462
Query 106: 0.1191	at 0.60 0.3072
Query 107: 0.0069	at 0.70 0.2908
Query 108: 0.3995	at 0.80 0.2229
Query 109: 0.0018	at 0.90 0.1683
Query 111: 0.1977	at 1.00 0.1280
Query 112: 0.6560	
Query 113: 0.0000	Avg. prec. (non-interpolated) for all rel. documents 0.3310
Query 114: 0.6188	
Query 115: 0.3058	Precision:
Query 116: 0.3892	At 5 docs: 0.4095
Query 119: 0.8854	At 10 docs: 0.3214
Query 120: 0.4211	At 15 docs: 0.2921
Query 121: 0.5719	At 20 docs: 0.2631
Query 122: 0.0123	At 30 docs: 0.2302
Query 123: 0.5137	At 100 docs: 0.1221
Query 124: 0.0023	At 200 docs: 0.0727
Query 125: 0.8750	At 500 docs: 0.0328
Query 126: 0.0000	At 1000 docs: 0.0168
Query 128: 0.0282	
Query 129: 0.0402	R-Precision (prec. after R (=num_rel) docs. retrieved):
Query 130: 0.5286	Exact: 0.3046
Query 131: 0.5140	
Query 133: 0.1075	
Query 134: 0.6905	
Query 135: 0.1830	
Query 136: 0.1000	
Query 137: 0.0069	
Query 138: 0.5072	
Query 139: 0.0079	
Query 140: 0.3602	

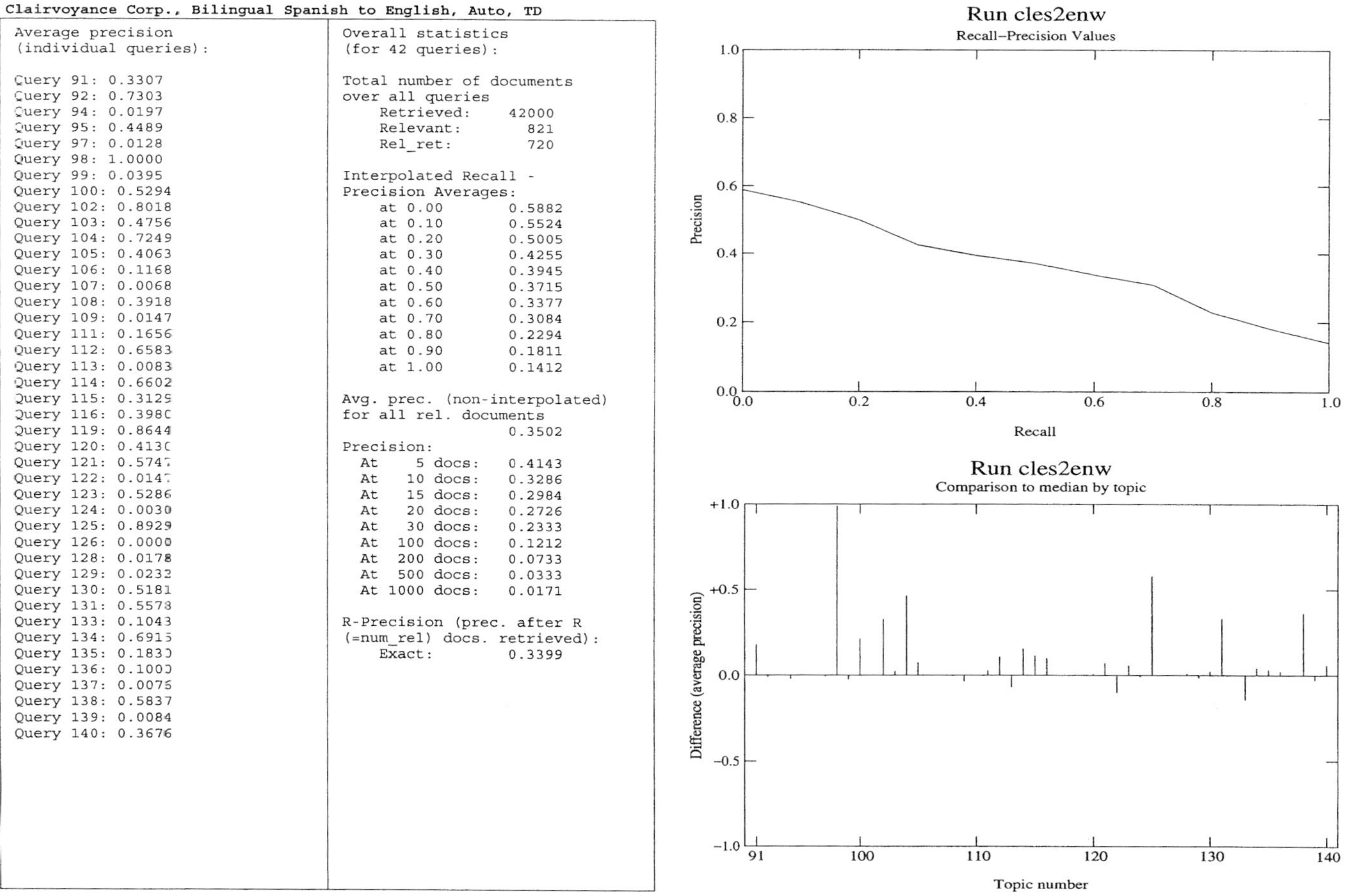

Clairvoyance Corp., Bilingual Spanish to English, Auto, TD

Average precision (individual queries):

Query	Average precision
Query 91:	0.3307
Query 92:	0.7303
Query 94:	0.0197
Query 95:	0.4489
Query 97:	0.0128
Query 98:	1.0000
Query 99:	0.0395
Query 100:	0.5294
Query 102:	0.8018
Query 103:	0.4756
Query 104:	0.7249
Query 105:	0.4063
Query 106:	0.1168
Query 107:	0.0068
Query 108:	0.3918
Query 109:	0.0147
Query 111:	0.1656
Query 112:	0.6583
Query 113:	0.0083
Query 114:	0.6602
Query 115:	0.3129
Query 116:	0.3980
Query 119:	0.8644
Query 120:	0.4130
Query 121:	0.5747
Query 122:	0.0147
Query 123:	0.5286
Query 124:	0.0030
Query 125:	0.8929
Query 126:	0.0000
Query 128:	0.0178
Query 129:	0.0232
Query 130:	0.5181
Query 131:	0.5578
Query 133:	0.1043
Query 134:	0.6915
Query 135:	0.1830
Query 136:	0.1000
Query 137:	0.0075
Query 138:	0.5837
Query 139:	0.0084
Query 140:	0.3676

Overall statistics (for 42 queries):

Total number of documents over all queries

Retrieved:	42000
Relevant:	821
Rel_ret:	720

Interpolated Recall - Precision Averages:

at 0.00	0.5882
at 0.10	0.5524
at 0.20	0.5005
at 0.30	0.4255
at 0.40	0.3945
at 0.50	0.3715
at 0.60	0.3377
at 0.70	0.3084
at 0.80	0.2294
at 0.90	0.1811
at 1.00	0.1412

Avg. prec. (non-interpolated) for all rel. documents 0.3502

Precision:

At 5 docs:	0.4143
At 10 docs:	0.3286
At 15 docs:	0.2984
At 20 docs:	0.2726
At 30 docs:	0.2333
At 100 docs:	0.1212
At 200 docs:	0.0733
At 500 docs:	0.0333
At 1000 docs:	0.0171

R-Precision (prec. after R (=num_rel) docs. retrieved):
Exact: 0.3399

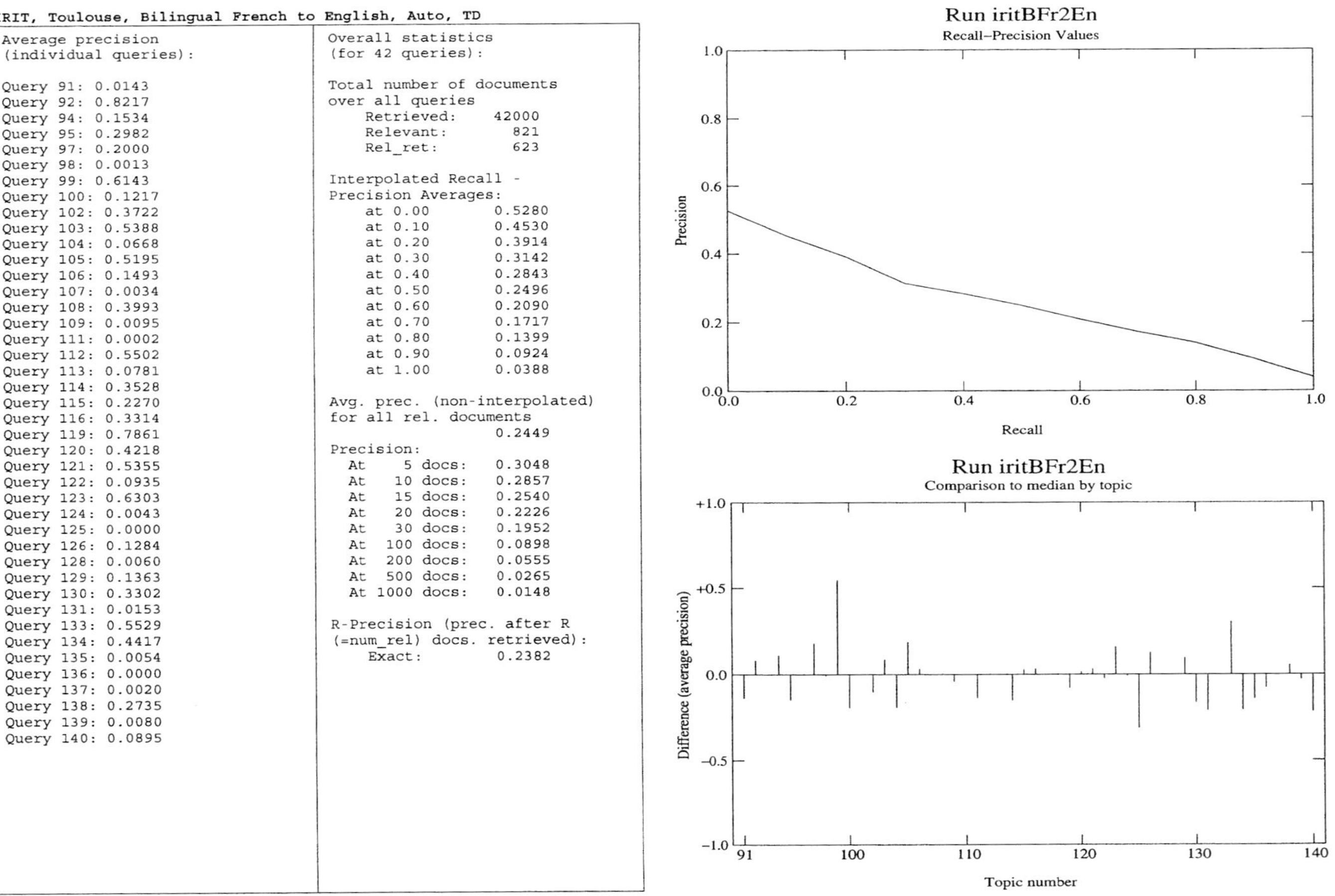

IRIT, Toulouse, Bilingual French to English, Auto, TD

Average precision (individual queries):	Overall statistics (for 42 queries):
Query 91: 0.0143	Total number of documents over all queries
Query 92: 0.8217	Retrieved: 42000
Query 94: 0.1534	Relevant: 821
Query 95: 0.2982	Rel_ret: 623
Query 97: 0.2000	
Query 98: 0.0013	Interpolated Recall - Precision Averages:
Query 99: 0.6143	at 0.00 0.5280
Query 100: 0.1217	at 0.10 0.4530
Query 102: 0.3722	at 0.20 0.3914
Query 103: 0.5388	at 0.30 0.3142
Query 104: 0.0668	at 0.40 0.2843
Query 105: 0.5195	at 0.50 0.2496
Query 106: 0.1493	at 0.60 0.2090
Query 107: 0.0034	at 0.70 0.1717
Query 108: 0.3993	at 0.80 0.1399
Query 109: 0.0095	at 0.90 0.0924
Query 111: 0.0002	at 1.00 0.0388
Query 112: 0.5502	
Query 113: 0.0781	Avg. prec. (non-interpolated) for all rel. documents 0.2449
Query 114: 0.3528	
Query 115: 0.2270	Precision:
Query 116: 0.3314	At 5 docs: 0.3048
Query 119: 0.7861	At 10 docs: 0.2857
Query 120: 0.4218	At 15 docs: 0.2540
Query 121: 0.5355	At 20 docs: 0.2226
Query 122: 0.0935	At 30 docs: 0.1952
Query 123: 0.6303	At 100 docs: 0.0898
Query 124: 0.0043	At 200 docs: 0.0555
Query 125: 0.0000	At 500 docs: 0.0265
Query 126: 0.1284	At 1000 docs: 0.0148
Query 128: 0.0060	
Query 129: 0.1363	R-Precision (prec. after R (=num_rel) docs. retrieved):
Query 130: 0.3302	Exact: 0.2382
Query 131: 0.0153	
Query 133: 0.5529	
Query 134: 0.4417	
Query 135: 0.0054	
Query 136: 0.0000	
Query 137: 0.0020	
Query 138: 0.2735	
Query 139: 0.0080	
Query 140: 0.0895	

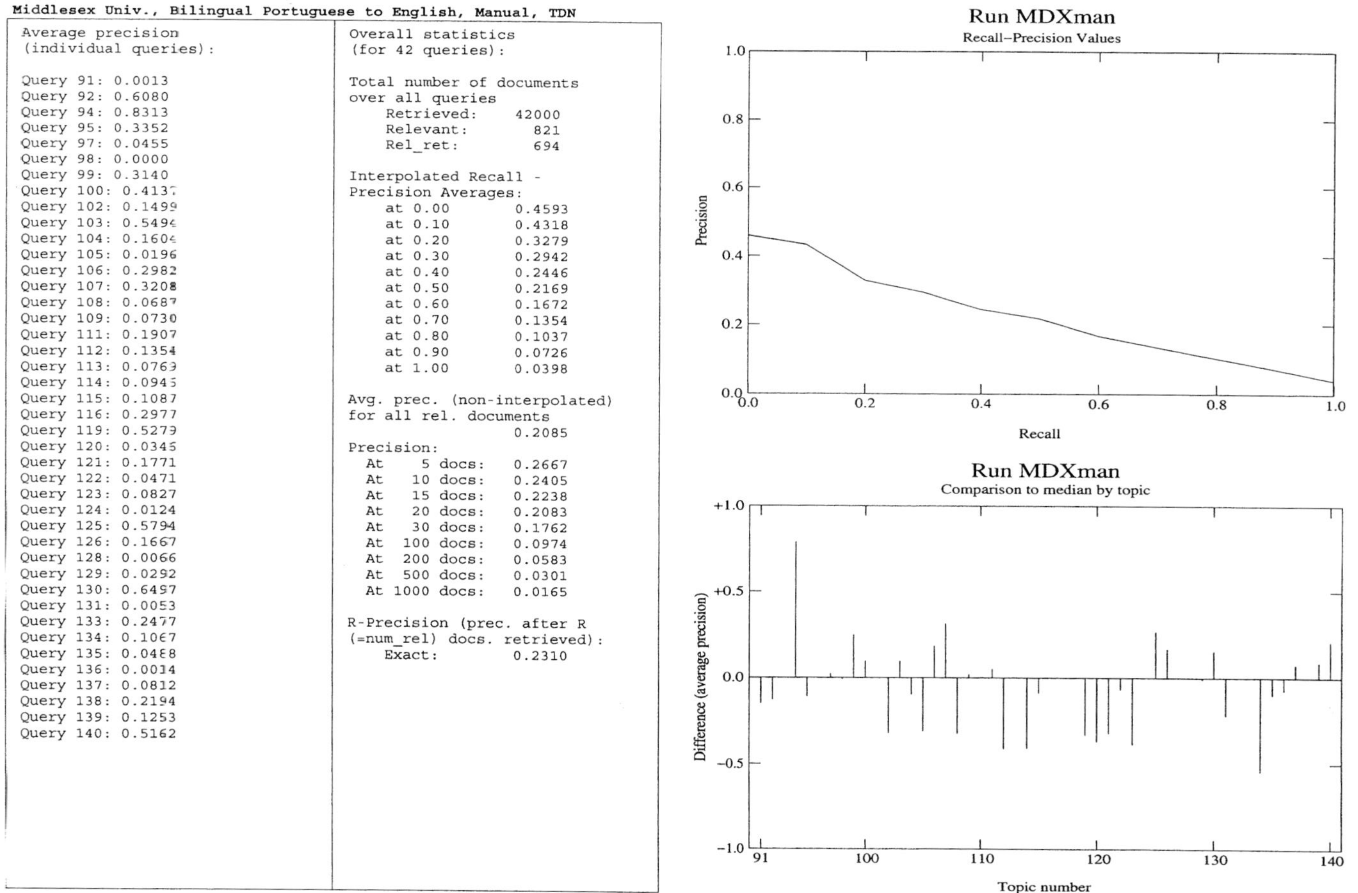

Middlesex Univ., Bilingual Portuguese to English, Manual, TDN

```
Average precision               Overall statistics
(individual queries):           (for 42 queries):

Query 91: 0.0013                Total number of documents
Query 92: 0.6080                over all queries
Query 94: 0.8313                    Retrieved:     42000
Query 95: 0.3352                    Relevant:        821
Query 97: 0.0455                    Rel_ret:         694
Query 98: 0.0000
Query 99: 0.3140                Interpolated Recall -
Query 100: 0.4137               Precision Averages:
Query 102: 0.1499                   at 0.00        0.4593
Query 103: 0.5494                   at 0.10        0.4318
Query 104: 0.1604                   at 0.20        0.3279
Query 105: 0.0196                   at 0.30        0.2942
Query 106: 0.2982                   at 0.40        0.2446
Query 107: 0.3208                   at 0.50        0.2169
Query 108: 0.0687                   at 0.60        0.1672
Query 109: 0.0730                   at 0.70        0.1354
Query 111: 0.1907                   at 0.80        0.1037
Query 112: 0.1354                   at 0.90        0.0726
Query 113: 0.0769                   at 1.00        0.0398
Query 114: 0.0945
Query 115: 0.1087               Avg. prec. (non-interpolated)
Query 116: 0.2977               for all rel. documents
Query 119: 0.5279                                  0.2085
Query 120: 0.0345               Precision:
Query 121: 0.1771                 At    5 docs:    0.2667
Query 122: 0.0471                 At   10 docs:    0.2405
Query 123: 0.0827                 At   15 docs:    0.2238
Query 124: 0.0124                 At   20 docs:    0.2083
Query 125: 0.5794                 At   30 docs:    0.1762
Query 126: 0.1667                 At  100 docs:    0.0974
Query 128: 0.0066                 At  200 docs:    0.0583
Query 129: 0.0292                 At  500 docs:    0.0301
Query 130: 0.6457                 At 1000 docs:    0.0165
Query 131: 0.0053
Query 133: 0.2477               R-Precision (prec. after R
Query 134: 0.1067               (=num_rel) docs. retrieved):
Query 135: 0.0488                   Exact:         0.2310
Query 136: 0.0014
Query 137: 0.0812
Query 138: 0.2194
Query 139: 0.1253
Query 140: 0.5162
```

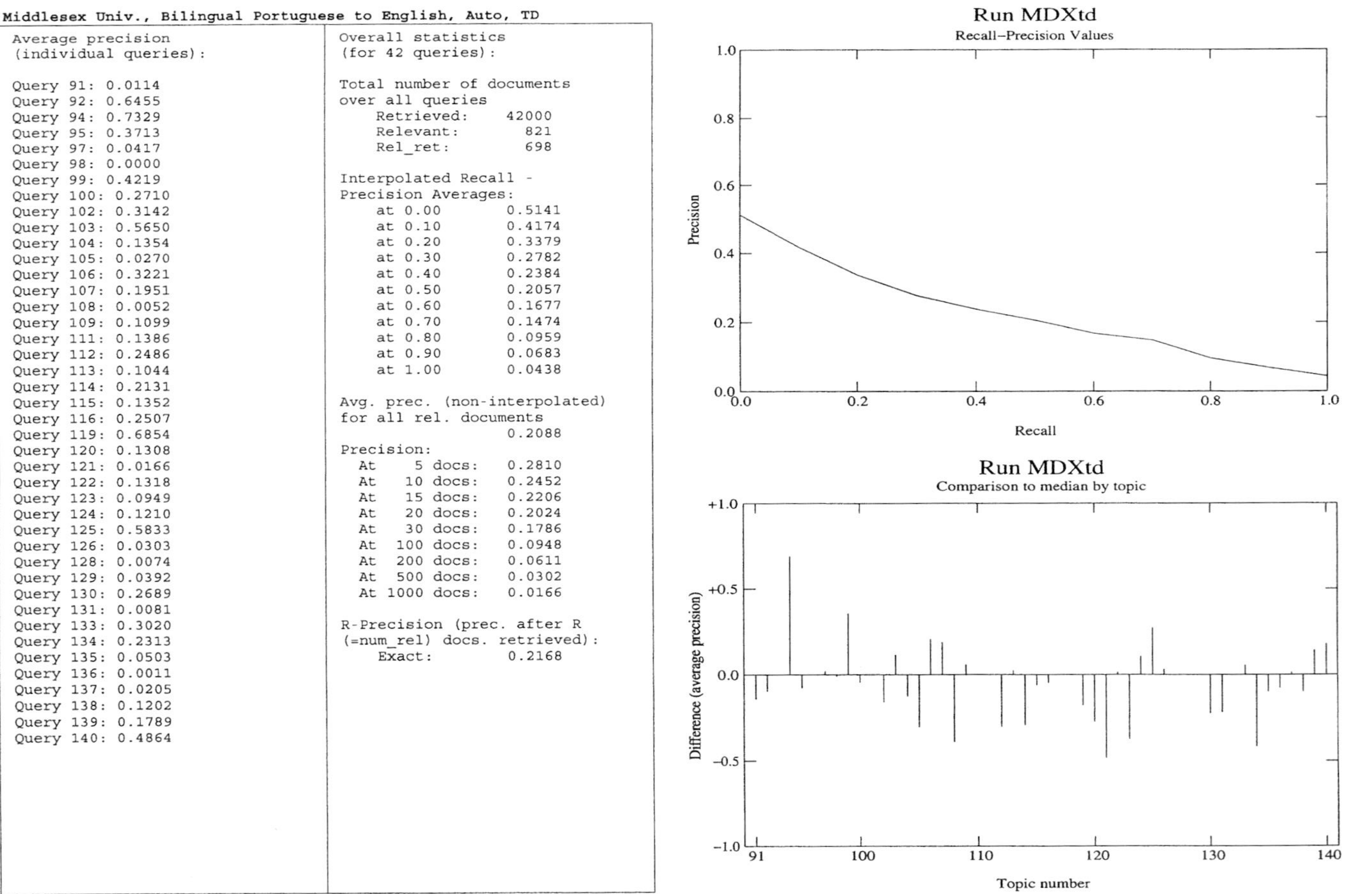

Middlesex Univ., Bilingual Portuguese to English, Auto, TD

Average precision (individual queries):	Overall statistics (for 42 queries):
Query 91: 0.0114 Query 92: 0.6455 Query 94: 0.7329 Query 95: 0.3713 Query 97: 0.0417 Query 98: 0.0000 Query 99: 0.4219 Query 100: 0.2710 Query 102: 0.3142 Query 103: 0.5650 Query 104: 0.1354 Query 105: 0.0270 Query 106: 0.3221 Query 107: 0.1951 Query 108: 0.0052 Query 109: 0.1099 Query 111: 0.1386 Query 112: 0.2486 Query 113: 0.1044 Query 114: 0.2131 Query 115: 0.1352 Query 116: 0.2507 Query 119: 0.6854 Query 120: 0.1308 Query 121: 0.0166 Query 122: 0.1318 Query 123: 0.0949 Query 124: 0.1210 Query 125: 0.5833 Query 126: 0.0303 Query 128: 0.0074 Query 129: 0.0392 Query 130: 0.2689 Query 131: 0.0081 Query 133: 0.3020 Query 134: 0.2313 Query 135: 0.0503 Query 136: 0.0011 Query 137: 0.0205 Query 138: 0.1202 Query 139: 0.1789 Query 140: 0.4864	Total number of documents over all queries Retrieved: 42000 Relevant: 821 Rel_ret: 698 Interpolated Recall - Precision Averages: at 0.00 0.5141 at 0.10 0.4174 at 0.20 0.3379 at 0.30 0.2782 at 0.40 0.2384 at 0.50 0.2057 at 0.60 0.1677 at 0.70 0.1474 at 0.80 0.0959 at 0.90 0.0683 at 1.00 0.0438 Avg. prec. (non-interpolated) for all rel. documents 0.2088 Precision: At 5 docs: 0.2810 At 10 docs: 0.2452 At 15 docs: 0.2206 At 20 docs: 0.2024 At 30 docs: 0.1786 At 100 docs: 0.0948 At 200 docs: 0.0611 At 500 docs: 0.0302 At 1000 docs: 0.0166 R-Precision (prec. after R (=num_rel) docs. retrieved): Exact: 0.2168

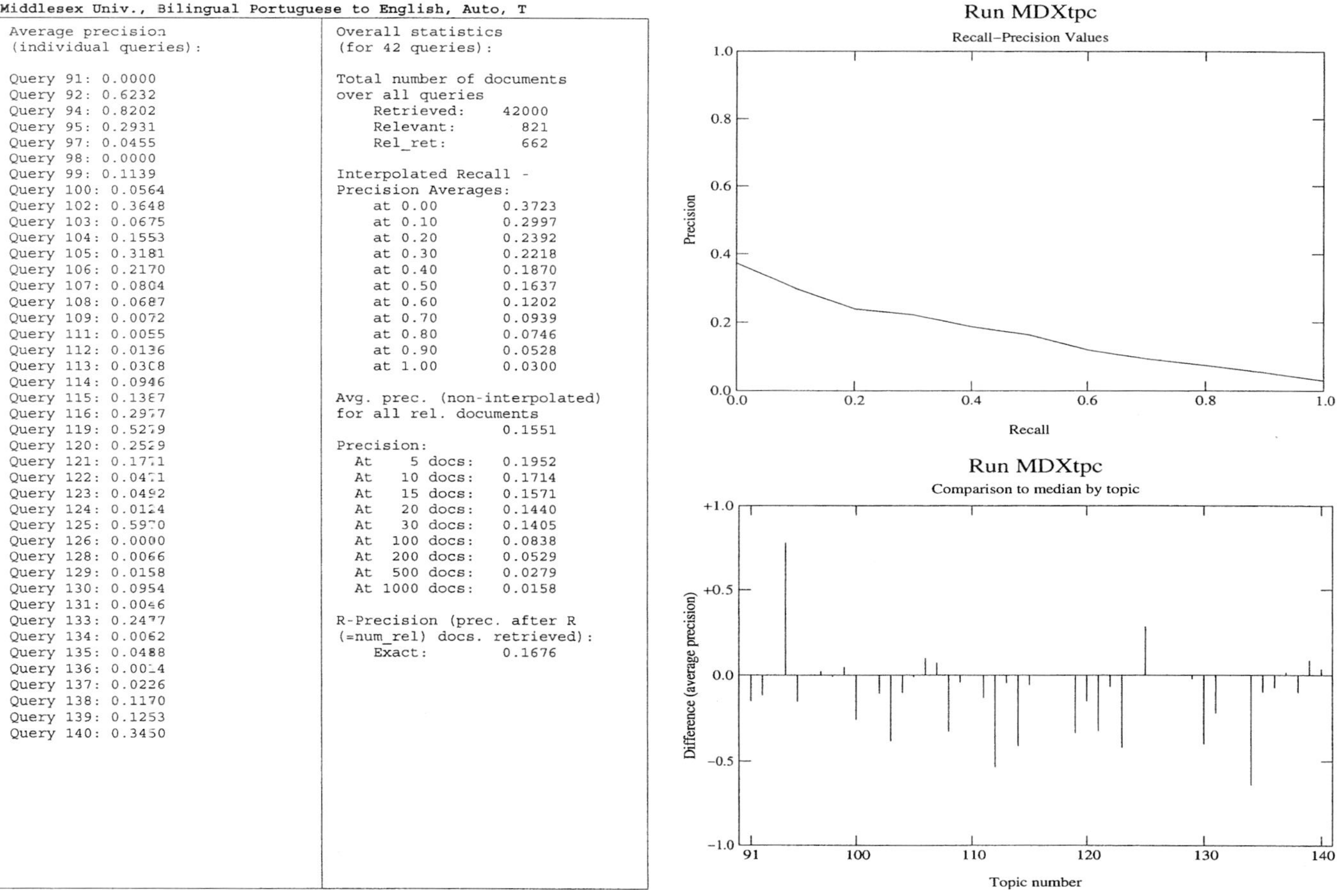

```
Middlesex Univ., Bilingual Portuguese to English, Auto, T

Average precision
(individual queries):

Query 91: 0.0000
Query 92: 0.6232
Query 94: 0.8202
Query 95: 0.2931
Query 97: 0.0455
Query 98: 0.0000
Query 99: 0.1139
Query 100: 0.0564
Query 102: 0.3648
Query 103: 0.0675
Query 104: 0.1553
Query 105: 0.3181
Query 106: 0.2170
Query 107: 0.0804
Query 108: 0.0687
Query 109: 0.0072
Query 111: 0.0055
Query 112: 0.0136
Query 113: 0.0308
Query 114: 0.0946
Query 115: 0.1387
Query 116: 0.2977
Query 119: 0.5279
Query 120: 0.2529
Query 121: 0.1771
Query 122: 0.0471
Query 123: 0.0492
Query 124: 0.0124
Query 125: 0.5970
Query 126: 0.0000
Query 128: 0.0066
Query 129: 0.0158
Query 130: 0.0954
Query 131: 0.0046
Query 133: 0.2477
Query 134: 0.0062
Query 135: 0.0488
Query 136: 0.0014
Query 137: 0.0226
Query 138: 0.1170
Query 139: 0.1253
Query 140: 0.3450

Overall statistics
(for 42 queries):

Total number of documents
over all queries
    Retrieved:    42000
    Relevant:       821
    Rel_ret:        662

Interpolated Recall -
Precision Averages:
    at 0.00        0.3723
    at 0.10        0.2997
    at 0.20        0.2392
    at 0.30        0.2218
    at 0.40        0.1870
    at 0.50        0.1637
    at 0.60        0.1202
    at 0.70        0.0939
    at 0.80        0.0746
    at 0.90        0.0528
    at 1.00        0.0300

Avg. prec. (non-interpolated)
for all rel. documents
                   0.1551
Precision:
  At    5 docs:    0.1952
  At   10 docs:    0.1714
  At   15 docs:    0.1571
  At   20 docs:    0.1440
  At   30 docs:    0.1405
  At  100 docs:    0.0838
  At  200 docs:    0.0529
  At  500 docs:    0.0279
  At 1000 docs:    0.0158

R-Precision (prec. after R
(=num_rel) docs. retrieved):
    Exact:         0.1676
```

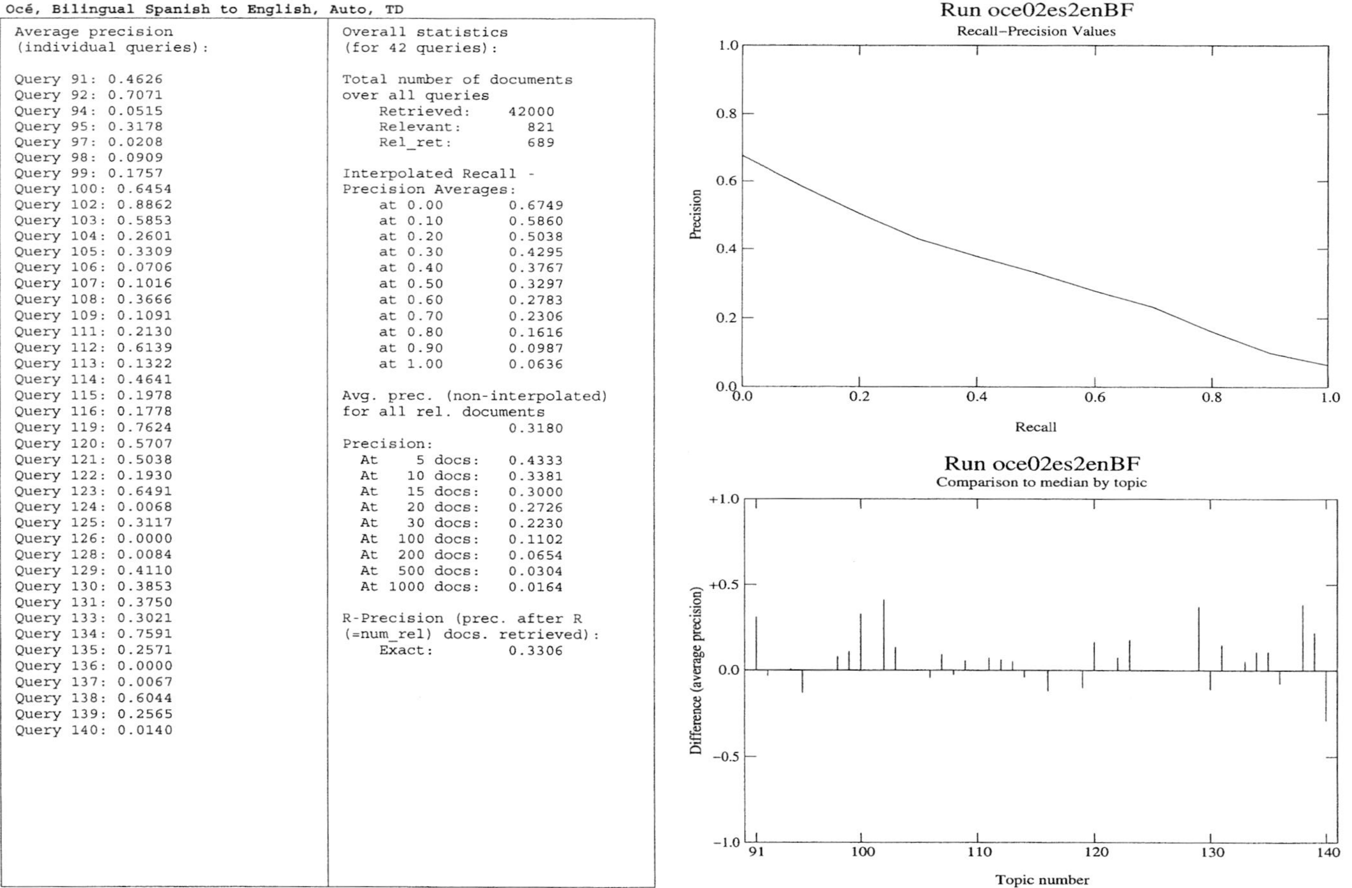

Océ, Bilingual Spanish to English, Auto, TD

Average precision (individual queries):	Overall statistics (for 42 queries):
Query 91: 0.4626	Total number of documents over all queries
Query 92: 0.7071	Retrieved: 42000
Query 94: 0.0515	Relevant: 821
Query 95: 0.3178	Rel_ret: 689
Query 97: 0.0208	
Query 98: 0.0909	Interpolated Recall - Precision Averages:
Query 99: 0.1757	at 0.00 0.6749
Query 100: 0.6454	at 0.10 0.5860
Query 102: 0.8862	at 0.20 0.5038
Query 103: 0.5853	at 0.30 0.4295
Query 104: 0.2601	at 0.40 0.3767
Query 105: 0.3309	at 0.50 0.3297
Query 106: 0.0706	at 0.60 0.2783
Query 107: 0.1016	at 0.70 0.2306
Query 108: 0.3666	at 0.80 0.1616
Query 109: 0.1091	at 0.90 0.0987
Query 111: 0.2130	at 1.00 0.0636
Query 112: 0.6139	
Query 113: 0.1322	Avg. prec. (non-interpolated) for all rel. documents 0.3180
Query 114: 0.4641	
Query 115: 0.1978	Precision:
Query 116: 0.1778	At 5 docs: 0.4333
Query 119: 0.7624	At 10 docs: 0.3381
Query 120: 0.5707	At 15 docs: 0.3000
Query 121: 0.5038	At 20 docs: 0.2726
Query 122: 0.1930	At 30 docs: 0.2230
Query 123: 0.6491	At 100 docs: 0.1102
Query 124: 0.0068	At 200 docs: 0.0654
Query 125: 0.3117	At 500 docs: 0.0304
Query 126: 0.0000	At 1000 docs: 0.0164
Query 128: 0.0084	
Query 129: 0.4110	R-Precision (prec. after R (=num_rel) docs. retrieved):
Query 130: 0.3853	Exact: 0.3306
Query 131: 0.3750	
Query 133: 0.3021	
Query 134: 0.7591	
Query 135: 0.2571	
Query 136: 0.0000	
Query 137: 0.0067	
Query 138: 0.6044	
Query 139: 0.2565	
Query 140: 0.0140	

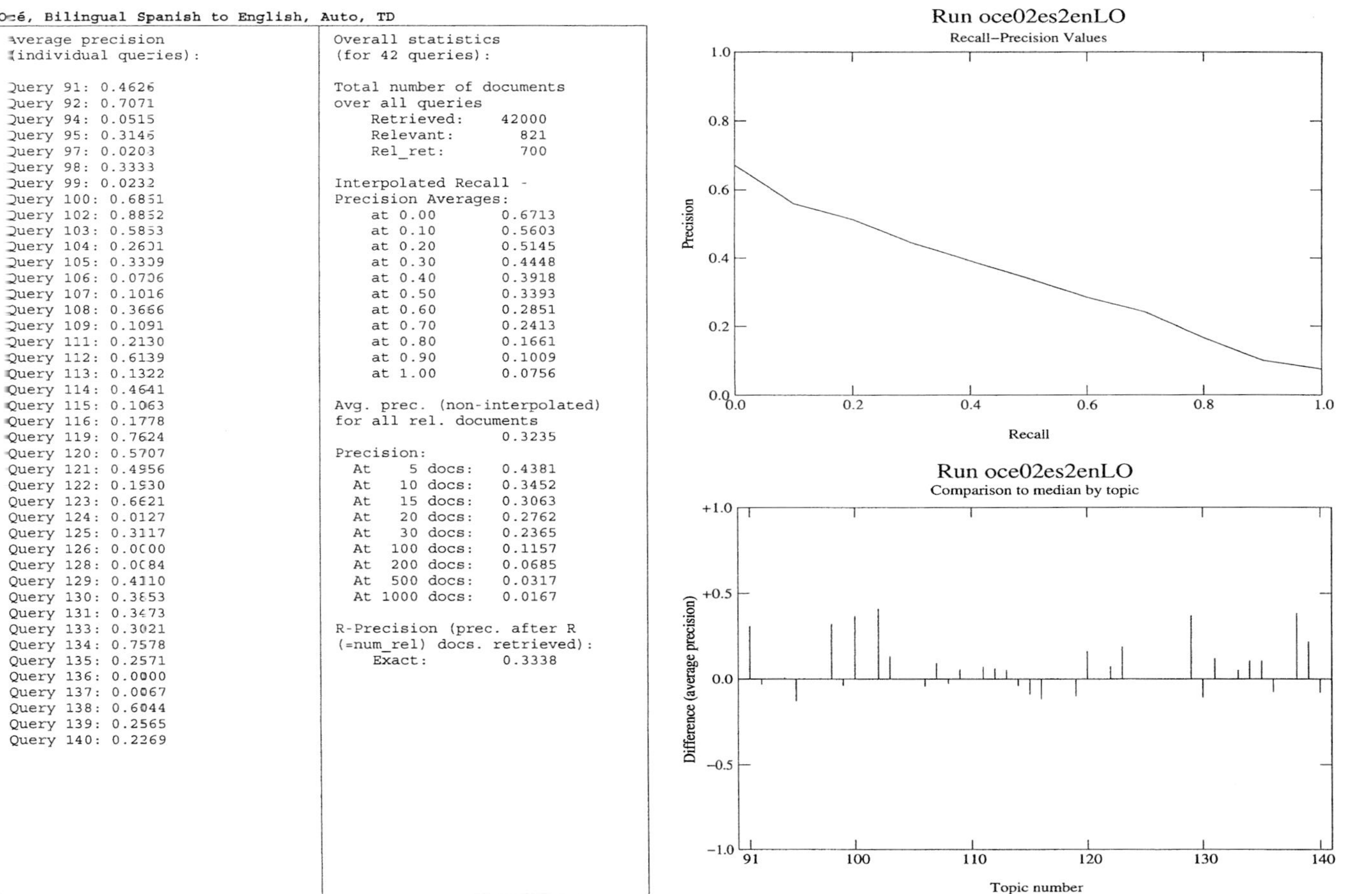

Océ, Bilingual Spanish to English, Auto, TD

```
Average precision                 Overall statistics
(individual queries):             (for 42 queries):

Query 91: 0.4626                  Total number of documents
Query 92: 0.7071                  over all queries
Query 94: 0.0515                      Retrieved:    42000
Query 95: 0.3146                      Relevant:       821
Query 97: 0.0203                      Rel_ret:        700
Query 98: 0.3333
Query 99: 0.0232                  Interpolated Recall -
Query 100: 0.6851                 Precision Averages:
Query 102: 0.8852                     at 0.00       0.6713
Query 103: 0.5853                     at 0.10       0.5603
Query 104: 0.2601                     at 0.20       0.5145
Query 105: 0.3309                     at 0.30       0.4448
Query 106: 0.0706                     at 0.40       0.3918
Query 107: 0.1016                     at 0.50       0.3393
Query 108: 0.3666                     at 0.60       0.2851
Query 109: 0.1091                     at 0.70       0.2413
Query 111: 0.2130                     at 0.80       0.1661
Query 112: 0.6139                     at 0.90       0.1009
Query 113: 0.1322                     at 1.00       0.0756
Query 114: 0.4641
Query 115: 0.1063                 Avg. prec. (non-interpolated)
Query 116: 0.1778                 for all rel. documents
Query 119: 0.7624                                   0.3235
Query 120: 0.5707                 Precision:
Query 121: 0.4956                   At    5 docs:   0.4381
Query 122: 0.1930                   At   10 docs:   0.3452
Query 123: 0.6621                   At   15 docs:   0.3063
Query 124: 0.0127                   At   20 docs:   0.2762
Query 125: 0.3117                   At   30 docs:   0.2365
Query 126: 0.0000                   At  100 docs:   0.1157
Query 128: 0.0084                   At  200 docs:   0.0685
Query 129: 0.4110                   At  500 docs:   0.0317
Query 130: 0.3853                   At 1000 docs:   0.0167
Query 131: 0.3473
Query 133: 0.3021                 R-Precision (prec. after R
Query 134: 0.7578                 (=num_rel) docs. retrieved):
Query 135: 0.2571                     Exact:        0.3338
Query 136: 0.0000
Query 137: 0.0067
Query 138: 0.6044
Query 139: 0.2565
Query 140: 0.2269
```

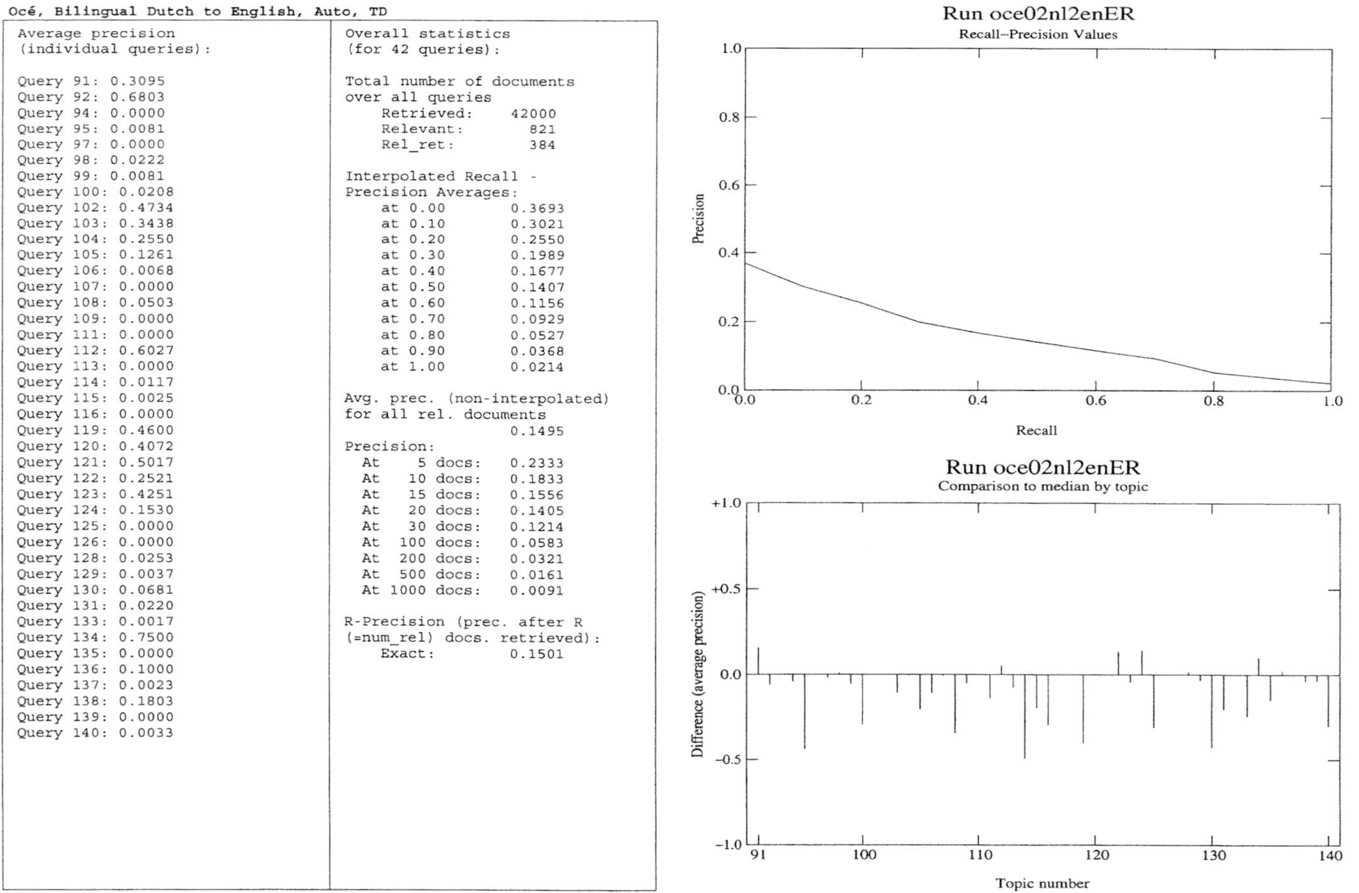

Océ, Bilingual Dutch to English, Auto, TD

```
Average precision              Overall statistics
(individual queries):          (for 42 queries):

Query 91: 0.3095               Total number of documents
Query 92: 0.6803               over all queries
Query 94: 0.0000                   Retrieved:    42000
Query 95: 0.0081                   Relevant:       821
Query 97: 0.0000                   Rel_ret:        384
Query 98: 0.0222
Query 99: 0.0081               Interpolated Recall -
Query 100: 0.0208              Precision Averages:
Query 102: 0.4734                  at 0.00       0.3693
Query 103: 0.3438                  at 0.10       0.3021
Query 104: 0.2550                  at 0.20       0.2550
Query 105: 0.1261                  at 0.30       0.1989
Query 106: 0.0068                  at 0.40       0.1677
Query 107: 0.0000                  at 0.50       0.1407
Query 108: 0.0503                  at 0.60       0.1156
Query 109: 0.0000                  at 0.70       0.0929
Query 111: 0.0000                  at 0.80       0.0527
Query 112: 0.6027                  at 0.90       0.0368
Query 113: 0.0000                  at 1.00       0.0214
Query 114: 0.0117
Query 115: 0.0025              Avg. prec. (non-interpolated)
Query 116: 0.0000              for all rel. documents
Query 119: 0.4600                                0.1495
Query 120: 0.4072              Precision:
Query 121: 0.5017                At    5 docs:   0.2333
Query 122: 0.2521                At   10 docs:   0.1833
Query 123: 0.4251                At   15 docs:   0.1556
Query 124: 0.1530                At   20 docs:   0.1405
Query 125: 0.0000                At   30 docs:   0.1214
Query 126: 0.0000                At  100 docs:   0.0583
Query 128: 0.0253                At  200 docs:   0.0321
Query 129: 0.0037                At  500 docs:   0.0161
Query 130: 0.0681                At 1000 docs:   0.0091
Query 131: 0.0220
Query 133: 0.0017              R-Precision (prec. after R
Query 134: 0.7500              (=num_rel) docs. retrieved):
Query 135: 0.0000                  Exact:        0.1501
Query 136: 0.1000
Query 137: 0.0023
Query 138: 0.1803
Query 139: 0.0000
Query 140: 0.0033
```

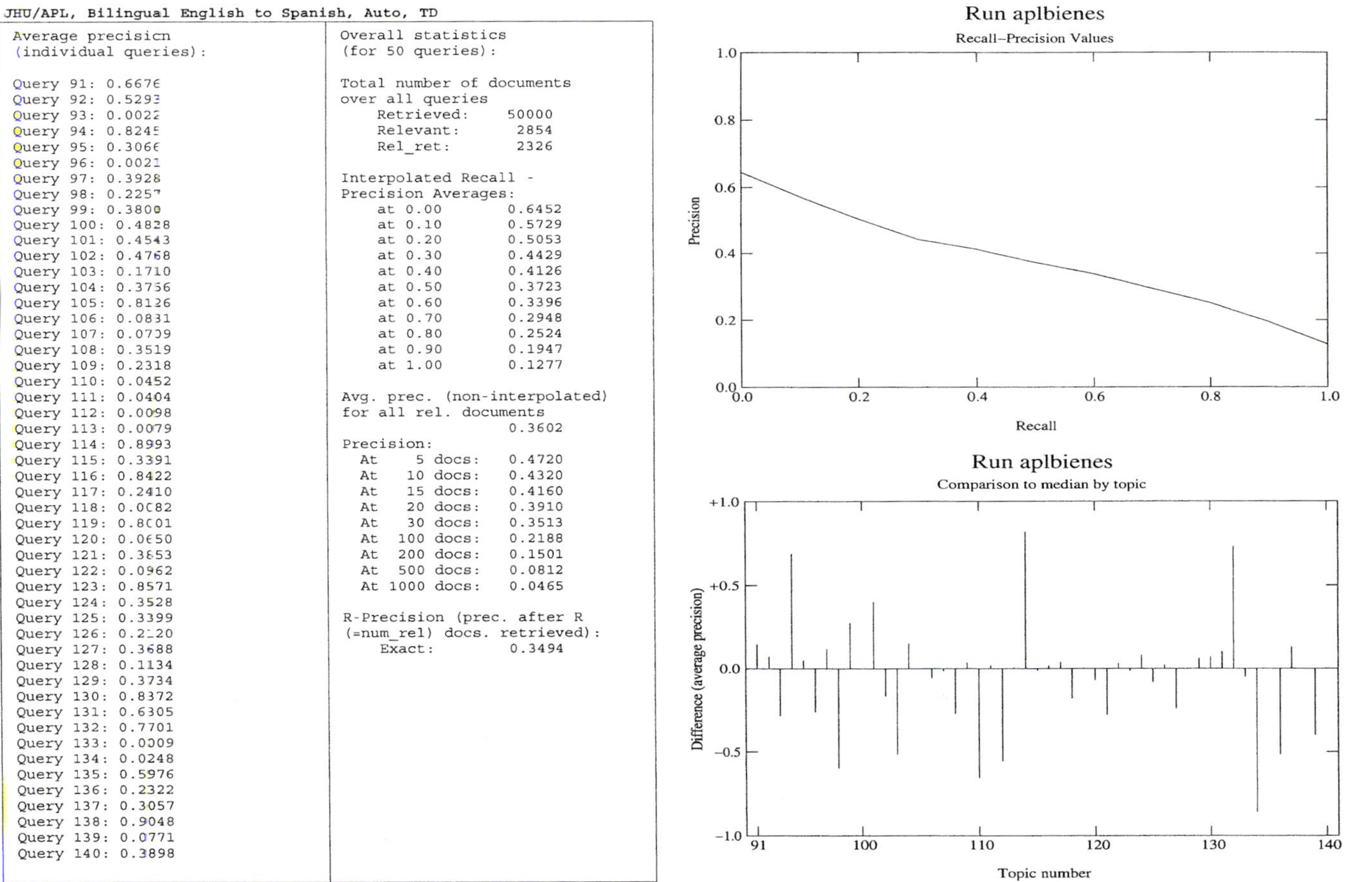

JHU/APL, Bilingual English to Spanish, Auto, TD

```
Average precision                 Overall statistics
(individual queries):             (for 50 queries):

Query 91: 0.6676                  Total number of documents
Query 92: 0.5293                  over all queries
Query 93: 0.0022                      Retrieved:     50000
Query 94: 0.8245                      Relevant:       2854
Query 95: 0.3066                      Rel_ret:        2326
Query 96: 0.0021
Query 97: 0.3928                  Interpolated Recall -
Query 98: 0.2257                  Precision Averages:
Query 99: 0.3800                      at 0.00        0.6452
Query 100: 0.4828                     at 0.10        0.5729
Query 101: 0.4543                     at 0.20        0.5053
Query 102: 0.4768                     at 0.30        0.4429
Query 103: 0.1710                     at 0.40        0.4126
Query 104: 0.3756                     at 0.50        0.3723
Query 105: 0.8126                     at 0.60        0.3396
Query 106: 0.0831                     at 0.70        0.2948
Query 107: 0.0709                     at 0.80        0.2524
Query 108: 0.3519                     at 0.90        0.1947
Query 109: 0.2318                     at 1.00        0.1277
Query 110: 0.0452
Query 111: 0.0404                 Avg. prec. (non-interpolated)
Query 112: 0.0098                 for all rel. documents
Query 113: 0.0079                                    0.3602
Query 114: 0.8993                 Precision:
Query 115: 0.3391                   At    5 docs:    0.4720
Query 116: 0.8422                   At   10 docs:    0.4320
Query 117: 0.2410                   At   15 docs:    0.4160
Query 118: 0.0082                   At   20 docs:    0.3910
Query 119: 0.8001                   At   30 docs:    0.3513
Query 120: 0.0650                   At  100 docs:    0.2188
Query 121: 0.3853                   At  200 docs:    0.1501
Query 122: 0.0962                   At  500 docs:    0.0812
Query 123: 0.8571                   At 1000 docs:    0.0465
Query 124: 0.3528
Query 125: 0.3399                 R-Precision (prec. after R
Query 126: 0.2120                 (=num_rel) docs. retrieved):
Query 127: 0.3688                     Exact:         0.3494
Query 128: 0.1134
Query 129: 0.3734
Query 130: 0.8372
Query 131: 0.6305
Query 132: 0.7701
Query 133: 0.0009
Query 134: 0.0248
Query 135: 0.5976
Query 136: 0.2322
Query 137: 0.3057
Query 138: 0.9048
Query 139: 0.0771
Query 140: 0.3898
```

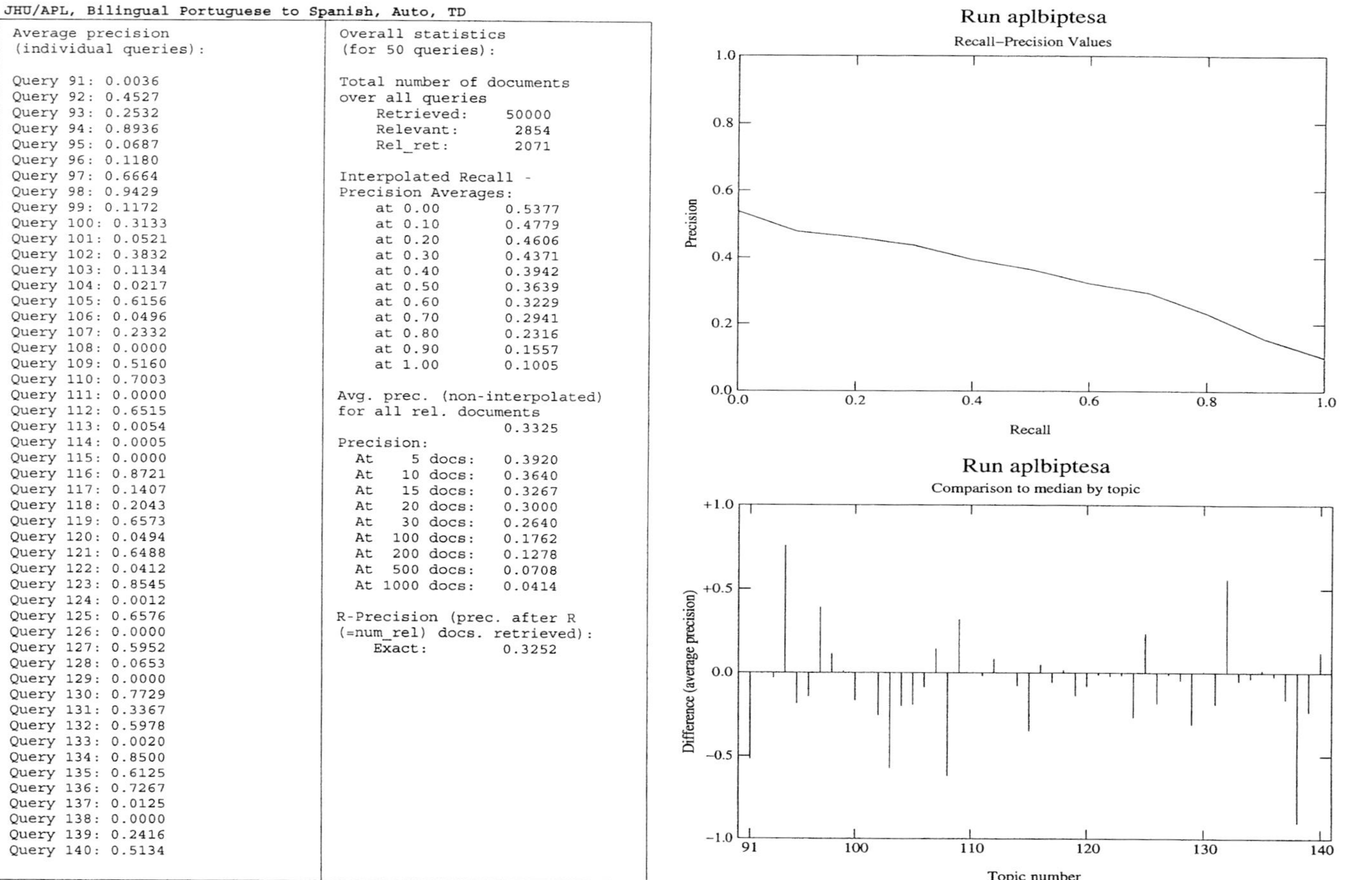

JHU/APL, Bilingual Portuguese to Spanish, Auto, TD

Average precision (individual queries):

Query	Average precision
Query 91:	0.0036
Query 92:	0.4527
Query 93:	0.2532
Query 94:	0.8936
Query 95:	0.0687
Query 96:	0.1180
Query 97:	0.6664
Query 98:	0.9429
Query 99:	0.1172
Query 100:	0.3133
Query 101:	0.0521
Query 102:	0.3832
Query 103:	0.1134
Query 104:	0.0217
Query 105:	0.6156
Query 106:	0.0496
Query 107:	0.2332
Query 108:	0.0000
Query 109:	0.5160
Query 110:	0.7003
Query 111:	0.0000
Query 112:	0.6515
Query 113:	0.0054
Query 114:	0.0005
Query 115:	0.0000
Query 116:	0.8721
Query 117:	0.1407
Query 118:	0.2043
Query 119:	0.6573
Query 120:	0.0494
Query 121:	0.6488
Query 122:	0.0412
Query 123:	0.8545
Query 124:	0.0012
Query 125:	0.6576
Query 126:	0.0000
Query 127:	0.5952
Query 128:	0.0653
Query 129:	0.0000
Query 130:	0.7729
Query 131:	0.3367
Query 132:	0.5978
Query 133:	0.0020
Query 134:	0.8500
Query 135:	0.6125
Query 136:	0.7267
Query 137:	0.0125
Query 138:	0.0000
Query 139:	0.2416
Query 140:	0.5134

Overall statistics (for 50 queries):

Total number of documents over all queries

Retrieved:	50000
Relevant:	2854
Rel_ret:	2071

Interpolated Recall - Precision Averages:

at 0.00	0.5377
at 0.10	0.4779
at 0.20	0.4606
at 0.30	0.4371
at 0.40	0.3942
at 0.50	0.3639
at 0.60	0.3229
at 0.70	0.2941
at 0.80	0.2316
at 0.90	0.1557
at 1.00	0.1005

Avg. prec. (non-interpolated) for all rel. documents 0.3325

Precision:

At 5 docs:	0.3920
At 10 docs:	0.3640
At 15 docs:	0.3267
At 20 docs:	0.3000
At 30 docs:	0.2640
At 100 docs:	0.1762
At 200 docs:	0.1278
At 500 docs:	0.0708
At 1000 docs:	0.0414

R-Precision (prec. after R (=num_rel) docs. retrieved):
Exact: 0.3252

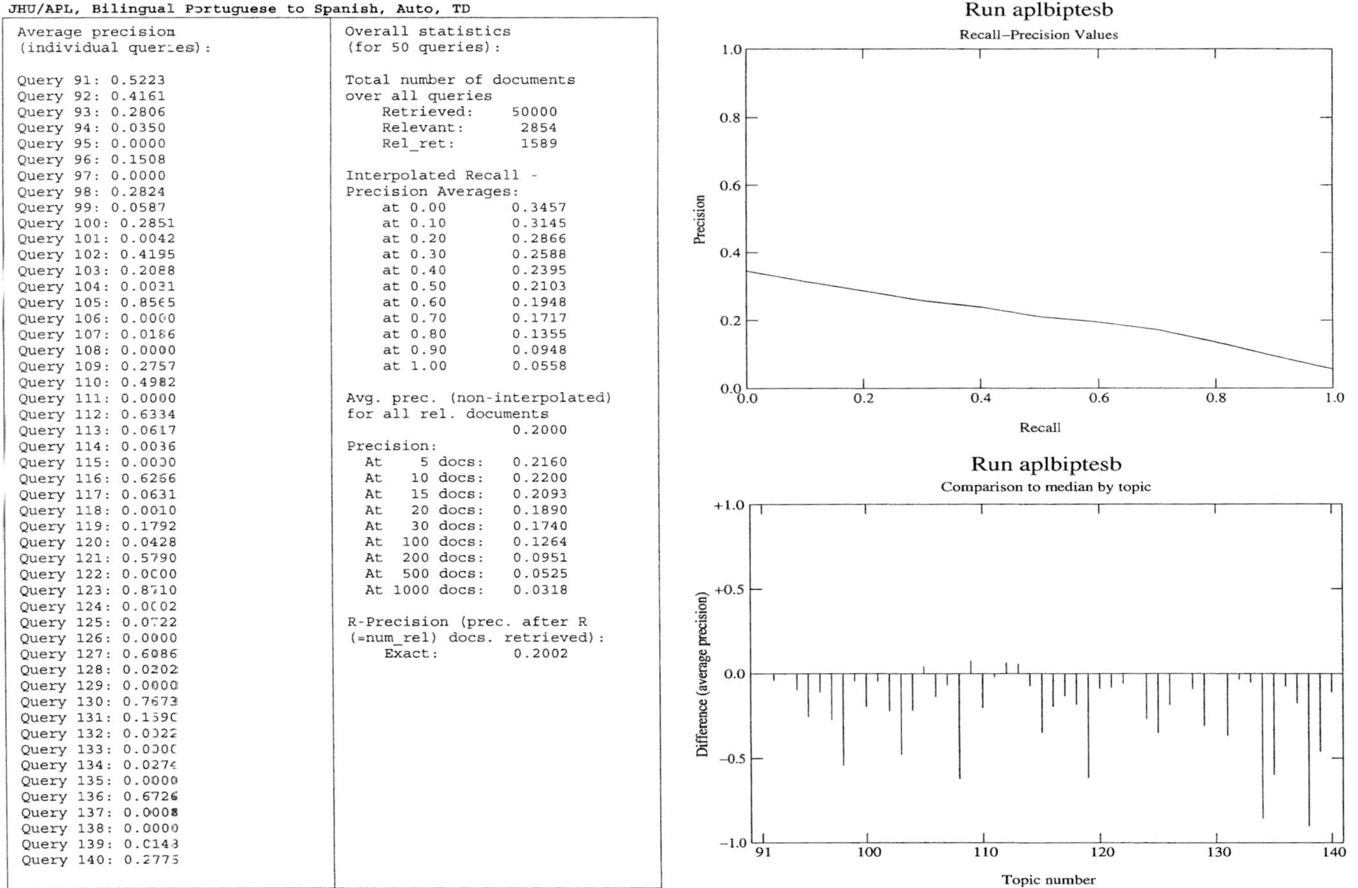

JHU/APL, Bilingual Portuguese to Spanish, Auto, TD

Average precision (individual queries):	Overall statistics (for 50 queries):
Query 91: 0.5223	Total number of documents over all queries
Query 92: 0.4161	Retrieved: 50000
Query 93: 0.2806	Relevant: 2854
Query 94: 0.0350	Rel_ret: 1589
Query 95: 0.0000	
Query 96: 0.1508	Interpolated Recall - Precision Averages:
Query 97: 0.0000	at 0.00 0.3457
Query 98: 0.2824	at 0.10 0.3145
Query 99: 0.0587	at 0.20 0.2866
Query 100: 0.2851	at 0.30 0.2588
Query 101: 0.0042	at 0.40 0.2395
Query 102: 0.4195	at 0.50 0.2103
Query 103: 0.2088	at 0.60 0.1948
Query 104: 0.0031	at 0.70 0.1717
Query 105: 0.8565	at 0.80 0.1355
Query 106: 0.0000	at 0.90 0.0948
Query 107: 0.0186	at 1.00 0.0558
Query 108: 0.0000	
Query 109: 0.2757	Avg. prec. (non-interpolated) for all rel. documents
Query 110: 0.4982	0.2000
Query 111: 0.0000	Precision:
Query 112: 0.6334	At 5 docs: 0.2160
Query 113: 0.0617	At 10 docs: 0.2200
Query 114: 0.0036	At 15 docs: 0.2093
Query 115: 0.0030	At 20 docs: 0.1890
Query 116: 0.6256	At 30 docs: 0.1740
Query 117: 0.0631	At 100 docs: 0.1264
Query 118: 0.0010	At 200 docs: 0.0951
Query 119: 0.1792	At 500 docs: 0.0525
Query 120: 0.0428	At 1000 docs: 0.0318
Query 121: 0.5790	
Query 122: 0.0000	R-Precision (prec. after R (=num_rel) docs. retrieved):
Query 123: 0.8710	Exact: 0.2002
Query 124: 0.0002	
Query 125: 0.0722	
Query 126: 0.0000	
Query 127: 0.6086	
Query 128: 0.0202	
Query 129: 0.0000	
Query 130: 0.7673	
Query 131: 0.1590	
Query 132: 0.0022	
Query 133: 0.0000	
Query 134: 0.0274	
Query 135: 0.0000	
Query 136: 0.6726	
Query 137: 0.0008	
Query 138: 0.0000	
Query 139: 0.0143	
Query 140: 0.2775	

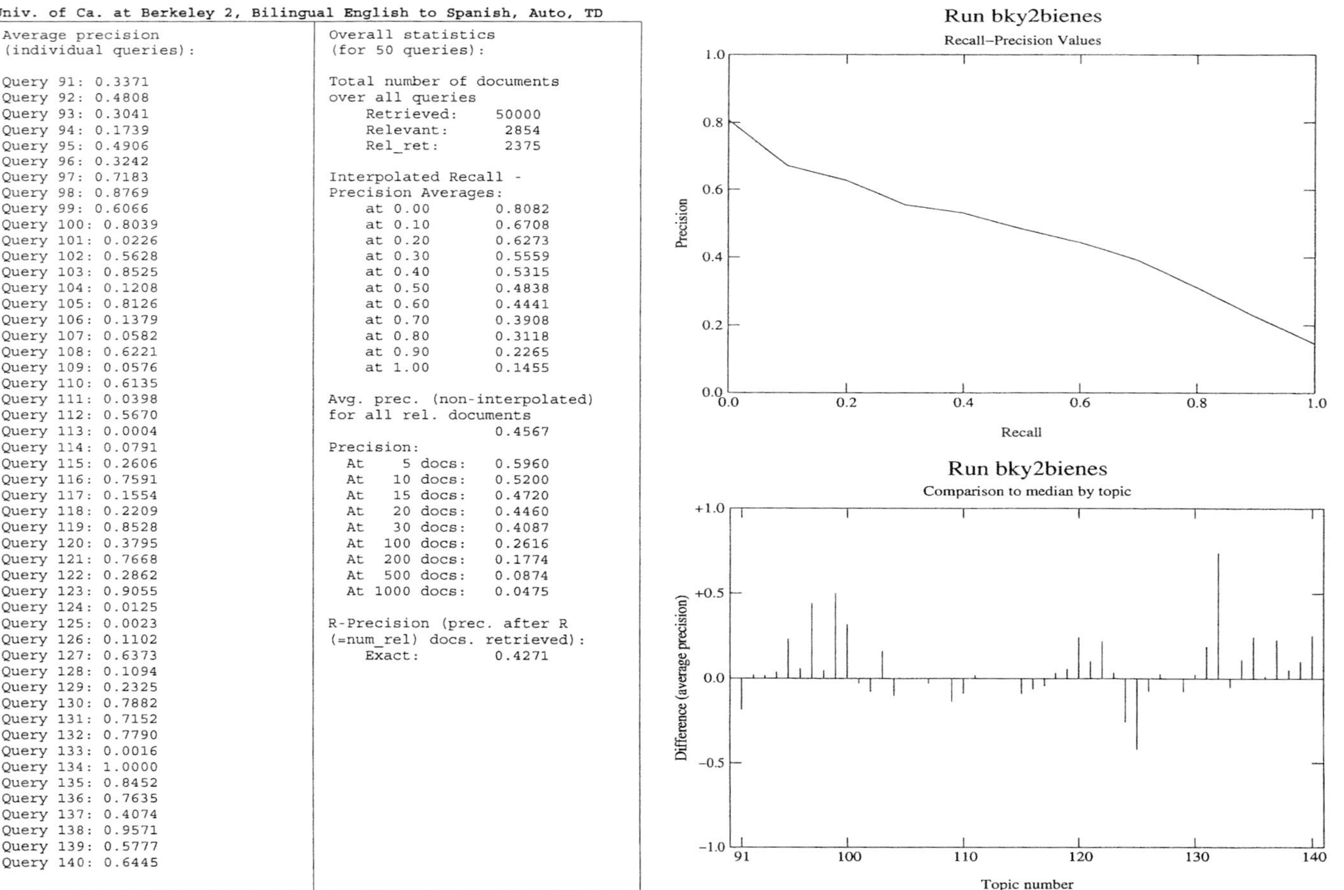

Univ. of Ca. at Berkeley 2, Bilingual English to Spanish, Auto, TD

```
Average precision                 Overall statistics
(individual queries):             (for 50 queries):

Query 91: 0.3371                  Total number of documents
Query 92: 0.4808                  over all queries
Query 93: 0.3041                      Retrieved:     50000
Query 94: 0.1739                      Relevant:       2854
Query 95: 0.4906                      Rel_ret:        2375
Query 96: 0.3242
Query 97: 0.7183                  Interpolated Recall -
Query 98: 0.8769                  Precision Averages:
Query 99: 0.6066                      at 0.00        0.8082
Query 100: 0.8039                     at 0.10        0.6708
Query 101: 0.0226                     at 0.20        0.6273
Query 102: 0.5628                     at 0.30        0.5559
Query 103: 0.8525                     at 0.40        0.5315
Query 104: 0.1208                     at 0.50        0.4838
Query 105: 0.8126                     at 0.60        0.4441
Query 106: 0.1379                     at 0.70        0.3908
Query 107: 0.0582                     at 0.80        0.3118
Query 108: 0.6221                     at 0.90        0.2265
Query 109: 0.0576                     at 1.00        0.1455
Query 110: 0.6135
Query 111: 0.0398                 Avg. prec. (non-interpolated)
Query 112: 0.5670                 for all rel. documents
Query 113: 0.0004                                    0.4567
Query 114: 0.0791                 Precision:
Query 115: 0.2606                   At    5 docs:    0.5960
Query 116: 0.7591                   At   10 docs:    0.5200
Query 117: 0.1554                   At   15 docs:    0.4720
Query 118: 0.2209                   At   20 docs:    0.4460
Query 119: 0.8528                   At   30 docs:    0.4087
Query 120: 0.3795                   At  100 docs:    0.2616
Query 121: 0.7668                   At  200 docs:    0.1774
Query 122: 0.2862                   At  500 docs:    0.0874
Query 123: 0.9055                   At 1000 docs:    0.0475
Query 124: 0.0125
Query 125: 0.0023                 R-Precision (prec. after R
Query 126: 0.1102                 (=num_rel) docs. retrieved):
Query 127: 0.6373                     Exact:         0.4271
Query 128: 0.1094
Query 129: 0.2325
Query 130: 0.7882
Query 131: 0.7152
Query 132: 0.7790
Query 133: 0.0016
Query 134: 1.0000
Query 135: 0.8452
Query 136: 0.7635
Query 137: 0.4074
Query 138: 0.9571
Query 139: 0.5777
Query 140: 0.6445
```

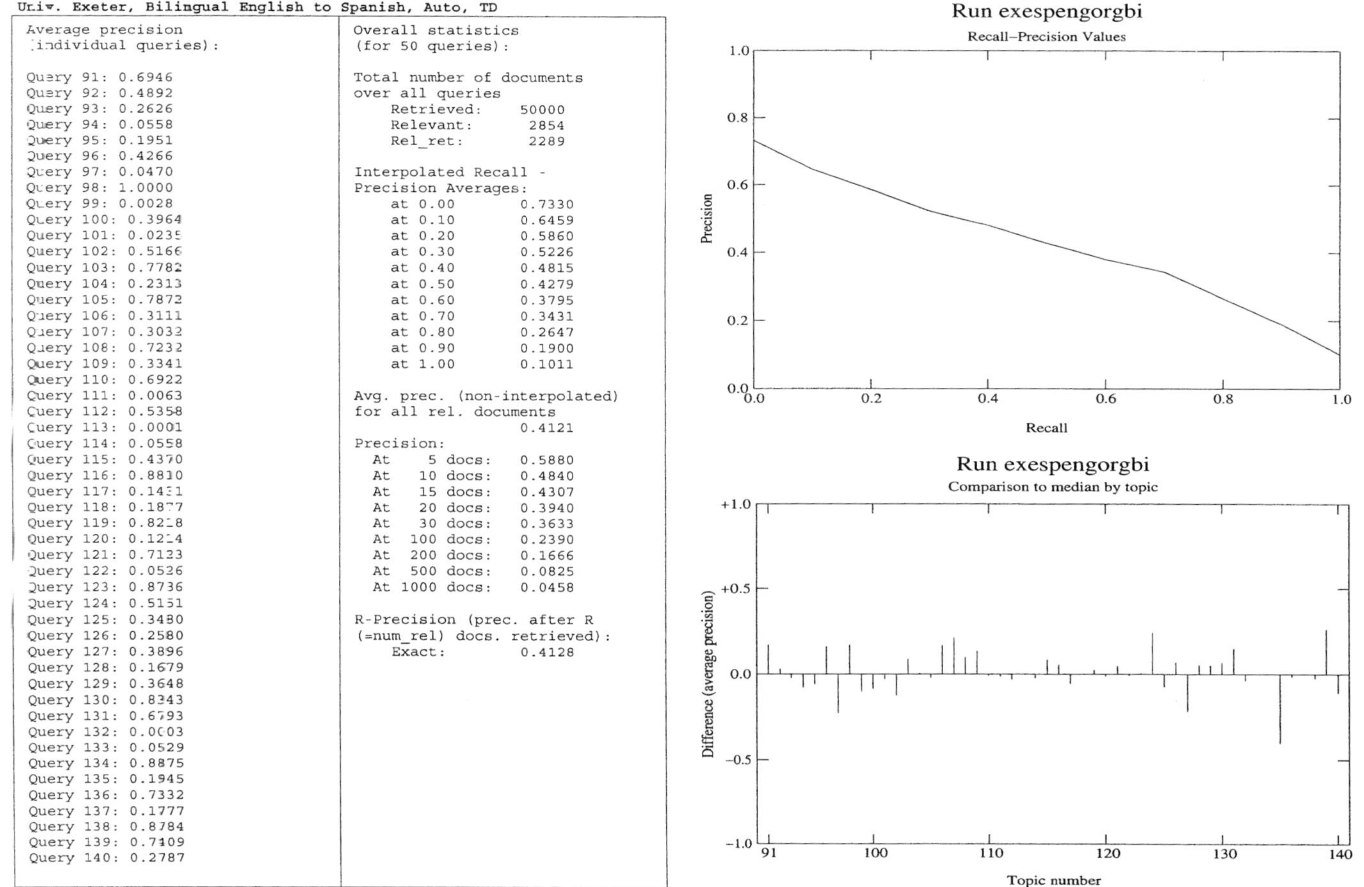

Univ. Exeter, Bilingual English to Spanish, Auto, TD

Average precision (individual queries):	Overall statistics (for 50 queries):
Query 91: 0.6946	Total number of documents over all queries
Query 92: 0.4892	Retrieved: 50000
Query 93: 0.2626	Relevant: 2854
Query 94: 0.0558	Rel_ret: 2289
Query 95: 0.1951	
Query 96: 0.4266	Interpolated Recall - Precision Averages:
Query 97: 0.0470	at 0.00 0.7330
Query 98: 1.0000	at 0.10 0.6459
Query 99: 0.0028	at 0.20 0.5860
Query 100: 0.3964	at 0.30 0.5226
Query 101: 0.0235	at 0.40 0.4815
Query 102: 0.5166	at 0.50 0.4279
Query 103: 0.7782	at 0.60 0.3795
Query 104: 0.2313	at 0.70 0.3431
Query 105: 0.7872	at 0.80 0.2647
Query 106: 0.3111	at 0.90 0.1900
Query 107: 0.3032	at 1.00 0.1011
Query 108: 0.7232	
Query 109: 0.3341	Avg. prec. (non-interpolated) for all rel. documents 0.4121
Query 110: 0.6922	
Query 111: 0.0063	Precision:
Query 112: 0.5358	At 5 docs: 0.5880
Query 113: 0.0001	At 10 docs: 0.4840
Query 114: 0.0558	At 15 docs: 0.4307
Query 115: 0.4370	At 20 docs: 0.3940
Query 116: 0.8810	At 30 docs: 0.3633
Query 117: 0.1431	At 100 docs: 0.2390
Query 118: 0.1877	At 200 docs: 0.1666
Query 119: 0.8218	At 500 docs: 0.0825
Query 120: 0.1214	At 1000 docs: 0.0458
Query 121: 0.7123	
Query 122: 0.0526	R-Precision (prec. after R (=num_rel) docs. retrieved):
Query 123: 0.8736	Exact: 0.4128
Query 124: 0.5151	
Query 125: 0.3480	
Query 126: 0.2580	
Query 127: 0.3896	
Query 128: 0.1679	
Query 129: 0.3648	
Query 130: 0.8343	
Query 131: 0.6793	
Query 132: 0.0003	
Query 133: 0.0529	
Query 134: 0.8875	
Query 135: 0.1945	
Query 136: 0.7332	
Query 137: 0.1777	
Query 138: 0.8784	
Query 139: 0.7109	
Query 140: 0.2787	

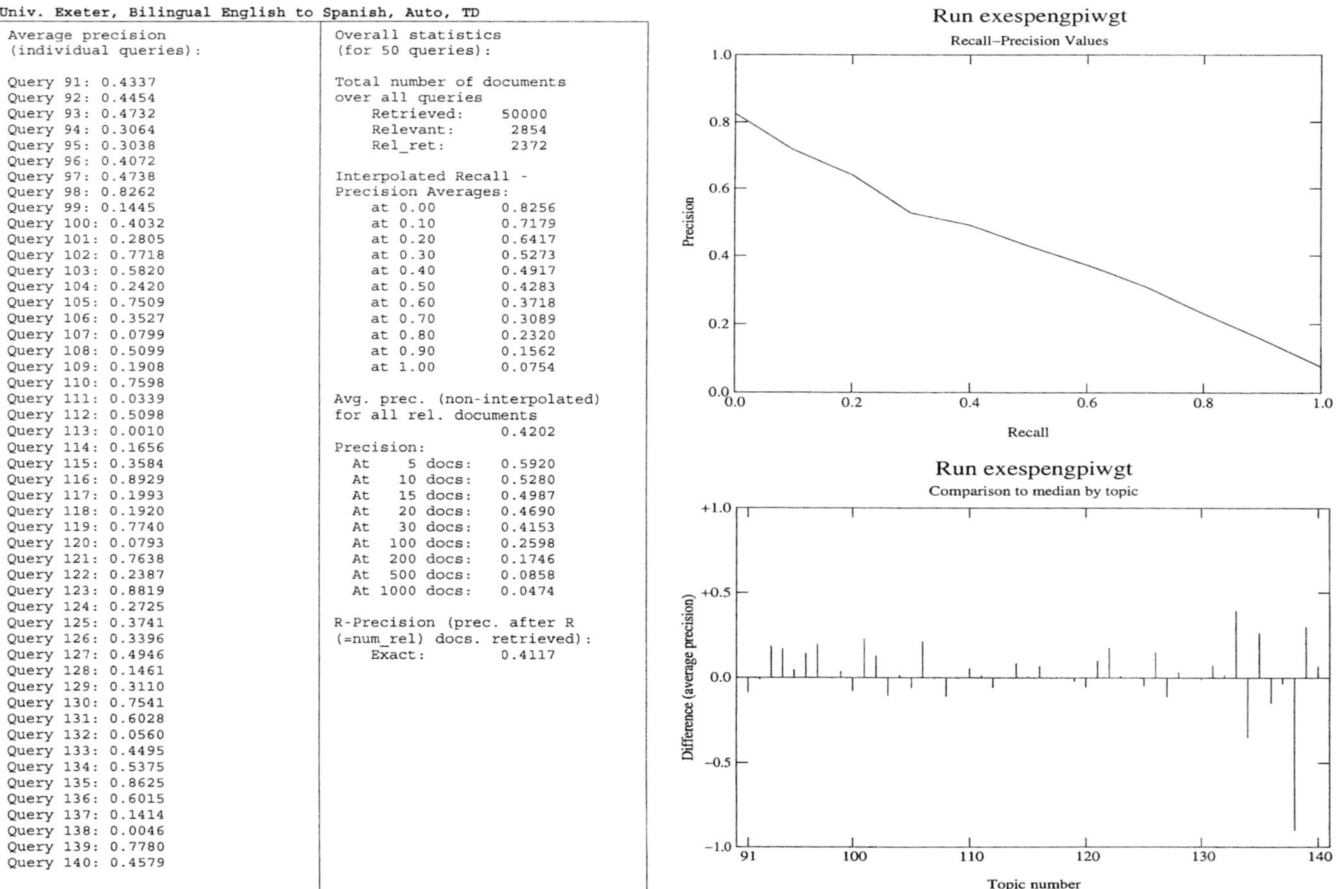

Univ. Exeter, Bilingual English to Spanish, Auto, TD

```
Average precision               Overall statistics
(individual queries):           (for 50 queries):

Query 91: 0.4337                Total number of documents
Query 92: 0.4454                over all queries
Query 93: 0.4732                    Retrieved:    50000
Query 94: 0.3064                    Relevant:      2854
Query 95: 0.3038                    Rel_ret:       2372
Query 96: 0.4072
Query 97: 0.4738                Interpolated Recall -
Query 98: 0.8262                Precision Averages:
Query 99: 0.1445                    at 0.00       0.8256
Query 100: 0.4032                   at 0.10       0.7179
Query 101: 0.2805                   at 0.20       0.6417
Query 102: 0.7718                   at 0.30       0.5273
Query 103: 0.5820                   at 0.40       0.4917
Query 104: 0.2420                   at 0.50       0.4283
Query 105: 0.7509                   at 0.60       0.3718
Query 106: 0.3527                   at 0.70       0.3089
Query 107: 0.0799                   at 0.80       0.2320
Query 108: 0.5099                   at 0.90       0.1562
Query 109: 0.1908                   at 1.00       0.0754
Query 110: 0.7598
Query 111: 0.0339               Avg. prec. (non-interpolated)
Query 112: 0.5098               for all rel. documents
Query 113: 0.0010                                 0.4202
Query 114: 0.1656               Precision:
Query 115: 0.3584                 At    5 docs:   0.5920
Query 116: 0.8929                 At   10 docs:   0.5280
Query 117: 0.1993                 At   15 docs:   0.4987
Query 118: 0.1920                 At   20 docs:   0.4690
Query 119: 0.7740                 At   30 docs:   0.4153
Query 120: 0.0793                 At  100 docs:   0.2598
Query 121: 0.7638                 At  200 docs:   0.1746
Query 122: 0.2387                 At  500 docs:   0.0858
Query 123: 0.8819                 At 1000 docs:   0.0474
Query 124: 0.2725
Query 125: 0.3741               R-Precision (prec. after R
Query 126: 0.3396               (=num_rel) docs. retrieved):
Query 127: 0.4946                   Exact:        0.4117
Query 128: 0.1461
Query 129: 0.3110
Query 130: 0.7541
Query 131: 0.6028
Query 132: 0.0560
Query 133: 0.4495
Query 134: 0.5375
Query 135: 0.8625
Query 136: 0.6015
Query 137: 0.1414
Query 138: 0.0046
Query 139: 0.7780
Query 140: 0.4579
```

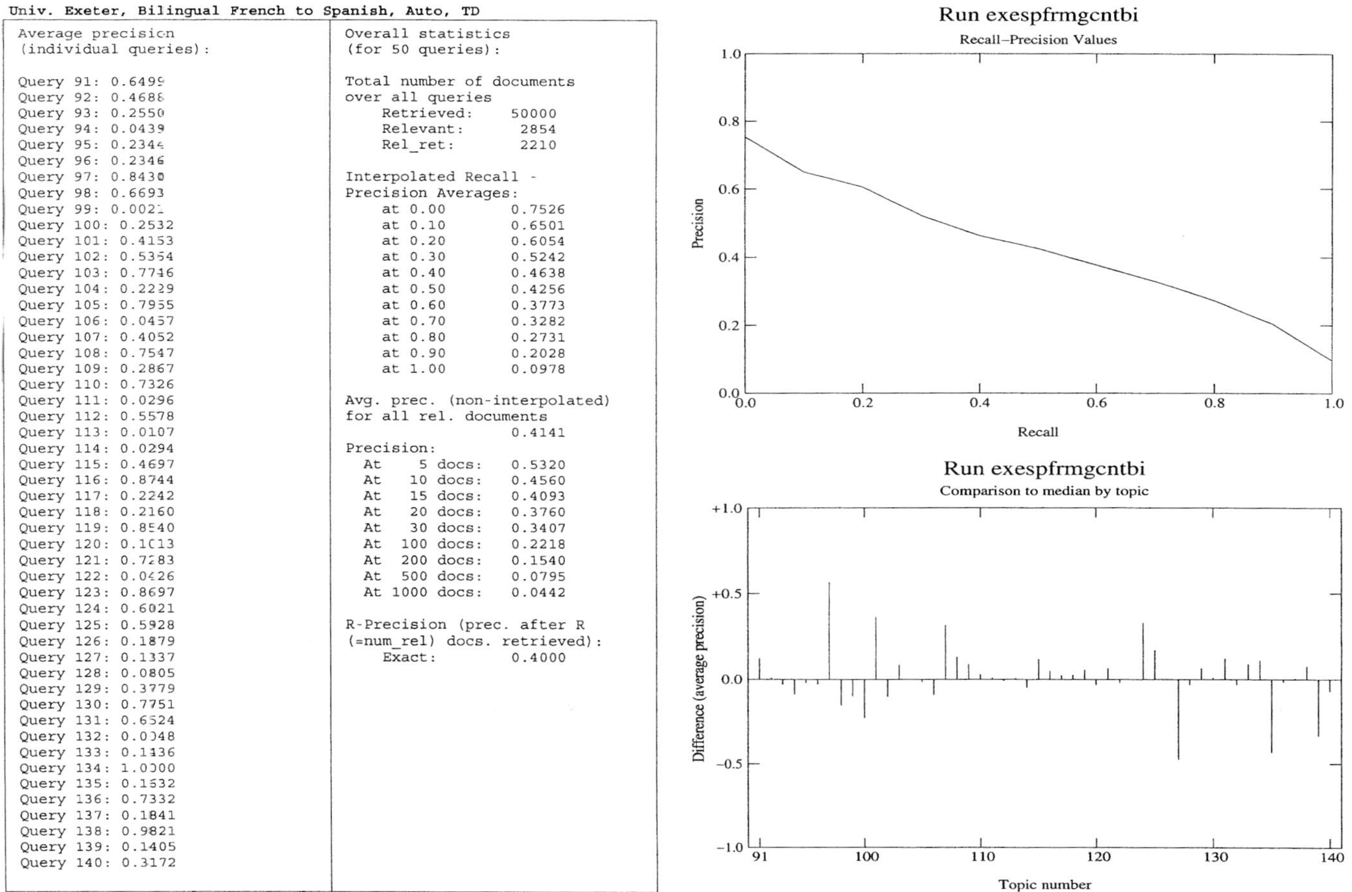

Univ. Exeter, Bilingual French to Spanish, Auto, TD

```
Average precision                 Overall statistics
(individual queries):             (for 50 queries):

Query 91: 0.6499                  Total number of documents
Query 92: 0.4688                  over all queries
Query 93: 0.2550                      Retrieved:    50000
Query 94: 0.0439                      Relevant:      2854
Query 95: 0.2344                      Rel_ret:       2210
Query 96: 0.2346
Query 97: 0.8430                  Interpolated Recall -
Query 98: 0.6693                  Precision Averages:
Query 99: 0.0021                      at 0.00        0.7526
Query 100: 0.2532                     at 0.10        0.6501
Query 101: 0.4153                     at 0.20        0.6054
Query 102: 0.5354                     at 0.30        0.5242
Query 103: 0.7746                     at 0.40        0.4638
Query 104: 0.2229                     at 0.50        0.4256
Query 105: 0.7955                     at 0.60        0.3773
Query 106: 0.0457                     at 0.70        0.3282
Query 107: 0.4052                     at 0.80        0.2731
Query 108: 0.7547                     at 0.90        0.2028
Query 109: 0.2867                     at 1.00        0.0978
Query 110: 0.7326
Query 111: 0.0296                 Avg. prec. (non-interpolated)
Query 112: 0.5578                 for all rel. documents
Query 113: 0.0107                                    0.4141
Query 114: 0.0294                 Precision:
Query 115: 0.4697                   At    5 docs:    0.5320
Query 116: 0.8744                   At   10 docs:    0.4560
Query 117: 0.2242                   At   15 docs:    0.4093
Query 118: 0.2160                   At   20 docs:    0.3760
Query 119: 0.8540                   At   30 docs:    0.3407
Query 120: 0.1013                   At  100 docs:    0.2218
Query 121: 0.7283                   At  200 docs:    0.1540
Query 122: 0.0426                   At  500 docs:    0.0795
Query 123: 0.8697                   At 1000 docs:    0.0442
Query 124: 0.6021
Query 125: 0.5928                 R-Precision (prec. after R
Query 126: 0.1879                 (=num_rel) docs. retrieved):
Query 127: 0.1337                     Exact:         0.4000
Query 128: 0.0805
Query 129: 0.3779
Query 130: 0.7751
Query 131: 0.6524
Query 132: 0.0048
Query 133: 0.1136
Query 134: 1.0000
Query 135: 0.1532
Query 136: 0.7332
Query 137: 0.1841
Query 138: 0.9821
Query 139: 0.1405
Query 140: 0.3172
```

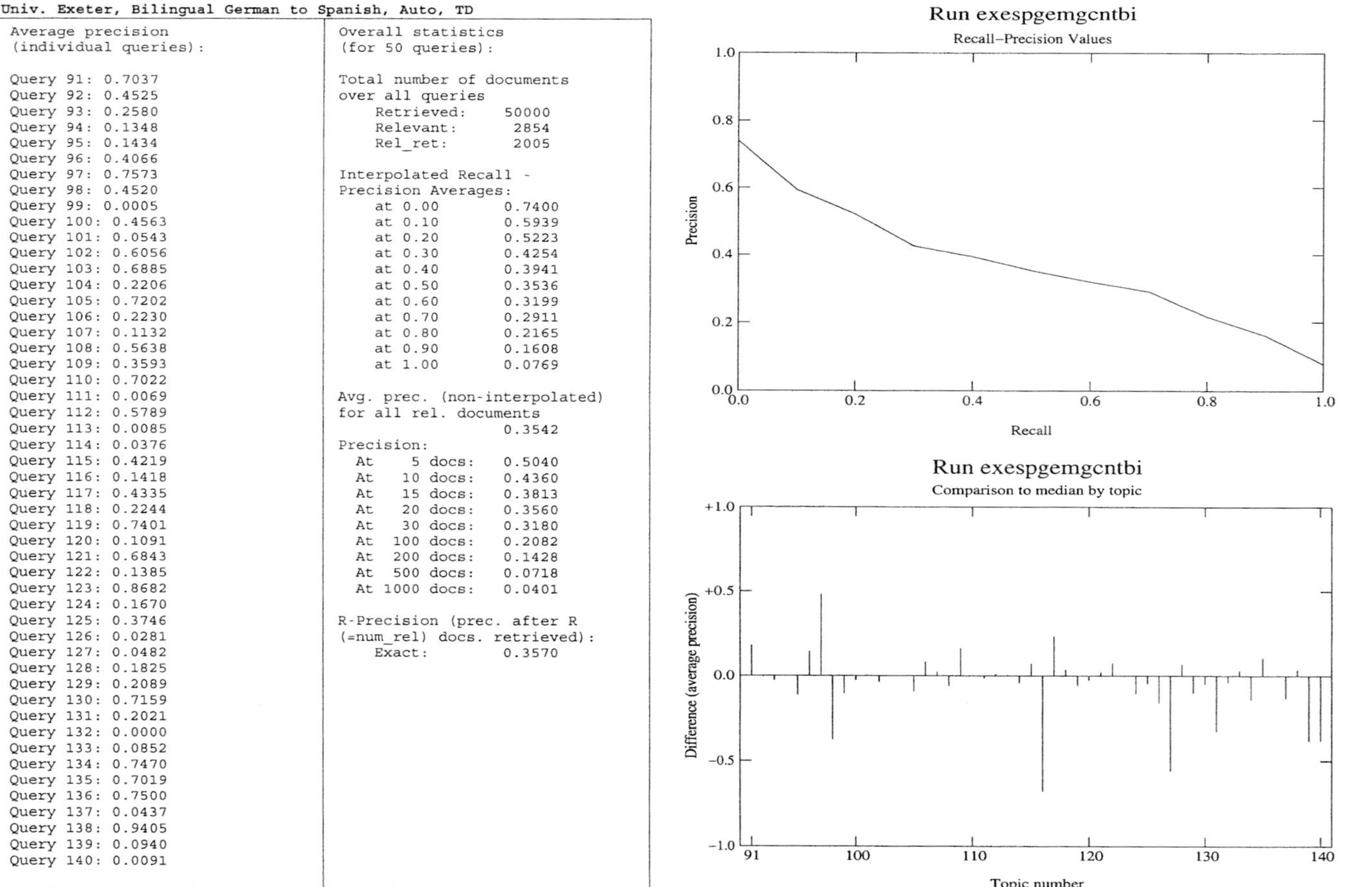

Univ. Exeter, Bilingual German to Spanish, Auto, TD

```
Average precision                 Overall statistics
(individual queries):             (for 50 queries):

Query 91: 0.7037                  Total number of documents
Query 92: 0.4525                  over all queries
Query 93: 0.2580                      Retrieved:     50000
Query 94: 0.1348                      Relevant:       2854
Query 95: 0.1434                      Rel_ret:        2005
Query 96: 0.4066
Query 97: 0.7573                  Interpolated Recall -
Query 98: 0.4520                  Precision Averages:
Query 99: 0.0005                      at 0.00        0.7400
Query 100: 0.4563                     at 0.10        0.5939
Query 101: 0.0543                     at 0.20        0.5223
Query 102: 0.6056                     at 0.30        0.4254
Query 103: 0.6885                     at 0.40        0.3941
Query 104: 0.2206                     at 0.50        0.3536
Query 105: 0.7202                     at 0.60        0.3199
Query 106: 0.2230                     at 0.70        0.2911
Query 107: 0.1132                     at 0.80        0.2165
Query 108: 0.5638                     at 0.90        0.1608
Query 109: 0.3593                     at 1.00        0.0769
Query 110: 0.7022
Query 111: 0.0069                 Avg. prec. (non-interpolated)
Query 112: 0.5789                 for all rel. documents
Query 113: 0.0085                                    0.3542
Query 114: 0.0376                 Precision:
Query 115: 0.4219                   At    5 docs:    0.5040
Query 116: 0.1418                   At   10 docs:    0.4360
Query 117: 0.4335                   At   15 docs:    0.3813
Query 118: 0.2244                   At   20 docs:    0.3560
Query 119: 0.7401                   At   30 docs:    0.3180
Query 120: 0.1091                   At  100 docs:    0.2082
Query 121: 0.6843                   At  200 docs:    0.1428
Query 122: 0.1385                   At  500 docs:    0.0718
Query 123: 0.8682                   At 1000 docs:    0.0401
Query 124: 0.1670
Query 125: 0.3746                 R-Precision (prec. after R
Query 126: 0.0281                 (=num_rel) docs. retrieved):
Query 127: 0.0482                     Exact:         0.3570
Query 128: 0.1825
Query 129: 0.2089
Query 130: 0.7159
Query 131: 0.2021
Query 132: 0.0000
Query 133: 0.0852
Query 134: 0.7470
Query 135: 0.7019
Query 136: 0.7500
Query 137: 0.0437
Query 138: 0.9405
Query 139: 0.0940
Query 140: 0.0091
```

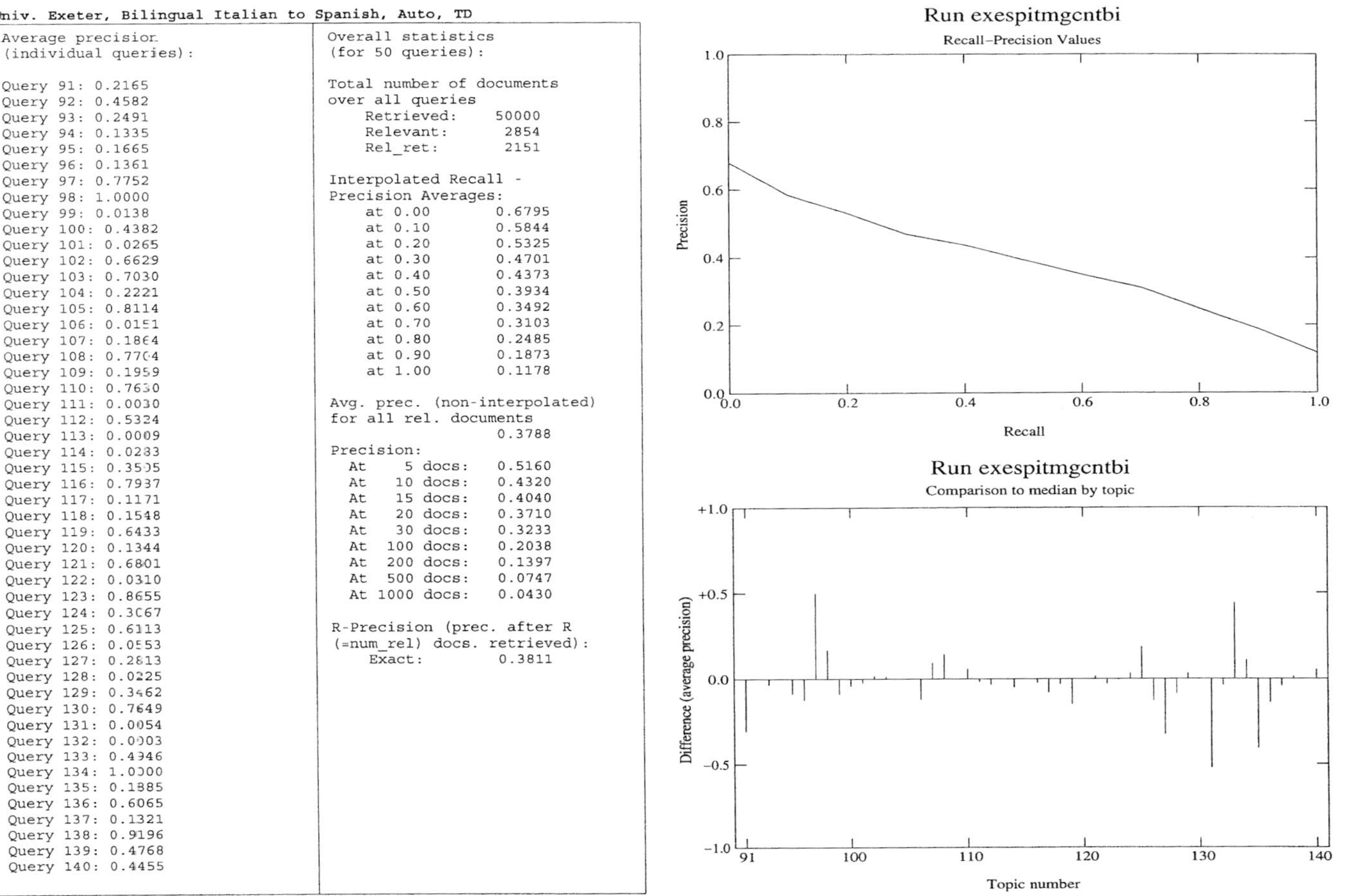

Univ. Exeter, Bilingual Italian to Spanish, Auto, TD

Average precision
(individual queries):

Query	Average precision
Query 91:	0.2165
Query 92:	0.4582
Query 93:	0.2491
Query 94:	0.1335
Query 95:	0.1665
Query 96:	0.1361
Query 97:	0.7752
Query 98:	1.0000
Query 99:	0.0138
Query 100:	0.4382
Query 101:	0.0265
Query 102:	0.6629
Query 103:	0.7030
Query 104:	0.2221
Query 105:	0.8114
Query 106:	0.0151
Query 107:	0.1864
Query 108:	0.7704
Query 109:	0.1959
Query 110:	0.7630
Query 111:	0.0030
Query 112:	0.5324
Query 113:	0.0009
Query 114:	0.0283
Query 115:	0.3505
Query 116:	0.7937
Query 117:	0.1171
Query 118:	0.1548
Query 119:	0.6433
Query 120:	0.1344
Query 121:	0.6801
Query 122:	0.0310
Query 123:	0.8655
Query 124:	0.3067
Query 125:	0.6113
Query 126:	0.0553
Query 127:	0.2813
Query 128:	0.0225
Query 129:	0.3462
Query 130:	0.7649
Query 131:	0.0054
Query 132:	0.0003
Query 133:	0.4946
Query 134:	1.0000
Query 135:	0.1885
Query 136:	0.6065
Query 137:	0.1321
Query 138:	0.9196
Query 139:	0.4768
Query 140:	0.4455

Overall statistics
(for 50 queries):

Total number of documents
over all queries

Retrieved:	50000
Relevant:	2854
Rel_ret:	2151

Interpolated Recall -
Precision Averages:

at 0.00	0.6795
at 0.10	0.5844
at 0.20	0.5325
at 0.30	0.4701
at 0.40	0.4373
at 0.50	0.3934
at 0.60	0.3492
at 0.70	0.3103
at 0.80	0.2485
at 0.90	0.1873
at 1.00	0.1178

Avg. prec. (non-interpolated)
for all rel. documents
0.3788

Precision:

At 5 docs:	0.5160
At 10 docs:	0.4320
At 15 docs:	0.4040
At 20 docs:	0.3710
At 30 docs:	0.3233
At 100 docs:	0.2038
At 200 docs:	0.1397
At 500 docs:	0.0747
At 1000 docs:	0.0430

R-Precision (prec. after R
(=num_rel) docs. retrieved):
Exact: 0.3811

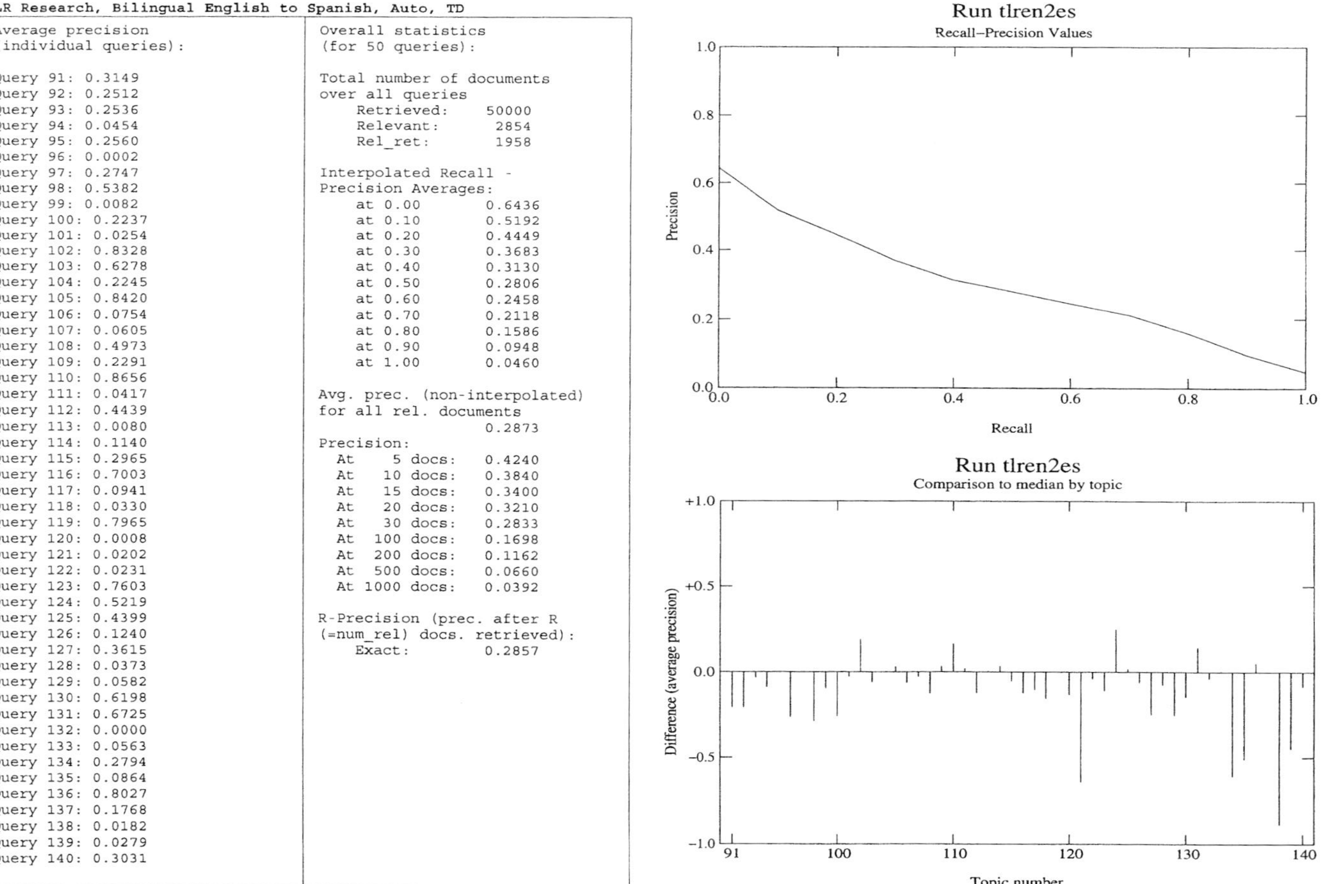

TLR Research, Bilingual English to Spanish, Auto, TD

Average precision (individual queries):	Overall statistics (for 50 queries):	
Query 91: 0.3149	Total number of documents over all queries	
Query 92: 0.2512	Retrieved:	50000
Query 93: 0.2536	Relevant:	2854
Query 94: 0.0454	Rel_ret:	1958
Query 95: 0.2560		
Query 96: 0.0002	Interpolated Recall - Precision Averages:	
Query 97: 0.2747	at 0.00	0.6436
Query 98: 0.5382	at 0.10	0.5192
Query 99: 0.0082	at 0.20	0.4449
Query 100: 0.2237	at 0.30	0.3683
Query 101: 0.0254	at 0.40	0.3130
Query 102: 0.8328	at 0.50	0.2806
Query 103: 0.6278	at 0.60	0.2458
Query 104: 0.2245	at 0.70	0.2118
Query 105: 0.8420	at 0.80	0.1586
Query 106: 0.0754	at 0.90	0.0948
Query 107: 0.0605	at 1.00	0.0460
Query 108: 0.4973		
Query 109: 0.2291	Avg. prec. (non-interpolated) for all rel. documents	0.2873
Query 110: 0.8656	Precision:	
Query 111: 0.0417	At 5 docs:	0.4240
Query 112: 0.4439	At 10 docs:	0.3840
Query 113: 0.0080	At 15 docs:	0.3400
Query 114: 0.1140	At 20 docs:	0.3210
Query 115: 0.2965	At 30 docs:	0.2833
Query 116: 0.7003	At 100 docs:	0.1698
Query 117: 0.0941	At 200 docs:	0.1162
Query 118: 0.0330	At 500 docs:	0.0660
Query 119: 0.7965	At 1000 docs:	0.0392
Query 120: 0.0008		
Query 121: 0.0202	R-Precision (prec. after R (=num_rel) docs. retrieved):	
Query 122: 0.0231	Exact:	0.2857
Query 123: 0.7603		
Query 124: 0.5219		
Query 125: 0.4399		
Query 126: 0.1240		
Query 127: 0.3615		
Query 128: 0.0373		
Query 129: 0.0582		
Query 130: 0.6198		
Query 131: 0.6725		
Query 132: 0.0000		
Query 133: 0.0563		
Query 134: 0.2794		
Query 135: 0.0864		
Query 136: 0.8027		
Query 137: 0.1768		
Query 138: 0.0182		
Query 139: 0.0279		
Query 140: 0.3031		

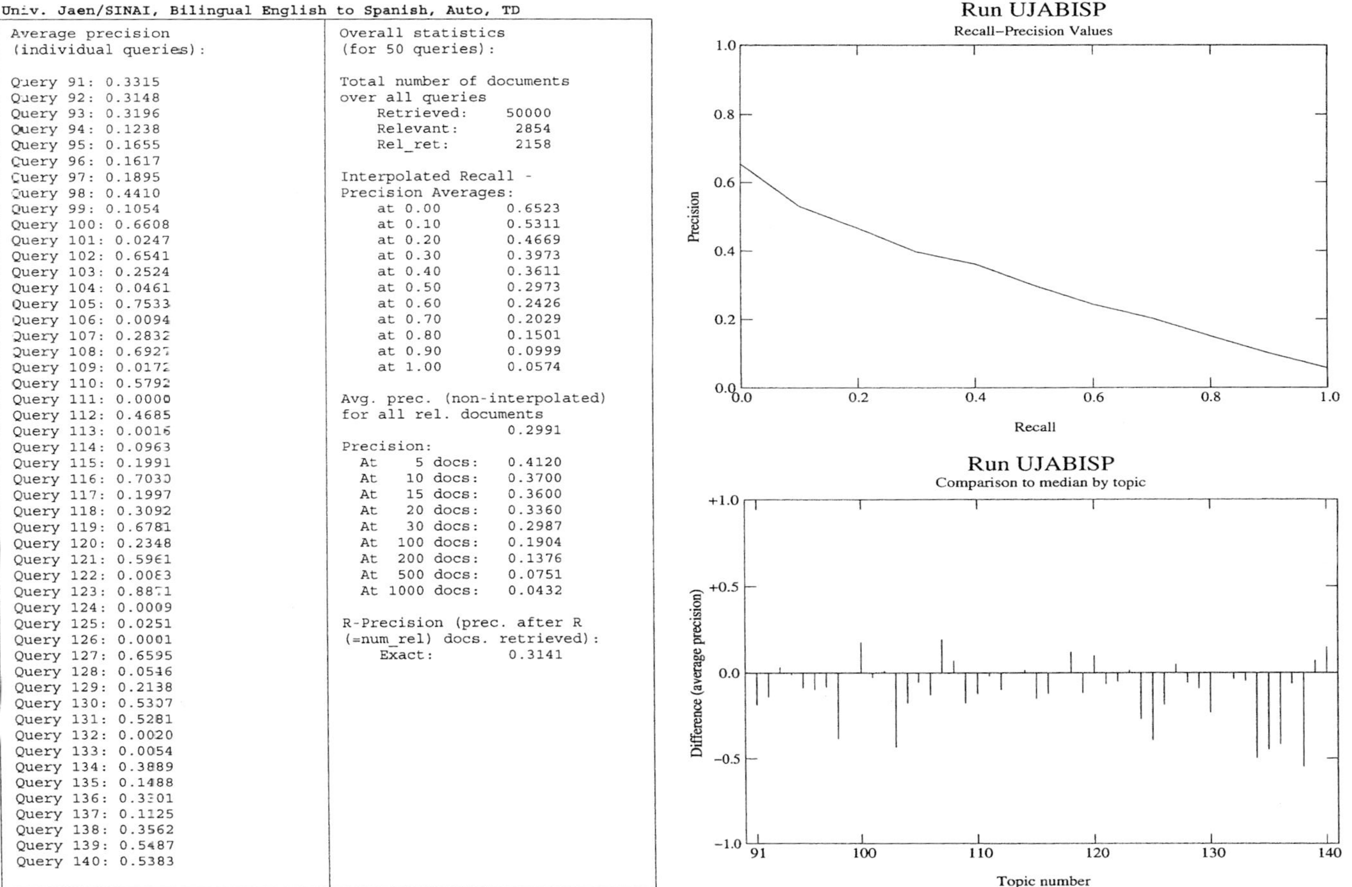

```
Univ. Jaen/SINAI, Bilingual English to Spanish, Auto, TD
Average precision              Overall statistics
(individual queries):          (for 50 queries):

Query 91: 0.3315               Total number of documents
Query 92: 0.3148               over all queries
Query 93: 0.3196                   Retrieved:     50000
Query 94: 0.1238                   Relevant:       2854
Query 95: 0.1655                   Rel_ret:        2158
Query 96: 0.1617
Query 97: 0.1895               Interpolated Recall -
Query 98: 0.4410               Precision Averages:
Query 99: 0.1054                   at 0.00        0.6523
Query 100: 0.6608                  at 0.10        0.5311
Query 101: 0.0247                  at 0.20        0.4669
Query 102: 0.6541                  at 0.30        0.3973
Query 103: 0.2524                  at 0.40        0.3611
Query 104: 0.0461                  at 0.50        0.2973
Query 105: 0.7533                  at 0.60        0.2426
Query 106: 0.0094                  at 0.70        0.2029
Query 107: 0.2832                  at 0.80        0.1501
Query 108: 0.6927                  at 0.90        0.0999
Query 109: 0.0172                  at 1.00        0.0574
Query 110: 0.5792
Query 111: 0.0000              Avg. prec. (non-interpolated)
Query 112: 0.4685              for all rel. documents
Query 113: 0.0016                                 0.2991
Query 114: 0.0963              Precision:
Query 115: 0.1991                At    5 docs:    0.4120
Query 116: 0.7030                At   10 docs:    0.3700
Query 117: 0.1997                At   15 docs:    0.3600
Query 118: 0.3092                At   20 docs:    0.3360
Query 119: 0.6781                At   30 docs:    0.2987
Query 120: 0.2348                At  100 docs:    0.1904
Query 121: 0.5961                At  200 docs:    0.1376
Query 122: 0.0083                At  500 docs:    0.0751
Query 123: 0.8871                At 1000 docs:    0.0432
Query 124: 0.0009
Query 125: 0.0251              R-Precision (prec. after R
Query 126: 0.0001              (=num_rel) docs. retrieved):
Query 127: 0.6595                  Exact:         0.3141
Query 128: 0.0546
Query 129: 0.2138
Query 130: 0.5307
Query 131: 0.5281
Query 132: 0.0020
Query 133: 0.0054
Query 134: 0.3889
Query 135: 0.1488
Query 136: 0.3301
Query 137: 0.1125
Query 138: 0.3562
Query 139: 0.5487
Query 140: 0.5383
```

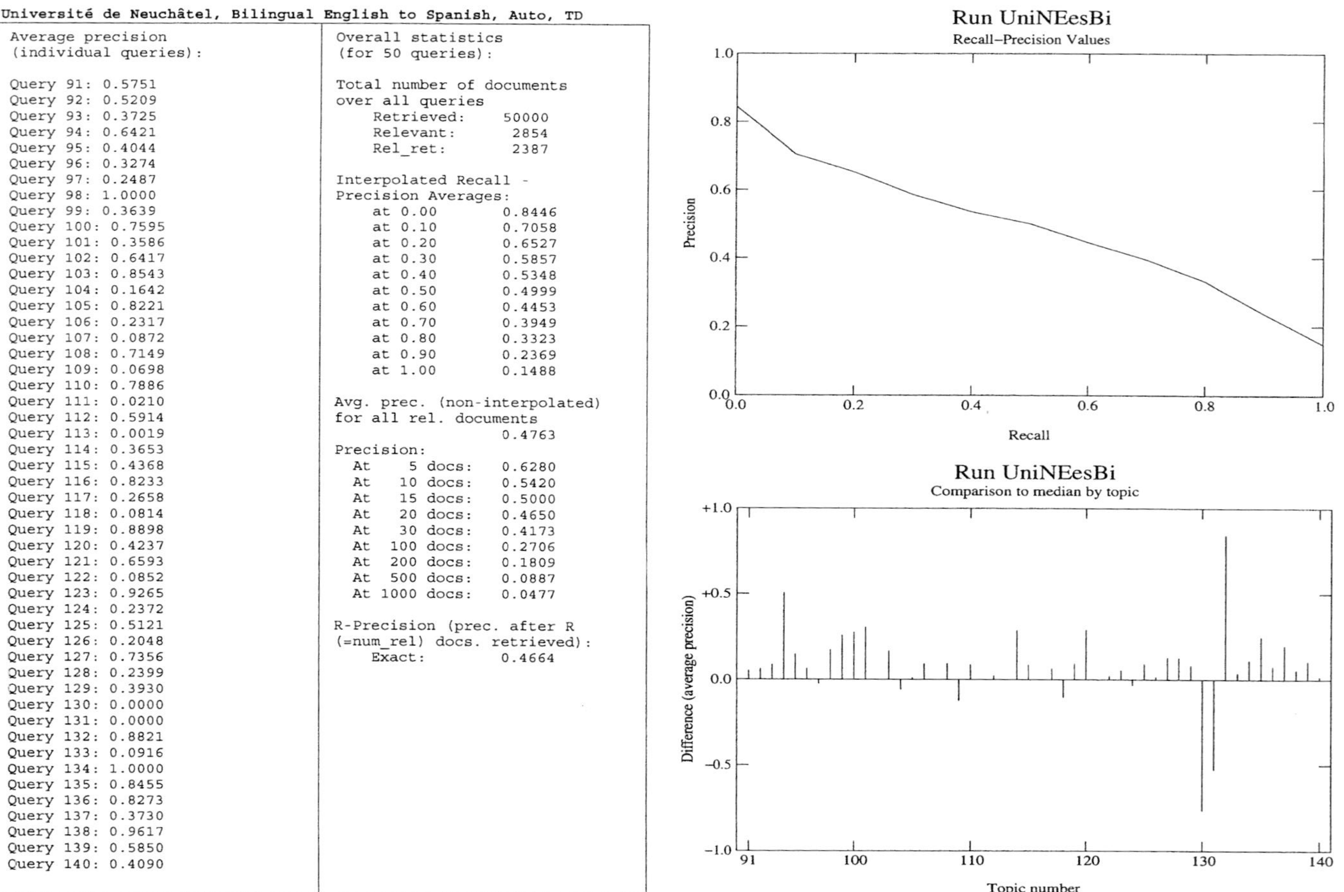

Université de Neuchâtel, Bilingual English to Spanish, Auto, TD

Average precision (individual queries):	Overall statistics (for 50 queries):
Query 91: 0.5751	Total number of documents over all queries
Query 92: 0.5209	Retrieved: 50000
Query 93: 0.3725	Relevant: 2854
Query 94: 0.6421	Rel_ret: 2387
Query 95: 0.4044	
Query 96: 0.3274	Interpolated Recall - Precision Averages:
Query 97: 0.2487	at 0.00 0.8446
Query 98: 1.0000	at 0.10 0.7058
Query 99: 0.3639	at 0.20 0.6527
Query 100: 0.7595	at 0.30 0.5857
Query 101: 0.3586	at 0.40 0.5348
Query 102: 0.6417	at 0.50 0.4999
Query 103: 0.8543	at 0.60 0.4453
Query 104: 0.1642	at 0.70 0.3949
Query 105: 0.8221	at 0.80 0.3323
Query 106: 0.2317	at 0.90 0.2369
Query 107: 0.0872	at 1.00 0.1488
Query 108: 0.7149	
Query 109: 0.0698	Avg. prec. (non-interpolated) for all rel. documents 0.4763
Query 110: 0.7886	Precision:
Query 111: 0.0210	At 5 docs: 0.6280
Query 112: 0.5914	At 10 docs: 0.5420
Query 113: 0.0019	At 15 docs: 0.5000
Query 114: 0.3653	At 20 docs: 0.4650
Query 115: 0.4368	At 30 docs: 0.4173
Query 116: 0.8233	At 100 docs: 0.2706
Query 117: 0.2658	At 200 docs: 0.1809
Query 118: 0.0814	At 500 docs: 0.0887
Query 119: 0.8898	At 1000 docs: 0.0477
Query 120: 0.4237	
Query 121: 0.6593	R-Precision (prec. after R (=num_rel) docs. retrieved):
Query 122: 0.0852	Exact: 0.4664
Query 123: 0.9265	
Query 124: 0.2372	
Query 125: 0.5121	
Query 126: 0.2048	
Query 127: 0.7356	
Query 128: 0.2399	
Query 129: 0.3930	
Query 130: 0.0000	
Query 131: 0.0000	
Query 132: 0.8821	
Query 133: 0.0916	
Query 134: 1.0000	
Query 135: 0.8455	
Query 136: 0.8273	
Query 137: 0.3730	
Query 138: 0.9617	
Query 139: 0.5850	
Query 140: 0.4090	

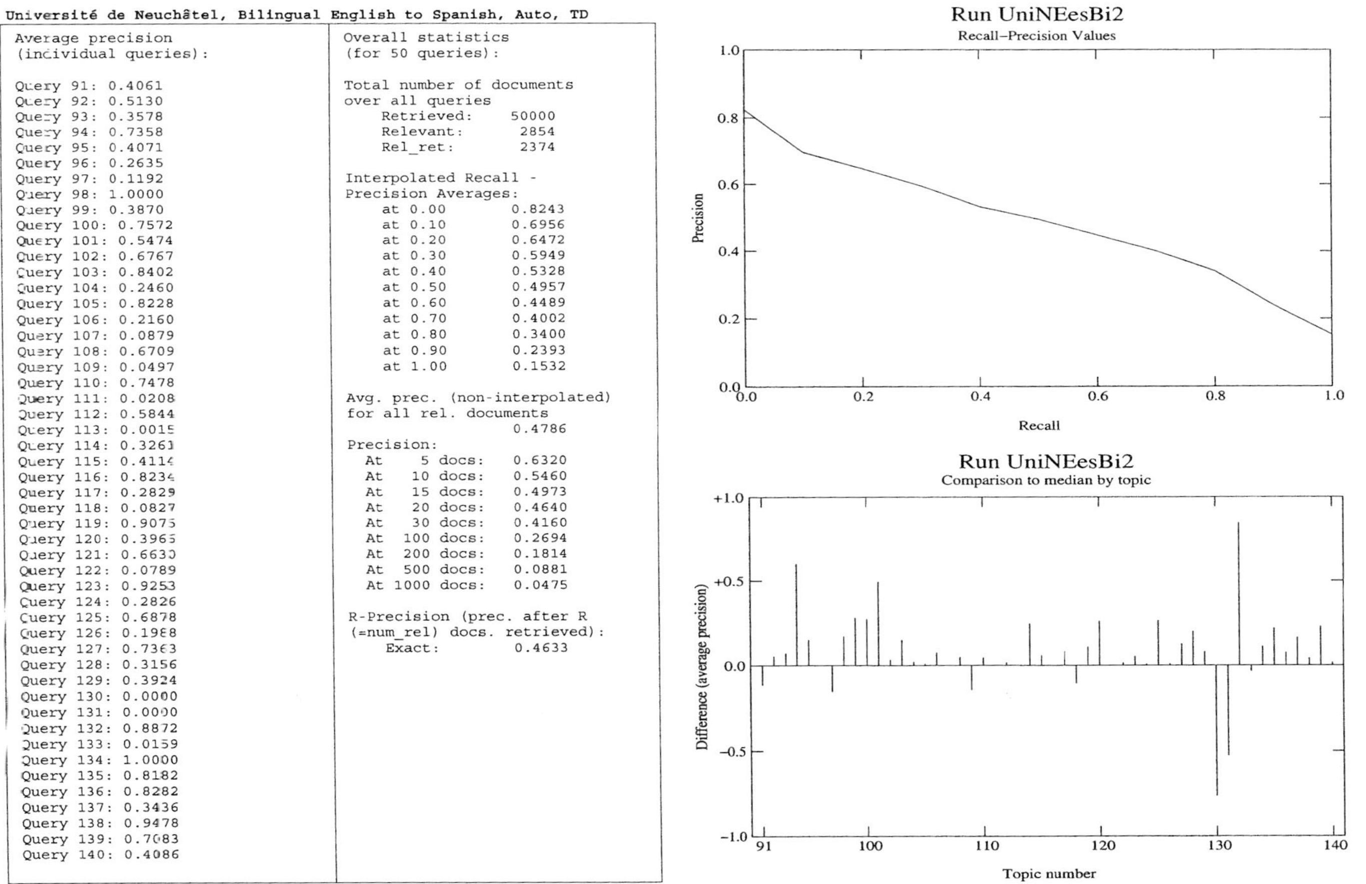

Université de Neuchâtel, Bilingual English to Spanish, Auto, TD

```
Average precision                  Overall statistics
(individual queries):              (for 50 queries):

Query 91: 0.4061                   Total number of documents
Query 92: 0.5130                   over all queries
Query 93: 0.3578                       Retrieved:     50000
Query 94: 0.7358                       Relevant:       2854
Query 95: 0.4071                       Rel_ret:        2374
Query 96: 0.2635
Query 97: 0.1192                   Interpolated Recall -
Query 98: 1.0000                   Precision Averages:
Query 99: 0.3870                       at 0.00        0.8243
Query 100: 0.7572                      at 0.10        0.6956
Query 101: 0.5474                      at 0.20        0.6472
Query 102: 0.6767                      at 0.30        0.5949
Query 103: 0.8402                      at 0.40        0.5328
Query 104: 0.2460                      at 0.50        0.4957
Query 105: 0.8228                      at 0.60        0.4489
Query 106: 0.2160                      at 0.70        0.4002
Query 107: 0.0879                      at 0.80        0.3400
Query 108: 0.6709                      at 0.90        0.2393
Query 109: 0.0497                      at 1.00        0.1532
Query 110: 0.7478
Query 111: 0.0208                  Avg. prec. (non-interpolated)
Query 112: 0.5844                  for all rel. documents
Query 113: 0.0015                                     0.4786
Query 114: 0.3261                  Precision:
Query 115: 0.4114                    At    5 docs:    0.6320
Query 116: 0.8234                    At   10 docs:    0.5460
Query 117: 0.2829                    At   15 docs:    0.4973
Query 118: 0.0827                    At   20 docs:    0.4640
Query 119: 0.9075                    At   30 docs:    0.4160
Query 120: 0.3965                    At  100 docs:    0.2694
Query 121: 0.6630                    At  200 docs:    0.1814
Query 122: 0.0789                    At  500 docs:    0.0881
Query 123: 0.9253                    At 1000 docs:    0.0475
Query 124: 0.2826
Query 125: 0.6878                  R-Precision (prec. after R
Query 126: 0.1988                  (=num_rel) docs. retrieved):
Query 127: 0.7363                      Exact:         0.4633
Query 128: 0.3156
Query 129: 0.3924
Query 130: 0.0000
Query 131: 0.0000
Query 132: 0.8872
Query 133: 0.0159
Query 134: 1.0000
Query 135: 0.8182
Query 136: 0.8282
Query 137: 0.3436
Query 138: 0.9478
Query 139: 0.7083
Query 140: 0.4086
```

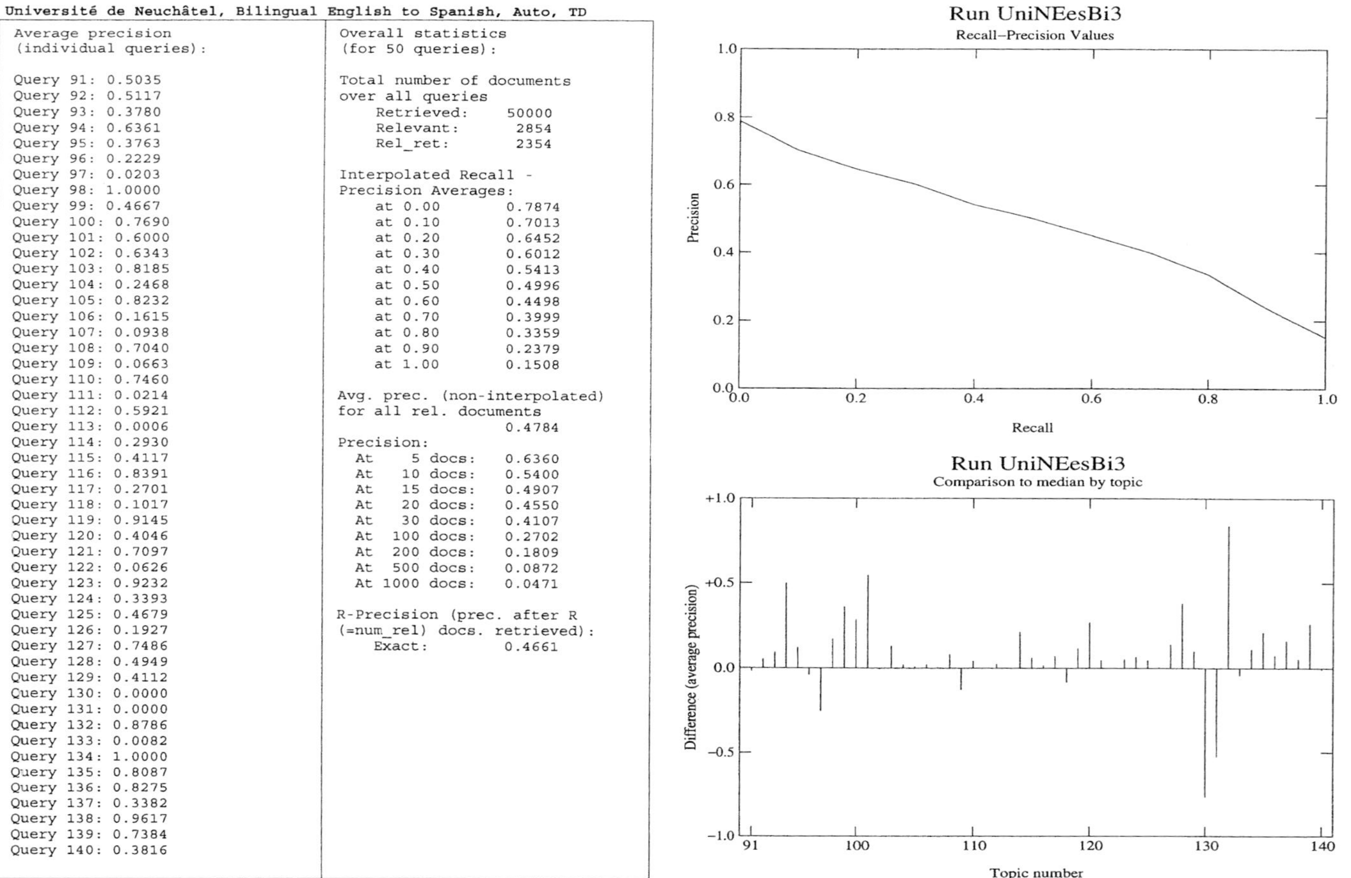

Université de Neuchâtel, Bilingual English to Spanish, Auto, TD

```
Average precision                  Overall statistics
(individual queries):              (for 50 queries):

Query 91: 0.5035                   Total number of documents
Query 92: 0.5117                   over all queries
Query 93: 0.3780                       Retrieved:     50000
Query 94: 0.6361                       Relevant:       2854
Query 95: 0.3763                       Rel_ret:        2354
Query 96: 0.2229
Query 97: 0.0203                   Interpolated Recall -
Query 98: 1.0000                   Precision Averages:
Query 99: 0.4667                       at 0.00         0.7874
Query 100: 0.7690                      at 0.10         0.7013
Query 101: 0.6000                      at 0.20         0.6452
Query 102: 0.6343                      at 0.30         0.6012
Query 103: 0.8185                      at 0.40         0.5413
Query 104: 0.2468                      at 0.50         0.4996
Query 105: 0.8232                      at 0.60         0.4498
Query 106: 0.1615                      at 0.70         0.3999
Query 107: 0.0938                      at 0.80         0.3359
Query 108: 0.7040                      at 0.90         0.2379
Query 109: 0.0663                      at 1.00         0.1508
Query 110: 0.7460
Query 111: 0.0214                  Avg. prec. (non-interpolated)
Query 112: 0.5921                  for all rel. documents
Query 113: 0.0006                                      0.4784
Query 114: 0.2930                  Precision:
Query 115: 0.4117                    At    5 docs:     0.6360
Query 116: 0.8391                    At   10 docs:     0.5400
Query 117: 0.2701                    At   15 docs:     0.4907
Query 118: 0.1017                    At   20 docs:     0.4550
Query 119: 0.9145                    At   30 docs:     0.4107
Query 120: 0.4046                    At  100 docs:     0.2702
Query 121: 0.7097                    At  200 docs:     0.1809
Query 122: 0.0626                    At  500 docs:     0.0872
Query 123: 0.9232                    At 1000 docs:     0.0471
Query 124: 0.3393
Query 125: 0.4679                  R-Precision (prec. after R
Query 126: 0.1927                  (=num_rel) docs. retrieved):
Query 127: 0.7486                      Exact:          0.4661
Query 128: 0.4949
Query 129: 0.4112
Query 130: 0.0000
Query 131: 0.0000
Query 132: 0.8786
Query 133: 0.0082
Query 134: 1.0000
Query 135: 0.8087
Query 136: 0.8275
Query 137: 0.3382
Query 138: 0.9617
Query 139: 0.7384
Query 140: 0.3816
```

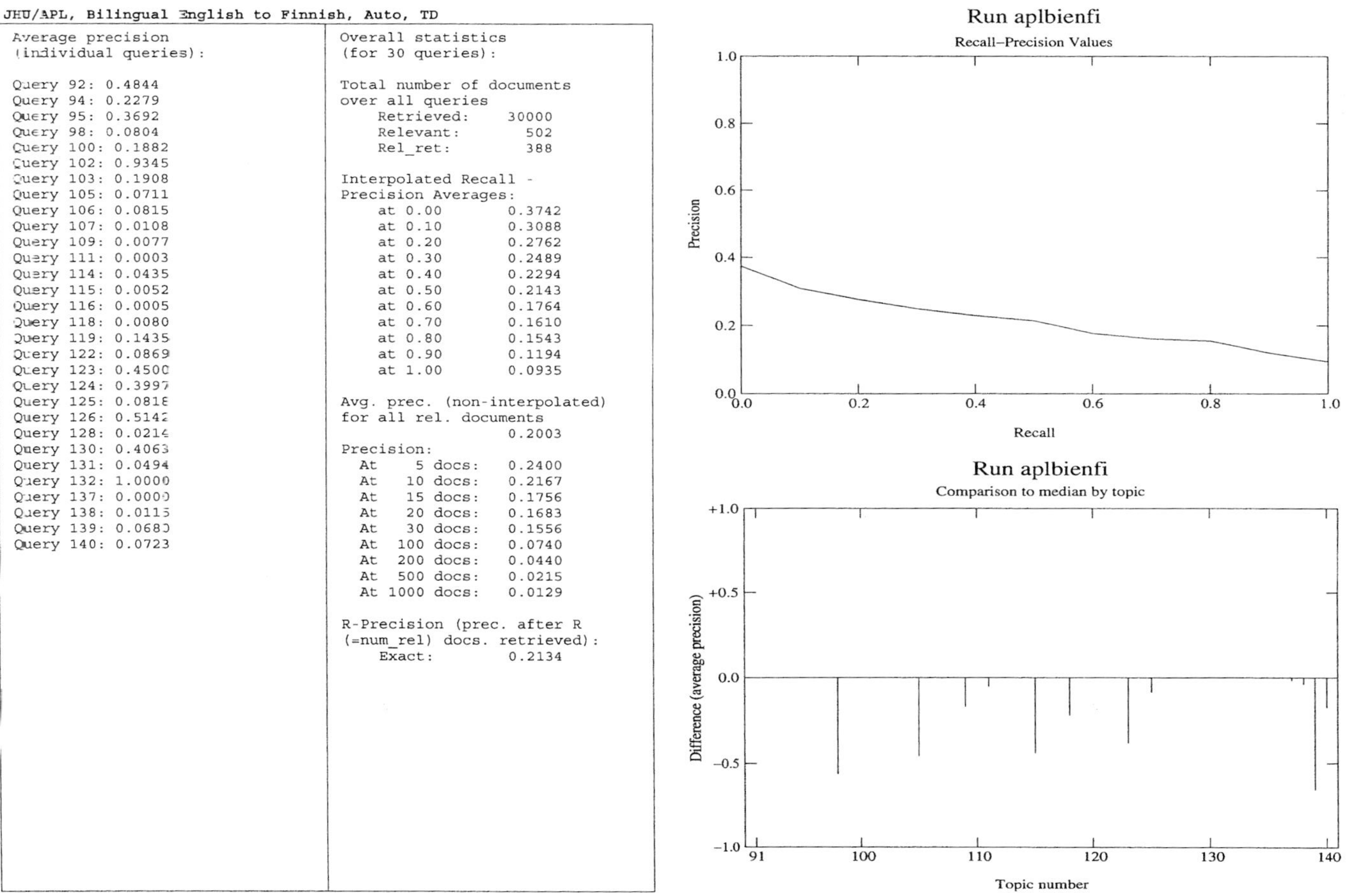

JHU/APL, Bilingual English to Finnish, Auto, TD

```
Average precision                 Overall statistics
(individual queries):             (for 30 queries):

Query 92: 0.4844                  Total number of documents
Query 94: 0.2279                  over all queries
Query 95: 0.3692                      Retrieved:    30000
Query 98: 0.0804                      Relevant:       502
Query 100: 0.1882                     Rel_ret:        388
Query 102: 0.9345
Query 103: 0.1908                 Interpolated Recall -
Query 105: 0.0711                 Precision Averages:
Query 106: 0.0815                     at 0.00       0.3742
Query 107: 0.0108                     at 0.10       0.3088
Query 109: 0.0077                     at 0.20       0.2762
Query 111: 0.0003                     at 0.30       0.2489
Query 114: 0.0435                     at 0.40       0.2294
Query 115: 0.0052                     at 0.50       0.2143
Query 116: 0.0005                     at 0.60       0.1764
Query 118: 0.0080                     at 0.70       0.1610
Query 119: 0.1435                     at 0.80       0.1543
Query 122: 0.0869                     at 0.90       0.1194
Query 123: 0.4500                     at 1.00       0.0935
Query 124: 0.3997
Query 125: 0.0818                 Avg. prec. (non-interpolated)
Query 126: 0.5142                 for all rel. documents
Query 128: 0.0214                                   0.2003
Query 130: 0.4063                 Precision:
Query 131: 0.0494                   At    5 docs:   0.2400
Query 132: 1.0000                   At   10 docs:   0.2167
Query 137: 0.0000                   At   15 docs:   0.1756
Query 138: 0.0115                   At   20 docs:   0.1683
Query 139: 0.0680                   At   30 docs:   0.1556
Query 140: 0.0723                   At  100 docs:   0.0740
                                    At  200 docs:   0.0440
                                    At  500 docs:   0.0215
                                    At 1000 docs:   0.0129

                                  R-Precision (prec. after R
                                  (=num_rel) docs. retrieved):
                                      Exact:        0.2134
```

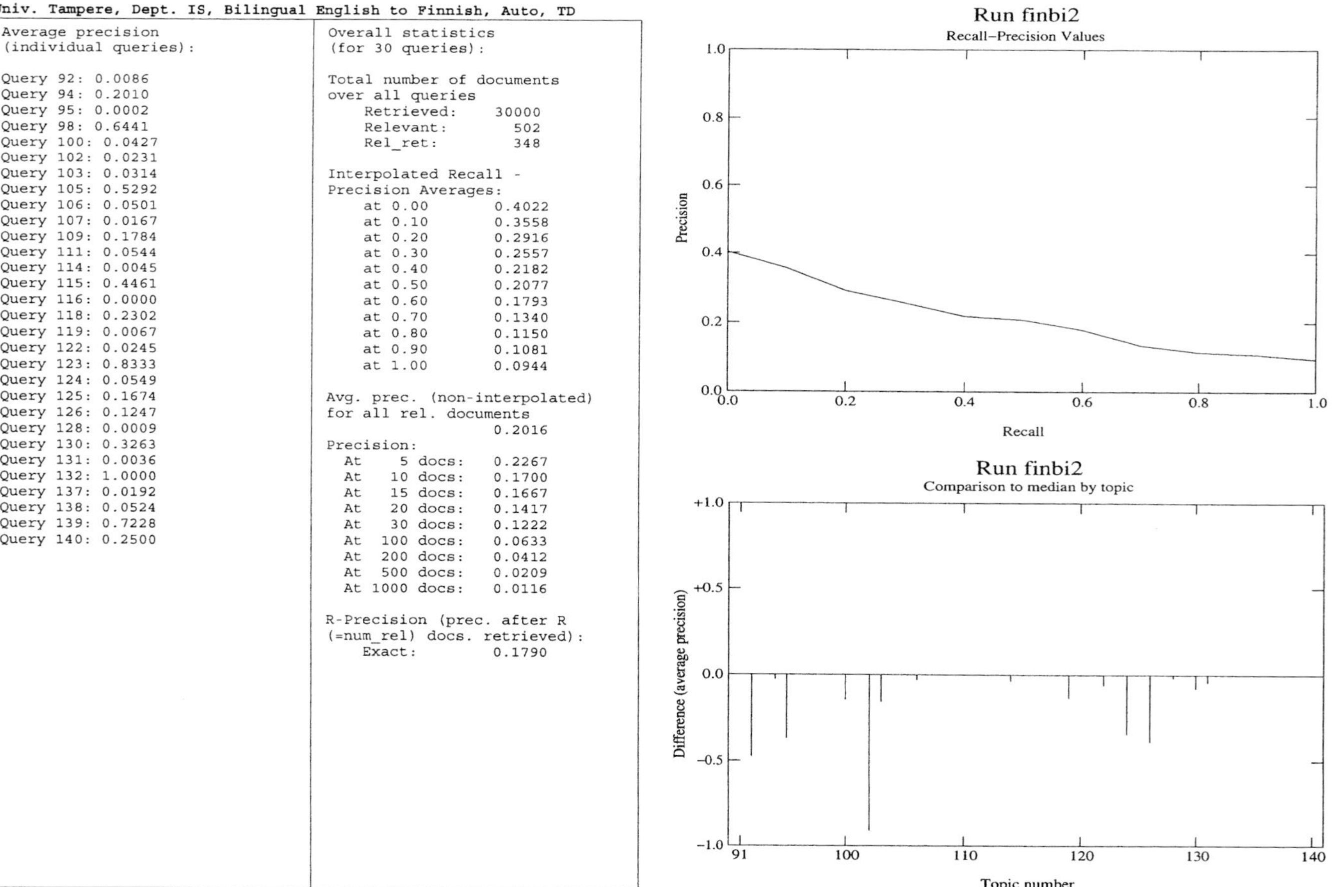

```
Univ. Tampere, Dept. IS, Bilingual English to Finnish, Auto, TD

Average precision              Overall statistics
(individual queries):          (for 30 queries):

Query 92: 0.0086               Total number of documents
Query 94: 0.2010               over all queries
Query 95: 0.0002                   Retrieved:    30000
Query 98: 0.6441                   Relevant:       502
Query 100: 0.0427                  Rel_ret:        348
Query 102: 0.0231
Query 103: 0.0314              Interpolated Recall -
Query 105: 0.5292              Precision Averages:
Query 106: 0.0501                  at 0.00       0.4022
Query 107: 0.0167                  at 0.10       0.3558
Query 109: 0.1784                  at 0.20       0.2916
Query 111: 0.0544                  at 0.30       0.2557
Query 114: 0.0045                  at 0.40       0.2182
Query 115: 0.4461                  at 0.50       0.2077
Query 116: 0.0000                  at 0.60       0.1793
Query 118: 0.2302                  at 0.70       0.1340
Query 119: 0.0067                  at 0.80       0.1150
Query 122: 0.0245                  at 0.90       0.1081
Query 123: 0.8333                  at 1.00       0.0944
Query 124: 0.0549
Query 125: 0.1674              Avg. prec. (non-interpolated)
Query 126: 0.1247              for all rel. documents
Query 128: 0.0009                                0.2016
Query 130: 0.3263              Precision:
Query 131: 0.0036                At    5 docs:   0.2267
Query 132: 1.0000                At   10 docs:   0.1700
Query 137: 0.0192                At   15 docs:   0.1667
Query 138: 0.0524                At   20 docs:   0.1417
Query 139: 0.7228                At   30 docs:   0.1222
Query 140: 0.2500                At  100 docs:   0.0633
                                 At  200 docs:   0.0412
                                 At  500 docs:   0.0209
                                 At 1000 docs:   0.0116

                               R-Precision (prec. after R
                               (=num_rel) docs. retrieved):
                                   Exact:        0.1790
```

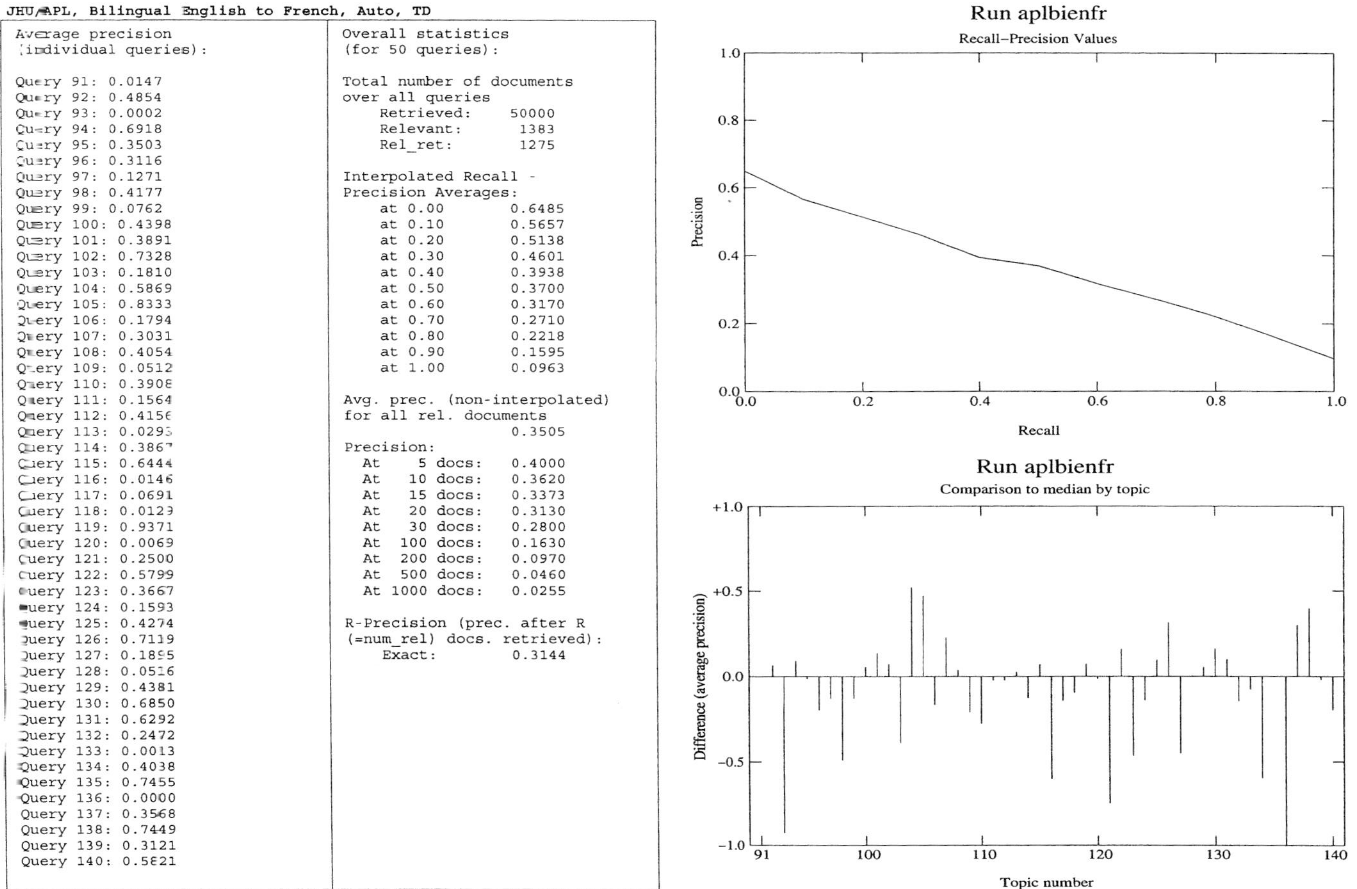

JHU/APL, Bilingual English to French, Auto, TD

Average precision (individual queries):

Query 91: 0.0147
Query 92: 0.4854
Query 93: 0.0002
Query 94: 0.6918
Query 95: 0.3503
Query 96: 0.3116
Query 97: 0.1271
Query 98: 0.4177
Query 99: 0.0762
Query 100: 0.4398
Query 101: 0.3891
Query 102: 0.7328
Query 103: 0.1810
Query 104: 0.5869
Query 105: 0.8333
Query 106: 0.1794
Query 107: 0.3031
Query 108: 0.4054
Query 109: 0.0512
Query 110: 0.3908
Query 111: 0.1564
Query 112: 0.4156
Query 113: 0.0293
Query 114: 0.3867
Query 115: 0.6444
Query 116: 0.0146
Query 117: 0.0691
Query 118: 0.0123
Query 119: 0.9371
Query 120: 0.0069
Query 121: 0.2500
Query 122: 0.5799
Query 123: 0.3667
Query 124: 0.1593
Query 125: 0.4274
Query 126: 0.7119
Query 127: 0.1895
Query 128: 0.0516
Query 129: 0.4381
Query 130: 0.6850
Query 131: 0.6292
Query 132: 0.2472
Query 133: 0.0013
Query 134: 0.4038
Query 135: 0.7455
Query 136: 0.0000
Query 137: 0.3568
Query 138: 0.7449
Query 139: 0.3121
Query 140: 0.5821

Overall statistics (for 50 queries):

Total number of documents over all queries
Retrieved: 50000
Relevant: 1383
Rel_ret: 1275

Interpolated Recall - Precision Averages:

at 0.00	0.6485
at 0.10	0.5657
at 0.20	0.5138
at 0.30	0.4601
at 0.40	0.3938
at 0.50	0.3700
at 0.60	0.3170
at 0.70	0.2710
at 0.80	0.2218
at 0.90	0.1595
at 1.00	0.0963

Avg. prec. (non-interpolated) for all rel. documents 0.3505

Precision:

At 5 docs:	0.4000
At 10 docs:	0.3620
At 15 docs:	0.3373
At 20 docs:	0.3130
At 30 docs:	0.2800
At 100 docs:	0.1630
At 200 docs:	0.0970
At 500 docs:	0.0460
At 1000 docs:	0.0255

R-Precision (prec. after R (=num_rel) docs. retrieved):
Exact: 0.3144

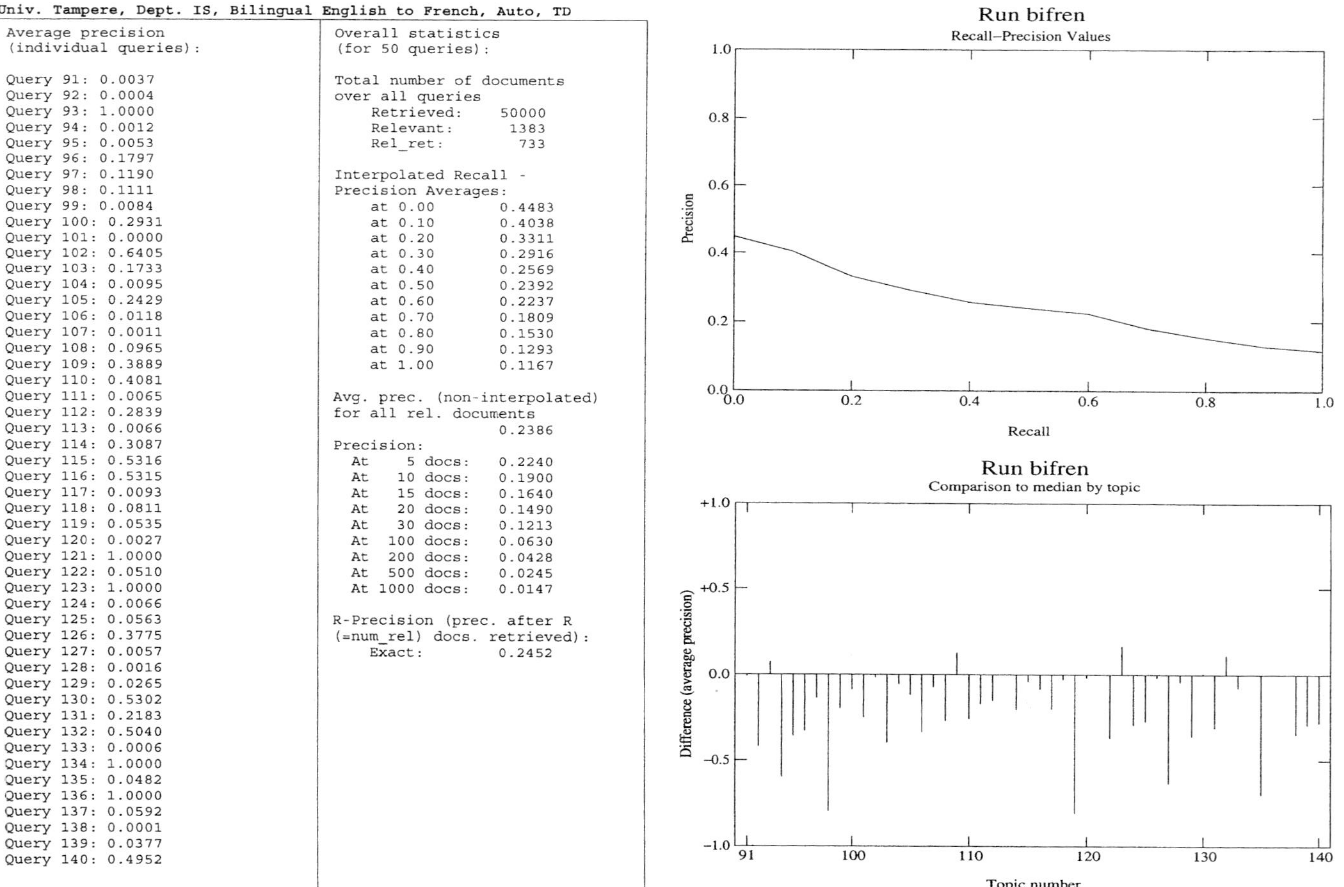

Univ. Tampere, Dept. IS, Bilingual English to French, Auto, TD

Average precision (individual queries):	Overall statistics (for 50 queries):
Query 91: 0.0037	Total number of documents over all queries
Query 92: 0.0004	Retrieved: 50000
Query 93: 1.0000	Relevant: 1383
Query 94: 0.0012	Rel_ret: 733
Query 95: 0.0053	
Query 96: 0.1797	Interpolated Recall - Precision Averages:
Query 97: 0.1190	at 0.00 0.4483
Query 98: 0.1111	at 0.10 0.4038
Query 99: 0.0084	at 0.20 0.3311
Query 100: 0.2931	at 0.30 0.2916
Query 101: 0.0000	at 0.40 0.2569
Query 102: 0.6405	at 0.50 0.2392
Query 103: 0.1733	at 0.60 0.2237
Query 104: 0.0095	at 0.70 0.1809
Query 105: 0.2429	at 0.80 0.1530
Query 106: 0.0118	at 0.90 0.1293
Query 107: 0.0011	at 1.00 0.1167
Query 108: 0.0965	
Query 109: 0.3889	Avg. prec. (non-interpolated) for all rel. documents
Query 110: 0.4081	0.2386
Query 111: 0.0065	Precision:
Query 112: 0.2839	At 5 docs: 0.2240
Query 113: 0.0066	At 10 docs: 0.1900
Query 114: 0.3087	At 15 docs: 0.1640
Query 115: 0.5316	At 20 docs: 0.1490
Query 116: 0.5315	At 30 docs: 0.1213
Query 117: 0.0093	At 100 docs: 0.0630
Query 118: 0.0811	At 200 docs: 0.0428
Query 119: 0.0535	At 500 docs: 0.0245
Query 120: 0.0027	At 1000 docs: 0.0147
Query 121: 1.0000	
Query 122: 0.0510	R-Precision (prec. after R (=num_rel) docs. retrieved):
Query 123: 1.0000	Exact: 0.2452
Query 124: 0.0066	
Query 125: 0.0563	
Query 126: 0.3775	
Query 127: 0.0057	
Query 128: 0.0016	
Query 129: 0.0265	
Query 130: 0.5302	
Query 131: 0.2183	
Query 132: 0.5040	
Query 133: 0.0006	
Query 134: 1.0000	
Query 135: 0.0482	
Query 136: 1.0000	
Query 137: 0.0592	
Query 138: 0.0001	
Query 139: 0.0377	
Query 140: 0.4952	

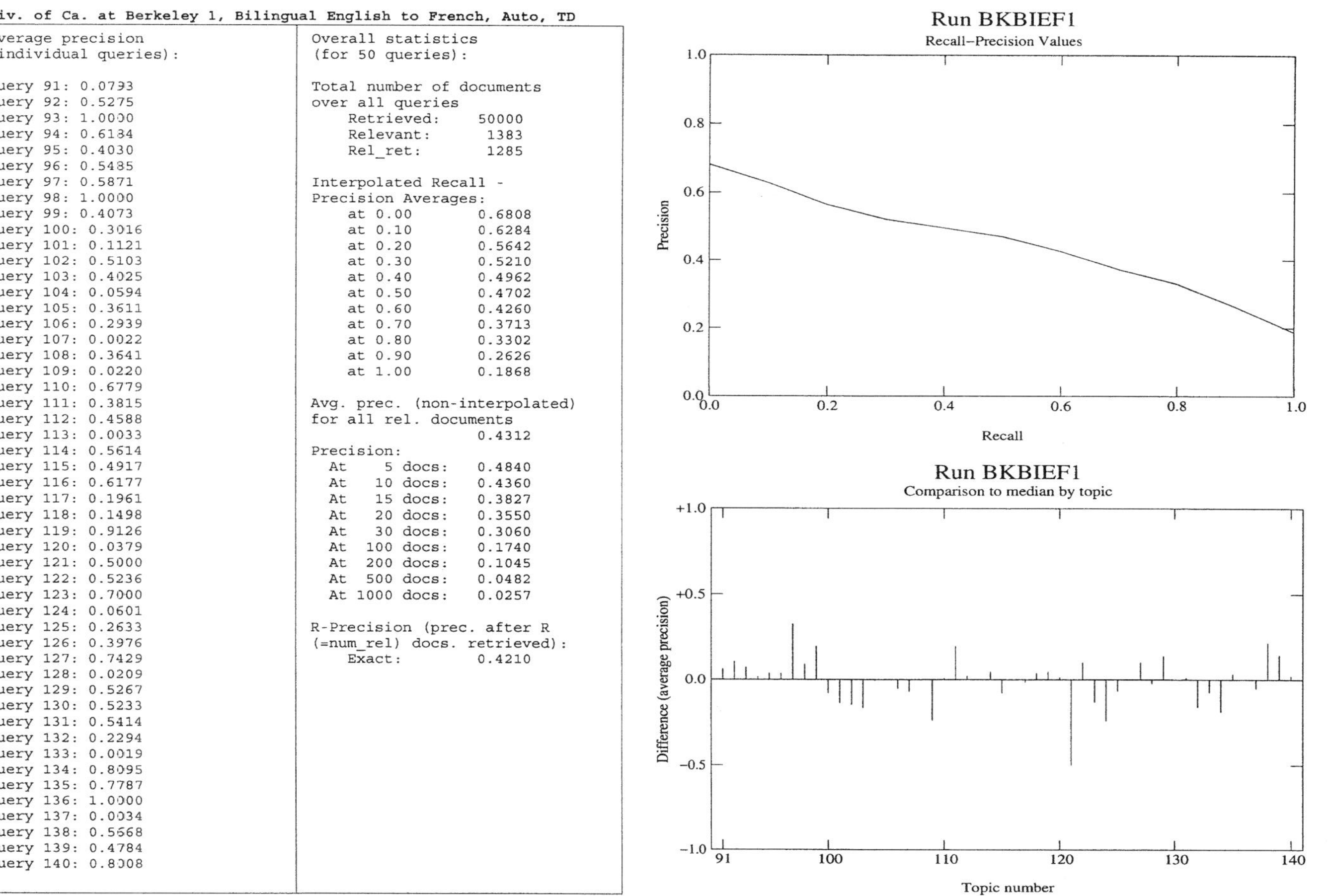

Univ. of Ca. at Berkeley 1, Bilingual English to French, Auto, TD

```
Average precision
(individual queries):

Query 91: 0.0793
Query 92: 0.5275
Query 93: 1.0000
Query 94: 0.6134
Query 95: 0.4030
Query 96: 0.5485
Query 97: 0.5871
Query 98: 1.0000
Query 99: 0.4073
Query 100: 0.3016
Query 101: 0.1121
Query 102: 0.5103
Query 103: 0.4025
Query 104: 0.0594
Query 105: 0.3611
Query 106: 0.2939
Query 107: 0.0022
Query 108: 0.3641
Query 109: 0.0220
Query 110: 0.6779
Query 111: 0.3815
Query 112: 0.4588
Query 113: 0.0033
Query 114: 0.5614
Query 115: 0.4917
Query 116: 0.6177
Query 117: 0.1961
Query 118: 0.1498
Query 119: 0.9126
Query 120: 0.0379
Query 121: 0.5000
Query 122: 0.5236
Query 123: 0.7000
Query 124: 0.0601
Query 125: 0.2633
Query 126: 0.3976
Query 127: 0.7429
Query 128: 0.0209
Query 129: 0.5267
Query 130: 0.5233
Query 131: 0.5414
Query 132: 0.2294
Query 133: 0.0019
Query 134: 0.8095
Query 135: 0.7787
Query 136: 1.0000
Query 137: 0.0034
Query 138: 0.5568
Query 139: 0.4784
Query 140: 0.8008
```

```
Overall statistics
(for 50 queries):

Total number of documents
over all queries
    Retrieved:     50000
    Relevant:       1383
    Rel_ret:        1285

Interpolated Recall -
Precision Averages:
    at 0.00        0.6808
    at 0.10        0.6284
    at 0.20        0.5642
    at 0.30        0.5210
    at 0.40        0.4962
    at 0.50        0.4702
    at 0.60        0.4260
    at 0.70        0.3713
    at 0.80        0.3302
    at 0.90        0.2626
    at 1.00        0.1868

Avg. prec. (non-interpolated)
for all rel. documents
                   0.4312
Precision:
  At    5 docs:    0.4840
  At   10 docs:    0.4360
  At   15 docs:    0.3827
  At   20 docs:    0.3550
  At   30 docs:    0.3060
  At  100 docs:    0.1740
  At  200 docs:    0.1045
  At  500 docs:    0.0482
  At 1000 docs:    0.0257

R-Precision (prec. after R
(=num_rel) docs. retrieved):
    Exact:         0.4210
```

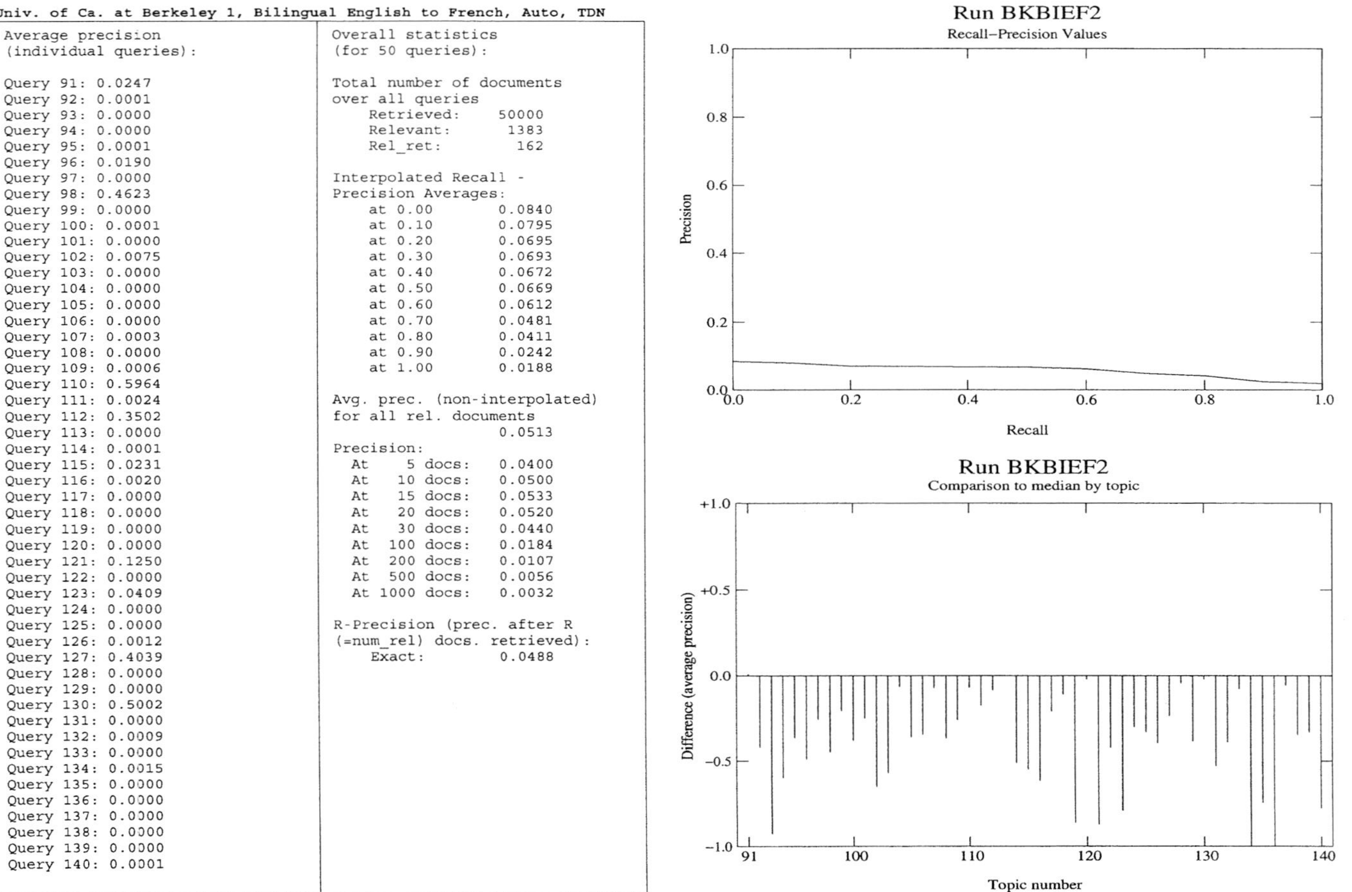

Univ. of Ca. at Berkeley 1, Bilingual English to French, Auto, TDN

Average precision (individual queries):	Overall statistics (for 50 queries):
Query 91: 0.0247	Total number of documents over all queries
Query 92: 0.0001	Retrieved: 50000
Query 93: 0.0000	Relevant: 1383
Query 94: 0.0000	Rel_ret: 162
Query 95: 0.0001	
Query 96: 0.0190	Interpolated Recall - Precision Averages:
Query 97: 0.0000	at 0.00 0.0840
Query 98: 0.4623	at 0.10 0.0795
Query 99: 0.0000	at 0.20 0.0695
Query 100: 0.0001	at 0.30 0.0693
Query 101: 0.0000	at 0.40 0.0672
Query 102: 0.0075	at 0.50 0.0669
Query 103: 0.0000	at 0.60 0.0612
Query 104: 0.0000	at 0.70 0.0481
Query 105: 0.0000	at 0.80 0.0411
Query 106: 0.0000	at 0.90 0.0242
Query 107: 0.0003	at 1.00 0.0188
Query 108: 0.0000	
Query 109: 0.0006	Avg. prec. (non-interpolated) for all rel. documents 0.0513
Query 110: 0.5964	
Query 111: 0.0024	Precision:
Query 112: 0.3502	At 5 docs: 0.0400
Query 113: 0.0000	At 10 docs: 0.0500
Query 114: 0.0001	At 15 docs: 0.0533
Query 115: 0.0231	At 20 docs: 0.0520
Query 116: 0.0020	At 30 docs: 0.0440
Query 117: 0.0000	At 100 docs: 0.0184
Query 118: 0.0000	At 200 docs: 0.0107
Query 119: 0.0000	At 500 docs: 0.0056
Query 120: 0.0000	At 1000 docs: 0.0032
Query 121: 0.1250	
Query 122: 0.0000	R-Precision (prec. after R (=num_rel) docs. retrieved):
Query 123: 0.0409	Exact: 0.0488
Query 124: 0.0000	
Query 125: 0.0000	
Query 126: 0.0012	
Query 127: 0.4039	
Query 128: 0.0000	
Query 129: 0.0000	
Query 130: 0.5002	
Query 131: 0.0000	
Query 132: 0.0009	
Query 133: 0.0000	
Query 134: 0.0015	
Query 135: 0.0000	
Query 136: 0.0000	
Query 137: 0.0000	
Query 138: 0.0000	
Query 139: 0.0000	
Query 140: 0.0001	

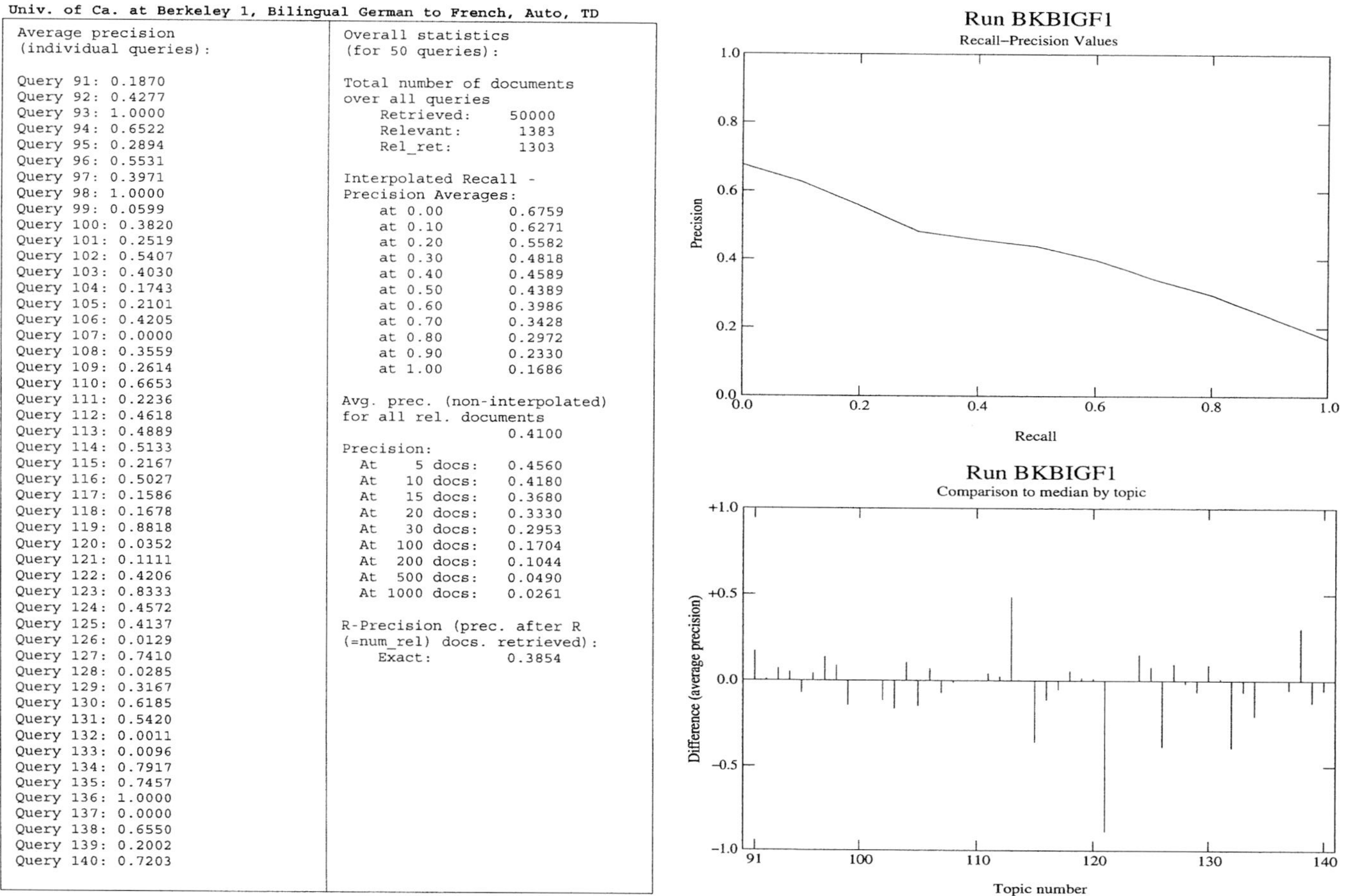

Univ. of Ca. at Berkeley 1, Bilingual German to French, Auto, TD

```
Average precision                 Overall statistics
(individual queries):             (for 50 queries):

Query 91: 0.1870                  Total number of documents
Query 92: 0.4277                  over all queries
Query 93: 1.0000                      Retrieved:     50000
Query 94: 0.6522                      Relevant:       1383
Query 95: 0.2894                      Rel_ret:        1303
Query 96: 0.5531
Query 97: 0.3971                  Interpolated Recall -
Query 98: 1.0000                  Precision Averages:
Query 99: 0.0599                      at 0.00        0.6759
Query 100: 0.3820                     at 0.10        0.6271
Query 101: 0.2519                     at 0.20        0.5582
Query 102: 0.5407                     at 0.30        0.4818
Query 103: 0.4030                     at 0.40        0.4589
Query 104: 0.1743                     at 0.50        0.4389
Query 105: 0.2101                     at 0.60        0.3986
Query 106: 0.4205                     at 0.70        0.3428
Query 107: 0.0000                     at 0.80        0.2972
Query 108: 0.3559                     at 0.90        0.2330
Query 109: 0.2614                     at 1.00        0.1686
Query 110: 0.6653
Query 111: 0.2236                 Avg. prec. (non-interpolated)
Query 112: 0.4618                 for all rel. documents
Query 113: 0.4889                                    0.4100
Query 114: 0.5133                 Precision:
Query 115: 0.2167                   At    5 docs:    0.4560
Query 116: 0.5027                   At   10 docs:    0.4180
Query 117: 0.1586                   At   15 docs:    0.3680
Query 118: 0.1678                   At   20 docs:    0.3330
Query 119: 0.8818                   At   30 docs:    0.2953
Query 120: 0.0352                   At  100 docs:    0.1704
Query 121: 0.1111                   At  200 docs:    0.1044
Query 122: 0.4206                   At  500 docs:    0.0490
Query 123: 0.8333                   At 1000 docs:    0.0261
Query 124: 0.4572
Query 125: 0.4137                 R-Precision (prec. after R
Query 126: 0.0129                 (=num_rel) docs. retrieved):
Query 127: 0.7410                     Exact:         0.3854
Query 128: 0.0285
Query 129: 0.3167
Query 130: 0.6185
Query 131: 0.5420
Query 132: 0.0011
Query 133: 0.0096
Query 134: 0.7917
Query 135: 0.7457
Query 136: 1.0000
Query 137: 0.0000
Query 138: 0.6550
Query 139: 0.2002
Query 140: 0.7203
```

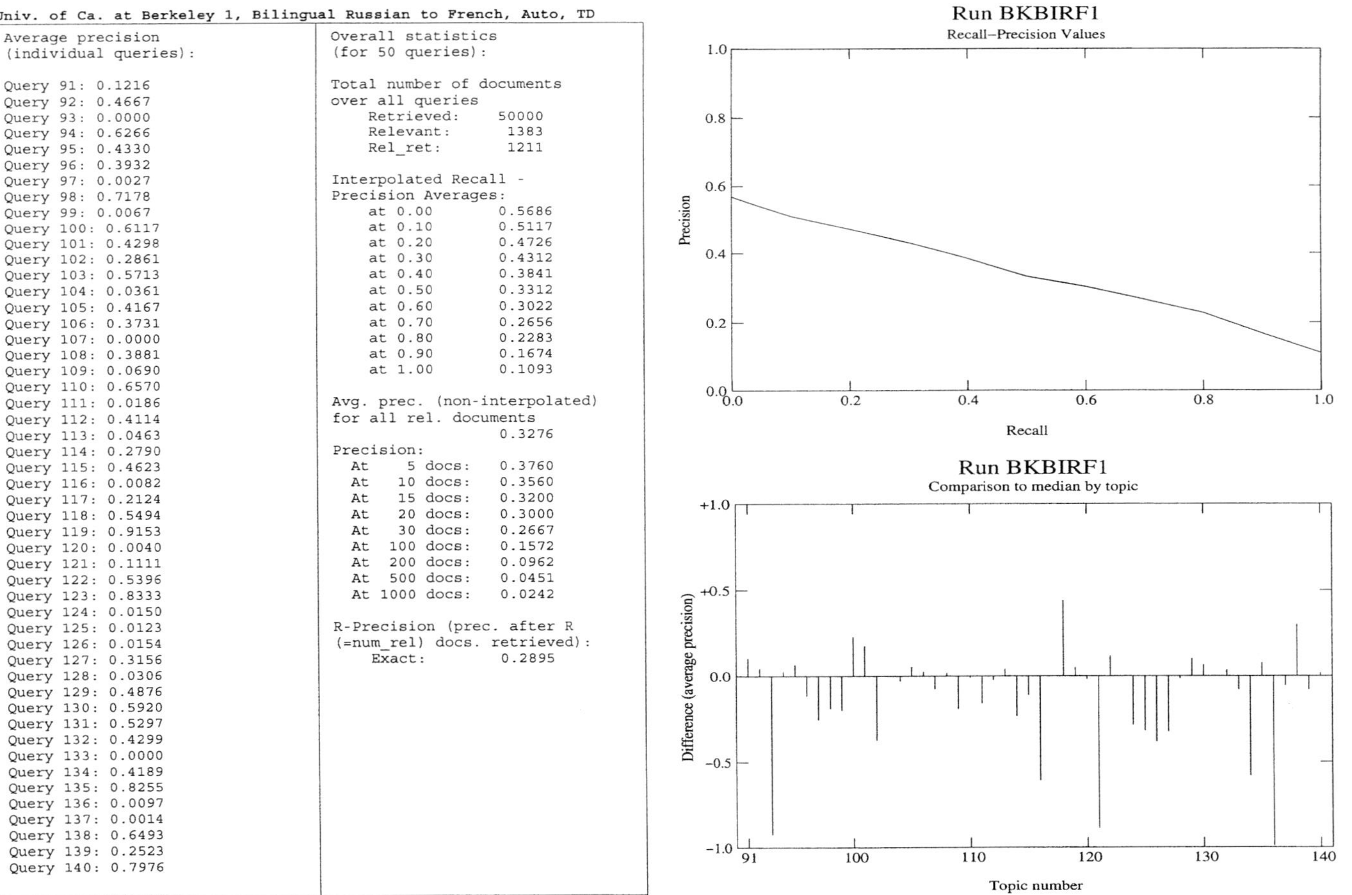

Univ. of Ca. at Berkeley 1, Bilingual Russian to French, Auto, TD

```
Average precision                 Overall statistics
(individual queries):             (for 50 queries):

Query 91: 0.1216                  Total number of documents
Query 92: 0.4667                  over all queries
Query 93: 0.0000                      Retrieved:    50000
Query 94: 0.6266                      Relevant:      1383
Query 95: 0.4330                      Rel_ret:       1211
Query 96: 0.3932
Query 97: 0.0027                  Interpolated Recall -
Query 98: 0.7178                  Precision Averages:
Query 99: 0.0067                      at 0.00        0.5686
Query 100: 0.6117                     at 0.10        0.5117
Query 101: 0.4298                     at 0.20        0.4726
Query 102: 0.2861                     at 0.30        0.4312
Query 103: 0.5713                     at 0.40        0.3841
Query 104: 0.0361                     at 0.50        0.3312
Query 105: 0.4167                     at 0.60        0.3022
Query 106: 0.3731                     at 0.70        0.2656
Query 107: 0.0000                     at 0.80        0.2283
Query 108: 0.3881                     at 0.90        0.1674
Query 109: 0.0690                     at 1.00        0.1093
Query 110: 0.6570
Query 111: 0.0186                 Avg. prec. (non-interpolated)
Query 112: 0.4114                 for all rel. documents
Query 113: 0.0463                                    0.3276
Query 114: 0.2790                 Precision:
Query 115: 0.4623                   At    5 docs:    0.3760
Query 116: 0.0082                   At   10 docs:    0.3560
Query 117: 0.2124                   At   15 docs:    0.3200
Query 118: 0.5494                   At   20 docs:    0.3000
Query 119: 0.9153                   At   30 docs:    0.2667
Query 120: 0.0040                   At  100 docs:    0.1572
Query 121: 0.1111                   At  200 docs:    0.0962
Query 122: 0.5396                   At  500 docs:    0.0451
Query 123: 0.8333                   At 1000 docs:    0.0242
Query 124: 0.0150
Query 125: 0.0123                 R-Precision (prec. after R
Query 126: 0.0154                 (=num_rel) docs. retrieved):
Query 127: 0.3156                     Exact:         0.2895
Query 128: 0.0306
Query 129: 0.4876
Query 130: 0.5920
Query 131: 0.5297
Query 132: 0.4299
Query 133: 0.0000
Query 134: 0.4189
Query 135: 0.8255
Query 136: 0.0097
Query 137: 0.0014
Query 138: 0.6493
Query 139: 0.2523
Query 140: 0.7976
```

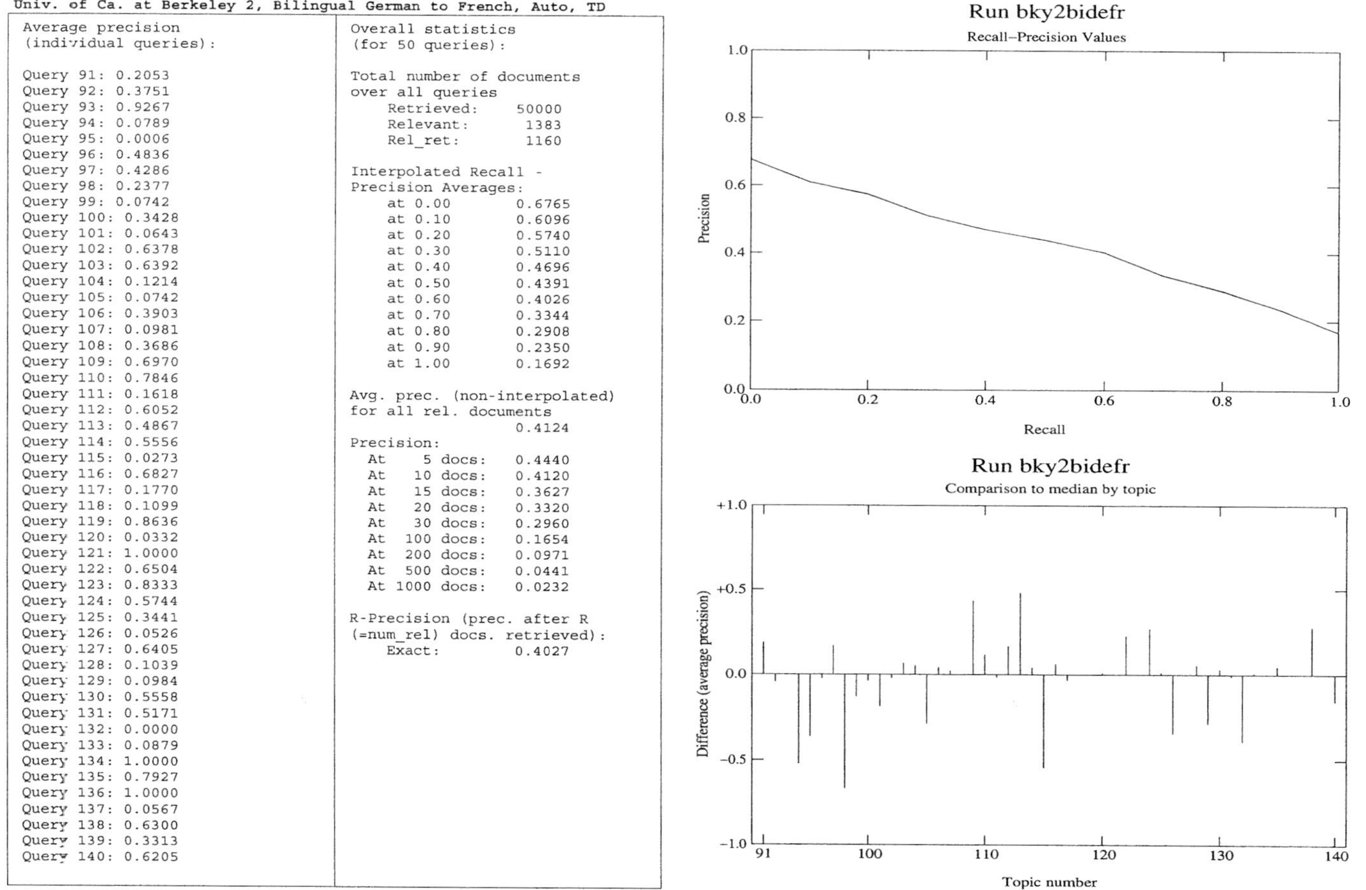

Univ. of Ca. at Berkeley 2, Bilingual German to French, Auto, TD

```
Average precision                  Overall statistics
(individual queries):              (for 50 queries):

Query 91: 0.2053                   Total number of documents
Query 92: 0.3751                   over all queries
Query 93: 0.9267                       Retrieved:     50000
Query 94: 0.0789                       Relevant:       1383
Query 95: 0.0006                       Rel_ret:        1160
Query 96: 0.4836
Query 97: 0.4286                   Interpolated Recall -
Query 98: 0.2377                   Precision Averages:
Query 99: 0.0742                       at 0.00        0.6765
Query 100: 0.3428                      at 0.10        0.6096
Query 101: 0.0643                      at 0.20        0.5740
Query 102: 0.6378                      at 0.30        0.5110
Query 103: 0.6392                      at 0.40        0.4696
Query 104: 0.1214                      at 0.50        0.4391
Query 105: 0.0742                      at 0.60        0.4026
Query 106: 0.3903                      at 0.70        0.3344
Query 107: 0.0981                      at 0.80        0.2908
Query 108: 0.3686                      at 0.90        0.2350
Query 109: 0.6970                      at 1.00        0.1692
Query 110: 0.7846
Query 111: 0.1618                  Avg. prec. (non-interpolated)
Query 112: 0.6052                  for all rel. documents
Query 113: 0.4867                                     0.4124
Query 114: 0.5556                  Precision:
Query 115: 0.0273                    At    5 docs:    0.4440
Query 116: 0.6827                    At   10 docs:    0.4120
Query 117: 0.1770                    At   15 docs:    0.3627
Query 118: 0.1099                    At   20 docs:    0.3320
Query 119: 0.8636                    At   30 docs:    0.2960
Query 120: 0.0332                    At  100 docs:    0.1654
Query 121: 1.0000                    At  200 docs:    0.0971
Query 122: 0.6504                    At  500 docs:    0.0441
Query 123: 0.8333                    At 1000 docs:    0.0232
Query 124: 0.5744
Query 125: 0.3441                  R-Precision (prec. after R
Query 126: 0.0526                  (=num_rel) docs. retrieved):
Query 127: 0.6405                      Exact:         0.4027
Query 128: 0.1039
Query 129: 0.0984
Query 130: 0.5558
Query 131: 0.5171
Query 132: 0.0000
Query 133: 0.0879
Query 134: 1.0000
Query 135: 0.7927
Query 136: 1.0000
Query 137: 0.0567
Query 138: 0.6300
Query 139: 0.3313
Query 140: 0.6205
```

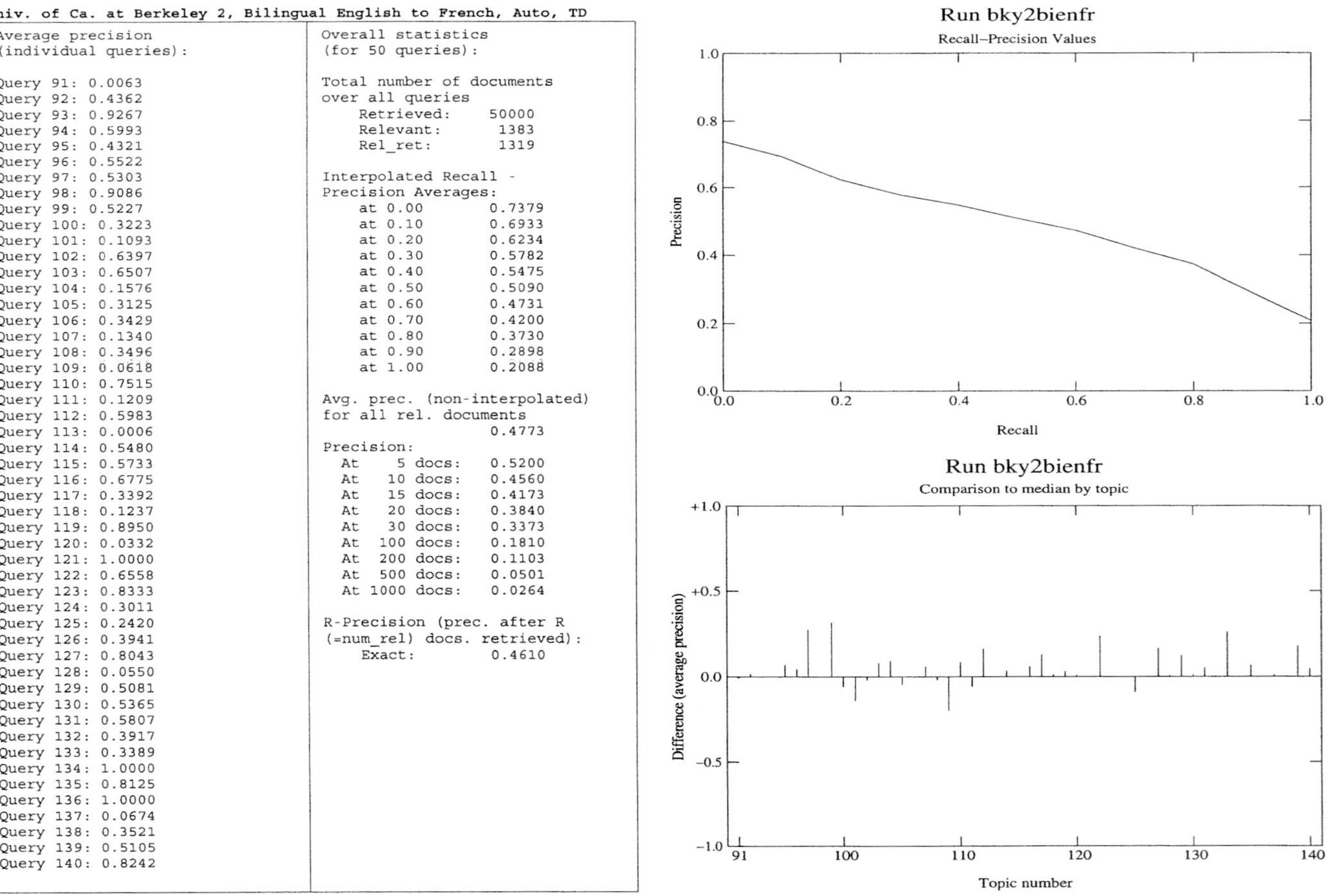

Univ. of Ca. at Berkeley 2, Bilingual English to French, Auto, TD

```
Average precision                 Overall statistics
(individual queries):             (for 50 queries):

Query 91: 0.0063                  Total number of documents
Query 92: 0.4362                  over all queries
Query 93: 0.9267                      Retrieved:    50000
Query 94: 0.5993                      Relevant:      1383
Query 95: 0.4321                      Rel_ret:       1319
Query 96: 0.5522
Query 97: 0.5303                  Interpolated Recall -
Query 98: 0.9086                  Precision Averages:
Query 99: 0.5227                      at 0.00        0.7379
Query 100: 0.3223                     at 0.10        0.6933
Query 101: 0.1093                     at 0.20        0.6234
Query 102: 0.6397                     at 0.30        0.5782
Query 103: 0.6507                     at 0.40        0.5475
Query 104: 0.1576                     at 0.50        0.5090
Query 105: 0.3125                     at 0.60        0.4731
Query 106: 0.3429                     at 0.70        0.4200
Query 107: 0.1340                     at 0.80        0.3730
Query 108: 0.3496                     at 0.90        0.2898
Query 109: 0.0618                     at 1.00        0.2088
Query 110: 0.7515
Query 111: 0.1209                 Avg. prec. (non-interpolated)
Query 112: 0.5983                 for all rel. documents
Query 113: 0.0006                                    0.4773
Query 114: 0.5480                 Precision:
Query 115: 0.5733                   At    5 docs:    0.5200
Query 116: 0.6775                   At   10 docs:    0.4560
Query 117: 0.3392                   At   15 docs:    0.4173
Query 118: 0.1237                   At   20 docs:    0.3840
Query 119: 0.8950                   At   30 docs:    0.3373
Query 120: 0.0332                   At  100 docs:    0.1810
Query 121: 1.0000                   At  200 docs:    0.1103
Query 122: 0.6558                   At  500 docs:    0.0501
Query 123: 0.8333                   At 1000 docs:    0.0264
Query 124: 0.3011
Query 125: 0.2420                 R-Precision (prec. after R
Query 126: 0.3941                 (=num_rel) docs. retrieved):
Query 127: 0.8043                     Exact:         0.4610
Query 128: 0.0550
Query 129: 0.5081
Query 130: 0.5365
Query 131: 0.5807
Query 132: 0.3917
Query 133: 0.3389
Query 134: 1.0000
Query 135: 0.8125
Query 136: 1.0000
Query 137: 0.0674
Query 138: 0.3521
Query 139: 0.5105
Query 140: 0.8242
```

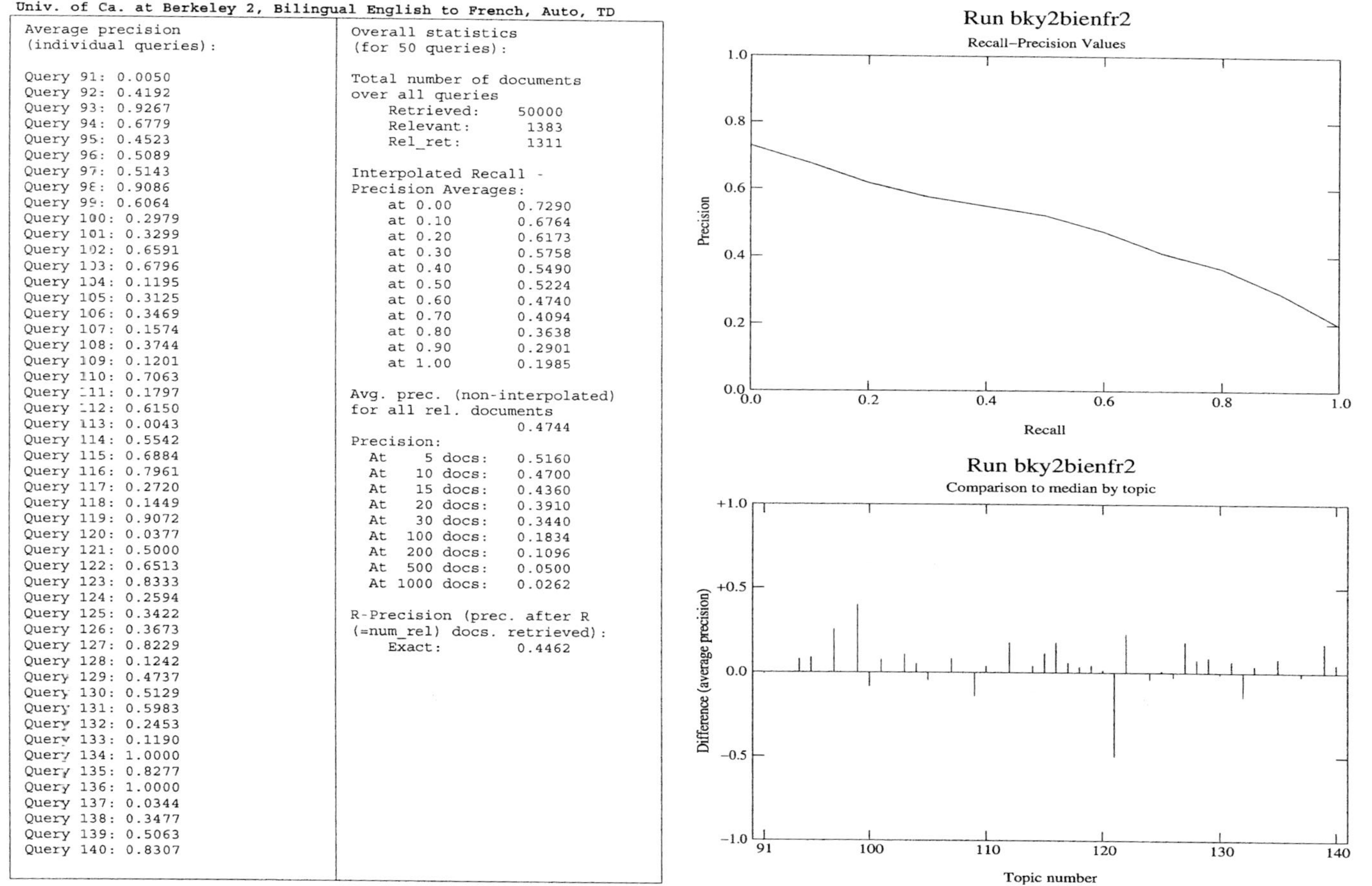

Univ. of Ca. at Berkeley 2, Bilingual English to French, Auto, TD

Average precision (individual queries):	Overall statistics (for 50 queries):
Query 91: 0.0050	Total number of documents over all queries
Query 92: 0.4192	Retrieved: 50000
Query 93: 0.9267	Relevant: 1383
Query 94: 0.6779	Rel_ret: 1311
Query 95: 0.4523	
Query 96: 0.5089	Interpolated Recall - Precision Averages:
Query 97: 0.5143	at 0.00 0.7290
Query 98: 0.9086	at 0.10 0.6764
Query 99: 0.6064	at 0.20 0.6173
Query 100: 0.2979	at 0.30 0.5758
Query 101: 0.3299	at 0.40 0.5490
Query 102: 0.6591	at 0.50 0.5224
Query 103: 0.6796	at 0.60 0.4740
Query 104: 0.1195	at 0.70 0.4094
Query 105: 0.3125	at 0.80 0.3638
Query 106: 0.3469	at 0.90 0.2901
Query 107: 0.1574	at 1.00 0.1985
Query 108: 0.3744	
Query 109: 0.1201	Avg. prec. (non-interpolated) for all rel. documents 0.4744
Query 110: 0.7063	
Query 111: 0.1797	Precision:
Query 112: 0.6150	At 5 docs: 0.5160
Query 113: 0.0043	At 10 docs: 0.4700
Query 114: 0.5542	At 15 docs: 0.4360
Query 115: 0.6884	At 20 docs: 0.3910
Query 116: 0.7961	At 30 docs: 0.3440
Query 117: 0.2720	At 100 docs: 0.1834
Query 118: 0.1449	At 200 docs: 0.1096
Query 119: 0.9072	At 500 docs: 0.0500
Query 120: 0.0377	At 1000 docs: 0.0262
Query 121: 0.5000	
Query 122: 0.6513	R-Precision (prec. after R (=num_rel) docs. retrieved):
Query 123: 0.8333	Exact: 0.4462
Query 124: 0.2594	
Query 125: 0.3422	
Query 126: 0.3673	
Query 127: 0.8229	
Query 128: 0.1242	
Query 129: 0.4737	
Query 130: 0.5129	
Query 131: 0.5983	
Query 132: 0.2453	
Query 133: 0.1190	
Query 134: 1.0000	
Query 135: 0.8277	
Query 136: 1.0000	
Query 137: 0.0344	
Query 138: 0.3477	
Query 139: 0.5063	
Query 140: 0.8307	

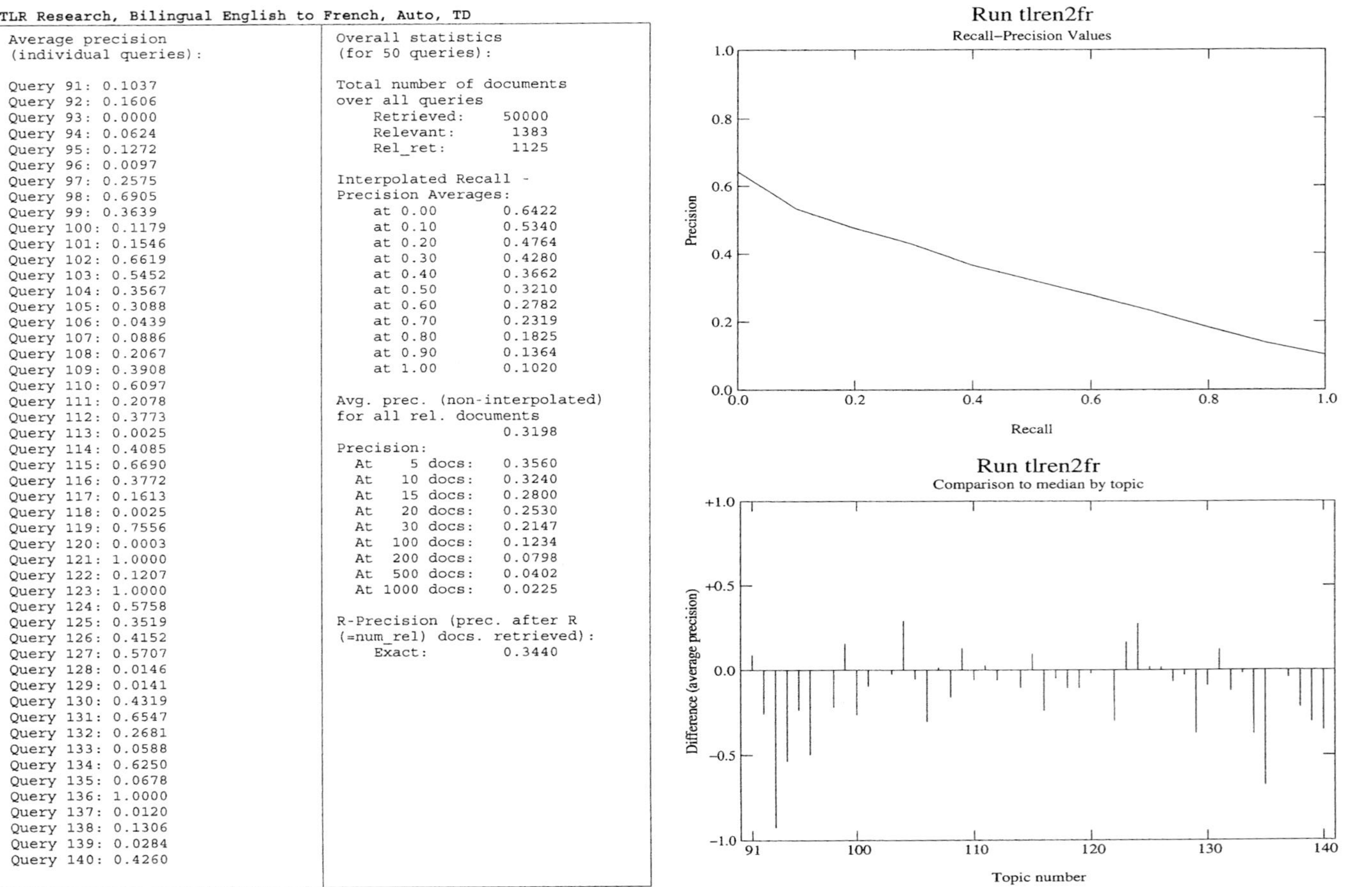

TLR Research, Bilingual English to French, Auto, TD

```
Average precision            Overall statistics
(individual queries):        (for 50 queries):

Query  91: 0.1037            Total number of documents
Query  92: 0.1606            over all queries
Query  93: 0.0000              Retrieved:     50000
Query  94: 0.0624              Relevant:       1383
Query  95: 0.1272              Rel_ret:        1125
Query  96: 0.0097
Query  97: 0.2575            Interpolated Recall -
Query  98: 0.6905            Precision Averages:
Query  99: 0.3639                at 0.00      0.6422
Query 100: 0.1179                at 0.10      0.5340
Query 101: 0.1546                at 0.20      0.4764
Query 102: 0.6619                at 0.30      0.4280
Query 103: 0.5452                at 0.40      0.3662
Query 104: 0.3567                at 0.50      0.3210
Query 105: 0.3088                at 0.60      0.2782
Query 106: 0.0439                at 0.70      0.2319
Query 107: 0.0886                at 0.80      0.1825
Query 108: 0.2067                at 0.90      0.1364
Query 109: 0.3908                at 1.00      0.1020
Query 110: 0.6097
Query 111: 0.2078            Avg. prec. (non-interpolated)
Query 112: 0.3773            for all rel. documents
Query 113: 0.0025                             0.3198
Query 114: 0.4085
Query 115: 0.6690            Precision:
Query 116: 0.3772              At    5 docs:  0.3560
Query 117: 0.1613              At   10 docs:  0.3240
Query 118: 0.0025              At   15 docs:  0.2800
Query 119: 0.7556              At   20 docs:  0.2530
Query 120: 0.0003              At   30 docs:  0.2147
Query 121: 1.0000              At  100 docs:  0.1234
Query 122: 0.1207              At  200 docs:  0.0798
Query 123: 1.0000              At  500 docs:  0.0402
Query 124: 0.5758              At 1000 docs:  0.0225
Query 125: 0.3519
Query 126: 0.4152            R-Precision (prec. after R
Query 127: 0.5707            (=num_rel) docs. retrieved):
Query 128: 0.0146                Exact:       0.3440
Query 129: 0.0141
Query 130: 0.4319
Query 131: 0.6547
Query 132: 0.2681
Query 133: 0.0588
Query 134: 0.6250
Query 135: 0.0678
Query 136: 1.0000
Query 137: 0.0120
Query 138: 0.1306
Query 139: 0.0284
Query 140: 0.4260
```

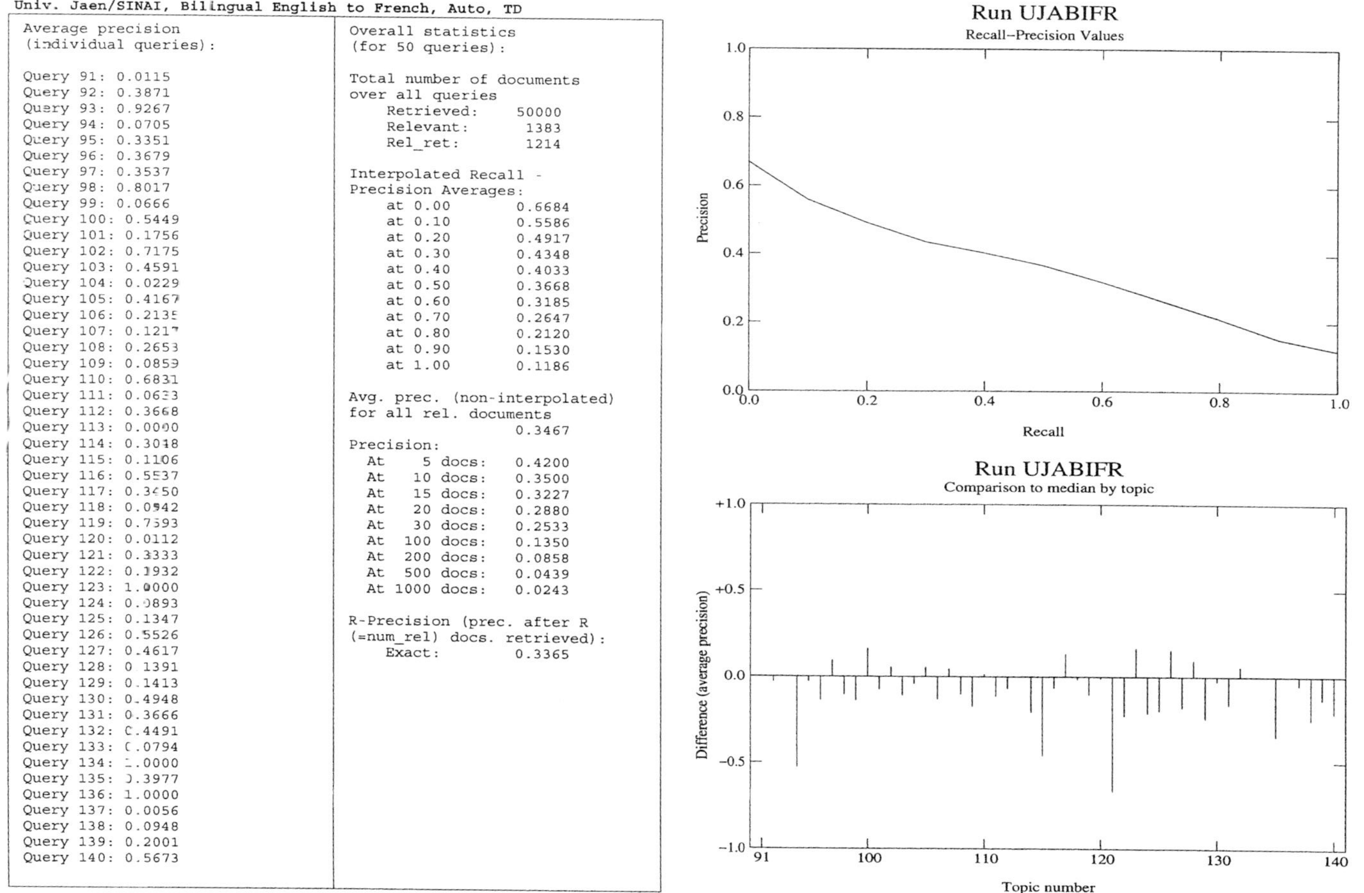

Univ. Jaen/SINAI, Bilingual English to French, Auto, TD

Average precision (individual queries):

Query	Average precision
Query 91:	0.0115
Query 92:	0.3871
Query 93:	0.9267
Query 94:	0.0705
Query 95:	0.3351
Query 96:	0.3679
Query 97:	0.3537
Query 98:	0.8017
Query 99:	0.0666
Query 100:	0.5449
Query 101:	0.1756
Query 102:	0.7175
Query 103:	0.4591
Query 104:	0.0229
Query 105:	0.4167
Query 106:	0.2135
Query 107:	0.1217
Query 108:	0.2653
Query 109:	0.0859
Query 110:	0.6831
Query 111:	0.0633
Query 112:	0.3668
Query 113:	0.0000
Query 114:	0.3048
Query 115:	0.1106
Query 116:	0.5537
Query 117:	0.3450
Query 118:	0.0942
Query 119:	0.7593
Query 120:	0.0112
Query 121:	0.3333
Query 122:	0.1932
Query 123:	1.0000
Query 124:	0.0893
Query 125:	0.1347
Query 126:	0.5526
Query 127:	0.4617
Query 128:	0.1391
Query 129:	0.1413
Query 130:	0.4948
Query 131:	0.3666
Query 132:	0.4491
Query 133:	0.0794
Query 134:	1.0000
Query 135:	0.3977
Query 136:	1.0000
Query 137:	0.0056
Query 138:	0.0948
Query 139:	0.2001
Query 140:	0.5673

Overall statistics (for 50 queries):

Total number of documents over all queries

Retrieved:	50000
Relevant:	1383
Rel_ret:	1214

Interpolated Recall - Precision Averages:

at 0.00	0.6684
at 0.10	0.5586
at 0.20	0.4917
at 0.30	0.4348
at 0.40	0.4033
at 0.50	0.3668
at 0.60	0.3185
at 0.70	0.2647
at 0.80	0.2120
at 0.90	0.1530
at 1.00	0.1186

Avg. prec. (non-interpolated) for all rel. documents 0.3467

Precision:

At 5 docs:	0.4200
At 10 docs:	0.3500
At 15 docs:	0.3227
At 20 docs:	0.2880
At 30 docs:	0.2533
At 100 docs:	0.1350
At 200 docs:	0.0858
At 500 docs:	0.0439
At 1000 docs:	0.0243

R-Precision (prec. after R (=num_rel) docs. retrieved):
Exact: 0.3365

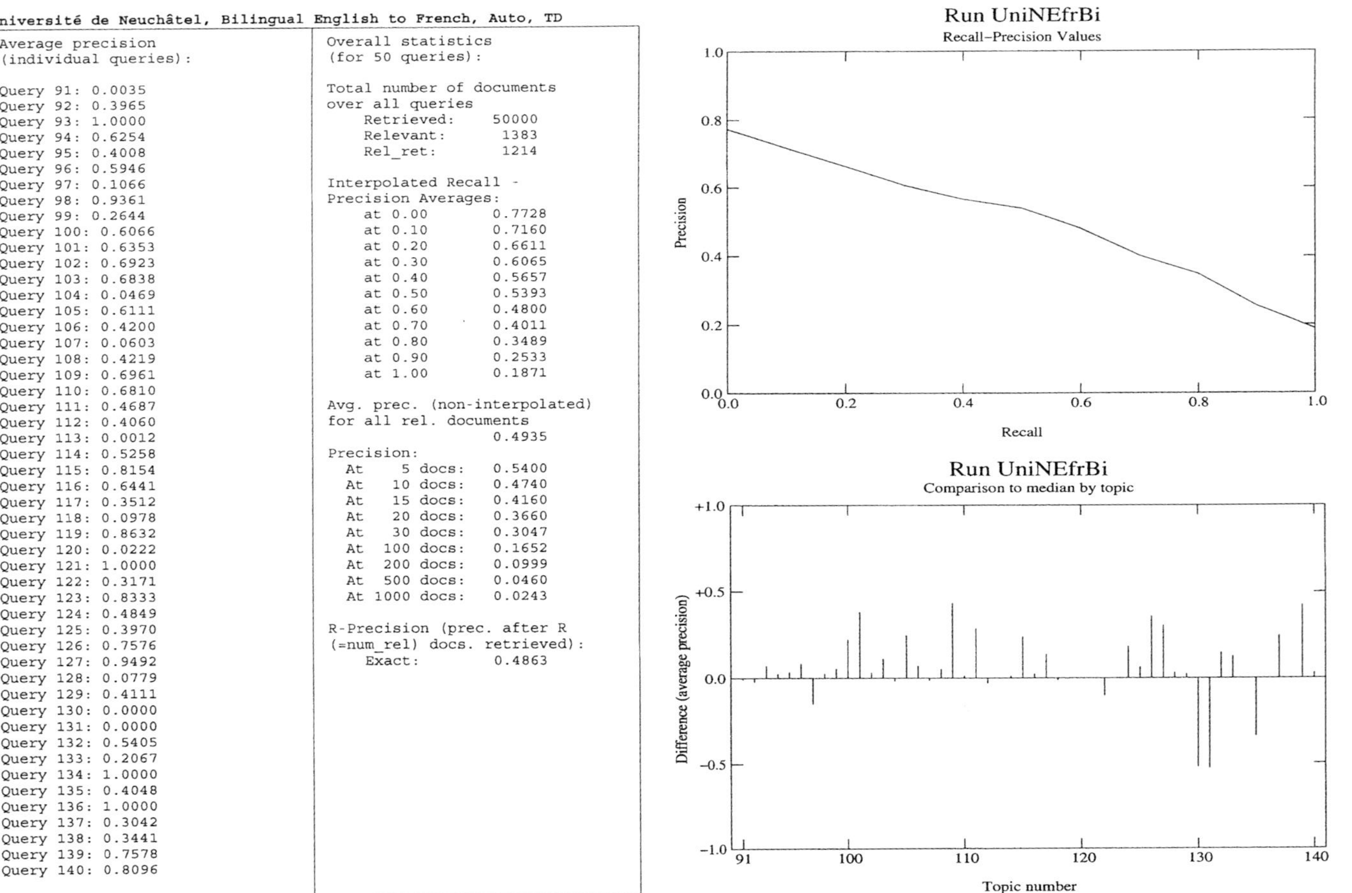

Université de Neuchâtel, Bilingual English to French, Auto, TD

Average precision (individual queries):	Overall statistics (for 50 queries):
Query 91: 0.0035	Total number of documents over all queries
Query 92: 0.3965	Retrieved: 50000
Query 93: 1.0000	Relevant: 1383
Query 94: 0.6254	Rel_ret: 1214
Query 95: 0.4008	
Query 96: 0.5946	Interpolated Recall - Precision Averages:
Query 97: 0.1066	at 0.00 0.7728
Query 98: 0.9361	at 0.10 0.7160
Query 99: 0.2644	at 0.20 0.6611
Query 100: 0.6066	at 0.30 0.6065
Query 101: 0.6353	at 0.40 0.5657
Query 102: 0.6923	at 0.50 0.5393
Query 103: 0.6838	at 0.60 0.4800
Query 104: 0.0469	at 0.70 0.4011
Query 105: 0.6111	at 0.80 0.3489
Query 106: 0.4200	at 0.90 0.2533
Query 107: 0.0603	at 1.00 0.1871
Query 108: 0.4219	
Query 109: 0.6961	Avg. prec. (non-interpolated) for all rel. documents 0.4935
Query 110: 0.6810	
Query 111: 0.4687	Precision:
Query 112: 0.4060	At 5 docs: 0.5400
Query 113: 0.0012	At 10 docs: 0.4740
Query 114: 0.5258	At 15 docs: 0.4160
Query 115: 0.8154	At 20 docs: 0.3660
Query 116: 0.6441	At 30 docs: 0.3047
Query 117: 0.3512	At 100 docs: 0.1652
Query 118: 0.0978	At 200 docs: 0.0999
Query 119: 0.8632	At 500 docs: 0.0460
Query 120: 0.0222	At 1000 docs: 0.0243
Query 121: 1.0000	
Query 122: 0.3171	R-Precision (prec. after R (=num_rel) docs. retrieved):
Query 123: 0.8333	Exact: 0.4863
Query 124: 0.4849	
Query 125: 0.3970	
Query 126: 0.7576	
Query 127: 0.9492	
Query 128: 0.0779	
Query 129: 0.4111	
Query 130: 0.0000	
Query 131: 0.0000	
Query 132: 0.5405	
Query 133: 0.2067	
Query 134: 1.0000	
Query 135: 0.4048	
Query 136: 1.0000	
Query 137: 0.3042	
Query 138: 0.3441	
Query 139: 0.7578	
Query 140: 0.8096	

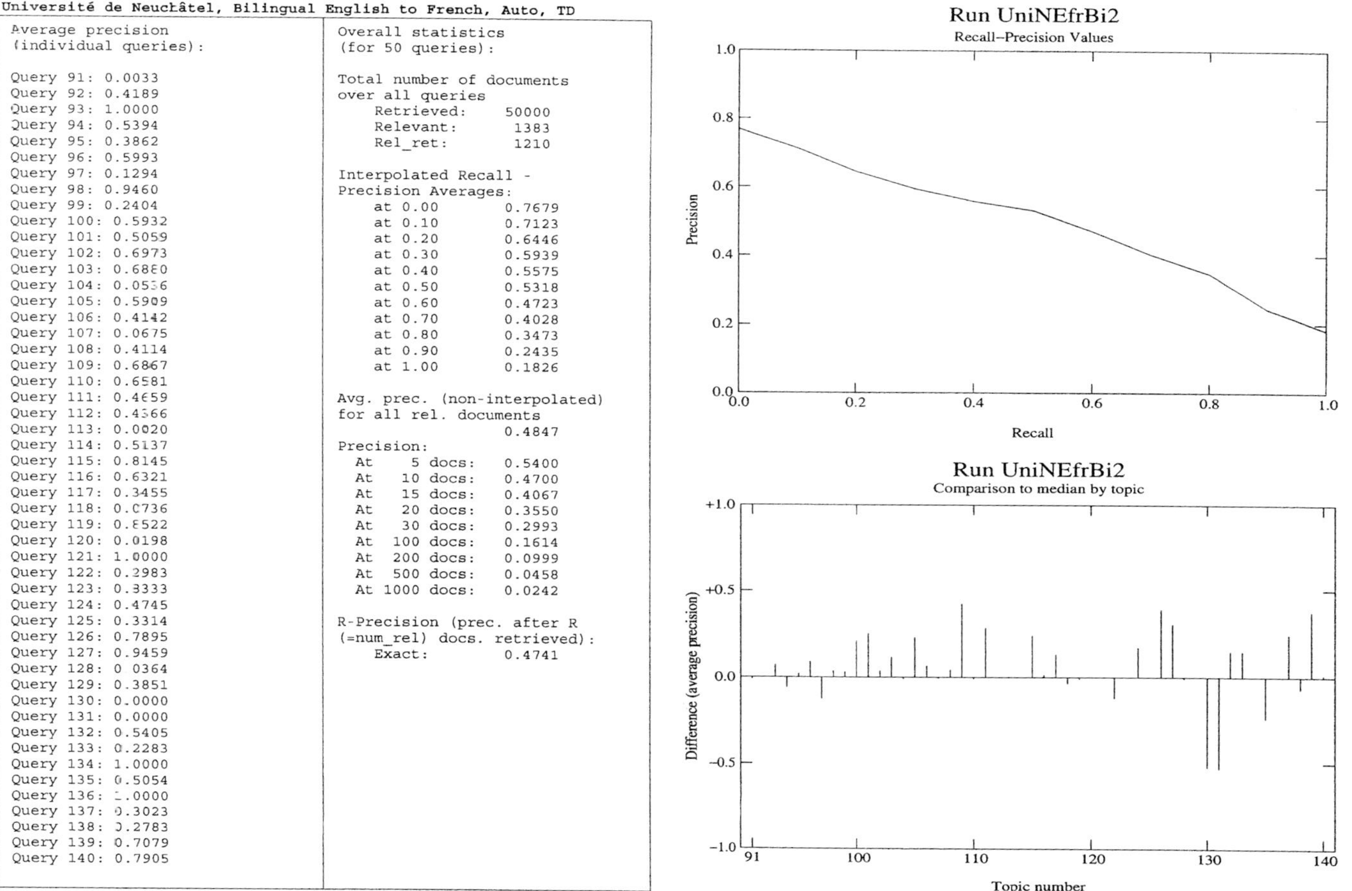

Université de Neuchâtel, Bilingual English to French, Auto, TD

Average precision (individual queries):

Query	Average precision
Query 91:	0.0033
Query 92:	0.4189
Query 93:	1.0000
Query 94:	0.5394
Query 95:	0.3862
Query 96:	0.5993
Query 97:	0.1294
Query 98:	0.9460
Query 99:	0.2404
Query 100:	0.5932
Query 101:	0.5059
Query 102:	0.6973
Query 103:	0.6880
Query 104:	0.0536
Query 105:	0.5909
Query 106:	0.4142
Query 107:	0.0675
Query 108:	0.4114
Query 109:	0.6867
Query 110:	0.6581
Query 111:	0.4659
Query 112:	0.4366
Query 113:	0.0020
Query 114:	0.5137
Query 115:	0.8145
Query 116:	0.6321
Query 117:	0.3455
Query 118:	0.0736
Query 119:	0.8522
Query 120:	0.0198
Query 121:	1.0000
Query 122:	0.2983
Query 123:	0.3333
Query 124:	0.4745
Query 125:	0.3314
Query 126:	0.7895
Query 127:	0.9459
Query 128:	0.0364
Query 129:	0.3851
Query 130:	0.0000
Query 131:	0.0000
Query 132:	0.5405
Query 133:	0.2283
Query 134:	1.0000
Query 135:	0.5054
Query 136:	1.0000
Query 137:	0.3023
Query 138:	0.2783
Query 139:	0.7079
Query 140:	0.7905

Overall statistics (for 50 queries):

Total number of documents over all queries

Retrieved:	50000
Relevant:	1383
Rel_ret:	1210

Interpolated Recall - Precision Averages:

at 0.00	0.7679
at 0.10	0.7123
at 0.20	0.6446
at 0.30	0.5939
at 0.40	0.5575
at 0.50	0.5318
at 0.60	0.4723
at 0.70	0.4028
at 0.80	0.3473
at 0.90	0.2435
at 1.00	0.1826

Avg. prec. (non-interpolated) for all rel. documents 0.4847

Precision:

At 5 docs:	0.5400
At 10 docs:	0.4700
At 15 docs:	0.4067
At 20 docs:	0.3550
At 30 docs:	0.2993
At 100 docs:	0.1614
At 200 docs:	0.0999
At 500 docs:	0.0458
At 1000 docs:	0.0242

R-Precision (prec. after R (=num_rel) docs. retrieved):
Exact: 0.4741

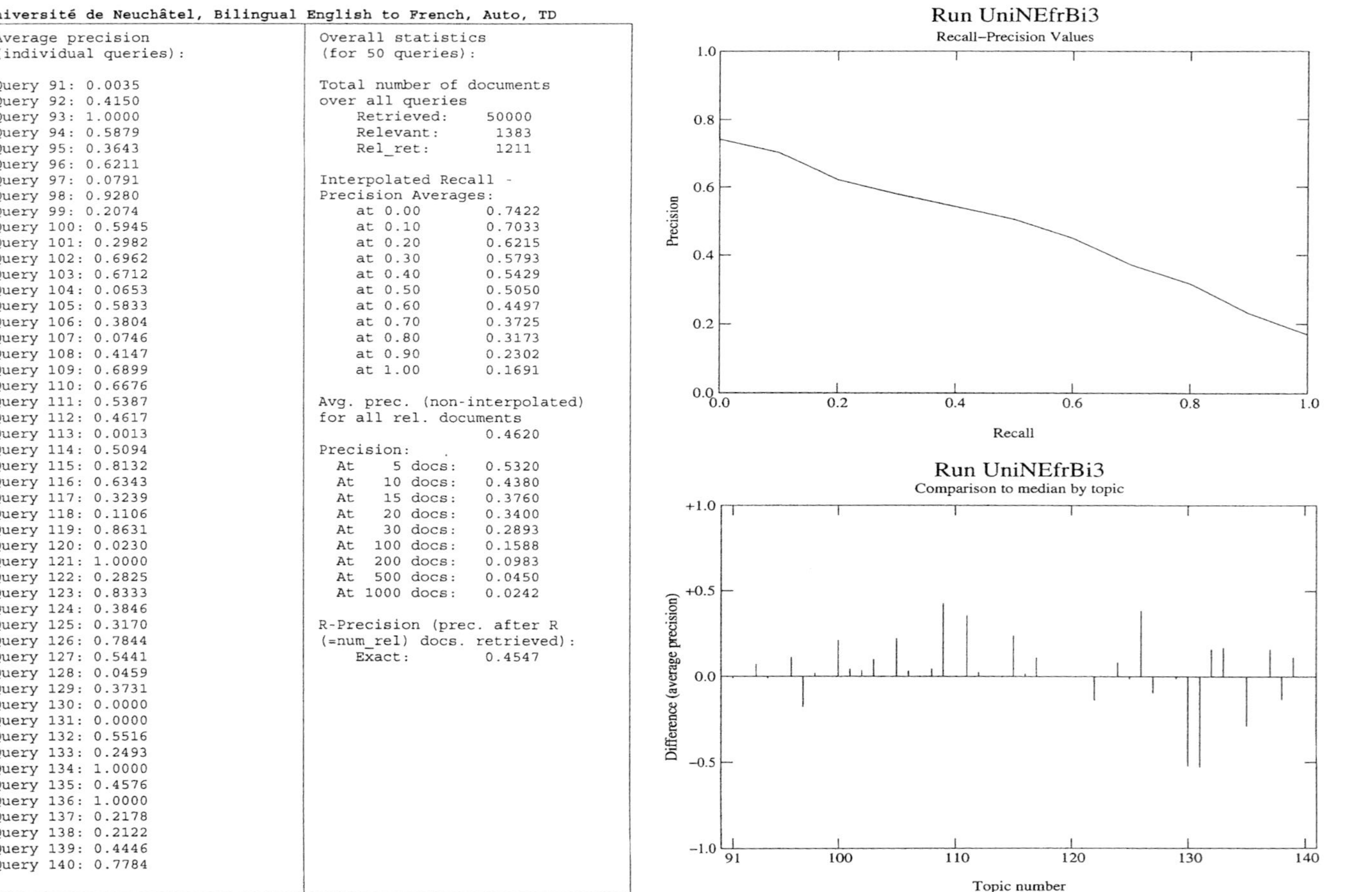

Université de Neuchâtel, Bilingual English to French, Auto, TD

```
Average precision                Overall statistics
(individual queries):            (for 50 queries):

Query 91: 0.0035                 Total number of documents
Query 92: 0.4150                 over all queries
Query 93: 1.0000                     Retrieved:    50000
Query 94: 0.5879                     Relevant:      1383
Query 95: 0.3643                     Rel_ret:       1211
Query 96: 0.6211
Query 97: 0.0791                 Interpolated Recall -
Query 98: 0.9280                 Precision Averages:
Query 99: 0.2074                     at 0.00       0.7422
Query 100: 0.5945                    at 0.10       0.7033
Query 101: 0.2982                    at 0.20       0.6215
Query 102: 0.6962                    at 0.30       0.5793
Query 103: 0.6712                    at 0.40       0.5429
Query 104: 0.0653                    at 0.50       0.5050
Query 105: 0.5833                    at 0.60       0.4497
Query 106: 0.3804                    at 0.70       0.3725
Query 107: 0.0746                    at 0.80       0.3173
Query 108: 0.4147                    at 0.90       0.2302
Query 109: 0.6899                    at 1.00       0.1691
Query 110: 0.6676
Query 111: 0.5387                Avg. prec. (non-interpolated)
Query 112: 0.4617                for all rel. documents
Query 113: 0.0013                                  0.4620
Query 114: 0.5094                Precision:
Query 115: 0.8132                  At    5 docs:   0.5320
Query 116: 0.6343                  At   10 docs:   0.4380
Query 117: 0.3239                  At   15 docs:   0.3760
Query 118: 0.1106                  At   20 docs:   0.3400
Query 119: 0.8631                  At   30 docs:   0.2893
Query 120: 0.0230                  At  100 docs:   0.1588
Query 121: 1.0000                  At  200 docs:   0.0983
Query 122: 0.2825                  At  500 docs:   0.0450
Query 123: 0.8333                  At 1000 docs:   0.0242
Query 124: 0.3846
Query 125: 0.3170                R-Precision (prec. after R
Query 126: 0.7844                (=num_rel) docs. retrieved):
Query 127: 0.5441                    Exact:        0.4547
Query 128: 0.0459
Query 129: 0.3731
Query 130: 0.0000
Query 131: 0.0000
Query 132: 0.5516
Query 133: 0.2493
Query 134: 1.0000
Query 135: 0.4576
Query 136: 1.0000
Query 137: 0.2178
Query 138: 0.2122
Query 139: 0.4446
Query 140: 0.7784
```

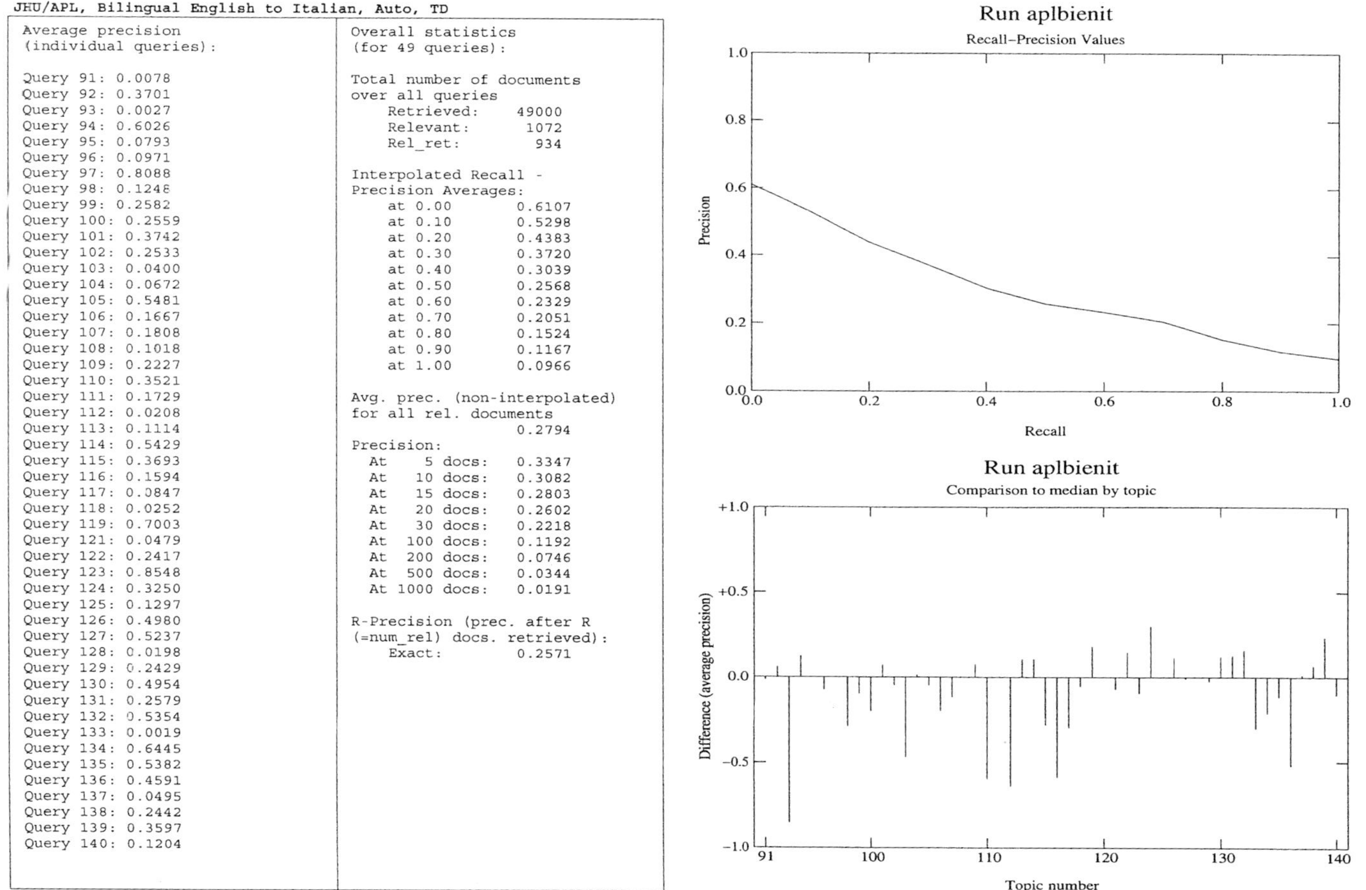

JHU/APL, Bilingual English to Italian, Auto, TD

Average precision (individual queries):	Overall statistics (for 49 queries):
Query 91: 0.0078	Total number of documents over all queries
Query 92: 0.3701	Retrieved: 49000
Query 93: 0.0027	Relevant: 1072
Query 94: 0.6026	Rel_ret: 934
Query 95: 0.0793	
Query 96: 0.0971	Interpolated Recall - Precision Averages:
Query 97: 0.8088	at 0.00 0.6107
Query 98: 0.1248	at 0.10 0.5298
Query 99: 0.2582	at 0.20 0.4383
Query 100: 0.2559	at 0.30 0.3720
Query 101: 0.3742	at 0.40 0.3039
Query 102: 0.2533	at 0.50 0.2568
Query 103: 0.0400	at 0.60 0.2329
Query 104: 0.0672	at 0.70 0.2051
Query 105: 0.5481	at 0.80 0.1524
Query 106: 0.1667	at 0.90 0.1167
Query 107: 0.1808	at 1.00 0.0966
Query 108: 0.1018	
Query 109: 0.2227	Avg. prec. (non-interpolated) for all rel. documents 0.2794
Query 110: 0.3521	
Query 111: 0.1729	Precision:
Query 112: 0.0208	At 5 docs: 0.3347
Query 113: 0.1114	At 10 docs: 0.3082
Query 114: 0.5429	At 15 docs: 0.2803
Query 115: 0.3693	At 20 docs: 0.2602
Query 116: 0.1594	At 30 docs: 0.2218
Query 117: 0.0847	At 100 docs: 0.1192
Query 118: 0.0252	At 200 docs: 0.0746
Query 119: 0.7003	At 500 docs: 0.0344
Query 121: 0.0479	At 1000 docs: 0.0191
Query 122: 0.2417	
Query 123: 0.8548	R-Precision (prec. after R (=num_rel) docs. retrieved):
Query 124: 0.3250	Exact: 0.2571
Query 125: 0.1297	
Query 126: 0.4980	
Query 127: 0.5237	
Query 128: 0.0198	
Query 129: 0.2429	
Query 130: 0.4954	
Query 131: 0.2579	
Query 132: 0.5354	
Query 133: 0.0019	
Query 134: 0.6445	
Query 135: 0.5382	
Query 136: 0.4591	
Query 137: 0.0495	
Query 138: 0.2442	
Query 139: 0.3597	
Query 140: 0.1204	

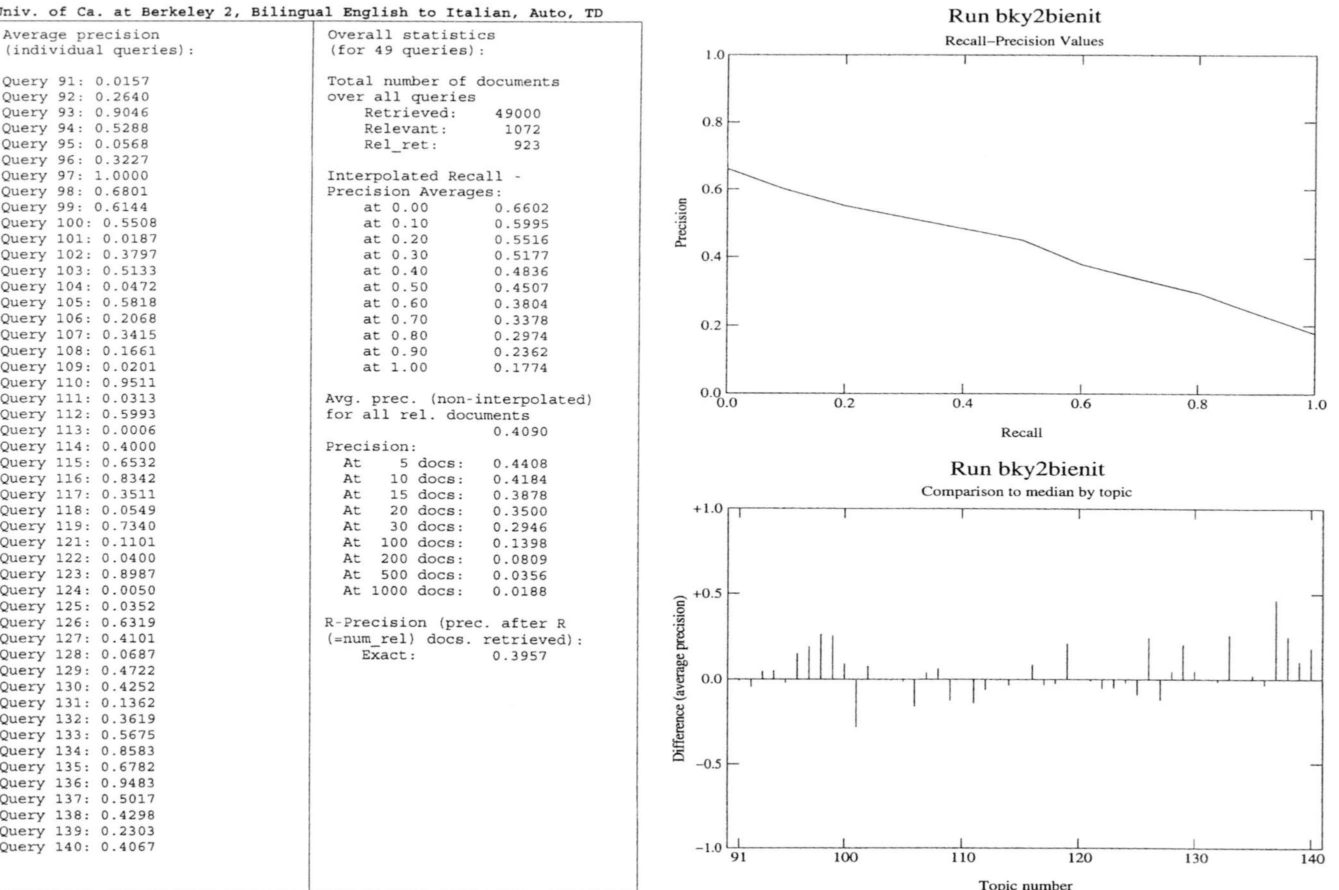

Univ. of Ca. at Berkeley 2, Bilingual English to Italian, Auto, TD

Average precision (individual queries):	Overall statistics (for 49 queries):
Query 91: 0.0157	Total number of documents over all queries
Query 92: 0.2640	Retrieved: 49000
Query 93: 0.9046	Relevant: 1072
Query 94: 0.5288	Rel_ret: 923
Query 95: 0.0568	
Query 96: 0.3227	Interpolated Recall - Precision Averages:
Query 97: 1.0000	at 0.00 0.6602
Query 98: 0.6801	at 0.10 0.5995
Query 99: 0.6144	at 0.20 0.5516
Query 100: 0.5508	at 0.30 0.5177
Query 101: 0.0187	at 0.40 0.4836
Query 102: 0.3797	at 0.50 0.4507
Query 103: 0.5133	at 0.60 0.3804
Query 104: 0.0472	at 0.70 0.3378
Query 105: 0.5818	at 0.80 0.2974
Query 106: 0.2068	at 0.90 0.2362
Query 107: 0.3415	at 1.00 0.1774
Query 108: 0.1661	
Query 109: 0.0201	Avg. prec. (non-interpolated) for all rel. documents 0.4090
Query 110: 0.9511	
Query 111: 0.0313	Precision:
Query 112: 0.5993	At 5 docs: 0.4408
Query 113: 0.0006	At 10 docs: 0.4184
Query 114: 0.4000	At 15 docs: 0.3878
Query 115: 0.6532	At 20 docs: 0.3500
Query 116: 0.8342	At 30 docs: 0.2946
Query 117: 0.3511	At 100 docs: 0.1398
Query 118: 0.0549	At 200 docs: 0.0809
Query 119: 0.7340	At 500 docs: 0.0356
Query 121: 0.1101	At 1000 docs: 0.0188
Query 122: 0.0400	
Query 123: 0.8987	R-Precision (prec. after R (=num_rel) docs. retrieved):
Query 124: 0.0050	Exact: 0.3957
Query 125: 0.0352	
Query 126: 0.6319	
Query 127: 0.4101	
Query 128: 0.0687	
Query 129: 0.4722	
Query 130: 0.4252	
Query 131: 0.1362	
Query 132: 0.3619	
Query 133: 0.5675	
Query 134: 0.8583	
Query 135: 0.6782	
Query 136: 0.9483	
Query 137: 0.5017	
Query 138: 0.4298	
Query 139: 0.2303	
Query 140: 0.4067	

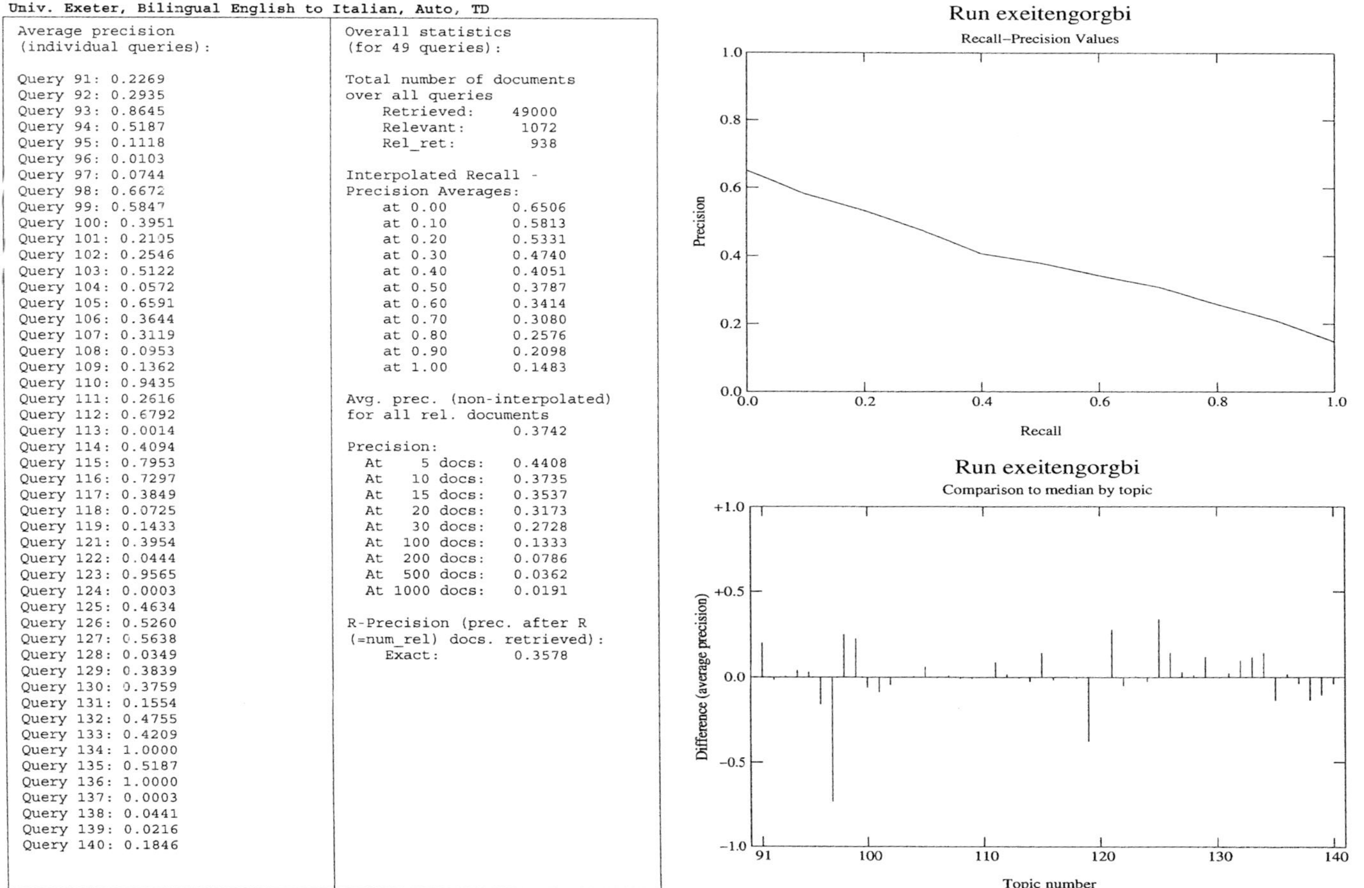

Univ. Exeter, Bilingual English to Italian, Auto, TD

Average precision (individual queries):	Overall statistics (for 49 queries):
Query 91: 0.2269	Total number of documents over all queries
Query 92: 0.2935	Retrieved: 49000
Query 93: 0.8645	Relevant: 1072
Query 94: 0.5187	Rel_ret: 938
Query 95: 0.1118	
Query 96: 0.0103	Interpolated Recall - Precision Averages:
Query 97: 0.0744	at 0.00 0.6506
Query 98: 0.6672	at 0.10 0.5813
Query 99: 0.5847	at 0.20 0.5331
Query 100: 0.3951	at 0.30 0.4740
Query 101: 0.2105	at 0.40 0.4051
Query 102: 0.2546	at 0.50 0.3787
Query 103: 0.5122	at 0.60 0.3414
Query 104: 0.0572	at 0.70 0.3080
Query 105: 0.6591	at 0.80 0.2576
Query 106: 0.3644	at 0.90 0.2098
Query 107: 0.3119	at 1.00 0.1483
Query 108: 0.0953	
Query 109: 0.1362	Avg. prec. (non-interpolated) for all rel. documents 0.3742
Query 110: 0.9435	Precision:
Query 111: 0.2616	At 5 docs: 0.4408
Query 112: 0.6792	At 10 docs: 0.3735
Query 113: 0.0014	At 15 docs: 0.3537
Query 114: 0.4094	At 20 docs: 0.3173
Query 115: 0.7953	At 30 docs: 0.2728
Query 116: 0.7297	At 100 docs: 0.1333
Query 117: 0.3849	At 200 docs: 0.0786
Query 118: 0.0725	At 500 docs: 0.0362
Query 119: 0.1433	At 1000 docs: 0.0191
Query 121: 0.3954	
Query 122: 0.0444	R-Precision (prec. after R (=num_rel) docs. retrieved):
Query 123: 0.9565	Exact: 0.3578
Query 124: 0.0003	
Query 125: 0.4634	
Query 126: 0.5260	
Query 127: 0.5638	
Query 128: 0.0349	
Query 129: 0.3839	
Query 130: 0.3759	
Query 131: 0.1554	
Query 132: 0.4755	
Query 133: 0.4209	
Query 134: 1.0000	
Query 135: 0.5187	
Query 136: 1.0000	
Query 137: 0.0003	
Query 138: 0.0441	
Query 139: 0.0216	
Query 140: 0.1846	

Univ. Exeter, Bilingual English to Italian, Auto, TD

```
Average precision                 Overall statistics
(individual queries):             (for 49 queries):

Query 91: 0.0898                  Total number of documents
Query 92: 0.3508                  over all queries
Query 93: 0.9253                      Retrieved:     49000
Query 94: 0.4767                      Relevant:       1072
Query 95: 0.1675                      Rel_ret:         968
Query 96: 0.1488
Query 97: 1.0000                  Interpolated Recall -
Query 98: 0.4775                  Precision Averages:
Query 99: 0.3585                      at 0.00        0.7289
Query 100: 0.4737                     at 0.10        0.6610
Query 101: 0.3011                     at 0.20        0.5817
Query 102: 0.2591                     at 0.30        0.4730
Query 103: 0.1648                     at 0.40        0.4231
Query 104: 0.0871                     at 0.50        0.4072
Query 105: 0.6369                     at 0.60        0.3696
Query 106: 0.4082                     at 0.70        0.3157
Query 107: 0.3504                     at 0.80        0.2682
Query 108: 0.0681                     at 0.90        0.2260
Query 109: 0.3354                     at 1.00        0.1672
Query 110: 0.9453
Query 111: 0.3198                 Avg. prec. (non-interpolated)
Query 112: 0.5277                 for all rel. documents
Query 113: 0.0013                                    0.3994
Query 114: 0.4274                 Precision:
Query 115: 0.6546                   At    5 docs:    0.4694
Query 116: 0.7465                   At   10 docs:    0.4204
Query 117: 0.1736                   At   15 docs:    0.3850
Query 118: 0.1227                   At   20 docs:    0.3500
Query 119: 0.5511                   At   30 docs:    0.2946
Query 121: 0.4244                   At  100 docs:    0.1402
Query 122: 0.1008                   At  200 docs:    0.0817
Query 123: 0.8345                   At  500 docs:    0.0372
Query 124: 0.1305                   At 1000 docs:    0.0198
Query 125: 0.4161
Query 126: 0.3446                 R-Precision (prec. after R
Query 127: 0.5577                 (=num_rel) docs. retrieved):
Query 128: 0.0148                     Exact:         0.3772
Query 129: 0.4648
Query 130: 0.3325
Query 131: 0.1775
Query 132: 0.3111
Query 133: 0.5548
Query 134: 0.7714
Query 135: 0.8853
Query 136: 0.9833
Query 137: 0.0000
Query 138: 0.0041
Query 139: 0.2321
Query 140: 0.4817
```

Run exeitengpiwgt

Recall–Precision Values

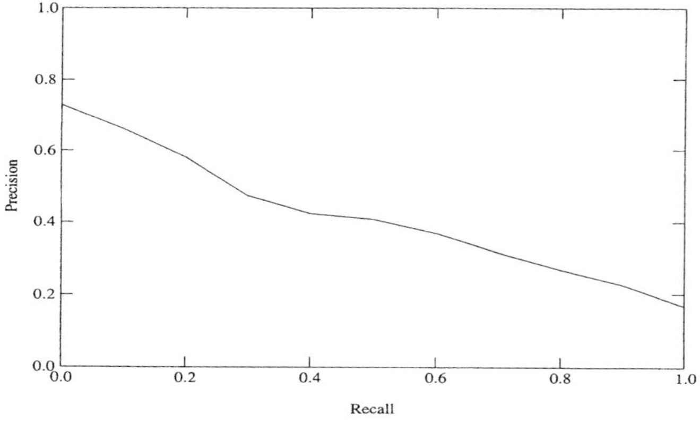

Run exeitengpiwgt

Comparison to median by topic

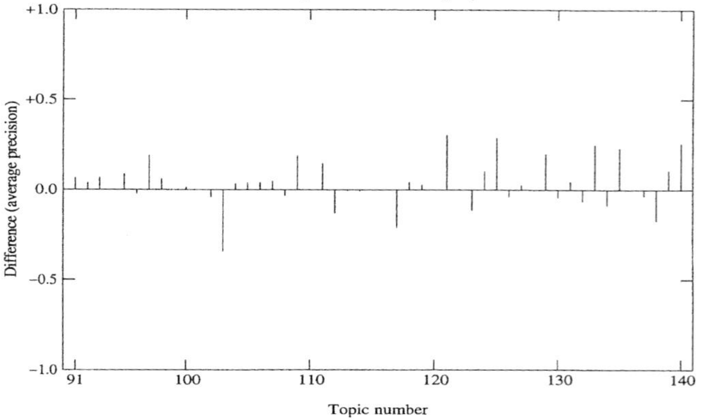

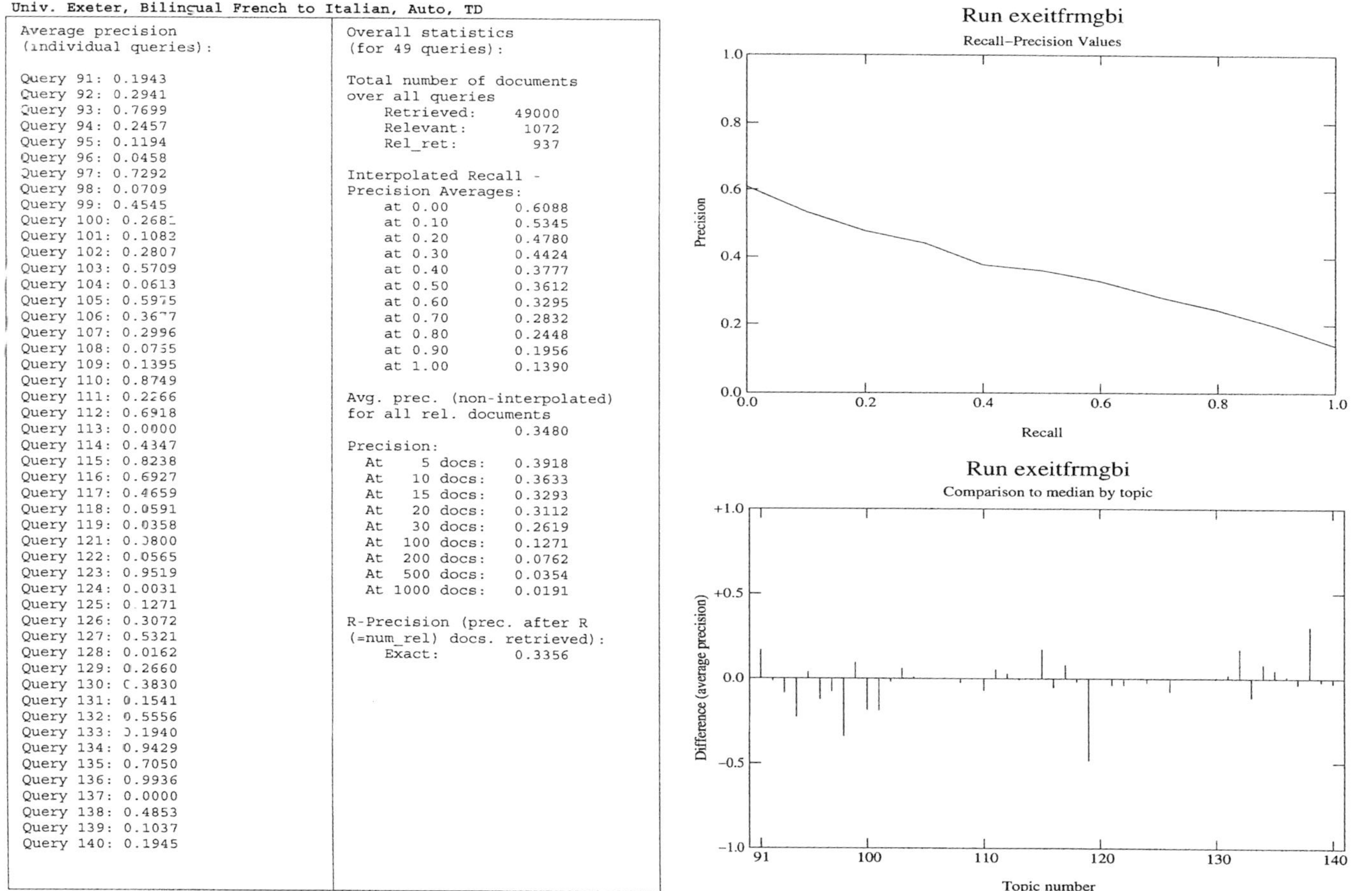

Univ. Exeter, Bilingual French to Italian, Auto, TD

```
Average precision                Overall statistics
(individual queries):            (for 49 queries):

Query 91: 0.1943                 Total number of documents
Query 92: 0.2941                 over all queries
Query 93: 0.7699                     Retrieved:     49000
Query 94: 0.2457                     Relevant:       1072
Query 95: 0.1194                     Rel_ret:         937
Query 96: 0.0458
Query 97: 0.7292                 Interpolated Recall -
Query 98: 0.0709                 Precision Averages:
Query 99: 0.4545                     at 0.00        0.6088
Query 100: 0.2681                    at 0.10        0.5345
Query 101: 0.1082                    at 0.20        0.4780
Query 102: 0.2807                    at 0.30        0.4424
Query 103: 0.5709                    at 0.40        0.3777
Query 104: 0.0613                    at 0.50        0.3612
Query 105: 0.5975                    at 0.60        0.3295
Query 106: 0.3677                    at 0.70        0.2832
Query 107: 0.2996                    at 0.80        0.2448
Query 108: 0.0755                    at 0.90        0.1956
Query 109: 0.1395                    at 1.00        0.1390
Query 110: 0.8749
Query 111: 0.2266                Avg. prec. (non-interpolated)
Query 112: 0.6918                for all rel. documents
Query 113: 0.0000                                   0.3480
Query 114: 0.4347                Precision:
Query 115: 0.8238                  At    5 docs:    0.3918
Query 116: 0.6927                  At   10 docs:    0.3633
Query 117: 0.4659                  At   15 docs:    0.3293
Query 118: 0.0591                  At   20 docs:    0.3112
Query 119: 0.0358                  At   30 docs:    0.2619
Query 121: 0.3800                  At  100 docs:    0.1271
Query 122: 0.0565                  At  200 docs:    0.0762
Query 123: 0.9519                  At  500 docs:    0.0354
Query 124: 0.0031                  At 1000 docs:    0.0191
Query 125: 0.1271
Query 126: 0.3072                R-Precision (prec. after R
Query 127: 0.5321                (=num_rel) docs. retrieved):
Query 128: 0.0162                    Exact:         0.3356
Query 129: 0.2660
Query 130: 0.3830
Query 131: 0.1541
Query 132: 0.5556
Query 133: 0.1940
Query 134: 0.9429
Query 135: 0.7050
Query 136: 0.9936
Query 137: 0.0000
Query 138: 0.4853
Query 139: 0.1037
Query 140: 0.1945
```

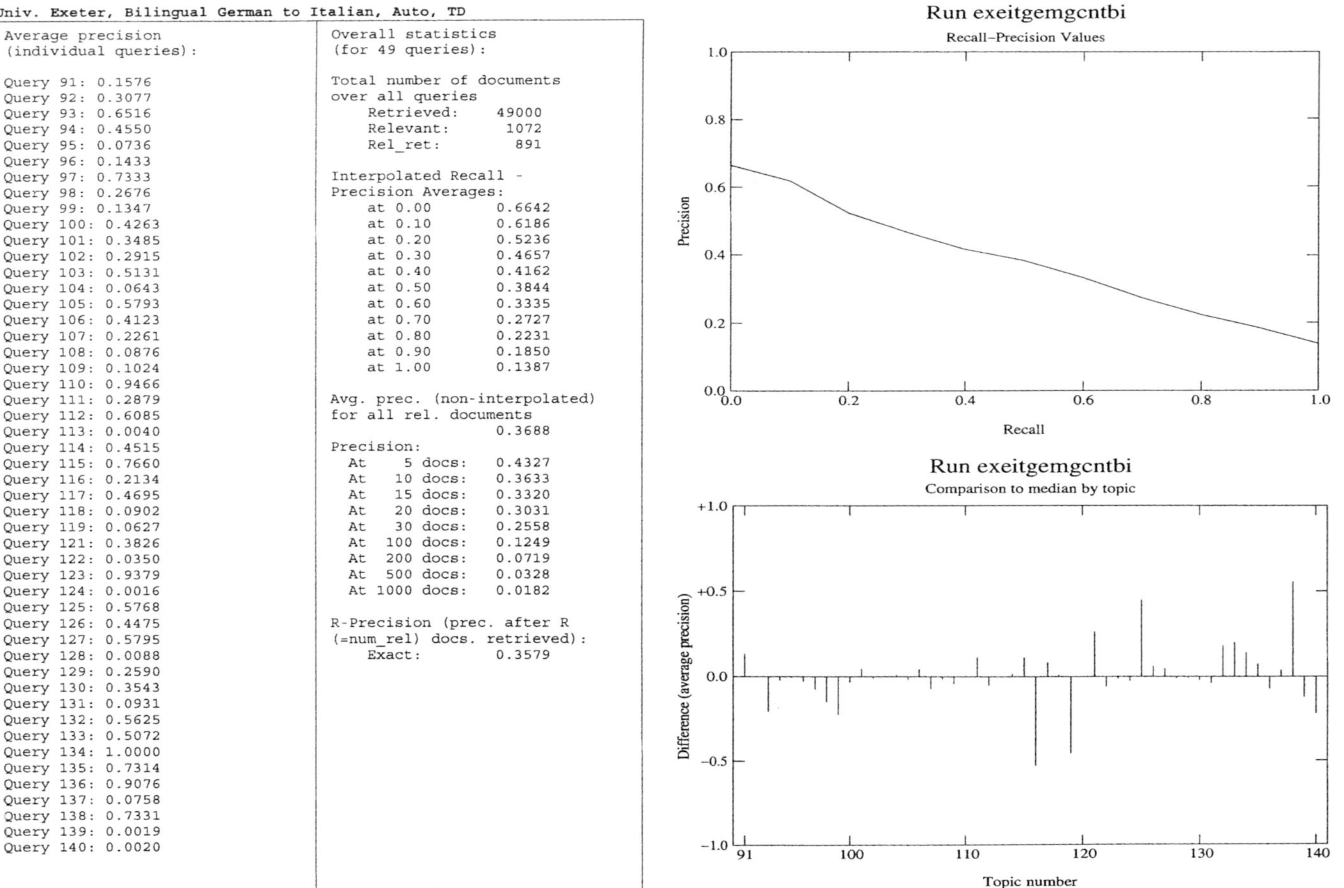

Univ. Exeter, Bilingual German to Italian, Auto, TD

```
Average precision              Overall statistics
(individual queries):          (for 49 queries):

Query 91: 0.1576               Total number of documents
Query 92: 0.3077               over all queries
Query 93: 0.6516                   Retrieved:    49000
Query 94: 0.4550                   Relevant:      1072
Query 95: 0.0736                   Rel_ret:        891
Query 96: 0.1433
Query 97: 0.7333               Interpolated Recall -
Query 98: 0.2676               Precision Averages:
Query 99: 0.1347                   at 0.00       0.6642
Query 100: 0.4263                  at 0.10       0.6186
Query 101: 0.3485                  at 0.20       0.5236
Query 102: 0.2915                  at 0.30       0.4657
Query 103: 0.5131                  at 0.40       0.4162
Query 104: 0.0643                  at 0.50       0.3844
Query 105: 0.5793                  at 0.60       0.3335
Query 106: 0.4123                  at 0.70       0.2727
Query 107: 0.2261                  at 0.80       0.2231
Query 108: 0.0876                  at 0.90       0.1850
Query 109: 0.1024                  at 1.00       0.1387
Query 110: 0.9466
Query 111: 0.2879              Avg. prec. (non-interpolated)
Query 112: 0.6085              for all rel. documents
Query 113: 0.0040                                0.3688
Query 114: 0.4515              Precision:
Query 115: 0.7660                At    5 docs:   0.4327
Query 116: 0.2134                At   10 docs:   0.3633
Query 117: 0.4695                At   15 docs:   0.3320
Query 118: 0.0902                At   20 docs:   0.3031
Query 119: 0.0627                At   30 docs:   0.2558
Query 121: 0.3826                At  100 docs:   0.1249
Query 122: 0.0350                At  200 docs:   0.0719
Query 123: 0.9379                At  500 docs:   0.0328
Query 124: 0.0016                At 1000 docs:   0.0182
Query 125: 0.5768
Query 126: 0.4475              R-Precision (prec. after R
Query 127: 0.5795              (=num_rel) docs. retrieved):
Query 128: 0.0088                  Exact:        0.3579
Query 129: 0.2590
Query 130: 0.3543
Query 131: 0.0931
Query 132: 0.5625
Query 133: 0.5072
Query 134: 1.0000
Query 135: 0.7314
Query 136: 0.9076
Query 137: 0.0758
Query 138: 0.7331
Query 139: 0.0019
Query 140: 0.0020
```

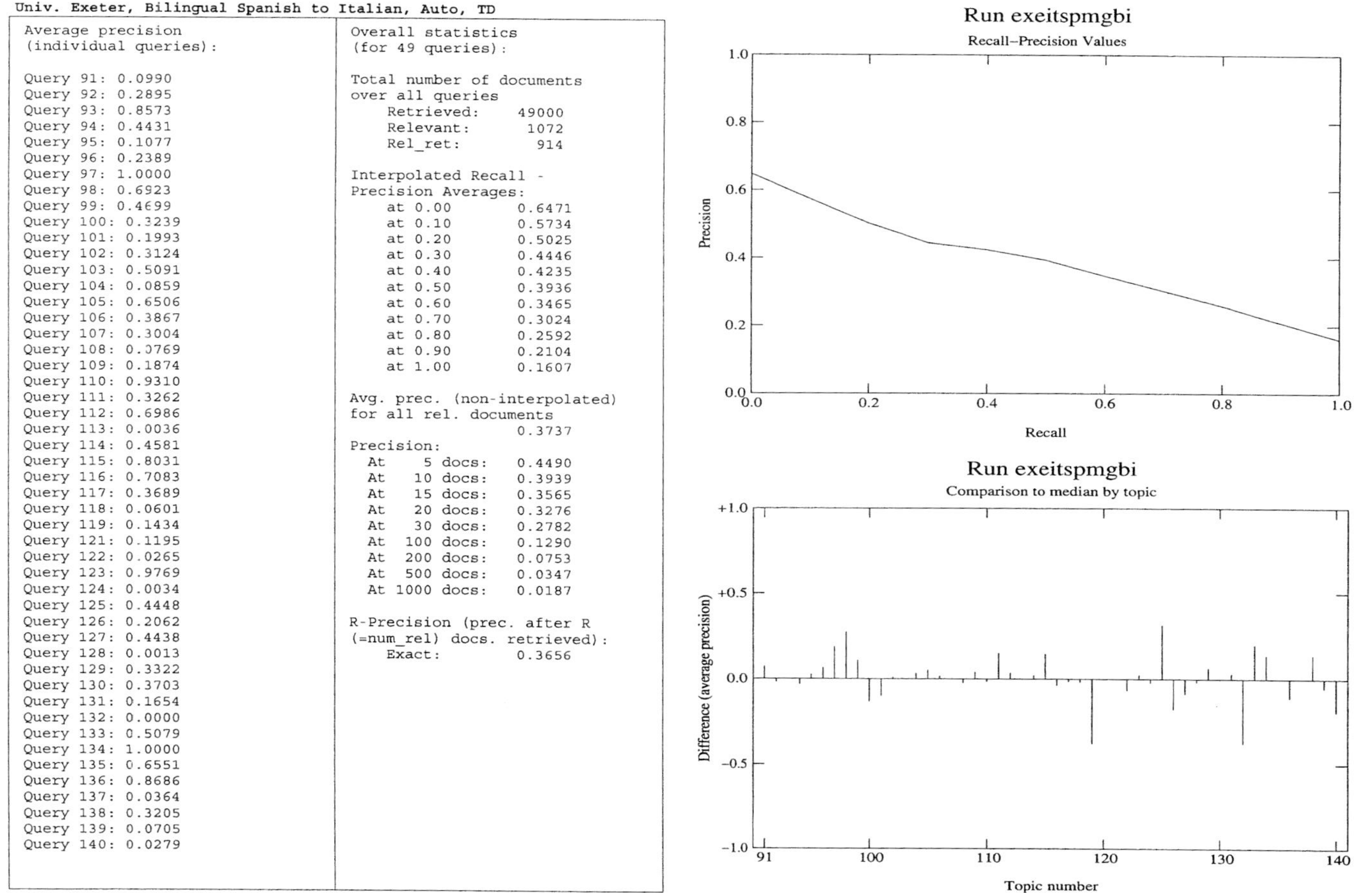

Univ. Exeter, Bilingual Spanish to Italian, Auto, TD

Average precision
(individual queries):

Query 91: 0.0990
Query 92: 0.2895
Query 93: 0.8573
Query 94: 0.4431
Query 95: 0.1077
Query 96: 0.2389
Query 97: 1.0000
Query 98: 0.6923
Query 99: 0.4699
Query 100: 0.3239
Query 101: 0.1993
Query 102: 0.3124
Query 103: 0.5091
Query 104: 0.0859
Query 105: 0.6506
Query 106: 0.3867
Query 107: 0.3004
Query 108: 0.0769
Query 109: 0.1874
Query 110: 0.9310
Query 111: 0.3262
Query 112: 0.6986
Query 113: 0.0036
Query 114: 0.4581
Query 115: 0.8031
Query 116: 0.7083
Query 117: 0.3689
Query 118: 0.0601
Query 119: 0.1434
Query 121: 0.1195
Query 122: 0.0265
Query 123: 0.9769
Query 124: 0.0034
Query 125: 0.4448
Query 126: 0.2062
Query 127: 0.4438
Query 128: 0.0013
Query 129: 0.3322
Query 130: 0.3703
Query 131: 0.1654
Query 132: 0.0000
Query 133: 0.5079
Query 134: 1.0000
Query 135: 0.6551
Query 136: 0.8686
Query 137: 0.0364
Query 138: 0.3205
Query 139: 0.0705
Query 140: 0.0279

Overall statistics
(for 49 queries):

Total number of documents
over all queries
Retrieved: 49000
Relevant: 1072
Rel_ret: 914

Interpolated Recall -
Precision Averages:
at 0.00 0.6471
at 0.10 0.5734
at 0.20 0.5025
at 0.30 0.4446
at 0.40 0.4235
at 0.50 0.3936
at 0.60 0.3465
at 0.70 0.3024
at 0.80 0.2592
at 0.90 0.2104
at 1.00 0.1607

Avg. prec. (non-interpolated)
for all rel. documents
0.3737

Precision:
At 5 docs: 0.4490
At 10 docs: 0.3939
At 15 docs: 0.3565
At 20 docs: 0.3276
At 30 docs: 0.2782
At 100 docs: 0.1290
At 200 docs: 0.0753
At 500 docs: 0.0347
At 1000 docs: 0.0187

R-Precision (prec. after R
(=num_rel) docs. retrieved):
Exact: 0.3656

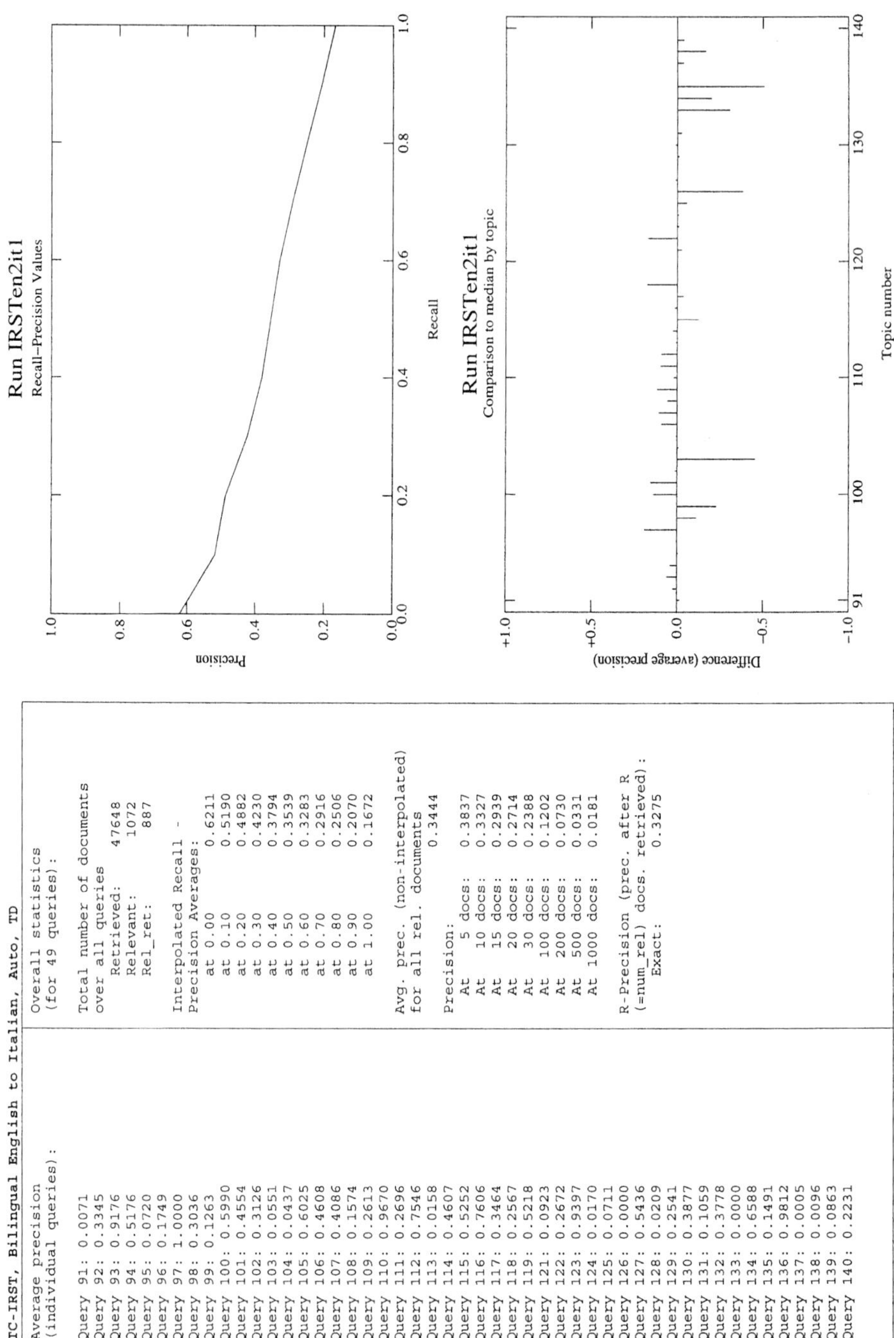

```
ITC-IRST, Bilingual English to Italian, Auto, TD

Average precision
 (individual queries):

Query 91: 0.0071
Query 92: 0.3345
Query 93: 0.9176
Query 94: 0.5176
Query 95: 0.0720
Query 96: 0.1749
Query 97: 1.0000
Query 98: 0.3036
Query 99: 0.1263
Query 100: 0.5990
Query 101: 0.4554
Query 102: 0.3126
Query 103: 0.0551
Query 104: 0.0437
Query 105: 0.6025
Query 106: 0.4608
Query 107: 0.4086
Query 108: 0.1574
Query 109: 0.2613
Query 110: 0.9670
Query 111: 0.2696
Query 112: 0.7546
Query 113: 0.0158
Query 114: 0.4607
Query 115: 0.5252
Query 116: 0.7606
Query 117: 0.3464
Query 118: 0.2567
Query 119: 0.5218
Query 121: 0.0923
Query 122: 0.2672
Query 123: 0.9397
Query 124: 0.0170
Query 125: 0.0711
Query 126: 0.0000
Query 127: 0.5436
Query 128: 0.0209
Query 129: 0.2541
Query 130: 0.3877
Query 131: 0.1059
Query 132: 0.3778
Query 133: 0.0000
Query 134: 0.6588
Query 135: 0.1491
Query 136: 0.9812
Query 137: 0.0005
Query 138: 0.0096
Query 139: 0.0863
Query 140: 0.2231

Overall statistics
(for 49 queries):

Total number of documents
over all queries
    Retrieved:     47648
    Relevant:       1072
    Rel_ret:         887

Interpolated Recall -
Precision Averages:
    at 0.00        0.6211
    at 0.10        0.5190
    at 0.20        0.4882
    at 0.30        0.4230
    at 0.40        0.3794
    at 0.50        0.3539
    at 0.60        0.3283
    at 0.70        0.2916
    at 0.80        0.2506
    at 0.90        0.2070
    at 1.00        0.1672

Avg. prec. (non-interpolated)
for all rel. documents
                   0.3444

Precision:
  At    5 docs:    0.3837
  At   10 docs:    0.3327
  At   15 docs:    0.2939
  At   20 docs:    0.2714
  At   30 docs:    0.2388
  At  100 docs:    0.1202
  At  200 docs:    0.0730
  At  500 docs:    0.0331
  At 1000 docs:    0.0181

R-Precision (prec. after R
(=num_rel) docs. retrieved):
    Exact:         0.3275
```

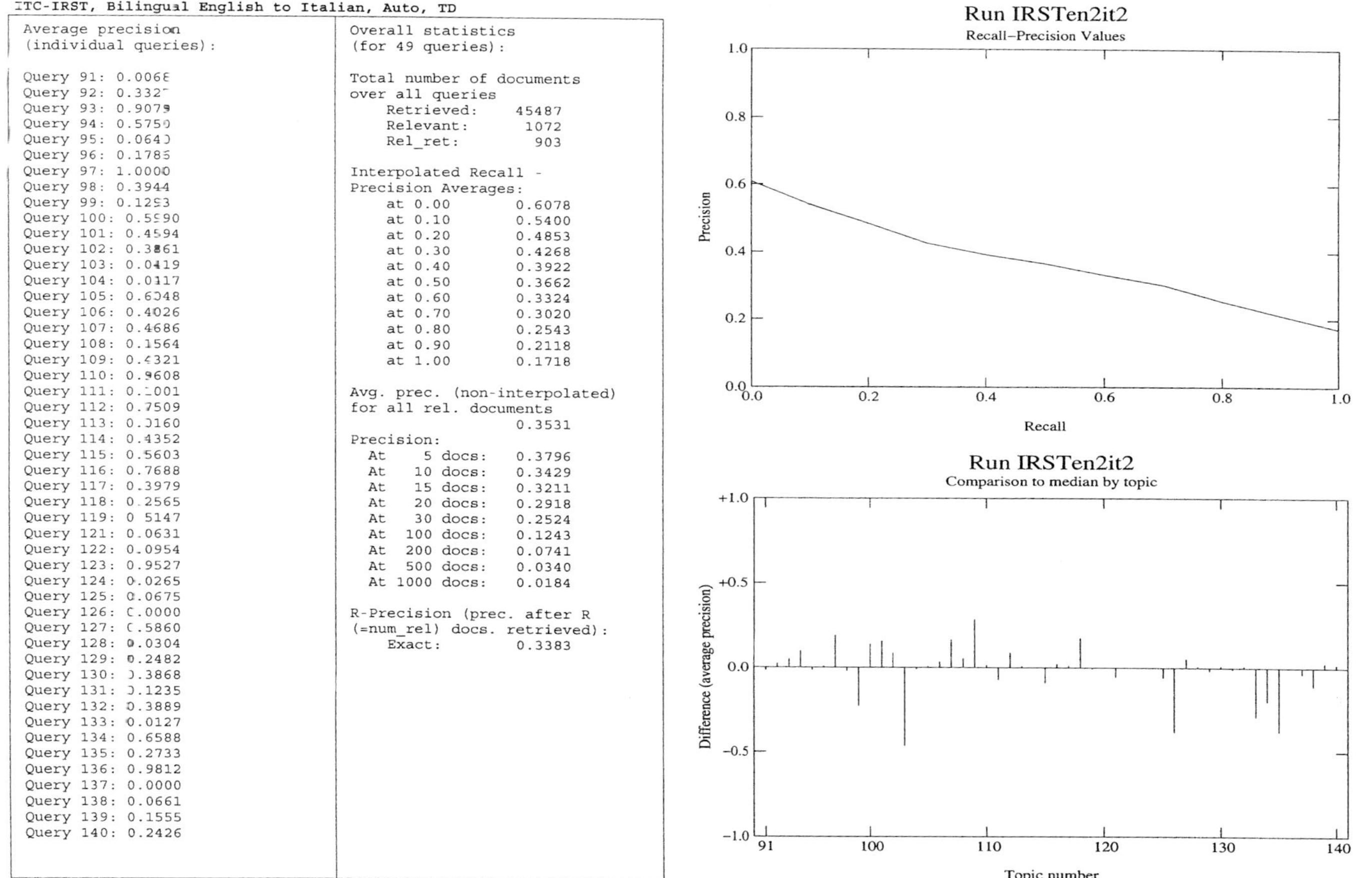

ITC-IRST, Bilingual English to Italian, Auto, TD

Average precision (individual queries):

Query	Average precision
Query 91:	0.0068
Query 92:	0.3327
Query 93:	0.9079
Query 94:	0.5750
Query 95:	0.0640
Query 96:	0.1785
Query 97:	1.0000
Query 98:	0.3944
Query 99:	0.1253
Query 100:	0.5590
Query 101:	0.4594
Query 102:	0.3861
Query 103:	0.0419
Query 104:	0.0117
Query 105:	0.6048
Query 106:	0.4026
Query 107:	0.4686
Query 108:	0.1564
Query 109:	0.4321
Query 110:	0.9608
Query 111:	0.1001
Query 112:	0.7509
Query 113:	0.0160
Query 114:	0.4352
Query 115:	0.5603
Query 116:	0.7688
Query 117:	0.3979
Query 118:	0.2565
Query 119:	0.5147
Query 121:	0.0631
Query 122:	0.0954
Query 123:	0.9527
Query 124:	0.0265
Query 125:	0.0675
Query 126:	0.0000
Query 127:	0.5860
Query 128:	0.0304
Query 129:	0.2482
Query 130:	0.3868
Query 131:	0.1235
Query 132:	0.3889
Query 133:	0.0127
Query 134:	0.6588
Query 135:	0.2733
Query 136:	0.9812
Query 137:	0.0000
Query 138:	0.0661
Query 139:	0.1555
Query 140:	0.2426

Overall statistics (for 49 queries):

Total number of documents over all queries

Retrieved:	45487
Relevant:	1072
Rel_ret:	903

Interpolated Recall - Precision Averages:

at 0.00	0.6078
at 0.10	0.5400
at 0.20	0.4853
at 0.30	0.4268
at 0.40	0.3922
at 0.50	0.3662
at 0.60	0.3324
at 0.70	0.3020
at 0.80	0.2543
at 0.90	0.2118
at 1.00	0.1718

Avg. prec. (non-interpolated) for all rel. documents 0.3531

Precision:

At 5 docs:	0.3796
At 10 docs:	0.3429
At 15 docs:	0.3211
At 20 docs:	0.2918
At 30 docs:	0.2524
At 100 docs:	0.1243
At 200 docs:	0.0741
At 500 docs:	0.0340
At 1000 docs:	0.0184

R-Precision (prec. after R (=num_rel) docs. retrieved):
Exact: 0.3383

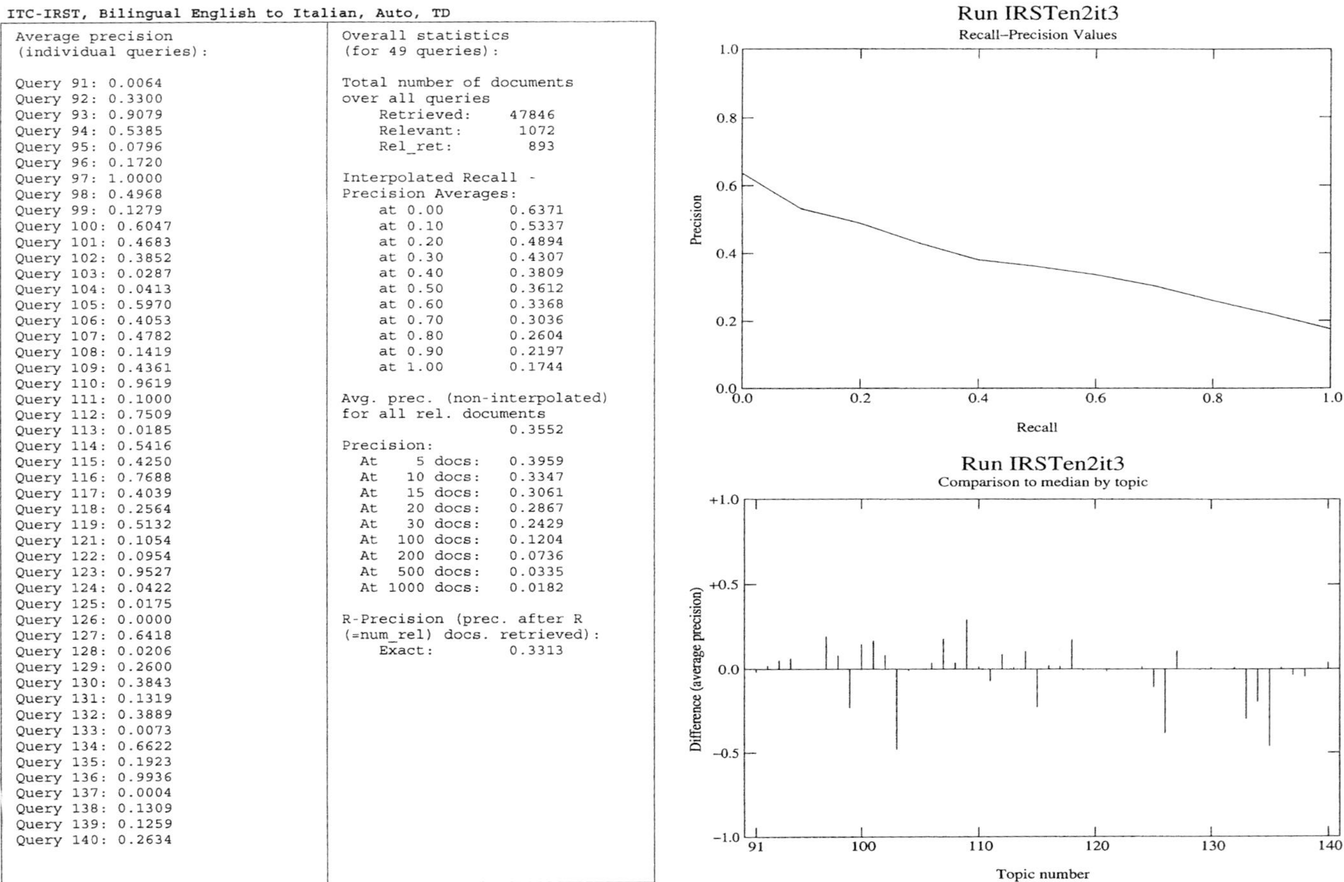

ITC-IRST, Bilingual English to Italian, Auto, TD

```
Average precision                Overall statistics
(individual queries):            (for 49 queries):

Query 91: 0.0064                 Total number of documents
Query 92: 0.3300                 over all queries
Query 93: 0.9079                     Retrieved:     47846
Query 94: 0.5385                     Relevant:       1072
Query 95: 0.0796                     Rel_ret:         893
Query 96: 0.1720
Query 97: 1.0000                 Interpolated Recall -
Query 98: 0.4968                 Precision Averages:
Query 99: 0.1279                     at 0.00        0.6371
Query 100: 0.6047                    at 0.10        0.5337
Query 101: 0.4683                    at 0.20        0.4894
Query 102: 0.3852                    at 0.30        0.4307
Query 103: 0.0287                    at 0.40        0.3809
Query 104: 0.0413                    at 0.50        0.3612
Query 105: 0.5970                    at 0.60        0.3368
Query 106: 0.4053                    at 0.70        0.3036
Query 107: 0.4782                    at 0.80        0.2604
Query 108: 0.1419                    at 0.90        0.2197
Query 109: 0.4361                    at 1.00        0.1744
Query 110: 0.9619
Query 111: 0.1000                Avg. prec. (non-interpolated)
Query 112: 0.7509                for all rel. documents
Query 113: 0.0185                                   0.3552
Query 114: 0.5416                Precision:
Query 115: 0.4250                  At    5 docs:    0.3959
Query 116: 0.7688                  At   10 docs:    0.3347
Query 117: 0.4039                  At   15 docs:    0.3061
Query 118: 0.2564                  At   20 docs:    0.2867
Query 119: 0.5132                  At   30 docs:    0.2429
Query 121: 0.1054                  At  100 docs:    0.1204
Query 122: 0.0954                  At  200 docs:    0.0736
Query 123: 0.9527                  At  500 docs:    0.0335
Query 124: 0.0422                  At 1000 docs:    0.0182
Query 125: 0.0175
Query 126: 0.0000                R-Precision (prec. after R
Query 127: 0.6418                (=num_rel) docs. retrieved):
Query 128: 0.0206                    Exact:         0.3313
Query 129: 0.2600
Query 130: 0.3843
Query 131: 0.1319
Query 132: 0.3889
Query 133: 0.0073
Query 134: 0.6622
Query 135: 0.1923
Query 136: 0.9936
Query 137: 0.0004
Query 138: 0.1309
Query 139: 0.1259
Query 140: 0.2634
```

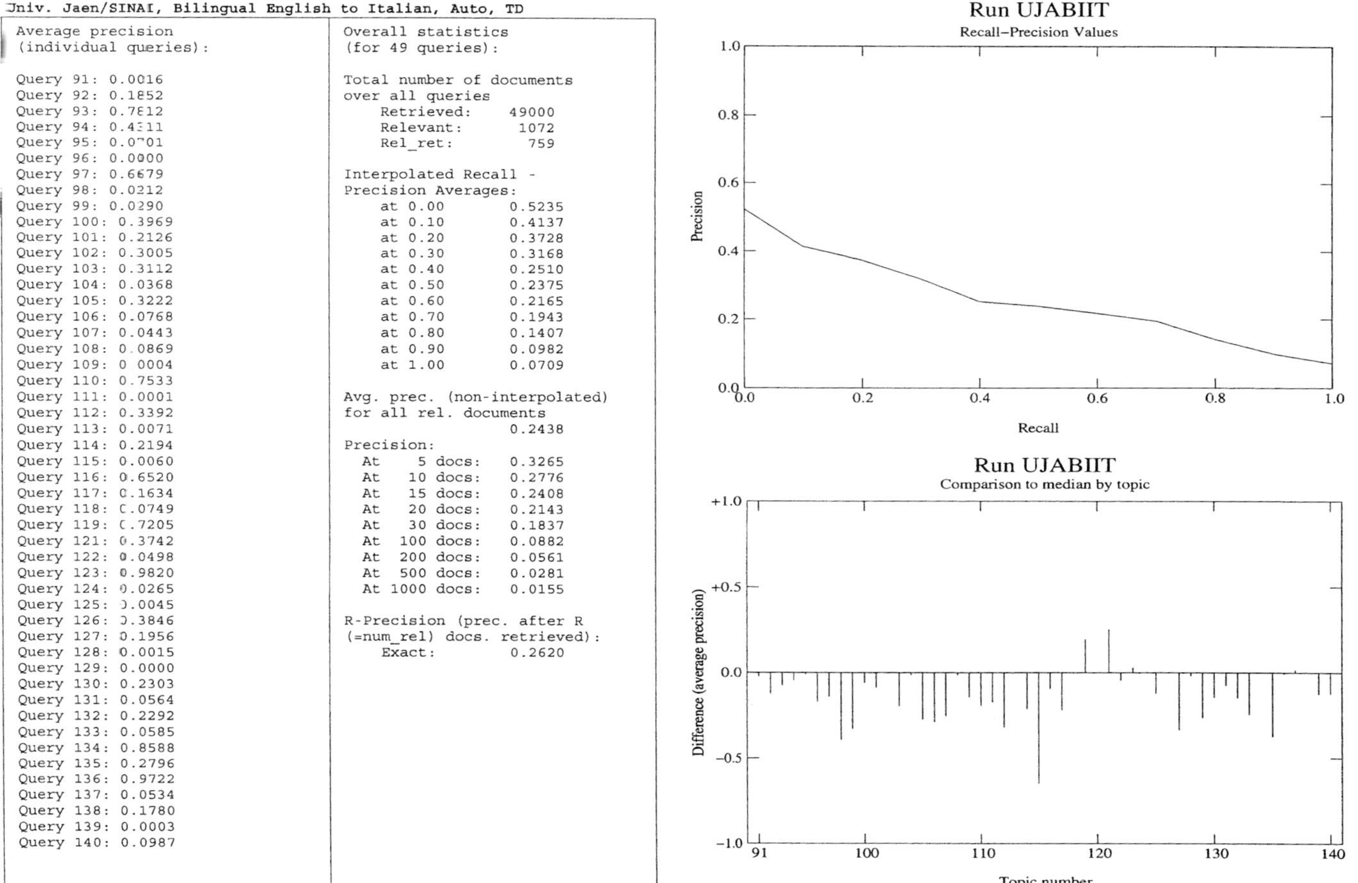

Univ. Jaen/SINAI, Bilingual English to Italian, Auto, TD

Average precision (individual queries):	Overall statistics (for 49 queries):
Query 91: 0.0016	Total number of documents over all queries
Query 92: 0.1852	Retrieved: 49000
Query 93: 0.7812	Relevant: 1072
Query 94: 0.4311	Rel_ret: 759
Query 95: 0.0701	
Query 96: 0.0000	Interpolated Recall - Precision Averages:
Query 97: 0.6679	at 0.00 0.5235
Query 98: 0.0212	at 0.10 0.4137
Query 99: 0.0290	at 0.20 0.3728
Query 100: 0.3969	at 0.30 0.3168
Query 101: 0.2126	at 0.40 0.2510
Query 102: 0.3005	at 0.50 0.2375
Query 103: 0.3112	at 0.60 0.2165
Query 104: 0.0368	at 0.70 0.1943
Query 105: 0.3222	at 0.80 0.1407
Query 106: 0.0768	at 0.90 0.0982
Query 107: 0.0443	at 1.00 0.0709
Query 108: 0.0869	
Query 109: 0.0004	Avg. prec. (non-interpolated) for all rel. documents 0.2438
Query 110: 0.7533	
Query 111: 0.0001	Precision:
Query 112: 0.3392	At 5 docs: 0.3265
Query 113: 0.0071	At 10 docs: 0.2776
Query 114: 0.2194	At 15 docs: 0.2408
Query 115: 0.0060	At 20 docs: 0.2143
Query 116: 0.6520	At 30 docs: 0.1837
Query 117: 0.1634	At 100 docs: 0.0882
Query 118: 0.0749	At 200 docs: 0.0561
Query 119: 0.7205	At 500 docs: 0.0281
Query 121: 0.3742	At 1000 docs: 0.0155
Query 122: 0.0498	
Query 123: 0.9820	R-Precision (prec. after R (=num_rel) docs. retrieved):
Query 124: 0.0265	Exact: 0.2620
Query 125: 0.0045	
Query 126: 0.3846	
Query 127: 0.1956	
Query 128: 0.0015	
Query 129: 0.0000	
Query 130: 0.2303	
Query 131: 0.0564	
Query 132: 0.2292	
Query 133: 0.0585	
Query 134: 0.8588	
Query 135: 0.2796	
Query 136: 0.9722	
Query 137: 0.0534	
Query 138: 0.1780	
Query 139: 0.0003	
Query 140: 0.0987	

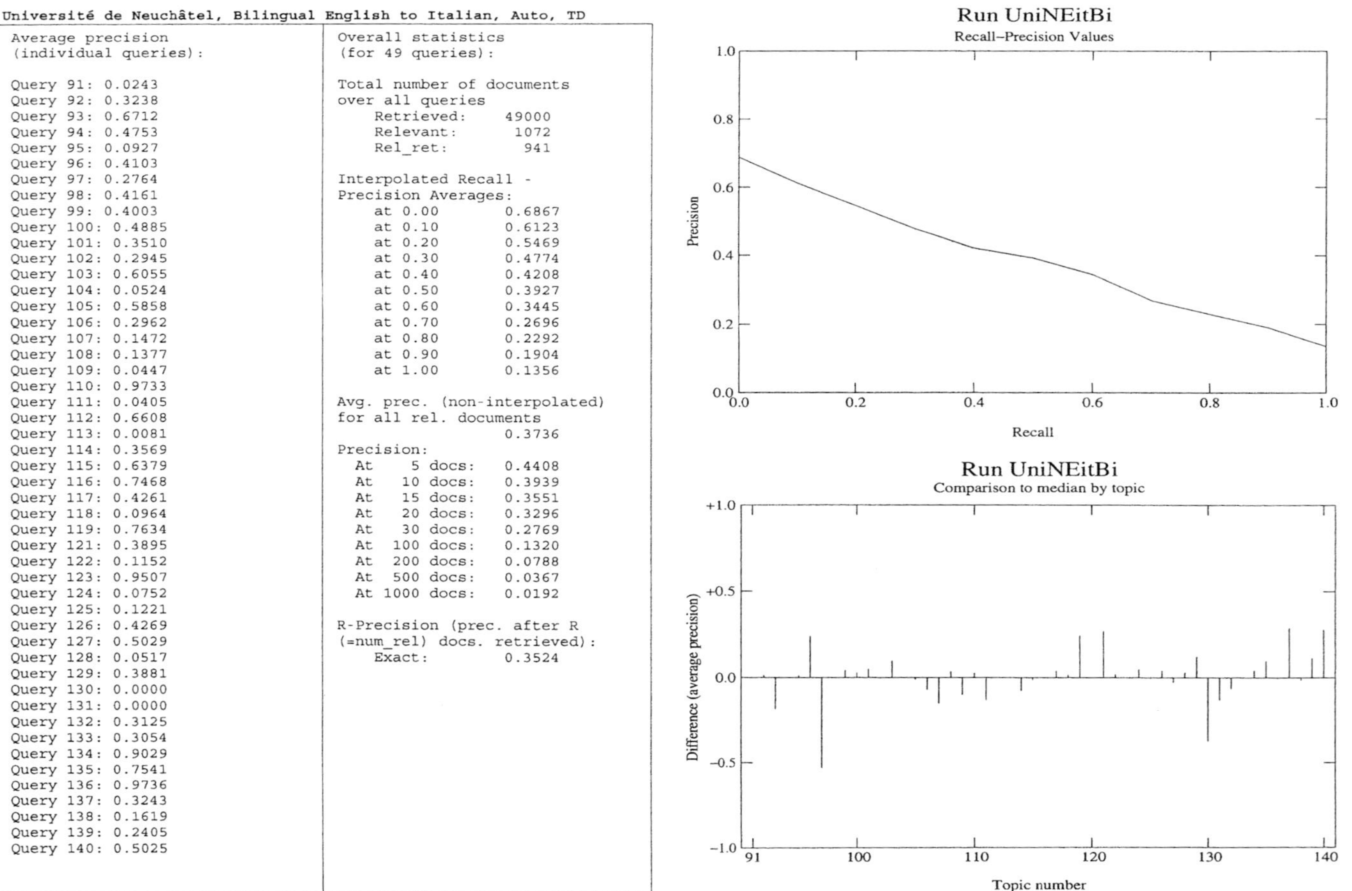

Université de Neuchâtel, Bilingual English to Italian, Auto, TD

```
Average precision               Overall statistics
(individual queries):           (for 49 queries):

Query 91: 0.0243                Total number of documents
Query 92: 0.3238                over all queries
Query 93: 0.6712                    Retrieved:     49000
Query 94: 0.4753                    Relevant:       1072
Query 95: 0.0927                    Rel_ret:         941
Query 96: 0.4103
Query 97: 0.2764                Interpolated Recall -
Query 98: 0.4161                Precision Averages:
Query 99: 0.4003                    at 0.00        0.6867
Query 100: 0.4885                   at 0.10        0.6123
Query 101: 0.3510                   at 0.20        0.5469
Query 102: 0.2945                   at 0.30        0.4774
Query 103: 0.6055                   at 0.40        0.4208
Query 104: 0.0524                   at 0.50        0.3927
Query 105: 0.5858                   at 0.60        0.3445
Query 106: 0.2962                   at 0.70        0.2696
Query 107: 0.1472                   at 0.80        0.2292
Query 108: 0.1377                   at 0.90        0.1904
Query 109: 0.0447                   at 1.00        0.1356
Query 110: 0.9733
Query 111: 0.0405               Avg. prec. (non-interpolated)
Query 112: 0.6608               for all rel. documents
Query 113: 0.0081                                  0.3736
Query 114: 0.3569               Precision:
Query 115: 0.6379                 At    5 docs:    0.4408
Query 116: 0.7468                 At   10 docs:    0.3939
Query 117: 0.4261                 At   15 docs:    0.3551
Query 118: 0.0964                 At   20 docs:    0.3296
Query 119: 0.7634                 At   30 docs:    0.2769
Query 121: 0.3895                 At  100 docs:    0.1320
Query 122: 0.1152                 At  200 docs:    0.0788
Query 123: 0.9507                 At  500 docs:    0.0367
Query 124: 0.0752                 At 1000 docs:    0.0192
Query 125: 0.1221
Query 126: 0.4269               R-Precision (prec. after R
Query 127: 0.5029               (=num_rel) docs. retrieved):
Query 128: 0.0517                   Exact:         0.3524
Query 129: 0.3881
Query 130: 0.0000
Query 131: 0.0000
Query 132: 0.3125
Query 133: 0.3054
Query 134: 0.9029
Query 135: 0.7541
Query 136: 0.9736
Query 137: 0.3243
Query 138: 0.1619
Query 139: 0.2405
Query 140: 0.5025
```

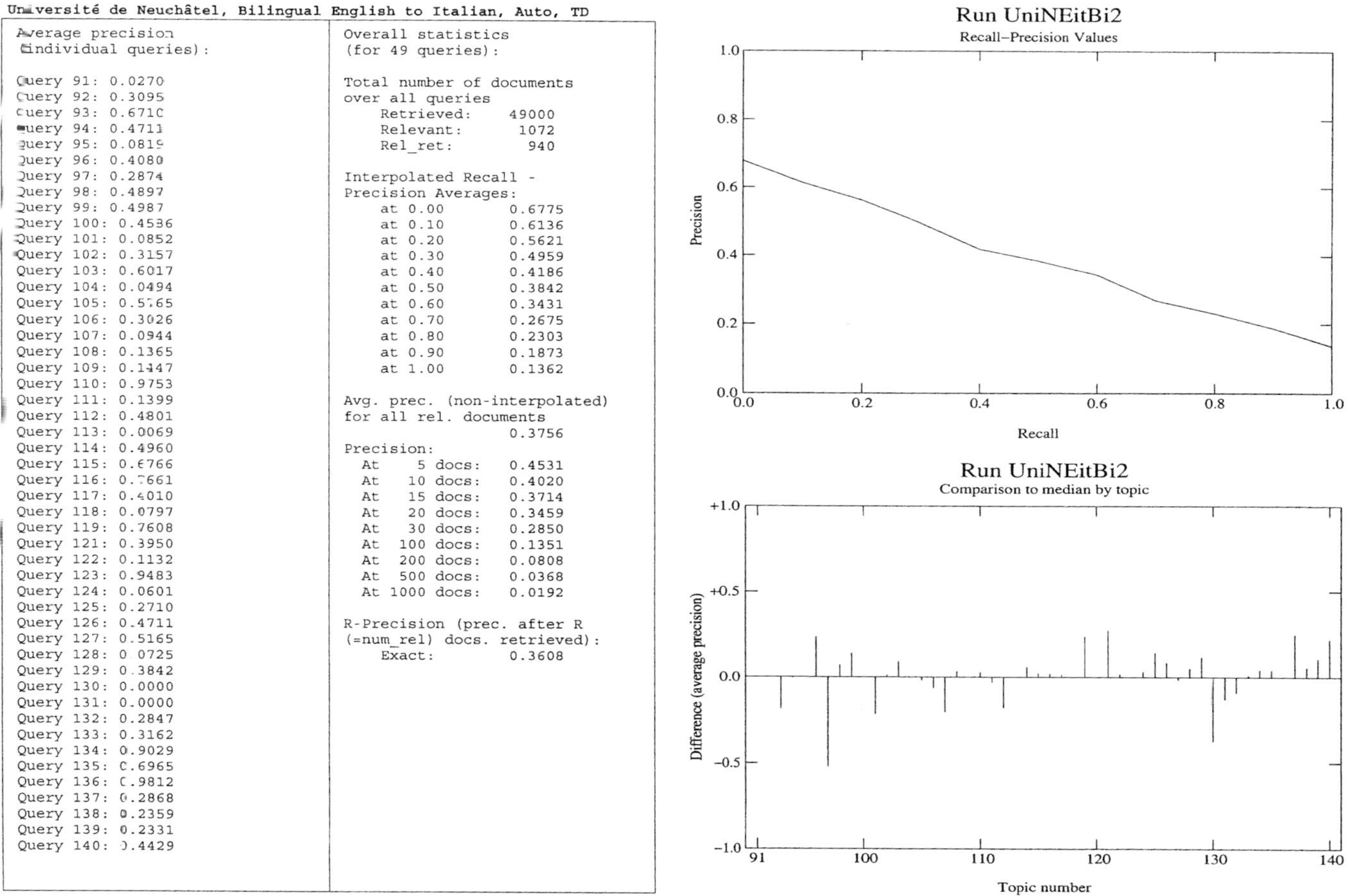

Université de Neuchâtel, Bilingual English to Italian, Auto, TD

```
Average precision
(individual queries):

Query 91: 0.0270
Query 92: 0.3095
Query 93: 0.6710
Query 94: 0.4711
Query 95: 0.0819
Query 96: 0.4080
Query 97: 0.2874
Query 98: 0.4897
Query 99: 0.4987
Query 100: 0.4536
Query 101: 0.0852
Query 102: 0.3157
Query 103: 0.6017
Query 104: 0.0494
Query 105: 0.5765
Query 106: 0.3026
Query 107: 0.0944
Query 108: 0.1365
Query 109: 0.1447
Query 110: 0.9753
Query 111: 0.1399
Query 112: 0.4801
Query 113: 0.0069
Query 114: 0.4960
Query 115: 0.6766
Query 116: 0.7661
Query 117: 0.4010
Query 118: 0.0797
Query 119: 0.7608
Query 121: 0.3950
Query 122: 0.1132
Query 123: 0.9483
Query 124: 0.0601
Query 125: 0.2710
Query 126: 0.4711
Query 127: 0.5165
Query 128: 0.0725
Query 129: 0.3842
Query 130: 0.0000
Query 131: 0.0000
Query 132: 0.2847
Query 133: 0.3162
Query 134: 0.9029
Query 135: 0.6965
Query 136: 0.9812
Query 137: 0.2868
Query 138: 0.2359
Query 139: 0.2331
Query 140: 0.4429
```

```
Overall statistics
(for 49 queries):

Total number of documents
over all queries
    Retrieved:    49000
    Relevant:      1072
    Rel_ret:        940

Interpolated Recall -
Precision Averages:
    at 0.00        0.6775
    at 0.10        0.6136
    at 0.20        0.5621
    at 0.30        0.4959
    at 0.40        0.4186
    at 0.50        0.3842
    at 0.60        0.3431
    at 0.70        0.2675
    at 0.80        0.2303
    at 0.90        0.1873
    at 1.00        0.1362

Avg. prec. (non-interpolated)
for all rel. documents
                   0.3756
Precision:
  At    5 docs:    0.4531
  At   10 docs:    0.4020
  At   15 docs:    0.3714
  At   20 docs:    0.3459
  At   30 docs:    0.2850
  At  100 docs:    0.1351
  At  200 docs:    0.0808
  At  500 docs:    0.0368
  At 1000 docs:    0.0192

R-Precision (prec. after R
(=num_rel) docs. retrieved):
    Exact:         0.3608
```

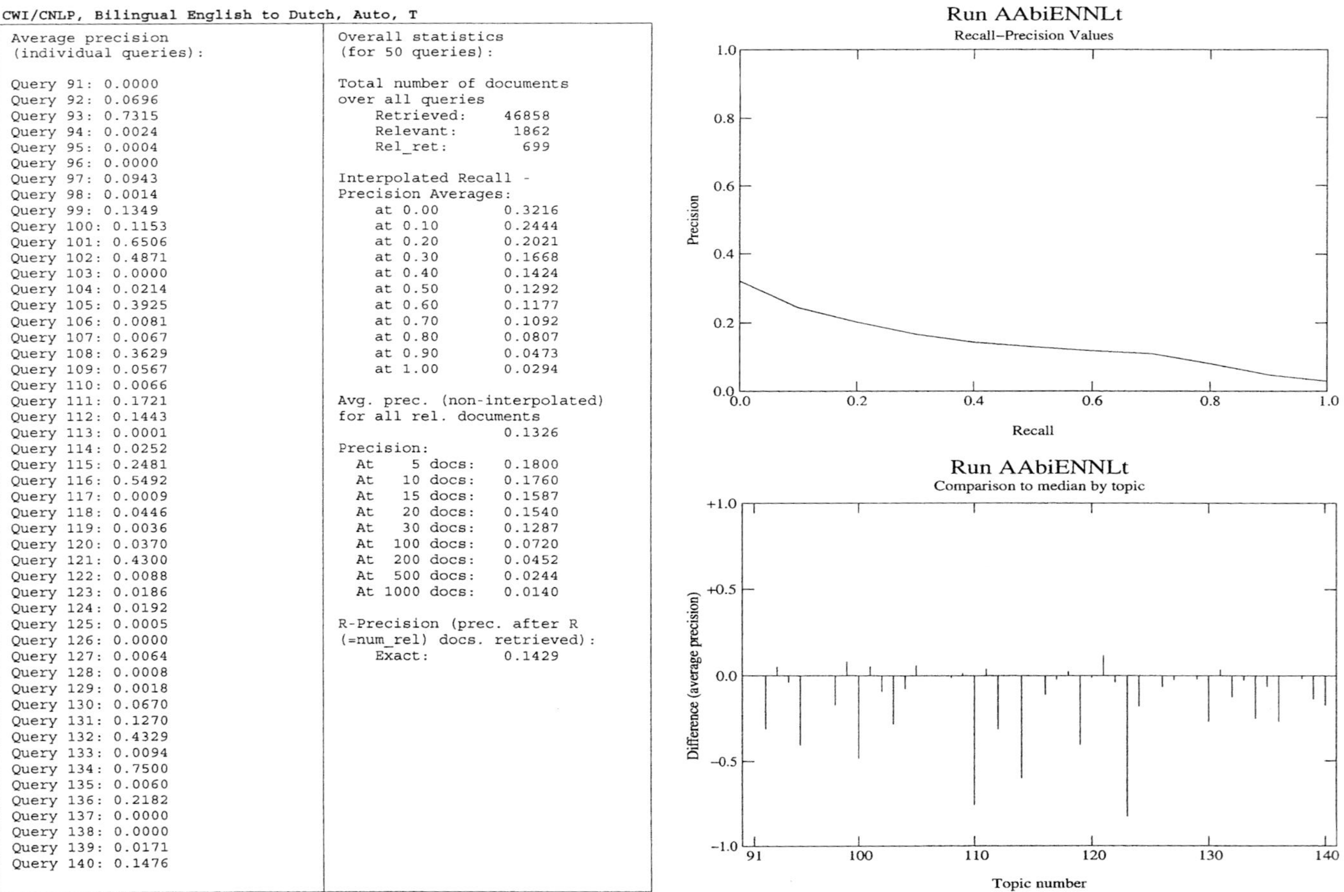

CWI/CNLP, Bilingual English to Dutch, Auto, T

Average precision (individual queries):	Overall statistics (for 50 queries):
Query 91: 0.0000	Total number of documents over all queries
Query 92: 0.0696	Retrieved: 46858
Query 93: 0.7315	Relevant: 1862
Query 94: 0.0024	Rel_ret: 699
Query 95: 0.0004	
Query 96: 0.0000	Interpolated Recall - Precision Averages:
Query 97: 0.0943	at 0.00 0.3216
Query 98: 0.0014	at 0.10 0.2444
Query 99: 0.1349	at 0.20 0.2021
Query 100: 0.1153	at 0.30 0.1668
Query 101: 0.6506	at 0.40 0.1424
Query 102: 0.4871	at 0.50 0.1292
Query 103: 0.0000	at 0.60 0.1177
Query 104: 0.0214	at 0.70 0.1092
Query 105: 0.3925	at 0.80 0.0807
Query 106: 0.0081	at 0.90 0.0473
Query 107: 0.0067	at 1.00 0.0294
Query 108: 0.3629	
Query 109: 0.0567	Avg. prec. (non-interpolated) for all rel. documents 0.1326
Query 110: 0.0066	
Query 111: 0.1721	Precision:
Query 112: 0.1443	At 5 docs: 0.1800
Query 113: 0.0001	At 10 docs: 0.1760
Query 114: 0.0252	At 15 docs: 0.1587
Query 115: 0.2481	At 20 docs: 0.1540
Query 116: 0.5492	At 30 docs: 0.1287
Query 117: 0.0009	At 100 docs: 0.0720
Query 118: 0.0446	At 200 docs: 0.0452
Query 119: 0.0036	At 500 docs: 0.0244
Query 120: 0.0370	At 1000 docs: 0.0140
Query 121: 0.4300	
Query 122: 0.0088	R-Precision (prec. after R (=num_rel) docs. retrieved):
Query 123: 0.0186	Exact: 0.1429
Query 124: 0.0192	
Query 125: 0.0005	
Query 126: 0.0000	
Query 127: 0.0064	
Query 128: 0.0008	
Query 129: 0.0018	
Query 130: 0.0670	
Query 131: 0.1270	
Query 132: 0.4329	
Query 133: 0.0094	
Query 134: 0.7500	
Query 135: 0.0060	
Query 136: 0.2182	
Query 137: 0.0000	
Query 138: 0.0000	
Query 139: 0.0171	
Query 140: 0.1476	

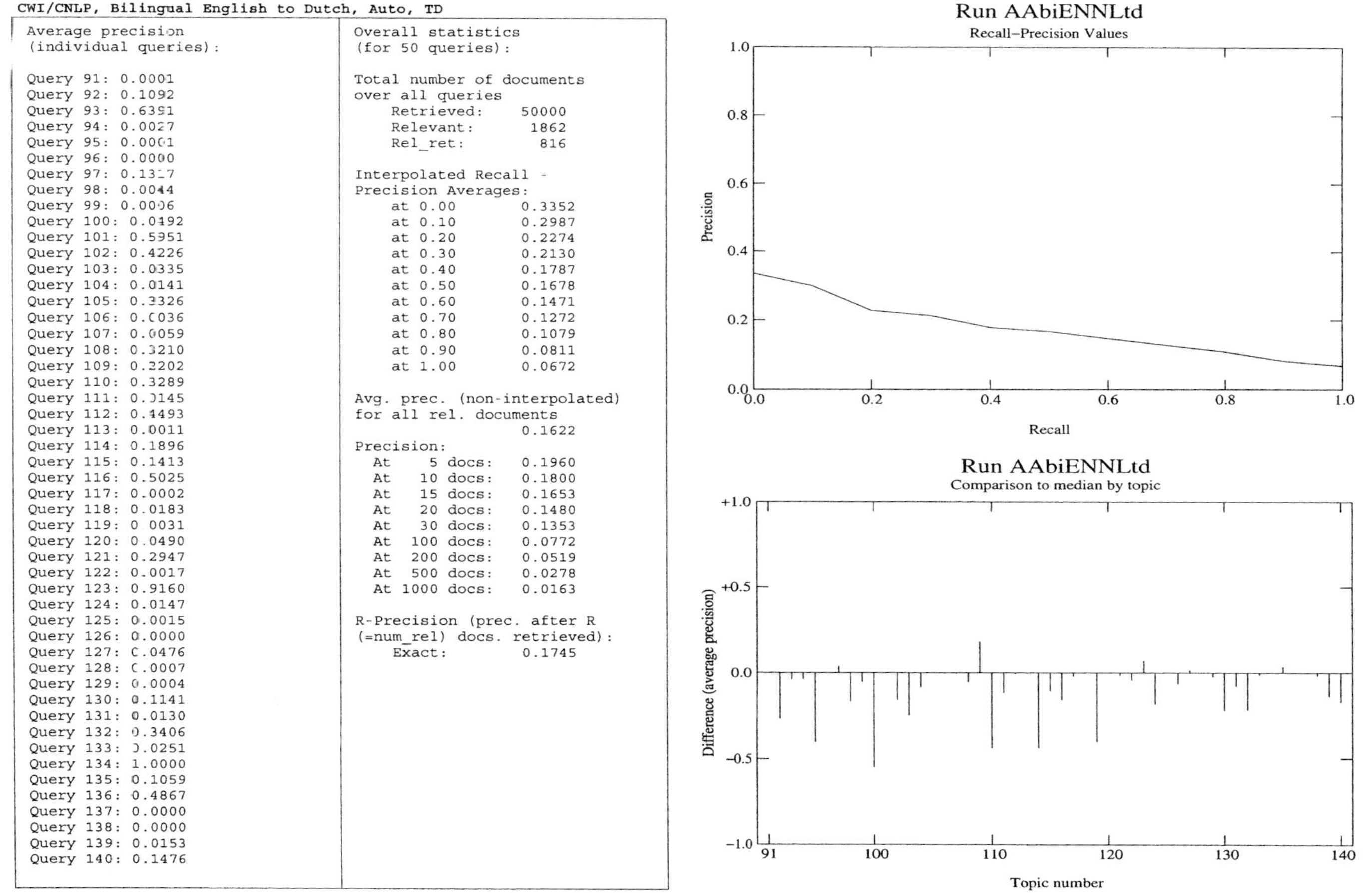

CWI/CNLP, Bilingual English to Dutch, Auto, TD

```
Average precision                Overall statistics
(individual queries):            (for 50 queries):

Query 91: 0.0001                 Total number of documents
Query 92: 0.1092                 over all queries
Query 93: 0.6391                     Retrieved:    50000
Query 94: 0.0027                     Relevant:      1862
Query 95: 0.0001                     Rel_ret:        816
Query 96: 0.0000
Query 97: 0.1317                 Interpolated Recall -
Query 98: 0.0044                 Precision Averages:
Query 99: 0.0006                     at 0.00        0.3352
Query 100: 0.0492                    at 0.10        0.2987
Query 101: 0.5951                    at 0.20        0.2274
Query 102: 0.4226                    at 0.30        0.2130
Query 103: 0.0335                    at 0.40        0.1787
Query 104: 0.0141                    at 0.50        0.1678
Query 105: 0.3326                    at 0.60        0.1471
Query 106: 0.0036                    at 0.70        0.1272
Query 107: 0.0059                    at 0.80        0.1079
Query 108: 0.3210                    at 0.90        0.0811
Query 109: 0.2202                    at 1.00        0.0672
Query 110: 0.3289
Query 111: 0.0145                Avg. prec. (non-interpolated)
Query 112: 0.4493                for all rel. documents
Query 113: 0.0011                                   0.1622
Query 114: 0.1896                Precision:
Query 115: 0.1413                  At    5 docs:    0.1960
Query 116: 0.5025                  At   10 docs:    0.1800
Query 117: 0.0002                  At   15 docs:    0.1653
Query 118: 0.0183                  At   20 docs:    0.1480
Query 119: 0.0031                  At   30 docs:    0.1353
Query 120: 0.0490                  At  100 docs:    0.0772
Query 121: 0.2947                  At  200 docs:    0.0519
Query 122: 0.0017                  At  500 docs:    0.0278
Query 123: 0.9160                  At 1000 docs:    0.0163
Query 124: 0.0147
Query 125: 0.0015                R-Precision (prec. after R
Query 126: 0.0000                (=num_rel) docs. retrieved):
Query 127: 0.0476                    Exact:         0.1745
Query 128: 0.0007
Query 129: 0.0004
Query 130: 0.1141
Query 131: 0.0130
Query 132: 0.3406
Query 133: 0.0251
Query 134: 1.0000
Query 135: 0.1059
Query 136: 0.4867
Query 137: 0.0000
Query 138: 0.0000
Query 139: 0.0153
Query 140: 0.1476
```

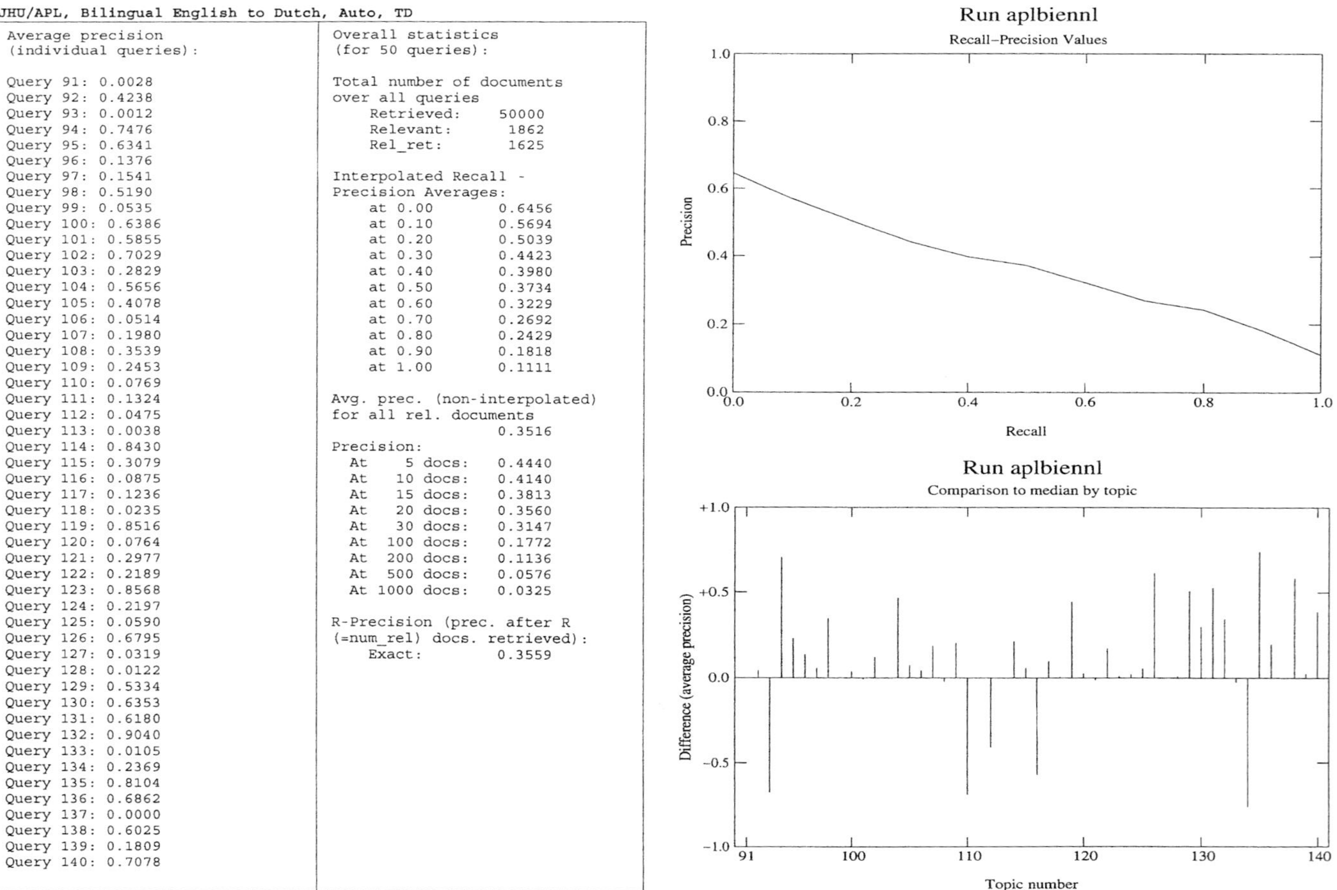

JHU/APL, Bilingual English to Dutch, Auto, TD

Average precision (individual queries):	Overall statistics (for 50 queries):
Query 91: 0.0028	Total number of documents over all queries
Query 92: 0.4238	Retrieved: 50000
Query 93: 0.0012	Relevant: 1862
Query 94: 0.7476	Rel_ret: 1625
Query 95: 0.6341	
Query 96: 0.1376	Interpolated Recall - Precision Averages:
Query 97: 0.1541	at 0.00 0.6456
Query 98: 0.5190	at 0.10 0.5694
Query 99: 0.0535	at 0.20 0.5039
Query 100: 0.6386	at 0.30 0.4423
Query 101: 0.5855	at 0.40 0.3980
Query 102: 0.7029	at 0.50 0.3734
Query 103: 0.2829	at 0.60 0.3229
Query 104: 0.5656	at 0.70 0.2692
Query 105: 0.4078	at 0.80 0.2429
Query 106: 0.0514	at 0.90 0.1818
Query 107: 0.1980	at 1.00 0.1111
Query 108: 0.3539	
Query 109: 0.2453	Avg. prec. (non-interpolated) for all rel. documents 0.3516
Query 110: 0.0769	
Query 111: 0.1324	Precision:
Query 112: 0.0475	At 5 docs: 0.4440
Query 113: 0.0038	At 10 docs: 0.4140
Query 114: 0.8430	At 15 docs: 0.3813
Query 115: 0.3079	At 20 docs: 0.3560
Query 116: 0.0875	At 30 docs: 0.3147
Query 117: 0.1236	At 100 docs: 0.1772
Query 118: 0.0235	At 200 docs: 0.1136
Query 119: 0.8516	At 500 docs: 0.0576
Query 120: 0.0764	At 1000 docs: 0.0325
Query 121: 0.2977	
Query 122: 0.2189	R-Precision (prec. after R (=num_rel) docs. retrieved):
Query 123: 0.8568	Exact: 0.3559
Query 124: 0.2197	
Query 125: 0.0590	
Query 126: 0.6795	
Query 127: 0.0319	
Query 128: 0.0122	
Query 129: 0.5334	
Query 130: 0.6353	
Query 131: 0.6180	
Query 132: 0.9040	
Query 133: 0.0105	
Query 134: 0.2369	
Query 135: 0.8104	
Query 136: 0.6862	
Query 137: 0.0000	
Query 138: 0.6025	
Query 139: 0.1809	
Query 140: 0.7078	

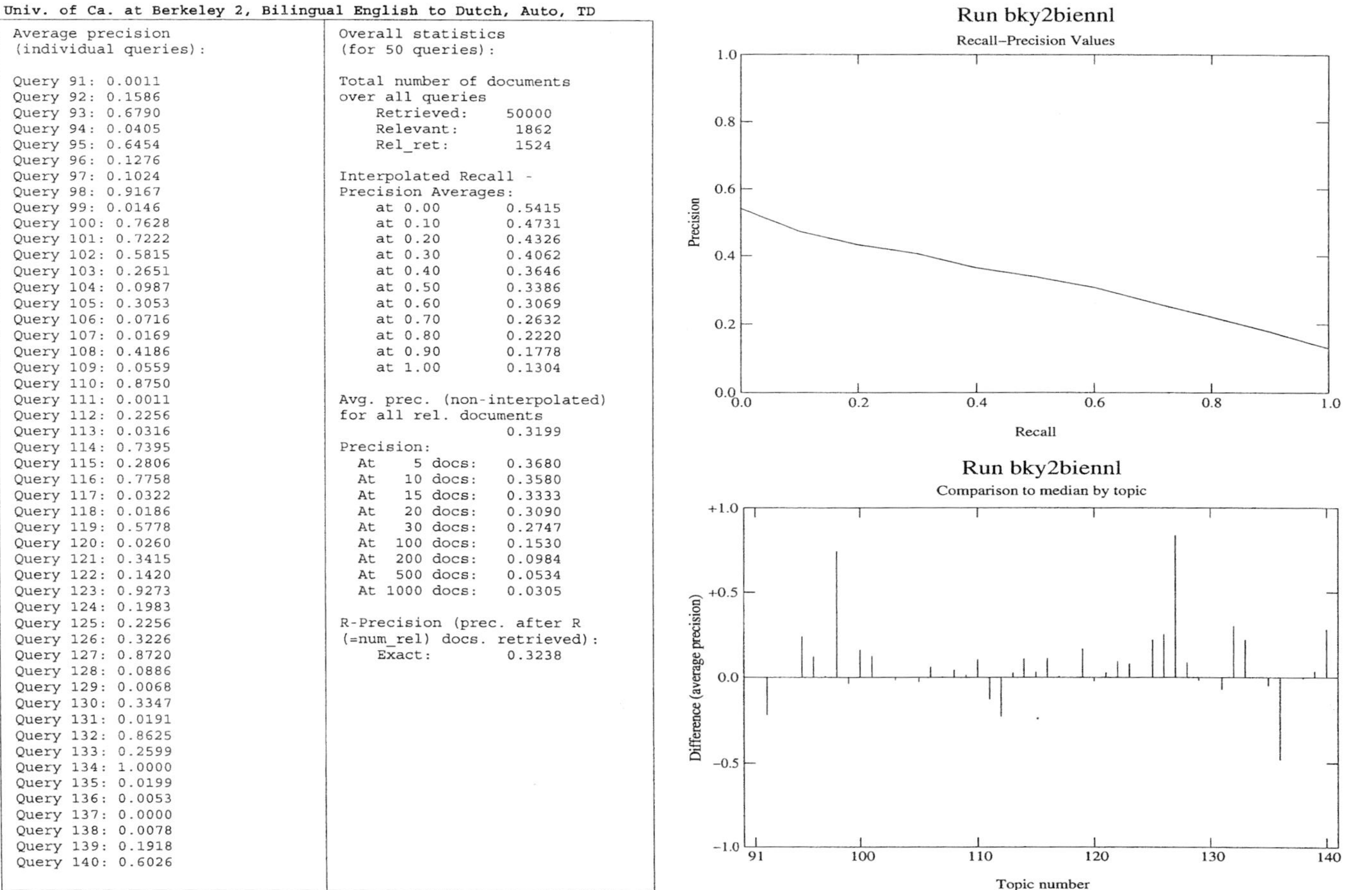

Univ. of Ca. at Berkeley 2, Bilingual English to Dutch, Auto, TD

Average precision (individual queries):	Overall statistics (for 50 queries):
Query 91: 0.0011	Total number of documents over all queries
Query 92: 0.1586	Retrieved: 50000
Query 93: 0.6790	Relevant: 1862
Query 94: 0.0405	Rel_ret: 1524
Query 95: 0.6454	
Query 96: 0.1276	Interpolated Recall - Precision Averages:
Query 97: 0.1024	at 0.00 0.5415
Query 98: 0.9167	at 0.10 0.4731
Query 99: 0.0146	at 0.20 0.4326
Query 100: 0.7628	at 0.30 0.4062
Query 101: 0.7222	at 0.40 0.3646
Query 102: 0.5815	at 0.50 0.3386
Query 103: 0.2651	at 0.60 0.3069
Query 104: 0.0987	at 0.70 0.2632
Query 105: 0.3053	at 0.80 0.2220
Query 106: 0.0716	at 0.90 0.1778
Query 107: 0.0169	at 1.00 0.1304
Query 108: 0.4186	
Query 109: 0.0559	Avg. prec. (non-interpolated) for all rel. documents 0.3199
Query 110: 0.8750	
Query 111: 0.0011	Precision:
Query 112: 0.2256	At 5 docs: 0.3680
Query 113: 0.0316	At 10 docs: 0.3580
Query 114: 0.7395	At 15 docs: 0.3333
Query 115: 0.2806	At 20 docs: 0.3090
Query 116: 0.7758	At 30 docs: 0.2747
Query 117: 0.0322	At 100 docs: 0.1530
Query 118: 0.0186	At 200 docs: 0.0984
Query 119: 0.5778	At 500 docs: 0.0534
Query 120: 0.0260	At 1000 docs: 0.0305
Query 121: 0.3415	
Query 122: 0.1420	R-Precision (prec. after R (=num_rel) docs. retrieved):
Query 123: 0.9273	Exact: 0.3238
Query 124: 0.1983	
Query 125: 0.2256	
Query 126: 0.3226	
Query 127: 0.8720	
Query 128: 0.0886	
Query 129: 0.0068	
Query 130: 0.3347	
Query 131: 0.0191	
Query 132: 0.8625	
Query 133: 0.2599	
Query 134: 1.0000	
Query 135: 0.0199	
Query 136: 0.0053	
Query 137: 0.0000	
Query 138: 0.0078	
Query 139: 0.1918	
Query 140: 0.6026	

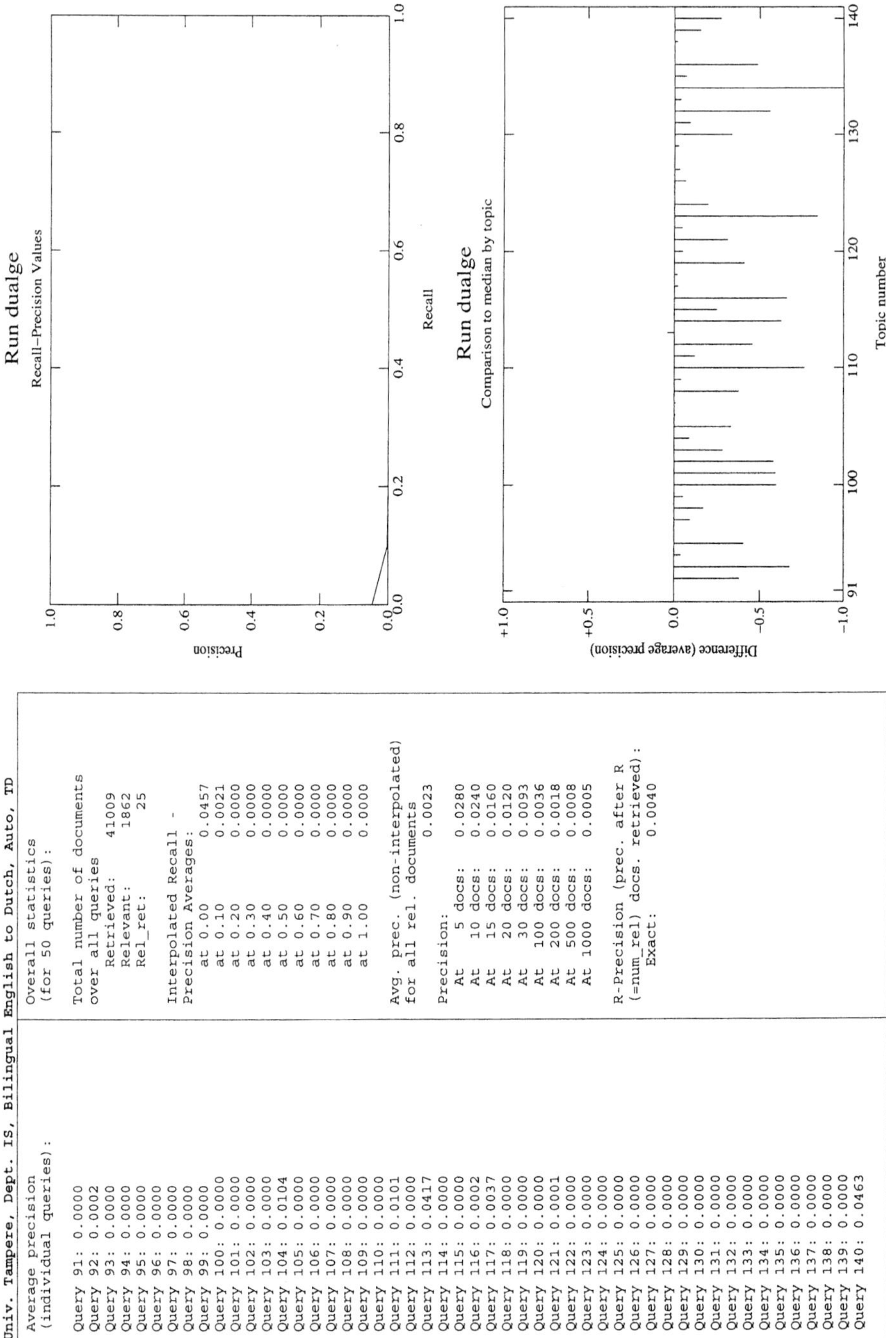

Univ. Tampere, Dept. IS, Bilingual English to Dutch, Auto, TD

```
Average precision              Overall statistics
(individual queries):          (for 50 queries):

Query 91: 0.0000               Total number of documents
Query 92: 0.0002               over all queries
Query 93: 0.0000                 Retrieved:    41009
Query 94: 0.0000                 Relevant:      1862
Query 95: 0.0000                 Rel_ret:         25
Query 96: 0.0000
Query 97: 0.0000               Interpolated Recall -
Query 98: 0.0000               Precision Averages:
Query 99: 0.0000                 at 0.00       0.0457
Query 100: 0.0000                at 0.10       0.0021
Query 101: 0.0000                at 0.20       0.0000
Query 102: 0.0000                at 0.30       0.0000
Query 103: 0.0000                at 0.40       0.0000
Query 104: 0.0104                at 0.50       0.0000
Query 105: 0.0000                at 0.60       0.0000
Query 106: 0.0000                at 0.70       0.0000
Query 107: 0.0000                at 0.80       0.0000
Query 108: 0.0000                at 0.90       0.0000
Query 109: 0.0000                at 1.00       0.0000
Query 110: 0.0000
Query 111: 0.0101              Avg. prec. (non-interpolated)
Query 112: 0.0000              for all rel. documents
Query 113: 0.0417                              0.0023
Query 114: 0.0000
Query 115: 0.0000              Precision:
Query 116: 0.0002                At    5 docs:   0.0280
Query 117: 0.0037                At   10 docs:   0.0240
Query 118: 0.0000                At   15 docs:   0.0160
Query 119: 0.0000                At   20 docs:   0.0120
Query 120: 0.0000                At   30 docs:   0.0093
Query 121: 0.0001                At  100 docs:   0.0036
Query 122: 0.0000                At  200 docs:   0.0018
Query 123: 0.0000                At  500 docs:   0.0008
Query 124: 0.0000                At 1000 docs:   0.0005
Query 125: 0.0000
Query 126: 0.0000              R-Precision (prec. after R
Query 127: 0.0000              (=num_rel) docs. retrieved):
Query 128: 0.0000                Exact:         0.0040
Query 129: 0.0000
Query 130: 0.0000
Query 131: 0.0000
Query 132: 0.0000
Query 133: 0.0000
Query 134: 0.0000
Query 135: 0.0000
Query 136: 0.0000
Query 137: 0.0000
Query 138: 0.0000
Query 139: 0.0000
Query 140: 0.0463
```

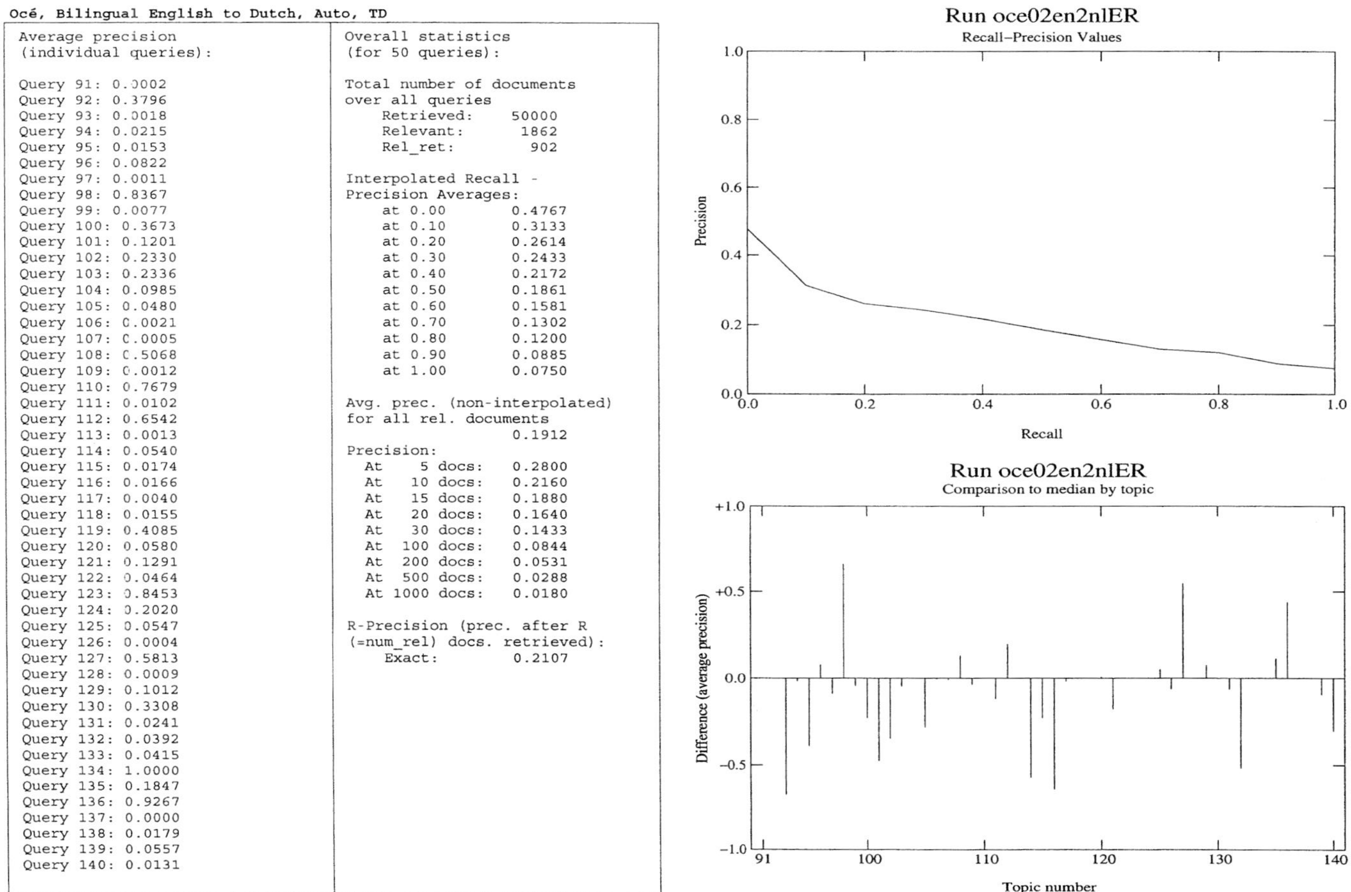

Océ, Bilingual English to Dutch, Auto, TD

Average precision (individual queries):	Overall statistics (for 50 queries):
Query 91: 0.0002	Total number of documents over all queries
Query 92: 0.3796	Retrieved: 50000
Query 93: 0.0018	Relevant: 1862
Query 94: 0.0215	Rel_ret: 902
Query 95: 0.0153	
Query 96: 0.0822	Interpolated Recall - Precision Averages:
Query 97: 0.0011	at 0.00 0.4767
Query 98: 0.8367	at 0.10 0.3133
Query 99: 0.0077	at 0.20 0.2614
Query 100: 0.3673	at 0.30 0.2433
Query 101: 0.1201	at 0.40 0.2172
Query 102: 0.2330	at 0.50 0.1861
Query 103: 0.2336	at 0.60 0.1581
Query 104: 0.0985	at 0.70 0.1302
Query 105: 0.0480	at 0.80 0.1200
Query 106: 0.0021	at 0.90 0.0885
Query 107: 0.0005	at 1.00 0.0750
Query 108: 0.5068	
Query 109: 0.0012	Avg. prec. (non-interpolated) for all rel. documents 0.1912
Query 110: 0.7679	Precision:
Query 111: 0.0102	At 5 docs: 0.2800
Query 112: 0.6542	At 10 docs: 0.2160
Query 113: 0.0013	At 15 docs: 0.1880
Query 114: 0.0540	At 20 docs: 0.1640
Query 115: 0.0174	At 30 docs: 0.1433
Query 116: 0.0166	At 100 docs: 0.0844
Query 117: 0.0040	At 200 docs: 0.0531
Query 118: 0.0155	At 500 docs: 0.0288
Query 119: 0.4085	At 1000 docs: 0.0180
Query 120: 0.0580	
Query 121: 0.1291	R-Precision (prec. after R (=num_rel) docs. retrieved):
Query 122: 0.0464	Exact: 0.2107
Query 123: 0.8453	
Query 124: 0.2020	
Query 125: 0.0547	
Query 126: 0.0004	
Query 127: 0.5813	
Query 128: 0.0009	
Query 129: 0.1012	
Query 130: 0.3308	
Query 131: 0.0241	
Query 132: 0.0392	
Query 133: 0.0415	
Query 134: 1.0000	
Query 135: 0.1847	
Query 136: 0.9267	
Query 137: 0.0000	
Query 138: 0.0179	
Query 139: 0.0557	
Query 140: 0.0131	

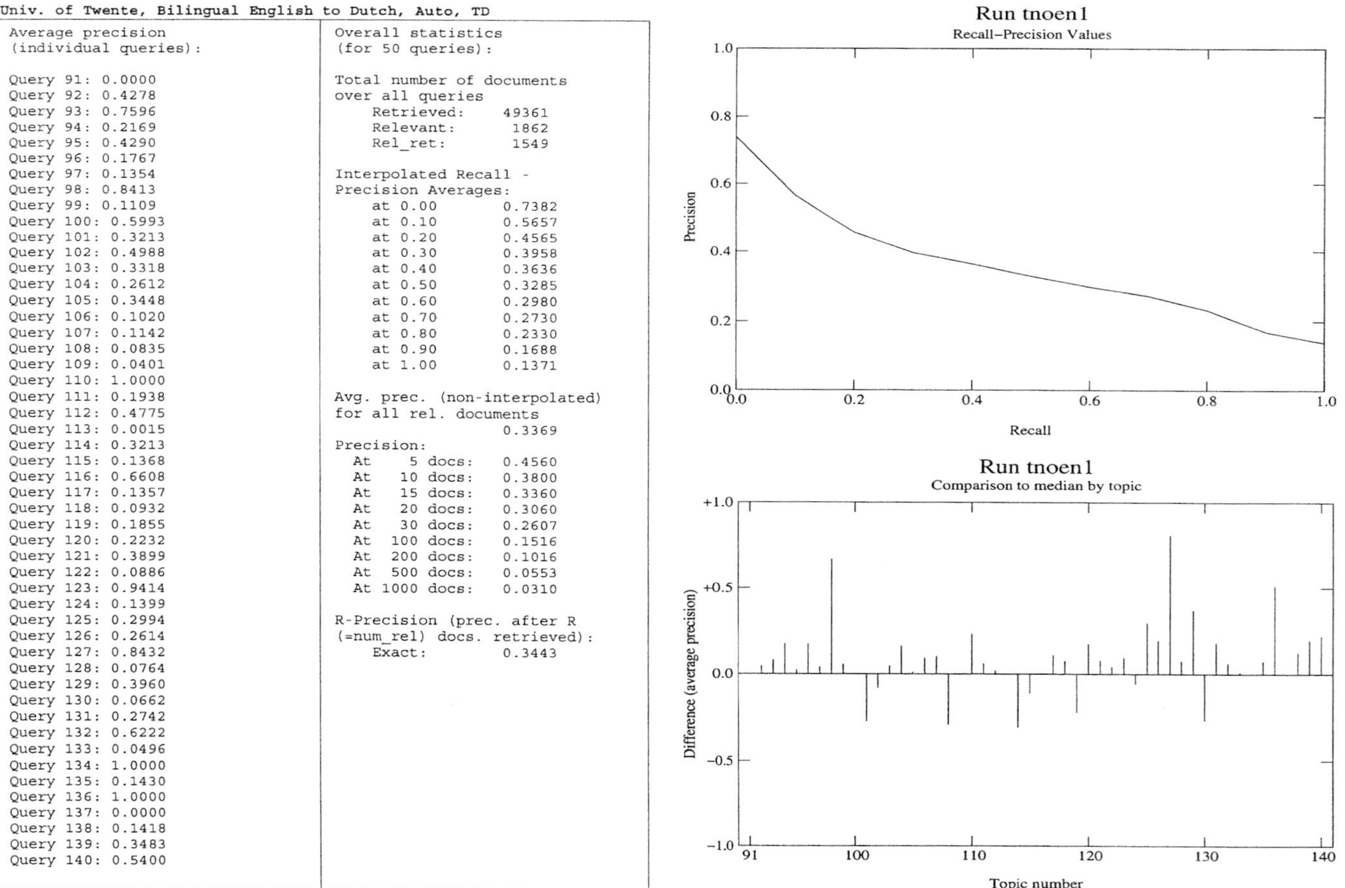

```
Univ. of Twente, Bilingual English to Dutch, Auto, TD

Average precision              Overall statistics
(individual queries):          (for 50 queries):

Query 91: 0.0000               Total number of documents
Query 92: 0.4278               over all queries
Query 93: 0.7596                   Retrieved:    49361
Query 94: 0.2169                   Relevant:      1862
Query 95: 0.4290                   Rel_ret:       1549
Query 96: 0.1767
Query 97: 0.1354               Interpolated Recall -
Query 98: 0.8413               Precision Averages:
Query 99: 0.1109                   at 0.00        0.7382
Query 100: 0.5993                  at 0.10        0.5657
Query 101: 0.3213                  at 0.20        0.4565
Query 102: 0.4988                  at 0.30        0.3958
Query 103: 0.3318                  at 0.40        0.3636
Query 104: 0.2612                  at 0.50        0.3285
Query 105: 0.3448                  at 0.60        0.2980
Query 106: 0.1020                  at 0.70        0.2730
Query 107: 0.1142                  at 0.80        0.2330
Query 108: 0.0835                  at 0.90        0.1688
Query 109: 0.0401                  at 1.00        0.1371
Query 110: 1.0000
Query 111: 0.1938              Avg. prec. (non-interpolated)
Query 112: 0.4775              for all rel. documents
Query 113: 0.0015                                 0.3369
Query 114: 0.3213              Precision:
Query 115: 0.1368                At    5 docs:    0.4560
Query 116: 0.6608                At   10 docs:    0.3800
Query 117: 0.1357                At   15 docs:    0.3360
Query 118: 0.0932                At   20 docs:    0.3060
Query 119: 0.1855                At   30 docs:    0.2607
Query 120: 0.2232                At  100 docs:    0.1516
Query 121: 0.3899                At  200 docs:    0.1016
Query 122: 0.0886                At  500 docs:    0.0553
Query 123: 0.9414                At 1000 docs:    0.0310
Query 124: 0.1399
Query 125: 0.2994              R-Precision (prec. after R
Query 126: 0.2614              (=num_rel) docs. retrieved):
Query 127: 0.8432                  Exact:         0.3443
Query 128: 0.0764
Query 129: 0.3960
Query 130: 0.0662
Query 131: 0.2742
Query 132: 0.6222
Query 133: 0.0496
Query 134: 1.0000
Query 135: 0.1430
Query 136: 1.0000
Query 137: 0.0000
Query 138: 0.1418
Query 139: 0.3483
Query 140: 0.5400
```

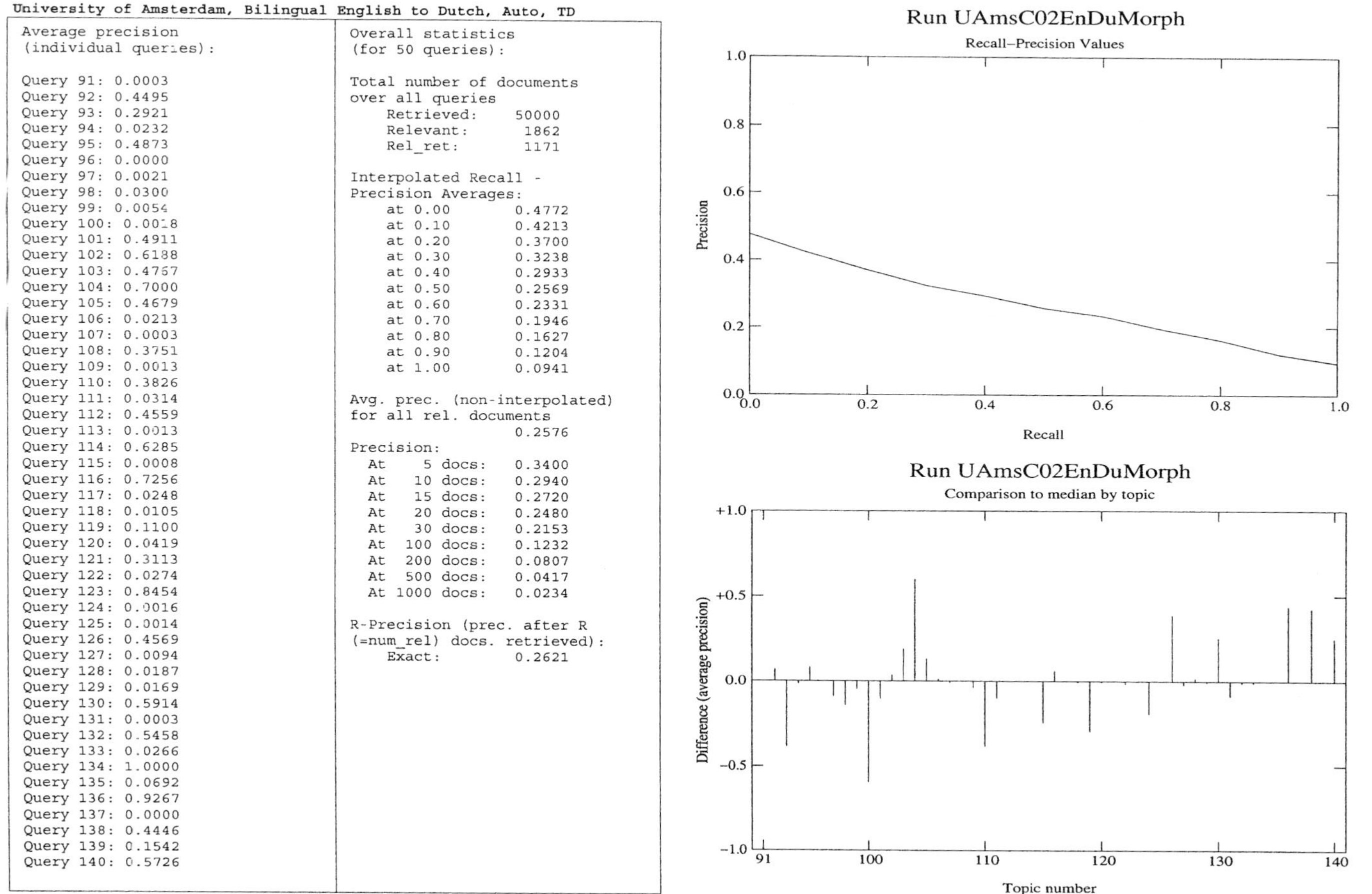

University of Amsterdam, Bilingual English to Dutch, Auto, TD

Average precision (individual queries):	Overall statistics (for 50 queries):
Query 91: 0.0003	Total number of documents over all queries
Query 92: 0.4495	Retrieved: 50000
Query 93: 0.2921	Relevant: 1862
Query 94: 0.0232	Rel_ret: 1171
Query 95: 0.4873	
Query 96: 0.0000	Interpolated Recall - Precision Averages:
Query 97: 0.0021	at 0.00 0.4772
Query 98: 0.0300	at 0.10 0.4213
Query 99: 0.0054	at 0.20 0.3700
Query 100: 0.0018	at 0.30 0.3238
Query 101: 0.4911	at 0.40 0.2933
Query 102: 0.6188	at 0.50 0.2569
Query 103: 0.4767	at 0.60 0.2331
Query 104: 0.7000	at 0.70 0.1946
Query 105: 0.4679	at 0.80 0.1627
Query 106: 0.0213	at 0.90 0.1204
Query 107: 0.0003	at 1.00 0.0941
Query 108: 0.3751	
Query 109: 0.0013	Avg. prec. (non-interpolated) for all rel. documents 0.2576
Query 110: 0.3826	
Query 111: 0.0314	Precision:
Query 112: 0.4559	At 5 docs: 0.3400
Query 113: 0.0013	At 10 docs: 0.2940
Query 114: 0.6285	At 15 docs: 0.2720
Query 115: 0.0008	At 20 docs: 0.2480
Query 116: 0.7256	At 30 docs: 0.2153
Query 117: 0.0248	At 100 docs: 0.1232
Query 118: 0.0105	At 200 docs: 0.0807
Query 119: 0.1100	At 500 docs: 0.0417
Query 120: 0.0419	At 1000 docs: 0.0234
Query 121: 0.3113	
Query 122: 0.0274	R-Precision (prec. after R (=num_rel) docs. retrieved):
Query 123: 0.8454	Exact: 0.2621
Query 124: 0.0016	
Query 125: 0.0014	
Query 126: 0.4569	
Query 127: 0.0094	
Query 128: 0.0187	
Query 129: 0.0169	
Query 130: 0.5914	
Query 131: 0.0003	
Query 132: 0.5458	
Query 133: 0.0266	
Query 134: 1.0000	
Query 135: 0.0692	
Query 136: 0.9267	
Query 137: 0.0000	
Query 138: 0.4446	
Query 139: 0.1542	
Query 140: 0.5726	

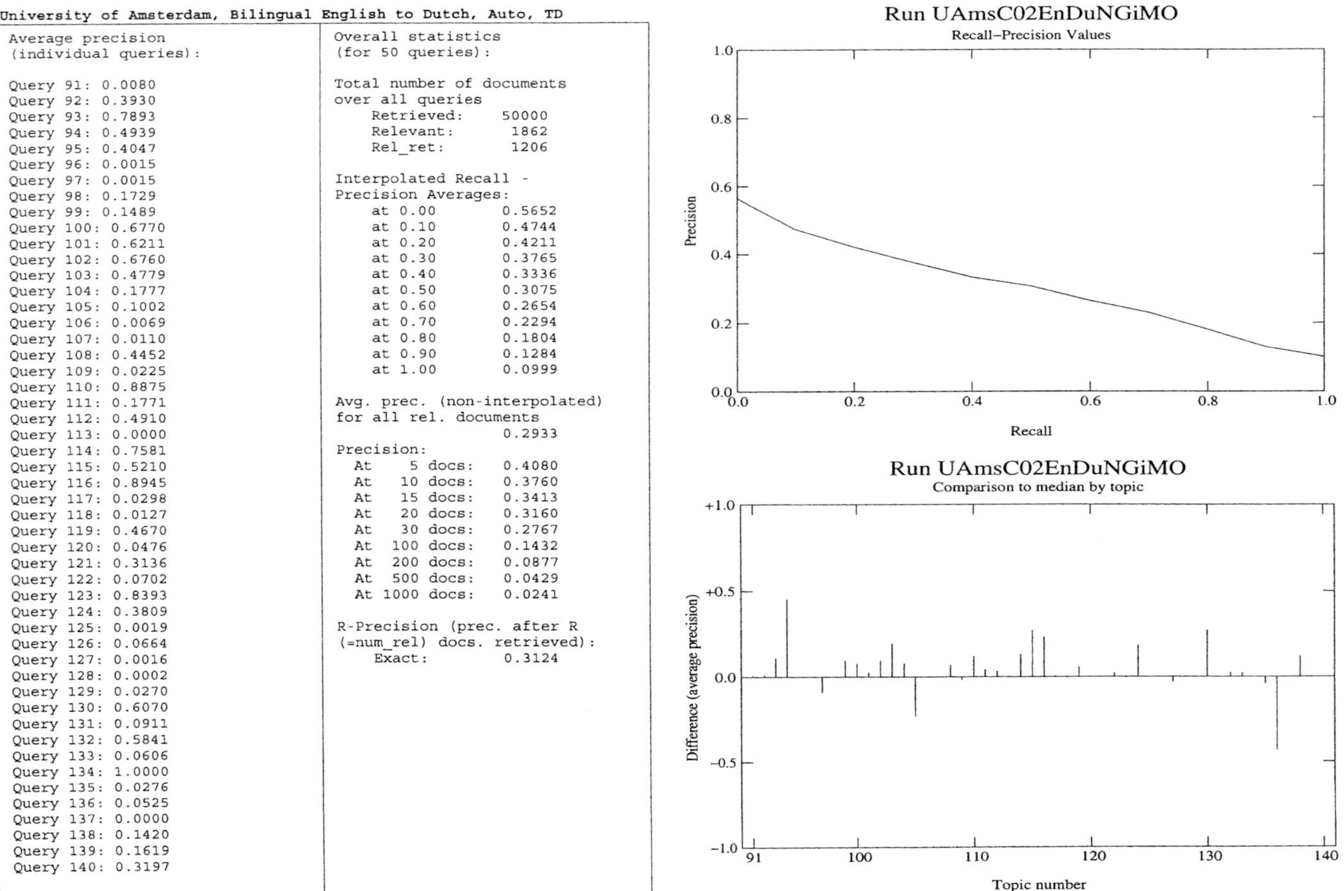

University of Amsterdam, Bilingual English to Dutch, Auto, TD

```
Average precision              Overall statistics
(individual queries):          (for 50 queries):

Query 91: 0.0080               Total number of documents
Query 92: 0.3930               over all queries
Query 93: 0.7893                   Retrieved:    50000
Query 94: 0.4939                   Relevant:      1862
Query 95: 0.4047                   Rel_ret:       1206
Query 96: 0.0015
Query 97: 0.0015               Interpolated Recall -
Query 98: 0.1729               Precision Averages:
Query 99: 0.1489                   at 0.00       0.5652
Query 100: 0.6770                  at 0.10       0.4744
Query 101: 0.6211                  at 0.20       0.4211
Query 102: 0.6760                  at 0.30       0.3765
Query 103: 0.4779                  at 0.40       0.3336
Query 104: 0.1777                  at 0.50       0.3075
Query 105: 0.1002                  at 0.60       0.2654
Query 106: 0.0069                  at 0.70       0.2294
Query 107: 0.0110                  at 0.80       0.1804
Query 108: 0.4452                  at 0.90       0.1284
Query 109: 0.0225                  at 1.00       0.0999
Query 110: 0.8875
Query 111: 0.1771              Avg. prec. (non-interpolated)
Query 112: 0.4910              for all rel. documents
Query 113: 0.0000                                0.2933
Query 114: 0.7581              Precision:
Query 115: 0.5210                At    5 docs:   0.4080
Query 116: 0.8945                At   10 docs:   0.3760
Query 117: 0.0298                At   15 docs:   0.3413
Query 118: 0.0127                At   20 docs:   0.3160
Query 119: 0.4670                At   30 docs:   0.2767
Query 120: 0.0476                At  100 docs:   0.1432
Query 121: 0.3136                At  200 docs:   0.0877
Query 122: 0.0702                At  500 docs:   0.0429
Query 123: 0.8393                At 1000 docs:   0.0241
Query 124: 0.3809
Query 125: 0.0019              R-Precision (prec. after R
Query 126: 0.0664              (=num_rel) docs. retrieved):
Query 127: 0.0016                  Exact:        0.3124
Query 128: 0.0002
Query 129: 0.0270
Query 130: 0.6070
Query 131: 0.0911
Query 132: 0.5841
Query 133: 0.0606
Query 134: 1.0000
Query 135: 0.0276
Query 136: 0.0525
Query 137: 0.0000
Query 138: 0.1420
Query 139: 0.1619
Query 140: 0.3197
```

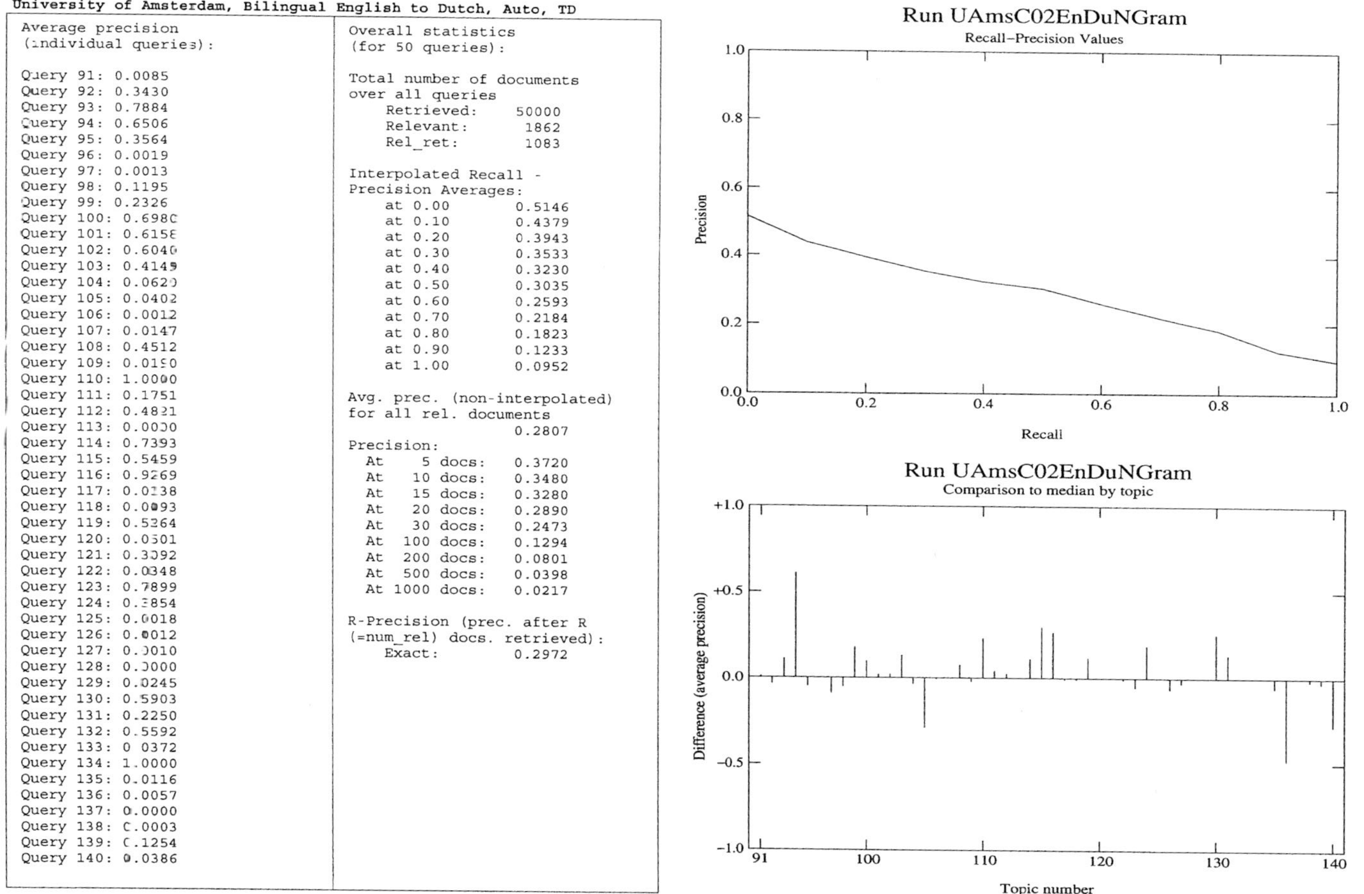

University of Amsterdam, Bilingual English to Dutch, Auto, TD

Average precision (individual queries):

Query	Average precision
Query 91:	0.0085
Query 92:	0.3430
Query 93:	0.7884
Query 94:	0.6506
Query 95:	0.3564
Query 96:	0.0019
Query 97:	0.0013
Query 98:	0.1195
Query 99:	0.2326
Query 100:	0.6980
Query 101:	0.6158
Query 102:	0.6040
Query 103:	0.4149
Query 104:	0.0620
Query 105:	0.0402
Query 106:	0.0012
Query 107:	0.0147
Query 108:	0.4512
Query 109:	0.0190
Query 110:	1.0000
Query 111:	0.1751
Query 112:	0.4821
Query 113:	0.0000
Query 114:	0.7393
Query 115:	0.5459
Query 116:	0.9269
Query 117:	0.0138
Query 118:	0.0093
Query 119:	0.5264
Query 120:	0.0501
Query 121:	0.3092
Query 122:	0.0348
Query 123:	0.7899
Query 124:	0.3854
Query 125:	0.0018
Query 126:	0.0012
Query 127:	0.0010
Query 128:	0.0000
Query 129:	0.0245
Query 130:	0.5903
Query 131:	0.2250
Query 132:	0.5592
Query 133:	0.0372
Query 134:	1.0000
Query 135:	0.0116
Query 136:	0.0057
Query 137:	0.0000
Query 138:	0.0003
Query 139:	0.1254
Query 140:	0.0386

Overall statistics (for 50 queries):

Total number of documents over all queries

Retrieved:	50000
Relevant:	1862
Rel_ret:	1083

Interpolated Recall - Precision Averages:

at 0.00	0.5146
at 0.10	0.4379
at 0.20	0.3943
at 0.30	0.3533
at 0.40	0.3230
at 0.50	0.3035
at 0.60	0.2593
at 0.70	0.2184
at 0.80	0.1823
at 0.90	0.1233
at 1.00	0.0952

Avg. prec. (non-interpolated) for all rel. documents 0.2807

Precision:

At 5 docs:	0.3720
At 10 docs:	0.3480
At 15 docs:	0.3280
At 20 docs:	0.2890
At 30 docs:	0.2473
At 100 docs:	0.1294
At 200 docs:	0.0801
At 500 docs:	0.0398
At 1000 docs:	0.0217

R-Precision (prec. after R (=num_rel) docs. retrieved):
Exact: 0.2972

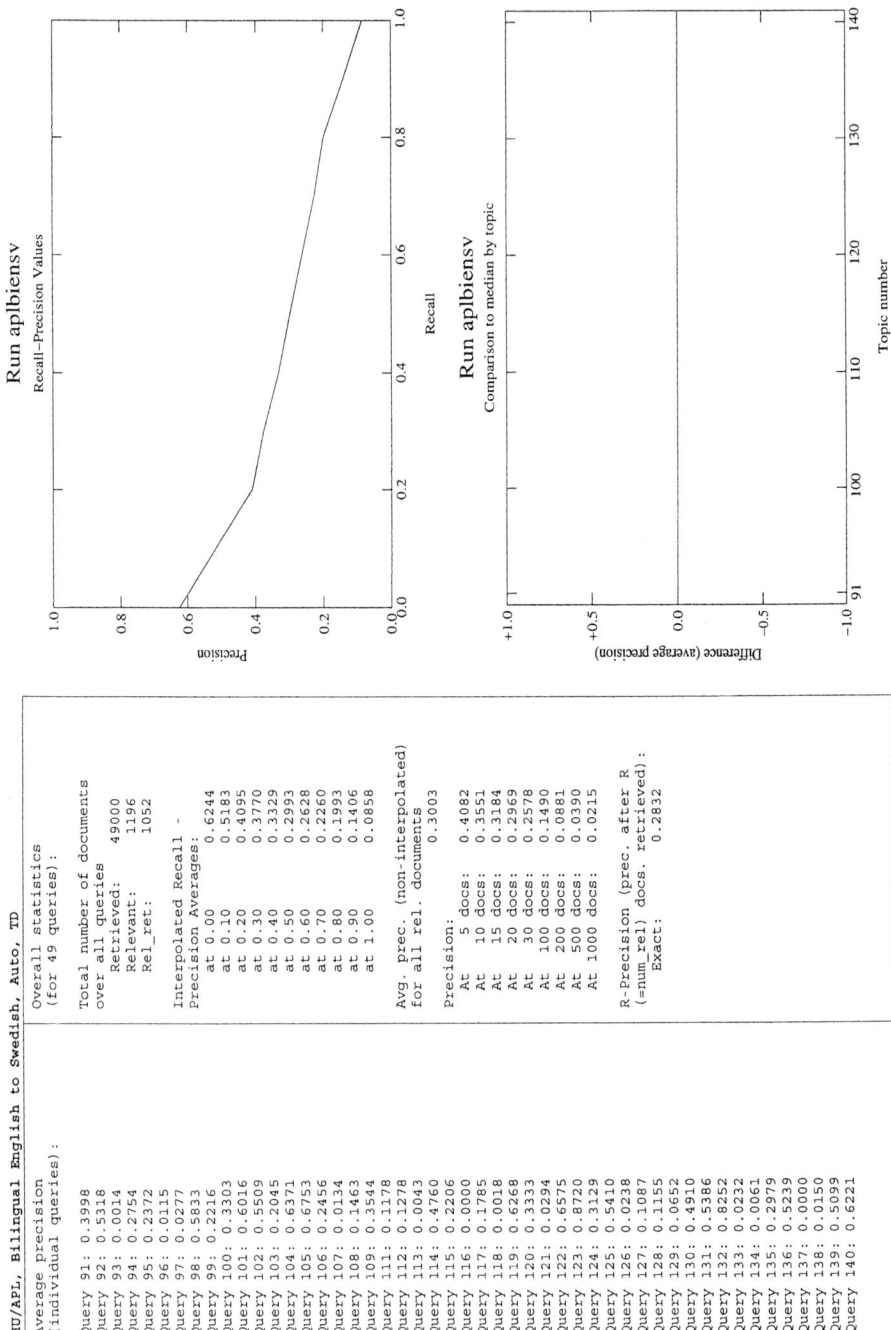

JHU/APL, Bilingual English to Swedish, Auto, TD

```
Average precision                Overall statistics
(individual queries):            (for 49 queries):

Query 91: 0.3998                 Total number of documents
Query 92: 0.5318                 over all queries
Query 93: 0.0014                     Retrieved:    49000
Query 94: 0.2754                     Relevant:      1196
Query 95: 0.2372                     Rel_ret:       1052
Query 96: 0.0115
Query 97: 0.0277                 Interpolated Recall -
Query 98: 0.5833                 Precision Averages:
Query 99: 0.2216                     at 0.00       0.6244
Query 100: 0.3303                    at 0.10       0.5183
Query 101: 0.6016                    at 0.20       0.4095
Query 102: 0.5509                    at 0.30       0.3770
Query 103: 0.2045                    at 0.40       0.3329
Query 104: 0.6371                    at 0.50       0.2993
Query 105: 0.6753                    at 0.60       0.2628
Query 106: 0.2456                    at 0.70       0.2260
Query 107: 0.0134                    at 0.80       0.1993
Query 108: 0.1463                    at 0.90       0.1406
Query 109: 0.3544                    at 1.00       0.0858
Query 111: 0.1178
Query 112: 0.1278                Avg. prec. (non-interpolated)
Query 113: 0.0043                for all rel. documents
Query 114: 0.4760                                  0.3003
Query 115: 0.2206                Precision:
Query 116: 0.0000                  At    5 docs:   0.4082
Query 117: 0.1785                  At   10 docs:   0.3551
Query 118: 0.0018                  At   15 docs:   0.3184
Query 119: 0.6268                  At   20 docs:   0.2969
Query 120: 0.3333                  At   30 docs:   0.2578
Query 121: 0.0294                  At  100 docs:   0.1490
Query 122: 0.6575                  At  200 docs:   0.0881
Query 123: 0.8720                  At  500 docs:   0.0390
Query 124: 0.3129                  At 1000 docs:   0.0215
Query 125: 0.5410
Query 126: 0.0238                R-Precision (prec. after R
Query 127: 0.1087                (=num_rel) docs. retrieved):
Query 128: 0.1155                    Exact:        0.2832
Query 129: 0.0652
Query 130: 0.4910
Query 131: 0.5386
Query 132: 0.8252
Query 133: 0.0232
Query 134: 0.0061
Query 135: 0.2979
Query 136: 0.5239
Query 137: 0.0000
Query 138: 0.0150
Query 139: 0.5099
Query 140: 0.6221
```

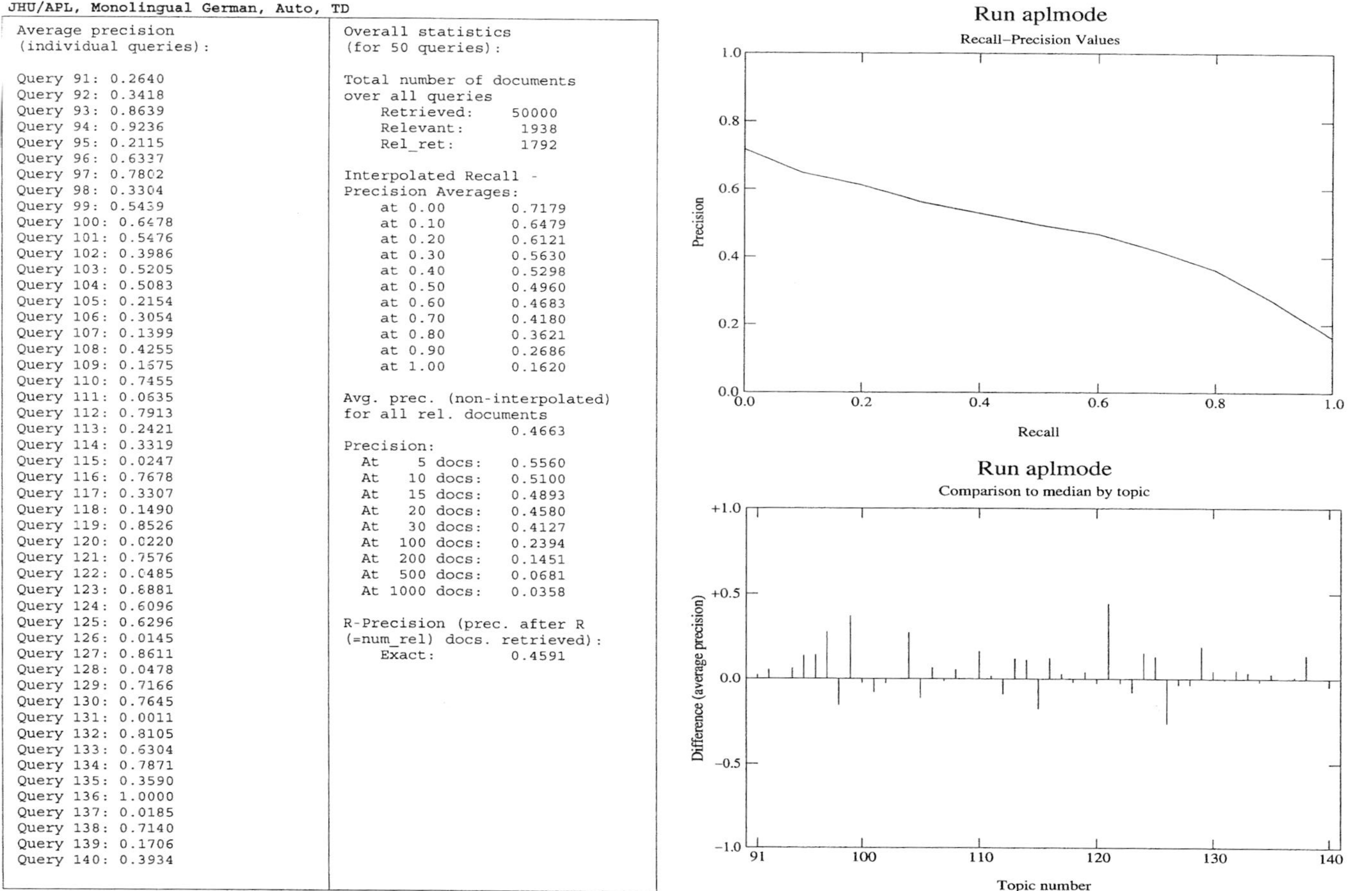

JHU/APL, Monolingual German, Auto, TD

Average precision (individual queries):	Overall statistics (for 50 queries):
Query 91: 0.2640	Total number of documents over all queries
Query 92: 0.3418	Retrieved: 50000
Query 93: 0.8639	Relevant: 1938
Query 94: 0.9236	Rel_ret: 1792
Query 95: 0.2115	
Query 96: 0.6337	Interpolated Recall - Precision Averages:
Query 97: 0.7802	at 0.00 0.7179
Query 98: 0.3304	at 0.10 0.6479
Query 99: 0.5439	at 0.20 0.6121
Query 100: 0.6478	at 0.30 0.5630
Query 101: 0.5476	at 0.40 0.5298
Query 102: 0.3986	at 0.50 0.4960
Query 103: 0.5205	at 0.60 0.4683
Query 104: 0.5083	at 0.70 0.4180
Query 105: 0.2154	at 0.80 0.3621
Query 106: 0.3054	at 0.90 0.2686
Query 107: 0.1399	at 1.00 0.1620
Query 108: 0.4255	
Query 109: 0.1675	Avg. prec. (non-interpolated) for all rel. documents 0.4663
Query 110: 0.7455	
Query 111: 0.0635	Precision:
Query 112: 0.7913	At 5 docs: 0.5560
Query 113: 0.2421	At 10 docs: 0.5100
Query 114: 0.3319	At 15 docs: 0.4893
Query 115: 0.0247	At 20 docs: 0.4580
Query 116: 0.7678	At 30 docs: 0.4127
Query 117: 0.3307	At 100 docs: 0.2394
Query 118: 0.1490	At 200 docs: 0.1451
Query 119: 0.8526	At 500 docs: 0.0681
Query 120: 0.0220	At 1000 docs: 0.0358
Query 121: 0.7576	
Query 122: 0.0485	R-Precision (prec. after R (=num_rel) docs. retrieved):
Query 123: 0.8881	Exact: 0.4591
Query 124: 0.6096	
Query 125: 0.6296	
Query 126: 0.0145	
Query 127: 0.8611	
Query 128: 0.0478	
Query 129: 0.7166	
Query 130: 0.7645	
Query 131: 0.0011	
Query 132: 0.8105	
Query 133: 0.6304	
Query 134: 0.7871	
Query 135: 0.3590	
Query 136: 1.0000	
Query 137: 0.0185	
Query 138: 0.7140	
Query 139: 0.1706	
Query 140: 0.3934	

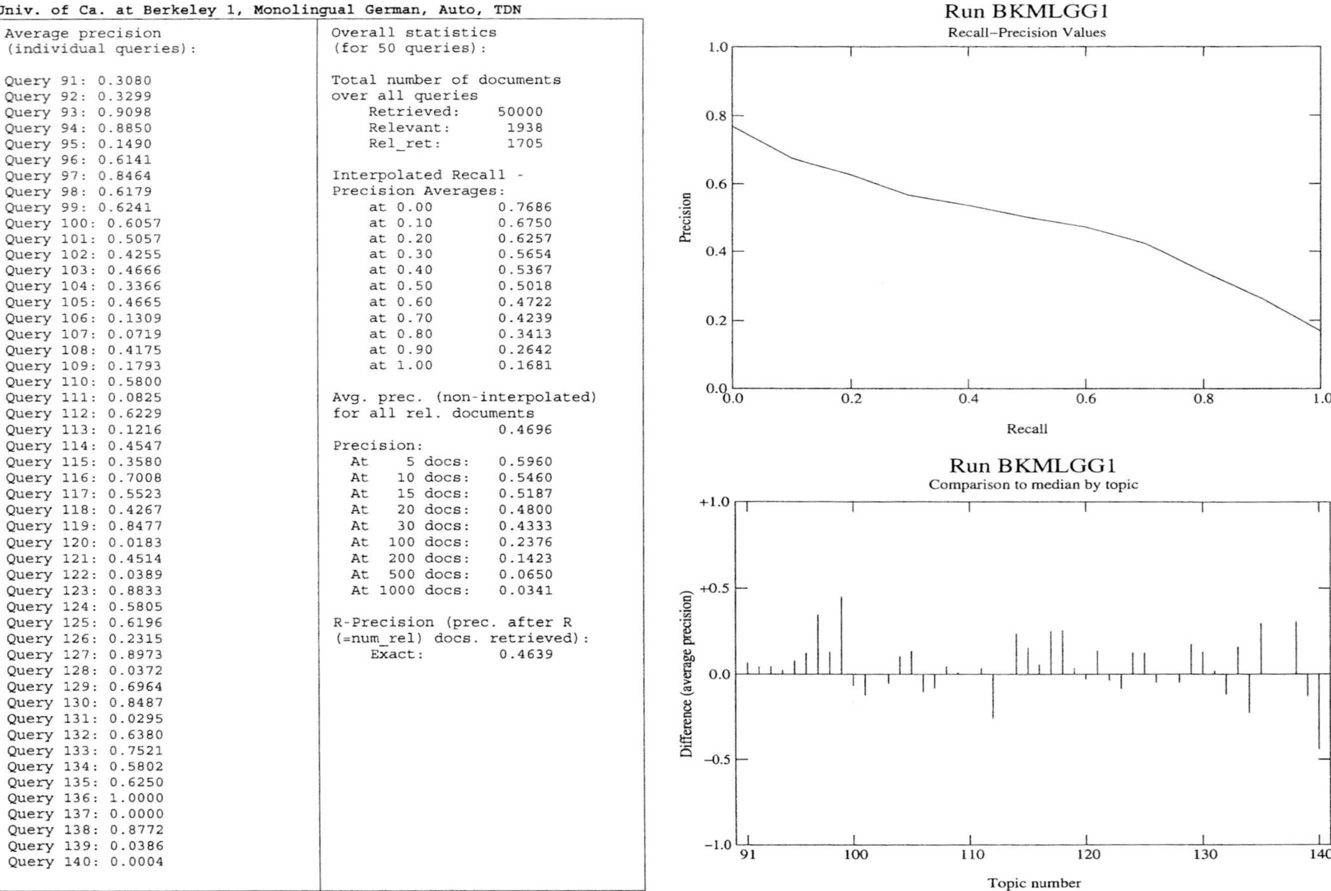

Univ. of Ca. at Berkeley 1, Monolingual German, Auto, TDN

```
Average precision          Overall statistics
(individual queries):      (for 50 queries):

Query 91: 0.3080           Total number of documents
Query 92: 0.3299           over all queries
Query 93: 0.9098               Retrieved:     50000
Query 94: 0.8850               Relevant:       1938
Query 95: 0.1490               Rel_ret:        1705
Query 96: 0.6141
Query 97: 0.8464           Interpolated Recall -
Query 98: 0.6179           Precision Averages:
Query 99: 0.6241               at 0.00        0.7686
Query 100: 0.6057              at 0.10        0.6750
Query 101: 0.5057              at 0.20        0.6257
Query 102: 0.4255              at 0.30        0.5654
Query 103: 0.4666              at 0.40        0.5367
Query 104: 0.3366              at 0.50        0.5018
Query 105: 0.4665              at 0.60        0.4722
Query 106: 0.1309              at 0.70        0.4239
Query 107: 0.0719              at 0.80        0.3413
Query 108: 0.4175              at 0.90        0.2642
Query 109: 0.1793              at 1.00        0.1681
Query 110: 0.5800
Query 111: 0.0825          Avg. prec. (non-interpolated)
Query 112: 0.6229          for all rel. documents
Query 113: 0.1216                             0.4696
Query 114: 0.4547          Precision:
Query 115: 0.3580            At    5 docs:    0.5960
Query 116: 0.7008            At   10 docs:    0.5460
Query 117: 0.5523            At   15 docs:    0.5187
Query 118: 0.4267            At   20 docs:    0.4800
Query 119: 0.8477            At   30 docs:    0.4333
Query 120: 0.0183            At  100 docs:    0.2376
Query 121: 0.4514            At  200 docs:    0.1423
Query 122: 0.0389            At  500 docs:    0.0650
Query 123: 0.8833            At 1000 docs:    0.0341
Query 124: 0.5805
Query 125: 0.6196          R-Precision (prec. after R
Query 126: 0.2315          (=num_rel) docs. retrieved):
Query 127: 0.8973              Exact:         0.4639
Query 128: 0.0372
Query 129: 0.6964
Query 130: 0.8487
Query 131: 0.0295
Query 132: 0.6380
Query 133: 0.7521
Query 134: 0.5802
Query 135: 0.6250
Query 136: 1.0000
Query 137: 0.0000
Query 138: 0.8772
Query 139: 0.0386
Query 140: 0.0004
```

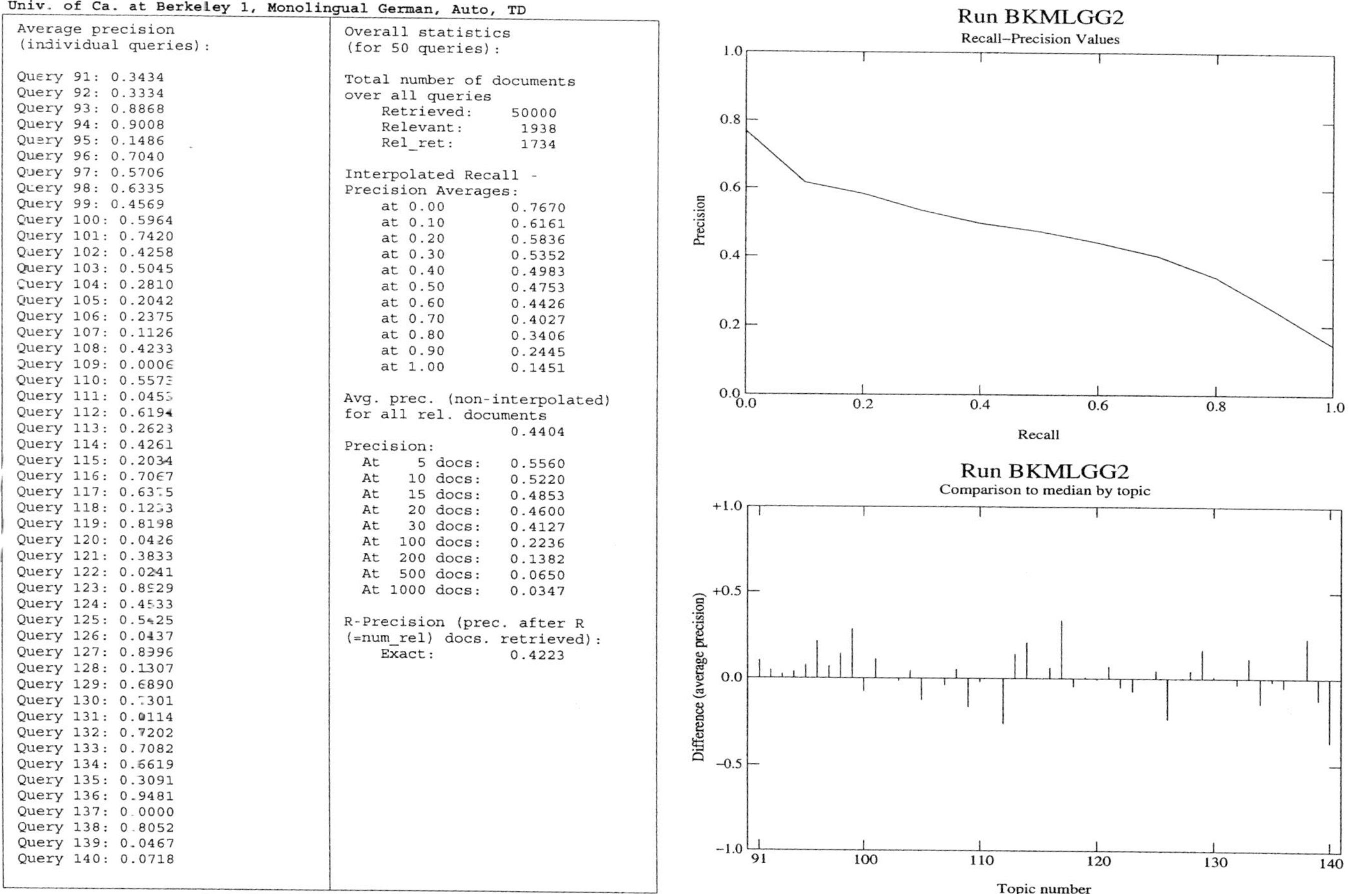

Univ. of Ca. at Berkeley 1, Monolingual German, Auto, TD

Average precision (individual queries):

Query	Average precision
Query 91:	0.3434
Query 92:	0.3334
Query 93:	0.8868
Query 94:	0.9008
Query 95:	0.1486
Query 96:	0.7040
Query 97:	0.5706
Query 98:	0.6335
Query 99:	0.4569
Query 100:	0.5964
Query 101:	0.7420
Query 102:	0.4258
Query 103:	0.5045
Query 104:	0.2810
Query 105:	0.2042
Query 106:	0.2375
Query 107:	0.1126
Query 108:	0.4233
Query 109:	0.0006
Query 110:	0.5573
Query 111:	0.0453
Query 112:	0.6194
Query 113:	0.2623
Query 114:	0.4261
Query 115:	0.2034
Query 116:	0.7067
Query 117:	0.6375
Query 118:	0.1233
Query 119:	0.8198
Query 120:	0.0426
Query 121:	0.3833
Query 122:	0.0241
Query 123:	0.8929
Query 124:	0.4533
Query 125:	0.5425
Query 126:	0.0437
Query 127:	0.8996
Query 128:	0.1307
Query 129:	0.6890
Query 130:	0.7301
Query 131:	0.0114
Query 132:	0.7202
Query 133:	0.7082
Query 134:	0.6619
Query 135:	0.3091
Query 136:	0.9481
Query 137:	0.0000
Query 138:	0.8052
Query 139:	0.0467
Query 140:	0.0718

Overall statistics (for 50 queries):

Total number of documents over all queries

Retrieved:	50000
Relevant:	1938
Rel_ret:	1734

Interpolated Recall - Precision Averages:

at 0.00	0.7670
at 0.10	0.6161
at 0.20	0.5836
at 0.30	0.5352
at 0.40	0.4983
at 0.50	0.4753
at 0.60	0.4426
at 0.70	0.4027
at 0.80	0.3406
at 0.90	0.2445
at 1.00	0.1451

Avg. prec. (non-interpolated) for all rel. documents 0.4404

Precision:

At 5 docs:	0.5560
At 10 docs:	0.5220
At 15 docs:	0.4853
At 20 docs:	0.4600
At 30 docs:	0.4127
At 100 docs:	0.2236
At 200 docs:	0.1382
At 500 docs:	0.0650
At 1000 docs:	0.0347

R-Precision (prec. after R (=num_rel) docs. retrieved):
Exact: 0.4223

Univ. of Ca. at Berkeley 2, Monolingual German, Auto, TD

```
Average precision                 Overall statistics
(individual queries):             (for 50 queries):

Query 91: 0.3621                  Total number of documents
Query 92: 0.3485                  over all queries
Query 93: 0.8289                      Retrieved:     50000
Query 94: 0.8517                      Relevant:       1938
Query 95: 0.1451                      Rel_ret:        1807
Query 96: 0.4631
Query 97: 0.6372                  Interpolated Recall -
Query 98: 0.6020                  Precision Averages:
Query 99: 0.1539                      at 0.00        0.8308
Query 100: 0.7521                     at 0.10        0.7349
Query 101: 0.8186                     at 0.20        0.6989
Query 102: 0.4513                     at 0.30        0.6489
Query 103: 0.6436                     at 0.40        0.6043
Query 104: 0.1337                     at 0.50        0.5675
Query 105: 0.6399                     at 0.60        0.5202
Query 106: 0.3993                     at 0.70        0.4705
Query 107: 0.6462                     at 0.80        0.3898
Query 108: 0.4214                     at 0.90        0.2884
Query 109: 0.5214                     at 1.00        0.1735
Query 110: 0.4726
Query 111: 0.0428                 Avg. prec. (non-interpolated)
Query 112: 0.9250                 for all rel. documents
Query 113: 0.1856                                    0.5234
Query 114: 0.3313                 Precision:
Query 115: 0.5274                   At    5 docs:    0.6480
Query 116: 0.6150                   At   10 docs:    0.5800
Query 117: 0.5123                   At   15 docs:    0.5467
Query 118: 0.1200                   At   20 docs:    0.5130
Query 119: 0.8392                   At   30 docs:    0.4573
Query 120: 0.0382                   At  100 docs:    0.2562
Query 121: 0.3131                   At  200 docs:    0.1532
Query 122: 0.4119                   At  500 docs:    0.0691
Query 123: 0.9821                   At 1000 docs:    0.0361
Query 124: 0.4723
Query 125: 0.4944                 R-Precision (prec. after R
Query 126: 0.2901                 (=num_rel) docs. retrieved):
Query 127: 0.9090                     Exact:         0.5218
Query 128: 0.0745
Query 129: 0.6987
Query 130: 0.7174
Query 131: 0.0518
Query 132: 0.7160
Query 133: 0.5812
Query 134: 0.8231
Query 135: 0.7314
Query 136: 1.0000
Query 137: 1.0000
Query 138: 0.5224
Query 139: 0.3670
Query 140: 0.5857
```

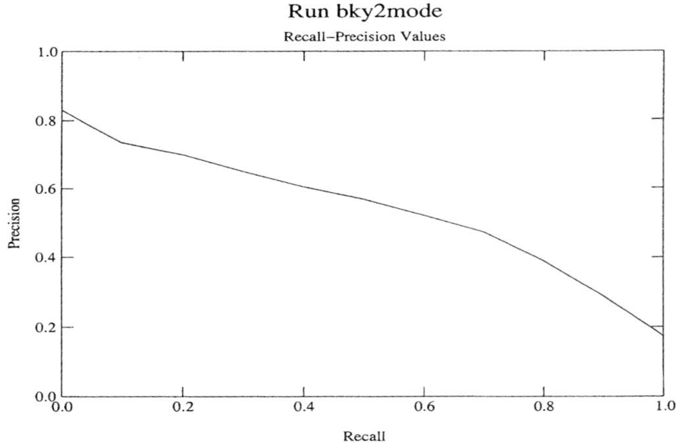

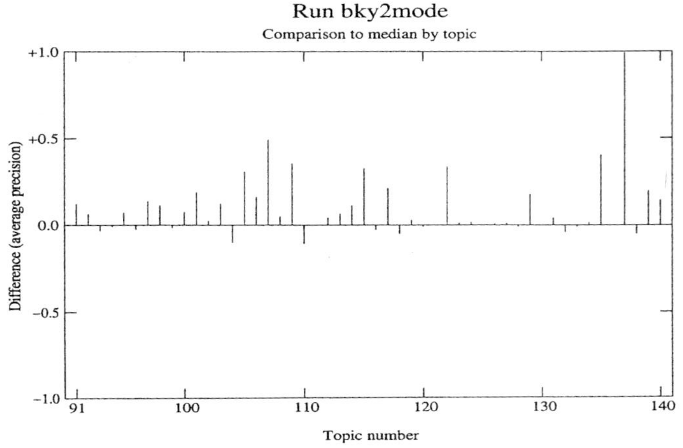

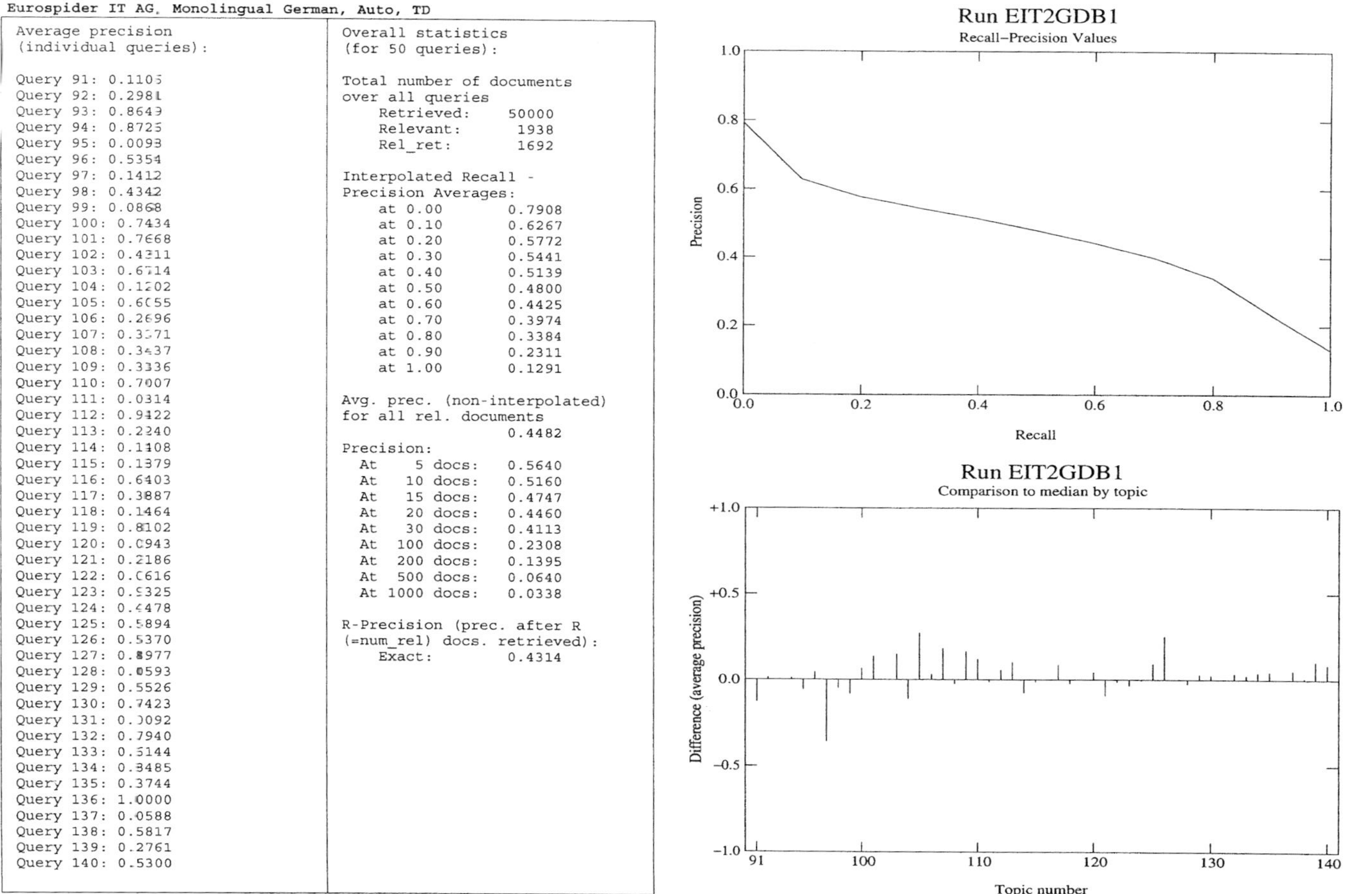

Eurospider IT AG, Monolingual German, Auto, TD

```
Average precision                 Overall statistics
(individual queries):             (for 50 queries):

Query 91: 0.1105                  Total number of documents
Query 92: 0.2981                  over all queries
Query 93: 0.8649                      Retrieved:     50000
Query 94: 0.8725                      Relevant:       1938
Query 95: 0.0093                      Rel_ret:        1692
Query 96: 0.5354
Query 97: 0.1412                  Interpolated Recall -
Query 98: 0.4342                  Precision Averages:
Query 99: 0.0868                      at 0.00        0.7908
Query 100: 0.7434                     at 0.10        0.6267
Query 101: 0.7668                     at 0.20        0.5772
Query 102: 0.4311                     at 0.30        0.5441
Query 103: 0.6714                     at 0.40        0.5139
Query 104: 0.1202                     at 0.50        0.4800
Query 105: 0.6055                     at 0.60        0.4425
Query 106: 0.2696                     at 0.70        0.3974
Query 107: 0.3371                     at 0.80        0.3384
Query 108: 0.3437                     at 0.90        0.2311
Query 109: 0.3336                     at 1.00        0.1291
Query 110: 0.7007
Query 111: 0.0314                 Avg. prec. (non-interpolated)
Query 112: 0.9422                 for all rel. documents
Query 113: 0.2240                                    0.4482
Query 114: 0.1108                 Precision:
Query 115: 0.1379                   At    5 docs:    0.5640
Query 116: 0.6403                   At   10 docs:    0.5160
Query 117: 0.3887                   At   15 docs:    0.4747
Query 118: 0.1464                   At   20 docs:    0.4460
Query 119: 0.8102                   At   30 docs:    0.4113
Query 120: 0.0943                   At  100 docs:    0.2308
Query 121: 0.2186                   At  200 docs:    0.1395
Query 122: 0.0616                   At  500 docs:    0.0640
Query 123: 0.9325                   At 1000 docs:    0.0338
Query 124: 0.4478
Query 125: 0.5894                 R-Precision (prec. after R
Query 126: 0.5370                 (=num_rel) docs. retrieved):
Query 127: 0.8977                     Exact:         0.4314
Query 128: 0.0593
Query 129: 0.5526
Query 130: 0.7423
Query 131: 0.0092
Query 132: 0.7940
Query 133: 0.5144
Query 134: 0.3485
Query 135: 0.3744
Query 136: 1.0000
Query 137: 0.0588
Query 138: 0.5817
Query 139: 0.2761
Query 140: 0.5300
```

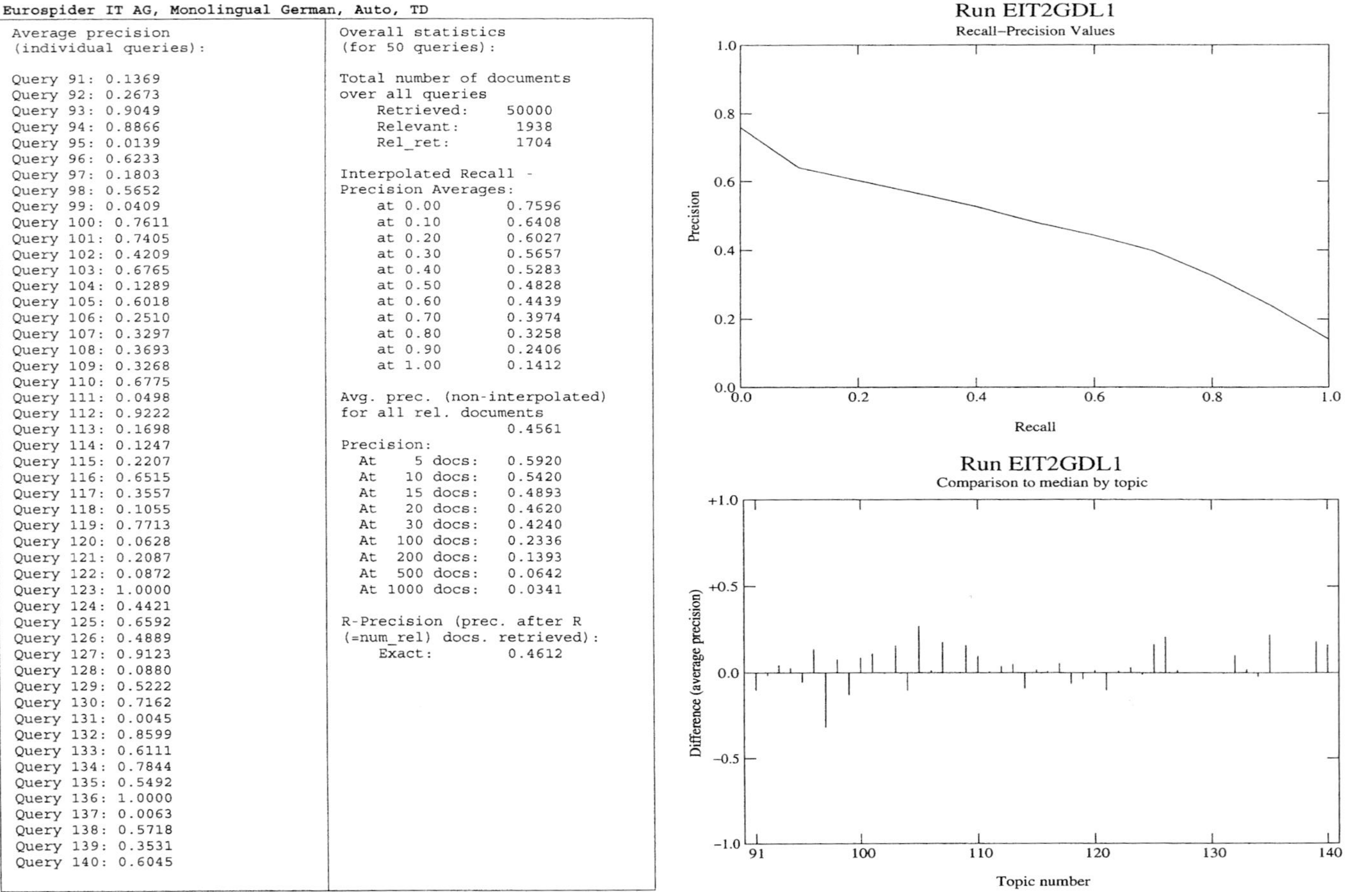

Eurospider IT AG, Monolingual German, Auto, TD

```
Average precision                 Overall statistics
(individual queries):             (for 50 queries):

Query 91: 0.1369                  Total number of documents
Query 92: 0.2673                  over all queries
Query 93: 0.9049                      Retrieved:    50000
Query 94: 0.8866                      Relevant:      1938
Query 95: 0.0139                      Rel_ret:       1704
Query 96: 0.6233
Query 97: 0.1803                  Interpolated Recall -
Query 98: 0.5652                  Precision Averages:
Query 99: 0.0409                      at 0.00       0.7596
Query 100: 0.7611                     at 0.10       0.6408
Query 101: 0.7405                     at 0.20       0.6027
Query 102: 0.4209                     at 0.30       0.5657
Query 103: 0.6765                     at 0.40       0.5283
Query 104: 0.1289                     at 0.50       0.4828
Query 105: 0.6018                     at 0.60       0.4439
Query 106: 0.2510                     at 0.70       0.3974
Query 107: 0.3297                     at 0.80       0.3258
Query 108: 0.3693                     at 0.90       0.2406
Query 109: 0.3268                     at 1.00       0.1412
Query 110: 0.6775
Query 111: 0.0498                 Avg. prec. (non-interpolated)
Query 112: 0.9222                 for all rel. documents
Query 113: 0.1698                                   0.4561
Query 114: 0.1247                 Precision:
Query 115: 0.2207                   At    5 docs:   0.5920
Query 116: 0.6515                   At   10 docs:   0.5420
Query 117: 0.3557                   At   15 docs:   0.4893
Query 118: 0.1055                   At   20 docs:   0.4620
Query 119: 0.7713                   At   30 docs:   0.4240
Query 120: 0.0628                   At  100 docs:   0.2336
Query 121: 0.2087                   At  200 docs:   0.1393
Query 122: 0.0872                   At  500 docs:   0.0642
Query 123: 1.0000                   At 1000 docs:   0.0341
Query 124: 0.4421
Query 125: 0.6592                 R-Precision (prec. after R
Query 126: 0.4889                 (=num_rel) docs. retrieved):
Query 127: 0.9123                     Exact:        0.4612
Query 128: 0.0880
Query 129: 0.5222
Query 130: 0.7162
Query 131: 0.0045
Query 132: 0.8599
Query 133: 0.6111
Query 134: 0.7844
Query 135: 0.5492
Query 136: 1.0000
Query 137: 0.0063
Query 138: 0.5718
Query 139: 0.3531
Query 140: 0.6045
```

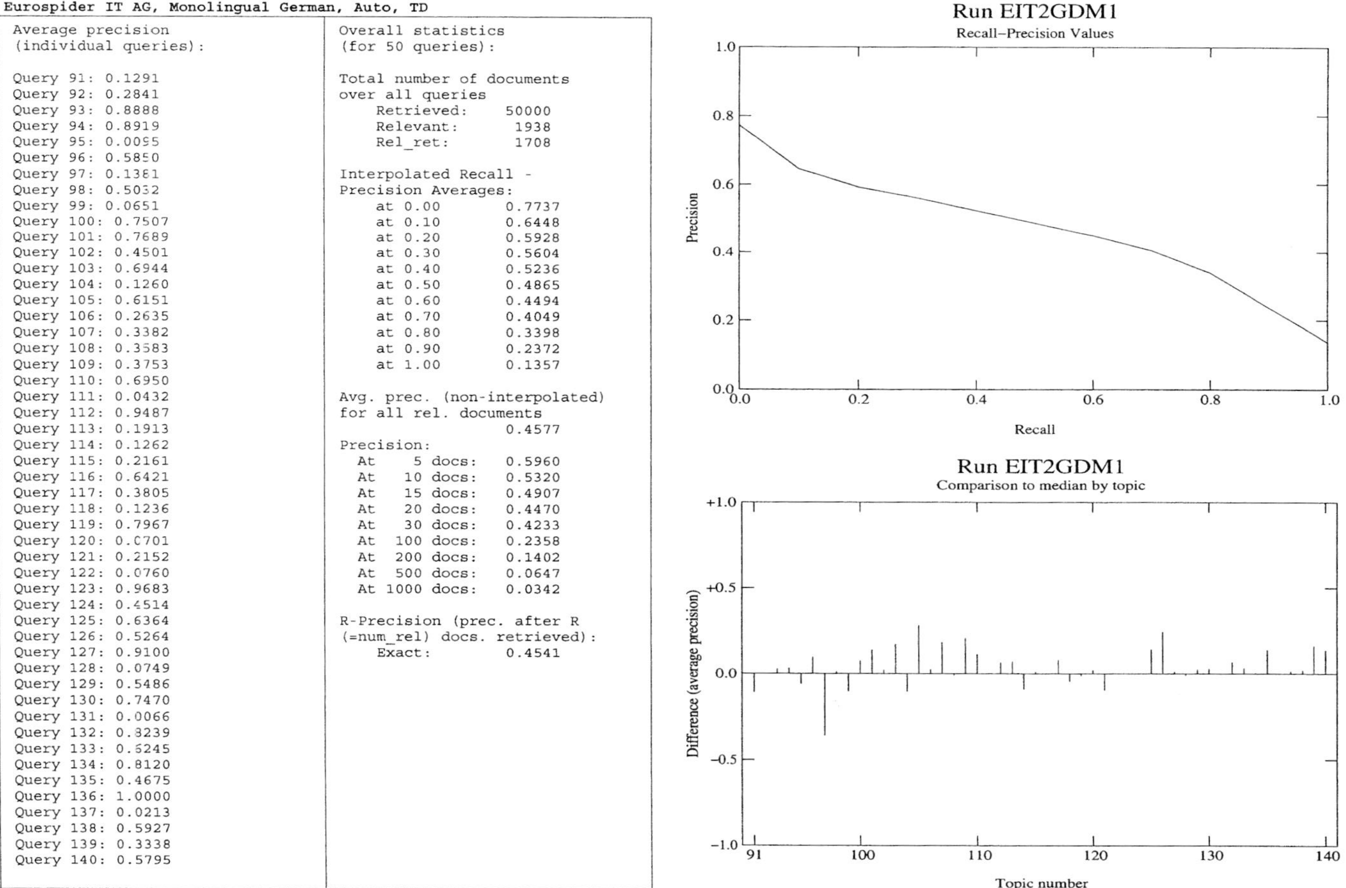

Eurospider IT AG, Monolingual German, Auto, TD

```
Average precision                 Overall statistics
(individual queries):             (for 50 queries):

Query 91: 0.1291                  Total number of documents
Query 92: 0.2841                  over all queries
Query 93: 0.8888                      Retrieved:    50000
Query 94: 0.8919                      Relevant:      1938
Query 95: 0.0095                      Rel_ret:       1708
Query 96: 0.5850
Query 97: 0.1381                  Interpolated Recall -
Query 98: 0.5032                  Precision Averages:
Query 99: 0.0651                      at 0.00        0.7737
Query 100: 0.7507                     at 0.10        0.6448
Query 101: 0.7689                     at 0.20        0.5928
Query 102: 0.4501                     at 0.30        0.5604
Query 103: 0.6944                     at 0.40        0.5236
Query 104: 0.1260                     at 0.50        0.4865
Query 105: 0.6151                     at 0.60        0.4494
Query 106: 0.2635                     at 0.70        0.4049
Query 107: 0.3382                     at 0.80        0.3398
Query 108: 0.3583                     at 0.90        0.2372
Query 109: 0.3753                     at 1.00        0.1357
Query 110: 0.6950
Query 111: 0.0432                 Avg. prec. (non-interpolated)
Query 112: 0.9487                 for all rel. documents
Query 113: 0.1913                                    0.4577
Query 114: 0.1262                 Precision:
Query 115: 0.2161                   At    5 docs:    0.5960
Query 116: 0.6421                   At   10 docs:    0.5320
Query 117: 0.3805                   At   15 docs:    0.4907
Query 118: 0.1236                   At   20 docs:    0.4470
Query 119: 0.7967                   At   30 docs:    0.4233
Query 120: 0.0701                   At  100 docs:    0.2358
Query 121: 0.2152                   At  200 docs:    0.1402
Query 122: 0.0760                   At  500 docs:    0.0647
Query 123: 0.9683                   At 1000 docs:    0.0342
Query 124: 0.4514
Query 125: 0.6364                 R-Precision (prec. after R
Query 126: 0.5264                 (=num_rel) docs. retrieved):
Query 127: 0.9100                     Exact:         0.4541
Query 128: 0.0749
Query 129: 0.5486
Query 130: 0.7470
Query 131: 0.0066
Query 132: 0.3239
Query 133: 0.5245
Query 134: 0.8120
Query 135: 0.4675
Query 136: 1.0000
Query 137: 0.0213
Query 138: 0.5927
Query 139: 0.3338
Query 140: 0.5795
```

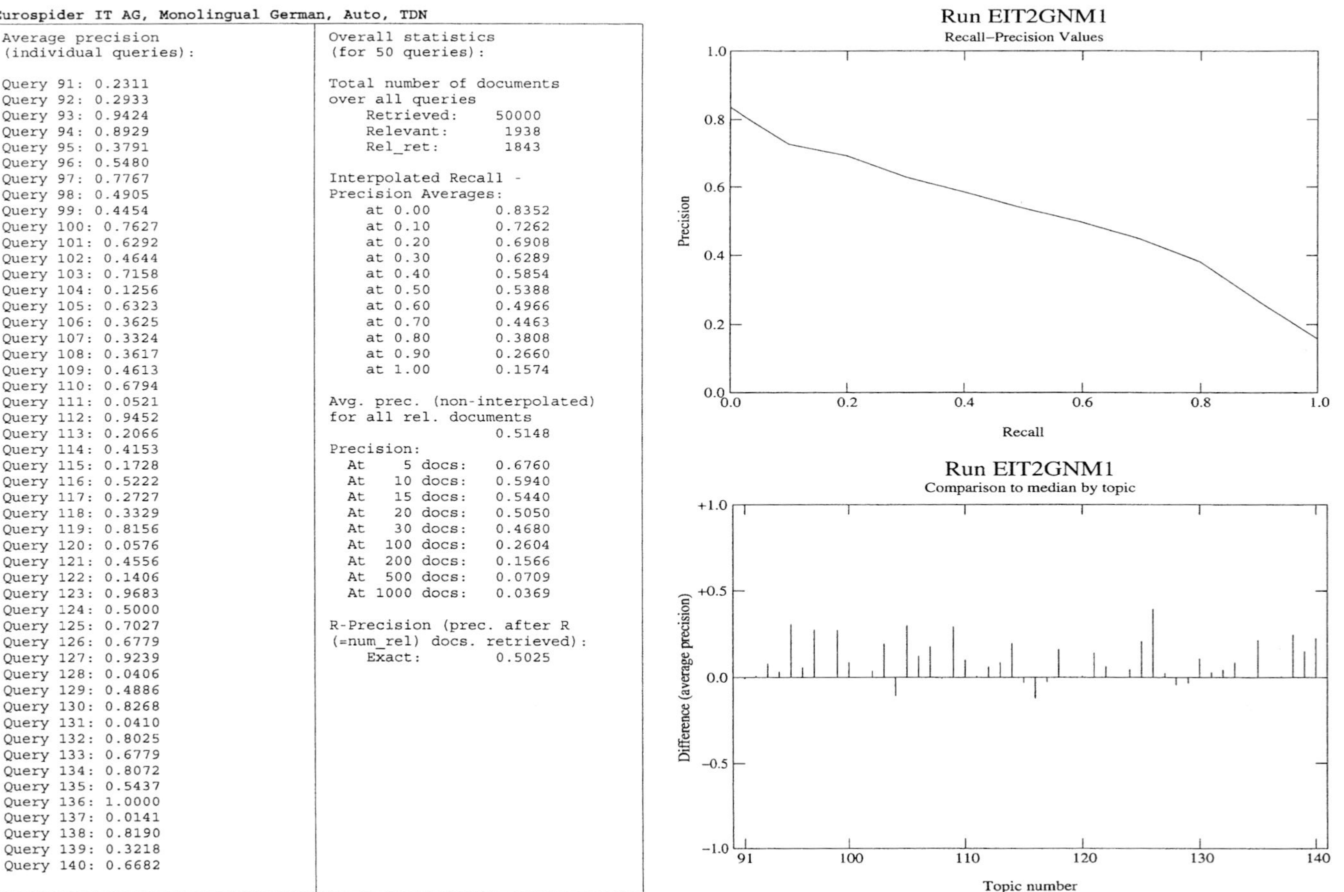

Eurospider IT AG, Monolingual German, Auto, TDN

```
Average precision                 Overall statistics
(individual queries):             (for 50 queries):

Query 91: 0.2311                  Total number of documents
Query 92: 0.2933                  over all queries
Query 93: 0.9424                      Retrieved:    50000
Query 94: 0.8929                      Relevant:      1938
Query 95: 0.3791                      Rel_ret:       1843
Query 96: 0.5480
Query 97: 0.7767                  Interpolated Recall -
Query 98: 0.4905                  Precision Averages:
Query 99: 0.4454                      at 0.00        0.8352
Query 100: 0.7627                     at 0.10        0.7262
Query 101: 0.6292                     at 0.20        0.6908
Query 102: 0.4644                     at 0.30        0.6289
Query 103: 0.7158                     at 0.40        0.5854
Query 104: 0.1256                     at 0.50        0.5388
Query 105: 0.6323                     at 0.60        0.4966
Query 106: 0.3625                     at 0.70        0.4463
Query 107: 0.3324                     at 0.80        0.3808
Query 108: 0.3617                     at 0.90        0.2660
Query 109: 0.4613                     at 1.00        0.1574
Query 110: 0.6794
Query 111: 0.0521                 Avg. prec. (non-interpolated)
Query 112: 0.9452                 for all rel. documents
Query 113: 0.2066                                    0.5148
Query 114: 0.4153                 Precision:
Query 115: 0.1728                   At    5 docs:    0.6760
Query 116: 0.5222                   At   10 docs:    0.5940
Query 117: 0.2727                   At   15 docs:    0.5440
Query 118: 0.3329                   At   20 docs:    0.5050
Query 119: 0.8156                   At   30 docs:    0.4680
Query 120: 0.0576                   At  100 docs:    0.2604
Query 121: 0.4556                   At  200 docs:    0.1566
Query 122: 0.1406                   At  500 docs:    0.0709
Query 123: 0.9683                   At 1000 docs:    0.0369
Query 124: 0.5000
Query 125: 0.7027                 R-Precision (prec. after R
Query 126: 0.6779                 (=num_rel) docs. retrieved):
Query 127: 0.9239                     Exact:         0.5025
Query 128: 0.0406
Query 129: 0.4886
Query 130: 0.8268
Query 131: 0.0410
Query 132: 0.8025
Query 133: 0.6779
Query 134: 0.8072
Query 135: 0.5437
Query 136: 1.0000
Query 137: 0.0141
Query 138: 0.8190
Query 139: 0.3218
Query 140: 0.6682
```

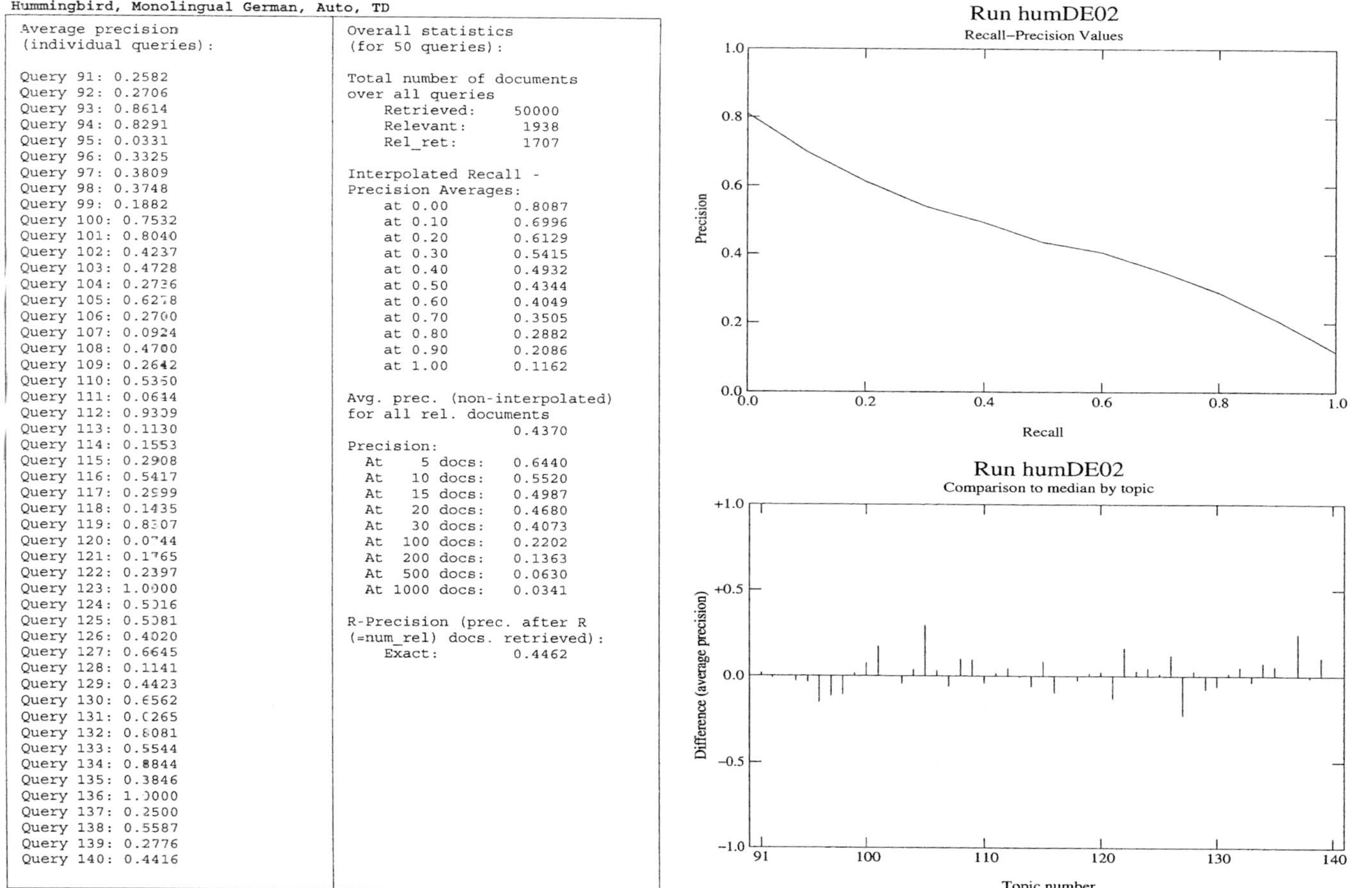

Hummingbird, Monolingual German, Auto, TD

Average precision (individual queries):

Query	Average precision
Query 91:	0.2582
Query 92:	0.2706
Query 93:	0.8614
Query 94:	0.8291
Query 95:	0.0331
Query 96:	0.3325
Query 97:	0.3809
Query 98:	0.3748
Query 99:	0.1882
Query 100:	0.7532
Query 101:	0.8040
Query 102:	0.4237
Query 103:	0.4728
Query 104:	0.2736
Query 105:	0.6278
Query 106:	0.2700
Query 107:	0.0924
Query 108:	0.4700
Query 109:	0.2642
Query 110:	0.5350
Query 111:	0.0644
Query 112:	0.9339
Query 113:	0.1130
Query 114:	0.1553
Query 115:	0.2908
Query 116:	0.5417
Query 117:	0.2599
Query 118:	0.1435
Query 119:	0.8307
Query 120:	0.0744
Query 121:	0.1765
Query 122:	0.2397
Query 123:	1.0000
Query 124:	0.5016
Query 125:	0.5081
Query 126:	0.4020
Query 127:	0.6645
Query 128:	0.1141
Query 129:	0.4423
Query 130:	0.6562
Query 131:	0.0265
Query 132:	0.8081
Query 133:	0.5544
Query 134:	0.8844
Query 135:	0.3846
Query 136:	1.0000
Query 137:	0.2500
Query 138:	0.5587
Query 139:	0.2776
Query 140:	0.4416

Overall statistics (for 50 queries):

Total number of documents over all queries

Retrieved:	50000
Relevant:	1938
Rel_ret:	1707

Interpolated Recall - Precision Averages:

at 0.00	0.8087
at 0.10	0.6996
at 0.20	0.6129
at 0.30	0.5415
at 0.40	0.4932
at 0.50	0.4344
at 0.60	0.4049
at 0.70	0.3505
at 0.80	0.2882
at 0.90	0.2086
at 1.00	0.1162

Avg. prec. (non-interpolated) for all rel. documents
0.4370

Precision:

At 5 docs:	0.6440
At 10 docs:	0.5520
At 15 docs:	0.4987
At 20 docs:	0.4680
At 30 docs:	0.4073
At 100 docs:	0.2202
At 200 docs:	0.1363
At 500 docs:	0.0630
At 1000 docs:	0.0341

R-Precision (prec. after R (=num_rel) docs. retrieved):
Exact: 0.4462

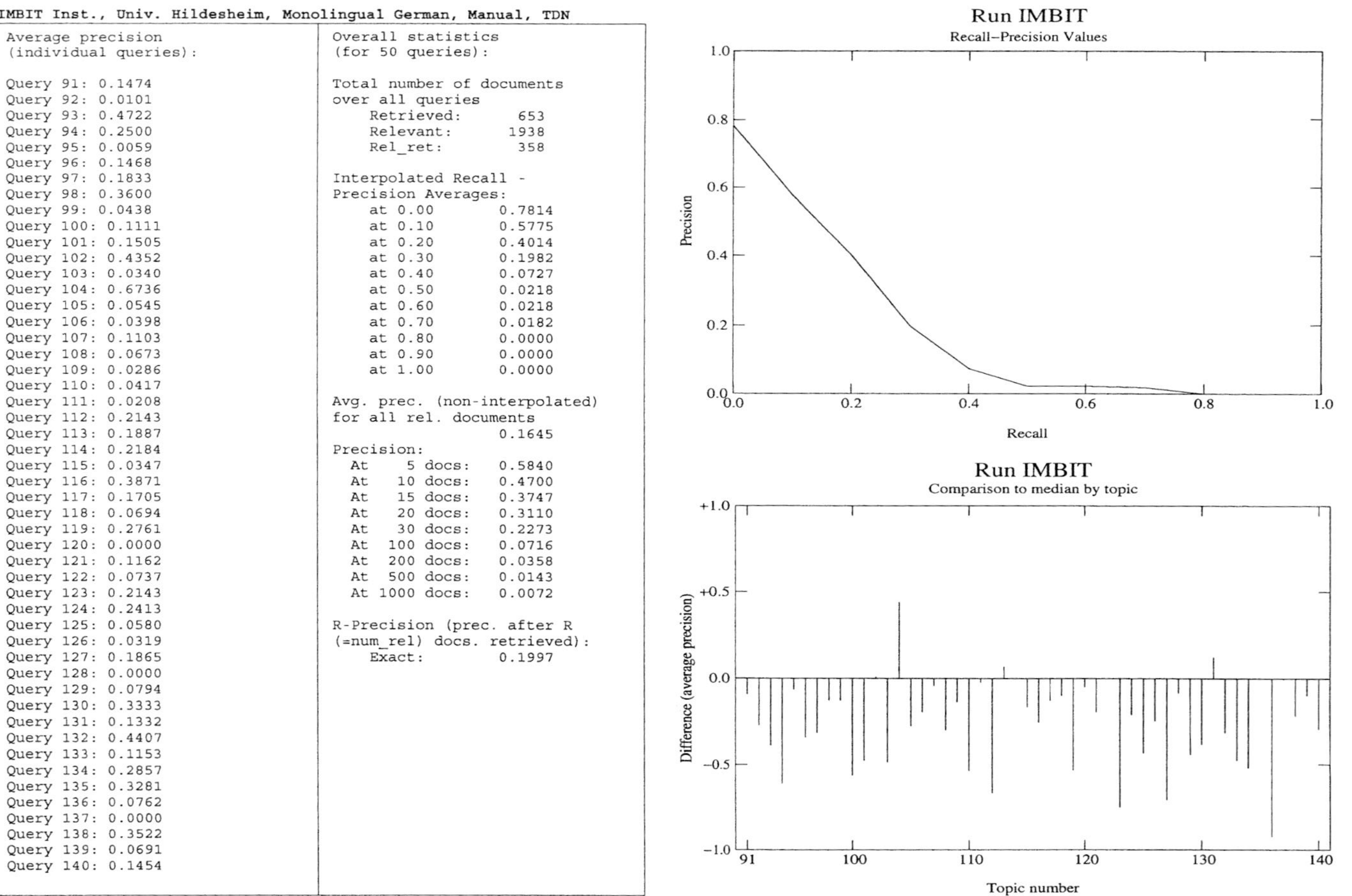

IMBIT Inst., Univ. Hildesheim, Monolingual German, Manual, TDN

Average precision (individual queries):	Overall statistics (for 50 queries):
Query 91: 0.1474	Total number of documents over all queries
Query 92: 0.0101	Retrieved: 653
Query 93: 0.4722	Relevant: 1938
Query 94: 0.2500	Rel_ret: 358
Query 95: 0.0059	
Query 96: 0.1468	Interpolated Recall - Precision Averages:
Query 97: 0.1833	at 0.00 0.7814
Query 98: 0.3600	at 0.10 0.5775
Query 99: 0.0438	at 0.20 0.4014
Query 100: 0.1111	at 0.30 0.1982
Query 101: 0.1505	at 0.40 0.0727
Query 102: 0.4352	at 0.50 0.0218
Query 103: 0.0340	at 0.60 0.0218
Query 104: 0.6736	at 0.70 0.0182
Query 105: 0.0545	at 0.80 0.0000
Query 106: 0.0398	at 0.90 0.0000
Query 107: 0.1103	at 1.00 0.0000
Query 108: 0.0673	
Query 109: 0.0286	Avg. prec. (non-interpolated) for all rel. documents
Query 110: 0.0417	0.1645
Query 111: 0.0208	
Query 112: 0.2143	Precision:
Query 113: 0.1887	At 5 docs: 0.5840
Query 114: 0.2184	At 10 docs: 0.4700
Query 115: 0.0347	At 15 docs: 0.3747
Query 116: 0.3871	At 20 docs: 0.3110
Query 117: 0.1705	At 30 docs: 0.2273
Query 118: 0.0694	At 100 docs: 0.0716
Query 119: 0.2761	At 200 docs: 0.0358
Query 120: 0.0000	At 500 docs: 0.0143
Query 121: 0.1162	At 1000 docs: 0.0072
Query 122: 0.0737	
Query 123: 0.2143	R-Precision (prec. after R (=num_rel) docs. retrieved):
Query 124: 0.2413	Exact: 0.1997
Query 125: 0.0580	
Query 126: 0.0319	
Query 127: 0.1865	
Query 128: 0.0000	
Query 129: 0.0794	
Query 130: 0.3333	
Query 131: 0.1332	
Query 132: 0.4407	
Query 133: 0.1153	
Query 134: 0.2857	
Query 135: 0.3281	
Query 136: 0.0762	
Query 137: 0.0000	
Query 138: 0.3522	
Query 139: 0.0691	
Query 140: 0.1454	

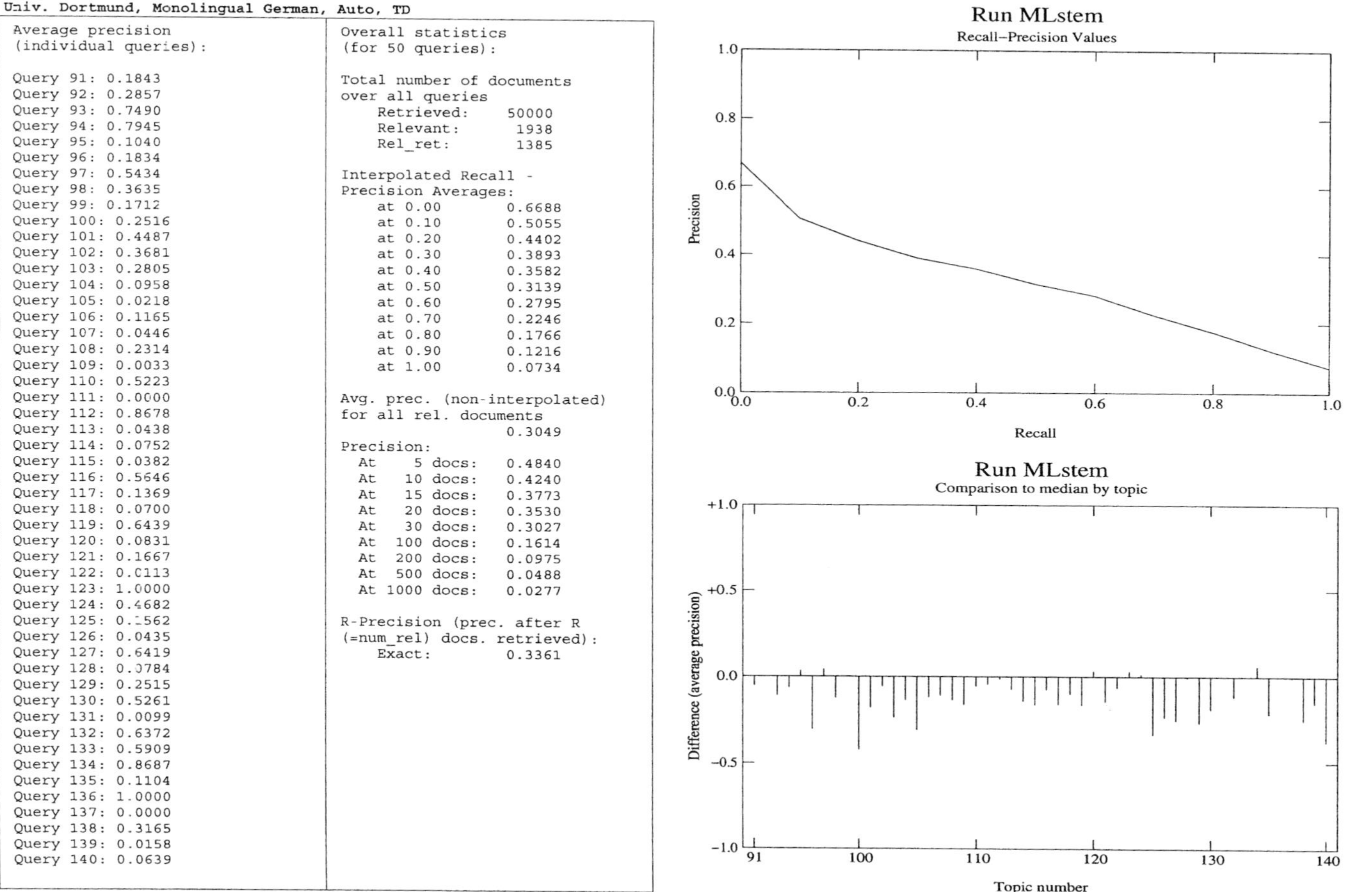

Univ. Dortmund, Monolingual German, Auto, TD

Average precision (individual queries):	Overall statistics (for 50 queries):
Query 91: 0.1843	Total number of documents over all queries
Query 92: 0.2857	Retrieved: 50000
Query 93: 0.7490	Relevant: 1938
Query 94: 0.7945	Rel_ret: 1385
Query 95: 0.1040	
Query 96: 0.1834	Interpolated Recall - Precision Averages:
Query 97: 0.5434	at 0.00 0.6688
Query 98: 0.3635	at 0.10 0.5055
Query 99: 0.1712	at 0.20 0.4402
Query 100: 0.2516	at 0.30 0.3893
Query 101: 0.4487	at 0.40 0.3582
Query 102: 0.3681	at 0.50 0.3139
Query 103: 0.2805	at 0.60 0.2795
Query 104: 0.0958	at 0.70 0.2246
Query 105: 0.0218	at 0.80 0.1766
Query 106: 0.1165	at 0.90 0.1216
Query 107: 0.0446	at 1.00 0.0734
Query 108: 0.2314	
Query 109: 0.0033	Avg. prec. (non-interpolated) for all rel. documents
Query 110: 0.5223	0.3049
Query 111: 0.0000	Precision:
Query 112: 0.8678	At 5 docs: 0.4840
Query 113: 0.0438	At 10 docs: 0.4240
Query 114: 0.0752	At 15 docs: 0.3773
Query 115: 0.0382	At 20 docs: 0.3530
Query 116: 0.5646	At 30 docs: 0.3027
Query 117: 0.1369	At 100 docs: 0.1614
Query 118: 0.0700	At 200 docs: 0.0975
Query 119: 0.6439	At 500 docs: 0.0488
Query 120: 0.0831	At 1000 docs: 0.0277
Query 121: 0.1667	
Query 122: 0.0113	R-Precision (prec. after R (=num_rel) docs. retrieved):
Query 123: 1.0000	Exact: 0.3361
Query 124: 0.4682	
Query 125: 0.1562	
Query 126: 0.0435	
Query 127: 0.6419	
Query 128: 0.0784	
Query 129: 0.2515	
Query 130: 0.5261	
Query 131: 0.0099	
Query 132: 0.6372	
Query 133: 0.5909	
Query 134: 0.8687	
Query 135: 0.1104	
Query 136: 1.0000	
Query 137: 0.0000	
Query 138: 0.3165	
Query 139: 0.0158	
Query 140: 0.0639	

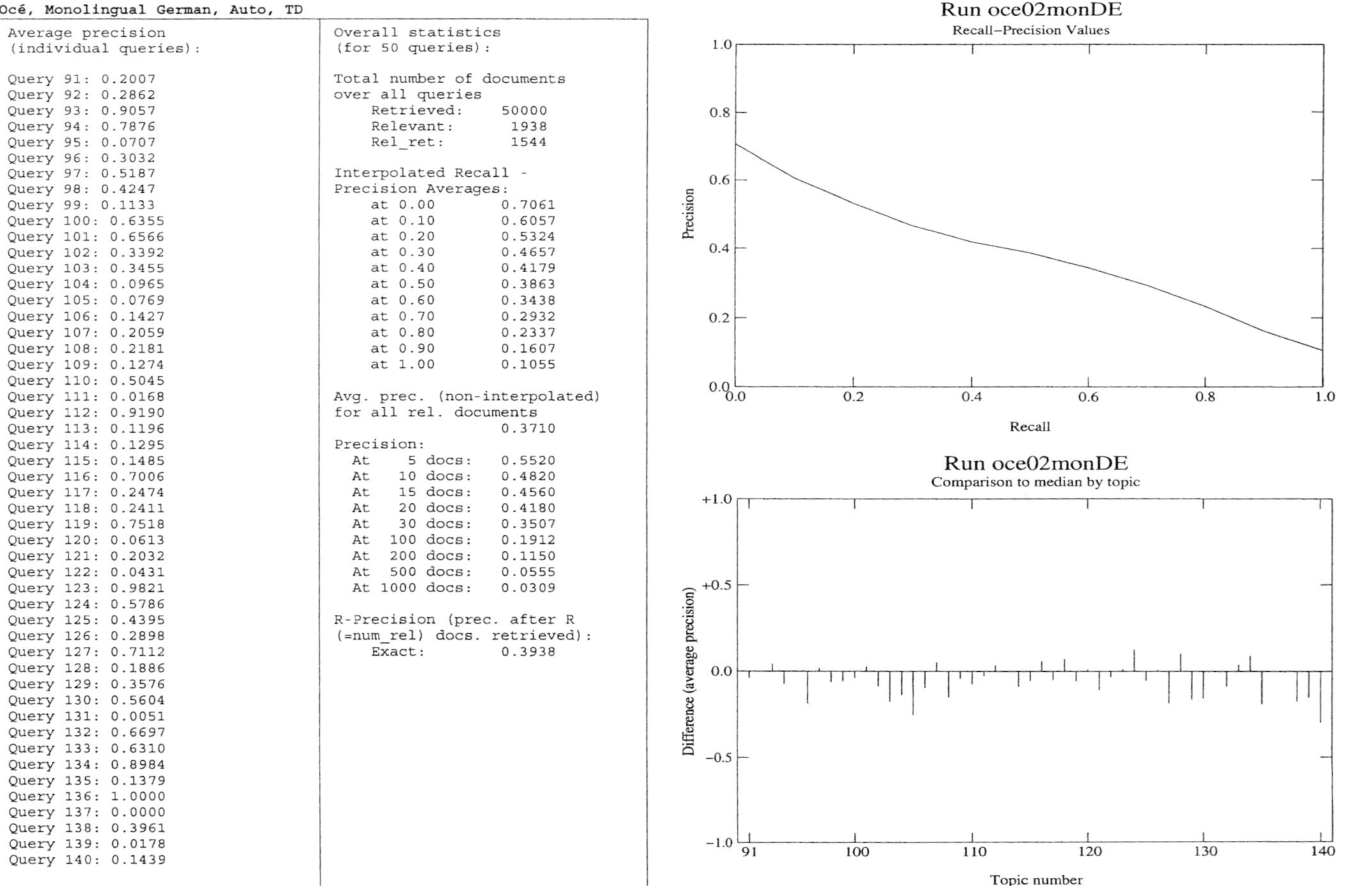

Océ, Monolingual German, Auto, TD

Average precision (individual queries):	Overall statistics (for 50 queries):
Query 91: 0.2007	Total number of documents over all queries
Query 92: 0.2862	Retrieved: 50000
Query 93: 0.9057	Relevant: 1938
Query 94: 0.7876	Rel_ret: 1544
Query 95: 0.0707	
Query 96: 0.3032	Interpolated Recall - Precision Averages:
Query 97: 0.5187	at 0.00 0.7061
Query 98: 0.4247	at 0.10 0.6057
Query 99: 0.1133	at 0.20 0.5324
Query 100: 0.6355	at 0.30 0.4657
Query 101: 0.6566	at 0.40 0.4179
Query 102: 0.3392	at 0.50 0.3863
Query 103: 0.3455	at 0.60 0.3438
Query 104: 0.0965	at 0.70 0.2932
Query 105: 0.0769	at 0.80 0.2337
Query 106: 0.1427	at 0.90 0.1607
Query 107: 0.2059	at 1.00 0.1055
Query 108: 0.2181	
Query 109: 0.1274	Avg. prec. (non-interpolated) for all rel. documents 0.3710
Query 110: 0.5045	
Query 111: 0.0168	Precision:
Query 112: 0.9190	At 5 docs: 0.5520
Query 113: 0.1196	At 10 docs: 0.4820
Query 114: 0.1295	At 15 docs: 0.4560
Query 115: 0.1485	At 20 docs: 0.4180
Query 116: 0.7006	At 30 docs: 0.3507
Query 117: 0.2474	At 100 docs: 0.1912
Query 118: 0.2411	At 200 docs: 0.1150
Query 119: 0.7518	At 500 docs: 0.0555
Query 120: 0.0613	At 1000 docs: 0.0309
Query 121: 0.2032	
Query 122: 0.0431	R-Precision (prec. after R (=num_rel) docs. retrieved):
Query 123: 0.9821	Exact: 0.3938
Query 124: 0.5786	
Query 125: 0.4395	
Query 126: 0.2898	
Query 127: 0.7112	
Query 128: 0.1886	
Query 129: 0.3576	
Query 130: 0.5604	
Query 131: 0.0051	
Query 132: 0.6697	
Query 133: 0.6310	
Query 134: 0.8984	
Query 135: 0.1379	
Query 136: 1.0000	
Query 137: 0.0000	
Query 138: 0.3961	
Query 139: 0.0178	
Query 140: 0.1439	

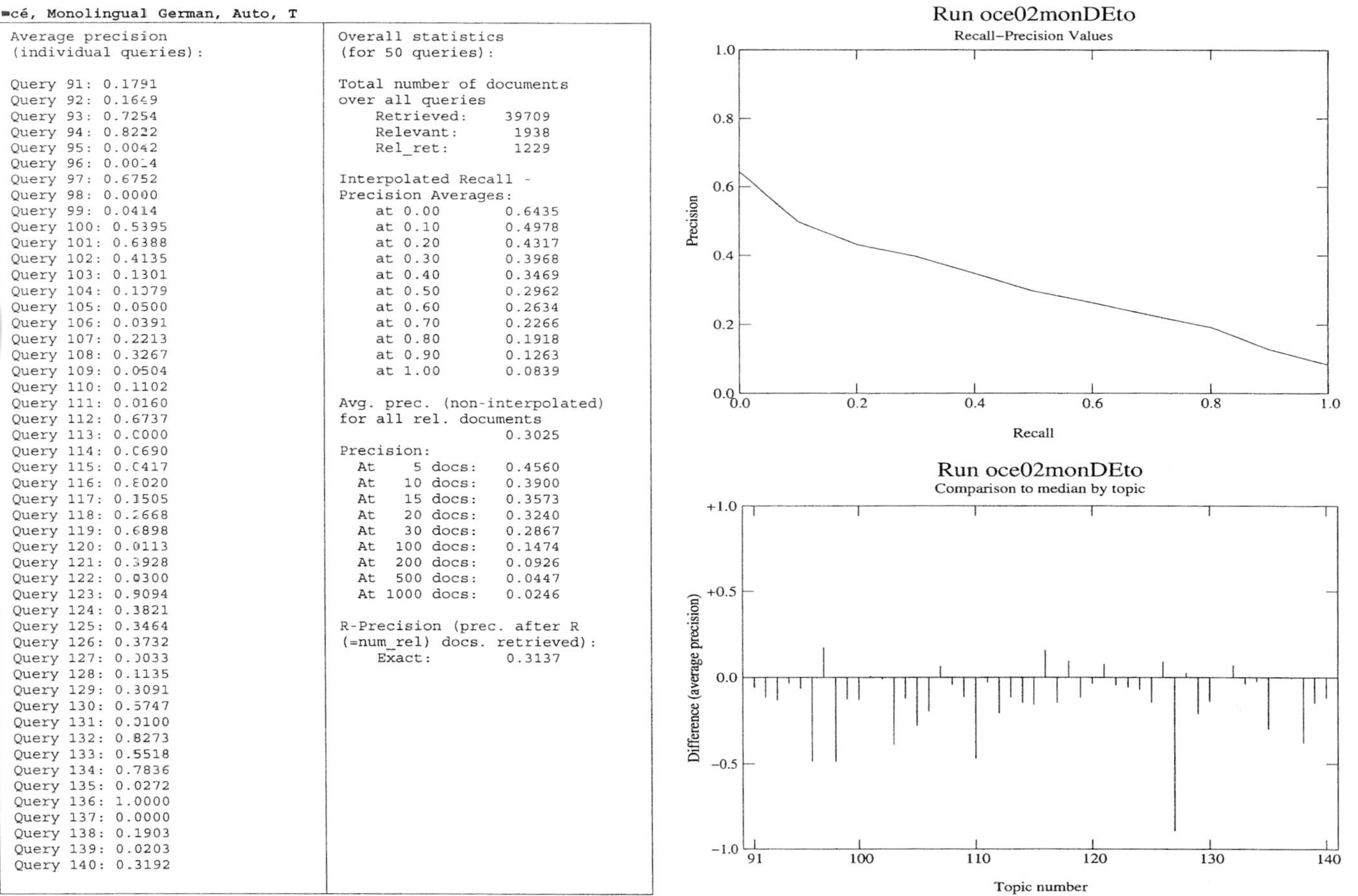

```
cé, Monolingual German, Auto, T

Average precision                Overall statistics
(individual queries):            (for 50 queries):

Query 91: 0.1791                 Total number of documents
Query 92: 0.1649                 over all queries
Query 93: 0.7254                     Retrieved:    39709
Query 94: 0.8222                     Relevant:      1938
Query 95: 0.0042                     Rel_ret:       1229
Query 96: 0.0014
Query 97: 0.6752                 Interpolated Recall -
Query 98: 0.0000                 Precision Averages:
Query 99: 0.0414                     at 0.00        0.6435
Query 100: 0.5395                    at 0.10        0.4978
Query 101: 0.6388                    at 0.20        0.4317
Query 102: 0.4135                    at 0.30        0.3968
Query 103: 0.1301                    at 0.40        0.3469
Query 104: 0.1079                    at 0.50        0.2962
Query 105: 0.0500                    at 0.60        0.2634
Query 106: 0.0391                    at 0.70        0.2266
Query 107: 0.2213                    at 0.80        0.1918
Query 108: 0.3267                    at 0.90        0.1263
Query 109: 0.0504                    at 1.00        0.0839
Query 110: 0.1102
Query 111: 0.0160                Avg. prec. (non-interpolated)
Query 112: 0.6737                for all rel. documents
Query 113: 0.0000                                   0.3025
Query 114: 0.0690                Precision:
Query 115: 0.0417                  At    5 docs:    0.4560
Query 116: 0.8020                  At   10 docs:    0.3900
Query 117: 0.1505                  At   15 docs:    0.3573
Query 118: 0.2668                  At   20 docs:    0.3240
Query 119: 0.6898                  At   30 docs:    0.2867
Query 120: 0.0113                  At  100 docs:    0.1474
Query 121: 0.3928                  At  200 docs:    0.0926
Query 122: 0.0300                  At  500 docs:    0.0447
Query 123: 0.9094                  At 1000 docs:    0.0246
Query 124: 0.3821
Query 125: 0.3464                R-Precision (prec. after R
Query 126: 0.3732                (=num_rel) docs. retrieved):
Query 127: 0.0033                    Exact:         0.3137
Query 128: 0.1135
Query 129: 0.3091
Query 130: 0.5747
Query 131: 0.0100
Query 132: 0.8273
Query 133: 0.5518
Query 134: 0.7836
Query 135: 0.0272
Query 136: 1.0000
Query 137: 0.0000
Query 138: 0.1903
Query 139: 0.0203
Query 140: 0.3192
```

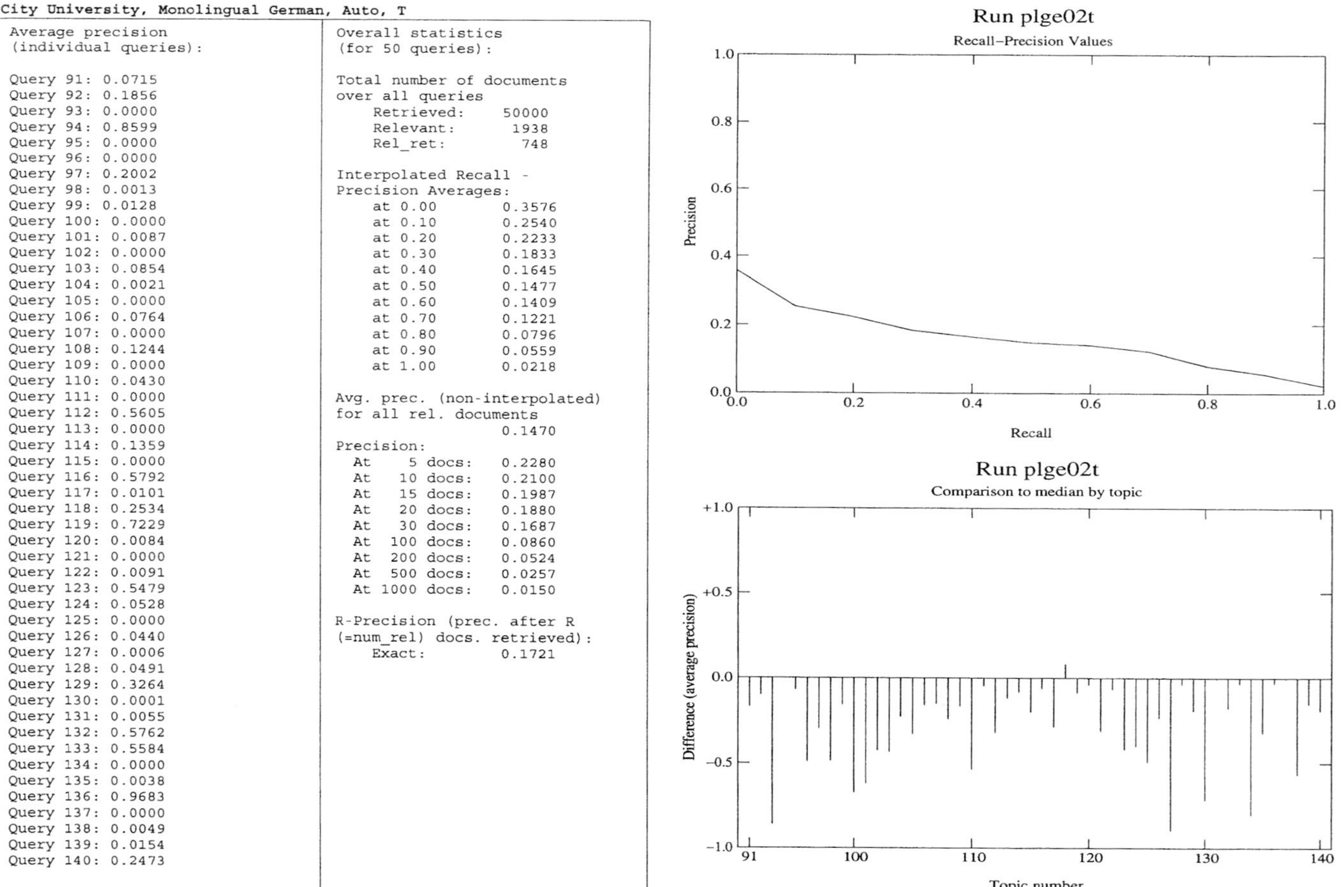

City University, Monolingual German, Auto, T

Average precision (individual queries):	Overall statistics (for 50 queries):
Query 91: 0.0715	Total number of documents over all queries
Query 92: 0.1856	Retrieved: 50000
Query 93: 0.0000	Relevant: 1938
Query 94: 0.8599	Rel_ret: 748
Query 95: 0.0000	
Query 96: 0.0000	Interpolated Recall - Precision Averages:
Query 97: 0.2002	at 0.00 0.3576
Query 98: 0.0013	at 0.10 0.2540
Query 99: 0.0128	at 0.20 0.2233
Query 100: 0.0000	at 0.30 0.1833
Query 101: 0.0087	at 0.40 0.1645
Query 102: 0.0000	at 0.50 0.1477
Query 103: 0.0854	at 0.60 0.1409
Query 104: 0.0021	at 0.70 0.1221
Query 105: 0.0000	at 0.80 0.0796
Query 106: 0.0764	at 0.90 0.0559
Query 107: 0.0000	at 1.00 0.0218
Query 108: 0.1244	
Query 109: 0.0000	Avg. prec. (non-interpolated) for all rel. documents 0.1470
Query 110: 0.0430	
Query 111: 0.0000	Precision:
Query 112: 0.5605	At 5 docs: 0.2280
Query 113: 0.0000	At 10 docs: 0.2100
Query 114: 0.1359	At 15 docs: 0.1987
Query 115: 0.0000	At 20 docs: 0.1880
Query 116: 0.5792	At 30 docs: 0.1687
Query 117: 0.0101	At 100 docs: 0.0860
Query 118: 0.2534	At 200 docs: 0.0524
Query 119: 0.7229	At 500 docs: 0.0257
Query 120: 0.0084	At 1000 docs: 0.0150
Query 121: 0.0000	
Query 122: 0.0091	R-Precision (prec. after R (=num_rel) docs. retrieved):
Query 123: 0.5479	Exact: 0.1721
Query 124: 0.0528	
Query 125: 0.0000	
Query 126: 0.0440	
Query 127: 0.0006	
Query 128: 0.0491	
Query 129: 0.3264	
Query 130: 0.0001	
Query 131: 0.0055	
Query 132: 0.5762	
Query 133: 0.5584	
Query 134: 0.0000	
Query 135: 0.0038	
Query 136: 0.9683	
Query 137: 0.0000	
Query 138: 0.0049	
Query 139: 0.0154	
Query 140: 0.2473	

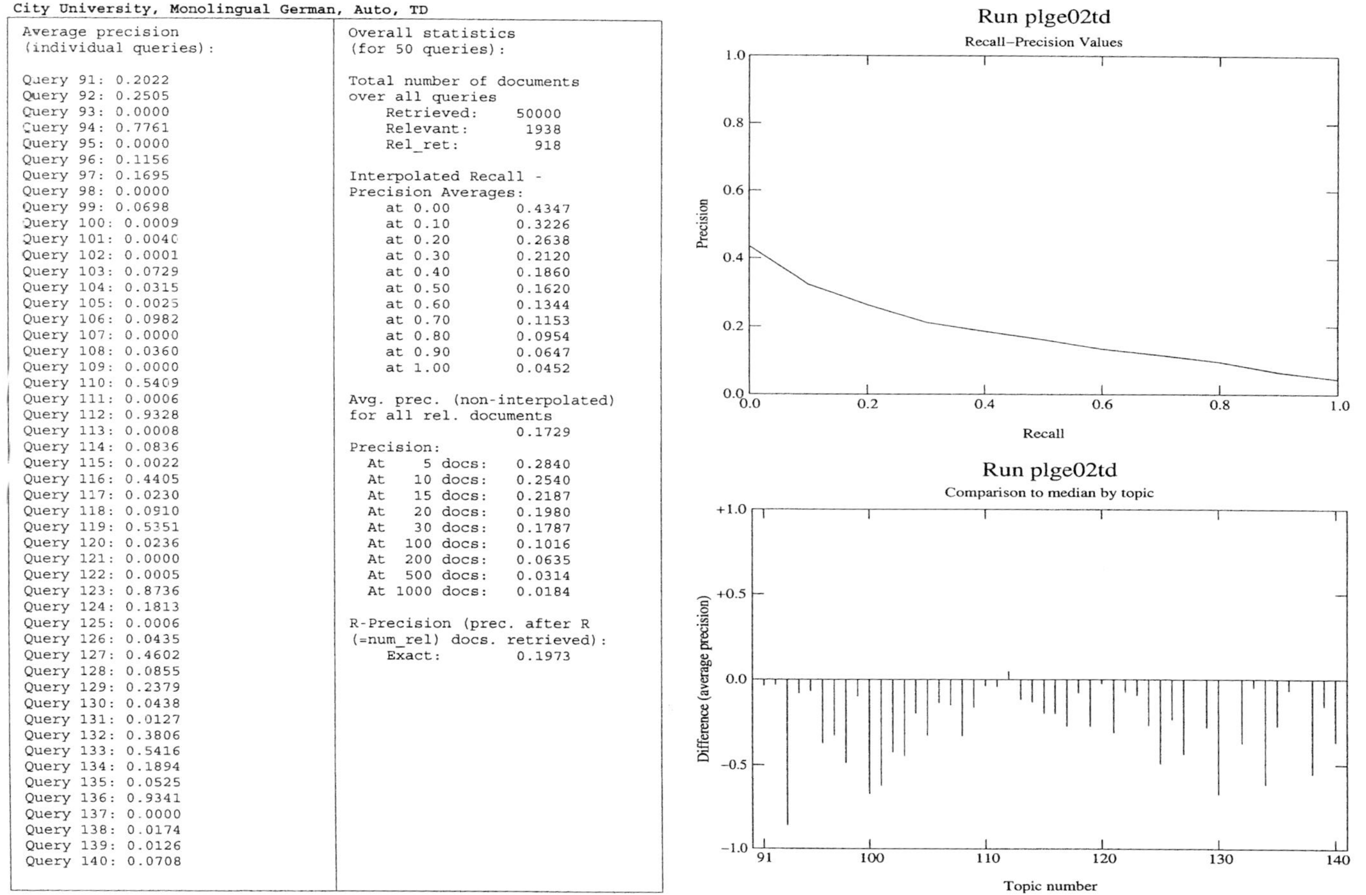

City University, Monolingual German, Auto, TD

Average precision (individual queries):	Overall statistics (for 50 queries):
Query 91: 0.2022 Query 92: 0.2505 Query 93: 0.0000 Query 94: 0.7761 Query 95: 0.0000 Query 96: 0.1156 Query 97: 0.1695 Query 98: 0.0000 Query 99: 0.0698 Query 100: 0.0009 Query 101: 0.0040 Query 102: 0.0001 Query 103: 0.0729 Query 104: 0.0315 Query 105: 0.0025 Query 106: 0.0982 Query 107: 0.0000 Query 108: 0.0360 Query 109: 0.0000 Query 110: 0.5409 Query 111: 0.0006 Query 112: 0.9328 Query 113: 0.0008 Query 114: 0.0836 Query 115: 0.0022 Query 116: 0.4405 Query 117: 0.0230 Query 118: 0.0910 Query 119: 0.5351 Query 120: 0.0236 Query 121: 0.0000 Query 122: 0.0005 Query 123: 0.8736 Query 124: 0.1813 Query 125: 0.0006 Query 126: 0.0435 Query 127: 0.4602 Query 128: 0.0855 Query 129: 0.2379 Query 130: 0.0438 Query 131: 0.0127 Query 132: 0.3806 Query 133: 0.5416 Query 134: 0.1894 Query 135: 0.0525 Query 136: 0.9341 Query 137: 0.0000 Query 138: 0.0174 Query 139: 0.0126 Query 140: 0.0708	Total number of documents over all queries Retrieved: 50000 Relevant: 1938 Rel_ret: 918 Interpolated Recall - Precision Averages: at 0.00 0.4347 at 0.10 0.3226 at 0.20 0.2638 at 0.30 0.2120 at 0.40 0.1860 at 0.50 0.1620 at 0.60 0.1344 at 0.70 0.1153 at 0.80 0.0954 at 0.90 0.0647 at 1.00 0.0452 Avg. prec. (non-interpolated) for all rel. documents 0.1729 Precision: At 5 docs: 0.2840 At 10 docs: 0.2540 At 15 docs: 0.2187 At 20 docs: 0.1980 At 30 docs: 0.1787 At 100 docs: 0.1016 At 200 docs: 0.0635 At 500 docs: 0.0314 At 1000 docs: 0.0184 R-Precision (prec. after R (=num_rel) docs. retrieved): Exact: 0.1973

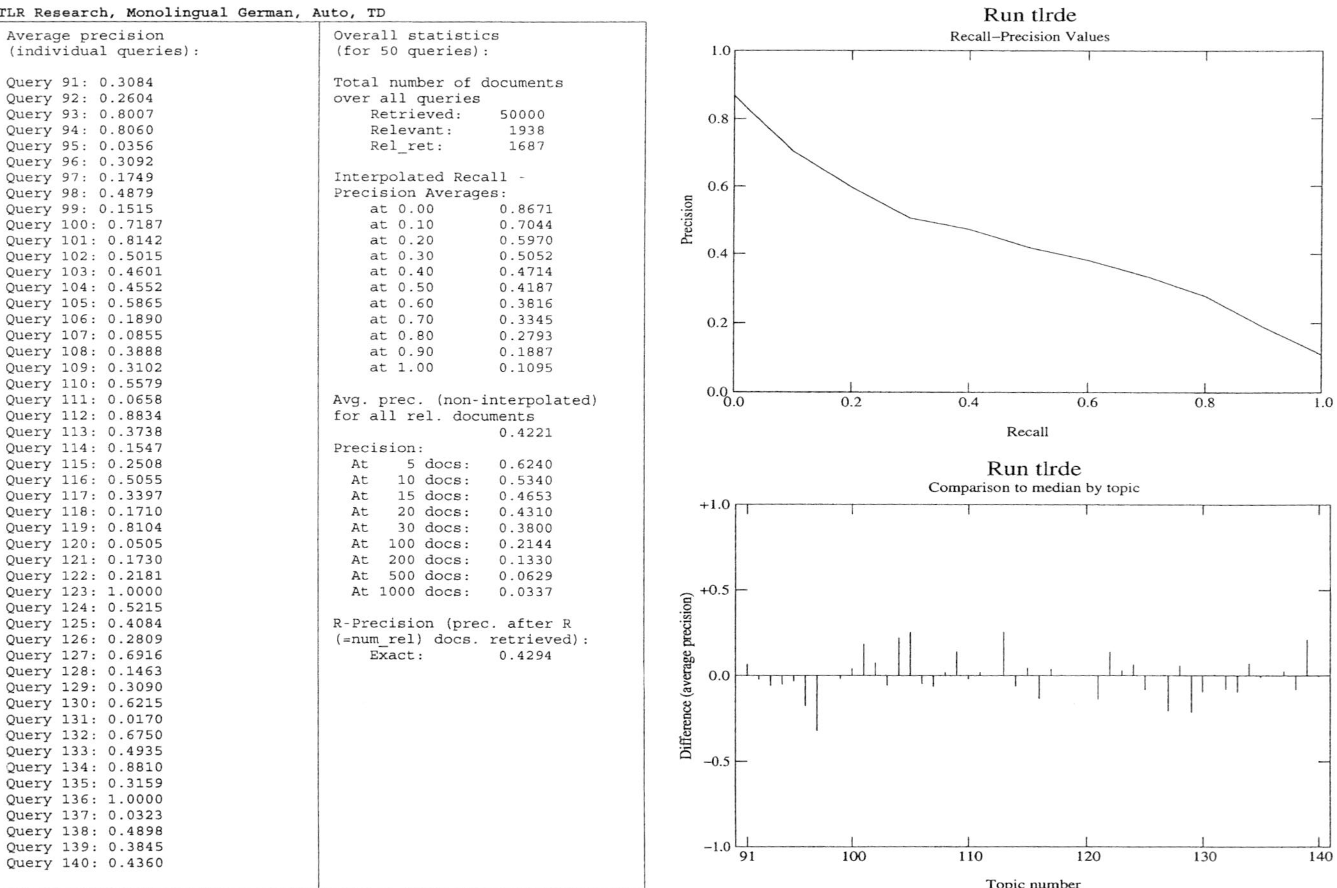

TLR Research, Monolingual German, Auto, TD

Average precision (individual queries):	Overall statistics (for 50 queries):
Query 91: 0.3084	Total number of documents over all queries
Query 92: 0.2604	Retrieved: 50000
Query 93: 0.8007	Relevant: 1938
Query 94: 0.8060	Rel_ret: 1687
Query 95: 0.0356	
Query 96: 0.3092	Interpolated Recall - Precision Averages:
Query 97: 0.1749	at 0.00 0.8671
Query 98: 0.4879	at 0.10 0.7044
Query 99: 0.1515	at 0.20 0.5970
Query 100: 0.7187	at 0.30 0.5052
Query 101: 0.8142	at 0.40 0.4714
Query 102: 0.5015	at 0.50 0.4187
Query 103: 0.4601	at 0.60 0.3816
Query 104: 0.4552	at 0.70 0.3345
Query 105: 0.5865	at 0.80 0.2793
Query 106: 0.1890	at 0.90 0.1887
Query 107: 0.0855	at 1.00 0.1095
Query 108: 0.3888	
Query 109: 0.3102	Avg. prec. (non-interpolated) for all rel. documents 0.4221
Query 110: 0.5579	
Query 111: 0.0658	Precision:
Query 112: 0.8834	At 5 docs: 0.6240
Query 113: 0.3738	At 10 docs: 0.5340
Query 114: 0.1547	At 15 docs: 0.4653
Query 115: 0.2508	At 20 docs: 0.4310
Query 116: 0.5055	At 30 docs: 0.3800
Query 117: 0.3397	At 100 docs: 0.2144
Query 118: 0.1710	At 200 docs: 0.1330
Query 119: 0.8104	At 500 docs: 0.0629
Query 120: 0.0505	At 1000 docs: 0.0337
Query 121: 0.1730	
Query 122: 0.2181	R-Precision (prec. after R (=num_rel) docs. retrieved):
Query 123: 1.0000	Exact: 0.4294
Query 124: 0.5215	
Query 125: 0.4084	
Query 126: 0.2809	
Query 127: 0.6916	
Query 128: 0.1463	
Query 129: 0.3090	
Query 130: 0.6215	
Query 131: 0.0170	
Query 132: 0.6750	
Query 133: 0.4935	
Query 134: 0.8810	
Query 135: 0.3159	
Query 136: 1.0000	
Query 137: 0.0323	
Query 138: 0.4898	
Query 139: 0.3845	
Query 140: 0.4360	

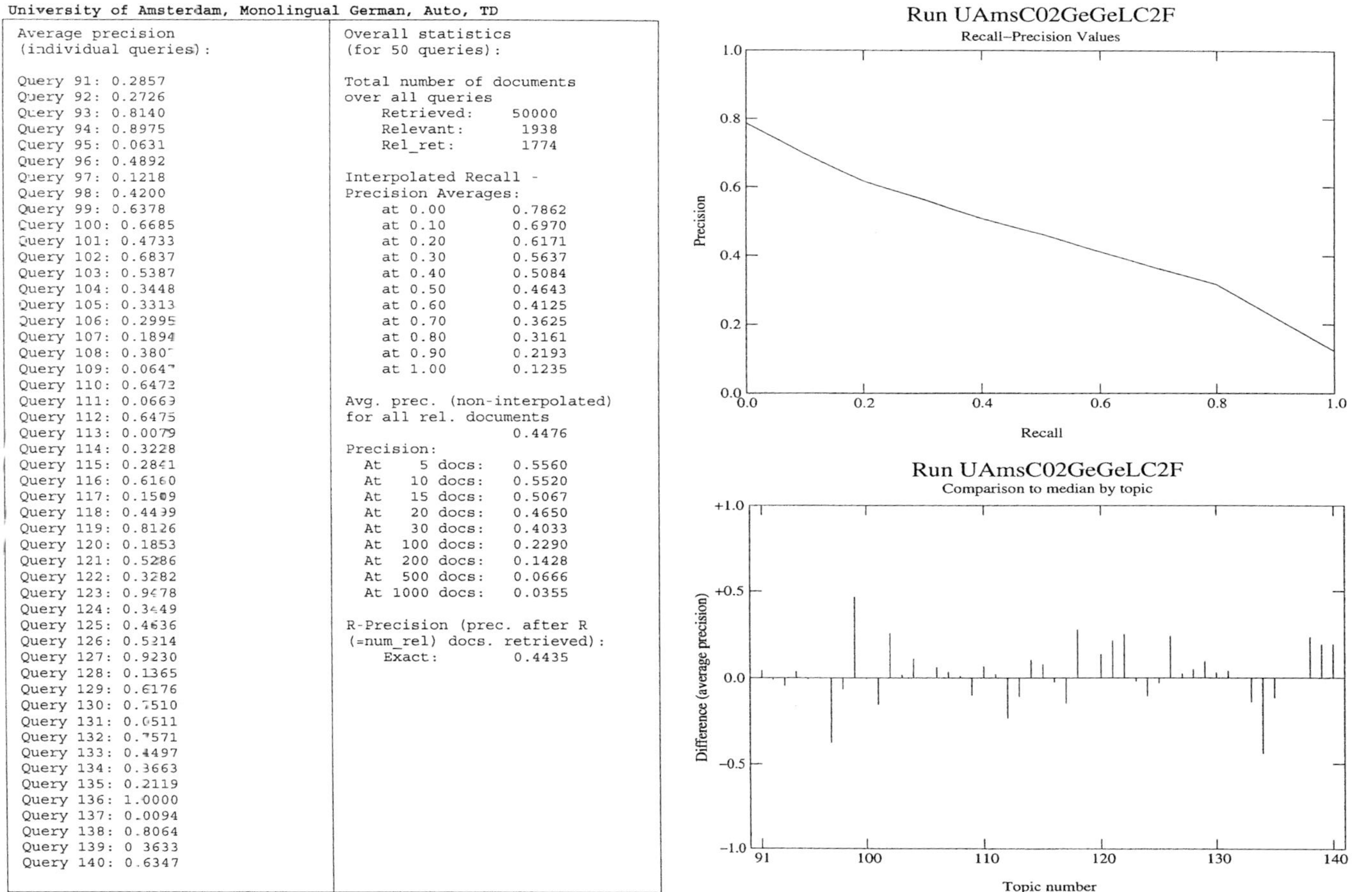

University of Amsterdam, Monolingual German, Auto, TD

Average precision (individual queries):	Overall statistics (for 50 queries):
Query 91: 0.2857	Total number of documents over all queries
Query 92: 0.2726	Retrieved: 50000
Query 93: 0.8140	Relevant: 1938
Query 94: 0.8975	Rel_ret: 1774
Query 95: 0.0631	
Query 96: 0.4892	Interpolated Recall - Precision Averages:
Query 97: 0.1218	at 0.00 0.7862
Query 98: 0.4200	at 0.10 0.6970
Query 99: 0.6378	at 0.20 0.6171
Query 100: 0.6685	at 0.30 0.5637
Query 101: 0.4733	at 0.40 0.5084
Query 102: 0.6837	at 0.50 0.4643
Query 103: 0.5387	at 0.60 0.4125
Query 104: 0.3448	at 0.70 0.3625
Query 105: 0.3313	at 0.80 0.3161
Query 106: 0.2995	at 0.90 0.2193
Query 107: 0.1894	at 1.00 0.1235
Query 108: 0.3807	
Query 109: 0.0647	Avg. prec. (non-interpolated) for all rel. documents 0.4476
Query 110: 0.6473	
Query 111: 0.0669	Precision:
Query 112: 0.6475	At 5 docs: 0.5560
Query 113: 0.0079	At 10 docs: 0.5520
Query 114: 0.3228	At 15 docs: 0.5067
Query 115: 0.2841	At 20 docs: 0.4650
Query 116: 0.6160	At 30 docs: 0.4033
Query 117: 0.1509	At 100 docs: 0.2290
Query 118: 0.4439	At 200 docs: 0.1428
Query 119: 0.8126	At 500 docs: 0.0666
Query 120: 0.1853	At 1000 docs: 0.0355
Query 121: 0.5286	
Query 122: 0.3282	R-Precision (prec. after R (=num_rel) docs. retrieved):
Query 123: 0.9478	Exact: 0.4435
Query 124: 0.3449	
Query 125: 0.4636	
Query 126: 0.5214	
Query 127: 0.9230	
Query 128: 0.1365	
Query 129: 0.6176	
Query 130: 0.7510	
Query 131: 0.0511	
Query 132: 0.7571	
Query 133: 0.4497	
Query 134: 0.3663	
Query 135: 0.2119	
Query 136: 1.0000	
Query 137: 0.0094	
Query 138: 0.8064	
Query 139: 0.3633	
Query 140: 0.6347	

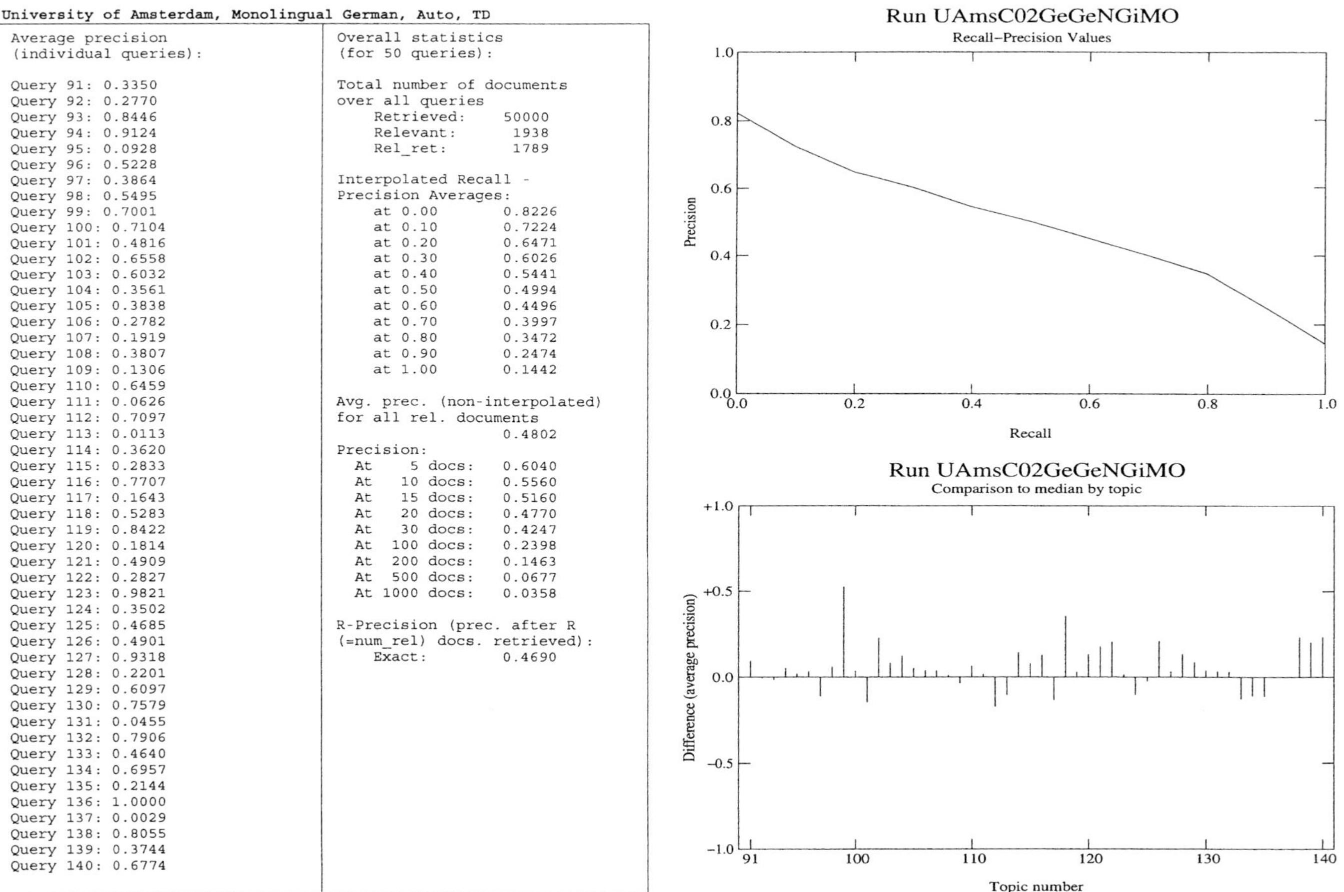

University of Amsterdam, Monolingual German, Auto, TD

```
Average precision                Overall statistics
(individual queries):            (for 50 queries):

Query 91: 0.3350                 Total number of documents
Query 92: 0.2770                 over all queries
Query 93: 0.8446                     Retrieved:    50000
Query 94: 0.9124                     Relevant:      1938
Query 95: 0.0928                     Rel_ret:       1789
Query 96: 0.5228
Query 97: 0.3864                 Interpolated Recall -
Query 98: 0.5495                 Precision Averages:
Query 99: 0.7001                     at 0.00       0.8226
Query 100: 0.7104                    at 0.10       0.7224
Query 101: 0.4816                    at 0.20       0.6471
Query 102: 0.6558                    at 0.30       0.6026
Query 103: 0.6032                    at 0.40       0.5441
Query 104: 0.3561                    at 0.50       0.4994
Query 105: 0.3838                    at 0.60       0.4496
Query 106: 0.2782                    at 0.70       0.3997
Query 107: 0.1919                    at 0.80       0.3472
Query 108: 0.3807                    at 0.90       0.2474
Query 109: 0.1306                    at 1.00       0.1442
Query 110: 0.6459
Query 111: 0.0626                Avg. prec. (non-interpolated)
Query 112: 0.7097                for all rel. documents
Query 113: 0.0113                                  0.4802
Query 114: 0.3620                Precision:
Query 115: 0.2833                  At    5 docs:   0.6040
Query 116: 0.7707                  At   10 docs:   0.5560
Query 117: 0.1643                  At   15 docs:   0.5160
Query 118: 0.5283                  At   20 docs:   0.4770
Query 119: 0.8422                  At   30 docs:   0.4247
Query 120: 0.1814                  At  100 docs:   0.2398
Query 121: 0.4909                  At  200 docs:   0.1463
Query 122: 0.2827                  At  500 docs:   0.0677
Query 123: 0.9821                  At 1000 docs:   0.0358
Query 124: 0.3502
Query 125: 0.4685                R-Precision (prec. after R
Query 126: 0.4901                (=num_rel) docs. retrieved):
Query 127: 0.9318                    Exact:        0.4690
Query 128: 0.2201
Query 129: 0.6097
Query 130: 0.7579
Query 131: 0.0455
Query 132: 0.7906
Query 133: 0.4640
Query 134: 0.6957
Query 135: 0.2144
Query 136: 1.0000
Query 137: 0.0029
Query 138: 0.8055
Query 139: 0.3744
Query 140: 0.6774
```

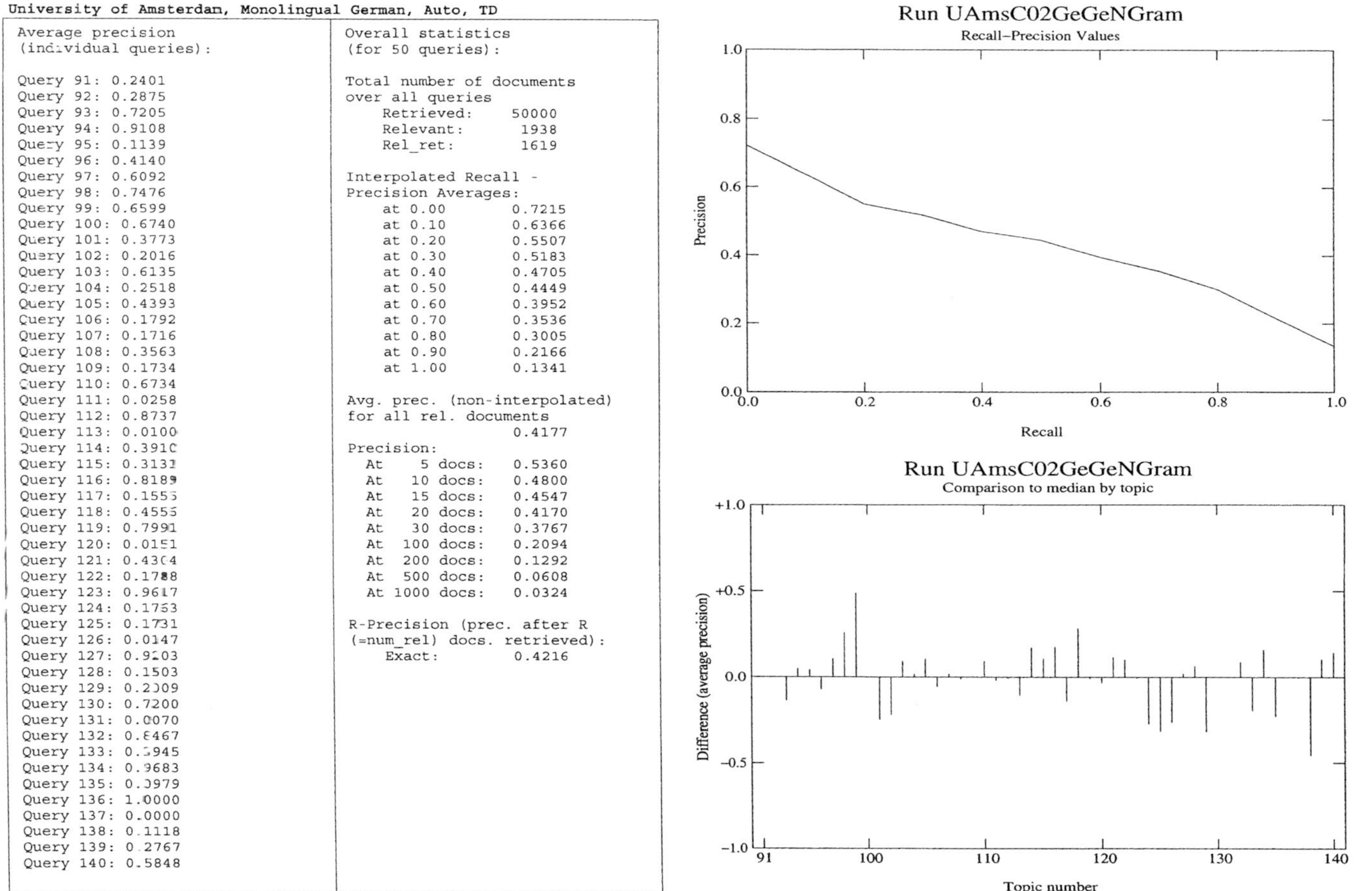

```
University of Amsterdam, Monolingual German, Auto, TD

Average precision                 Overall statistics
(individual queries):             (for 50 queries):

Query 91: 0.2401                  Total number of documents
Query 92: 0.2875                  over all queries
Query 93: 0.7205                      Retrieved:    50000
Query 94: 0.9108                      Relevant:      1938
Query 95: 0.1139                      Rel_ret:       1619
Query 96: 0.4140
Query 97: 0.6092                  Interpolated Recall -
Query 98: 0.7476                  Precision Averages:
Query 99: 0.6599                      at 0.00       0.7215
Query 100: 0.6740                     at 0.10       0.6366
Query 101: 0.3773                     at 0.20       0.5507
Query 102: 0.2016                     at 0.30       0.5183
Query 103: 0.6135                     at 0.40       0.4705
Query 104: 0.2518                     at 0.50       0.4449
Query 105: 0.4393                     at 0.60       0.3952
Query 106: 0.1792                     at 0.70       0.3536
Query 107: 0.1716                     at 0.80       0.3005
Query 108: 0.3563                     at 0.90       0.2166
Query 109: 0.1734                     at 1.00       0.1341
Query 110: 0.6734
Query 111: 0.0258                 Avg. prec. (non-interpolated)
Query 112: 0.8737                 for all rel. documents
Query 113: 0.0100                                   0.4177
Query 114: 0.3910                 Precision:
Query 115: 0.3131                   At    5 docs:   0.5360
Query 116: 0.8189                   At   10 docs:   0.4800
Query 117: 0.1555                   At   15 docs:   0.4547
Query 118: 0.4555                   At   20 docs:   0.4170
Query 119: 0.7991                   At   30 docs:   0.3767
Query 120: 0.0151                   At  100 docs:   0.2094
Query 121: 0.4304                   At  200 docs:   0.1292
Query 122: 0.1788                   At  500 docs:   0.0608
Query 123: 0.9617                   At 1000 docs:   0.0324
Query 124: 0.1753
Query 125: 0.1731                 R-Precision (prec. after R
Query 126: 0.0147                 (=num_rel) docs. retrieved):
Query 127: 0.9203                     Exact:        0.4216
Query 128: 0.1503
Query 129: 0.2009
Query 130: 0.7200
Query 131: 0.0070
Query 132: 0.8467
Query 133: 0.5945
Query 134: 0.9683
Query 135: 0.0979
Query 136: 1.0000
Query 137: 0.0000
Query 138: 0.1118
Query 139: 0.2767
Query 140: 0.5848
```

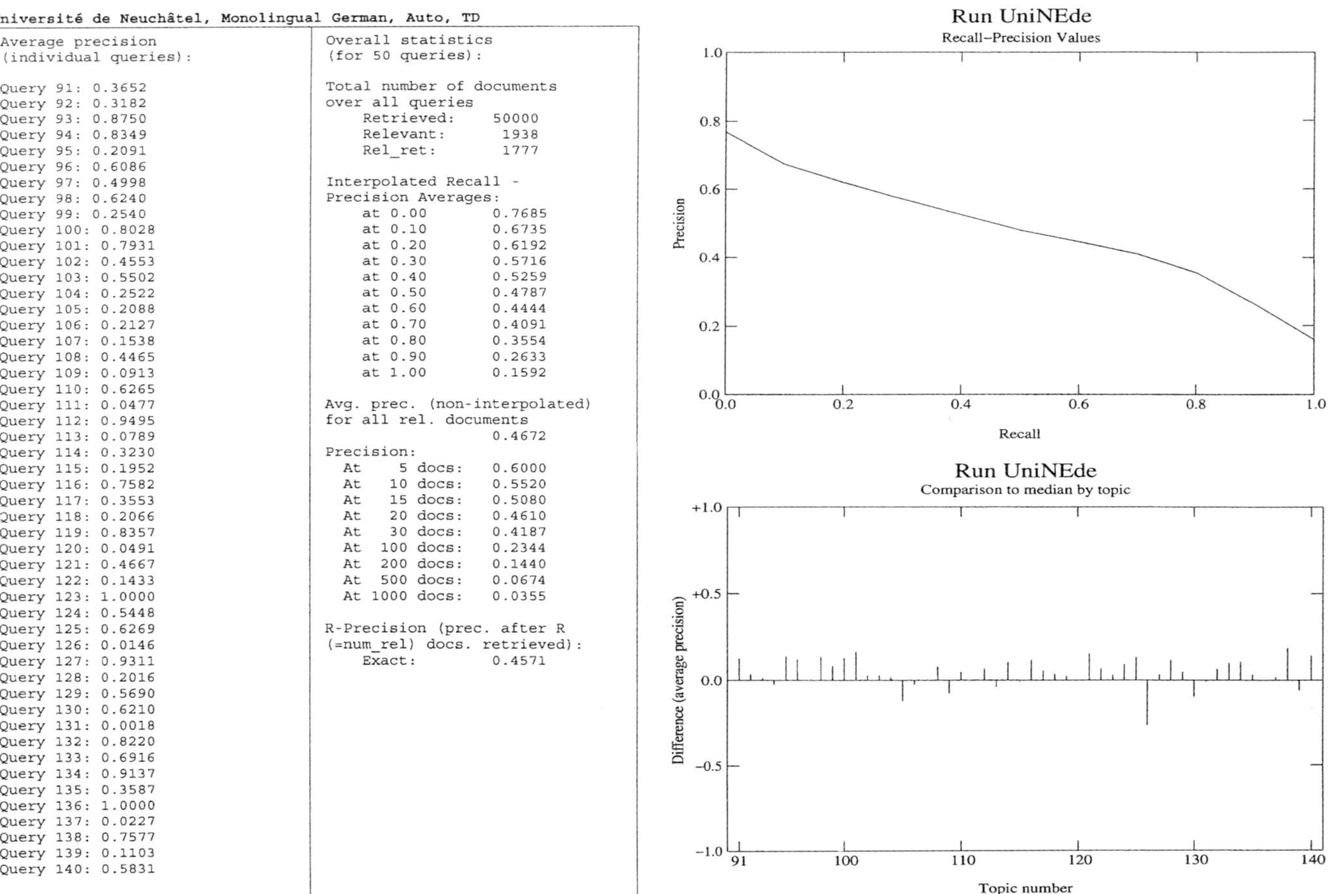

Université de Neuchâtel, Monolingual German, Auto, TD

```
Average precision              Overall statistics
(individual queries):          (for 50 queries):

Query 91: 0.3652               Total number of documents
Query 92: 0.3182               over all queries
Query 93: 0.8750                   Retrieved:    50000
Query 94: 0.8349                   Relevant:      1938
Query 95: 0.2091                   Rel_ret:       1777
Query 96: 0.6086
Query 97: 0.4998               Interpolated Recall -
Query 98: 0.6240               Precision Averages:
Query 99: 0.2540                   at 0.00        0.7685
Query 100: 0.8028                  at 0.10        0.6735
Query 101: 0.7931                  at 0.20        0.6192
Query 102: 0.4553                  at 0.30        0.5716
Query 103: 0.5502                  at 0.40        0.5259
Query 104: 0.2522                  at 0.50        0.4787
Query 105: 0.2088                  at 0.60        0.4444
Query 106: 0.2127                  at 0.70        0.4091
Query 107: 0.1538                  at 0.80        0.3554
Query 108: 0.4465                  at 0.90        0.2633
Query 109: 0.0913                  at 1.00        0.1592
Query 110: 0.6265
Query 111: 0.0477              Avg. prec. (non-interpolated)
Query 112: 0.9495              for all rel. documents
Query 113: 0.0789                                 0.4672
Query 114: 0.3230              Precision:
Query 115: 0.1952                At     5 docs:   0.6000
Query 116: 0.7582                At    10 docs:   0.5520
Query 117: 0.3553                At    15 docs:   0.5080
Query 118: 0.2066                At    20 docs:   0.4610
Query 119: 0.8357                At    30 docs:   0.4187
Query 120: 0.0491                At   100 docs:   0.2344
Query 121: 0.4667                At   200 docs:   0.1440
Query 122: 0.1433                At   500 docs:   0.0674
Query 123: 1.0000                At  1000 docs:   0.0355
Query 124: 0.5448
Query 125: 0.6269              R-Precision (prec. after R
Query 126: 0.0146              (=num_rel) docs. retrieved):
Query 127: 0.9311                  Exact:         0.4571
Query 128: 0.2016
Query 129: 0.5690
Query 130: 0.6210
Query 131: 0.0018
Query 132: 0.8220
Query 133: 0.6916
Query 134: 0.9137
Query 135: 0.3587
Query 136: 1.0000
Query 137: 0.0227
Query 138: 0.7577
Query 139: 0.1103
Query 140: 0.5831
```

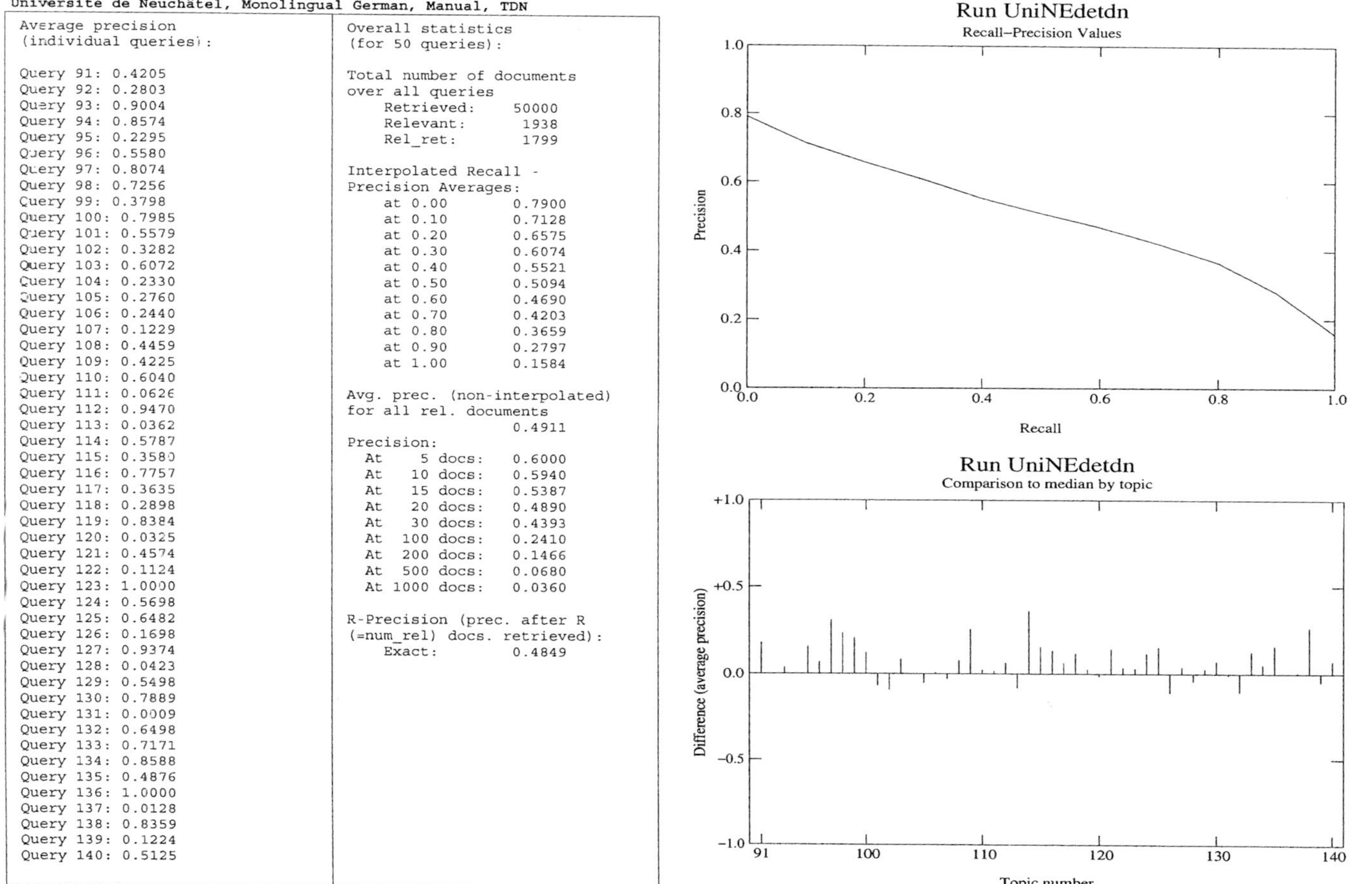

Université de Neuchâtel, Monolingual German, Manual, TDN

Average precision (individual queries):

Query	Average precision
Query 91:	0.4205
Query 92:	0.2803
Query 93:	0.9004
Query 94:	0.8574
Query 95:	0.2295
Query 96:	0.5580
Query 97:	0.8074
Query 98:	0.7256
Query 99:	0.3798
Query 100:	0.7985
Query 101:	0.5579
Query 102:	0.3282
Query 103:	0.6072
Query 104:	0.2330
Query 105:	0.2760
Query 106:	0.2440
Query 107:	0.1229
Query 108:	0.4459
Query 109:	0.4225
Query 110:	0.6040
Query 111:	0.0626
Query 112:	0.9470
Query 113:	0.0362
Query 114:	0.5787
Query 115:	0.3580
Query 116:	0.7757
Query 117:	0.3635
Query 118:	0.2898
Query 119:	0.8384
Query 120:	0.0325
Query 121:	0.4574
Query 122:	0.1124
Query 123:	1.0000
Query 124:	0.5698
Query 125:	0.6482
Query 126:	0.1698
Query 127:	0.9374
Query 128:	0.0423
Query 129:	0.5498
Query 130:	0.7889
Query 131:	0.0009
Query 132:	0.6498
Query 133:	0.7171
Query 134:	0.8588
Query 135:	0.4876
Query 136:	1.0000
Query 137:	0.0128
Query 138:	0.8359
Query 139:	0.1224
Query 140:	0.5125

Overall statistics (for 50 queries):

Total number of documents over all queries

Retrieved:	50000
Relevant:	1938
Rel_ret:	1799

Interpolated Recall - Precision Averages:

at 0.00	0.7900
at 0.10	0.7128
at 0.20	0.6575
at 0.30	0.6074
at 0.40	0.5521
at 0.50	0.5094
at 0.60	0.4690
at 0.70	0.4203
at 0.80	0.3659
at 0.90	0.2797
at 1.00	0.1584

Avg. prec. (non-interpolated) for all rel. documents 0.4911

Precision:

At 5 docs:	0.6000
At 10 docs:	0.5940
At 15 docs:	0.5387
At 20 docs:	0.4890
At 30 docs:	0.4393
At 100 docs:	0.2410
At 200 docs:	0.1466
At 500 docs:	0.0680
At 1000 docs:	0.0360

R-Precision (prec. after R (=num_rel) docs. retrieved):
Exact: 0.4849

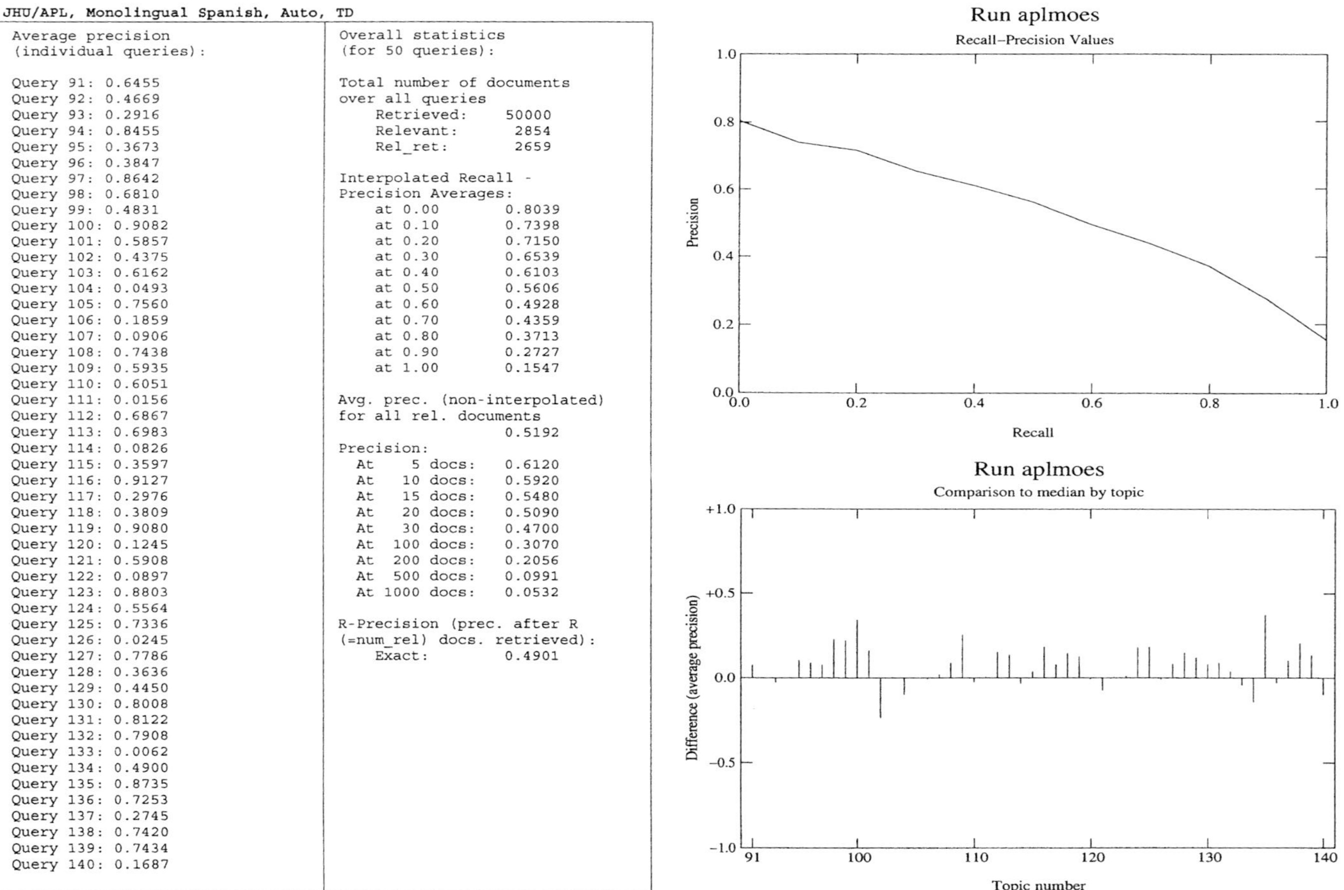

JHU/APL, Monolingual Spanish, Auto, TD

```
Average precision                 Overall statistics
(individual queries):             (for 50 queries):

Query 91: 0.6455                  Total number of documents
Query 92: 0.4669                  over all queries
Query 93: 0.2916                      Retrieved:    50000
Query 94: 0.8455                      Relevant:      2854
Query 95: 0.3673                      Rel_ret:       2659
Query 96: 0.3847
Query 97: 0.8642                  Interpolated Recall -
Query 98: 0.6810                  Precision Averages:
Query 99: 0.4831                      at 0.00       0.8039
Query 100: 0.9082                     at 0.10       0.7398
Query 101: 0.5857                     at 0.20       0.7150
Query 102: 0.4375                     at 0.30       0.6539
Query 103: 0.6162                     at 0.40       0.6103
Query 104: 0.0493                     at 0.50       0.5606
Query 105: 0.7560                     at 0.60       0.4928
Query 106: 0.1859                     at 0.70       0.4359
Query 107: 0.0906                     at 0.80       0.3713
Query 108: 0.7438                     at 0.90       0.2727
Query 109: 0.5935                     at 1.00       0.1547
Query 110: 0.6051
Query 111: 0.0156                 Avg. prec. (non-interpolated)
Query 112: 0.6867                 for all rel. documents
Query 113: 0.6983                                   0.5192
Query 114: 0.0826                 Precision:
Query 115: 0.3597                   At    5 docs:   0.6120
Query 116: 0.9127                   At   10 docs:   0.5920
Query 117: 0.2976                   At   15 docs:   0.5480
Query 118: 0.3809                   At   20 docs:   0.5090
Query 119: 0.9080                   At   30 docs:   0.4700
Query 120: 0.1245                   At  100 docs:   0.3070
Query 121: 0.5908                   At  200 docs:   0.2056
Query 122: 0.0897                   At  500 docs:   0.0991
Query 123: 0.8803                   At 1000 docs:   0.0532
Query 124: 0.5564
Query 125: 0.7336                 R-Precision (prec. after R
Query 126: 0.0245                 (=num_rel) docs. retrieved):
Query 127: 0.7786                     Exact:        0.4901
Query 128: 0.3636
Query 129: 0.4450
Query 130: 0.8008
Query 131: 0.8122
Query 132: 0.7908
Query 133: 0.0062
Query 134: 0.4900
Query 135: 0.8735
Query 136: 0.7253
Query 137: 0.2745
Query 138: 0.7420
Query 139: 0.7434
Query 140: 0.1687
```

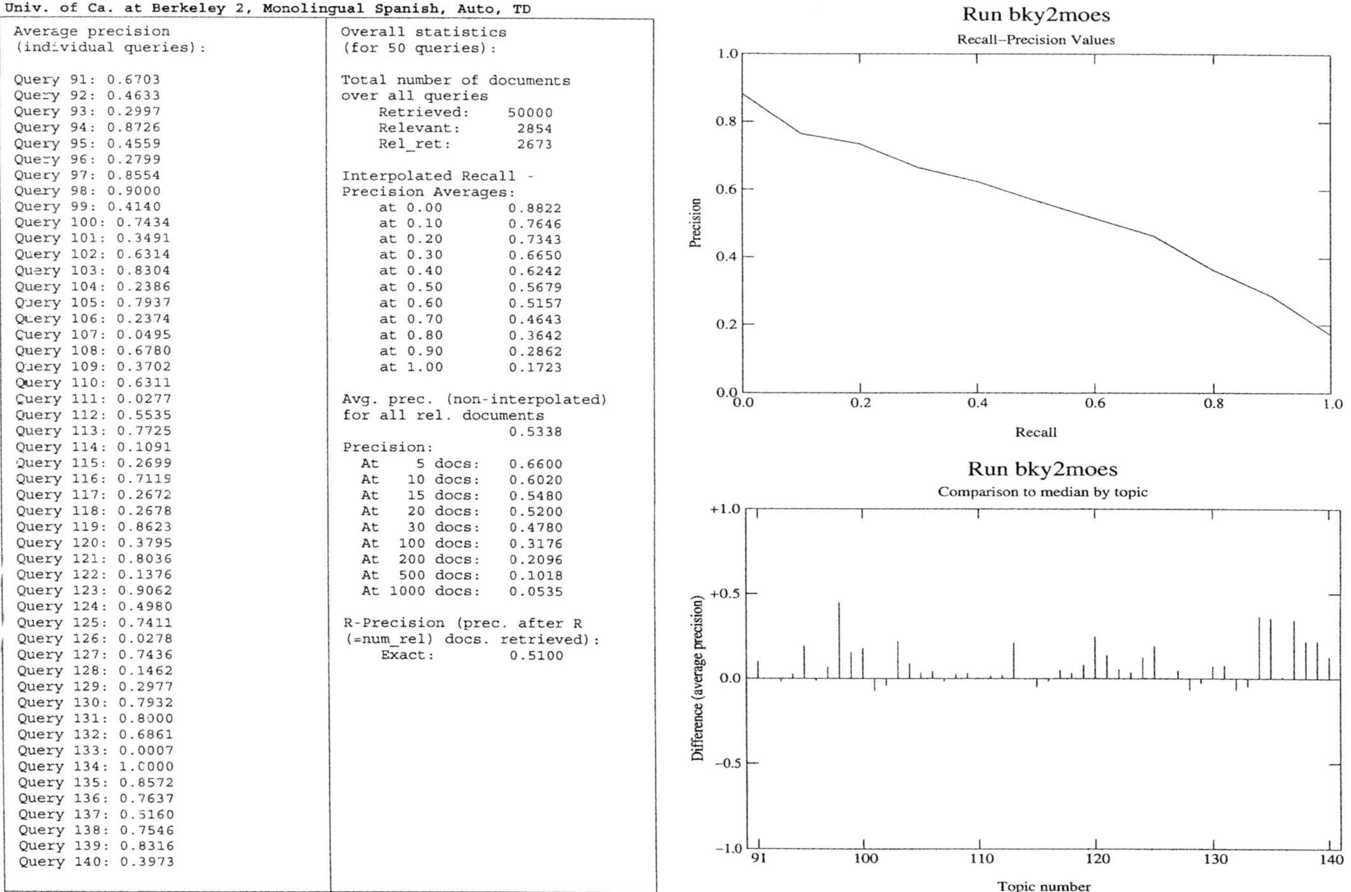

Univ. of Ca. at Berkeley 2, Monolingual Spanish, Auto, TD

Average precision (individual queries):

Query	Average precision
Query 91:	0.6703
Query 92:	0.4633
Query 93:	0.2997
Query 94:	0.8726
Query 95:	0.4559
Query 96:	0.2799
Query 97:	0.8554
Query 98:	0.9000
Query 99:	0.4140
Query 100:	0.7434
Query 101:	0.3491
Query 102:	0.6314
Query 103:	0.8304
Query 104:	0.2386
Query 105:	0.7937
Query 106:	0.2374
Query 107:	0.0495
Query 108:	0.6780
Query 109:	0.3702
Query 110:	0.6311
Query 111:	0.0277
Query 112:	0.5535
Query 113:	0.7725
Query 114:	0.1091
Query 115:	0.2699
Query 116:	0.7119
Query 117:	0.2672
Query 118:	0.2678
Query 119:	0.8623
Query 120:	0.3795
Query 121:	0.8036
Query 122:	0.1376
Query 123:	0.9062
Query 124:	0.4980
Query 125:	0.7411
Query 126:	0.0278
Query 127:	0.7436
Query 128:	0.1462
Query 129:	0.2977
Query 130:	0.7932
Query 131:	0.8000
Query 132:	0.6861
Query 133:	0.0007
Query 134:	1.0000
Query 135:	0.8572
Query 136:	0.7637
Query 137:	0.5160
Query 138:	0.7546
Query 139:	0.8316
Query 140:	0.3973

Overall statistics (for 50 queries):

Total number of documents over all queries

Retrieved:	50000
Relevant:	2854
Rel_ret:	2673

Interpolated Recall - Precision Averages:

at 0.00	0.8822
at 0.10	0.7646
at 0.20	0.7343
at 0.30	0.6650
at 0.40	0.6242
at 0.50	0.5679
at 0.60	0.5157
at 0.70	0.4643
at 0.80	0.3642
at 0.90	0.2862
at 1.00	0.1723

Avg. prec. (non-interpolated) for all rel. documents 0.5338

Precision:

At 5 docs:	0.6600
At 10 docs:	0.6020
At 15 docs:	0.5480
At 20 docs:	0.5200
At 30 docs:	0.4780
At 100 docs:	0.3176
At 200 docs:	0.2096
At 500 docs:	0.1018
At 1000 docs:	0.0535

R-Precision (prec. after R (=num_rel) docs. retrieved):
Exact: 0.5100

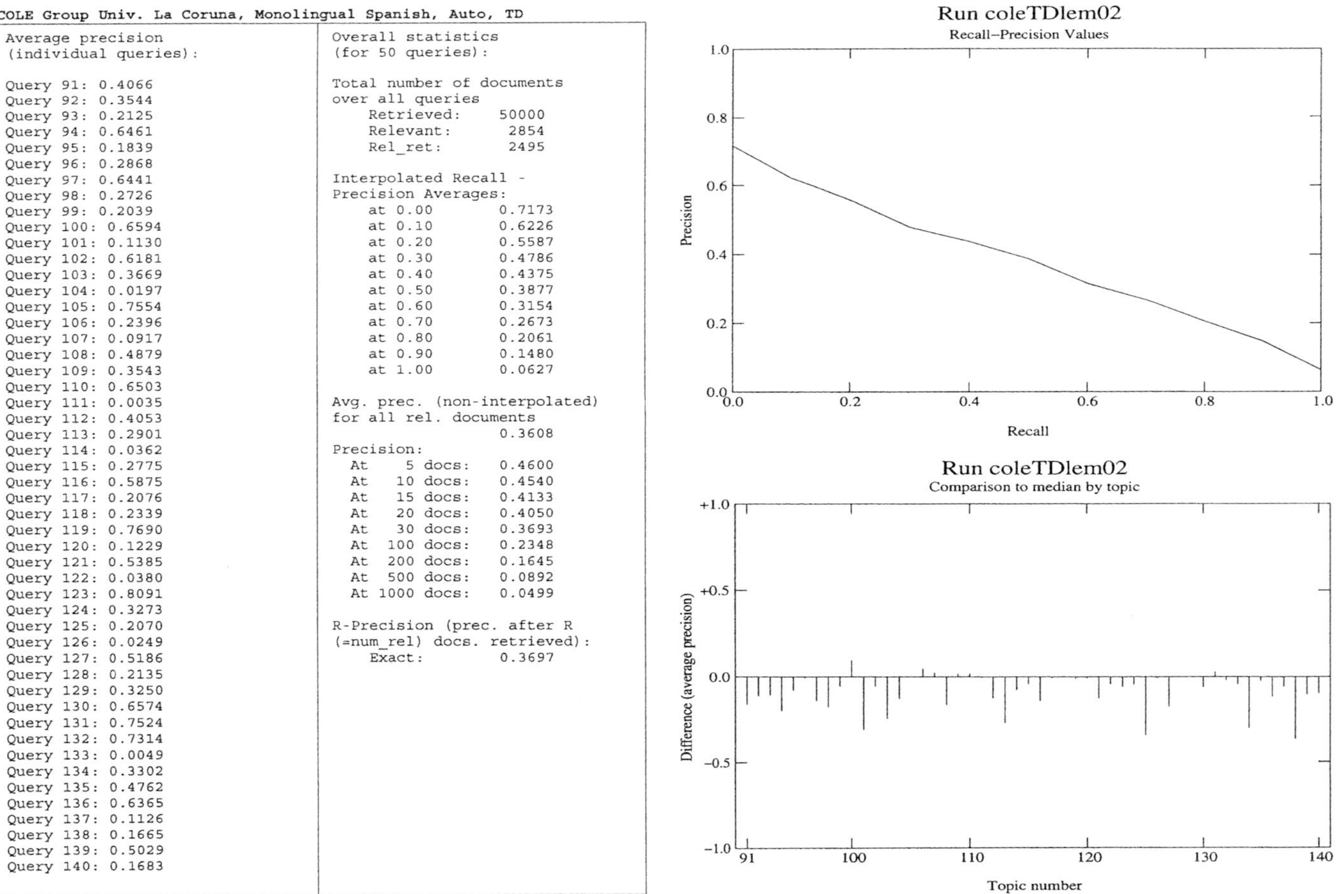

COLE Group Univ. La Coruna, Monolingual Spanish, Auto, TD

```
Average precision              Overall statistics
(individual queries):          (for 50 queries):

Query 91: 0.4066               Total number of documents
Query 92: 0.3544               over all queries
Query 93: 0.2125                   Retrieved:     50000
Query 94: 0.6461                   Relevant:       2854
Query 95: 0.1839                   Rel_ret:        2495
Query 96: 0.2868
Query 97: 0.6441               Interpolated Recall -
Query 98: 0.2726               Precision Averages:
Query 99: 0.2039                   at 0.00        0.7173
Query 100: 0.6594                  at 0.10        0.6226
Query 101: 0.1130                  at 0.20        0.5587
Query 102: 0.6181                  at 0.30        0.4786
Query 103: 0.3669                  at 0.40        0.4375
Query 104: 0.0197                  at 0.50        0.3877
Query 105: 0.7554                  at 0.60        0.3154
Query 106: 0.2396                  at 0.70        0.2673
Query 107: 0.0917                  at 0.80        0.2061
Query 108: 0.4879                  at 0.90        0.1480
Query 109: 0.3543                  at 1.00        0.0627
Query 110: 0.6503
Query 111: 0.0035              Avg. prec. (non-interpolated)
Query 112: 0.4053              for all rel. documents
Query 113: 0.2901                                 0.3608
Query 114: 0.0362              Precision:
Query 115: 0.2775                At    5 docs:    0.4600
Query 116: 0.5875                At   10 docs:    0.4540
Query 117: 0.2076                At   15 docs:    0.4133
Query 118: 0.2339                At   20 docs:    0.4050
Query 119: 0.7690                At   30 docs:    0.3693
Query 120: 0.1229                At  100 docs:    0.2348
Query 121: 0.5385                At  200 docs:    0.1645
Query 122: 0.0380                At  500 docs:    0.0892
Query 123: 0.8091                At 1000 docs:    0.0499
Query 124: 0.3273
Query 125: 0.2070              R-Precision (prec. after R
Query 126: 0.0249              (=num_rel) docs. retrieved):
Query 127: 0.5186                  Exact:         0.3697
Query 128: 0.2135
Query 129: 0.3250
Query 130: 0.6574
Query 131: 0.7524
Query 132: 0.7314
Query 133: 0.0049
Query 134: 0.3302
Query 135: 0.4762
Query 136: 0.6365
Query 137: 0.1126
Query 138: 0.1665
Query 139: 0.5029
Query 140: 0.1683
```

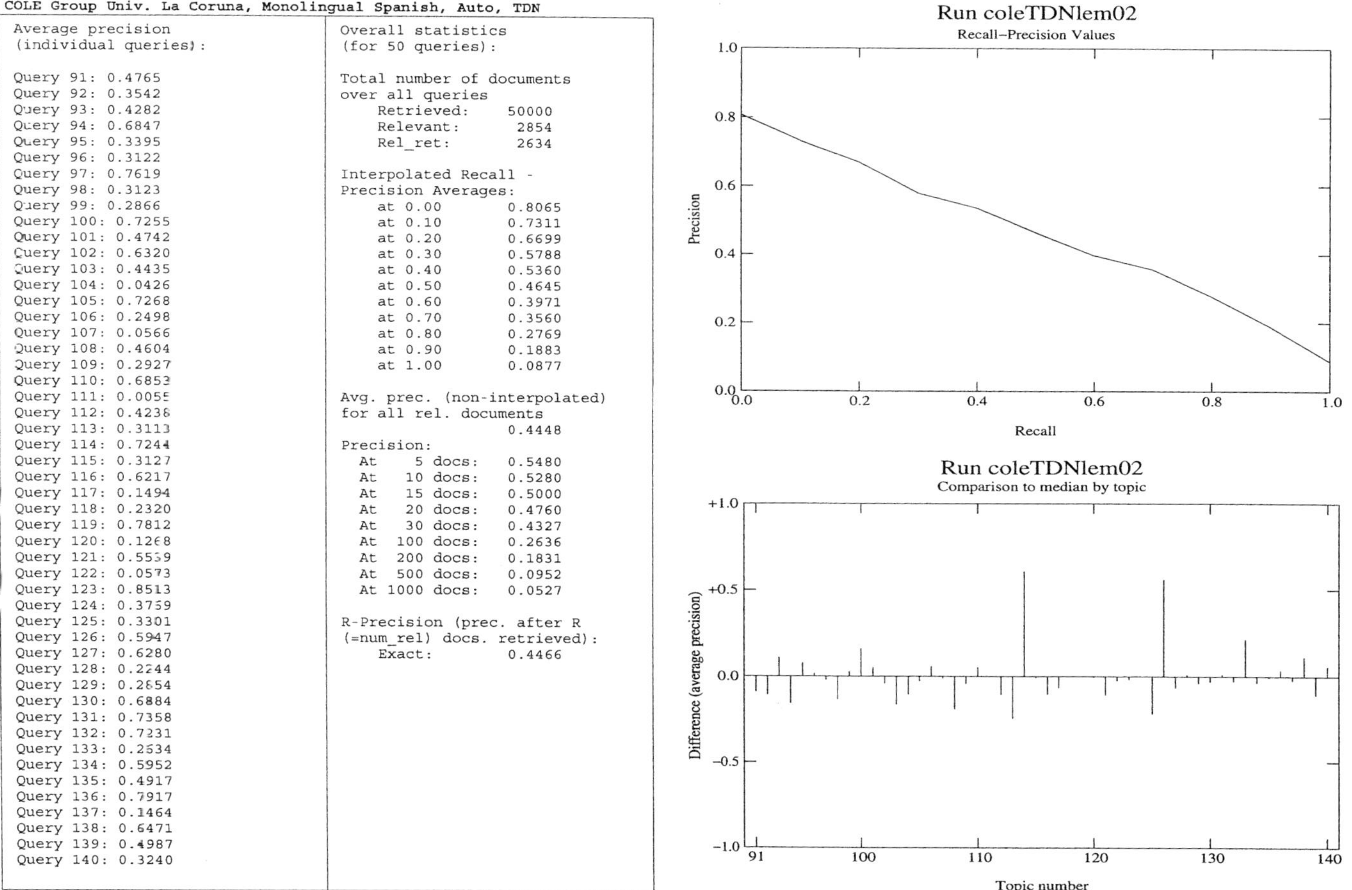

COLE Group Univ. La Coruna, Monolingual Spanish, Auto, TDN

```
Average precision                 Overall statistics
(individual queries):             (for 50 queries):

Query 91: 0.4765                  Total number of documents
Query 92: 0.3542                  over all queries
Query 93: 0.4282                      Retrieved:     50000
Query 94: 0.6847                      Relevant:       2854
Query 95: 0.3395                      Rel_ret:        2634
Query 96: 0.3122
Query 97: 0.7619                  Interpolated Recall -
Query 98: 0.3123                  Precision Averages:
Query 99: 0.2866                      at 0.00        0.8065
Query 100: 0.7255                     at 0.10        0.7311
Query 101: 0.4742                     at 0.20        0.6699
Query 102: 0.6320                     at 0.30        0.5788
Query 103: 0.4435                     at 0.40        0.5360
Query 104: 0.0426                     at 0.50        0.4645
Query 105: 0.7268                     at 0.60        0.3971
Query 106: 0.2498                     at 0.70        0.3560
Query 107: 0.0566                     at 0.80        0.2769
Query 108: 0.4604                     at 0.90        0.1883
Query 109: 0.2927                     at 1.00        0.0877
Query 110: 0.6853
Query 111: 0.0055                 Avg. prec. (non-interpolated)
Query 112: 0.4238                 for all rel. documents
Query 113: 0.3113                                    0.4448
Query 114: 0.7244                 Precision:
Query 115: 0.3127                   At    5 docs:    0.5480
Query 116: 0.6217                   At   10 docs:    0.5280
Query 117: 0.1494                   At   15 docs:    0.5000
Query 118: 0.2320                   At   20 docs:    0.4760
Query 119: 0.7812                   At   30 docs:    0.4327
Query 120: 0.1268                   At  100 docs:    0.2636
Query 121: 0.5559                   At  200 docs:    0.1831
Query 122: 0.0573                   At  500 docs:    0.0952
Query 123: 0.8513                   At 1000 docs:    0.0527
Query 124: 0.3759
Query 125: 0.3301                 R-Precision (prec. after R
Query 126: 0.5947                 (=num_rel) docs. retrieved):
Query 127: 0.6280                     Exact:         0.4466
Query 128: 0.2244
Query 129: 0.2654
Query 130: 0.6884
Query 131: 0.7358
Query 132: 0.7231
Query 133: 0.2534
Query 134: 0.5952
Query 135: 0.4917
Query 136: 0.7917
Query 137: 0.1464
Query 138: 0.6471
Query 139: 0.4987
Query 140: 0.3240
```

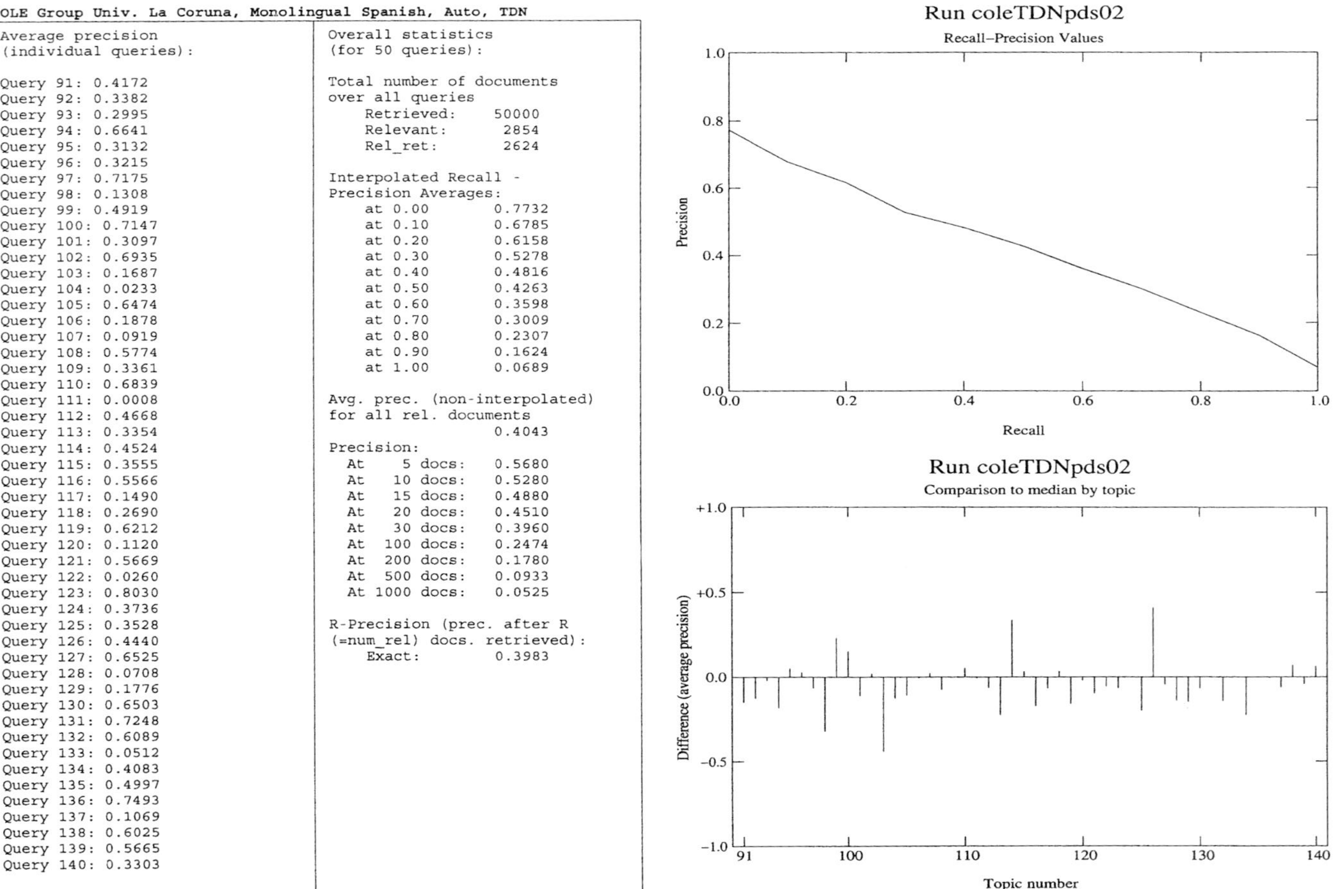

COLE Group Univ. La Coruna, Monolingual Spanish, Auto, TDN

```
Average precision                Overall statistics
(individual queries):            (for 50 queries):

Query 91: 0.4172                 Total number of documents
Query 92: 0.3382                 over all queries
Query 93: 0.2995                     Retrieved:    50000
Query 94: 0.6641                     Relevant:      2854
Query 95: 0.3132                     Rel_ret:       2624
Query 96: 0.3215
Query 97: 0.7175                 Interpolated Recall -
Query 98: 0.1308                 Precision Averages:
Query 99: 0.4919                     at 0.00       0.7732
Query 100: 0.7147                    at 0.10       0.6785
Query 101: 0.3097                    at 0.20       0.6158
Query 102: 0.6935                    at 0.30       0.5278
Query 103: 0.1687                    at 0.40       0.4816
Query 104: 0.0233                    at 0.50       0.4263
Query 105: 0.6474                    at 0.60       0.3598
Query 106: 0.1878                    at 0.70       0.3009
Query 107: 0.0919                    at 0.80       0.2307
Query 108: 0.5774                    at 0.90       0.1624
Query 109: 0.3361                    at 1.00       0.0689
Query 110: 0.6839
Query 111: 0.0008                Avg. prec. (non-interpolated)
Query 112: 0.4668                for all rel. documents
Query 113: 0.3354                                  0.4043
Query 114: 0.4524                Precision:
Query 115: 0.3555                  At    5 docs:   0.5680
Query 116: 0.5566                  At   10 docs:   0.5280
Query 117: 0.1490                  At   15 docs:   0.4880
Query 118: 0.2690                  At   20 docs:   0.4510
Query 119: 0.6212                  At   30 docs:   0.3960
Query 120: 0.1120                  At  100 docs:   0.2474
Query 121: 0.5669                  At  200 docs:   0.1780
Query 122: 0.0260                  At  500 docs:   0.0933
Query 123: 0.8030                  At 1000 docs:   0.0525
Query 124: 0.3736
Query 125: 0.3528                R-Precision (prec. after R
Query 126: 0.4440                (=num_rel) docs. retrieved):
Query 127: 0.6525                    Exact:        0.3983
Query 128: 0.0708
Query 129: 0.1776
Query 130: 0.6503
Query 131: 0.7248
Query 132: 0.6089
Query 133: 0.0512
Query 134: 0.4083
Query 135: 0.4997
Query 136: 0.7493
Query 137: 0.1069
Query 138: 0.6025
Query 139: 0.5665
Query 140: 0.3303
```

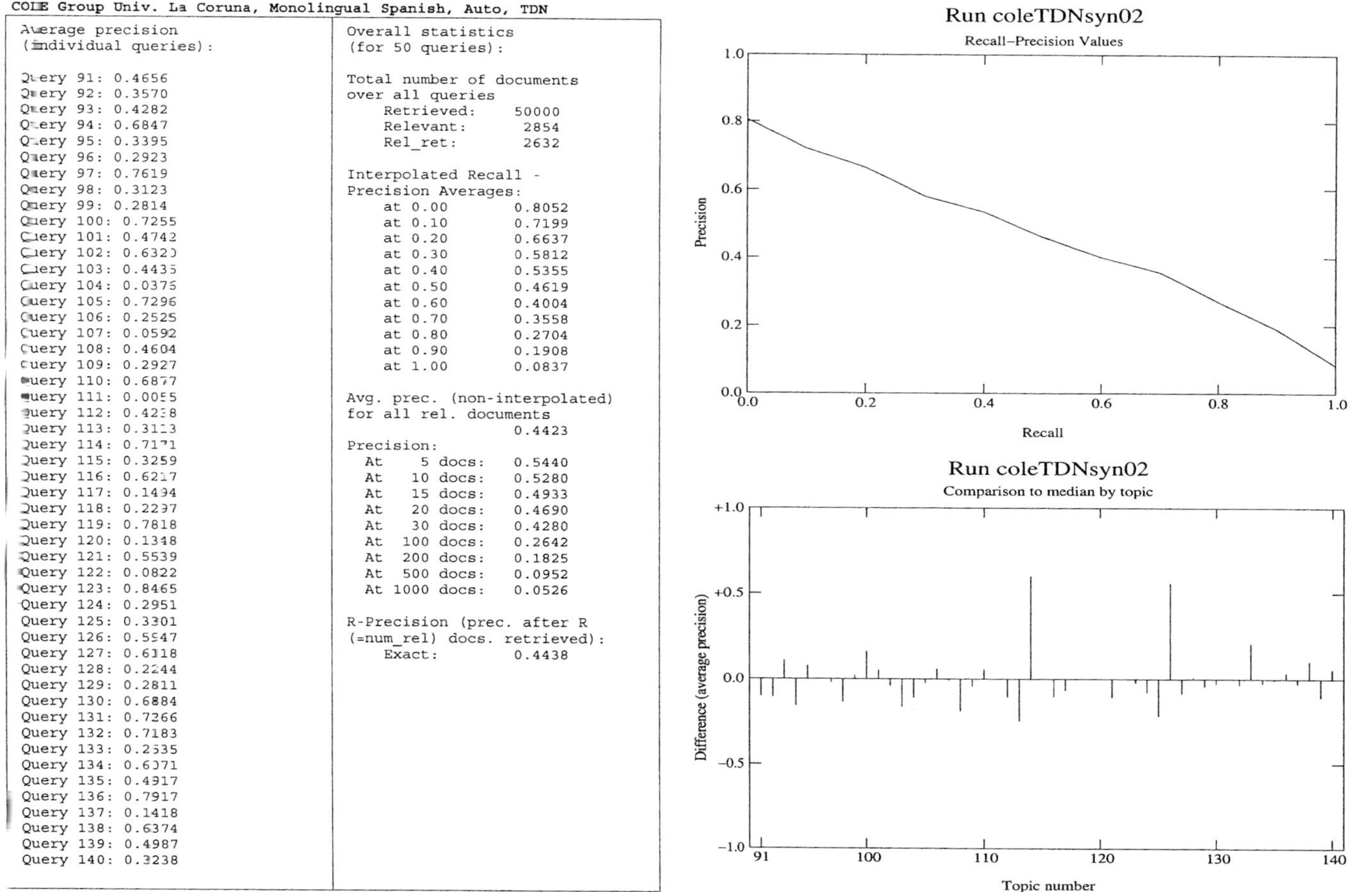

COLE Group Univ. La Coruna, Monolingual Spanish, Auto, TDN

Average precision (individual queries):	Overall statistics (for 50 queries):
Query 91: 0.4656	Total number of documents over all queries
Query 92: 0.3570	Retrieved: 50000
Query 93: 0.4282	Relevant: 2854
Query 94: 0.6847	Rel_ret: 2632
Query 95: 0.3395	
Query 96: 0.2923	Interpolated Recall - Precision Averages:
Query 97: 0.7619	at 0.00 0.8052
Query 98: 0.3123	at 0.10 0.7199
Query 99: 0.2814	at 0.20 0.6637
Query 100: 0.7255	at 0.30 0.5812
Query 101: 0.4742	at 0.40 0.5355
Query 102: 0.6320	at 0.50 0.4619
Query 103: 0.4435	at 0.60 0.4004
Query 104: 0.0375	at 0.70 0.3558
Query 105: 0.7296	at 0.80 0.2704
Query 106: 0.2525	at 0.90 0.1908
Query 107: 0.0592	at 1.00 0.0837
Query 108: 0.4604	
Query 109: 0.2927	Avg. prec. (non-interpolated) for all rel. documents 0.4423
Query 110: 0.6877	
Query 111: 0.0055	Precision:
Query 112: 0.4238	At 5 docs: 0.5440
Query 113: 0.3123	At 10 docs: 0.5280
Query 114: 0.7171	At 15 docs: 0.4933
Query 115: 0.3259	At 20 docs: 0.4690
Query 116: 0.6217	At 30 docs: 0.4280
Query 117: 0.1434	At 100 docs: 0.2642
Query 118: 0.2237	At 200 docs: 0.1825
Query 119: 0.7818	At 500 docs: 0.0952
Query 120: 0.1348	At 1000 docs: 0.0526
Query 121: 0.5539	
Query 122: 0.0822	R-Precision (prec. after R (=num_rel) docs. retrieved):
Query 123: 0.8465	Exact: 0.4438
Query 124: 0.2951	
Query 125: 0.3301	
Query 126: 0.5547	
Query 127: 0.6118	
Query 128: 0.2244	
Query 129: 0.2811	
Query 130: 0.6884	
Query 131: 0.7266	
Query 132: 0.7183	
Query 133: 0.2535	
Query 134: 0.6071	
Query 135: 0.4917	
Query 136: 0.7917	
Query 137: 0.1418	
Query 138: 0.6374	
Query 139: 0.4987	
Query 140: 0.3238	

Univ. Exeter, Monolingual Spanish, Auto, TD

Average precision (individual queries):	Overall statistics (for 50 queries):
Query 91: 0.5143	Total number of documents over all queries
Query 92: 0.4469	Retrieved: 50000
Query 93: 0.2640	Relevant: 2854
Query 94: 0.7357	Rel_ret: 2460
Query 95: 0.1823	
Query 96: 0.2946	Interpolated Recall - Precision Averages:
Query 97: 0.8294	at 0.00 0.8038
Query 98: 0.9667	at 0.10 0.7267
Query 99: 0.3588	at 0.20 0.6566
Query 100: 0.5819	at 0.30 0.5755
Query 101: 0.1489	at 0.40 0.5298
Query 102: 0.6141	at 0.50 0.4913
Query 103: 0.7593	at 0.60 0.4481
Query 104: 0.2242	at 0.70 0.4081
Query 105: 0.8155	at 0.80 0.3268
Query 106: 0.2170	at 0.90 0.2253
Query 107: 0.0983	at 1.00 0.1164
Query 108: 0.7479	
Query 109: 0.3481	Avg. prec. (non-interpolated) for all rel. documents 0.4684
Query 110: 0.7682	
Query 111: 0.0072	Precision:
Query 112: 0.5342	At 5 docs: 0.5880
Query 113: 0.3381	At 10 docs: 0.5400
Query 114: 0.0303	At 15 docs: 0.5000
Query 115: 0.4047	At 20 docs: 0.4730
Query 116: 0.8733	At 30 docs: 0.4173
Query 117: 0.2883	At 100 docs: 0.2766
Query 118: 0.2189	At 200 docs: 0.1878
Query 119: 0.7759	At 500 docs: 0.0912
Query 120: 0.1446	At 1000 docs: 0.0492
Query 121: 0.6649	
Query 122: 0.1062	R-Precision (prec. after R (=num_rel) docs. retrieved):
Query 123: 0.8587	Exact: 0.4555
Query 124: 0.1150	
Query 125: 0.6415	
Query 126: 0.0325	
Query 127: 0.6333	
Query 128: 0.0815	
Query 129: 0.3779	
Query 130: 0.7953	
Query 131: 0.7232	
Query 132: 0.7563	
Query 133: 0.0952	
Query 134: 0.9500	
Query 135: 0.3955	
Query 136: 0.7514	
Query 137: 0.1189	
Query 138: 0.6252	
Query 139: 0.8202	
Query 140: 0.3448	

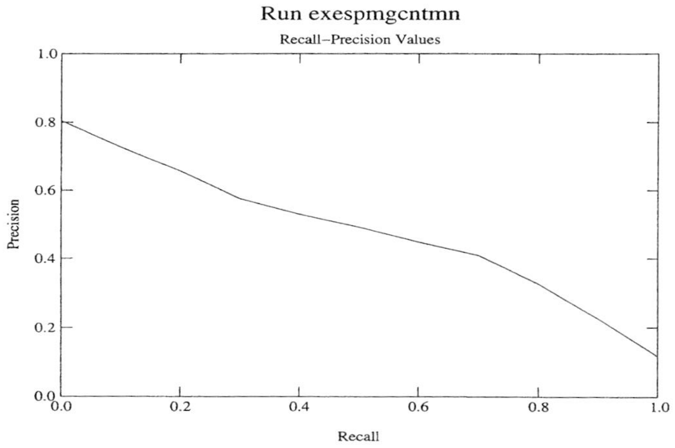

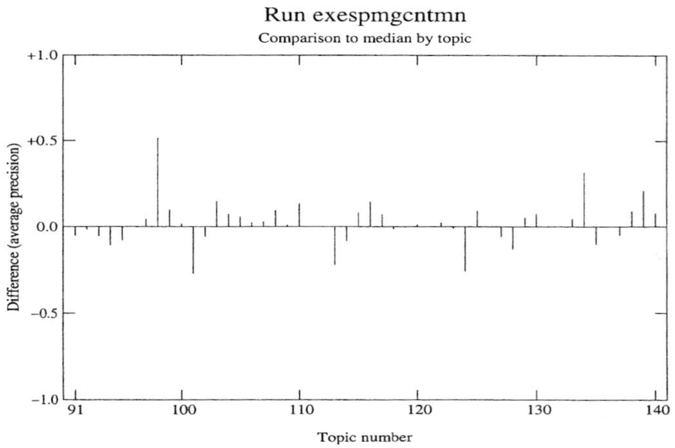

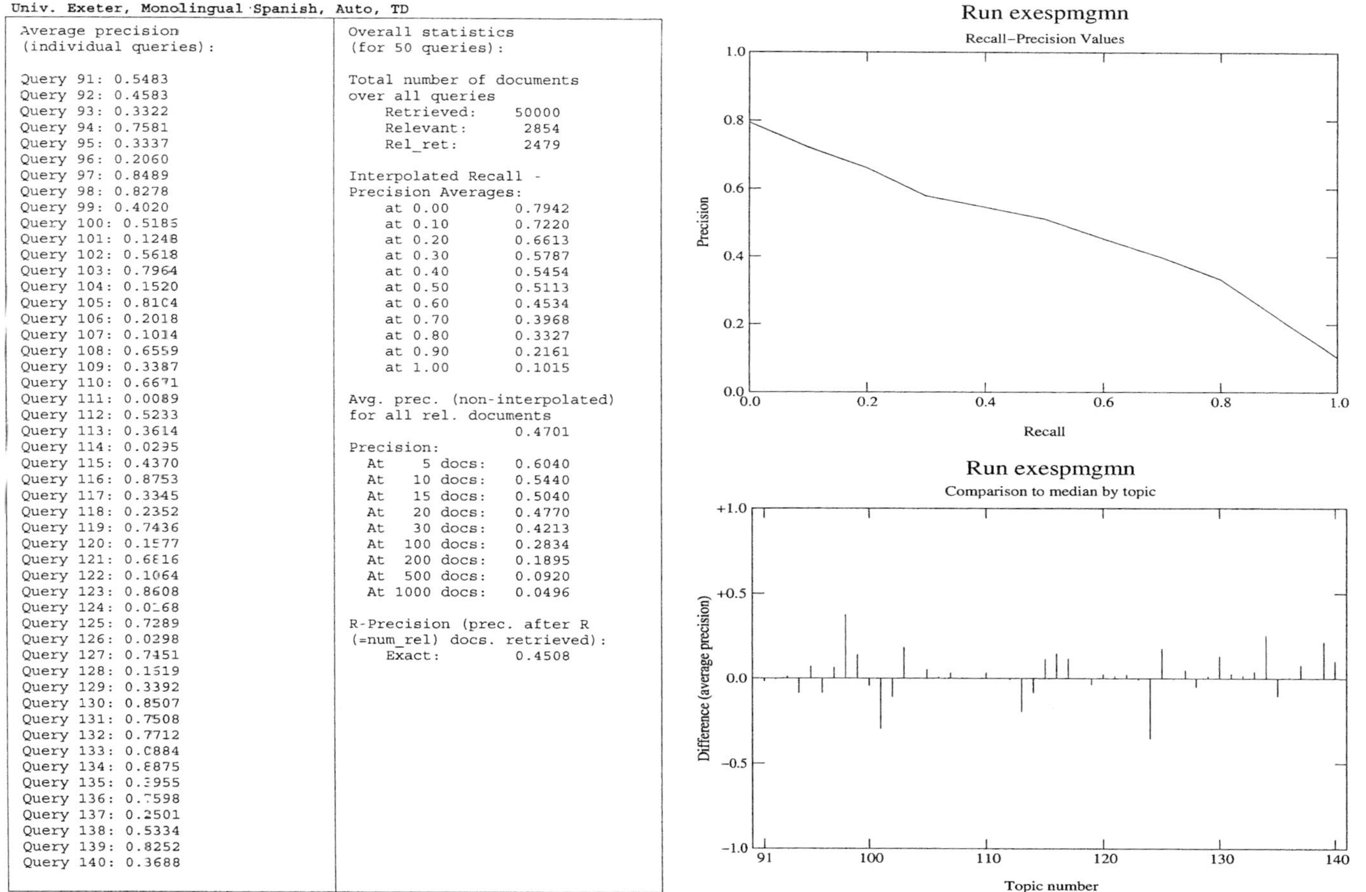

Univ. Exeter, Monolingual Spanish, Auto, TD

Average precision (individual queries):	Overall statistics (for 50 queries):
Query 91: 0.5483	Total number of documents over all queries
Query 92: 0.4583	Retrieved: 50000
Query 93: 0.3322	Relevant: 2854
Query 94: 0.7581	Rel_ret: 2479
Query 95: 0.3337	
Query 96: 0.2060	Interpolated Recall - Precision Averages:
Query 97: 0.8489	at 0.00 0.7942
Query 98: 0.8278	at 0.10 0.7220
Query 99: 0.4020	at 0.20 0.6613
Query 100: 0.5185	at 0.30 0.5787
Query 101: 0.1248	at 0.40 0.5454
Query 102: 0.5618	at 0.50 0.5113
Query 103: 0.7964	at 0.60 0.4534
Query 104: 0.1520	at 0.70 0.3968
Query 105: 0.8104	at 0.80 0.3327
Query 106: 0.2018	at 0.90 0.2161
Query 107: 0.1014	at 1.00 0.1015
Query 108: 0.6559	
Query 109: 0.3387	Avg. prec. (non-interpolated) for all rel. documents 0.4701
Query 110: 0.6671	
Query 111: 0.0089	Precision:
Query 112: 0.5233	At 5 docs: 0.6040
Query 113: 0.3614	At 10 docs: 0.5440
Query 114: 0.0295	At 15 docs: 0.5040
Query 115: 0.4370	At 20 docs: 0.4770
Query 116: 0.8753	At 30 docs: 0.4213
Query 117: 0.3345	At 100 docs: 0.2834
Query 118: 0.2352	At 200 docs: 0.1895
Query 119: 0.7436	At 500 docs: 0.0920
Query 120: 0.1577	At 1000 docs: 0.0496
Query 121: 0.6816	
Query 122: 0.1064	R-Precision (prec. after R (=num_rel) docs. retrieved):
Query 123: 0.8608	Exact: 0.4508
Query 124: 0.0168	
Query 125: 0.7289	
Query 126: 0.0298	
Query 127: 0.7451	
Query 128: 0.1519	
Query 129: 0.3392	
Query 130: 0.8507	
Query 131: 0.7508	
Query 132: 0.7712	
Query 133: 0.0884	
Query 134: 0.8875	
Query 135: 0.3955	
Query 136: 0.7598	
Query 137: 0.2501	
Query 138: 0.5334	
Query 139: 0.8252	
Query 140: 0.3688	

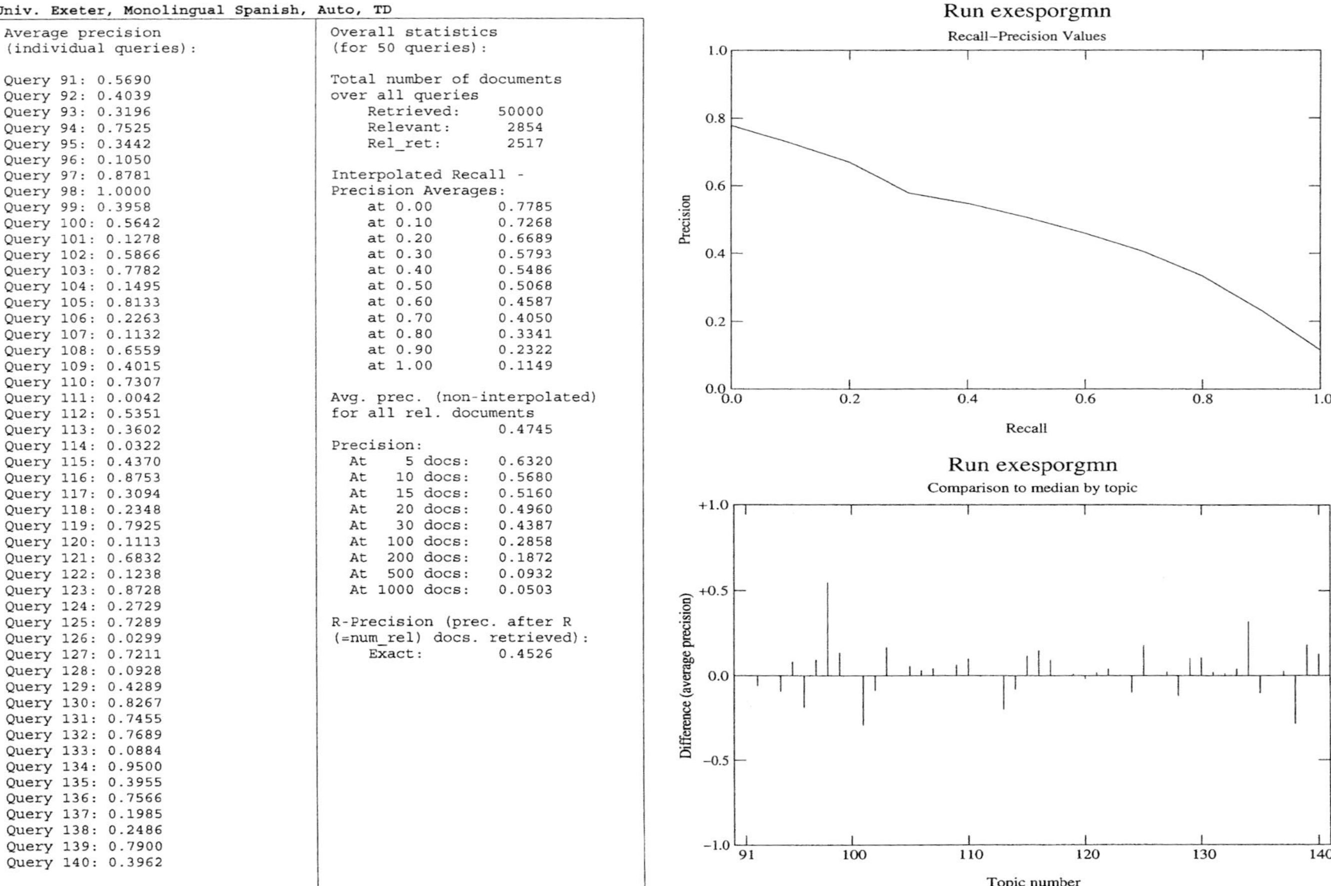

Univ. Exeter, Monolingual Spanish, Auto, TD

```
Average precision                Overall statistics
(individual queries):            (for 50 queries):

Query 91: 0.5690                 Total number of documents
Query 92: 0.4039                 over all queries
Query 93: 0.3196                     Retrieved:    50000
Query 94: 0.7525                     Relevant:      2854
Query 95: 0.3442                     Rel_ret:       2517
Query 96: 0.1050
Query 97: 0.8781                 Interpolated Recall -
Query 98: 1.0000                 Precision Averages:
Query 99: 0.3958                     at 0.00        0.7785
Query 100: 0.5642                    at 0.10        0.7268
Query 101: 0.1278                    at 0.20        0.6689
Query 102: 0.5866                    at 0.30        0.5793
Query 103: 0.7782                    at 0.40        0.5486
Query 104: 0.1495                    at 0.50        0.5068
Query 105: 0.8133                    at 0.60        0.4587
Query 106: 0.2263                    at 0.70        0.4050
Query 107: 0.1132                    at 0.80        0.3341
Query 108: 0.6559                    at 0.90        0.2322
Query 109: 0.4015                    at 1.00        0.1149
Query 110: 0.7307
Query 111: 0.0042                Avg. prec. (non-interpolated)
Query 112: 0.5351                for all rel. documents
Query 113: 0.3602                                   0.4745
Query 114: 0.0322                Precision:
Query 115: 0.4370                  At    5 docs:   0.6320
Query 116: 0.8753                  At   10 docs:   0.5680
Query 117: 0.3094                  At   15 docs:   0.5160
Query 118: 0.2348                  At   20 docs:   0.4960
Query 119: 0.7925                  At   30 docs:   0.4387
Query 120: 0.1113                  At  100 docs:   0.2858
Query 121: 0.6832                  At  200 docs:   0.1872
Query 122: 0.1238                  At  500 docs:   0.0932
Query 123: 0.8728                  At 1000 docs:   0.0503
Query 124: 0.2729
Query 125: 0.7289                R-Precision (prec. after R
Query 126: 0.0299                (=num_rel) docs. retrieved):
Query 127: 0.7211                    Exact:         0.4526
Query 128: 0.0928
Query 129: 0.4289
Query 130: 0.8267
Query 131: 0.7455
Query 132: 0.7689
Query 133: 0.0884
Query 134: 0.9500
Query 135: 0.3955
Query 136: 0.7566
Query 137: 0.1985
Query 138: 0.2486
Query 139: 0.7900
Query 140: 0.3962
```

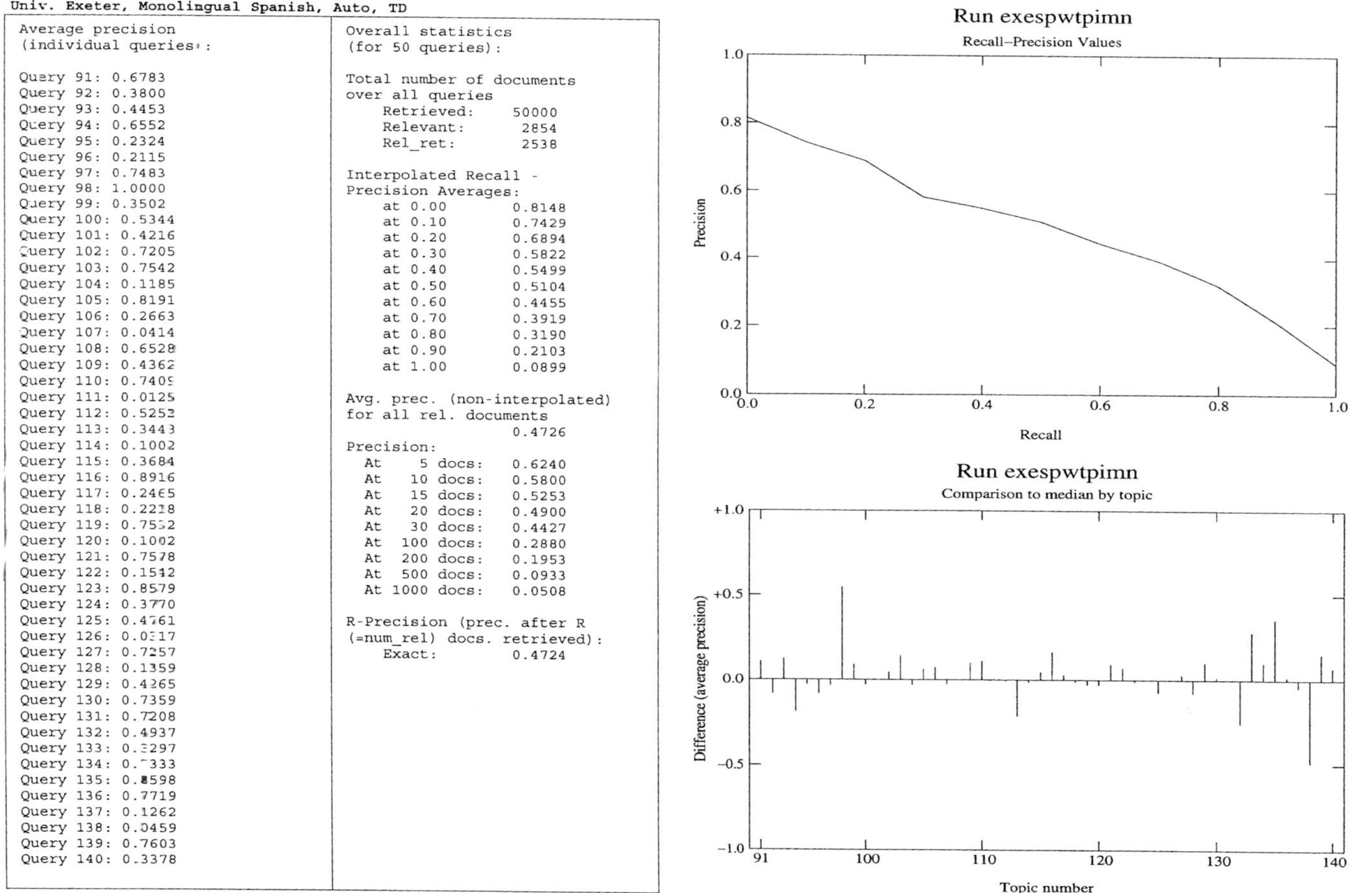

Univ. Exeter, Monolingual Spanish, Auto, TD

```
Average precision                 Overall statistics
(individual queries):             (for 50 queries):

Query 91: 0.6783                  Total number of documents
Query 92: 0.3800                  over all queries
Query 93: 0.4453                      Retrieved:     50000
Query 94: 0.6552                      Relevant:       2854
Query 95: 0.2324                      Rel_ret:        2538
Query 96: 0.2115
Query 97: 0.7483                  Interpolated Recall -
Query 98: 1.0000                  Precision Averages:
Query 99: 0.3502                      at 0.00        0.8148
Query 100: 0.5344                     at 0.10        0.7429
Query 101: 0.4216                     at 0.20        0.6894
Query 102: 0.7205                     at 0.30        0.5822
Query 103: 0.7542                     at 0.40        0.5499
Query 104: 0.1185                     at 0.50        0.5104
Query 105: 0.8191                     at 0.60        0.4455
Query 106: 0.2663                     at 0.70        0.3919
Query 107: 0.0414                     at 0.80        0.3190
Query 108: 0.6528                     at 0.90        0.2103
Query 109: 0.4362                     at 1.00        0.0899
Query 110: 0.7409
Query 111: 0.0125                 Avg. prec. (non-interpolated)
Query 112: 0.5252                 for all rel. documents
Query 113: 0.3443                                    0.4726
Query 114: 0.1002                 Precision:
Query 115: 0.3684                   At    5 docs:    0.6240
Query 116: 0.8916                   At   10 docs:    0.5800
Query 117: 0.2465                   At   15 docs:    0.5253
Query 118: 0.2218                   At   20 docs:    0.4900
Query 119: 0.7552                   At   30 docs:    0.4427
Query 120: 0.1002                   At  100 docs:    0.2880
Query 121: 0.7578                   At  200 docs:    0.1953
Query 122: 0.1542                   At  500 docs:    0.0933
Query 123: 0.8579                   At 1000 docs:    0.0508
Query 124: 0.3770
Query 125: 0.4761                 R-Precision (prec. after R
Query 126: 0.0317                 (=num_rel) docs. retrieved):
Query 127: 0.7257                     Exact:         0.4724
Query 128: 0.1359
Query 129: 0.4265
Query 130: 0.7359
Query 131: 0.7208
Query 132: 0.4937
Query 133: 0.3297
Query 134: 0.7333
Query 135: 0.8598
Query 136: 0.7719
Query 137: 0.1262
Query 138: 0.0459
Query 139: 0.7603
Query 140: 0.3378
```

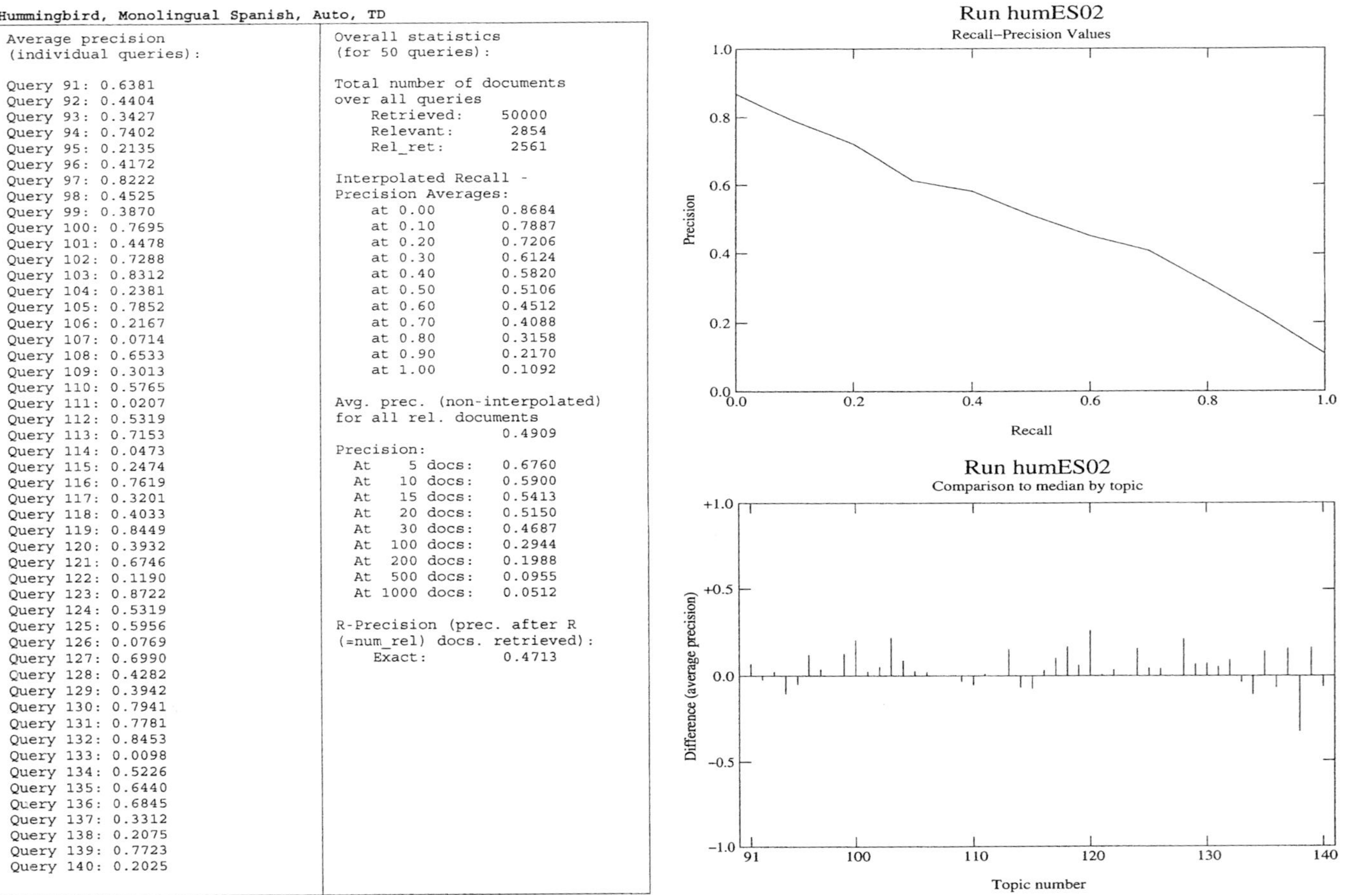

Hummingbird, Monolingual Spanish, Auto, TD

```
Average precision              Overall statistics
(individual queries):          (for 50 queries):

Query 91: 0.6381               Total number of documents
Query 92: 0.4404               over all queries
Query 93: 0.3427                  Retrieved:     50000
Query 94: 0.7402                  Relevant:       2854
Query 95: 0.2135                  Rel_ret:        2561
Query 96: 0.4172
Query 97: 0.8222               Interpolated Recall -
Query 98: 0.4525               Precision Averages:
Query 99: 0.3870                  at 0.00        0.8684
Query 100: 0.7695                 at 0.10        0.7887
Query 101: 0.4478                 at 0.20        0.7206
Query 102: 0.7288                 at 0.30        0.6124
Query 103: 0.8312                 at 0.40        0.5820
Query 104: 0.2381                 at 0.50        0.5106
Query 105: 0.7852                 at 0.60        0.4512
Query 106: 0.2167                 at 0.70        0.4088
Query 107: 0.0714                 at 0.80        0.3158
Query 108: 0.6533                 at 0.90        0.2170
Query 109: 0.3013                 at 1.00        0.1092
Query 110: 0.5765
Query 111: 0.0207              Avg. prec. (non-interpolated)
Query 112: 0.5319              for all rel. documents
Query 113: 0.7153                                0.4909
Query 114: 0.0473              Precision:
Query 115: 0.2474                At    5 docs:   0.6760
Query 116: 0.7619                At   10 docs:   0.5900
Query 117: 0.3201                At   15 docs:   0.5413
Query 118: 0.4033                At   20 docs:   0.5150
Query 119: 0.8449                At   30 docs:   0.4687
Query 120: 0.3932                At  100 docs:   0.2944
Query 121: 0.6746                At  200 docs:   0.1988
Query 122: 0.1190                At  500 docs:   0.0955
Query 123: 0.8722                At 1000 docs:   0.0512
Query 124: 0.5319
Query 125: 0.5956              R-Precision (prec. after R
Query 126: 0.0769              (=num_rel) docs. retrieved):
Query 127: 0.6990                  Exact:        0.4713
Query 128: 0.4282
Query 129: 0.3942
Query 130: 0.7941
Query 131: 0.7781
Query 132: 0.8453
Query 133: 0.0098
Query 134: 0.5226
Query 135: 0.6440
Query 136: 0.6845
Query 137: 0.3312
Query 138: 0.2075
Query 139: 0.7723
Query 140: 0.2025
```

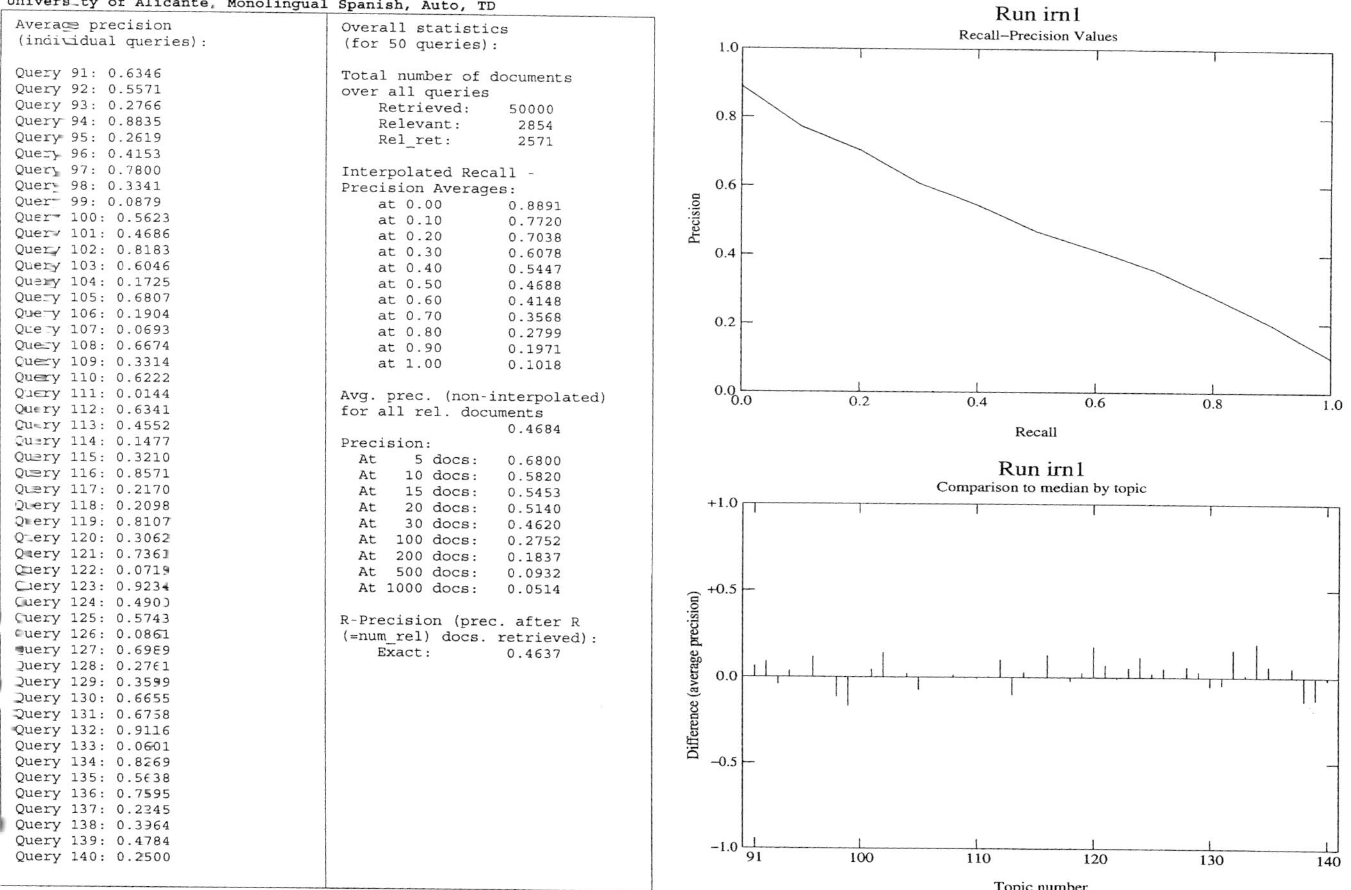

University of Alicante, Monolingual Spanish, Auto, TD

Average precision (individual queries):

Query	Average precision
Query 91:	0.6346
Query 92:	0.5571
Query 93:	0.2766
Query 94:	0.8835
Query 95:	0.2619
Query 96:	0.4153
Query 97:	0.7800
Query 98:	0.3341
Query 99:	0.0879
Query 100:	0.5623
Query 101:	0.4686
Query 102:	0.8183
Query 103:	0.6046
Query 104:	0.1725
Query 105:	0.6807
Query 106:	0.1904
Query 107:	0.0693
Query 108:	0.6674
Query 109:	0.3314
Query 110:	0.6222
Query 111:	0.0144
Query 112:	0.6341
Query 113:	0.4552
Query 114:	0.1477
Query 115:	0.3210
Query 116:	0.8571
Query 117:	0.2170
Query 118:	0.2098
Query 119:	0.8107
Query 120:	0.3062
Query 121:	0.7361
Query 122:	0.0719
Query 123:	0.9234
Query 124:	0.4900
Query 125:	0.5743
Query 126:	0.0861
Query 127:	0.6989
Query 128:	0.2761
Query 129:	0.3599
Query 130:	0.6655
Query 131:	0.6758
Query 132:	0.9116
Query 133:	0.0601
Query 134:	0.8269
Query 135:	0.5638
Query 136:	0.7595
Query 137:	0.2345
Query 138:	0.3364
Query 139:	0.4784
Query 140:	0.2500

Overall statistics (for 50 queries):

Total number of documents over all queries

Retrieved:	50000
Relevant:	2854
Rel_ret:	2571

Interpolated Recall - Precision Averages:

at 0.00	0.8891
at 0.10	0.7720
at 0.20	0.7038
at 0.30	0.6078
at 0.40	0.5447
at 0.50	0.4688
at 0.60	0.4148
at 0.70	0.3568
at 0.80	0.2799
at 0.90	0.1971
at 1.00	0.1018

Avg. prec. (non-interpolated) for all rel. documents 0.4684

Precision:

At 5 docs:	0.6800
At 10 docs:	0.5820
At 15 docs:	0.5453
At 20 docs:	0.5140
At 30 docs:	0.4620
At 100 docs:	0.2752
At 200 docs:	0.1837
At 500 docs:	0.0932
At 1000 docs:	0.0514

R-Precision (prec. after R (=num_rel) docs. retrieved):
Exact: 0.4637

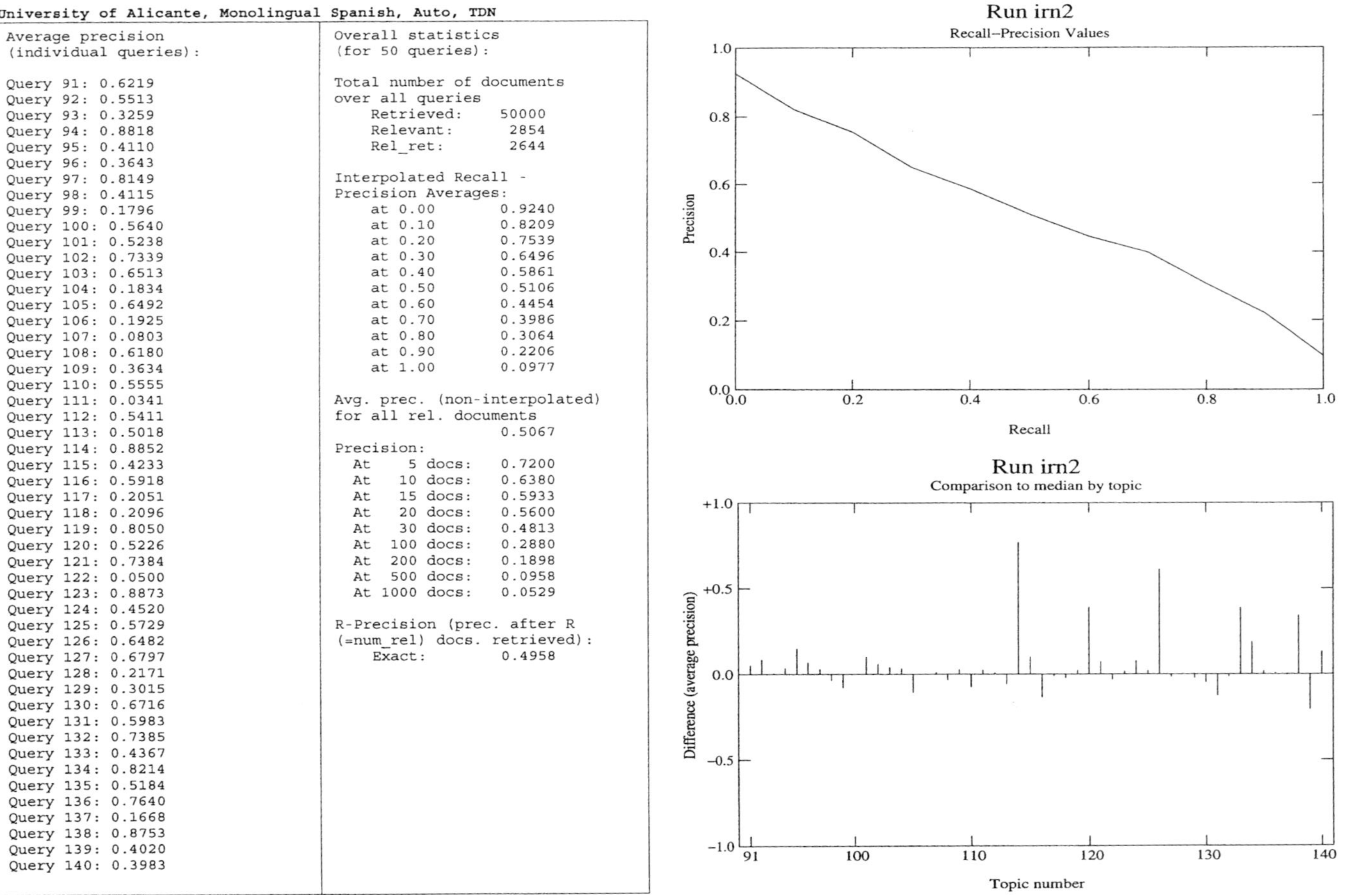

University of Alicante, Monolingual Spanish, Auto, TDN

Average precision (individual queries):

Query	Average precision
Query 91:	0.6219
Query 92:	0.5513
Query 93:	0.3259
Query 94:	0.8818
Query 95:	0.4110
Query 96:	0.3643
Query 97:	0.8149
Query 98:	0.4115
Query 99:	0.1796
Query 100:	0.5640
Query 101:	0.5238
Query 102:	0.7339
Query 103:	0.6513
Query 104:	0.1834
Query 105:	0.6492
Query 106:	0.1925
Query 107:	0.0803
Query 108:	0.6180
Query 109:	0.3634
Query 110:	0.5555
Query 111:	0.0341
Query 112:	0.5411
Query 113:	0.5018
Query 114:	0.8852
Query 115:	0.4233
Query 116:	0.5918
Query 117:	0.2051
Query 118:	0.2096
Query 119:	0.8050
Query 120:	0.5226
Query 121:	0.7384
Query 122:	0.0500
Query 123:	0.8873
Query 124:	0.4520
Query 125:	0.5729
Query 126:	0.6482
Query 127:	0.6797
Query 128:	0.2171
Query 129:	0.3015
Query 130:	0.6716
Query 131:	0.5983
Query 132:	0.7385
Query 133:	0.4367
Query 134:	0.8214
Query 135:	0.5184
Query 136:	0.7640
Query 137:	0.1668
Query 138:	0.8753
Query 139:	0.4020
Query 140:	0.3983

Overall statistics (for 50 queries):

Total number of documents over all queries

Retrieved:	50000
Relevant:	2854
Rel_ret:	2644

Interpolated Recall - Precision Averages:

at 0.00	0.9240
at 0.10	0.8209
at 0.20	0.7539
at 0.30	0.6496
at 0.40	0.5861
at 0.50	0.5106
at 0.60	0.4454
at 0.70	0.3986
at 0.80	0.3064
at 0.90	0.2206
at 1.00	0.0977

Avg. prec. (non-interpolated) for all rel. documents 0.5067

Precision:

At 5 docs:	0.7200
At 10 docs:	0.6380
At 15 docs:	0.5933
At 20 docs:	0.5600
At 30 docs:	0.4813
At 100 docs:	0.2880
At 200 docs:	0.1898
At 500 docs:	0.0958
At 1000 docs:	0.0529

R-Precision (prec. after R (=num_rel) docs. retrieved):
Exact: 0.4958

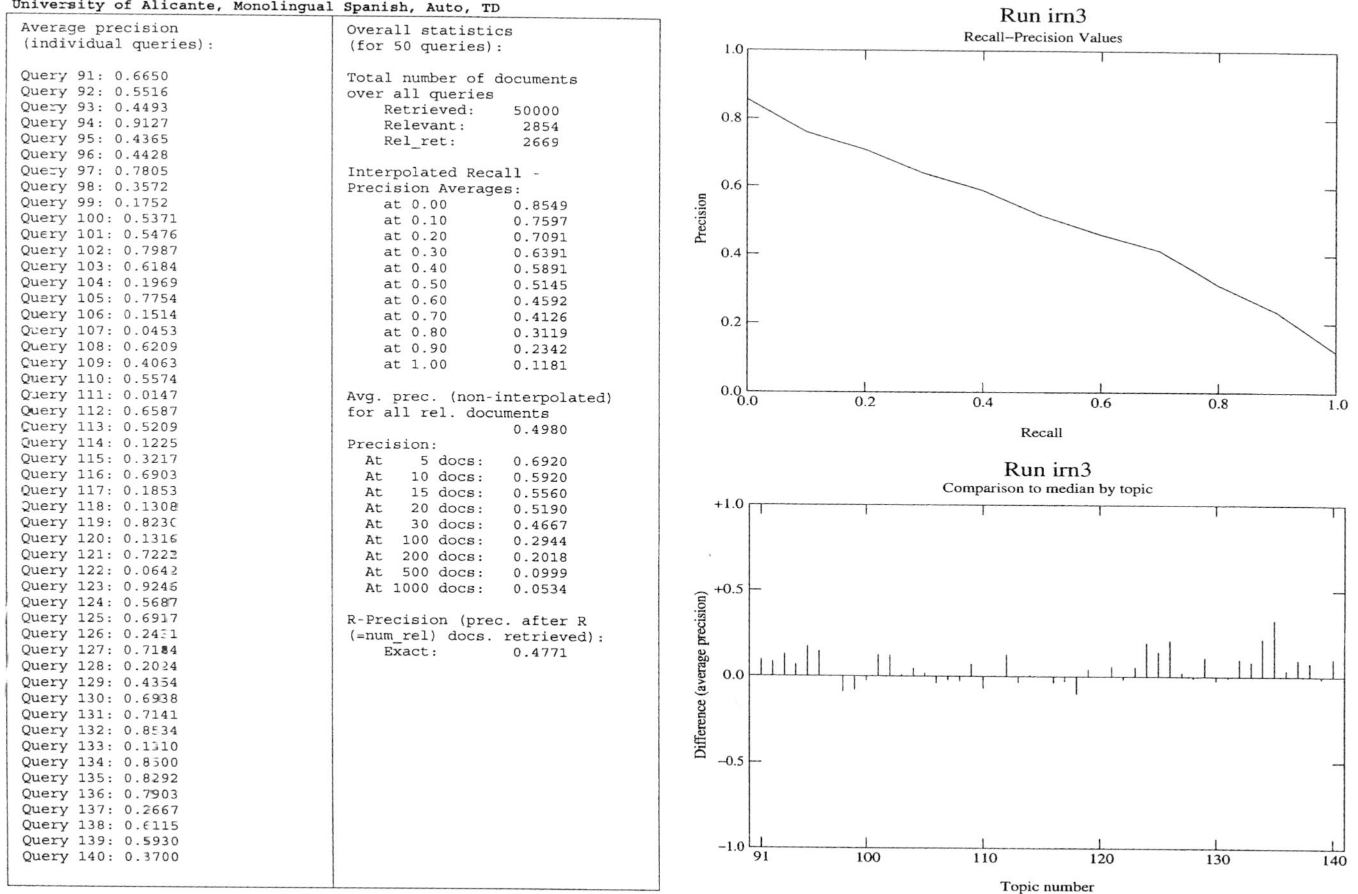

University of Alicante, Monolingual Spanish, Auto, TD

Average precision
(individual queries):

Query	Average precision
Query 91:	0.6650
Query 92:	0.5516
Query 93:	0.4493
Query 94:	0.9127
Query 95:	0.4365
Query 96:	0.4428
Query 97:	0.7805
Query 98:	0.3572
Query 99:	0.1752
Query 100:	0.5371
Query 101:	0.5476
Query 102:	0.7987
Query 103:	0.6184
Query 104:	0.1969
Query 105:	0.7754
Query 106:	0.1514
Query 107:	0.0453
Query 108:	0.6209
Query 109:	0.4063
Query 110:	0.5574
Query 111:	0.0147
Query 112:	0.6587
Query 113:	0.5209
Query 114:	0.1225
Query 115:	0.3217
Query 116:	0.6903
Query 117:	0.1853
Query 118:	0.1308
Query 119:	0.8230
Query 120:	0.1316
Query 121:	0.7223
Query 122:	0.0642
Query 123:	0.9246
Query 124:	0.5687
Query 125:	0.6917
Query 126:	0.2431
Query 127:	0.7184
Query 128:	0.2024
Query 129:	0.4354
Query 130:	0.6938
Query 131:	0.7141
Query 132:	0.8534
Query 133:	0.1310
Query 134:	0.8500
Query 135:	0.8292
Query 136:	0.7903
Query 137:	0.2667
Query 138:	0.6115
Query 139:	0.5930
Query 140:	0.3700

Overall statistics
(for 50 queries):

Total number of documents
over all queries

Retrieved:	50000
Relevant:	2854
Rel_ret:	2669

Interpolated Recall -
Precision Averages:

at 0.00	0.8549
at 0.10	0.7597
at 0.20	0.7091
at 0.30	0.6391
at 0.40	0.5891
at 0.50	0.5145
at 0.60	0.4592
at 0.70	0.4126
at 0.80	0.3119
at 0.90	0.2342
at 1.00	0.1181

Avg. prec. (non-interpolated)
for all rel. documents
0.4980

Precision:

At 5 docs:	0.6920
At 10 docs:	0.5920
At 15 docs:	0.5560
At 20 docs:	0.5190
At 30 docs:	0.4667
At 100 docs:	0.2944
At 200 docs:	0.2018
At 500 docs:	0.0999
At 1000 docs:	0.0534

R-Precision (prec. after R
(=num_rel) docs. retrieved):
Exact: 0.4771

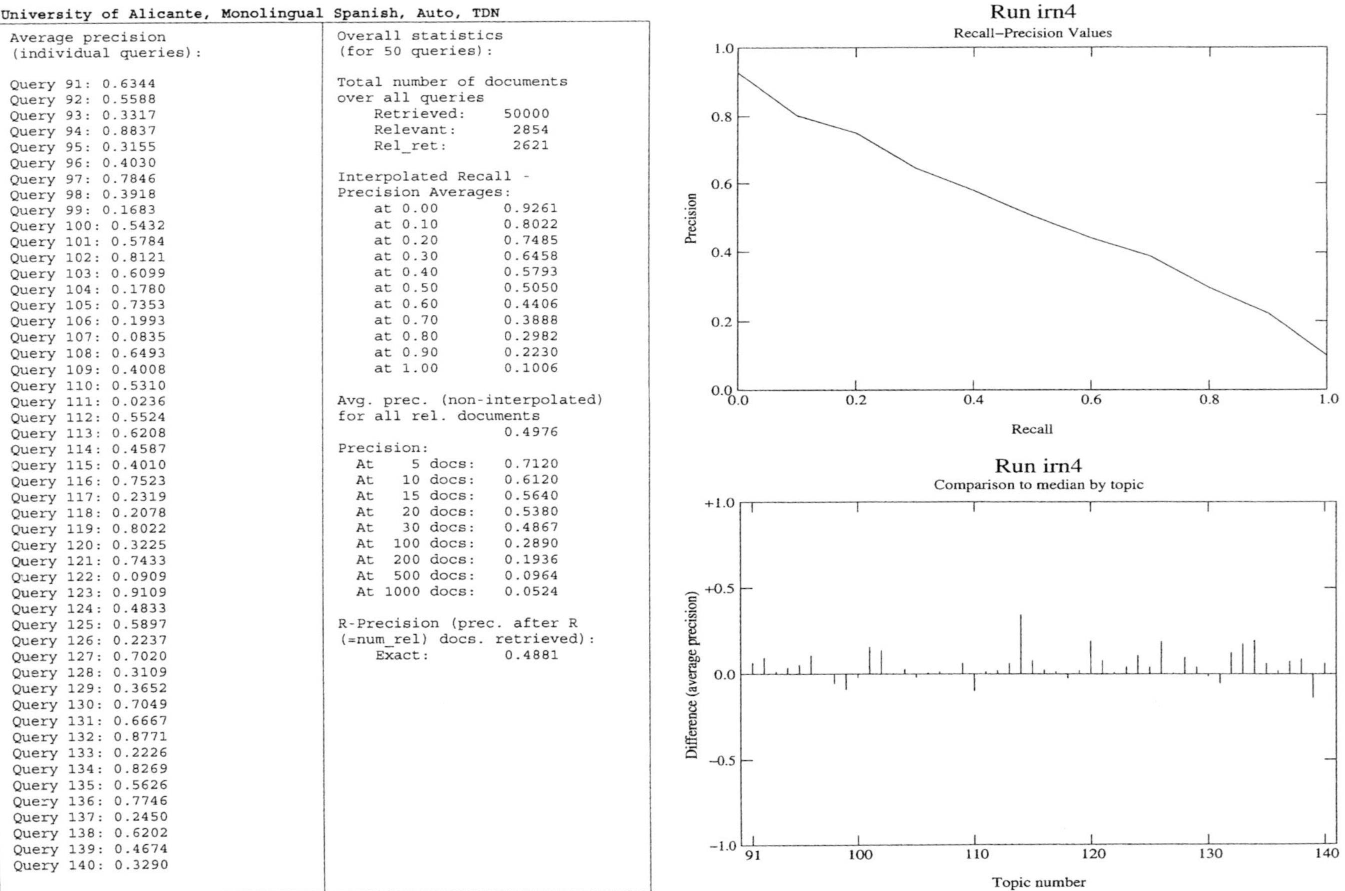

University of Alicante, Monolingual Spanish, Auto, TDN

```
Average precision                Overall statistics
(individual queries):            (for 50 queries):

Query 91: 0.6344                 Total number of documents
Query 92: 0.5588                 over all queries
Query 93: 0.3317                     Retrieved:    50000
Query 94: 0.8837                     Relevant:      2854
Query 95: 0.3155                     Rel_ret:       2621
Query 96: 0.4030
Query 97: 0.7846                 Interpolated Recall -
Query 98: 0.3918                 Precision Averages:
Query 99: 0.1683                     at 0.00       0.9261
Query 100: 0.5432                    at 0.10       0.8022
Query 101: 0.5784                    at 0.20       0.7485
Query 102: 0.8121                    at 0.30       0.6458
Query 103: 0.6099                    at 0.40       0.5793
Query 104: 0.1780                    at 0.50       0.5050
Query 105: 0.7353                    at 0.60       0.4406
Query 106: 0.1993                    at 0.70       0.3888
Query 107: 0.0835                    at 0.80       0.2982
Query 108: 0.6493                    at 0.90       0.2230
Query 109: 0.4008                    at 1.00       0.1006
Query 110: 0.5310
Query 111: 0.0236                Avg. prec. (non-interpolated)
Query 112: 0.5524                for all rel. documents
Query 113: 0.6208                                  0.4976
Query 114: 0.4587                Precision:
Query 115: 0.4010                  At    5 docs:   0.7120
Query 116: 0.7523                  At   10 docs:   0.6120
Query 117: 0.2319                  At   15 docs:   0.5640
Query 118: 0.2078                  At   20 docs:   0.5380
Query 119: 0.8022                  At   30 docs:   0.4867
Query 120: 0.3225                  At  100 docs:   0.2890
Query 121: 0.7433                  At  200 docs:   0.1936
Query 122: 0.0909                  At  500 docs:   0.0964
Query 123: 0.9109                  At 1000 docs:   0.0524
Query 124: 0.4833
Query 125: 0.5897                R-Precision (prec. after R
Query 126: 0.2237                (=num_rel) docs. retrieved):
Query 127: 0.7020                    Exact:        0.4881
Query 128: 0.3109
Query 129: 0.3652
Query 130: 0.7049
Query 131: 0.6667
Query 132: 0.8771
Query 133: 0.2226
Query 134: 0.8269
Query 135: 0.5626
Query 136: 0.7746
Query 137: 0.2450
Query 138: 0.6202
Query 139: 0.4674
Query 140: 0.3290
```

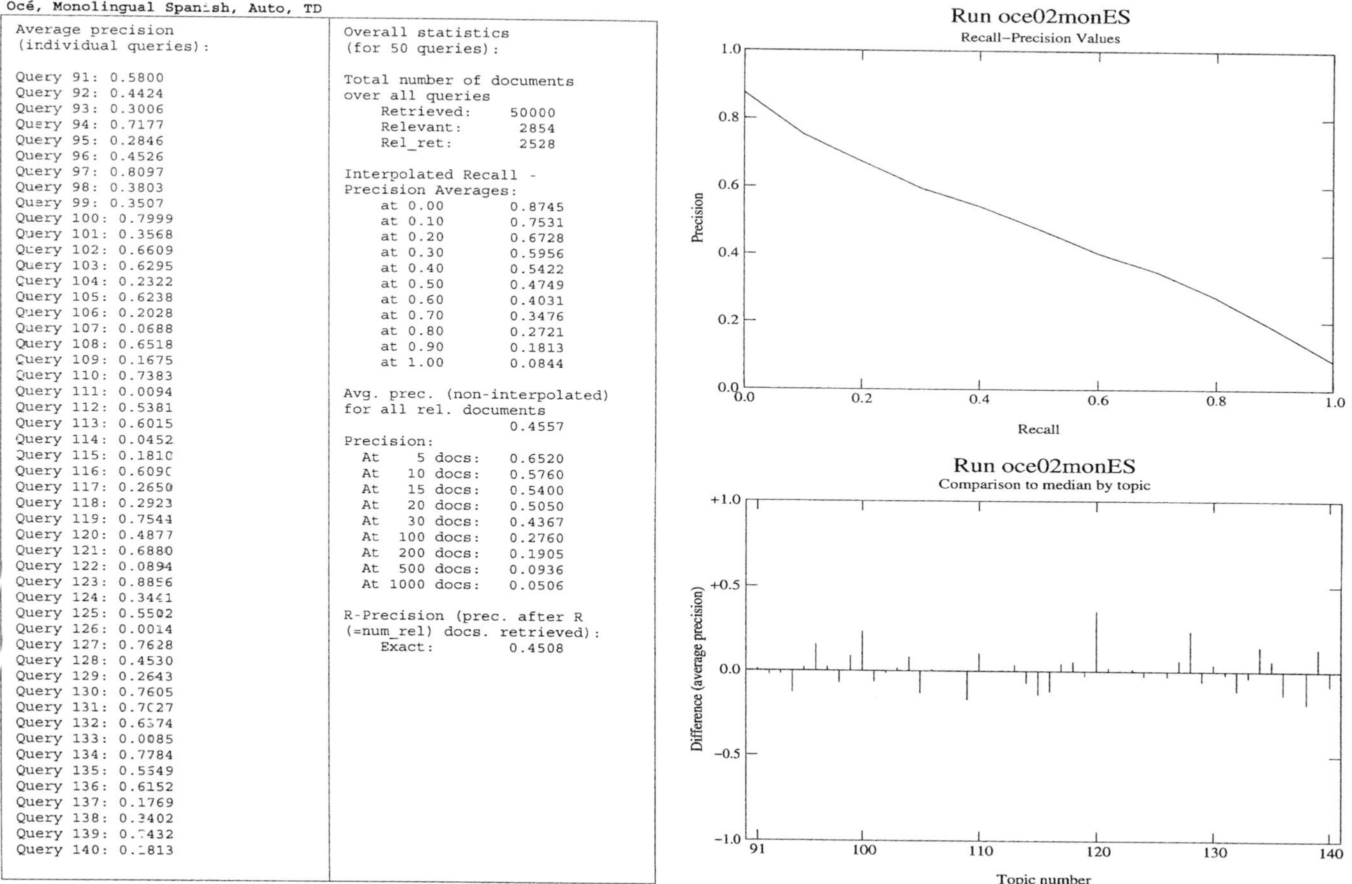

Océ, Monolingual Spanish, Auto, TD

Average precision
(individual queries):

Query 91: 0.5800
Query 92: 0.4424
Query 93: 0.3006
Query 94: 0.7177
Query 95: 0.2846
Query 96: 0.4526
Query 97: 0.8097
Query 98: 0.3803
Query 99: 0.3507
Query 100: 0.7999
Query 101: 0.3568
Query 102: 0.6609
Query 103: 0.6295
Query 104: 0.2322
Query 105: 0.6238
Query 106: 0.2028
Query 107: 0.0688
Query 108: 0.6518
Query 109: 0.1675
Query 110: 0.7383
Query 111: 0.0094
Query 112: 0.5381
Query 113: 0.6015
Query 114: 0.0452
Query 115: 0.1810
Query 116: 0.6090
Query 117: 0.2650
Query 118: 0.2923
Query 119: 0.7544
Query 120: 0.4877
Query 121: 0.6880
Query 122: 0.0894
Query 123: 0.8856
Query 124: 0.3441
Query 125: 0.5502
Query 126: 0.0014
Query 127: 0.7628
Query 128: 0.4530
Query 129: 0.2643
Query 130: 0.7605
Query 131: 0.7027
Query 132: 0.6374
Query 133: 0.0085
Query 134: 0.7784
Query 135: 0.5549
Query 136: 0.6152
Query 137: 0.1769
Query 138: 0.3402
Query 139: 0.7432
Query 140: 0.1813

Overall statistics
(for 50 queries):

Total number of documents
over all queries
Retrieved: 50000
Relevant: 2854
Rel_ret: 2528

Interpolated Recall -
Precision Averages:
at 0.00 0.8745
at 0.10 0.7531
at 0.20 0.6728
at 0.30 0.5956
at 0.40 0.5422
at 0.50 0.4749
at 0.60 0.4031
at 0.70 0.3476
at 0.80 0.2721
at 0.90 0.1813
at 1.00 0.0844

Avg. prec. (non-interpolated)
for all rel. documents
0.4557

Precision:
At 5 docs: 0.6520
At 10 docs: 0.5760
At 15 docs: 0.5400
At 20 docs: 0.5050
At 30 docs: 0.4367
At 100 docs: 0.2760
At 200 docs: 0.1905
At 500 docs: 0.0936
At 1000 docs: 0.0506

R-Precision (prec. after R
(=num_rel) docs. retrieved):
Exact: 0.4508

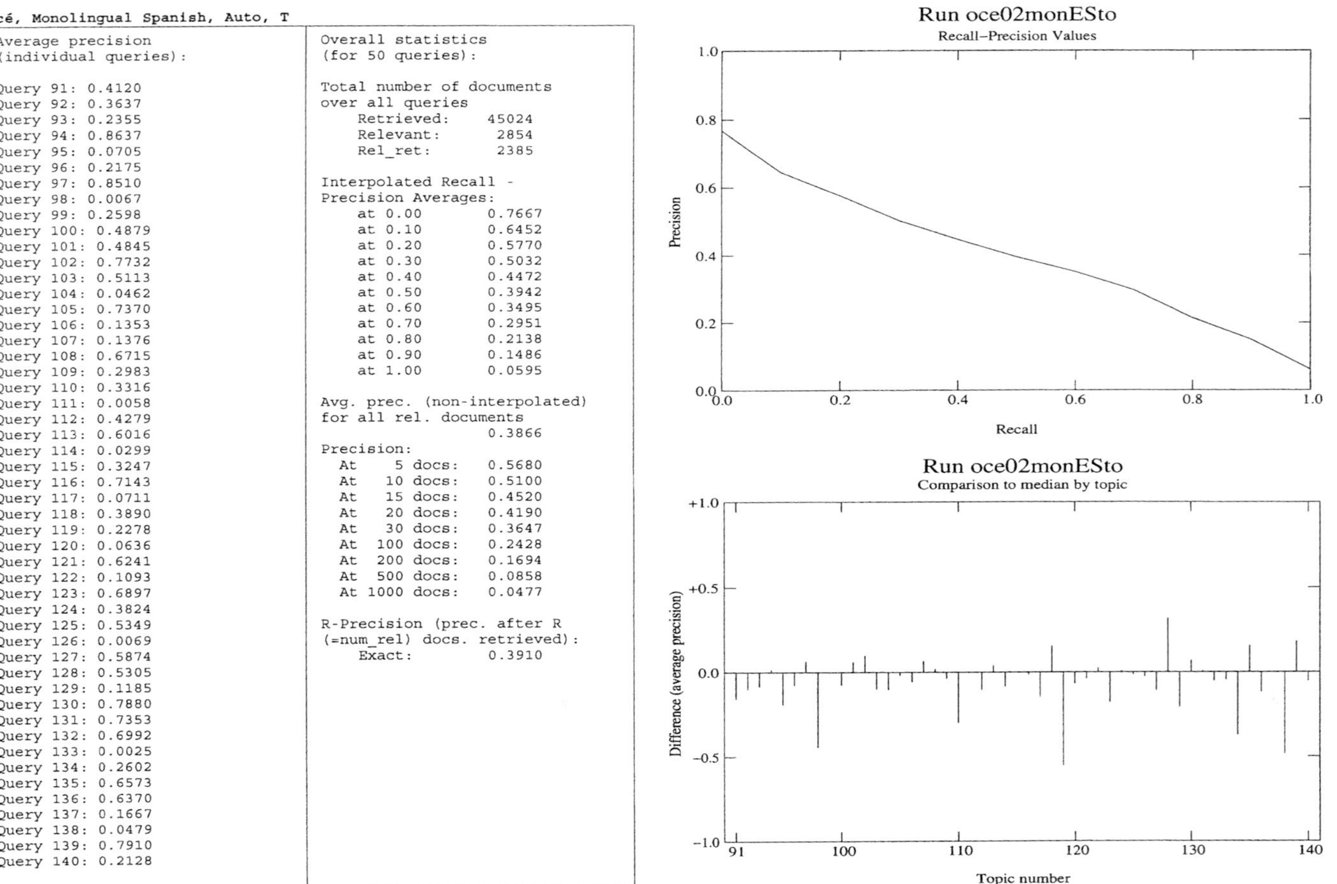

Océ, Monolingual Spanish, Auto, T

Average precision
(individual queries):

Query 91: 0.4120
Query 92: 0.3637
Query 93: 0.2355
Query 94: 0.8637
Query 95: 0.0705
Query 96: 0.2175
Query 97: 0.8510
Query 98: 0.0067
Query 99: 0.2598
Query 100: 0.4879
Query 101: 0.4845
Query 102: 0.7732
Query 103: 0.5113
Query 104: 0.0462
Query 105: 0.7370
Query 106: 0.1353
Query 107: 0.1376
Query 108: 0.6715
Query 109: 0.2983
Query 110: 0.3316
Query 111: 0.0058
Query 112: 0.4279
Query 113: 0.6016
Query 114: 0.0299
Query 115: 0.3247
Query 116: 0.7143
Query 117: 0.0711
Query 118: 0.3890
Query 119: 0.2278
Query 120: 0.0636
Query 121: 0.6241
Query 122: 0.1093
Query 123: 0.6897
Query 124: 0.3824
Query 125: 0.5349
Query 126: 0.0069
Query 127: 0.5874
Query 128: 0.5305
Query 129: 0.1185
Query 130: 0.7880
Query 131: 0.7353
Query 132: 0.6992
Query 133: 0.0025
Query 134: 0.2602
Query 135: 0.6573
Query 136: 0.6370
Query 137: 0.1667
Query 138: 0.0479
Query 139: 0.7910
Query 140: 0.2128

Overall statistics
(for 50 queries):

Total number of documents
over all queries
Retrieved: 45024
Relevant: 2854
Rel_ret: 2385

Interpolated Recall -
Precision Averages:
at 0.00 0.7667
at 0.10 0.6452
at 0.20 0.5770
at 0.30 0.5032
at 0.40 0.4472
at 0.50 0.3942
at 0.60 0.3495
at 0.70 0.2951
at 0.80 0.2138
at 0.90 0.1486
at 1.00 0.0595

Avg. prec. (non-interpolated)
for all rel. documents
0.3866

Precision:
At 5 docs: 0.5680
At 10 docs: 0.5100
At 15 docs: 0.4520
At 20 docs: 0.4190
At 30 docs: 0.3647
At 100 docs: 0.2428
At 200 docs: 0.1694
At 500 docs: 0.0858
At 1000 docs: 0.0477

R-Precision (prec. after R
(=num_rel) docs. retrieved):
Exact: 0.3910

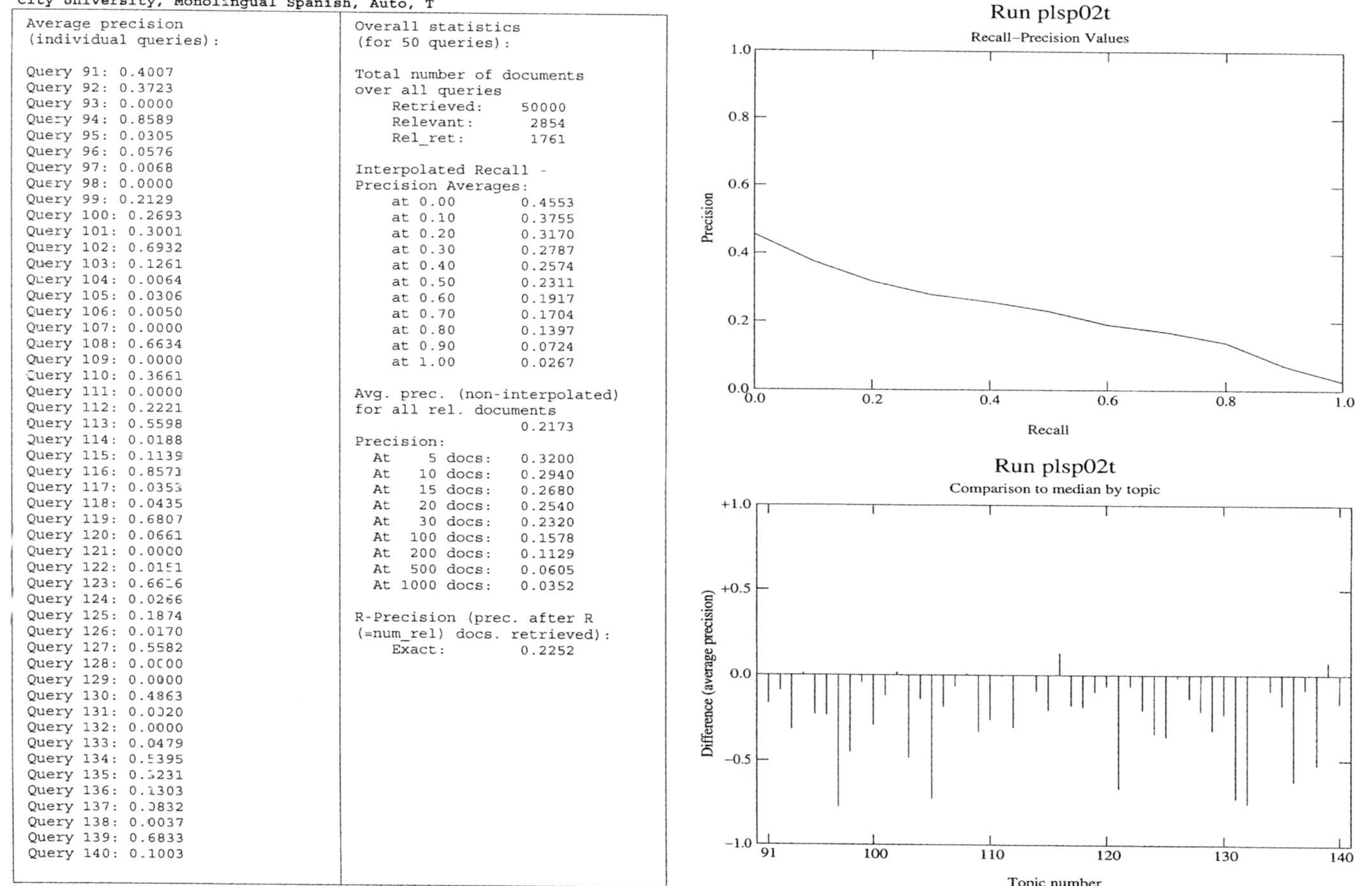

City University, Monolingual Spanish, Auto, T

```
Average precision              Overall statistics
(individual queries):          (for 50 queries):

Query 91: 0.4007               Total number of documents
Query 92: 0.3723               over all queries
Query 93: 0.0000                   Retrieved:    50000
Query 94: 0.8589                   Relevant:      2854
Query 95: 0.0305                   Rel_ret:       1761
Query 96: 0.0576
Query 97: 0.0068               Interpolated Recall -
Query 98: 0.0000               Precision Averages:
Query 99: 0.2129                   at 0.00      0.4553
Query 100: 0.2693                  at 0.10      0.3755
Query 101: 0.3001                  at 0.20      0.3170
Query 102: 0.6932                  at 0.30      0.2787
Query 103: 0.1261                  at 0.40      0.2574
Query 104: 0.0064                  at 0.50      0.2311
Query 105: 0.0306                  at 0.60      0.1917
Query 106: 0.0050                  at 0.70      0.1704
Query 107: 0.0000                  at 0.80      0.1397
Query 108: 0.6634                  at 0.90      0.0724
Query 109: 0.0000                  at 1.00      0.0267
Query 110: 0.3661
Query 111: 0.0000              Avg. prec. (non-interpolated)
Query 112: 0.2221              for all rel. documents
Query 113: 0.5598                               0.2173
Query 114: 0.0188              Precision:
Query 115: 0.1139                At    5 docs:   0.3200
Query 116: 0.8571                At   10 docs:   0.2940
Query 117: 0.0353                At   15 docs:   0.2680
Query 118: 0.0435                At   20 docs:   0.2540
Query 119: 0.6807                At   30 docs:   0.2320
Query 120: 0.0661                At  100 docs:   0.1578
Query 121: 0.0000                At  200 docs:   0.1129
Query 122: 0.0151                At  500 docs:   0.0605
Query 123: 0.6616                At 1000 docs:   0.0352
Query 124: 0.0266
Query 125: 0.1874              R-Precision (prec. after R
Query 126: 0.0170              (=num_rel) docs. retrieved):
Query 127: 0.5582                  Exact:       0.2252
Query 128: 0.0000
Query 129: 0.0000
Query 130: 0.4863
Query 131: 0.0020
Query 132: 0.0000
Query 133: 0.0479
Query 134: 0.5395
Query 135: 0.5231
Query 136: 0.1303
Query 137: 0.0832
Query 138: 0.0037
Query 139: 0.6833
Query 140: 0.1003
```

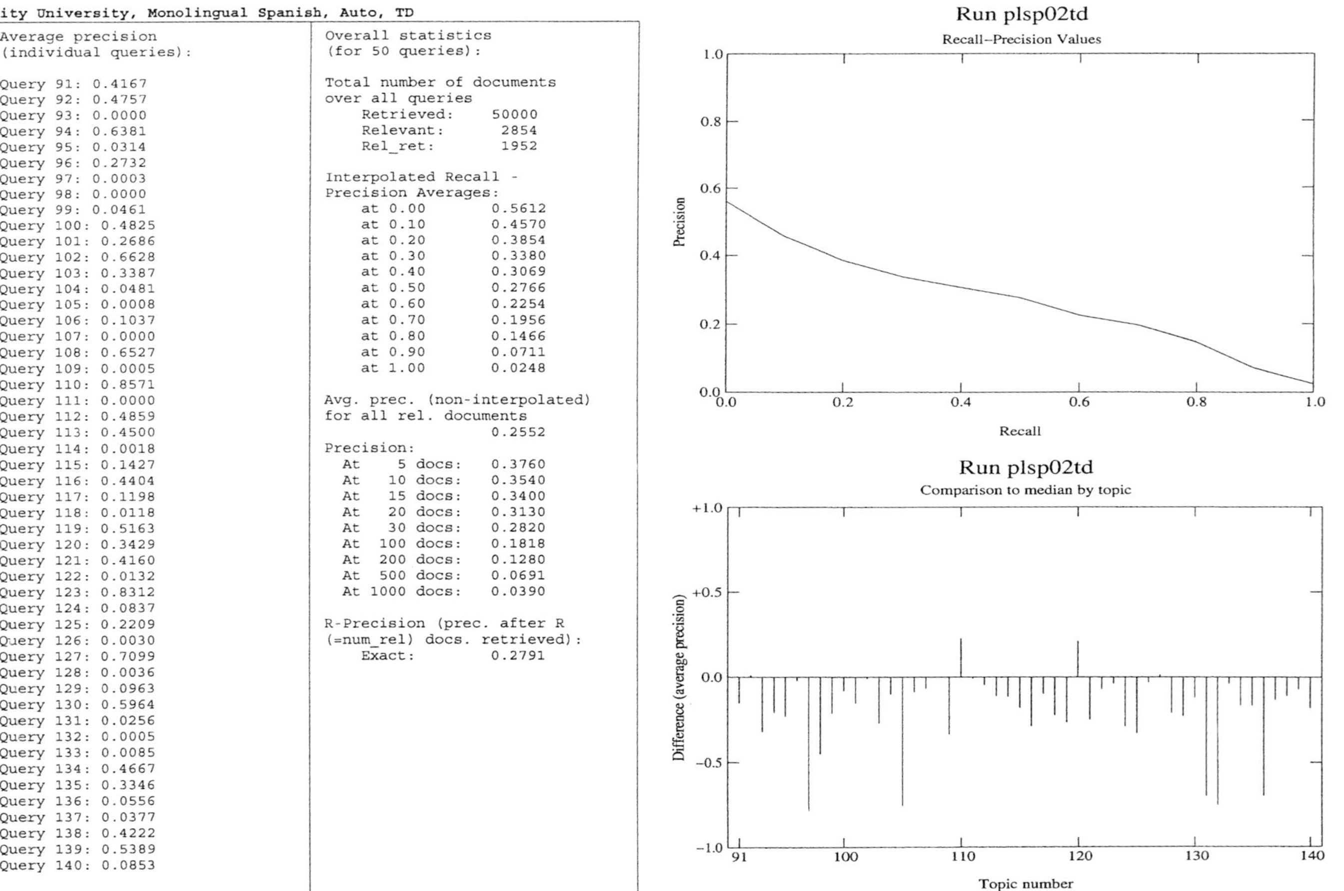

City University, Monolingual Spanish, Auto, TD

Average precision (individual queries):

Query	Average precision
Query 91:	0.4167
Query 92:	0.4757
Query 93:	0.0000
Query 94:	0.6381
Query 95:	0.0314
Query 96:	0.2732
Query 97:	0.0003
Query 98:	0.0000
Query 99:	0.0461
Query 100:	0.4825
Query 101:	0.2686
Query 102:	0.6628
Query 103:	0.3387
Query 104:	0.0481
Query 105:	0.0008
Query 106:	0.1037
Query 107:	0.0000
Query 108:	0.6527
Query 109:	0.0005
Query 110:	0.8571
Query 111:	0.0000
Query 112:	0.4859
Query 113:	0.4500
Query 114:	0.0018
Query 115:	0.1427
Query 116:	0.4404
Query 117:	0.1198
Query 118:	0.0118
Query 119:	0.5163
Query 120:	0.3429
Query 121:	0.4160
Query 122:	0.0132
Query 123:	0.8312
Query 124:	0.0837
Query 125:	0.2209
Query 126:	0.0030
Query 127:	0.7099
Query 128:	0.0036
Query 129:	0.0963
Query 130:	0.5964
Query 131:	0.0256
Query 132:	0.0005
Query 133:	0.0085
Query 134:	0.4667
Query 135:	0.3346
Query 136:	0.0556
Query 137:	0.0377
Query 138:	0.4222
Query 139:	0.5389
Query 140:	0.0853

Overall statistics (for 50 queries):

Total number of documents over all queries

Retrieved:	50000
Relevant:	2854
Rel_ret:	1952

Interpolated Recall - Precision Averages:

at 0.00	0.5612
at 0.10	0.4570
at 0.20	0.3854
at 0.30	0.3380
at 0.40	0.3069
at 0.50	0.2766
at 0.60	0.2254
at 0.70	0.1956
at 0.80	0.1466
at 0.90	0.0711
at 1.00	0.0248

Avg. prec. (non-interpolated) for all rel. documents 0.2552

Precision:

At 5 docs:	0.3760
At 10 docs:	0.3540
At 15 docs:	0.3400
At 20 docs:	0.3130
At 30 docs:	0.2820
At 100 docs:	0.1818
At 200 docs:	0.1280
At 500 docs:	0.0691
At 1000 docs:	0.0390

R-Precision (prec. after R (=num_rel) docs. retrieved):
Exact: 0.2791

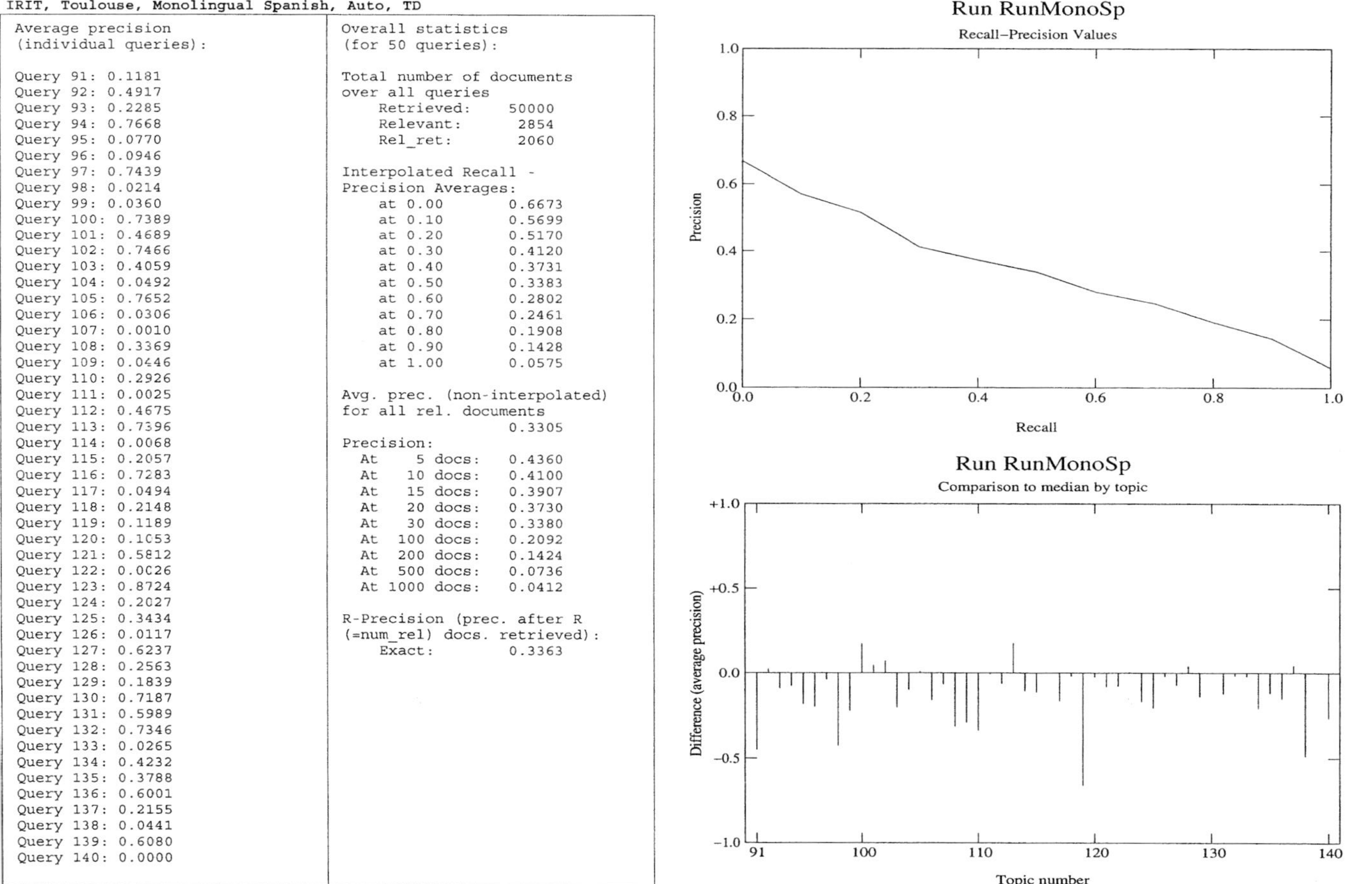

IRIT, Toulouse, Monolingual Spanish, Auto, TD

Average precision
(individual queries):

Query 91: 0.1181
Query 92: 0.4917
Query 93: 0.2285
Query 94: 0.7668
Query 95: 0.0770
Query 96: 0.0946
Query 97: 0.7439
Query 98: 0.0214
Query 99: 0.0360
Query 100: 0.7389
Query 101: 0.4689
Query 102: 0.7466
Query 103: 0.4059
Query 104: 0.0492
Query 105: 0.7652
Query 106: 0.0306
Query 107: 0.0010
Query 108: 0.3369
Query 109: 0.0446
Query 110: 0.2926
Query 111: 0.0025
Query 112: 0.4675
Query 113: 0.7396
Query 114: 0.0068
Query 115: 0.2057
Query 116: 0.7283
Query 117: 0.0494
Query 118: 0.2148
Query 119: 0.1189
Query 120: 0.1053
Query 121: 0.5812
Query 122: 0.0026
Query 123: 0.8724
Query 124: 0.2027
Query 125: 0.3434
Query 126: 0.0117
Query 127: 0.6237
Query 128: 0.2563
Query 129: 0.1839
Query 130: 0.7187
Query 131: 0.5989
Query 132: 0.7346
Query 133: 0.0265
Query 134: 0.4232
Query 135: 0.3788
Query 136: 0.6001
Query 137: 0.2155
Query 138: 0.0441
Query 139: 0.6080
Query 140: 0.0000

Overall statistics
(for 50 queries):

Total number of documents
over all queries
Retrieved: 50000
Relevant: 2854
Rel_ret: 2060

Interpolated Recall -
Precision Averages:
at 0.00 0.6673
at 0.10 0.5699
at 0.20 0.5170
at 0.30 0.4120
at 0.40 0.3731
at 0.50 0.3383
at 0.60 0.2802
at 0.70 0.2461
at 0.80 0.1908
at 0.90 0.1428
at 1.00 0.0575

Avg. prec. (non-interpolated)
for all rel. documents
0.3305

Precision:
At 5 docs: 0.4360
At 10 docs: 0.4100
At 15 docs: 0.3907
At 20 docs: 0.3730
At 30 docs: 0.3380
At 100 docs: 0.2092
At 200 docs: 0.1424
At 500 docs: 0.0736
At 1000 docs: 0.0412

R-Precision (prec. after R
(=num_rel) docs. retrieved):
Exact: 0.3363

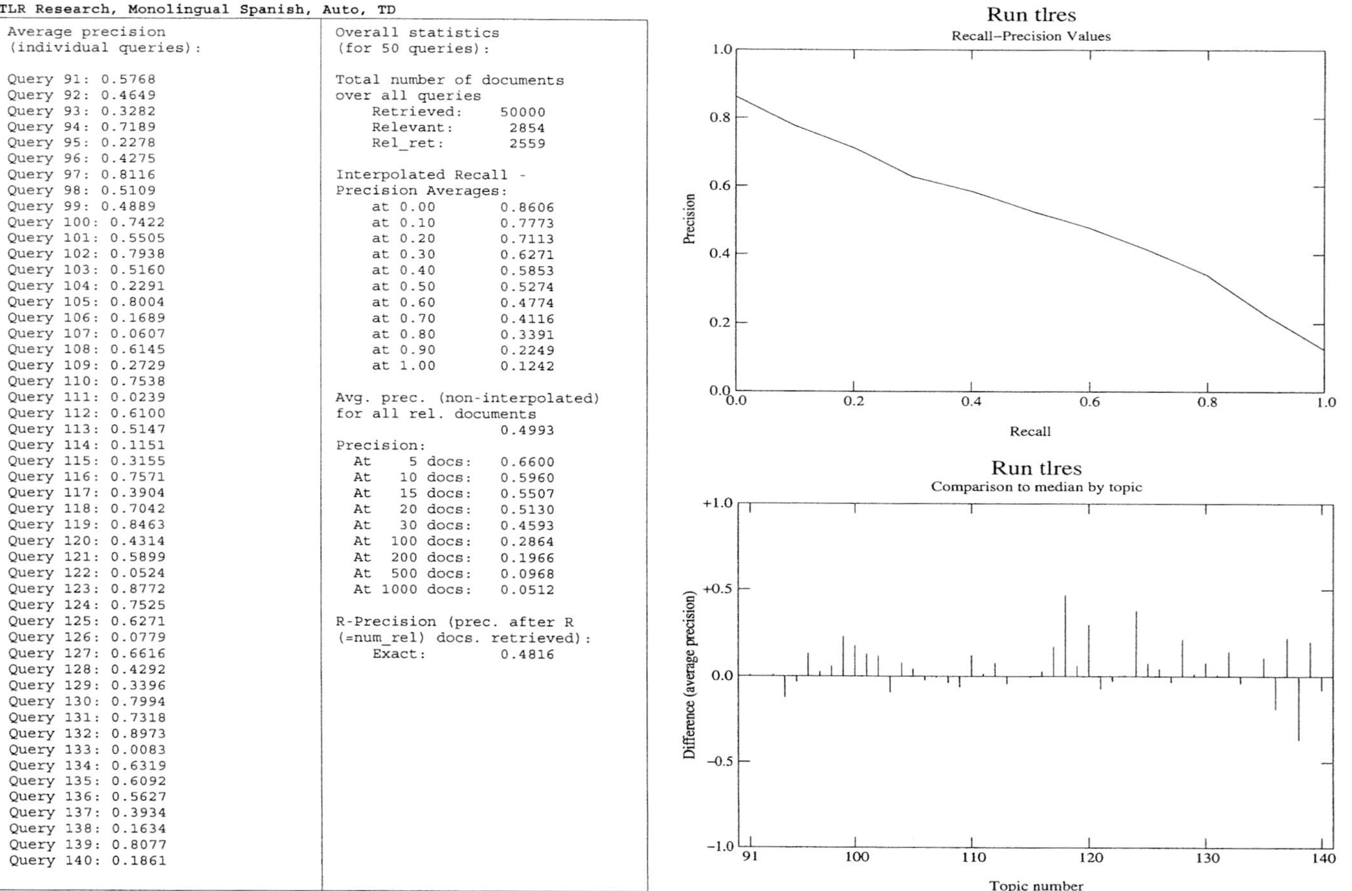

TLR Research, Monolingual Spanish, Auto, TD

```
Average precision                Overall statistics
(individual queries):            (for 50 queries):

Query 91: 0.5768                 Total number of documents
Query 92: 0.4649                 over all queries
Query 93: 0.3282                     Retrieved:     50000
Query 94: 0.7189                     Relevant:       2854
Query 95: 0.2278                     Rel_ret:        2559
Query 96: 0.4275
Query 97: 0.8116                 Interpolated Recall -
Query 98: 0.5109                 Precision Averages:
Query 99: 0.4889                     at 0.00        0.8606
Query 100: 0.7422                    at 0.10        0.7773
Query 101: 0.5505                    at 0.20        0.7113
Query 102: 0.7938                    at 0.30        0.6271
Query 103: 0.5160                    at 0.40        0.5853
Query 104: 0.2291                    at 0.50        0.5274
Query 105: 0.8004                    at 0.60        0.4774
Query 106: 0.1689                    at 0.70        0.4116
Query 107: 0.0607                    at 0.80        0.3391
Query 108: 0.6145                    at 0.90        0.2249
Query 109: 0.2729                    at 1.00        0.1242
Query 110: 0.7538
Query 111: 0.0239                Avg. prec. (non-interpolated)
Query 112: 0.6100                for all rel. documents
Query 113: 0.5147                                   0.4993
Query 114: 0.1151                Precision:
Query 115: 0.3155                  At    5 docs:    0.6600
Query 116: 0.7571                  At   10 docs:    0.5960
Query 117: 0.3904                  At   15 docs:    0.5507
Query 118: 0.7042                  At   20 docs:    0.5130
Query 119: 0.8463                  At   30 docs:    0.4593
Query 120: 0.4314                  At  100 docs:    0.2864
Query 121: 0.5899                  At  200 docs:    0.1966
Query 122: 0.0524                  At  500 docs:    0.0968
Query 123: 0.8772                  At 1000 docs:    0.0512
Query 124: 0.7525
Query 125: 0.6271                R-Precision (prec. after R
Query 126: 0.0779                (=num_rel) docs. retrieved):
Query 127: 0.6616                    Exact:         0.4816
Query 128: 0.4292
Query 129: 0.3396
Query 130: 0.7994
Query 131: 0.7318
Query 132: 0.8973
Query 133: 0.0083
Query 134: 0.6319
Query 135: 0.6092
Query 136: 0.5627
Query 137: 0.3934
Query 138: 0.1634
Query 139: 0.8077
Query 140: 0.1861
```

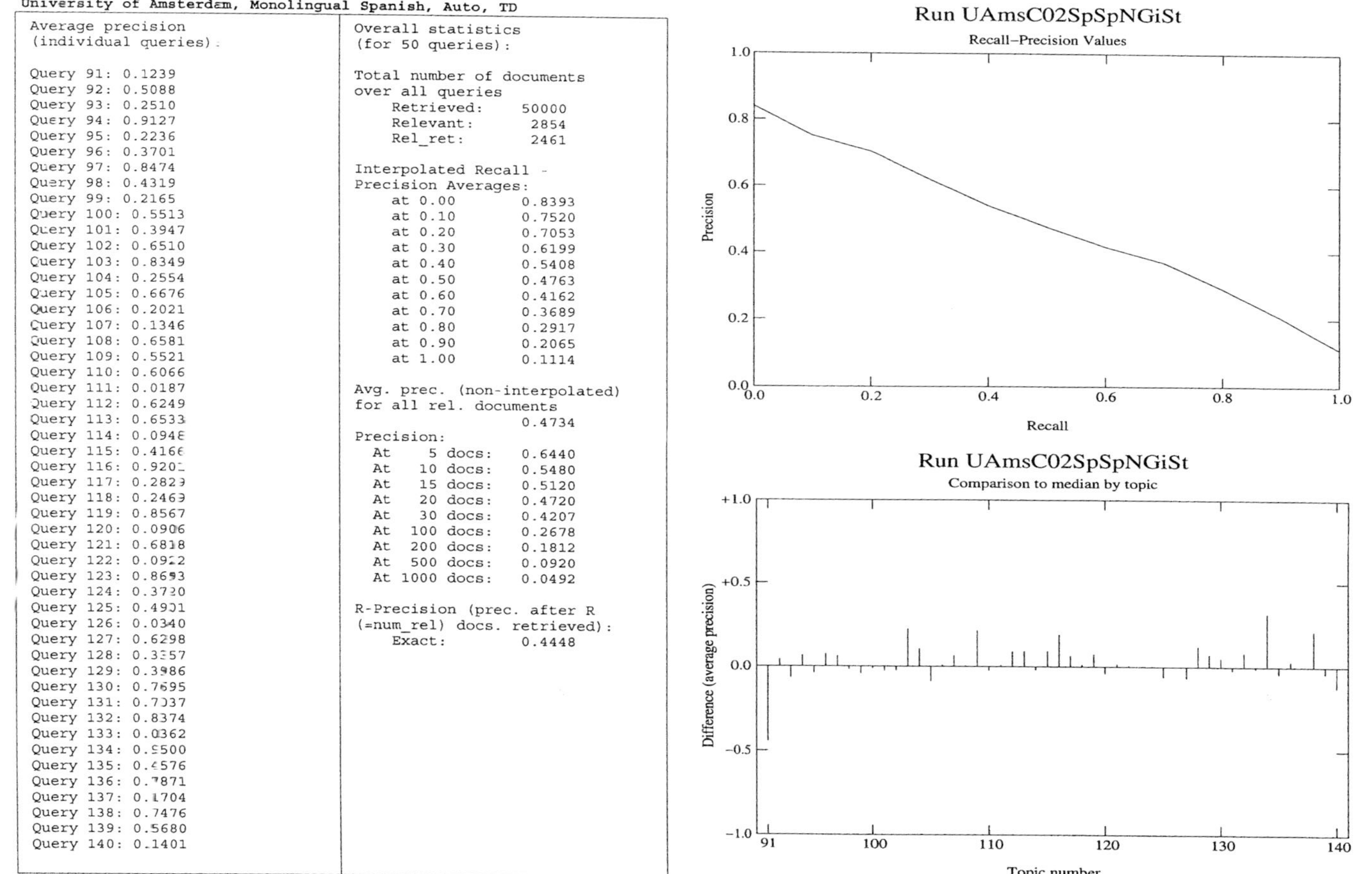

University of Amsterdam, Monolingual Spanish, Auto, TD

Average precision (individual queries):	Overall statistics (for 50 queries):
Query 91: 0.1239 Query 92: 0.5088 Query 93: 0.2510 Query 94: 0.9127 Query 95: 0.2236 Query 96: 0.3701 Query 97: 0.8474 Query 98: 0.4319 Query 99: 0.2165 Query 100: 0.5513 Query 101: 0.3947 Query 102: 0.6510 Query 103: 0.8349 Query 104: 0.2554 Query 105: 0.6676 Query 106: 0.2021 Query 107: 0.1346 Query 108: 0.6581 Query 109: 0.5521 Query 110: 0.6066 Query 111: 0.0187 Query 112: 0.6249 Query 113: 0.6533 Query 114: 0.0948 Query 115: 0.4166 Query 116: 0.9201 Query 117: 0.2829 Query 118: 0.2469 Query 119: 0.8567 Query 120: 0.0906 Query 121: 0.6818 Query 122: 0.0922 Query 123: 0.8693 Query 124: 0.3720 Query 125: 0.4901 Query 126: 0.0340 Query 127: 0.6298 Query 128: 0.3357 Query 129: 0.3986 Query 130: 0.7695 Query 131: 0.7037 Query 132: 0.8374 Query 133: 0.0362 Query 134: 0.9500 Query 135: 0.4576 Query 136: 0.7871 Query 137: 0.1704 Query 138: 0.7476 Query 139: 0.5680 Query 140: 0.1401	Total number of documents over all queries Retrieved: 50000 Relevant: 2854 Rel_ret: 2461 Interpolated Recall - Precision Averages: at 0.00 0.8393 at 0.10 0.7520 at 0.20 0.7053 at 0.30 0.6199 at 0.40 0.5408 at 0.50 0.4763 at 0.60 0.4162 at 0.70 0.3689 at 0.80 0.2917 at 0.90 0.2065 at 1.00 0.1114 Avg. prec. (non-interpolated) for all rel. documents 0.4734 Precision: At 5 docs: 0.6440 At 10 docs: 0.5480 At 15 docs: 0.5120 At 20 docs: 0.4720 At 30 docs: 0.4207 At 100 docs: 0.2678 At 200 docs: 0.1812 At 500 docs: 0.0920 At 1000 docs: 0.0492 R-Precision (prec. after R (=num_rel) docs. retrieved): Exact: 0.4448

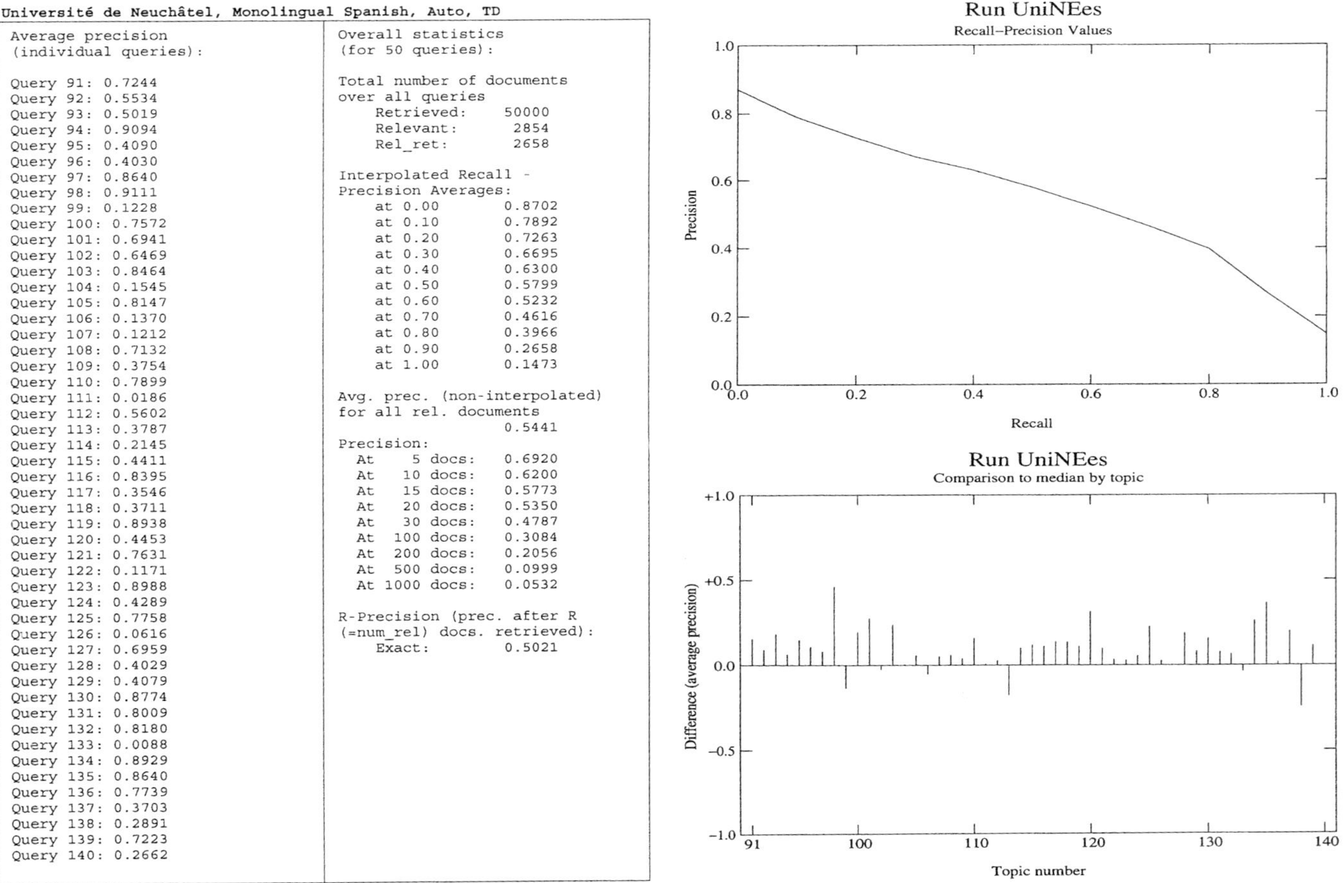

Université de Neuchâtel, Monolingual Spanish, Auto, TD

Average precision
(individual queries):

Query 91: 0.7244
Query 92: 0.5534
Query 93: 0.5019
Query 94: 0.9094
Query 95: 0.4090
Query 96: 0.4030
Query 97: 0.8640
Query 98: 0.9111
Query 99: 0.1228
Query 100: 0.7572
Query 101: 0.6941
Query 102: 0.6469
Query 103: 0.8464
Query 104: 0.1545
Query 105: 0.8147
Query 106: 0.1370
Query 107: 0.1212
Query 108: 0.7132
Query 109: 0.3754
Query 110: 0.7899
Query 111: 0.0186
Query 112: 0.5602
Query 113: 0.3787
Query 114: 0.2145
Query 115: 0.4411
Query 116: 0.8395
Query 117: 0.3546
Query 118: 0.3711
Query 119: 0.8938
Query 120: 0.4453
Query 121: 0.7631
Query 122: 0.1171
Query 123: 0.8988
Query 124: 0.4289
Query 125: 0.7758
Query 126: 0.0616
Query 127: 0.6959
Query 128: 0.4029
Query 129: 0.4079
Query 130: 0.8774
Query 131: 0.8009
Query 132: 0.8180
Query 133: 0.0088
Query 134: 0.8929
Query 135: 0.8640
Query 136: 0.7739
Query 137: 0.3703
Query 138: 0.2891
Query 139: 0.7223
Query 140: 0.2662

Overall statistics
(for 50 queries):

Total number of documents
over all queries
Retrieved: 50000
Relevant: 2854
Rel_ret: 2658

Interpolated Recall -
Precision Averages:
at 0.00 0.8702
at 0.10 0.7892
at 0.20 0.7263
at 0.30 0.6695
at 0.40 0.6300
at 0.50 0.5799
at 0.60 0.5232
at 0.70 0.4616
at 0.80 0.3966
at 0.90 0.2658
at 1.00 0.1473

Avg. prec. (non-interpolated)
for all rel. documents
0.5441

Precision:
At 5 docs: 0.6920
At 10 docs: 0.6200
At 15 docs: 0.5773
At 20 docs: 0.5350
At 30 docs: 0.4787
At 100 docs: 0.3084
At 200 docs: 0.2056
At 500 docs: 0.0999
At 1000 docs: 0.0532

R-Precision (prec. after R
(=num_rel) docs. retrieved):
Exact: 0.5021

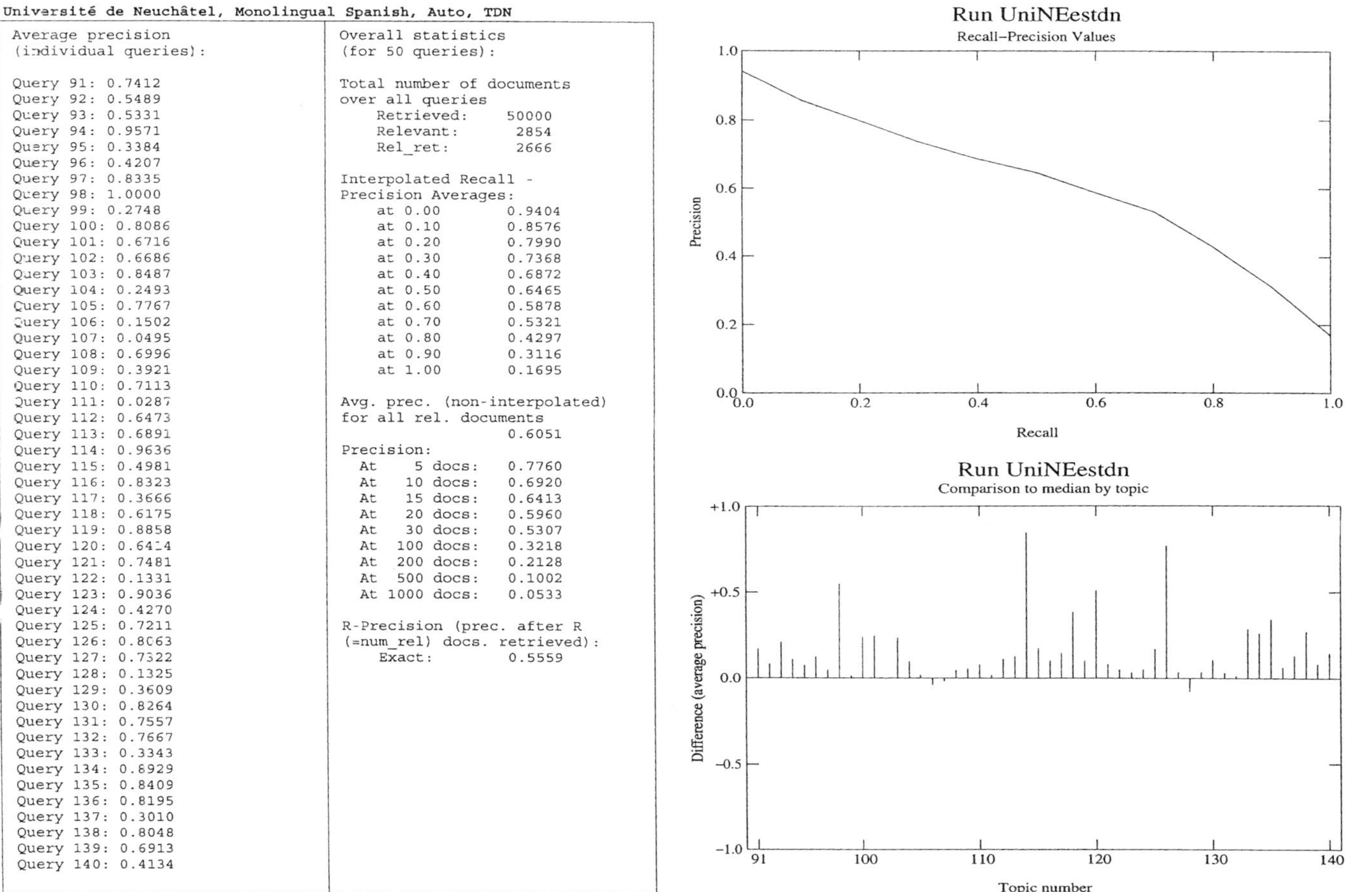

Université de Neuchâtel, Monolingual Spanish, Auto, TDN

```
Average precision                Overall statistics
(individual queries):            (for 50 queries):

Query 91: 0.7412                 Total number of documents
Query 92: 0.5489                 over all queries
Query 93: 0.5331                     Retrieved:    50000
Query 94: 0.9571                     Relevant:      2854
Query 95: 0.3384                     Rel_ret:       2666
Query 96: 0.4207
Query 97: 0.8335                 Interpolated Recall -
Query 98: 1.0000                 Precision Averages:
Query 99: 0.2748                     at 0.00       0.9404
Query 100: 0.8086                    at 0.10       0.8576
Query 101: 0.6716                    at 0.20       0.7990
Query 102: 0.6686                    at 0.30       0.7368
Query 103: 0.8487                    at 0.40       0.6872
Query 104: 0.2493                    at 0.50       0.6465
Query 105: 0.7767                    at 0.60       0.5878
Query 106: 0.1502                    at 0.70       0.5321
Query 107: 0.0495                    at 0.80       0.4297
Query 108: 0.6996                    at 0.90       0.3116
Query 109: 0.3921                    at 1.00       0.1695
Query 110: 0.7113
Query 111: 0.0287                Avg. prec. (non-interpolated)
Query 112: 0.6473                for all rel. documents
Query 113: 0.6891                                  0.6051
Query 114: 0.9636                Precision:
Query 115: 0.4981                  At    5 docs:   0.7760
Query 116: 0.8323                  At   10 docs:   0.6920
Query 117: 0.3666                  At   15 docs:   0.6413
Query 118: 0.6175                  At   20 docs:   0.5960
Query 119: 0.8858                  At   30 docs:   0.5307
Query 120: 0.6414                  At  100 docs:   0.3218
Query 121: 0.7481                  At  200 docs:   0.2128
Query 122: 0.1331                  At  500 docs:   0.1002
Query 123: 0.9036                  At 1000 docs:   0.0533
Query 124: 0.4270
Query 125: 0.7211                R-Precision (prec. after R
Query 126: 0.8063                (=num_rel) docs. retrieved):
Query 127: 0.7322                    Exact:        0.5559
Query 128: 0.1325
Query 129: 0.3609
Query 130: 0.8264
Query 131: 0.7557
Query 132: 0.7667
Query 133: 0.3343
Query 134: 0.6929
Query 135: 0.8409
Query 136: 0.8195
Query 137: 0.3010
Query 138: 0.8048
Query 139: 0.6913
Query 140: 0.4134
```

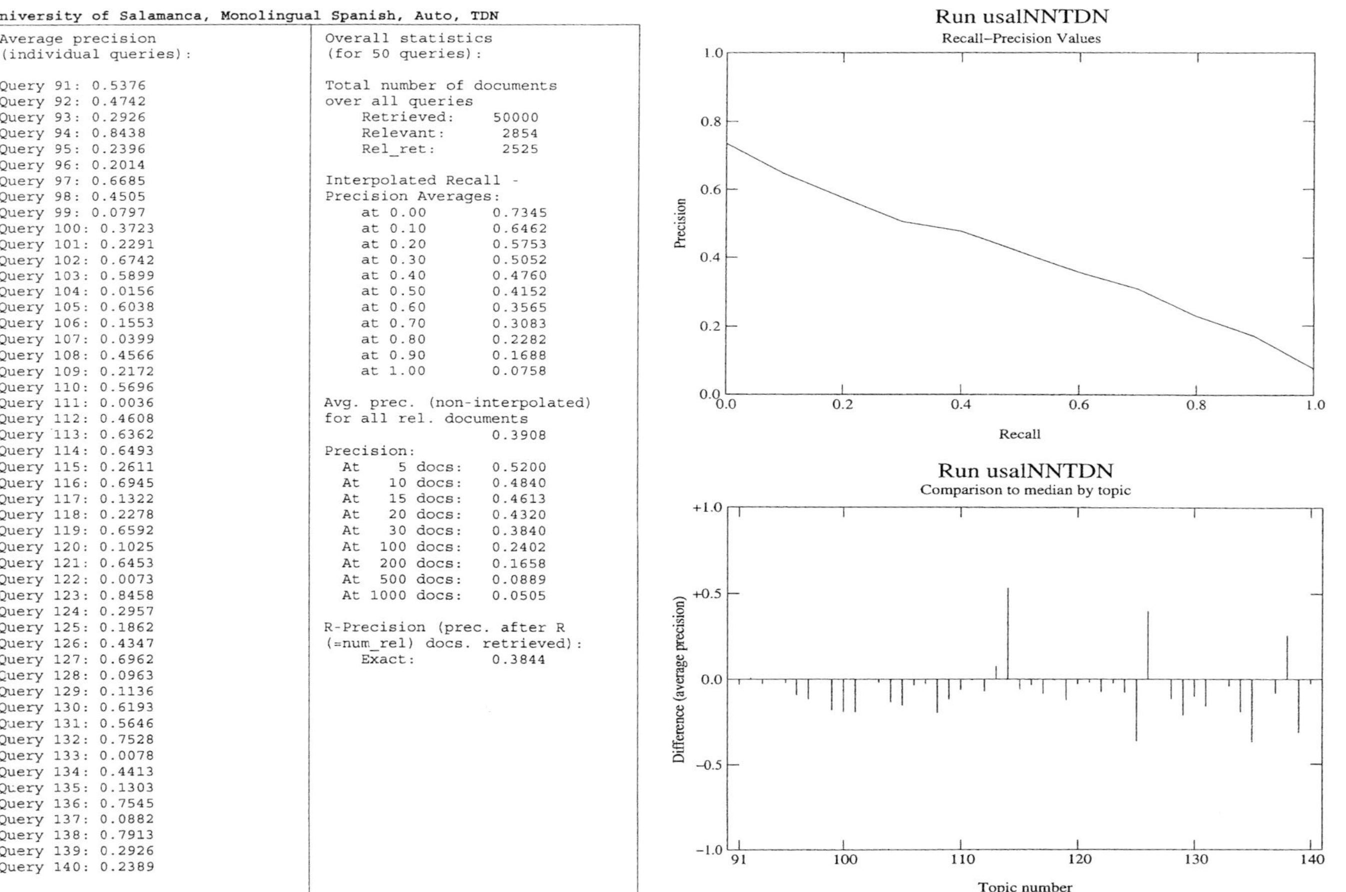

University of Salamanca, Monolingual Spanish, Auto, TDN

```
Average precision                  Overall statistics
(individual queries):              (for 50 queries):

Query 91: 0.5376                   Total number of documents
Query 92: 0.4742                   over all queries
Query 93: 0.2926                       Retrieved:    50000
Query 94: 0.8438                       Relevant:      2854
Query 95: 0.2396                       Rel_ret:       2525
Query 96: 0.2014
Query 97: 0.6685                   Interpolated Recall -
Query 98: 0.4505                   Precision Averages:
Query 99: 0.0797                       at 0.00       0.7345
Query 100: 0.3723                      at 0.10       0.6462
Query 101: 0.2291                      at 0.20       0.5753
Query 102: 0.6742                      at 0.30       0.5052
Query 103: 0.5899                      at 0.40       0.4760
Query 104: 0.0156                      at 0.50       0.4152
Query 105: 0.6038                      at 0.60       0.3565
Query 106: 0.1553                      at 0.70       0.3083
Query 107: 0.0399                      at 0.80       0.2282
Query 108: 0.4566                      at 0.90       0.1688
Query 109: 0.2172                      at 1.00       0.0758
Query 110: 0.5696
Query 111: 0.0036                  Avg. prec. (non-interpolated)
Query 112: 0.4608                  for all rel. documents
Query 113: 0.6362                                    0.3908
Query 114: 0.6493                  Precision:
Query 115: 0.2611                    At    5 docs:   0.5200
Query 116: 0.6945                    At   10 docs:   0.4840
Query 117: 0.1322                    At   15 docs:   0.4613
Query 118: 0.2278                    At   20 docs:   0.4320
Query 119: 0.6592                    At   30 docs:   0.3840
Query 120: 0.1025                    At  100 docs:   0.2402
Query 121: 0.6453                    At  200 docs:   0.1658
Query 122: 0.0073                    At  500 docs:   0.0889
Query 123: 0.8458                    At 1000 docs:   0.0505
Query 124: 0.2957
Query 125: 0.1862                  R-Precision (prec. after R
Query 126: 0.4347                  (=num_rel) docs. retrieved):
Query 127: 0.6962                      Exact:        0.3844
Query 128: 0.0963
Query 129: 0.1136
Query 130: 0.6193
Query 131: 0.5646
Query 132: 0.7528
Query 133: 0.0078
Query 134: 0.4413
Query 135: 0.1303
Query 136: 0.7545
Query 137: 0.0882
Query 138: 0.7913
Query 139: 0.2926
Query 140: 0.2389
```

University of Salamanca, Monolingual Spanish, Auto, T

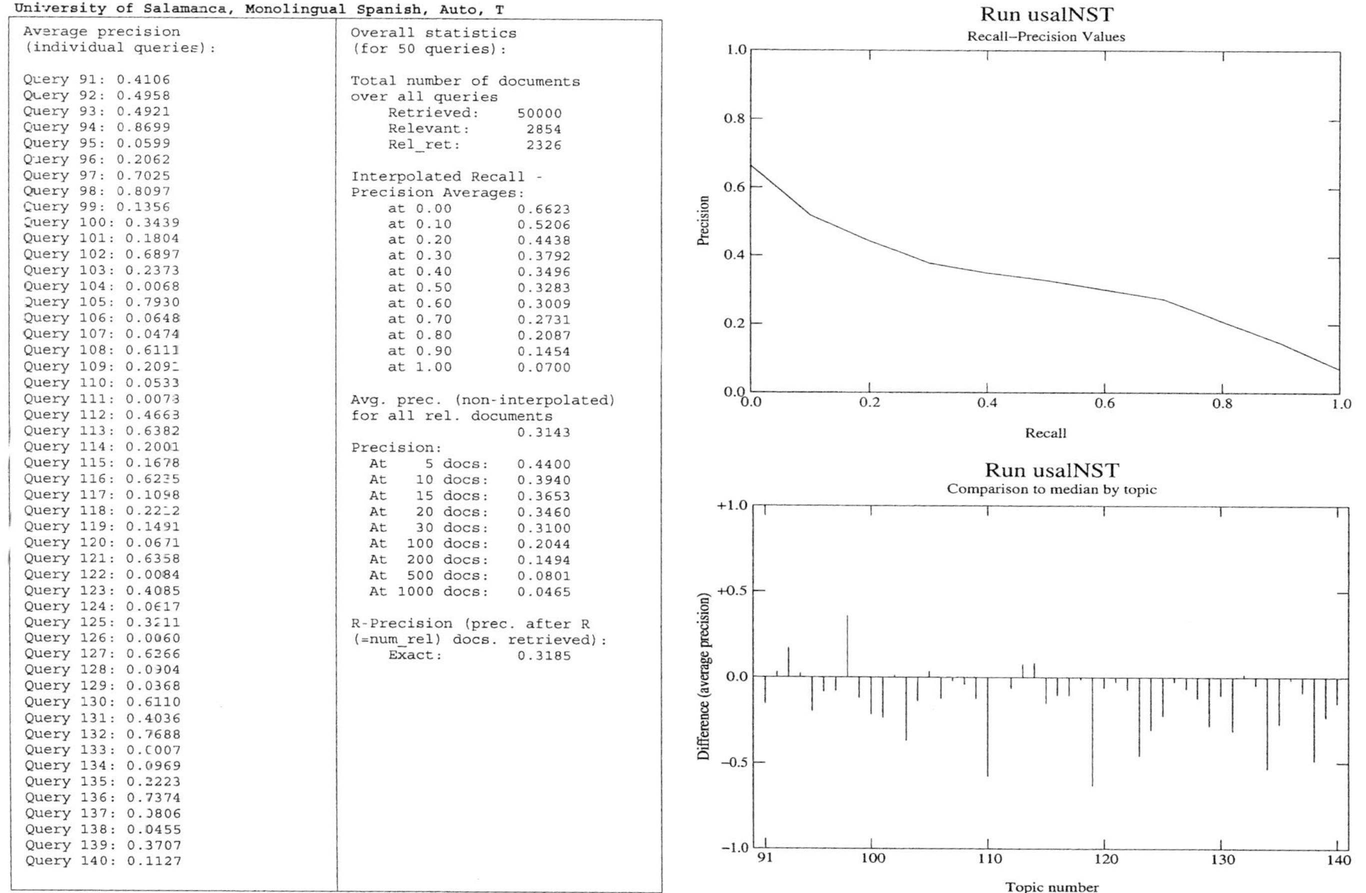

Average precision (individual queries):

Query	Average precision
Query 91:	0.4106
Query 92:	0.4958
Query 93:	0.4921
Query 94:	0.8699
Query 95:	0.0599
Query 96:	0.2062
Query 97:	0.7025
Query 98:	0.8097
Query 99:	0.1356
Query 100:	0.3439
Query 101:	0.1804
Query 102:	0.6897
Query 103:	0.2373
Query 104:	0.0068
Query 105:	0.7930
Query 106:	0.0648
Query 107:	0.0474
Query 108:	0.6111
Query 109:	0.2091
Query 110:	0.0533
Query 111:	0.0073
Query 112:	0.4663
Query 113:	0.6382
Query 114:	0.2001
Query 115:	0.1678
Query 116:	0.6235
Query 117:	0.1098
Query 118:	0.2212
Query 119:	0.1491
Query 120:	0.0671
Query 121:	0.6358
Query 122:	0.0084
Query 123:	0.4085
Query 124:	0.0617
Query 125:	0.3211
Query 126:	0.0060
Query 127:	0.6266
Query 128:	0.0304
Query 129:	0.0368
Query 130:	0.6110
Query 131:	0.4036
Query 132:	0.7688
Query 133:	0.0007
Query 134:	0.0969
Query 135:	0.2223
Query 136:	0.7374
Query 137:	0.0806
Query 138:	0.0455
Query 139:	0.3707
Query 140:	0.1127

Overall statistics (for 50 queries):

Total number of documents over all queries

Retrieved:	50000
Relevant:	2854
Rel_ret:	2326

Interpolated Recall - Precision Averages:

at 0.00	0.6623
at 0.10	0.5206
at 0.20	0.4438
at 0.30	0.3792
at 0.40	0.3496
at 0.50	0.3283
at 0.60	0.3009
at 0.70	0.2731
at 0.80	0.2087
at 0.90	0.1454
at 1.00	0.0700

Avg. prec. (non-interpolated) for all rel. documents 0.3143

Precision:

At 5 docs:	0.4400
At 10 docs:	0.3940
At 15 docs:	0.3653
At 20 docs:	0.3460
At 30 docs:	0.3100
At 100 docs:	0.2044
At 200 docs:	0.1494
At 500 docs:	0.0801
At 1000 docs:	0.0465

R-Precision (prec. after R (=num_rel) docs. retrieved):
Exact: 0.3185

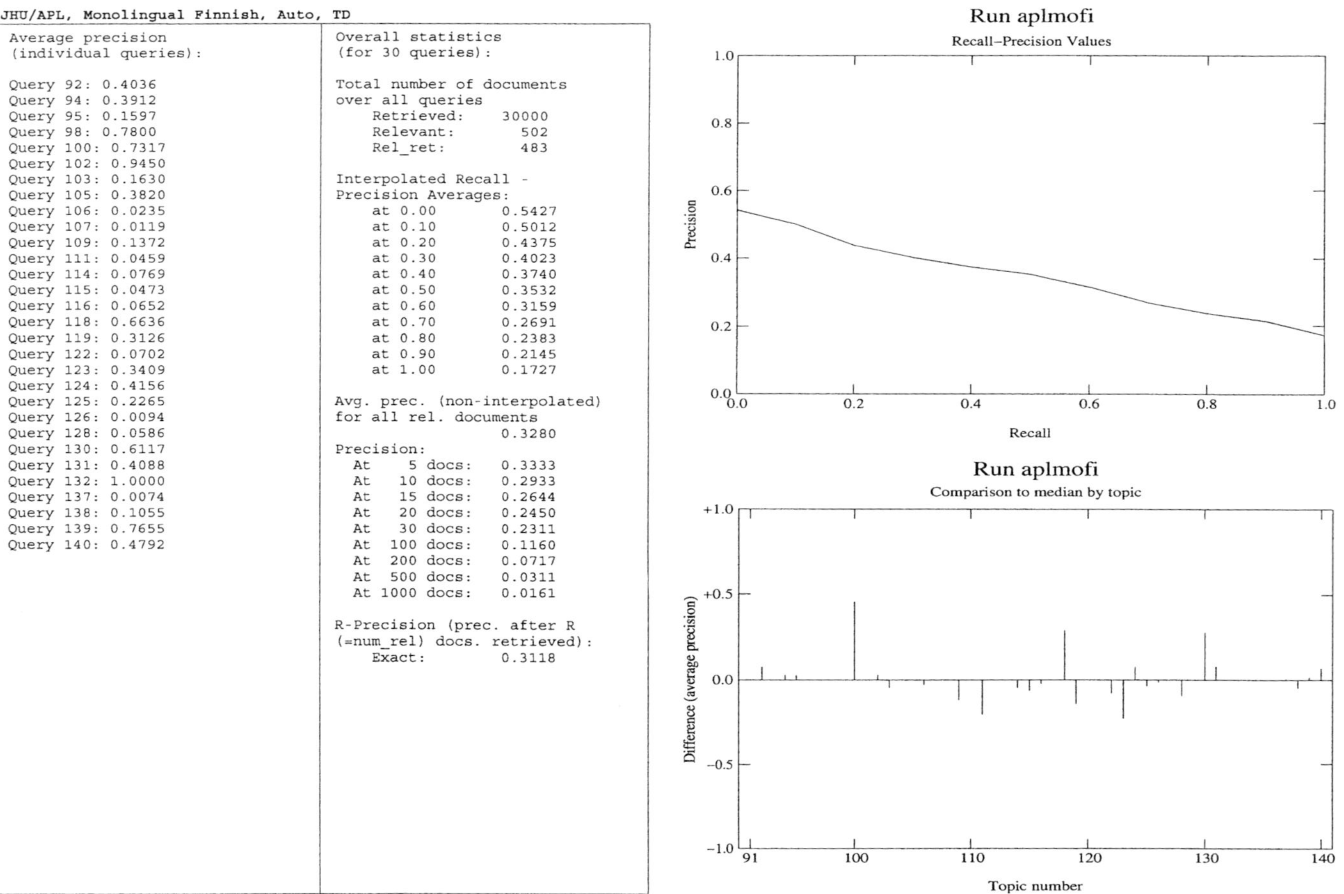

JHU/APL, Monolingual Finnish, Auto, TD

```
Average precision                Overall statistics
(individual queries):            (for 30 queries):

Query 92: 0.4036                 Total number of documents
Query 94: 0.3912                 over all queries
Query 95: 0.1597                     Retrieved:    30000
Query 98: 0.7800                     Relevant:       502
Query 100: 0.7317                    Rel_ret:        483
Query 102: 0.9450
Query 103: 0.1630                Interpolated Recall -
Query 105: 0.3820                Precision Averages:
Query 106: 0.0235                    at 0.00        0.5427
Query 107: 0.0119                    at 0.10        0.5012
Query 109: 0.1372                    at 0.20        0.4375
Query 111: 0.0459                    at 0.30        0.4023
Query 114: 0.0769                    at 0.40        0.3740
Query 115: 0.0473                    at 0.50        0.3532
Query 116: 0.0652                    at 0.60        0.3159
Query 118: 0.6636                    at 0.70        0.2691
Query 119: 0.3126                    at 0.80        0.2383
Query 122: 0.0702                    at 0.90        0.2145
Query 123: 0.3409                    at 1.00        0.1727
Query 124: 0.4156
Query 125: 0.2265                Avg. prec. (non-interpolated)
Query 126: 0.0094                for all rel. documents
Query 128: 0.0586                                   0.3280
Query 130: 0.6117                Precision:
Query 131: 0.4088                  At    5 docs:    0.3333
Query 132: 1.0000                  At   10 docs:    0.2933
Query 137: 0.0074                  At   15 docs:    0.2644
Query 138: 0.1055                  At   20 docs:    0.2450
Query 139: 0.7655                  At   30 docs:    0.2311
Query 140: 0.4792                  At  100 docs:    0.1160
                                   At  200 docs:    0.0717
                                   At  500 docs:    0.0311
                                   At 1000 docs:    0.0161

                                 R-Precision (prec. after R
                                 (=num_rel) docs. retrieved):
                                     Exact:         0.3118
```

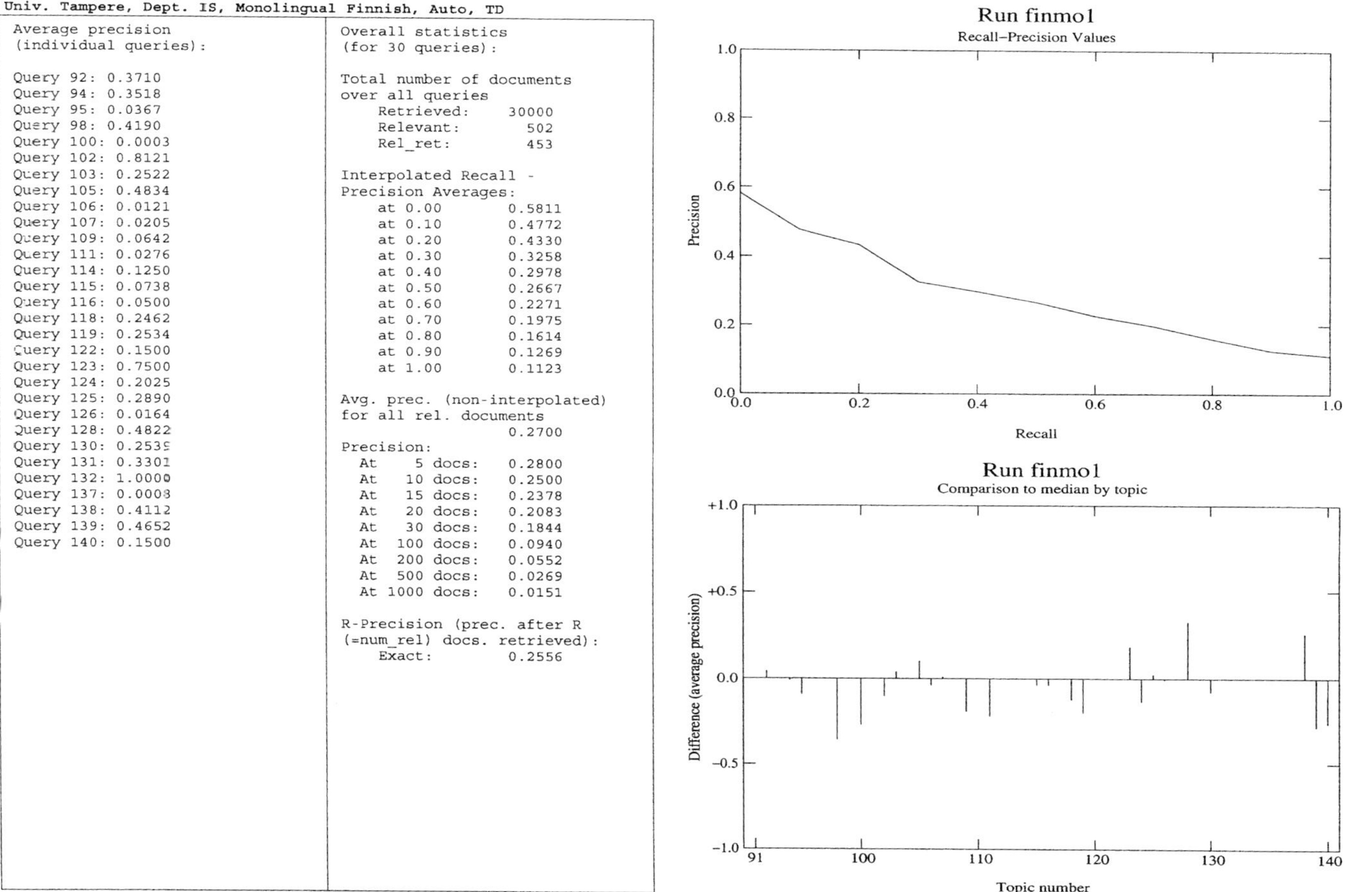

Univ. Tampere, Dept. IS, Monolingual Finnish, Auto, TD

```
Average precision                 Overall statistics
(individual queries):             (for 30 queries):

Query 92: 0.3710                  Total number of documents
Query 94: 0.3518                  over all queries
Query 95: 0.0367                      Retrieved:    30000
Query 98: 0.4190                      Relevant:       502
Query 100: 0.0003                     Rel_ret:        453
Query 102: 0.8121
Query 103: 0.2522                 Interpolated Recall -
Query 105: 0.4834                 Precision Averages:
Query 106: 0.0121                     at 0.00       0.5811
Query 107: 0.0205                     at 0.10       0.4772
Query 109: 0.0642                     at 0.20       0.4330
Query 111: 0.0276                     at 0.30       0.3258
Query 114: 0.1250                     at 0.40       0.2978
Query 115: 0.0738                     at 0.50       0.2667
Query 116: 0.0500                     at 0.60       0.2271
Query 118: 0.2462                     at 0.70       0.1975
Query 119: 0.2534                     at 0.80       0.1614
Query 122: 0.1500                     at 0.90       0.1269
Query 123: 0.7500                     at 1.00       0.1123
Query 124: 0.2025
Query 125: 0.2890                 Avg. prec. (non-interpolated)
Query 126: 0.0164                 for all rel. documents
Query 128: 0.4822                                   0.2700
Query 130: 0.2539                 Precision:
Query 131: 0.3301                   At    5 docs:   0.2800
Query 132: 1.0000                   At   10 docs:   0.2500
Query 137: 0.0008                   At   15 docs:   0.2378
Query 138: 0.4112                   At   20 docs:   0.2083
Query 139: 0.4652                   At   30 docs:   0.1844
Query 140: 0.1500                   At  100 docs:   0.0940
                                    At  200 docs:   0.0552
                                    At  500 docs:   0.0269
                                    At 1000 docs:   0.0151

                                  R-Precision (prec. after R
                                  (=num_rel) docs. retrieved):
                                      Exact:        0.2556
```

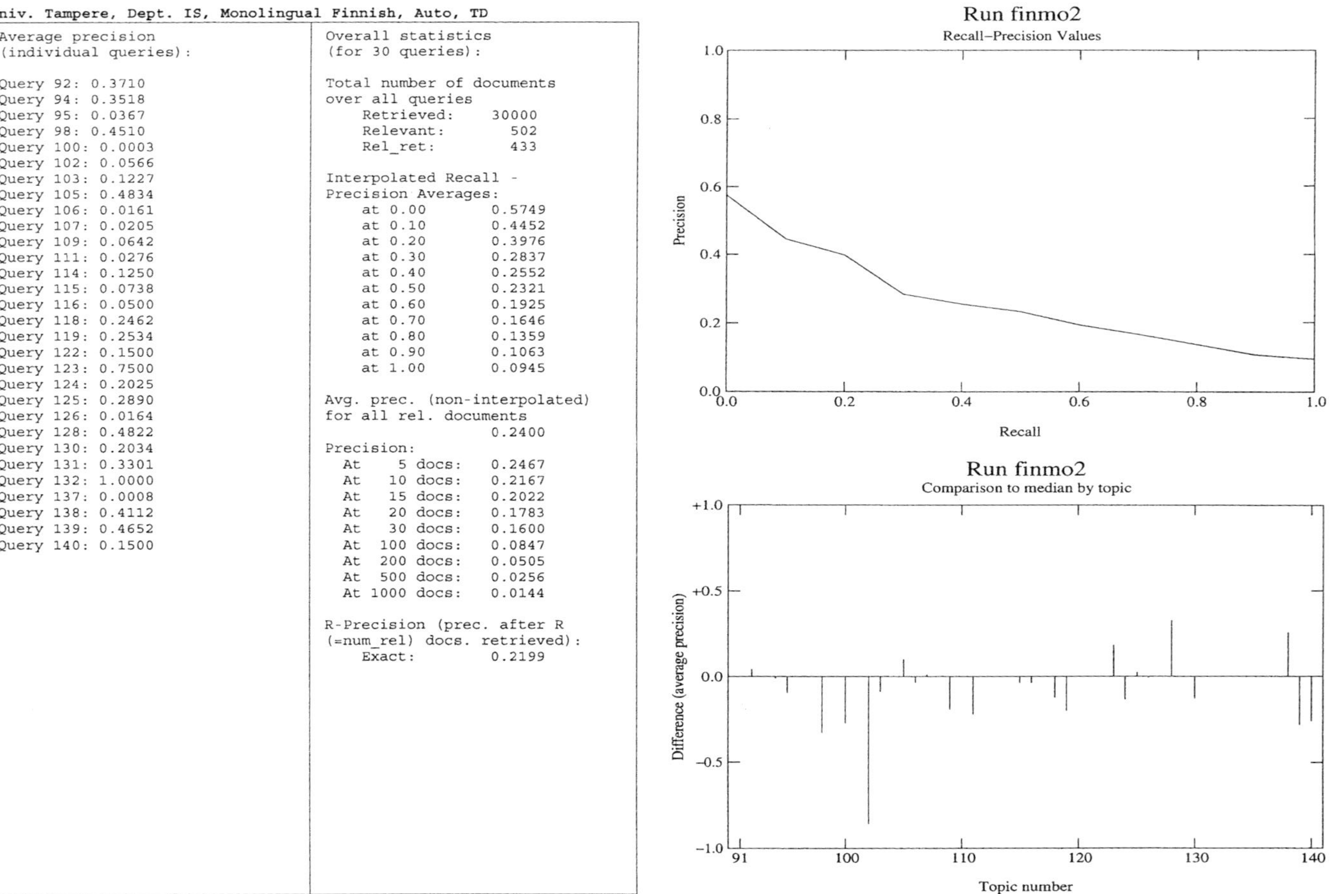

Univ. Tampere, Dept. IS, Monolingual Finnish, Auto, TD

```
Average precision            Overall statistics
(individual queries):        (for 30 queries):

Query  92: 0.3710            Total number of documents
Query  94: 0.3518            over all queries
Query  95: 0.0367              Retrieved:   30000
Query  98: 0.4510              Relevant:      502
Query 100: 0.0003              Rel_ret:       433
Query 102: 0.0566
Query 103: 0.1227            Interpolated Recall -
Query 105: 0.4834            Precision Averages:
Query 106: 0.0161              at 0.00      0.5749
Query 107: 0.0205              at 0.10      0.4452
Query 109: 0.0642              at 0.20      0.3976
Query 111: 0.0276              at 0.30      0.2837
Query 114: 0.1250              at 0.40      0.2552
Query 115: 0.0738              at 0.50      0.2321
Query 116: 0.0500              at 0.60      0.1925
Query 118: 0.2462              at 0.70      0.1646
Query 119: 0.2534              at 0.80      0.1359
Query 122: 0.1500              at 0.90      0.1063
Query 123: 0.7500              at 1.00      0.0945
Query 124: 0.2025
Query 125: 0.2890            Avg. prec. (non-interpolated)
Query 126: 0.0164            for all rel. documents
Query 128: 0.4822                           0.2400
Query 130: 0.2034
Query 131: 0.3301            Precision:
Query 132: 1.0000              At    5 docs:  0.2467
Query 137: 0.0008              At   10 docs:  0.2167
Query 138: 0.4112              At   15 docs:  0.2022
Query 139: 0.4652              At   20 docs:  0.1783
Query 140: 0.1500              At   30 docs:  0.1600
                               At  100 docs:  0.0847
                               At  200 docs:  0.0505
                               At  500 docs:  0.0256
                               At 1000 docs:  0.0144

                             R-Precision (prec. after R
                             (=num_rel) docs. retrieved):
                               Exact:         0.2199
```

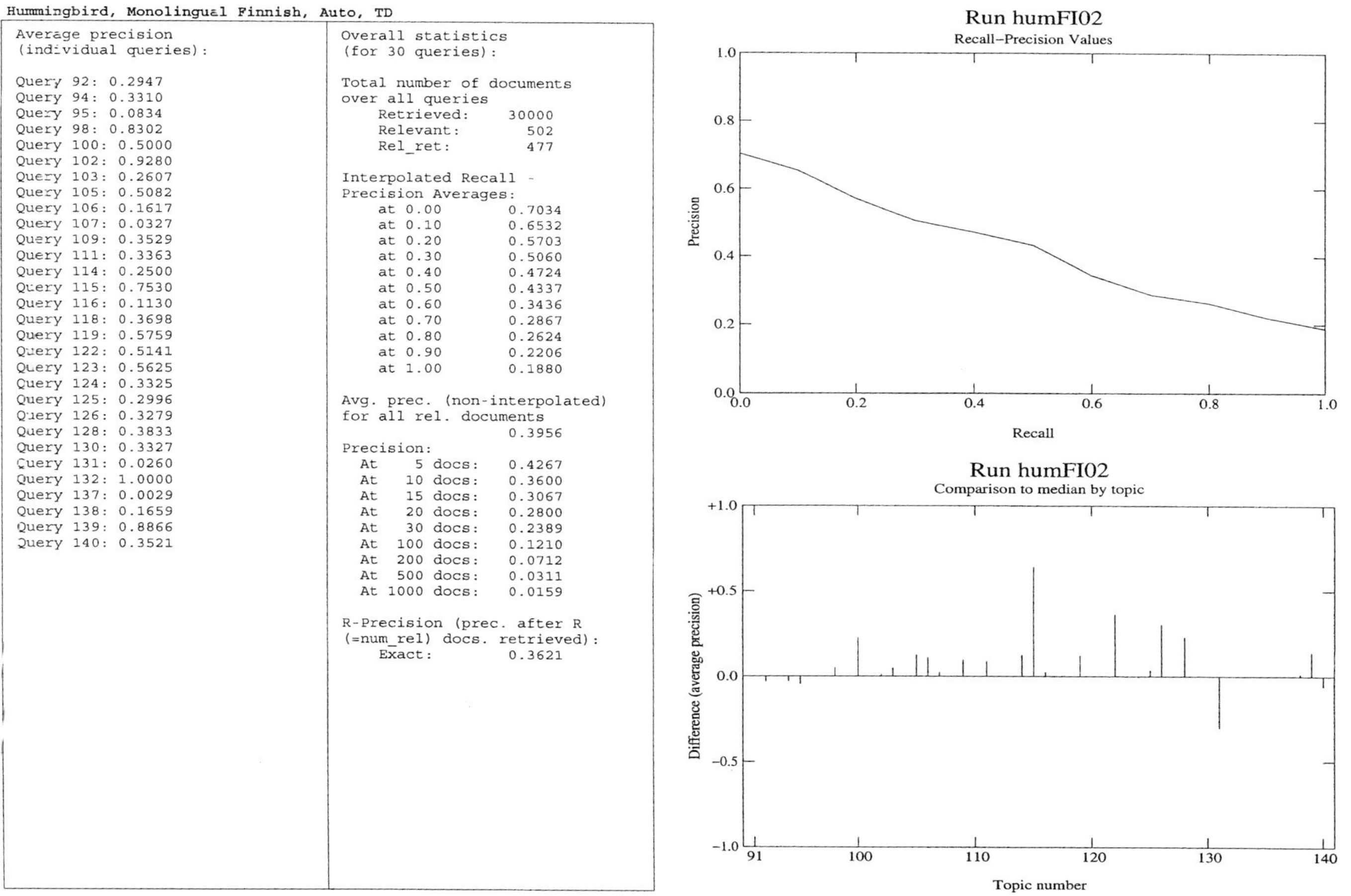

Hummingbird, Monolingual Finnish, Auto, TD

```
Average precision                 Overall statistics
(individual queries):             (for 30 queries):

Query 92: 0.2947                  Total number of documents
Query 94: 0.3310                  over all queries
Query 95: 0.0834                      Retrieved:     30000
Query 98: 0.8302                      Relevant:        502
Query 100: 0.5000                     Rel_ret:         477
Query 102: 0.9280
Query 103: 0.2607                 Interpolated Recall -
Query 105: 0.5082                 Precision Averages:
Query 106: 0.1617                     at 0.00        0.7034
Query 107: 0.0327                     at 0.10        0.6532
Query 109: 0.3529                     at 0.20        0.5703
Query 111: 0.3363                     at 0.30        0.5060
Query 114: 0.2500                     at 0.40        0.4724
Query 115: 0.7530                     at 0.50        0.4337
Query 116: 0.1130                     at 0.60        0.3436
Query 118: 0.3698                     at 0.70        0.2867
Query 119: 0.5759                     at 0.80        0.2624
Query 122: 0.5141                     at 0.90        0.2206
Query 123: 0.5625                     at 1.00        0.1880
Query 124: 0.3325
Query 125: 0.2996                 Avg. prec. (non-interpolated)
Query 126: 0.3279                 for all rel. documents
Query 128: 0.3833                                    0.3956
Query 130: 0.3327                 Precision:
Query 131: 0.0260                   At    5 docs:    0.4267
Query 132: 1.0000                   At   10 docs:    0.3600
Query 137: 0.0029                   At   15 docs:    0.3067
Query 138: 0.1659                   At   20 docs:    0.2800
Query 139: 0.8866                   At   30 docs:    0.2389
Query 140: 0.3521                   At  100 docs:    0.1210
                                    At  200 docs:    0.0712
                                    At  500 docs:    0.0311
                                    At 1000 docs:    0.0159

                                  R-Precision (prec. after R
                                  (=num_rel) docs. retrieved):
                                      Exact:         0.3621
```

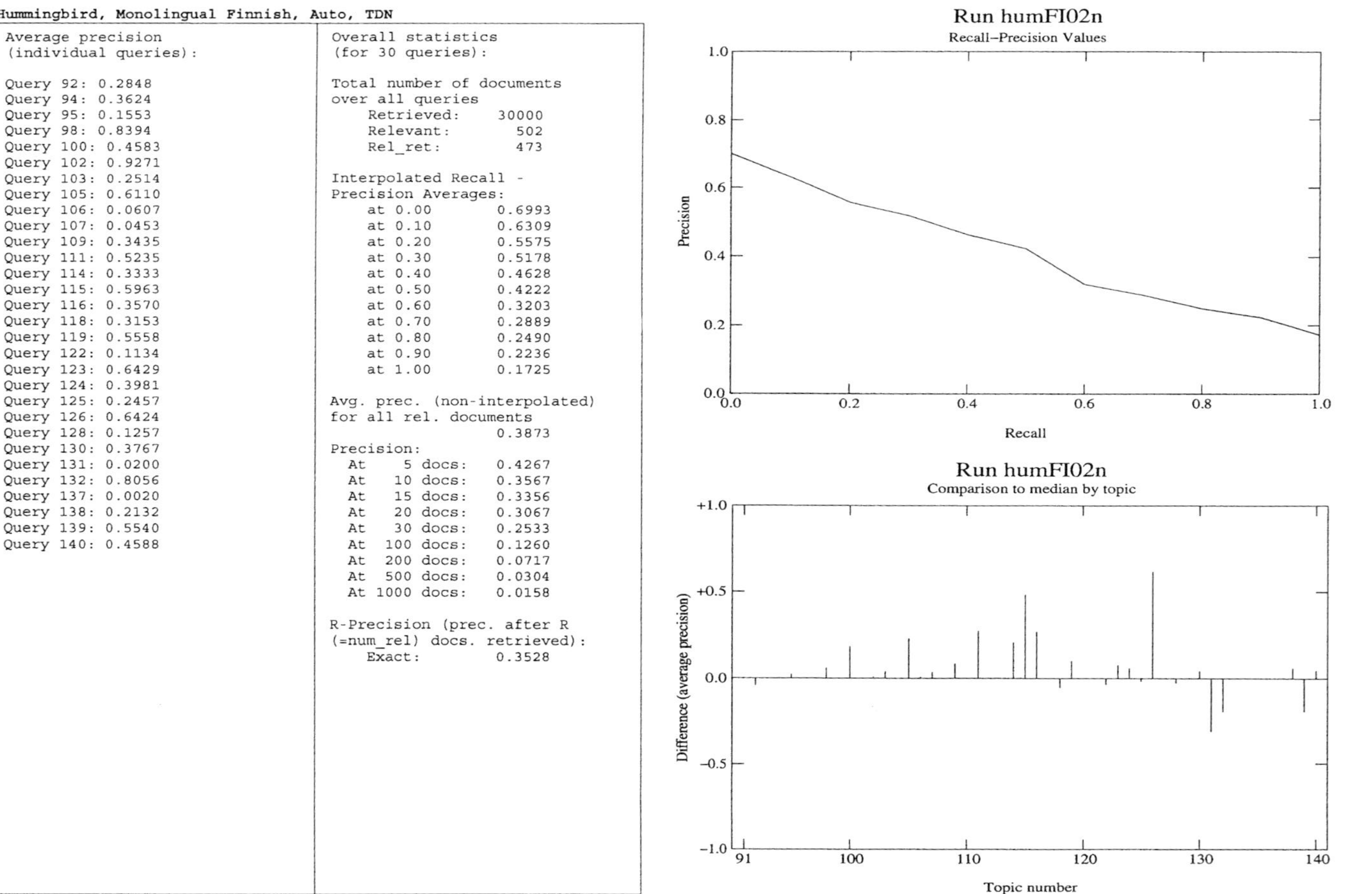

Hummingbird, Monolingual Finnish, Auto, TDN

```
Average precision
(individual queries):

Query 92: 0.2848
Query 94: 0.3624
Query 95: 0.1553
Query 98: 0.8394
Query 100: 0.4583
Query 102: 0.9271
Query 103: 0.2514
Query 105: 0.6110
Query 106: 0.0607
Query 107: 0.0453
Query 109: 0.3435
Query 111: 0.5235
Query 114: 0.3333
Query 115: 0.5963
Query 116: 0.3570
Query 118: 0.3153
Query 119: 0.5558
Query 122: 0.1134
Query 123: 0.6429
Query 124: 0.3981
Query 125: 0.2457
Query 126: 0.6424
Query 128: 0.1257
Query 130: 0.3767
Query 131: 0.0200
Query 132: 0.8056
Query 137: 0.0020
Query 138: 0.2132
Query 139: 0.5540
Query 140: 0.4588
```

```
Overall statistics
(for 30 queries):

Total number of documents
over all queries
    Retrieved:     30000
    Relevant:        502
    Rel_ret:         473

Interpolated Recall -
Precision Averages:
    at 0.00        0.6993
    at 0.10        0.6309
    at 0.20        0.5575
    at 0.30        0.5178
    at 0.40        0.4628
    at 0.50        0.4222
    at 0.60        0.3203
    at 0.70        0.2889
    at 0.80        0.2490
    at 0.90        0.2236
    at 1.00        0.1725

Avg. prec. (non-interpolated)
for all rel. documents
                   0.3873
Precision:
  At    5 docs:    0.4267
  At   10 docs:    0.3567
  At   15 docs:    0.3356
  At   20 docs:    0.3067
  At   30 docs:    0.2533
  At  100 docs:    0.1260
  At  200 docs:    0.0717
  At  500 docs:    0.0304
  At 1000 docs:    0.0158

R-Precision (prec. after R
(=num_rel) docs. retrieved):
    Exact:         0.3528
```

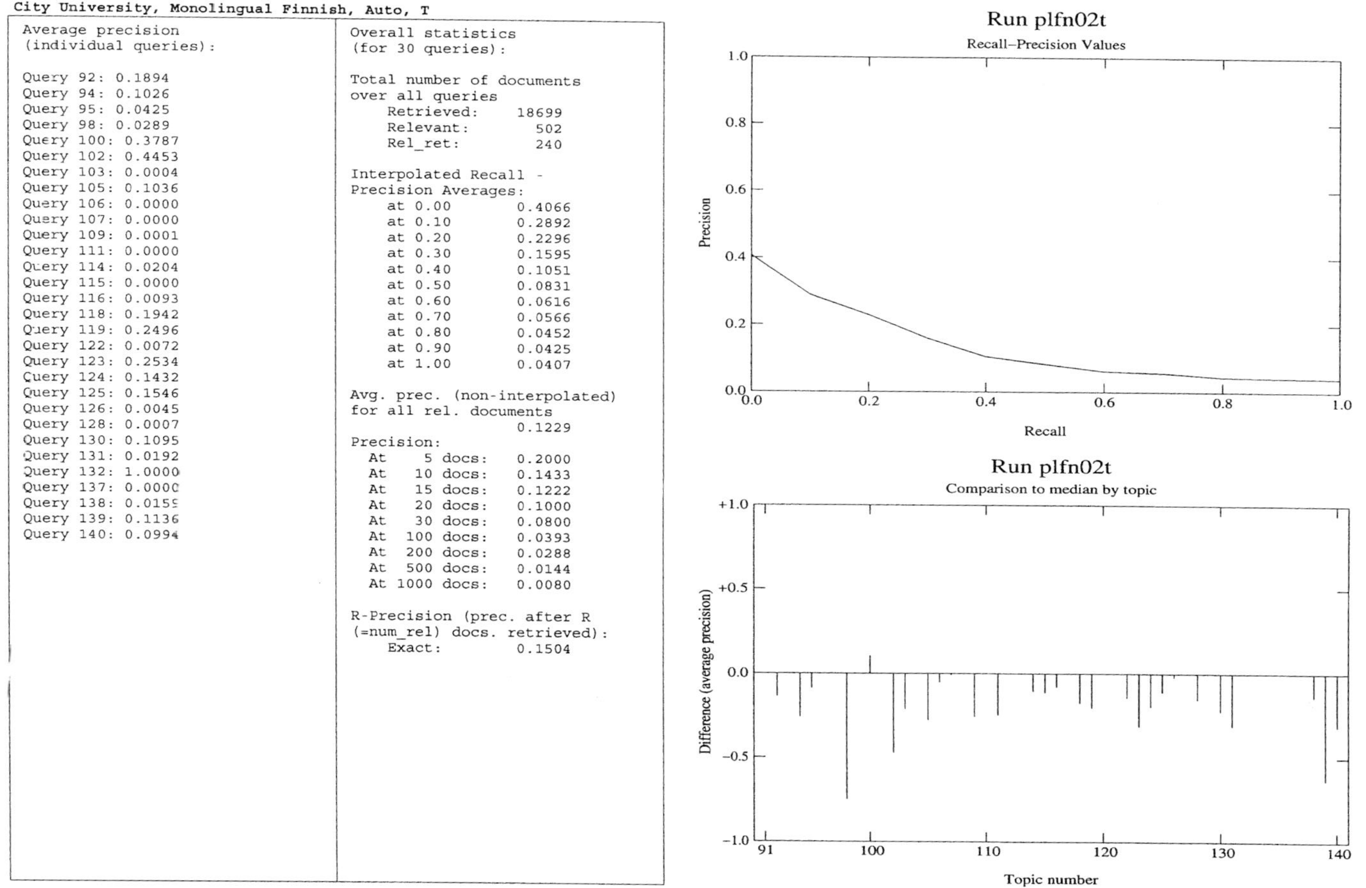

City University, Monolingual Finnish, Auto, T

```
Average precision              Overall statistics
(individual queries):          (for 30 queries):

Query 92: 0.1894               Total number of documents
Query 94: 0.1026               over all queries
Query 95: 0.0425                   Retrieved:     18699
Query 98: 0.0289                   Relevant:        502
Query 100: 0.3787                  Rel_ret:         240
Query 102: 0.4453
Query 103: 0.0004              Interpolated Recall -
Query 105: 0.1036              Precision Averages:
Query 106: 0.0000                  at 0.00        0.4066
Query 107: 0.0000                  at 0.10        0.2892
Query 109: 0.0001                  at 0.20        0.2296
Query 111: 0.0000                  at 0.30        0.1595
Query 114: 0.0204                  at 0.40        0.1051
Query 115: 0.0000                  at 0.50        0.0831
Query 116: 0.0093                  at 0.60        0.0616
Query 118: 0.1942                  at 0.70        0.0566
Query 119: 0.2496                  at 0.80        0.0452
Query 122: 0.0072                  at 0.90        0.0425
Query 123: 0.2534                  at 1.00        0.0407
Query 124: 0.1432
Query 125: 0.1546              Avg. prec. (non-interpolated)
Query 126: 0.0045              for all rel. documents
Query 128: 0.0007                                 0.1229
Query 130: 0.1095              Precision:
Query 131: 0.0192                At    5 docs:    0.2000
Query 132: 1.0000                At   10 docs:    0.1433
Query 137: 0.0000                At   15 docs:    0.1222
Query 138: 0.0159                At   20 docs:    0.1000
Query 139: 0.1136                At   30 docs:    0.0800
Query 140: 0.0994                At  100 docs:    0.0393
                                 At  200 docs:    0.0288
                                 At  500 docs:    0.0144
                                 At 1000 docs:    0.0080

                               R-Precision (prec. after R
                               (=num_rel) docs. retrieved):
                                   Exact:         0.1504
```

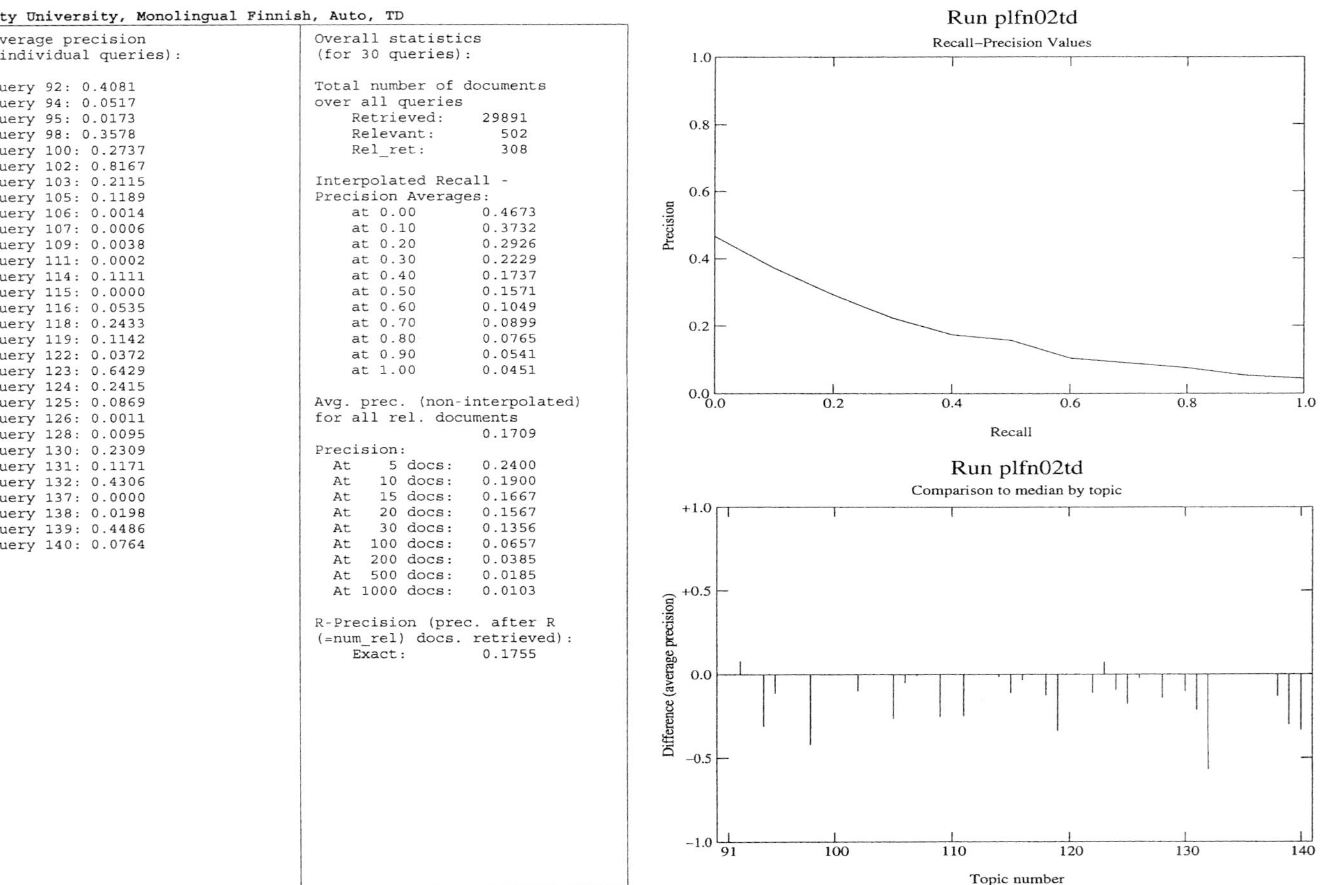

City University, Monolingual Finnish, Auto, TD

```
Average precision               Overall statistics
(individual queries):           (for 30 queries):

Query 92: 0.4081                Total number of documents
Query 94: 0.0517                over all queries
Query 95: 0.0173                    Retrieved:    29891
Query 98: 0.3578                    Relevant:       502
Query 100: 0.2737                   Rel_ret:        308
Query 102: 0.8167
Query 103: 0.2115               Interpolated Recall -
Query 105: 0.1189               Precision Averages:
Query 106: 0.0014                   at 0.00        0.4673
Query 107: 0.0006                   at 0.10        0.3732
Query 109: 0.0038                   at 0.20        0.2926
Query 111: 0.0002                   at 0.30        0.2229
Query 114: 0.1111                   at 0.40        0.1737
Query 115: 0.0000                   at 0.50        0.1571
Query 116: 0.0535                   at 0.60        0.1049
Query 118: 0.2433                   at 0.70        0.0899
Query 119: 0.1142                   at 0.80        0.0765
Query 122: 0.0372                   at 0.90        0.0541
Query 123: 0.6429                   at 1.00        0.0451
Query 124: 0.2415
Query 125: 0.0869               Avg. prec. (non-interpolated)
Query 126: 0.0011               for all rel. documents
Query 128: 0.0095                                  0.1709
Query 130: 0.2309               Precision:
Query 131: 0.1171                 At    5 docs:    0.2400
Query 132: 0.4306                 At   10 docs:    0.1900
Query 137: 0.0000                 At   15 docs:    0.1667
Query 138: 0.0198                 At   20 docs:    0.1567
Query 139: 0.4486                 At   30 docs:    0.1356
Query 140: 0.0764                 At  100 docs:    0.0657
                                  At  200 docs:    0.0385
                                  At  500 docs:    0.0185
                                  At 1000 docs:    0.0103

                                R-Precision (prec. after R
                                (=num_rel) docs. retrieved):
                                    Exact:         0.1755
```

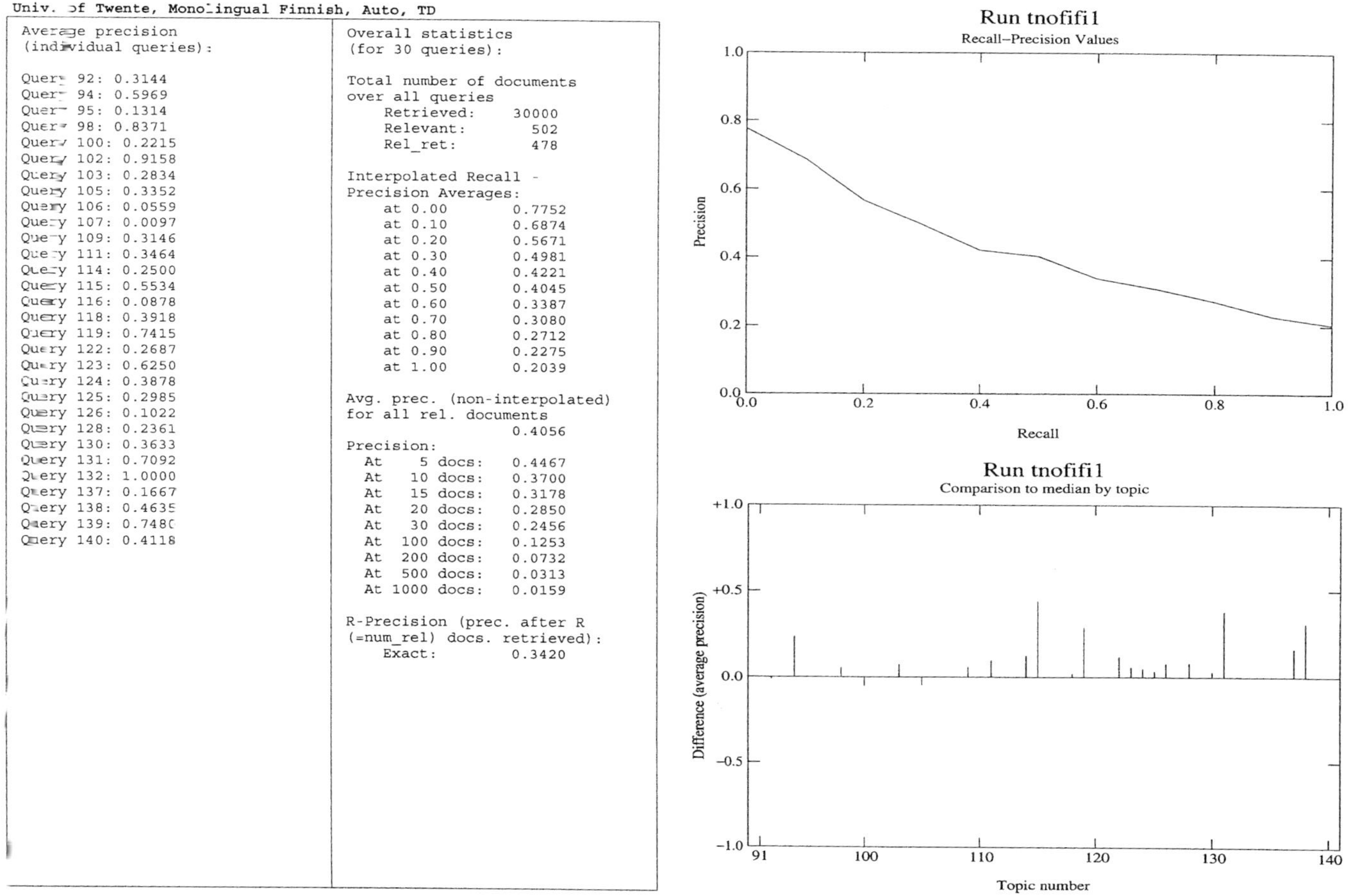

Univ. of Twente, Monolingual Finnish, Auto, TD

```
Average precision                Overall statistics
(individual queries):            (for 30 queries):

Query  92: 0.3144                Total number of documents
Query  94: 0.5969                over all queries
Query  95: 0.1314                    Retrieved:     30000
Query  98: 0.8371                    Relevant:        502
Query 100: 0.2215                    Rel_ret:         478
Query 102: 0.9158
Query 103: 0.2834                Interpolated Recall -
Query 105: 0.3352                Precision Averages:
Query 106: 0.0559                    at 0.00        0.7752
Query 107: 0.0097                    at 0.10        0.6874
Query 109: 0.3146                    at 0.20        0.5671
Query 111: 0.3464                    at 0.30        0.4981
Query 114: 0.2500                    at 0.40        0.4221
Query 115: 0.5534                    at 0.50        0.4045
Query 116: 0.0878                    at 0.60        0.3387
Query 118: 0.3918                    at 0.70        0.3080
Query 119: 0.7415                    at 0.80        0.2712
Query 122: 0.2687                    at 0.90        0.2275
Query 123: 0.6250                    at 1.00        0.2039
Query 124: 0.3878
Query 125: 0.2985                Avg. prec. (non-interpolated)
Query 126: 0.1022                for all rel. documents
Query 128: 0.2361                                   0.4056
Query 130: 0.3633                Precision:
Query 131: 0.7092                  At    5 docs:    0.4467
Query 132: 1.0000                  At   10 docs:    0.3700
Query 137: 0.1667                  At   15 docs:    0.3178
Query 138: 0.4635                  At   20 docs:    0.2850
Query 139: 0.7480                  At   30 docs:    0.2456
Query 140: 0.4118                  At  100 docs:    0.1253
                                   At  200 docs:    0.0732
                                   At  500 docs:    0.0313
                                   At 1000 docs:    0.0159

                                 R-Precision (prec. after R
                                 (=num_rel) docs. retrieved):
                                     Exact:         0.3420
```

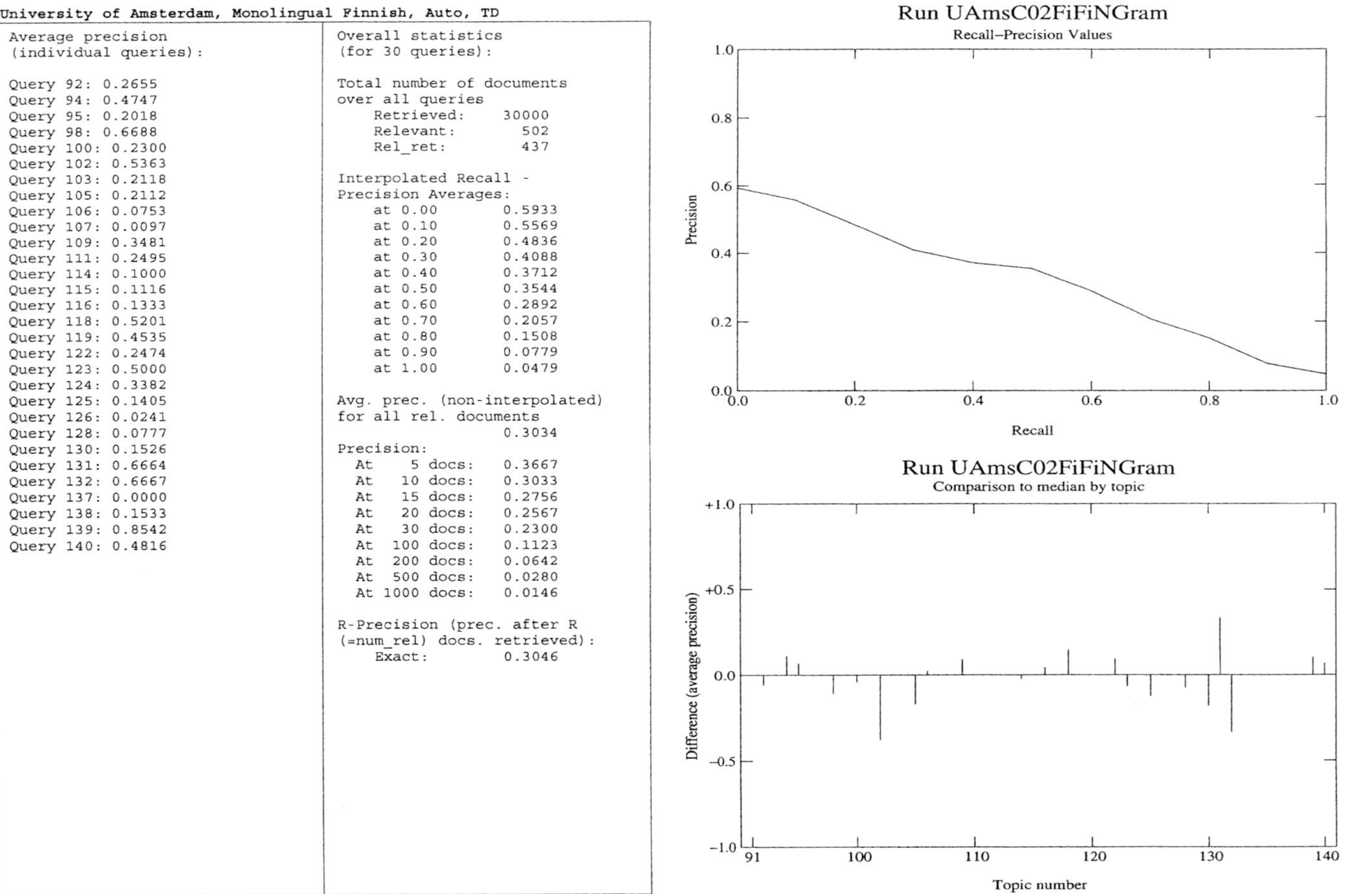

University of Amsterdam, Monolingual Finnish, Auto, TD

Average precision (individual queries):

Query 92: 0.2655
Query 94: 0.4747
Query 95: 0.2018
Query 98: 0.6688
Query 100: 0.2300
Query 102: 0.5363
Query 103: 0.2118
Query 105: 0.2112
Query 106: 0.0753
Query 107: 0.0097
Query 109: 0.3481
Query 111: 0.2495
Query 114: 0.1000
Query 115: 0.1116
Query 116: 0.1333
Query 118: 0.5201
Query 119: 0.4535
Query 122: 0.2474
Query 123: 0.5000
Query 124: 0.3382
Query 125: 0.1405
Query 126: 0.0241
Query 128: 0.0777
Query 130: 0.1526
Query 131: 0.6664
Query 132: 0.6667
Query 137: 0.0000
Query 138: 0.1533
Query 139: 0.8542
Query 140: 0.4816

Overall statistics (for 30 queries):

Total number of documents over all queries
Retrieved: 30000
Relevant: 502
Rel_ret: 437

Interpolated Recall - Precision Averages:
at 0.00 0.5933
at 0.10 0.5569
at 0.20 0.4836
at 0.30 0.4088
at 0.40 0.3712
at 0.50 0.3544
at 0.60 0.2892
at 0.70 0.2057
at 0.80 0.1508
at 0.90 0.0779
at 1.00 0.0479

Avg. prec. (non-interpolated) for all rel. documents
0.3034

Precision:
At 5 docs: 0.3667
At 10 docs: 0.3033
At 15 docs: 0.2756
At 20 docs: 0.2567
At 30 docs: 0.2300
At 100 docs: 0.1123
At 200 docs: 0.0642
At 500 docs: 0.0280
At 1000 docs: 0.0146

R-Precision (prec. after R (=num_rel) docs. retrieved):
Exact: 0.3046

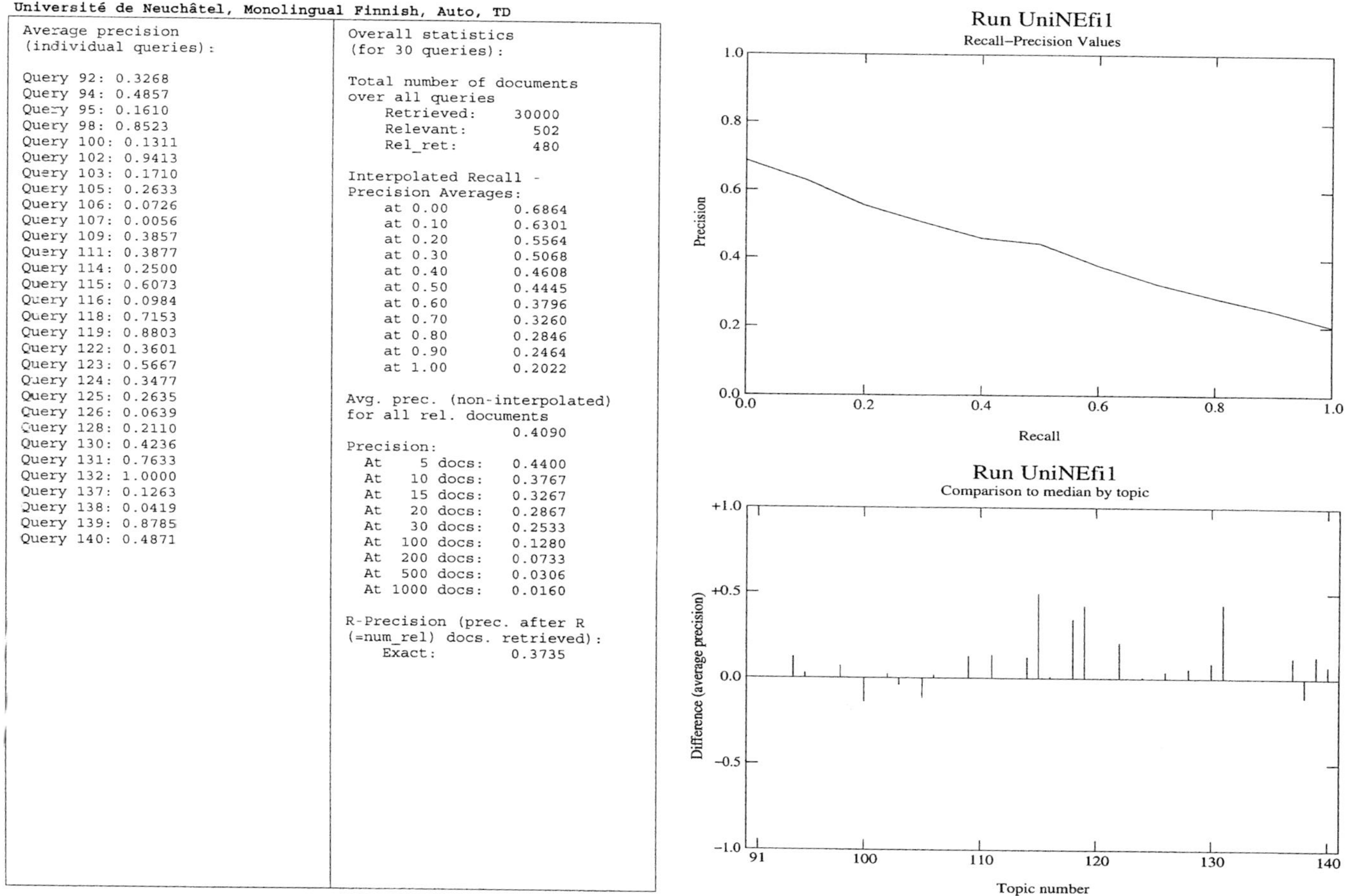

Université de Neuchâtel, Monolingual Finnish, Auto, TD

```
Average precision
(individual queries):

Query 92: 0.3268
Query 94: 0.4857
Query 95: 0.1610
Query 98: 0.8523
Query 100: 0.1311
Query 102: 0.9413
Query 103: 0.1710
Query 105: 0.2633
Query 106: 0.0726
Query 107: 0.0056
Query 109: 0.3857
Query 111: 0.3877
Query 114: 0.2500
Query 115: 0.6073
Query 116: 0.0984
Query 118: 0.7153
Query 119: 0.8803
Query 122: 0.3601
Query 123: 0.5667
Query 124: 0.3477
Query 125: 0.2635
Query 126: 0.0639
Query 128: 0.2110
Query 130: 0.4236
Query 131: 0.7633
Query 132: 1.0000
Query 137: 0.1263
Query 138: 0.0419
Query 139: 0.8785
Query 140: 0.4871
```

```
Overall statistics
(for 30 queries):

Total number of documents
over all queries
    Retrieved:    30000
    Relevant:       502
    Rel_ret:        480

Interpolated Recall -
Precision Averages:
    at 0.00       0.6864
    at 0.10       0.6301
    at 0.20       0.5564
    at 0.30       0.5068
    at 0.40       0.4608
    at 0.50       0.4445
    at 0.60       0.3796
    at 0.70       0.3260
    at 0.80       0.2846
    at 0.90       0.2464
    at 1.00       0.2022

Avg. prec. (non-interpolated)
for all rel. documents
                  0.4090
Precision:
  At    5 docs:   0.4400
  At   10 docs:   0.3767
  At   15 docs:   0.3267
  At   20 docs:   0.2867
  At   30 docs:   0.2533
  At  100 docs:   0.1280
  At  200 docs:   0.0733
  At  500 docs:   0.0306
  At 1000 docs:   0.0160

R-Precision (prec. after R
(=num_rel) docs. retrieved):
    Exact:        0.3735
```

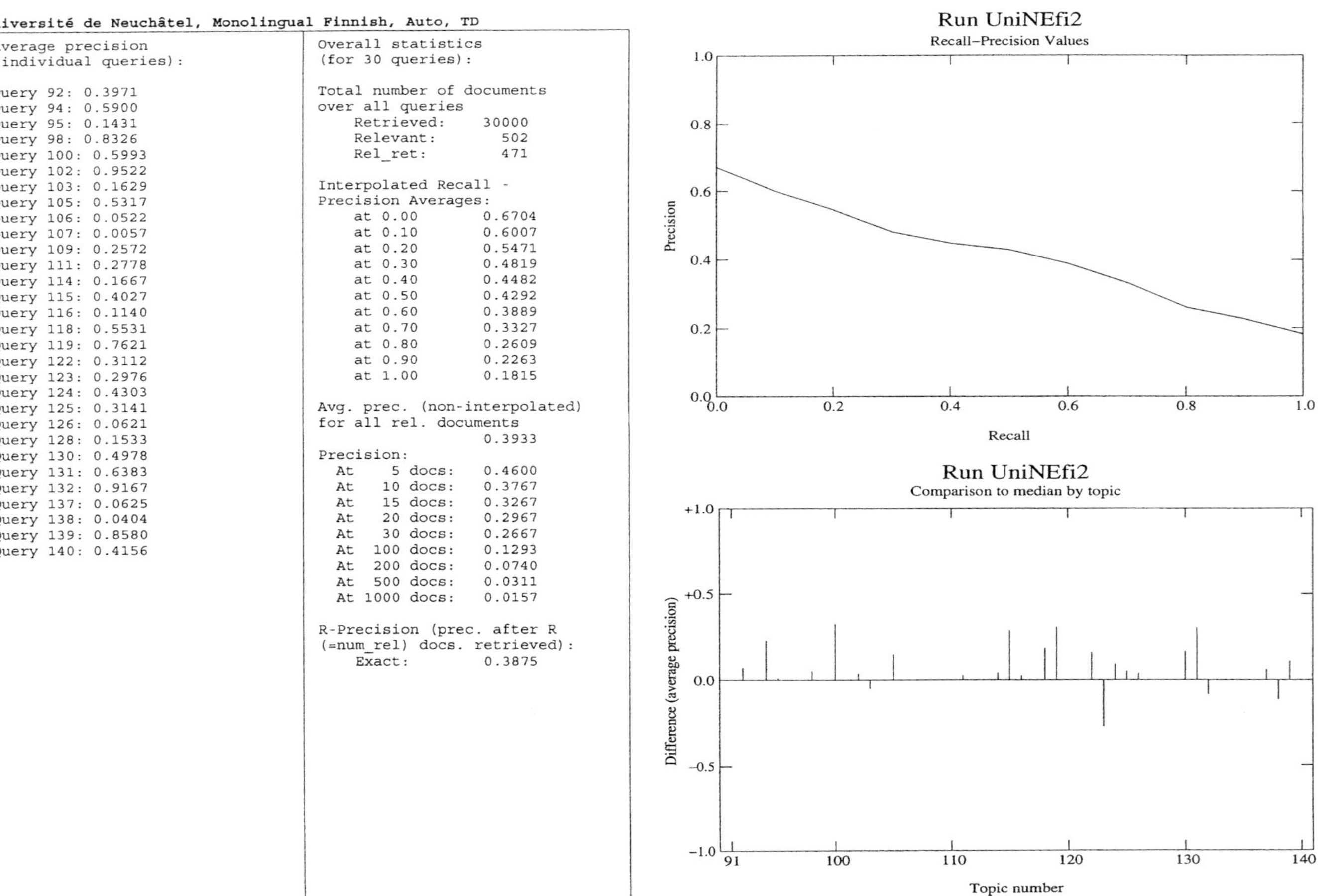

Université de Neuchâtel, Monolingual Finnish, Auto, TD

```
Average precision               Overall statistics
(individual queries):           (for 30 queries):

Query 92: 0.3971                Total number of documents
Query 94: 0.5900                over all queries
Query 95: 0.1431                    Retrieved:    30000
Query 98: 0.8326                    Relevant:       502
Query 100: 0.5993                   Rel_ret:        471
Query 102: 0.9522
Query 103: 0.1629               Interpolated Recall -
Query 105: 0.5317               Precision Averages:
Query 106: 0.0522                   at 0.00       0.6704
Query 107: 0.0057                   at 0.10       0.6007
Query 109: 0.2572                   at 0.20       0.5471
Query 111: 0.2778                   at 0.30       0.4819
Query 114: 0.1667                   at 0.40       0.4482
Query 115: 0.4027                   at 0.50       0.4292
Query 116: 0.1140                   at 0.60       0.3889
Query 118: 0.5531                   at 0.70       0.3327
Query 119: 0.7621                   at 0.80       0.2609
Query 122: 0.3112                   at 0.90       0.2263
Query 123: 0.2976                   at 1.00       0.1815
Query 124: 0.4303
Query 125: 0.3141               Avg. prec. (non-interpolated)
Query 126: 0.0621               for all rel. documents
Query 128: 0.1533                                 0.3933
Query 130: 0.4978               Precision:
Query 131: 0.6383                 At    5 docs:   0.4600
Query 132: 0.9167                 At   10 docs:   0.3767
Query 137: 0.0625                 At   15 docs:   0.3267
Query 138: 0.0404                 At   20 docs:   0.2967
Query 139: 0.8580                 At   30 docs:   0.2667
Query 140: 0.4156                 At  100 docs:   0.1293
                                  At  200 docs:   0.0740
                                  At  500 docs:   0.0311
                                  At 1000 docs:   0.0157

                                R-Precision (prec. after R
                                (=num_rel) docs. retrieved):
                                    Exact:        0.3875
```

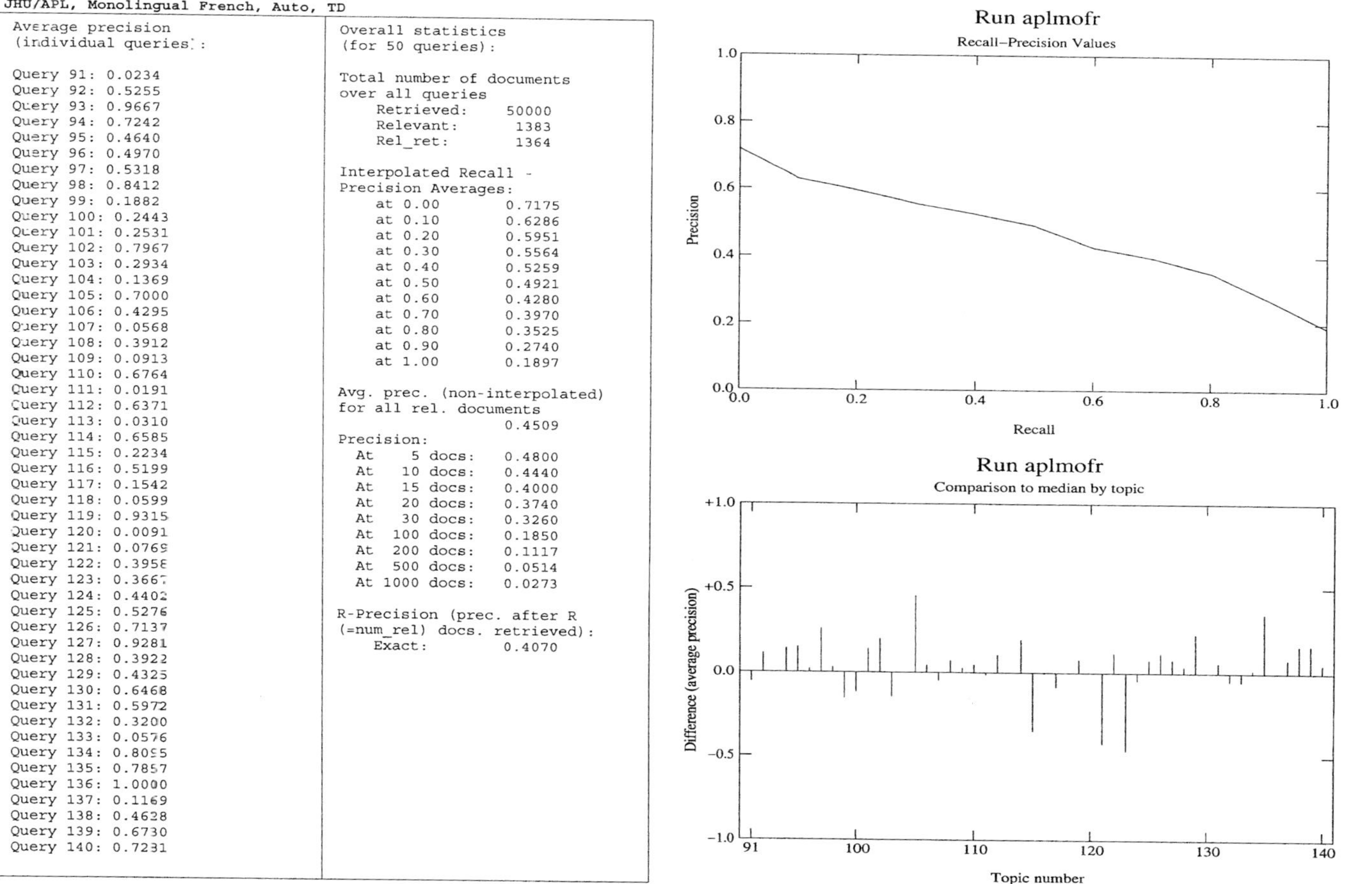

JHU/APL, Monolingual French, Auto, TD

```
Average precision                 Overall statistics
(individual queries):             (for 50 queries):

Query 91: 0.0234                  Total number of documents
Query 92: 0.5255                  over all queries
Query 93: 0.9667                      Retrieved:    50000
Query 94: 0.7242                      Relevant:      1383
Query 95: 0.4640                      Rel_ret:       1364
Query 96: 0.4970
Query 97: 0.5318                  Interpolated Recall -
Query 98: 0.8412                  Precision Averages:
Query 99: 0.1882                      at 0.00       0.7175
Query 100: 0.2443                     at 0.10       0.6286
Query 101: 0.2531                     at 0.20       0.5951
Query 102: 0.7967                     at 0.30       0.5564
Query 103: 0.2934                     at 0.40       0.5259
Query 104: 0.1369                     at 0.50       0.4921
Query 105: 0.7000                     at 0.60       0.4280
Query 106: 0.4295                     at 0.70       0.3970
Query 107: 0.0568                     at 0.80       0.3525
Query 108: 0.3912                     at 0.90       0.2740
Query 109: 0.0913                     at 1.00       0.1897
Query 110: 0.6764
Query 111: 0.0191                 Avg. prec. (non-interpolated)
Query 112: 0.6371                 for all rel. documents
Query 113: 0.0310                                   0.4509
Query 114: 0.6585                 Precision:
Query 115: 0.2234                   At    5 docs:   0.4800
Query 116: 0.5199                   At   10 docs:   0.4440
Query 117: 0.1542                   At   15 docs:   0.4000
Query 118: 0.0599                   At   20 docs:   0.3740
Query 119: 0.9315                   At   30 docs:   0.3260
Query 120: 0.0091                   At  100 docs:   0.1850
Query 121: 0.0769                   At  200 docs:   0.1117
Query 122: 0.3958                   At  500 docs:   0.0514
Query 123: 0.3667                   At 1000 docs:   0.0273
Query 124: 0.4402
Query 125: 0.5276                 R-Precision (prec. after R
Query 126: 0.7137                 (=num_rel) docs. retrieved):
Query 127: 0.9281                     Exact:        0.4070
Query 128: 0.3922
Query 129: 0.4325
Query 130: 0.6468
Query 131: 0.5972
Query 132: 0.3200
Query 133: 0.0576
Query 134: 0.8095
Query 135: 0.7857
Query 136: 1.0000
Query 137: 0.1169
Query 138: 0.4628
Query 139: 0.6730
Query 140: 0.7231
```

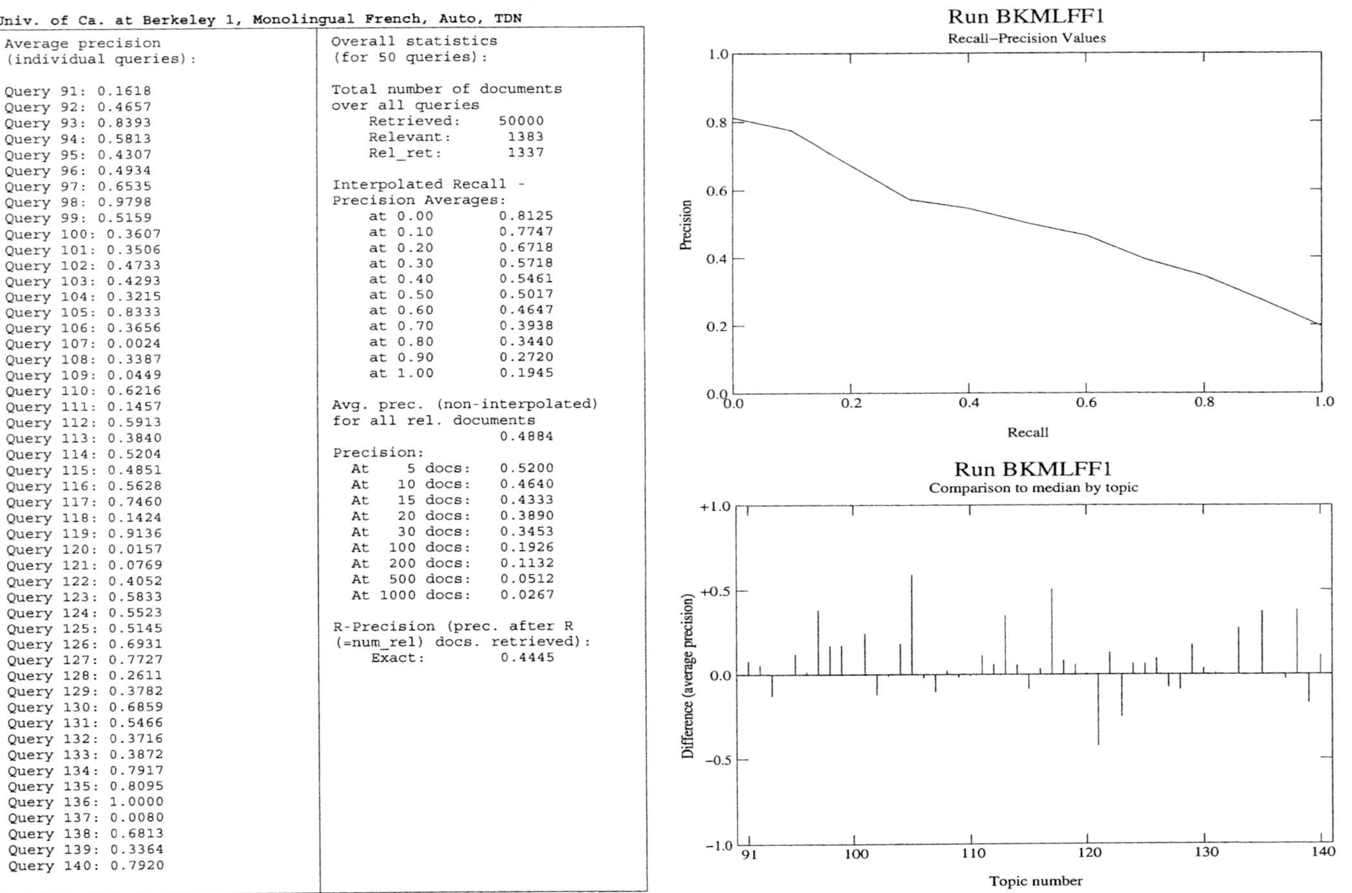

Univ. of Ca. at Berkeley 1, Monolingual French, Auto, TDN

Average precision
(individual queries):

Query 91: 0.1618
Query 92: 0.4657
Query 93: 0.8393
Query 94: 0.5813
Query 95: 0.4307
Query 96: 0.4934
Query 97: 0.6535
Query 98: 0.9798
Query 99: 0.5159
Query 100: 0.3607
Query 101: 0.3506
Query 102: 0.4733
Query 103: 0.4293
Query 104: 0.3215
Query 105: 0.8333
Query 106: 0.3656
Query 107: 0.0024
Query 108: 0.3387
Query 109: 0.0449
Query 110: 0.6216
Query 111: 0.1457
Query 112: 0.5913
Query 113: 0.3840
Query 114: 0.5204
Query 115: 0.4851
Query 116: 0.5628
Query 117: 0.7460
Query 118: 0.1424
Query 119: 0.9136
Query 120: 0.0157
Query 121: 0.0769
Query 122: 0.4052
Query 123: 0.5833
Query 124: 0.5523
Query 125: 0.5145
Query 126: 0.6931
Query 127: 0.7727
Query 128: 0.2611
Query 129: 0.3782
Query 130: 0.6859
Query 131: 0.5466
Query 132: 0.3716
Query 133: 0.3872
Query 134: 0.7917
Query 135: 0.8095
Query 136: 1.0000
Query 137: 0.0080
Query 138: 0.6813
Query 139: 0.3364
Query 140: 0.7920

Overall statistics
(for 50 queries):

Total number of documents
over all queries
Retrieved: 50000
Relevant: 1383
Rel_ret: 1337

Interpolated Recall -
Precision Averages:
at 0.00 0.8125
at 0.10 0.7747
at 0.20 0.6718
at 0.30 0.5718
at 0.40 0.5461
at 0.50 0.5017
at 0.60 0.4647
at 0.70 0.3938
at 0.80 0.3440
at 0.90 0.2720
at 1.00 0.1945

Avg. prec. (non-interpolated)
for all rel. documents
0.4884

Precision:
At 5 docs: 0.5200
At 10 docs: 0.4640
At 15 docs: 0.4333
At 20 docs: 0.3890
At 30 docs: 0.3453
At 100 docs: 0.1926
At 200 docs: 0.1132
At 500 docs: 0.0512
At 1000 docs: 0.0267

R-Precision (prec. after R
(=num_rel) docs. retrieved):
Exact: 0.4445

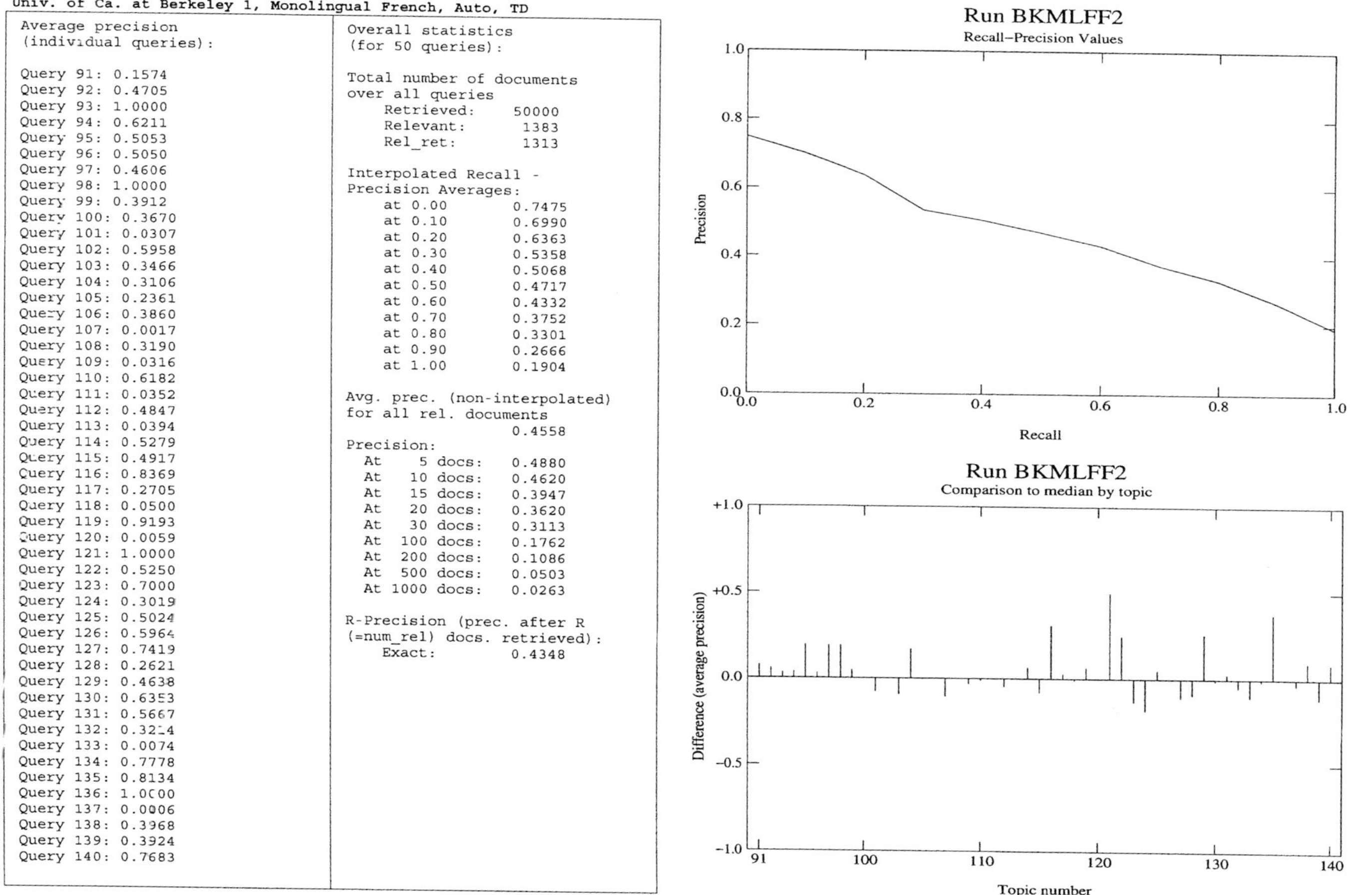

Univ. of Ca. at Berkeley 1, Monolingual French, Auto, TD

```
Average precision               Overall statistics
(individual queries):           (for 50 queries):

Query 91: 0.1574                Total number of documents
Query 92: 0.4705                over all queries
Query 93: 1.0000                    Retrieved:     50000
Query 94: 0.6211                    Relevant:       1383
Query 95: 0.5053                    Rel_ret:        1313
Query 96: 0.5050
Query 97: 0.4606                Interpolated Recall -
Query 98: 1.0000                Precision Averages:
Query 99: 0.3912                    at 0.00        0.7475
Query 100: 0.3670                   at 0.10        0.6990
Query 101: 0.0307                   at 0.20        0.6363
Query 102: 0.5958                   at 0.30        0.5358
Query 103: 0.3466                   at 0.40        0.5068
Query 104: 0.3106                   at 0.50        0.4717
Query 105: 0.2361                   at 0.60        0.4332
Query 106: 0.3860                   at 0.70        0.3752
Query 107: 0.0017                   at 0.80        0.3301
Query 108: 0.3190                   at 0.90        0.2666
Query 109: 0.0316                   at 1.00        0.1904
Query 110: 0.6182
Query 111: 0.0352               Avg. prec. (non-interpolated)
Query 112: 0.4847               for all rel. documents
Query 113: 0.0394                                  0.4558
Query 114: 0.5279               Precision:
Query 115: 0.4917                 At    5 docs:    0.4880
Query 116: 0.8369                 At   10 docs:    0.4620
Query 117: 0.2705                 At   15 docs:    0.3947
Query 118: 0.0500                 At   20 docs:    0.3620
Query 119: 0.9193                 At   30 docs:    0.3113
Query 120: 0.0059                 At  100 docs:    0.1762
Query 121: 1.0000                 At  200 docs:    0.1086
Query 122: 0.5250                 At  500 docs:    0.0503
Query 123: 0.7000                 At 1000 docs:    0.0263
Query 124: 0.3019
Query 125: 0.5024               R-Precision (prec. after R
Query 126: 0.5964               (=num_rel) docs. retrieved):
Query 127: 0.7419                   Exact:         0.4348
Query 128: 0.2621
Query 129: 0.4638
Query 130: 0.6353
Query 131: 0.5667
Query 132: 0.3214
Query 133: 0.0074
Query 134: 0.7778
Query 135: 0.8134
Query 136: 1.0000
Query 137: 0.0006
Query 138: 0.3968
Query 139: 0.3924
Query 140: 0.7683
```

Univ. of Ca. at Berkeley 2, Monolingual French, Auto, TD

```
Average precision                Overall statistics
(individual queries):            (for 50 queries):

Query 91: 0.2224                 Total number of documents
Query 92: 0.4334                 over all queries
Query 93: 0.9267                     Retrieved:     50000
Query 94: 0.5928                     Relevant:       1383
Query 95: 0.5886                     Rel_ret:        1354
Query 96: 0.5370
Query 97: 0.4999                 Interpolated Recall -
Query 98: 0.9086                 Precision Averages:
Query 99: 0.6372                     at 0.00        0.7915
Query 100: 0.3899                    at 0.10        0.7270
Query 101: 0.0643                    at 0.20        0.6835
Query 102: 0.6971                    at 0.30        0.6353
Query 103: 0.5443                    at 0.40        0.5985
Query 104: 0.0997                    at 0.50        0.5661
Query 105: 0.3250                    at 0.60        0.5106
Query 106: 0.4773                    at 0.70        0.4696
Query 107: 0.4787                    at 0.80        0.4047
Query 108: 0.3371                    at 0.90        0.3197
Query 109: 0.0944                    at 1.00        0.2019
Query 110: 0.6143
Query 111: 0.0178                Avg. prec. (non-interpolated)
Query 112: 0.6019                for all rel. documents
Query 113: 0.0376                                   0.5191
Query 114: 0.4982                Precision:
Query 115: 0.5733                  At    5 docs:   0.5640
Query 116: 0.8363                  At   10 docs:   0.4980
Query 117: 0.3124                  At   15 docs:   0.4520
Query 118: 0.0266                  At   20 docs:   0.4170
Query 119: 0.9151                  At   30 docs:   0.3653
Query 120: 0.0182                  At  100 docs:   0.1986
Query 121: 1.0000                  At  200 docs:   0.1158
Query 122: 0.7194                  At  500 docs:   0.0524
Query 123: 0.8333                  At 1000 docs:   0.0271
Query 124: 0.5278
Query 125: 0.4500                R-Precision (prec. after R
Query 126: 0.4911                (=num_rel) docs. retrieved):
Query 127: 0.9187                    Exact:          0.4996
Query 128: 0.4994
Query 129: 0.4725
Query 130: 0.7017
Query 131: 0.5307
Query 132: 0.3735
Query 133: 0.4996
Query 134: 1.0000
Query 135: 0.7846
Query 136: 1.0000
Query 137: 0.0063
Query 138: 0.3593
Query 139: 0.6812
Query 140: 0.8008
```

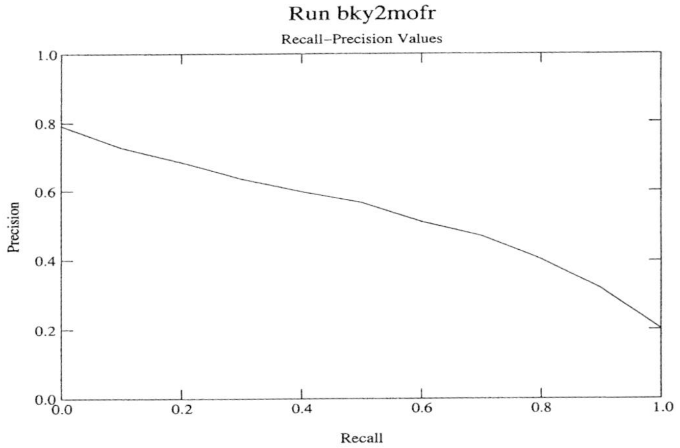

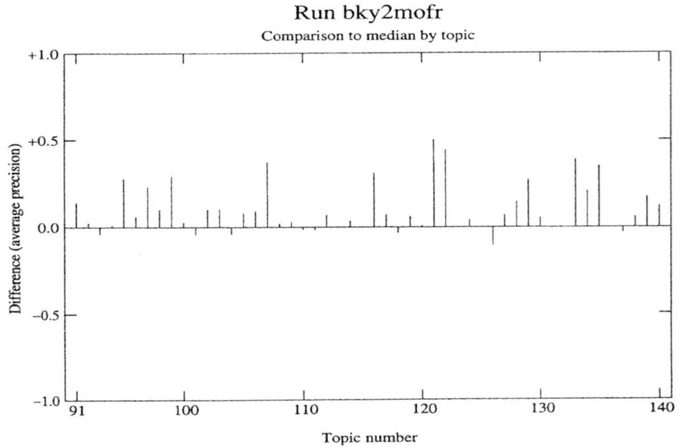

Run bky2mofr

Recall–Precision Values

Precision: 0.0 0.2 0.4 0.6 0.8 1.0

Recall: 0.0 0.2 0.4 0.6 0.8 1.0

Run bky2mofr

Comparison to median by topic

Difference (average precision): +1.0 +0.5 0.0 −0.5 −1.0

Topic number: 91 100 110 120 130 140

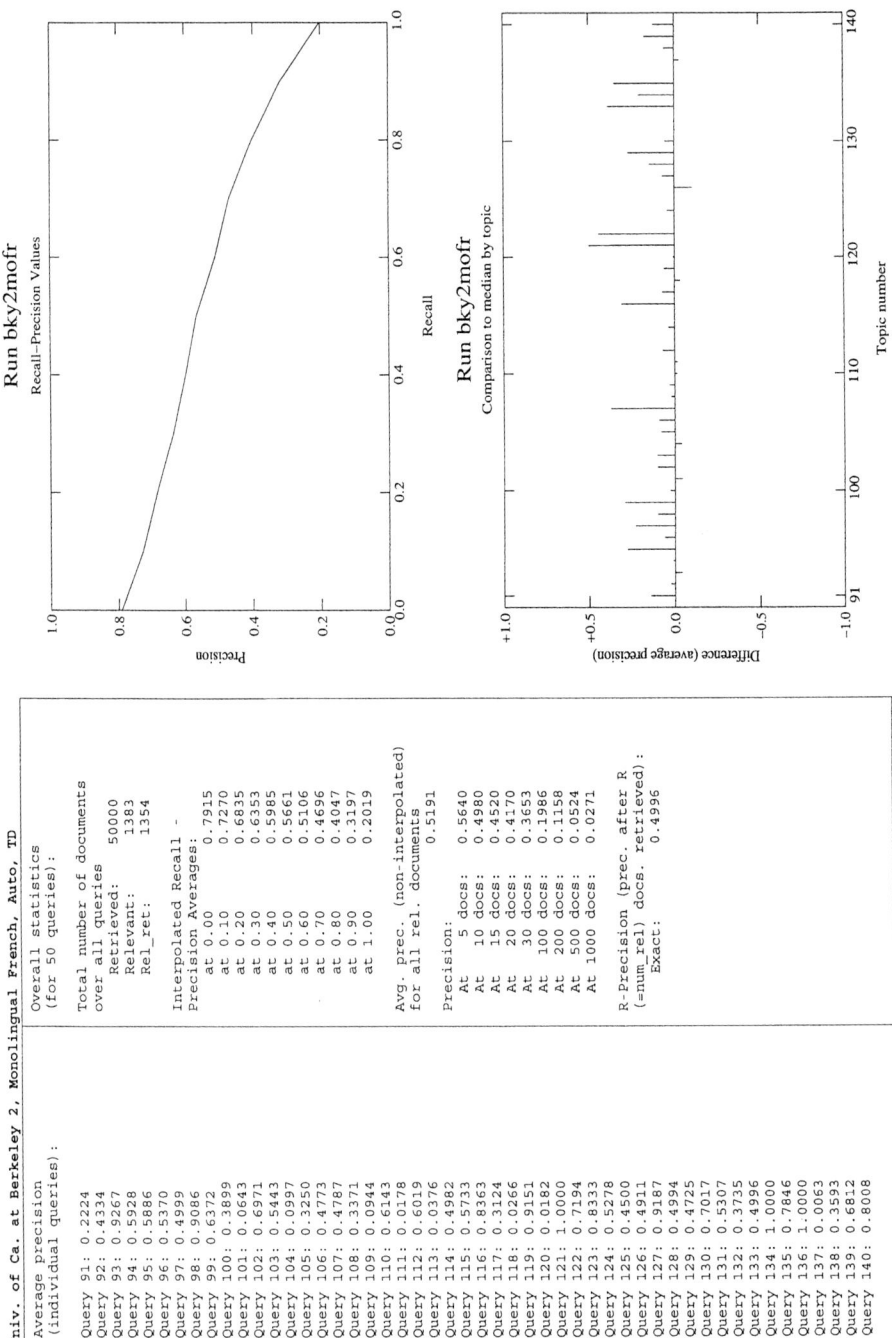

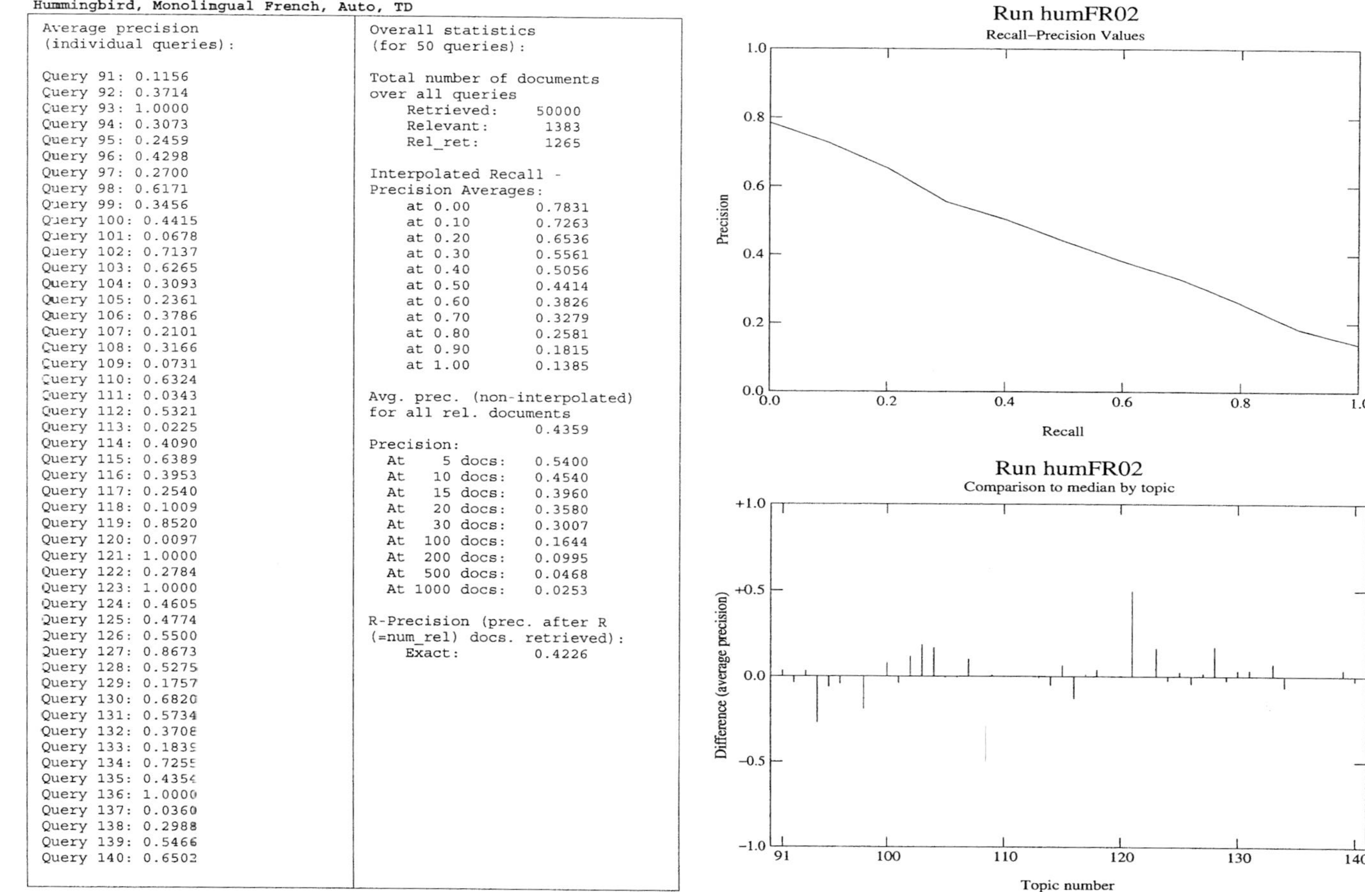

Hummingbird, Monolingual French, Auto, TD

Average precision (individual queries):	Overall statistics (for 50 queries):	
Query 91: 0.1156	Total number of documents over all queries	
Query 92: 0.3714	Retrieved:	50000
Query 93: 1.0000	Relevant:	1383
Query 94: 0.3073	Rel_ret:	1265
Query 95: 0.2459	Interpolated Recall - Precision Averages:	
Query 96: 0.4298	at 0.00	0.7831
Query 97: 0.2700	at 0.10	0.7263
Query 98: 0.6171	at 0.20	0.6536
Query 99: 0.3456	at 0.30	0.5561
Query 100: 0.4415	at 0.40	0.5056
Query 101: 0.0678	at 0.50	0.4414
Query 102: 0.7137	at 0.60	0.3826
Query 103: 0.6265	at 0.70	0.3279
Query 104: 0.3093	at 0.80	0.2581
Query 105: 0.2361	at 0.90	0.1815
Query 106: 0.3786	at 1.00	0.1385
Query 107: 0.2101	Avg. prec. (non-interpolated) for all rel. documents	0.4359
Query 108: 0.3166	Precision:	
Query 109: 0.0731	At 5 docs:	0.5400
Query 110: 0.6324	At 10 docs:	0.4540
Query 111: 0.0343	At 15 docs:	0.3960
Query 112: 0.5321	At 20 docs:	0.3580
Query 113: 0.0225	At 30 docs:	0.3007
Query 114: 0.4090	At 100 docs:	0.1644
Query 115: 0.6389	At 200 docs:	0.0995
Query 116: 0.3953	At 500 docs:	0.0468
Query 117: 0.2540	At 1000 docs:	0.0253
Query 118: 0.1009	R-Precision (prec. after R (=num_rel) docs. retrieved):	
Query 119: 0.8520	Exact:	0.4226
Query 120: 0.0097		
Query 121: 1.0000		
Query 122: 0.2784		
Query 123: 1.0000		
Query 124: 0.4605		
Query 125: 0.4774		
Query 126: 0.5500		
Query 127: 0.8673		
Query 128: 0.5275		
Query 129: 0.1757		
Query 130: 0.6820		
Query 131: 0.5734		
Query 132: 0.3708		
Query 133: 0.1839		
Query 134: 0.7255		
Query 135: 0.4354		
Query 136: 1.0000		
Query 137: 0.0360		
Query 138: 0.2988		
Query 139: 0.5466		
Query 140: 0.6502		

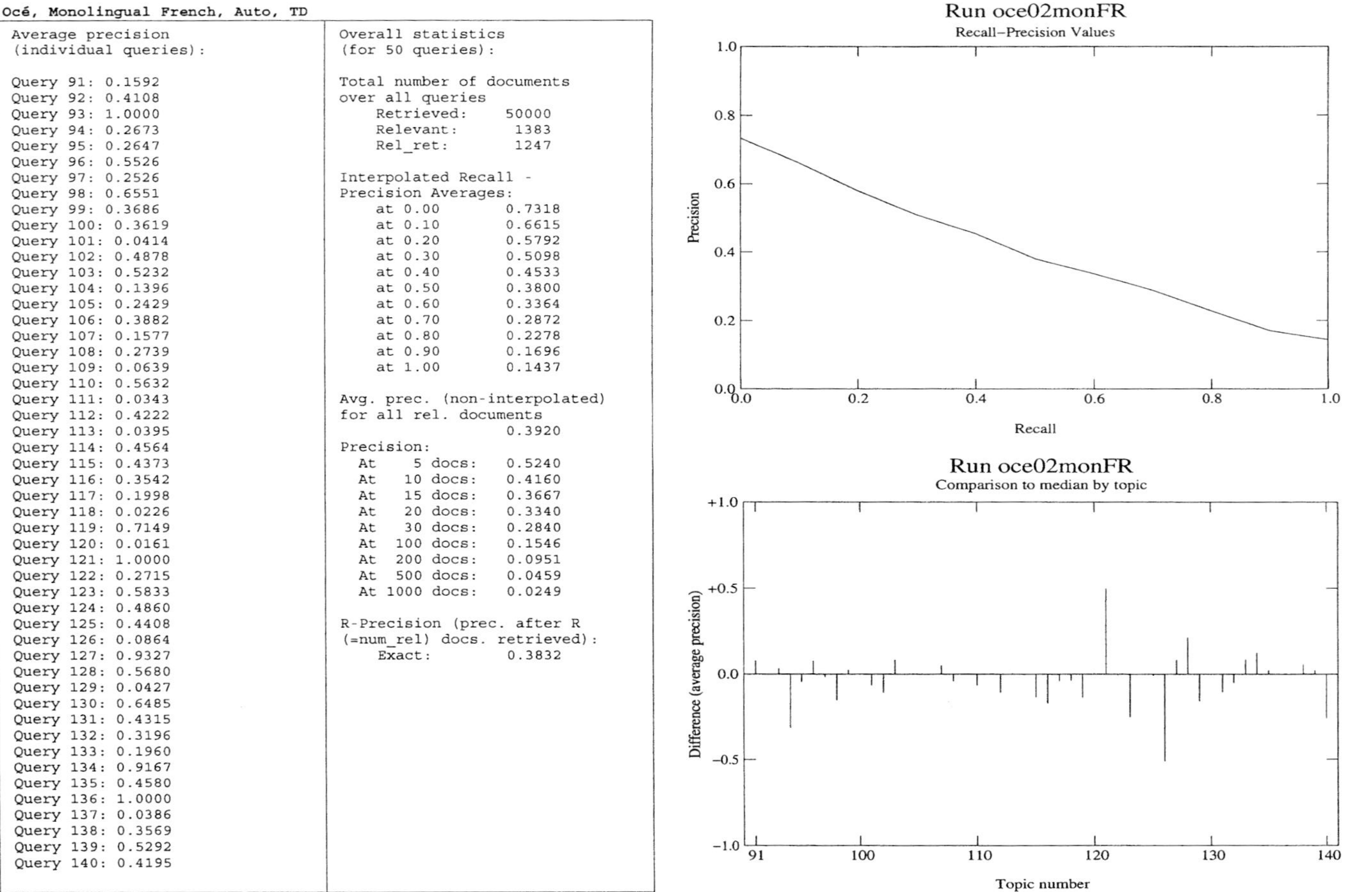

Océ, Monolingual French, Auto, TD

```
Average precision
(individual queries):

Query 91: 0.1592
Query 92: 0.4108
Query 93: 1.0000
Query 94: 0.2673
Query 95: 0.2647
Query 96: 0.5526
Query 97: 0.2526
Query 98: 0.6551
Query 99: 0.3686
Query 100: 0.3619
Query 101: 0.0414
Query 102: 0.4878
Query 103: 0.5232
Query 104: 0.1396
Query 105: 0.2429
Query 106: 0.3882
Query 107: 0.1577
Query 108: 0.2739
Query 109: 0.0639
Query 110: 0.5632
Query 111: 0.0343
Query 112: 0.4222
Query 113: 0.0395
Query 114: 0.4564
Query 115: 0.4373
Query 116: 0.3542
Query 117: 0.1998
Query 118: 0.0226
Query 119: 0.7149
Query 120: 0.0161
Query 121: 1.0000
Query 122: 0.2715
Query 123: 0.5833
Query 124: 0.4860
Query 125: 0.4408
Query 126: 0.0864
Query 127: 0.9327
Query 128: 0.5680
Query 129: 0.0427
Query 130: 0.6485
Query 131: 0.4315
Query 132: 0.3196
Query 133: 0.1960
Query 134: 0.9167
Query 135: 0.4580
Query 136: 1.0000
Query 137: 0.0386
Query 138: 0.3569
Query 139: 0.5292
Query 140: 0.4195
```

```
Overall statistics
(for 50 queries):

Total number of documents
over all queries
    Retrieved:     50000
    Relevant:       1383
    Rel_ret:        1247

Interpolated Recall -
Precision Averages:
    at 0.00        0.7318
    at 0.10        0.6615
    at 0.20        0.5792
    at 0.30        0.5098
    at 0.40        0.4533
    at 0.50        0.3800
    at 0.60        0.3364
    at 0.70        0.2872
    at 0.80        0.2278
    at 0.90        0.1696
    at 1.00        0.1437

Avg. prec. (non-interpolated)
for all rel. documents
                   0.3920
Precision:
  At    5 docs:    0.5240
  At   10 docs:    0.4160
  At   15 docs:    0.3667
  At   20 docs:    0.3340
  At   30 docs:    0.2840
  At  100 docs:    0.1546
  At  200 docs:    0.0951
  At  500 docs:    0.0459
  At 1000 docs:    0.0249

R-Precision (prec. after R
(=num_rel) docs. retrieved):
    Exact:         0.3832
```

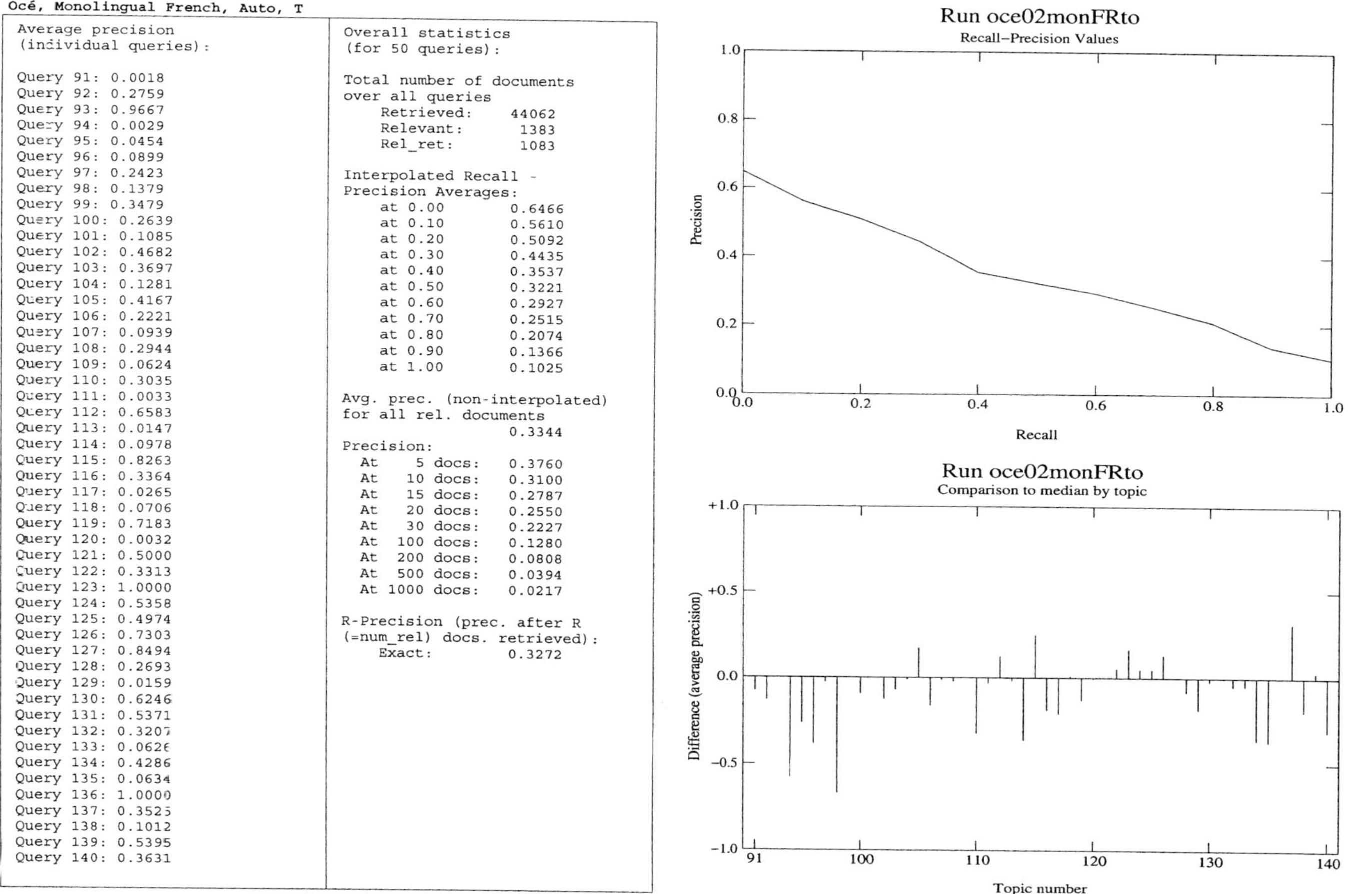

Océ, Monolingual French, Auto, T

Average precision (individual queries):	Overall statistics (for 50 queries):
Query 91: 0.0018	Total number of documents over all queries
Query 92: 0.2759	Retrieved: 44062
Query 93: 0.9667	Relevant: 1383
Query 94: 0.0029	Rel_ret: 1083
Query 95: 0.0454	
Query 96: 0.0899	Interpolated Recall - Precision Averages:
Query 97: 0.2423	at 0.00 0.6466
Query 98: 0.1379	at 0.10 0.5610
Query 99: 0.3479	at 0.20 0.5092
Query 100: 0.2639	at 0.30 0.4435
Query 101: 0.1085	at 0.40 0.3537
Query 102: 0.4682	at 0.50 0.3221
Query 103: 0.3697	at 0.60 0.2927
Query 104: 0.1281	at 0.70 0.2515
Query 105: 0.4167	at 0.80 0.2074
Query 106: 0.2221	at 0.90 0.1366
Query 107: 0.0939	at 1.00 0.1025
Query 108: 0.2944	
Query 109: 0.0624	Avg. prec. (non-interpolated) for all rel. documents 0.3344
Query 110: 0.3035	
Query 111: 0.0033	Precision:
Query 112: 0.6583	At 5 docs: 0.3760
Query 113: 0.0147	At 10 docs: 0.3100
Query 114: 0.0978	At 15 docs: 0.2787
Query 115: 0.8263	At 20 docs: 0.2550
Query 116: 0.3364	At 30 docs: 0.2227
Query 117: 0.0265	At 100 docs: 0.1280
Query 118: 0.0706	At 200 docs: 0.0808
Query 119: 0.7183	At 500 docs: 0.0394
Query 120: 0.0032	At 1000 docs: 0.0217
Query 121: 0.5000	
Query 122: 0.3313	R-Precision (prec. after R (=num_rel) docs. retrieved):
Query 123: 1.0000	Exact: 0.3272
Query 124: 0.5358	
Query 125: 0.4974	
Query 126: 0.7303	
Query 127: 0.8494	
Query 128: 0.2693	
Query 129: 0.0159	
Query 130: 0.6246	
Query 131: 0.5371	
Query 132: 0.3207	
Query 133: 0.0626	
Query 134: 0.4286	
Query 135: 0.0634	
Query 136: 1.0000	
Query 137: 0.3525	
Query 138: 0.1012	
Query 139: 0.5395	
Query 140: 0.3631	

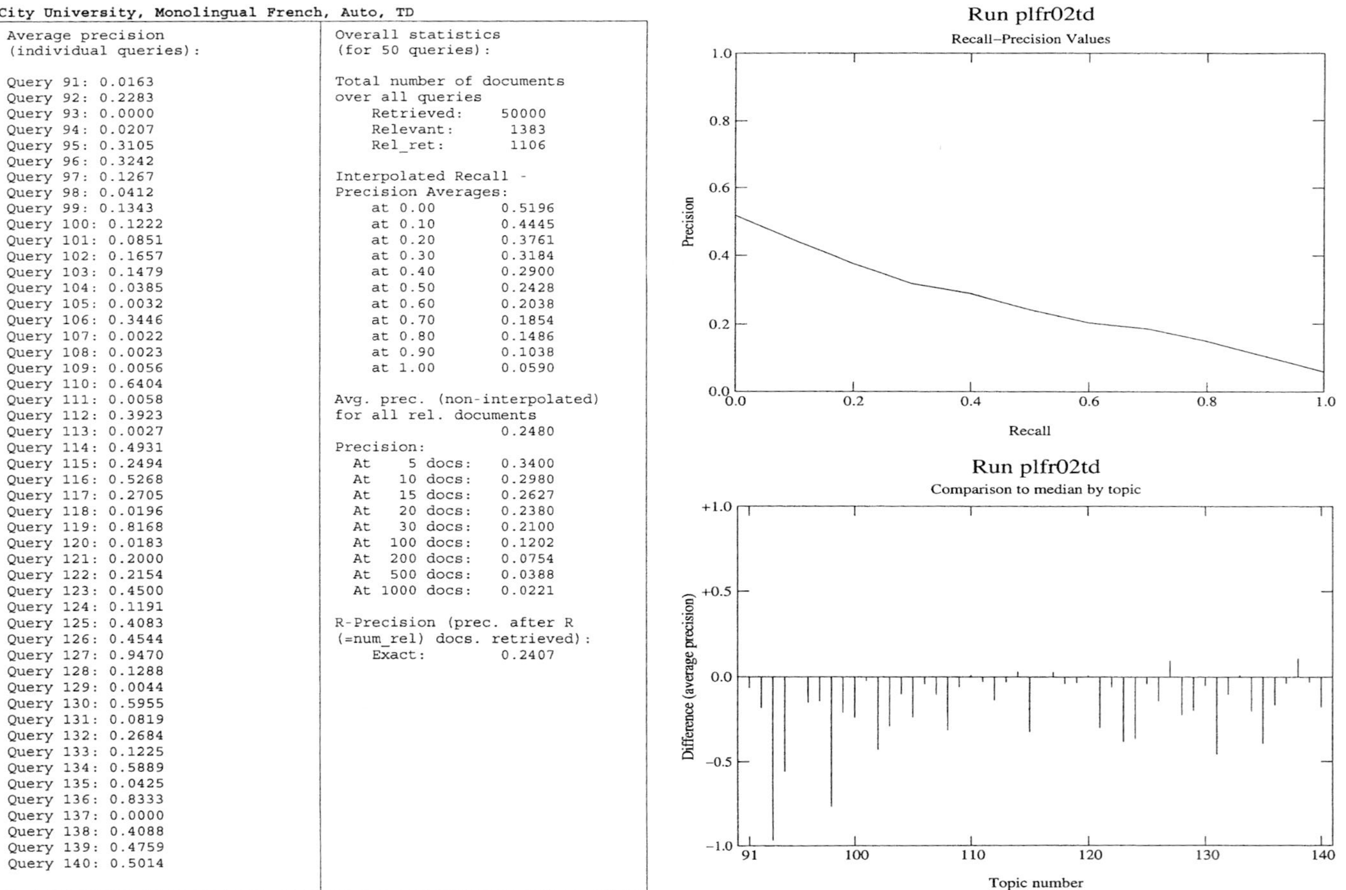

City University, Monolingual French, Auto, TD

```
Average precision                Overall statistics
(individual queries):            (for 50 queries):

Query 91: 0.0163                 Total number of documents
Query 92: 0.2283                 over all queries
Query 93: 0.0000                     Retrieved:    50000
Query 94: 0.0207                     Relevant:      1383
Query 95: 0.3105                     Rel_ret:       1106
Query 96: 0.3242
Query 97: 0.1267                 Interpolated Recall -
Query 98: 0.0412                 Precision Averages:
Query 99: 0.1343                     at 0.00       0.5196
Query 100: 0.1222                    at 0.10       0.4445
Query 101: 0.0851                    at 0.20       0.3761
Query 102: 0.1657                    at 0.30       0.3184
Query 103: 0.1479                    at 0.40       0.2900
Query 104: 0.0385                    at 0.50       0.2428
Query 105: 0.0032                    at 0.60       0.2038
Query 106: 0.3446                    at 0.70       0.1854
Query 107: 0.0022                    at 0.80       0.1486
Query 108: 0.0023                    at 0.90       0.1038
Query 109: 0.0056                    at 1.00       0.0590
Query 110: 0.6404
Query 111: 0.0058                Avg. prec. (non-interpolated)
Query 112: 0.3923                for all rel. documents
Query 113: 0.0027                                  0.2480
Query 114: 0.4931                Precision:
Query 115: 0.2494                  At    5 docs:   0.3400
Query 116: 0.5268                  At   10 docs:   0.2980
Query 117: 0.2705                  At   15 docs:   0.2627
Query 118: 0.0196                  At   20 docs:   0.2380
Query 119: 0.8168                  At   30 docs:   0.2100
Query 120: 0.0183                  At  100 docs:   0.1202
Query 121: 0.2000                  At  200 docs:   0.0754
Query 122: 0.2154                  At  500 docs:   0.0388
Query 123: 0.4500                  At 1000 docs:   0.0221
Query 124: 0.1191
Query 125: 0.4083                R-Precision (prec. after R
Query 126: 0.4544                (=num_rel) docs. retrieved):
Query 127: 0.9470                    Exact:        0.2407
Query 128: 0.1288
Query 129: 0.0044
Query 130: 0.5955
Query 131: 0.0819
Query 132: 0.2684
Query 133: 0.1225
Query 134: 0.5889
Query 135: 0.0425
Query 136: 0.8333
Query 137: 0.0000
Query 138: 0.4088
Query 139: 0.4759
Query 140: 0.5014
```

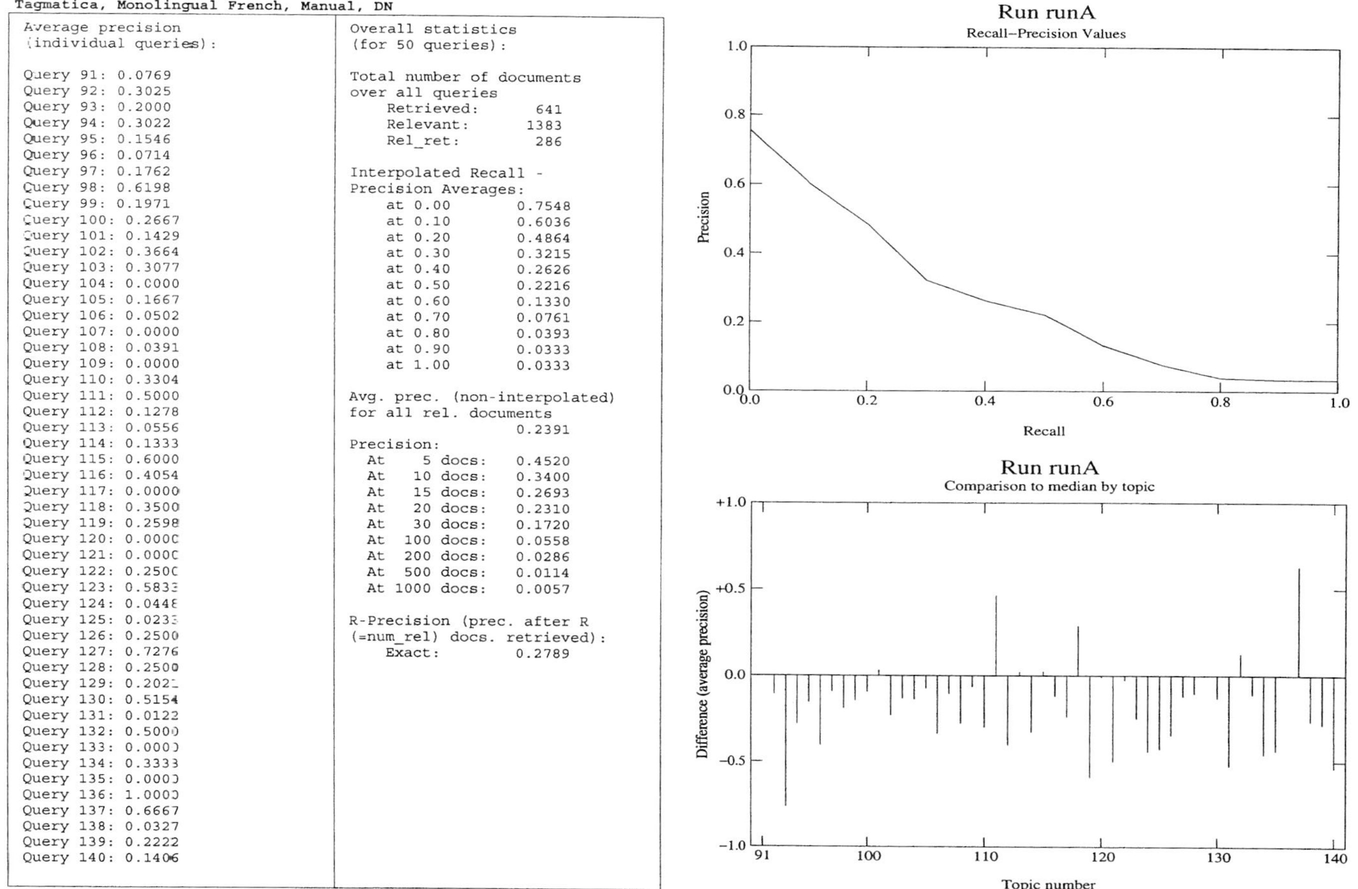

Tagmatica, Monolingual French, Manual, DN

```
Average precision                Overall statistics
(individual queries):            (for 50 queries):

Query 91: 0.0769                 Total number of documents
Query 92: 0.3025                 over all queries
Query 93: 0.2000                     Retrieved:        641
Query 94: 0.3022                     Relevant:        1383
Query 95: 0.1546                     Rel_ret:          286
Query 96: 0.0714
Query 97: 0.1762                 Interpolated Recall -
Query 98: 0.6198                 Precision Averages:
Query 99: 0.1971                     at 0.00         0.7548
Query 100: 0.2667                    at 0.10         0.6036
Query 101: 0.1429                    at 0.20         0.4864
Query 102: 0.3664                    at 0.30         0.3215
Query 103: 0.3077                    at 0.40         0.2626
Query 104: 0.0000                    at 0.50         0.2216
Query 105: 0.1667                    at 0.60         0.1330
Query 106: 0.0502                    at 0.70         0.0761
Query 107: 0.0000                    at 0.80         0.0393
Query 108: 0.0391                    at 0.90         0.0333
Query 109: 0.0000                    at 1.00         0.0333
Query 110: 0.3304
Query 111: 0.5000                Avg. prec. (non-interpolated)
Query 112: 0.1278                for all rel. documents
Query 113: 0.0556                                    0.2391
Query 114: 0.1333                Precision:
Query 115: 0.6000                  At    5 docs:     0.4520
Query 116: 0.4054                  At   10 docs:     0.3400
Query 117: 0.0000                  At   15 docs:     0.2693
Query 118: 0.3500                  At   20 docs:     0.2310
Query 119: 0.2598                  At   30 docs:     0.1720
Query 120: 0.0000                  At  100 docs:     0.0558
Query 121: 0.0000                  At  200 docs:     0.0286
Query 122: 0.2500                  At  500 docs:     0.0114
Query 123: 0.5833                  At 1000 docs:     0.0057
Query 124: 0.0448
Query 125: 0.0233                R-Precision (prec. after R
Query 126: 0.2500                (=num_rel) docs. retrieved):
Query 127: 0.7276                    Exact:          0.2789
Query 128: 0.2500
Query 129: 0.2021
Query 130: 0.5154
Query 131: 0.0122
Query 132: 0.5000
Query 133: 0.0000
Query 134: 0.3333
Query 135: 0.0000
Query 136: 1.0000
Query 137: 0.6667
Query 138: 0.0327
Query 139: 0.2222
Query 140: 0.1406
```

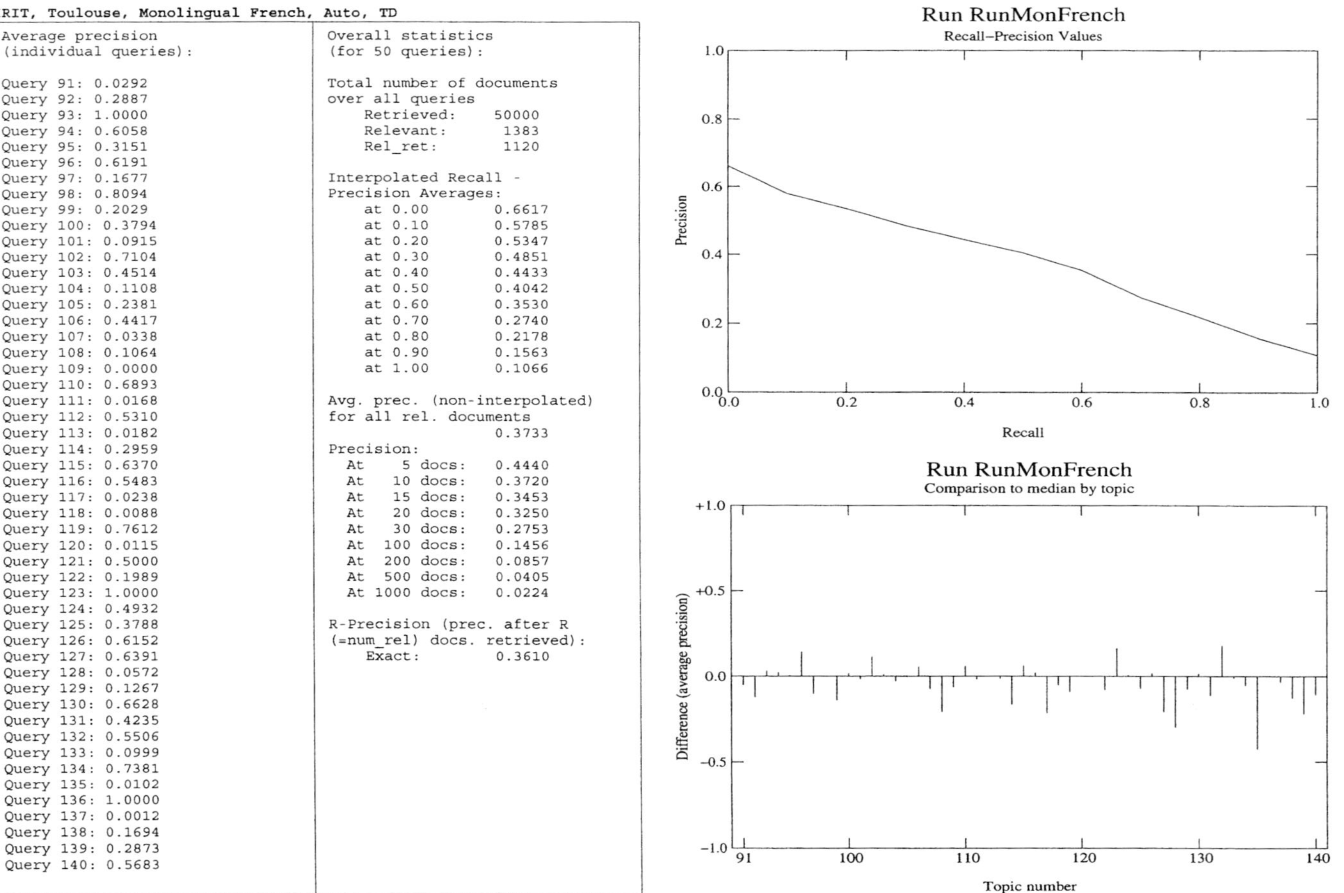

IRIT, Toulouse, Monolingual French, Auto, TD

```
Average precision                Overall statistics
(individual queries):            (for 50 queries):

Query 91: 0.0292                 Total number of documents
Query 92: 0.2887                 over all queries
Query 93: 1.0000                     Retrieved:    50000
Query 94: 0.6058                     Relevant:      1383
Query 95: 0.3151                     Rel_ret:       1120
Query 96: 0.6191
Query 97: 0.1677                 Interpolated Recall -
Query 98: 0.8094                 Precision Averages:
Query 99: 0.2029                     at 0.00       0.6617
Query 100: 0.3794                    at 0.10       0.5785
Query 101: 0.0915                    at 0.20       0.5347
Query 102: 0.7104                    at 0.30       0.4851
Query 103: 0.4514                    at 0.40       0.4433
Query 104: 0.1108                    at 0.50       0.4042
Query 105: 0.2381                    at 0.60       0.3530
Query 106: 0.4417                    at 0.70       0.2740
Query 107: 0.0338                    at 0.80       0.2178
Query 108: 0.1064                    at 0.90       0.1563
Query 109: 0.0000                    at 1.00       0.1066
Query 110: 0.6893
Query 111: 0.0168                Avg. prec. (non-interpolated)
Query 112: 0.5310                for all rel. documents
Query 113: 0.0182                                  0.3733
Query 114: 0.2959                Precision:
Query 115: 0.6370                  At    5 docs:   0.4440
Query 116: 0.5483                  At   10 docs:   0.3720
Query 117: 0.0238                  At   15 docs:   0.3453
Query 118: 0.0088                  At   20 docs:   0.3250
Query 119: 0.7612                  At   30 docs:   0.2753
Query 120: 0.0115                  At  100 docs:   0.1456
Query 121: 0.5000                  At  200 docs:   0.0857
Query 122: 0.1989                  At  500 docs:   0.0405
Query 123: 1.0000                  At 1000 docs:   0.0224
Query 124: 0.4932
Query 125: 0.3788                R-Precision (prec. after R
Query 126: 0.6152                (=num_rel) docs. retrieved):
Query 127: 0.6391                    Exact:        0.3610
Query 128: 0.0572
Query 129: 0.1267
Query 130: 0.6628
Query 131: 0.4235
Query 132: 0.5506
Query 133: 0.0999
Query 134: 0.7381
Query 135: 0.0102
Query 136: 1.0000
Query 137: 0.0012
Query 138: 0.1694
Query 139: 0.2873
Query 140: 0.5683
```

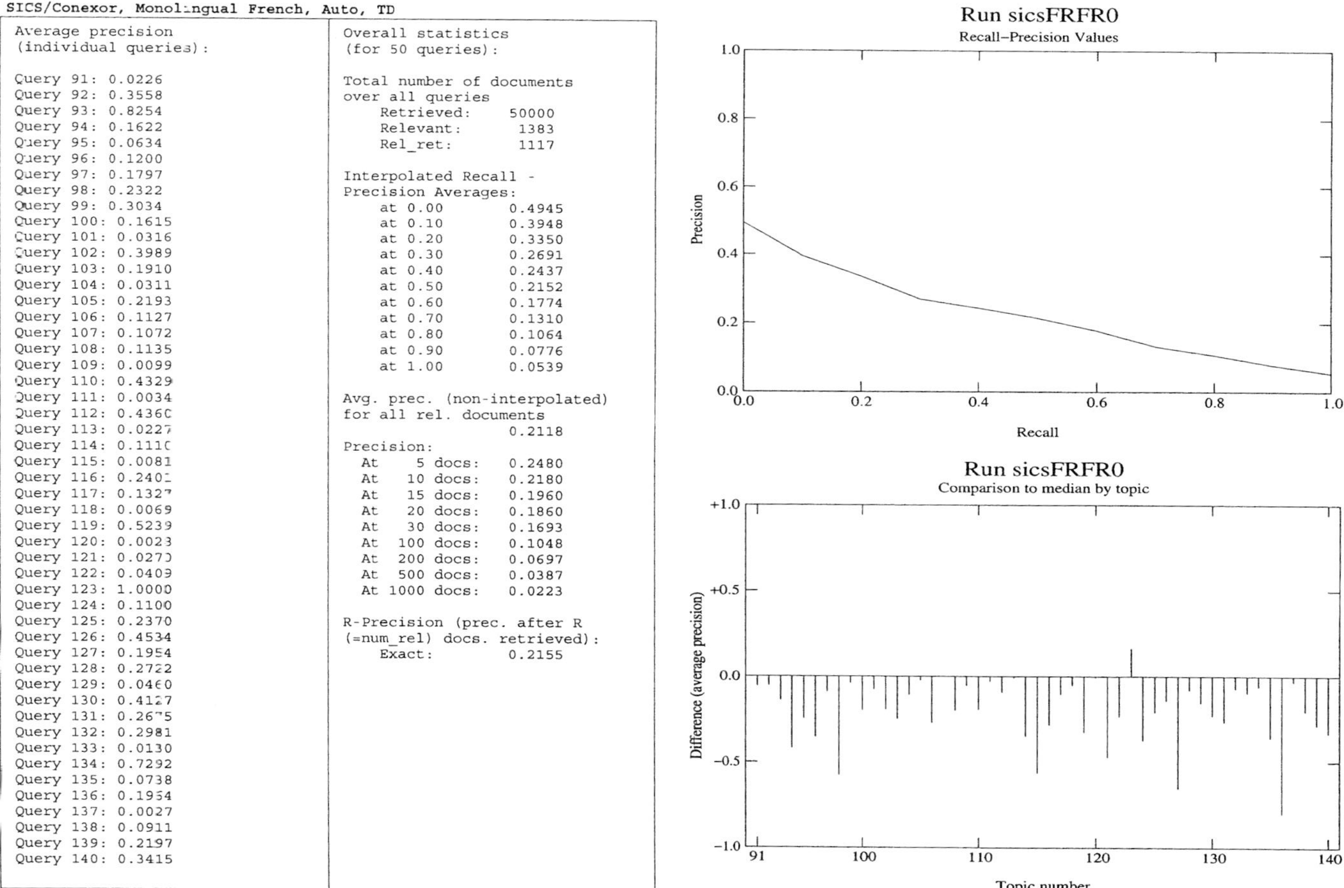

SICS/Conexor, Monolingual French, Auto, TD

```
Average precision                 Overall statistics
(individual queries):             (for 50 queries):

Query 91: 0.0226                  Total number of documents
Query 92: 0.3558                  over all queries
Query 93: 0.8254                      Retrieved:     50000
Query 94: 0.1622                      Relevant:       1383
Query 95: 0.0634                      Rel_ret:        1117
Query 96: 0.1200
Query 97: 0.1797                  Interpolated Recall -
Query 98: 0.2322                  Precision Averages:
Query 99: 0.3034                      at 0.00        0.4945
Query 100: 0.1615                     at 0.10        0.3948
Query 101: 0.0316                     at 0.20        0.3350
Query 102: 0.3989                     at 0.30        0.2691
Query 103: 0.1910                     at 0.40        0.2437
Query 104: 0.0311                     at 0.50        0.2152
Query 105: 0.2193                     at 0.60        0.1774
Query 106: 0.1127                     at 0.70        0.1310
Query 107: 0.1072                     at 0.80        0.1064
Query 108: 0.1135                     at 0.90        0.0776
Query 109: 0.0099                     at 1.00        0.0539
Query 110: 0.4329
Query 111: 0.0034                 Avg. prec. (non-interpolated)
Query 112: 0.4360                 for all rel. documents
Query 113: 0.0227                                    0.2118
Query 114: 0.1110                 Precision:
Query 115: 0.0081                   At    5 docs:    0.2480
Query 116: 0.2401                   At   10 docs:    0.2180
Query 117: 0.1327                   At   15 docs:    0.1960
Query 118: 0.0069                   At   20 docs:    0.1860
Query 119: 0.5239                   At   30 docs:    0.1693
Query 120: 0.0023                   At  100 docs:    0.1048
Query 121: 0.0270                   At  200 docs:    0.0697
Query 122: 0.0409                   At  500 docs:    0.0387
Query 123: 1.0000                   At 1000 docs:    0.0223
Query 124: 0.1100
Query 125: 0.2370                 R-Precision (prec. after R
Query 126: 0.4534                 (=num_rel) docs. retrieved):
Query 127: 0.1954                     Exact:         0.2155
Query 128: 0.2722
Query 129: 0.0460
Query 130: 0.4127
Query 131: 0.2675
Query 132: 0.2981
Query 133: 0.0130
Query 134: 0.7292
Query 135: 0.0738
Query 136: 0.1954
Query 137: 0.0027
Query 138: 0.0911
Query 139: 0.2197
Query 140: 0.3415
```

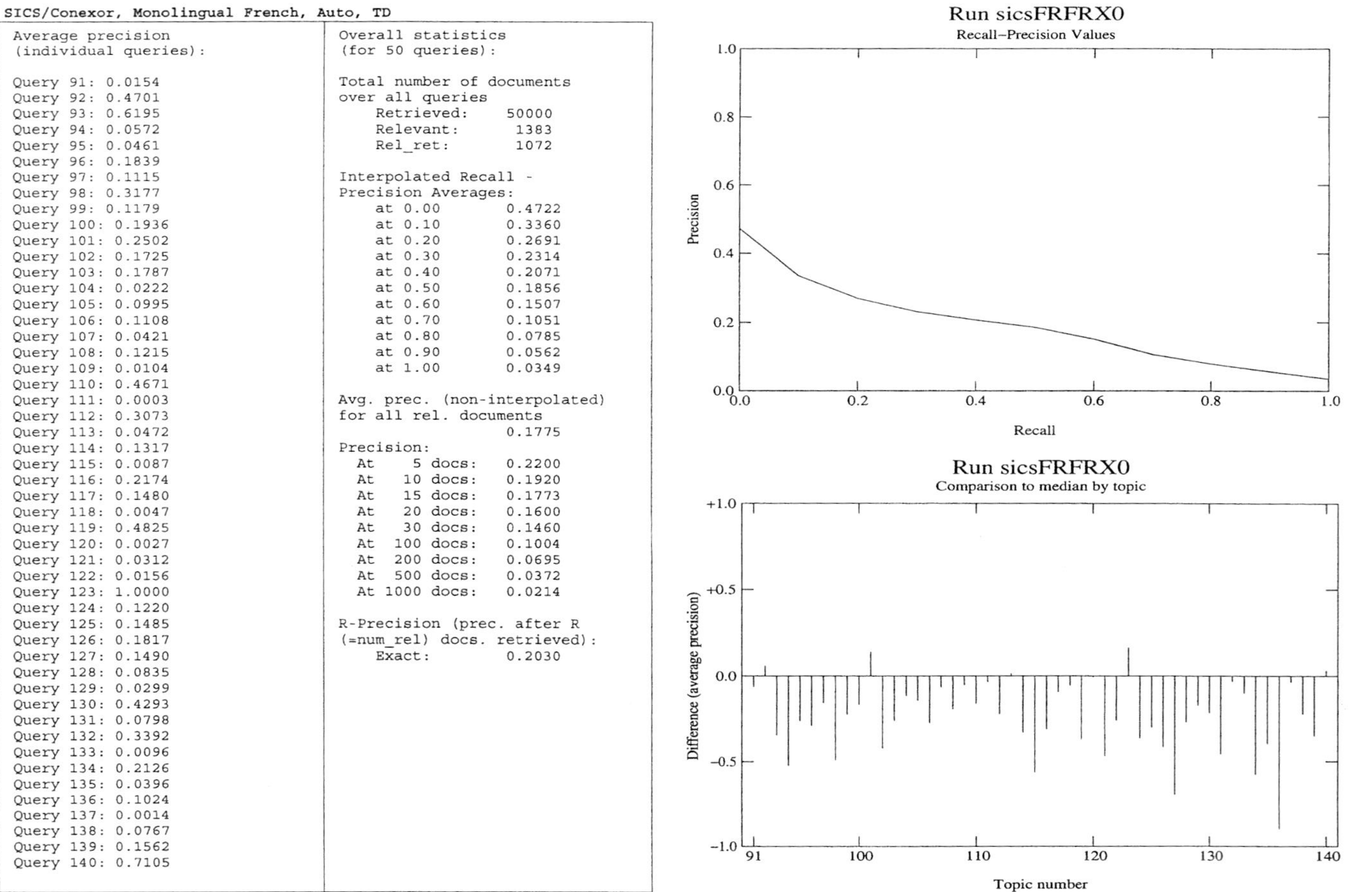

SICS/Conexor, Monolingual French, Auto, TD

```
Average precision                 Overall statistics
(individual queries):             (for 50 queries):

Query 91: 0.0154                  Total number of documents
Query 92: 0.4701                  over all queries
Query 93: 0.6195                      Retrieved:    50000
Query 94: 0.0572                      Relevant:      1383
Query 95: 0.0461                      Rel_ret:       1072
Query 96: 0.1839
Query 97: 0.1115                  Interpolated Recall -
Query 98: 0.3177                  Precision Averages:
Query 99: 0.1179                      at 0.00       0.4722
Query 100: 0.1936                     at 0.10       0.3360
Query 101: 0.2502                     at 0.20       0.2691
Query 102: 0.1725                     at 0.30       0.2314
Query 103: 0.1787                     at 0.40       0.2071
Query 104: 0.0222                     at 0.50       0.1856
Query 105: 0.0995                     at 0.60       0.1507
Query 106: 0.1108                     at 0.70       0.1051
Query 107: 0.0421                     at 0.80       0.0785
Query 108: 0.1215                     at 0.90       0.0562
Query 109: 0.0104                     at 1.00       0.0349
Query 110: 0.4671
Query 111: 0.0003                 Avg. prec. (non-interpolated)
Query 112: 0.3073                 for all rel. documents
Query 113: 0.0472                                   0.1775
Query 114: 0.1317                 Precision:
Query 115: 0.0087                   At    5 docs:   0.2200
Query 116: 0.2174                   At   10 docs:   0.1920
Query 117: 0.1480                   At   15 docs:   0.1773
Query 118: 0.0047                   At   20 docs:   0.1600
Query 119: 0.4825                   At   30 docs:   0.1460
Query 120: 0.0027                   At  100 docs:   0.1004
Query 121: 0.0312                   At  200 docs:   0.0695
Query 122: 0.0156                   At  500 docs:   0.0372
Query 123: 1.0000                   At 1000 docs:   0.0214
Query 124: 0.1220
Query 125: 0.1485                 R-Precision (prec. after R
Query 126: 0.1817                 (=num_rel) docs. retrieved):
Query 127: 0.1490                     Exact:        0.2030
Query 128: 0.0835
Query 129: 0.0299
Query 130: 0.4293
Query 131: 0.0798
Query 132: 0.3392
Query 133: 0.0096
Query 134: 0.2126
Query 135: 0.0396
Query 136: 0.1024
Query 137: 0.0014
Query 138: 0.0767
Query 139: 0.1562
Query 140: 0.7105
```

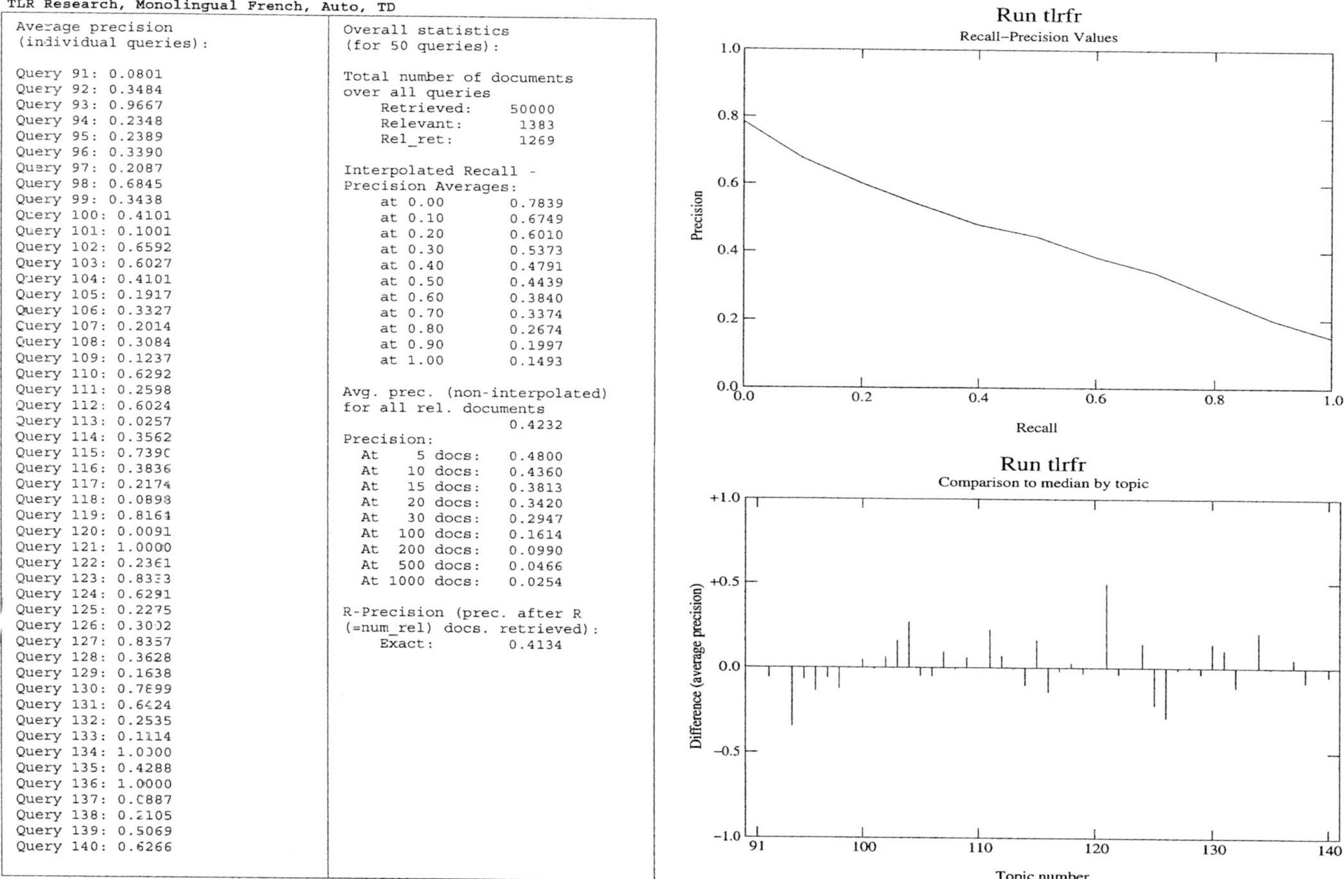

TLR Research, Monolingual French, Auto, TD

Average precision (individual queries):	Overall statistics (for 50 queries):
Query 91: 0.0801	Total number of documents over all queries
Query 92: 0.3484	Retrieved: 50000
Query 93: 0.9667	Relevant: 1383
Query 94: 0.2348	Rel_ret: 1269
Query 95: 0.2389	
Query 96: 0.3390	Interpolated Recall - Precision Averages:
Query 97: 0.2087	at 0.00 0.7839
Query 98: 0.6845	at 0.10 0.6749
Query 99: 0.3438	at 0.20 0.6010
Query 100: 0.4101	at 0.30 0.5373
Query 101: 0.1001	at 0.40 0.4791
Query 102: 0.6592	at 0.50 0.4439
Query 103: 0.6027	at 0.60 0.3840
Query 104: 0.4101	at 0.70 0.3374
Query 105: 0.1917	at 0.80 0.2674
Query 106: 0.3327	at 0.90 0.1997
Query 107: 0.2014	at 1.00 0.1493
Query 108: 0.3084	
Query 109: 0.1237	Avg. prec. (non-interpolated) for all rel. documents 0.4232
Query 110: 0.6292	
Query 111: 0.2598	Precision:
Query 112: 0.6024	At 5 docs: 0.4800
Query 113: 0.0257	At 10 docs: 0.4360
Query 114: 0.3562	At 15 docs: 0.3813
Query 115: 0.7390	At 20 docs: 0.3420
Query 116: 0.3836	At 30 docs: 0.2947
Query 117: 0.2174	At 100 docs: 0.1614
Query 118: 0.0898	At 200 docs: 0.0990
Query 119: 0.8164	At 500 docs: 0.0466
Query 120: 0.0091	At 1000 docs: 0.0254
Query 121: 1.0000	
Query 122: 0.2361	R-Precision (prec. after R (=num_rel) docs. retrieved):
Query 123: 0.8333	Exact: 0.4134
Query 124: 0.6291	
Query 125: 0.2275	
Query 126: 0.3002	
Query 127: 0.8357	
Query 128: 0.3628	
Query 129: 0.1638	
Query 130: 0.7899	
Query 131: 0.6424	
Query 132: 0.2535	
Query 133: 0.1114	
Query 134: 1.0000	
Query 135: 0.4288	
Query 136: 1.0000	
Query 137: 0.0887	
Query 138: 0.2105	
Query 139: 0.5069	
Query 140: 0.6266	

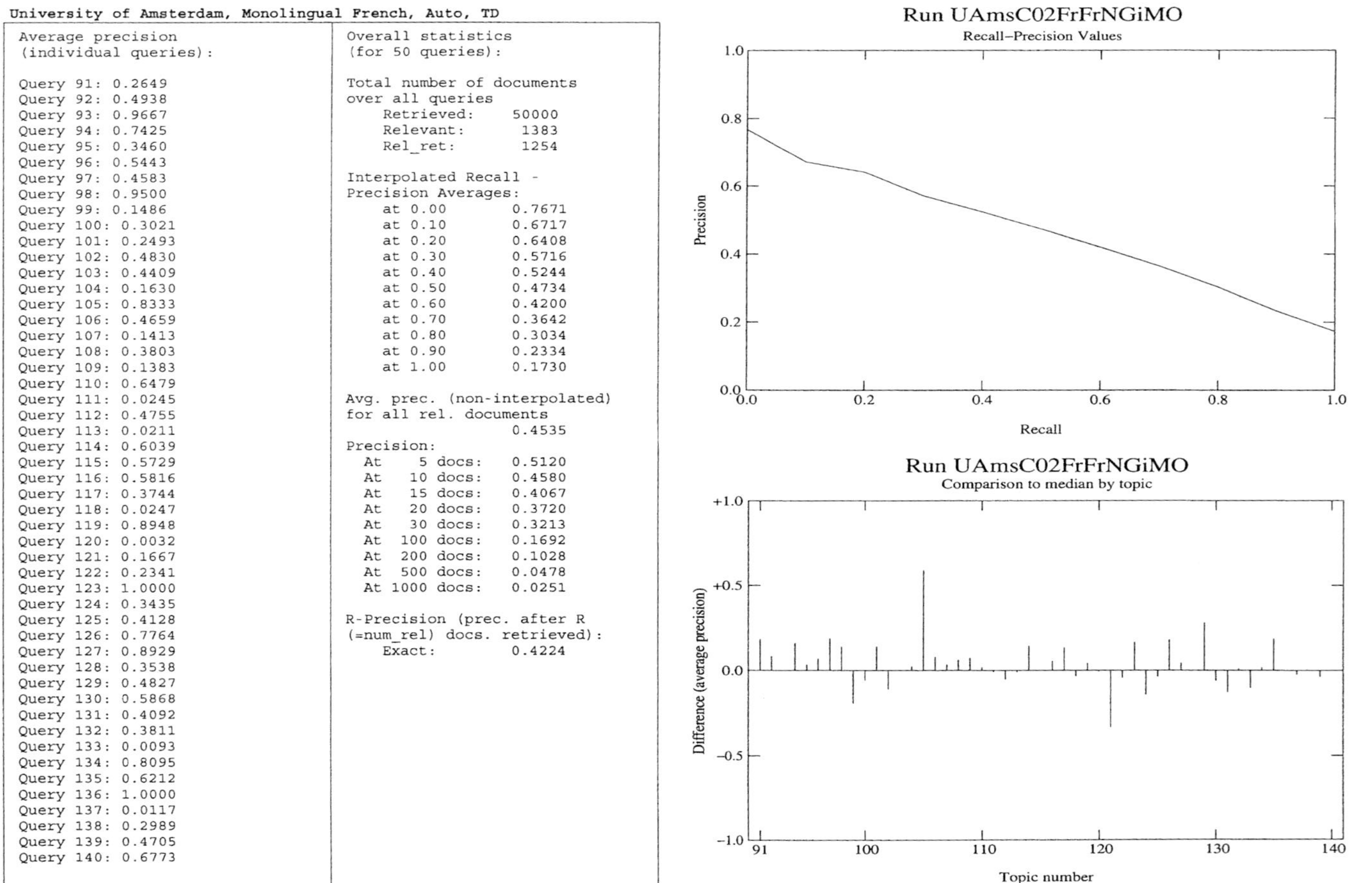

University of Amsterdam, Monolingual French, Auto, TD

Average precision (individual queries):	Overall statistics (for 50 queries):
Query 91: 0.2649 Query 92: 0.4938 Query 93: 0.9667 Query 94: 0.7425 Query 95: 0.3460 Query 96: 0.5443 Query 97: 0.4583 Query 98: 0.9500 Query 99: 0.1486 Query 100: 0.3021 Query 101: 0.2493 Query 102: 0.4830 Query 103: 0.4409 Query 104: 0.1630 Query 105: 0.8333 Query 106: 0.4659 Query 107: 0.1413 Query 108: 0.3803 Query 109: 0.1383 Query 110: 0.6479 Query 111: 0.0245 Query 112: 0.4755 Query 113: 0.0211 Query 114: 0.6039 Query 115: 0.5729 Query 116: 0.5816 Query 117: 0.3744 Query 118: 0.0247 Query 119: 0.8948 Query 120: 0.0032 Query 121: 0.1667 Query 122: 0.2341 Query 123: 1.0000 Query 124: 0.3435 Query 125: 0.4128 Query 126: 0.7764 Query 127: 0.8929 Query 128: 0.3538 Query 129: 0.4827 Query 130: 0.5868 Query 131: 0.4092 Query 132: 0.3811 Query 133: 0.0093 Query 134: 0.8095 Query 135: 0.6212 Query 136: 1.0000 Query 137: 0.0117 Query 138: 0.2989 Query 139: 0.4705 Query 140: 0.6773	Total number of documents over all queries Retrieved: 50000 Relevant: 1383 Rel_ret: 1254 Interpolated Recall - Precision Averages: at 0.00 0.7671 at 0.10 0.6717 at 0.20 0.6408 at 0.30 0.5716 at 0.40 0.5244 at 0.50 0.4734 at 0.60 0.4200 at 0.70 0.3642 at 0.80 0.3034 at 0.90 0.2334 at 1.00 0.1730 Avg. prec. (non-interpolated) for all rel. documents 0.4535 Precision: At 5 docs: 0.5120 At 10 docs: 0.4580 At 15 docs: 0.4067 At 20 docs: 0.3720 At 30 docs: 0.3213 At 100 docs: 0.1692 At 200 docs: 0.1028 At 500 docs: 0.0478 At 1000 docs: 0.0251 R-Precision (prec. after R (=num_rel) docs. retrieved): Exact: 0.4224

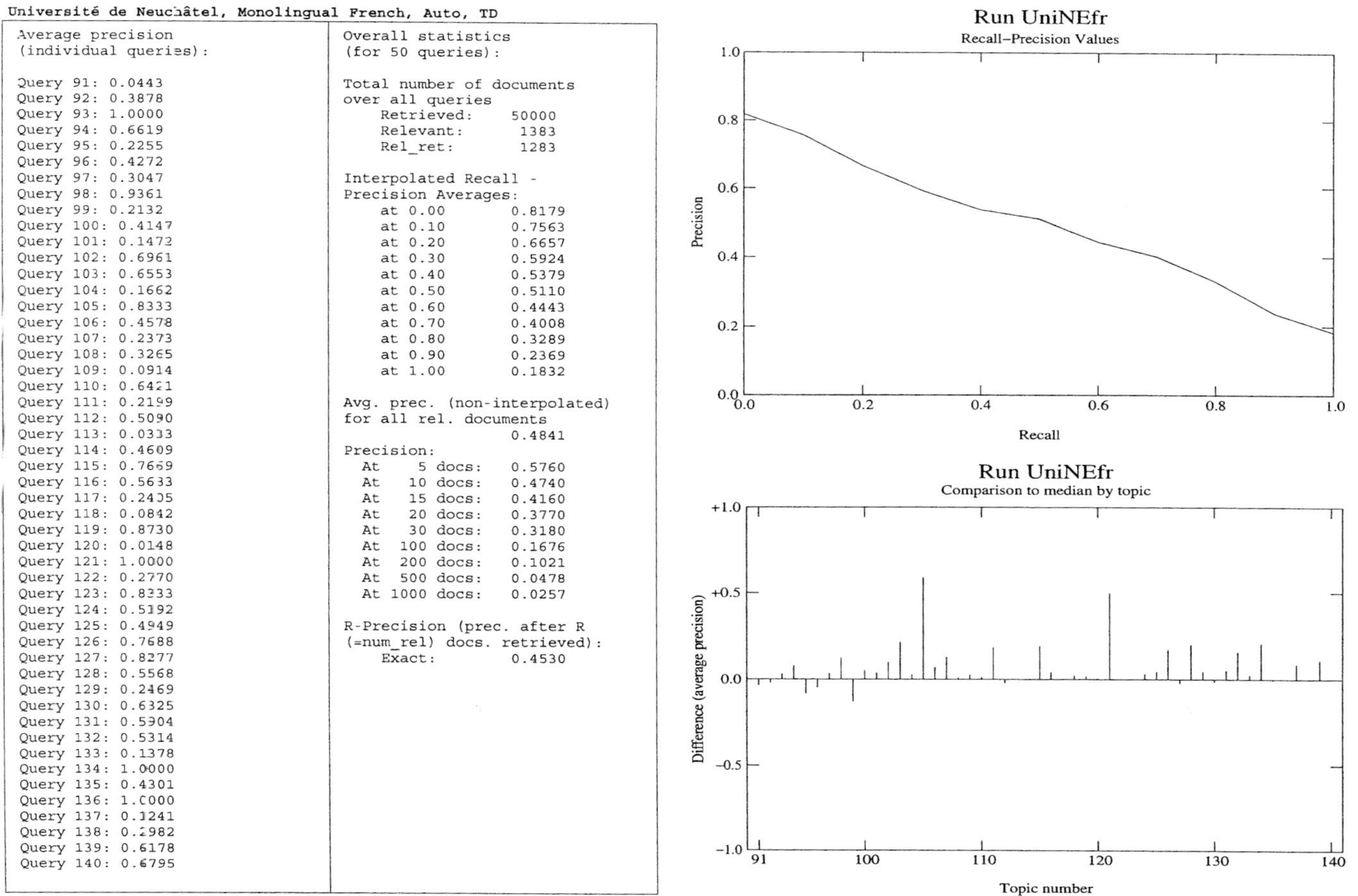

Université de Neuchâtel, Monolingual French, Auto, TD

Average precision (individual queries):	Overall statistics (for 50 queries):
Query 91: 0.0443	Total number of documents over all queries
Query 92: 0.3878	Retrieved: 50000
Query 93: 1.0000	Relevant: 1383
Query 94: 0.6619	Rel_ret: 1283
Query 95: 0.2255	
Query 96: 0.4272	Interpolated Recall - Precision Averages:
Query 97: 0.3047	at 0.00 0.8179
Query 98: 0.9361	at 0.10 0.7563
Query 99: 0.2132	at 0.20 0.6657
Query 100: 0.4147	at 0.30 0.5924
Query 101: 0.1472	at 0.40 0.5379
Query 102: 0.6961	at 0.50 0.5110
Query 103: 0.6553	at 0.60 0.4443
Query 104: 0.1662	at 0.70 0.4008
Query 105: 0.8333	at 0.80 0.3289
Query 106: 0.4578	at 0.90 0.2369
Query 107: 0.2373	at 1.00 0.1832
Query 108: 0.3265	
Query 109: 0.0914	Avg. prec. (non-interpolated) for all rel. documents 0.4841
Query 110: 0.6421	
Query 111: 0.2199	Precision:
Query 112: 0.5090	At 5 docs: 0.5760
Query 113: 0.0333	At 10 docs: 0.4740
Query 114: 0.4609	At 15 docs: 0.4160
Query 115: 0.7669	At 20 docs: 0.3770
Query 116: 0.5633	At 30 docs: 0.3180
Query 117: 0.2405	At 100 docs: 0.1676
Query 118: 0.0842	At 200 docs: 0.1021
Query 119: 0.8730	At 500 docs: 0.0478
Query 120: 0.0148	At 1000 docs: 0.0257
Query 121: 1.0000	
Query 122: 0.2770	R-Precision (prec. after R (=num_rel) docs. retrieved):
Query 123: 0.8333	Exact: 0.4530
Query 124: 0.5192	
Query 125: 0.4949	
Query 126: 0.7688	
Query 127: 0.8277	
Query 128: 0.5568	
Query 129: 0.2469	
Query 130: 0.6325	
Query 131: 0.5904	
Query 132: 0.5314	
Query 133: 0.1378	
Query 134: 1.0000	
Query 135: 0.4301	
Query 136: 1.0000	
Query 137: 0.1241	
Query 138: 0.2982	
Query 139: 0.6178	
Query 140: 0.6795	

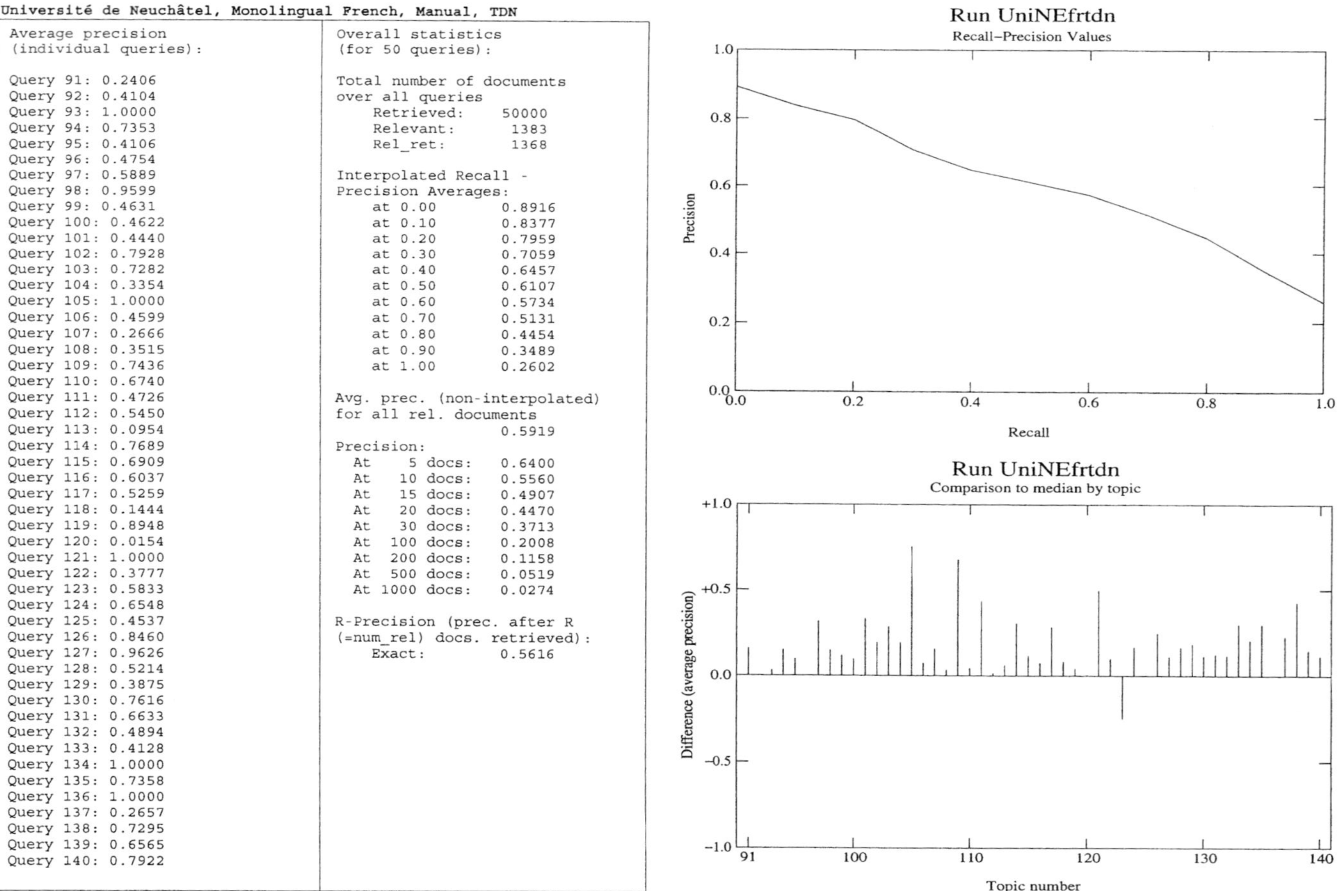

Université de Neuchâtel, Monolingual French, Manual, TDN

Average precision (individual queries):	Overall statistics (for 50 queries):
Query 91: 0.2406	Total number of documents over all queries
Query 92: 0.4104	Retrieved: 50000
Query 93: 1.0000	Relevant: 1383
Query 94: 0.7353	Rel_ret: 1368
Query 95: 0.4106	
Query 96: 0.4754	Interpolated Recall - Precision Averages:
Query 97: 0.5889	at 0.00 0.8916
Query 98: 0.9599	at 0.10 0.8377
Query 99: 0.4631	at 0.20 0.7959
Query 100: 0.4622	at 0.30 0.7059
Query 101: 0.4440	at 0.40 0.6457
Query 102: 0.7928	at 0.50 0.6107
Query 103: 0.7282	at 0.60 0.5734
Query 104: 0.3354	at 0.70 0.5131
Query 105: 1.0000	at 0.80 0.4454
Query 106: 0.4599	at 0.90 0.3489
Query 107: 0.2666	at 1.00 0.2602
Query 108: 0.3515	
Query 109: 0.7436	Avg. prec. (non-interpolated) for all rel. documents 0.5919
Query 110: 0.6740	
Query 111: 0.4726	Precision:
Query 112: 0.5450	At 5 docs: 0.6400
Query 113: 0.0954	At 10 docs: 0.5560
Query 114: 0.7689	At 15 docs: 0.4907
Query 115: 0.6909	At 20 docs: 0.4470
Query 116: 0.6037	At 30 docs: 0.3713
Query 117: 0.5259	At 100 docs: 0.2008
Query 118: 0.1444	At 200 docs: 0.1158
Query 119: 0.8948	At 500 docs: 0.0519
Query 120: 0.0154	At 1000 docs: 0.0274
Query 121: 1.0000	
Query 122: 0.3777	R-Precision (prec. after R (=num_rel) docs. retrieved):
Query 123: 0.5833	Exact: 0.5616
Query 124: 0.6548	
Query 125: 0.4537	
Query 126: 0.8460	
Query 127: 0.9626	
Query 128: 0.5214	
Query 129: 0.3875	
Query 130: 0.7616	
Query 131: 0.6633	
Query 132: 0.4894	
Query 133: 0.4128	
Query 134: 1.0000	
Query 135: 0.7358	
Query 136: 1.0000	
Query 137: 0.2657	
Query 138: 0.7295	
Query 139: 0.6565	
Query 140: 0.7922	

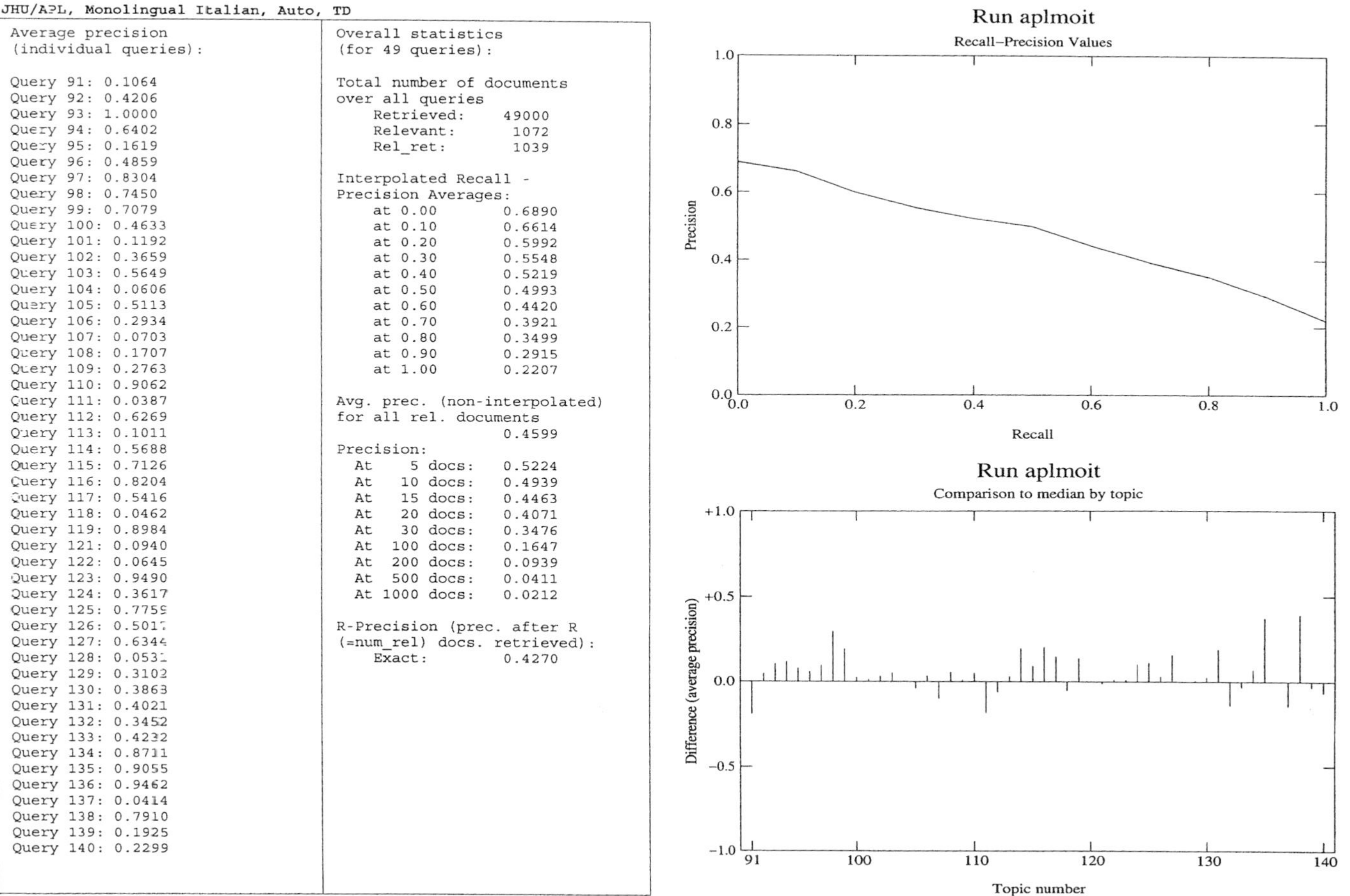

JHU/APL, Monolingual Italian, Auto, TD

Average precision (individual queries):	Overall statistics (for 49 queries):
Query 91: 0.1064	Total number of documents over all queries
Query 92: 0.4206	Retrieved: 49000
Query 93: 1.0000	Relevant: 1072
Query 94: 0.6402	Rel_ret: 1039
Query 95: 0.1619	
Query 96: 0.4859	Interpolated Recall - Precision Averages:
Query 97: 0.8304	at 0.00 0.6890
Query 98: 0.7450	at 0.10 0.6614
Query 99: 0.7079	at 0.20 0.5992
Query 100: 0.4633	at 0.30 0.5548
Query 101: 0.1192	at 0.40 0.5219
Query 102: 0.3659	at 0.50 0.4993
Query 103: 0.5649	at 0.60 0.4420
Query 104: 0.0606	at 0.70 0.3921
Query 105: 0.5113	at 0.80 0.3499
Query 106: 0.2934	at 0.90 0.2915
Query 107: 0.0703	at 1.00 0.2207
Query 108: 0.1707	
Query 109: 0.2763	Avg. prec. (non-interpolated) for all rel. documents 0.4599
Query 110: 0.9062	
Query 111: 0.0387	Precision:
Query 112: 0.6269	At 5 docs: 0.5224
Query 113: 0.1011	At 10 docs: 0.4939
Query 114: 0.5688	At 15 docs: 0.4463
Query 115: 0.7126	At 20 docs: 0.4071
Query 116: 0.8204	At 30 docs: 0.3476
Query 117: 0.5416	At 100 docs: 0.1647
Query 118: 0.0462	At 200 docs: 0.0939
Query 119: 0.8984	At 500 docs: 0.0411
Query 121: 0.0940	At 1000 docs: 0.0212
Query 122: 0.0645	
Query 123: 0.9490	R-Precision (prec. after R (=num_rel) docs. retrieved):
Query 124: 0.3617	Exact: 0.4270
Query 125: 0.7759	
Query 126: 0.5017	
Query 127: 0.6344	
Query 128: 0.0531	
Query 129: 0.3102	
Query 130: 0.3863	
Query 131: 0.4021	
Query 132: 0.3452	
Query 133: 0.4232	
Query 134: 0.8711	
Query 135: 0.9055	
Query 136: 0.9462	
Query 137: 0.0414	
Query 138: 0.7910	
Query 139: 0.1925	
Query 140: 0.2299	

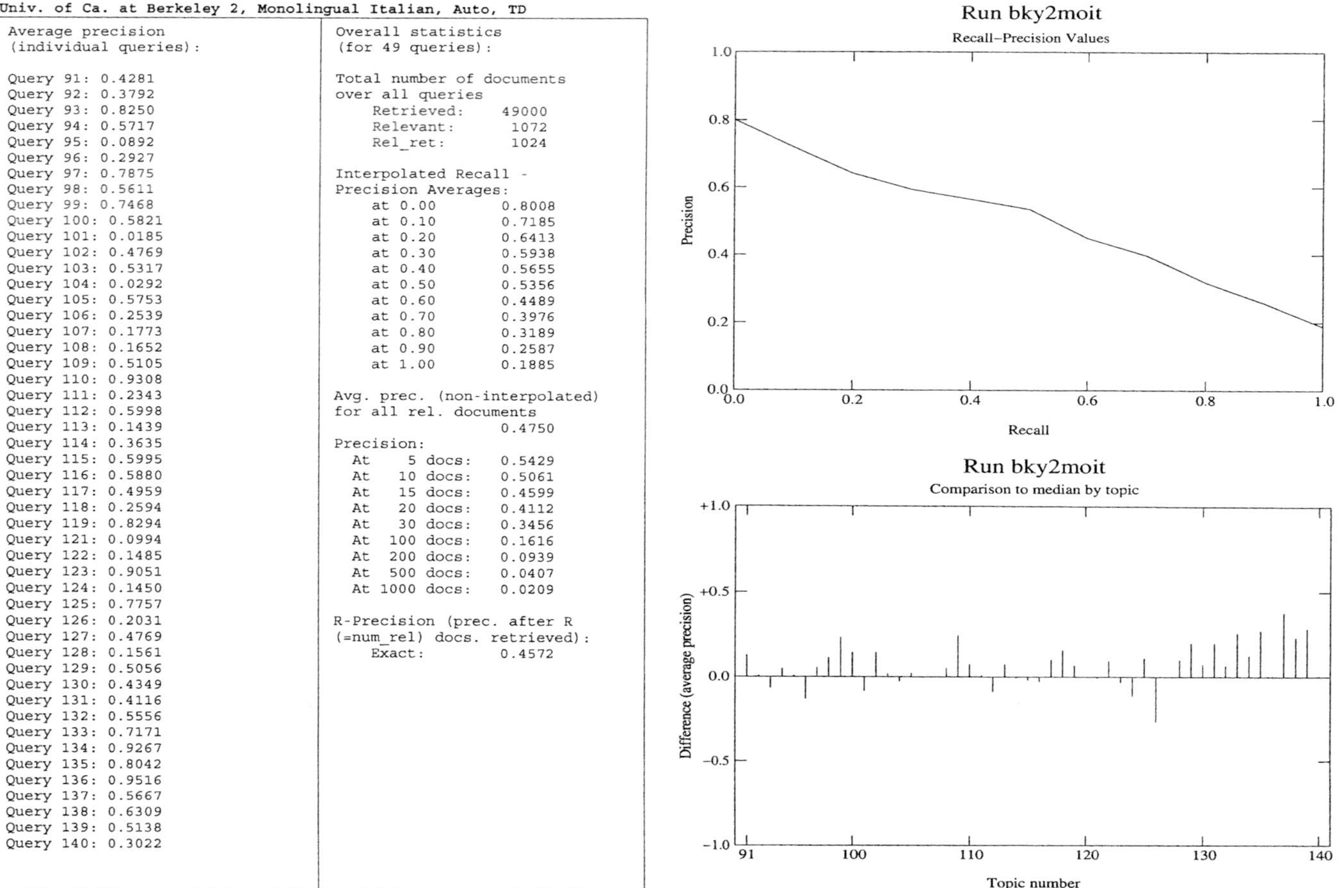

Univ. of Ca. at Berkeley 2, Monolingual Italian, Auto, TD

```
Average precision                Overall statistics
(individual queries):            (for 49 queries):

Query 91: 0.4281                 Total number of documents
Query 92: 0.3792                 over all queries
Query 93: 0.8250                     Retrieved:    49000
Query 94: 0.5717                     Relevant:      1072
Query 95: 0.0892                     Rel_ret:       1024
Query 96: 0.2927
Query 97: 0.7875                 Interpolated Recall -
Query 98: 0.5611                 Precision Averages:
Query 99: 0.7468                     at 0.00        0.8008
Query 100: 0.5821                    at 0.10        0.7185
Query 101: 0.0185                    at 0.20        0.6413
Query 102: 0.4769                    at 0.30        0.5938
Query 103: 0.5317                    at 0.40        0.5655
Query 104: 0.0292                    at 0.50        0.5356
Query 105: 0.5753                    at 0.60        0.4489
Query 106: 0.2539                    at 0.70        0.3976
Query 107: 0.1773                    at 0.80        0.3189
Query 108: 0.1652                    at 0.90        0.2587
Query 109: 0.5105                    at 1.00        0.1885
Query 110: 0.9308
Query 111: 0.2343                Avg. prec. (non-interpolated)
Query 112: 0.5998                for all rel. documents
Query 113: 0.1439                                   0.4750
Query 114: 0.3635                Precision:
Query 115: 0.5995                  At    5 docs:    0.5429
Query 116: 0.5880                  At   10 docs:    0.5061
Query 117: 0.4959                  At   15 docs:    0.4599
Query 118: 0.2594                  At   20 docs:    0.4112
Query 119: 0.8294                  At   30 docs:    0.3456
Query 121: 0.0994                  At  100 docs:    0.1616
Query 122: 0.1485                  At  200 docs:    0.0939
Query 123: 0.9051                  At  500 docs:    0.0407
Query 124: 0.1450                  At 1000 docs:    0.0209
Query 125: 0.7757
Query 126: 0.2031                R-Precision (prec. after R
Query 127: 0.4769                (=num_rel) docs. retrieved):
Query 128: 0.1561                    Exact:         0.4572
Query 129: 0.5056
Query 130: 0.4349
Query 131: 0.4116
Query 132: 0.5556
Query 133: 0.7171
Query 134: 0.9267
Query 135: 0.8042
Query 136: 0.9516
Query 137: 0.5667
Query 138: 0.6309
Query 139: 0.5138
Query 140: 0.3022
```

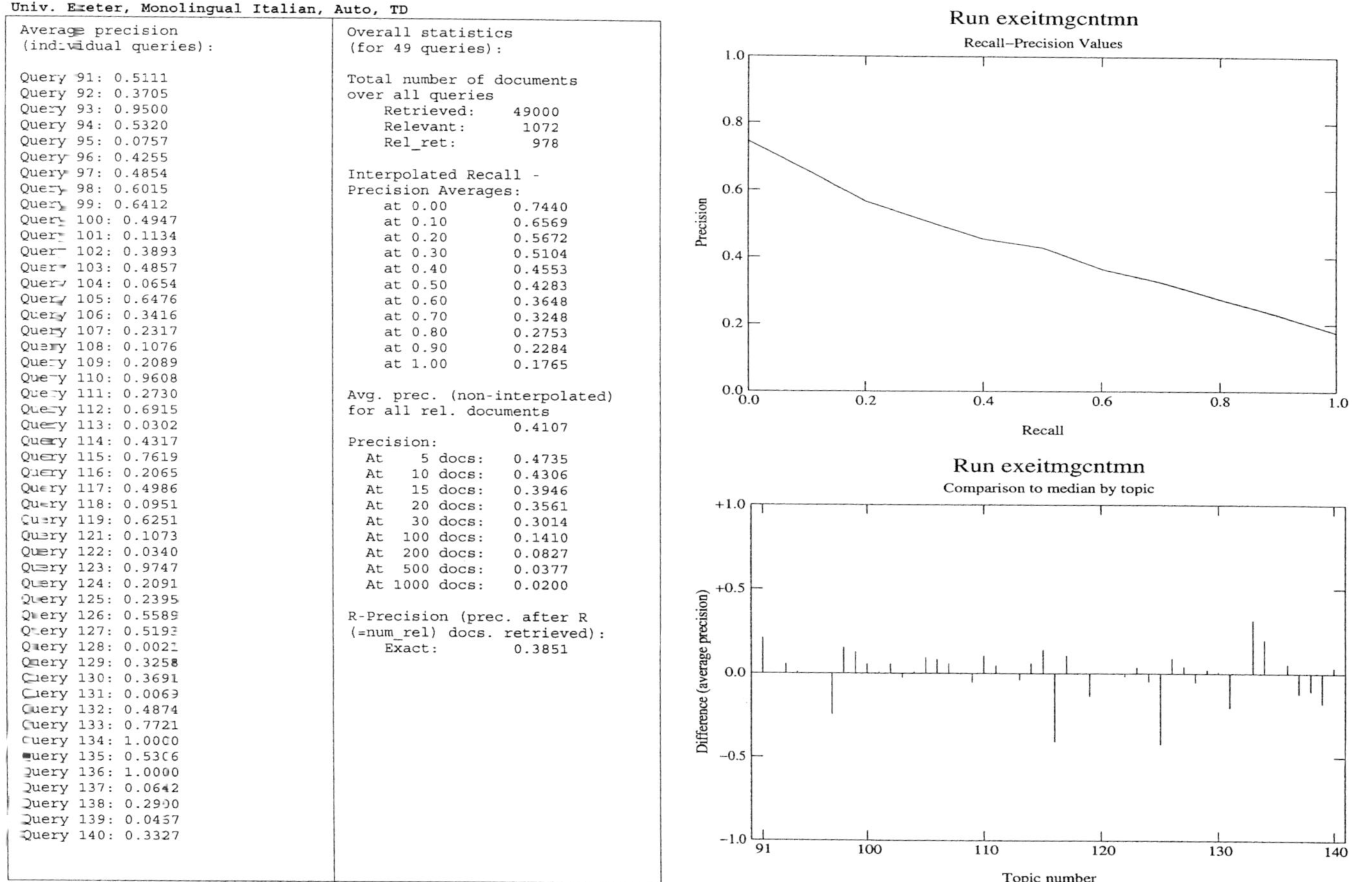

Univ. Exeter, Monolingual Italian, Auto, TD

Average precision (individual queries):	Overall statistics (for 49 queries):
Query 91: 0.5111	Total number of documents over all queries
Query 92: 0.3705	Retrieved: 49000
Query 93: 0.9500	Relevant: 1072
Query 94: 0.5320	Rel_ret: 978
Query 95: 0.0757	
Query 96: 0.4255	Interpolated Recall - Precision Averages:
Query 97: 0.4854	at 0.00 0.7440
Query 98: 0.6015	at 0.10 0.6569
Query 99: 0.6412	at 0.20 0.5672
Query 100: 0.4947	at 0.30 0.5104
Query 101: 0.1134	at 0.40 0.4553
Query 102: 0.3893	at 0.50 0.4283
Query 103: 0.4857	at 0.60 0.3648
Query 104: 0.0654	at 0.70 0.3248
Query 105: 0.6476	at 0.80 0.2753
Query 106: 0.3416	at 0.90 0.2284
Query 107: 0.2317	at 1.00 0.1765
Query 108: 0.1076	
Query 109: 0.2089	Avg. prec. (non-interpolated) for all rel. documents 0.4107
Query 110: 0.9608	
Query 111: 0.2730	Precision:
Query 112: 0.6915	At 5 docs: 0.4735
Query 113: 0.0302	At 10 docs: 0.4306
Query 114: 0.4317	At 15 docs: 0.3946
Query 115: 0.7619	At 20 docs: 0.3561
Query 116: 0.2065	At 30 docs: 0.3014
Query 117: 0.4986	At 100 docs: 0.1410
Query 118: 0.0951	At 200 docs: 0.0827
Query 119: 0.6251	At 500 docs: 0.0377
Query 121: 0.1073	At 1000 docs: 0.0200
Query 122: 0.0340	
Query 123: 0.9747	R-Precision (prec. after R (=num_rel) docs. retrieved):
Query 124: 0.2091	Exact: 0.3851
Query 125: 0.2395	
Query 126: 0.5589	
Query 127: 0.5193	
Query 128: 0.0021	
Query 129: 0.3258	
Query 130: 0.3691	
Query 131: 0.0069	
Query 132: 0.4874	
Query 133: 0.7721	
Query 134: 1.0000	
Query 135: 0.5306	
Query 136: 1.0000	
Query 137: 0.0642	
Query 138: 0.2900	
Query 139: 0.0457	
Query 140: 0.3327	

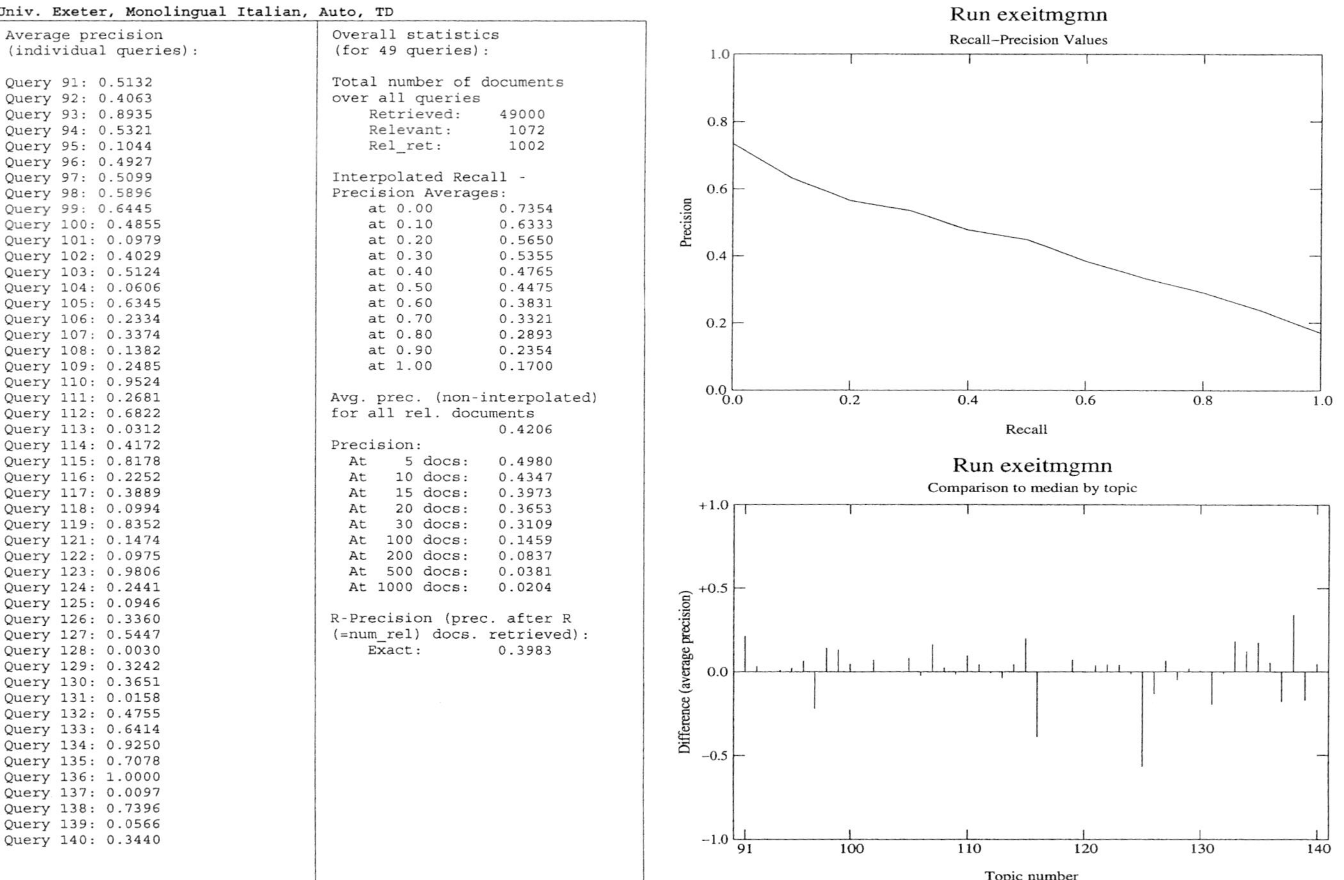

Univ. Exeter, Monolingual Italian, Auto, TD

```
Average precision               Overall statistics
(individual queries):           (for 49 queries):

Query 91: 0.5132                Total number of documents
Query 92: 0.4063                over all queries
Query 93: 0.8935                    Retrieved:    49000
Query 94: 0.5321                    Relevant:      1072
Query 95: 0.1044                    Rel_ret:       1002
Query 96: 0.4927
Query 97: 0.5099                Interpolated Recall -
Query 98: 0.5896                Precision Averages:
Query 99: 0.6445                    at 0.00       0.7354
Query 100: 0.4855                   at 0.10       0.6333
Query 101: 0.0979                   at 0.20       0.5650
Query 102: 0.4029                   at 0.30       0.5355
Query 103: 0.5124                   at 0.40       0.4765
Query 104: 0.0606                   at 0.50       0.4475
Query 105: 0.6345                   at 0.60       0.3831
Query 106: 0.2334                   at 0.70       0.3321
Query 107: 0.3374                   at 0.80       0.2893
Query 108: 0.1382                   at 0.90       0.2354
Query 109: 0.2485                   at 1.00       0.1700
Query 110: 0.9524
Query 111: 0.2681               Avg. prec. (non-interpolated)
Query 112: 0.6822               for all rel. documents
Query 113: 0.0312                                 0.4206
Query 114: 0.4172               Precision:
Query 115: 0.8178                 At    5 docs:   0.4980
Query 116: 0.2252                 At   10 docs:   0.4347
Query 117: 0.3889                 At   15 docs:   0.3973
Query 118: 0.0994                 At   20 docs:   0.3653
Query 119: 0.8352                 At   30 docs:   0.3109
Query 121: 0.1474                 At  100 docs:   0.1459
Query 122: 0.0975                 At  200 docs:   0.0837
Query 123: 0.9806                 At  500 docs:   0.0381
Query 124: 0.2441                 At 1000 docs:   0.0204
Query 125: 0.0946
Query 126: 0.3360               R-Precision (prec. after R
Query 127: 0.5447               (=num_rel) docs. retrieved):
Query 128: 0.0030                   Exact:        0.3983
Query 129: 0.3242
Query 130: 0.3651
Query 131: 0.0158
Query 132: 0.4755
Query 133: 0.6414
Query 134: 0.9250
Query 135: 0.7078
Query 136: 1.0000
Query 137: 0.0097
Query 138: 0.7396
Query 139: 0.0566
Query 140: 0.3440
```

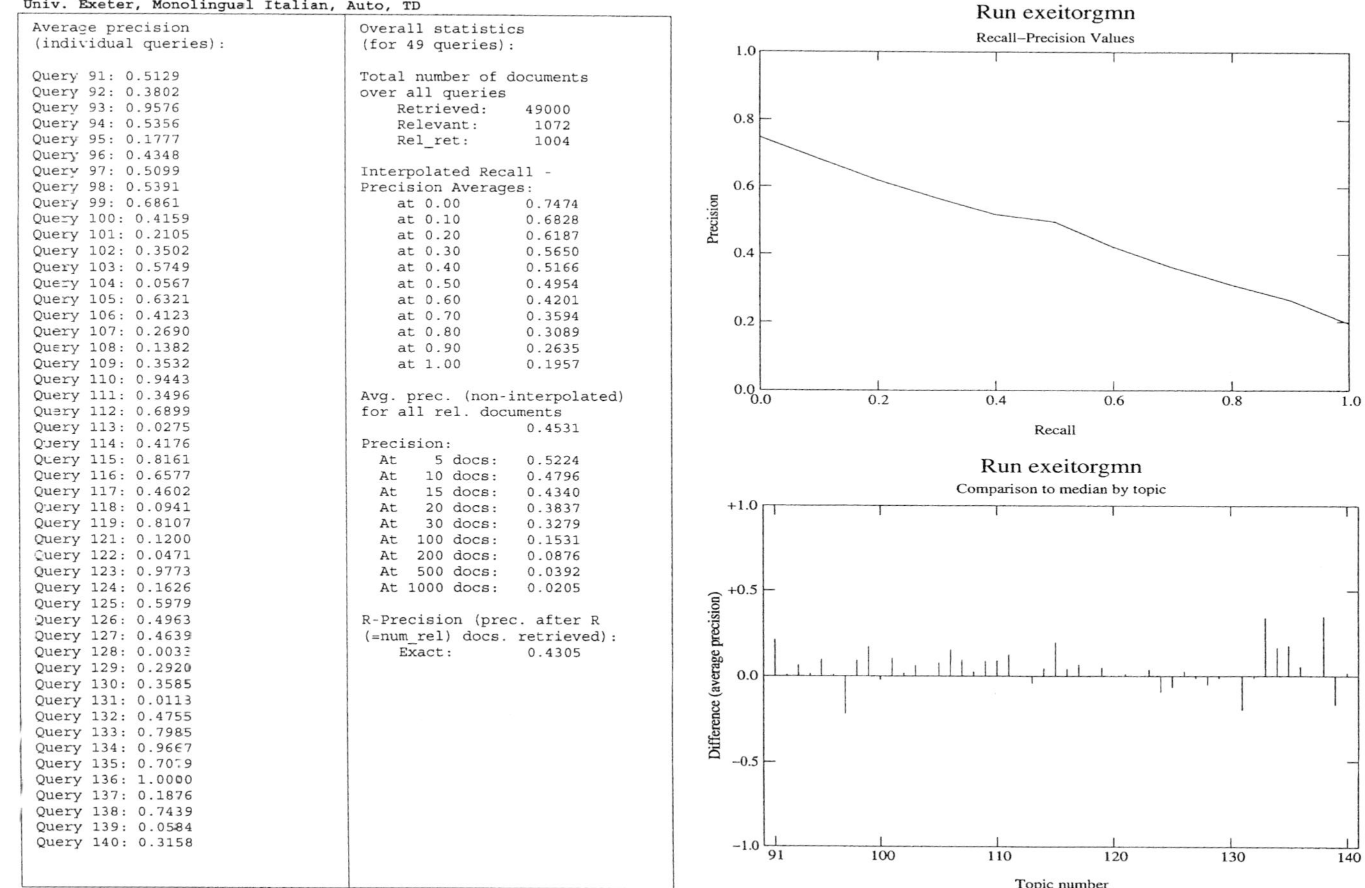

Univ. Exeter, Monolingual Italian, Auto, TD

```
Average precision              Overall statistics
(individual queries):          (for 49 queries):

Query 91: 0.5129               Total number of documents
Query 92: 0.3802               over all queries
Query 93: 0.9576                   Retrieved:    49000
Query 94: 0.5356                   Relevant:      1072
Query 95: 0.1777                   Rel_ret:       1004
Query 96: 0.4348
Query 97: 0.5099               Interpolated Recall -
Query 98: 0.5391               Precision Averages:
Query 99: 0.6861                   at 0.00       0.7474
Query 100: 0.4159                  at 0.10       0.6828
Query 101: 0.2105                  at 0.20       0.6187
Query 102: 0.3502                  at 0.30       0.5650
Query 103: 0.5749                  at 0.40       0.5166
Query 104: 0.0567                  at 0.50       0.4954
Query 105: 0.6321                  at 0.60       0.4201
Query 106: 0.4123                  at 0.70       0.3594
Query 107: 0.2690                  at 0.80       0.3089
Query 108: 0.1382                  at 0.90       0.2635
Query 109: 0.3532                  at 1.00       0.1957
Query 110: 0.9443
Query 111: 0.3496              Avg. prec. (non-interpolated)
Query 112: 0.6899              for all rel. documents
Query 113: 0.0275                                0.4531
Query 114: 0.4176              Precision:
Query 115: 0.8161                At    5 docs:   0.5224
Query 116: 0.6577                At   10 docs:   0.4796
Query 117: 0.4602                At   15 docs:   0.4340
Query 118: 0.0941                At   20 docs:   0.3837
Query 119: 0.8107                At   30 docs:   0.3279
Query 121: 0.1200                At  100 docs:   0.1531
Query 122: 0.0471                At  200 docs:   0.0876
Query 123: 0.9773                At  500 docs:   0.0392
Query 124: 0.1626                At 1000 docs:   0.0205
Query 125: 0.5979
Query 126: 0.4963              R-Precision (prec. after R
Query 127: 0.4639              (=num_rel) docs. retrieved):
Query 128: 0.0033                  Exact:        0.4305
Query 129: 0.2920
Query 130: 0.3585
Query 131: 0.0113
Query 132: 0.4755
Query 133: 0.7985
Query 134: 0.9667
Query 135: 0.7079
Query 136: 1.0000
Query 137: 0.1876
Query 138: 0.7439
Query 139: 0.0584
Query 140: 0.3158
```

Univ. Exeter, Monolingual Italian, Auto, TD

Average precision
(individual queries):

Query	Average precision
Query 91:	0.5189
Query 92:	0.3483
Query 93:	0.9008
Query 94:	0.5181
Query 95:	0.1401
Query 96:	0.4120
Query 97:	0.4702
Query 98:	0.2949
Query 99:	0.4699
Query 100:	0.4968
Query 101:	0.1652
Query 102:	0.2800
Query 103:	0.4996
Query 104:	0.0850
Query 105:	0.6909
Query 106:	0.2627
Query 107:	0.2716
Query 108:	0.0829
Query 109:	0.2165
Query 110:	0.9299
Query 111:	0.4274
Query 112:	0.6194
Query 113:	0.0199
Query 114:	0.3872
Query 115:	0.6925
Query 116:	0.7614
Query 117:	0.3918
Query 118:	0.1365
Query 119:	0.7605
Query 121:	0.2381
Query 122:	0.0868
Query 123:	0.9642
Query 124:	0.1219
Query 125:	0.3837
Query 126:	0.4325
Query 127:	0.4476
Query 128:	0.0056
Query 129:	0.3708
Query 130:	0.2994
Query 131:	0.0126
Query 132:	0.5111
Query 133:	0.7631
Query 134:	0.9250
Query 135:	0.8445
Query 136:	0.8420
Query 137:	0.0865
Query 138:	0.2250
Query 139:	0.0615
Query 140:	0.4156

Overall statistics
(for 49 queries):

Total number of documents
over all queries

Retrieved:	49000
Relevant:	1072
Rel_ret:	993

Interpolated Recall -
Precision Averages:

at 0.00	0.7364
at 0.10	0.6732
at 0.20	0.5748
at 0.30	0.5070
at 0.40	0.4590
at 0.50	0.4308
at 0.60	0.3684
at 0.70	0.3301
at 0.80	0.2836
at 0.90	0.2203
at 1.00	0.1641

Avg. prec. (non-interpolated)
for all rel. documents
0.4141

Precision:

At 5 docs:	0.4939
At 10 docs:	0.4347
At 15 docs:	0.3850
At 20 docs:	0.3561
At 30 docs:	0.3102
At 100 docs:	0.1455
At 200 docs:	0.0850
At 500 docs:	0.0385
At 1000 docs:	0.0203

R-Precision (prec. after R
(=num_rel) docs. retrieved):
Exact: 0.3963

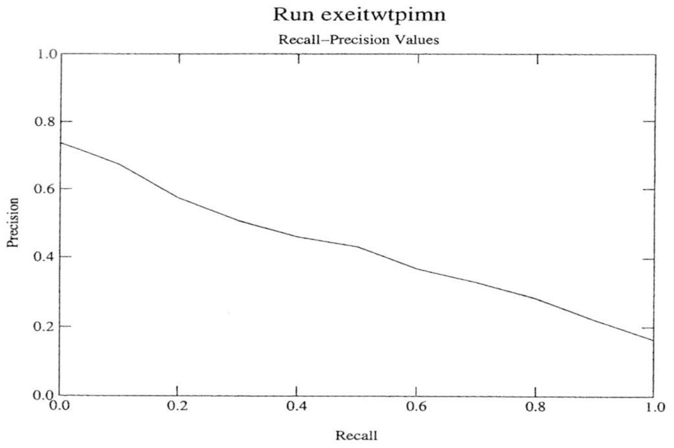

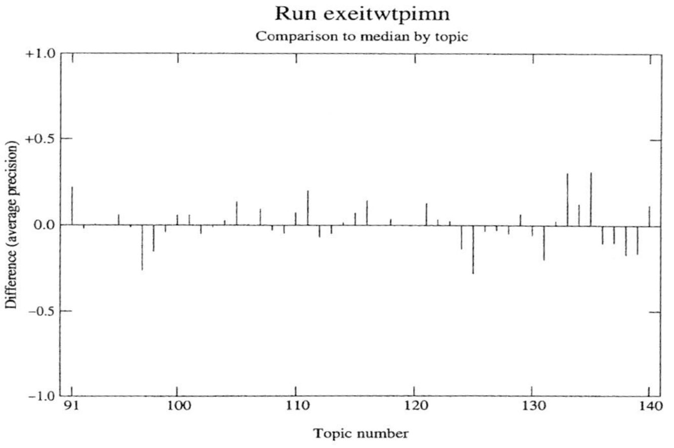

Run exeitwtpimn
Recall–Precision Values

Precision: 0.0 0.2 0.4 0.6 0.8 1.0
Recall: 0.0 0.2 0.4 0.6 0.8 1.0

Run exeitwtpimn
Comparison to median by topic

Difference (average precision): −1.0 −0.5 0.0 +0.5 +1.0
Topic number: 91 100 110 120 130 140

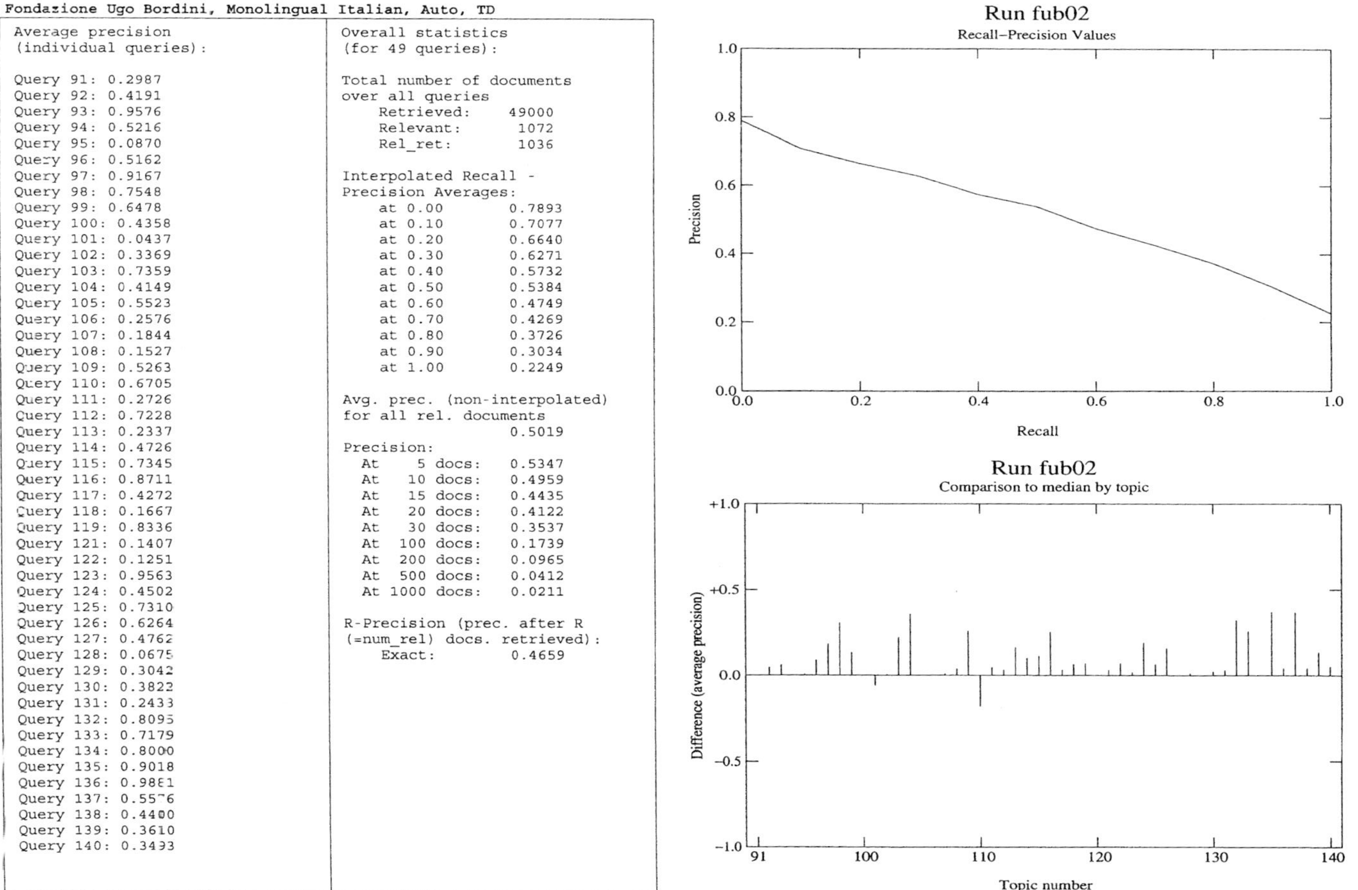

Fondazione Ugo Bordini, Monolingual Italian, Auto, TD

```
Average precision               Overall statistics
(individual queries):           (for 49 queries):

Query 91: 0.2987                Total number of documents
Query 92: 0.4191                over all queries
Query 93: 0.9576                    Retrieved:     49000
Query 94: 0.5216                    Relevant:       1072
Query 95: 0.0870                    Rel_ret:        1036
Query 96: 0.5162
Query 97: 0.9167                Interpolated Recall -
Query 98: 0.7548                Precision Averages:
Query 99: 0.6478                    at 0.00        0.7893
Query 100: 0.4358                   at 0.10        0.7077
Query 101: 0.0437                   at 0.20        0.6640
Query 102: 0.3369                   at 0.30        0.6271
Query 103: 0.7359                   at 0.40        0.5732
Query 104: 0.4149                   at 0.50        0.5384
Query 105: 0.5523                   at 0.60        0.4749
Query 106: 0.2576                   at 0.70        0.4269
Query 107: 0.1844                   at 0.80        0.3726
Query 108: 0.1527                   at 0.90        0.3034
Query 109: 0.5263                   at 1.00        0.2249
Query 110: 0.6705
Query 111: 0.2726               Avg. prec. (non-interpolated)
Query 112: 0.7228               for all rel. documents
Query 113: 0.2337                                  0.5019
Query 114: 0.4726               Precision:
Query 115: 0.7345                 At    5 docs:    0.5347
Query 116: 0.8711                 At   10 docs:    0.4959
Query 117: 0.4272                 At   15 docs:    0.4435
Query 118: 0.1667                 At   20 docs:    0.4122
Query 119: 0.8336                 At   30 docs:    0.3537
Query 121: 0.1407                 At  100 docs:    0.1739
Query 122: 0.1251                 At  200 docs:    0.0965
Query 123: 0.9563                 At  500 docs:    0.0412
Query 124: 0.4502                 At 1000 docs:    0.0211
Query 125: 0.7310
Query 126: 0.6264               R-Precision (prec. after R
Query 127: 0.4762               (=num_rel) docs. retrieved):
Query 128: 0.0675                   Exact:         0.4659
Query 129: 0.3042
Query 130: 0.3822
Query 131: 0.2433
Query 132: 0.8095
Query 133: 0.7179
Query 134: 0.8000
Query 135: 0.9018
Query 136: 0.9881
Query 137: 0.5576
Query 138: 0.4400
Query 139: 0.3610
Query 140: 0.3493
```

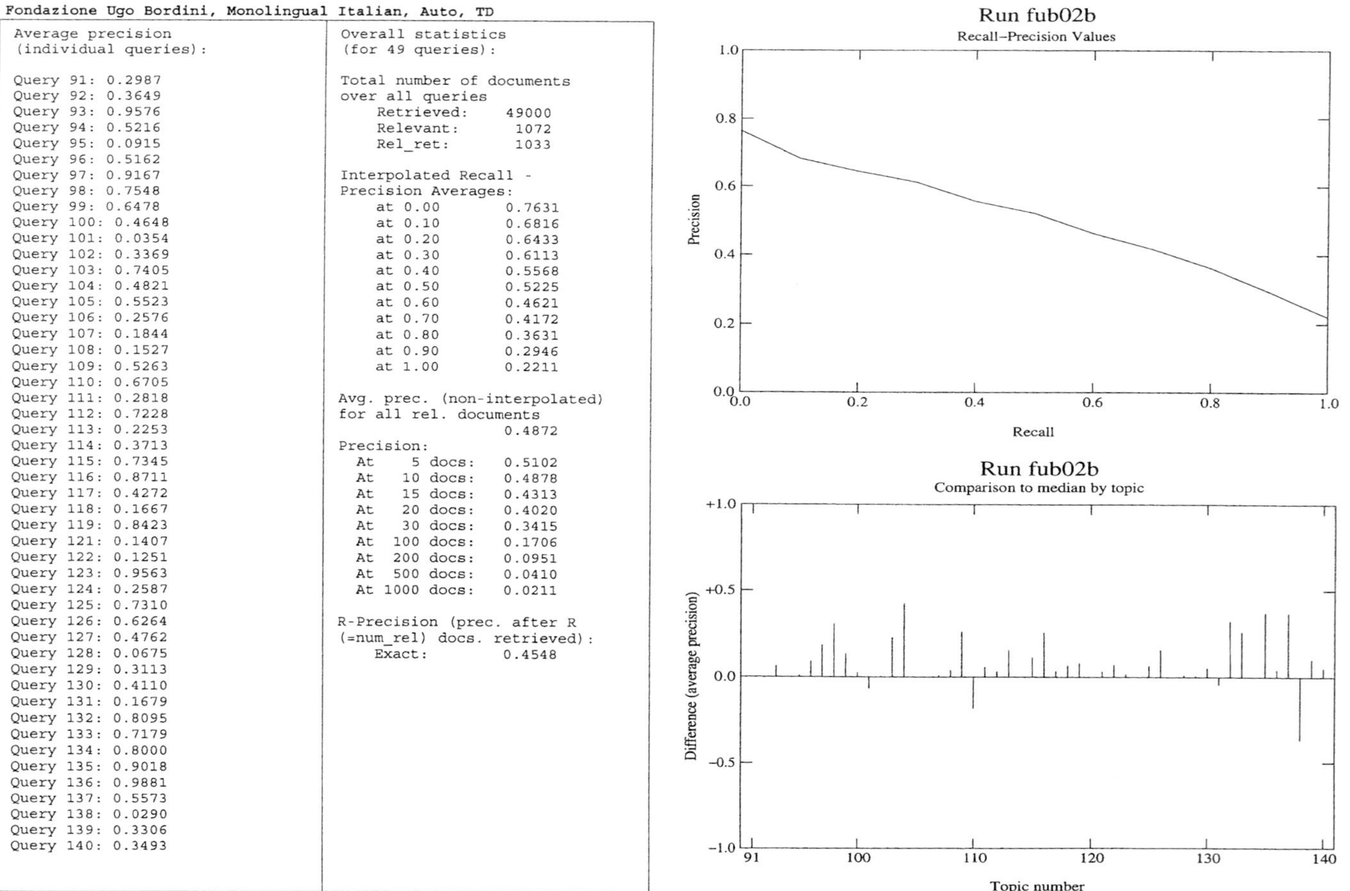

Fondazione Ugo Bordini, Monolingual Italian, Auto, TD

Average precision (individual queries):	Overall statistics (for 49 queries):
Query 91: 0.2987	Total number of documents over all queries
Query 92: 0.3649	Retrieved: 49000
Query 93: 0.9576	Relevant: 1072
Query 94: 0.5216	Rel_ret: 1033
Query 95: 0.0915	
Query 96: 0.5162	Interpolated Recall - Precision Averages:
Query 97: 0.9167	at 0.00 0.7631
Query 98: 0.7548	at 0.10 0.6816
Query 99: 0.6478	at 0.20 0.6433
Query 100: 0.4648	at 0.30 0.6113
Query 101: 0.0354	at 0.40 0.5568
Query 102: 0.3369	at 0.50 0.5225
Query 103: 0.7405	at 0.60 0.4621
Query 104: 0.4821	at 0.70 0.4172
Query 105: 0.5523	at 0.80 0.3631
Query 106: 0.2576	at 0.90 0.2946
Query 107: 0.1844	at 1.00 0.2211
Query 108: 0.1527	
Query 109: 0.5263	Avg. prec. (non-interpolated) for all rel. documents 0.4872
Query 110: 0.6705	
Query 111: 0.2818	Precision:
Query 112: 0.7228	At 5 docs: 0.5102
Query 113: 0.2253	At 10 docs: 0.4878
Query 114: 0.3713	At 15 docs: 0.4313
Query 115: 0.7345	At 20 docs: 0.4020
Query 116: 0.8711	At 30 docs: 0.3415
Query 117: 0.4272	At 100 docs: 0.1706
Query 118: 0.1667	At 200 docs: 0.0951
Query 119: 0.8423	At 500 docs: 0.0410
Query 121: 0.1407	At 1000 docs: 0.0211
Query 122: 0.1251	
Query 123: 0.9563	R-Precision (prec. after R (=num_rel) docs. retrieved):
Query 124: 0.2587	Exact: 0.4548
Query 125: 0.7310	
Query 126: 0.6264	
Query 127: 0.4762	
Query 128: 0.0675	
Query 129: 0.3113	
Query 130: 0.4110	
Query 131: 0.1679	
Query 132: 0.8095	
Query 133: 0.7179	
Query 134: 0.8000	
Query 135: 0.9018	
Query 136: 0.9881	
Query 137: 0.5573	
Query 138: 0.0290	
Query 139: 0.3306	
Query 140: 0.3493	

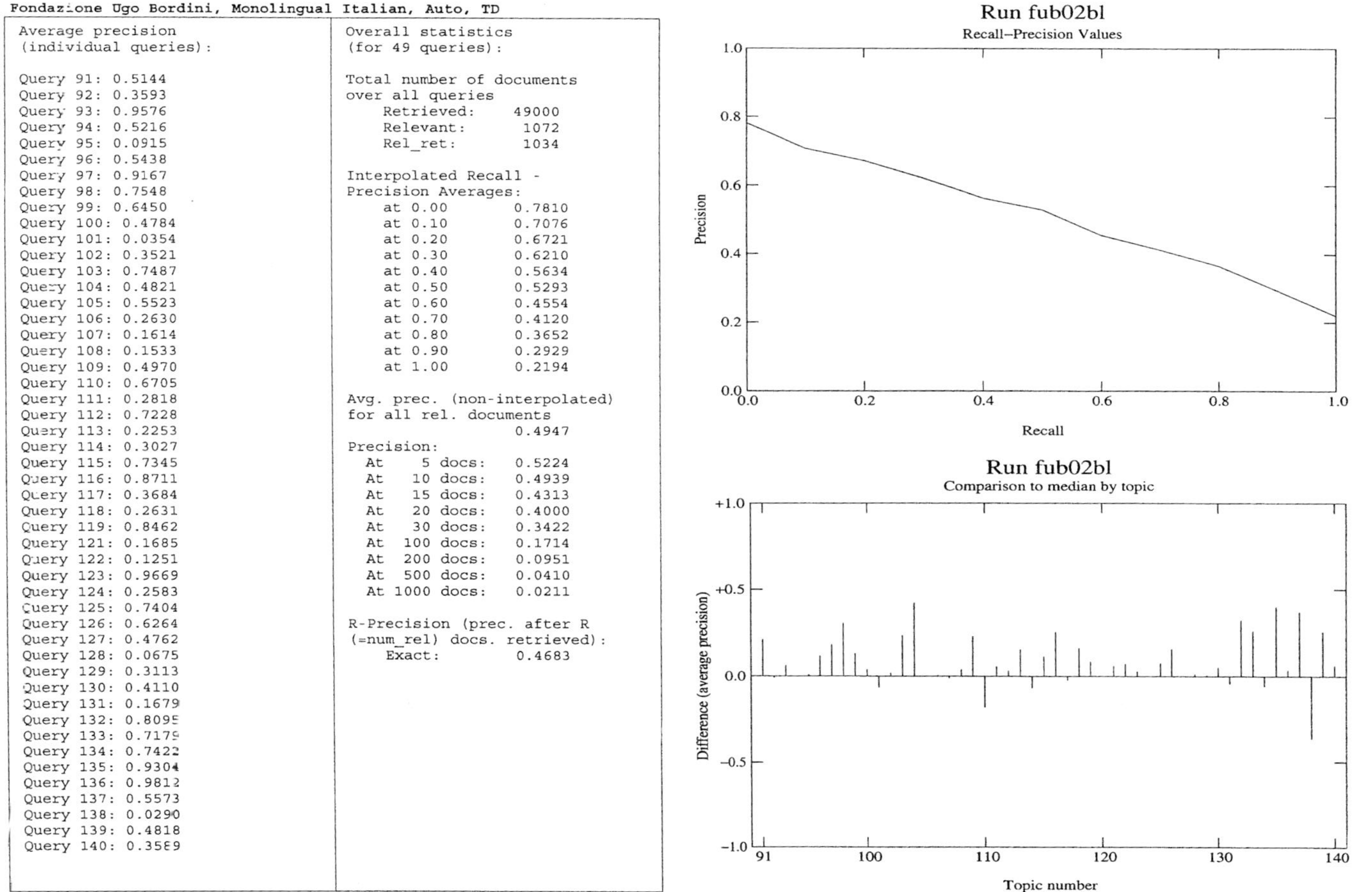

Fondazione Ugo Bordini, Monolingual Italian, Auto, TD

```
Average precision              Overall statistics
(individual queries):          (for 49 queries):

Query 91: 0.5144               Total number of documents
Query 92: 0.3593               over all queries
Query 93: 0.9576                   Retrieved:    49000
Query 94: 0.5216                   Relevant:      1072
Query 95: 0.0915                   Rel_ret:       1034
Query 96: 0.5438
Query 97: 0.9167               Interpolated Recall -
Query 98: 0.7548               Precision Averages:
Query 99: 0.6450                   at 0.00        0.7810
Query 100: 0.4784                  at 0.10        0.7076
Query 101: 0.0354                  at 0.20        0.6721
Query 102: 0.3521                  at 0.30        0.6210
Query 103: 0.7487                  at 0.40        0.5634
Query 104: 0.4821                  at 0.50        0.5293
Query 105: 0.5523                  at 0.60        0.4554
Query 106: 0.2630                  at 0.70        0.4120
Query 107: 0.1614                  at 0.80        0.3652
Query 108: 0.1533                  at 0.90        0.2929
Query 109: 0.4970                  at 1.00        0.2194
Query 110: 0.6705
Query 111: 0.2818              Avg. prec. (non-interpolated)
Query 112: 0.7228              for all rel. documents
Query 113: 0.2253                                 0.4947
Query 114: 0.3027              Precision:
Query 115: 0.7345                At    5 docs:    0.5224
Query 116: 0.8711                At   10 docs:    0.4939
Query 117: 0.3684                At   15 docs:    0.4313
Query 118: 0.2631                At   20 docs:    0.4000
Query 119: 0.8462                At   30 docs:    0.3422
Query 121: 0.1685                At  100 docs:    0.1714
Query 122: 0.1251                At  200 docs:    0.0951
Query 123: 0.9669                At  500 docs:    0.0410
Query 124: 0.2583                At 1000 docs:    0.0211
Query 125: 0.7404
Query 126: 0.6264              R-Precision (prec. after R
Query 127: 0.4762              (=num_rel) docs. retrieved):
Query 128: 0.0675                 Exact:          0.4683
Query 129: 0.3113
Query 130: 0.4110
Query 131: 0.1679
Query 132: 0.8095
Query 133: 0.7179
Query 134: 0.7422
Query 135: 0.9304
Query 136: 0.9812
Query 137: 0.5573
Query 138: 0.0290
Query 139: 0.4818
Query 140: 0.3589
```

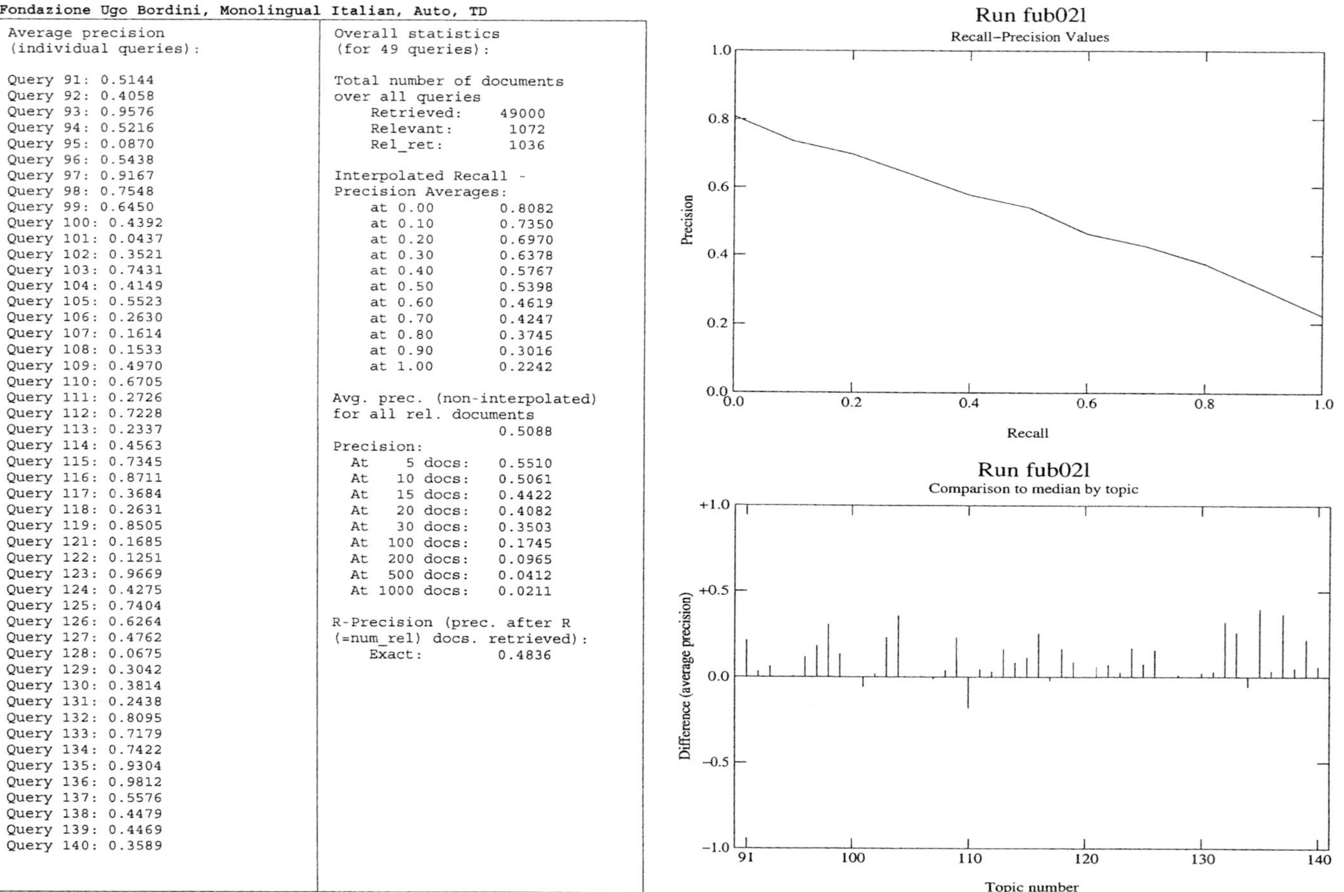

Fondazione Ugo Bordini, Monolingual Italian, Auto, TD

```
Average precision                Overall statistics
(individual queries):            (for 49 queries):

Query 91: 0.5144                 Total number of documents
Query 92: 0.4058                 over all queries
Query 93: 0.9576                     Retrieved:    49000
Query 94: 0.5216                     Relevant:      1072
Query 95: 0.0870                     Rel_ret:       1036
Query 96: 0.5438
Query 97: 0.9167                 Interpolated Recall -
Query 98: 0.7548                 Precision Averages:
Query 99: 0.6450                     at 0.00         0.8082
Query 100: 0.4392                    at 0.10         0.7350
Query 101: 0.0437                    at 0.20         0.6970
Query 102: 0.3521                    at 0.30         0.6378
Query 103: 0.7431                    at 0.40         0.5767
Query 104: 0.4149                    at 0.50         0.5398
Query 105: 0.5523                    at 0.60         0.4619
Query 106: 0.2630                    at 0.70         0.4247
Query 107: 0.1614                    at 0.80         0.3745
Query 108: 0.1533                    at 0.90         0.3016
Query 109: 0.4970                    at 1.00         0.2242
Query 110: 0.6705
Query 111: 0.2726                Avg. prec. (non-interpolated)
Query 112: 0.7228                for all rel. documents
Query 113: 0.2337                                    0.5088
Query 114: 0.4563                Precision:
Query 115: 0.7345                  At    5 docs:     0.5510
Query 116: 0.8711                  At   10 docs:     0.5061
Query 117: 0.3684                  At   15 docs:     0.4422
Query 118: 0.2631                  At   20 docs:     0.4082
Query 119: 0.8505                  At   30 docs:     0.3503
Query 121: 0.1685                  At  100 docs:     0.1745
Query 122: 0.1251                  At  200 docs:     0.0965
Query 123: 0.9669                  At  500 docs:     0.0412
Query 124: 0.4275                  At 1000 docs:     0.0211
Query 125: 0.7404
Query 126: 0.6264                R-Precision (prec. after R
Query 127: 0.4762                (=num_rel) docs. retrieved):
Query 128: 0.0675                    Exact:          0.4836
Query 129: 0.3042
Query 130: 0.3814
Query 131: 0.2438
Query 132: 0.8095
Query 133: 0.7179
Query 134: 0.7422
Query 135: 0.9304
Query 136: 0.9812
Query 137: 0.5576
Query 138: 0.4479
Query 139: 0.4469
Query 140: 0.3589
```

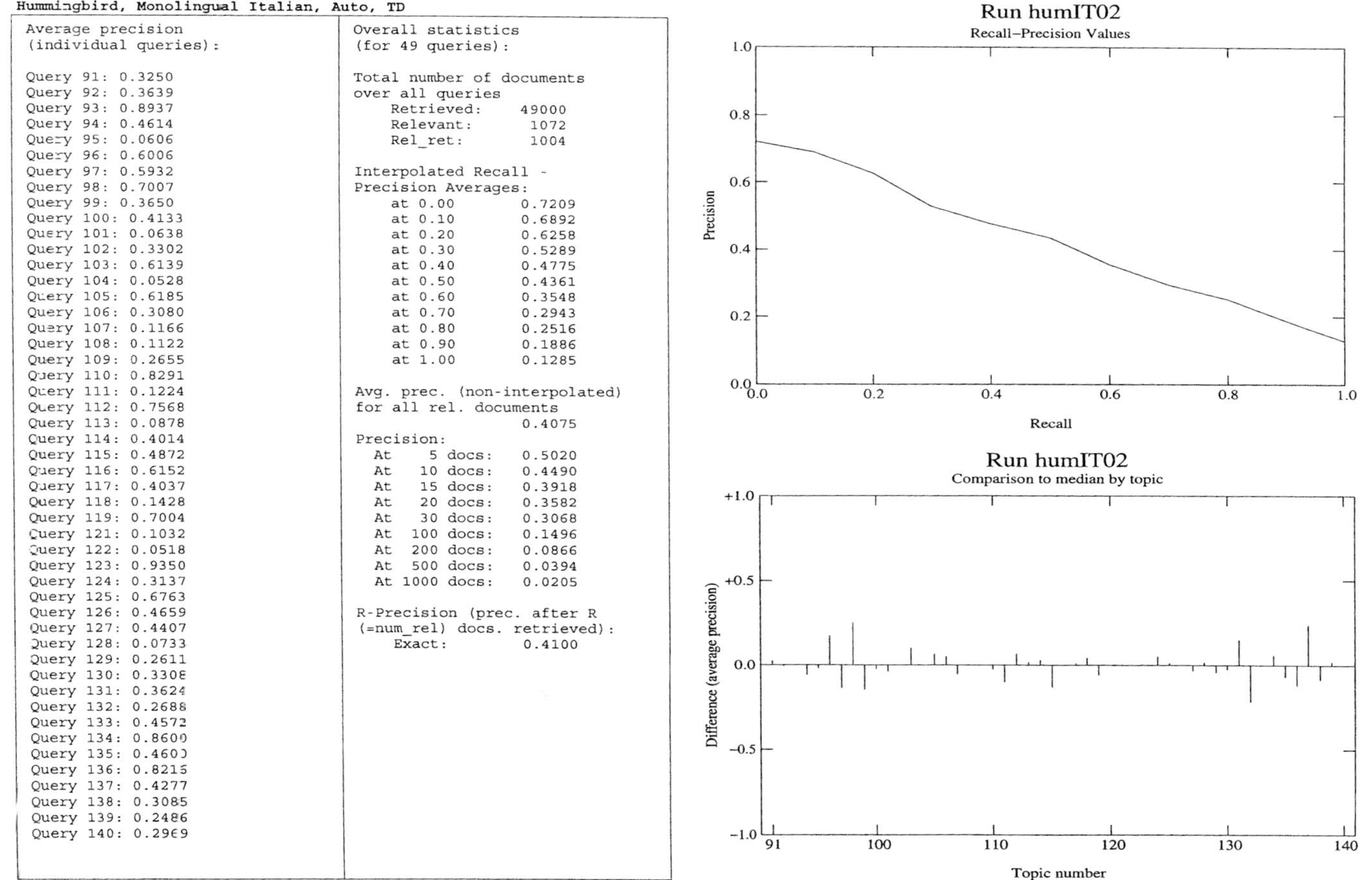

Hummingbird, Monolingual Italian, Auto, TD

```
Average precision              Overall statistics
(individual queries):          (for 49 queries):

Query 91: 0.3250               Total number of documents
Query 92: 0.3639               over all queries
Query 93: 0.8937                   Retrieved:    49000
Query 94: 0.4614                   Relevant:      1072
Query 95: 0.0606                   Rel_ret:       1004
Query 96: 0.6006
Query 97: 0.5932               Interpolated Recall -
Query 98: 0.7007               Precision Averages:
Query 99: 0.3650                   at 0.00       0.7209
Query 100: 0.4133                  at 0.10       0.6892
Query 101: 0.0638                  at 0.20       0.6258
Query 102: 0.3302                  at 0.30       0.5289
Query 103: 0.6139                  at 0.40       0.4775
Query 104: 0.0528                  at 0.50       0.4361
Query 105: 0.6185                  at 0.60       0.3548
Query 106: 0.3080                  at 0.70       0.2943
Query 107: 0.1166                  at 0.80       0.2516
Query 108: 0.1122                  at 0.90       0.1886
Query 109: 0.2655                  at 1.00       0.1285
Query 110: 0.8291
Query 111: 0.1224              Avg. prec. (non-interpolated)
Query 112: 0.7568              for all rel. documents
Query 113: 0.0878                                0.4075
Query 114: 0.4014              Precision:
Query 115: 0.4872                At    5 docs:   0.5020
Query 116: 0.6152                At   10 docs:   0.4490
Query 117: 0.4037                At   15 docs:   0.3918
Query 118: 0.1428                At   20 docs:   0.3582
Query 119: 0.7004                At   30 docs:   0.3068
Query 121: 0.1032                At  100 docs:   0.1496
Query 122: 0.0518                At  200 docs:   0.0866
Query 123: 0.9350                At  500 docs:   0.0394
Query 124: 0.3137                At 1000 docs:   0.0205
Query 125: 0.6763
Query 126: 0.4659              R-Precision (prec. after R
Query 127: 0.4407              (=num_rel) docs. retrieved):
Query 128: 0.0733                  Exact:        0.4100
Query 129: 0.2611
Query 130: 0.3308
Query 131: 0.3624
Query 132: 0.2688
Query 133: 0.4572
Query 134: 0.8600
Query 135: 0.4600
Query 136: 0.8215
Query 137: 0.4277
Query 138: 0.3085
Query 139: 0.2486
Query 140: 0.2969
```

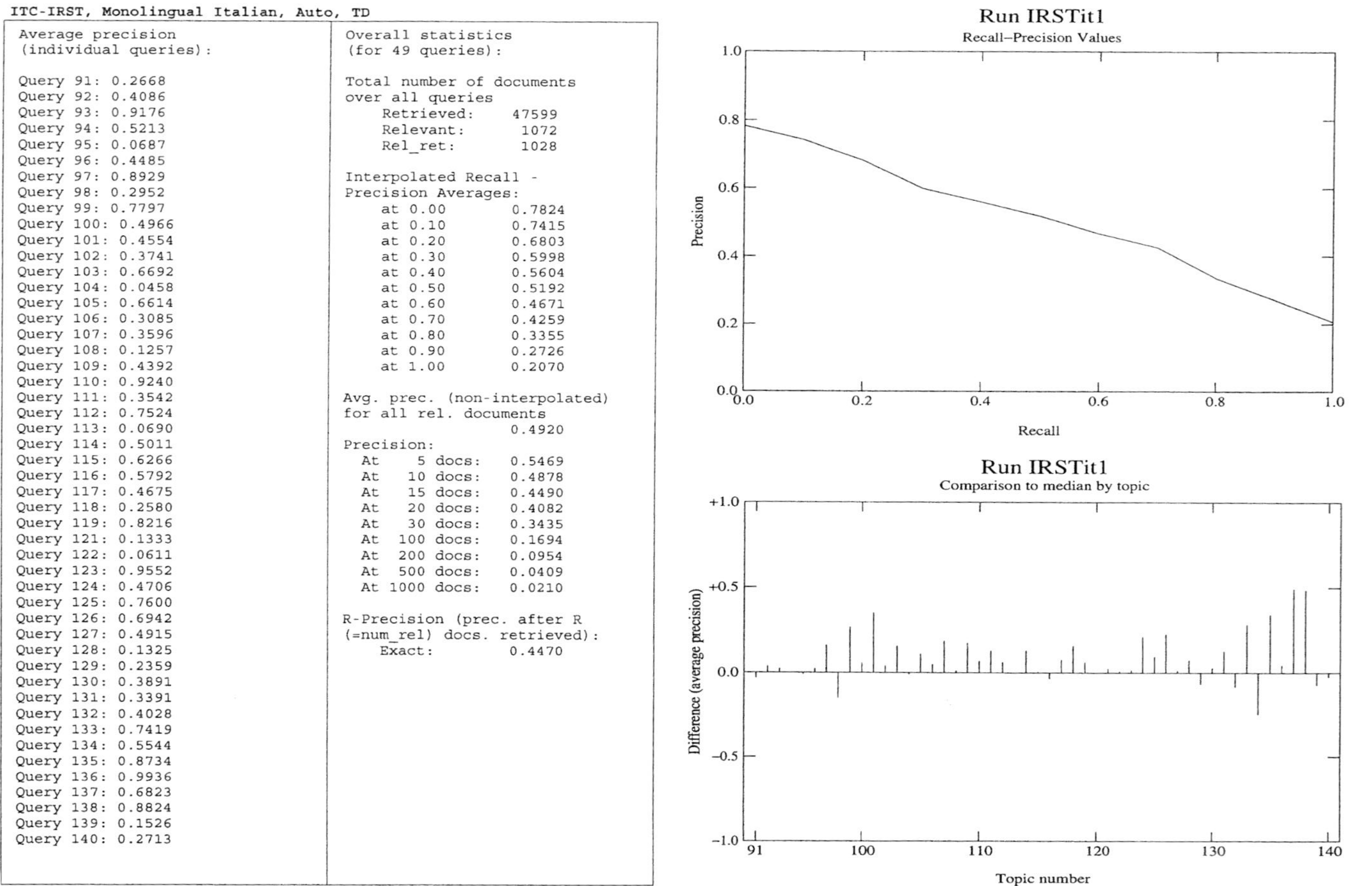

ITC-IRST, Monolingual Italian, Auto, TD

Average precision (individual queries):	Overall statistics (for 49 queries):
Query 91: 0.2668	Total number of documents over all queries
Query 92: 0.4086	Retrieved: 47599
Query 93: 0.9176	Relevant: 1072
Query 94: 0.5213	Rel_ret: 1028
Query 95: 0.0687	
Query 96: 0.4485	Interpolated Recall - Precision Averages:
Query 97: 0.8929	at 0.00 0.7824
Query 98: 0.2952	at 0.10 0.7415
Query 99: 0.7797	at 0.20 0.6803
Query 100: 0.4966	at 0.30 0.5998
Query 101: 0.4554	at 0.40 0.5604
Query 102: 0.3741	at 0.50 0.5192
Query 103: 0.6692	at 0.60 0.4671
Query 104: 0.0458	at 0.70 0.4259
Query 105: 0.6614	at 0.80 0.3355
Query 106: 0.3085	at 0.90 0.2726
Query 107: 0.3596	at 1.00 0.2070
Query 108: 0.1257	
Query 109: 0.4392	Avg. prec. (non-interpolated) for all rel. documents 0.4920
Query 110: 0.9240	
Query 111: 0.3542	Precision:
Query 112: 0.7524	At 5 docs: 0.5469
Query 113: 0.0690	At 10 docs: 0.4878
Query 114: 0.5011	At 15 docs: 0.4490
Query 115: 0.6266	At 20 docs: 0.4082
Query 116: 0.5792	At 30 docs: 0.3435
Query 117: 0.4675	At 100 docs: 0.1694
Query 118: 0.2580	At 200 docs: 0.0954
Query 119: 0.8216	At 500 docs: 0.0409
Query 121: 0.1333	At 1000 docs: 0.0210
Query 122: 0.0611	
Query 123: 0.9552	R-Precision (prec. after R (=num_rel) docs. retrieved):
Query 124: 0.4706	Exact: 0.4470
Query 125: 0.7600	
Query 126: 0.6942	
Query 127: 0.4915	
Query 128: 0.1325	
Query 129: 0.2359	
Query 130: 0.3891	
Query 131: 0.3391	
Query 132: 0.4028	
Query 133: 0.7419	
Query 134: 0.5544	
Query 135: 0.8734	
Query 136: 0.9936	
Query 137: 0.6823	
Query 138: 0.8824	
Query 139: 0.1526	
Query 140: 0.2713	

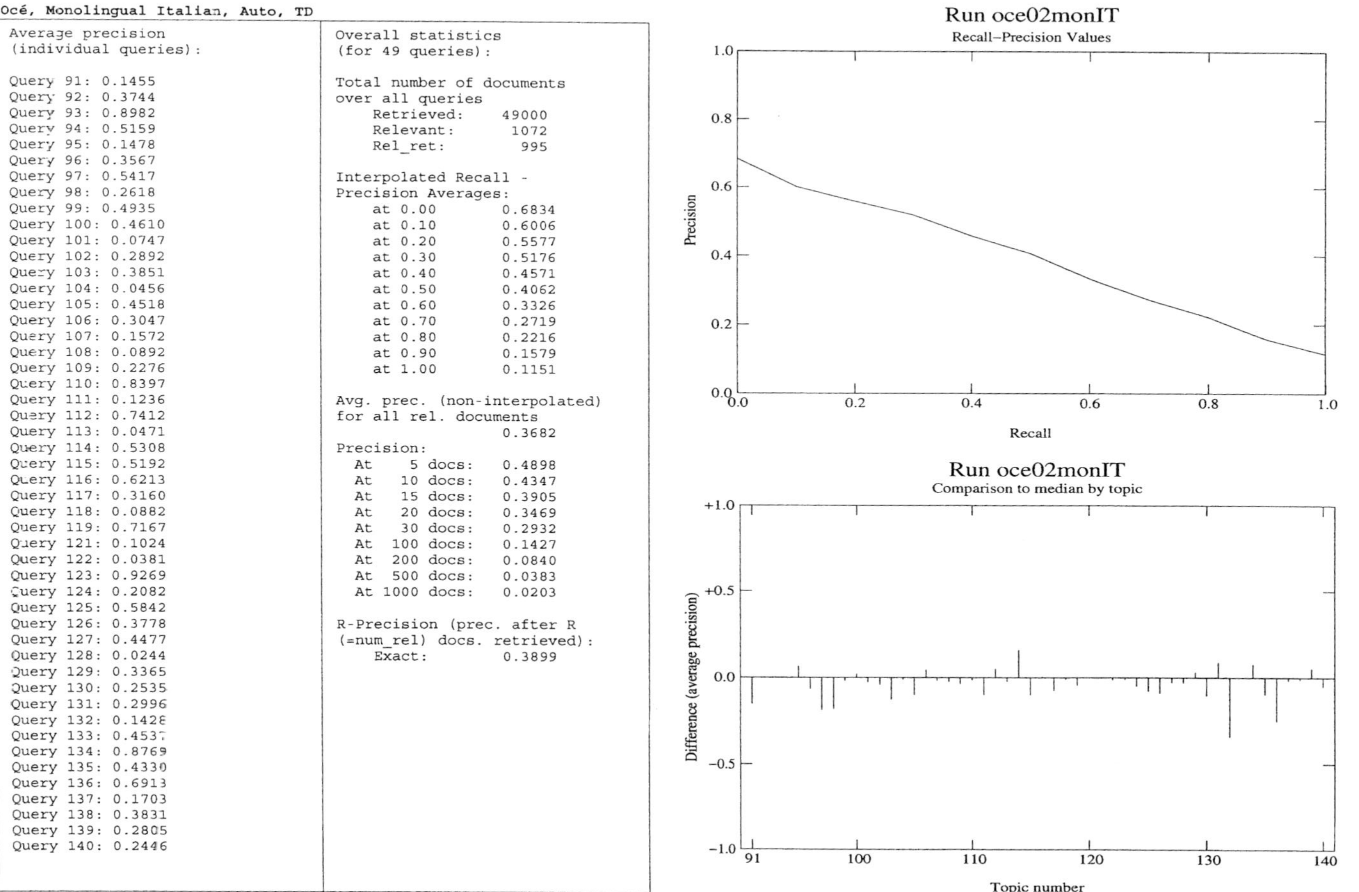

Océ, Monolingual Italian, Auto, TD

```
Average precision                 Overall statistics
(individual queries):             (for 49 queries):

Query 91: 0.1455                  Total number of documents
Query 92: 0.3744                  over all queries
Query 93: 0.8982                      Retrieved:    49000
Query 94: 0.5159                      Relevant:      1072
Query 95: 0.1478                      Rel_ret:        995
Query 96: 0.3567
Query 97: 0.5417                  Interpolated Recall -
Query 98: 0.2618                  Precision Averages:
Query 99: 0.4935                      at 0.00        0.6834
Query 100: 0.4610                     at 0.10        0.6006
Query 101: 0.0747                     at 0.20        0.5577
Query 102: 0.2892                     at 0.30        0.5176
Query 103: 0.3851                     at 0.40        0.4571
Query 104: 0.0456                     at 0.50        0.4062
Query 105: 0.4518                     at 0.60        0.3326
Query 106: 0.3047                     at 0.70        0.2719
Query 107: 0.1572                     at 0.80        0.2216
Query 108: 0.0892                     at 0.90        0.1579
Query 109: 0.2276                     at 1.00        0.1151
Query 110: 0.8397
Query 111: 0.1236                 Avg. prec. (non-interpolated)
Query 112: 0.7412                 for all rel. documents
Query 113: 0.0471                                    0.3682
Query 114: 0.5308                 Precision:
Query 115: 0.5192                   At    5 docs:    0.4898
Query 116: 0.6213                   At   10 docs:    0.4347
Query 117: 0.3160                   At   15 docs:    0.3905
Query 118: 0.0882                   At   20 docs:    0.3469
Query 119: 0.7167                   At   30 docs:    0.2932
Query 121: 0.1024                   At  100 docs:    0.1427
Query 122: 0.0381                   At  200 docs:    0.0840
Query 123: 0.9269                   At  500 docs:    0.0383
Query 124: 0.2082                   At 1000 docs:    0.0203
Query 125: 0.5842
Query 126: 0.3778                 R-Precision (prec. after R
Query 127: 0.4477                 (=num_rel) docs. retrieved):
Query 128: 0.0244                     Exact:         0.3899
Query 129: 0.3365
Query 130: 0.2535
Query 131: 0.2996
Query 132: 0.1428
Query 133: 0.4537
Query 134: 0.8769
Query 135: 0.4330
Query 136: 0.6913
Query 137: 0.1703
Query 138: 0.3831
Query 139: 0.2805
Query 140: 0.2446
```

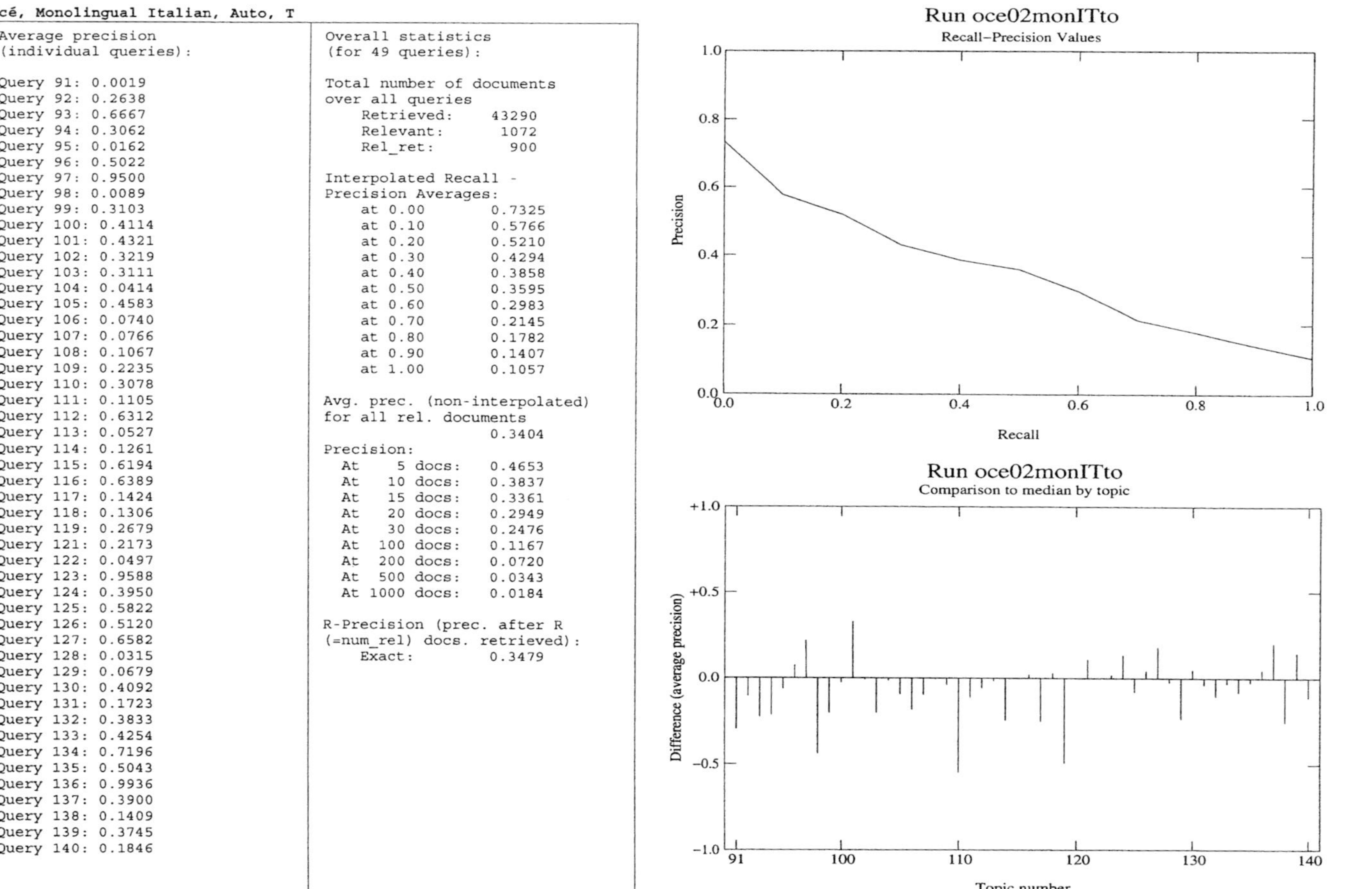

Océ, Monolingual Italian, Auto, T

```
Average precision                 Overall statistics
(individual queries):             (for 49 queries):

Query 91: 0.0019                  Total number of documents
Query 92: 0.2638                  over all queries
Query 93: 0.6667                      Retrieved:     43290
Query 94: 0.3062                      Relevant:       1072
Query 95: 0.0162                      Rel_ret:         900
Query 96: 0.5022
Query 97: 0.9500                  Interpolated Recall -
Query 98: 0.0089                  Precision Averages:
Query 99: 0.3103                      at 0.00         0.7325
Query 100: 0.4114                     at 0.10         0.5766
Query 101: 0.4321                     at 0.20         0.5210
Query 102: 0.3219                     at 0.30         0.4294
Query 103: 0.3111                     at 0.40         0.3858
Query 104: 0.0414                     at 0.50         0.3595
Query 105: 0.4583                     at 0.60         0.2983
Query 106: 0.0740                     at 0.70         0.2145
Query 107: 0.0766                     at 0.80         0.1782
Query 108: 0.1067                     at 0.90         0.1407
Query 109: 0.2235                     at 1.00         0.1057
Query 110: 0.3078
Query 111: 0.1105                 Avg. prec. (non-interpolated)
Query 112: 0.6312                 for all rel. documents
Query 113: 0.0527                                     0.3404
Query 114: 0.1261                 Precision:
Query 115: 0.6194                   At    5 docs:     0.4653
Query 116: 0.6389                   At   10 docs:     0.3837
Query 117: 0.1424                   At   15 docs:     0.3361
Query 118: 0.1306                   At   20 docs:     0.2949
Query 119: 0.2679                   At   30 docs:     0.2476
Query 121: 0.2173                   At  100 docs:     0.1167
Query 122: 0.0497                   At  200 docs:     0.0720
Query 123: 0.9588                   At  500 docs:     0.0343
Query 124: 0.3950                   At 1000 docs:     0.0184
Query 125: 0.5822
Query 126: 0.5120                 R-Precision (prec. after R
Query 127: 0.6582                 (=num_rel) docs. retrieved):
Query 128: 0.0315                     Exact:          0.3479
Query 129: 0.0679
Query 130: 0.4092
Query 131: 0.1723
Query 132: 0.3833
Query 133: 0.4254
Query 134: 0.7196
Query 135: 0.5043
Query 136: 0.9936
Query 137: 0.3900
Query 138: 0.1409
Query 139: 0.3745
Query 140: 0.1846
```

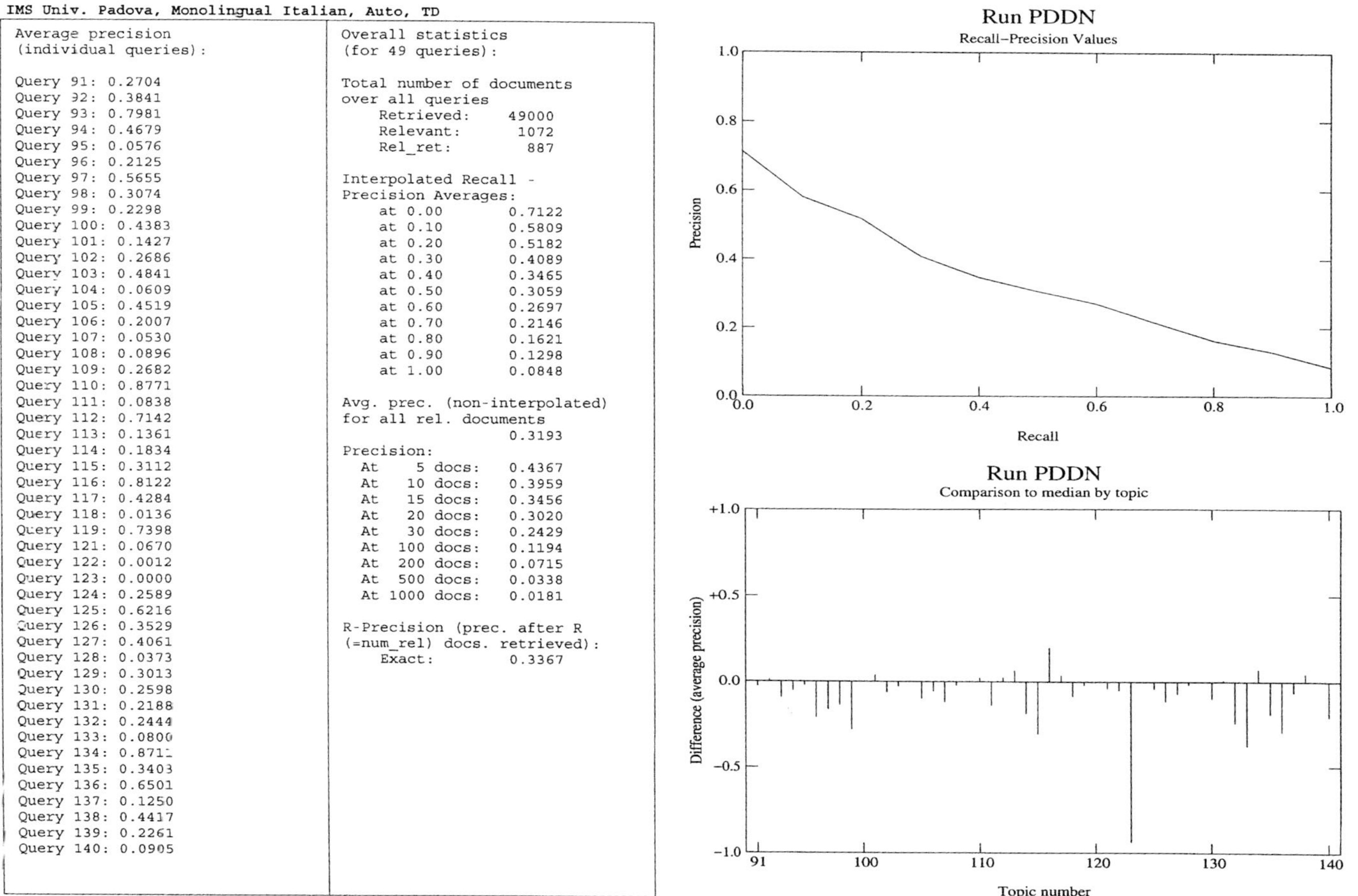

IMS Univ. Padova, Monolingual Italian, Auto, TD

Average precision (individual queries):	Overall statistics (for 49 queries):
Query 91: 0.2704	Total number of documents over all queries
Query 92: 0.3841	Retrieved: 49000
Query 93: 0.7981	Relevant: 1072
Query 94: 0.4679	Rel_ret: 887
Query 95: 0.0576	
Query 96: 0.2125	Interpolated Recall - Precision Averages:
Query 97: 0.5655	at 0.00 0.7122
Query 98: 0.3074	at 0.10 0.5809
Query 99: 0.2298	at 0.20 0.5182
Query 100: 0.4383	at 0.30 0.4089
Query 101: 0.1427	at 0.40 0.3465
Query 102: 0.2686	at 0.50 0.3059
Query 103: 0.4841	at 0.60 0.2697
Query 104: 0.0609	at 0.70 0.2146
Query 105: 0.4519	at 0.80 0.1621
Query 106: 0.2007	at 0.90 0.1298
Query 107: 0.0530	at 1.00 0.0848
Query 108: 0.0896	
Query 109: 0.2682	Avg. prec. (non-interpolated) for all rel. documents 0.3193
Query 110: 0.8771	
Query 111: 0.0838	Precision:
Query 112: 0.7142	At 5 docs: 0.4367
Query 113: 0.1361	At 10 docs: 0.3959
Query 114: 0.1834	At 15 docs: 0.3456
Query 115: 0.3112	At 20 docs: 0.3020
Query 116: 0.8122	At 30 docs: 0.2429
Query 117: 0.4284	At 100 docs: 0.1194
Query 118: 0.0136	At 200 docs: 0.0715
Query 119: 0.7398	At 500 docs: 0.0338
Query 121: 0.0670	At 1000 docs: 0.0181
Query 122: 0.0012	
Query 123: 0.0000	R-Precision (prec. after R (=num_rel) docs. retrieved):
Query 124: 0.2589	Exact: 0.3367
Query 125: 0.6216	
Query 126: 0.3529	
Query 127: 0.4061	
Query 128: 0.0373	
Query 129: 0.3013	
Query 130: 0.2598	
Query 131: 0.2188	
Query 132: 0.2444	
Query 133: 0.0800	
Query 134: 0.8711	
Query 135: 0.3403	
Query 136: 0.6501	
Query 137: 0.1250	
Query 138: 0.4417	
Query 139: 0.2261	
Query 140: 0.0905	

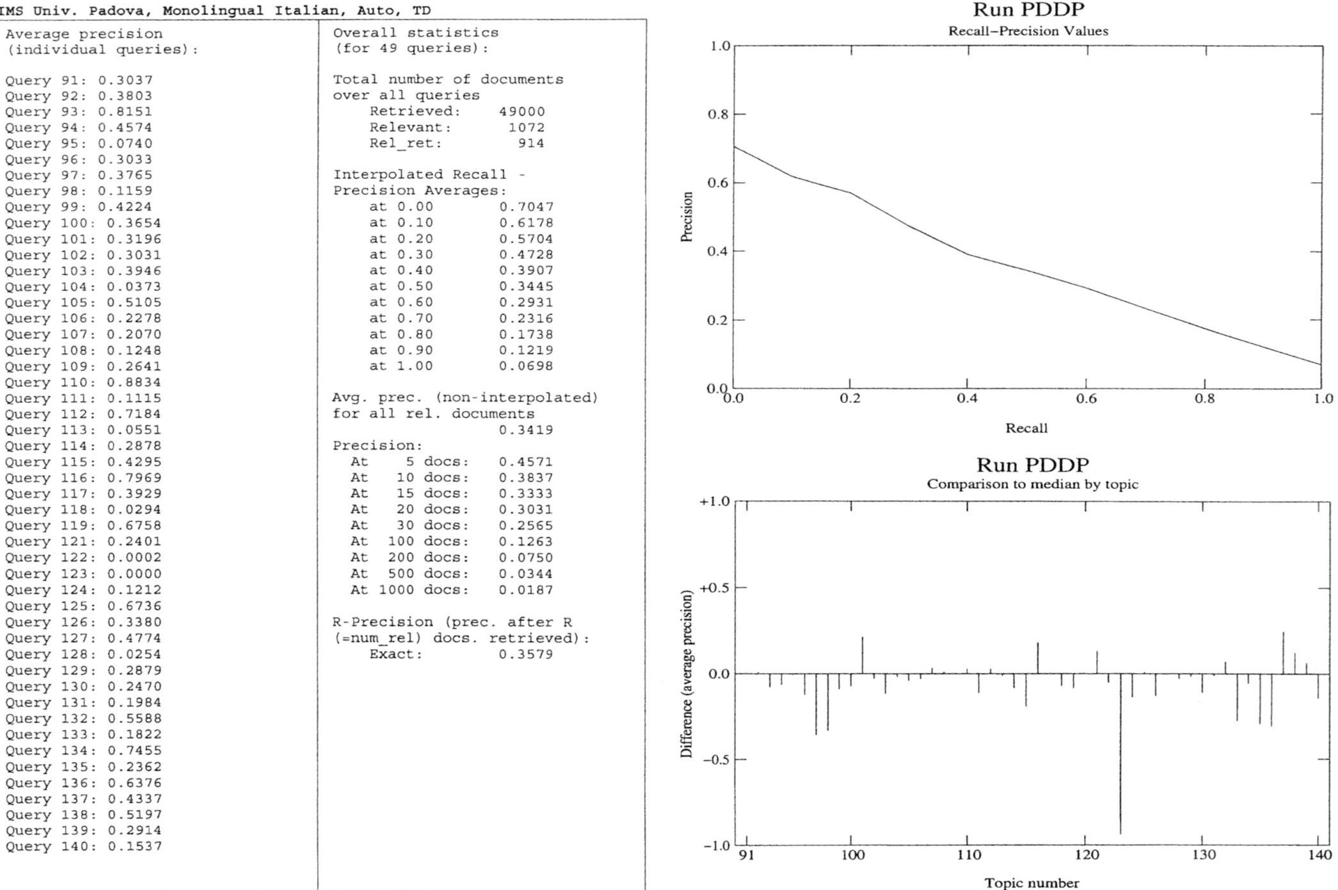

IMS Univ. Padova, Monolingual Italian, Auto, TD

Average precision
(individual queries):

Query 91: 0.3037
Query 92: 0.3803
Query 93: 0.8151
Query 94: 0.4574
Query 95: 0.0740
Query 96: 0.3033
Query 97: 0.3765
Query 98: 0.1159
Query 99: 0.4224
Query 100: 0.3654
Query 101: 0.3196
Query 102: 0.3031
Query 103: 0.3946
Query 104: 0.0373
Query 105: 0.5105
Query 106: 0.2278
Query 107: 0.2070
Query 108: 0.1248
Query 109: 0.2641
Query 110: 0.8834
Query 111: 0.1115
Query 112: 0.7184
Query 113: 0.0551
Query 114: 0.2878
Query 115: 0.4295
Query 116: 0.7969
Query 117: 0.3929
Query 118: 0.0294
Query 119: 0.6758
Query 121: 0.2401
Query 122: 0.0002
Query 123: 0.0000
Query 124: 0.1212
Query 125: 0.6736
Query 126: 0.3380
Query 127: 0.4774
Query 128: 0.0254
Query 129: 0.2879
Query 130: 0.2470
Query 131: 0.1984
Query 132: 0.5588
Query 133: 0.1822
Query 134: 0.7455
Query 135: 0.2362
Query 136: 0.6376
Query 137: 0.4337
Query 138: 0.5197
Query 139: 0.2914
Query 140: 0.1537

Overall statistics
(for 49 queries):

Total number of documents
over all queries
Retrieved: 49000
Relevant: 1072
Rel_ret: 914

Interpolated Recall -
Precision Averages:
at 0.00 0.7047
at 0.10 0.6178
at 0.20 0.5704
at 0.30 0.4728
at 0.40 0.3907
at 0.50 0.3445
at 0.60 0.2931
at 0.70 0.2316
at 0.80 0.1738
at 0.90 0.1219
at 1.00 0.0698

Avg. prec. (non-interpolated)
for all rel. documents
0.3419

Precision:
At 5 docs: 0.4571
At 10 docs: 0.3837
At 15 docs: 0.3333
At 20 docs: 0.3031
At 30 docs: 0.2565
At 100 docs: 0.1263
At 200 docs: 0.0750
At 500 docs: 0.0344
At 1000 docs: 0.0187

R-Precision (prec. after R
(=num_rel) docs. retrieved):
Exact: 0.3579

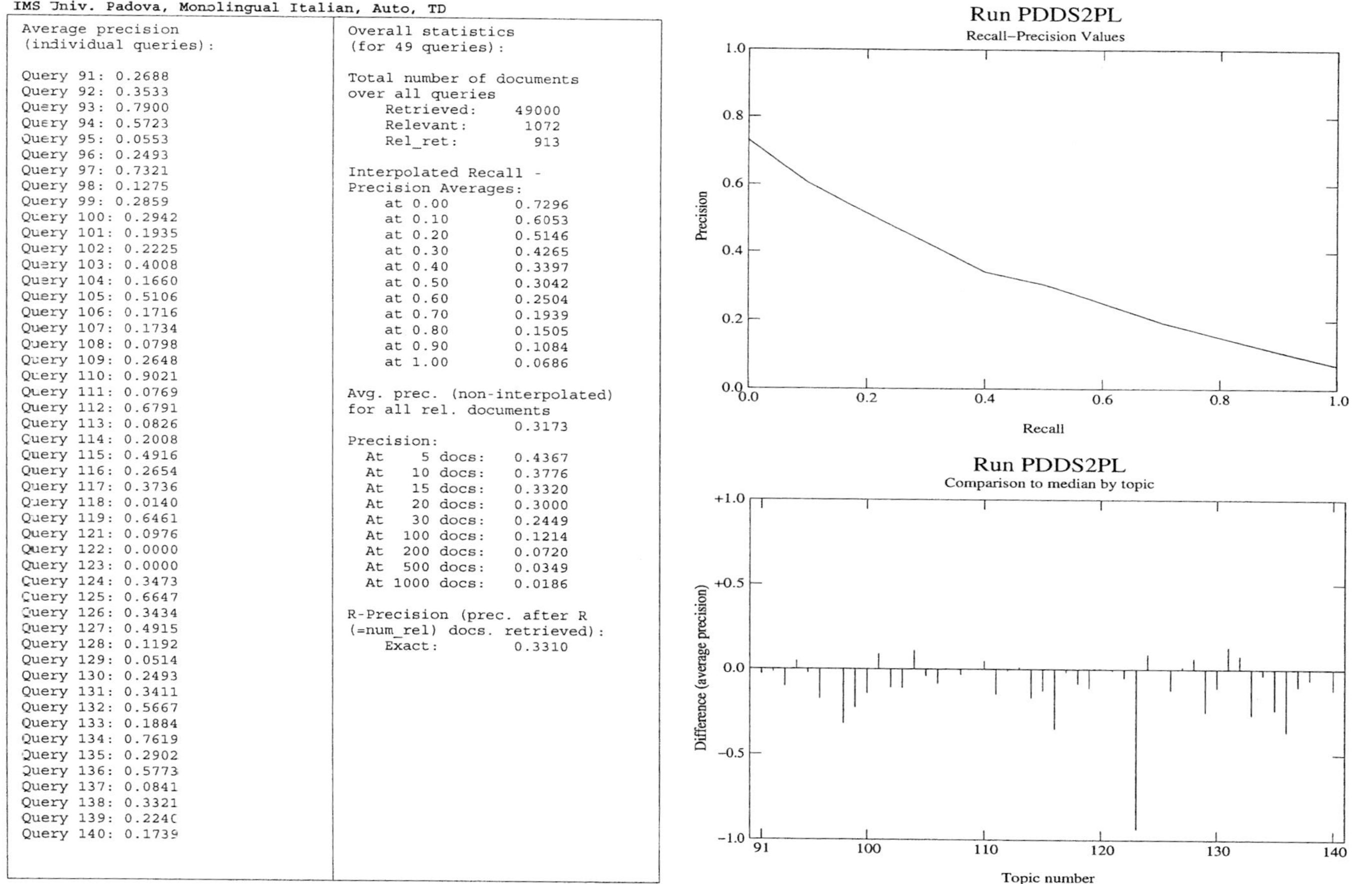

IMS Univ. Padova, Monolingual Italian, Auto, TD

```
Average precision                  Overall statistics
(individual queries):              (for 49 queries):

Query 91: 0.2688                   Total number of documents
Query 92: 0.3533                   over all queries
Query 93: 0.7900                       Retrieved:     49000
Query 94: 0.5723                       Relevant:       1072
Query 95: 0.0553                       Rel_ret:         913
Query 96: 0.2493
Query 97: 0.7321                   Interpolated Recall -
Query 98: 0.1275                   Precision Averages:
Query 99: 0.2859                       at 0.00        0.7296
Query 100: 0.2942                      at 0.10        0.6053
Query 101: 0.1935                      at 0.20        0.5146
Query 102: 0.2225                      at 0.30        0.4265
Query 103: 0.4008                      at 0.40        0.3397
Query 104: 0.1660                      at 0.50        0.3042
Query 105: 0.5106                      at 0.60        0.2504
Query 106: 0.1716                      at 0.70        0.1939
Query 107: 0.1734                      at 0.80        0.1505
Query 108: 0.0798                      at 0.90        0.1084
Query 109: 0.2648                      at 1.00        0.0686
Query 110: 0.9021
Query 111: 0.0769                  Avg. prec. (non-interpolated)
Query 112: 0.6791                  for all rel. documents
Query 113: 0.0826                                     0.3173
Query 114: 0.2008                  Precision:
Query 115: 0.4916                    At    5 docs:    0.4367
Query 116: 0.2654                    At   10 docs:    0.3776
Query 117: 0.3736                    At   15 docs:    0.3320
Query 118: 0.0140                    At   20 docs:    0.3000
Query 119: 0.6461                    At   30 docs:    0.2449
Query 121: 0.0976                    At  100 docs:    0.1214
Query 122: 0.0000                    At  200 docs:    0.0720
Query 123: 0.0000                    At  500 docs:    0.0349
Query 124: 0.3473                    At 1000 docs:    0.0186
Query 125: 0.6647
Query 126: 0.3434                  R-Precision (prec. after R
Query 127: 0.4915                  (=num_rel) docs. retrieved):
Query 128: 0.1192                      Exact:         0.3310
Query 129: 0.0514
Query 130: 0.2493
Query 131: 0.3411
Query 132: 0.5667
Query 133: 0.1884
Query 134: 0.7619
Query 135: 0.2902
Query 136: 0.5773
Query 137: 0.0841
Query 138: 0.3321
Query 139: 0.2240
Query 140: 0.1739
```

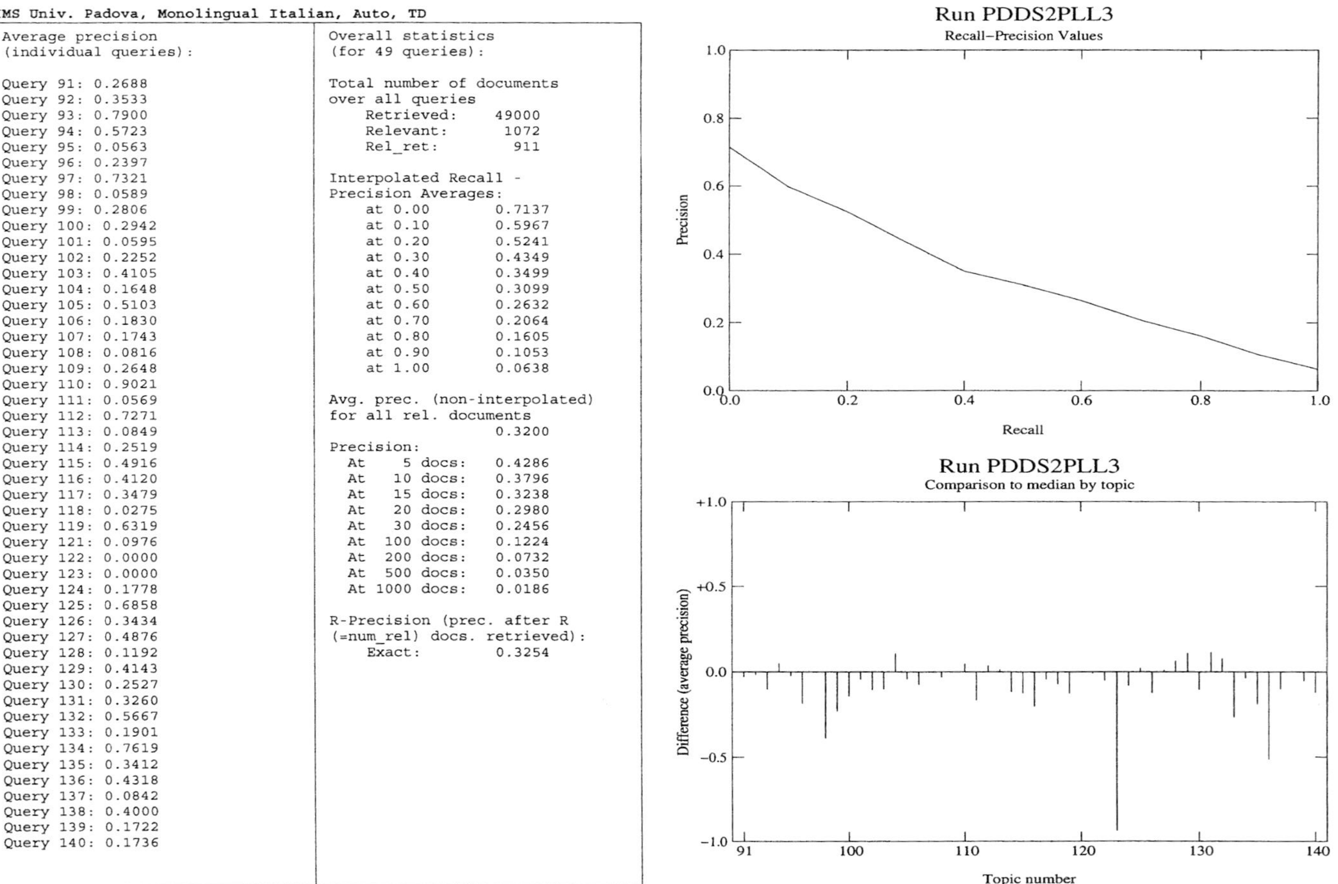

IMS Univ. Padova, Monolingual Italian, Auto, TD

```
Average precision                Overall statistics
(individual queries):            (for 49 queries):

Query 91: 0.2688                 Total number of documents
Query 92: 0.3533                 over all queries
Query 93: 0.7900                     Retrieved:    49000
Query 94: 0.5723                     Relevant:      1072
Query 95: 0.0563                     Rel_ret:        911
Query 96: 0.2397
Query 97: 0.7321                 Interpolated Recall -
Query 98: 0.0589                 Precision Averages:
Query 99: 0.2806                     at 0.00       0.7137
Query 100: 0.2942                    at 0.10       0.5967
Query 101: 0.0595                    at 0.20       0.5241
Query 102: 0.2252                    at 0.30       0.4349
Query 103: 0.4105                    at 0.40       0.3499
Query 104: 0.1648                    at 0.50       0.3099
Query 105: 0.5103                    at 0.60       0.2632
Query 106: 0.1830                    at 0.70       0.2064
Query 107: 0.1743                    at 0.80       0.1605
Query 108: 0.0816                    at 0.90       0.1053
Query 109: 0.2648                    at 1.00       0.0638
Query 110: 0.9021
Query 111: 0.0569                Avg. prec. (non-interpolated)
Query 112: 0.7271                for all rel. documents
Query 113: 0.0849                                  0.3200
Query 114: 0.2519                Precision:
Query 115: 0.4916                  At    5 docs:   0.4286
Query 116: 0.4120                  At   10 docs:   0.3796
Query 117: 0.3479                  At   15 docs:   0.3238
Query 118: 0.0275                  At   20 docs:   0.2980
Query 119: 0.6319                  At   30 docs:   0.2456
Query 121: 0.0976                  At  100 docs:   0.1224
Query 122: 0.0000                  At  200 docs:   0.0732
Query 123: 0.0000                  At  500 docs:   0.0350
Query 124: 0.1778                  At 1000 docs:   0.0186
Query 125: 0.6858
Query 126: 0.3434                R-Precision (prec. after R
Query 127: 0.4876                (=num_rel) docs. retrieved):
Query 128: 0.1192                    Exact:        0.3254
Query 129: 0.4143
Query 130: 0.2527
Query 131: 0.3260
Query 132: 0.5667
Query 133: 0.1901
Query 134: 0.7619
Query 135: 0.3412
Query 136: 0.4318
Query 137: 0.0842
Query 138: 0.4000
Query 139: 0.1722
Query 140: 0.1736
```

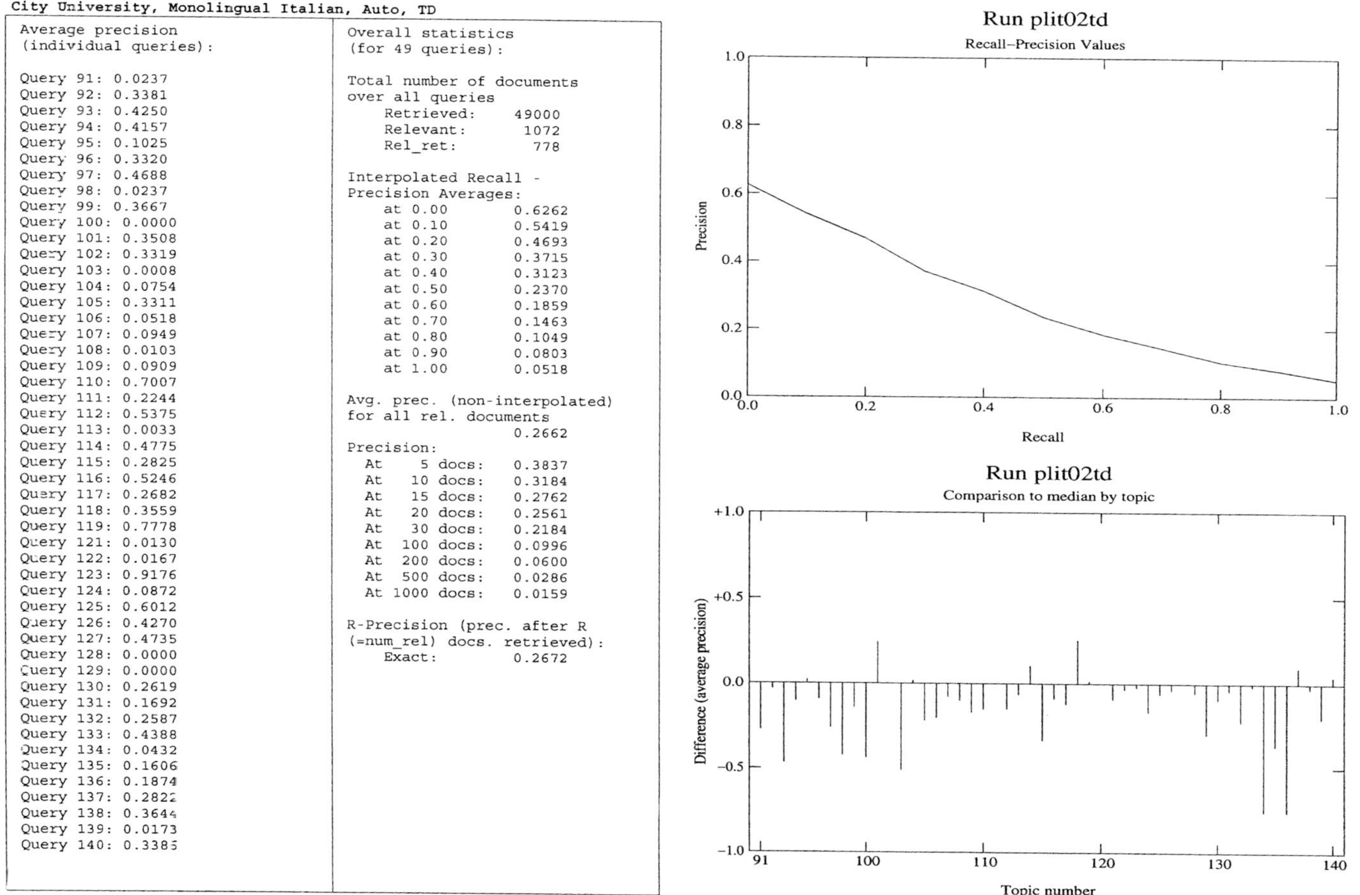

City University, Monolingual Italian, Auto, TD

```
Average precision                Overall statistics
(individual queries):            (for 49 queries):

Query 91: 0.0237                 Total number of documents
Query 92: 0.3381                 over all queries
Query 93: 0.4250                     Retrieved:     49000
Query 94: 0.4157                     Relevant:       1072
Query 95: 0.1025                     Rel_ret:         778
Query 96: 0.3320
Query 97: 0.4688                 Interpolated Recall -
Query 98: 0.0237                 Precision Averages:
Query 99: 0.3667                     at 0.00        0.6262
Query 100: 0.0000                    at 0.10        0.5419
Query 101: 0.3508                    at 0.20        0.4693
Query 102: 0.3319                    at 0.30        0.3715
Query 103: 0.0008                    at 0.40        0.3123
Query 104: 0.0754                    at 0.50        0.2370
Query 105: 0.3311                    at 0.60        0.1859
Query 106: 0.0518                    at 0.70        0.1463
Query 107: 0.0949                    at 0.80        0.1049
Query 108: 0.0103                    at 0.90        0.0803
Query 109: 0.0909                    at 1.00        0.0518
Query 110: 0.7007
Query 111: 0.2244                Avg. prec. (non-interpolated)
Query 112: 0.5375                for all rel. documents
Query 113: 0.0033                                   0.2662
Query 114: 0.4775                Precision:
Query 115: 0.2825                  At    5 docs:    0.3837
Query 116: 0.5246                  At   10 docs:    0.3184
Query 117: 0.2682                  At   15 docs:    0.2762
Query 118: 0.3559                  At   20 docs:    0.2561
Query 119: 0.7778                  At   30 docs:    0.2184
Query 121: 0.0130                  At  100 docs:    0.0996
Query 122: 0.0167                  At  200 docs:    0.0600
Query 123: 0.9176                  At  500 docs:    0.0286
Query 124: 0.0872                  At 1000 docs:    0.0159
Query 125: 0.6012
Query 126: 0.4270                R-Precision (prec. after R
Query 127: 0.4735                (=num_rel) docs. retrieved):
Query 128: 0.0000                    Exact:         0.2672
Query 129: 0.0000
Query 130: 0.2619
Query 131: 0.1692
Query 132: 0.2587
Query 133: 0.4388
Query 134: 0.0432
Query 135: 0.1606
Query 136: 0.1874
Query 137: 0.2822
Query 138: 0.3644
Query 139: 0.0173
Query 140: 0.3385
```

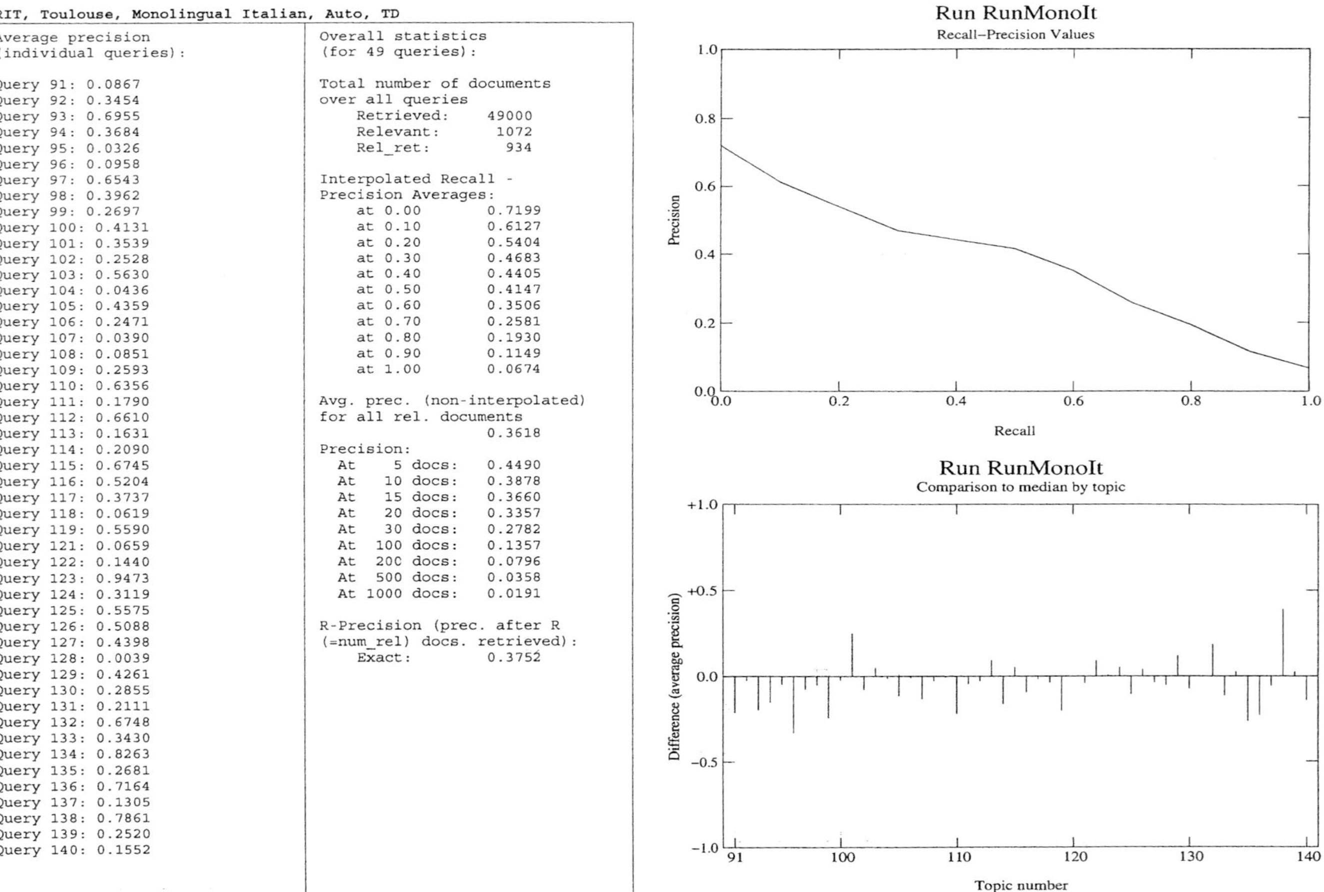

IRIT, Toulouse, Monolingual Italian, Auto, TD

```
Average precision              Overall statistics
(individual queries):          (for 49 queries):

Query 91: 0.0867               Total number of documents
Query 92: 0.3454               over all queries
Query 93: 0.6955                   Retrieved:    49000
Query 94: 0.3684                   Relevant:      1072
Query 95: 0.0326                   Rel_ret:        934
Query 96: 0.0958
Query 97: 0.6543               Interpolated Recall -
Query 98: 0.3962               Precision Averages:
Query 99: 0.2697                   at 0.00        0.7199
Query 100: 0.4131                  at 0.10        0.6127
Query 101: 0.3539                  at 0.20        0.5404
Query 102: 0.2528                  at 0.30        0.4683
Query 103: 0.5630                  at 0.40        0.4405
Query 104: 0.0436                  at 0.50        0.4147
Query 105: 0.4359                  at 0.60        0.3506
Query 106: 0.2471                  at 0.70        0.2581
Query 107: 0.0390                  at 0.80        0.1930
Query 108: 0.0851                  at 0.90        0.1149
Query 109: 0.2593                  at 1.00        0.0674
Query 110: 0.6356
Query 111: 0.1790              Avg. prec. (non-interpolated)
Query 112: 0.6610              for all rel. documents
Query 113: 0.1631                                 0.3618
Query 114: 0.2090              Precision:
Query 115: 0.6745                At     5 docs:   0.4490
Query 116: 0.5204                At    10 docs:   0.3878
Query 117: 0.3737                At    15 docs:   0.3660
Query 118: 0.0619                At    20 docs:   0.3357
Query 119: 0.5590                At    30 docs:   0.2782
Query 121: 0.0659                At   100 docs:   0.1357
Query 122: 0.1440                At   200 docs:   0.0796
Query 123: 0.9473                At   500 docs:   0.0358
Query 124: 0.3119                At  1000 docs:   0.0191
Query 125: 0.5575
Query 126: 0.5088              R-Precision (prec. after R
Query 127: 0.4398              (=num_rel) docs. retrieved):
Query 128: 0.0039                  Exact:         0.3752
Query 129: 0.4261
Query 130: 0.2855
Query 131: 0.2111
Query 132: 0.6748
Query 133: 0.3430
Query 134: 0.8263
Query 135: 0.2681
Query 136: 0.7164
Query 137: 0.1305
Query 138: 0.7861
Query 139: 0.2520
Query 140: 0.1552
```

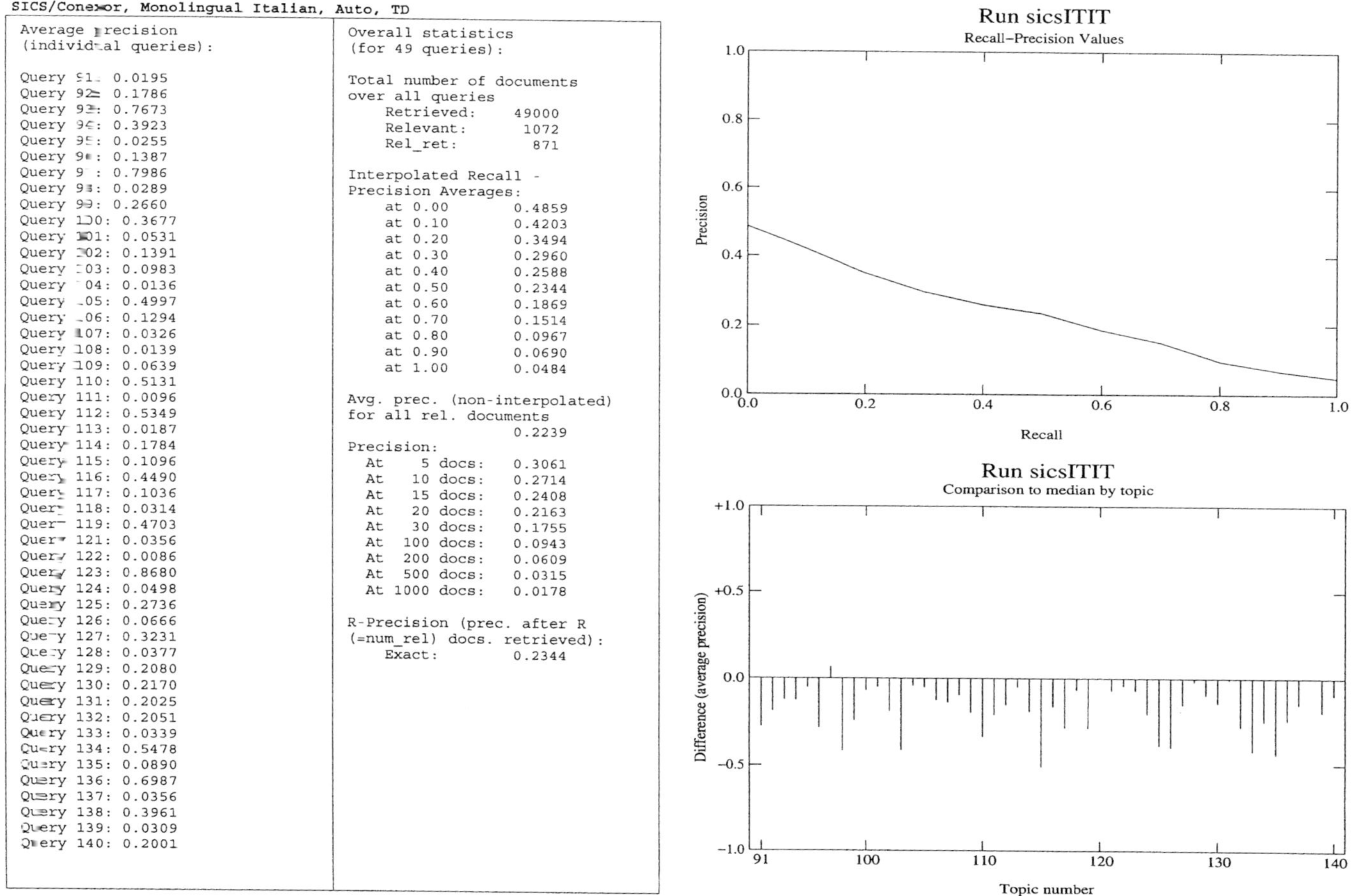

SICS/Conexor, Monolingual Italian, Auto, TD

```
Average precision                 Overall statistics
(individual queries):             (for 49 queries):

Query 91: 0.0195                  Total number of documents
Query 92: 0.1786                  over all queries
Query 93: 0.7673                      Retrieved:     49000
Query 94: 0.3923                      Relevant:       1072
Query 95: 0.0255                      Rel_ret:         871
Query 96: 0.1387
Query 97: 0.7986                  Interpolated Recall -
Query 98: 0.0289                  Precision Averages:
Query 99: 0.2660                      at 0.00        0.4859
Query 100: 0.3677                     at 0.10        0.4203
Query 101: 0.0531                     at 0.20        0.3494
Query 102: 0.1391                     at 0.30        0.2960
Query 103: 0.0983                     at 0.40        0.2588
Query 104: 0.0136                     at 0.50        0.2344
Query 105: 0.4997                     at 0.60        0.1869
Query 106: 0.1294                     at 0.70        0.1514
Query 107: 0.0326                     at 0.80        0.0967
Query 108: 0.0139                     at 0.90        0.0690
Query 109: 0.0639                     at 1.00        0.0484
Query 110: 0.5131
Query 111: 0.0096                 Avg. prec. (non-interpolated)
Query 112: 0.5349                 for all rel. documents
Query 113: 0.0187                                    0.2239
Query 114: 0.1784                 Precision:
Query 115: 0.1096                   At    5 docs:    0.3061
Query 116: 0.4490                   At   10 docs:    0.2714
Query 117: 0.1036                   At   15 docs:    0.2408
Query 118: 0.0314                   At   20 docs:    0.2163
Query 119: 0.4703                   At   30 docs:    0.1755
Query 121: 0.0356                   At  100 docs:    0.0943
Query 122: 0.0086                   At  200 docs:    0.0609
Query 123: 0.8680                   At  500 docs:    0.0315
Query 124: 0.0498                   At 1000 docs:    0.0178
Query 125: 0.2736
Query 126: 0.0666                 R-Precision (prec. after R
Query 127: 0.3231                 (=num_rel) docs. retrieved):
Query 128: 0.0377                     Exact:         0.2344
Query 129: 0.2080
Query 130: 0.2170
Query 131: 0.2025
Query 132: 0.2051
Query 133: 0.0339
Query 134: 0.5478
Query 135: 0.0890
Query 136: 0.6987
Query 137: 0.0356
Query 138: 0.3961
Query 139: 0.0309
Query 140: 0.2001
```

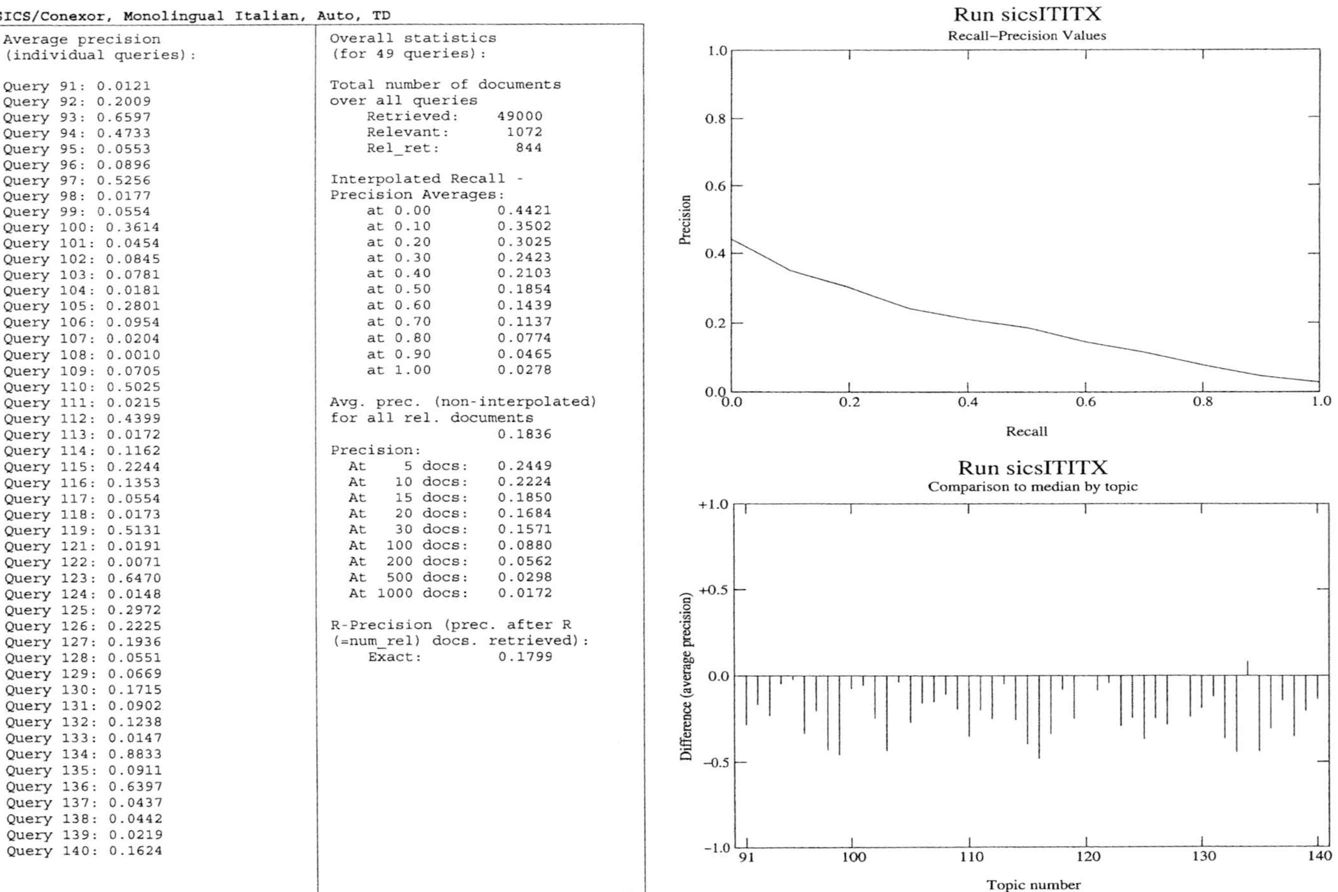

SICS/Conexor, Monolingual Italian, Auto, TD

```
Average precision                 Overall statistics
(individual queries):             (for 49 queries):

Query 91: 0.0121                  Total number of documents
Query 92: 0.2009                  over all queries
Query 93: 0.6597                      Retrieved:     49000
Query 94: 0.4733                      Relevant:       1072
Query 95: 0.0553                      Rel_ret:         844
Query 96: 0.0896
Query 97: 0.5256                  Interpolated Recall -
Query 98: 0.0177                  Precision Averages:
Query 99: 0.0554                      at 0.00        0.4421
Query 100: 0.3614                     at 0.10        0.3502
Query 101: 0.0454                     at 0.20        0.3025
Query 102: 0.0845                     at 0.30        0.2423
Query 103: 0.0781                     at 0.40        0.2103
Query 104: 0.0181                     at 0.50        0.1854
Query 105: 0.2801                     at 0.60        0.1439
Query 106: 0.0954                     at 0.70        0.1137
Query 107: 0.0204                     at 0.80        0.0774
Query 108: 0.0010                     at 0.90        0.0465
Query 109: 0.0705                     at 1.00        0.0278
Query 110: 0.5025
Query 111: 0.0215                 Avg. prec. (non-interpolated)
Query 112: 0.4399                 for all rel. documents
Query 113: 0.0172                                    0.1836
Query 114: 0.1162                 Precision:
Query 115: 0.2244                   At    5 docs:    0.2449
Query 116: 0.1353                   At   10 docs:    0.2224
Query 117: 0.0554                   At   15 docs:    0.1850
Query 118: 0.0173                   At   20 docs:    0.1684
Query 119: 0.5131                   At   30 docs:    0.1571
Query 121: 0.0191                   At  100 docs:    0.0880
Query 122: 0.0071                   At  200 docs:    0.0562
Query 123: 0.6470                   At  500 docs:    0.0298
Query 124: 0.0148                   At 1000 docs:    0.0172
Query 125: 0.2972
Query 126: 0.2225                 R-Precision (prec. after R
Query 127: 0.1936                 (=num_rel) docs. retrieved):
Query 128: 0.0551                     Exact:         0.1799
Query 129: 0.0669
Query 130: 0.1715
Query 131: 0.0902
Query 132: 0.1238
Query 133: 0.0147
Query 134: 0.8833
Query 135: 0.0911
Query 136: 0.6397
Query 137: 0.0437
Query 138: 0.0442
Query 139: 0.0219
Query 140: 0.1624
```

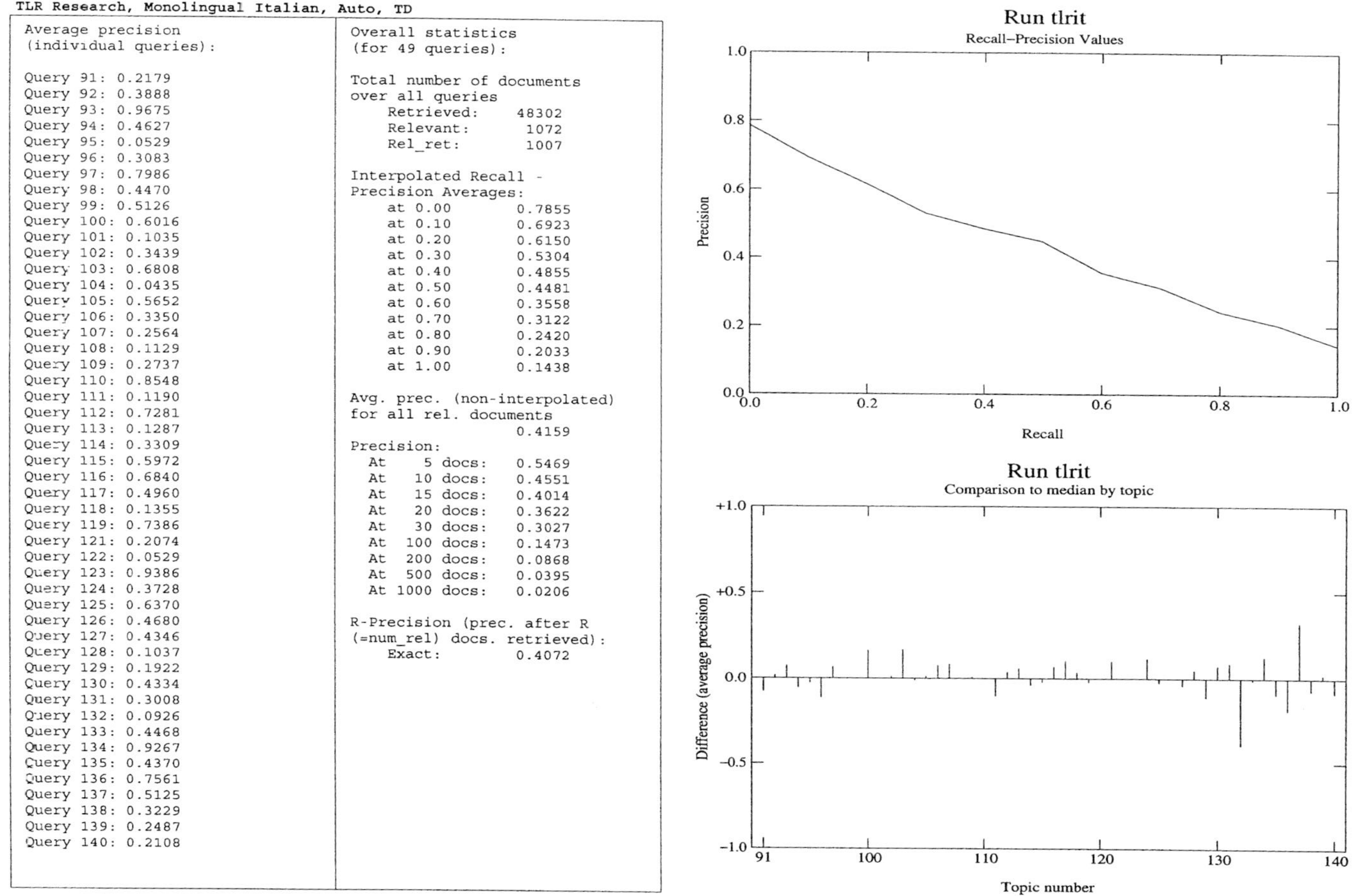

TLR Research, Monolingual Italian, Auto, TD

```
Average precision                  Overall statistics
(individual queries):              (for 49 queries):

Query 91: 0.2179                   Total number of documents
Query 92: 0.3888                   over all queries
Query 93: 0.9675                       Retrieved:     48302
Query 94: 0.4627                       Relevant:       1072
Query 95: 0.0529                       Rel_ret:        1007
Query 96: 0.3083
Query 97: 0.7986                   Interpolated Recall -
Query 98: 0.4470                   Precision Averages:
Query 99: 0.5126                       at 0.00        0.7855
Query 100: 0.6016                      at 0.10        0.6923
Query 101: 0.1035                      at 0.20        0.6150
Query 102: 0.3439                      at 0.30        0.5304
Query 103: 0.6808                      at 0.40        0.4855
Query 104: 0.0435                      at 0.50        0.4481
Query 105: 0.5652                      at 0.60        0.3558
Query 106: 0.3350                      at 0.70        0.3122
Query 107: 0.2564                      at 0.80        0.2420
Query 108: 0.1129                      at 0.90        0.2033
Query 109: 0.2737                      at 1.00        0.1438
Query 110: 0.8548
Query 111: 0.1190                  Avg. prec. (non-interpolated)
Query 112: 0.7281                  for all rel. documents
Query 113: 0.1287                                     0.4159
Query 114: 0.3309                  Precision:
Query 115: 0.5972                    At    5 docs:    0.5469
Query 116: 0.6840                    At   10 docs:    0.4551
Query 117: 0.4960                    At   15 docs:    0.4014
Query 118: 0.1355                    At   20 docs:    0.3622
Query 119: 0.7386                    At   30 docs:    0.3027
Query 121: 0.2074                    At  100 docs:    0.1473
Query 122: 0.0529                    At  200 docs:    0.0868
Query 123: 0.9386                    At  500 docs:    0.0395
Query 124: 0.3728                    At 1000 docs:    0.0206
Query 125: 0.6370
Query 126: 0.4680                  R-Precision (prec. after R
Query 127: 0.4346                  (=num_rel) docs. retrieved):
Query 128: 0.1037                      Exact:         0.4072
Query 129: 0.1922
Query 130: 0.4334
Query 131: 0.3008
Query 132: 0.0926
Query 133: 0.4468
Query 134: 0.9267
Query 135: 0.4370
Query 136: 0.7561
Query 137: 0.5125
Query 138: 0.3229
Query 139: 0.2487
Query 140: 0.2108
```

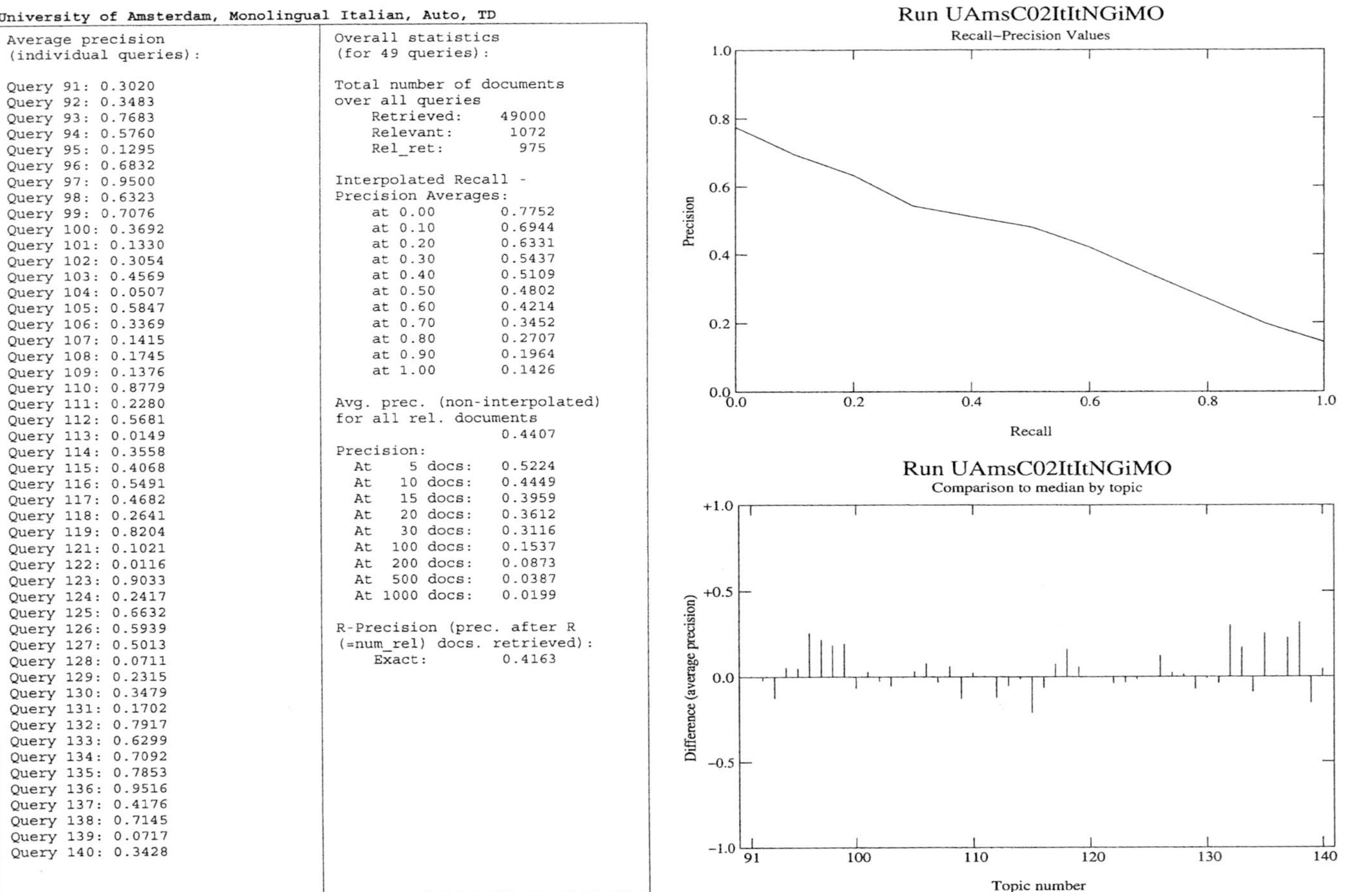

University of Amsterdam, Monolingual Italian, Auto, TD

Average precision (individual queries):	Overall statistics (for 49 queries):
Query 91: 0.3020	Total number of documents over all queries
Query 92: 0.3483	Retrieved: 49000
Query 93: 0.7683	Relevant: 1072
Query 94: 0.5760	Rel_ret: 975
Query 95: 0.1295	
Query 96: 0.6832	Interpolated Recall - Precision Averages:
Query 97: 0.9500	at 0.00 0.7752
Query 98: 0.6323	at 0.10 0.6944
Query 99: 0.7076	at 0.20 0.6331
Query 100: 0.3692	at 0.30 0.5437
Query 101: 0.1330	at 0.40 0.5109
Query 102: 0.3054	at 0.50 0.4802
Query 103: 0.4569	at 0.60 0.4214
Query 104: 0.0507	at 0.70 0.3452
Query 105: 0.5847	at 0.80 0.2707
Query 106: 0.3369	at 0.90 0.1964
Query 107: 0.1415	at 1.00 0.1426
Query 108: 0.1745	
Query 109: 0.1376	Avg. prec. (non-interpolated) for all rel. documents
Query 110: 0.8779	0.4407
Query 111: 0.2280	Precision:
Query 112: 0.5681	At 5 docs: 0.5224
Query 113: 0.0149	At 10 docs: 0.4449
Query 114: 0.3558	At 15 docs: 0.3959
Query 115: 0.4068	At 20 docs: 0.3612
Query 116: 0.5491	At 30 docs: 0.3116
Query 117: 0.4682	At 100 docs: 0.1537
Query 118: 0.2641	At 200 docs: 0.0873
Query 119: 0.8204	At 500 docs: 0.0387
Query 121: 0.1021	At 1000 docs: 0.0199
Query 122: 0.0116	
Query 123: 0.9033	R-Precision (prec. after R (=num_rel) docs. retrieved):
Query 124: 0.2417	Exact: 0.4163
Query 125: 0.6632	
Query 126: 0.5939	
Query 127: 0.5013	
Query 128: 0.0711	
Query 129: 0.2315	
Query 130: 0.3479	
Query 131: 0.1702	
Query 132: 0.7917	
Query 133: 0.6299	
Query 134: 0.7092	
Query 135: 0.7853	
Query 136: 0.9516	
Query 137: 0.4176	
Query 138: 0.7145	
Query 139: 0.0717	
Query 140: 0.3428	

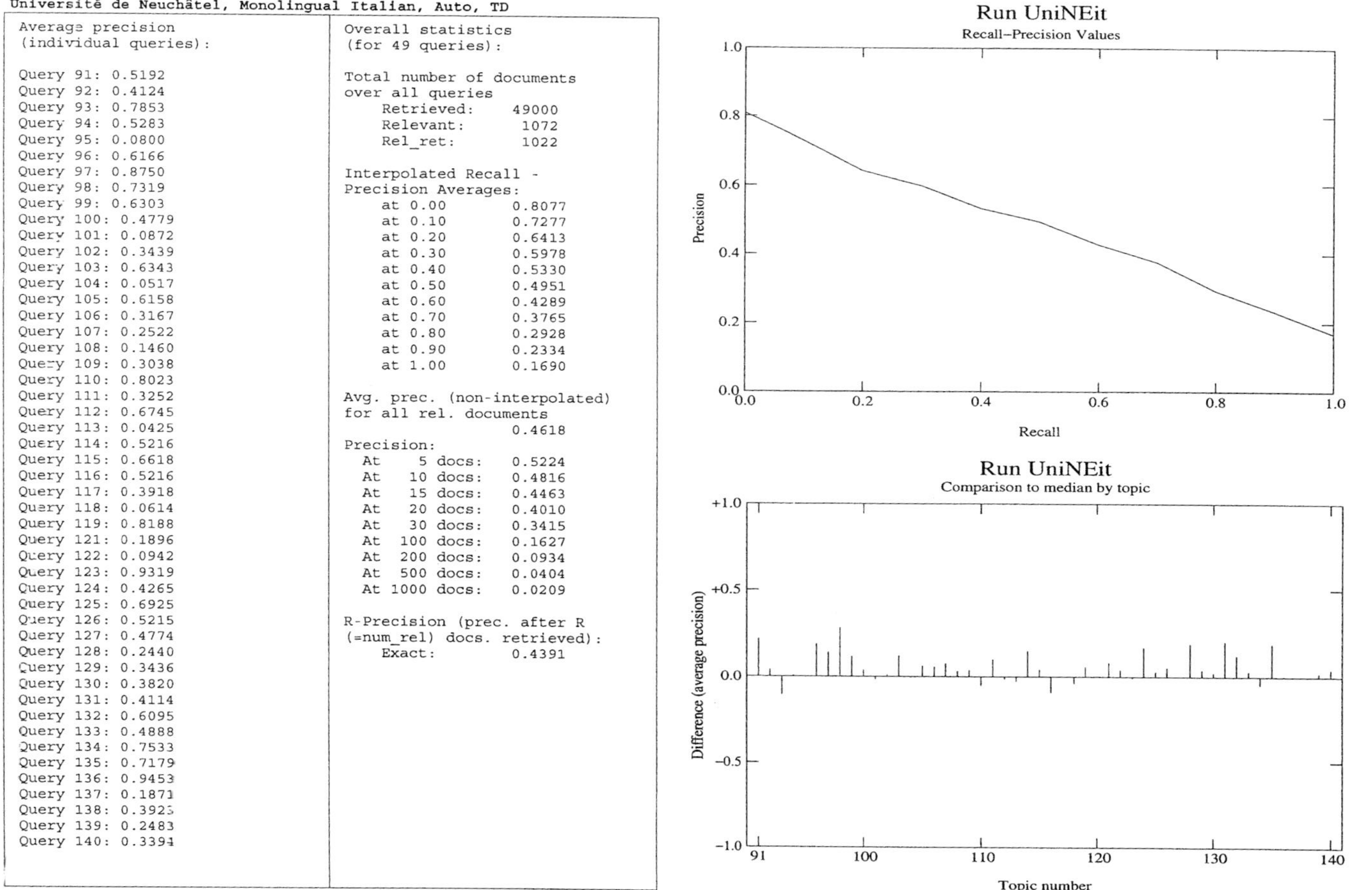

Université de Neuchâtel, Monolingual Italian, Auto, TD

Average precision (individual queries):	Overall statistics (for 49 queries):
Query 91: 0.5192	Total number of documents over all queries
Query 92: 0.4124	Retrieved: 49000
Query 93: 0.7853	Relevant: 1072
Query 94: 0.5283	Rel_ret: 1022
Query 95: 0.0800	
Query 96: 0.6166	Interpolated Recall - Precision Averages:
Query 97: 0.8750	at 0.00 0.8077
Query 98: 0.7319	at 0.10 0.7277
Query 99: 0.6303	at 0.20 0.6413
Query 100: 0.4779	at 0.30 0.5978
Query 101: 0.0872	at 0.40 0.5330
Query 102: 0.3439	at 0.50 0.4951
Query 103: 0.6343	at 0.60 0.4289
Query 104: 0.0517	at 0.70 0.3765
Query 105: 0.6158	at 0.80 0.2928
Query 106: 0.3167	at 0.90 0.2334
Query 107: 0.2522	at 1.00 0.1690
Query 108: 0.1460	
Query 109: 0.3038	Avg. prec. (non-interpolated) for all rel. documents 0.4618
Query 110: 0.8023	
Query 111: 0.3252	Precision:
Query 112: 0.6745	At 5 docs: 0.5224
Query 113: 0.0425	At 10 docs: 0.4816
Query 114: 0.5216	At 15 docs: 0.4463
Query 115: 0.6618	At 20 docs: 0.4010
Query 116: 0.5216	At 30 docs: 0.3415
Query 117: 0.3918	At 100 docs: 0.1627
Query 118: 0.0614	At 200 docs: 0.0934
Query 119: 0.8188	At 500 docs: 0.0404
Query 121: 0.1896	At 1000 docs: 0.0209
Query 122: 0.0942	
Query 123: 0.9319	R-Precision (prec. after R (=num_rel) docs. retrieved):
Query 124: 0.4265	Exact: 0.4391
Query 125: 0.6925	
Query 126: 0.5215	
Query 127: 0.4774	
Query 128: 0.2440	
Query 129: 0.3436	
Query 130: 0.3820	
Query 131: 0.4114	
Query 132: 0.6095	
Query 133: 0.4888	
Query 134: 0.7533	
Query 135: 0.7179	
Query 136: 0.9453	
Query 137: 0.1871	
Query 138: 0.3923	
Query 139: 0.2483	
Query 140: 0.3394	

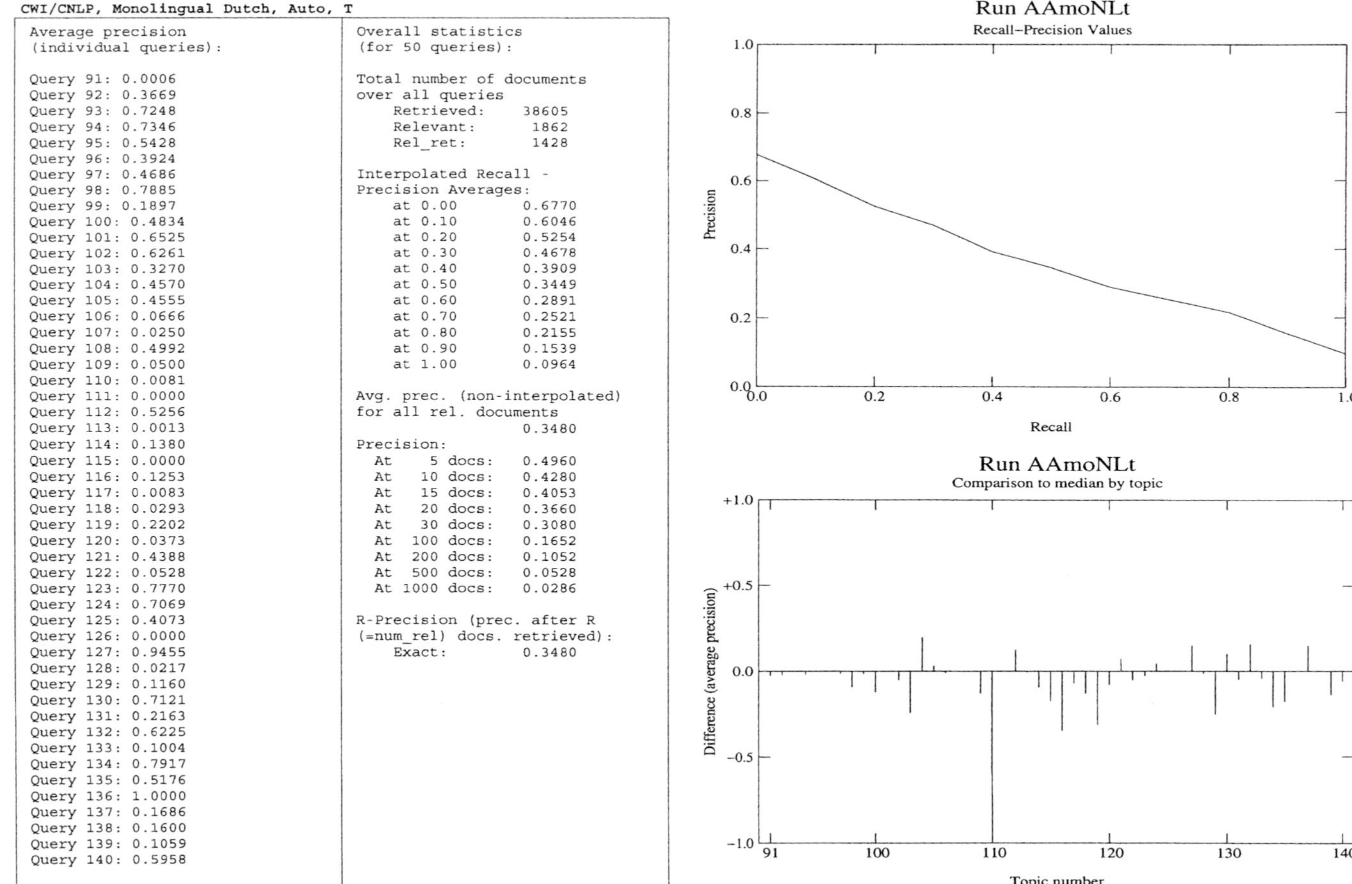

CWI/CNLP, Monolingual Dutch, Auto, T

```
Average precision                 Overall statistics
(individual queries):             (for 50 queries):

Query 91: 0.0006                  Total number of documents
Query 92: 0.3669                  over all queries
Query 93: 0.7248                      Retrieved:    38605
Query 94: 0.7346                      Relevant:      1862
Query 95: 0.5428                      Rel_ret:       1428
Query 96: 0.3924
Query 97: 0.4686                  Interpolated Recall -
Query 98: 0.7885                  Precision Averages:
Query 99: 0.1897                      at 0.00        0.6770
Query 100: 0.4834                     at 0.10        0.6046
Query 101: 0.6525                     at 0.20        0.5254
Query 102: 0.6261                     at 0.30        0.4678
Query 103: 0.3270                     at 0.40        0.3909
Query 104: 0.4570                     at 0.50        0.3449
Query 105: 0.4555                     at 0.60        0.2891
Query 106: 0.0666                     at 0.70        0.2521
Query 107: 0.0250                     at 0.80        0.2155
Query 108: 0.4992                     at 0.90        0.1539
Query 109: 0.0500                     at 1.00        0.0964
Query 110: 0.0081
Query 111: 0.0000                 Avg. prec. (non-interpolated)
Query 112: 0.5256                 for all rel. documents
Query 113: 0.0013                                    0.3480
Query 114: 0.1380                 Precision:
Query 115: 0.0000                   At    5 docs:    0.4960
Query 116: 0.1253                   At   10 docs:    0.4280
Query 117: 0.0083                   At   15 docs:    0.4053
Query 118: 0.0293                   At   20 docs:    0.3660
Query 119: 0.2202                   At   30 docs:    0.3080
Query 120: 0.0373                   At  100 docs:    0.1652
Query 121: 0.4388                   At  200 docs:    0.1052
Query 122: 0.0528                   At  500 docs:    0.0528
Query 123: 0.7770                   At 1000 docs:    0.0286
Query 124: 0.7069
Query 125: 0.4073                 R-Precision (prec. after R
Query 126: 0.0000                 (=num_rel) docs. retrieved):
Query 127: 0.9455                     Exact:         0.3480
Query 128: 0.0217
Query 129: 0.1160
Query 130: 0.7121
Query 131: 0.2163
Query 132: 0.6225
Query 133: 0.1004
Query 134: 0.7917
Query 135: 0.5176
Query 136: 1.0000
Query 137: 0.1686
Query 138: 0.1600
Query 139: 0.1059
Query 140: 0.5958
```

CWI/CNLP, Monolingual Dutch, Auto, TD

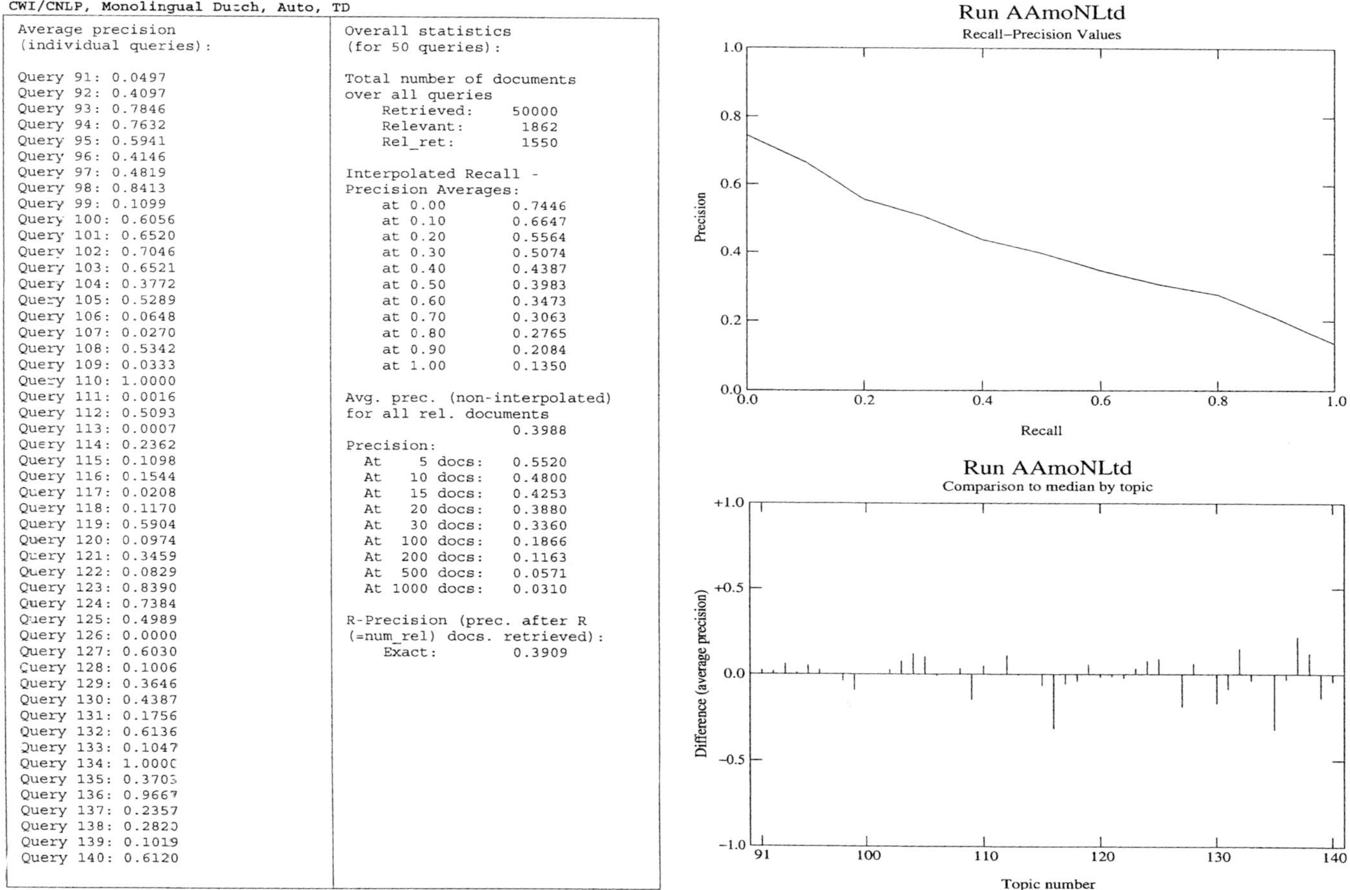

Average precision (individual queries):	Overall statistics (for 50 queries):
Query 91: 0.0497	Total number of documents over all queries
Query 92: 0.4097	Retrieved: 50000
Query 93: 0.7846	Relevant: 1862
Query 94: 0.7632	Rel_ret: 1550
Query 95: 0.5941	
Query 96: 0.4146	Interpolated Recall - Precision Averages:
Query 97: 0.4819	at 0.00 0.7446
Query 98: 0.8413	at 0.10 0.6647
Query 99: 0.1099	at 0.20 0.5564
Query 100: 0.6056	at 0.30 0.5074
Query 101: 0.6520	at 0.40 0.4387
Query 102: 0.7046	at 0.50 0.3983
Query 103: 0.6521	at 0.60 0.3473
Query 104: 0.3772	at 0.70 0.3063
Query 105: 0.5289	at 0.80 0.2765
Query 106: 0.0648	at 0.90 0.2084
Query 107: 0.0270	at 1.00 0.1350
Query 108: 0.5342	
Query 109: 0.0333	Avg. prec. (non-interpolated) for all rel. documents 0.3988
Query 110: 1.0000	
Query 111: 0.0016	Precision:
Query 112: 0.5093	At 5 docs: 0.5520
Query 113: 0.0007	At 10 docs: 0.4800
Query 114: 0.2362	At 15 docs: 0.4253
Query 115: 0.1098	At 20 docs: 0.3880
Query 116: 0.1544	At 30 docs: 0.3360
Query 117: 0.0208	At 100 docs: 0.1866
Query 118: 0.1170	At 200 docs: 0.1163
Query 119: 0.5904	At 500 docs: 0.0571
Query 120: 0.0974	At 1000 docs: 0.0310
Query 121: 0.3459	
Query 122: 0.0829	R-Precision (prec. after R (=num_rel) docs. retrieved):
Query 123: 0.8390	Exact: 0.3909
Query 124: 0.7384	
Query 125: 0.4989	
Query 126: 0.0000	
Query 127: 0.6030	
Query 128: 0.1006	
Query 129: 0.3646	
Query 130: 0.4387	
Query 131: 0.1756	
Query 132: 0.6136	
Query 133: 0.1047	
Query 134: 1.0000	
Query 135: 0.3703	
Query 136: 0.9667	
Query 137: 0.2357	
Query 138: 0.2820	
Query 139: 0.1019	
Query 140: 0.6120	

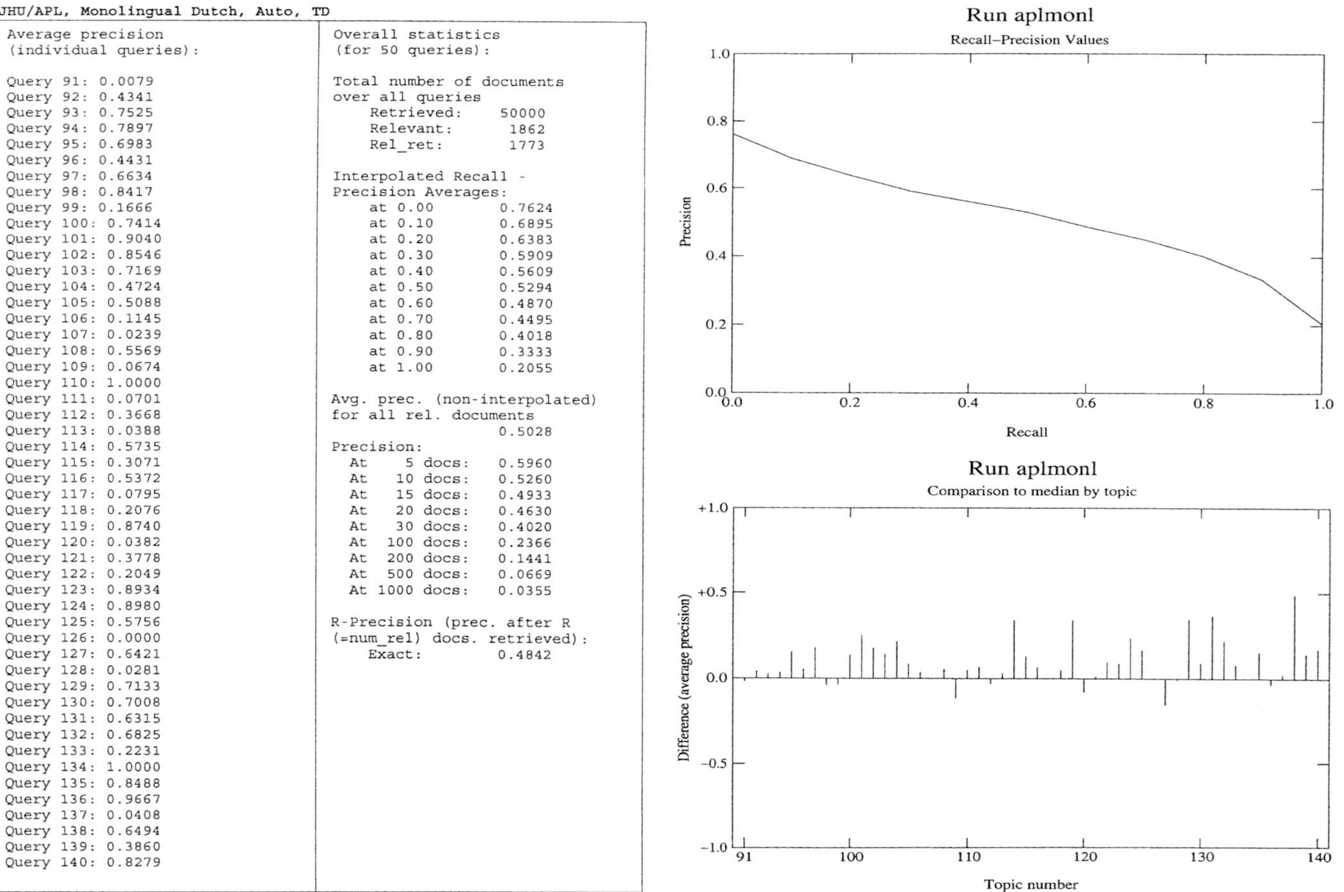

JHU/APL, Monolingual Dutch, Auto, TD

```
Average precision                 Overall statistics
(individual queries):             (for 50 queries):

Query 91: 0.0079                  Total number of documents
Query 92: 0.4341                  over all queries
Query 93: 0.7525                      Retrieved:    50000
Query 94: 0.7897                      Relevant:      1862
Query 95: 0.6983                      Rel_ret:       1773
Query 96: 0.4431
Query 97: 0.6634                  Interpolated Recall -
Query 98: 0.8417                  Precision Averages:
Query 99: 0.1666                      at 0.00       0.7624
Query 100: 0.7414                     at 0.10       0.6895
Query 101: 0.9040                     at 0.20       0.6383
Query 102: 0.8546                     at 0.30       0.5909
Query 103: 0.7169                     at 0.40       0.5609
Query 104: 0.4724                     at 0.50       0.5294
Query 105: 0.5088                     at 0.60       0.4870
Query 106: 0.1145                     at 0.70       0.4495
Query 107: 0.0239                     at 0.80       0.4018
Query 108: 0.5569                     at 0.90       0.3333
Query 109: 0.0674                     at 1.00       0.2055
Query 110: 1.0000
Query 111: 0.0701                 Avg. prec. (non-interpolated)
Query 112: 0.3668                 for all rel. documents
Query 113: 0.0388                                   0.5028
Query 114: 0.5735                 Precision:
Query 115: 0.3071                   At    5 docs:   0.5960
Query 116: 0.5372                   At   10 docs:   0.5260
Query 117: 0.0795                   At   15 docs:   0.4933
Query 118: 0.2076                   At   20 docs:   0.4630
Query 119: 0.8740                   At   30 docs:   0.4020
Query 120: 0.0382                   At  100 docs:   0.2366
Query 121: 0.3778                   At  200 docs:   0.1441
Query 122: 0.2049                   At  500 docs:   0.0669
Query 123: 0.8934                   At 1000 docs:   0.0355
Query 124: 0.8980
Query 125: 0.5756                 R-Precision (prec. after R
Query 126: 0.0000                 (=num_rel) docs. retrieved):
Query 127: 0.6421                     Exact:        0.4842
Query 128: 0.0281
Query 129: 0.7133
Query 130: 0.7008
Query 131: 0.6315
Query 132: 0.6825
Query 133: 0.2231
Query 134: 1.0000
Query 135: 0.8488
Query 136: 0.9667
Query 137: 0.0408
Query 138: 0.6494
Query 139: 0.3860
Query 140: 0.8279
```

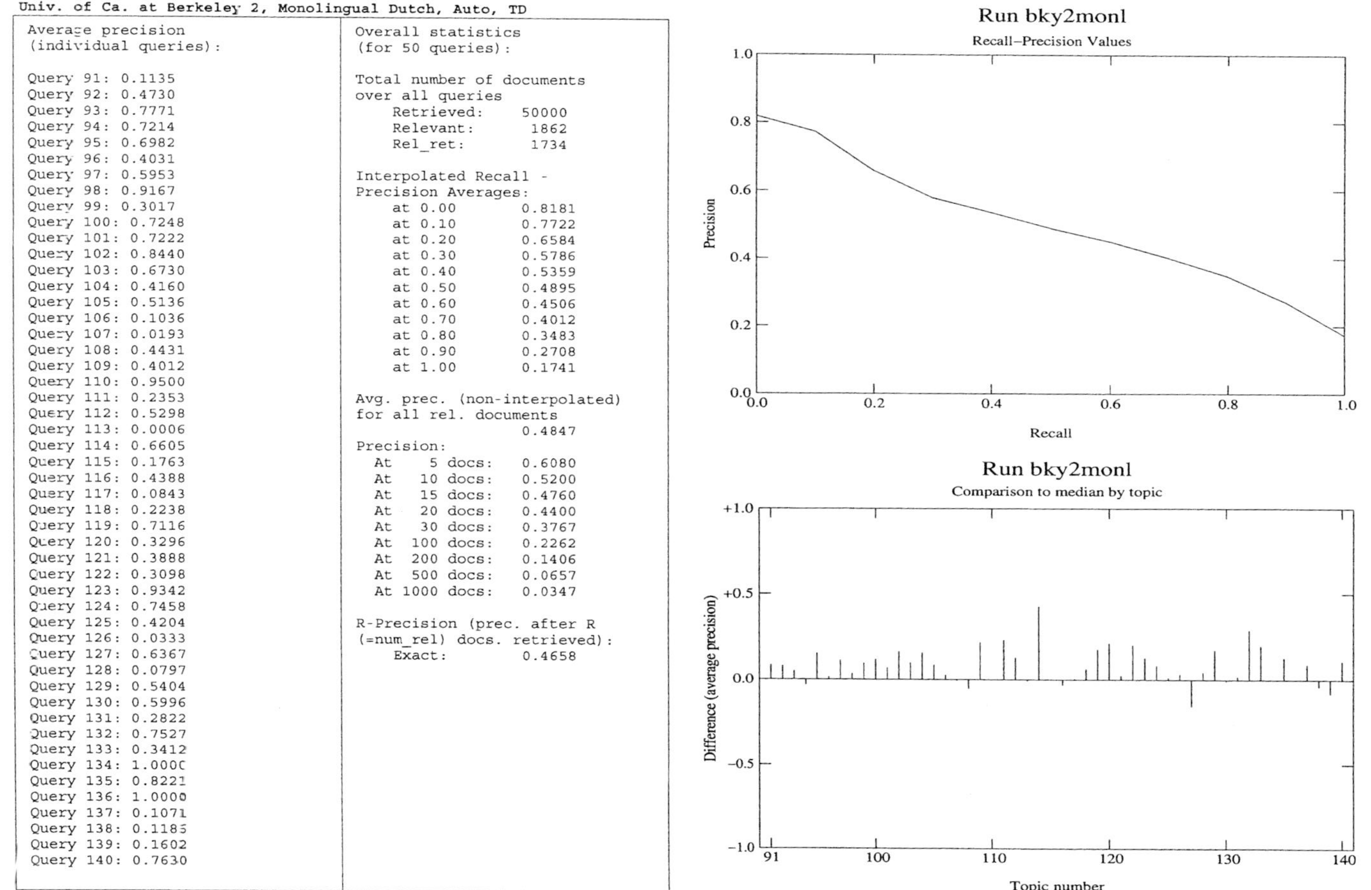

Univ. of Ca. at Berkeley 2, Monolingual Dutch, Auto, TD

```
Average precision                 Overall statistics
(individual queries):             (for 50 queries):

Query 91: 0.1135                  Total number of documents
Query 92: 0.4730                  over all queries
Query 93: 0.7771                      Retrieved:     50000
Query 94: 0.7214                      Relevant:       1862
Query 95: 0.6982                      Rel_ret:        1734
Query 96: 0.4031
Query 97: 0.5953                  Interpolated Recall -
Query 98: 0.9167                  Precision Averages:
Query 99: 0.3017                      at 0.00        0.8181
Query 100: 0.7248                     at 0.10        0.7722
Query 101: 0.7222                     at 0.20        0.6584
Query 102: 0.8440                     at 0.30        0.5786
Query 103: 0.6730                     at 0.40        0.5359
Query 104: 0.4160                     at 0.50        0.4895
Query 105: 0.5136                     at 0.60        0.4506
Query 106: 0.1036                     at 0.70        0.4012
Query 107: 0.0193                     at 0.80        0.3483
Query 108: 0.4431                     at 0.90        0.2708
Query 109: 0.4012                     at 1.00        0.1741
Query 110: 0.9500
Query 111: 0.2353                 Avg. prec. (non-interpolated)
Query 112: 0.5298                 for all rel. documents
Query 113: 0.0006                                    0.4847
Query 114: 0.6605                 Precision:
Query 115: 0.1763                   At    5 docs:    0.6080
Query 116: 0.4388                   At   10 docs:    0.5200
Query 117: 0.0843                   At   15 docs:    0.4760
Query 118: 0.2238                   At   20 docs:    0.4400
Query 119: 0.7116                   At   30 docs:    0.3767
Query 120: 0.3296                   At  100 docs:    0.2262
Query 121: 0.3888                   At  200 docs:    0.1406
Query 122: 0.3098                   At  500 docs:    0.0657
Query 123: 0.9342                   At 1000 docs:    0.0347
Query 124: 0.7458
Query 125: 0.4204                 R-Precision (prec. after R
Query 126: 0.0333                 (=num_rel) docs. retrieved):
Query 127: 0.6367                     Exact:         0.4658
Query 128: 0.0797
Query 129: 0.5404
Query 130: 0.5996
Query 131: 0.2822
Query 132: 0.7527
Query 133: 0.3412
Query 134: 1.0000
Query 135: 0.8221
Query 136: 1.0000
Query 137: 0.1071
Query 138: 0.1185
Query 139: 0.1602
Query 140: 0.7630
```

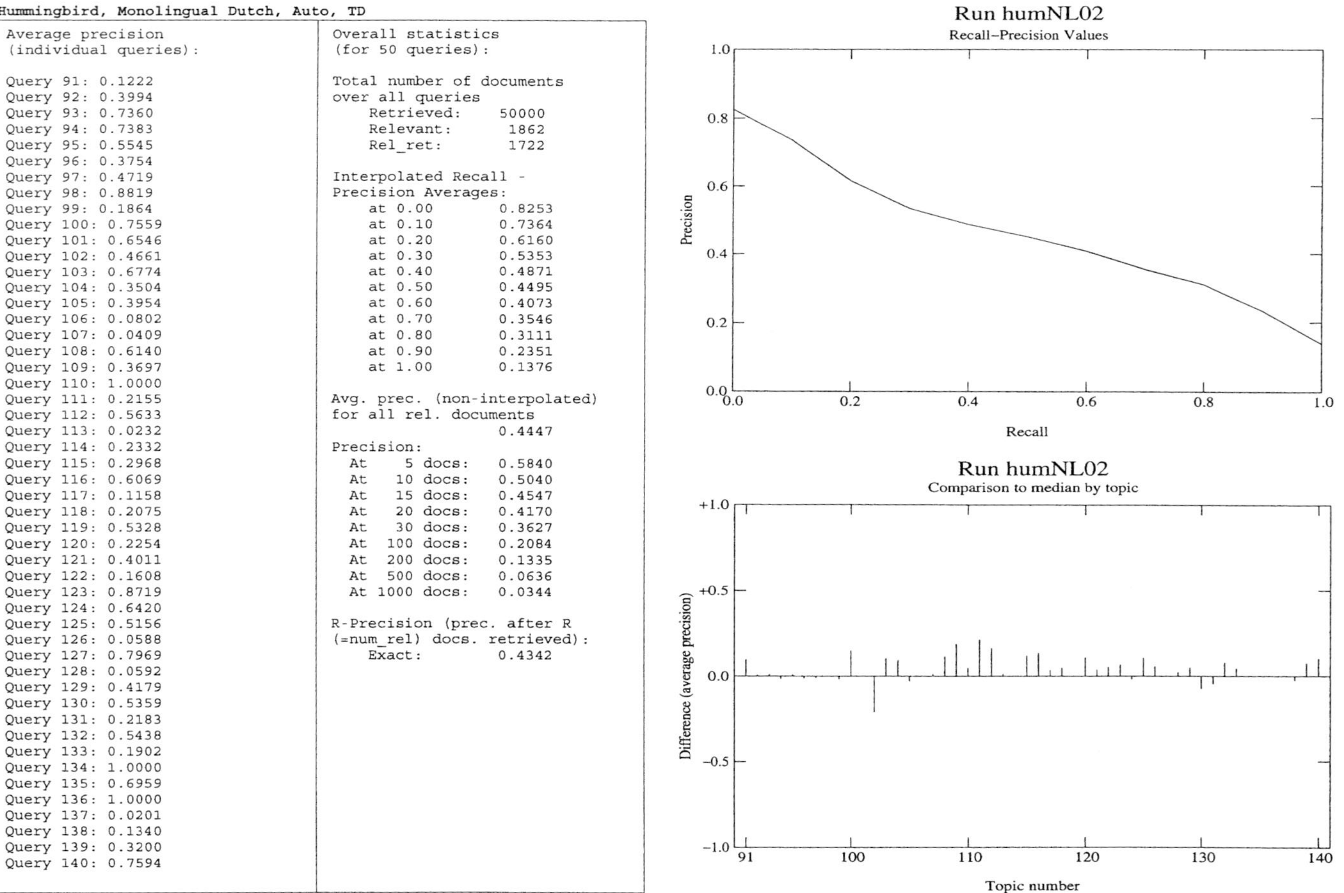

Hummingbird, Monolingual Dutch, Auto, TD

```
Average precision                Overall statistics
(individual queries):            (for 50 queries):

Query 91: 0.1222                 Total number of documents
Query 92: 0.3994                 over all queries
Query 93: 0.7360                     Retrieved:    50000
Query 94: 0.7383                     Relevant:      1862
Query 95: 0.5545                     Rel_ret:       1722
Query 96: 0.3754
Query 97: 0.4719                 Interpolated Recall -
Query 98: 0.8819                 Precision Averages:
Query 99: 0.1864                     at 0.00       0.8253
Query 100: 0.7559                    at 0.10       0.7364
Query 101: 0.6546                    at 0.20       0.6160
Query 102: 0.4661                    at 0.30       0.5353
Query 103: 0.6774                    at 0.40       0.4871
Query 104: 0.3504                    at 0.50       0.4495
Query 105: 0.3954                    at 0.60       0.4073
Query 106: 0.0802                    at 0.70       0.3546
Query 107: 0.0409                    at 0.80       0.3111
Query 108: 0.6140                    at 0.90       0.2351
Query 109: 0.3697                    at 1.00       0.1376
Query 110: 1.0000
Query 111: 0.2155                Avg. prec. (non-interpolated)
Query 112: 0.5633                for all rel. documents
Query 113: 0.0232                                  0.4447
Query 114: 0.2332                Precision:
Query 115: 0.2968                  At    5 docs:   0.5840
Query 116: 0.6069                  At   10 docs:   0.5040
Query 117: 0.1158                  At   15 docs:   0.4547
Query 118: 0.2075                  At   20 docs:   0.4170
Query 119: 0.5328                  At   30 docs:   0.3627
Query 120: 0.2254                  At  100 docs:   0.2084
Query 121: 0.4011                  At  200 docs:   0.1335
Query 122: 0.1608                  At  500 docs:   0.0636
Query 123: 0.8719                  At 1000 docs:   0.0344
Query 124: 0.6420
Query 125: 0.5156                R-Precision (prec. after R
Query 126: 0.0588                (=num_rel) docs. retrieved):
Query 127: 0.7969                    Exact:        0.4342
Query 128: 0.0592
Query 129: 0.4179
Query 130: 0.5359
Query 131: 0.2183
Query 132: 0.5438
Query 133: 0.1902
Query 134: 1.0000
Query 135: 0.6959
Query 136: 1.0000
Query 137: 0.0201
Query 138: 0.1340
Query 139: 0.3200
Query 140: 0.7594
```

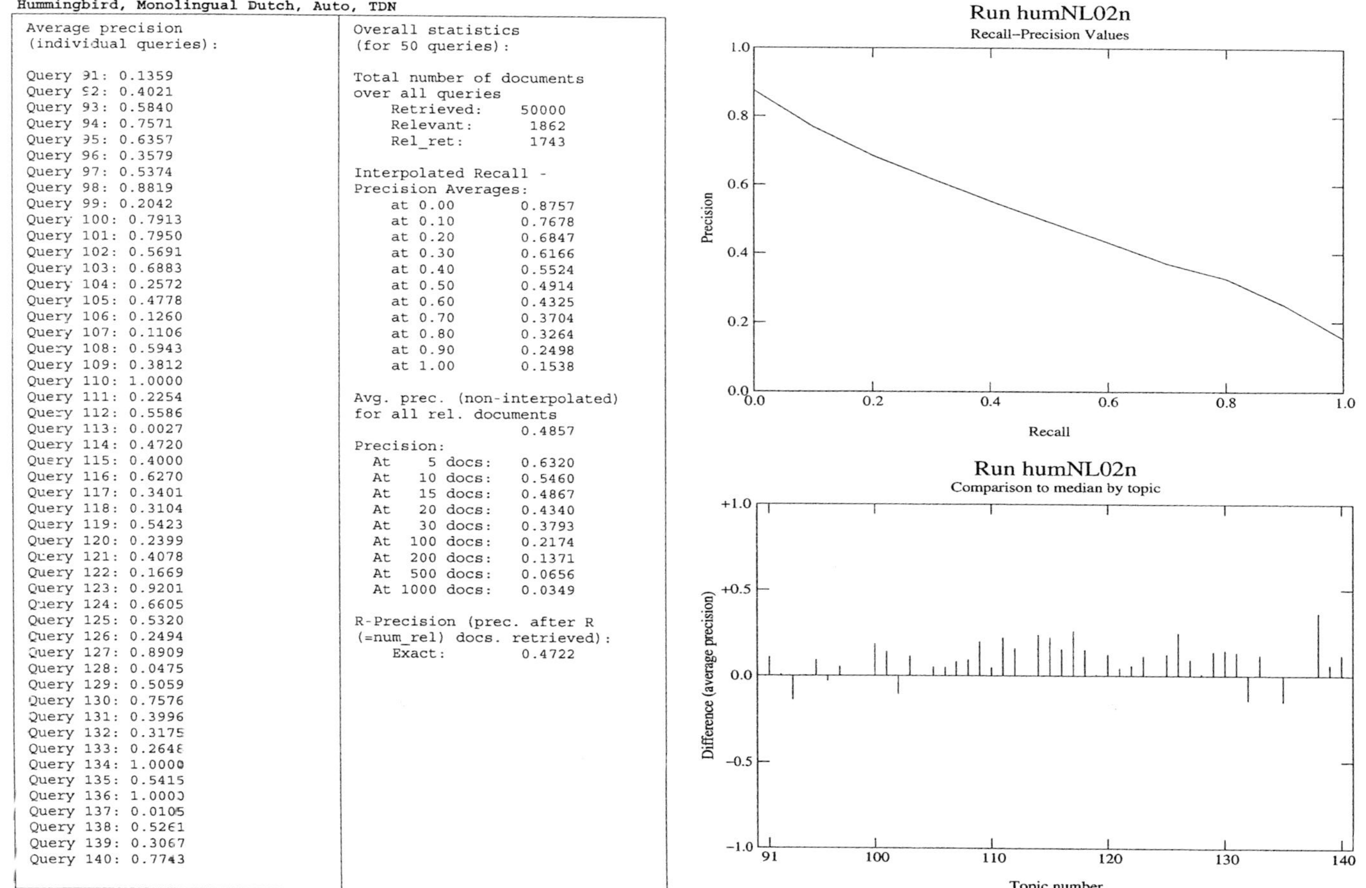

Hummingbird, Monolingual Dutch, Auto, TDN

Average precision (individual queries):

Query	Average precision
Query 91:	0.1359
Query 92:	0.4021
Query 93:	0.5840
Query 94:	0.7571
Query 95:	0.6357
Query 96:	0.3579
Query 97:	0.5374
Query 98:	0.8819
Query 99:	0.2042
Query 100:	0.7913
Query 101:	0.7950
Query 102:	0.5691
Query 103:	0.6883
Query 104:	0.2572
Query 105:	0.4778
Query 106:	0.1260
Query 107:	0.1106
Query 108:	0.5943
Query 109:	0.3812
Query 110:	1.0000
Query 111:	0.2254
Query 112:	0.5586
Query 113:	0.0027
Query 114:	0.4720
Query 115:	0.4000
Query 116:	0.6270
Query 117:	0.3401
Query 118:	0.3104
Query 119:	0.5423
Query 120:	0.2399
Query 121:	0.4078
Query 122:	0.1669
Query 123:	0.9201
Query 124:	0.6605
Query 125:	0.5320
Query 126:	0.2494
Query 127:	0.8909
Query 128:	0.0475
Query 129:	0.5059
Query 130:	0.7576
Query 131:	0.3996
Query 132:	0.3175
Query 133:	0.2648
Query 134:	1.0000
Query 135:	0.5415
Query 136:	1.0000
Query 137:	0.0105
Query 138:	0.5261
Query 139:	0.3067
Query 140:	0.7743

Overall statistics (for 50 queries):

Total number of documents over all queries

Retrieved:	50000
Relevant:	1862
Rel_ret:	1743

Interpolated Recall - Precision Averages:

at 0.00	0.8757
at 0.10	0.7678
at 0.20	0.6847
at 0.30	0.6166
at 0.40	0.5524
at 0.50	0.4914
at 0.60	0.4325
at 0.70	0.3704
at 0.80	0.3264
at 0.90	0.2498
at 1.00	0.1538

Avg. prec. (non-interpolated) for all rel. documents 0.4857

Precision:

At 5 docs:	0.6320
At 10 docs:	0.5460
At 15 docs:	0.4867
At 20 docs:	0.4340
At 30 docs:	0.3793
At 100 docs:	0.2174
At 200 docs:	0.1371
At 500 docs:	0.0656
At 1000 docs:	0.0349

R-Precision (prec. after R (=num_rel) docs. retrieved):

Exact:	0.4722

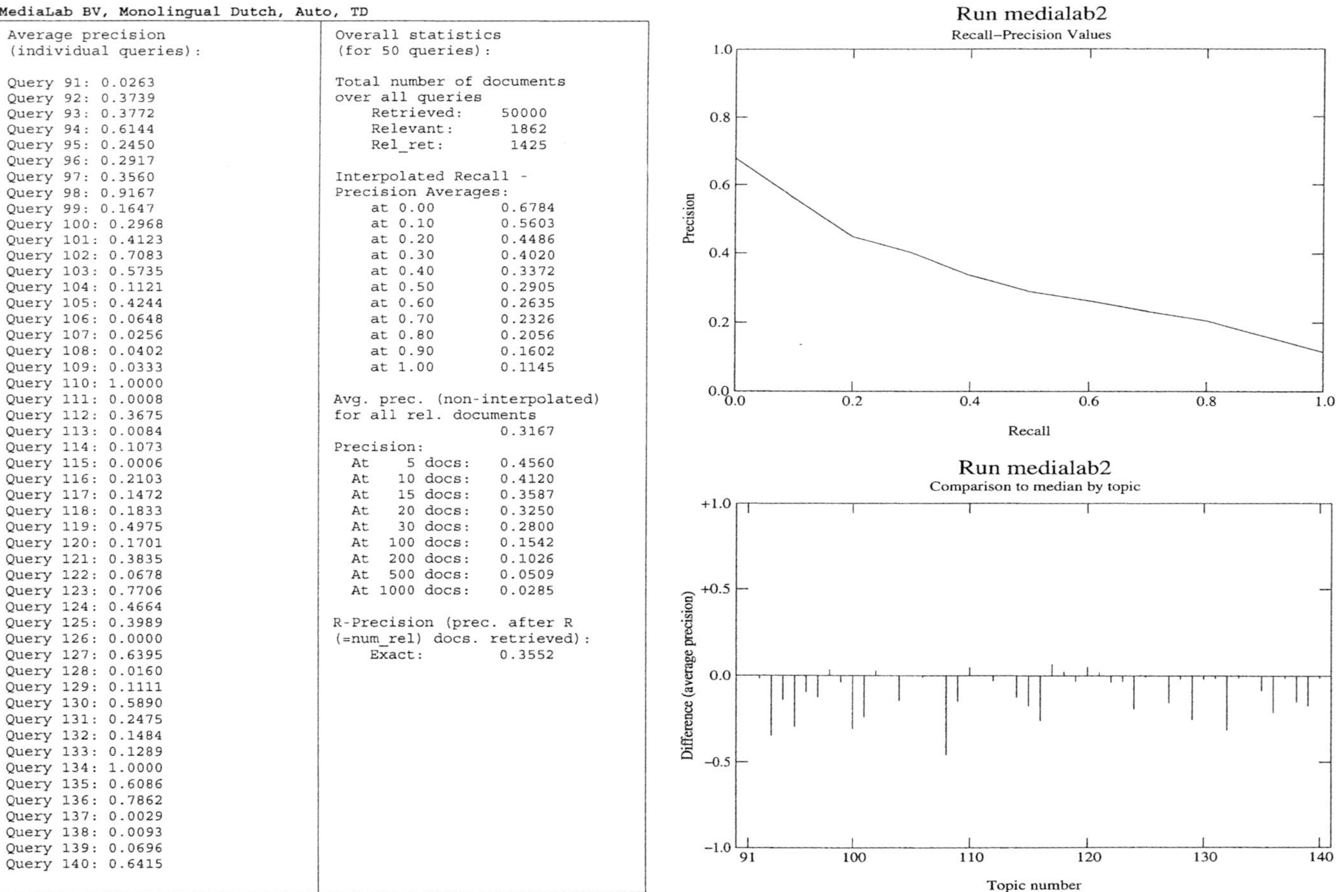

MediaLab BV, Monolingual Dutch, Auto, TD

Average precision
(individual queries):

Query 91: 0.0263
Query 92: 0.3739
Query 93: 0.3772
Query 94: 0.6144
Query 95: 0.2450
Query 96: 0.2917
Query 97: 0.3560
Query 98: 0.9167
Query 99: 0.1647
Query 100: 0.2968
Query 101: 0.4123
Query 102: 0.7083
Query 103: 0.5735
Query 104: 0.1121
Query 105: 0.4244
Query 106: 0.0648
Query 107: 0.0256
Query 108: 0.0402
Query 109: 0.0333
Query 110: 1.0000
Query 111: 0.0008
Query 112: 0.3675
Query 113: 0.0084
Query 114: 0.1073
Query 115: 0.0006
Query 116: 0.2103
Query 117: 0.1472
Query 118: 0.1833
Query 119: 0.4975
Query 120: 0.1701
Query 121: 0.3835
Query 122: 0.0678
Query 123: 0.7706
Query 124: 0.4664
Query 125: 0.3989
Query 126: 0.0000
Query 127: 0.6395
Query 128: 0.0160
Query 129: 0.1111
Query 130: 0.5890
Query 131: 0.2475
Query 132: 0.1484
Query 133: 0.1289
Query 134: 1.0000
Query 135: 0.6086
Query 136: 0.7862
Query 137: 0.0029
Query 138: 0.0093
Query 139: 0.0696
Query 140: 0.6415

Overall statistics
(for 50 queries):

Total number of documents
over all queries
Retrieved: 50000
Relevant: 1862
Rel_ret: 1425

Interpolated Recall -
Precision Averages:
at 0.00 0.6784
at 0.10 0.5603
at 0.20 0.4486
at 0.30 0.4020
at 0.40 0.3372
at 0.50 0.2905
at 0.60 0.2635
at 0.70 0.2326
at 0.80 0.2056
at 0.90 0.1602
at 1.00 0.1145

Avg. prec. (non-interpolated)
for all rel. documents
0.3167

Precision:
At 5 docs: 0.4560
At 10 docs: 0.4120
At 15 docs: 0.3587
At 20 docs: 0.3250
At 30 docs: 0.2800
At 100 docs: 0.1542
At 200 docs: 0.1026
At 500 docs: 0.0509
At 1000 docs: 0.0285

R-Precision (prec. after R
(=num_rel) docs. retrieved):
Exact: 0.3552

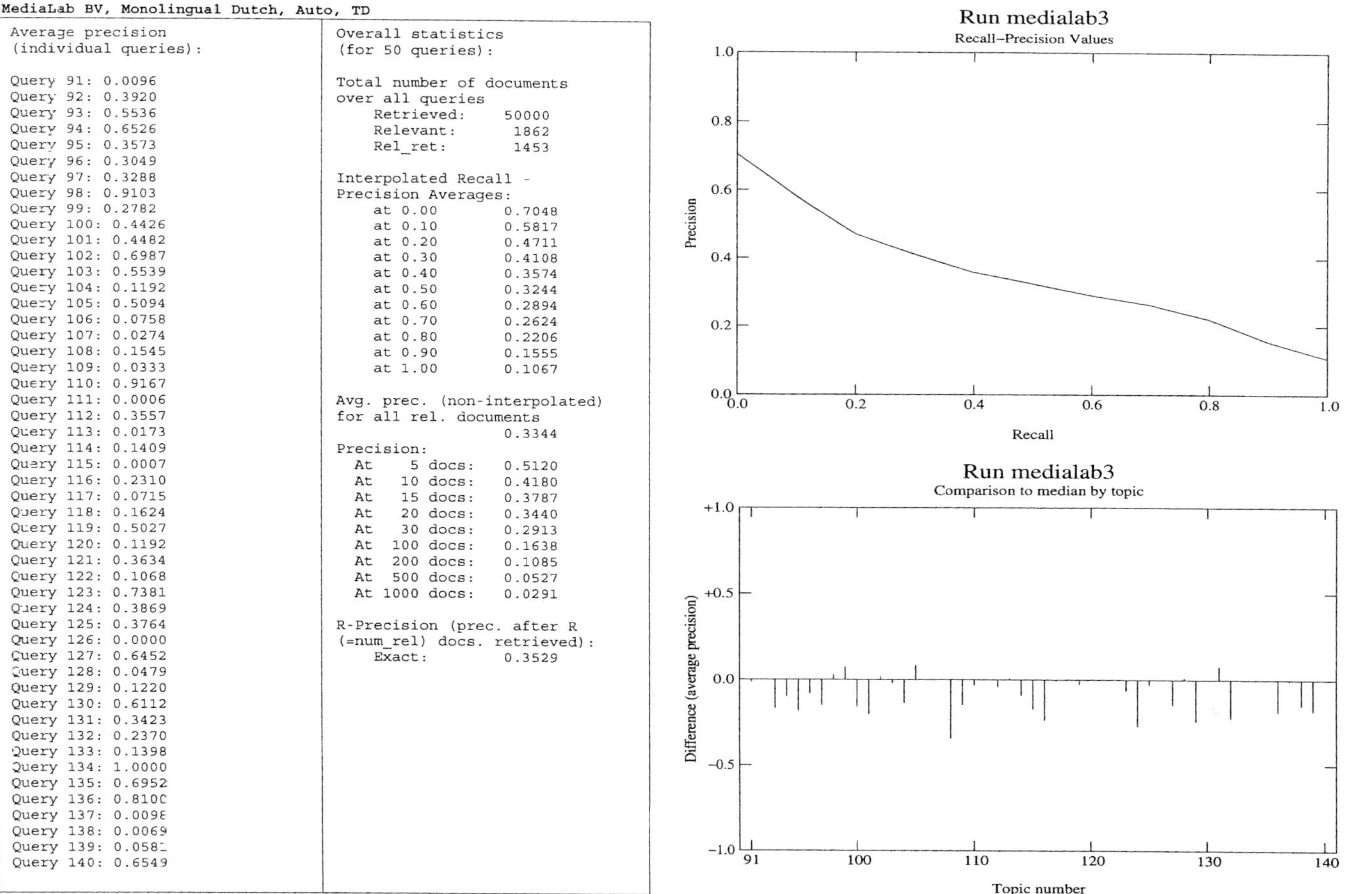

MediaLab BV, Monolingual Dutch, Auto, TD

Average precision
(individual queries):

Query 91: 0.0096
Query 92: 0.3920
Query 93: 0.5536
Query 94: 0.6526
Query 95: 0.3573
Query 96: 0.3049
Query 97: 0.3288
Query 98: 0.9103
Query 99: 0.2782
Query 100: 0.4426
Query 101: 0.4482
Query 102: 0.6987
Query 103: 0.5539
Query 104: 0.1192
Query 105: 0.5094
Query 106: 0.0758
Query 107: 0.0274
Query 108: 0.1545
Query 109: 0.0333
Query 110: 0.9167
Query 111: 0.0006
Query 112: 0.3557
Query 113: 0.0173
Query 114: 0.1409
Query 115: 0.0007
Query 116: 0.2310
Query 117: 0.0715
Query 118: 0.1624
Query 119: 0.5027
Query 120: 0.1192
Query 121: 0.3634
Query 122: 0.1068
Query 123: 0.7381
Query 124: 0.3869
Query 125: 0.3764
Query 126: 0.0000
Query 127: 0.6452
Query 128: 0.0479
Query 129: 0.1220
Query 130: 0.6112
Query 131: 0.3423
Query 132: 0.2370
Query 133: 0.1398
Query 134: 1.0000
Query 135: 0.6952
Query 136: 0.8100
Query 137: 0.0098
Query 138: 0.0069
Query 139: 0.0581
Query 140: 0.6549

Overall statistics
(for 50 queries):

Total number of documents
over all queries
Retrieved: 50000
Relevant: 1862
Rel_ret: 1453

Interpolated Recall -
Precision Averages:
at 0.00 0.7048
at 0.10 0.5817
at 0.20 0.4711
at 0.30 0.4108
at 0.40 0.3574
at 0.50 0.3244
at 0.60 0.2894
at 0.70 0.2624
at 0.80 0.2206
at 0.90 0.1555
at 1.00 0.1067

Avg. prec. (non-interpolated)
for all rel. documents
0.3344

Precision:
At 5 docs: 0.5120
At 10 docs: 0.4180
At 15 docs: 0.3787
At 20 docs: 0.3440
At 30 docs: 0.2913
At 100 docs: 0.1638
At 200 docs: 0.1085
At 500 docs: 0.0527
At 1000 docs: 0.0291

R-Precision (prec. after R
(=num_rel) docs. retrieved):
Exact: 0.3529

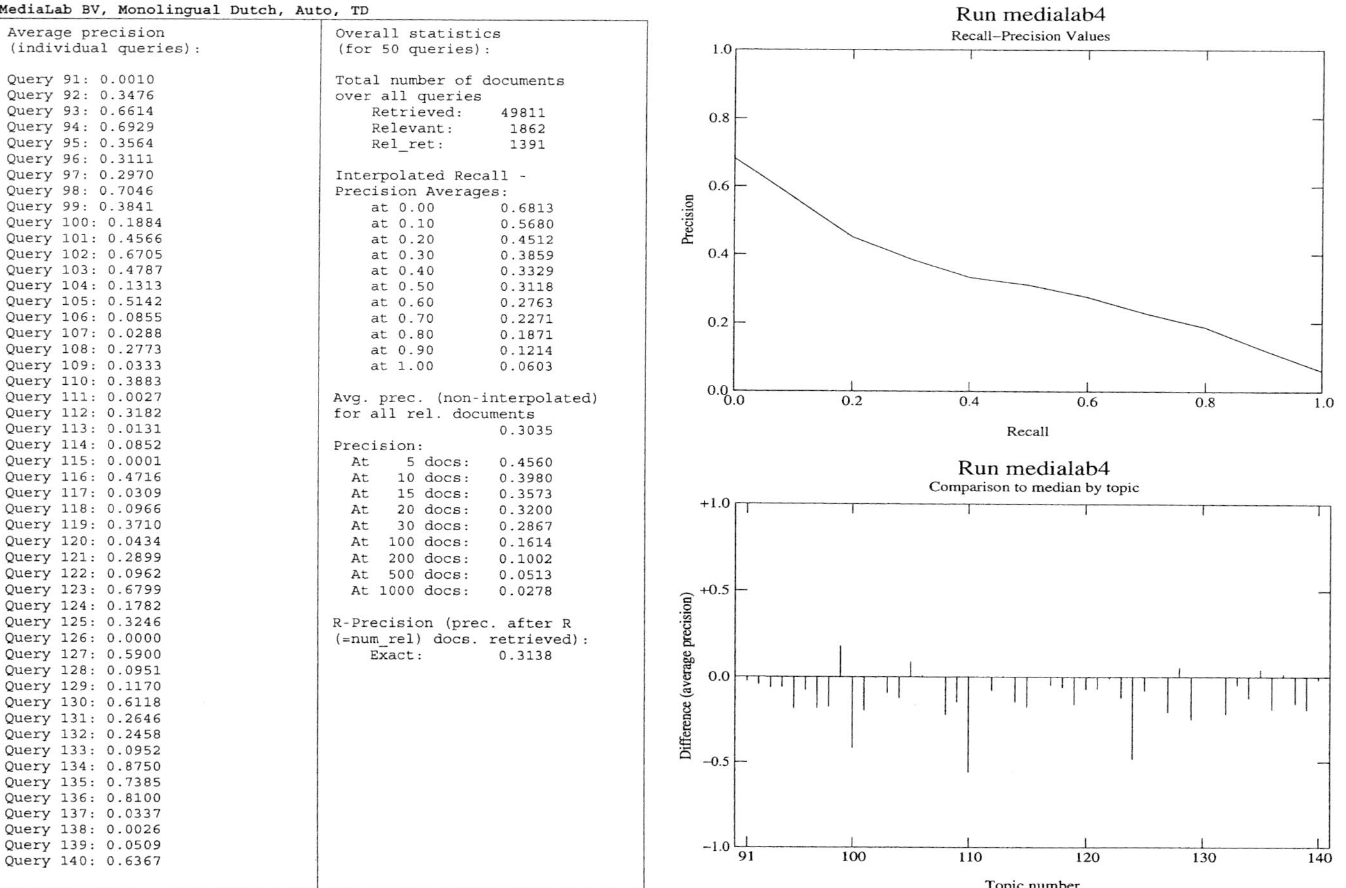

MediaLab BV, Monolingual Dutch, Auto, TD

Average precision (individual queries):	
Query 91:	0.0010
Query 92:	0.3476
Query 93:	0.6614
Query 94:	0.6929
Query 95:	0.3564
Query 96:	0.3111
Query 97:	0.2970
Query 98:	0.7046
Query 99:	0.3841
Query 100:	0.1884
Query 101:	0.4566
Query 102:	0.6705
Query 103:	0.4787
Query 104:	0.1313
Query 105:	0.5142
Query 106:	0.0855
Query 107:	0.0288
Query 108:	0.2773
Query 109:	0.0333
Query 110:	0.3883
Query 111:	0.0027
Query 112:	0.3182
Query 113:	0.0131
Query 114:	0.0852
Query 115:	0.0001
Query 116:	0.4716
Query 117:	0.0309
Query 118:	0.0966
Query 119:	0.3710
Query 120:	0.0434
Query 121:	0.2899
Query 122:	0.0962
Query 123:	0.6799
Query 124:	0.1782
Query 125:	0.3246
Query 126:	0.0000
Query 127:	0.5900
Query 128:	0.0951
Query 129:	0.1170
Query 130:	0.6118
Query 131:	0.2646
Query 132:	0.2458
Query 133:	0.0952
Query 134:	0.8750
Query 135:	0.7385
Query 136:	0.8100
Query 137:	0.0337
Query 138:	0.0026
Query 139:	0.0509
Query 140:	0.6367

Overall statistics (for 50 queries):	
Total number of documents over all queries	
Retrieved:	49811
Relevant:	1862
Rel_ret:	1391
Interpolated Recall - Precision Averages:	
at 0.00	0.6813
at 0.10	0.5680
at 0.20	0.4512
at 0.30	0.3859
at 0.40	0.3329
at 0.50	0.3118
at 0.60	0.2763
at 0.70	0.2271
at 0.80	0.1871
at 0.90	0.1214
at 1.00	0.0603
Avg. prec. (non-interpolated) for all rel. documents	0.3035
Precision:	
At 5 docs:	0.4560
At 10 docs:	0.3980
At 15 docs:	0.3573
At 20 docs:	0.3200
At 30 docs:	0.2867
At 100 docs:	0.1614
At 200 docs:	0.1002
At 500 docs:	0.0513
At 1000 docs:	0.0278
R-Precision (prec. after R (=num_rel) docs. retrieved):	
Exact:	0.3138

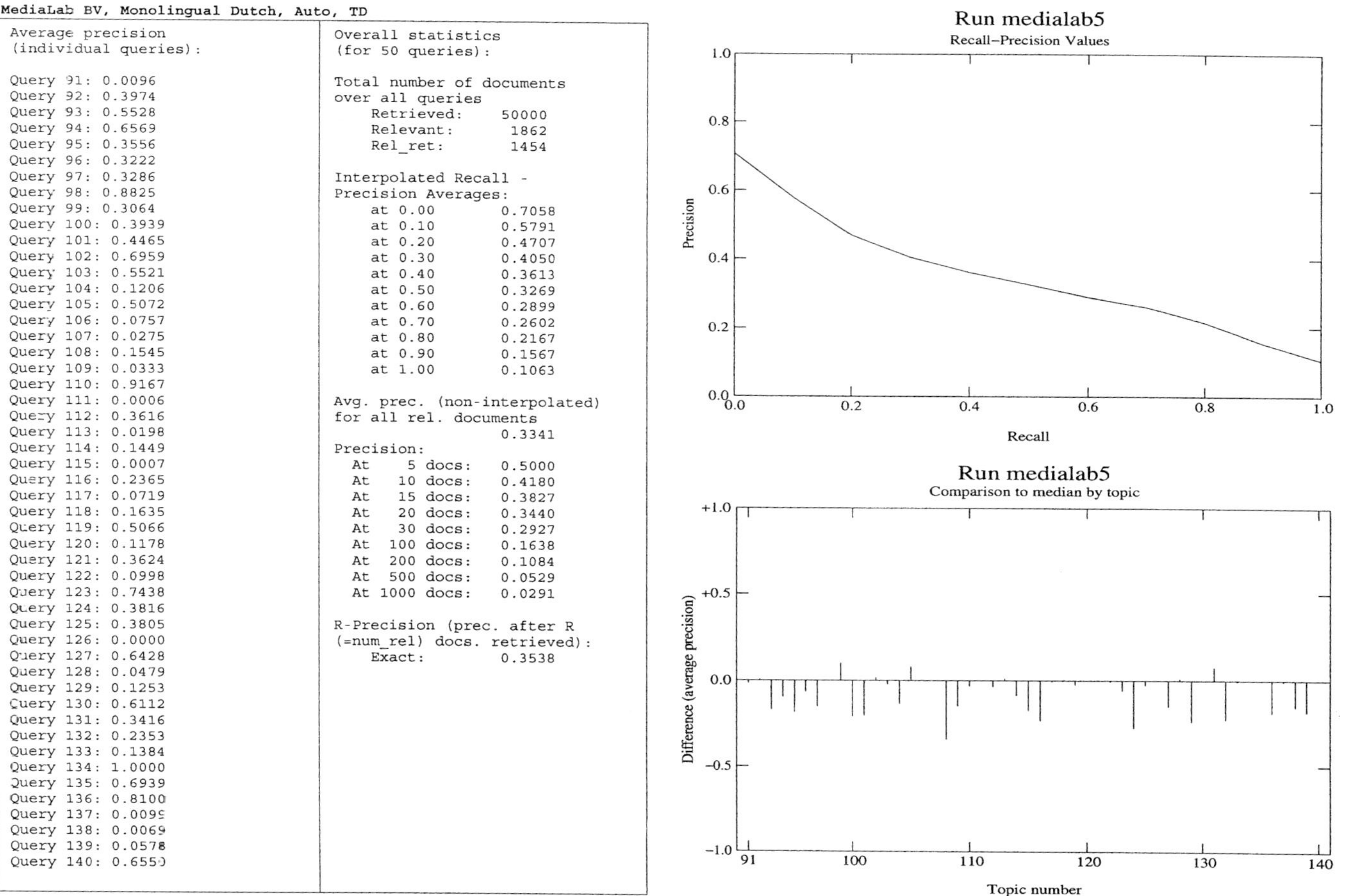

MediaLab BV, Monolingual Dutch, Auto, TD

```
Average precision                Overall statistics
(individual queries):            (for 50 queries):

Query 91: 0.0096                 Total number of documents
Query 92: 0.3974                 over all queries
Query 93: 0.5528                     Retrieved:    50000
Query 94: 0.6569                     Relevant:      1862
Query 95: 0.3556                     Rel_ret:       1454
Query 96: 0.3222
Query 97: 0.3286                 Interpolated Recall -
Query 98: 0.8825                 Precision Averages:
Query 99: 0.3064                     at 0.00        0.7058
Query 100: 0.3939                    at 0.10        0.5791
Query 101: 0.4465                    at 0.20        0.4707
Query 102: 0.6959                    at 0.30        0.4050
Query 103: 0.5521                    at 0.40        0.3613
Query 104: 0.1206                    at 0.50        0.3269
Query 105: 0.5072                    at 0.60        0.2899
Query 106: 0.0757                    at 0.70        0.2602
Query 107: 0.0275                    at 0.80        0.2167
Query 108: 0.1545                    at 0.90        0.1567
Query 109: 0.0333                    at 1.00        0.1063
Query 110: 0.9167
Query 111: 0.0006                Avg. prec. (non-interpolated)
Query 112: 0.3616                for all rel. documents
Query 113: 0.0198                                   0.3341
Query 114: 0.1449                Precision:
Query 115: 0.0007                  At    5 docs:    0.5000
Query 116: 0.2365                  At   10 docs:    0.4180
Query 117: 0.0719                  At   15 docs:    0.3827
Query 118: 0.1635                  At   20 docs:    0.3440
Query 119: 0.5066                  At   30 docs:    0.2927
Query 120: 0.1178                  At  100 docs:    0.1638
Query 121: 0.3624                  At  200 docs:    0.1084
Query 122: 0.0998                  At  500 docs:    0.0529
Query 123: 0.7438                  At 1000 docs:    0.0291
Query 124: 0.3816
Query 125: 0.3805                R-Precision (prec. after R
Query 126: 0.0000                (=num_rel) docs. retrieved):
Query 127: 0.6428                    Exact:         0.3538
Query 128: 0.0479
Query 129: 0.1253
Query 130: 0.6112
Query 131: 0.3416
Query 132: 0.2353
Query 133: 0.1384
Query 134: 1.0000
Query 135: 0.6939
Query 136: 0.8100
Query 137: 0.0099
Query 138: 0.0069
Query 139: 0.0578
Query 140: 0.6550
```

Océ, Monolingual Dutch, Auto, TD

```
Average precision                 Overall statistics
(individual queries):             (for 50 queries):

Query 91: 0.1776                  Total number of documents
Query 92: 0.3688                  over all queries
Query 93: 0.7182                      Retrieved:    50000
Query 94: 0.5059                      Relevant:      1862
Query 95: 0.1883                      Rel_ret:       1538
Query 96: 0.2415
Query 97: 0.4858                  Interpolated Recall -
Query 98: 0.8819                  Precision Averages:
Query 99: 0.1796                      at 0.00       0.7852
Query 100: 0.7166                     at 0.10       0.6649
Query 101: 0.5918                     at 0.20       0.5454
Query 102: 0.4521                     at 0.30       0.4913
Query 103: 0.5443                     at 0.40       0.4306
Query 104: 0.1999                     at 0.50       0.3841
Query 105: 0.2089                     at 0.60       0.3442
Query 106: 0.0807                     at 0.70       0.2980
Query 107: 0.0441                     at 0.80       0.2579
Query 108: 0.5301                     at 0.90       0.1936
Query 109: 0.3382                     at 1.00       0.1299
Query 110: 1.0000
Query 111: 0.0014                 Avg. prec. (non-interpolated)
Query 112: 0.5090                 for all rel. documents
Query 113: 0.0076                                   0.3919
Query 114: 0.2155                 Precision:
Query 115: 0.4457                   At    5 docs:   0.5480
Query 116: 0.0706                   At   10 docs:   0.4640
Query 117: 0.0434                   At   15 docs:   0.4187
Query 118: 0.0938                   At   20 docs:   0.3790
Query 119: 0.6461                   At   30 docs:   0.3220
Query 120: 0.3073                   At  100 docs:   0.1790
Query 121: 0.3526                   At  200 docs:   0.1141
Query 122: 0.1056                   At  500 docs:   0.0561
Query 123: 0.8328                   At 1000 docs:   0.0308
Query 124: 0.6711
Query 125: 0.5206                 R-Precision (prec. after R
Query 126: 0.0697                 (=num_rel) docs. retrieved):
Query 127: 0.8395                     Exact:        0.3957
Query 128: 0.0206
Query 129: 0.4672
Query 130: 0.5561
Query 131: 0.1603
Query 132: 0.2284
Query 133: 0.1717
Query 134: 1.0000
Query 135: 0.6382
Query 136: 1.0000
Query 137: 0.0019
Query 138: 0.2139
Query 139: 0.3639
Query 140: 0.5844
```

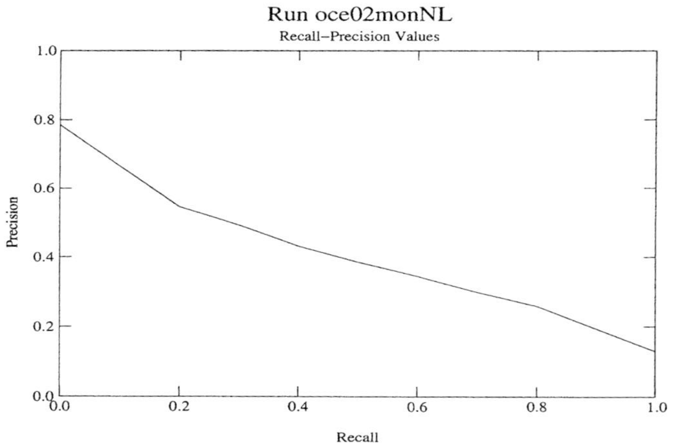

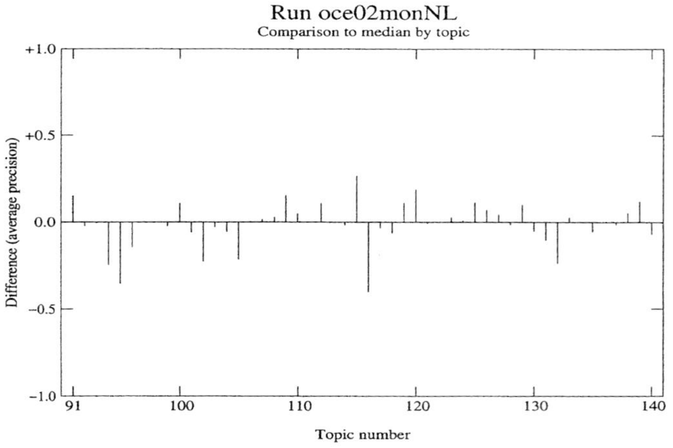

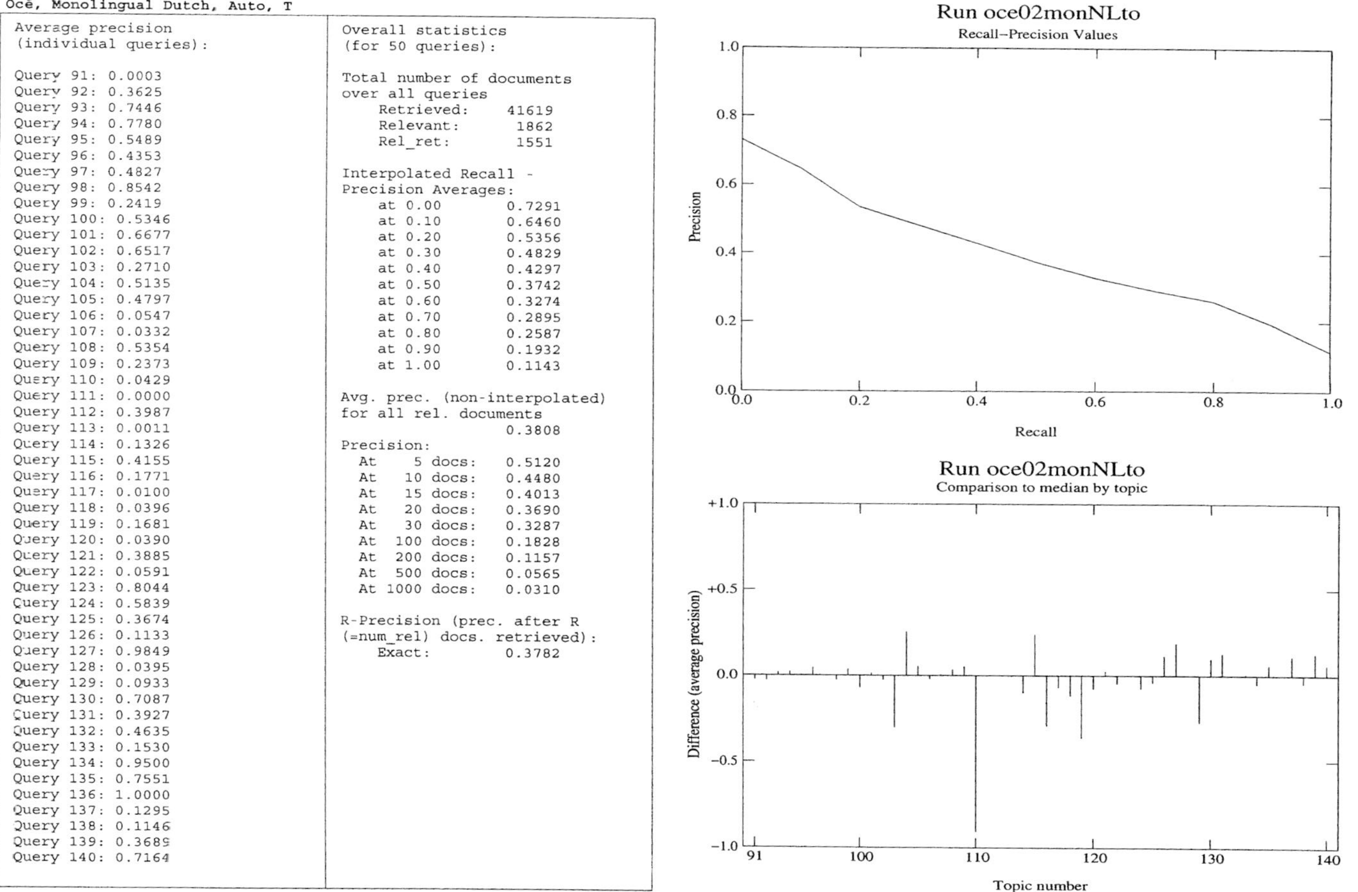

Océ, Monolingual Dutch, Auto, T

```
Average precision              Overall statistics
(individual queries):          (for 50 queries):

Query 91: 0.0003               Total number of documents
Query 92: 0.3625               over all queries
Query 93: 0.7446                   Retrieved:    41619
Query 94: 0.7780                   Relevant:      1862
Query 95: 0.5489                   Rel_ret:       1551
Query 96: 0.4353
Query 97: 0.4827               Interpolated Recall -
Query 98: 0.8542               Precision Averages:
Query 99: 0.2419                   at 0.00       0.7291
Query 100: 0.5346                  at 0.10       0.6460
Query 101: 0.6677                  at 0.20       0.5356
Query 102: 0.6517                  at 0.30       0.4829
Query 103: 0.2710                  at 0.40       0.4297
Query 104: 0.5135                  at 0.50       0.3742
Query 105: 0.4797                  at 0.60       0.3274
Query 106: 0.0547                  at 0.70       0.2895
Query 107: 0.0332                  at 0.80       0.2587
Query 108: 0.5354                  at 0.90       0.1932
Query 109: 0.2373                  at 1.00       0.1143
Query 110: 0.0429
Query 111: 0.0000              Avg. prec. (non-interpolated)
Query 112: 0.3987              for all rel. documents
Query 113: 0.0011                                0.3808
Query 114: 0.1326              Precision:
Query 115: 0.4155                At    5 docs:   0.5120
Query 116: 0.1771                At   10 docs:   0.4480
Query 117: 0.0100                At   15 docs:   0.4013
Query 118: 0.0396                At   20 docs:   0.3690
Query 119: 0.1681                At   30 docs:   0.3287
Query 120: 0.0390                At  100 docs:   0.1828
Query 121: 0.3885                At  200 docs:   0.1157
Query 122: 0.0591                At  500 docs:   0.0565
Query 123: 0.8044                At 1000 docs:   0.0310
Query 124: 0.5839
Query 125: 0.3674              R-Precision (prec. after R
Query 126: 0.1133              (=num_rel) docs. retrieved):
Query 127: 0.9849                  Exact:        0.3782
Query 128: 0.0395
Query 129: 0.0933
Query 130: 0.7087
Query 131: 0.3927
Query 132: 0.4635
Query 133: 0.1530
Query 134: 0.9500
Query 135: 0.7551
Query 136: 1.0000
Query 137: 0.1295
Query 138: 0.1146
Query 139: 0.3689
Query 140: 0.7164
```

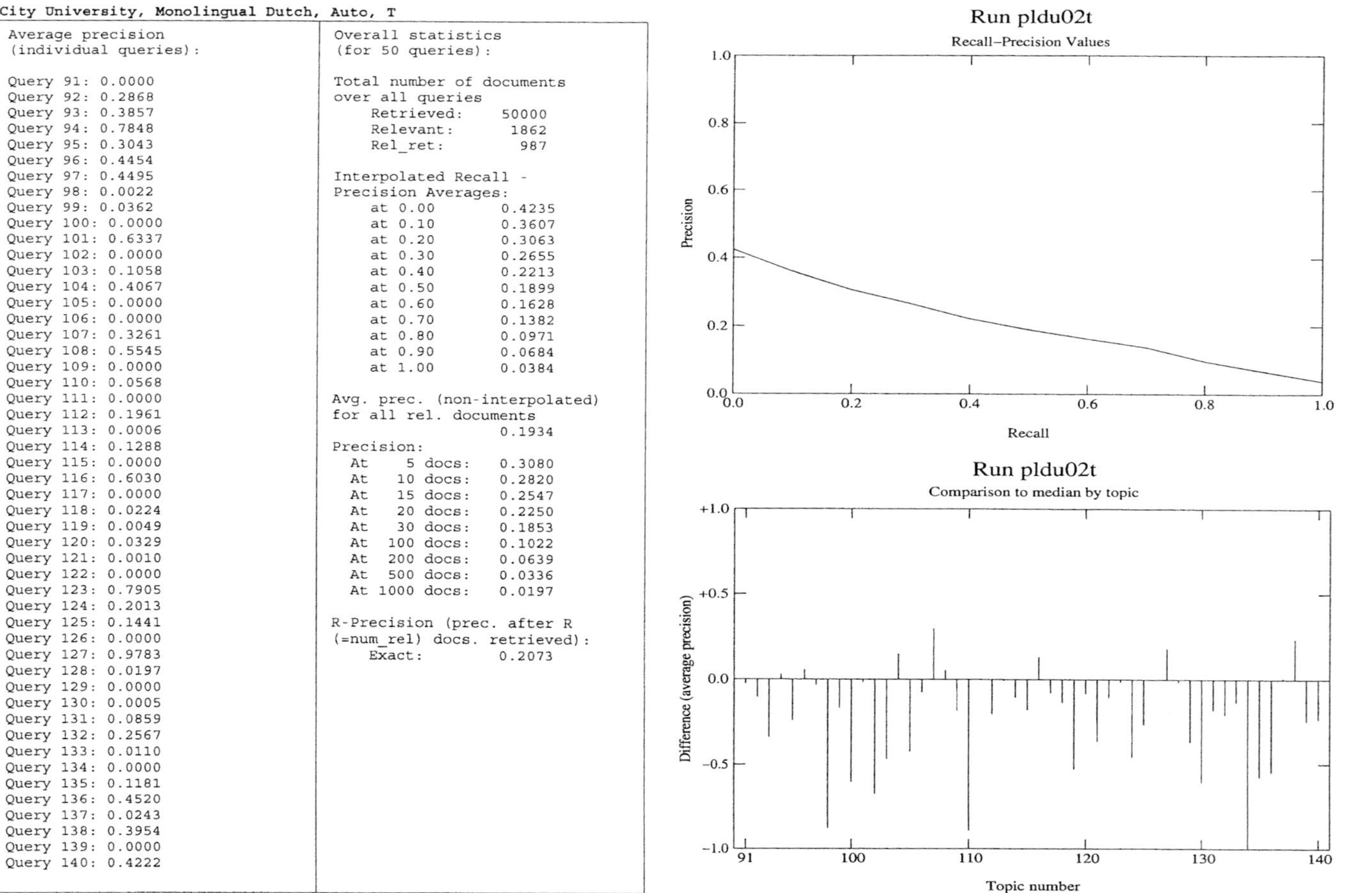

City University, Monolingual Dutch, Auto, T

Average precision (individual queries):	Overall statistics (for 50 queries):
Query 91: 0.0000	Total number of documents over all queries
Query 92: 0.2868	Retrieved: 50000
Query 93: 0.3857	Relevant: 1862
Query 94: 0.7848	Rel_ret: 987
Query 95: 0.3043	
Query 96: 0.4454	Interpolated Recall - Precision Averages:
Query 97: 0.4495	at 0.00 0.4235
Query 98: 0.0022	at 0.10 0.3607
Query 99: 0.0362	at 0.20 0.3063
Query 100: 0.0000	at 0.30 0.2655
Query 101: 0.6337	at 0.40 0.2213
Query 102: 0.0000	at 0.50 0.1899
Query 103: 0.1058	at 0.60 0.1628
Query 104: 0.4067	at 0.70 0.1382
Query 105: 0.0000	at 0.80 0.0971
Query 106: 0.0000	at 0.90 0.0684
Query 107: 0.3261	at 1.00 0.0384
Query 108: 0.5545	
Query 109: 0.0000	Avg. prec. (non-interpolated) for all rel. documents
Query 110: 0.0568	0.1934
Query 111: 0.0000	Precision:
Query 112: 0.1961	At 5 docs: 0.3080
Query 113: 0.0006	At 10 docs: 0.2820
Query 114: 0.1288	At 15 docs: 0.2547
Query 115: 0.0000	At 20 docs: 0.2250
Query 116: 0.6030	At 30 docs: 0.1853
Query 117: 0.0000	At 100 docs: 0.1022
Query 118: 0.0224	At 200 docs: 0.0639
Query 119: 0.0049	At 500 docs: 0.0336
Query 120: 0.0329	At 1000 docs: 0.0197
Query 121: 0.0010	
Query 122: 0.0000	R-Precision (prec. after R (=num_rel) docs. retrieved):
Query 123: 0.7905	Exact: 0.2073
Query 124: 0.2013	
Query 125: 0.1441	
Query 126: 0.0000	
Query 127: 0.9783	
Query 128: 0.0197	
Query 129: 0.0000	
Query 130: 0.0005	
Query 131: 0.0859	
Query 132: 0.2567	
Query 133: 0.0110	
Query 134: 0.0000	
Query 135: 0.1181	
Query 136: 0.4520	
Query 137: 0.0243	
Query 138: 0.3954	
Query 139: 0.0000	
Query 140: 0.4222	

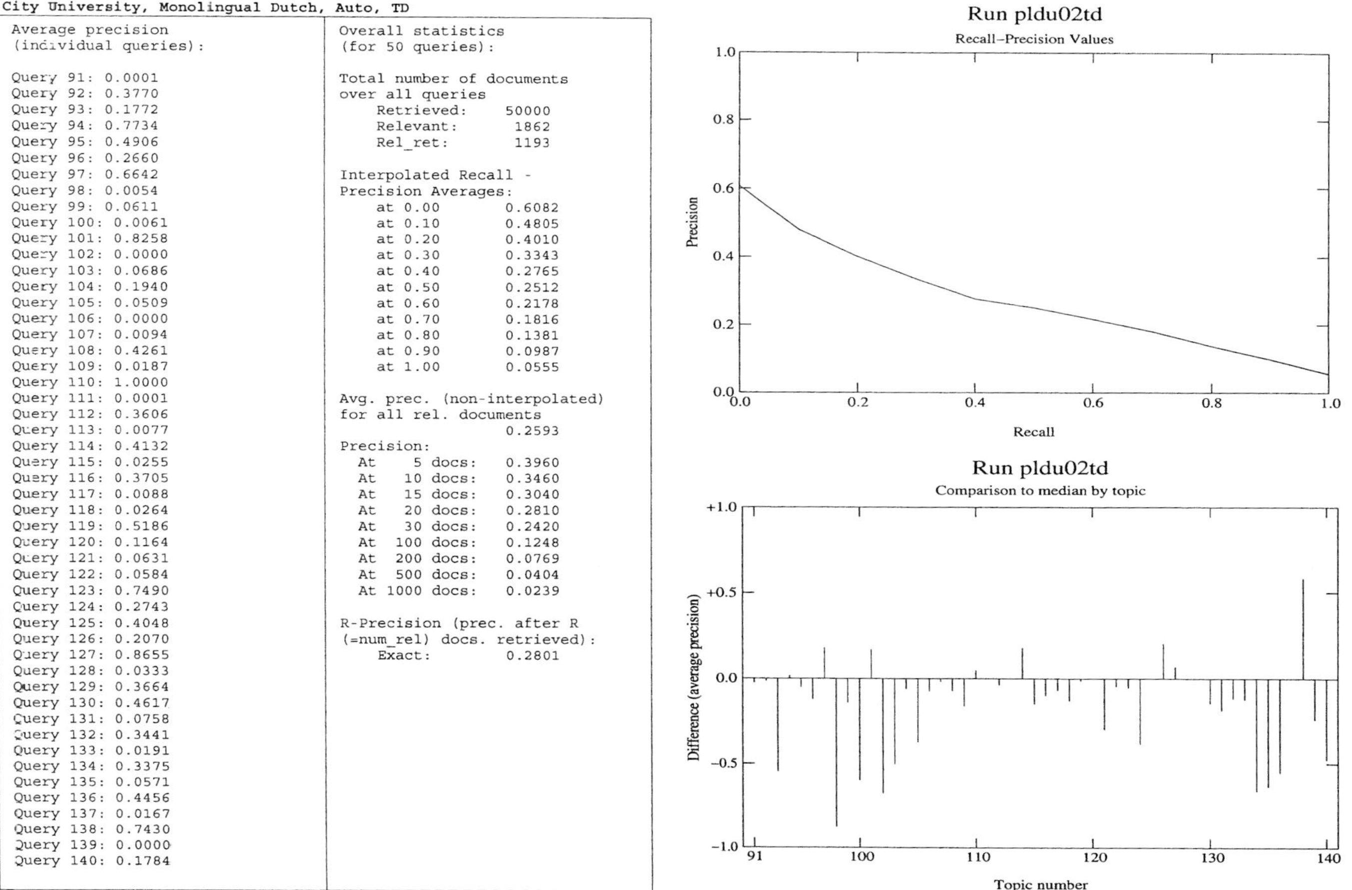

City University, Monolingual Dutch, Auto, TD

```
Average precision                Overall statistics
(individual queries):            (for 50 queries):

Query 91: 0.0001                 Total number of documents
Query 92: 0.3770                 over all queries
Query 93: 0.1772                     Retrieved:    50000
Query 94: 0.7734                     Relevant:      1862
Query 95: 0.4906                     Rel_ret:       1193
Query 96: 0.2660
Query 97: 0.6642                 Interpolated Recall -
Query 98: 0.0054                 Precision Averages:
Query 99: 0.0611                     at 0.00       0.6082
Query 100: 0.0061                    at 0.10       0.4805
Query 101: 0.8258                    at 0.20       0.4010
Query 102: 0.0000                    at 0.30       0.3343
Query 103: 0.0686                    at 0.40       0.2765
Query 104: 0.1940                    at 0.50       0.2512
Query 105: 0.0509                    at 0.60       0.2178
Query 106: 0.0000                    at 0.70       0.1816
Query 107: 0.0094                    at 0.80       0.1381
Query 108: 0.4261                    at 0.90       0.0987
Query 109: 0.0187                    at 1.00       0.0555
Query 110: 1.0000
Query 111: 0.0001                Avg. prec. (non-interpolated)
Query 112: 0.3606                for all rel. documents
Query 113: 0.0077                                  0.2593
Query 114: 0.4132                Precision:
Query 115: 0.0255                  At    5 docs:   0.3960
Query 116: 0.3705                  At   10 docs:   0.3460
Query 117: 0.0088                  At   15 docs:   0.3040
Query 118: 0.0264                  At   20 docs:   0.2810
Query 119: 0.5186                  At   30 docs:   0.2420
Query 120: 0.1164                  At  100 docs:   0.1248
Query 121: 0.0631                  At  200 docs:   0.0769
Query 122: 0.0584                  At  500 docs:   0.0404
Query 123: 0.7490                  At 1000 docs:   0.0239
Query 124: 0.2743
Query 125: 0.4048                R-Precision (prec. after R
Query 126: 0.2070                (=num_rel) docs. retrieved):
Query 127: 0.8655                    Exact:        0.2801
Query 128: 0.0333
Query 129: 0.3664
Query 130: 0.4617
Query 131: 0.0758
Query 132: 0.3441
Query 133: 0.0191
Query 134: 0.3375
Query 135: 0.0571
Query 136: 0.4456
Query 137: 0.0167
Query 138: 0.7430
Query 139: 0.0000
Query 140: 0.1784
```

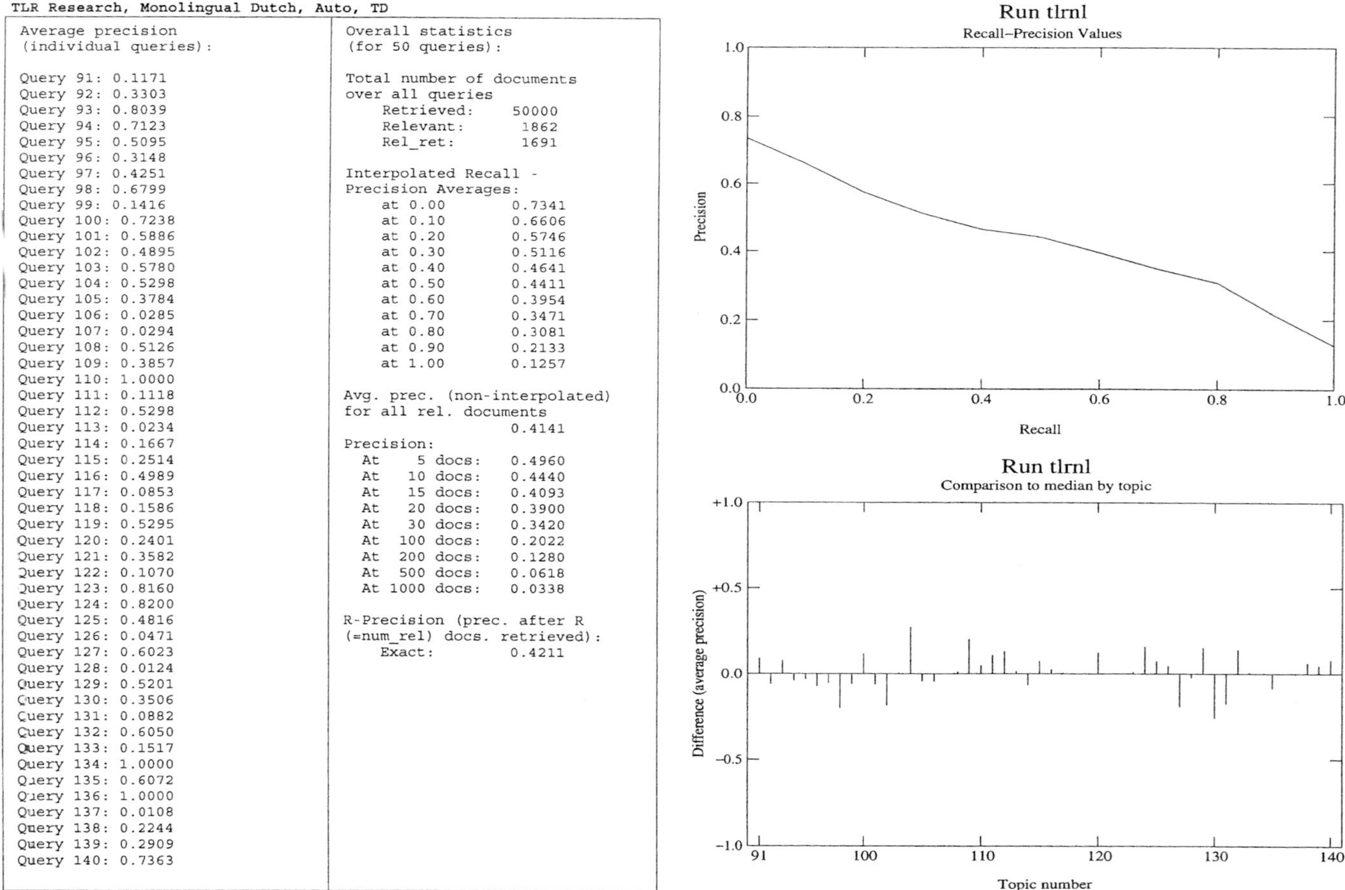

TLR Research, Monolingual Dutch, Auto, TD

```
Average precision               Overall statistics
(individual queries):           (for 50 queries):

Query 91: 0.1171                Total number of documents
Query 92: 0.3303                over all queries
Query 93: 0.8039                    Retrieved:     50000
Query 94: 0.7123                    Relevant:       1862
Query 95: 0.5095                    Rel_ret:        1691
Query 96: 0.3148
Query 97: 0.4251                Interpolated Recall -
Query 98: 0.6799                Precision Averages:
Query 99: 0.1416                    at 0.00         0.7341
Query 100: 0.7238                   at 0.10         0.6606
Query 101: 0.5886                   at 0.20         0.5746
Query 102: 0.4895                   at 0.30         0.5116
Query 103: 0.5780                   at 0.40         0.4641
Query 104: 0.5298                   at 0.50         0.4411
Query 105: 0.3784                   at 0.60         0.3954
Query 106: 0.0285                   at 0.70         0.3471
Query 107: 0.0294                   at 0.80         0.3081
Query 108: 0.5126                   at 0.90         0.2133
Query 109: 0.3857                   at 1.00         0.1257
Query 110: 1.0000
Query 111: 0.1118               Avg. prec. (non-interpolated)
Query 112: 0.5298               for all rel. documents
Query 113: 0.0234                                   0.4141
Query 114: 0.1667               Precision:
Query 115: 0.2514                 At    5 docs:     0.4960
Query 116: 0.4989                 At   10 docs:     0.4440
Query 117: 0.0853                 At   15 docs:     0.4093
Query 118: 0.1586                 At   20 docs:     0.3900
Query 119: 0.5295                 At   30 docs:     0.3420
Query 120: 0.2401                 At  100 docs:     0.2022
Query 121: 0.3582                 At  200 docs:     0.1280
Query 122: 0.1070                 At  500 docs:     0.0618
Query 123: 0.8160                 At 1000 docs:     0.0338
Query 124: 0.8200
Query 125: 0.4816               R-Precision (prec. after R
Query 126: 0.0471               (=num_rel) docs. retrieved):
Query 127: 0.6023                   Exact:          0.4211
Query 128: 0.0124
Query 129: 0.5201
Query 130: 0.3506
Query 131: 0.0882
Query 132: 0.6050
Query 133: 0.1517
Query 134: 1.0000
Query 135: 0.6072
Query 136: 1.0000
Query 137: 0.0108
Query 138: 0.2244
Query 139: 0.2909
Query 140: 0.7363
```

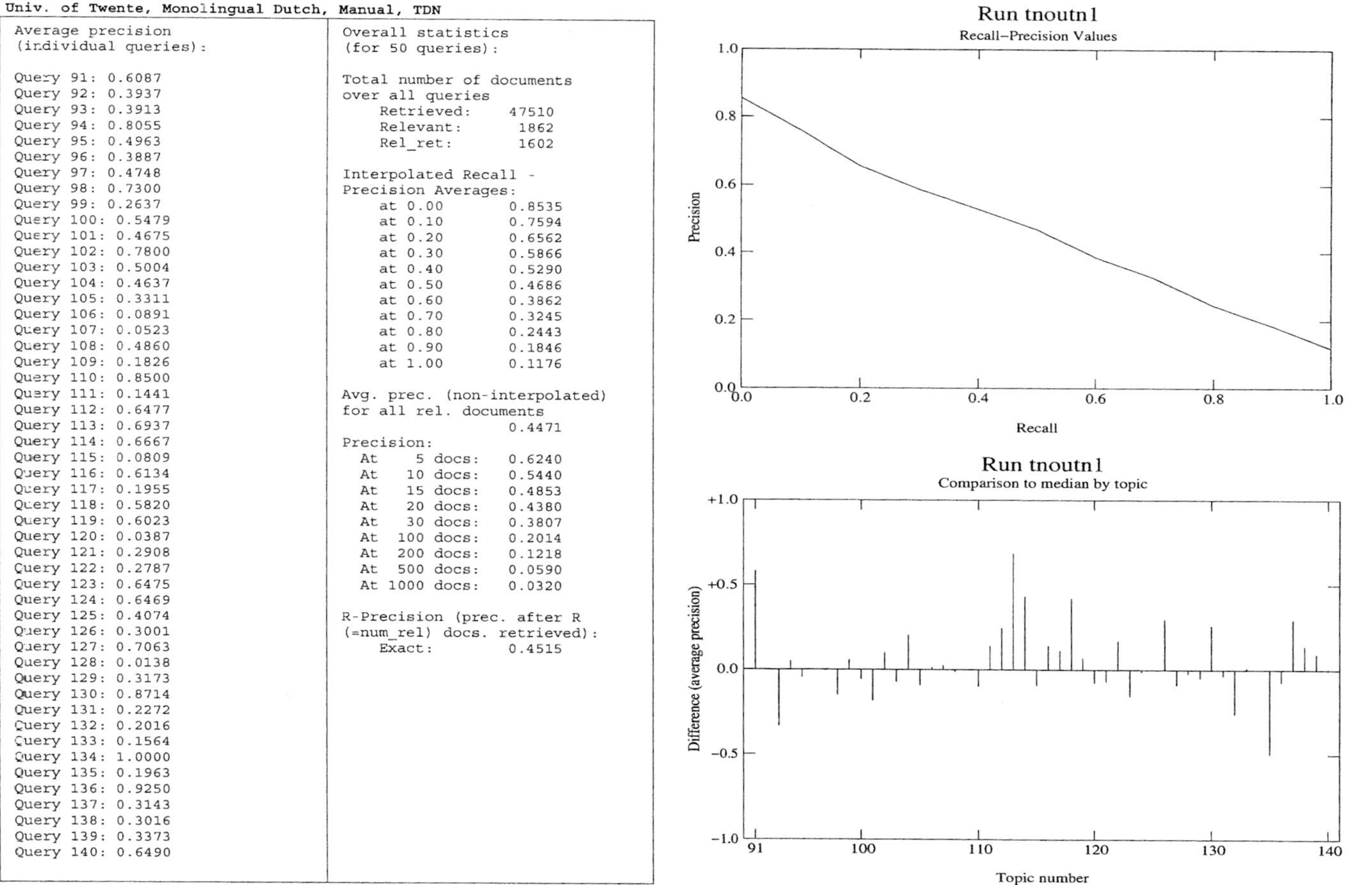

Univ. of Twente, Monolingual Dutch, Manual, TDN

Average precision (individual queries):	Overall statistics (for 50 queries):
Query 91: 0.6087	Total number of documents over all queries
Query 92: 0.3937	Retrieved: 47510
Query 93: 0.3913	Relevant: 1862
Query 94: 0.8055	Rel_ret: 1602
Query 95: 0.4963	
Query 96: 0.3887	Interpolated Recall - Precision Averages:
Query 97: 0.4748	at 0.00 0.8535
Query 98: 0.7300	at 0.10 0.7594
Query 99: 0.2637	at 0.20 0.6562
Query 100: 0.5479	at 0.30 0.5866
Query 101: 0.4675	at 0.40 0.5290
Query 102: 0.7800	at 0.50 0.4686
Query 103: 0.5004	at 0.60 0.3862
Query 104: 0.4637	at 0.70 0.3245
Query 105: 0.3311	at 0.80 0.2443
Query 106: 0.0891	at 0.90 0.1846
Query 107: 0.0523	at 1.00 0.1176
Query 108: 0.4860	
Query 109: 0.1826	Avg. prec. (non-interpolated) for all rel. documents 0.4471
Query 110: 0.8500	
Query 111: 0.1441	Precision:
Query 112: 0.6477	At 5 docs: 0.6240
Query 113: 0.6937	At 10 docs: 0.5440
Query 114: 0.6667	At 15 docs: 0.4853
Query 115: 0.0809	At 20 docs: 0.4380
Query 116: 0.6134	At 30 docs: 0.3807
Query 117: 0.1955	At 100 docs: 0.2014
Query 118: 0.5820	At 200 docs: 0.1218
Query 119: 0.6023	At 500 docs: 0.0590
Query 120: 0.0387	At 1000 docs: 0.0320
Query 121: 0.2908	
Query 122: 0.2787	R-Precision (prec. after R (=num_rel) docs. retrieved):
Query 123: 0.6475	Exact: 0.4515
Query 124: 0.6469	
Query 125: 0.4074	
Query 126: 0.3001	
Query 127: 0.7063	
Query 128: 0.0138	
Query 129: 0.3173	
Query 130: 0.8714	
Query 131: 0.2272	
Query 132: 0.2016	
Query 133: 0.1564	
Query 134: 1.0000	
Query 135: 0.1963	
Query 136: 0.9250	
Query 137: 0.3143	
Query 138: 0.3016	
Query 139: 0.3373	
Query 140: 0.6490	

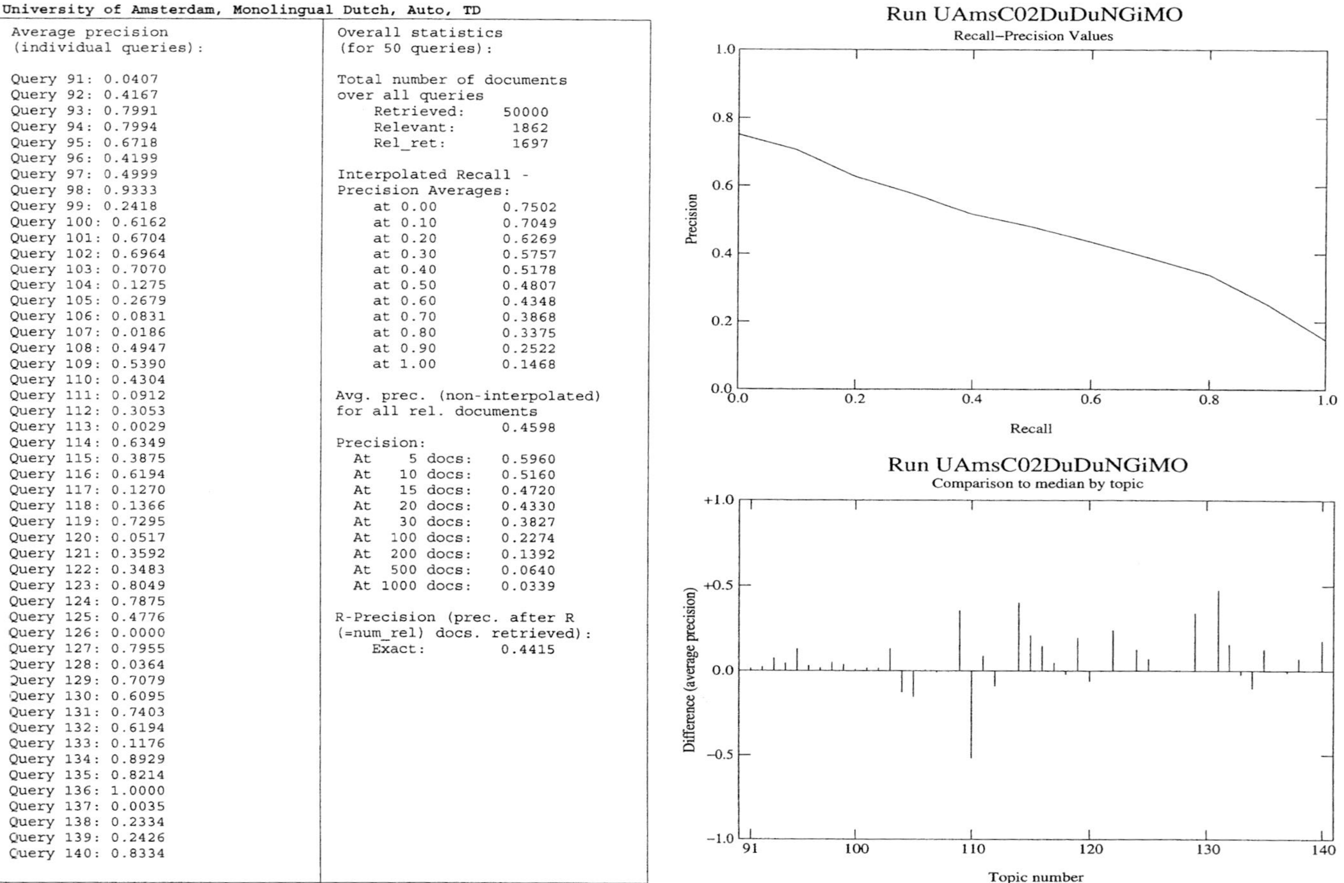

University of Amsterdam, Monolingual Dutch, Auto, TD

Average precision (individual queries):

Query	Average precision
Query 91:	0.0407
Query 92:	0.4167
Query 93:	0.7991
Query 94:	0.7994
Query 95:	0.6718
Query 96:	0.4199
Query 97:	0.4999
Query 98:	0.9333
Query 99:	0.2418
Query 100:	0.6162
Query 101:	0.6704
Query 102:	0.6964
Query 103:	0.7070
Query 104:	0.1275
Query 105:	0.2679
Query 106:	0.0831
Query 107:	0.0186
Query 108:	0.4947
Query 109:	0.5390
Query 110:	0.4304
Query 111:	0.0912
Query 112:	0.3053
Query 113:	0.0029
Query 114:	0.6349
Query 115:	0.3875
Query 116:	0.6194
Query 117:	0.1270
Query 118:	0.1366
Query 119:	0.7295
Query 120:	0.0517
Query 121:	0.3592
Query 122:	0.3483
Query 123:	0.8049
Query 124:	0.7875
Query 125:	0.4776
Query 126:	0.0000
Query 127:	0.7955
Query 128:	0.0364
Query 129:	0.7079
Query 130:	0.6095
Query 131:	0.7403
Query 132:	0.6194
Query 133:	0.1176
Query 134:	0.8929
Query 135:	0.8214
Query 136:	1.0000
Query 137:	0.0035
Query 138:	0.2334
Query 139:	0.2426
Query 140:	0.8334

Overall statistics (for 50 queries):

Total number of documents over all queries

Retrieved:	50000
Relevant:	1862
Rel_ret:	1697

Interpolated Recall - Precision Averages:

at 0.00	0.7502
at 0.10	0.7049
at 0.20	0.6269
at 0.30	0.5757
at 0.40	0.5178
at 0.50	0.4807
at 0.60	0.4348
at 0.70	0.3868
at 0.80	0.3375
at 0.90	0.2522
at 1.00	0.1468

Avg. prec. (non-interpolated) for all rel. documents 0.4598

Precision:

At 5 docs:	0.5960
At 10 docs:	0.5160
At 15 docs:	0.4720
At 20 docs:	0.4330
At 30 docs:	0.3827
At 100 docs:	0.2274
At 200 docs:	0.1392
At 500 docs:	0.0640
At 1000 docs:	0.0339

R-Precision (prec. after R (=num_rel) docs. retrieved):
Exact: 0.4415

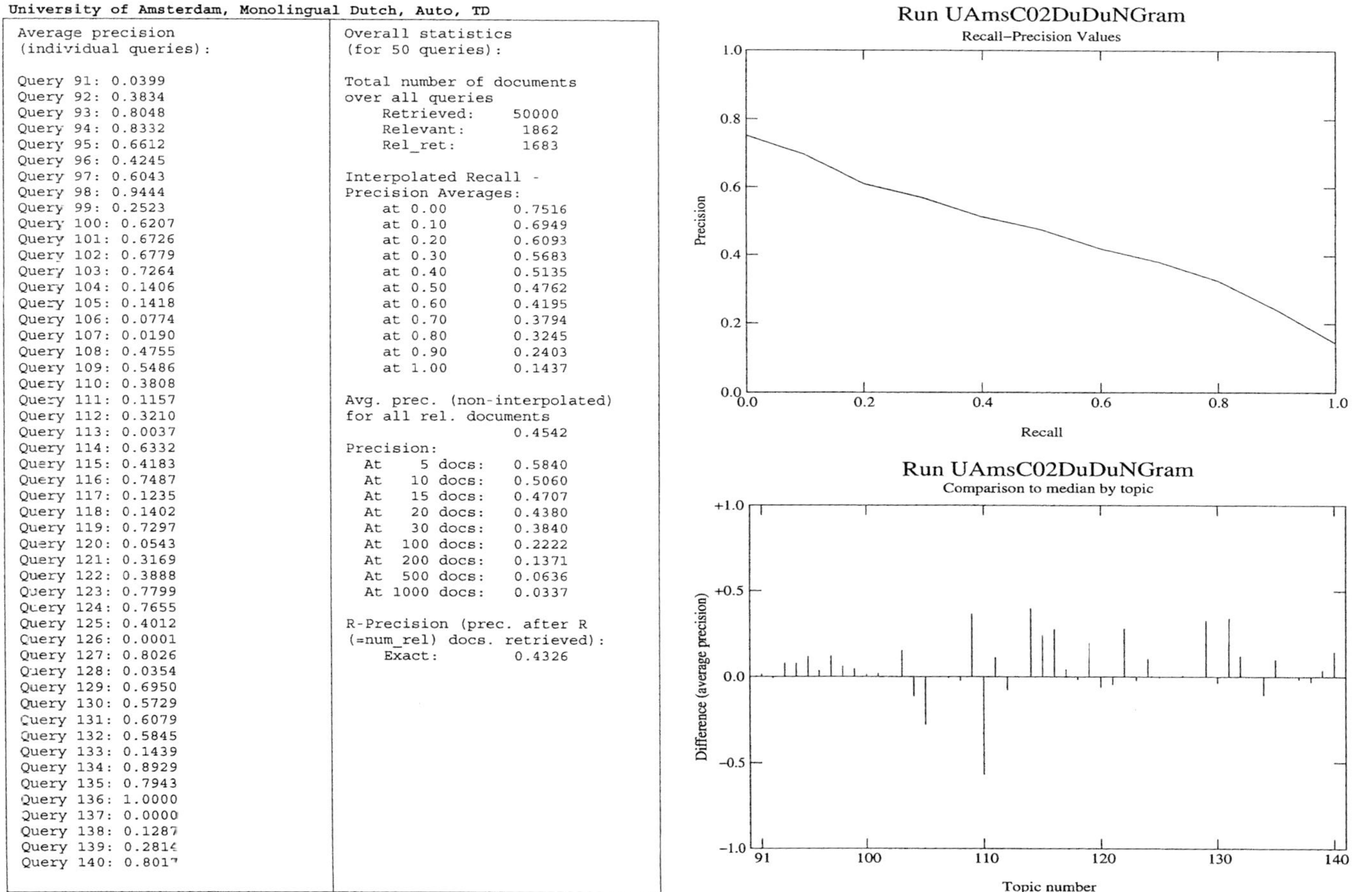

University of Amsterdam, Monolingual Dutch, Auto, TD

Average precision (individual queries):

Query	Average precision
Query 91:	0.0399
Query 92:	0.3834
Query 93:	0.8048
Query 94:	0.8332
Query 95:	0.6612
Query 96:	0.4245
Query 97:	0.6043
Query 98:	0.9444
Query 99:	0.2523
Query 100:	0.6207
Query 101:	0.6726
Query 102:	0.6779
Query 103:	0.7264
Query 104:	0.1406
Query 105:	0.1418
Query 106:	0.0774
Query 107:	0.0190
Query 108:	0.4755
Query 109:	0.5486
Query 110:	0.3808
Query 111:	0.1157
Query 112:	0.3210
Query 113:	0.0037
Query 114:	0.6332
Query 115:	0.4183
Query 116:	0.7487
Query 117:	0.1235
Query 118:	0.1402
Query 119:	0.7297
Query 120:	0.0543
Query 121:	0.3169
Query 122:	0.3888
Query 123:	0.7799
Query 124:	0.7655
Query 125:	0.4012
Query 126:	0.0001
Query 127:	0.8026
Query 128:	0.0354
Query 129:	0.6950
Query 130:	0.5729
Query 131:	0.6079
Query 132:	0.5845
Query 133:	0.1439
Query 134:	0.8929
Query 135:	0.7943
Query 136:	1.0000
Query 137:	0.0000
Query 138:	0.1287
Query 139:	0.2814
Query 140:	0.8017

Overall statistics (for 50 queries):

Total number of documents over all queries

Retrieved:	50000
Relevant:	1862
Rel_ret:	1683

Interpolated Recall - Precision Averages:

at 0.00	0.7516
at 0.10	0.6949
at 0.20	0.6093
at 0.30	0.5683
at 0.40	0.5135
at 0.50	0.4762
at 0.60	0.4195
at 0.70	0.3794
at 0.80	0.3245
at 0.90	0.2403
at 1.00	0.1437

Avg. prec. (non-interpolated) for all rel. documents 0.4542

Precision:

At 5 docs:	0.5840
At 10 docs:	0.5060
At 15 docs:	0.4707
At 20 docs:	0.4380
At 30 docs:	0.3840
At 100 docs:	0.2222
At 200 docs:	0.1371
At 500 docs:	0.0636
At 1000 docs:	0.0337

R-Precision (prec. after R (=num_rel) docs. retrieved):
Exact: 0.4326

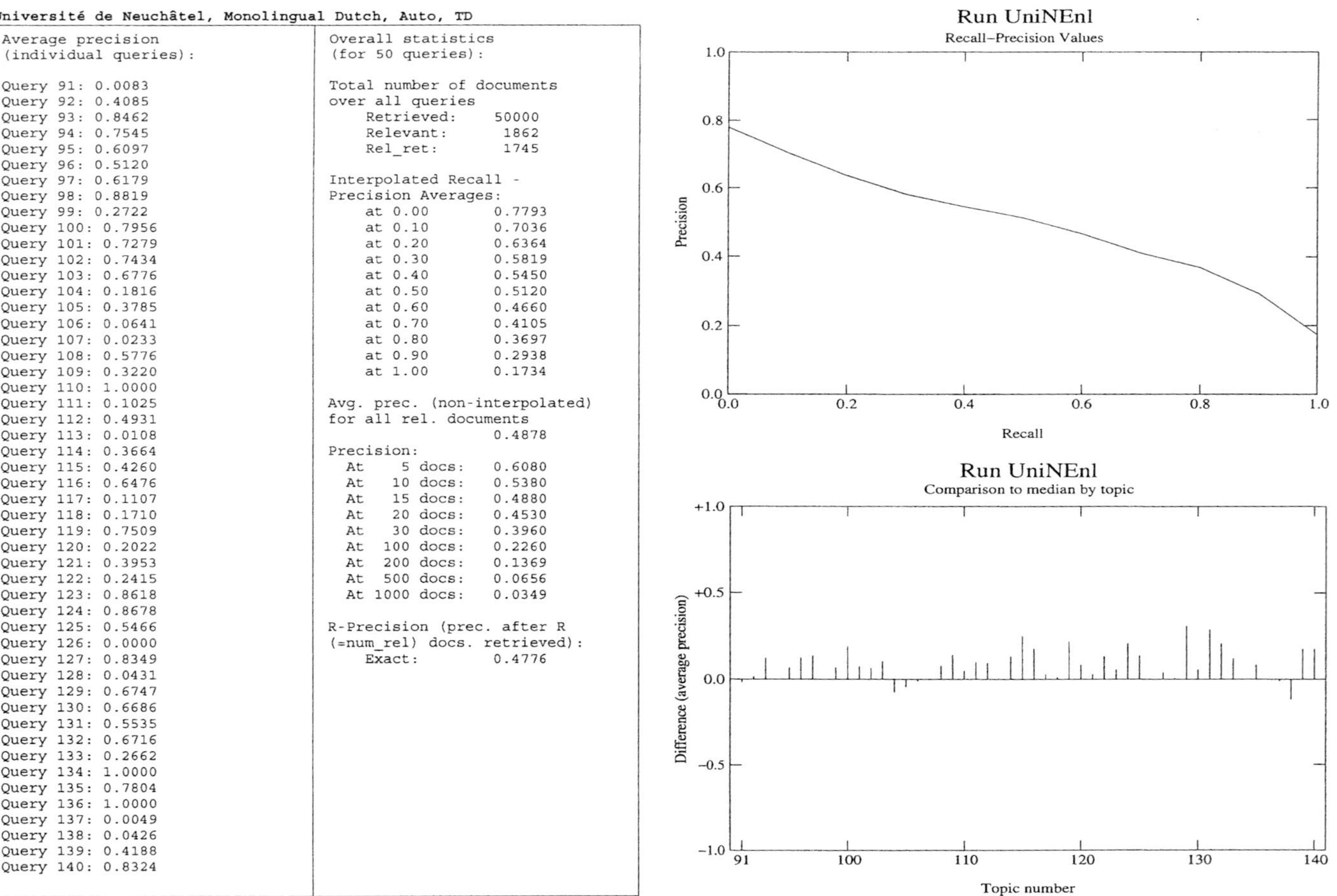

Université de Neuchâtel, Monolingual Dutch, Auto, TD

```
Average precision            Overall statistics
(individual queries):        (for 50 queries):

Query 91: 0.0083             Total number of documents
Query 92: 0.4085             over all queries
Query 93: 0.8462                 Retrieved:    50000
Query 94: 0.7545                 Relevant:      1862
Query 95: 0.6097                 Rel_ret:       1745
Query 96: 0.5120
Query 97: 0.6179             Interpolated Recall -
Query 98: 0.8819             Precision Averages:
Query 99: 0.2722                 at 0.00       0.7793
Query 100: 0.7956                at 0.10       0.7036
Query 101: 0.7279                at 0.20       0.6364
Query 102: 0.7434                at 0.30       0.5819
Query 103: 0.6776                at 0.40       0.5450
Query 104: 0.1816                at 0.50       0.5120
Query 105: 0.3785                at 0.60       0.4660
Query 106: 0.0641                at 0.70       0.4105
Query 107: 0.0233                at 0.80       0.3697
Query 108: 0.5776                at 0.90       0.2938
Query 109: 0.3220                at 1.00       0.1734
Query 110: 1.0000
Query 111: 0.1025            Avg. prec. (non-interpolated)
Query 112: 0.4931            for all rel. documents
Query 113: 0.0108                              0.4878
Query 114: 0.3664            Precision:
Query 115: 0.4260              At    5 docs:   0.6080
Query 116: 0.6476              At   10 docs:   0.5380
Query 117: 0.1107              At   15 docs:   0.4880
Query 118: 0.1710              At   20 docs:   0.4530
Query 119: 0.7509              At   30 docs:   0.3960
Query 120: 0.2022              At  100 docs:   0.2260
Query 121: 0.3953              At  200 docs:   0.1369
Query 122: 0.2415              At  500 docs:   0.0656
Query 123: 0.8618              At 1000 docs:   0.0349
Query 124: 0.8678
Query 125: 0.5466            R-Precision (prec. after R
Query 126: 0.0000            (=num_rel) docs. retrieved):
Query 127: 0.8349                Exact:        0.4776
Query 128: 0.0431
Query 129: 0.6747
Query 130: 0.6686
Query 131: 0.5535
Query 132: 0.6716
Query 133: 0.2662
Query 134: 1.0000
Query 135: 0.7804
Query 136: 1.0000
Query 137: 0.0049
Query 138: 0.0426
Query 139: 0.4188
Query 140: 0.8324
```

JHU/AFL, Monolingual Swedish, Auto, TD

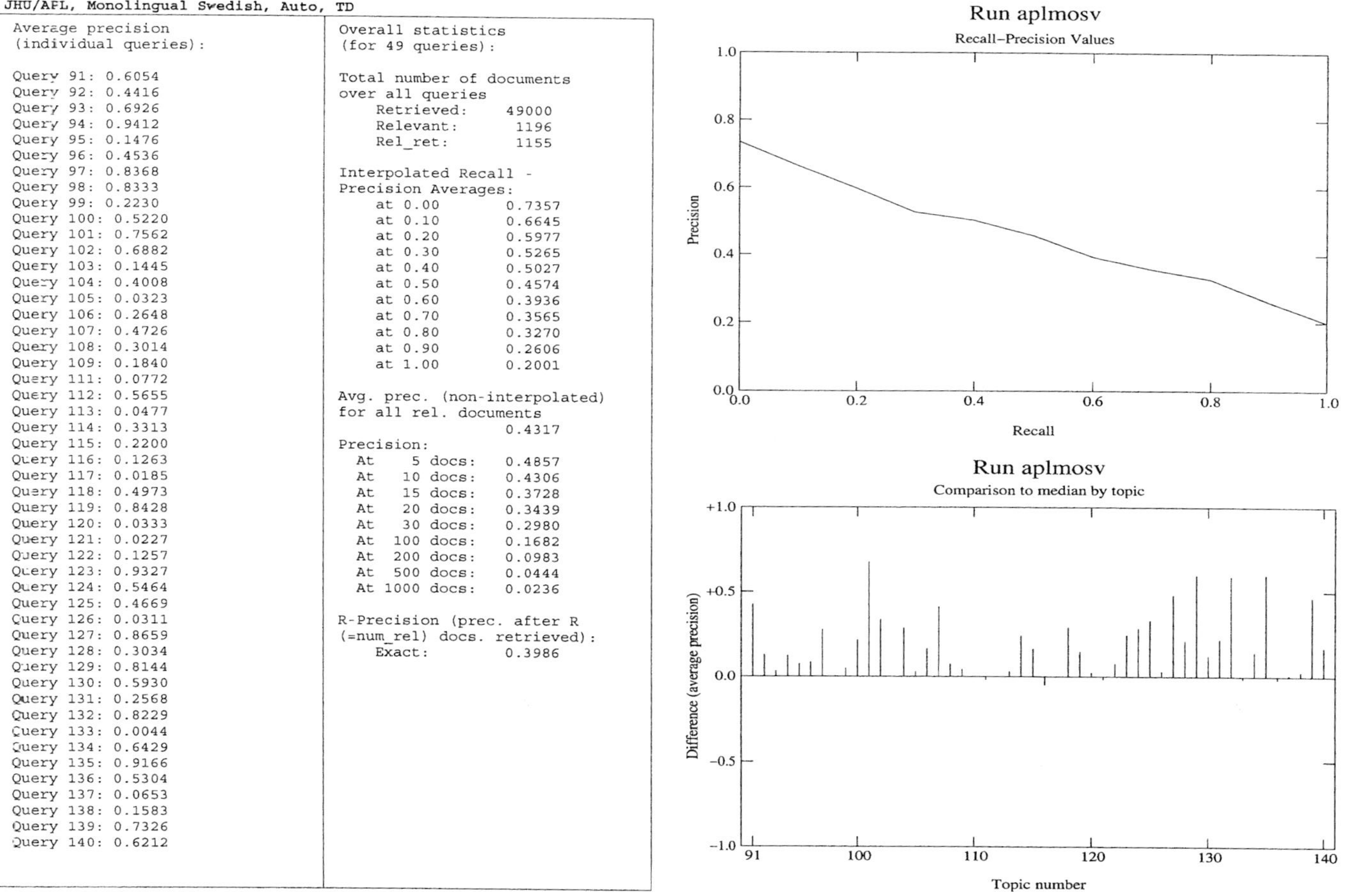

Average precision (individual queries):	Overall statistics (for 49 queries):
Query 91: 0.6054	Total number of documents over all queries
Query 92: 0.4416	Retrieved: 49000
Query 93: 0.6926	Relevant: 1196
Query 94: 0.9412	Rel_ret: 1155
Query 95: 0.1476	
Query 96: 0.4536	Interpolated Recall - Precision Averages:
Query 97: 0.8368	at 0.00 0.7357
Query 98: 0.8333	at 0.10 0.6645
Query 99: 0.2230	at 0.20 0.5977
Query 100: 0.5220	at 0.30 0.5265
Query 101: 0.7562	at 0.40 0.5027
Query 102: 0.6882	at 0.50 0.4574
Query 103: 0.1445	at 0.60 0.3936
Query 104: 0.4008	at 0.70 0.3565
Query 105: 0.0323	at 0.80 0.3270
Query 106: 0.2648	at 0.90 0.2606
Query 107: 0.4726	at 1.00 0.2001
Query 108: 0.3014	
Query 109: 0.1840	Avg. prec. (non-interpolated) for all rel. documents 0.4317
Query 111: 0.0772	
Query 112: 0.5655	Precision:
Query 113: 0.0477	At 5 docs: 0.4857
Query 114: 0.3313	At 10 docs: 0.4306
Query 115: 0.2200	At 15 docs: 0.3728
Query 116: 0.1263	At 20 docs: 0.3439
Query 117: 0.0185	At 30 docs: 0.2980
Query 118: 0.4973	At 100 docs: 0.1682
Query 119: 0.8428	At 200 docs: 0.0983
Query 120: 0.0333	At 500 docs: 0.0444
Query 121: 0.0227	At 1000 docs: 0.0236
Query 122: 0.1257	
Query 123: 0.9327	R-Precision (prec. after R (=num_rel) docs. retrieved):
Query 124: 0.5464	Exact: 0.3986
Query 125: 0.4669	
Query 126: 0.0311	
Query 127: 0.8659	
Query 128: 0.3034	
Query 129: 0.8144	
Query 130: 0.5930	
Query 131: 0.2568	
Query 132: 0.8229	
Query 133: 0.0044	
Query 134: 0.6429	
Query 135: 0.9166	
Query 136: 0.5304	
Query 137: 0.0653	
Query 138: 0.1583	
Query 139: 0.7326	
Query 140: 0.6212	

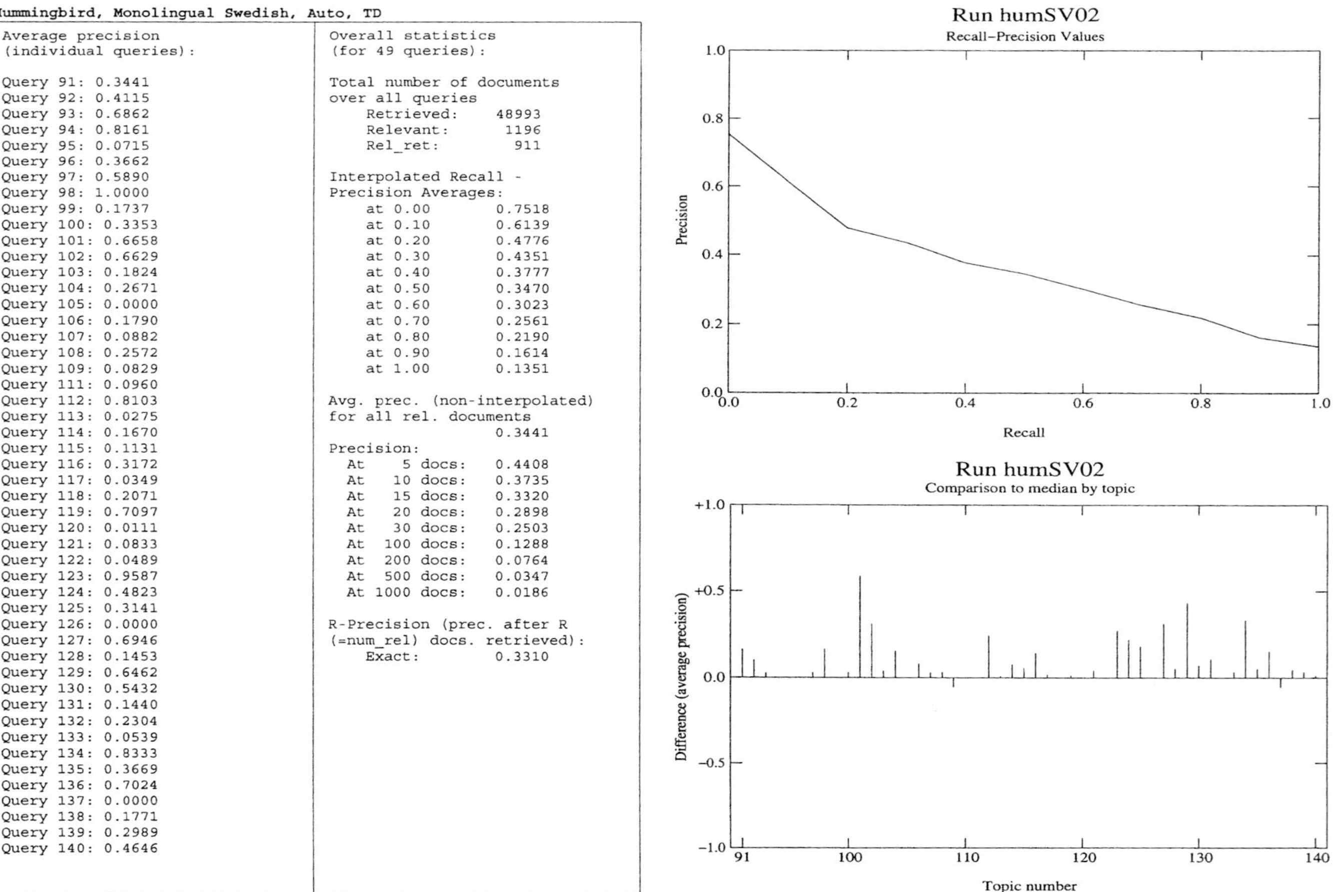

Hummingbird, Monolingual Swedish, Auto, TD

```
Average precision                   Overall statistics
(individual queries):               (for 49 queries):

Query 91: 0.3441                    Total number of documents
Query 92: 0.4115                    over all queries
Query 93: 0.6862                        Retrieved:    48993
Query 94: 0.8161                        Relevant:      1196
Query 95: 0.0715                        Rel_ret:        911
Query 96: 0.3662
Query 97: 0.5890                    Interpolated Recall -
Query 98: 1.0000                    Precision Averages:
Query 99: 0.1737                        at 0.00       0.7518
Query 100: 0.3353                       at 0.10       0.6139
Query 101: 0.6658                       at 0.20       0.4776
Query 102: 0.6629                       at 0.30       0.4351
Query 103: 0.1824                       at 0.40       0.3777
Query 104: 0.2671                       at 0.50       0.3470
Query 105: 0.0000                       at 0.60       0.3023
Query 106: 0.1790                       at 0.70       0.2561
Query 107: 0.0882                       at 0.80       0.2190
Query 108: 0.2572                       at 0.90       0.1614
Query 109: 0.0829                       at 1.00       0.1351
Query 111: 0.0960
Query 112: 0.8103                   Avg. prec. (non-interpolated)
Query 113: 0.0275                   for all rel. documents
Query 114: 0.1670                                     0.3441
Query 115: 0.1131                   Precision:
Query 116: 0.3172                     At    5 docs:   0.4408
Query 117: 0.0349                     At   10 docs:   0.3735
Query 118: 0.2071                     At   15 docs:   0.3320
Query 119: 0.7097                     At   20 docs:   0.2898
Query 120: 0.0111                     At   30 docs:   0.2503
Query 121: 0.0833                     At  100 docs:   0.1288
Query 122: 0.0489                     At  200 docs:   0.0764
Query 123: 0.9587                     At  500 docs:   0.0347
Query 124: 0.4823                     At 1000 docs:   0.0186
Query 125: 0.3141
Query 126: 0.0000                   R-Precision (prec. after R
Query 127: 0.6946                   (=num_rel) docs. retrieved):
Query 128: 0.1453                       Exact:        0.3310
Query 129: 0.6462
Query 130: 0.5432
Query 131: 0.1440
Query 132: 0.2304
Query 133: 0.0539
Query 134: 0.8333
Query 135: 0.3669
Query 136: 0.7024
Query 137: 0.0000
Query 138: 0.1771
Query 139: 0.2989
Query 140: 0.4646
```

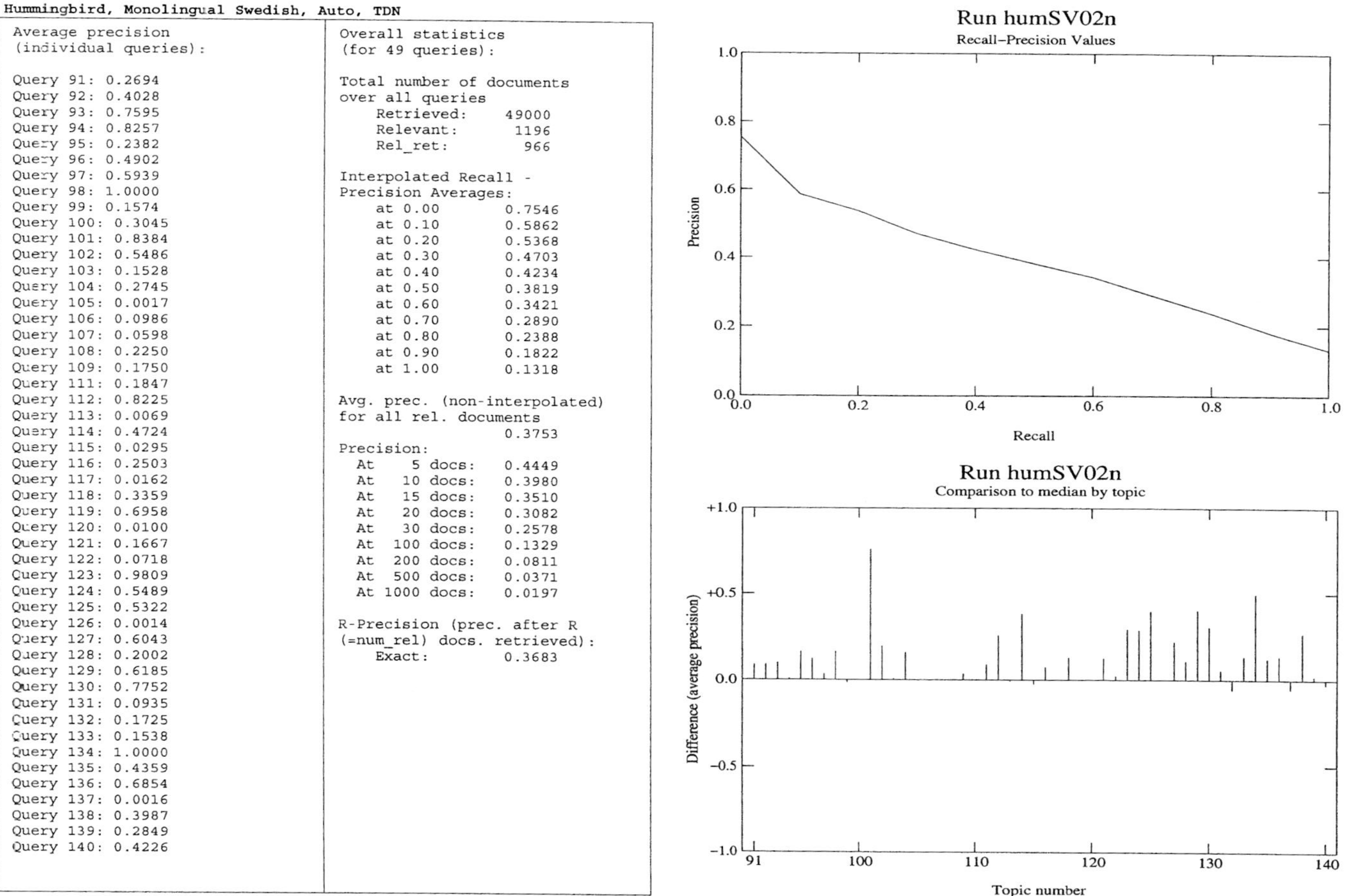

Hummingbird, Monolingual Swedish, Auto, TDN

Average precision (individual queries):	Overall statistics (for 49 queries):
Query 91: 0.2694 Query 92: 0.4028 Query 93: 0.7595 Query 94: 0.8257 Query 95: 0.2382 Query 96: 0.4902 Query 97: 0.5939 Query 98: 1.0000 Query 99: 0.1574 Query 100: 0.3045 Query 101: 0.8384 Query 102: 0.5486 Query 103: 0.1528 Query 104: 0.2745 Query 105: 0.0017 Query 106: 0.0986 Query 107: 0.0598 Query 108: 0.2250 Query 109: 0.1750 Query 111: 0.1847 Query 112: 0.8225 Query 113: 0.0069 Query 114: 0.4724 Query 115: 0.0295 Query 116: 0.2503 Query 117: 0.0162 Query 118: 0.3359 Query 119: 0.6958 Query 120: 0.0100 Query 121: 0.1667 Query 122: 0.0718 Query 123: 0.9809 Query 124: 0.5489 Query 125: 0.5322 Query 126: 0.0014 Query 127: 0.6043 Query 128: 0.2002 Query 129: 0.6185 Query 130: 0.7752 Query 131: 0.0935 Query 132: 0.1725 Query 133: 0.1538 Query 134: 1.0000 Query 135: 0.4359 Query 136: 0.6854 Query 137: 0.0016 Query 138: 0.3987 Query 139: 0.2849 Query 140: 0.4226	Total number of documents over all queries Retrieved: 49000 Relevant: 1196 Rel_ret: 966 Interpolated Recall - Precision Averages: at 0.00 0.7546 at 0.10 0.5862 at 0.20 0.5368 at 0.30 0.4703 at 0.40 0.4234 at 0.50 0.3819 at 0.60 0.3421 at 0.70 0.2890 at 0.80 0.2388 at 0.90 0.1822 at 1.00 0.1318 Avg. prec. (non-interpolated) for all rel. documents 0.3753 Precision: At 5 docs: 0.4449 At 10 docs: 0.3980 At 15 docs: 0.3510 At 20 docs: 0.3082 At 30 docs: 0.2578 At 100 docs: 0.1329 At 200 docs: 0.0811 At 500 docs: 0.0371 At 1000 docs: 0.0197 R-Precision (prec. after R (=num_rel) docs. retrieved): Exact: 0.3683

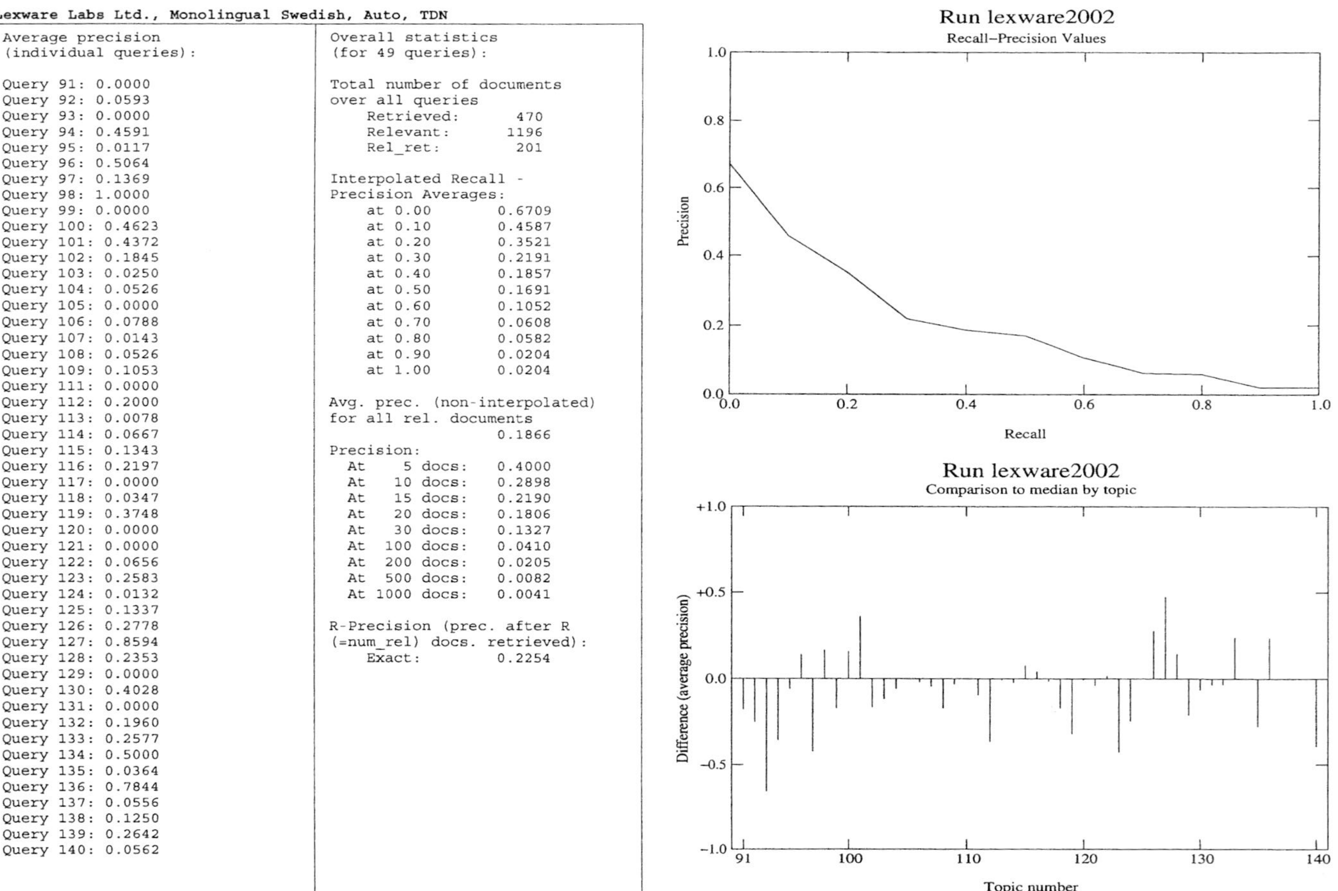

Lexware Labs Ltd., Monolingual Swedish, Auto, TDN

Average precision (individual queries):	Overall statistics (for 49 queries):
Query 91: 0.0000 Query 92: 0.0593 Query 93: 0.0000 Query 94: 0.4591 Query 95: 0.0117 Query 96: 0.5064 Query 97: 0.1369 Query 98: 1.0000 Query 99: 0.0000 Query 100: 0.4623 Query 101: 0.4372 Query 102: 0.1845 Query 103: 0.0250 Query 104: 0.0526 Query 105: 0.0000 Query 106: 0.0788 Query 107: 0.0143 Query 108: 0.0526 Query 109: 0.1053 Query 111: 0.0000 Query 112: 0.2000 Query 113: 0.0078 Query 114: 0.0667 Query 115: 0.1343 Query 116: 0.2197 Query 117: 0.0000 Query 118: 0.0347 Query 119: 0.3748 Query 120: 0.0000 Query 121: 0.0000 Query 122: 0.0656 Query 123: 0.2583 Query 124: 0.0132 Query 125: 0.1337 Query 126: 0.2778 Query 127: 0.8594 Query 128: 0.2353 Query 129: 0.0000 Query 130: 0.4028 Query 131: 0.0000 Query 132: 0.1960 Query 133: 0.2577 Query 134: 0.5000 Query 135: 0.0364 Query 136: 0.7844 Query 137: 0.0556 Query 138: 0.1250 Query 139: 0.2642 Query 140: 0.0562	Total number of documents over all queries Retrieved: 470 Relevant: 1196 Rel_ret: 201 Interpolated Recall - Precision Averages: at 0.00 0.6709 at 0.10 0.4587 at 0.20 0.3521 at 0.30 0.2191 at 0.40 0.1857 at 0.50 0.1691 at 0.60 0.1052 at 0.70 0.0608 at 0.80 0.0582 at 0.90 0.0204 at 1.00 0.0204 Avg. prec. (non-interpolated) for all rel. documents 0.1866 Precision: At 5 docs: 0.4000 At 10 docs: 0.2898 At 15 docs: 0.2190 At 20 docs: 0.1806 At 30 docs: 0.1327 At 100 docs: 0.0410 At 200 docs: 0.0205 At 500 docs: 0.0082 At 1000 docs: 0.0041 R-Precision (prec. after R (=num_rel) docs. retrieved): Exact: 0.2254

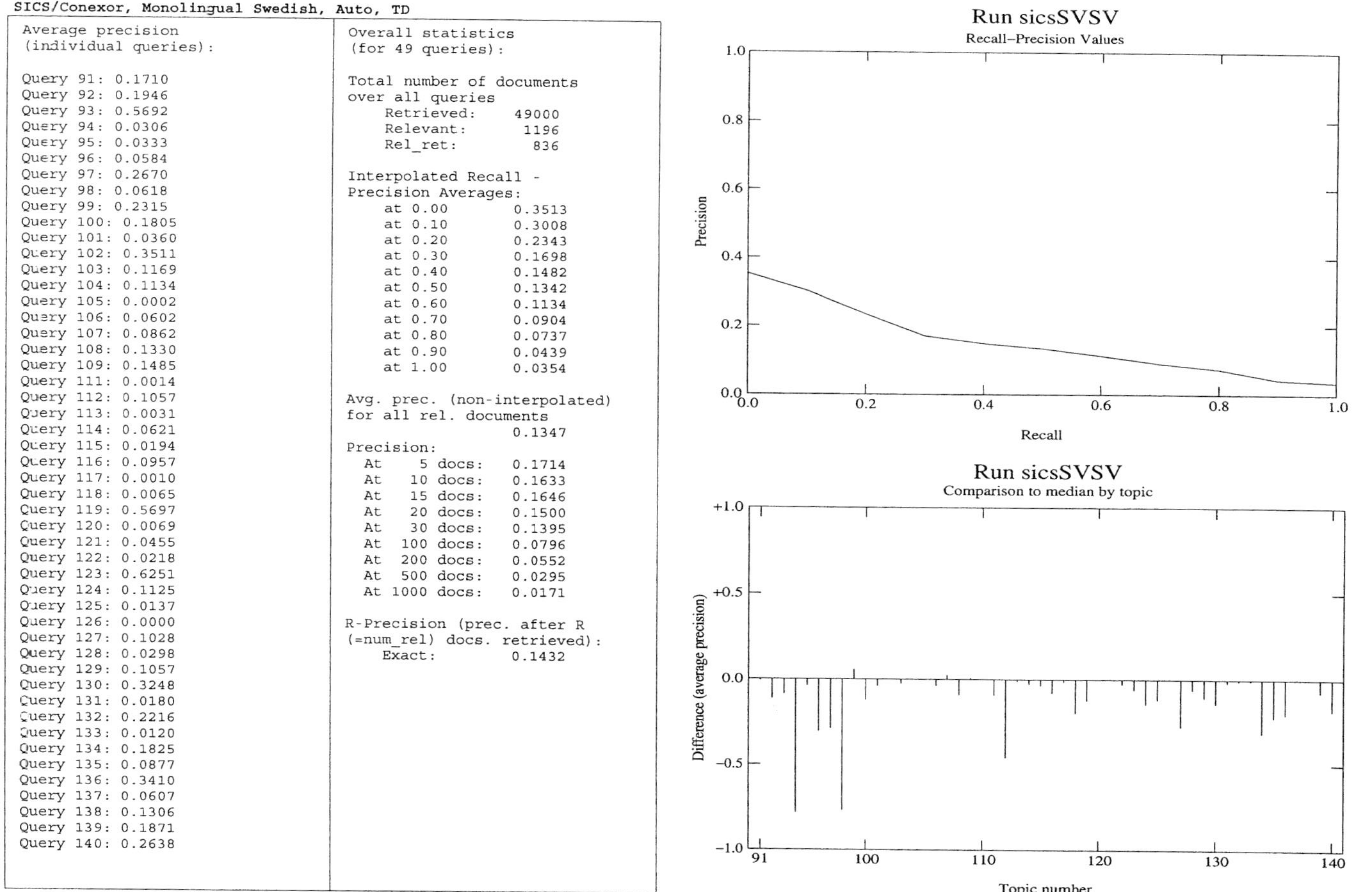

SICS/Conexor, Monolingual Swedish, Auto, TD

```
Average precision                Overall statistics
(individual queries):            (for 49 queries):

Query 91: 0.1710                 Total number of documents
Query 92: 0.1946                 over all queries
Query 93: 0.5692                     Retrieved:    49000
Query 94: 0.0306                     Relevant:      1196
Query 95: 0.0333                     Rel_ret:        836
Query 96: 0.0584
Query 97: 0.2670                 Interpolated Recall -
Query 98: 0.0618                 Precision Averages:
Query 99: 0.2315                     at 0.00       0.3513
Query 100: 0.1805                    at 0.10       0.3008
Query 101: 0.0360                    at 0.20       0.2343
Query 102: 0.3511                    at 0.30       0.1698
Query 103: 0.1169                    at 0.40       0.1482
Query 104: 0.1134                    at 0.50       0.1342
Query 105: 0.0002                    at 0.60       0.1134
Query 106: 0.0602                    at 0.70       0.0904
Query 107: 0.0862                    at 0.80       0.0737
Query 108: 0.1330                    at 0.90       0.0439
Query 109: 0.1485                    at 1.00       0.0354
Query 111: 0.0014
Query 112: 0.1057                Avg. prec. (non-interpolated)
Query 113: 0.0031                for all rel. documents
Query 114: 0.0621                                  0.1347
Query 115: 0.0194                Precision:
Query 116: 0.0957                  At    5 docs:   0.1714
Query 117: 0.0010                  At   10 docs:   0.1633
Query 118: 0.0065                  At   15 docs:   0.1646
Query 119: 0.5697                  At   20 docs:   0.1500
Query 120: 0.0069                  At   30 docs:   0.1395
Query 121: 0.0455                  At  100 docs:   0.0796
Query 122: 0.0218                  At  200 docs:   0.0552
Query 123: 0.6251                  At  500 docs:   0.0295
Query 124: 0.1125                  At 1000 docs:   0.0171
Query 125: 0.0137
Query 126: 0.0000                R-Precision (prec. after R
Query 127: 0.1028                (=num_rel) docs. retrieved):
Query 128: 0.0298                    Exact:        0.1432
Query 129: 0.1057
Query 130: 0.3248
Query 131: 0.0180
Query 132: 0.2216
Query 133: 0.0120
Query 134: 0.1825
Query 135: 0.0877
Query 136: 0.3410
Query 137: 0.0607
Query 138: 0.1306
Query 139: 0.1871
Query 140: 0.2638
```

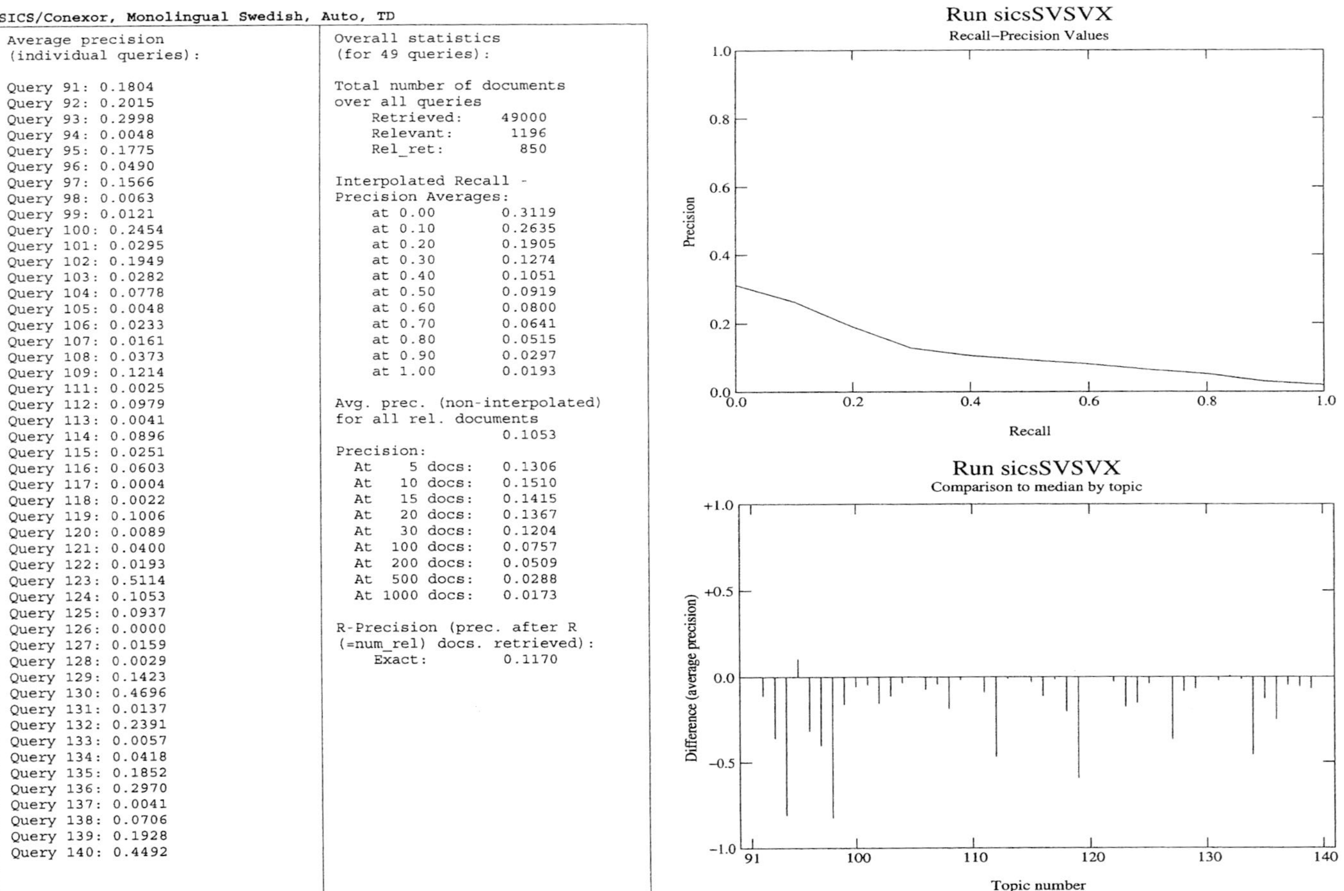

SICS/Conexor, Monolingual Swedish, Auto, TD

```
Average precision                 Overall statistics
(individual queries):             (for 49 queries):

Query 91: 0.1804                  Total number of documents
Query 92: 0.2015                  over all queries
Query 93: 0.2998                      Retrieved:    49000
Query 94: 0.0048                      Relevant:      1196
Query 95: 0.1775                      Rel_ret:        850
Query 96: 0.0490
Query 97: 0.1566                  Interpolated Recall -
Query 98: 0.0063                  Precision Averages:
Query 99: 0.0121                      at 0.00        0.3119
Query 100: 0.2454                     at 0.10        0.2635
Query 101: 0.0295                     at 0.20        0.1905
Query 102: 0.1949                     at 0.30        0.1274
Query 103: 0.0282                     at 0.40        0.1051
Query 104: 0.0778                     at 0.50        0.0919
Query 105: 0.0048                     at 0.60        0.0800
Query 106: 0.0233                     at 0.70        0.0641
Query 107: 0.0161                     at 0.80        0.0515
Query 108: 0.0373                     at 0.90        0.0297
Query 109: 0.1214                     at 1.00        0.0193
Query 111: 0.0025
Query 112: 0.0979                 Avg. prec. (non-interpolated)
Query 113: 0.0041                 for all rel. documents
Query 114: 0.0896                                    0.1053
Query 115: 0.0251                 Precision:
Query 116: 0.0603                   At    5 docs:    0.1306
Query 117: 0.0004                   At   10 docs:    0.1510
Query 118: 0.0022                   At   15 docs:    0.1415
Query 119: 0.1006                   At   20 docs:    0.1367
Query 120: 0.0089                   At   30 docs:    0.1204
Query 121: 0.0400                   At  100 docs:    0.0757
Query 122: 0.0193                   At  200 docs:    0.0509
Query 123: 0.5114                   At  500 docs:    0.0288
Query 124: 0.1053                   At 1000 docs:    0.0173
Query 125: 0.0937
Query 126: 0.0000                 R-Precision (prec. after R
Query 127: 0.0159                 (=num_rel) docs. retrieved):
Query 128: 0.0029                     Exact:         0.1170
Query 129: 0.1423
Query 130: 0.4696
Query 131: 0.0137
Query 132: 0.2391
Query 133: 0.0057
Query 134: 0.0418
Query 135: 0.1852
Query 136: 0.2970
Query 137: 0.0041
Query 138: 0.0706
Query 139: 0.1928
Query 140: 0.4492
```

Run sicsSVSVX

Recall–Precision Values

Run sicsSVSVX

Comparison to median by topic

SICS/Conexor, Monolingual Swedish, Auto, T

```
Average precision                 Overall statistics
(individual queries):             (for 49 queries):

Query 91: 0.0909                  Total number of documents
Query 92: 0.0240                  over all queries
Query 93: 0.6593                      Retrieved:     1796
Query 94: 0.5610                      Relevant:      1196
Query 95: 0.0144                      Rel_ret:        190
Query 96: 0.0556
Query 97: 0.1429                  Interpolated Recall -
Query 98: 0.5000                  Precision Averages:
Query 99: 0.0833                      at 0.00        0.5394
Query 100: 0.0385                     at 0.10        0.3046
Query 101: 0.0083                     at 0.20        0.1873
Query 102: 0.0761                     at 0.30        0.1154
Query 103: 0.0500                     at 0.40        0.1102
Query 104: 0.0787                     at 0.50        0.1029
Query 105: 0.0000                     at 0.60        0.0364
Query 106: 0.0707                     at 0.70        0.0350
Query 107: 0.0333                     at 0.80        0.0340
Query 108: 0.0357                     at 0.90        0.0290
Query 109: 0.1930                     at 1.00        0.0290
Query 111: 0.2364
Query 112: 0.1345                 Avg. prec. (non-interpolated)
Query 113: 0.0166                 for all rel. documents
Query 114: 0.0383                                    0.1143
Query 115: 0.0556                 Precision:
Query 116: 0.1757                   At    5 docs:    0.2408
Query 117: 0.0108                   At   10 docs:    0.1816
Query 118: 0.2000                   At   15 docs:    0.1293
Query 119: 0.0556                   At   20 docs:    0.1051
Query 120: 0.0086                   At   30 docs:    0.0762
Query 121: 0.0000                   At  100 docs:    0.0290
Query 122: 0.0000                   At  200 docs:    0.0160
Query 123: 0.0000                   At  500 docs:    0.0076
Query 124: 0.0263                   At 1000 docs:    0.0039
Query 125: 0.0290
Query 126: 0.0000                 R-Precision (prec. after R
Query 127: 0.0000                 (=num_rel) docs. retrieved):
Query 128: 0.0075                     Exact:         0.1331
Query 129: 0.0000
Query 130: 0.0000
Query 131: 0.0000
Query 132: 0.0222
Query 133: 0.0000
Query 134: 0.5000
Query 135: 0.0364
Query 136: 0.5423
Query 137: 0.1667
Query 138: 0.1250
Query 139: 0.0000
Query 140: 0.4976
```

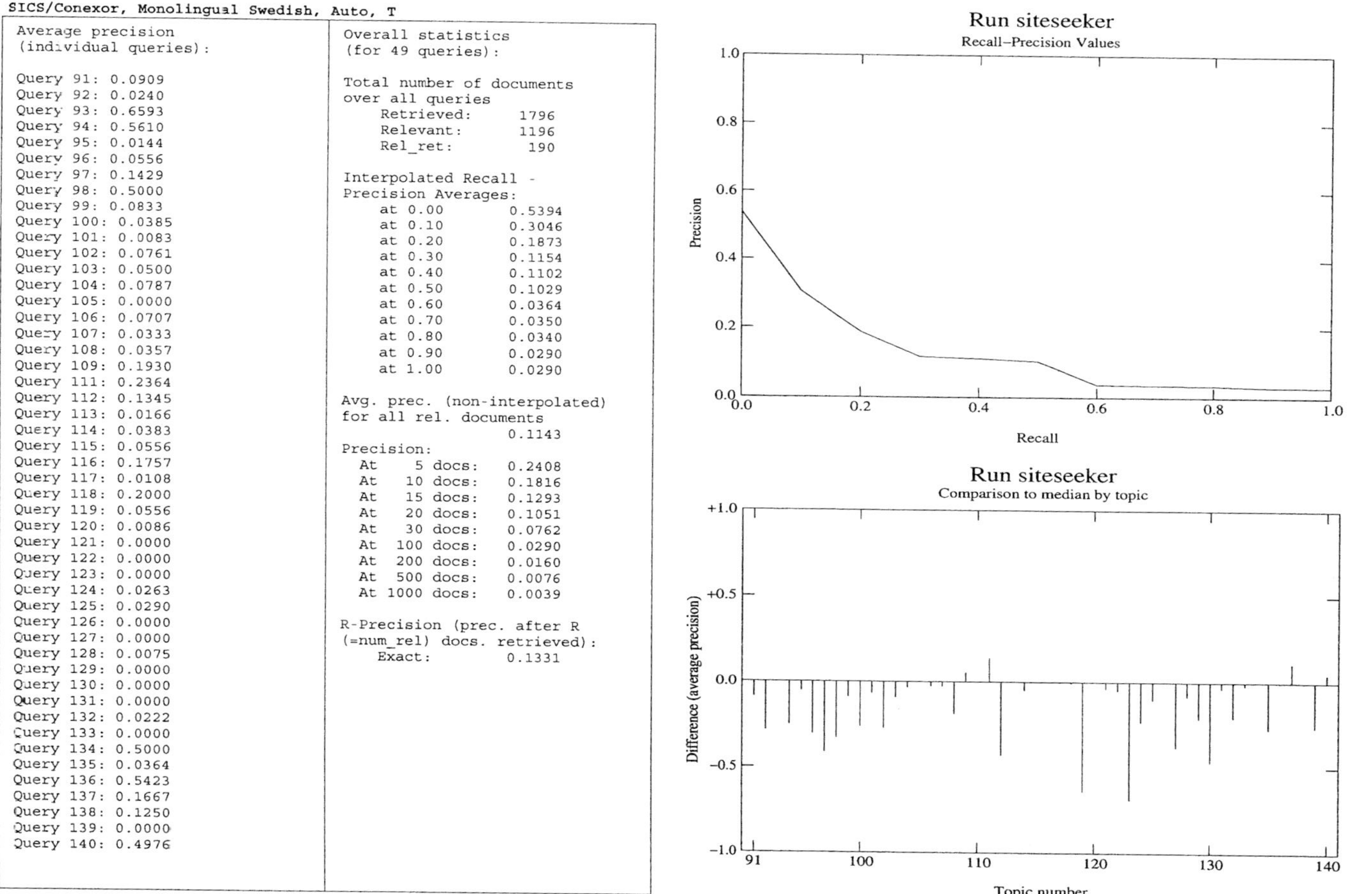

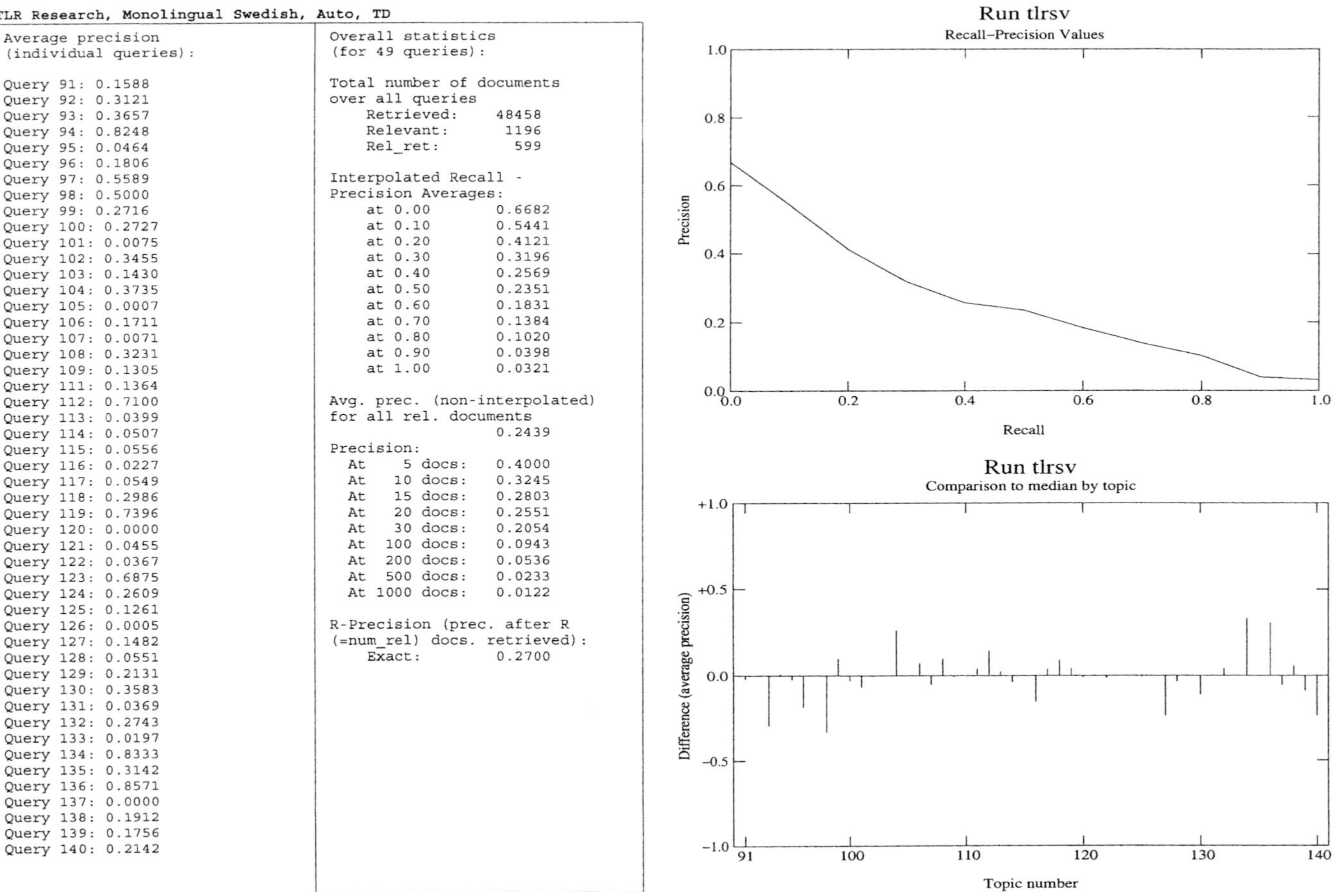

TLR Research, Monolingual Swedish, Auto, TD

Average precision (individual queries):	Overall statistics (for 49 queries):
Query 91: 0.1588	Total number of documents over all queries
Query 92: 0.3121	Retrieved: 48458
Query 93: 0.3657	Relevant: 1196
Query 94: 0.8248	Rel_ret: 599
Query 95: 0.0464	
Query 96: 0.1806	Interpolated Recall - Precision Averages:
Query 97: 0.5589	at 0.00 0.6682
Query 98: 0.5000	at 0.10 0.5441
Query 99: 0.2716	at 0.20 0.4121
Query 100: 0.2727	at 0.30 0.3196
Query 101: 0.0075	at 0.40 0.2569
Query 102: 0.3455	at 0.50 0.2351
Query 103: 0.1430	at 0.60 0.1831
Query 104: 0.3735	at 0.70 0.1384
Query 105: 0.0007	at 0.80 0.1020
Query 106: 0.1711	at 0.90 0.0398
Query 107: 0.0071	at 1.00 0.0321
Query 108: 0.3231	
Query 109: 0.1305	Avg. prec. (non-interpolated) for all rel. documents 0.2439
Query 111: 0.1364	
Query 112: 0.7100	Precision:
Query 113: 0.0399	At 5 docs: 0.4000
Query 114: 0.0507	At 10 docs: 0.3245
Query 115: 0.0556	At 15 docs: 0.2803
Query 116: 0.0227	At 20 docs: 0.2551
Query 117: 0.0549	At 30 docs: 0.2054
Query 118: 0.2986	At 100 docs: 0.0943
Query 119: 0.7396	At 200 docs: 0.0536
Query 120: 0.0000	At 500 docs: 0.0233
Query 121: 0.0455	At 1000 docs: 0.0122
Query 122: 0.0367	
Query 123: 0.6875	R-Precision (prec. after R (=num_rel) docs. retrieved):
Query 124: 0.2609	Exact: 0.2700
Query 125: 0.1261	
Query 126: 0.0005	
Query 127: 0.1482	
Query 128: 0.0551	
Query 129: 0.2131	
Query 130: 0.3583	
Query 131: 0.0369	
Query 132: 0.2743	
Query 133: 0.0197	
Query 134: 0.8333	
Query 135: 0.3142	
Query 136: 0.8571	
Query 137: 0.0000	
Query 138: 0.1912	
Query 139: 0.1756	
Query 140: 0.2142	

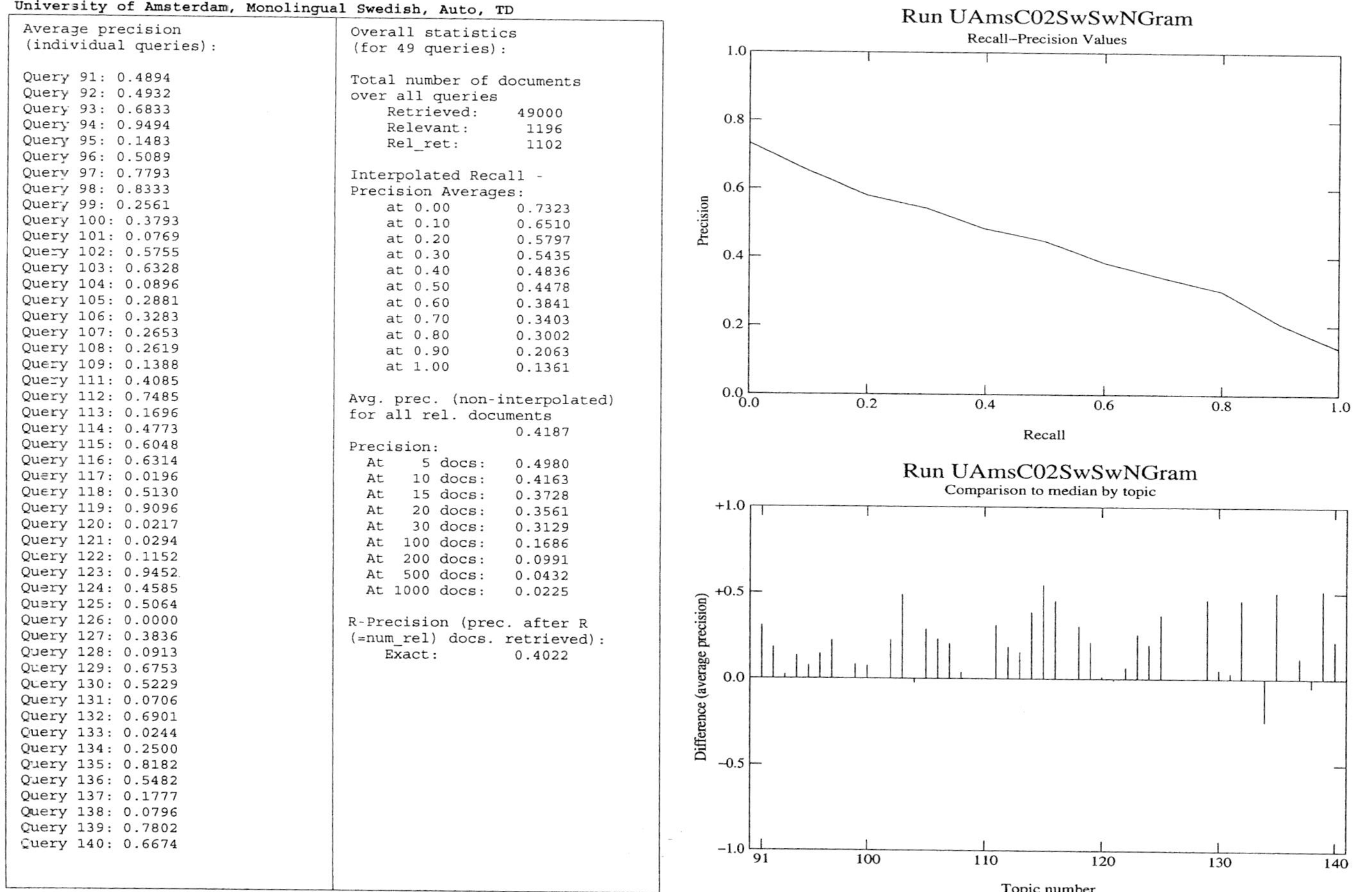

University of Amsterdam, Monolingual Swedish, Auto, TD

Average precision (individual queries):	Overall statistics (for 49 queries):
Query 91: 0.4894	Total number of documents over all queries
Query 92: 0.4932	Retrieved: 49000
Query 93: 0.6833	Relevant: 1196
Query 94: 0.9494	Rel_ret: 1102
Query 95: 0.1483	
Query 96: 0.5089	Interpolated Recall - Precision Averages:
Query 97: 0.7793	at 0.00 0.7323
Query 98: 0.8333	at 0.10 0.6510
Query 99: 0.2561	at 0.20 0.5797
Query 100: 0.3793	at 0.30 0.5435
Query 101: 0.0769	at 0.40 0.4836
Query 102: 0.5755	at 0.50 0.4478
Query 103: 0.6328	at 0.60 0.3841
Query 104: 0.0896	at 0.70 0.3403
Query 105: 0.2881	at 0.80 0.3002
Query 106: 0.3283	at 0.90 0.2063
Query 107: 0.2653	at 1.00 0.1361
Query 108: 0.2619	
Query 109: 0.1388	Avg. prec. (non-interpolated) for all rel. documents 0.4187
Query 111: 0.4085	
Query 112: 0.7485	Precision:
Query 113: 0.1696	At 5 docs: 0.4980
Query 114: 0.4773	At 10 docs: 0.4163
Query 115: 0.6048	At 15 docs: 0.3728
Query 116: 0.6314	At 20 docs: 0.3561
Query 117: 0.0196	At 30 docs: 0.3129
Query 118: 0.5130	At 100 docs: 0.1686
Query 119: 0.9096	At 200 docs: 0.0991
Query 120: 0.0217	At 500 docs: 0.0432
Query 121: 0.0294	At 1000 docs: 0.0225
Query 122: 0.1152	
Query 123: 0.9452	R-Precision (prec. after R (=num_rel) docs. retrieved):
Query 124: 0.4585	Exact: 0.4022
Query 125: 0.5064	
Query 126: 0.0000	
Query 127: 0.3836	
Query 128: 0.0913	
Query 129: 0.6753	
Query 130: 0.5229	
Query 131: 0.0706	
Query 132: 0.6901	
Query 133: 0.0244	
Query 134: 0.2500	
Query 135: 0.8182	
Query 136: 0.5482	
Query 137: 0.1777	
Query 138: 0.0796	
Query 139: 0.7802	
Query 140: 0.6674	

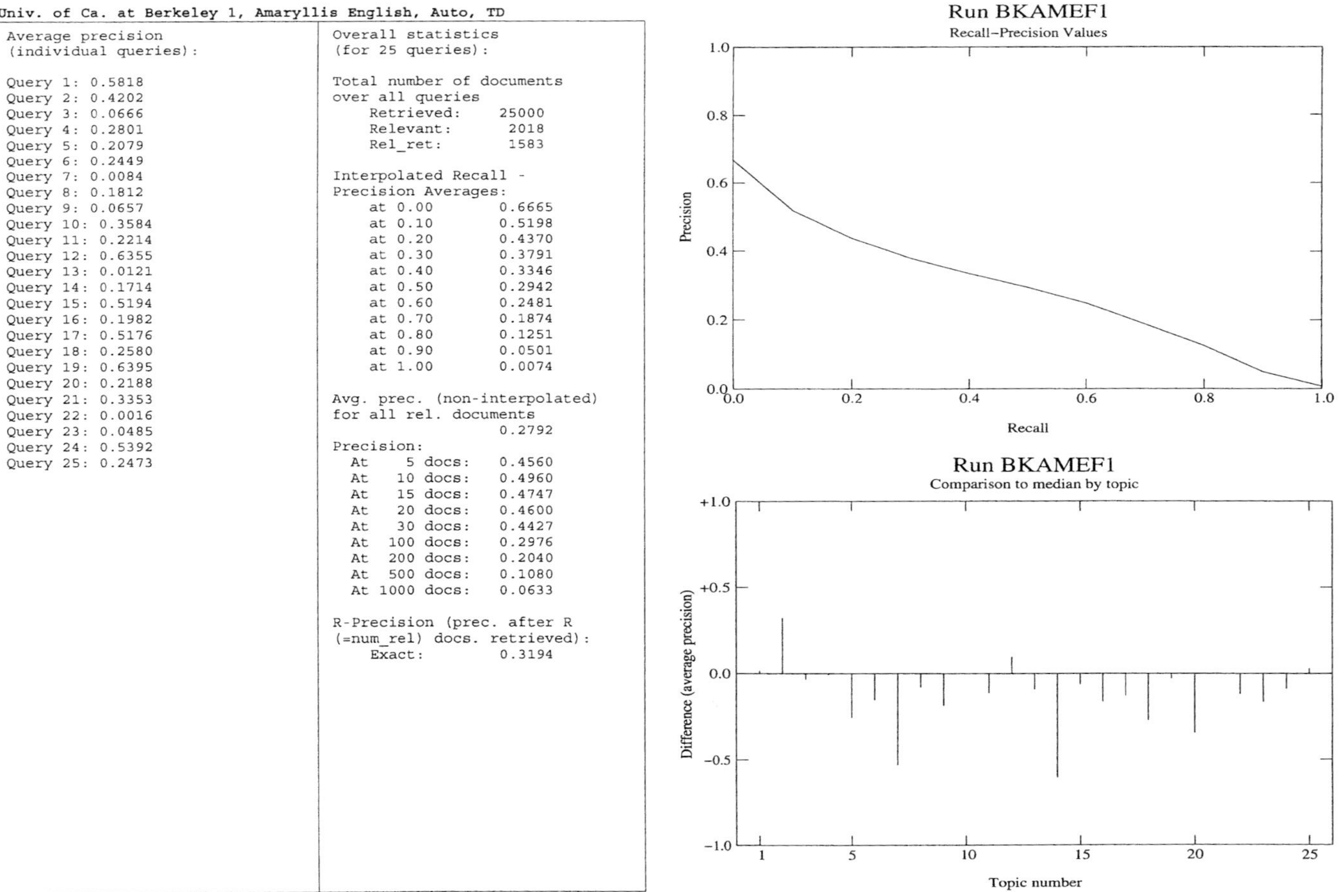

Univ. of Ca. at Berkeley 1, Amaryllis English, Auto, TD

Average precision (individual queries):

Query	Average precision
Query 1:	0.5818
Query 2:	0.4202
Query 3:	0.0666
Query 4:	0.2801
Query 5:	0.2079
Query 6:	0.2449
Query 7:	0.0084
Query 8:	0.1812
Query 9:	0.0657
Query 10:	0.3584
Query 11:	0.2214
Query 12:	0.6355
Query 13:	0.0121
Query 14:	0.1714
Query 15:	0.5194
Query 16:	0.1982
Query 17:	0.5176
Query 18:	0.2580
Query 19:	0.6395
Query 20:	0.2188
Query 21:	0.3353
Query 22:	0.0016
Query 23:	0.0485
Query 24:	0.5392
Query 25:	0.2473

Overall statistics (for 25 queries):

Total number of documents over all queries	
Retrieved:	25000
Relevant:	2018
Rel_ret:	1583
Interpolated Recall - Precision Averages:	
at 0.00	0.6665
at 0.10	0.5198
at 0.20	0.4370
at 0.30	0.3791
at 0.40	0.3346
at 0.50	0.2942
at 0.60	0.2481
at 0.70	0.1874
at 0.80	0.1251
at 0.90	0.0501
at 1.00	0.0074
Avg. prec. (non-interpolated) for all rel. documents	0.2792
Precision:	
At 5 docs:	0.4560
At 10 docs:	0.4960
At 15 docs:	0.4747
At 20 docs:	0.4600
At 30 docs:	0.4427
At 100 docs:	0.2976
At 200 docs:	0.2040
At 500 docs:	0.1080
At 1000 docs:	0.0633
R-Precision (prec. after R (=num_rel) docs. retrieved):	
Exact:	0.3194

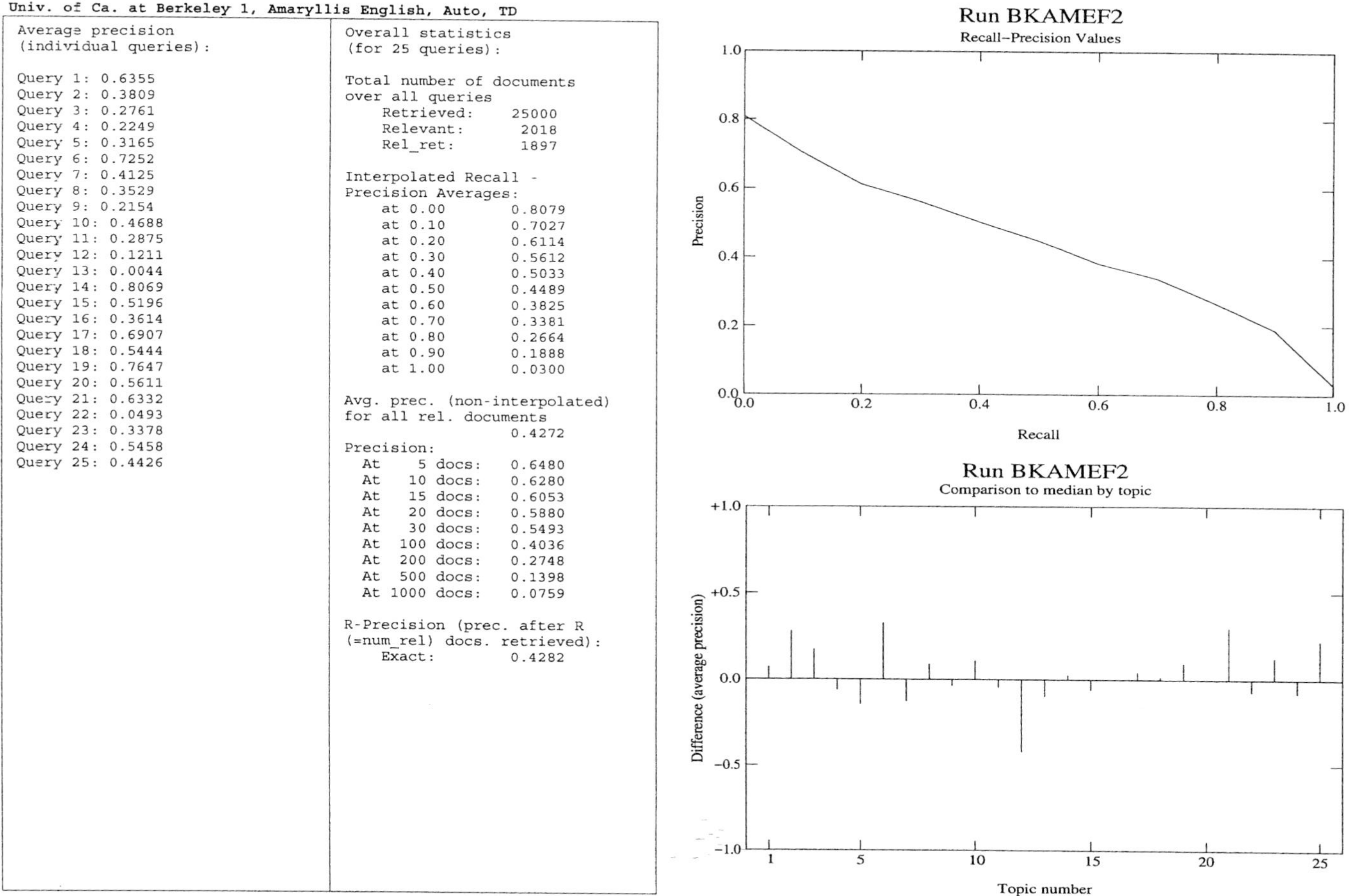

Univ. of Ca. at Berkeley 1, Amaryllis English, Auto, TD

Average precision (individual queries):

Query	Average precision
Query 1:	0.6355
Query 2:	0.3809
Query 3:	0.2761
Query 4:	0.2249
Query 5:	0.3165
Query 6:	0.7252
Query 7:	0.4125
Query 8:	0.3529
Query 9:	0.2154
Query 10:	0.4688
Query 11:	0.2875
Query 12:	0.1211
Query 13:	0.0044
Query 14:	0.8069
Query 15:	0.5196
Query 16:	0.3614
Query 17:	0.6907
Query 18:	0.5444
Query 19:	0.7647
Query 20:	0.5611
Query 21:	0.6332
Query 22:	0.0493
Query 23:	0.3378
Query 24:	0.5458
Query 25:	0.4426

Overall statistics (for 25 queries):

Total number of documents over all queries

Retrieved:	25000
Relevant:	2018
Rel_ret:	1897

Interpolated Recall - Precision Averages:

at 0.00	0.8079
at 0.10	0.7027
at 0.20	0.6114
at 0.30	0.5612
at 0.40	0.5033
at 0.50	0.4489
at 0.60	0.3825
at 0.70	0.3381
at 0.80	0.2664
at 0.90	0.1888
at 1.00	0.0300

Avg. prec. (non-interpolated) for all rel. documents 0.4272

Precision:

At 5 docs:	0.6480
At 10 docs:	0.6280
At 15 docs:	0.6053
At 20 docs:	0.5880
At 30 docs:	0.5493
At 100 docs:	0.4036
At 200 docs:	0.2748
At 500 docs:	0.1398
At 1000 docs:	0.0759

R-Precision (prec. after R (=num_rel) docs. retrieved):
Exact: 0.4282

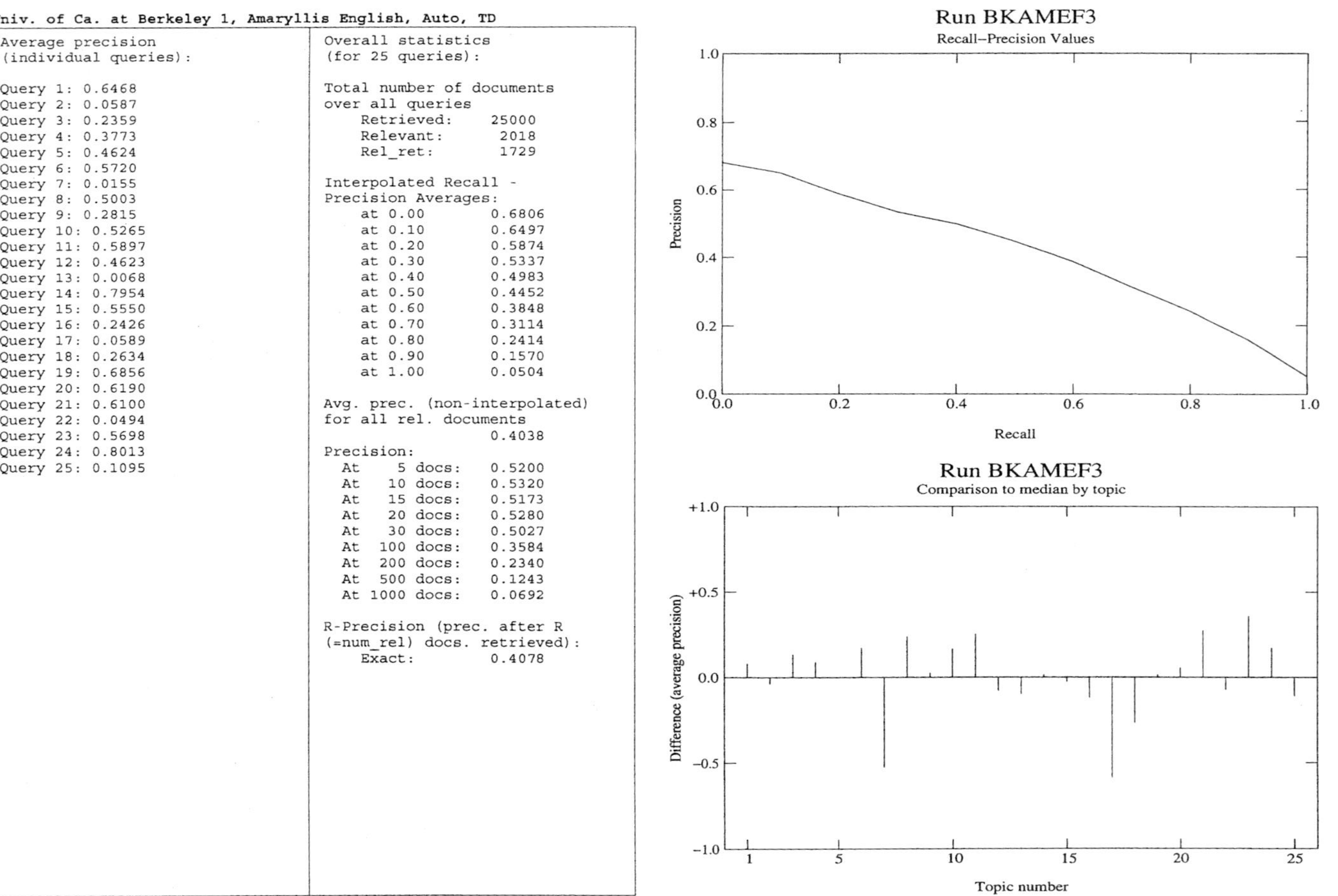

Univ. of Ca. at Berkeley 1, Amaryllis English, Auto, TD

```
Average precision                  Overall statistics
(individual queries):              (for 25 queries):

Query 1: 0.6468                    Total number of documents
Query 2: 0.0587                    over all queries
Query 3: 0.2359                        Retrieved:    25000
Query 4: 0.3773                        Relevant:      2018
Query 5: 0.4624                        Rel_ret:       1729
Query 6: 0.5720
Query 7: 0.0155                    Interpolated Recall -
Query 8: 0.5003                    Precision Averages:
Query 9: 0.2815                        at 0.00        0.6806
Query 10: 0.5265                       at 0.10        0.6497
Query 11: 0.5897                       at 0.20        0.5874
Query 12: 0.4623                       at 0.30        0.5337
Query 13: 0.0068                       at 0.40        0.4983
Query 14: 0.7954                       at 0.50        0.4452
Query 15: 0.5550                       at 0.60        0.3848
Query 16: 0.2426                       at 0.70        0.3114
Query 17: 0.0589                       at 0.80        0.2414
Query 18: 0.2634                       at 0.90        0.1570
Query 19: 0.6856                       at 1.00        0.0504
Query 20: 0.6190
Query 21: 0.6100                   Avg. prec. (non-interpolated)
Query 22: 0.0494                   for all rel. documents
Query 23: 0.5698                                      0.4038
Query 24: 0.8013                   Precision:
Query 25: 0.1095                     At    5 docs:    0.5200
                                     At   10 docs:    0.5320
                                     At   15 docs:    0.5173
                                     At   20 docs:    0.5280
                                     At   30 docs:    0.5027
                                     At  100 docs:    0.3584
                                     At  200 docs:    0.2340
                                     At  500 docs:    0.1243
                                     At 1000 docs:    0.0692

                                   R-Precision (prec. after R
                                   (=num_rel) docs. retrieved):
                                       Exact:         0.4078
```

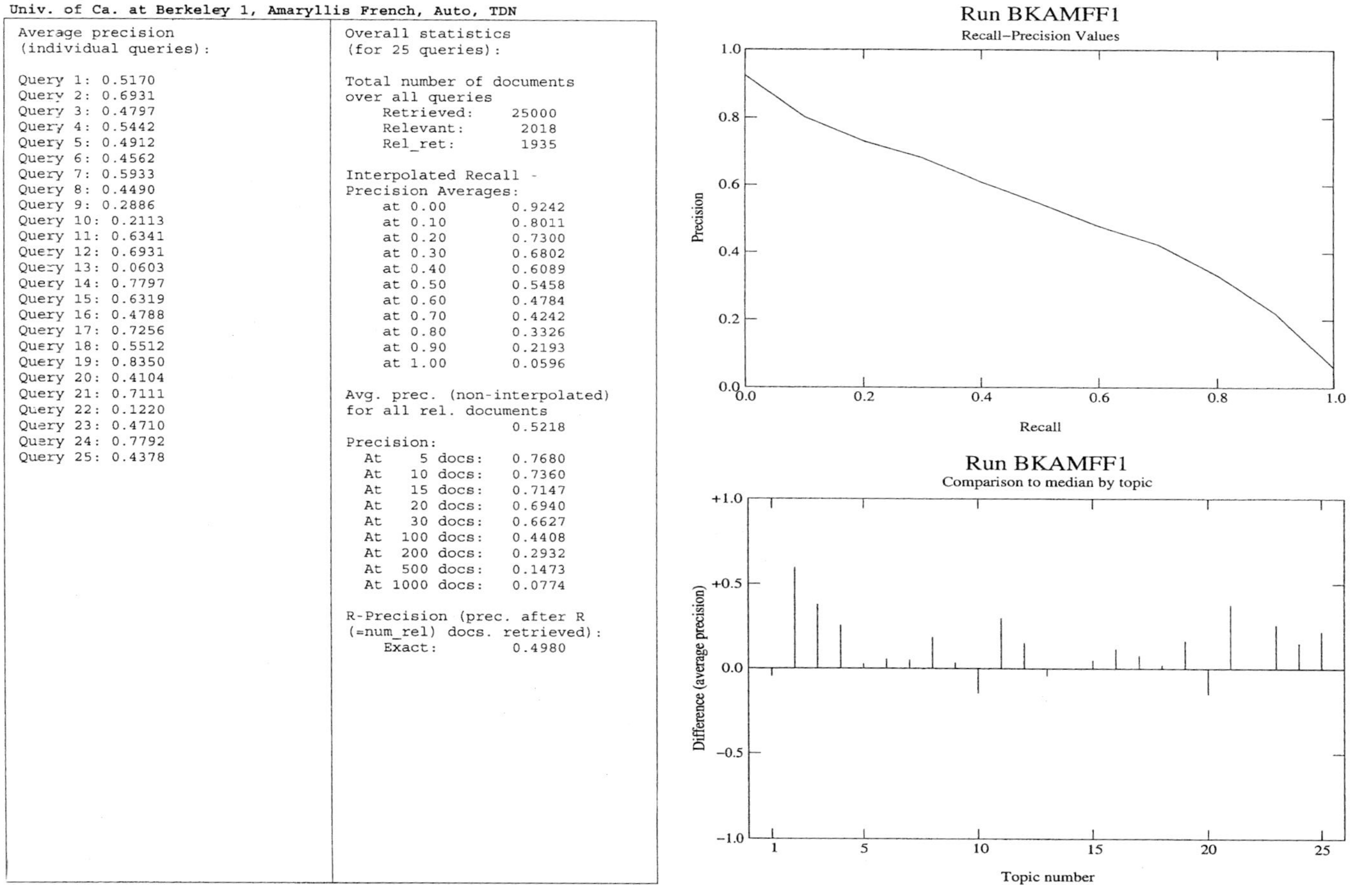

Univ. of Ca. at Berkeley 1, Amaryllis French, Auto, TDN

Average precision (individual queries):	Overall statistics (for 25 queries):	
Query 1: 0.5170	Total number of documents over all queries	
Query 2: 0.6931	Retrieved:	25000
Query 3: 0.4797	Relevant:	2018
Query 4: 0.5442	Rel_ret:	1935
Query 5: 0.4912	Interpolated Recall - Precision Averages:	
Query 6: 0.4562	at 0.00	0.9242
Query 7: 0.5933	at 0.10	0.8011
Query 8: 0.4490	at 0.20	0.7300
Query 9: 0.2886	at 0.30	0.6802
Query 10: 0.2113	at 0.40	0.6089
Query 11: 0.6341	at 0.50	0.5458
Query 12: 0.6931	at 0.60	0.4784
Query 13: 0.0603	at 0.70	0.4242
Query 14: 0.7797	at 0.80	0.3326
Query 15: 0.6319	at 0.90	0.2193
Query 16: 0.4788	at 1.00	0.0596
Query 17: 0.7256	Avg. prec. (non-interpolated) for all rel. documents	0.5218
Query 18: 0.5512	Precision:	
Query 19: 0.8350	At 5 docs:	0.7680
Query 20: 0.4104	At 10 docs:	0.7360
Query 21: 0.7111	At 15 docs:	0.7147
Query 22: 0.1220	At 20 docs:	0.6940
Query 23: 0.4710	At 30 docs:	0.6627
Query 24: 0.7792	At 100 docs:	0.4408
Query 25: 0.4378	At 200 docs:	0.2932
	At 500 docs:	0.1473
	At 1000 docs:	0.0774
	R-Precision (prec. after R (=num_rel) docs. retrieved):	
	Exact:	0.4980

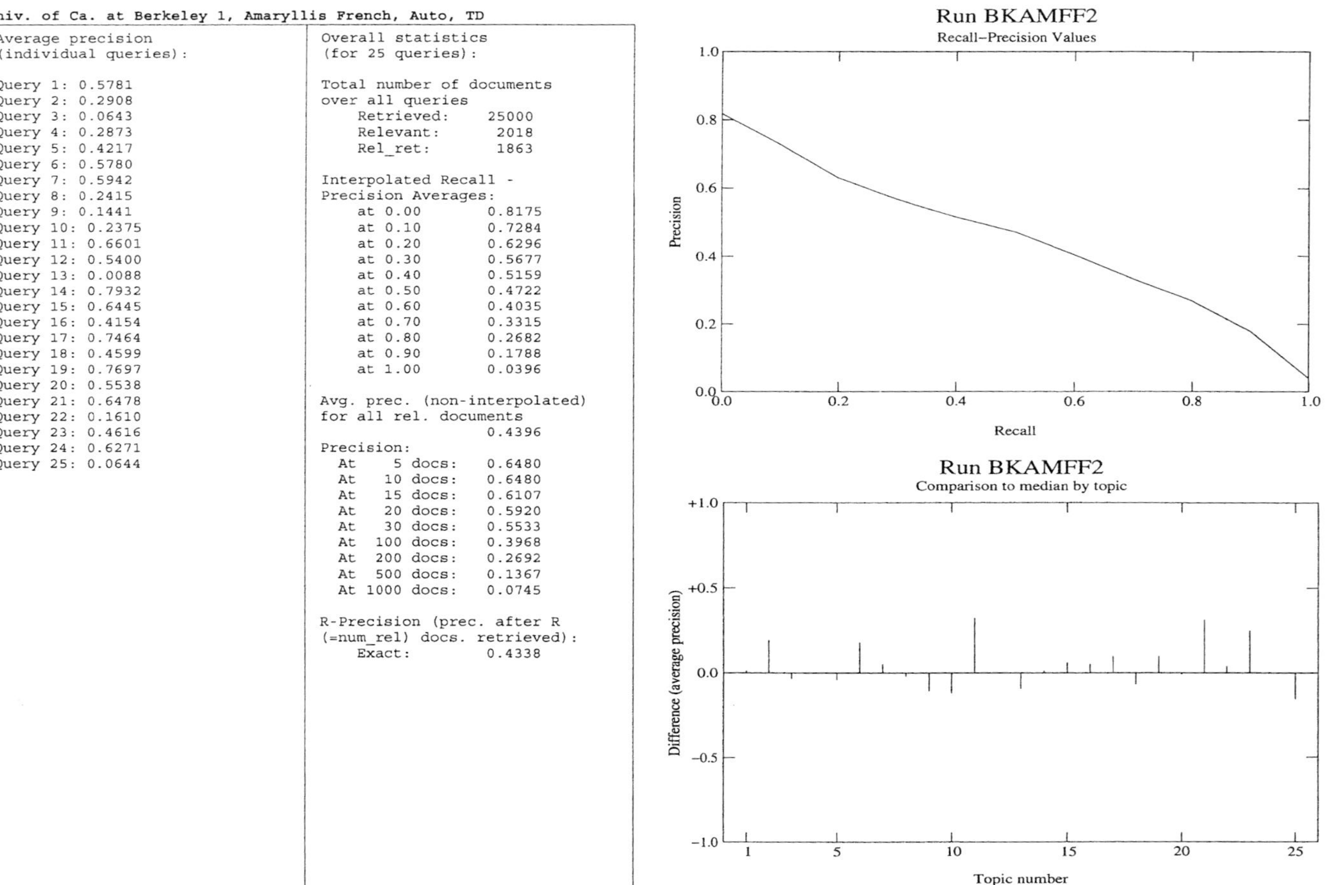

Univ. of Ca. at Berkeley 1, Amaryllis French, Auto, TD

Average precision (individual queries):	Overall statistics (for 25 queries):
Query 1: 0.5781	Total number of documents over all queries
Query 2: 0.2908	Retrieved: 25000
Query 3: 0.0643	Relevant: 2018
Query 4: 0.2873	Rel_ret: 1863
Query 5: 0.4217	
Query 6: 0.5780	Interpolated Recall - Precision Averages:
Query 7: 0.5942	at 0.00 0.8175
Query 8: 0.2415	at 0.10 0.7284
Query 9: 0.1441	at 0.20 0.6296
Query 10: 0.2375	at 0.30 0.5677
Query 11: 0.6601	at 0.40 0.5159
Query 12: 0.5400	at 0.50 0.4722
Query 13: 0.0088	at 0.60 0.4035
Query 14: 0.7932	at 0.70 0.3315
Query 15: 0.6445	at 0.80 0.2682
Query 16: 0.4154	at 0.90 0.1788
Query 17: 0.7464	at 1.00 0.0396
Query 18: 0.4599	
Query 19: 0.7697	Avg. prec. (non-interpolated) for all rel. documents 0.4396
Query 20: 0.5538	Precision:
Query 21: 0.6478	At 5 docs: 0.6480
Query 22: 0.1610	At 10 docs: 0.6480
Query 23: 0.4616	At 15 docs: 0.6107
Query 24: 0.6271	At 20 docs: 0.5920
Query 25: 0.0644	At 30 docs: 0.5533
	At 100 docs: 0.3968
	At 200 docs: 0.2692
	At 500 docs: 0.1367
	At 1000 docs: 0.0745
	R-Precision (prec. after R (=num_rel) docs. retrieved):
	Exact: 0.4338

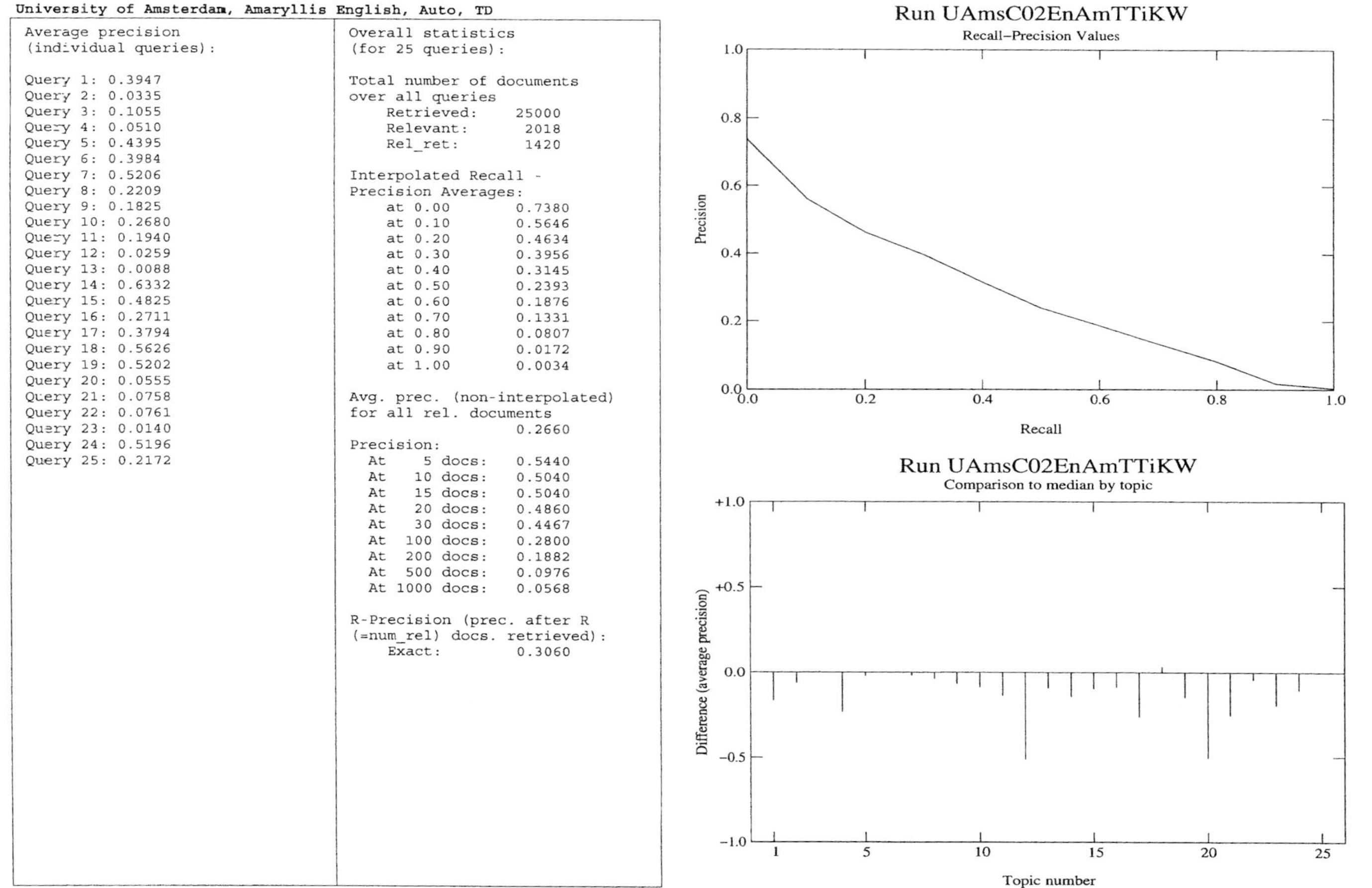

University of Amsterdam, Amaryllis English, Auto, TD

Average precision (individual queries):	Overall statistics (for 25 queries):
Query 1: 0.3947	Total number of documents over all queries
Query 2: 0.0335	Retrieved: 25000
Query 3: 0.1055	Relevant: 2018
Query 4: 0.0510	Rel_ret: 1420
Query 5: 0.4395	
Query 6: 0.3984	Interpolated Recall - Precision Averages:
Query 7: 0.5206	at 0.00 0.7380
Query 8: 0.2209	at 0.10 0.5646
Query 9: 0.1825	at 0.20 0.4634
Query 10: 0.2680	at 0.30 0.3956
Query 11: 0.1940	at 0.40 0.3145
Query 12: 0.0259	at 0.50 0.2393
Query 13: 0.0088	at 0.60 0.1876
Query 14: 0.6332	at 0.70 0.1331
Query 15: 0.4825	at 0.80 0.0807
Query 16: 0.2711	at 0.90 0.0172
Query 17: 0.3794	at 1.00 0.0034
Query 18: 0.5626	
Query 19: 0.5202	Avg. prec. (non-interpolated) for all rel. documents 0.2660
Query 20: 0.0555	Precision:
Query 21: 0.0758	At 5 docs: 0.5440
Query 22: 0.0761	At 10 docs: 0.5040
Query 23: 0.0140	At 15 docs: 0.5040
Query 24: 0.5196	At 20 docs: 0.4860
Query 25: 0.2172	At 30 docs: 0.4467
	At 100 docs: 0.2800
	At 200 docs: 0.1882
	At 500 docs: 0.0976
	At 1000 docs: 0.0568
	R-Precision (prec. after R (=num_rel) docs. retrieved):
	Exact: 0.3060

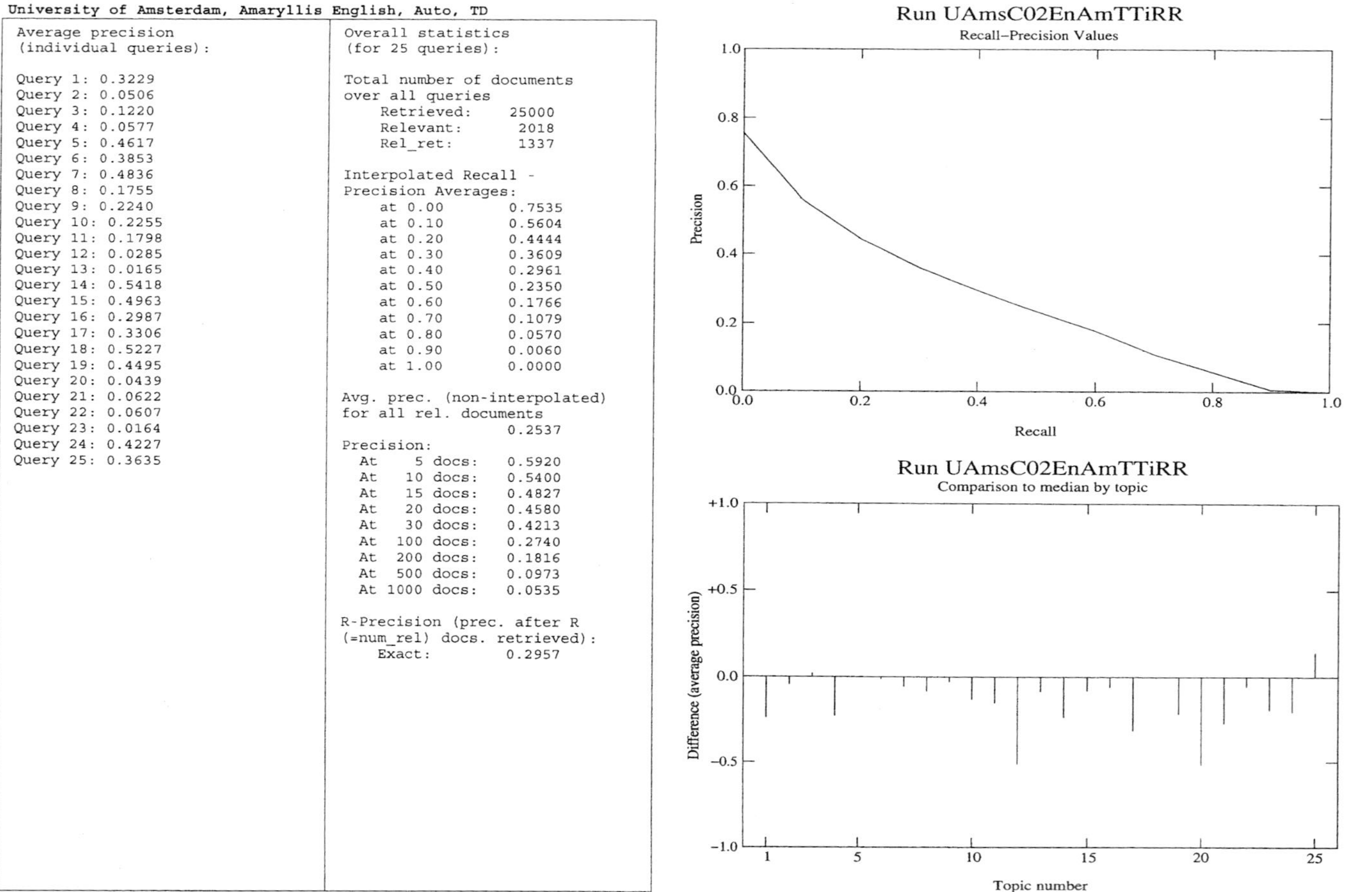

University of Amsterdam, Amaryllis English, Auto, TD

Average precision (individual queries):	Overall statistics (for 25 queries):
Query 1: 0.3229	Total number of documents over all queries
Query 2: 0.0506	Retrieved: 25000
Query 3: 0.1220	Relevant: 2018
Query 4: 0.0577	Rel_ret: 1337
Query 5: 0.4617	
Query 6: 0.3853	Interpolated Recall - Precision Averages:
Query 7: 0.4836	at 0.00 0.7535
Query 8: 0.1755	at 0.10 0.5604
Query 9: 0.2240	at 0.20 0.4444
Query 10: 0.2255	at 0.30 0.3609
Query 11: 0.1798	at 0.40 0.2961
Query 12: 0.0285	at 0.50 0.2350
Query 13: 0.0165	at 0.60 0.1766
Query 14: 0.5418	at 0.70 0.1079
Query 15: 0.4963	at 0.80 0.0570
Query 16: 0.2987	at 0.90 0.0060
Query 17: 0.3306	at 1.00 0.0000
Query 18: 0.5227	
Query 19: 0.4495	Avg. prec. (non-interpolated) for all rel. documents 0.2537
Query 20: 0.0439	Precision:
Query 21: 0.0622	At 5 docs: 0.5920
Query 22: 0.0607	At 10 docs: 0.5400
Query 23: 0.0164	At 15 docs: 0.4827
Query 24: 0.4227	At 20 docs: 0.4580
Query 25: 0.3635	At 30 docs: 0.4213
	At 100 docs: 0.2740
	At 200 docs: 0.1816
	At 500 docs: 0.0973
	At 1000 docs: 0.0535
	R-Precision (prec. after R (=num_rel) docs. retrieved):
	Exact: 0.2957

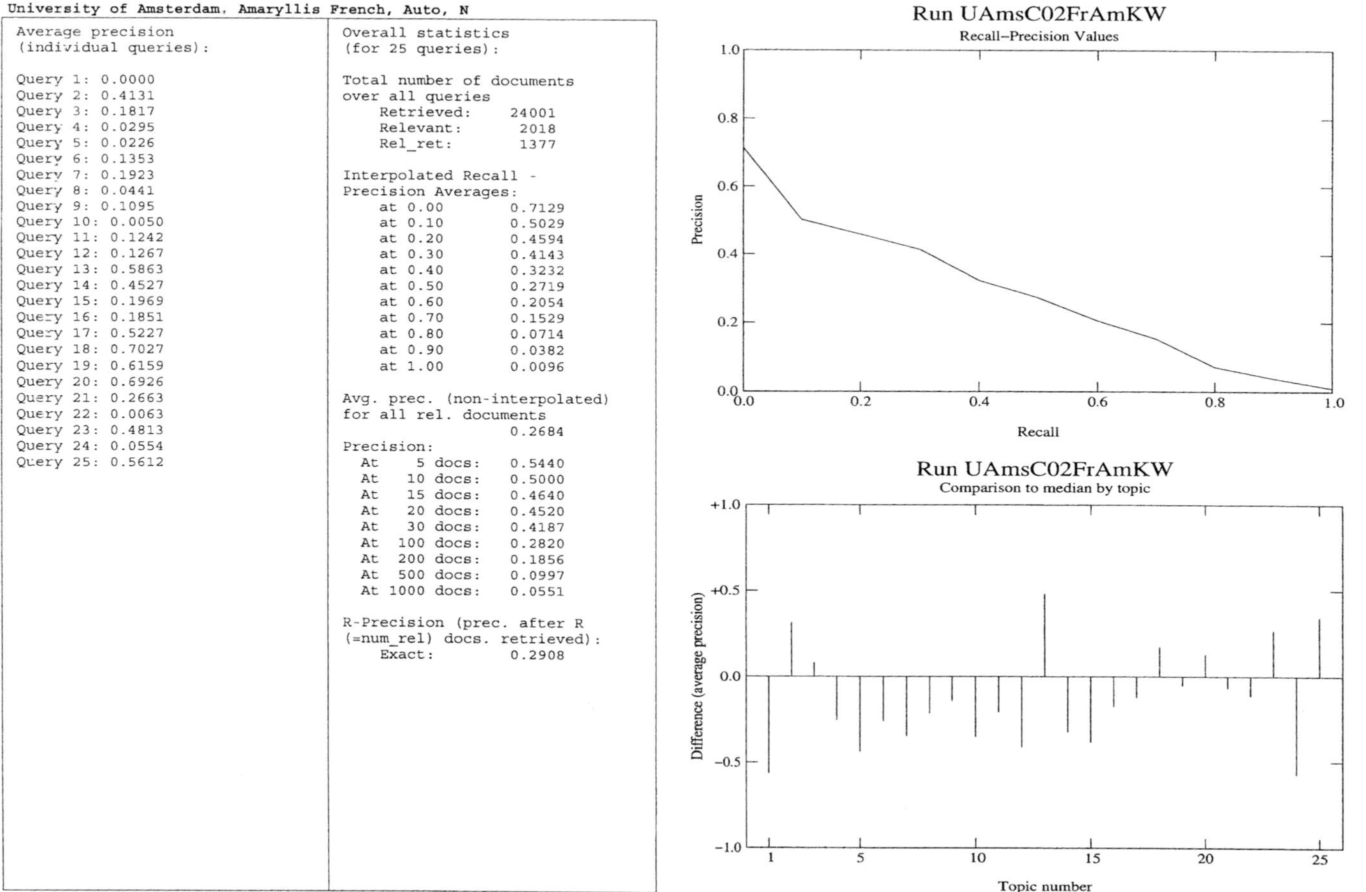

University of Amsterdam, Amaryllis French, Auto, N

```
Average precision              Overall statistics
(individual queries):          (for 25 queries):

Query 1: 0.0000                Total number of documents
Query 2: 0.4131                over all queries
Query 3: 0.1817                    Retrieved:    24001
Query 4: 0.0295                    Relevant:      2018
Query 5: 0.0226                    Rel_ret:       1377
Query 6: 0.1353
Query 7: 0.1923                Interpolated Recall -
Query 8: 0.0441                Precision Averages:
Query 9: 0.1095                    at 0.00       0.7129
Query 10: 0.0050                   at 0.10       0.5029
Query 11: 0.1242                   at 0.20       0.4594
Query 12: 0.1267                   at 0.30       0.4143
Query 13: 0.5863                   at 0.40       0.3232
Query 14: 0.4527                   at 0.50       0.2719
Query 15: 0.1969                   at 0.60       0.2054
Query 16: 0.1851                   at 0.70       0.1529
Query 17: 0.5227                   at 0.80       0.0714
Query 18: 0.7027                   at 0.90       0.0382
Query 19: 0.6159                   at 1.00       0.0096
Query 20: 0.6926
Query 21: 0.2663               Avg. prec. (non-interpolated)
Query 22: 0.0063               for all rel. documents
Query 23: 0.4813                                 0.2684
Query 24: 0.0554               Precision:
Query 25: 0.5612                 At    5 docs:   0.5440
                                 At   10 docs:   0.5000
                                 At   15 docs:   0.4640
                                 At   20 docs:   0.4520
                                 At   30 docs:   0.4187
                                 At  100 docs:   0.2820
                                 At  200 docs:   0.1856
                                 At  500 docs:   0.0997
                                 At 1000 docs:   0.0551

                               R-Precision (prec. after R
                               (=num_rel) docs. retrieved):
                                   Exact:        0.2908
```

University of Amsterdam, Amaryllis French, Auto, TD

Average precision (individual queries):	Overall statistics (for 25 queries):
Query 1: 0.5640 Query 2: 0.0738 Query 3: 0.0309 Query 4: 0.1649 Query 5: 0.4790 Query 6: 0.3455 Query 7: 0.5088 Query 8: 0.1045 Query 9: 0.2122 Query 10: 0.2109 Query 11: 0.2212 Query 12: 0.1673 Query 13: 0.1040 Query 14: 0.5554 Query 15: 0.5244 Query 16: 0.3371 Query 17: 0.3245 Query 18: 0.4244 Query 19: 0.2675 Query 20: 0.3664 Query 21: 0.0397 Query 22: 0.1470 Query 23: 0.0104 Query 24: 0.4368 Query 25: 0.0806	Total number of documents over all queries Retrieved: 25000 Relevant: 2018 Rel_ret: 1423 Interpolated Recall - Precision Averages: at 0.00 0.7464 at 0.10 0.5504 at 0.20 0.4724 at 0.30 0.3875 at 0.40 0.3357 at 0.50 0.2631 at 0.60 0.1935 at 0.70 0.1148 at 0.80 0.0714 at 0.90 0.0213 at 1.00 0.0000 Avg. prec. (non-interpolated) for all rel. documents 0.2681 Precision: At 5 docs: 0.5280 At 10 docs: 0.5200 At 15 docs: 0.5013 At 20 docs: 0.4800 At 30 docs: 0.4453 At 100 docs: 0.2920 At 200 docs: 0.1936 At 500 docs: 0.1000 At 1000 docs: 0.0569 R-Precision (prec. after R (=num_rel) docs. retrieved): Exact: 0.3211

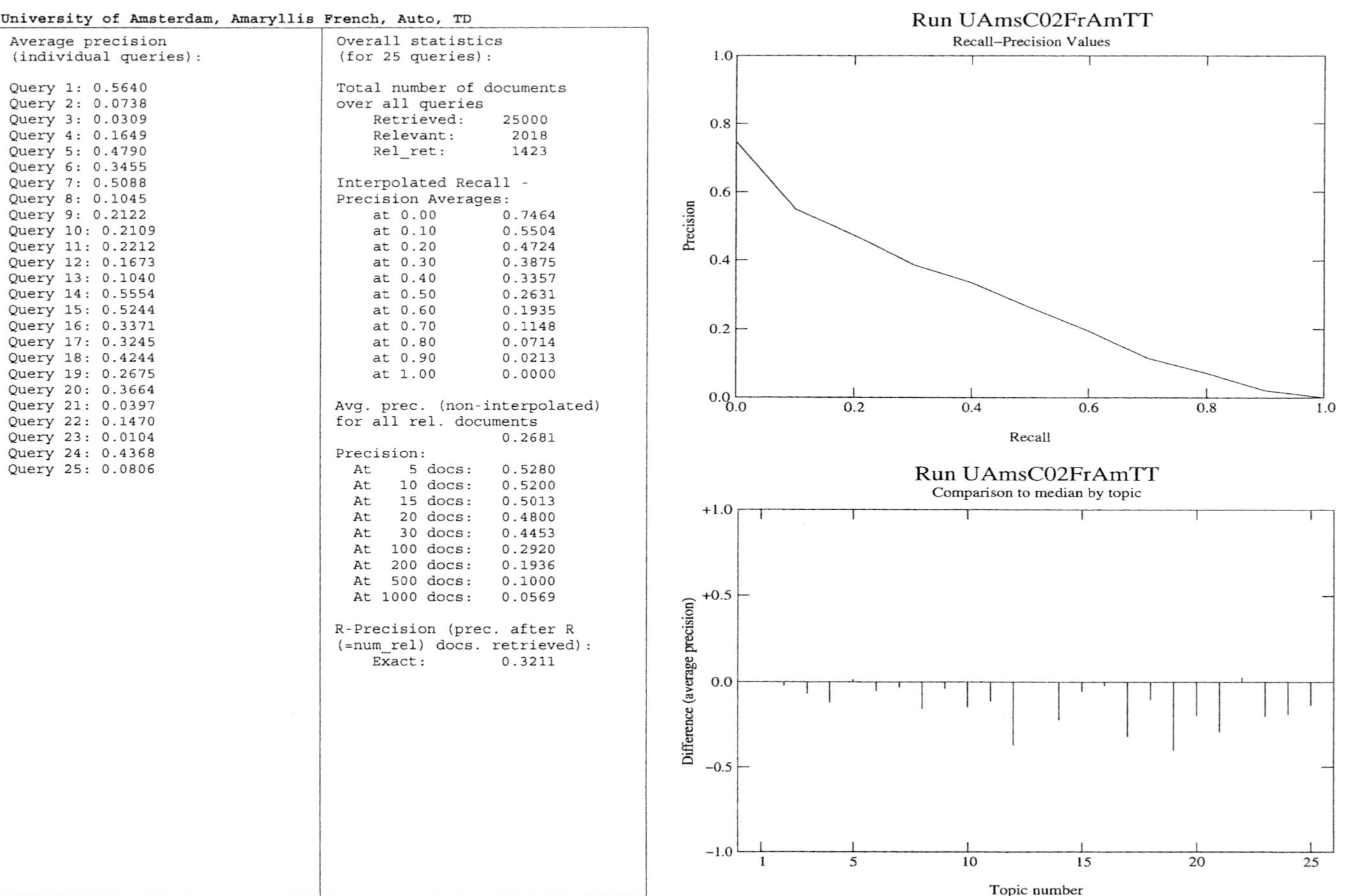

University of Amsterdam, Amaryllis French, Auto, TDN

Average precision (individual queries):	Overall statistics (for 25 queries):
Query 1: 0.5640	Total number of documents over all queries
Query 2: 0.1006	Retrieved: 25000
Query 3: 0.0872	Relevant: 2018
Query 4: 0.2535	Rel_ret: 1606
Query 5: 0.4954	
Query 6: 0.3542	Interpolated Recall - Precision Averages:
Query 7: 0.5413	at 0.00 0.8460
Query 8: 0.1259	at 0.10 0.6878
Query 9: 0.2529	at 0.20 0.5517
Query 10: 0.1993	at 0.30 0.4649
Query 11: 0.3343	at 0.40 0.4100
Query 12: 0.1989	at 0.50 0.3511
Query 13: 0.2239	at 0.60 0.2631
Query 14: 0.7168	at 0.70 0.1729
Query 15: 0.5811	at 0.80 0.1129
Query 16: 0.3532	at 0.90 0.0532
Query 17: 0.4554	at 1.00 0.0108
Query 18: 0.5277	
Query 19: 0.4847	Avg. prec. (non-interpolated) for all rel. documents 0.3401
Query 20: 0.4974	Precision:
Query 21: 0.0502	At 5 docs: 0.6640
Query 22: 0.1367	At 10 docs: 0.6120
Query 23: 0.1488	At 15 docs: 0.5867
Query 24: 0.4482	At 20 docs: 0.5460
Query 25: 0.3710	At 30 docs: 0.5027
	At 100 docs: 0.3412
	At 200 docs: 0.2308
	At 500 docs: 0.1150
	At 1000 docs: 0.0642
	R-Precision (prec. after R (=num_rel) docs. retrieved):
	Exact: 0.3837

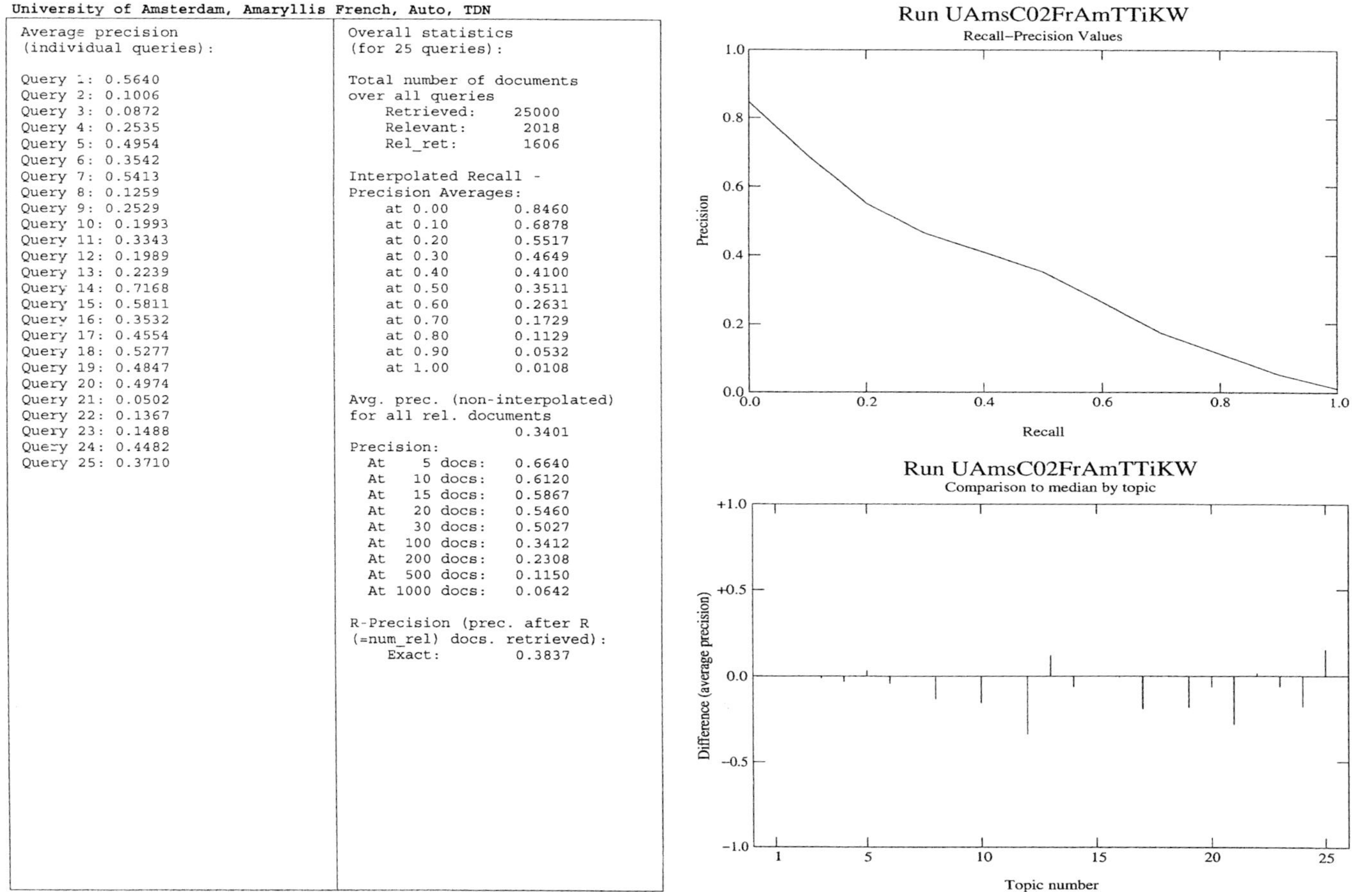

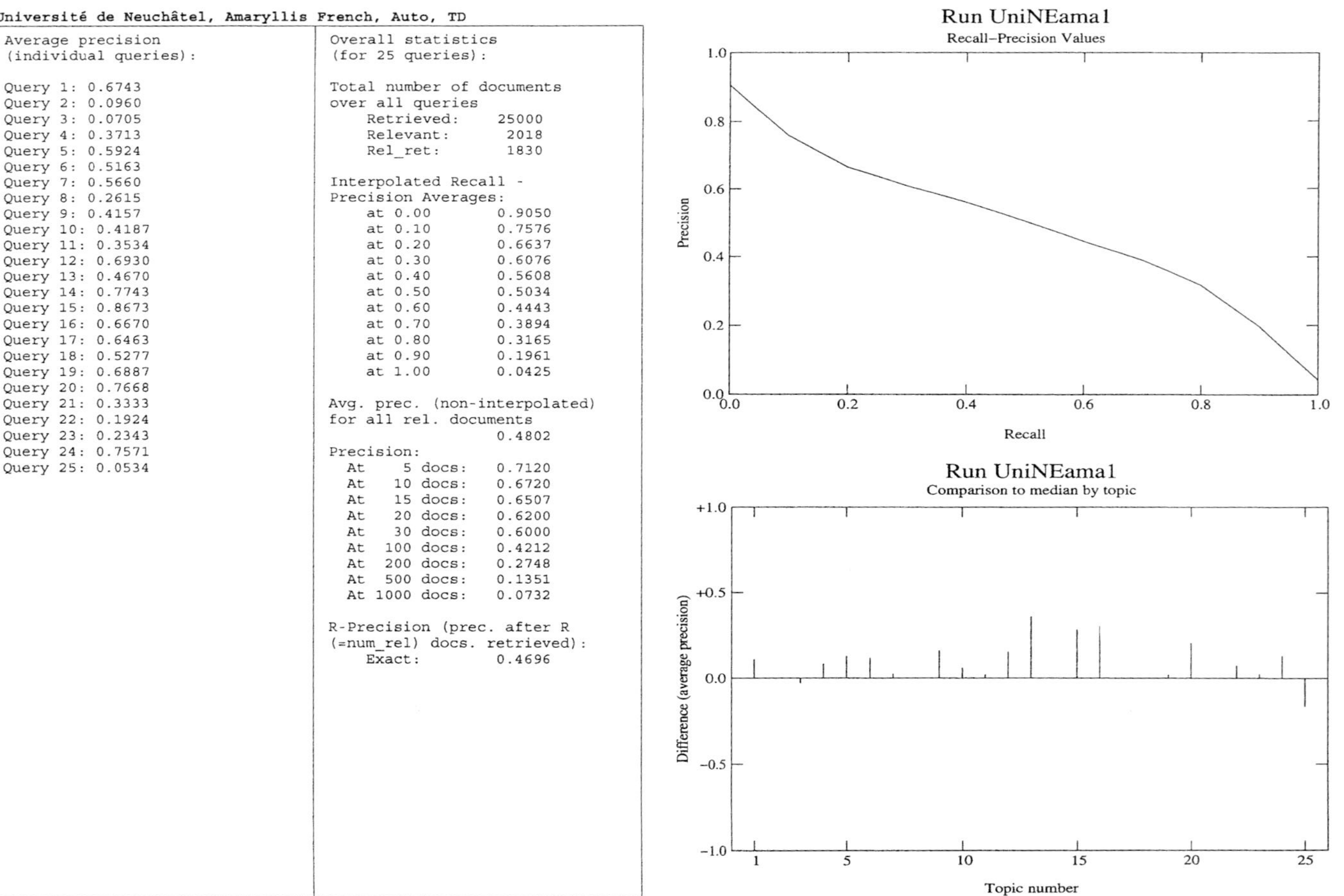

Université de Neuchâtel, Amaryllis French, Auto, TD

Average precision (individual queries):	Overall statistics (for 25 queries):
Query 1: 0.6743	Total number of documents over all queries
Query 2: 0.0960	Retrieved: 25000
Query 3: 0.0705	Relevant: 2018
Query 4: 0.3713	Rel_ret: 1830
Query 5: 0.5924	
Query 6: 0.5163	Interpolated Recall - Precision Averages:
Query 7: 0.5660	at 0.00 0.9050
Query 8: 0.2615	at 0.10 0.7576
Query 9: 0.4157	at 0.20 0.6637
Query 10: 0.4187	at 0.30 0.6076
Query 11: 0.3534	at 0.40 0.5608
Query 12: 0.6930	at 0.50 0.5034
Query 13: 0.4670	at 0.60 0.4443
Query 14: 0.7743	at 0.70 0.3894
Query 15: 0.8673	at 0.80 0.3165
Query 16: 0.6670	at 0.90 0.1961
Query 17: 0.6463	at 1.00 0.0425
Query 18: 0.5277	
Query 19: 0.6887	Avg. prec. (non-interpolated) for all rel. documents 0.4802
Query 20: 0.7668	Precision:
Query 21: 0.3333	At 5 docs: 0.7120
Query 22: 0.1924	At 10 docs: 0.6720
Query 23: 0.2343	At 15 docs: 0.6507
Query 24: 0.7571	At 20 docs: 0.6200
Query 25: 0.0534	At 30 docs: 0.6000
	At 100 docs: 0.4212
	At 200 docs: 0.2748
	At 500 docs: 0.1351
	At 1000 docs: 0.0732
	R-Precision (prec. after R (=num_rel) docs. retrieved):
	Exact: 0.4696

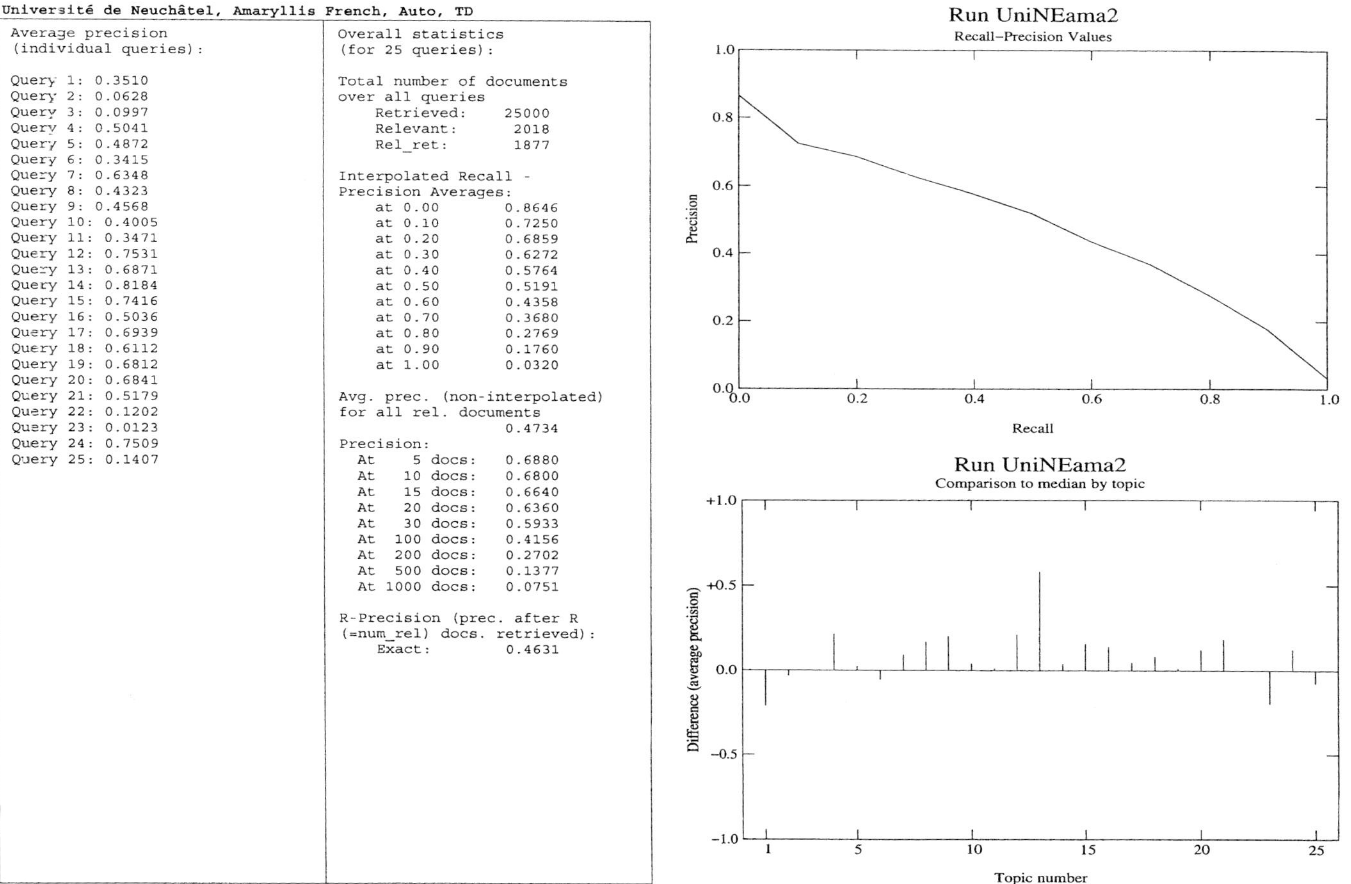

Université de Neuchâtel, Amaryllis French, Auto, TD

Average precision (individual queries):	Overall statistics (for 25 queries):
Query 1: 0.3510	Total number of documents over all queries
Query 2: 0.0628	Retrieved: 25000
Query 3: 0.0997	Relevant: 2018
Query 4: 0.5041	Rel_ret: 1877
Query 5: 0.4872	
Query 6: 0.3415	Interpolated Recall - Precision Averages:
Query 7: 0.6348	at 0.00 0.8646
Query 8: 0.4323	at 0.10 0.7250
Query 9: 0.4568	at 0.20 0.6859
Query 10: 0.4005	at 0.30 0.6272
Query 11: 0.3471	at 0.40 0.5764
Query 12: 0.7531	at 0.50 0.5191
Query 13: 0.6871	at 0.60 0.4358
Query 14: 0.8184	at 0.70 0.3680
Query 15: 0.7416	at 0.80 0.2769
Query 16: 0.5036	at 0.90 0.1760
Query 17: 0.6939	at 1.00 0.0320
Query 18: 0.6112	
Query 19: 0.6812	Avg. prec. (non-interpolated) for all rel. documents 0.4734
Query 20: 0.6841	Precision:
Query 21: 0.5179	At 5 docs: 0.6880
Query 22: 0.1202	At 10 docs: 0.6800
Query 23: 0.0123	At 15 docs: 0.6640
Query 24: 0.7509	At 20 docs: 0.6360
Query 25: 0.1407	At 30 docs: 0.5933
	At 100 docs: 0.4156
	At 200 docs: 0.2702
	At 500 docs: 0.1377
	At 1000 docs: 0.0751
	R-Precision (prec. after R (=num_rel) docs. retrieved):
	Exact: 0.4631

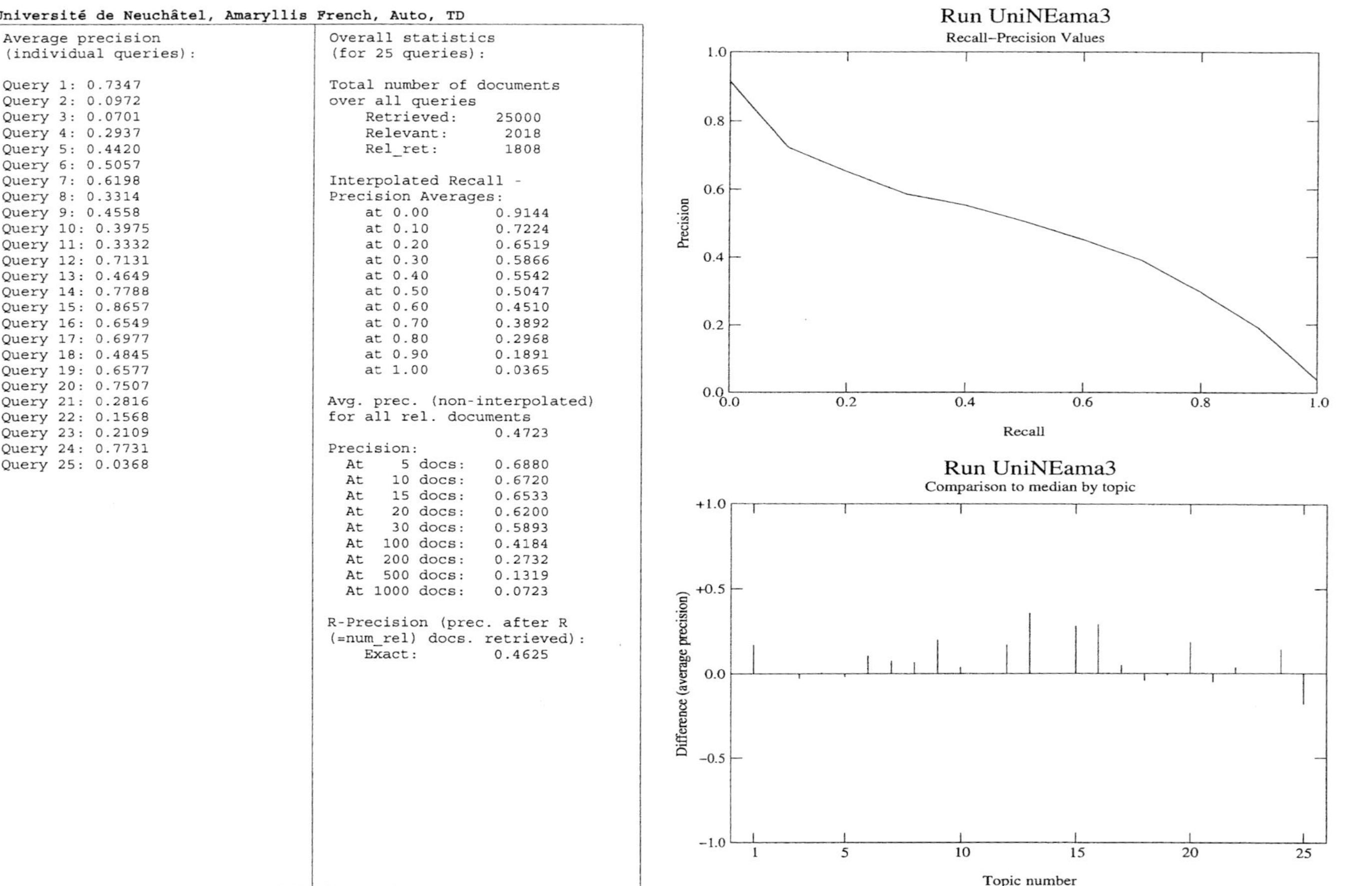

Université de Neuchâtel, Amaryllis French, Auto, TD

```
Average precision              Overall statistics
(individual queries):          (for 25 queries):

Query 1: 0.7347                Total number of documents
Query 2: 0.0972                over all queries
Query 3: 0.0701                    Retrieved:    25000
Query 4: 0.2937                    Relevant:      2018
Query 5: 0.4420                    Rel_ret:       1808
Query 6: 0.5057
Query 7: 0.6198                Interpolated Recall -
Query 8: 0.3314                Precision Averages:
Query 9: 0.4558                    at 0.00       0.9144
Query 10: 0.3975                   at 0.10       0.7224
Query 11: 0.3332                   at 0.20       0.6519
Query 12: 0.7131                   at 0.30       0.5866
Query 13: 0.4649                   at 0.40       0.5542
Query 14: 0.7788                   at 0.50       0.5047
Query 15: 0.8657                   at 0.60       0.4510
Query 16: 0.6549                   at 0.70       0.3892
Query 17: 0.6977                   at 0.80       0.2968
Query 18: 0.4845                   at 0.90       0.1891
Query 19: 0.6577                   at 1.00       0.0365
Query 20: 0.7507
Query 21: 0.2816               Avg. prec. (non-interpolated)
Query 22: 0.1568               for all rel. documents
Query 23: 0.2109                                 0.4723
Query 24: 0.7731               Precision:
Query 25: 0.0368                 At    5 docs:   0.6880
                                 At   10 docs:   0.6720
                                 At   15 docs:   0.6533
                                 At   20 docs:   0.6200
                                 At   30 docs:   0.5893
                                 At  100 docs:   0.4184
                                 At  200 docs:   0.2732
                                 At  500 docs:   0.1319
                                 At 1000 docs:   0.0723

                               R-Precision (prec. after R
                               (=num_rel) docs. retrieved):
                                   Exact:        0.4625
```

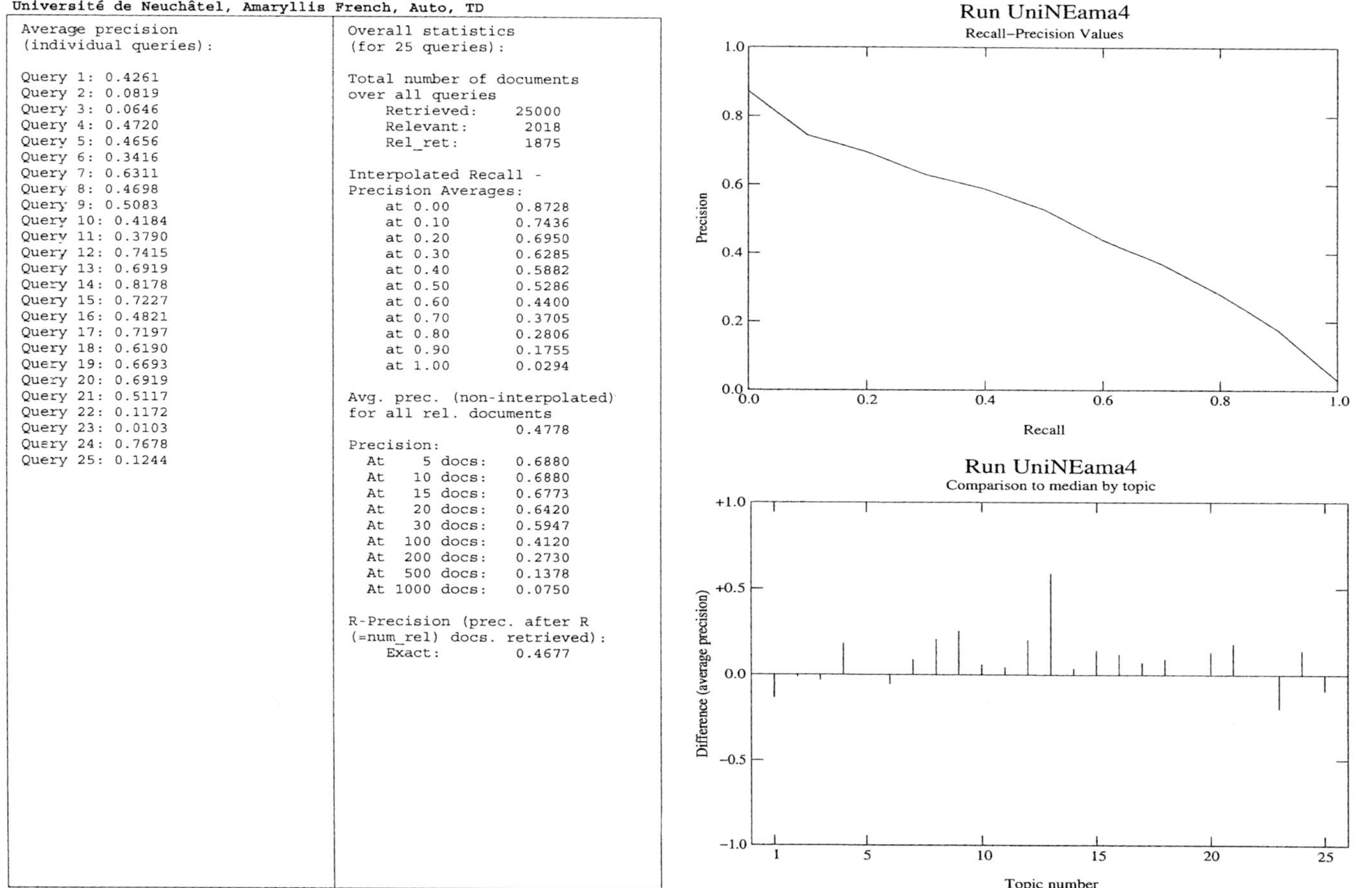

Université de Neuchâtel, Amaryllis French, Auto, TD

Average precision (individual queries):	Overall statistics (for 25 queries):
Query 1: 0.4261	Total number of documents over all queries
Query 2: 0.0819	Retrieved: 25000
Query 3: 0.0646	Relevant: 2018
Query 4: 0.4720	Rel_ret: 1875
Query 5: 0.4656	
Query 6: 0.3416	Interpolated Recall - Precision Averages:
Query 7: 0.6311	at 0.00 0.8728
Query 8: 0.4698	at 0.10 0.7436
Query 9: 0.5083	at 0.20 0.6950
Query 10: 0.4184	at 0.30 0.6285
Query 11: 0.3790	at 0.40 0.5882
Query 12: 0.7415	at 0.50 0.5286
Query 13: 0.6919	at 0.60 0.4400
Query 14: 0.8178	at 0.70 0.3705
Query 15: 0.7227	at 0.80 0.2806
Query 16: 0.4821	at 0.90 0.1755
Query 17: 0.7197	at 1.00 0.0294
Query 18: 0.6190	
Query 19: 0.6693	Avg. prec. (non-interpolated) for all rel. documents 0.4778
Query 20: 0.6919	
Query 21: 0.5117	Precision:
Query 22: 0.1172	At 5 docs: 0.6880
Query 23: 0.0103	At 10 docs: 0.6880
Query 24: 0.7678	At 15 docs: 0.6773
Query 25: 0.1244	At 20 docs: 0.6420
	At 30 docs: 0.5947
	At 100 docs: 0.4120
	At 200 docs: 0.2730
	At 500 docs: 0.1378
	At 1000 docs: 0.0750
	R-Precision (prec. after R (=num_rel) docs. retrieved):
	Exact: 0.4677

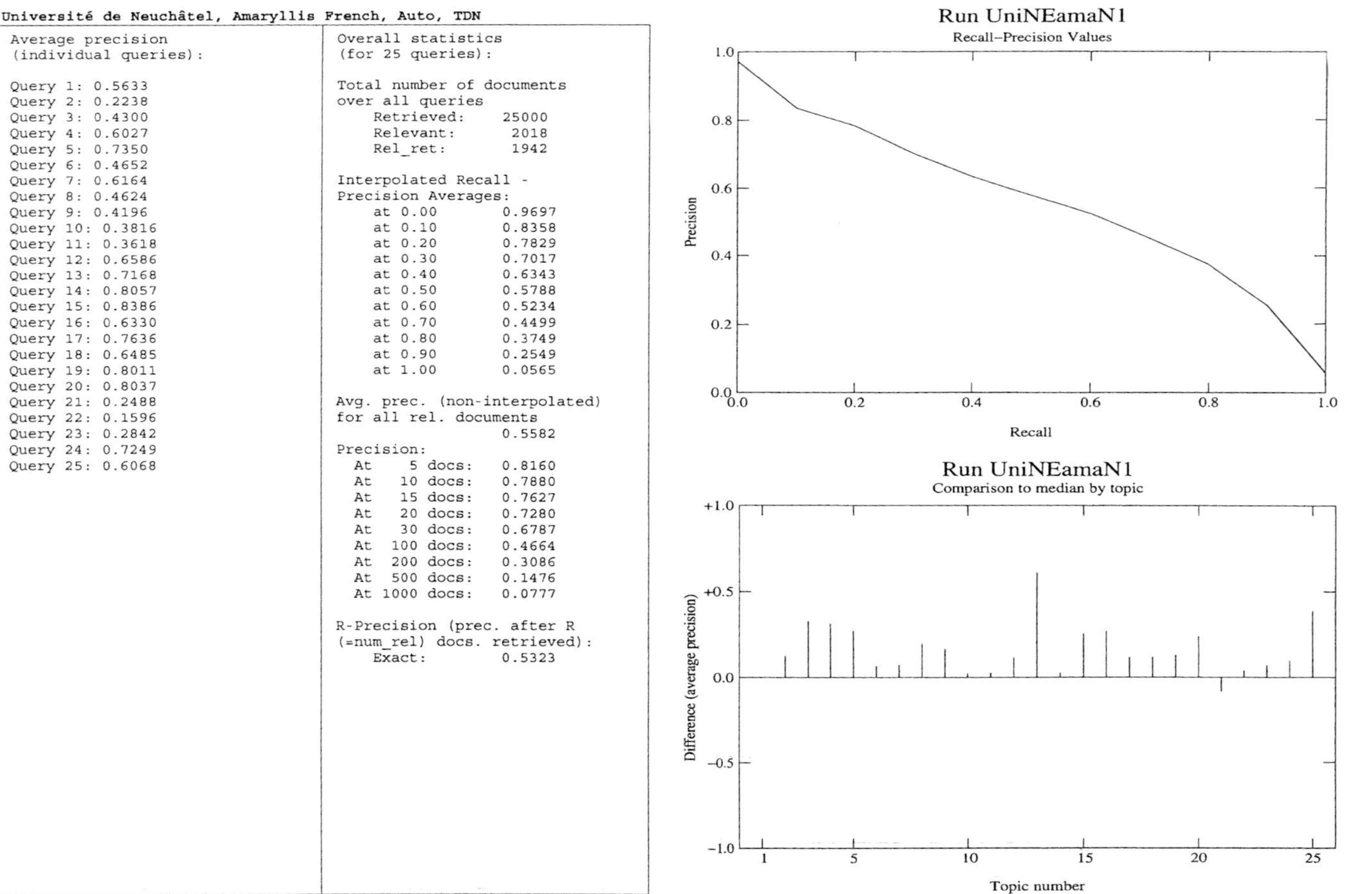

Université de Neuchâtel, Amaryllis French, Auto, TDN

```
Average precision
(individual queries):

Query 1: 0.5633
Query 2: 0.2238
Query 3: 0.4300
Query 4: 0.6027
Query 5: 0.7350
Query 6: 0.4652
Query 7: 0.6164
Query 8: 0.4624
Query 9: 0.4196
Query 10: 0.3816
Query 11: 0.3618
Query 12: 0.6586
Query 13: 0.7168
Query 14: 0.8057
Query 15: 0.8386
Query 16: 0.6330
Query 17: 0.7636
Query 18: 0.6485
Query 19: 0.8011
Query 20: 0.8037
Query 21: 0.2488
Query 22: 0.1596
Query 23: 0.2842
Query 24: 0.7249
Query 25: 0.6068
```

```
Overall statistics
(for 25 queries):

Total number of documents
over all queries
    Retrieved:    25000
    Relevant:      2018
    Rel_ret:       1942

Interpolated Recall -
Precision Averages:
    at 0.00       0.9697
    at 0.10       0.8358
    at 0.20       0.7829
    at 0.30       0.7017
    at 0.40       0.6343
    at 0.50       0.5788
    at 0.60       0.5234
    at 0.70       0.4499
    at 0.80       0.3749
    at 0.90       0.2549
    at 1.00       0.0565

Avg. prec. (non-interpolated)
for all rel. documents
                  0.5582
Precision:
  At    5 docs:   0.8160
  At   10 docs:   0.7880
  At   15 docs:   0.7627
  At   20 docs:   0.7280
  At   30 docs:   0.6787
  At  100 docs:   0.4664
  At  200 docs:   0.3086
  At  500 docs:   0.1476
  At 1000 docs:   0.0777

R-Precision (prec. after R
(=num_rel) docs. retrieved):
    Exact:        0.5323
```

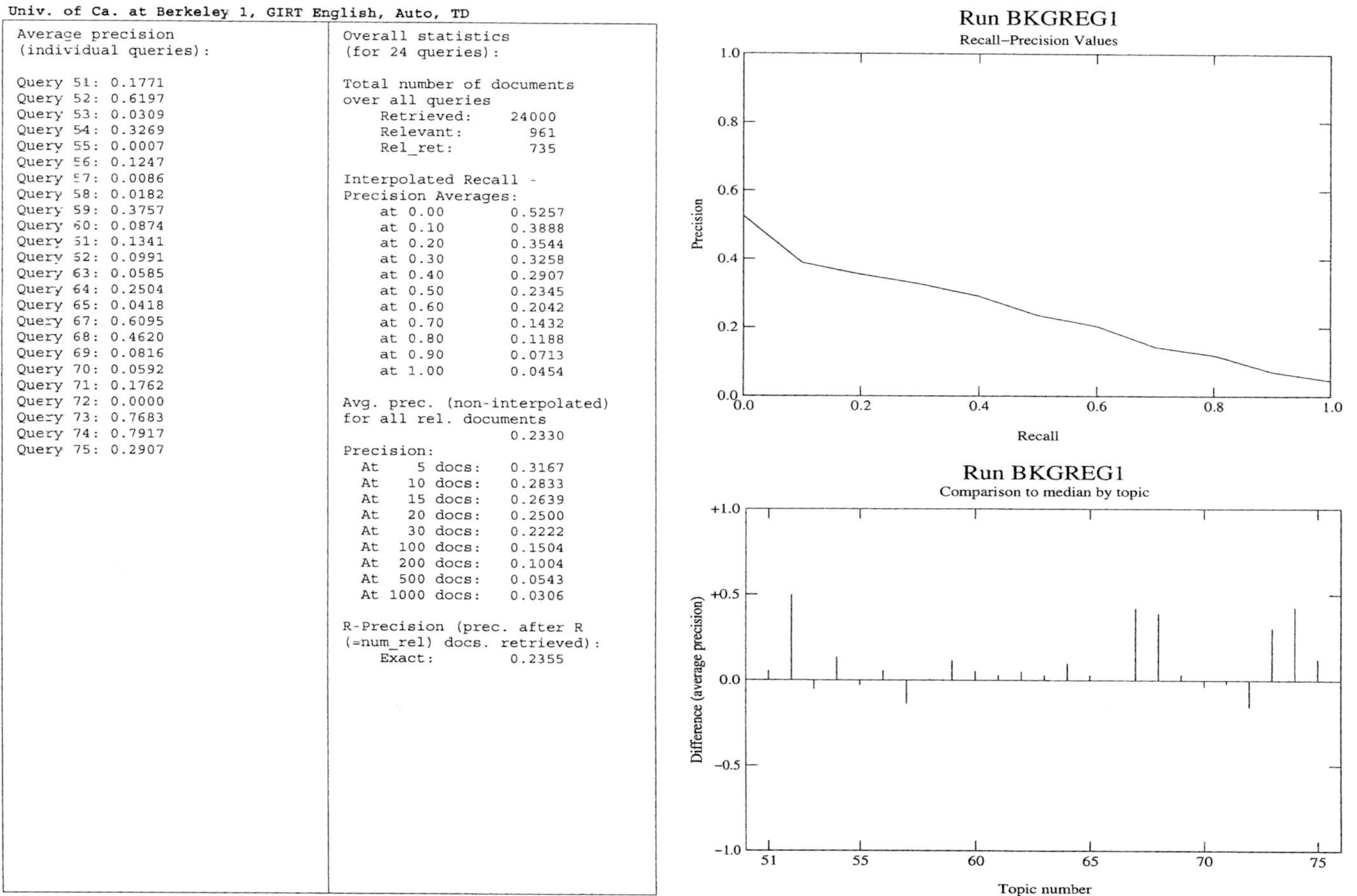

Univ. of Ca. at Berkeley 1, GIRT English, Auto, TD

Average precision (individual queries):	Overall statistics (for 24 queries):
Query 51: 0.1771	Total number of documents over all queries
Query 52: 0.6197	Retrieved: 24000
Query 53: 0.0309	Relevant: 961
Query 54: 0.3269	Rel_ret: 735
Query 55: 0.0007	
Query 56: 0.1247	Interpolated Recall - Precision Averages:
Query 57: 0.0086	at 0.00 0.5257
Query 58: 0.0182	at 0.10 0.3888
Query 59: 0.3757	at 0.20 0.3544
Query 60: 0.0874	at 0.30 0.3258
Query 61: 0.1341	at 0.40 0.2907
Query 62: 0.0991	at 0.50 0.2345
Query 63: 0.0585	at 0.60 0.2042
Query 64: 0.2504	at 0.70 0.1432
Query 65: 0.0418	at 0.80 0.1188
Query 67: 0.6095	at 0.90 0.0713
Query 68: 0.4620	at 1.00 0.0454
Query 69: 0.0816	
Query 70: 0.0592	Avg. prec. (non-interpolated) for all rel. documents 0.2330
Query 71: 0.1762	
Query 72: 0.0000	Precision:
Query 73: 0.7683	At 5 docs: 0.3167
Query 74: 0.7917	At 10 docs: 0.2833
Query 75: 0.2907	At 15 docs: 0.2639
	At 20 docs: 0.2500
	At 30 docs: 0.2222
	At 100 docs: 0.1504
	At 200 docs: 0.1004
	At 500 docs: 0.0543
	At 1000 docs: 0.0306
	R-Precision (prec. after R (=num_rel) docs. retrieved):
	Exact: 0.2355

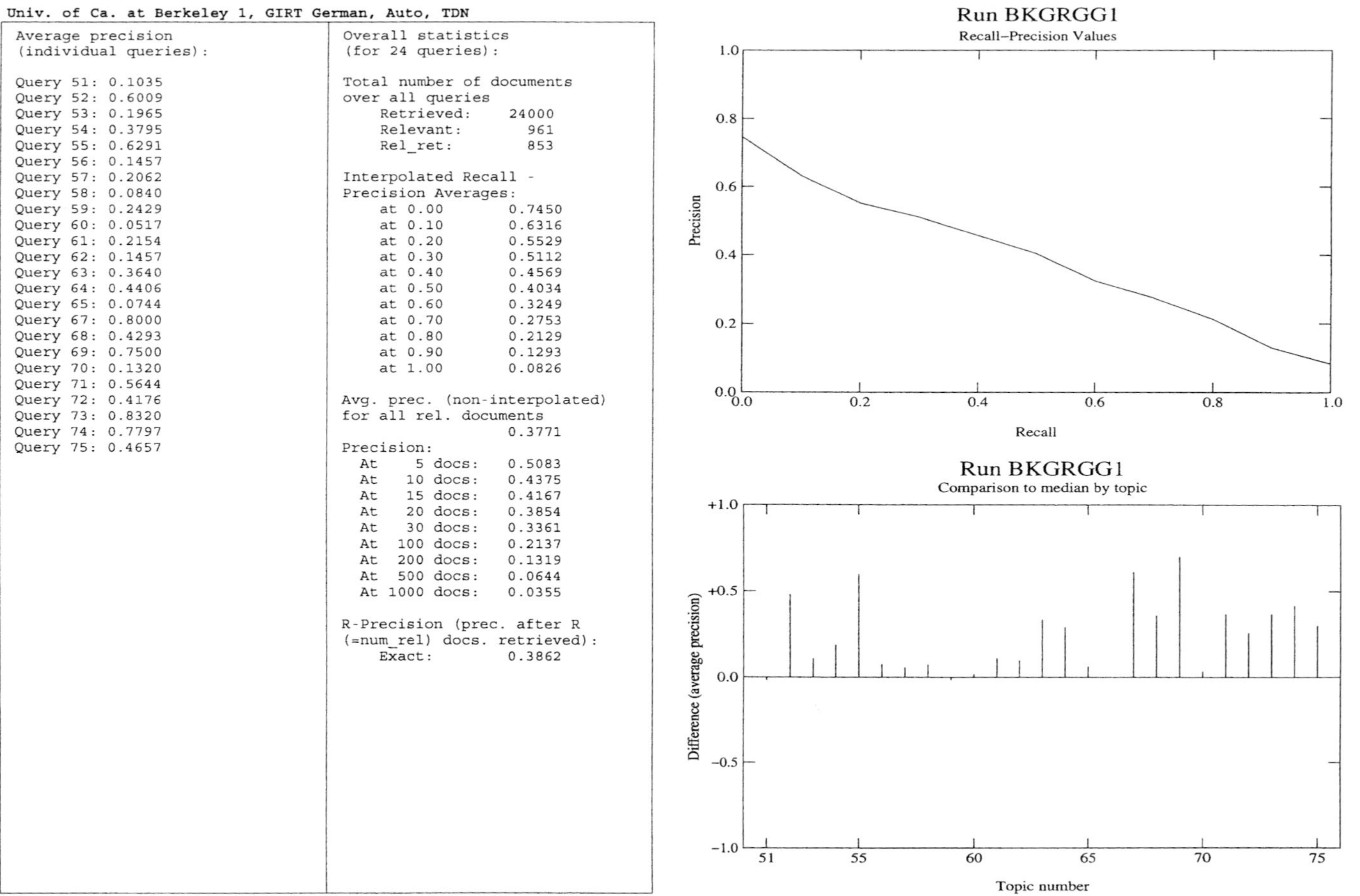

Univ. of Ca. at Berkeley 1, GIRT German, Auto, TDN

Average precision (individual queries):	Overall statistics (for 24 queries):
Query 51: 0.1035	Total number of documents over all queries
Query 52: 0.6009	Retrieved: 24000
Query 53: 0.1965	Relevant: 961
Query 54: 0.3795	Rel_ret: 853
Query 55: 0.6291	
Query 56: 0.1457	Interpolated Recall - Precision Averages:
Query 57: 0.2062	at 0.00 0.7450
Query 58: 0.0840	at 0.10 0.6316
Query 59: 0.2429	at 0.20 0.5529
Query 60: 0.0517	at 0.30 0.5112
Query 61: 0.2154	at 0.40 0.4569
Query 62: 0.1457	at 0.50 0.4034
Query 63: 0.3640	at 0.60 0.3249
Query 64: 0.4406	at 0.70 0.2753
Query 65: 0.0744	at 0.80 0.2129
Query 67: 0.8000	at 0.90 0.1293
Query 68: 0.4293	at 1.00 0.0826
Query 69: 0.7500	
Query 70: 0.1320	Avg. prec. (non-interpolated) for all rel. documents 0.3771
Query 71: 0.5644	Precision:
Query 72: 0.4176	At 5 docs: 0.5083
Query 73: 0.8320	At 10 docs: 0.4375
Query 74: 0.7797	At 15 docs: 0.4167
Query 75: 0.4657	At 20 docs: 0.3854
	At 30 docs: 0.3361
	At 100 docs: 0.2137
	At 200 docs: 0.1319
	At 500 docs: 0.0644
	At 1000 docs: 0.0355
	R-Precision (prec. after R (=num_rel) docs. retrieved):
	Exact: 0.3862

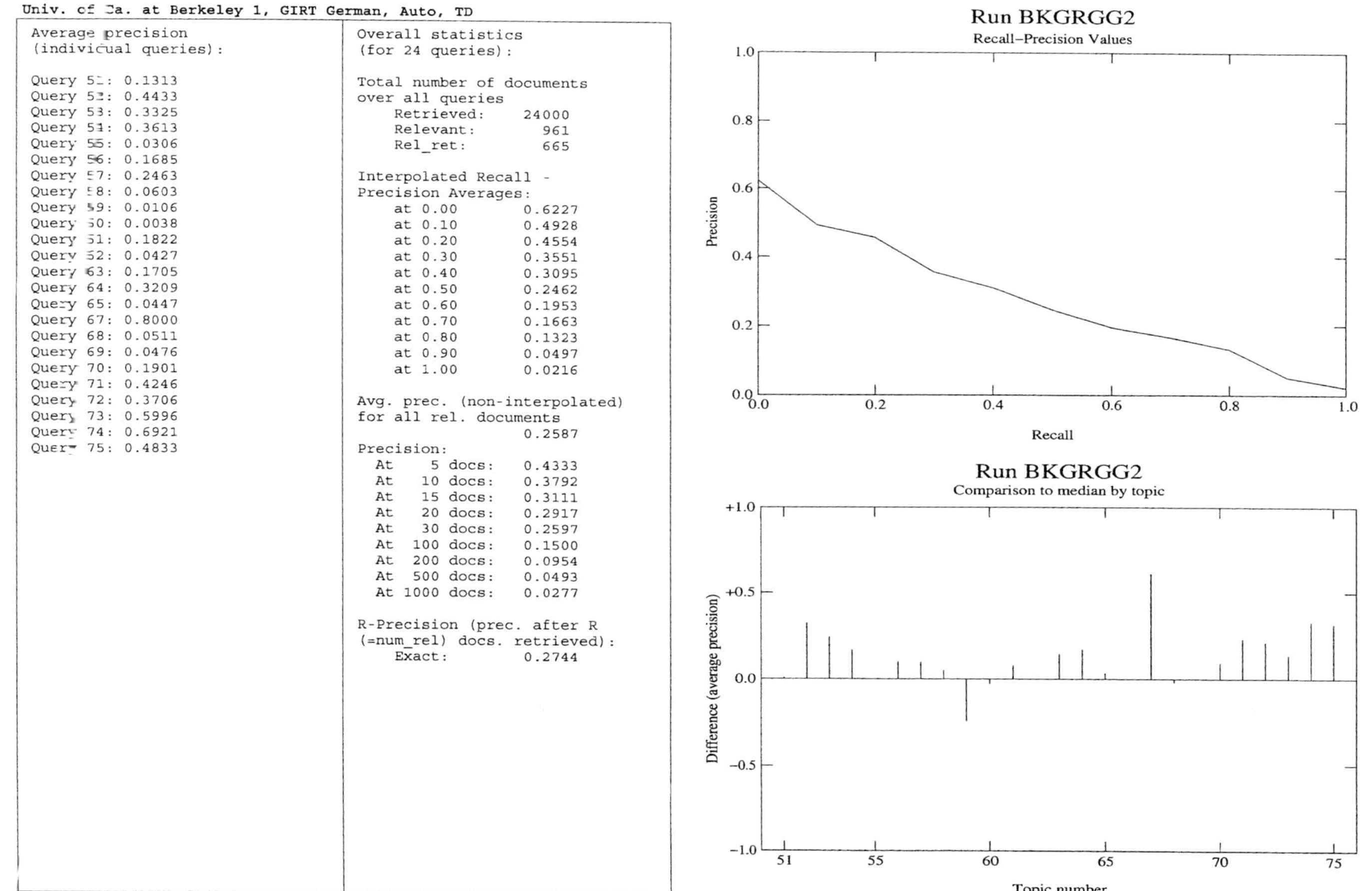

Univ. of Ca. at Berkeley 1, GIRT German, Auto, TD

```
Average precision            Overall statistics
(individual queries):        (for 24 queries):

Query 51: 0.1313             Total number of documents
Query 52: 0.4433             over all queries
Query 53: 0.3325                 Retrieved:    24000
Query 54: 0.3613                 Relevant:       961
Query 55: 0.0306                 Rel_ret:        665
Query 56: 0.1685
Query 57: 0.2463             Interpolated Recall -
Query 58: 0.0603             Precision Averages:
Query 59: 0.0106                 at 0.00       0.6227
Query 60: 0.0038                 at 0.10       0.4928
Query 61: 0.1822                 at 0.20       0.4554
Query 62: 0.0427                 at 0.30       0.3551
Query 63: 0.1705                 at 0.40       0.3095
Query 64: 0.3209                 at 0.50       0.2462
Query 65: 0.0447                 at 0.60       0.1953
Query 67: 0.8000                 at 0.70       0.1663
Query 68: 0.0511                 at 0.80       0.1323
Query 69: 0.0476                 at 0.90       0.0497
Query 70: 0.1901                 at 1.00       0.0216
Query 71: 0.4246
Query 72: 0.3706             Avg. prec. (non-interpolated)
Query 73: 0.5996             for all rel. documents
Query 74: 0.6921                               0.2587
Query 75: 0.4833             Precision:
                               At    5 docs:   0.4333
                               At   10 docs:   0.3792
                               At   15 docs:   0.3111
                               At   20 docs:   0.2917
                               At   30 docs:   0.2597
                               At  100 docs:   0.1500
                               At  200 docs:   0.0954
                               At  500 docs:   0.0493
                               At 1000 docs:   0.0277

                             R-Precision (prec. after R
                             (=num_rel) docs. retrieved):
                                 Exact:        0.2744
```

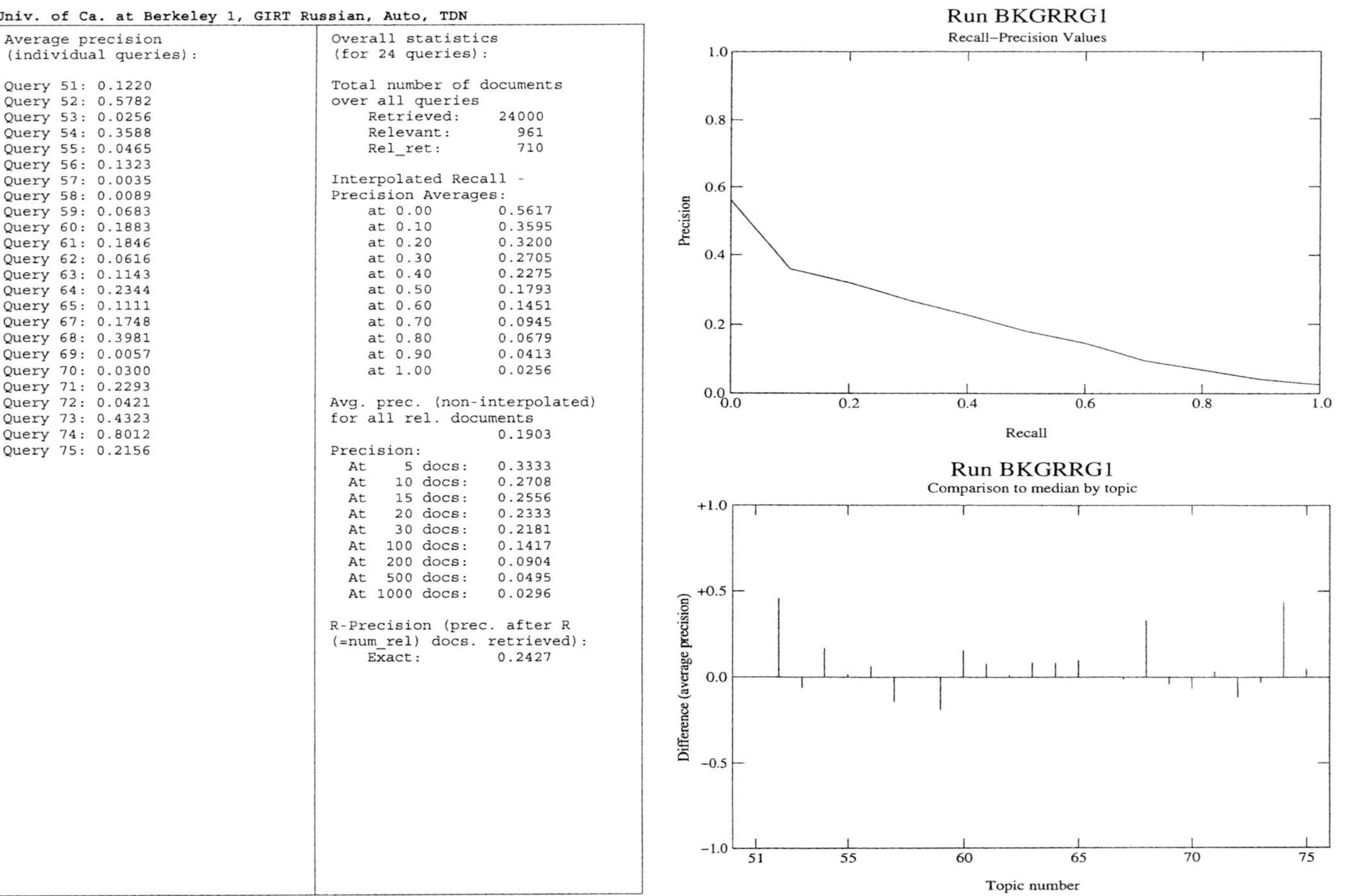

Univ. of Ca. at Berkeley 1, GIRT Russian, Auto, TDN

Average precision (individual queries):	Overall statistics (for 24 queries):	
Query 51: 0.1220	Total number of documents over all queries	
Query 52: 0.5782	Retrieved:	24000
Query 53: 0.0256	Relevant:	961
Query 54: 0.3588	Rel_ret:	710
Query 55: 0.0465		
Query 56: 0.1323	Interpolated Recall - Precision Averages:	
Query 57: 0.0035	at 0.00	0.5617
Query 58: 0.0089	at 0.10	0.3595
Query 59: 0.0683	at 0.20	0.3200
Query 60: 0.1883	at 0.30	0.2705
Query 61: 0.1846	at 0.40	0.2275
Query 62: 0.0616	at 0.50	0.1793
Query 63: 0.1143	at 0.60	0.1451
Query 64: 0.2344	at 0.70	0.0945
Query 65: 0.1111	at 0.80	0.0679
Query 67: 0.1748	at 0.90	0.0413
Query 68: 0.3981	at 1.00	0.0256
Query 69: 0.0057		
Query 70: 0.0300	Avg. prec. (non-interpolated) for all rel. documents	0.1903
Query 71: 0.2293		
Query 72: 0.0421	Precision:	
Query 73: 0.4323	At 5 docs:	0.3333
Query 74: 0.8012	At 10 docs:	0.2708
Query 75: 0.2156	At 15 docs:	0.2556
	At 20 docs:	0.2333
	At 30 docs:	0.2181
	At 100 docs:	0.1417
	At 200 docs:	0.0904
	At 500 docs:	0.0495
	At 1000 docs:	0.0296
	R-Precision (prec. after R (=num_rel) docs. retrieved):	
	Exact:	0.2427

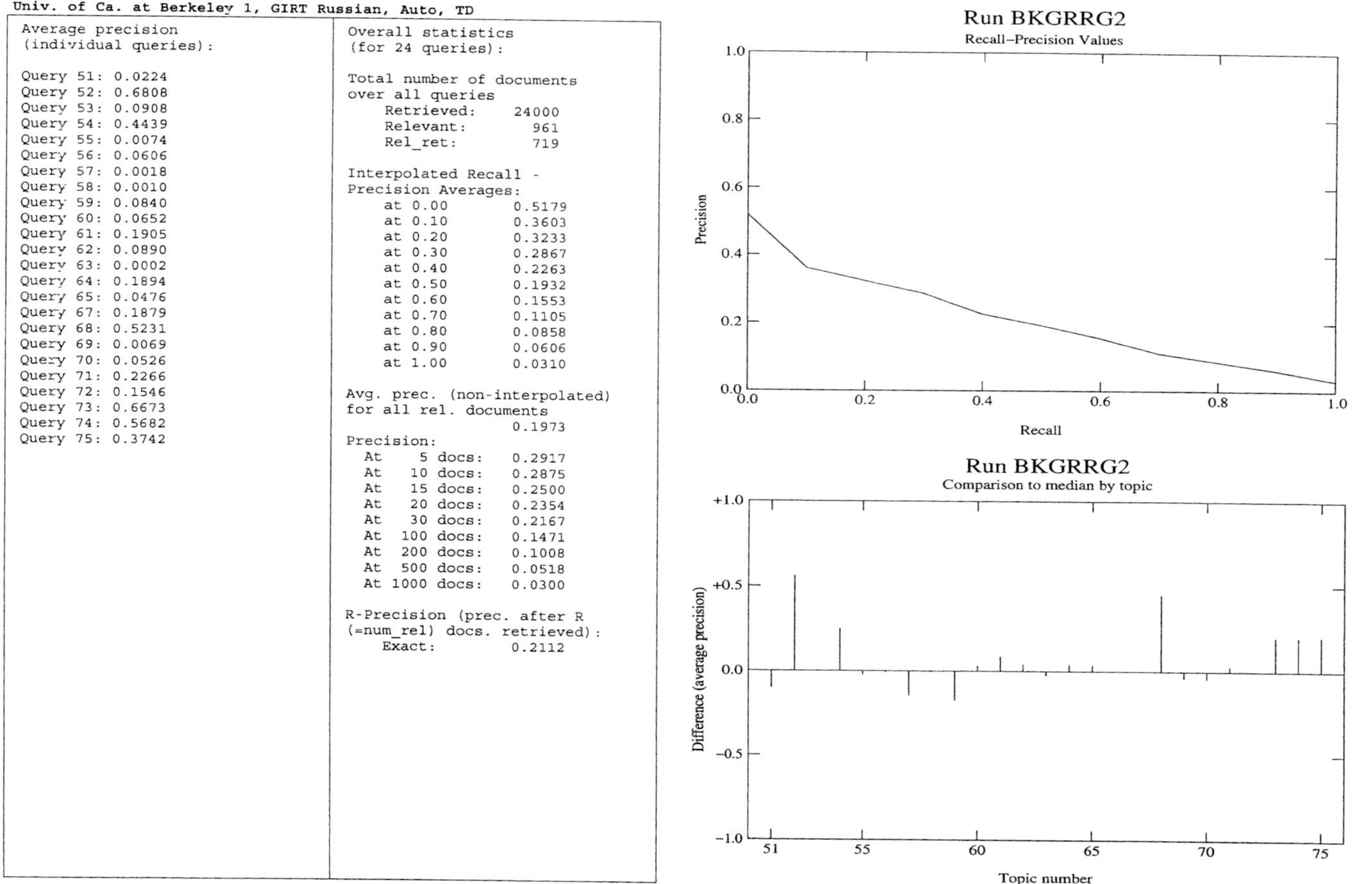

Univ. of Ca. at Berkeley 1, GIRT Russian, Auto, TD

```
Average precision                Overall statistics
(individual queries):            (for 24 queries):

Query 51: 0.0224                 Total number of documents
Query 52: 0.6808                 over all queries
Query 53: 0.0908                     Retrieved:    24000
Query 54: 0.4439                     Relevant:       961
Query 55: 0.0074                     Rel_ret:        719
Query 56: 0.0606
Query 57: 0.0018                 Interpolated Recall -
Query 58: 0.0010                 Precision Averages:
Query 59: 0.0840                     at 0.00       0.5179
Query 60: 0.0652                     at 0.10       0.3603
Query 61: 0.1905                     at 0.20       0.3233
Query 62: 0.0890                     at 0.30       0.2867
Query 63: 0.0002                     at 0.40       0.2263
Query 64: 0.1894                     at 0.50       0.1932
Query 65: 0.0476                     at 0.60       0.1553
Query 67: 0.1879                     at 0.70       0.1105
Query 68: 0.5231                     at 0.80       0.0858
Query 69: 0.0069                     at 0.90       0.0606
Query 70: 0.0526                     at 1.00       0.0310
Query 71: 0.2266
Query 72: 0.1546                 Avg. prec. (non-interpolated)
Query 73: 0.6673                 for all rel. documents
Query 74: 0.5682                                   0.1973
Query 75: 0.3742                 Precision:
                                   At    5 docs:   0.2917
                                   At   10 docs:   0.2875
                                   At   15 docs:   0.2500
                                   At   20 docs:   0.2354
                                   At   30 docs:   0.2167
                                   At  100 docs:   0.1471
                                   At  200 docs:   0.1008
                                   At  500 docs:   0.0518
                                   At 1000 docs:   0.0300

                                 R-Precision (prec. after R
                                 (=num_rel) docs. retrieved):
                                     Exact:        0.2112
```

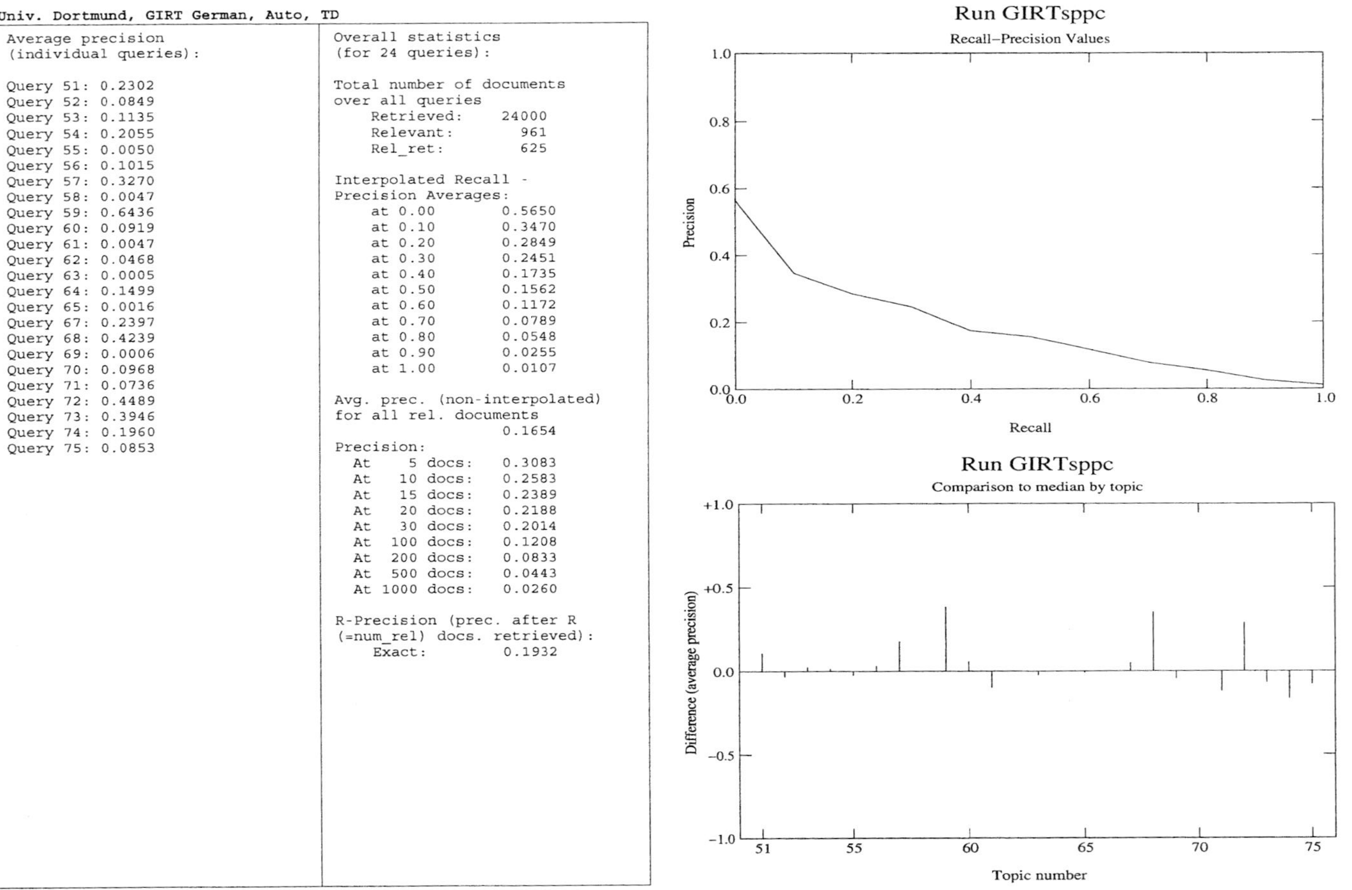

Univ. Dortmund, GIRT German, Auto, TD

```
Average precision                Overall statistics
(individual queries):            (for 24 queries):

Query 51: 0.2302                 Total number of documents
Query 52: 0.0849                 over all queries
Query 53: 0.1135                     Retrieved:     24000
Query 54: 0.2055                     Relevant:        961
Query 55: 0.0050                     Rel_ret:         625
Query 56: 0.1015
Query 57: 0.3270                 Interpolated Recall -
Query 58: 0.0047                 Precision Averages:
Query 59: 0.6436                     at 0.00        0.5650
Query 60: 0.0919                     at 0.10        0.3470
Query 61: 0.0047                     at 0.20        0.2849
Query 62: 0.0468                     at 0.30        0.2451
Query 63: 0.0005                     at 0.40        0.1735
Query 64: 0.1499                     at 0.50        0.1562
Query 65: 0.0016                     at 0.60        0.1172
Query 67: 0.2397                     at 0.70        0.0789
Query 68: 0.4239                     at 0.80        0.0548
Query 69: 0.0006                     at 0.90        0.0255
Query 70: 0.0968                     at 1.00        0.0107
Query 71: 0.0736
Query 72: 0.4489                 Avg. prec. (non-interpolated)
Query 73: 0.3946                 for all rel. documents
Query 74: 0.1960                                    0.1654
Query 75: 0.0853                 Precision:
                                   At    5 docs:   0.3083
                                   At   10 docs:   0.2583
                                   At   15 docs:   0.2389
                                   At   20 docs:   0.2188
                                   At   30 docs:   0.2014
                                   At  100 docs:   0.1208
                                   At  200 docs:   0.0833
                                   At  500 docs:   0.0443
                                   At 1000 docs:   0.0260

                                 R-Precision (prec. after R
                                 (=num_rel) docs. retrieved):
                                     Exact:         0.1932
```

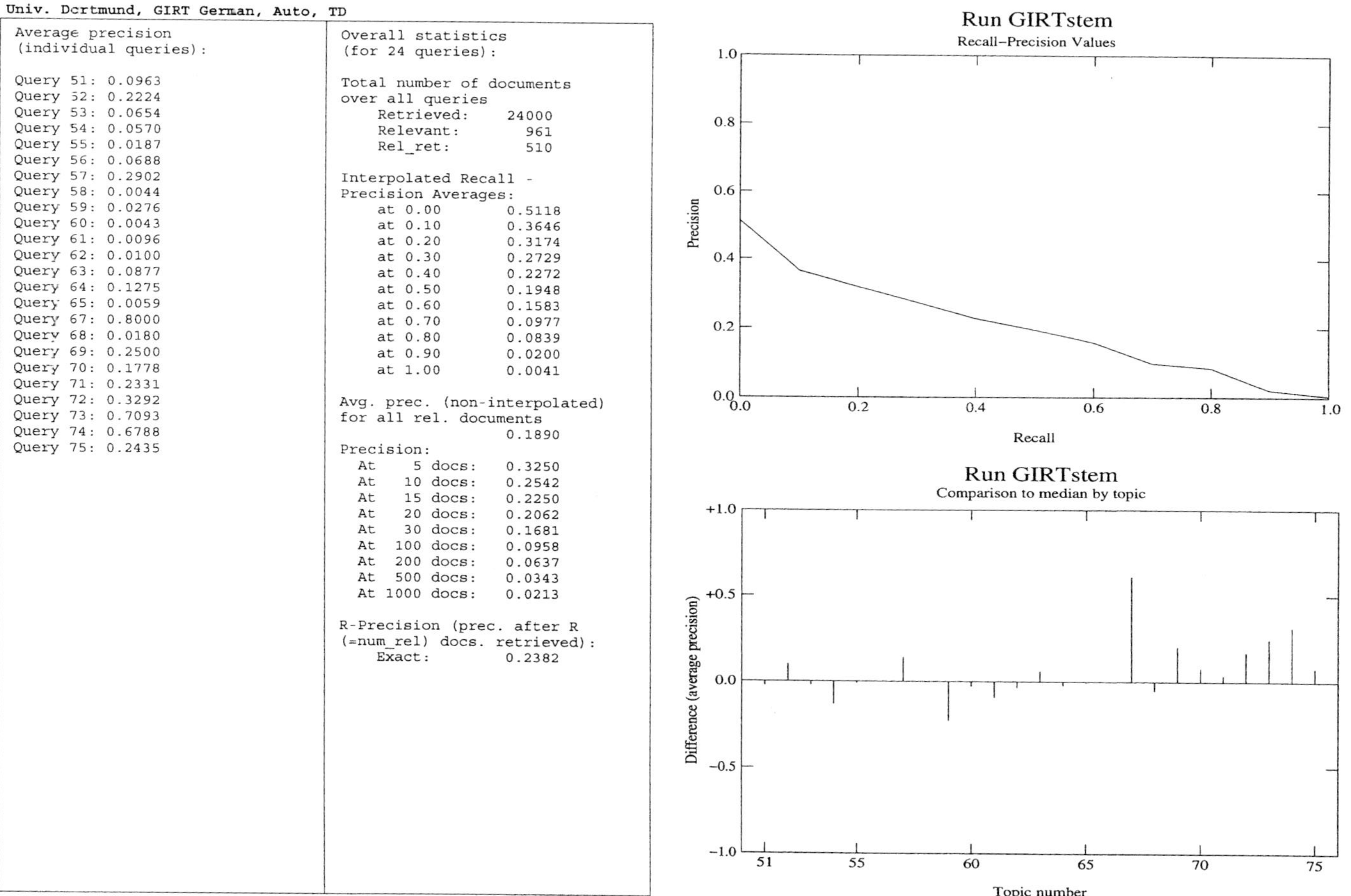

Univ. Dortmund, GIRT German, Auto, TD

```
Average precision                Overall statistics
(individual queries):            (for 24 queries):

Query 51: 0.0963                 Total number of documents
Query 52: 0.2224                 over all queries
Query 53: 0.0654                     Retrieved:     24000
Query 54: 0.0570                     Relevant:        961
Query 55: 0.0187                     Rel_ret:         510
Query 56: 0.0688
Query 57: 0.2902                 Interpolated Recall -
Query 58: 0.0044                 Precision Averages:
Query 59: 0.0276                     at 0.00         0.5118
Query 60: 0.0043                     at 0.10         0.3646
Query 61: 0.0096                     at 0.20         0.3174
Query 62: 0.0100                     at 0.30         0.2729
Query 63: 0.0877                     at 0.40         0.2272
Query 64: 0.1275                     at 0.50         0.1948
Query 65: 0.0059                     at 0.60         0.1583
Query 67: 0.8000                     at 0.70         0.0977
Query 68: 0.0180                     at 0.80         0.0839
Query 69: 0.2500                     at 0.90         0.0200
Query 70: 0.1778                     at 1.00         0.0041
Query 71: 0.2331
Query 72: 0.3292                 Avg. prec. (non-interpolated)
Query 73: 0.7093                 for all rel. documents
Query 74: 0.6788                                     0.1890
Query 75: 0.2435                 Precision:
                                   At    5 docs:     0.3250
                                   At   10 docs:     0.2542
                                   At   15 docs:     0.2250
                                   At   20 docs:     0.2062
                                   At   30 docs:     0.1681
                                   At  100 docs:     0.0958
                                   At  200 docs:     0.0637
                                   At  500 docs:     0.0343
                                   At 1000 docs:     0.0213

                                 R-Precision (prec. after R
                                 (=num_rel) docs. retrieved):
                                     Exact:          0.2382
```

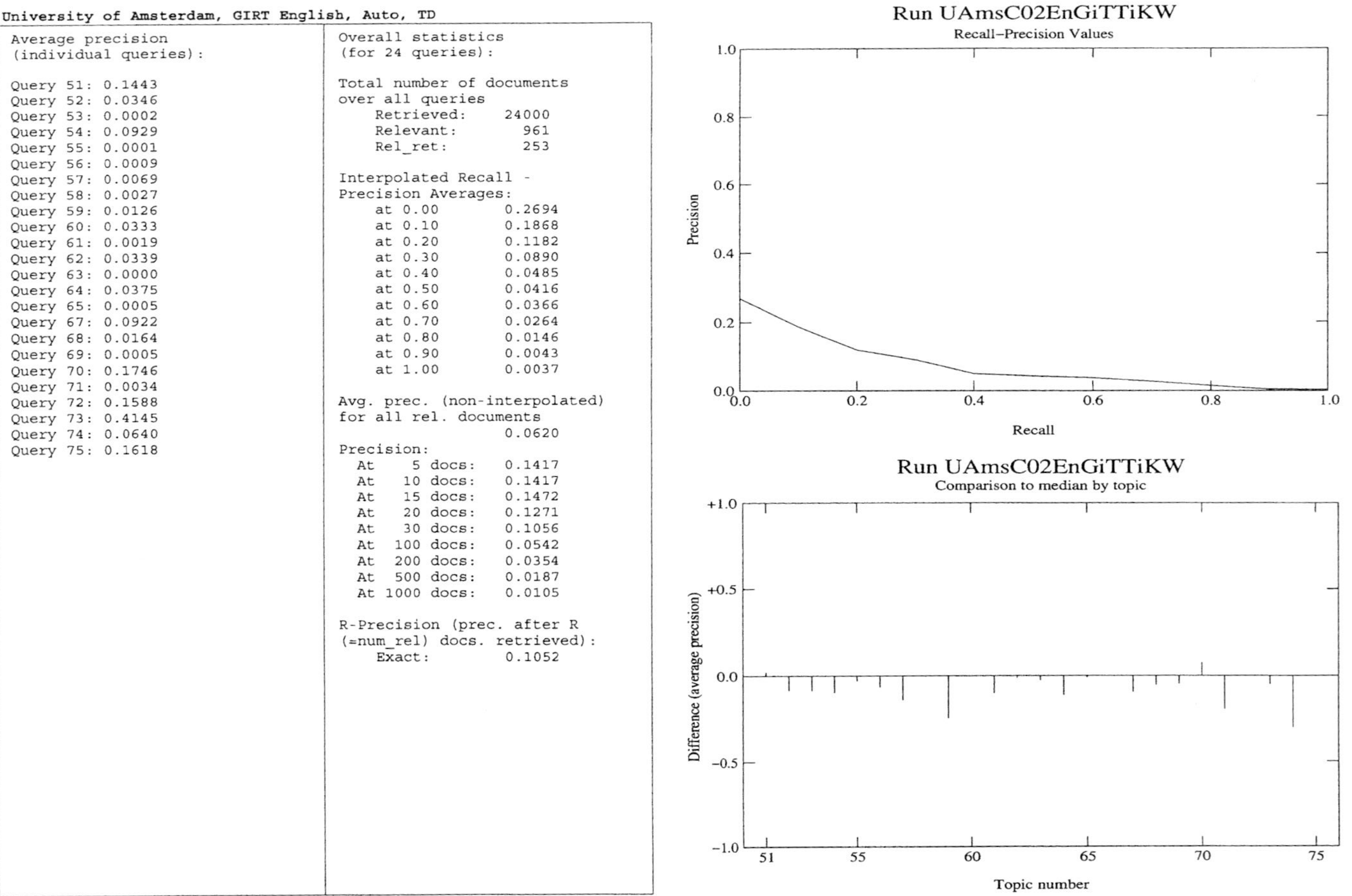

University of Amsterdam, GIRT English, Auto, TD

```
Average precision              Overall statistics
(individual queries):          (for 24 queries):

Query 51: 0.1443               Total number of documents
Query 52: 0.0346               over all queries
Query 53: 0.0002                 Retrieved:     24000
Query 54: 0.0929                 Relevant:        961
Query 55: 0.0001                 Rel_ret:         253
Query 56: 0.0009
Query 57: 0.0069               Interpolated Recall -
Query 58: 0.0027               Precision Averages:
Query 59: 0.0126                 at 0.00       0.2694
Query 60: 0.0333                 at 0.10       0.1868
Query 61: 0.0019                 at 0.20       0.1182
Query 62: 0.0339                 at 0.30       0.0890
Query 63: 0.0000                 at 0.40       0.0485
Query 64: 0.0375                 at 0.50       0.0416
Query 65: 0.0005                 at 0.60       0.0366
Query 67: 0.0922                 at 0.70       0.0264
Query 68: 0.0164                 at 0.80       0.0146
Query 69: 0.0005                 at 0.90       0.0043
Query 70: 0.1746                 at 1.00       0.0037
Query 71: 0.0034
Query 72: 0.1588               Avg. prec. (non-interpolated)
Query 73: 0.4145               for all rel. documents
Query 74: 0.0640                               0.0620
Query 75: 0.1618               Precision:
                                 At    5 docs:  0.1417
                                 At   10 docs:  0.1417
                                 At   15 docs:  0.1472
                                 At   20 docs:  0.1271
                                 At   30 docs:  0.1056
                                 At  100 docs:  0.0542
                                 At  200 docs:  0.0354
                                 At  500 docs:  0.0187
                                 At 1000 docs:  0.0105

                               R-Precision (prec. after R
                               (=num_rel) docs. retrieved):
                                   Exact:       0.1052
```

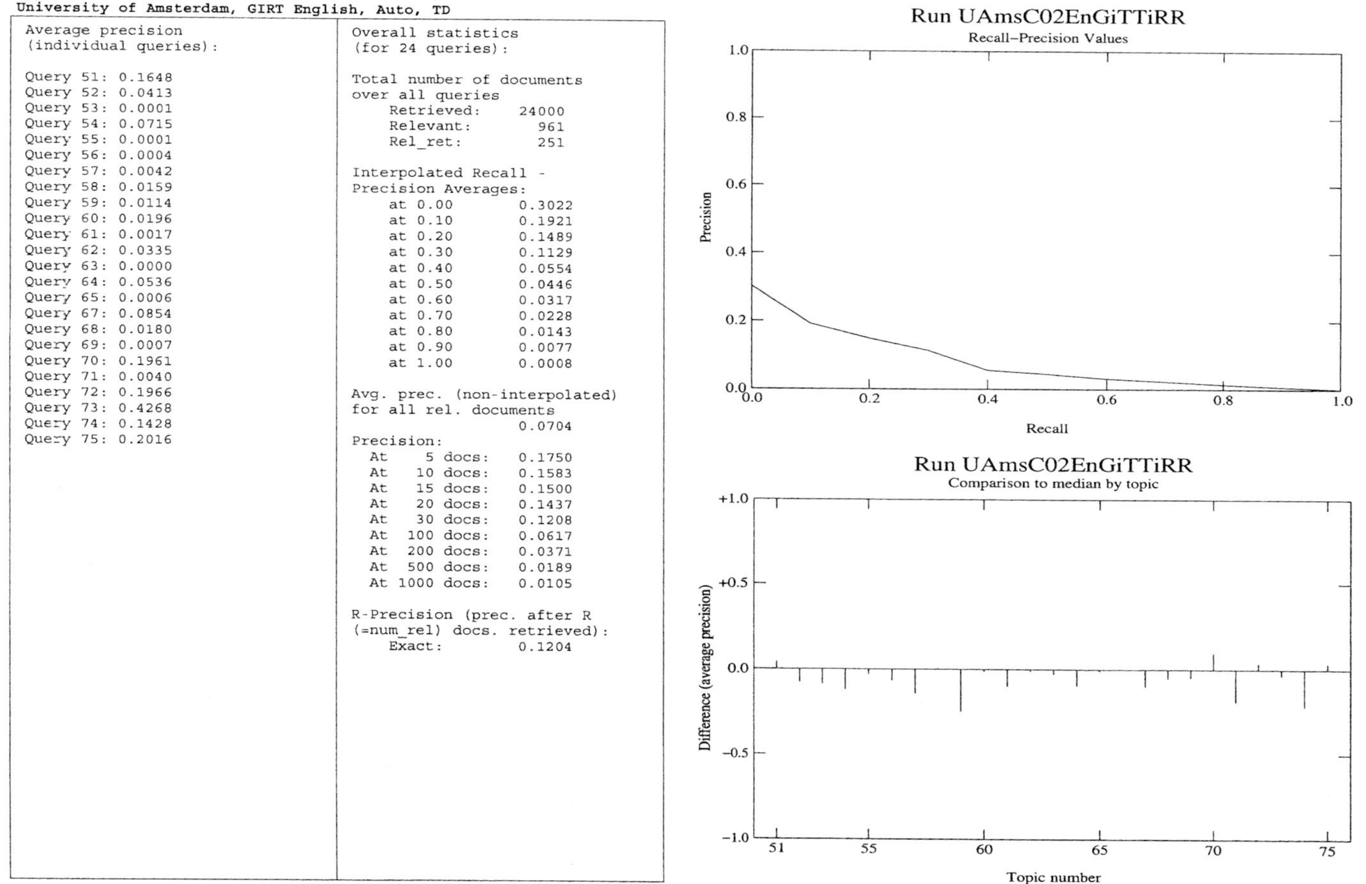

University of Amsterdam, GIRT English, Auto, TD

```
Average precision                 Overall statistics
(individual queries):             (for 24 queries):

Query 51: 0.1648                  Total number of documents
Query 52: 0.0413                  over all queries
Query 53: 0.0001                      Retrieved:     24000
Query 54: 0.0715                      Relevant:        961
Query 55: 0.0001                      Rel_ret:         251
Query 56: 0.0004
Query 57: 0.0042                  Interpolated Recall -
Query 58: 0.0159                  Precision Averages:
Query 59: 0.0114                      at 0.00         0.3022
Query 60: 0.0196                      at 0.10         0.1921
Query 61: 0.0017                      at 0.20         0.1489
Query 62: 0.0335                      at 0.30         0.1129
Query 63: 0.0000                      at 0.40         0.0554
Query 64: 0.0536                      at 0.50         0.0446
Query 65: 0.0006                      at 0.60         0.0317
Query 67: 0.0854                      at 0.70         0.0228
Query 68: 0.0180                      at 0.80         0.0143
Query 69: 0.0007                      at 0.90         0.0077
Query 70: 0.1961                      at 1.00         0.0008
Query 71: 0.0040
Query 72: 0.1966                  Avg. prec. (non-interpolated)
Query 73: 0.4268                  for all rel. documents
Query 74: 0.1428                                      0.0704
Query 75: 0.2016                  Precision:
                                    At    5 docs:     0.1750
                                    At   10 docs:     0.1583
                                    At   15 docs:     0.1500
                                    At   20 docs:     0.1437
                                    At   30 docs:     0.1208
                                    At  100 docs:     0.0617
                                    At  200 docs:     0.0371
                                    At  500 docs:     0.0189
                                    At 1000 docs:     0.0105

                                  R-Precision (prec. after R
                                  (=num_rel) docs. retrieved):
                                      Exact:          0.1204
```

Run UAmsC02EnGiTTiRR

Recall–Precision Values

Run UAmsC02EnGiTTiRR

Comparison to median by topic

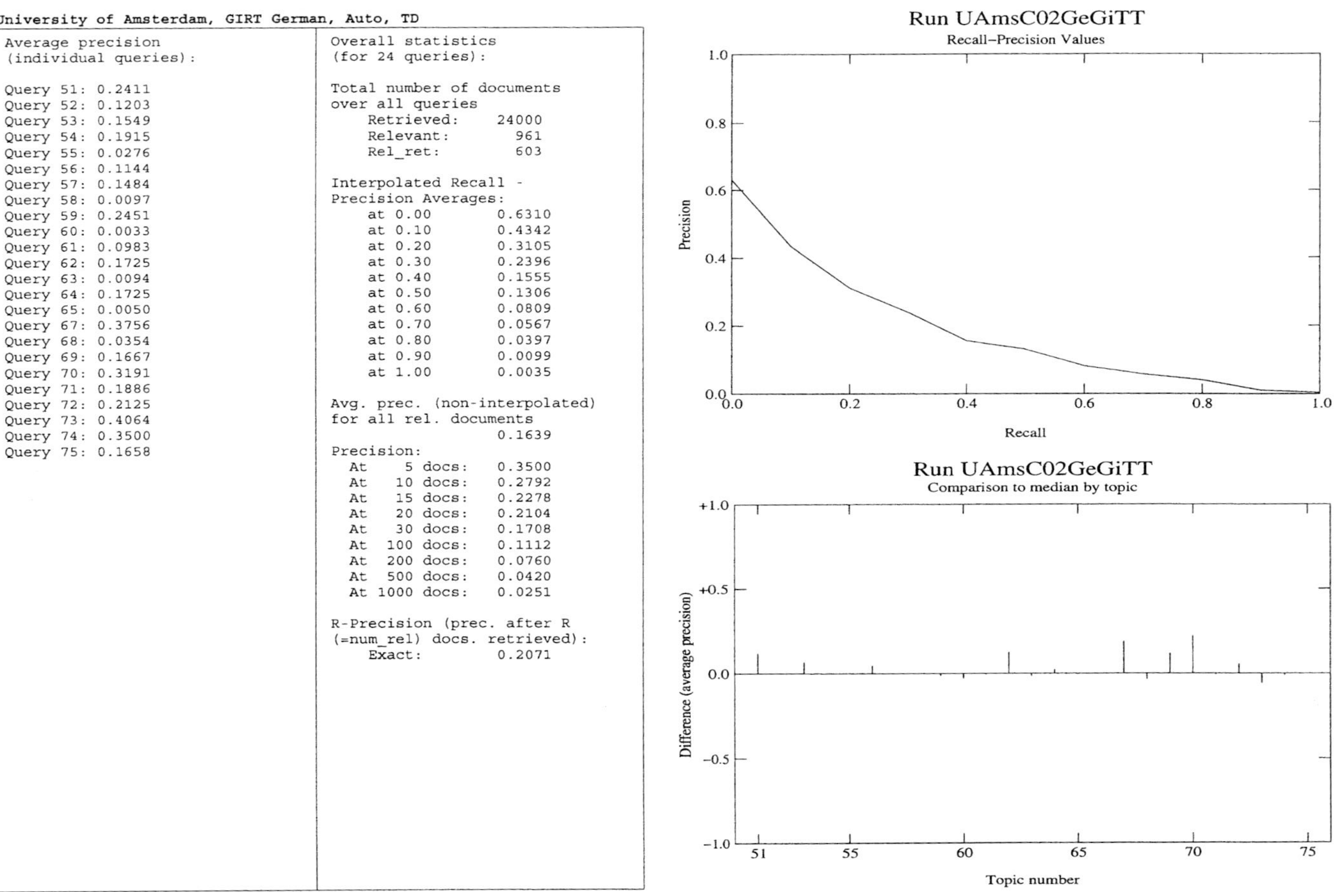

University of Amsterdam, GIRT German, Auto, TD

```
Average precision
(individual queries):

Query 51: 0.2411
Query 52: 0.1203
Query 53: 0.1549
Query 54: 0.1915
Query 55: 0.0276
Query 56: 0.1144
Query 57: 0.1484
Query 58: 0.0097
Query 59: 0.2451
Query 60: 0.0033
Query 61: 0.0983
Query 62: 0.1725
Query 63: 0.0094
Query 64: 0.1725
Query 65: 0.0050
Query 67: 0.3756
Query 68: 0.0354
Query 69: 0.1667
Query 70: 0.3191
Query 71: 0.1886
Query 72: 0.2125
Query 73: 0.4064
Query 74: 0.3500
Query 75: 0.1658
```

```
Overall statistics
(for 24 queries):

Total number of documents
over all queries
    Retrieved:     24000
    Relevant:        961
    Rel_ret:         603

Interpolated Recall -
Precision Averages:
    at 0.00        0.6310
    at 0.10        0.4342
    at 0.20        0.3105
    at 0.30        0.2396
    at 0.40        0.1555
    at 0.50        0.1306
    at 0.60        0.0809
    at 0.70        0.0567
    at 0.80        0.0397
    at 0.90        0.0099
    at 1.00        0.0035

Avg. prec. (non-interpolated)
for all rel. documents
                   0.1639
Precision:
  At    5 docs:    0.3500
  At   10 docs:    0.2792
  At   15 docs:    0.2278
  At   20 docs:    0.2104
  At   30 docs:    0.1708
  At  100 docs:    0.1112
  At  200 docs:    0.0760
  At  500 docs:    0.0420
  At 1000 docs:    0.0251

R-Precision (prec. after R
(=num_rel) docs. retrieved):
    Exact:         0.2071
```

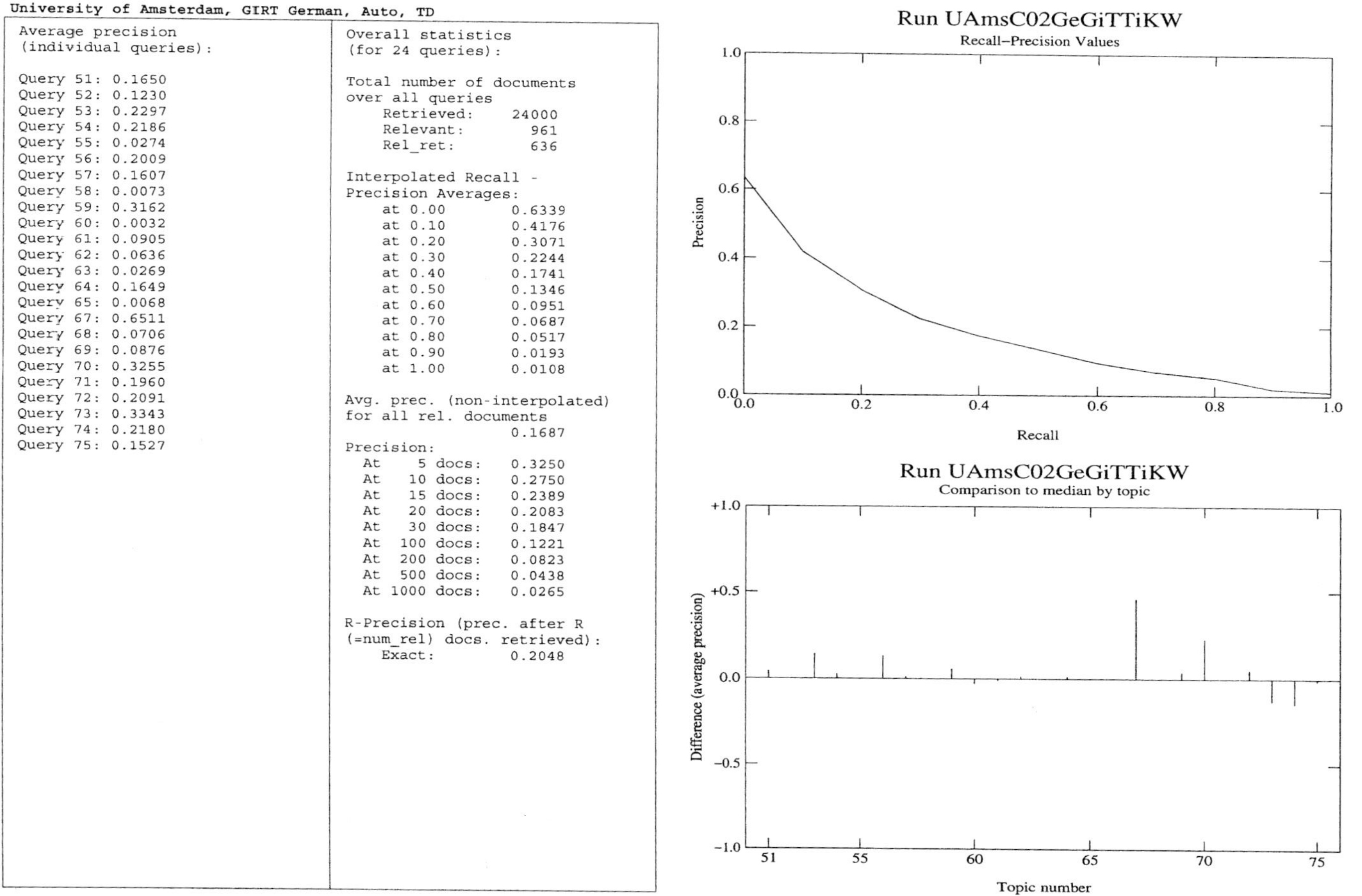

University of Amsterdam, GIRT German, Auto, TD

```
Average precision                 Overall statistics
(individual queries):             (for 24 queries):

Query 51: 0.1650                  Total number of documents
Query 52: 0.1230                  over all queries
Query 53: 0.2297                      Retrieved:     24000
Query 54: 0.2186                      Relevant:        961
Query 55: 0.0274                      Rel_ret:         636
Query 56: 0.2009
Query 57: 0.1607                  Interpolated Recall -
Query 58: 0.0073                  Precision Averages:
Query 59: 0.3162                      at 0.00        0.6339
Query 60: 0.0032                      at 0.10        0.4176
Query 61: 0.0905                      at 0.20        0.3071
Query 62: 0.0636                      at 0.30        0.2244
Query 63: 0.0269                      at 0.40        0.1741
Query 64: 0.1649                      at 0.50        0.1346
Query 65: 0.0068                      at 0.60        0.0951
Query 67: 0.6511                      at 0.70        0.0687
Query 68: 0.0706                      at 0.80        0.0517
Query 69: 0.0876                      at 0.90        0.0193
Query 70: 0.3255                      at 1.00        0.0108
Query 71: 0.1960
Query 72: 0.2091                  Avg. prec. (non-interpolated)
Query 73: 0.3343                  for all rel. documents
Query 74: 0.2180                                     0.1687
Query 75: 0.1527                  Precision:
                                    At    5 docs:    0.3250
                                    At   10 docs:    0.2750
                                    At   15 docs:    0.2389
                                    At   20 docs:    0.2083
                                    At   30 docs:    0.1847
                                    At  100 docs:    0.1221
                                    At  200 docs:    0.0823
                                    At  500 docs:    0.0438
                                    At 1000 docs:    0.0265

                                  R-Precision (prec. after R
                                  (=num_rel) docs. retrieved):
                                      Exact:         0.2048
```

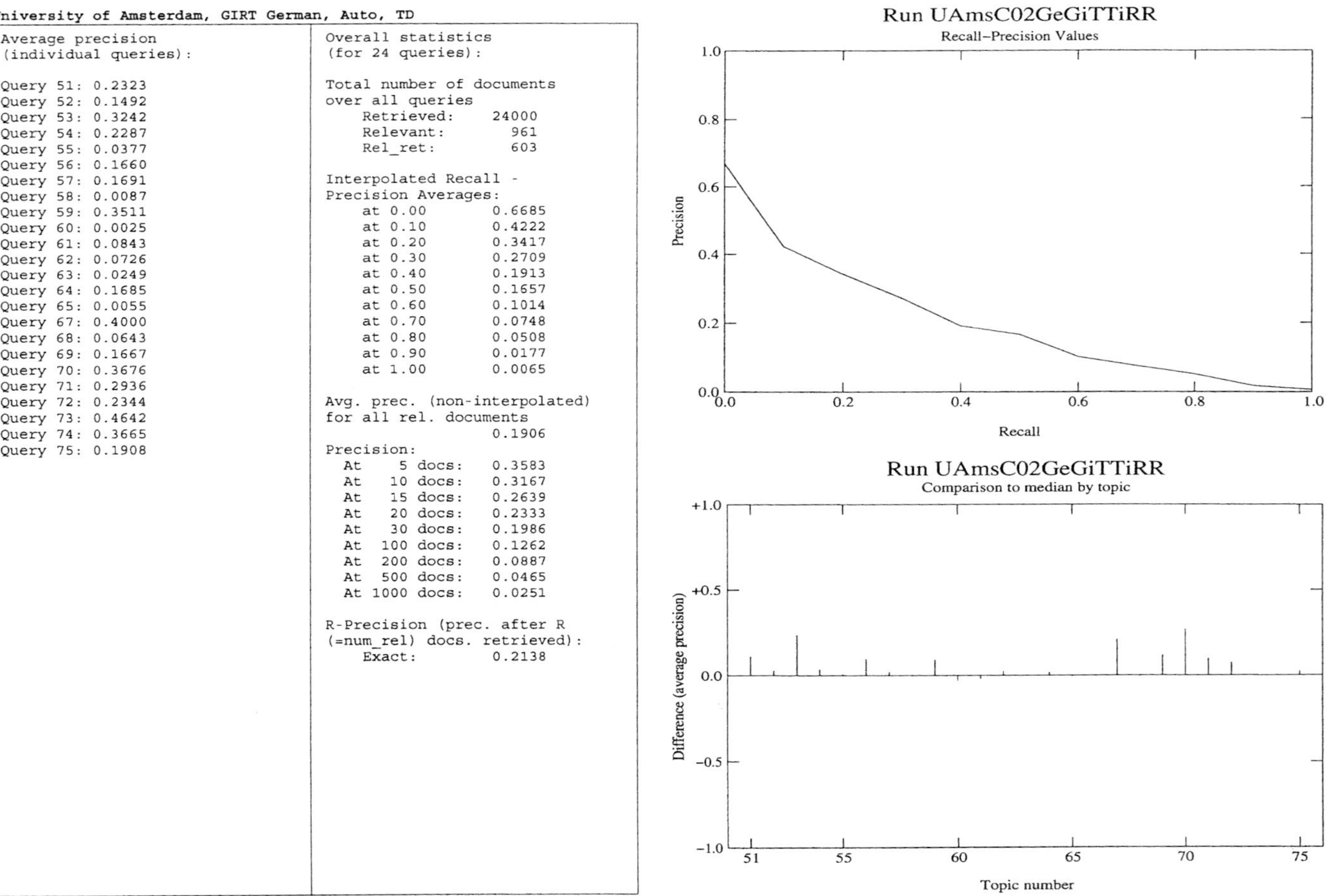

University of Amsterdam, GIRT German, Auto, TD

Average precision (individual queries):	Overall statistics (for 24 queries):
Query 51: 0.2323	Total number of documents over all queries
Query 52: 0.1492	Retrieved: 24000
Query 53: 0.3242	Relevant: 961
Query 54: 0.2287	Rel_ret: 603
Query 55: 0.0377	
Query 56: 0.1660	Interpolated Recall - Precision Averages:
Query 57: 0.1691	at 0.00 0.6685
Query 58: 0.0087	at 0.10 0.4222
Query 59: 0.3511	at 0.20 0.3417
Query 60: 0.0025	at 0.30 0.2709
Query 61: 0.0843	at 0.40 0.1913
Query 62: 0.0726	at 0.50 0.1657
Query 63: 0.0249	at 0.60 0.1014
Query 64: 0.1685	at 0.70 0.0748
Query 65: 0.0055	at 0.80 0.0508
Query 67: 0.4000	at 0.90 0.0177
Query 68: 0.0643	at 1.00 0.0065
Query 69: 0.1667	
Query 70: 0.3676	Avg. prec. (non-interpolated) for all rel. documents 0.1906
Query 71: 0.2936	
Query 72: 0.2344	Precision:
Query 73: 0.4642	At 5 docs: 0.3583
Query 74: 0.3665	At 10 docs: 0.3167
Query 75: 0.1908	At 15 docs: 0.2639
	At 20 docs: 0.2333
	At 30 docs: 0.1986
	At 100 docs: 0.1262
	At 200 docs: 0.0887
	At 500 docs: 0.0465
	At 1000 docs: 0.0251
	R-Precision (prec. after R (=num_rel) docs. retrieved):
	Exact: 0.2138

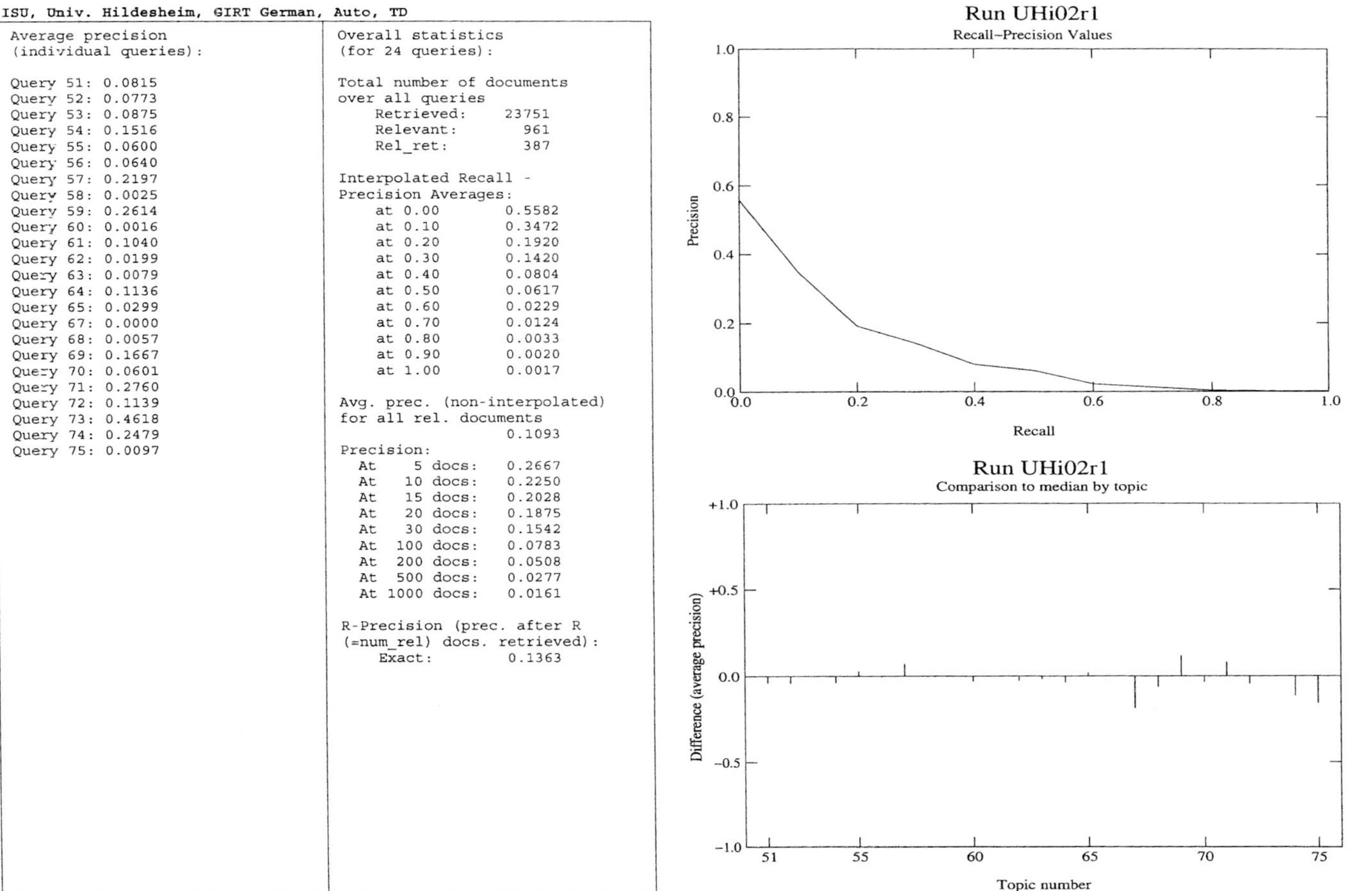

ISU, Univ. Hildesheim, GIRT German, Auto, TD

Average precision (individual queries):	Overall statistics (for 24 queries):
Query 51: 0.0815	Total number of documents over all queries
Query 52: 0.0773	Retrieved: 23751
Query 53: 0.0875	Relevant: 961
Query 54: 0.1516	Rel_ret: 387
Query 55: 0.0600	
Query 56: 0.0640	Interpolated Recall - Precision Averages:
Query 57: 0.2197	at 0.00 0.5582
Query 58: 0.0025	at 0.10 0.3472
Query 59: 0.2614	at 0.20 0.1920
Query 60: 0.0016	at 0.30 0.1420
Query 61: 0.1040	at 0.40 0.0804
Query 62: 0.0199	at 0.50 0.0617
Query 63: 0.0079	at 0.60 0.0229
Query 64: 0.1136	at 0.70 0.0124
Query 65: 0.0299	at 0.80 0.0033
Query 67: 0.0000	at 0.90 0.0020
Query 68: 0.0057	at 1.00 0.0017
Query 69: 0.1667	
Query 70: 0.0601	Avg. prec. (non-interpolated) for all rel. documents 0.1093
Query 71: 0.2760	Precision:
Query 72: 0.1139	At 5 docs: 0.2667
Query 73: 0.4618	At 10 docs: 0.2250
Query 74: 0.2479	At 15 docs: 0.2028
Query 75: 0.0097	At 20 docs: 0.1875
	At 30 docs: 0.1542
	At 100 docs: 0.0783
	At 200 docs: 0.0508
	At 500 docs: 0.0277
	At 1000 docs: 0.0161
	R-Precision (prec. after R (=num_rel) docs. retrieved):
	Exact: 0.1363

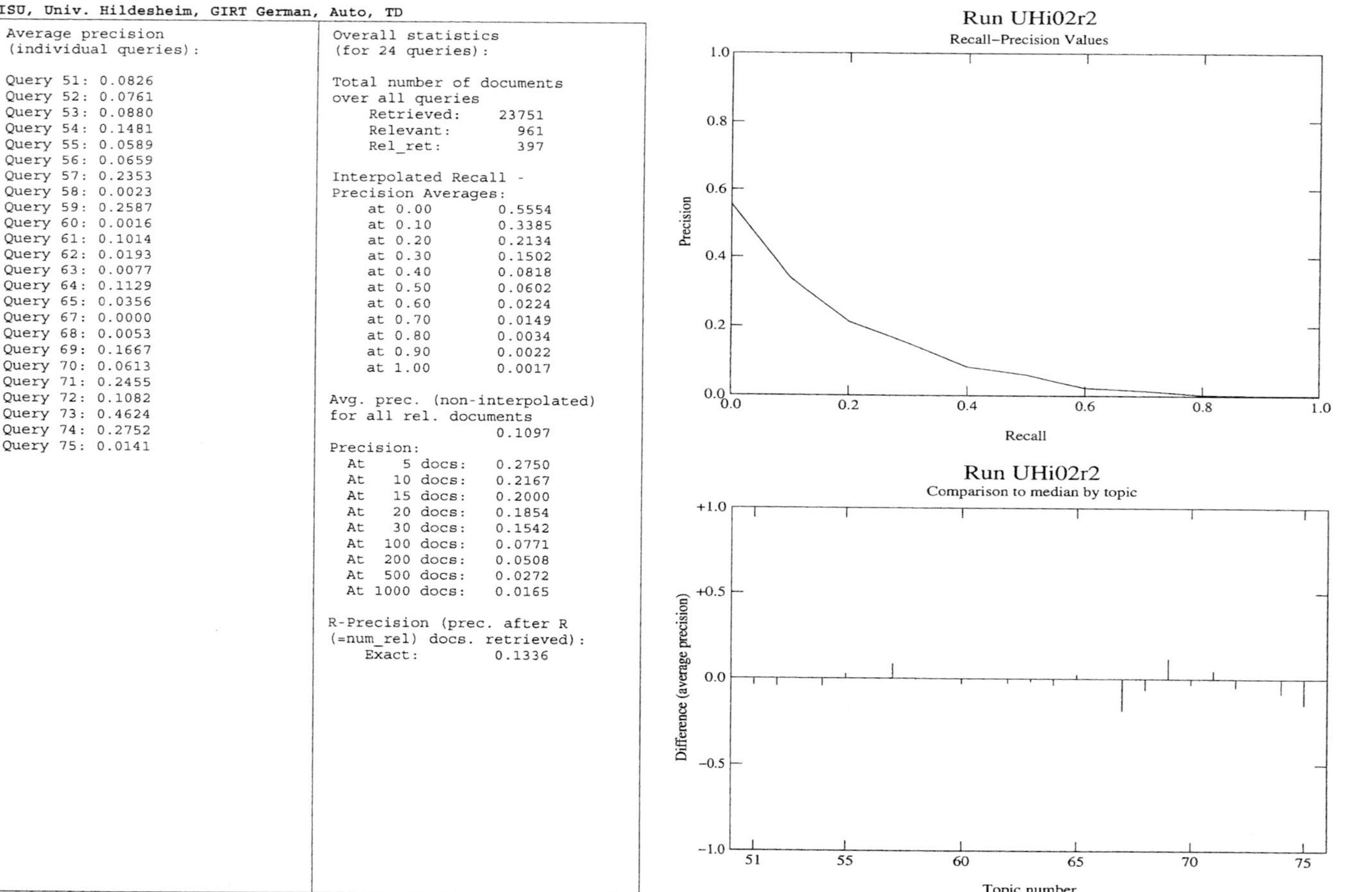

ISU, Univ. Hildesheim, GIRT German, Auto, TD

Average precision (individual queries):	Overall statistics (for 24 queries):	
Query 51: 0.0826	Total number of documents over all queries	
Query 52: 0.0761	Retrieved:	23751
Query 53: 0.0880	Relevant:	961
Query 54: 0.1481	Rel_ret:	397
Query 55: 0.0589	Interpolated Recall - Precision Averages:	
Query 56: 0.0659	at 0.00	0.5554
Query 57: 0.2353	at 0.10	0.3385
Query 58: 0.0023	at 0.20	0.2134
Query 59: 0.2587	at 0.30	0.1502
Query 60: 0.0016	at 0.40	0.0818
Query 61: 0.1014	at 0.50	0.0602
Query 62: 0.0193	at 0.60	0.0224
Query 63: 0.0077	at 0.70	0.0149
Query 64: 0.1129	at 0.80	0.0034
Query 65: 0.0356	at 0.90	0.0022
Query 67: 0.0000	at 1.00	0.0017
Query 68: 0.0053	Avg. prec. (non-interpolated) for all rel. documents	0.1097
Query 69: 0.1667	Precision:	
Query 70: 0.0613	At 5 docs:	0.2750
Query 71: 0.2455	At 10 docs:	0.2167
Query 72: 0.1082	At 15 docs:	0.2000
Query 73: 0.4624	At 20 docs:	0.1854
Query 74: 0.2752	At 30 docs:	0.1542
Query 75: 0.0141	At 100 docs:	0.0771
	At 200 docs:	0.0508
	At 500 docs:	0.0272
	At 1000 docs:	0.0165
	R-Precision (prec. after R (=num_rel) docs. retrieved): Exact:	0.1336

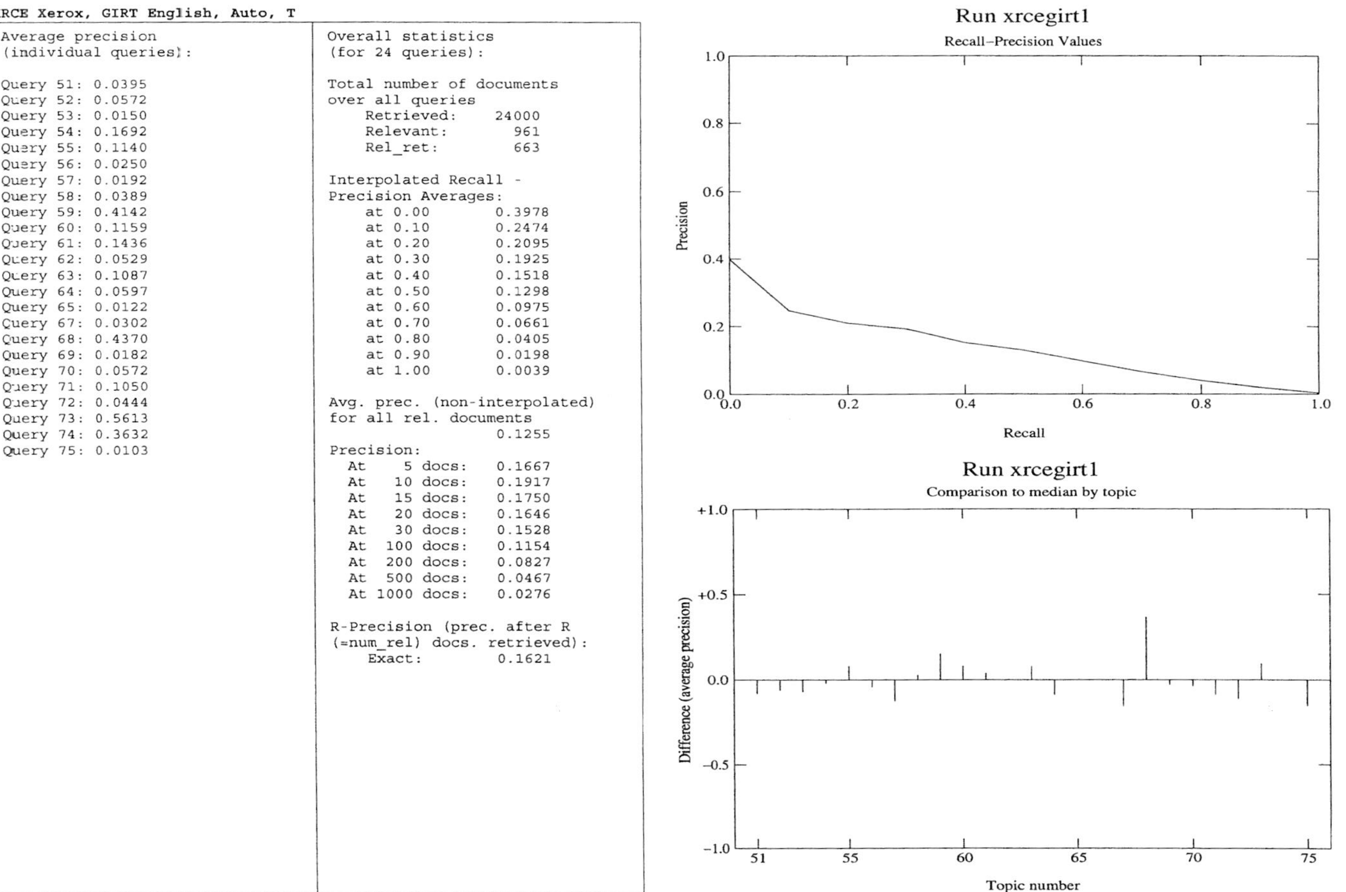

XRCE Xerox, GIRT English, Auto, T

Average precision (individual queries):	Overall statistics (for 24 queries):
Query 51: 0.0395	Total number of documents over all queries
Query 52: 0.0572	Retrieved: 24000
Query 53: 0.0150	Relevant: 961
Query 54: 0.1692	Rel_ret: 663
Query 55: 0.1140	
Query 56: 0.0250	Interpolated Recall - Precision Averages:
Query 57: 0.0192	at 0.00 0.3978
Query 58: 0.0389	at 0.10 0.2474
Query 59: 0.4142	at 0.20 0.2095
Query 60: 0.1159	at 0.30 0.1925
Query 61: 0.1436	at 0.40 0.1518
Query 62: 0.0529	at 0.50 0.1298
Query 63: 0.1087	at 0.60 0.0975
Query 64: 0.0597	at 0.70 0.0661
Query 65: 0.0122	at 0.80 0.0405
Query 67: 0.0302	at 0.90 0.0198
Query 68: 0.4370	at 1.00 0.0039
Query 69: 0.0182	
Query 70: 0.0572	Avg. prec. (non-interpolated) for all rel. documents 0.1255
Query 71: 0.1050	Precision:
Query 72: 0.0444	At 5 docs: 0.1667
Query 73: 0.5613	At 10 docs: 0.1917
Query 74: 0.3632	At 15 docs: 0.1750
Query 75: 0.0103	At 20 docs: 0.1646
	At 30 docs: 0.1528
	At 100 docs: 0.1154
	At 200 docs: 0.0827
	At 500 docs: 0.0467
	At 1000 docs: 0.0276
	R-Precision (prec. after R (=num_rel) docs. retrieved):
	Exact: 0.1621

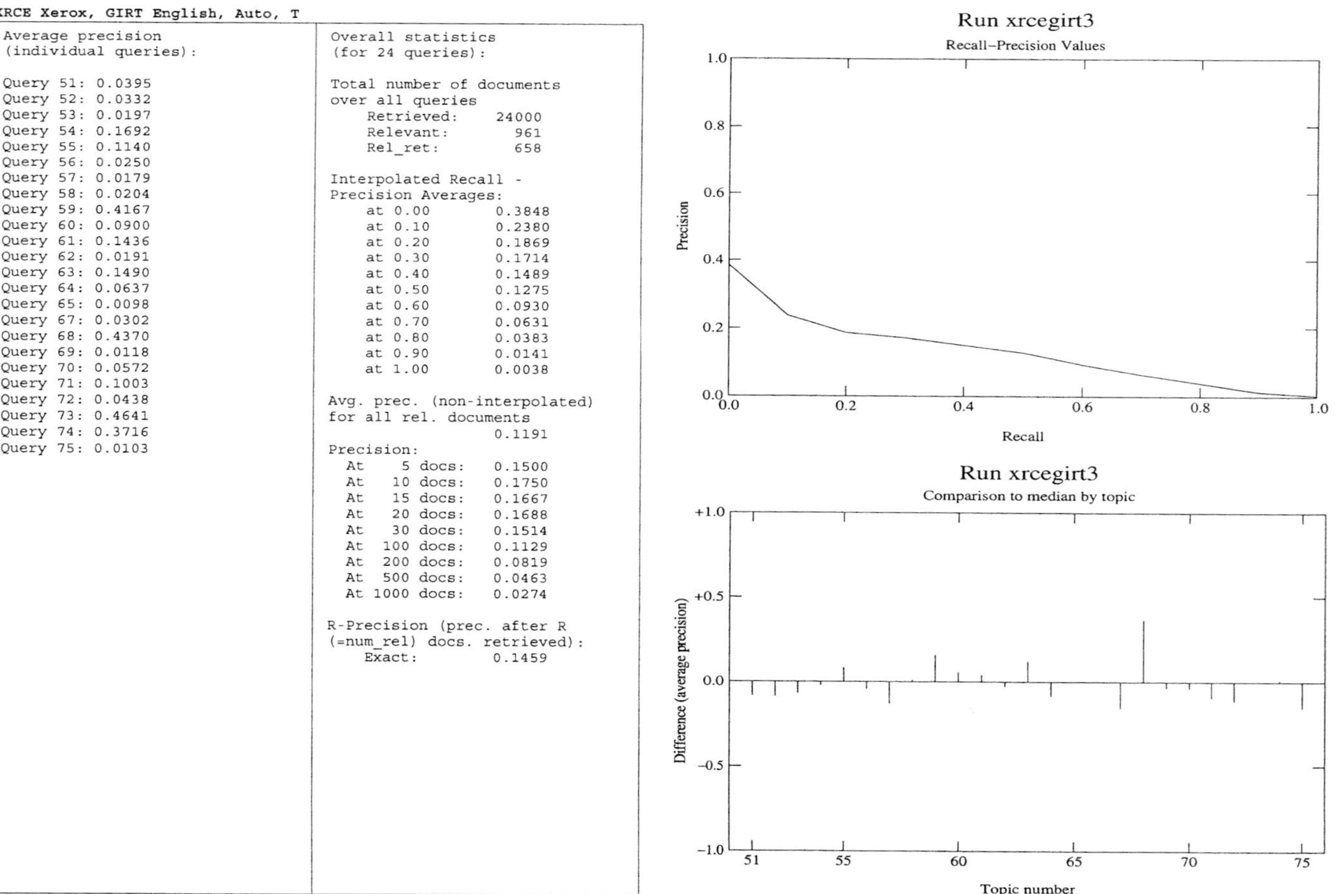

XRCE Xerox, GIRT English, Auto, T

```
Average precision                  Overall statistics
(individual queries):              (for 24 queries):

Query 51: 0.0395                   Total number of documents
Query 52: 0.0332                   over all queries
Query 53: 0.0197                       Retrieved:    24000
Query 54: 0.1692                       Relevant:       961
Query 55: 0.1140                       Rel_ret:        658
Query 56: 0.0250
Query 57: 0.0179                   Interpolated Recall -
Query 58: 0.0204                   Precision Averages:
Query 59: 0.4167                       at 0.00        0.3848
Query 60: 0.0900                       at 0.10        0.2380
Query 61: 0.1436                       at 0.20        0.1869
Query 62: 0.0191                       at 0.30        0.1714
Query 63: 0.1490                       at 0.40        0.1489
Query 64: 0.0637                       at 0.50        0.1275
Query 65: 0.0098                       at 0.60        0.0930
Query 67: 0.0302                       at 0.70        0.0631
Query 68: 0.4370                       at 0.80        0.0383
Query 69: 0.0118                       at 0.90        0.0141
Query 70: 0.0572                       at 1.00        0.0038
Query 71: 0.1003
Query 72: 0.0438                   Avg. prec. (non-interpolated)
Query 73: 0.4641                   for all rel. documents
Query 74: 0.3716                                      0.1191
Query 75: 0.0103                   Precision:
                                     At    5 docs:    0.1500
                                     At   10 docs:    0.1750
                                     At   15 docs:    0.1667
                                     At   20 docs:    0.1688
                                     At   30 docs:    0.1514
                                     At  100 docs:    0.1129
                                     At  200 docs:    0.0819
                                     At  500 docs:    0.0463
                                     At 1000 docs:    0.0274

                                   R-Precision (prec. after R
                                   (=num_rel) docs. retrieved):
                                       Exact:         0.1459
```

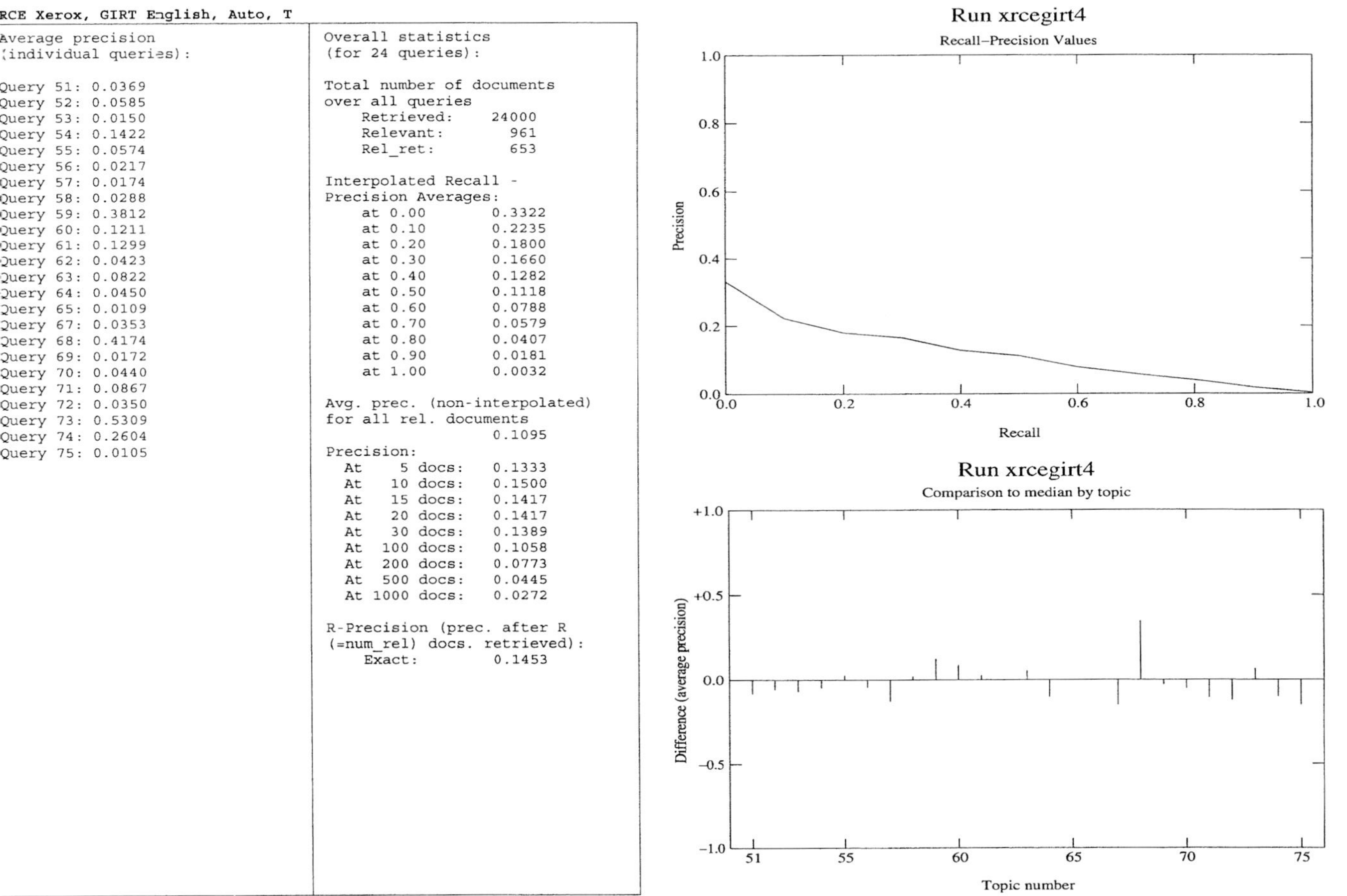

XRCE Xerox, GIRT English, Auto, T

```
Average precision
(individual queries):

Query 51: 0.0369
Query 52: 0.0585
Query 53: 0.0150
Query 54: 0.1422
Query 55: 0.0574
Query 56: 0.0217
Query 57: 0.0174
Query 58: 0.0288
Query 59: 0.3812
Query 60: 0.1211
Query 61: 0.1299
Query 62: 0.0423
Query 63: 0.0822
Query 64: 0.0450
Query 65: 0.0109
Query 67: 0.0353
Query 68: 0.4174
Query 69: 0.0172
Query 70: 0.0440
Query 71: 0.0867
Query 72: 0.0350
Query 73: 0.5309
Query 74: 0.2604
Query 75: 0.0105
```

```
Overall statistics
(for 24 queries):

Total number of documents
over all queries
    Retrieved:    24000
    Relevant:       961
    Rel_ret:        653

Interpolated Recall -
Precision Averages:
    at 0.00       0.3322
    at 0.10       0.2235
    at 0.20       0.1800
    at 0.30       0.1660
    at 0.40       0.1282
    at 0.50       0.1118
    at 0.60       0.0788
    at 0.70       0.0579
    at 0.80       0.0407
    at 0.90       0.0181
    at 1.00       0.0032

Avg. prec. (non-interpolated)
for all rel. documents
                  0.1095
Precision:
  At    5 docs:   0.1333
  At   10 docs:   0.1500
  At   15 docs:   0.1417
  At   20 docs:   0.1417
  At   30 docs:   0.1389
  At  100 docs:   0.1058
  At  200 docs:   0.0773
  At  500 docs:   0.0445
  At 1000 docs:   0.0272

R-Precision (prec. after R
(=num_rel) docs. retrieved):
    Exact:        0.1453
```

Author Index

Lecture Notes in Computer Science

For information about Vols. 1–2780
please contact your bookseller or Springer-Verlag

Vol. 2781: B. Michaelis, G. Krell (Eds.), Pattern Recognition. Proceedings, 2003. XVII, 621 pages. 2003.

Vol. 2782: M. Klusch, A. Omicini, S. Ossowski, H. Laamanen (Eds.), Cooperative Information Agents VII. Proceedings, 2003. XI, 345 pages. 2003. (Subseries LNAI).

Vol. 2783: W. Zhou, P. Nicholson, B. Corbitt, J. Fong (Eds.), Advances in Web-Based Learning – ICWL 2003. Proceedings, 2003. XV, 552 pages. 2003.

Vol. 2784: M. Genero, F. Grandi, W.-J. van den Heuvel, J. Krogstie, K. Lyytinen, H.C. Mayr, J. Nelson, A. Olivé, M. Piattini, G. Poels, J. Roddick, K. Siau, M. Yoshikawa, E.S.K. Yu (Eds.), Advanced Conceptual Modeling Techniques. Revised Papers, 2003. XVIII, 452 pages. 2003.

Vol. 2785: C. Peters, M. Braschler, J. Gonzalo, M. Kluck (Eds.), Advances in Cross-Language Information Retrieval. Revised Papers, 2003. XI, 828 pages. 2003.

Vol. 2786: F. Oquendo (Ed.), Software Process Technology. Proceedings, 2003. X, 173 pages. 2003.

Vol. 2787: J. Timmis, P. Bentley, E. Hart (Eds.), Artificial Immune Systems. Proceedings, 2003. XI, 299 pages. 2003.

Vol. 2788: S. Anderson, M. Felici, B. Littlewood (Eds.), Computer Safety, Reliability, and Security. Proceedings, 2003. XIX, 426 pages. 2003.

Vol. 2789: L. Böszörményi, P. Schojer (Eds.), Modular Programming Languages. Proceedings, 2003. XIII, 271 pages. 2003.

Vol. 2790: H. Kosch, L. Böszörményi, H. Hellwagner (Eds.), Euro-Par 2003 Parallel Processing. Proceedings, 2003. XXXV, 1320 pages. 2003.

Vol. 2792: T. Rist, R. Aylett, D. Ballin, J. Rickel (Eds.), Intelligent Virtual Agents. Proceedings, 2003. XV, 364 pages. 2003. (Subseries LNAI).

Vol. 2793: R. Backhouse, J. Gibbons (Eds.), Generic Programming. IX, 223 pages. 2003.

Vol. 2794: P. Kemper, W. H. Sanders (Eds.), Computer Performance Evaluation. Proceedings, 2003. X, 309 pages. 2003.

Vol. 2795: L. Chittaro (Ed.), Human-Computer Interaction with Mobile Devices and Services. Proceedings, 2003. XV, 494 pages. 2003.

Vol. 2796: M. Cialdea Mayer, F. Pirri (Eds.), Automated Reasoning with Analytic Tableaux and Related Methods. Proceedings, 2003. X, 271 pages. 2003. (Subseries LNAI).

Vol. 2798: L. Kalinichenko, R. Manthey, B. Thalheim, U. Wloka (Eds.), Advances in Databases and Information Systems. Proceedings, 2003. XIII, 431 pages. 2003.

Vol. 2799: J.J. Chico, E. Macii (Eds.), Integrated Circuit and System Design. Proceedings, 2003. XVII, 631 pages. 2003.

Vol. 2801: W. Banzhaf, T. Christaller, P. Dittrich, J.T. Kim, J. Ziegler (Eds.), Advances in Artificial Life. Proceedings, 2003. XVI, 905 pages. 2003. (Subseries LNAI).

Vol. 2803: M. Baaz, J.A. Makowsky (Eds.), Computer Science Logic. Proceedings, 2003. XII, 589 pages. 2003.

Vol. 2804: M. Bernardo, P. Inverardi (Eds.), Formal Methods for Software Architectures. Proceedings, 2003. VII, 287 pages. 2003.

Vol. 2805: K. Araki, S. Gnesi, D. Mandrioli (Eds.), FME 2003: Formal Methods. Proceedings, 2003. XVII, 942 pages. 2003.

Vol. 2806: J. Favela, D. Decouchant (Eds.), Groupware: Design, Implementation, and Use. Proceedings, 2003. XII, 382 pages. 2003.

Vol. 2807: V. Matoušek, P. Mautner (Eds.), Text, Speech and Dialogue. Proceedings, 2003. XIII, 426 pages. 2003. (Subseries LNAI).

Vol. 2808: E. Snekkenes, D. Gollmann (Eds.), Computer Security – ESORICS 2003. Proceedings, 2003. X, 345 pages. 2003.

Vol. 2810: M.R. Berthold, H.-J. Lenz, E. Bradley, R. Kruse, C. Borgelt (Eds.), Advances in Intelligent Data Analysis V. Proceedings, 2003. XV, 624 pages. 2003.

Vol. 2811: G. Karlsson, M.I. Smirnov (Eds.), Quality for All. Proceedings, 2003. XII, 295 pages. 2003.

Vol. 2812: G. Benson, R. Page (Eds.), Algorithms in Bioinformatics. Proceedings, 2003. X, 528 pages. 2003. (Subseries LNBI).

Vol. 2813: I.-Y. Song, S.W. Liddle, T.W. Ling, P. Scheuermann (Eds.), Conceptual Modeling – ER 2003. Proceedings, 2003. XIX, 584 pages. 2003.

Vol. 2814: M.A. Jeusfeld, Ó. Pastor (Eds.), Conceptual Modeling for Novel Application Domains. Proceedings, 2003. XVI, 410 pages. 2003.

Vol. 2815: Y. Lindell, Composition of Secure Multi-Party Protocols. XVI, 192 pages. 2003.

Vol. 2816: B. Stiller, G. Carle, M. Karsten, P. Reichl (Eds.), Group Communications and Charges. Proceedings, 2003. XIII, 354 pages. 2003.

Vol. 2817: D. Konstantas, M. Leonard, Y. Pigneur, S. Patel (Eds.), Object-Oriented Information Systems. Proceedings, 2003. XII, 426 pages. 2003.

Vol. 2818: H. Blanken, T. Grabs, H.-J. Schek, R. Schenkel, G. Weikum (Eds.), Intelligent Search on XML Data. XVII, 319 pages. 2003.

Vol. 2819: B. Benatallah, M.-C. Shan (Eds.), Technologies for E-Services. Proceedings, 2003. X, 203 pages. 2003.

Vol. 2820: G. Vigna, E. Jonsson, C. Kruegel (Eds.), Recent Advances in Intrusion Detection. Proceedings, 2003. X, 239 pages. 2003.

Vol. 2821: A. Günter, R. Kruse, B. Neumann (Eds.), KI 2003: Advances in Artificial Intelligence. Proceedings, 2003. XII, 662 pages. 2003. (Subseries LNAI).

Vol. 2822: N. Bianchi-Berthouze (Ed.), Databases in Networked Information Systems. Proceedings, 2003. X, 271 pages. 2003.

Vol. 2823: A. Omondi, S. Sedukhin (Eds.), Advances in Computer Systems Architecture. Proceedings, 2003. XIII, 409 pages. 2003.

Vol. 2824: Z. Bellahsène, A.B. Chaudhri, E. Rahm, M. Rys, R. Unland (Eds.), Database and XML Technologies. Proceedings, 2003. X, 283 pages. 2003.

Vol. 2825: W. Kuhn, M. Worboys, S. Timpf (Eds.), Spatial Information Theory. Proceedings, 2003. XI, 399 pages. 2003.

Vol. 2826: A. Krall (Ed.), Software and Compilers for Embedded Systems. Proceedings, 2003. XI, 403 pages. 2003.

Vol. 2827: A. Albrecht, K. Steinhöfel (Eds.), Stochastic Algorithms: Foundations and Applications. Proceedings, 2003. VIII, 167 pages. 2003.

Vol. 2828: A. Lioy, D. Mazzocchi (Eds.), Communications and Multimedia Security. Proceedings, 2003. VIII, 265 pages. 2003.

Vol. 2829: A. Cappelli, F. Turini (Eds.), AI*IA 2003: Advances in Artificial Intelligence. Proceedings, 2003. XIV, 552 pages. 2003. (Subseries LNAI).

Vol. 2830: F. Pfenning, Y. Smaragdakis (Eds.), Generative Programming and Component Engineering. Proceedings, 2003. IX, 397 pages. 2003.

Vol. 2831: M. Schillo, M. Klusch, J. Müller, H. Tianfield (Eds.), Multiagent System Technologies. Proceedings, 2003. X, 229 pages. 2003. (Subseries LNAI).

Vol. 2832: G. Di Battista, U. Zwick (Eds.), Algorithms – ESA 2003. Proceedings, 2003. XIV, 790 pages. 2003.

Vol. 2833: F. Rossi (Ed.), Principles and Practice of Constraint Programming – CP 2003. Proceedings, 2003. XIX, 1005 pages. 2003.

Vol. 2834: X. Zhou, S. Jähnichen, M. Xu, J. Cao (Eds.), Advanced Parallel Processing Technologies. Proceedings, 2003. XIV, 679 pages. 2003.

Vol. 2835: T. Horváth, A. Yamamoto (Eds.), Inductive Logic Programming. Proceedings, 2003. X, 401 pages. 2003. (Subseries LNAI).

Vol. 2836: S. Qing, D. Gollmann, J. Zhou (Eds.), Information and Communications Security. Proceedings, 2003. XI, 416 pages. 2003.

Vol. 2837: N. Lavrač, D. Gamberger, H. Blockeel, L. Todorovski (Eds.), Machine Learning: ECML 2003. Proceedings, 2003. XVI, 504 pages. 2003. (Subseries LNAI).

Vol. 2838: N. Lavrač, D. Gamberger, L. Todorovski, H. Blockeel (Eds.), Knowledge Discovery in Databases: PKDD 2003. Proceedings, 2003. XVI, 508 pages. 2003. (Subseries LNAI).

Vol. 2839: A. Marshall, N. Agoulmine (Eds.), Management of Multimedia Networks and Services. Proceedings, 2003. XIV, 532 pages. 2003.

Vol. 2840: J. Dongarra, D. Laforenza, S. Orlando (Eds.), Recent Advances in Parallel Virtual Machine and Message Passing Interface. Proceedings, 2003. XVIII, 693 pages. 2003.

…l. 2841: C. Blundo, C. Laneve (Eds.), Theoretical Com-… Science. Proceedings, 2003. XI, 397 pages. 2003.

…42: R. Gavaldà, K.P. Jantke, E. Takimoto (Eds.), …ic Learning Theory. Proceedings, 2003. XI, 313 … (Subseries LNAI).

…rieser, Y. Tanaka, A. Yamamoto (Eds.), … Proceedings, 2003. XII, 504 pages. …AI).

Vol. 2844: J.A. Jorge, N.J. Nunes, J.F. e Cunha (Eds.), Interactive Systems. Revised Papers, 2003. XIII, 429 pages. 2003.

Vol. 2846: J. Zhou, M. Yung, Y. Han (Eds.), Applied Cryptography and Network Security. Proceedings, 2003. XI, 436 pages. 2003.

Vol. 2847: R. de Lemos, T.S. Weber, J.B. Camargo Jr. (Eds.), Dependable Computing. Proceedings, 2003. XIV, 371 pages. 2003.

Vol. 2848: F.E. Fich (Ed.), Distributed Computing. Proceedings, 2003. X, 367 pages. 2003.

Vol. 2849: N. García, J.M. Martínez, L. Salgado (Eds.), Visual Content Processing and Representation. Proceedings, 2003. XII, 352 pages. 2003.

Vol. 2850: M.Y. Vardi, A. Voronkov (Eds.), Logic for Programming, Artificial Intelligence, and Reasoning. Proceedings, 2003. XIII, 437 pages. 2003. (Subseries LNAI)

Vol. 2851: C. Boyd, W. Mao (Eds.), Information Security. Proceedings, 2003. XI, 443 pages. 2003.

Vol. 2852: F.S. de Boer, M.M. Bonsangue, S. Graf, W.-P. de Roever (Eds.), Formal Methods for Components and Objects. Revised Lectures, 2003. VIII, 509 pages. 2003.

Vol. 2853: M. Jeckle, L.-J. Zhang (Eds.), Web Services – ICWS-Europe 2003. Proceedings, 2003. VIII, 227 pages. 2003.

Vol. 2855: R. Alur, I. Lee (Eds.), Embedded Software. Proceedings, 2003. X, 373 pages. 2003.

Vol. 2856: M. Smirnov, E. Biersack, C. Blondia, O. Bonaventure, O. Casals, G. Karlsson, George Pavlou, B. Quoitin, J. Roberts, I. Stavrakakis, B. Stiller, P. Trimintzios, P. Van Mieghem (Eds.), Quality of Future Internet Services. IX, 293 pages. 2003.

Vol. 2857: M.A. Nascimento, E.S. de Moura, A.L. Oliveira (Eds.), String Processing and Information Retrieval. Proceedings, 2003. XI, 379 pages. 2003.

Vol. 2858: A. Veidenbaum, K. Joe, H. Amano, H. Aiso (Eds.), High Performance Computing. Proceedings, 2003. XV, 566 pages. 2003.

Vol. 2859: B. Apolloni, M. Marinaro, R. Tagliaferri (Eds.), Neural Nets. Proceedings, 2003. X, 376 pages. 2003.

Vol. 2863: P. Stevens, J. Whittle, G. Booch (Eds.), «UML» 2003 – The Unified Modeling Language. Proceedings, 2003. XIV, 415 pages. 2003.

Vol. 2864: A.K. Dey, A. Schmidt, J.F. McCarthy (Eds.), UbiComp 2003: Ubiquitous Computing. Proceedings, 2003. XVII, 368 pages. 2003.

Vol. 2865: S. Pierre, M. Barbeau, E. Kranakis (Eds.), Ad-Hoc, Mobile, and Wireless Networks. Proceedings, 2003. X, 293 pages. 2003.

Vol. 2868: P. Perner, R. Brause, H.-G. Holzhütter (Eds.), Medical Data Analysis. Proceedings, 2003. VIII, 127 pages. 2003.

Vol. 2870: D. Fensel, K. Sycara, J. Mylopoulos (Eds.), The Semantic Web - ISWC 2003. Proceedings, 2003. XV, 931 pages. 2003.

Vol. 2871: N. Zhong, Z.W. Raś, S. Tsumoto, E. Suzuki (Eds.), Foundations of Intelligent Systems. Proceedings, 2003. XV, 697 pages. 2003. (Subseries LNAI)

Vol. 2881: E. Horlait, T. Magedanz, R.H. Glitho (Eds.), Mobile Agents for Telecommunication Applications. Proceedings, 2003. IX, 297 pages. 2003.